Lecture Notes in Computer Science 2805
Edited by G. Goos, J. Hartmanis, and J. van Leeuwen

Springer
Berlin
Heidelberg
New York
Hong Kong
London
Milan
Paris
Tokyo

Keijiro Araki Stefania Gnesi
Dino Mandrioli (Eds.)

FME 2003: Formal Methods

International Symposium of Formal Methods Europe
Pisa, Italy, September 8-14, 2003
Proceedings

 Springer

Volume Editors

Keijiro Araki
Kyushu University
Department of Computer Science and Communication Engineering
Graduate School of Information Science and Electrical Engineering
6-10-1-Hakozaki, Higashi-ku, Fukuoka 812-8581, Japan
E-mail: araki@csce.kyushu-u.ac.jp

Stefania Gnesi
Istituto di Scienze e Tecnologie della Informazione
Via Moruzzi 1, 56124 Pisa, Italy
E-mail: gnesi@iei.pi.cnr.it

Dino Mandrioli
Politecnico di Milano
Dipartimento di Elettronica e Informazione
Piazza Leonardo Da Vinci 32, 20133 Milano, Italy
E-mail: mandrioli@elet.polimi.it

Cataloging-in-Publication Data applied for

A catalog record for this book is available from the Library of Congress

Bibliographic information published by Die Deutsche Bibliothek
Die Deutsche Bibliothek lists this publication in the Deutsche Nationalbibliografie;
detailed bibliographic data is available in the Internet at <http://dnb.ddb.de>.

CR Subject Classification (1998): F.3, D.2, D.3, D.1, J.1, K.6, F.4.1

ISSN 0302-9743
ISBN 3-540-40828-2 Springer-Verlag Berlin Heidelberg New York

This work is subject to copyright. All rights are reserved, whether the whole or part of the material is
concerned, specifically the rights of translation, reprinting, re-use of illustrations, recitation, broadcasting,
reproduction on microfilms or in any other way, and storage in data banks. Duplication of this publication
or parts thereof is permitted only under the provisions of the German Copyright Law of September 9, 1965,
in its current version, and permission for use must always be obtained from Springer-Verlag. Violations are
liable for prosecution under the German Copyright Law.

Springer-Verlag Berlin Heidelberg New York
a member of BertelsmannSpringer Science+Business Media GmbH

http://www.springer.de

© Springer-Verlag Berlin Heidelberg 2003
Printed in Germany

Typesetting: Camera-ready by author, data conversion by Steingräber Satztechnik GmbH
Printed on acid-free paper   SPIN 10949801   06/3142   5 4 3 2 1 0

Preface

This volume contains the proceedings of FM 2003, the 12th International Formal Methods Europe Symposium which was held in Pisa, Italy on September 8–14, 2003. Formal Methods Europe (FME, www.fmeurope.org) is an independent association which aims to stimulate the use of and research on formal methods for system development. FME conferences began with a VDM Europe symposium in 1987. Since then, the meetings have grown and have been held about once every 18 months. Throughout the years the symposia have been notably successful in bringing together researchers, tool developers, vendors, and users, both from academia and from industry.

Unlike previous symposia in the series, FM 2003 was not given a specific theme. Rather, its main goal could be synthesized as "widening the scope." Indeed, the organizers aimed at enlarging the audience and impact of the symposium along several directions. Dropping the suffix 'E' from the title of the conference reflects the wish to welcome participation and contribution from every country; also, contributions from outside the traditional Formal Methods community were solicited. The recent innovation of including an Industrial Day as an important part of the symposium shows the strong commitment to involve industrial people more and more within the Formal Methods community. Even the traditional and rather fuzzy borderline between "software engineering formal methods" and methods and formalisms exploited in different fields of engineering was somewhat challenged. This is in recognition of the increasing need to look at and to understand systems (often hybrid systems) in their entirety: something that should have a higher priority than focusing on the specific software issues that in most cases just relate to a component of the whole system.

All in all we can claim to have made significant steps towards our goal of widening our scope, although, certainly, many challenges are still open. In particular, we were very happy with the paper submissions: 144 papers were submitted from 27 countries of all continents. Submitted papers were of both theoretical and applicative nature, and were overall of high quality. Not only were the 44 accepted papers selected according to our traditional high standards, but the Program Committee board also recognized significant potential contributions in many papers that had to be rejected, mostly due to their fairly preliminary development stage. Four of the 44 accepted papers were selected for presentation during the Industry Day. Besides the refereed papers, these proceedings include contributions from the following invited speakers: Kouichi Kishida, Brian Randell, Gerard Holzmann, and Jean-Raymond Abrial. Finally, we emphasize the importance and quality of numerous satellite events: besides the Industry Day, eight tutorials, seven workshops, and a rich tool fair completed the program of the symposium. Enjoy reading!

September 2003   Keijiro Araki, Stefania Gnesi and Dino Mandrioli

Organization

FM 2003 was organized by Formal Methods Europe, the Institute for Informatics Science and Technology (ISTI) of the National Research Council of Italy, and CoLogNet.

Conference Chairs

General Chair	Stefania Gnesi (ISTI-CNR, I)
Program Co-chairs	Keijiro Araki (Kyushu University, J)
	Dino Mandrioli (Politecnico di Milano, I)
Organizing Committee Chair	Alessandro Fantechi (Università di Firenze, I)
Publicity Chair	Vinicio Lami (ISTI-CNR, I)
Tool Exhibition Chair	Tiziana Margaria (Universität Dortmund, and Metaframe, D)
Tutorials Chair	Mieke Massink (ISTI-CNR, I)
Workshops Chair	Tommaso Bolognesi (ISTI-CNR, I)

Program Committee

Dominique Bolignano	Trusted Logic, France
Jonathan Bowen	South Bank Univ., London, UK
Lubos Brim	Masaryk Univ., Brno, Czech Republic
Han-Myung Chang	Nanzan Univ., Japan
Krzysztof Czarnecki	DaimlerChrysler Research Lab, Germany
Lars-Henrik Eriksson	Uppsala Univ., Sweden
Jose Fiadeiro	Leicester Univ., UK
John Fitzgerald	Transitive Technologies Ltd., UK
Kokichi Futatsugi	JAIST, Japan
Chris George	UNU/IIST, Macao
Connie Heitmeyer	NRL, USA
Shusaku Iida	Senshu Univ., Japan
Mehdi Jazayeri	Technical Univ., Vienna, Austria
Kyo-Chul Kang	POSTECH, Korea
Shmuel Katz	Technion, Israel
Shigeru Kusakabe	Kyushu Univ., Japan
Diego Latella	ISTI-CNR, Pisa, Italy
Yves Ledru	IMAG Grenoble, France
Raimondas Lencevicius	Nokia, USA
Peter Lindsay	Queensland Univ., Australia
Shaoying Liu	Hosei Univ., Japan
Peter Löhr	Freie Univ., Berlin, Germany

Tom Maibaum   King's College London, UK
Huaikou Miao   Shanghai Univ., China
Nico Plat   West Consulting, The Netherlands
Harald Ruess   SRI, USA
Shin Sahara   JFITS, Japan
Pierluigi San Pietro Politecnico di Milano, Italy
Jim Woodcock   Kent Univ., Canterbury, UK
Pamela Zave   AT&T Labs, USA

External Referees

The Program Committee members and the external referees listed below did an excellent job in managing an unexpectedly high number of submissions under the usual pressure of strict deadlines. All papers were refereed by at least three reviewers. Reports were thorough, detailed, and rich with constructive suggestions even when rejection was recommended. Both PC members and external referees further contributed to the active and intense "e-discussion" that led to the final decision. We are very happy to acknowledge such a superb contribution to the quality of these proceedings.

Referees

Nazareno Aguirre
Bernhard K. Aicherning
Myla Archer
James M. Armstrong
Jos Baeten
Luciano Baresi
Jiri Barnat
Maurice ter Beek
Saddek Bensalem
Neil Bergmann
Pierre Berlioux
Roxane Bernier
Didier Bert
Denis Besnard
Gustavo Betarte
Ramesh Bharadwaj
Jonathan Billington
Tommaso Bolognesi
Sylvain Boulmé
Juan C. Burguillo Rial
Ana Cavalcanti
Ivana Cerna

Antonio Cerone
Yihai Chen
Judy Crow
Giampaolo Cugola
Paul Curzon
David Cyrluk
Zhe Dang
Leonardo de Moura
Lydie du Bousquet
Sophie Dupuy
Adolfo Duran
Giorgio Faconti
Alessandro Fantechi
Loe Feijs
Pascal Fenkam
Jean-Claude Fernandez
M.J. Fernández Iglesias
Colin Fidge
Torsten Fink
Leonardo Freitas
Eduardo Gimenez
Jan Friso Groote

Roland Groz
Orna Grumberg
Stefan Gruner
Gregoire Hamon
Ian Hayes
Simon Helsen
John Herbert
Michael G. Hinchey
Zhu Huibiao
Ralph D. Jeffords
He Jifeng
Cliff Jones
Joost-Pieter Katoen
Clemens Kerer
James Kirby
Manuel Koch
Andre Koster
Vishnu Kotrajaras
Pavel Krcal
Mojmir Kretinsky
G. Kwon
Regine Laleau

Rom Langerak
Kevin Lano
Gabriele Lenzini
Elizabeth Leonard
Xavier Leroy
Martin Leucker
Zhiming Liu
Jing Liu
Ling Liu
Antonia Lopes
Marco Lovere
Brendan Mahony
Mieke Massink
Franco Mazzanti
Kees Middelburg
Kim Moonjoo
Angelo Morzenti
Kazuki Munakata
Masaki Nakamura
Masahiro Nakano
John Nicholls
Kazuhiro Ogata

Jose Oliveira
Catherine Oriat
Sam Owre
Jun Pang
Tim Panton
Joachim Parrow
Erik Poll
Marie-Laure Potet
Matteo Pradella
Kees Pronk
Shengchao Qin
Andrew Rae
Murali Rangarajan
Anders P. Ravn
M. Reza Mousavi
Jean-Luc Richier
S. Riddle
Jonathan Roberts
Matteo Rossi
Peter Y.A. Ryan
David Safranek
Fabio Schreiber

Takahiro Seino
Twittie Senivongse
N. Shankar
Yunfu Shen
Maria Sorea
Paola Spoletini
Ketil Stølen
Paul Strooper
Ashish Tiwari
Jan Tretmans
Hung Dang Van
Mario Verdicchio
Marcel Verhoef
Gerald Weber
Michel Wermelinger
Jacco Wesselius
Jan Wessels
Luke Wildman
Kirsten Winter
Jianwen Xiang
Tang Xinbei
Jitka Zidkova

Sponsoring Institutions

Formal Methods Europe
www.fmeurope.org

ISTI-CNR
www.isti.cnr.it

CoLogNET
www.eurice.de/colognet

Ercim
www.ercim.org

Microsoft
www.microsoft.com

TESS-COM Italia I-Logix
www.tess-com.it

Telelogic Technologies
www.telelogic.com

EPSON

Epson
www.epson.com

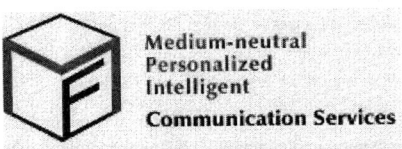

Metaframe
www.metaframe.de

DataPort
www.dataport.it

Table of Contents

Invited Speakers

Looking Back to the Future 1
  Kouichi Kishida

Past, Present, and Future of SRA Implementation of CafeOBJ (Annex) ... 7
  Toshimi Sawada, Kouichi Kishida, Kokichi Futatsugi

On Failures and Faults 18
  Brian Randell

Trends in Software Verification 40
  Gerard J. Holzmann

Event Based Sequential Program Development:
Application to Constructing a Pointer Program 51
  Jean-Raymond Abrial

I-Day

Proving the Shalls 75
  Steven P. Miller, Alan C. Tribble, Mats P.E. Heimdahl

Adaptable Translator of B Specifications to Embedded C Programs ... 94
  *Didier Bert, Sylvain Boulmé, Marie-Laure Potet,
  Antoine Requet, Laurent Voisin*

Integrating Model-Checking Architectural Analysis and Validation
in a Real Software Life-Cycle 114
  *Daniele Compare, Paola Inverardi,
  Patrizio Pelliccione, Alessandra Sebastiani*

Lessons Learned from a Successful Implementation of Formal Methods
in an Industrial Project 133
  Alan Wassyng, Mark Lawford

Control Systems and Industrial Applications

Determining the Specification of a Control System
from That of Its Environment 154
  Ian J. Hayes, Michael A. Jackson, Cliff B. Jones

Managerial Issues for the Consideration and Use of Formal Methods 170
 Donna C. Stidolph, James Whitehead

Verifying Emulation of Legacy Mission Computer Systems 187
 Colin J. Fidge

Improving Safety Assessment of Complex Systems:
An Industrial Case Study 208
 Marco Bozzano, Antonella Cavallo, Massimo Cifaldi, Laura Valacca,
 Adolfo Villafiorita

Communications System Verification

Compositional Verification of an ATM Protocol 223
 Vlad Rusu

Proving the Correctness of Simpson's 4-Slot ACM
Using an Assertional Rely-Guarantee Proof Method 244
 Neil Henderson

Synthesis and Verification of Constraints in the PGM Protocol 264
 Marc Boyer, Mihaela Sighireanu

Co-specification and Compilers

Mapping Statecharts to Verilog for Hardware/Software Co-specification ... 282
 Shengchao Qin, Wei-Ngan Chin

A Strategy for Compiling Classes, Inheritance, and Dynamic Binding 301
 Adolfo Duran, Ana Cavalcanti, Augusto Sampaio

Composition

A Semantic Foundation for TCOZ in Unifying Theories of Programming .. 321
 Shengchao Qin, Jin Song Dong, Wei-Ngan Chin

Refinement and Verification of Synchronized Component-Based Systems .. 341
 Olga Kouchnarenko, Arnaud Lanoix

Certifying and Synthesizing Membership Equational Proofs 359
 Grigore Roşu, Steven Eker, Patrick Lincoln, José Meseguer

Team Automata Satisfying Compositionality 381
 Maurice H. ter Beek, Jetty Kleijn

Composing Invariants 401
 Michel Charpentier

Java, Object Orientation and Modularity

Java Applet Correctness: A Developer-Oriented Approach 422
  Lilian Burdy, Antoine Requet, Jean-Louis Lanet

Improving JML: For a Safer and More Effective Language 440
  Patrice Chalin

Using Abstractions for Heuristic State Space Exploration
of Reactive Object-Oriented Systems 462
  Marc Lettrari

A Formal Framework for Modular Synchronous System Design 482
  Maria-Cristina V. Marinescu, Martin C. Rinard

Model Checking

Generating Counterexamples for Multi-valued Model-Checking 503
  Arie Gurfinkel, Marsha Chechik

Combining Real-Time Model-Checking and Fault Tree Analysis 522
  Andreas Schäfer

Model-Checking TRIO Specifications in SPIN 542
  Angelo Morzenti, Matteo Pradella, Pierluigi San Pietro, Paola Spoletini

Computing Meta-transitions
for Linear Transition Systems with Polynomials 562
  Julien Musset, Michaël Rusinowitch

Translation-Based Compositional Reasoning for Software Systems 582
  Fei Xie, James C. Browne, Robert P. Kurshan

Watchdog Transformations for Property-Oriented Model-Checking 600
  Michael Goldsmith, Nick Moffat, Bill Roscoe,
  Tim Whitworth, Irfan Zakiuddin

Parallel Process

A *Circus* Semantics for Ravenscar Protected Objects 617
  Diyaa-Addein Atiya, Steve King, Jim C.P. Woodcock

Constructing Deadlock Free Event-Based Applications:
A Rely/Guarantee Approach 636
  Pascal Fenkam, Harald Gall, Mehdi Jazayeri

A General Approach to Deadlock Freedom Verification
for Software Architectures... 658
   Alessandro Aldini, Marco Bernardo

Taking *Alloy* to the Movies 678
   *Marcelo F. Frias, Carlos G. López Pombo, Gabriel A. Baum,
   Nazareno M. Aguirre, Tom Maibaum*

Interacting State Machines for Mobility 698
   Thomas A. Kuhn, David von Oheimb

Composing Temporal-Logic Specifications with Machine Assistance 719
   Jei-Wen Teng, Yih-Kuen Tsay

Program Checking and Testing

Model Checking FTA 739
   Andreas Thums, Gerhard Schellhorn

Program Checking with Certificates: Separating Correctness-Critical Code 758
   Sabine Glesner

Reification of Executable Test Scripts in Formal Specification-Based
Test Generation: The Java Card Transaction Mechanism Case Study 778
   Fabrice Bouquet, Bruno Legeard

Checking and Reasoning about Semantic Web through Alloy 796
   Jin Song Dong, Jing Sun, Hai Wang

B Method

Structuring Retrenchments in B by Decomposition 814
   Michael Poppleton, Richard Banach

Design of an Automatic Prover Dedicated
to the Refinement of Database Applications 834
   Amel Mammar, Régine Laleau

ProB: A Model Checker for B 855
   Michael Leuschel, Michael Butler

Security

SAT-Based Model-Checking of Security Protocols
Using Planning Graph Analysis 875
   Alessandro Armando, Luca Compagna, Pierre Ganty

Correctness of Source-Level Safety Policies 894
    Ewen Denney, Bernd Fischer

A Topological Characterization of TCP/IP Security 914
    Giovanni Vigna

Author Index **941**

Looking Back to the Future
Thoughts on Paradigm Shift in Software Development

Kouichi Kishida

SRA-KTL, 3-12, Yotsuya, Shinjuku-ku, Tokyo 164-0004, Japan,
k2@sra.co.jp

Abstract. During the short history of Computer Science and Software Engineering, there have been proposed many development methods or paradigms: such as structured design, object orientation, etc,, etc. The same situation will be found when we look into also short history of formal development methods.It looks like people are following the same pattern of evolution of human thinking in other fields.

About a decade ago, I noticed the similarity of conceptual framework of Confucian philosophy and those of software engineering: for example, similarity between Confucian theory of *rectification of names* and the hierarchical mode of thinking in object orientation. Since then, I have surveyed the history of Confucianism and found a young philosopher in early 18th century in Japan: Mr. Nakamoto Tominaga. His observation about important role of *Add-on* principle in the evolution process of philosophy seems very useful when we consider and evaluate practical value of various software development paradigms including formal methods.

According to a classic metaphor in poetry, time flows in the direction of *from future to past*. So, if we want to think about our future, at first we should look back into the past.

Keywords: software engineering, paradigm shift, formal method, object orientation, philosophical thoughts

1 Introduction

About 2,500 years ago, Confucious said, on the bank of Yellow River, as follows:

It is what passes like that indeed,
Not stopping day and night

Time flows without stopping as he said.

But, which direction? According to the detailed analysis by George Lakof[1], when time is treated as moving object in poetical metaphor the direction of the movement is *towards us*: namely, from the future to the past. We can see nothing in the future in front of us, but there are too many mamemories or stories left behind us.

2 Strange Conceptual Similarity

In the spring of 1990, I visited the head quarter of Eureka Software Factory Project n Berlin, where I chanced to come across a technical report written by Professor Trygve Reenskaug, a description of his own version of an object oriented design/analysis method[2]. In passing, this Norwegian professor indicated that, in his mind, a 19th century German philosopher Max Weber was the true *father* of O-O methods. Weber's concept of the *ideal* bureaucracy has key characteristics in common with O-O:

(1) emphasis on form,
(2) concept of hierarchy,
(3) specialization of tasks,
(4) specified sphere of competence, and
(5) established norm of conduct for each layer in hierarchy.

This left my thoughts spinning; I made a mental time trip back floating to 2 thousands years ago. One of the Confucian philosophers Hsun-tzu (BC 298–238) was then writing a considered essay on rectification of names. He described therein a systematic hierarchy of concepts and their names (in O-O terminology, relationship between meta-class, class, instance, etc.):

> Then names are given to things. Similar things are given the same name and different things are given different names. When simple name (e.g. horse) is sufficient, the simple name is used. When it is not sufficient, then a compound name (e.g. white horse) is used. When simple and compound concepts do not conflict, then the general name (e.g. horse in general) may be used. ... For although the myriad things are innumerable, sometimes we want to speak of the as a whole and so we call them *things*. It is a great general name.

Confucius himself speculated about this issue a little differently. It is called as "the principle for the rectification of names":

> If names are not rectified,
>   then language will not be in accord with truth.
> If language is not in accord with truth,
>   then things cannot be accomplished.
> If things cannot be accomplished,
>   then rites and music will not flourish.
> If rites and music do not flourish,
>   then the punishment will not be just.
> If punishment is not just,
>   then the people will not know how to move their hands or feet.
> Therefore, the superior man will give only names that can be described in speech, and say only what can be carried out in practice.

What might this have to do with software project management? Well, apply the thought using this simple conversion table:

Names	⟷	Concepts
Language	⟷	Process Model
Things	⟷	Projects
Rites	⟷	Development Methods
Music	⟷	Tools/Environment
Punishment	⟷	Management
People	⟷	Programmers
Hands/Feet	⟷	Development Activities

Also, the starting paragraph of "The Book of Great Learning", edited by a famous Neo-Confucian philosopher of 16th century Zhu-Xi, says:

If you want to conquer the world,
   at first you must govern your state properly.
To govern a state,
   at first you must regulate your family.
To regulate your family,
   at first you must cultivate yourself.
To cultivate yourself,
   at first you must rectify your mind.
To rectify your mind,
   at first you must make your will sincere.
To make your will sincere,
   at first you must expand your knowledge.
To expand your knowledge,
   at first you must study various objects around you.

This hierarchical structure of self-management discipline is almost same as the framework of CMM-TSP-PSP for software process improvement today.

3   A Linguistic Turn in Edo

18th–19th century was a kind of Golden Age in the history of Japanese philosophy. A number of unique philosophers developed their own thoughts. Unfortunately, after Meiji revolution in late 19 century, importance of those intellectual achievements were almost forgotten in the huge socio-cultural wave of Westernization.

The biggest name was Mr. Sorai Ogiu (1666–1728). After following Neo-Confucian way of thinking, he made a kind of linguistic turn when he became 50 years old and proposed a radically new approach to Confucian studies.

Sorai criticized Neo-Confucianist that they had too much stressed on metaphysics, philosophical idealism and personal cultivation. After careful comparative study of Six Classics (Book of History, Odes, Rites, etc) and Four Books

(Analects, Mencious, Great Learning, Doctorine of Mean), he concluded that Tao (Cofucian *Way*) should be considered in sociological context rather than as discipline for personal cultivation.

In his major work "Bendo" (Distinguishing the Way), he wrote:

– The Way of Confucious is the Way of Sacred Kings.

In this metaphorical statement, he tried to say that:

> The fundamental concept of the Way is too abstract and difficult to understand for ordinary people. So, Sacred Kings in legendary ancient times invented Rites-and-Musics as an implementation example of the Way, which people easy to understand and practice. But those were invented to fit with people's culture in their times, they do not fit into contemporary situation. We should only inherit the spirit of the Way and think about our own version of Rites-and-Musics.

Paraphrasing into software engineering terms, the Way for software process improvement is now implemented as a set of KPAs in CMM, and the Way of object orientation is implemented as various class libraries for several application domains.

4 One Step Further to Paradigm Shift

Japan in Edo period (under Tokugawa Shogun's administration) was two-centered society: Edo (Tokyo) was the center of politics, and Naniwa (Osaka) was the center of commerce. Sorai Ogiu was a typical figure representing samurai culture in Edo.

In early 18th century, 5 rich merchants in Naniwa jointly established a private academy for philosophical study to strengthen the cultural foundation of their commercial business. This school, Kaitokudo, became a good incubation base of civilian philosophy and produced a number of excellent scholars[3].

Kaitokudo people inherited Sorai Ogiu's linguistic approach (the first school master was a friend of Sorai) and later somehow against him and over-rode his theory. The front runner of this school was Mr. Nakamoto Tominaga (1715–1746).

Until he died at the age of 31, he published 3 books. The first book (collection of critical comments on Cofucianism) was lost. So, there remain only 2 books: "Shutsujogo-Go" ("Words after Enlightenment"; written in classic Chinese), and "Okina-no-Fume" ("Memorandum of an Old-man"; written in plain Japanese). The first book is an analysis of the long history of Buddhism from outsider's viewpoint. The second one is a comparative review of three major religions: Buddhism, Confucianism, and Japanese Shinto.

These 2 books were almost neglected while Nakamoto was alive, because the author was just a young unknown scholar with no fame. They have been forgotten for longtime until a famous historian of Kyoto University (Prof. Konan Naito) found them in early 19th century and re-evaluated the intellectual value of Nakamoto's work.

Nakamoto carefully studied the huge volumes of Buddhism scriptures and also Confucian classics, then he found the *Add-on Principle* in the evolving history of those religious thinking. He noticed that every new religious sect has come into the history with some bright idea to distinguish their uniqueness from existing other sects and authorize their theory. This principle also works in other area of human thinking. Let's think about various software methods and how they are claiming their authority and uniqueness.

He also pointed out that 3 important characteristics in religious or philosophical discourses: trends of the time, ethnic taste, and style of representation.

The first one is easy to understand: every thinker was influenced by the trend of their time somehow, In our terms, structured programming is a discourse of late 1960s, and XP is clearly a baby of early 21th century.

As for the second characteristics *ethnicity of thoughts*, Nakamoto claimed that Buddhism reflects taste of *magic* in Indian culture, Confucianism reflects taste of *rhetoric* in Chinese culture, and Shinto reflects taste of *simplicity* in Japanese culture. In our terms, formal method people like mathematics very much, and OO community has a strange taste for poetical metaphor, etc.

Presentation style of discourses depends on time and ethnic factors. Nakamoto classified 5 categories of presentation styles, and those are considered very useful for the linguistic analysis of human discourses of any kind.

5 From Thinking to Practice

In the final chapter of "Okina-no-Fume", Nakamoto wrote an important message:

– The Way is *the way of sincere practice*, that's all.

This definition over-rides Sorai's these *The Way is the way of sacred kings*. Nakamoto criticized that the many Confucian discussion so far have been made only for debates among them. He stressed that the real purpose of philosophical discourses is just for sincere practice of the Way.

Unfortunately, this message have been overlooked even by the people who appraised Nakamoto's work, because they evaluated him just as a unique historian who were little ahead of the age.

In our short history of software engineering, there have been proposed a variety of brave new development methods with some *add-on* features to supersede their forerunners. It is true if we focus our concern into the area of formal methods.

But how about the situation, from the viewpoint of *sincere practice*?

We need to concentrate our effort more into the practice than inventing new methods or techniques. To enforce the practice, it is necessary to provide some tools/environments (rites/musics) supporting industrial practitioners. That is the reason why SRA have been developing **CafeOBJ** software systems in cooperation with academic researchers[1]. Our effort is still not yet completed, but I

---

[1] A brief historical overview of **CafeOBJ** and its characteristic features are given in the annex of this paper.

believe that we are on the proper way to the application of the method for the industrial use in the real world.

6 Concluding Remark

Time flows in the direction of the future to the past. We can not see anything in front of us, but many useful memories are left in the past. To make our future really meaningful for us, we need to look back into the past with the mind of *sincere practice*.

References

1. George Lakoff and Mark Turner, *More than Cool Reason – A Field Guide to Poetic Metaphor*, University of Chicago Press, 1989.
2. Trygve Reenskaug, *A Methodology for the Design and Description of Complex, Object-Oriented Systems*, Senter for Industriforskning, Oslo, 1988.
3. Tetsuo Najita, *Visions of Virtue in Tokugawa Japan: The Kaitokudo – Merchant Academy of Osaka*, University of Hawaii Press, 1998.

Past, Present, and Future of SRA Implementation of CafeOBJ
Annex

Toshimi Sawada[1], Kouichi Kishida[1], and Kokichi Futatsugi[2]

[1] SRA-KTL,
3-12, Yotsuya, Shinjuku-ku, Tokyo 164-0004, Japan,
{sawada,k2}@sra.co.jp
[2] Japan Advanced Institute of Science and Technology,
1-1 Asahidai, Tatsunokuchi, Ishikawa 923-1292, Japan,
kokichi@jaist.ac.jp

1 Background

CafeOBJ is a formal language for specifying or defining models of real problems, and also for analyzing and/or verifying the properties of the models [1, 8, 7]. It is based on algebraic specification techniques and is a member of OBJ [6, 14, 19] language family.

The concept of CafeOBJ was first conceived around 1990 at ETL[1] as a successor of the OBJ language. The design and development of CafeOBJ was conducted under the leadership of Professor Futatsugi of JAIST for more than 10 years. The development activities of CafeOBJ are mainly supported by several public research funds including the ones from IPA[2] and MEXT[3]. A large part of the current implementation of CafeOBJ was done by SRA (Software Research Associate, Inc.) who participated the CafeOBJ project from the very beginning.

This annex gives a brief history of the SRA implementation of CafeOBJ, its current status, and its future perspective. This annex is prepared for explaining a specific contribution of the SRA (a Tokyo based software company) to the community of formal methods.

2 Paradigms Underlie CafeOBJ

Multiple Paradigms

CafeOBJ offers multiple underlining logics which allows users to select a suitable representation scheme of their specific problem domains. Besides, these logics can be combined in a seamless manner. That is, users can use multiple logics (paradigms) at the same time, e.g., specifying abstract data types for a static

---

[1] Electrotechnical Laboratories, Tsukuba, Japan
[2] Information Technology Promotion Agency Japan, Tokyo, Japan
[3] Ministry of Education, Culture, Sports, Science and Technology, Japan

part of a system and describing dynamic behavior of the system in a form of state transition. This is one of the most powerful features of the language.

According to each logic, it provides the following basic ways of specifying systems:

Equational Specification
This is a traditional way of specifying ADT in algebraic specification framework constituting the logical basis of the language. Other features are built on top of it.

Rewriting Logic Specification
CafeOBJ adopts a simplified version[4] of Meseguer's rewriting logic (RWL) [22, 23] specification framework. This is a (non-trivial) extension of traditional algebraic specification towards concurrency and provides many different models of concurrency in a natural and simple way.

Behavioral Specification
This framework is based on coherent hidden algebra [3, 17], an another generalization of traditional algebraic specification. In this way of specification, we characterize how systems behave, not how they are implemented.

These should be understood in their combination rather than as separated paradigms. CafeOBJ supports each of the above directly by corresponding language constructs. This multi-paradigm approach has an elegant mathematical semantics based on multiple institutions and is fully described in [1, 2].

Object-Orientation

CafeOBJ does *not* provide object-orientation as primary paradigm of the language; there are no specific language constructs for denoting classes or objects, e.t.c. Object-orientation is, however, a derived feature of the language; it can be obtained easily through rewriting logic and/or behavioral specification.

Based on rewriting logic, object orientated concurrent computations are modeled as a collection of objects/messages and reactions between them [22, 23]. Overall configuration is represented as a set of objects and messages; objects and messages themselves are represented by ordinal data types, possibly by record-like structures representing internal structures of objects and messages. Concurrent computations are described by rewriting rules which non-deterministically defines the next configurations of the current one.

By using behavioral specification based on coherent hidden algebra, one can represent how objects or systems behave without mentioning their internal structures [1, 3, 4, 8]. This modeling scheme is more faithful to the principle of state encapsulation. In many situations we encounter, it is very handy and useful to describe the behavior of a system or an object by just specifying the changes of interested observable values of them. This is naturally achieved by behavioral specification of CafeOBJ.

---

[4] CafeOBJ does not fully support labeled RWL.

Of course, one can use both approaches in combined manner. Yet, this is not studied well until now, but the combination seems to provide a quite powerful method for formally specified dynamic system description and its verification.

Powerful Module System

One of the most promising and important application of algebraic specification is to prepare *generic reusable modules* and to compose them for specific requirement [5, 9, 10, 30]. Parameterized programming already realized in OBJ is powerful programming method for preparation and composition of generic reusable modules [15, 19]. CafeOBJ inherited this feature from OBJ, and its theory is updated to multi-paradigm situations mentioned in the above. One of the consequences is the ability of providing more powerful style of specification that results from the combination of parameterized programming and seamlessly incorporated multiple logics. This will provide a promising semantic framework for component based software constructions [20].

Powerful Type System

CafeOBJ has a type system that allows subtypes based on *order-sorted algebra* [16, 29]. This provides rigorous notion of type checking and exception handling with syntactic flexibility and it also gives CafeOBJ a syntactic flexibility comparable to that of untyped languages, while preserving the advantage of strong typing.

3 The Past – A Brief History of SRA Implementation

In this section we give a brief historical overview of the SRA implementation of CafeOBJ.

3.1 The First Implementation

The first version was developed during 1992-1995 under the leadership of Professor Futatsugi of JAIST. This task was carried as a rather small project (2 to 3 workers) with the help of public research fund of IPA. At this stage, the core language is almost a refinement of OBJ3, including mix-fix syntax, sub typing by ordered sorts, modules with parameterized programming. Additionally, it supports a subset of rewriting logic [22, 23] by introducing a language construct *rewrite rule* (the language and its operational semantics was described by order sorted rewriting logic.)

This was the first language implementation which incorporates full support of traditional order-sorted equational logic with powerful module system and rewriting logic that provides an ability of declarative description of dynamic concurrent system behaviors á la Maude.

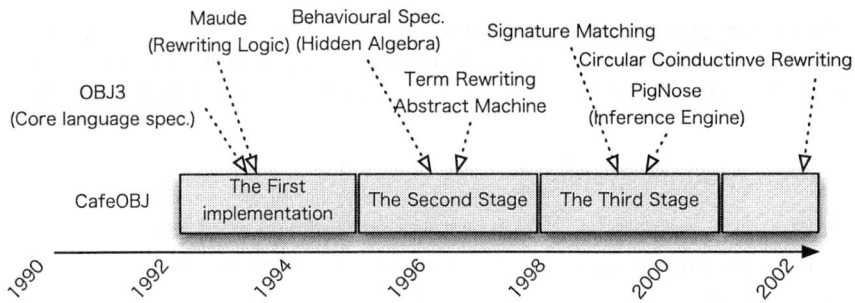

Fig. 1. History of SRA implementation

3.2 The Second Stage

At 1996 a three years project was started, also with the support of IPA and Professor Futatsugi as the leader. The target of the project was to provides an environment for supporting the system (mainly software but not only) development process at several levels, including prototyping, specification and formal verification. It embraced CafeOBJ as the core language of the system with its SRA implementation. This project was carried out by the international team including JAIST, Univ. of Tokyo., Mitsubishi Research Institute (MRI), Nihon Unisys, Hitachi, SRI, UCSD and SRA (not exhaustive)[5].

During the project, the language itself and its implementation was refined and advanced in several ways. One of the most important feature was incorporating behavioral specification based on coherent hidden algebra [3] which provides us another notion of object-orientation. CafeOBJ directly supports behavioral specification and its proof theory through newly introduced language constructs, such as hidden sorts, behavioral operations and behavioral axioms. The system also provided basic supports for coinductive verification methods.

As a result, CafeOBJ preserves the distinctive useful features of OBJ3, and adds new features for coherent hidden algebra, rewriting logic, and their combinations with order sorted algebra. According to a selection of a logic or combinations of logics, system provides different kinds of specification paradigms in a seamless manner.

The SRA implementation supports all of the features described in the report [1], with a minor limitation of parameterized specification realization which may not be so important for practical use. Other important results includes a translator from a specification to an operationally equivalent term rewriting system (TRS) definition. Besides, the translated TRS can be compiled and executed on the fly by *term rewriting engine* which runs as an external process communicating with CafeOBJ system.

---

[5] SRI (Stanford Research), UCSD (Univ. California, San Diego) and LMUM (Univ. Munchen) participated from abroad. You can find more detailed explanation of this project in [11].

3.3 The Third Stage

From 1999 to 2001, a project which aims to practical utilization of formal methods in the are of software component search was formed and carried out by the collaboration of JAIST, Nihon Unisys, Mitsubishi Research Institute and SRA. The project was also supported by IPA and headed by Professor Futatsugi. In this project, we developed search engines for software components hosted by object request brokers (ORBs). Behavioral specification based on coherent hidden algebra was used to allow search by functionalities rather than syntactic features [26].

As mentioned in 3.2, CafeOBJ system had been developed as a language system directly supporting behavioral specifications. The resultant SRA implementation is decided to be used as a core language of this project of component search. During this project, several new features are added to it for supporting automation of the search. A signature matching mechanism was introduced as a new command for the aid of syntactic search of components which produces all possible specification morphisms and they can be used later for further semantical checking, such as refinement verification. System also provides a safety model checking facility (described briefly in later). The verification and model checking are performed by using an inference engine (called PigNose [24, 25]) built on top of CafeOBJ system which will be described in the next section.

4 The Present – Current SRA Implementation

The system has been maintained and is still growing. Recent development includes more additional tools that support coinductive proof of behavioral specification such as an implementation of circular coinductive rewriting [18]. In this section, we show an organizational view of our current implementation. The most recent version can be obtained from ftp://ftp.sra.co.jp/pub/lang/CafeOBJ/.

4.1 Overall View

Figure 2 shows the main system components of the SRA implementation.

In figure 2, "CafeOBJ interpreter" is the component representing the whole system. It is essentially an interpreter of CafeOBJ language, and performs simple interactive sessions with users via terminal I/O, or with external systems through "CafeMaster". CafeMaster provides multiple many to many sessions between several CafeOBJ interpreters and other systems (including human) through TCP/IP port.

The interpreter has an ability of translating specifications to operationally equivalent term rewriting system (TRS) definitions. "TRS compiler" accepts a definition of a TRS and compiles it into *machine code* of "TRAM(Term Rewriting Abstract Machine) runtime system" which performs (order-sorted) term rewriting (modulo ACI) very efficiently (more than 10 times faster than the

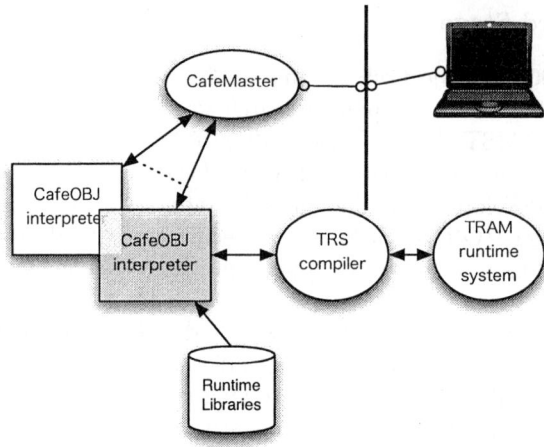

Fig. 2. Components of CafeOBJ System

rewriting of the interpreter). TRS definitions generated by CafeOBJ interpreter have full operational informations of corresponding specifications, but only a subset of them are supported by TRAM. Especially, behavioral specifications are not *executable* in TRAM, while the interpreter offers full operation.

In the sequel, we will set our focus on the interpreter only, and describe its construct in some detail.

4.2 CafeOBJ Interpreter

The interpreter acts like a traditional 'read-eval-print' loop of Lisp interpreter. It accepts full CafeOBJ language, and additionally it provides many useful commands including not only several syntactic checking commands like type checkers and browsers/inspectors of specifications and their constructs but also many semantical tools, such as a varieties of *execution* commands for each logic which performs deductions in a form of term rewriting with special treatments of the corresponding logic. There also exist very powerful term rewriting stepper and tracer which eases debugging of specifications, and a group of commands which supports writing and checking proof scores and verification of specifications.

As showed in the Figure 3, the interpreter consists of 3 major components: (1) **CafeOBJ**, (2) **Chaos** and (3) **PigNose**.

CafeOBJ

This component provides the full language with the syntax defined in [1]. It consists of (a) Listener and (b) Top level Parser: Listener accepts inputs from user or other systems then translates them into representations of the system's intermediate language by consulting to Toplevel Parser. This is essentially a set

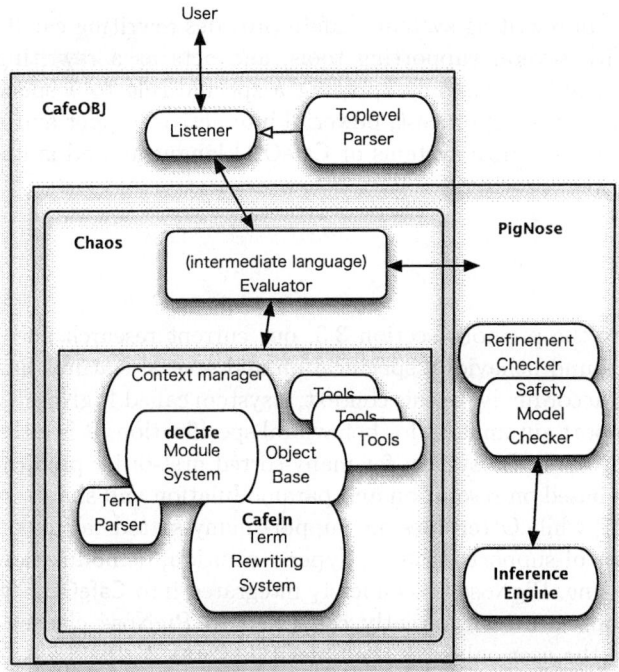

Fig. 3. Main constructs of CafeOBJ interpreter

of abstract syntax trees of CafeOBJ language constructs and commands with associated *evaluators* and *printers*. Listener passes them to Chaos(system kernel) and get the results from it then print them out.

Chaos

This component is the kernel of the system, and is a group of several components each of which provides specific functionality working in cooperative manner. Given a sentence represented in the intermediate language from CafeOBJ component, Evaluator invokes the associated function with a context given by Context manager. In CafeOBJ system, everything runs within some particular context, that is, a CafeOBJ module. Context manager keeps track of the current context (module) and setups appropriate runtime environment.

Invoked functions perform various tasks according to their associated language constructs or commands, such as making semantic objects which will be stored in Object Base, performing term rewriting within a module, showing constructs of a module, etc. Evaluating a module declaration requires parsing of axioms contained in it. This task is done by the Term Parser that accepts full context free grammar. Several kinds of module importations and parameterized module mechanisms are handled by the component deCafe, that also generates a corresponding term rewriting system.

Given a term rewriting system, CafeIn provides rewriting capabilities of various kinds with several supporting tools, and acts as a rewriting laboratory. These tools include commands applying a specific rule to a specific part of a term, tracer of rewriting process, powerful interactive stepper and so on. CafeIn supports all of the logical systems of CafeOBJ language, and is used as a basic engine of theorem proving.

PigNose

As implied by the previous section 3.3, our current research and development focus is set around behavioral specification and several features has been added to the system accordingly. In this context, a system called PigNose was developed aiming to support automation for behavioral specification. It is a theorem prover built on top of CafeOBJ system for many-sorted first-order predicate logic with equality. It is based on resolution and paramodulation and shares many features with Otter [21] while Otter does not support many-sorted calculus. The features include the set of support strategy, hyper-resolution, demodulation and atomic formula rewriting. PigNose is seamlessly integrated into CafeOBJ system in that CafeOBJ axioms are transparently converted to PigNose clauses for theorem proving while the user only sees the CafeOBJ syntax.

Users can invoke the theorem prover for checking provability of the implication formulas. There provided several commands and parameters that set inference strategies and behavior of the engine. Since the task of first-order theorem proving is not decidable in general, it must be terminated when exceeding the predefined limit of computational resources such as the number of generated clauses and the time spent, in which case the result is reported as "unprovable". These limitations can also be specified by a set of commands and parameters.

PigNose also provides two special purpose semantic checkers that uses the power of the inference engine. The one is for refinement verification, and the another is for safety model checking [24, 25].

5 The Future

Formal methods are still expected to improve the practice of software engineering. No doubt formal methods should be better supported by formal specification languages equipped with formal reasoning capability.

CafeOBJ is a formal specification language equipped with verification capability (reduction and resolution engines) based on algebraic techniques. It is an executable wide spectrum language based on multiple logical foundations; mainly based on initial and hidden algebras. Static aspects of systems are specified in terms of initial algebras, and dynamic aspects of systems are specified in terms of hidden algebras.

CafeOBJ is the first algebraic specification language which incorporates observational (or behavioral) specifications based on coherent hidden algebras in a serious way. Observational specifications in CafeOBJ can be seen as a nice combination of static and dynamic specifications, and facilitate natural and transparent specification and verification of complex systems.

There are several levels in using CafeOBJ system as an interactive proof-checker or verifier; the followings are three important ones:

- **Proof Assistant:** Users (human beings) write mathematical proofs in natural language based on specifications in CafeOBJ, and some crucial calculations are passed to the systems to assist necessary logical inferences/calculations.
- **Proof Score Executor:** Users write proof scores in CafeOBJ and CafeOBJ system execute the proof scores; if the result of the executions are as expected, the users can be confident that the specified systems have properties at issue.
- **Automatic Verifier or Model Checker:** Users write assertions which should be proved, and CafeOBJ system verifies the assertions automatically. Usually, PigNose resolution engine is used and the users are supposed to set several parameters of the resolution engine appropriately.

Each of these tree level has its own merit and demerit, and should be chosen depending on problems to be solved and situations. One of the unique features of the current SRA implementation is that it can provide smooth transition between these three levels of proof checking.

Based on extensive experiences of using the current SRA implementation of CafeOBJ for specifying and verifying systems [4, 12, 13, 27, 28, 20], we have a positive observation that the system is usable as a well balanced light weighted specification and verification tools. We are planning to continue the improvement of CafeOBJ language and its implementation, and hope that it will become a fundamental modeling and verification tool for software einginners.

References

1. Razvan Diaconescu and Kokichi Futatsugi: "CafeOBJ *Report*: The Language, Proof Techniques, and Methodologies for Object?]Oriented Algebraic Specification", World Scientific, Vol. 6 of AMAST Series in Computing (ISBN981-02-3513-5), 1998. (174pages)
2. Razvan Diaconescu and Kokichi Futatsugi: Logical Foundations of CafeOBJ, Theoretical Computer Science, 285, pp 289–318, 2002.
3. Razvan Diaconescu and Kokichi Futatsugi: Behavioural Coherence in Object-Oriented Algebraic Specification, Journal of Universal Computer Science, Vol.6, No.1, pp.74-96, 2000.
4. Razvan Diaconescu, Kokichi Futatsugi, Shusaku Iida: Component-based Algebraic Specification and Verification in CafeOBJ, Lecture Notes in Computer Science, 1708, pp.1644-1663, 1999.
5. Kokichi Futatsugi: "Hierarchical Software Development in HISP", in *Computer Science and Technologies 1982*, ed. Kitagawa,T., Japan Annual Review in Electronics, Computers and Telecommunications Series, OHMSHA/North-Holland, pp.151–174, 1982.

6. Kokichi Futatsugi: "An Overview of OBJ2", Proc. of Franco-Japanese Symp. on Programming of Future Generation Computers, Tokyo, Oct. 1986, published as *Programming of Future Generation Computers*, ed. Fuchi,K. and Nivat,M., North-Holland, 1988, pp.139–160.
7. Kokichi Futatsugi: "Trends in Formal Specification Methods based on Algebraic Specification Techniques – from Abstract Data Types to Software Processes: A Personal Perspective –", Proceedings of the International Conference of Information Technology to Commemorating the 30th Anniversary of the Information Processing Society of Japan (InfoJapan'90), October 1990, pp.59-66.
8. Kokichi Futatsugi: Formal Methods in CafeOBJ, Lecture Notes in Computer Science, 2441, pp.1-20, 2002.
9. Kokichi Futatsugi and Koji Okada: "Specification Writing as Construction of hierarchically Structured Clusters of Operators", Proc. of IFIP Congress 80, Tokyo, Oct. 1980, pp. 287–292.
10. Kokichi Futatsugi and Koji Okada: "A Hierarchical Structuring Method for Functional Software Systems", Proc. of the 6th ICSE, pp.393–402, 1982.
11. Kokichi Futatsugi and Ataru Nakagawa: "An Overview of CAFE Specification Environment – an algebraic approach for creating,verifying, and maintaining formal specifications over networks", Proc. Pst Intl. Conf. on Formal Engineering Methods,pp.170-181, IEEE, 1997.
12. Kokichi Futatsugi, Joseph Goguen, Jose Meseguer, editors: "OBJ/CafeOBJ/Maude at Formal Methods '99", The Theta Foundation, Bucharest, Romania, (ISBN 973-99097-1-X), 1999, 241 pages.
13. Kokichi Futatsugi, Aataru Nakagawa, Tetsuo Tamai, editors: "CAFE: An Industiral-Strength Algebraic Formal Method", Elsevier, 2000. (xiv+194 pages)
14. Futatsugi,K., Goguen,J.A., Jouannaud,J.-P., and Meseguer,J., "Principles of OBJ2", Proceedings of the 12th ACM Symposium on Principles of Programming Languages, ACM, 1985, pp.52-66.
15. Futatsugi,K., Goguen,J.A., Meseguer,J.,and Okada,K., "Parameterized Programming in OBJ2", Proc. of the 9th ICSE, IEEE, 1987, pp.51–60.
16. Joseph A. Goguen and Jose Meseguer: "Order-Sorted Algebra I: Equational Deduction for Multiple Inheritance, Overloading, Exceptions and Partial Operations", Theoretical Computer Science, Vol 105, No. 2, pp.217-273, 1992.
17. Joseph Goguen and Grant Malcolm: "A hidden agenda", Theoretical Computer Science, Vol. 245, No. 1, pp. 55–101, 2000.
18. Goguen,J.A., Lin,K., Rosu,G., "Circular Coinductive Rewriting" in Proceedings, Automated Software Enginnering 00, IEEE, 2000, pp.123–131.
19. Joseh Goguen, Timoth Winkler, Jose Meseguer, Kokichi Futatsugi, and Jean-Perre Jouannaud: "Introducing OBJ", in Joseph Goguen and Grant Malcolm, editors, "Software Engineering with OBJ", Kluwer Academic Publishers, pp.3–167, 2000.
20. Michihiro Matsumoto and Kokichi Futatsugi: Highly Reliable Component-Based Software Development by using Algebraic Behavioral Specification, Proceedings of ICFEM'2000, IEEE CS Press, pp.35-43, 2000.
21. McCune, W.: OTTER 3.0 Reference Manual and Guide.
    http://www-unix.mcs.anl.gov/AR/otter/
22. Jose Meseguer: "A logical theory of cuncurrent objects", In *ECOOP-OOPSLA'90 Conference on Object-Oriented Programming*, ACM, pp.101-115, 1990.
23. Jose Meseguer: "Conditional rewriting logic as a unified model of cuncurrency", Theoretical Computer Science, 96, pp.73-155, 1992.

24. Akira Mori and Kokichi Futatsugi: Verifying Behavioural Specifications in CafeOBJ Environment. Proc. of *World Congress on Formal Methods FM'99, Lecture Notes in Computer Science* **1709**, 1625–1643, 1999.
25. Akira Mori and Kokichi Futatsugi: CafeOBJ as a tool for behavioral system specification, in Proc. of Symposium on Software Security 2002, Springer LNCS, 2002.
26. Akira Mori, Toshimi Sawada, Kokichi Futatsugi, Akishi Seo, and Masaki Ishiguro: Software Component Search based on Behavioral Specification, Proc . of International Symposium on Future Software Technology, ISFST'2001, November, 2001.
27. Kazuhiro Ogata and Kokichi Futatsugi: Flaw and modification of the iKP electronic payment protocols, Information Processing Letters, 2002.
28. Kazuhiro Ogata and Kokichi Futatsugi: Formal analysis of the iKP electric payment protocols, in Proc. of Symposium on Software Security 2002, Springer LNCS, 2002.
29. Smolka,G., Nutt,W. Goguen,J., and Meseguer,J., "Order-Sorted Equational Computation" *Resolution of Equations in Algebraic Structures, Vol 2., Rewriting Techniques*, eds H. Aït-Kaci and M. Nivat, Academic Press, Inc., pp.297–368, 1989.
30. Srinivas,Y.V., Jülling,R., "SPECWARE: Formal Support for Composing Software" Tech. Reprot KES.U.94.5, Kestrel Institute, 1994.

On Failures and Faults[1]

Brian Randell

School of Computing Science
University of Newcastle upon Tyne

Abstract. Real computer-based systems fail, and hence are often far less dependable than their owners and users need and desire. Individuals, organisations and indeed the world at large are becoming more dependent on such systems, so there has been much work on trying to gain increased understanding of the many and varied types of faults that need to be prevented or tolerated in order to reduce the probability and severity of system failures. In this paper I analyze the concept of system faults and failures, and discuss the assumptions that are often made by computing system designers regarding faults, and a number of continuing research issues related to fault tolerance.

Keywords: Dependability, formal concepts, fault assumptions.

1 On Fault-Tolerant Computing

The direct origins of modern fault-tolerant computing lie in John von Neumann's influential work in the early 1950s on "Probabilistic Logic and the Synthesis of Reliable Organisms from Unreliable Components" [22]. In the 1950s and 1960s much work was done on hardware fault tolerance, from the (widespread) use of error detecting and correcting codes, to the more exotic realms of replicated processors, automatic reconfiguration, etc., used in highly demanding environments, e.g. in aerospace. However, in the software world, the notion of dependability was still equated to that of correctness – indeed, of perfecting the software development process.

In 1968 I participated in the first NATO Software Engineering Conference at Garmisch in Bavaria [17]. The participants constituted a broad international cross-section of industry, government and academia. What was special and novel about this conference was the readiness of these participants to face up to the at times very serious faults in the whole process by means of which software was then specified, designed, implemented and deployed. The impact of this conference, particularly on many of the attendees, was therefore immense. For example, both Edsger Dijkstra and I later went on record as to how the discussions at this conference on the "software crisis" had strongly influenced our thinking and our subsequent research activities. In his case the discussions prompted his study of formal approaches to producing high quality, indeed formally validated, programs. In my case they led me to the belief that large software systems would essentially always contain residual design faults and,

---

[1] Much of this paper is based closely on some of the material in my BCS/IEE 1999 Turing Memorial Lecture [19].

following my move to Newcastle soon after the Garmisch Conference, to the then novel and controversial idea that it was worth trying to find means by which such systems could nevertheless be made adequately reliable. (As I've remarked before, our respective choices of research problems suitably reflect our relative skills as programmers.)

A detailed study that I and my colleagues were commissioned to make in 1970 of a number of large on-line computer systems confirmed that software faults were a major cause of undependability in these systems, and more importantly, resulted in our finding that:

(i) a significant fraction of the code in these systems was aimed at detecting and recovering from errors caused by hardware and operational faults,
(ii) this code was ad hoc and limited in its capability, e.g. concerning the possibility of concurrent faults, or of further errors being detected while error recovery was already being attempted, yet
(iii) nevertheless, somewhat fortuitously, these error recovery facilities did in fact help to provide a useful measure of software fault tolerance.

This study marked the start of a still-continuing, and indeed now greatly-expanded, programme of research at Newcastle on system dependability, and in particular fault tolerance (for various types of fault), which has been funded by a succession of research grants from UK and European government sources, and from industry. The subject of fault tolerance continues, even thirty years later, to fascinate me – my aim in this talk is to try to explain why.

2 On Dependability Concepts

The concept of a "fault" is surprisingly subtle – or, as I would prefer to put it, "gloriously recursive". Indeed, clarifying the concepts related to dependability is difficult – and hence vitally important – when one is talking about systems in which

(i) there is potential confusion regarding the placement and nature of system boundaries
(ii) the very complexity of the systems (and their specification, if they have one) is a major problem,
(iii) judgements as to possible causes or consequences of failure can be very subtle, and
(iv) there are (fallible) provisions for preventing faults from causing failures.

From early on in our work at Newcastle on software fault tolerance we realised the inadequacy, with regard to residual design faults, of the definitions of terms such as fault and error used at that time by hardware designers. The problem was that they took as the basis of their definitions a set of terms for a few well-known forms of fault, such as "stuck-at-zero" faults, "bridging" faults, etc. This approach did not seem at all appropriate for thinking about residual design faults, given the huge variety, and the lack of any useful classification, of such faults. In fact, we eventually realised that we could achieve the generality we needed by starting not from faults, but from the concept of a system "failure" [20].

The ensuing generality of our definitions led us to start using the term "reliability" in a much broader sense than was then common, since a system might fail in all sorts of ways – it might deliver the wrong results, work too slowly, fail to protect confidential information, lead to someone's death, or whatever. Our overgeneralisation of the term "reliability" was not well received, and it was a French colleague, Jean-Claude Laprie of LAAS-CNRS, who came to our linguistic rescue by proposing the use of the term "dependability" [13] for the concept underlying our broadened definition. The term dependability thus can be seen as including, as special cases, such properties as availability, reliability, safety, confidentiality, integrity, etc. These are illustrated in Figure 1, taken from [14], as being attributes of dependability.

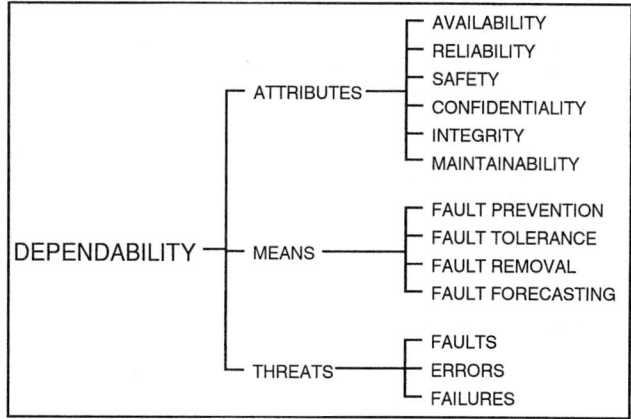

Fig. 1. The dependability tree

Quoting from the latest published version of the dependability definitions [3][2].

> "A system **failure** occurs when the delivered service deviates from fulfilling the system **function**, the latter being what the system is *aimed at.*."

The phrase "what the system is aimed at" is a means of avoiding reference to a system "specification" – since it is not unusual for a system's lack of dependability to be due to inadequacies in its documented specification. (I return to the issue of inadequate specifications below.)

Systems of interest will possess an internal state:

> "An **error** is that part of the system state which is *liable to lead to subsequent failure*: an error affecting the service is an indication that a failure occurs or has occurred. The *adjudged or hypothesised cause* of an error is a **fault**."

Note that an error may be judged to have multiple causes, and does not necessarily lead to a failure – for example error recovery might be attempted successfully and failure averted.

---

[2] A revised edition of the definitions in [13] and [14].

"A failure occurs when an error 'passes through' the system-user interface and affects the service delivered by the system – a system of course being composed of components which are themselves systems. Thus the manifestation of failures, faults and errors follows a "fundamental chain":

$$\ldots \to \text{failure} \to \text{fault} \to \text{error} \to \text{failure} \to \text{fault} \to \ldots"$$

One example of this fundamental chain is as follows:

"the result of a programmer's error is a (dormant) fault in the written software (faulty instruction(s) or data); upon activation (invoking the component where the fault resides and triggering the faulty instruction, instruction sequence or data by an appropriate input pattern) the fault becomes active and produces an error; if and when the erroneous data affect the delivered service (in value and/or in timing of their delivery), a failure occurs." [12].

The recognition of the importance of this chain – which takes the form of

$$\ldots \to \text{event} \to \text{cause} \to \text{state} \to \text{event} \to \text{cause} \to \ldots$$

led to a great increase in our ability to understand, and to design means of ameliorating, all sorts of complex manifestations of undependability. This chain can go from one system to:

(i) some enclosing system of which it is a component,
(ii) another essentially separate system with which it is deployed, or from
(iii) a further system(s) that it creates

Let me illustrate some of these possibilities by a further example:

A fighter plane crashed killing the pilot – it turned out that it had for a period before this failure (i.e. the crash) been calculating its position erroneously, and that this was due to it having been fitted with the wrong (albeit correctly functioning) inertial navigation subsystem. One could describe this as the fault. In fact, this fault had arisen as the result of a failure of the (largely human) system responsible for maintaining the plane. But this failure (i.e. the act of installing the wrong inertial navigation subsystem) could in part be blamed on a much earlier failure of the system that had specified and designed the whole plane maintenance system; it had created a situation in which two functionally distinct inertial navigation subsystems had identical mechanical interfaces, and catalogue numbers that differed by only one in the least significant digit! This was surely a situation that was a positive invitation to disaster. In fact it was eventually determined that the erroneous catalogue number had been generated as a result of a hitherto un-noticed failure by the computerised inventory control system. This failure was due to the fact that an overflow had occurred from a quantity field into the catalogue number field, in a COBOL program that contained no checks against overflow. So, here we have a whole set of different systems, and a complicated chain, in which failures in one system constituted faults in other systems that created erroneous states which were not corrected but instead led to further failures.

This did actually happen. The good news is that the overall inventory control process, which was part-manual, part-automated, was in other respects so well designed and managed that it was possible to determine when the overflow had occurred and which other planes also had been fitted with the wrong inertial navigation subsystem – so other impending fatalities were averted. In fact, some of the most important sources of the whole subject of database transactions and integrity controls derive in large part from this work, which was carried out by C.T. Davies, first for the U.S. Air Force, and later at IBM, and led to the creation of the very influential "spheres of control" concept [6].

The wording that has been in use for some time as a definition of computer system dependability *per se* is:

> **Dependability** is defined as that property of a computer system such that *reliance can justifiably be placed on the service* it delivers. (The service delivered by a system is its behaviour *as it is perceptible* by its user(s); a user is another system (human or physical) which *interacts* with the former.)"

I now feel it possible, and worthwhile, to improve on the definition of "failure" in order to make explicit the judgement that is involved, and to use this more directly in the definition of dependability. First the alternative definition of failure:

> A given system, operating in some particular environment (a wider system), may fail in the sense that some other system makes, or could in principle have made, a *judgement* that the activity or inactivity of the given system constitutes **failure**.

The second system, the judgemental system, may be an automated system, a human being, the relevant judicial authority or whatever. (It may or may not have a documented system specification to guide it.) Different judgemental systems might, of course, come to different decisions regarding the given system. Moreover, such a judgemental system might itself fail – in the eyes of some other judgemental system – a possibility that is well understood by the legal system, with its hierarchy of courts. So, we can have a (recursive) notion of "failure" which is defined merely in terms of what are taken as the fundamental, dictionary-defined, concepts of "system" and "judgement", and which clearly is a relative rather than an absolute notion. So then is the concept of dependability:

> The concept of **dependability** can be simply defined as "the quality or characteristic of being dependable", where the adjective "dependable" is attributed to a system whose failures are judged sufficiently rare or insignificant.

It should be noted that these definitions, and the four basic means of obtaining and establishing high dependability, namely fault prevention, fault tolerance, fault removal and fault forecasting, are as applicable to human and industrial systems, as they are to computer systems. In particular they are applicable to the part-manual part-automated systems, i.e. "computer-based systems", including those that are used to design and implement computer systems. This generality, and the explicit role given to judgement, are important given the subtleties that are sometimes involved in identifying the exact boundaries of the various systems of concern, of resolving disagreements regarding the acceptability of a system's specified and/or actual behaviour, and of determining how blame should be apportioned after a system fails.

2.1 Concept Formalisation

In fact, since a first version of this discussion was published [19], my colleague Cliff Jones has, to my great delight, taken up very seriously the problem of providing a formalisation of these basic dependability concepts. I have long regretted the lack of such a formalisation, since I recall how much benefit I, at least, obtained from my collaboration many years ago with Jim Horning on a paper for Computing Surveys on process structuring concepts [10]. (This paper interlaced informal and formal definitions of a large number of concepts related to processes, process combination and process abstraction, using a few rather basic mathematical concepts, such as sets, sequences, relations, and functions.) Subsequently, much of my research, in particular my recent involvement in work on Co-ordinated Atomic Actions (see below), has been greatly helped by the efforts of my more formal colleagues,

The formalisation of the basic dependability concepts in [11] is introduced in the following terms:

> "The idea here is to offer definitions of [the terms *fault, error, failure*] with respect to a particular notion of what constitutes a system. . . . The intention here is not to offer formalism for its own sake. In fact the details of the particular notation, etc., are unimportant. The hope is that understanding can be increased by employing a firm foundation. [. . .] some interesting relationships between systems are explored. The propagation of *fault, error, failure* chains where one system is *built on* another system are well-understood. Many of the failure propagation systems of interest in socio-technical systems arise when one system is *created by* another. Lastly, the idea of one system being *deployed with* another is considered."

The systems that are dealt with are thus both technical and socio-technical (e.g. computer-based) systems, and include systems (e.g. "real-time" control systems) that are linked to processes that evolve autonomously. The formalism Cliff uses is in fact VDM, though he points out that Z and B would be equally appropriate.

One of the main divergences between Cliff and myself concerns the role played by a "specification". Quoting again from his paper:

> "[My view] is that the judgement that a system fails can only be made against a specification. What if the "specification is wrong"? Presumably, this means that the specification is in some sense inappropriate; the specification might be precise, but it can be seen to result in faults and failures in a bigger system. For example, a specification might state that a developer can assume that the user might respond in one micro-second but failing to so do can result in fatal consequences. The developer writes a program which "times out"

after one micro-second and an accident occurs. It surely is not right to say that the software system (which meets its specification) is failing. Nor of course is it reasonable to blame "operator error" with such an unreasonable assumption. The only reasonable conclusion is that it is an earlier system which exhibited erroneous behaviour: the act of producing the silly specification is the failure that caused a fault in the combined system of software and operator. The judgement that a specification is "silly" must of course be made by another (external) system. A similar argument can be made for missing specifications: an engineering process requires a reference point."

I remain to be convinced on this point. I have seen systems whose facilities and interfaces are so intuitive and well-chosen that users can immediately understand how to operate them, and have to turn to the manual, assuming there is one, only in extremis. Moreover, they can with little difficulty recognize any such failures as do occur as being failures by their inconsistency with respect to other aspects of the perceived behaviour of the system. On the other hand, in my experience specifications of large computer or computer-based systems are rarely complete, in the sense that one can guarantee that any implementation that satisfies the specification will be regarded as fully satisfactory by the people who are in a position to judge the system. Rather, specifications should act as constraints, possibly extremely detailed constraints, that enable one to state various (pre-conceived) ways in which a system would be regarded as inadequate.

The notion of the superiority of such "negative" specifications is in fact one of the important ideas in Alexander's very influential book "Notes on the Synthesis of Form" [1]:

". . . every design problem begins with an effort to achieve fitness between two entities: the form in question and its context. The form is the solution to the problem; the context defines the problem. In other words, when we speak of design, the real object of discussion is not the form alone, but the ensemble comprising the form and its context. Good fit is a desired property of this ensemble which relates to some particular division of the ensemble into form and context. . . . It seems as though in practice the concept of good fit, describing only the absence of such failures and hence leaving us nothing concrete to refer to in explanation, can only be explained indirectly; it is, in practice, the disjunction of all possible misfits.

In the case of a design problem which is truly problematical, we . . . have no intrinsic way of reducing the potentially infinite set of requirements to finite terms. Yet for practical reasons we do need some way of picking a finite set from the infinite set of possible ones. In the case of requirements, no sensible way of picking this finite set presents itself. From a purely descriptive standpoint we have no way of knowing which of the infinitely many relations between form and context to include, and which ones to leave out. But if we think of the requirements from a negative point of view, as misfits, there is a simple way of picking a finite set. This is because it is through misfit that the problem originally brings itself to our attention. We take just those relations between form and context which obtrude most strongly, which demand attention most clearly, which seem most likely to go wrong. We cannot do better than this. . . .

In the case of a real design problem, even our conviction that there is such a thing as fit to be achieved is curiously flimsy and insubstantial. We are searching for some kind of harmony between two intangibles; a form which we have not yet designed, and a context we cannot properly describe. The only reason we have for thinking that there must be some kind of fit to be achieved between them is that we can detect incongruities, or negative instances of it.

Such detection of course involves judgement – both while the design is being created, and for any resulting real (i.e. fallible) system, while this system is deployed. Hence my view is that system specifications are, at least conceptually, just a valuable adjunct to an authoritative judgement system. (An analogy I would make is to the notion of a contract – normally one would expect this to be written and signed – but in some situations and environments a handshake will be equally acceptable and indeed binding in law.) But in practice, as stated in [11], "it is difficult to see how an engineering process can be used to create a system where there is no initial notion of specifying the required properties of the to-be-created artefact". One can hardly rely entirely on some scheme of having all the designers continuously interrogating a judge throughout the design process! However, with regard to dependability concept definitions, I still prefer to avoid involving reference to a specification.

For example, Cliff's specification-oriented approach led him to the following definition of the notion of an error: "An error is present when the state of a system is inconsistent with that required by the specification". In contrast, the definition I am used to is: "An error is that part of the system state that may cause a subsequent failure: a failure occurs when an error reaches the service interface and alters the service." No doubt this definition could be clarified through formalisation, but I feel this should be done using judgement rather than specification as a starting point.

This is because, in my view, there will often be considerable subjective judgement involved in identifying errors, particularly errors due to design faults in complex software. Once a fault has been activated, all subsequent state transitions up to the occurrence of a failure are to be regarded as errors. However, identifying the fault occurrence involves deciding which instruction, or set of instructions, is incorrect or missing, i.e. how the faulty program compares with "the" correct program. But there could be several, equally sensible ways of correcting a program, and hence identifications of the location of "the" fault in the code, the moment when it was activated, and its subsequent errors – and it is not evident that a specification could or should be so detailed as to provide means of adjudicating between these different equally-correct programs.

A rather different situation, also illustrating the distinction between these two definitions of error, is that of a system failure which comes to be regarded as due to some earlier failure of another system, either one it is deployed with, or one it was created by. The state of the given system prior to its failure will be erroneous by the definition that I favour. This is the case even if is decided that the given system was correctly processing the faulty inputs it received, or is correctly interpreting the faulty design that it incorporates, (so that its state is in all probability consistent with its specification, should one have been documented).

Nevertheless, despite such differences of approach, I very much welcome Cliff's contribution to the development and fomalisation of dependability concepts, and hope to contribute to extending it to deal with further basic dependability concepts. One such is that of "dependence" – which, perhaps surprisingly, has not been dealt with in the standard accounts of dependability concepts and terminology, so is the main point I deal with next.

2.2 Dependence, Trust and Confidence

It is commonplace to say that the dependability of a system should suffice for the dependence being placed on that system. What we term the "dependence of system A on system B" is thus a measure of the impact of B's undependability on A's dependability. Clearly, this can vary from total dependence (any failure of B will cause A to fail) to complete independence (B cannot cause A to fail). In other words, dependence can be defined as a measure of the difference between the dependability that A would have, were B to be totally dependable, with that which A has in the presence of the actual (presumably less than fully dependable) B.

If there is reason to believe that B's dependability is insufficient for A's required dependability, the former must be enhanced, and/or A's dependence reduced, and/or additional means of fault tolerance introduced "between" A and B, e.g. in the form of a "wrapper".

The concept of dependence leads on to those of "trust" and "confidence", two terms that are much in current vogue in the EU IST Programme. (Another word in common use in some circles is "trustworthiness" – which I in fact regard as being synonomous with "dependability.") In my view, trust can very conveniently be defined as "accepted dependence" – i.e. the dependence (say of A on B) allied to a judgement that this level of dependence is acceptable. Such a judgement (made by or on behalf of A) about B is possibly explicit, and even laid down in a contract between A and B, but might be only implicit, even unthinking. Indeed it might even be unwilling – in that A has no alternative option but to put its trust in B.

Thus to the extent that A trusts B, it need not assume responsibility for, i.e. provide means of tolerating, B's failures. (The question of whether it is capable of doing this is another matter.). Indeed, turning things around, the extent to which A fails to provide means of tolerating B's faults is a measure of A's (perhaps unthinking or unwilling) trust in B.

Thus the notion of trust is applicable to technical or socio-technical systems, as well as to humans. A distinction between trust and confidence is that the former leads to the act of becoming dependent, the latter is inapplicable to technical systems, since it concerns how some human, or group of humans, might feel about this act. A system which provides evidence which can be used to attempt to justify A's trust in B, i.e. to provide confidence regarding A's dependence on B, can itself of course fail. One type of failure of such a confidence-building system (which might be system A itself), produces an underestimate of A's dependence on B, which could lead to a decision to avoid using B, even though B is adequately dependable. What is normally a more serious type of failure of a confidence-building system puts A at unacceptable risk of failing due to a failure of B, i.e. of a "trusted" system turning out to be "untrustworthy".

2.3 Concepts and Terminology

This continued interest that I and a number of people involved in dependability research take in concepts and definitions perhaps seems rather pedantic, though I believe it is fully justified. One reason of course is the subtleties involved, and the need to clarify them. Another is the fact that a number of what are essentially dependability concepts are being re-invented (sometimes rather incompetently), or at least re-named, in numerous research communities, which variously categorise their area of interest as safety, survivability, trustworthiness, security, critical infrastructure protection, information survivability, or whatever.

The issue of whether the different research communities use a common set of terms is much less important than their failure to recognise that they are concerning themselves with (different facets of) the same concept. One consequence is that they are not getting as much advantage from each other's insights and advances as they might. However, regardless of the terminology employed, I believe it is very important to have, and to use, some term for the general concept, i.e. that which is associated with a *fully general notion of failure* as opposed to one which is restricted in some way to particular types, causes or consequences of failure. (I also believe it is essential to have separate terms for the three essentially different concepts named here *"fault"*, *"error"* and *"failure"* – since otherwise one cannot deal properly with the complexities (and realities) of failure-prone components, being assembled together in possibly incorrect ways, so resulting in failure-prone systems.) Only when this is done will, I believe, the researchers take an adequately general approach to the problems that they are attempting to tackle. And if I manage to put over only one point in this lecture – this is the one I hope it will be.

In fact, time and time again it seems to me that muddled thinking about dependability-related notions has been a barrier to progress – most recently I have been alerted to this in the work of the "intrusion detection" research community. This community concerns itself with a major aspect of the problem of protecting computer networks and networked computers from hackers. As some of the researchers involved have admitted, the community has got itself into very confused and confusing debates as it tries to expand its horizons beyond the problem of merely detecting the fact that some hacker is, or has recently been, intruding into a system. I will return to this topic later.

3 On Fault Classification

As I have indicated, the faults that might affect a computer-based system are many and varied. A detailed classification is provided by Laprie [14], the first part of which is summarised in Figure 2.

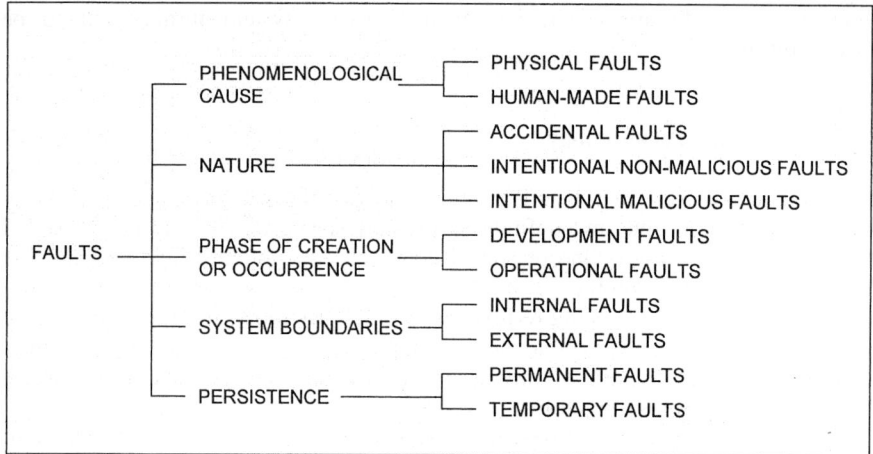

Fig. 2. Fault classification

The actual application of this classification itself involves judgement. For example, is a hardware component that occasionally fails as a result of electronic interference suffering temporary operational physical faults, or should one regard it as having been provided with inadequate shielding, i.e. regard the situation as being due to a permanent human-made development fault? Nevertheless, such classifications can provide useful guidance, in particular with regard to planning means of fault prevention, tolerance, diagnosis, and removal, based on the designer's assumptions about likely faults. Actual automated fault tolerance strategies can however make only limited use of such classifications, depending on the extent to which faults can be quickly and accurately recognised as belonging to a class for which some specialised fault tolerance measure is particularly appropriate. This is often not feasible – for example, it is often difficult to be sure whether the immediate cause of an error is an operational hardware fault or a residual software design fault, so if both possibilities are to be allowed for a very general fault tolerance strategy must be employed.

Logical, or qualitative, classification is however just a starting point. All work on system dependability is, or at any rate should be, guided by considerations of relative probabilities. There is little point, for example, in providing a parity bit with each byte being transmitted over a network if the most common form of fault causes long bursts of errors. Similarly, there is little point employing expensive and time-consuming code verification tools if in a particular application domain virtually all the significant failures arise from inadequate system specifications. The success with which one can design a system that will achieve some required level fault of tolerance therefore depends on the quality of the statistics that are available, or of the statistical assumptions made by the designers, concerning the faults that will occur.

In principle, and often in practice, one can have relatively accurate statistics concerning operational hardware faults, detailed enough to provide very useful guidance as to what specific fault tolerance measures are needed where, and what ones are not worth their cost. When it comes to residual design faults, such statistics as are available are too imprecise to be of much use, so fault tolerance provisions have to be very general. Thus one of the motivations behind the original recovery

```
            ensure    acceptance test
            by        primary alternate
            else by   alternate 2
                          .
                          .
            else by   alternate n
            else      error
```

Fig. 3. The Recovery Block Structure

block scheme [9] was to provide means of error recovery that would work (almost) no matter what fault existed where in the suspect program.

With the program structuring scheme that we developed this was the case so long as the underlying recovery and control mechanism was not corrupted. However, the degree to which the error recovery mechanism could be used to provide successful fault tolerance, i.e., enable the program to continue and produce satisfactory results, of course depended on the adequacy of the programmer-supplied error detection measures (such as acceptance tests) and last-ditch alternate blocks. Our first demonstration recovery block system involved a fault-tolerant application program containing a complete acceptance test and final alternate block, running on a simulated machine which completely confined programs within their allotted resources. We then provided visitors with means of making arbitrary changes to the code of any or all of the alternate blocks (other than the final one) in the running application program – the challenge to them being to find some means of preventing the program from producing correct results. Within a short period of time this demonstration system had been honed to the point where no visitors were able to subvert it. This demonstration was a very compelling one.

The demonstration in fact indicated that when the concern is with the possibility of malicious faults the only sensible thing is to assume that the situation is statistically as bad as could be imagined – that faults occur at locations, in circumstances, and with a frequency, that are essentially "pessimal" from a designer's viewpoint. (The term "pessimal" is in fact not in the dictionary, though its meaning, and the need for such a word, are I claim both self-evident.) I will return to the problems of tolerating malicious faults later.

4 On Fault Assumptions

The problems of preventing faults in systems from leading to system failures vary greatly in difficulty depending on the (it is hoped justified) assumptions that the designers make about the nature as well as the frequency of the faults, and the effectiveness of the fault tolerance mechanisms that are employed. For example, one might choose to assume that operational hardware faults can be cost-effectively masked (i.e. hidden) by the use of hardware replication and voting, and that any residual software design faults can be adequately masked by the use of design diversity, i.e. using N-version programming. In such circumstances error recovery is not needed. In many realistic situations, however, if the likelihood of a failure is to be kept within acceptable bounds, error recovery facilities will have to be provided, in addition to whatever fault prevention and fault masking techniques are used.

In a decentralised system, i.e. one whose activity can be usefully modelled by a set of partly independent threads of control, the problems of error recovery will vary greatly depending on what design assumptions can be justified. For example, if the designer concerns him/herself simply with a distributed database system and disallows (i.e. ignores) the possibility of undetected invalid inputs or outputs, the errors that have to be recovered from will essentially all be ones that are wholly within the computer system. In this situation backward error recovery (i.e. recovery to an earlier, it is hoped error-free, state) will suffice, and be readily implementable, such is the nature of computer storage. If such a system is serving the needs of a set of essentially independent users, competing against each other to access and perhaps update the database, then the now extensive literature on database transaction processing and protocols can provide a fertile source of well-engineered, and mathematically well-founded, solutions to such problems [8].

However, the multiple activities in a decentralised system will often not simply be competing against each other for access to some shared internal resource, but rather will on occasion at least be attempting to co-operate with each other, in small or large groups, in pursuit of some common goal. This will make the provision of backward error recovery more complicated than is the case in basic transaction-oriented systems. And the problem of avoiding the "domino effect"[20], in which a single fault can lead to a whole sequence of rollbacks, will be much harder if one cannot disallow (i.e. ignore) the possibility of undetected invalid communications between activities.

When a system of interacting threads employs backward recovery, each thread will be continually establishing and discarding checkpoints, and may also on occasion need to restore its state to one given in a previously established checkpoint. But if interactions are not controlled, and appropriately co-ordinated with checkpoint management, then the rollback of one thread can result in a cascade of rollbacks that could push all the threads back to their beginnings.

However, the domino effect would not occur if it could safely be assumed that data was fully validated before it was output, i.e. was transmitted from one thread to another. (Similarly, the effect would be avoided if a thread could validate its inputs fully.) Such an assumption is in effect made in simple transaction-based systems, in which outputs are allowed to occur only after a transaction has been "committed". Moreover, in such systems the notion of commitment is regarded as absolute, so that once the commitment has been made, there is no going back, i.e. there is no provision

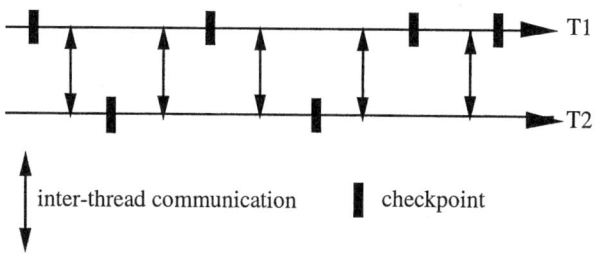

Fig. 4. The domino effect

for the possibility that an output was invalid. The notion of nested transactions can be used to limit the amount of activity that has to be abandoned when backward recovery (of small inner transactions) is invoked. However, this notion typically still assumes that there are absolute "outermost" transactions, and that outputs to the world outside the database system, e.g. to the users, that take place after such outermost transactions end must be presumed to be valid.

The conversation scheme [4] provides a means of co-ordinating the recovery provisions of interacting threads so as to avoid the domino effect, without making assumptions regarding output or input validation. Figure 5 shows an example where three threads communicate within a conversation and the threads T1 and T2 communicate within a nested conversation. (Not all of these threads need represent activity inside a computer – some might represent activity in its environment.) Communication can only take place between threads that are participating in a conversation together, so while T1 and T2 are in their inner conversation they cannot damage or be damaged by T3.

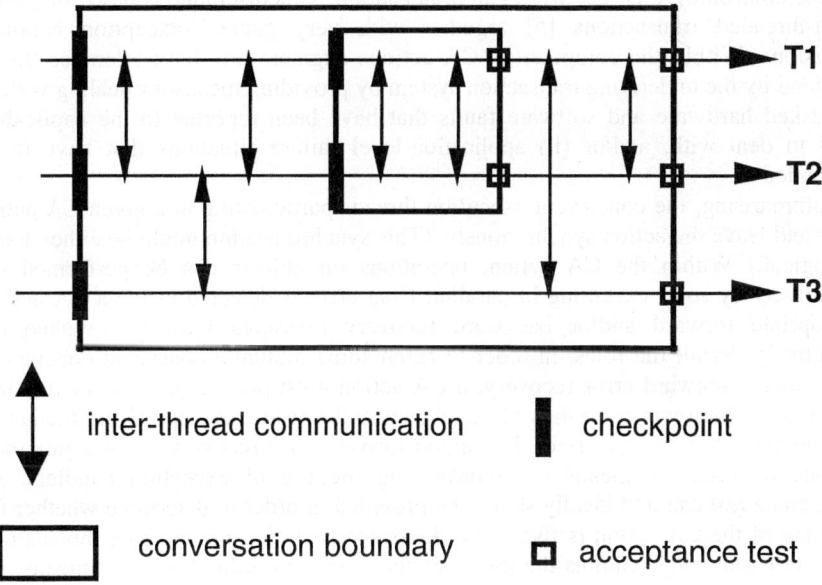

Fig. 5. Nested conversations

The operation of a conversation is as follows: (i) on entry to a conversation a thread establishes a checkpoint; (ii) if an error is detected by any thread then all the participating threads must restore their checkpoints; (iii) after restoration all threads then attempt to make further progress; and (iv) all threads leave the conversation together, only if all pass any acceptance tests that are provided. (If this is not possible, the conversation fails – a situation that causes the enclosing conversation to invoke backward error recovery at its level.)

Both transactions and conversations are examples of atomic actions [16], in that viewed from the outside, they appear to perform their activity as a single indivisible action. (In practice transaction-support systems also implement other properties, such as "durability", i.e. a guarantee that the results produced by completed transactions will not be lost as a result of a computer hardware fault.) And both rely on backward error recovery.

However, systems are usually not made up just of computers – rather they will also involve other entities (e.g. devices and humans) which in many cases will not be able to simply forget some of their recent activity, and so simply go straight back to an exact earlier state when told that an error has been detected. Thus forward error recovery (the typical programming mechanism for which is exception handling), rather than backward recovery will have to be used. Each of these complications individually makes the task of error recovery more difficult, and together they make it much more challenging. This in fact is the topic that I and colleagues have concentrated on these last few years.

Our Co-ordinated Atomic (CA) Action scheme [23] was arrived at as a result of work on extending the conversation concept so as to allow for the use of forward error recovery, and to allow for both co-operative and competitive concurrency. CA actions can be regarded as providing a discipline, both for programming computers and for controlling their use within an organisation. This discipline is based on nested multi-threaded transactions [5] together with very general exception handling provisions. Within the computer(s), CA actions augment any fault tolerance that is provided by the underlying transaction system by providing means for dealing with (i) unmasked hardware and software faults that have been reported to the application level to deal with, and/or (ii) application-level failure situations that have to be responded to.

Summarising, the concurrent execution threads participating in a given CA action enter and leave the action synchronously. (This synchronisation might be either actual or logical.) Within the CA action, operations on objects can be performed co-operatively by *roles* executing in parallel. If an error is detected inside a CA action, appropriate forward and/or backward recovery measures must be invoked co-operatively, by all the roles, in order to reach some mutually consistent conclusion. To support backward error recovery, a CA action must provide a recovery line that co-ordinates the recovery points of the objects and threads participating in the action so as to avoid the domino effect. To support forward error recovery, a CA action must provide an effective means of co-ordinating the use of exception handlers. An *acceptance test* can and ideally should be provided in order to determine whether the outcome of the CA action is successful. Error recovery for participating threads of a CA action generally requires the use of explicit error co-ordination mechanisms, i.e. exception handling or backward error recovery within the CA action; objects that are external to the CA action and so can be shared with other actions and threads must provide their own error co-ordination mechanisms and behave atomically with respect to other CA actions and threads.

Figure 6 shows an example in which two concurrent threads enter a CA action in order to play the corresponding roles. Within the CA action the two concurrent roles communicate with each other and manipulate the external objects co-operatively in pursuit of some common goal – portrayed in the Figure by the arrow from Role 1 to Role 2. However, during the execution of the CA action, an exception e is raised by Role 2. Role 1 is then informed of the exception and both roles transfer control to their respective exception handlers H1 and H2 for this particular exception, which then attempt to perform forward error recovery. (When multiple exceptions are raised within an action, a resolution algorithm based on an exception resolution graph [4,

27] is used to identify the appropriate "covering" exception, and hence the set of exception handlers to be used in this situation.) The effects of erroneous operations on external objects are repaired, if possible, by putting the objects into new correct states so that the CA action is able to exit with an acceptable outcome. The two threads leave the CA action synchronously at the end of the action.

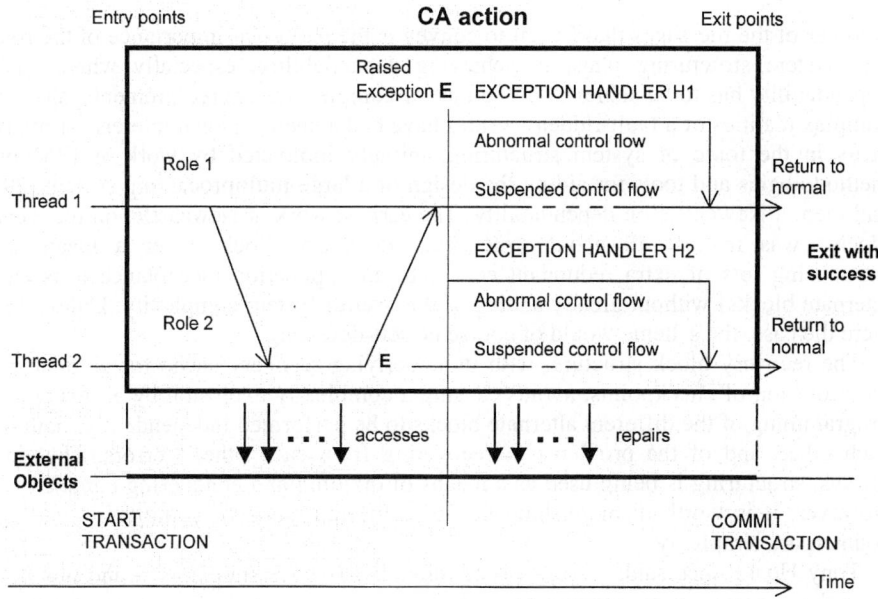

Fig. 6. Example of a CA Action

In general, the desired effect of performing a CA action is specified by an acceptance test. The effect only becomes visible if the test is passed. The acceptance test allows both a normal outcome and one or more exceptional (or degraded) outcomes, with each exceptional outcome signalling a specified exception to the surrounding environment (typically a larger CA action).

We have in recent years, with colleagues in several EU-funded research projects, investigated the advantages and limitations of this approach to structuring systems so as to facilitate the design and validation of sophisticated error recovery, through a series of detailed case studies. Publications describing these include [21, 24-26, 28].

However, my purpose in describing this particular line of development in fault tolerance was not so much to argue the merits of CA actions, but rather to illustrate the crucial role that a designer's choice of fault assumptions should make in directing the subsequent design activity. (For example, the vast majority of research, and practice, in the distributed systems world assumes that a computer fails by crashing – i.e. is a "fail-silent" device, despite the existence of evidence that this is by no means always the case.) The crucial nature of this choice applies not only when one is considering the fault assumptions underlying the design of a fault-tolerant computer, but also the merits of a particular system design, implementation and validation process. (Which if any aspects of this process can justifiably be assumed to be faultless – the specification, the compiler, the formal validation?) Yet all too often, inadequate attention is paid to identifying and justifying a set of fault assumptions – this indeed is one of the major messages I want to put across in this talk.

5 On Structure

Another of the messages that I want to convey is the particular importance of the role that system structuring plays in achieving dependability, especially where such dependability has to be achieved in the face of complex system requirements, and the complex realities of a fault-ridden world. I have had a keen personal interest for many years in the topic of system structuring, initially motivated by work at IBM on methodologies and tools for aiding the design of a large multiprocessing system [29] and then at Newcastle on dependability. The earliest work at Newcastle, on recovery blocks, was in fact all about structuring. Recovery blocks offer a means of introducing lots of extra redundant code into an application (acceptance tests and alternate blocks) without greatly adding to the overall system complexity. Unless this were the case, the scheme would of course be self-defeating.

The recovery block structure, with its underlying recovery cache for automating the provision of checkpoints, avoids causing a complexity explosion by allowing the programming of the different alternate blocks to be performed independently, both of each other, and of the problems of recovering from each other's errors. Thus, as always, structuring is being used as a means of dividing and conquering complexity. However, it is worth distinguishing between different sorts of complexity, and its counterpart, simplicity.

Tony Hoare once said: "The price of reliability is utter simplicity – and this is a price that major software manufacturers find too high to afford!" This is true, but so is Einstein's remark that: "Everything should be made as simple as possible, but not simpler"[3]

As I've discussed above, one can gain much simplicity by making assumptions as to the nature of the faults that will not occur (whether in system specification, design or operation). But this will be a spurious simplicity if the assumptions are false. Good system structuring allows one to deal with the added complexity that result from more realistic fault assumptions.

What is meant here by good structuring is not just the conventional characteristics, such as coupling and cohesion, that are used to determine the impact of structuring on performance, but also a characteristic which might be termed "strength". A strongly-structured system is one in which the structuring exists in the actual system, (as opposed to being used just in descriptions of, or the design for, a system) and helps to limit the impact of any faults – the analogy being to water-tight bulkheads in a ship.

For example, one of the standard (hardware) fault tolerance techniques is Triple Modular Redundancy (TMR) – figure 7 is a typical illustration, found in many textbooks, of part of an overall TMR system, involving a triplicated component and voter.

---

[3] As quoted in Reader's Digest (British edition), Vol 111, No 666, October 1977, p. 164. The German original is normally given as "Alles sollte so einfach wie möglich gemacht werden, aber nicht einfacher".

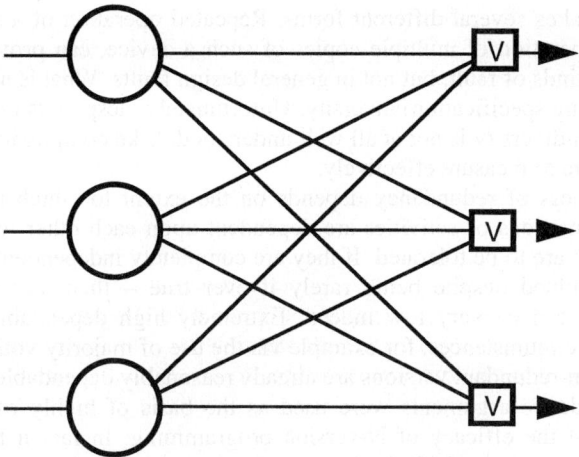

Fig. 7. Triple Modular Redundancy

One of the principal assumptions underlying TMR is that its structuring is strong. A majority vote that is obtained by collusion, whether accidental or deliberate, between two of the triplicated components or voters, is worthless. Thus it is essential that there to be good reason to assume that there is and can be no communication between these components or between these votes – that they are properly insulated from each other, that no-one has accidentally left a screw-driver across them, and – more subtly – that they are indeed wired together in the form shown in the Figure.

Taking a software example, it would be possible to use mere programming conventions to implement a recovery block-like approach. But the scheme is only truly effective if there are some effective means of enforcing the required separation between alternates, for example, so that one can have adequate reason to assume that a residual design fault in one alternate cannot impact any of the other alternates.

6 On Diversity

Rather than continue to develop this theme of the importance of system structuring, let me move on the topics of redundancy and diversity – which are much more specific to fault tolerance.

All fault tolerance involves the use of redundancy – of representation and/or activity – whose consistency can be checked. I have concentrated on what one might term "built-in" fault tolerance – but the system design process can also benefit from redundancy and consistency checking. For example, a system specification is likely to be improved (to the benefit of the dependability of the resulting system) if the specification is scrutinised by knowledgeable system designers who have the task of creating a system to match the specification. This opportunity is of course lost if this process is automated. And indeed, a recent experiment by Ross Anderson has convincingly shown the advantages of massive (human) redundancy, in developing security specifications [2].

Redundancy takes several different forms. Repeated operation of a single device, or the parallel operation of multiple copies of such a device, can provide means of tolerating some kinds of fault, but not in general design faults. What is needed for this is design (including specification) diversity. Unfortunately, despite its importance, the concept of design diversity is not at all well understood. Like complexity, it is hard to define, leave alone to measure effectively.

The effectiveness of redundancy depends on the extent to which the diversely-designed representations or activities are dependent upon each other with respect to types of fault that are to be tolerated. If they are completely independent – something that is often assumed despite being rarely if ever true – then the probability of coincident faults can be very low indeed. Extremely high dependability could be achieved in such circumstances, for example via the use of majority voting, assuming that the initial non-redundant versions are already reasonably dependable.

Such independence arguments were used as the basis of highly over-optimistic early estimates of the efficacy of N-version programming. In fact it turns out that there is a strong theoretical basis for the non-independence of faults in "independently-designed" software. As explained for example in [15], the demands placed upon systems by their environment can vary in 'difficulty', and this variation induces dependence upon the failure processes of different 'diverse' versions. Nevertheless, redundancy, including software design diversity, can provide considerable added dependability – though it is problematic to predict just how much, given the difficulty of assessing the degree of dependence, indeed the degree of diversity.

Just as deliberate use of diverse designs, or of diversity in the design process, can have significant benefits, accidental lack of diversity can have considerable dangers. This is well known in the world of biology, for example – but the phenomenon is also highly relevant in a computer world in which particular (ad hoc) standard platforms and protocols are becoming increasingly dominant. One might have thought that uniformity would lead to a reduction in complexity that would be very beneficial with respect to dependability – unfortunately life is not so simple. A nine hour outage, on 15 January 1990, of the long-distance phone system in the USA [18] was largely due to the fact that all the switches were of a single common design; and the impact of computer viruses is much greater now that so many people are using basically the same hardware and software.

So much for diversity. The topics that I have discussed so far, namely (i) fault concepts, classification and assumptions, (ii) system structuring, and (iii) redundancy and diversity, are to my mind the perennial central topics underlying the problem of achieving dependability from complex systems. I hope that I have succeeded in bringing out the fact these are a set of, so-to-speak, everlasting dependability research topics – ones that have been studied for years and yet still need much more study. However, let me now, against this background, devote the final part of my talk to a brief summary of one particular research issue in dependability that is I believe particularly topical.

7 Malicious Faults

Recently, some thirty years after we started thinking about design fault tolerance, I had a great sense of deja vu. This wass because I and my colleagues (this time not just in Newcastle, but also from several other research groups across Europe) were undertaking a EU-funded research project, to see whether we could extend the scope of fault tolerance technology (and in our case, ideas such as CA Actions) to cover a type of fault that hitherto has largely been regarded as one to be prevented and/or removed, rather than coped with automatically. This is the intentional malicious fault, arising from the nefarious activities of hackers and – much worse – corrupt insiders (including people who have systems administration roles).

Such protection is needed because the likely reality is that most large systems will have to be used even though it is known that they contain vulnerabilities. Some of these vulnerabilities might even have been identified already, but for some reason must be allowed to remain in the system; other vulnerabilities will be awaiting discovery – probably first by system hackers. Thus means for tolerating malicious faults are needed, not just for reporting detected intrusions to the management, if continuous service is needed from the system.

Over a decade ago I and a colleague, John Dobson, first started to think about this sort of problem, though we did not develop the idea extensively at the time. The main result of our work was a paper [7] whose title "Building reliable secure systems from unreliable insecure components" (a deliberate allusion to von Neumann) both neatly summed up our approach, and provoked one of the referees of the conference at which it was presented, the IEEE Oakland "Privacy and Security" conference, to describe it as "highly controversial" – though now I think the idea, or at least the aim, is more accepted.

Indeed, the recently-completed collaborative research project to which I alluded above, namely MAFTIA (standing for "Malicious- and Accidental- Fault-tolerant Internet Applications"), brought together teams working on encryption, intrusion detection, asynchronous distributed algorithms, rigorous evaluation and, of course, fault tolerance. The project's major innovation was a comprehensive approach for tolerating both accidental faults and malicious attacks in large-scale distributed systems, including attacks by external hackers and by corrupt insiders. However, this is a whole story in itself–full details can be found from the project's web-site, at:

http://www.newcastle.research.ec.org/maftia/

8 Concluding Remark

Much of this lecture has been aimed at trying to explain what I believe to be some of the most important issues of long term and continuing importance in dependability. But my fundamental aims in this lecture, implied by its title, have been first to argue how important it is to accept the reality of human fallibility and frailty, both in the design and the use of computer systems, and second to indicate various constructive approaches to trying to cope with this uncomfortable reality. If such an acceptance were more prevalent in the computer science community, it would I believe go some way toward improving our standing, and that of our subject, among the general public.

Acknowledgements

In this talk I have attempted to cover a wide variety of topics related to system dependability, and have been drawing not just on my own work but also on that of many colleagues, both past and present. Alluding to another famous quotation, let me say that though I do not claim to be able to see further than other people, I have stood on many people's shoulders. It is therefore a pleasure to acknowledge the great debt I owe to many colleagues at Newcastle and, especially in recent years, to colleagues in the ESPRIT PDCS and DeVa Projects, the IST MAFTIA and DSoS Projects, and the EPSRC Interdisciplinary Research Collaboration on the Dependability of Computer-Based Systems (DIRC).

References

1. Alexander, C. Notes on the Synthesis of Form. Harvard University Press, Cambridge, Mass., USA, 1964.
2. Anderson, R., How to Cheat at the Lottery (or, Massively Parallel Requirements Engineering). in Proc. Computer Security Applications Conference, (Phoenix, AZ, 1999).
3. Avizienis, A., Laprie, J.C. and Randell, B., Fundamental Concepts of Dependability. in Third IEEE Information Survivability Workshop, (Cambridge, Mass., 2000), Software Engineering Institute, Carnegie-Mellon University, Pittsburg, 7-12.
4. Campbell, R.H. and Randell, B. Error Recovery in Asynchronous Systems. IEEE Trans. Software Engineering, **SE-12** (8). 811-826.
5. Caughey, S.J., Little, M.C. and Shrivastava, S.K., Checked Transactions in an Asynchronous Message Passing Environment. in 1st IEEE International Symposium on Object-Oriented Real-time Distributed Computing, (Kyoto, 1998), 222-229.
6. Davies, C.T. Data processing spheres of control. IBM Systems Journal, **17** (2). 179-198.
7. Dobson, J.E. and Randell, B., Building Reliable Secure Systems out of Unreliable Insecure Components. in Proc. Conf. on Security and Privacy, (Oakland, 1986), IEEE.
8. Gray, J. and Reuter, A. Transaction Processing: Concepts and techniques. Morgan Kaufmann, 1993.
9. Horning, J.J., Lauer, H.C., Melliar-Smith, P.M. and Randell, B., A Program Structure for Error Detection and Recovery. in Proc. Conf. on Operating Systems, Theoretical and Practical Aspects (Lecture Notes in Computer Science, vol. 16), (IRIA, 1974), Springer Verlag, 171-187.
10. Horning, J.J. and Randell, B. Process Structuring. ACM Computing Surveys, **5** (1). 5-30.
11. Jones, C.B. A Formal Basis for some Dependability Notions. in Aichernig, B.K. and Maibaum, T. eds. Formal Methods at the Crossroads: from Panacea to Foundational Support, Springer-Verlag, 2003.
12. Laprie, J.C. (ed.), Dependability: Basic concepts and associated terminology. Springer-Verlag, 1991.
13. Laprie, J.C. (ed.), Dependability: Basic concepts and terminology — in English, French, German, Italian and Japanese. Springer-Verlag, Vienna, Austria, 1992.
14. Laprie, J.C., Dependable Computing: Concepts, Limits, Challenges. in 25th IEEE International Symposium on Fault-Tolerant Computing - Special Issue, (Pasadena, California, USA, 1995), IEEE, 42-54.

15. Littlewood, B. and Miller, D.R. Conceptual Modelling of Coincident Failures in Multi-Version Software. IEEE Trans. Software Engineering, **15** (12). 1596-1614.
16. Lomet, D.B. Process Structuring, Synchronization, and Recovery Using Atomic Actions. ACM SIGPLAN Notices, 12 (3). 128-137.
17. Naur, P. and Randell, B. (eds.). Software Engineering: Report of a conference sponsored by the NATO Science Committee, Garmisch, Germany, 7th to 11th October 1968. Scientific Affairs Division, NATO, Brussels, 1969.
18. Neumann, P. Computer Related Risks. Addison-Wesley, New York, 1995.
19. Randell, B. Facing up to Faults (Turing Memorial Lecture). Computer Journal, **43** (2). 95-106.
20. Randell, B. System Structure for Software Fault Tolerance. IEEE Trans. on Software Engineering, **SE-1** (2). 220-232.
21. Romanovsky, A., Xu, J. and Randell, B., Exception Handling in Object-Oriented Real-Time Distributed Systems. in Proc. 1st IEEE International Symposium on Object-Oriented Real-time Distributed Computing (ISORC'98), (Kyoto, Japan, 1998), 32-42.
22. von Neumann, J. Probabilistic Logic and the Synthesis of Reliable Organisms from Unreliable Components. in Shannon, C.E. and McCarthy, J. eds. Automata Studies, Princeton University Press, Princeton, NJ, 1956, 43-98.
23. Xu, J., Randell, B., Romanovsky, A., Stroud, R.J. and Wu, Z., Fault Tolerance in Concurrent Object-Oriented Software through Coordinated Error Recovery. in Proc. 25th Int. Symp. Fault-Tolerant Computing (FTCS-25), (Los Angeles, 1995), IEEE Computer Society Press.
24. Xu, J., Randell, B., Romanovsky, A., Stroud, R.J., Zorzo, A., Canver, E. and Henke, F.v., Developing Control Software for Production Cell II: Failure Analysis and System Design Using CA Actions. in FTCS-29, (Madison, USA, 1999), IEEE CS Press.
25. Xu, J., Randell, B., Romanovsky, A., Stroud, R.J., Zorzo, A.F., Canver, E. and Henke, F.v., Rigorous Development of a Safety-Critical System Based on Coordinated Atomic Actions. in Proc. 29th Int. Symp. Fault-Tolerant Computing (FTCS-29), (Madison, 1999), IEEE Computer Society Press.
26. Xu, J., Randell, B., Romanovsky, A., Stroud, R.J., Zorzo, A.F., Canver, E. and Henke, F.v. Rigorous development of an Embedded Fault-Tolerant System Based on Coordinated Atomic Actions. IEEE Trans. on Computers (Special Issue on Fault Tolerance), **51** (2). 164-179.
27. Xu, J., Romanovsky, A. and Randell, B., Co-ordinated Exception Handling in Distributed Object Systems: from Model to System Implementation. in Proc. 18th IEEE International Conference on Distributed Computing Systems, (Amsterdam, Netherlands, 1998), 12-21.
28. Zorzo, A.F., Romanovsky, A., J. Xu, B.R., Stroud, R.J. and Welch, I.S. Using Co-ordinated Atomic Actions to Design Complex Safety-Critical Systems: The Production Cell Case Study. Software — Practice & Experience, **29** (8). 677-697.
29. Zurcher, F.W. and Randell, B., Iterative Multi-Level modelling: A methodology for computer system design. in Proc. IFIP Congress 68, (Edinburgh, 1968), D138-D142.

Trends in Software Verification

Gerard J. Holzmann

JPL Laboratory for Reliable Software
California Institute of Technology
4800 Oak Grove Drive
Pasadena, CA 91006
gerard.j.holzmann@jpl.nasa.gov

Abstract. With the steady increase in computational power of general purpose computers, our ability to analyze routine software artifacts is also steadily increasing. As a result, we are witnessing a shift in emphasis from the verification of abstract hand-built models of code, towards the direct verification of implementation level code. This change in emphasis poses a new set of challenges in software verification. We explore some of them in this paper.

1 Introduction

In the last few years, we have seen a push towards the direct application of formal verification techniques to implementation level code, instead of to manually constructed high-level models of code. Although the direct application of, for instance, model checking techniques to implementation level code can significantly increase the computational requirements for a verification, the promise of this new approach is that it can eliminate the need for expert model builders and can place the power of automated verification techniques where it belongs: in the hands of programmers.

There are two general approaches to the software verification problem in this form.

- Mapping the implementation level description of the software artifact mechanically to the description language of an existing verification tool. The application is rewritten to match the requirements of a given verification tool.
- Developing a verification tool that can work directly on implementation level descriptions. The verification tool is rewritten to match the requirements of a given implementation language.

Examples of projects pursuing the first method include the first Java Pathfinder tool [5], the Bandera toolset [4], and the FeaVer toolset[1] [8], which all target the SPIN model checker[2] [7,10] as the main verification engine. Examples of projects pursuing the second method include the second version of the Java Pathfinder tool [2], Microsoft's Bebop toolset [1], and the Blast tool [6].

---

[1] http://cm.bell-labs.com/cm/cs/what/feaver
[2] http://spinroot.com/whatispin.html

Of the six projects mentioned, three target the Java programming language ([2,4,5]), and the remaining three target the C programming language. The two methods have different advantages and disadvantages. The first makes it possible to leverage the power of an existing tool, and to trust the validity of the verification process. The second method, on the other hand, makes it possible to leverage the efforts that have already been spent in the creation of the software artifacts and to trust their accuracy, rather than the accuracy of a newly developed translator. In other words: the first method tries to secure that the application is verified correctly, while the second method tries to secure that the correct application is verified. The most significant challenges that each method poses are as follows.

- The first method requires the construction of a model extractor that can convert implementation level program descriptions into detailed verification models that can be submitted to a model checker. To perform the conversion accurately, we need to be able to interpret the semantic content of the implementation level code (e.g., written in C) and convert it into equivalent representations in the verification model.
- The second method requires the construction of a verifier that can pass accurate judgements on the validity of a system execution. The construction of a comprehensive verification system for any formally defined language can be a significant challenge. Doing so for an implementation level language, that was not designed with verifiability in mind, can be even more challenging.

It would seem that both methods face significant hurdles, and are difficult to combine. As it turns out, though, many of the difficulties that are encountered by these two approaches can be overcome with a third technique. This technique is based on the use of embedded code statements inside a traditional model checker.

2 Embedding Code vs Translating Code

A model checker is programmed to systematically explore the reachable state space of a (model) system. As far as it is concerned, the world consists only of states, and state transformers. It renders its verdicts with the help of sets of boolean propositions on states and state sets. Within the model checker, a system state is defined as the set of control-flow points, and value assignments to data objects, where the data objects are restricted to the ones that are definable within the specification language. State transformers, similarly, are defined by the set of executable statements that are predefined in the specification language. So all the model checker does is to provide the user with a carefully designed language for the specification of systems of states and state transformers. There is a pleasing similarity here with a mathematical theory that is defined by a small set of axioms (the initial system state), a small set of rules of inference (state transformers), and a potentially much larger set of provable theorems (the reachable states).

A programming language, just like the specification language for a model checker, allows us to specify systems of states and state transformers. The main difference with a model checking language is that no provision is generally made to keep the system finite or to secure that the properties of the system remain decidable. We will postpone a discussion of the issue of decidability for now and consider just the notion that the purpose of a software application is merely to define systems of states and state transformers. The first strategy for model checking software systems that we mentioned above required us to translate the possibly unwieldy specification from a mainstream programming language into the more structured specification language of a model checker: replacing one system of states and state transformers with another. This is necessarily a hard problem since it will require us to faithfully map semantic concepts from one language into another.

Having recognized that, at least at some level of abstraction, both the programming language and the model checking language perform the same type of function, we may wonder if it would not be possible to use the programming language directly to define a system of states and state transformers and to let the model checker add only its checking engine. We can do so by *embedding* descriptions from the source programming language directly into the target model that will be verified by the model checker.

Doing so, we can combine the benefits of both approaches outlined above, while avoiding all the work that would be needed to solve the hard part of the problem in both domains. For the first approach this means that we can avoid having to develop a method that would allow us to provide an accurate interpretation of source C code, such that it can be mapped into the target language of the model checker. For the second approach it means that we can avoid having to develop an efficient model checking system for a new language from scratch.

SPIN is designed to generate a verification program in C, to perform the model checking task for a high-level system model. To do so, SPIN interprets the state descriptors and state transformers as the user specified them in PROMELA (the SPIN input language), and converts them into C code, thereby fixing their semantic interpretation. Rather than having a new translator convert native C code into PROMELA, and have SPIN convert the PROMELA code back into C, we can try to bypass the translation steps and use the original C code to define elements state transformers within the verifier directly. Ultimately, it is now the C compiler that determines the semantics of the C code, just like it does when we compile the application level code directly for execution.

To support these ideas, SPIN Version 4 introduced a small set of new language primitives.

The most important of these are: c_code, c_expr, and c_state.

- c_code   The c_code primitive allows us to include an arbitrary fragment of C code as a formal state transformer in a SPIN model.
- c_expr   The c_expr primitive can be used to evaluate an arbitrary C expression and to interpret the return value as a Boolean condition (non-zero meaning *true* and zero meaning *false*).
- c_state   The c_state primitive, finally, can be used to embed an arbitrary global or a local C data object into the state descriptor that is maintained by the model checker.

With the help of these three primitives it now becomes possible to build an accurate model of a large class of routine C applications with relatively little effort.

3 Separating Data and Control

It is of course not sufficient to simply encapsulate an entire C program and pass it to the model checker to execute: the model checker needs to be able to control the execution of the program. Consider, for instance, the execution of a concurrent system, with multiple threads of execution being able to access and modify a pool of shared data objects. There could well be race conditions in the code that depend on the particular access pattern that is followed: the specific interleaving of statement executions. Unless the model checker is in charge of these interleavings and can schedule the statement executions one by one, we may miss these errors. So by necessity we need to devise a system that can separate control and data. Control in a C program is defined with the help of control flow constructs such as the semi-colon (for sequential execution) the if-then-else statement (for conditional branching), the for- or while-loop (for iterations), and goto statements and labels (for unconditional branching). The control structure of a program can be visualized in a control-flow graph, where nodes represent control-flow states, and edges represent statement executions (i.e., the basic state transformers).

The SPIN extension exploits the fact that we can fairly easily separate the control aspects of a program from the data aspects. We can translate the control aspects, and leave the data aspects untouched, embedding them as-is into a verification model, so that their effect as state transformers is fully and accurately represented.

```
#include <stdio.h>

int
main(void)
{       int lower, upper, step;
        float fahr, celsius;

        lower = 0;
        upper = 300;
        step = 20;

        fahr = lower;
        while (fahr <= upper) {
                celsius = (5.0/9.0) * (fahr - 32.0);
                printf("%4.0f %6.1f\n", fahr, celsius);
                fahr = fahr + step;
        }
}
```

Fig. 1. Example C program.

MODEX

We designed a model extractor,[3] called MODEX, to convert simple C programs mechanically into SPIN models, following the principles given above. The model extractor derives the control flow graph of a program, using standard parsing

---
[3] http://cm.bell-labs.com/cm/cs/what/modex

techniques, it expresses the control-flow constructs of the source program into the corresponding control-flow constructs of SPIN's input language (a relatively straightforward procedure), and it embeds data declarations and basic statements into the model with the help of the new embedding primitives from SPIN. As a simple example, the model extractor can mechanically convert the C program shown in Figure 1 into the SPIN model that is shown in Figure 2.

The details of the model extraction process are not too important for this paper, but note that through the use of embedded declarations and embedded code the model checker can now access and manipulate floating point variables, even though SPIN itself does not support the associated data type. The two floating point variables fahr and celsius are embedded here into the state vector as local objects of the main process. The model extractor automatically arranges for the variable references to be prefixed with pointers into the appropriate part of the verifiers state descriptor, in such a way that any reference to, for instance, fahr becomes Pmain->fahr.

In a similar way we can generate models that use pointers, even function pointers, though there is no direct support for any of these language features at the SPIN level.

```
c_state "float fahr" "Local main"
c_state "float celsius" "Local main"

active proctype main()
{       int lower;
        int upper;
        int step;

        c_code { Pmain->lower=0; };
        c_code { Pmain->upper=300; };
        c_code { Pmain->step=20; };
        c_code { Pmain->fahr=Pmain->lower; };

        do
        :: c_expr { (Pmain->fahr <= Pmain->upper) };
           c_code { Pmain->celsius =
                        ((5.0/9.0)*(Pmain->fahr-32.0)); };
           c_code { Printf("%4.0f %6.1f\n",
                        Pmain->fahr, Pmain->celsius); };
           c_code { Pmain->fahr = (Pmain->fahr+Pmain->step); };
        :: else -> break
        od
}
```

Fig. 2. SPIN Model Corresponding to Figure 1.

There are limits to how much can be automated with this approach. Consider, for instance, how function calls, like printf in the example, are handled. Without special provision, MODEX considers a function call to be an atomic event, and the code that is generated will not return control to the model checker until the function is completely executed. This is the right policy for the printf call. To allow the model checker to look inside a function, though, we need to give additional instructions to the model extractor. This means that we still need to rely on human judgement to determine which functions need instrumenting, and which can be left alone.

To apply the model checking algorithm, the model checker must be able to set the application into any one of its reachable states. This means that the state descriptor that is maintained by the model checker must always contain a complete description of the (relevant part of the) state of the system. If any part is missing from this description, then that part of the system state will not get updated accurately when the verifier places the system into a new state.

A potential problem now exists if the application can maintain part of its system state external to the application. This can happen, for instance, if the application stores or reads data from the file system, if it communicates through live network connections with other systems, and even if it can dynamically allocate memory for new data objects. In the latter case, the memory allocator, maintaining heap memory, is an external resource where some of the relevant system state information is maintained.

All these issues can be resolved, but currently require some degree of user intervention into the model extraction process. A more detailed treatment of these issues can be found in [9,10].

4 Decidability

A SPIN verification model must satisfy two conditions to secure the decidability of the verification problem. First, the model must be self-contained. There can be no hidden assumptions, and no undefined components that contribute in any way to the behavior that is being verified. Second, the model must be bounded. This means that when an execution of the model is simulated, only a finite number of distinct system states can be reached. The number can be large, but it must be finite.

If verification models are specified in SPIN's native specification language PROMELA, then both fitness requirements are automatically satisfied. It is impossible to define a non-finite state SPIN model in PROMELA. All data objects are bounded, the capacity of all message channels is bounded, and there is a strict limit on the number of asynchronous process threads that can be created in a system execution. This secures the decidability of all correctness questions that can be expressed with SPIN, which if formally the class of ω-regular properties, and which includes the set of properties that can be defined in standard linear temporal logic [12].

But the same is not necessarily true for SPIN models that contain embedded C code. If the model is self-contained and bounded, decidability is retained. Reflect for a moment on how the model checker would recognize a runaway C program: one that lands itself in an infinite loop. First note that the model checker maintains a state descriptor in memory, recording all information that holds state information for the application. When the program starts executing an infinite loop, the model checker will detect that previously visited states are repeated in the execution. It can analyze the cycle for the potential violation of liveness properties, and complete its work normally. The cycle is merely a traversal of a strong component in the reachability graph of the system, which the verifier can recognize as it builds that graph.

If the application is not finite-state, it must be able to increase the size of the state descriptor without limit. If this happens, the verifier will sooner or later run out of its limited resources to track the execution, making complete verification impossible. In truth, the application itself, when run standalone, would encounter the same problem, and when it reaches the point where it exhausts the available system resources it too would have to abandon its execution. In real-life, at least to date, the deliberate design of a program that is fundamentally infinite state is not sensible. If it occurs, it is usually the result of a design error, and not a planned feature of a program.

The Halting Problem

But, how do we square this observation with the unsolvability of the *halting problem*, which is one of the best known results in theoretical computer science [14]. In rendering the proof for the unsolvability of the halting problem one normally does not distinguish infinite state programs from finite state ones. As an example, let us consider a popular variant of such a proof, as it was given by Christopher Strachey in 1965 [13], which is also used in [11].

Strachey's proof is by contradiction. Suppose we had a procedure, call it mc, that could determine for any given program p whether or not it would terminate if executed. The procedure mc(p,i) can then be used to return *true* if it determines that program p necessarily terminates on input i, and *false* it fails to terminate.[4] Naturally, we must assume that mc itself will always terminate in a finite amount of time, so it cannot simply run the program it is inspecting to determine the answer to its question. How precisely it does operate is undefined.

```
strachey(p,i)              /* program p, input i */
{
L:         if (mc(p,i))    /* true if p halts on i */
                goto L;    /* make strachey() loop */
           else
                exit(0);   /* else halt */
}
```

Fig. 3. Strachey's Construction.

Given the procedure mc we can now write the program shown in Figure 3. The program strachey(p,i) is designed to halt when the program p(i) does not, and vice versa.

All is well, untill we ask whether the program strachey(strachey,strachey) will terminates or loops. Clearly, it cannot do either. If it halts, then it must loop, and vice versa.

It is curious that this version of the proof has never been seriously challenged. First, note that the proof argument seems to be independent of the issue of finiteness, and would appear to apply equally to finite state and infinite state programs.

Strachey tacitly assumes in his argument that all programs either halt or loop. In practice, though, there is a third possibility: a program can fail. When a program attempts to divide by zero, or runs out of memory, it is forced to terminate by its environment: it fails. Program failure cannot simply be grouped into the category of program termination, because if this were the case we could apply Strachey's argument to the class of finite state programs.

---

[4] In Strachey's version of the proof, the required arguments to procedure mc() are omitted.

Given an upper-bound N bits on the amount of memory that a program can consume, we can derive an upper-bound on the number of reachable states it could generate when executed (trivially $2N$). If we declare that exceeding the upperbound of N bits of memory constitutes program termination as considered in Strachey's argument, then we can easily decide the outcome of mc(p,i) in finite time: we have to consider maximally $2N$ steps of the program. Within this number of steps the program must either terminate or loop.

We can use SPIN to solve the halting problem for finite state programs, using the model extraction procedure we have outlined before. To do so, we first write a UNIX® shell script that returns *true* if SPIN determines that a given model has at least one reachable endstate, and *false* if it does not.

```
#!/bin/sh
### filename: halts

echo -n "testing $1: "

spin -a $1                          # generate model
cc -DSAFETY -o pan pan.c            # compile it
./pan | grep "errors: 0"            # run it and grep stats
if $?                               # test exit status of grep
then
        echo "halts"
else
        echo "loops"
fi
```

We can try this on the Fahrenheit conversion model from Figure 2, to check if the scripts gives us the right answer.

```
$ ./halts fahrenheit.pml
halts
```

If we change the loop in this example into a non-terminating one, the script will accurately report that the model will now loop. So far so good. We can now invoke this script in a SPIN c_expr statement, in the devious manner envisioned by Strachey.

```
init {  /* filename: strachey */
        do
        :: c_expr { system("halts strachey") }  /* loop */
        :: else -> break                        /* halt */
        od;
        false /* block the execution */
}
```

Returning to Strachey's proof argument: what happens if we now execute

```
$ ./halts strachey
.....
```

After some reflection, aided by performing the actual experiment, we can see that the `halts` script ends up going into an infinite descent. Each time the model checker gets to the point where it needs to establish the executability of the `c_expr` statement, it needs to invoke the `halts` script once more and it must restart itself. This very construction then is *not* finite state. In reality, the infinite recursion cannot go on forever, since our machines are always finite. The process will stop when the maximum number of processes is exceeded, or a maximum recursion depth on nested system calls is exceeded, leading to a crash of the program. Because the `strachey` program is infinite state, it is firmly outside the scope of systems that can be verified with finitary methods. Note carefully that the infinite recursion is not caused by any particular choice we have made in the implementation of the `halts` script. Even if this script only needed to read the source text of the program before rendering a verdict on its termination properties, the same infinite descent would occur.

The executions of Strachey's impossible program, then neither leads to termination nor does it lead to looping: it leads to a failure. Strachey's program itself then belongs to the class of faulty programs (and there are many ways to construct those).

Note that if SPIN can be used to verify the termination properties of systems with up to N reachable states, it will itself need considerably more than N reachable states to perform this verification. Therefore, SPIN also could not be used to verify itself in another Strachey-like construction. There is much more that can be said on this topic though, cf. [10].

5 Conclusion

A practically useful software tool is usable by any normally skilled programmer, requiring no more tool-specific training than an ordinary language compiler. Since their inception, roughly twenty years ago, formal software verification systems have relied on the construction of a mathematical or computational model of an application, by a domain expert, which is then analyzed either manually or mechanically. Even the fully automated tools that operate in this domain come short of reaching the goal of practically useful software tools as long as they rely on human experts to construct the input models.

The emphasis of much of the work in the area of formal verification has therefore recently been placed by some groups on the automatic generation of logic models from implementation level code, and by others on the adaption of the verification tools themselves to work directly on implementation level code. We have shown that these two seemingly distinct approaches can effectively be combined, by allowing the embedding of implementation level code into higher-level logic models that can then be verified with existing model checking techniques. The technique we have described relies on the fact that we can separate the control aspects of a program from the data manipulation. The control aspects of a program can in most cases trivially be adapted to the syntax requirements of the logic model checker, while the data aspects (which are much harder to convert) can be embedded.

Limitations: There remain clear limitations to this approach. If *most* control aspects can easily be handled in this way, this does not mean that *all* will fit the default pattern. The use of function pointers in C programs, for instance, needs special care, as does the use of dynamic memory allocation, and access by a program to external sources of information. It may be possible to develop a methodology, though, by which cases such as these can be handled more or less routinely in the construction of a *test-harness* for the application to be verified. A beginning with such a development can be found in the user guide to the Bell Labs FeaVer system [9].

It is also clear that the model checker cannot defend itself fully against outright errors within code that is embedded inside the logic models that it analyzes. Consider, for instance, what happens if such code contains a divide-by-zero error, or dereferences a nil-pointer. A model extractor can be somewhat proactive, and instrument the embedded code with additional checks. Our MODEX tool, for instance, inserts an assertion before any pointer dereference operation, to make sure it is non-zero. Not all errors can be anticipated, and some can cause the model checker to crash, just like the application being verified. There is still benefit to the use of the model checker, even in these cases, since the model checker will be far more likely to find the cases where application code may crash, as part of its search process. A crashed model checking run, like a real execution, leaves a detailed trace of the steps in the program that led to the failure, making it possible to diagnose and repair the code.

Decidability Issues: The fact that we can do model checking on at least some categories of implementation level code may at first seem to conflict with long established decidability results, but can easily be seen to be bound by all familiar limits. Other approaches to the software verification problem, such as static analysis and approaches based on theorem proving methods, naturally share this fate. As we hope to have shown, though, the existence of these limits need not prevent us from building systems that are both practically useful, *and* reliable.

Acknowledgements

The research described in this paper was carried out at the Jet Propulsion Laboratory, California Institute of Technology, under a contract with the National Aeronautics and Space Administration.

References

1. T. Ball, R. Majumdar, T. Millstein, S.K. Rajamani, Automatic Predicate Abstraction of C Programs, Proc. PLDI 2001, f2SIGPLAN Notices, Vol. 36, No. 5, pp. 203-213.
2. G. Brat, K. Havelund, S. Park, W. Visser, Java PathFinder - A 2nd generation of a Java model checker, *Proc. Workshop on Advances in Verification*, Chicago, Ill., July 2000.
3. E.M. Clarke, O. Grumberg, and D. Peled, *Model checking*, MIT Press, January 2000.
4. J.C. Corbett, M.B. Dwyer, et al., Bandera: Extracting finite-state models from Java source code, *Proc. 22nd Int. Conf. on Software Engineering*, June 2000, pp. 439-448.
5. K. Havelund, and T. Pressburger, Model Checking Java Programs Using Java PathFinder, *Int. Journal on Software Tools for Technology Transfer*, Vol. 2, No. 4, April 2000, pp. 366-381.
6. T.A. Henzinger, R. Jhala, et al., Software Verification with Blast, Proc. 10th SPIN Workshop on Model Checking Software, LNCS 2648, Springer-Verlag, 2003.

7. G.J. Holzmann, The Model Checker SPIN, *IEEE Trans. on Software Engineering*, Vol. 23, No. 5, May 1997, pp. 279-295.
8. G.J. Holzmann, and M.H. Smith, An automated verification method for distributed systems software based on model extraction, *IEEE Trans. on Software Engineering*, Vol. 28, No. 4, April 2002, pp. 364-377.
9. G.J. Holzmann, and M.H. Smith, *FeaVer 1.0 User Guide*, Bell Labs, Dec. 2002, 64 pgs. Online document http://cm.bell-labs.com/cm/cs/what/modex/.
10. G.J. Holzmann, *The SPIN Model Checker: Primer and Reference Manual*, Addison-Wesley, ISBN 0-32122-862-6, August 2003.
11. M.L. Minsky, *Computation: Finite and Infinite Machines*, Prentice Hall, Englewood Cliffs, N.J., 1967.
12. A. Pnueli, The temporal logic of programs. *Proc. 18th IEEE Symp. on Foundations of Computer Science*, 1977, Providence, R.I., pp. 46-57.
13. C. Strachey, An impossible program, *Computer Journal*, Vol. 7, No. 4, Jan. 1965, p. 313.
14. A.M. Turing, On computable numbers, with an application to the Entscheidungsproblem, *Proc. London Mathematical Soc.*, Ser. 2-42, 1936, pp. 230-265.

Event Based Sequential Program Development: Application to Constructing a Pointer Program

Jean-Raymond Abrial

Consultant, Marseille, France,
jr@abrial.org

Abstract. In this article, I present an "event approach" used to formally develop sequential programs. It is based on the formalism of Action Systems [6] (and Guarded Commands [7]), which is is interesting because it involves a large number of pointer manipulations.

1 Introduction

Sequential programs (e.g. loops), when formally constructed, are usually developed gradually by means of a series of progressively more refined "sketches" starting with the formal specification and ending in the final program. Each such sketch is already (although often in a highly non-deterministic form) a monolithic description which resumes the final intended program in terms of a single formula. This is precisely that initial "formula", which is gradually transformed into the final program.

It is argued here that this might *not be the right approach*. After all, in order to prove a large formula, a logician usually breaks it down into various pieces, on which he performs some simple manipulations before putting them again together in a final proof. We would like to experiment with such a paradigm and thus possibly decide whether it is applicable to construct programs as well.

A sequential program is essentially made up of a number of individual assignments that are glued together by means of various constructs: sequential composition (;), loop (WHILE) and condition (IF), whose rôle is to explicitly *schedule* these assignments in a proper order so that the execution of the program can achieve its intended goal. Here is an example of a sequential program where the various assignments have been emphasized:

```
WHILE   j ≠ m   DO
    IF    g(j+1) > x    THEN
        j := j + 1
    ELSIF    k = j    THEN
        k, j := k + 1, j + 1
    ELSE
        k, j, g := k + 1, j + 1, swap (g, k + 1, j + 1)
    END
END ;
p := k
```

The idea we want to explore here is to completely separate, during the design, these individual assignments from their scheduling. This approach is thus essentially one by which we favor an initial implicit *distribution of computation* over a centralized explicit one. At a certain stage, the "program" is just made of a number of "naked" guarded commands (which we call here "events"), performing some actions under the control of certain guarding conditions. And at this point the synchronization of these events is not our concern. Thinking operationally, it is done *implicitly* by a hidden scheduler, which *may fire* an event once its guard holds. We can express as follows the various "naked" events corresponding to the previous example (the guard of each event is introduced by the keyword SELECT):

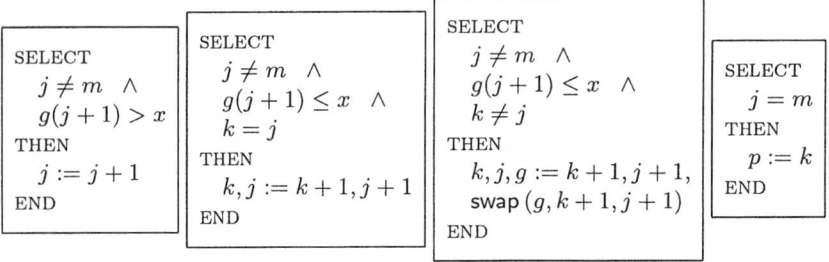

At the beginning of the development process, the event system is made of a single non-guarded event, which represents the specification of our future program. During the development process, other events might be added, which will be further refined together with the initial event. This is done in a certain disciplined manner as shown below. When all the individual pieces are "on the table" (this is the situation shown in the example), and only then, we start to be interested in their *explicit* scheduling. For this, we apply certain systematic rules whose rôle is to gradually *merge the events* and thus organize them into a single entity forming our final program. The application of these rules has the effect of gradually eliminating the various predicates making the guards. At the end of the development, it results in a single guardless final event (as the initial one).

What is interesting about this approach is that it gives us full freedom to refine small pieces of the future program, and also to create new ones, *without being disturbed by others* : the program is developed by means of small *independent* parts that so remain until they are eventually put together systematically at the end of the process.

The paper is organized in two parts. In the first one (section 2), the general framework of event systems is presented. In the second part (section 3) a complete example (inspired by the marking algorithm of Shorr and Waite) is presented.

2 Event System Concepts

2.1 Definition of an Event System: State and Events

An event system is first made of a *state*, which is defined by means of *constants* and *variables*. In practical terms, these constants and variables mainly show simple mathematical objects: sets, binary relations, functions, numbers etc. Moreover, they are constrained by some conditions expressing the *invariant properties* of the system.

Besides its state, an event system contains a number of *events* which show the way it may evolve. Each event is composed of a *guard* and an *action*. The guard is the necessary condition under which the event may occur. The action, as its name indicates, determines the way in which the state variables are going to evolve when the event occurs.

Once its guard holds, the occurrence of an event may be observed at any time (but may also never be observed). As soon as the guard does not hold however, the event cannot be observed. Events are *atomic* and when the guards of several events hold simultaneously then *at most one of them* may be observed. The choice of the elected event is non-deterministic. Practically speaking, an event, named xxx, is presented in one of the two following simple forms:

$$\text{xxx} \;\widehat{=}\; \text{SELECT } P(a,b,\ldots) \text{ THEN } S(a,b,\ldots) \text{ END} \quad\Big|\quad \text{xxx} \;\widehat{=}\; \text{BEGIN } S(a,b,\ldots) \text{ END}$$

where $P(a,b,\ldots)$ is a predicate denoting the guard, and $S(a,b,\ldots)$ is the action. The list $a,b,\ldots$ denotes some constants and variables of the state. Sometimes, the guard is simply missing and the event may thus take place at any time (this corresponds to the second form shown).

The action presents itself in the form of a simultaneous assignment of certain state variables $a,b,\ldots$ by certain expressions $E, F, \ldots$. Such expressions depend upon the state. It is to be noted that those variables which are not mentioned in the list $a,b,\ldots$ do not change. Such an action can be first written in one of the following two simple equivalent forms:

$$a,b,\ldots := E,F,\ldots \qquad\qquad a := E \;\|\; b := F \;\|\; \ldots$$

There exists however a more general form of action, which is the following:

$$\text{ANY } x,y,\ldots \text{ WHERE } Q(x,y,\ldots,a,b,\ldots) \text{ THEN } S(x,y,\ldots,a,b,\ldots) \text{ END}$$

where the identifiers $x,y,\ldots$ denotes some *constants that are local to the event*. These constants are constrained by the predicate $Q(x,y,\ldots,a,b,\ldots)$. The formula $S(x,y,\ldots,a,b,\ldots)$ denotes a simple deterministic action as above (multiple assignment). Notice that this *non-deterministic* action must be *feasible*. In other words, under the guard of the event, the following must hold:

$$\exists\,(x,y,\ldots)\cdot Q(x,y,\ldots,a,b,\ldots)$$

2.2 Consistency of an Event System

Once a system is built, one must prove that it is *consistent*. This is done by proving that each event of the system preserves the invariant. More precisely, it must be proved that the action associated to each event modifies the state variables in such a way that the corresponding new invariant holds under the hypothesis of the former invariant and of the guard of the event. For a system with state variable v, invariant $I(v)$, and an event of the form indicated on the left, the statement to be proved is the one indicated on the right:

$$\boxed{\text{SELECT } P(v) \text{ THEN } v := E(v) \text{ END}} \qquad \boxed{I(v) \land P(v) \;\Rightarrow\; I(E(v))}$$

2.3 Refining an Event System

Refining an event system consists of refining its state and its events. A concrete system (with regards to a more abstract one) has a state that should be related to that of the abstraction through a, so-called, *abstraction relation*, which is expressed in terms of an invariant $J(v, w)$ connecting the abstract state represented by the variables v and the concrete state represented by the variables w.

Each event of the abstract model is refined to one or more corresponding events of the concrete one. Informally speaking, a concrete event is said to refine its abstraction (1) when the guard of the former is stronger than that of the latter (guard strengthening), (2) and when the connecting invariant is preserved by the conjoined action of both events. In the case of an abstract event (left) and a corresponding concrete event (right) having the forms

$$\boxed{\text{SELECT } P(v) \text{ THEN } v := E(v) \text{ END}} \qquad \boxed{\text{SELECT } Q(w) \text{ THEN } w := F(w) \text{ END}}$$

then the statement to prove is the following (where $I(v)$ is the abstract invariant and $J(v, w)$ is the connecting invariant):

$$\boxed{I(v) \land J(v, w) \land Q(w) \;\Rightarrow\; P(v) \land J(E(v), F(w))}$$

Moreover, the concrete system must *not deadlock more often* than the abstract one. This is proved by stating that the disjunction of the abstract guards implies that of the concrete ones, formally:

$$\boxed{I(v) \land J(v, w) \land (P_1(v) \lor \ldots \lor P_n(v)) \;\Rightarrow\; Q_1(w) \lor \ldots \lor Q_n(w)}$$

where the P_i and Q_i denote the abstract and concrete guards respectively. Note that this statement could be split into n distinct statements.

2.4 Adding New Events in a Refinement

When refining an event system by another one, it is possible to *add new events*. Such events must be proved to refine the dummy event which does nothing (skip) in the abstraction. Moreover, a special proof must be performed, ensuring that the new events cannot collectively take control for ever. For this, a unique *variant expression* must be "decreased" by each new event. In the case of a new event of the following form:

$$\boxed{\text{SELECT } R(w) \text{ THEN } w := G(w) \text{ END}}$$

the following statement has thus to be proved:

$$\boxed{I(v) \wedge J(v,w) \;\Rightarrow\; V(w) \in \mathbb{N}}$$

$$\boxed{I(v) \wedge P(v) \wedge J(v,w) \;\Rightarrow\; J(v, G(w)) \wedge V(G(w)) < V(w)}$$

where $V(w)$ denotes the variant expression considered (here it is a natural number expression, but it can be more elaborate).

2.5 Special Properties of the Event System Used to Develop Sequential Programs

In this section, we shall express the specific properties that an event system used for sequential program development should satisfy. We shall also fix the *style* we shall adopt in our future program development.

(1) *At the beginning of a development*, our event system is first characterized by some *parameters*, say p, which denote some constant "input" of the future program. In other words they will not evolve when the future program is "run". The constant p are declared as follows:

$$\boxed{p \in S_p \;\wedge\; Pre\_condition(p)}$$

where S_p denotes the type of the parameters and $Pre\_condition(p)$ denotes a predicate defining a certain condition, which the *parameters* should satisfy (besides typing, of course). The initial system also has some variables, called here *results*. These variables are typed with S_r as follows:

$$\boxed{results \in S_r}$$

The initial event system contains only one event that can be fired any time: its guard is simply missing (hence it always holds). It involves the *results* and describes the characteristic properties of the outcome of the future program. Here is the most general form of this event:

$$
\begin{array}{|l|}
\hline
\textsf{aprog} \;\;\widehat{=} \\
\quad \text{BEGIN} \\
\qquad \text{ANY } r \text{ WHERE } r \in S_r \,\wedge\, Post\_condition(p,r) \text{ THEN } result := r \text{ END} \\
\quad \text{END} \\
\hline
\end{array}
$$

where S_r denotes the type of the *results* and $Post\_condition(p,r)$ denotes the final condition, which the program should satisfy. This condition involves the parameters p as well as the *results* r. The pre- and post- conditions together represent the *specification* of our program.

Notice that the initial system must contain another special event called init, which allows the initial value of *results* to freely "float" within its type as follows[1];

$$
\begin{array}{|l|}
\hline
\textsf{init} \;\;\widehat{=}\;\; \text{BEGIN } results :\in S_r \text{ END} \\
\hline
\end{array}
$$

(2) *During the development*, we perform various refinements of the initial event system. As a consequence, at each stage of the development, the current event system may contain more variables and more events.

(3) *At the end of the development*, and after applying some merging rules defined in the next section, one should obtain again a single event of the following form:

$$
\begin{array}{|l|}
\hline
\textsf{cprog} \;\;\widehat{=} \\
\quad \text{BEGIN} \\
\qquad Initialisation\;; \\
\qquad Program \\
\quad \text{END} \\
\hline
\end{array}
$$

where *Initialisation* corresponds to the last version of init and *Program* is the last version of aprog.

2.6 Merging Rules

We essentially have two merging rules, one for defining a conditional statement and the other one for defining a loop statement. Here are these rules:

$$
\begin{array}{|l|}
\hline
\text{SELECT } P \wedge Q \text{ THEN } S \text{ END} \\
\text{SELECT } P \wedge \neg Q \text{ THEN } T \text{ END} \\
\rightsquigarrow \\
\text{SELECT } P \text{ THEN} \\
\quad \text{IF } Q \text{ THEN } S \text{ ELSE } T \text{ END} \\
\text{END} \\
\hline
\end{array}
\qquad
\begin{array}{|l|}
\hline
\text{SELECT } P \wedge Q \text{ THEN } S \text{ END} \\
\text{SELECT } P \wedge \neg Q \text{ THEN } T \text{ END} \\
\rightsquigarrow \\
\text{SELECT } P \text{ THEN} \\
\quad \text{WHILE } Q \text{ DO } S \text{ END}\,;\, T \\
\text{END} \\
\hline
\end{array}
$$

---

[1] The construct $x :\in s$ is a shorthand for ANY y WHERE $y \in s$ THEN $x := y$ END.

These rules can be read as follows: if we have an event system where two events have forms corresponding to the ones shown in the antecedent of the rule, they can be merged into a single event corresponding to the consequent of the rule. Notice that both rules have the same "antecedent-events", so that the application of one or the other might be problematic. There is no confusion however as the rules have some *incompatible side conditions*:

- The second rule (that introducing WHILE) requires that the first antecedent event (that giving rise to the "body" S of the loop) appears at *one refinement level below that of the second one*. In this way, we are certain that there exists a variant ensuring that the loop terminates (see section 2.4). Moreover, *the first event must keep the common condition P invariant*. The merging event is considered to "appear" at the same level as the second antecedent event.
- The first rule (that introducing IF) is applicable when the second one is not. The merging event is considered to bear the same "level" as the smallest one. When the two merged events are not at the same level, the "merged variant" becomes the pair of both variants, which thus *decreases lexicographically*.

Note that in both rules, the common guard P is optional. If missing, the application of the rule results in a non-guarded event. The first rule may take a special form when one of the antecedent events has an IF form. It goes as follows:

```
SELECT   P ∧ Q   THEN   S   END
SELECT   P ∧ ¬Q  THEN
   IF   R   THEN   T   ELSE   U   END
END
⤳
SELECT   P   THEN
   IF   Q   THEN   S   ELSIF   R   THEN   T   ELSE   U   END
END
```

3 Example

The example we present in this section is inspired by the marking algorithm of Shorr and Waite. This algorithm has received a considerable attention in the literature, so that it is impossible to cite all references on the subject (a recent and interesting one is that of R. Bornat [5]). Given a graph and a certain point in it (called the "top"), the marking algorithm computes the image of this point under the transitive closure of the relation defining the graph. Informally, this algorithm is characterized by three properties:

1. It is is a graph traversal algorithm from the top.
2. The traversal is "depth-first".
3. The backtracking structure is stored within the graph itself.

3.1 A One Shot Specification

Let the graph be defined by a constant binary relation g built on a set N of nodes. Let c be the transitive closure of g (the required properties of c will appear in the next section). Let t be any node. The result r is a subset of N. The event mark computes in one shot the image of $\{t\}$ under c. **Fig.1** shows this marking performed in one shot[2].

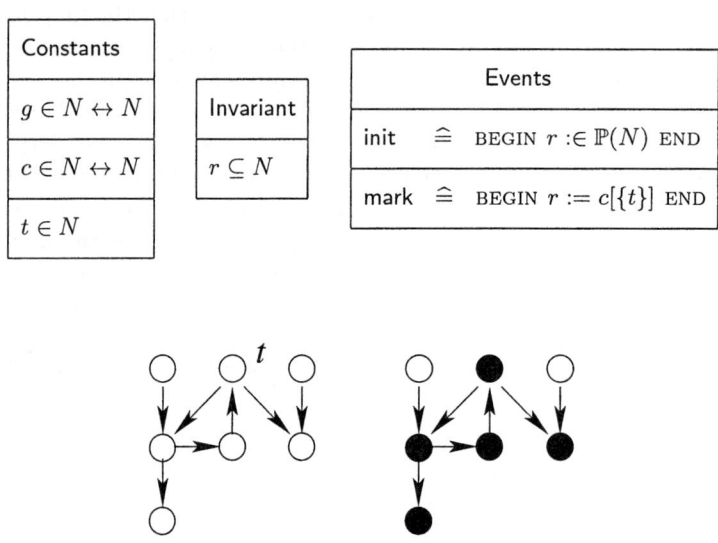

Fig. 1. Marking in one shot

3.2 Refinement 1: A Non-deterministic Loop

In this refinement, we introduce a new variables b (for "black"), which is a set of nodes, and a new event called prg1 (for "progress1"). The image of the set $\{t\}$ under the transitive closure c is now computed gradually. The node t is supposed to be in b, and the set b is supposed to be included in $c[\{t\}]$. It is set to the singleton $\{t\}$ in the init event[3]. The guard of event prg1 states that $g[b] - b$ is not empty. An element y of this set is thus chosen arbitrarily and put into the set b. The event mark is now guarded by the condition $g[b] \subseteq b$: in this case the closure $c[\{t\}]$ is exactly equal to the set b. **Fig.2** shows an animation of this non-deterministic algorithm.

---

[2] The main set-theoretic notations are summarized in the Appendix.
[3] In the event init, we have removed the initialisation of r in order to ease the reading.

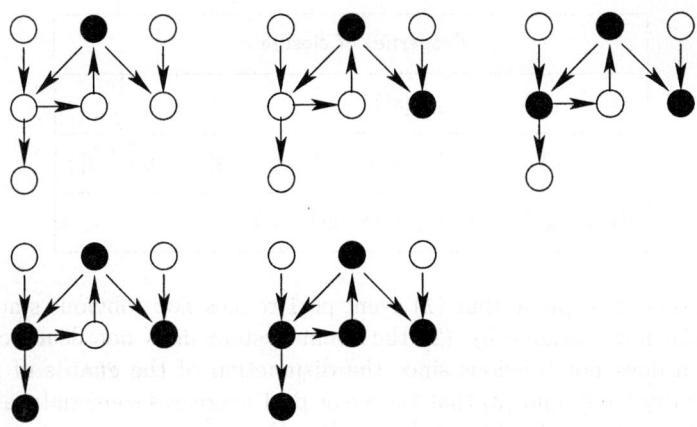

Fig. 2. A non-deterministic marking algorithm

Invariant
$b \subseteq N$
$t \in b$
$b \subseteq c[\{t\}]$

Events
init $\;\widehat{=}\;$ BEGIN $b := \{t\}$ END
prg1 $\;\widehat{=}\;$ SELECT $g[b] \not\subseteq b$ THEN ANY y WHERE $\quad y \in g[b] - b$ THEN $\quad b := b \cup \{y\}$ END END
mark $\;\widehat{=}\;$ SELECT $g[b] \subseteq b$ THEN $r := b$ END

In order to validate this refinement, we mainly need to prove that (1) the initialisation establishes the invariant $b \subseteq c[\{t\}]$, (2) the event prg1 maintains it, and (3) the concrete version of event mark refines its abstraction. After some elementary transformations, these amount to proving respectively:

To be proved
$\{t\} \subseteq c[\{t\}]$
$x, y \in g \;\wedge\; x \in c[\{t\}] \;\Rightarrow\; y \in c[\{t\}]$
$t \in b \;\wedge\; b \subseteq c[\{t\}] \;\wedge\; g[b] \subseteq b \;\Rightarrow\; c[\{t\}] \subseteq b$

For proving this, we only need the following well known properties of the closure c of g:

Properties of closure c
$\forall s \cdot (\, s \subseteq N \;\Rightarrow\; s \subseteq c[s] \,)$
$\forall (s, x, y) \cdot (\, s \subseteq N \;\wedge\; x, y \in g \;\wedge\; x \in c[s] \;\Rightarrow\; y \in c[s] \,)$
$\forall s \cdot (\, s \subseteq N \;\wedge\; g[s] \subseteq s \;\Rightarrow\; c[s] \subseteq s \,)$

We also need to prove that (1) event prg1 refines skip (obvious since it only involves the new variable b), (2) the event system does not deadlock as the abstraction does not (obvious since the disjunction of the guards of prg1 and mark is clearly true), and (3) that the event prg1 decreases some natural number quantity (take the cardinality of the set $N - b$).

3.3 Refinement 2: Making the Loop More Deterministic (Depth-First Marking)

This refinement contains the *first key decision* of the development. The idea is to constrain the previous non-deterministic algorithm to always move more deeply in the graph until one encounters either a terminal node or some previously encountered nodes. At this point, the algorithm backtracks to the previously visited node, and from there continues to explore the graph if possible, and so on. Note that there remains some non-determinacy in this algorithm as the choice of the branch to follow in a node is arbitrary. We introduce three variables in this refinement:

- First a, so-called, *current pointer* p. It always corresponds to a black node, from which we move to a deeper node in the graph. Initially p is set to the "top" node t.
- The second variable is a, so-called, *backtracking structure* f. It allows one to make p revisit the previous node when it cannot pursue further its depth-first graph traversal. The backtracking structure f has some interesting properties as shown in **Fig.3**: it is an injective function, it is made of black nodes only, its domain extended with $\{t\}$ is exactly its range extended with $\{p\}$, it has no cycle, and, when reversed, it is included in the graph g. Moreover, if we consider the image under g of the black nodes that are not in the backtracking structure, this image is made of black nodes only.
- The third variable is a *boolean* n which is used to detect the end of the loop. When equal to OK then $g[b]$ is included in b.

Fig. 3. The backtracking Structure

Invariant
$p \in b$
$f \in (b \cup \{p\}) - \{t\} \rightarrowtail (b \cup \{t\}) - \{p\}$

$\mathrm{dom}(f) \cup \{t\} = \mathrm{ran}(f) \cup \{p\}$
$\forall s \cdot (\, s \subseteq \mathrm{dom}(f) \cup \{t\} \,\wedge\, t \in s \,\wedge\, f^{-1}[s] \subseteq s \,\Rightarrow\, \mathrm{dom}(f) \cup \{t\} \subseteq s\,)$
$f^{-1} \subseteq g$
$g[b - (\mathrm{dom}(f) \cup \{t\})] \subseteq b$
$n \in \{OK, KO\}$
$n = OK \,\Rightarrow\, g[b] \subseteq b$

Two new events are introduced: **prg2** and **prg3**. Event **prg2** is doing the backtracking and event **prg3** is detecting the end of the loop (when p is equal to t and when there are no further nodes to explore from t). These events must decrease some natural number quantity (take the cardinality of f augmented with the encoding of n: 1 when KO, 0 when OK). Here are the events of this refinement:

		Events
init	$\widehat{=}$	BEGIN $b, p, f, n := \{t\}, t, \emptyset, KO$ END
prg1	$\widehat{=}$	SELECT $n = KO \,\wedge\, g[\{p\}] \not\subseteq b$ THEN ANY y WHERE $y \in g[\{p\}] - b$ THEN $b, p, f := b \cup \{y\}, y, f \cup \{y \mapsto p\}$ END END
prg2	$\widehat{=}$	SELECT $n = KO \,\wedge\, g[\{p\}] \subseteq b \,\wedge\, p \neq t$ THEN $p, f := f(p), \{p\} \triangleleft f$ END
prg3	$\widehat{=}$	SELECT $n = KO \,\wedge\, g[\{p\}] \subseteq b \,\wedge\, p = t$ THEN $n := OK$ END
mark	$\widehat{=}$	SELECT $n = OK$ THEN $r := b$ END

At this point, it might be interesting to apply the merging rules, just to have an idea of the abstract program we could obtain. Merging events **prg2** and **prg3** leads to the following:

$$\begin{array}{l}\mathsf{prg2\_3} \;\;\widehat{=}\\ \quad\text{SELECT } n = KO \,\wedge\, g[\{p\}] \subseteq b \text{ THEN}\\ \qquad\text{IF } p \neq t \text{ THEN}\\ \qquad\quad\boxed{p, f := f(p), \{p\} \triangleleft f}\\ \qquad\text{ELSE}\\ \qquad\quad\boxed{n := OK}\\ \qquad\text{END}\\ \quad\text{END}\end{array}$$

Now merging events prg1 and prg2_3 leads to the following (note that the WHILE merging rule is not applicable here since event prg2_3, which could be a potential candidate for the loop body since it appears one level below that of prg1, prg2_3 does not keep invariant the common guard $n = KO$):

$$\begin{array}{l}\mathsf{prg1\_2\_3} \;\;\widehat{=}\\ \quad\text{SELECT } n = KO \text{ THEN}\\ \qquad\text{IF } g[\{p\}] \not\subseteq b \text{ THEN}\\ \qquad\quad\boxed{\text{ANY } y \text{ WHERE } y \in g[\{p\}] - b \text{ THEN } b, p, f := b \cup \{y\}, y, f \cup \{y \mapsto p\} \text{ END}}\\ \qquad\text{ELSIF } q \neq t \text{ THEN}\\ \qquad\quad\boxed{p, f := f(p), \{p\} \triangleleft f}\\ \qquad\text{ELSE}\\ \qquad\quad\boxed{n := OK}\\ \qquad\text{END}\\ \quad\text{END}\end{array}$$

Merging finally events mark and prg1_2_3 leads to the following (we have no problem here applying the WHILE loop since there is no common remaining guard):

$$\begin{array}{l}\mathsf{mark\_prg1\_2\_3} \;\;\widehat{=}\\ \quad\text{WHILE } n = KO \text{ DO}\\ \qquad\text{IF } g[\{p\}] \not\subseteq b \text{ THEN}\\ \qquad\quad\boxed{\text{ANY } y \text{ WHERE } y \in g[\{p\}] - b \text{ THEN } b, p, f := b \cup \{y\}, y, f \cup \{y \mapsto p\} \text{ END}}\\ \qquad\text{ELSIF } q \neq t \text{ THEN}\\ \qquad\quad\boxed{p, f := f(p), \{p\} \triangleleft f}\\ \qquad\text{ELSE}\\ \qquad\quad\boxed{n := OK}\\ \qquad\text{END}\\ \quad\text{END ;}\\ \quad\boxed{r := b}\end{array}$$

By adding the init event, we obtain the following abstract program:

Event Based Sequential Program Development

$$\boxed{b,p,f,n := \{t\}, t, \emptyset, KO}\ ;$$
WHILE $n = KO$ DO
  IF $g[\{p\}] \not\subseteq b$ THEN
    $\boxed{\text{ANY } y \text{ WHERE } y \in g[\{p\}] - b \text{ THEN } b,p,f := b \cup \{y\}, y, f \cup \{y \mapsto p\} \text{ END}}$
  ELSIF $q \neq t$ THEN
    $\boxed{p, f := f(p), \{p\} \triangleleft f}$
  ELSE
    $\boxed{n := OK}$
  END
END ;
$\boxed{r := b}$

In **Fig.4**, you can see an animation of this abstract algorithm. Notice the current pointer (emphasized in grey, but it is also black!) and the backtracking structure situated next to the pointers forming the graph.

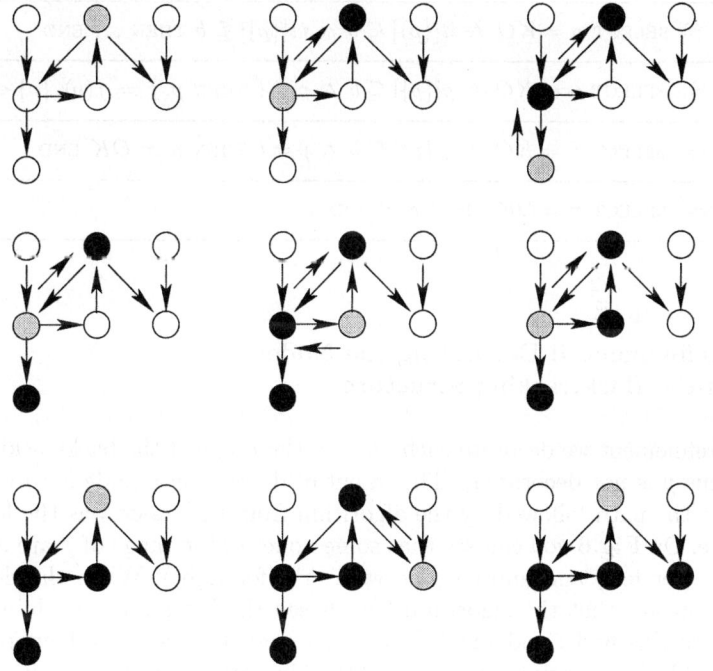

Fig. 4. A depth-first marking with backtracking structure and current point

3.4 Refinement 3: Specializing the Graph by Means of Two Partial Functions

In this refinement, we refine the constant relation g by two constant partial functions called lt (for 'left") and rt (for "right"). There are no changes in the variables. The event prg1 is refined by two events prg11 and prg12. They correspond to a left or right descent respectively. The algorithm is now completely deterministic: one first tries to move down along the left path then along the right one. **Fig.5.** shows an animation of this algorithm (we have represented the left arrows in white and the right ones in black).

Events	
init $\triangleq$	BEGIN $b, p, f, n := \{t\}, t, \emptyset, KO$ END
prg11 $\triangleq$	SELECT $n = KO \land lt[\{p\}] \not\subseteq b$ THEN $b, p, f := b \cup \{lt(p)\}, lt(p), f \cup \{lt(p) \mapsto p\}$ END
prg12 $\triangleq$	SELECT $n = KO \land lt[\{p\}] \subseteq b \land rt[\{p\}] \not\subseteq b$ THEN ... END
prg2 $\triangleq$	SELECT $n = KO \land g[\{p\}] \subseteq b \land p \neq t$ THEN $p, f := f(p), \{p\} \triangleleft f$ END
prg3 $\triangleq$	SELECT $n = KO \land g[\{p\}] \subseteq b \land p = t$ THEN $n := OK$ END
mark $\triangleq$	SELECT $n = OK$ THEN $r := b$ END

3.5 Refinement 4: Decorating the Nodes of the Backtracking Structure

In this refinement we decorate each node of the range of the backtracking structure (thus p is not decorated). The intent of decorating a node is to record the fact that the path followed by the algorithm from that node was the left or the right one. On **Fig.6** you can see that some nodes of the range of f are decorated with "l" (for left) and another one with "r" (for right). When the decoration is "l", it means that the algorithm has chosen the left pointer in doing further visits from this node, and similarly for the other direction. We have painted in white or black the pointer of the backtracking structure whose initial node is decorated "l" or "r" respectively.

We introduce two variables, called lft and rht, corresponding to the sets of decorated nodes. These sets form a partition of the range of f. Moreover by reversing a pointer of f which is ending in a node of lft we obtain a pointer of lt and similarly for the other direction. These properties are formalized in the following table:

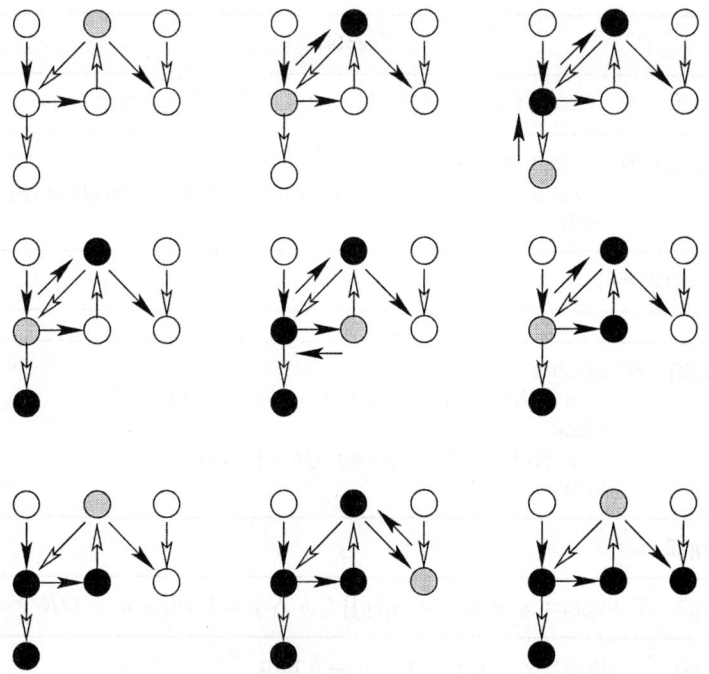

Fig. 5. Adding left and right pointers

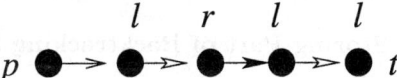

Fig. 6. Decorating the nodes (except first) and pointers (except first) of the backtracking structure f

Invariant
$lft \subseteq N$
$rht \subseteq N$
$lft \cup rht = \mathsf{ran}\,(f)$

Invariant
$lft \cap rht = \emptyset$
$lft \triangleleft f^{-1} \subseteq lt$
$rht \triangleleft f^{-1} \subseteq rt$

The event prg2 is refined by two events prg21 and prg22. They correspond to a left or right backtracking respectively. Here are the events of this refinement:

Events
init $\;\widehat{=}\;$ BEGIN $b, p, f, n, lft, rht := \{t\}, t, \emptyset, KO, \emptyset, \emptyset$ END
prg11 $\;\widehat{=}\;$ SELECT $n = KO \land lt[\{p\}] \not\subseteq b$ THEN $\quad b, p, f, lft := b \cup \{lt(p)\}, lt(p), f \cup \{lt(p) \mapsto p\}, lft \cup \{p\}$ END
prg12 $\;\widehat{=}\;$ ...

prg21 $\;\widehat{=}\;$ SELECT $\quad n = KO \land g[\{p\}] \subseteq b \land p \neq t \land f(p) \in lft$ THEN $\quad p, f, lft := f(p), \{p\} \triangleleft\!\!\!- f, lft - \{f(p)\}$ END
prg22 $\;\widehat{=}\;$ ...
prg3 $\;\widehat{=}\;$ SELECT $n = KO \land g[\{p\}] \subseteq b \land p = t$ THEN $n := OK$ END
mark $\;\widehat{=}\;$ SELECT $n = OK$ THEN $r := b$ END

3.6 Refinement 5: Storing Part of Backtracking Structure within the Graph

This refinement contains the *second key decision* of the development. This is the main idea of the Schorr and Waite paper: it consists in storing the backtracking structure in the graph itself, which is thus modified during the execution but recovers its initial setting at the end of it.

For this, we introduce two new variables called *ult* and *urt*. They represent the "dynamic" left and right pointers of the graph. The backtracking structure is now *almost* stored in *ult* and *urt*, "almost" because there remains the pair $p \mapsto f(p)$, which, when it exists, cannot be stored in the graph. For this, we define a new variable called h: it is a mini-function which is either empty or contains a single pair. Here are the definitions and properties of these variables:

Invariant
$ult \in N \nrightarrow N$
$urt \in N \nrightarrow N$
$h \in N \nrightarrow N$

Invariant
$ult = lft \triangleleft\!\!\!- lt \cup lft \triangleleft f$
$urt = rht \triangleleft\!\!\!- rt \cup rht \triangleleft f$
$h = \{p\} \triangleleft f$

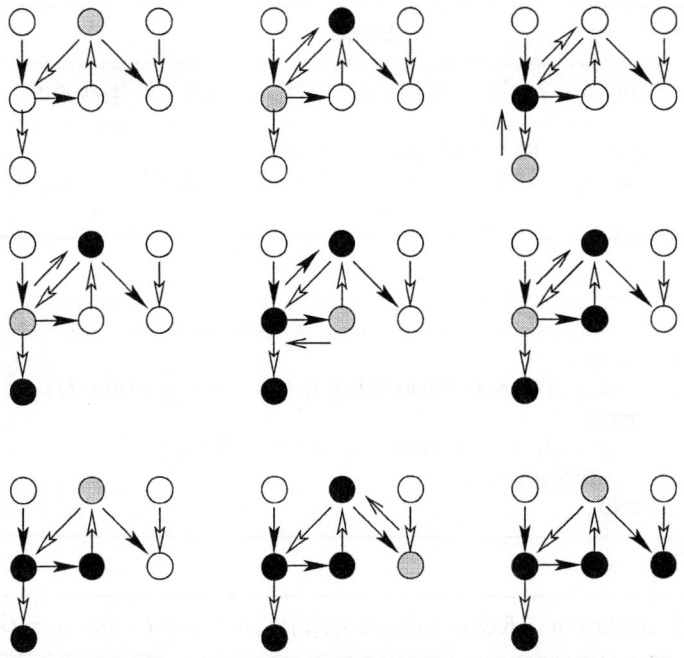

Fig. 7. Decorating the backtracking structure

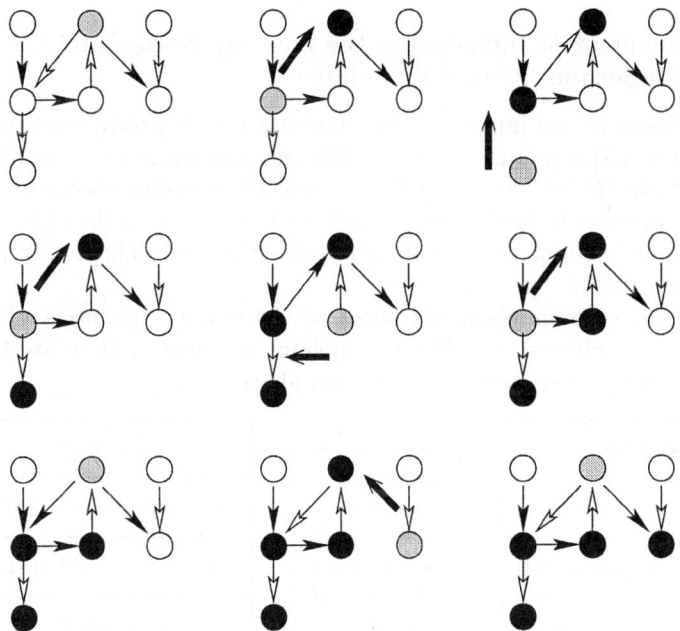

Fig. 8. Storing part of the backtracking structure within the graph (the remaining part is emphasized)

Events
init $\;\widehat{=}\;$ BEGIN $b, p, f, n, lft, rht, ult, urt := \{t\}, t, \emptyset, KO, \emptyset, \emptyset, lt, rt$ END
prg11 $\;\widehat{=}\;$ SELECT $n = KO \wedge ult[\{p\}] \not\subseteq b$ THEN $\quad b, p, h, lft, ult := b \cup \{ult(p)\}, ult(p), (\{p\} \triangleleft ult)^{-1}, lft \cup \{p\}, \{p\}\triangleleft ult \cup h$ END
prg12 $\;\widehat{=}\;$ ...

prg21 $\;\widehat{=}\;$ SELECT $\quad n = KO \wedge (ult \cup urt)[\{p\}] \subseteq b \wedge p \neq t \wedge h(p) \in lft$ THEN $\quad p, h, lft := h(p), \{h(p)\} \triangleleft ult, lft - \{h(p)\}\;\|$ $\quad ult(h(p)) := p$ END
prg22 $\;\widehat{=}\;$ ...
prg3 $\;\widehat{=}\;$ SELECT $n = KO \wedge (ult \cup urt)[\{p\}] \subseteq b \wedge p = t$ THEN $n := OK$ END
mark $\;\widehat{=}\;$ SELECT $n = OK$ THEN $r := b$ END

3.7 Refinement 6: Introducing the Dummy Node "nil" and a Second "Current" Pointer

In this refinement, we implement the mini-function h which, when non-empty, is made of a unique pair starting in p. The implementation is done by means of a second "sub-current" pointer q. In fact, when it is empty, then p is situated at the top, t. In order to implement the pair $p \mapsto h(p)$ even at the point t, we have no choice but introducing a "dummy" node, called nil. This is the purpose of this refinement.

This leads to a simple modification of the dynamic pointers ult and urt, which becomes vlt and vrt. The new pointer is called q. Here are the formal definitions and properties of these new variables:

Constants
$nil \in N$
$nil \notin \mathsf{dom}(lt) \cup \mathsf{dom}(rt)$
$nil \notin \mathsf{ran}(lt) \cup \mathsf{ran}(rt)$
$t \neq nil$

Invariant
$vlt \in N \nrightarrow N$
$vrt \in N \nrightarrow N$
$q \in N$

Invariant
$vlt = ult \Leftarrow (lft \triangleleft \{t \mapsto nil\})$
$vrt = urt \Leftarrow (rht \triangleleft \{t \mapsto nil\})$
$p = t \Rightarrow q = nil$
$p \neq t \Rightarrow q = h(t)$

Events
init $\triangleq$ BEGIN $b, p, q, n, lft, rht, vlt, vrt := \{t\}, t, nil, KO, \emptyset, \emptyset, lt, rt$ END
prg11 $\triangleq$ SELECT $n = KO \wedge vlt[\{p\}] \not\subseteq b$ THEN $b, p, q, lft := b \cup \{vlt(p)\}, vlt(p), p, lft \cup \{p\} \parallel vlt(p) := q$ END
prg12 $\triangleq$ ...

prg21 $\triangleq$ SELECT
    $n = KO \wedge (vlt \cup vrt)[\{p\}] \subseteq b \wedge p \neq t \wedge q \in lft$
THEN
    $p, q, lft := q, vlt(q), lft - \{q\} \parallel vlt(q) := p$
END

prg22 $\triangleq$ ...
prg3 $\triangleq$ SELECT $n = KO \wedge (vlt \cup vrt)[\{p\}] \subseteq b \wedge p = t$ THEN $n := OK$ END
mark $\triangleq$ SELECT $n = OK$ THEN $r := b$ END

3.8 Refinement 7: Making the Graph Functions Total

In this refinement we are making the two functions vlt and vrt total by introducing nil as a dummy value when they are not defined. For this we define two new constants ltp and rtp and two new variables wlt and wrt. They are as follows:

Constants	Invariant
$ltp \in N \to N$	$wlt \in N \to N$
$rtp \in N \to N$	$wrt \in N \to N$
$ltp = (N \times \{nil\}) \triangleleft lt$	$wlt = (N \times \{nil\}) \triangleleft vlt$
$rtp = (N \times \{nil\} \triangleleft rt$	$wrt = (N \times \{nil\} \triangleleft vrt$

init $\cong$	BEGIN $b, p, q, n, lft, rht, wlt, wrt := \{t\}, t, nil, KO, \emptyset, \emptyset, ltp, rtp$ END

prg11 $\cong$	SELECT $n = KO \land wlt(p) \neq nil \land wlt(p) \notin b$ THEN $\quad b, p, q, lft := b \cup \{wlt(p)\}, wlt(p), p, lft \cup \{p\} \parallel wlt(p) := q$ END

prg12 $\cong$	...

prg21 $\cong$	SELECT $\quad n = KO \land \neg(wlt(p) \neq nil \land wlt(p) \notin b) \land$ $\quad \neg(wrt(p) \neq nil \land wrt(p) \notin b) \land p \neq t \land q \in lft$ THEN $\quad p, q, lft := q, wlt(q), lft - \{q\} \parallel wlt(q) := p$ END

prg22 $\cong$	...

prg3 $\cong$	SELECT $\quad n = KO \land \neg(wlt(p) \neq nil \land wlt(p) \notin b) \land$ $\quad \neg(wrt(p) \neq nil \land wrt(p) \notin b) \land p = t$ THEN $\quad n := OK$ END

mark $\cong$	SELECT $n = OK$ THEN $r := b$ END

3.9 Refinement 8: Introducing Color and Direction

In this last refinement we encode the sets b, lft and rht. The first one, b, is encoded by means of a total function clr capable of taking two values, namely $BLACK$ and $WHITE$. The second and third sets are together encoded by means of a total function dir capable of taking two values, namely $LEFT$ and $RIGHT$. The verification of this refinement requires to prove that the pointer q is either in the set lft or in the set rht. Here are the definitions of these new variables:

Invariant
$clr \in NODE \rightarrow \{BLACK, WHITE\}$
$dir \in NODE \rightarrow \{LEFT, RIGHT\}$

Invariant
$b = clr^{-1}[\{BLACK\}]$
$lft \subseteq dir^{-1}[\{LEFT\}]$
$rht \subseteq dir^{-1}[\{RIGHT\}]$

init	$\triangleq$ BEGIN $p, q, n := t, nil, KO \parallel clr(t) := BLACK$ END

prg11	$\triangleq$ SELECT $n = KO \land wlt(p) \neq nil \land clr(wlt(p)) = WHITE$ THEN $clr(wlt(p)) := BLACK \parallel p, q := wlt(p), p \parallel$ $dir(p) := LEFT \parallel wlt(p) := q$ END

prg12	$\triangleq$ SELECT $n = KO \land \neg(wlt(p) \neq nil \land clr(wlt(p)) = WHITE) \land$ $wrt(p) \neq nil \land clr(wrt(p)) = WHITE$ THEN $clr(wrt(p)) := BLACK \parallel p, q := wrt(p), p \parallel$ $dir(p) := RIGHT \parallel wrt(p) := q$ END

prg21	$\triangleq$ SELECT $n = KO \land \neg(wlt(p) \neq nil \land clr(wlt(p)) = WHITE) \land$ $\neg(wrt(p) \neq nil \land clr(wrt(p)) = WHITE) \land p \neq t \land q \in lft$ THEN $p, q := q, wlt(q) \parallel wlt(q) := p$ END

prg22	$\triangleq$ SELECT $n = KO \land \neg(wlt(p) \neq nil \land clr(wlt(p)) = WHITE) \land$ $\neg(wrt(p) \neq nil \land clr(wrt(p)) = WHITE) \land p \neq t \land q \notin lft$ THEN $p, q := q, wrt(q) \parallel wrt(q) := p$ END

prg3	$\triangleq$ SELECT $n = KO \land \neg(wlt(p) \neq nil \land clr(wlt(p)) = WHITE) \land$ $\neg(wrt(p) \neq nil \land clr(wrt(p)) = WHITE) \land p = t$ THEN $n := OK$ END

mark	$\triangleq$ SELECT $n = OK$ THEN $r := clr^{-1}[\{BLACK\}]$ END

3.10 Obtaining the Final Program

Applying the merging rules in very much the same way as we have done it in section 3.3, leads to the following program. Note that we have not mentioned the mark event at the end of the program since our final purpose is just to change the colors of the relevant nodes. Also note that this program needs a few more obvious transformations in order to remove the various occurrences of the "$\parallel$" operators and replace them by ";". This would require the introduction of some local variables, and can be done on a purely syntactic basis.

$$
\begin{array}{l}
\boxed{\begin{array}{l} p,q,n := t, nil, KO \ \| \\ clr(t) := BLACK \end{array}} \ ; \\
\text{WHILE } n = KO \text{ DO} \\
\quad \text{IF } wlt(p) \neq nil \ \wedge \ clr(wlt(p)) = WHITE \text{ THEN} \\
\qquad \boxed{\begin{array}{l} clr(wlt(p)) := BLACK \ \| \\ p,q := wlt(p), p \ \| \\ dir(p) := LEFT \ \| \\ wlt(p) := q \end{array}} \\
\quad \text{ELSIF } wrt(p) \neq nil \ \wedge \ clr(wrt(p)) = WHITE \text{ THEN} \\
\qquad \boxed{\begin{array}{l} clr(wrt(p)) := BLACK \ \| \\ p,q := wrt(p), p \ \| \\ dir(p) := RIGHT \ \| \\ wrt(p) := q \end{array}} \\
\quad \text{ELSIF } p \neq t \text{ THEN} \\
\qquad \text{IF } dir(q) = LEFT \text{ THEN} \\
\qquad\quad \boxed{p,q := q, wlt(q) \ \| \ wlt(q) := p} \\
\qquad \text{ELSE} \\
\qquad\quad \boxed{p,q := q, wrt(q) \ \| \ wrt(q) := p} \\
\qquad \text{END} \\
\quad \text{ELSE} \\
\qquad \boxed{n := OK} \\
\quad \text{END} \\
\text{END}
\end{array}
$$

As can be seen, this algorithm is *very symmetric* with respect to the "left" and "right" directions. This was not the case with the original Schorr and Waite algorithm. An interesting outcome of the algorithm presented here is that it seems more efficient than the original one, where each marked node is visited three times. Here each marked node is visited once plus the number of outgoing pointers leading to genuine nodes that are not already marked. In the example shown, where we have five marked nodes, the original algorithm takes 15 iterations, whereas the one presented here takes only 9 iterations: two nodes are visited three times and three nodes are visited only once.

3.11 About Proofs

The development has been entirely proven with Atelier B [8], the tool associated with the B Method. In the following table, the statistical details of these proofs can be seen. It shows that approximatively 70% of the proofs are done automatically.

The interactive proofs have all been done with the new interface, "Click'n Prove" [3], which has recently been developed for Atelier B. Most of them are simple. A few of them, however, are technically (not mathematically) slightly more difficult. You can observe that, by the end of the development a larger proportion of proofs have to be done interactively: this is essentially due to the growing presence of useless hypotheses, which induce some noise and thus make the automatic prover less efficient. The interaction then essentially consists of *reducing the number of relevant hypotheses* and then launching the automatic prover.

Refinement Steps	Automatic	Interactive	Total
1. Non-deterministic Traversal	1	3	4
2. Depth-First Traversal	25	4	29
3. Introducing Left and Right Partial Functions	4	0	4
4. Decorating the Backtracking Structure	13	1	14
5. Storing the Backtracking Structure	24	8	32
6. Introducing "nil" and the Second Pointer	10	11	21
7. Making Left and Right Functions Total	26	13	26
8. Introducing Colors and Directions	12	11	23
TOTAL	108	45	153

4 Conclusion

We have presented an event-based approach to the development of sequential programs, and we have demonstrated it on a well-known non-trivial pointer program: the Schorr-Waite marking algorithm. Contrary to what is done usually, rather than proving it directly, we formally develop this program by means of a number of successive refinement steps. Note that the first two objectives of the Schorr-Waite algorithm (namely graph traversal from "top" and depth-first traversal) are reached after the first and second refinements, whereas the third one (storing the backtracking function in the graph) is obtained after the 5th and 6th refinements.

Acknowledgements

I would like to warmly thank D. Cansell and W. Stoddart for their very careful reading of this text.

References

1. H. Schorr and W.M. Waite. *An Efficient Machine-Independent Procedure for Garbage Collection in Various List Structures.* CACM Aug 1967
2. J.R. Abrial. *The B-Book – Assigning Programs to Meanings.* Cambridge University Press, 1996.
3. J.R. Abrial and D. Cansell *Click'n Prove: Interactive Proofs Within Set Theory* TPHOLs 2003.
4. J.R. Abrial, D. Cansell and D. Méry *A Mechanically Proved and Incremental Development of IEEE Tree Identify Protocol* Formal Aspect of Computing 14. 2003
5. R. Bornat. *Proving Pointer Programs in Hoare Logic.* In R. Backhouse and J. Oliveira, editors, *Mathematics of Program Construction (MPC 2000),* LNCS 1837. Springer-Varlag, 2000.
6. R.J.R Back and R. Kurki-Suonio. *Decentralization of Process Nets with Centralized Control* 2nd ACM SIGACT-SIGOPS Symposium on Principles of Distributed Computing. 1983.
7. E.W. Dijkstra *A Discipline of Programming* Prentice-Hall. 1976.
8. Clearsy *ATELIER B. User Manual.* Aix-en-Provence. 2001.

Appendix: Summary of Notations

Notation	Meaning
$\mathbb{P}(s)$	Set of subsets of s
$s \times t$	Cartesian product of s and t
$s \leftrightarrow t$	Set of binary relations from s to t. Same as $\mathbb{P}(s \times t)$
$r[s]$	Image of set s under binary relation r
$s \rightarrow\!\!\!\rightarrow t$	Set of partial functions from s to t
$s \rightarrowtail\!\!\!\rightarrow t$	Set of partial injections from s to t. Same as $(s \rightarrow\!\!\!\rightarrow t) \cap (t \rightarrow\!\!\!\rightarrow s)$
$s \triangleleft r$	Binary relation r reduced to pairs starting in set s
$s \triangleleft\!\!\!- r$	Binary relation r reduced to pairs not starting in set s
$a \mapsto b$	The pair made of a and b
$f \triangleleft\!\!\!- g$	Relation f overridden by relation g. Same as $(\text{dom}(g) \triangleleft\!\!\!- f) \cup g$
$f(x) := y$	Same as $f := f \triangleleft\!\!\!- \{x \mapsto y\}$

Proving the Shalls[1]

Steven P. Miller[1], Alan C. Tribble[1], and Mats P.E. Heimdahl[2]

[1] Rockwell Collins, 400 Collins Road NE,
Cedar Rapids, Iowa, 52498, USA
{spmiller, actribbl}@rockwellcollins.com

[2] Department of Computer Science and Engineering, University of Minnesota,
4-192 EE/CSci Bldg, 200 Union Street S.E., Minneapolis, Minnesota, 55455, USA
heimdahl@cs.umn.edu

Abstract. This paper describes an experiment conducted to determine how effectively formal methods could be used to capture and validate the requirements of a typical embedded system. A model of the mode logic of a Flight Guidance System was specified in the RSML^{-e} notation and translated into the NuSMV model checker and the PVS theorem prover. These tools were then used to verify several hundred properties of the RSML^{-e} model. In the process, several errors were discovered and corrected in the original model. This demonstrates that formal requirements models can be written for real problems and that formal analysis tools have matured to the point where they can be used to find errors before implementation. It also points out a clear relationship between requirements stated informally as "shalls", formal properties, and requirements models.

1 Introduction

Incomplete, inaccurate, ambiguous, and volatile requirements have plagued the software industry since its inception. In a 1987 article, Fred Brooks wrote [1]

> "The hardest single part of building a software system is deciding precisely what to build. No other part of the conceptual work is as difficult as establishing the detailed technical requirements... No other part of the work so cripples the resulting system if done wrong. No other part is as difficult to rectify later."

Studies have shown that the majority of software errors are made during requirements analysis, and that most of these errors are not found until the later phases of a project. Other studies have shown that the cost of fixing a requirements error grows dramatically the later in the product life cycle it is corrected [2], [3], [4], [5]. Researchers have also found that requirements errors are more likely to affect the safety of a system than errors introduced during design or implementation [6], [7].

---

[1] This project was partially funded by the NASA Langley Research Center under contract NCC1-01001 of the Aviation Safety Program.

The avionics industry has long recognized the need for better requirements, and has spearheaded the development of several methodologies for requirements specification. The Software Cost Reduction (SCR) methodology [8] was originally developed to specify the requirements for the A-7 aircraft [9]. It was later extended to the CoRE methodology by the Software Productivity Consortium [10] and used to specify the avionics requirements on the Lockheed C-130J [12]. The Requirements State Machine Language (RSML) notation was developed to specify the requirements for TCAS-II, a collision avoidance system installed on all commercial aircraft seating more than 30 passengers [13]. Even Statecharts, whose various derivatives make up one of the most widely accepted modeling notations in use today, has its roots in the avionics industry [13].

Despite this legacy, the requirements for most avionics systems are still specified using a combination of natural language and informal diagrams. In fact, in some ways, these efforts have actually increased the confusion about what requirements are and how they should be stated. Should requirements be captured as a list of "shall" statements written in a natural language? Or should requirements be expressed as mathematical models defining the relationship between the inputs and outputs as is done in SCR, CoRE, and RSML? Can the requirements of a system be completely stated with use cases? When does one cross the line between requirements analysis and design, and why does that matter?

This paper describes an experiment conducted by the Advanced Technology Center of Rockwell Collins, the Critical Systems Research Group at the University of Minnesota, and the NASA Langley Research Center to determine how far formal analysis could be pushed in an industrial example. In this exercise, a model of the mode logic of a Flight Guidance System was specified in the RSML^{-e} notation. While this model was representative in size and complexity of an actual system, it did not describe a fielded product. Translators were developed from RSML^{-e} to the NuSMV model checker and the PVS theorem prover. These tools were then used to verify several hundred properties of the RSML^{-e} model. In the process, several errors were discovered and corrected in the original RSML^{-e} model.

The results of this experiment are dramatic. They demonstrate that formal models can be written for real problems using notations acceptable to practicing engineers, and that formal analysis tools have matured to the point where they can be efficiently used to find errors before implementation. In previous experiments conducted by the authors using this example, only limited formal analysis was done on the model, or one model was used for specification and simulation while another model was created by hand for formal verification. For example, [14] describes the authors' experiences modeling the mode logic informally using the CoRE methodology [11] and the benefits that were gained from entering this model into the SCR* tool and using the consistency and completeness checks provided by SCR* [8]. In [16], a portion of the mode logic was modeled by hand in PVS and several properties were proven using the PVS theorem prover. In contrast, in this experiment, the same model was used for specification, review, and simulation, and automatically translated into other notations for formal verification. Also, all of the functional and safety requirements were formally verified in a clearly cost-effective manner.

Perhaps just as important, this experiment clarifies the relationship between requirements stated informally as shall statements, formal properties stated in notations such as predicate calculus and temporal logic, and requirements models written in notations such as RSML, SCR, or Statecharts. This is discussed in detail in Section 4.

2 Background Information

This section provides useful background information, including a description of the role of a Flight Guidance System in a modern aircraft and provides a brief overview of the RSML^{-e} notation, the NuSMV model checker, and the PVS theorem proving system.

2.1 Overview of a Flight Guidance System

A Flight Guidance System (FGS) is a component of the overall Flight Control System (FCS). It compares the measured state of an aircraft (position, speed, and attitude) to the desired state and generates pitch and roll guidance commands to minimize the difference between the measured and desired state. These guidance commands are both displayed to the pilot as guidance cues on the Primary Flight Display (PFD) and sent to the Autopilot (AP) that moves the control surfaces of the aircraft to achieve commanded pitch and roll.

The internal structure of the FGS can be broken down into the *mode logic* and the *flight control laws*. The flight control laws accept information about the aircraft's current and desired state and compute the pitch and roll guidance commands. The mode logic determines which lateral and vertical modes are armed and active at any given time. These in turn determine which flight control laws are generating guidance commands.

Our model of the FGS function includes identical left and right sides. In most modes, only one side is active and responds to pilot inputs and produces outputs. The inactive side simply copies its internal state from the active side, serving as a hot backup. In a few critical modes such as Approach and Go Around, both sides of the FGS are active and generate outputs that are compared before they are used.

We have used the mode logic of a FGS as an example in several previous studies [14], [15], [16], [17]. It is an excellent example because it is complex and representative of a class of problems frequently encountered in the design of embedded control systems.

2.2 The RSML^{-e} Specification Language

For this exercise, we specified the FGS mode logic using the RSML^{-e} notation, a derivative of RSML. RSML is a state-based specification language developed by Leveson's group at the University of California at Irvine as a language for specifying the behavior of process control systems [12]. One of the main design goals of RSML was readability and understandability by non-computer professionals such as end-users, engineers in the application domain, managers, and representatives from regulatory agencies. RSML was used to specify TCAS-II and this specification was ultimately adopted by the FAA as the official specification for TCAS-II.

RSML was heavily influenced by Statecharts [13] and uses a similar notion of explicit event propagation. In the course of developing the TCAS-II specification and the independent verification and validation effort, it became clear that the most common source of errors was this dependence on explicit events. To reduce this problem, the Critical Systems group at the University of Minnesota developed RSML^{-e} (RSML without events) [18]. As its name implies, RSML^{-e} eliminates the use of explicit events and is a synchronous language [19]. RSML^{-e} is similar to another derivative of RSML, SpecTRM-RL, developed by Safeware Engineering Corporation, but has a slightly different syntax and semantics and a different underlying philosophy of how the language should be used in the modeling tasks. An example of an RSML^{-e} specification can be found in [20].

2.3 The NuSMV Model Checker

NuSMV is a symbolic model checker developed as a joint project between the Formal Methods group in the Automated Reasoning System Division at the Instituto Trintino di Cultura (ITC) - Center for Scientific and Technological Research (IRST), the Mechanized Reasoning Groups at the University of Genova and the University of Trento in Italy, and the Model Checking group at Carnegie Mellon University in the United States. NuSMV is a re-implementation and extension of SMV [21], the first model checker based on Binary Decision Diagrams (BDDs). NuSMV has been designed to be an open architecture for model checking, which can be reliably used for the verification of industrial designs, as a core for custom verification tools, as a testbed for formal verification techniques, and applied to other research areas [22]. Properties to be verified in NuSMV are specified using either Computation Tree Logic (CTL) or Linear Time logic (LTL) [21].

2.4 The PVS Theorem Prover

PVS is an environment for specification and verification that has been developed at SRI International's Computer Science Laboratory. In comparison to other widely used verification systems such as HOL and the Boyer-Moore prover, the distinguishing characteristic of PVS is that it supports a highly expressive specification language with a highly effective interactive theorem prover in which most of the lower-level proof steps are automated. The system consists of a specification language, a parser, a type checker, and an interactive proof checker. The PVS specification language is based on higher-order logic with a richly expressive type system so that a number of semantic errors in specification can be caught during type checking. The PVS prover consists of a powerful collection of inference steps that can be used to reduce a proof goal to simpler subgoals that can be discharged automatically by the primitive proof steps of the prover. The primitive proof steps involve, among other things, the use of arithmetic and equality decision procedures, automatic rewriting, and BDD-based Boolean simplification. [23], [24].

3 The Requirements Analysis Process

In the next few sections, we describe the process we followed in eliciting, modeling, and analyzing the requirement of the FGS mode logic.

3.1 Requirements Elicitation

As in most projects, one of our first tasks was to develop an informal understanding of what the system was to do. A variety of techniques have been advocated for eliciting requirements, ranging from the traditional listing of shall statements to writing a concepts of operation document to the development of use cases. Since we were interested in injecting formal modeling into existing practices, we chose to start with the lowest common denominator, simply capturing the requirements as informal shall statements stored in a DOORS database[2]. Examples of a few such requirements for the FGS mode logic are shown in the left hand column of Table 1.

3.2 Requirements Modeling

Our next step was to create a formal statement of the black box behavior of the system. We were guided in this by a methodology developed at Rockwell Collins that was heavily based on the CoRE methodology developed by the Software Productivity Consortium [10], which is in turn based on the SCR methodology [8], [9].

This model was written in the RSML^{-e} language. One of the great advantages of executable specification languages such as RSML^{-e} or SCR is that they can be connected to a mock-up of their environment, provided inputs, and their behavior studied. This provides a very easy way for the developer to get immediate feedback about the model being created. We used this approach to continuously review the model under construction.

When completed, the RSML^{-e} model of the FGS mode logic consisted of 41 input variables, 16 small, tightly synchronized hierarchical finite state machines, 122 macro or function definitions, 29 output values, and was roughly 160 pages long. A detailed description of the model and its simulation environment is available in [25].

In the course of building the RSML^{-e} model, we found ourselves going back and modifying the original shall statements. Sometimes, they were just wrong. More of-

---

[2] DOORS (Dynamic Object Oriented Requirements System) by Telelogic is a commercial requirements management tool.

ten, their organization needed to be changed to provide clear traceability to the model. For example, in the original statement of the requirements, the conditions under which the mode annunciations and the flight director guidance cues would be turned on were combined in several shall statements. We found that the requirements were clearer if we broke these out as distinct groups of statements. Gradually, we realized that the revised shall statements were a clearer and improved description of the system. Maintaining even a coarse mapping between the shall statements and the RSML^{-e} model forced us to be more precise in writing down the shall statements.

3.3 Model Checking

As the model neared completion, the University of Minnesota team completed the first RSML^{-e} to NuSMV translator. This translator, described in [26], automatically converted the RSML^{-e} model to the specification language of the NuSMV model checker, a dialect of SMV. This made it possible for us to start formally checking our model.

We knew state space explosion would be a problem since we had included in the RSML^{-e} model a few integer input variables, such as the aircraft's altitude, and a few comparisons that depended on time. The state space explosion resulting from these few variables was indeed enough to make the verification of most properties infeasible using the earliest translators. While the University of Minnesota team was planning to develop algorithms that would reduce the size of the translated model through a variety of abstraction techniques, these extensions were not yet ready.

Fortunately, algorithms to deal with the time dependencies proved straightforward and were quickly implemented in the translator. To deal with the few remaining integer variables, we abstracted the model by hand by moving comparisons involving these variables (e.g., Altitude > PreSelectAlt + AltCapBias) into a different part of the specification and inputting the Boolean results directly into the model. Since there were only a few such computations, this took only a few hours to implement and did not significantly alter the specification. These changes reduced the state space of the model enough that we could check almost any property of the mode logic with the NuSMV model checker in a matter of minutes.

It was feasible to make these abstractions manually in this particular experiment because they were so few and so straightforward. In other domains, it is likely that the number of abstractions that would be needed would be too large to do reliably by hand. Ideally, these abstractions would be identified and made automatically during the translation process. Work is underway to add these capabilities to the RSML^{-e} to NuSMV translator.

At first, we focused on showing that our model satisfied the safety properties we had identified through a hazard analysis and fault tree analysis [17], [27]. However, it quickly became apparent that all of the original requirements, not just the safety properties, could be stated in CTL. As a result, we extended our verification to include all the shall statements captured during elicitation.

Our approach was to state each requirement as a CTL property over the translated model. Since there was a close correspondence between names in the RSML^{-e} model and the NuSMV model, this quickly became routine and most of the requirements could be translated by hand into CTL in a few minutes. A desirable future enhancement would be the development of a property specification language in RSML^{-e} so that the translator could translate the CTL properties automatically along with the NuSMV model.

All of the requirements could be specified with only two CTL formats. The first was simply a safety constraint that had to be maintained by all reachable states. For example, the requirement

> *If this side is active, the mode annunciations shall be on if and only if the onside FD cues are displayed, or the offside FD cues are displayed, or the AP is engaged*

was translated into the CTL property

```
AG(Is_This_Side_Active ->
    (Mode_Annunciations_On <->
        (Onside_FD_On | Offside_FD_On = TRUE |
         Is_AP_Engaged)))
```

where the AG operator states that the property must hold for all globally reachable states and the operators -> and <-> have their usual meaning of "implies" and "iff". Occasionally, the semantics of RSML^{-e} and CTL interacted in inelegant ways. For example the input variable Offside_FD_On in the above example could take on the values TRUE, FALSE, or UNDEFINED in RSML^{-e} and had to be explicitly compared with the value TRUE in CTL.

The second format was a constraint over a state and all possible next states. For example, the requirement

> *If the onside FD cues are off, the onside FD cues shall be displayed when the AP is engaged.*

was translated into the CTL property

```
AG((!Onside_FD_On & !Is_AP_Engaged)->
    AX(Is_AP_Engaged -> Onside_FD_On))
```

where the AX operator states the enclosed property must hold for all states reachable in the next step.

Only these two formats were needed because RSML^{-e} is a synchronous language in which each transition to the next system state is computed in a single atomic step. All the properties we were interested in could be stated as simple safety properties over a single state, or as a relationship describing how the system changed in a single step. These were sufficient to describe all the safety properties and functional requirements. If we had wanted to verify liveness properties, or if portions of the model had been allowed to evolve asynchronously, other temporal logic operators such as eventually (F), until (U), or release (R) would also have been needed [21].

Ultimately, all 281 properties originally stated informally in English were translated into CTL and checked using the NuSMV model checker. All 281 properties could be verified on a 2GHz Pentium 4 processor running Linux in less than an hour. To track the CTL properties, we modified the DOORS database to maintain both the informal and CTL versions of the requirements and to export a file that could be passed directly into the NuSMV model. This made it very easy to recheck the properties after the model was changed, though a simple "include" statement in the NuSMV language would have been very helpful. A few of the shall statements and their CTL properties are shown in Table 1.

Table 1. Sample of English Requirements and CTL Translation from DOORS Database

English Requirement	CTL Property
1. Mode Annunciations	
1.1 Selection	
If this side is active and the mode annunciations are off, the mode annunciations shall be turned on when the onside FD is turned on.	SPEC AG((!Mode_Annunciations_On & !Onside_FD_On) -> AX((Is_This_Side_Active = 1 & Onside_FD_On) -> Mode_Annunciations_On))
If this side is active and the mode annunciations are off, the mode annunciations shall be turned on when the offside FD is turned on.	SPEC AG((!Mode_Annunciations_On & Offside_FD_On = FALSE) -> AX((Is_This_Side_Active = 1 & Offside_FD_On = TRUE) -> Mode_Annunciations_On))
If this side is active and the mode annunciations are off, the mode annunciations shall be turned on when the AP is engaged.	SPEC AG((!Mode_Annunciations_On & !Is_AP_Engaged) -> AX((Is_This_Side_Active = 1 & Is_AP_Engaged) -> Mode_Annunciations_On))
1.2 Deselection	
If this side is active and the mode annunciations are on, the mode annunciations shall be turned off if the onside FD is off, the offside FD is off, and the AP is disengaged.	SPEC AG(Mode_Annunciations_On -> AX((Is_This_Side_Active = 1 & !Onside_FD_On & Offside_FD_On = FALSE & !Is_AP_Engaged) -> !Mode_Annunciations_On))
1.3 Operation	
The mode annunciations shall not be on at system power up.	(!Mode_Annunciations_On)
If this side is active the mode annunciations shall be on if and only if the onside FD cues are displayed, or the offside FD cues are displayed, or the AP is engaged.	AG(Is_This_Side_Active = 1 -> (Mode_Annunciations_On <-> (Onside_FD_On | Offside_FD_On = TRUE | Is_AP_Engaged)))

These properties are organized by a functional decomposition of the FGS that closely reflect how the FGS requirements have traditionally been organized. First, the ways in which a function can be selected are specified, followed by the ways in which the function can be deselected, finally followed by any invariants that must be maintained during the function's operation. Functions that can only be active when a "parent" function is active are nested in a natural outline structure.

The rationale for selecting this organization was to provide a clear bridge from the traditional specification of requirements to the formal statement of the properties. Practicing engineers accept this structure very well, and are usually intrigued by the clear mapping of informal shall statements to their formal properties.

3.4 Errors Found through Model Checking

Use of the model checker produced counter examples revealing several errors in the RSML^{-e} model of the mode logic that had not been discovered through simulation. For example, in trying to prove the requirement

> *If Heading Select mode is not selected, Heading Select mode shall be selected when the HDG switch is pressed on the Flight Control Panel.*

we discovered two ways in which this property was not true. First, if another event arrived at the same time as the HDG switch was pressed, that event could preempt the HDG switch event. Second, if this side of the FGS was not active, the HDG switch event was completely ignored by this side of the FGS. This led us to modify the requirement to state

> *If this side is active and Heading Select mode is not selected, Heading Select mode shall be selected when the HDG switch is pressed on the FCP (providing no higher priority event occurs at the same time).*

While longer and more difficult to read than the original statement, it has the advantage of being a more accurate description of the system's behavior. Of course, we also had to clearly define what a "higher priority" event was.

Clarifying whether the FGS needs to be active, while desirable, is a condition well understood by the engineers and the actual value of this clarification is probably minimal. However, we also discovered several ways in which important safety properties, such as having more than one mode active or having no mode active when a mode must be active, could be violated in our model. The model checker was relentless in tracking these scenarios down and presenting us with a counter example. Practicing engineers are well aware of the difficulty of identifying all such scenarios and have evolved a series of defensive coding practices to ensure that the safety properties are not violated. Model checking of the specification allows us to provide a rigorous analysis that the specification cannot violate these properties in the first place.

As one example, an entire class of errors was discovered that involved more than one input event arriving at the same time. This could occur for a variety of reasons. For example, the pilot might press a switch at the same time as the system captured a navigation source. Occasionally, these combinations would drive the model into an unsafe state.

There are several ways to deal with such simultaneous input events. SCR [8] makes the "one input assumption" mandating that only one input variable can change in any step. This makes reasoning about the specification simpler, but requires that the developer implement the system in such a way as to guarantee that only one input variable can change in each step. In a polling system, where all the inputs are sampled at periodic intervals, this can only be done by adding additional logic outside the specification that prioritizes multiple events and discards lower priority events or queues them for processing in subsequent steps.

RSML^{-e} normally makes a similar "one input message" assumption in which only one message is processed in each step, but any number of fields within the message are allowed to change in a single step. Since we were uncertain how communication with the outside world would ultimately be implemented, we selected an option in which all input messages (and hence all input variables) were read once on each step. This allowed for the possibility that all 41 input variables could change in the same step.

The problem was simplified somewhat in that only 21 of these input variables were of concern. The other 20 input variables provide state information from the other FGS used to set the state of the current FGS when it is the inactive (backup) side and had no impact on the system state when the current side was active. However, this still left 21 input variables that could change in a single step. To deal with this, we assigned a priority to each input event and only used the highest priority event in each step, ignoring the lower priority events. The logic to do this was localized in one part of the specification so that the only change to the main body of the specification was to replace the references of the form "When_Event_X" with references of the form "When_Event_X_Seen". In a few cases, such as the acquisition of a navigation signal, it was undesirable to simply ignore the event. In these cases, the specification was changed to depend on the condition itself rather than on the event of the condition becoming true. In this way, the condition would be processed in the first step in which a higher priority event did not preempt it. These changes effectively implemented a "one input assumption" within the RSM^{-e} specification.

In course of developing this prioritization, we realized that it was possible for some combinations of events to be processed in the same step as the order in which the events were processed did not matter. For example, an input that changed the active lateral mode could often (but not always) be processed in the same step as an input that changed the active vertical mode. In other words, a partial rather than a total order of the input events was acceptable. This partial order had three branches, with a maximum depth of eleven input events (i.e., eleven priorities) on a single branch. It was quite straightforward to understand, both by us and by the engineers who reviewed it for us. Since we could check both the safety and functional properties of the specification with NuSMV, we felt confident that the specified behavior was correct. However, without the power of formal verification, we would never have been able to convince ourselves that the safety properties of the system were still met.

The handling of multiple input events has been a recurring issue in our experiments, and appears to be a natural consequence of implementing a formal specification on an actual processor where system steps require a finite amount of time. On the one hand, it is impractical to ask human beings to reason about all possible combinations of inputs events in the main body of the specification. On the other hand, it is very difficult, if not impossible, to design systems that can guarantee that only one external input will change during a system step. Even interrupt driven systems must prioritize and queue external events that occur while a higher priority event is being handled. Our preference is to allow for the occurrence of multiple inputs, but to keep the logic that prioritizes the events separate from the logic that defines the processing of each individual event.

3.5 Theorem Proving

After verification of the mode logic with the NuSMV model checker was well underway, the University of Minnesota team completed the first version of the RSML^{-e} to PVS translator. This allowed us to start verifying properties using the PVS theorem prover.

In contrast to model checkers, theorem provers apply rules of inference to a specification in order to derive new properties of interest. Theorem provers are generally considered harder to use than model checkers, requiring more expertise on the part of the user. However, theorem provers are not limited by the size of the state space.

Even though we had been able to verify all the requirements against the RSML^{-e} model, we wanted to assess the use of PVS for a variety of reasons. First, we knew that not all problem domains would lend themselves to verification through model checking as well as the mode logic had. Models with very large or infinite state spaces would not be analyzable using model checking. We expected to encounter such problems when analyzing trajectories of aircraft relative to the flight plan. Also, the mode logic was already starting to strain the capabilities of NuSMV, and we were concerned that problems with larger state spaces would exceed its capabilities. For problems just at the limit of model checking, we speculated that theorem proving might even be more efficient than model checking. Finally, we had identified at least one class of properties, comparing the properties of two arbitrary states that were not temporally related to each other, that we were unable to state in CTL. An example of this was the property that any two arbitrary states with different mode configurations should have different annunciations to the pilots.

We started by using PVS to verify some of the properties already confirmed using NuSMV. Since the same RSML^{-e} model was used to generate the PVS specification as was used to generate the NuSMV model, the same handful of manual abstractions were present in the PVS specification even though they were probably not necessary for PVS. In the course of completing the proofs, it became clear that we needed to define and prove many simple properties of the FGS that could be used as automatic rewrite rules by PVS. This automated and simplified the more complex proofs we were interested in. For example, we followed the RSML^{-e} convention of assigning input variables the initial value of UNDEFINED. This prevents the model from making use of an initial value that does not reflect the actual environment around it, a common cause of safety errors in automated systems. As a consequence, all internal variables and functions dependent on those input variables included UNDEFINED in their range, even though guards in their definitions ensured they could never take on the value UNDEFINED. By defining and proving properties stating that these variables and functions were always defined, PVS was able to automatically resolve large portions of the proofs. As these libraries evolved, we realized that many of these properties, as well as several useful PVS strategies (scripts defining sequences of prover commands) could have been automatically produced by the translator. These were identified as enhancements for future versions of the translator.

With this infrastructure in place, some of proofs could be constructed in less than an hour. Others took several hours or even days, usually because they involved proving many other properties as intermediate lemmas. One surprise was that users proficient in PVS but unfamiliar with the FGS could usually complete a proof as quickly as someone familiar with the FGS. In fact, most of the proofs were completed by a graduate student with no avionics experience. The general process was to break the desired property down by case splits until a simple ASSERT or GRIND command could complete that branch of the proof tree. The structure of the proof s naturally reversed the dependency ordering defined in the RSML^{-e} specification. Many of the proofs could be simplified by introducing lemmas describing how intermediate values in the dependency graph changed, but identifying such lemmas seemed to require a sound understanding the FGS mode logic. As we gained experience, we started using the dependency map produced by the RSML^{-e} toolset to guide us in identifying these lemmas.

Another surprise was that while the proofs might take hours to construct, they usually executed in less than twenty seconds. This was significant since the time taken to prove similar properties using the NuSMV model checker had grown steadily with the size of the model. If the model had grown much larger, it is possible that the time to verify a property using model checking might have become prohibitive. The time required to run the PVS proofs seemed much less sensitive to the size of the model.

Since we had already completed the safety analysis of the mode logic using NuSMV, we decided to focus on using PVS to study the mode logic for potential forms of mode confusion. Mode confusion occurs when the operators of an automated system believe they are in a mode different than the one they are actually in and make inappropriate responses to the automation. Mode confusion can also occur when the operators do not fully understand the behavior of the automation, i.e., when the operators have a poor "mental model" of the automation. Numerous studies have shown that mode confusion is an important safety concern in automated systems such as modern avionics systems [28], [29], [30], [31].

In earlier work [32], [16], we had extended a taxonomy of design patterns indicative of potential sources of mode confusion originally developed by Nancy Leveson [33]. Other researchers have described ways in which formal analysis tools can be used to search specifications for such patterns [15], [34], [35], [36]. We decided to try using PVS to determine if there were patterns in our requirements model that might indicate potential sources of mode confusion. We were able to use PVS to search for ways that a system could enter and exit off normal modes, ignore pilot inputs, introduce unintended side effects, enter and exit hidden modes of operation, and provide insufficient feedback to the pilots [37]. While space does not permit a complete description, we do present here an example of how PVS was used to detect ignored pilot inputs.

The basic approach is to prove that each pilot input provides some visible change in the system state. For example, to prove that pressing the Flight Director (FD) switch always causes a change in the visible state, we attempt to prove the theorem

```
FD_Switch_Never_Ignored : Theorem
  verify((When_FD_Switch_Pressed AND
          No_Higher_Event_Than_FD_Switch)
         IMPLIES
            (Onside_FD_On /= PREV(Onside_FD_On)))
```

This theorem asserts that if the FD switch is pressed, and no higher priority event occurs at the same time, the onside FD guidance cues toggle on and off. Trying to prove this lemma leads to the following sequent that must be discharged in PVS

```
[-1]  *(Overspeed_Condition(s!1))
[-2]  *(Onside_FD(s!1))=*(Onside_FD(s!1-1))
[-3]  *(When_FD_Switch_Pressed(s!1))
[-4] *(No_Higher_Event_Than_FD_Switch(s!1))
[-5]  *(Onside_FD(s!1))=*(Onside_FD(s!1-1))
  |-------
[1]   *(Onside_FD(s!1-1)) = Off
[2]   s!1 = 0
```

As with all PVS sequents, we are allowed to assume that properties above the turnstile (|-------) are true and that at least one property from below the turnstile must be proven true to discharge the proof obligation. The current state is s!1 and the previous state is s!1-1.

This sequent requires us to prove that if the FD switch is pressed [-3] during an overspeed condition [-1] and no higher priority event occurs at the same time [-4] and the onside FD cues do not change value [-5] between state s!1-1 and s!1, then it must be true that the onside FD cues were off before the FD switch was pressed [1] or that the current state is the initial system state [2]. This is impossible to prove, indicating that the property we are trying to prove must be false.

The sequent provides us with a clue of what is wrong in that one way to complete the proof would be to show that an overspeed condition [-1] can not occur. This is also impossible, but review of the specification reveals that the FD switch is indeed ignored during an overspeed condition if the onside FD cues are on. To confirm that this is the problem, and to document this case of an ignored pilot input, we define a constraint

```
FD_Switch_Ignored_During_Overspeed: rCOND
  = (When_FD_Switch_Pressed AND
     Onside_FD_On AND Overspeed_Condition)
```

identifying the condition in which the FD switch is pressed, the onside FD is on, and an overspeed condition exists. We then use this to state an amended version of the theorem

```
FD_Switch_Never_Ignored : Theorem
  verify((When_FD_Switch_Pressed AND
          No_Higher_Event_Than_FD_Switch AND
          NOT FD_Switch_Ignored_During_Overspeed)
         IMPLIES
           (Onside_FD_On /= PREV(Onside_FD_On))))
```

stating that the FD switch is never ignored unless it is pressed during an overspeed condition while the FD cues are on. This proof completes without difficulty, taking a little under ten seconds to run.

In [15], we discuss how PVS was used to detect ignored pilot inputs in small, handcrafted models of the mode logic. We were not sure that we would be able to do similar proofs on PVS models translated from a much larger RSML^{-e} model of the mode logic. However, as this example shows, performing proofs over these models was no more difficult than doing them over the handcrafted models once the basic infrastructure was in place.

4 Observations on Specification Styles

There are at least two well-known styles of formal specification. In a *property*, or axiomatic, style of specification, one defines properties relating the operations of the type being specified without providing any information about the structure of the type itself. The common textbook example is the specification of a stack through equational specifications such as *top(push(s,e)) = e*.

In contrast, in a *constructive*, or model-based approach, one defines a new type in terms of primitive types and constructors provided by the specification language. For example, one might define a stack as a record consisting of an array *a* of the base type *e* and an integer *tos* representing the top of stack pointer. An operation such as *top* might then be defined as *top([a, tos]) = a(tos)*. That is, *top* returns the array element pointed at by *tos*.

The primary disadvantage of a constructive style of specification is that it biases the reader towards a particular implementation. In the example above, the specification strongly suggests that a stack *should* be implemented as a record containing an array and an integer. No such bias exists in the property style of specification since no information is provided about the structure of the type being defined. An advantage of a constructive style of specification is that it is used in common programming languages such as C and Ada and most engineers are immediately comfortable with it.

A property-oriented specification can be more difficult to understand and write. One also has to ensure that a property-oriented specification is *consistent* and *complete*. A specification is consistent if it always defines a single value for each operation on the same inputs (i.e., each operation is a *function*). A specification is complete if a result is specified for every set of inputs to an operation (i.e., each operation is a *total* function).

Most constructive specification languages are designed so that *only* complete and consistent specifications can be written. In fact, the textbook method for showing that a property oriented specification is consistent is to create a constructive model of it and prove that all the properties hold over that model. This establishes that at least one implementation of the specification exists and its properties must therefore be consistent.

The analogies to our two styles of requirements specification are obvious. Requirements written as shall statements in a natural language are simply informal property oriented specifications. In addition to the usual problems of ensuring completeness and consistency, they are also encumbered by the ambiguity of natural language. This helps to explain why developers working from requirements captured as informal shall statements usually complain of problems with completeness, consistency, and ambiguity.

In contrast, requirements captured using notations such as SCR and RSML actually are constructive models of the requirements. Due to the language constructs provided, they are inherently complete and consistent in the sense of defining a total function for each output. However, this also explains why a common reaction to such models is that they contain design decisions. In all honesty, they do suggest certain design decisions, even if nothing more than the names of internal variables that the customer does not care about.

These observations allow us to begin to address the questions raised in the introduction. Figure 1 illustrates a product life cycle paradigm often referred to as model-based development. This approach starts with informal techniques, such as writing shall statements in natural language or the development of use cases, to capture the requirements during the early, elicitation phase of the project.

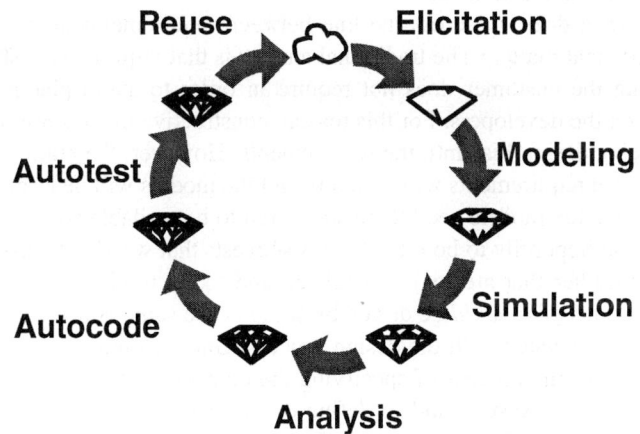

Fig. 1. Model Based Development Process Lifecycle

This is followed by the creation of a constructive model of the requirements that can be used to drive visualizations of the user interface so that the customer can simulate the requirements model and provide early feedback and validation. In the analysis phase, the informal statements are translated into properties over the model and proven to ensure their consistency and completeness. High-quality code generators and test case generators reduce much of the effort traditionally associated with coding and testing. Finally, since the models have been carefully developed so as to encapsulate key functions, selected components can be reused in the next project.

One of the questions posed in the introduction was whether requirements should be captured as a list of shall statements written in a natural language or whether they should be written as mathematical models defining the relationship between the inputs and outputs as is done in SCR, CoRE, and RSML. The observation that shall statements are just informal statements of the system properties suggests that perhaps they aren't such a bad first step. The very commonality of their use indicates they are a natural and intuitive way for designers to put their first thoughts on paper. The problem with shall statements has always been that inconsistencies, incompleteness, and ambiguities are not found until the later phases of the project. However, by developing a formal, constructive model of the requirements against which the informal shall statements can be verified, identification of these problems can be forced into the early modeling, simulation, and analysis phases of the project.

Another question raised was whether a system's requirements can be completely specified with use cases. While more structured than shall statements, as practiced today use cases normally lack a precise formal semantics and suffer from the same problems of inconsistency, incompleteness, and ambiguity as shall statements. While not part of this experiment, it seems reasonable that it should be possible to express use cases as a sequence of properties describing how the system responds to its stimuli, and these sequences verified through simulation and formal analysis. In this way, the consistency and completeness of use cases could be improved in the same manner as was done for shall statements.

Finally, when does one cross the line between requirements analysis and design, and why does that matter? The traditional answer is that requirements should not contain anything the customer does not require in order to avoid placing unnecessary constraints on the developers. For this reason, constructive models are often criticized for introducing design bias into the requirements. However, the reality is that for any real system, the requirements will be many and the models will be large and complex. Large and complex models need to be structured to be readable and robust in the face of change, and hopefully to be reused. This suggests that we *should* group portions of the model together that are logically related and likely to change together, and that requirements analysis *should* be driven by some of the same concerns that have traditionally been associated with the design process. Our preference is to define requirements analysis as the process of specifying the complete platform independent (logical) behavior of the system and to define design as the process of mapping of that behavior onto a specific (physical) platform. In this view, the requirements evolve from the informal definition gathered during elicitation to a formal, highly structured model suitable for the automatic generation of code and test cases.

5 Conclusions and Future Directions

We have described how a model of the requirements for the mode logic of a Flight Guidance System was created in the RSML^{-e} language from an initial set of requirements stated as shall statements written in English. Translators were used to automatically generate equivalent models of the mode logic in the NuSMV model checker and the PVS theorem prover. The original shall statements were then hand translated into properties over these models and proven to hold over these models.

The process of creating the RSML^{-e} model improved the informal requirements, and the process of proving the formal properties found errors in both the original requirements and the RSML^{-e} model. Our concerns about the difficulty of proving properties in the NuSMV and PVS models that were automatically generated from the RSML^{-e} models turned out to be unfounded. In fact, the ease with which these properties were verified leads us to conclude that formal methods tools are finally maturing to the point where they can be profitably used on industrial sized problems.

Several directions exist for further work, many of which are well known and have been proposed by others. We would like to explore translating use cases into sequences of properties than can be formally verified, just as was done with shall statements in this exercise. Stronger abstraction techniques are needed to increase the classes of problems that can be verified using model checkers. Better libraries and proof strategies are needed to make theorem proving less labor intensive. More work also needs to be done to identify proof strategies and properties that can be automatically generated from the model. Since many systems consist of synchronous components connected by asynchronous buses, work needs to be done to determine how properties that span models connected by asynchronous channels can be verified. Perhaps most important, these formal verification tools need to used on real problems with commercially supported modeling tools such as SCADE, Esterel, and Simulink.

Acknowledgements

The authors wish to acknowledge the ongoing support of this work by Ricky Butler, Kelly Hayhurst, and Celeste Bellcastro of the NASA Langley Research Center, the efforts of Mike Whalen, Anjali Joshi, Yunja Choi, Sanjai Rayadurgam, George Devaraj, and Dan O'Brien of the University of Minnesota in developing the technology described in this paper, and the insightful suggestions of the anonymous referees.

References

1. Brooks, F.: No Silver Bullet: Essence and Accidents of Software Engineering, IEEE Computer, April, 1987.
2. Boehm, B.: Software Engineering Economics, Prentice-Hall, Englewood Cliffs, NJ, 1981.
3. Davis, A.: Software Requirements (Revised): Object, Functions, and States, Prentice-Hall, Englewood Cliffs, NJ, 1993.

4. van Schouwen, A.: The A-7 Requirements Model: Re-examination for Real-Time Systems and an Application to Monitoring Systems, Technical Report 90-276, Queens University, Hamilton, Ontario, 1990.
5. Ramamoorthy, C., Prakesh, A., Tsai W., Usuda, Y.: Software Engineering: Problems and Perspectives, IEEE Computer, pages 191-209, October 1984.
6. Leveson, N.: Safeware: System Safety and Computers, Addison-Wesley Publishing Company: Reading, Massachusetts, 1995.
7. Lutz, R.: Analyzing Software Requirements Errors in Safety-Critical, Embedded, Systems, in IEEE International Symposium on Requirements Engineering, San Diego, CA, January 1993.
8. Heitmeyer, C., Jeffords,R., Labaw, B.: Automated Consistency Checking of Requirements Specification, ACM Transactions on Software Engineering and Methodology (TOSEM), 5(3):231-261, July 1996.
9. Parnas, D., Madey, J.: Functional Documentation for Computer Systems Engineering (Volume 2), Technical Report CRL 237, McMaster University, Hamilton, Ontario, September 1991.
10. Faulk, S., Brackett, J., Ward, P., Kirby, J.: The CoRE Method for Real-Time Requirements, IEEE Software, 9(5):22-33, September 1992.
11. Faulk, S., Finneran, L., Kirby, J., Shah, S., Sutton, J.: Experience Applying the CoRE Method to the Lockheed C-130J Software Requirements, in Proceedings of the Ninth Annual Conference on Computer Assurance, pages 3-8, Gaithersburg, MD, June 1994.
12. Leveson, N., Heimdahl, M., Hildreth, H., Reese, J.: Requirements Specifications for Process-Control Systems, IEEE Transactions on Software Engineering, 20(9):684-707, September 1994.
13. Harel, H., Naamad, A.:The STATEMATE Semantics of Statecharts, ACM Transactions on Software Engineering and Methodology, 5(4): 293-333, October, 1996.
14. Miller, S.: Specifying the Mode Logic of a Flight Guidance System in CoRE and SCR, in Proceedings of The Second Annual Workshop on Formal Methods in Software Practice (FMSP'98), Clearwater Beach, Florida, March 4-5, 1998
15. Butler, R., Miller, S., Potts, J., Carreno, V.: A Formal Methods Approach to the Analysis of Mode Confusion, in Proceedings of the 17th AIAA/IEEE Digital Avionics Systems Conference, Bellevue, WA, October 1998.
16. Miller, S, Tribble, A.:A Methodology for Improving Mode Awareness in Flight Guidance Design, in Proceedings of the 21st Digital Avionics Systems Conference (DASC'02), Irvine, CA, Oct. 2002.
17. Tribble, A., Lempia, D., Miller, S.: Software Safety Analysis of a Flight Guidance System, in Proceedings of the 21st Digital Avionics Systems Conference (DASC'02), Irvine, CA, Oct. 2002.
18. Thompson, J., Heimdahl, M., Miller, S.: Specification Based Prototyping for Embedded Systems, in Proceedings of the Seventh ACM SIGSOFT Symposium on the Foundations on Software Engineering, LNCS, Number 1687, September 1999.
19. Berry, G., Gonthier, G.: The Synchronous Programming Lanugage Esterel: Design, Semantics, and Implementation, Science of Computer Programming, 19:87-152, 1992.
20. Thompson, J., Heimdahl, M., Miller, S.: Specification Based Prototyping for Embedded Systems, in Proceedings of the Seventh ACM SIGSOFT Symposium on the Foundations on Software Engineering, LNCS, Number 1687, September 1999.
21. Clarke, E., Grumberg, O., Peled, P.: Model Checking, The MIT Press, Cambridge, Massachusetts, 2001.
22. Anonymous, NuSMV Home Page, http://nusmv.irst.itc.it/.

23. Owre, S., Rushby, J., Shankar, N., Henke, F.: Formal Verification for Fault-Tolerant Architectures: Prolegomena to the Design of PVS, IEEE Transactions on Software Engineering, Vol. 21, No. 2, pg. 107-125, February 1995.
24. Anonymous, PVS Home Page, http://www.csl.sri.com/projects/pvs/.
25. Miller, S., Tribble, A., Carlson, T., Danielson, E.: Flight Guidance System Requirements Specification Final Report, NASA Contractor Report, November 2001.
26. Heimdahl, M., Rayadurgam, S., Choi, Y., Joshi, A., Devaraj, G.: Proof and Model Checking Tools Final Report, NASA Contractor Report, November 2002.
27. Tribble, A.: FGS Safety Analysis Final Report, NASA Contractor Report, November 2002.
28. Billings, C.; Aviation Automation: the Search for a Human Centered Approach, Lawrence Erlbaum Associates, Inc., Mahwah, NJ, 1997.
29. Sarter, N.,Woods, D.:, Pilot Interaction with Cockpit Automation: Operational Experiences with the Flight Management System, The International Journal of Aviation Psychology, 2(4), pg. 303-31, 1992.
30. Sarter, N., Woods, D.: Pilot Interaction with Cockpit Automation II: An Experimental Study of Pilots' Model and Awareness of the Flight Management System, The International Journal of Aviation Psychology, 4(1), pg. 1-28, 1994.
31. Sarter, N., Woods, D.: "How in the World Did I Ever Get Into That Mode?": Mode Error and Awareness in Supervisory Control, Human Factors, 37(1), pg. 5-19, 1995.
32. Miller,S.: Taxonomy of Mode Confusion Sources Final Report, NASA Contractor Report, February 2001.
33. Leveson, N., et al, Analyzing Software Specifications for Mode Confusion Potential, in Proceedings of a Workshop on Human Error and System Development, C.W. Johnson, Editor, pg. 132-146, Glasgow, Scotland, March 1997.
34. Rushby, J.: Analyzing Cockpit Interfaces Using Formal Methods, Electronic Notes in Theoretical Computer Science, 43, URL: http://wwww.elsevier.nl/locate /entcs/volume43.html, 2001.
35. Rushby, J.: Using Model Checking to Help Discover Mode Confusions and Other Automation Surprises, in the Proceedings of the 3rd Workshop on Human Error, Safety, and System Development (HESSD'99), Liege, Belgium, June 7-8, 1999.
36. Rushby, J., Crow, J., Palmer, E.: An Automated Method to Detect Potential Mode Confusion, in the Proceedings of the 18th AIAA/IEEE Digital Avionics Systems Conference (DASC), St. Louis, MO, October 1999.
37. Miller, S., Joshi, A.: FGS Mode Awareness Final Report, NASA Contractor Report, November 2002.

Adaptable Translator of B Specifications to Embedded C Programs[*]

Didier Bert[3], Sylvain Boulmé[3], Marie-Laure Potet[3],
Antoine Requet[2], and Laurent Voisin[1]

[1] ClearSy, Aix-en-Provence, France,
Laurent.Voisin@clearsy.com
[2] Gemplus Research Labs, La Ciotat, France,
Antoine.Requet@gemplus.com
[3] Laboratoire Logiciels, Systèmes, Réseaux – LSR-IMAG – Grenoble, France,
{Didier.Bert,Sylvain Boulme,Marie-Laure.Potet}@imag.fr

Abstract. This paper presents the results of the RNTL BOM project, which aimed to develop an approach to generate efficient code from B formal developments. The target domain is smart card applications, in which memory and code size is an important factor. The results detailed in this paper are a new architecture of the translation process, a way to adapt the B_0 language in order to include types of the target language and a set of validated optimizations. An assessment of the proposed approach is given through a case study, relative to the development of a Java Card Virtual Machine environment.

Keywords. Code generation, embedded systems, B method, smart cards.

1 Introduction

Formal methods aim to produce zero-defect software, by controlling the whole software development process, from specifications to implementations. In top-down approaches, they start from high-level and abstract specifications, by describing the fundamental properties of the final product. Details and design choices are introduced in an incremental way. The correctness between two levels is insured by refinement proofs. When implementations are aimed, refinement leads to a last level which describes, in some way, the expected behavior. Implementations are generally stated in an appropriate sub-language of the specification language. The code generation process consists in two stages: formal implementations are translated into programs in a given programming language, and then these programs are compiled. This approach offers several advantages: the translation process is as simple as possible, and it can be validated in an

---

[*] This work has been supported by the French Ministry of Industry in the RNTL program (Réseau National des Technologies Logicielles), under project BOM (B with Optimized Memory), March 2001-March 2003.

easy way; secondly appropriate compilers can be used, as optimizing and/or certified compilers. The simplicity of the translation ensures traceability between the formal specification and the executed code.

Nevertheless all approaches which support formal development from specification to code must manage several constraining requirements, particularly in the domain of embedded software where specific properties on the code are expected, such as efficiency or memory size. First a compromise must be found between the expressiveness of the formal implementation language and the simplicity of the translation process. Another compromise is also necessary between the formal models, which generally favor the readability and the simplicity of the verification process, over the code efficiency. Finally it is not possible to define a unique translation process, which is proved adapted for all uses. A translation process is generally redefined depending on the range of products or target platforms.

The RNTL BOM project is supported by the French Ministry of Industry and involves two academic laboratories and two industrial partners: Gemplus who uses the B method for smart card applications and ClearSy who provides Atelier B. The aim was to develop a new translation approach to generate efficient code from B formal developments. The B method has been successfully applied for industrial projects, particularly in the domain of railway-automated systems [2]. For such applications adequate translators have been developed, thanks to the technique of the Vital Coded Processor which secures the execution process. In the domain of smart cards, Gemplus has used the B method for certification purposes [12, 13] or to develop correct code [10]. When implementations are expected, the generated code must meet the card's requirements. In particular the memory size is limited. For such applications, the Atelier B tool is not well-suited. Among others, the needs were to determine:
– soundness conditions to optimize parameter passing mechanisms and to perform operation inlining,
– a mechanism to integrate some basic C types in the last level of refinement.
– a new architecture of the translation process to easily adapt it with respect to target platforms.

The first requirement aims to optimize the memory size and to eliminate operation calls, introduced by the modeling process. The second requirement aims to give freedom to the developers to adjust at best their integer representation. The last one is crucial for the smart card domain where applications must be loaded on different platforms, with their own characteristics.

This paper describes how these requirements have been incorporated in the B method. Section 2 introduces some features of the B method which are important for the translation process. Conditions to optimize parameter passing are also presented. Section 3 presents the architecture and the various parts of the translation process. Section 4 explains how adaptability can be obtained at the level of the B_0 language and at the level of the translation process. Finally, Section 5 presents the result of a case study, relative to the development of a Java Card Virtual Machine environment. The code is compared with other translators and the impact of the optimization is assessed.

2 Some B Features

2.1 B Methodology

The B method supports a formal development approach in a top-down manner. In particular, data may be refined. That is expressed using a gluing invariant, linking "internal" data to "observed" data. Proof obligations guarantee that observable results are consistent with the higher levels of the specification. The last step of refinement is the implementation itself, written in a programming language called B_0. Moreover modular developments are also supported by the B method. Specifications can be composed and then refined separately.

The B_0 programming language is designed as a relatively low-level language. This choice has two advantages: it allows the developer to control the generated code (the code eventually executed), and it provides safety. Indeed, the job of the translator is simple and the final generated code uses only finite memory. In B_0, data-types (integers) are bound, there is no dynamic allocation, and no recursive call. Thus, it is theoretically (currently no tool performs this job) possible to bound statically the memory size needed by a B_0 program. On a checked development, the B method guarantees the total correctness of the development. It means that programs terminate and no runtime errors will occur on the generated code (if there is sufficient memory to run the program). More precisely:

- B_0 type-checking guarantees usual programming typing properties: right-hand side and left-hand side of an assignment get the same type and the type of actual parameters (input and output) is the same as the formal parameter ones.
- Proof obligations of "*well-definedness*" [3] guarantee that partial operators are soundly applied (arithmetic overflow, division by zero, access to array elements, etc.). That is verified by the proof that, in a call $f(e)$, the arguments e belong to the domain of the function f and that f and e are also well defined.
- *Well-definedness* guarantees also that values of variables always inhabit their declared type (i.e. variables are initialized before they are read).

2.2 Modularity of B Specifications

Specifications of large applications cannot be carried out in one block. The B language provides primitives to specify pieces of a problem, to develop them independently, and to compose them in such a way that the properties proved in a local part are preserved in the global development after composition.

High level specifications are expressed in MACHINE components. They declare the safety properties, which must be preserved in the final programs, the interface of the component (list of operations) and the specification of the internal state and of the operations. Machines are refined into REFINEMENT components and then in IMPLEMENTATION components which constitute the programming level. Machines or refinements can be built incrementally by including or by using other machines (clauses INCLUDES and USES).

Implementations can call operations of other machines which are imported (clause IMPORTS). This corresponds to a decomposition in layers. Finally a component can see another machine to share its services with other components (clause SEES). The opposite figure shows a typical B development. Each clause introduces specific syntactic restrictions to compose safely invariant and refinement proofs [5, 16] (in particular, variable sharing is strictly mastered).

Each component encapsulates an internal state made of variables, specified by a predicate called *invariant*. The link between the states of components connected by a refinement relation is performed by a *gluing invariant*. This invariant binds the variables at the higher level to the variables at the lower level. A particular case of binding consists in giving the same name to a variable in two adjacent levels. The gluing invariant is then the equality of the values of both variables. This principle of name

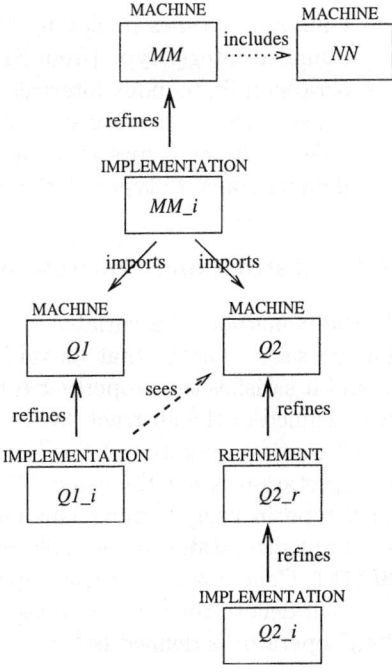

Fig. 1. A modular B development

equality is also allowed between two development chains. For instance, in the implementation MM_i, one can glue a name coming from MM with the same name in machine $Q2$. This mechanism is called *gluing by homonymy* and provides a facility to develop simpler models.

At the leaves of a B project, one finds either implementations, which can be translated directly, or *basic machines* the implementation of which is carried out in the target language. Those latter machines thus constitute the interface between B and non B parts of a project.

2.3 Abstract and Concrete Data

In the B language, there are two kinds of constants or variables (*data*): abstract data and concrete data. Abstract data consist in all the elements and sets that can be used in set theory, as defined in full B (integers, enumerated sets, cartesian products, power sets, relations, and so on). They are mainly used at the higher levels of specification (machines and first refinements). Concrete data are those which may be used in B_0, each time the data thus introduced will not be further refined in the development. It is the case for constants or variables at the implementation level but also for parameters and results of operations, which cannot be refined in B. Concrete data must match ordinary data types in usual programming language because they should be "implemented" directly in the target language. In the sequel concrete data types will be called "B_0 types". In standard B, they are the following ones:

- enumerated types (including the boolean type)
- bounded integer type (from MININT to MAXINT)
- arrays on finite index intervals where the type of elements is a concrete type (in set theory, they are similar to total functions)
- deferred types (types without representation). They will be represented by definite concrete types at the end of developments.

2.4 Abstract and Concrete Arithmetic

In the B method, if a variable is declared by $x \in$ INT (the predefined bounded integer set), it means that its value is an integer value in the mathematical set $\mathbb{Z}$ and it satisfies the property $x \in$ MININT .. MAXINT. An expression as "$x+1$" is well defined in the abstract levels, because 1 is a constant value in $\mathbb{Z}$ and $+$ is a mathematical operation defined in $\mathbb{Z} \times \mathbb{Z} \to \mathbb{Z}$. In the implementation level, the interpretation is not the same. The denotation INT becomes a B_0 type similar to a type in programming languages. The predefined operators $+$, $-$, etc. in the implementations are actually operations on this type, bounded by MININT .. MAXINT. Concrete and abstract operators are overloaded in the B language, but we shall denote the concrete ones by $+_0$, $-_0$, etc. to avoid confusion. Thus, the "$+_0$" operator is defined by[1]:

$$+_0 \triangleq \lambda(x,y) \cdot (\ x \in \mathsf{INT}\ \wedge\ y \in \mathsf{INT}\ \wedge\ x+y \in \mathsf{INT}\ |\ x+y\ )$$

Clearly, this definition contains a new restriction with respect to the mathematical $+$ operation, that is the operands and the result must satisfy the interval constraint. Thus, when refining abstract integers with concrete ones, *well-definedness* proof obligations ensure that no overflow will happen, even in intermediary results.

2.5 Parameter Passing

Parameter passing mechanisms are often the stumbling block of the semantics of programming languages. It is one of the crucial points for the correctness of program translation or compiling [11]. In this section, we show how the B theoretical parameter passing of the operations can be soundly translated into the classical parameter passing mechanisms of programming language. In the B language, operations are declared at the level of machines by a text of the form:

$$r \longleftarrow op\,(p) \triangleq \text{PRE}\ P\ \text{THEN}\ S\ \text{END}$$

where p is a list of formal input parameters and r is a list of formal output parameters. Predicate P is the precondition and S is the body of the operation. A call to the operation op is written as $v \longleftarrow op\,(e)$ where v is the list of actual output parameters (a variable list) and e is the list of actual input parameters

---

[1] In notation B, $\lambda x \cdot (\ P\ |\ E\ )$ is a function where the value is E iff parameter x satisfies predicate P (preconditions).

(an expression list). The semantics of the operation call is defined in the B-Book [1], by the following substitution rule, which means that r and p are respectively replaced by v and e in P and S:

$$v \longleftarrow op(e) \equiv [r, p := v, e] \text{ PRE } P \text{ THEN } S \text{ END} \qquad (1)$$

The syntactic restrictions of the call imply that v is a list of single variables without repetition (not array elements, for example) and that these variables do not occur in P and S (non aliasing). Definition (1) is well suitable for proofs, because proofs rely upon the specification of the operations where the state modification is atomic (i.e. specified in one step). But this rule is not an operational one because an operation call must indeed be translated by a call to the implementation of this operation. Rule (1) cannot be directly applied to the implementation, because operation bodies may contain sequencing of substitutions and while loops. So, it must be changed in the following equivalent rule, which can be applied to the implementation level:

$$v \longleftarrow op(e) \equiv \text{ PRE } [p := e] \, P \text{ THEN} \\ \text{VAR } p, r \text{ IN } p := e; S; v := r \text{ END} \\ \text{END} \qquad (2)$$

This rule is usually identified as *by copy* parameter passing. Here again, syntactic restrictions on variables allow deducing the new parameter passing rule:

$$v \longleftarrow op(e) \equiv \text{ PRE } [p := e] \, P \text{ THEN} \\ \text{VAR } p \text{ IN } p := e; [r := v] \, S \text{ END} \\ \text{END} \qquad (3)$$

The equivalence between (2) and (3) relies upon the fact that variables in list v do not occur in S. So, actual output parameters can be substituted into S, which is called *by reference* parameter passing. This rule is used by the regular translators of Atelier B. Moreover, it can be proved that input parameters can also be passed by reference, under the following condition:

Condition 1: [By-reference parameter passing condition] *Actual input parameters do not contain any occurrence of actual output parameters, nor any occurrence of variables that the operation works with.*

Under Condition 1, rule (1) can be applied to the bodies, also in the implementations. The proof of this condition is given in [15]. By this rule, no aliasing can appear between input parameters and output parameters or variables. Notice that calls of the form $op(x, x)$ do not introduce side effects, because input parameters cannot be assigned to. So, parameter passing in operation call in B can be done by reference if Condition 1 is satisfied. This is particularly useful in case of array parameters to avoid a copy of the value.

3 Translator Architecture

The translation process consists in transforming the B_0 part of a B project into a text written in C such that both texts (in B_0 and in C) are observationally equivalent, interpreted in their own semantics. To make B translator reusable for several targets, the translator is split into different parts as shown on Figure 2. In this architecture, tools *Flattener* and *Optimizer* are target-independent. The *Translator* tool must be customized for each new target language or for specific execution platforms.

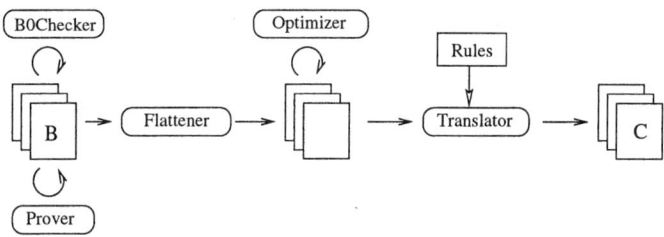

Fig. 2. Translator architecture

The *B0Checker* checks B_0 syntactical restrictions to fulfill the validity constraints determined for BOM translators. The *Flattener* produces compilation units called *flattened modules* (Section 3.1) from structured developments. Moreover, it renames identifiers in order to have a single name space for the whole project (like for instance in C). On the flattened modules, the *Optimizer* performs code transformations preserving the semantics (Section 3.2). At last, the *Translator* produces output files in the target language. For instance, for each flattened module, say *MM*, the BOM translator produces a header file MM.h and a code file MM.c (Section 3.3).

3.1 Modular Flattening of B Developments

A *module* is a chain of development starting from a machine and ending with the implementation of this machine, incremented by all the machines which are transitively included and used by the components of this chain. Relations between modules are only relations "sees" and "imports". The name of the root machine becomes the name of the module. A *flattened module* is obtained by gathering all the concrete data contained in a B original module. It contains concrete sets, concrete constants, concrete variables, initialization and operations of the implementation. Concrete data are equipped with their B_0 type. Figure 3 presents the modules of the development of Section 2.2 and the structure of the flattened modules.

To avoid *name clash* between identical names of different modules in a project, the flattener renames with a unique name each identifier in the B modules. Renaming is simply performed by prefixing all the names by the name of the module where they appear. This allows one to deal with a single name space for the whole project and makes the identifier generation in the target

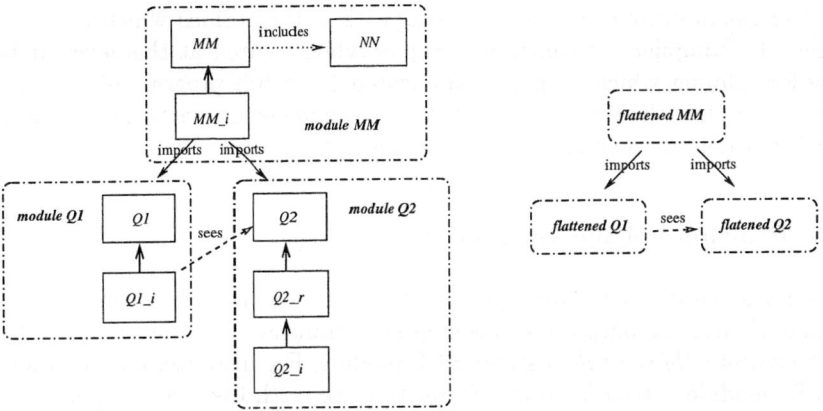

Fig. 3. B modules and flattened modules

language very easy: the renamed identifiers are kept as such in C. This provides also traceability: it is easy to know where each renamed identifier is defined.

However, the B language offers the ability to give the same name in different components to give rise to the same entity by homonymy rule, as explained in Section 2.2. After renaming, these names are no more the same. To solve this issue, a flattened module contains lists of pairs of names which have become different by renaming, but actually are the same. For more details, see the B reference manual and the report about renaming in the BOM project [9, 4]. Names which are paired in this list must be eventually represented by the same entity in the target language.

3.2 Global Optimization Phase

The global optimization phase contains two passes. The first one performs the *inlining* of operations. A pragma can be added to the source specifications in order to indicate to the optimizer which operations must be inlined. Inlining is safe thanks to condition 1 (section 2.5). As illustrated by the case study (section 5), this optimization is very useful, because the B method, as the other top-down methods, can lead to a great number of operations encapsulated in machines. Moreover, the decomposition of a development in small levels enhances the proving power of the tools by making the proofs shorter. By inlining, the number of calls is reduced, thus reducing the call stack and the execution time. Tools could be added at this stage to acquire more information on the effect of inlining and to tune the process according to determined objectives (memory size, execution time or stack size optimization).

The next optimization phase is complementary to the previous one. It consists in removing the operations which are not (or no more) called by the program. This is carried out by a simple examination of the call graph.

The global optimization phase deals with optimizations which are not performed by compilers or which are simpler when treated at this level. It is the case for inlining which is more complicated for a full programming language. Here we exploit the peculiarities of the B_0 language (in particular, there is no aliasing) to obtain a simpler and more efficient result.

3.3 Principles of the Translation

Like in a separate compilation process, the translation can be done a module at a time. Hence, the purpose of this step is to translate each flattened module in a *observationally equivalent* standard C module. For instance, an operation op_B of a B_0 module is translated in a C function op_C with the same name, such that given an instance C_B of the *context* of op_B and an instance C_C observationally equivalent to C_B, then op_C has a *behavior* observationally equivalent to op_B. Let us now make these notions precise.

- the behavior of an operation is characterized by the (abstract) function associating inputs parameters to output and the effect of the operation on the memory state.
- the context of a B_0 operation consists of all the names, visible by this operation, associated with their respective types. An instance of the context consists in associating to each name a value consistent with its declared type. In B_0, there is no aliasing: each state location is referred to by a unique identifier. State locations can be considered equivalent to their associated name.
- the observational equivalence is based on equivalence between B_0 values and C values. This equivalence on values is naturally extended on instances of context.

The observational equivalence between B_0 sets and C types is done as follows:

B_0 types	C types
Enumerated sets	Enumerated types
Basic integer sets	Predefined integer types
B_0 array types	C array types

The links between B_0 and C for integer values has been considered as crucial for the efficiency of the generated code and for the correctness of the translation. So, the solution chosen by the BOM project is to be able to interface very tightly the B_0 integer types and the C integer types. This interfacing is adaptable to various target platforms. More generally, this interfacing is a way to link B_0 types to the types of a given target language. This point is detailed in Section 4.2.

The links between B_0 arrays and C arrays is not straightforward. In B, arrays correspond to total functions whereas in C, they correspond to a contiguous zone of memory (coded as the beginning address of the array and its size). However, it is easy to do a semantical correspondence between an array element $t(i)$ in B and the value at the location t[i] in C.

4 Adaptability Means

Adaptability of the translator is achieved by two different techniques. The first one is the possibility to change the target language or to adapt the translation of the B syntactic constructions by the way of translation rules. The translator is thus a single interpreter, which applies the rules when they match the B texts in input, and produces the corresponding text in output. This point is developed in Section 4.1. The second one is the ability to connect a B_0 type with a corresponding type in the target language. Operations on these types are specified in basic machines, which have a direct implementation in the target language. Under the condition that the implementations of basic machines are correct with respect to their specification, then the correctness of the translator is preserved. We detail this mechanism in Section 4.2 on the example of the C integer types.

4.1 Translation Mechanism

The starting point of the translation is the language source syntax. To illustrate this, we give below the syntax of the definition of an operation. *F_Params* is a non-terminal notion which represents a sequence of formal parameters. We consider that there may be only one result parameter in *Op_Def* for the sake of simplicity. A formal parameter is a pair with the name of the parameter and its B_0 type. Square brackets are put around optional parts in the syntax.

$$Op\_Def \quad ::= \quad [\ (\ Idf : Idf\ ) <\!-\ ]\ Idf\ [\ (\ F\_Params\ )\ ]\ =\ Statement$$

The specification of the translator is the description of the links between the programs in the source language and programs in the target language. The translation is *complete* if all the correct[2] source programs can be translated. It is *sound* if the semantics of the translated programs is consistent with the semantics of the source programs. Generally, such a verification is very complex. Here, we are in a particular case because B_0 is very simple and the distance between B_0 and C is short. The translation can be specified for each input syntax rule, what ensures completeness, and the validation can be done inductively on the syntax of the language.

The translation is thus specified using a set of translation rules. Those rules are then interpreted by a tool developed specifically as part of the BOM project. That interpretor is built upon the Logic Solver provided with Atelier B[3]. In fact, the interpreter is a means to tailor the mechanisms provided by the Logic Solver (pattern-matching, term-rewriting, etc.) to the specific needs of translation. The translation rules are expressed by rewrite rules of the following form:

---

[2] Here "correct" means: syntactically correct, well-typed and proved.
[3] The Logic Solver is a general purpose formula manipulation tool that is used in the heart of the B prover.

operator name (pattern)	heading of the rule
& list of guards	optional conditions for applying the rule
=>	separator between antecedent and consequent
description of the result	effect of the rule

A pattern is a text (actually a tree) containing metavariables called *jokers*. For some input fragment, the interpreter tries to match the pattern of the rule with the input fragment, possibly deducing the value of some jokers. It then evaluates the guards. The rule is selected if the pattern matches the input fragment and the guards hold. Otherwise, it is skipped and the interpreter searches for an other rule further in the translator rule set. When a rule is selected, its consequent is evaluated, building the output of the translator as a side-effect.

Translation rules thus get a functional recursive form on the structure of the syntax tree. They may be defined conditionally. For example, an operation definition in B may get a result which is either a scalar value or an array value. In C, functions do not return array values. So, in the BOM project, we decided to consider the output array values as input array parameters, but to let the result as a returned value for the output scalar values. Such a condition can be done on the B_0 type of the result parameter. For example, an operation definition with one return parameter and without input parameters is translated by the conditional translation rules below. In that rules, V is the result variable of type T, I is the name of the operation and S is the body. They are jokers. Some operators are introduced to generate strings (e.g. Write) or to check conditions (e.g. Guard). Function tr_Proc_Sig(o,p) generates the heading of a C procedure with name o and parameters p and function tr_Func_Sig(t,o,p) generates the heading of a C function of type t, name o and parameters p. Finally, f_param is a constructor, which takes a pair of identifiers (a name and a type) and returns a list reduced to only one formal parameter.

```
tr_Oper( (V:T) <- I = S )
& Guard( IsArrayType(T) )
=>
tr_Proc_Sig(I,f_param(V,T)) & WriteLn("{") &
    Indent & tr_Stm(S) & Dedent &
WriteLn("}")

tr_Oper( (V:T) <- I = S )
& Guard( IsScalarType(T) )
=>
tr_Func_Sig(T,I,()) & WriteLn("{") & Indent &
    WriteLn("% %;", T, V) &
    tr_Stm(S) &
    WriteLn("return %;", V) & Dedent &
WriteLn("}")
```

The translator is flexible because the rules are written in one or more files that are interpreted. The classical approach is to describe a standard translation schema in a main file, and then to refine it by adding some rules in an auxiliary file. The rules in the auxiliary file are fetch first, then in case of failure, the rules of the main file are used. So, auxiliary files allow adaptation of the general translator to specific needs. If a developer wants to adapt the translator, he has to add new rules to the auxiliary file according to the characteristics of the target machine or of the C compiler. Obviously, these new rules must be certified to guarantee the validity of the whole translation process. The list of built-in commands of the translator is determined by the Atelier B provider (ClearSy) and the adaptation of the translator can be done by a developer (e.g. Gemplus).

4.2 Interface with C Integer Data Types

The principle is to associate a B_0 type to each C data type that are considered useful for the programming task. That means that some C data types (at least here the integers) are promoted from the target language into the B language. From a method point of view, if a user wants to generate C code, for example, he has to refine his abstract model towards a model where the integer values are exactly those provided by the C language. So, the correctness between the abstract level and the B_0 level is ensured by the proof obligations of the B method, while the translation between the last B_0 level and the C level is straightforward.

The promotion of the target data types into the B language is realized by *specifying* the former ones in the latter one. For the specification of C types in B, as for the validation of the translation rules, the ISO standard [19] has been followed. For the features which are considered as *implementation-dependent* by the standard, we chose to take the meaning usually adopted by C compilers. In these well-identified cases, a developer of a new translator must check that his own compiler respects the meaning formally specified by the BOM translator. An example of implementation-dependent behaviour is the overflow of an arithmetic operator on signed integers. We illustrate in the sequel the specification of some C integer types.

Following a common use, there exist several sizes for the integer values, each of them being able to contain either signed or unsigned representations. More formally, on a 16-bit architecture, the correspondence between both languages can be described as in the following table:

B_0 type	Formal range	C type attributes
t_int16	$-2^{15}..2^{15}-1$	int
t_int32	$-2^{31}..2^{31}-1$	long int
t_uint16	$0..2^{16}-1$	unsigned int
t_uint32	$0..2^{32}-1$	unsigned long int

The new type names are introduced in B by the declaration of concrete constants denoting the associated intervals in basic machines. These types are not compatible and conversions between them must be made explicit by the programmer (on the contrary to C). Several other constants can be added, like MIN_INT16, MAX_INT16, etc. as it was done for the standard integer type INT (Section 2.4).

Together with the B_0 types, C operations on integers must be specified in the basic machines. In project BOM, two B operations are defined for each C arithmetic operation. The first operation looks like standard B_0 arithmetic operation. It checks (by proof obligations) that the mathematical result is contained in the data type. The second one defines operations with overflow. In that case, a truncation is performed on the result. Notice that if the programmer uses the operation with truncation and if the refinement proofs of the implementation are done, then that means that whatever the result of the arithmetic operation, it is consistent with the abstract level.

For instance, the additions for signed or unsigned integers of size n with and without truncation are specified in B by the declarations:

$add\_int_n \;\hat{=}\; \lambda(x,y) \cdot (\; x \in t\_int_n \wedge y \in t\_int_n \wedge x + y \in t\_int_n \;|\; x + y \;)$
$add\_uint_n \;\hat{=}\; \lambda(x,y) \cdot (\; x \in t\_uint_n \wedge y \in t\_uint_n \wedge x + y \in t\_uint_n \;|\; x + y \;)$
$add\_int\_trunc_n \;\hat{=}\; \lambda(x,y) \cdot (\; x \in t\_int_n \wedge y \in t\_int_n$
$\qquad\qquad\qquad\qquad |\; ((x + y + 2^{n-1} + 2^n) \bmod 2^n) - 2^{n-1} \;)$
$add\_uint\_trunc_n \;\hat{=}\; \lambda(x,y) \cdot (\; x \in t\_uint_n \wedge y \in t\_uint_n \;|\; (x+y) \bmod 2^n \;)$

In these definitions, add_int and add_uint_trunc are the $+$ operator defined in the ISO-C standard, respectively on signed and unsigned integers. Function add_int_trunc is the $+$ operator usually implemented by the compilers in case of overflow. Function add_uint is provided by the BOM translator as an instance of add_uint_trunc in case of non overflow. The semantics of the non-truncating operator produces proof obligations much simpler to deal with.

5 A Case Study: The Java Card Virtual Machine

5.1 General Presentation

In the BOM project, a case study was chosen to assess the new translator of B specifications. The Java Card virtual machine is typically an application which must be embedded in smart cards and which has been intensively studied by Gemplus [17,8,10]. This case study completes a formal development of the Java Card byte code verifier using the B method[4] [7,6]. The subset of the JCVM specified and developed in B is large enough to be able to read the bytecode files of Java applets and to execute them. An application in Java was also written (an electronic purse) to test the embedded virtual machine. A complete JCVM contains four components: a loader, a linker, a Java Card Runtime Environment (JCRE) and an interpreter of bytecode. Only the last two components have been formally developed. For testing the machine, loading and linking is performed by an ad-hoc program. This is illustrated in Figure 4.

The specification written in B is about 10,000 lines long. To this part developed formally according to the B method, it is needed to add components developed outside the method, either to implement basic machines, or to interface the B components to low-level devices, or yet to simulate the underlying operating system (memory management, etc.). These components written in C

---
[4] Developed in the framework of the european project IST MATISSE, number IST-1999-11435.

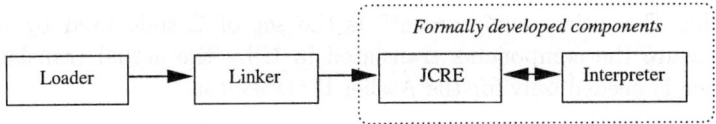

Fig. 4. Components of the Java Card Virtual Machine

are approximatively 5,000 lines long. One may consider that it constitutes a medium-size formal case study[5], but it is significant in the world of smart cards and embedded applications.

5.2 Analysis of the Case Study

In project BOM experiments, we compared four translation chains from B to C:

1. the translator provided by the actual version 3.6 of Atelier B,
2. a BOM translator without optimization and with a general set of translation rules. It translates data and programs in a standard manner and is referred to as BOM(G) (for *General*) in the paper,
3. a BOM translator, adapted for smart cards by the way of some specific translation rules, called BOM(C) (for *Cards*) and possibly optimizing the generated code by inlining, as explained in Section 3.2.
4. a prototype developed by Gemplus in the framework of the MATISSE project, called Simple C, dealing with a limited subset of B_0. Like BOM(C), it is adapted for smart cards but it does not perform inlining.

The aim of the fourth translator was to assess the feasibility of code generation for smart cards. The Java Card bytecode verifier has been embedded on a smart card [6] using this latter translator. The comparison of the results of the translations will be done in Section 5.4 with respect to these four translators. The components of the case study are presented in Figure 5. One can distinguish the following parts:

1. "Loader and linker" are the first modules (written in C) of the JCVM.
2. "Interface between B and C" is constituted of some C code which ensures the links between the C modules and the programs generated from the B developments.
3. "B components" is the part developed with the B method. It contains the JCRE module and the interpreter of Java Card bytecode.
4. "Basic B machines" are the machines which are no further developed in B. They provide interfaces with integer types and with system primitives.
5. "Basic C implementations" are the implementations of the basic B machines.
6. "Hardware abstraction" is the model in C of hardware components needed for the case study.

---

[5] By comparing to industrial B developments which can reach 100,000 lines of B code.

7. "Atelier B runtime environment" is the set of C code used by Atelier B to execute the components translated in C by the actual translator. This module is needed only for the Atelier B translator.

The "loader and linker" and the "Hardware abstraction" parts do not depend on the various translator versions of the case study. They will not be considered in the remainder of this paper. The "Interface between B and C" part differs between Atelier B, in which multi-instancing of machines is allowed, and the other translators. The case study contains nine basic B machines. They are implemented directly by C programs. The basic machine for integers does not generate specific C code. The "B components" part contains thirty components (twelve machines, twelve implementations and six refinements). Only implementations differ, due to the adaptation of the B_0 types.

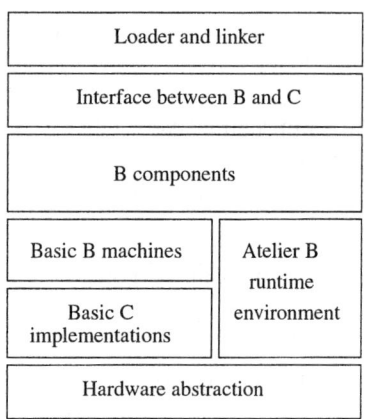

Fig. 5. Components involved in the case study

5.3 Compilation Chain and Characteristics of the Target Platforms

The translation chain can be represented as in Figure 6. "B files" and "Written by hand C files" are provided by the developer. The other files are generated by the tools. The size comparisons are done at the stage "Compiled files", i.e. size in byte of the object code. At this stage, the size of the various components is accessible for a detailed analysis (which is not the case in the binary file).

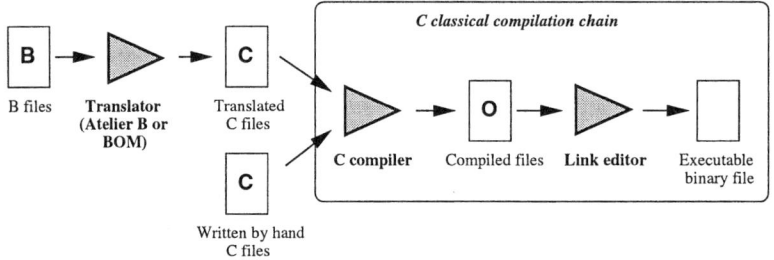

Fig. 6. Translation schema

Besides the four translation chains, we have experimented the translation for two target platforms with very different characteristics. By this way we can assess the efficiency of the BOM translator in several contexts. The chosen platforms are:

- An Atmel AVR 8-bit RISC microcontroler[6]. For this platform, the compiler used is the IAR one[7], and the optimizations are set to minimize code size. The code size presented corresponds to the size of the code given by the compiler plus the size of the constant data.
- The SmartMIPS[8], a 32-bit MIPS processor specially designed for smart cards. It is more representative of high-end next generation smart cards. For this platform, the compiler used is the MIPS SDE version of the gcc compiler. The mips16 instruction set is used, and the optimizations are set to reduce code size. For this platform, the size provided corresponds to the size of the "text" segment as given by the `sde-size` utility.

5.4 Comparisons between the Translators

The tables in Fig. 7 and Fig. 8 summarize the results of the code sizes generated by the various translators with respect to the two platforms. A detailed comparison is available in a BOM project report [18]. The measures are given respectively for the Atmel AVR and the SmartMIPS platforms. The "Gain" line displays the improvement in code size compared to the Atelier B generated code[9]

Atmel AVR	Atelier B	BOM(G)	BOM(C)	SimpleC
B Components	12,692	4,870	4,326	4,492
Basic B machines	2,970	140	140	677
Basic C implementations	726	726	726	726
Interface	1,606	24	24	20
Atelier B runtime env.	1,140			
Total	17,994	5,760	5,216	5,915
Gain	0 %	68 %	71 %	67 %

Fig. 7. Code sizes (bytes) for each translators (Atmel AVR platform)

In the case of the AVR platform, the BOM translators clearly outperforms the Atelier B one. The difference of code size between "Interface" and "Basic B machines" of table 7 is mainly due to the fact that the Atelier B translator allows multi-instancing of machines. Indeed, this feature requires to introduce in the generated code an internal representation (using C structures) of machine states. Therefore, machine initialization needs dynamic allocation and associated initialization code, and machine states are accessed using indirections. The difference between translated B machines is also partly due to the same reason. But the benefits of BOM translators and Simple C on the B components also come from the use of extended B_0 types (as explained in section 4.2), which are especially well suited to 8-bit platforms such as the Atmel AVR one.

---

[6] URL: http://www.atmel.com/products/AVR/.
[7] URL: http://www.iar.com.
[8] URL: http://www.mips.com/products/s2p12.html.
[9] For each column c, the gain is computed by: $\frac{(Total(AtelierB) - Total(c)) \times 100}{Total(AtelierB)}$.

SmartMIPS	Atelier B	BOM(G)	BOM(C)	SimpleC
B Components	9,686	7,630	5,018	6,916
Basic B machines	2,286	168	168	720
Basic C implementations	1,034	1,040	1,040	1,032
Interface	624	42	42	36
Atelier B runtime env.	588			
Total	14,218	8,880	6,268	8,704
Gain	0 %	38 %	56 %	39 %

Fig. 8. Code sizes (bytes) for each translator (SmartMIPS platform)

Atmel AVR	C implementation	BOM(C)	BOM(G)	Atelier B
Size JCRE	537	596	634	1,704
Overhead	0 %	11 %	18 %	217 %
SmartMIPS				
Size JCRE	536	588	652	904
Overhead	0 %	10 %	22 %	69 %

Fig. 9. Overhead with respect to a C program

As the SmartMIPS is a 32-bit platform, the Atelier B code is more adapted, and differences between the translators are tighter. Contrary to the AVR platform, using small integer types is less efficient than using the default 32-bit integer. Thus, both the Atelier B translator as well as the BOM translator uses 32-bit integers, reducing the gap between the translators. However, the overhead implied by the initialization of the machines still remains, and can be seen on the "Interface" and "Basic B machines" lines of table 8.

Another comparison can be done, even if they rely upon a little part of the case study. The component JCRE was written in C for the Gemplus prototype translator, because this translator was not able to deal with some B features used to specify this component. So, it is possible to compare the size of this component (after compilation) with the size of the translations from B to C of the same component. The summary is given in Fig. 9. The line "Overhead" displays the size overhead compared to the C implementation[10].

5.5 Main Results

Let us sum up now the results of this case study. BOM translators produce more efficient code than Atelier B. It is however not surprising, because the Atelier B generator does not generate very optimised code. BOM translators produce code which efficiency is comparable with the output of SimpleC, for which some parts are directly encoded in C due to the incompleteness of the prototype. It is an interesting result because Gemplus experiments have shown that SimpleC is compliant with smart cards requirements [7, 6]. Moreover, BOM translator has

---

[10] For each column c, the overhead is: $\frac{(size(c) - size(1)) \times 100}{size(1)}$.

	BOM(G)	BOM(C) without inlining	Gain	BOM(C) with inlining	Gain
AVR size	4,870	4,820	1.03 %	4,326	11.17 %
SmartMIPS size	7,630	7,572	0.76 %	5,018	33.60 %

Fig. 10. Code sizes (bytes) with and without optimizations

several important advantage over SimpleC. Indeed, SimpleC is an incomplete prototype which is not integrated with Atelier B. Moreover it does not offer any mechanism to adapt the translation process.

In regard to the points which are detailed in this paper, the B_0 type extension is interesting for code efficiency, as illustrated in the case of the Atmel AVR platform. Moreover, adding finer types at the level of the B_0 language offers a set of guarantees due to the proof process, in particular when operations without overflow are used. The main improvement in code efficiency is achieved by the optimization phase as illustrated in Fig. 10 for the part "B components".

Abstract models generally introduce operations to modularize specifications and the proof process, as explained in Section 3.2. Thus, inlining can improve implementations in a significant way, depending on the choice of the calls to be inlined. In the case study the gain is important because the interpretor abstract model contains a lot of operations which are called only once. After inlining, about a hundred of operations have been eliminated. Recall that inlining is valid only when condition 1 (Section 2.5) is fulfilled. In the case study, no restriction has been met by this condition.

Finally the adaptability of BOM translation rules allow a developer to optimize the translator for a given platform and for a given project. Indeed, some translation rules corresponding to a frequent form of code in the project can be made more efficient. In the case study, apart for C types, only few adaptations have been necessary.

6 Conclusion

The objectives of the BOM project were to carry out a translation chain from B specifications to C programs. The imposed constraints were that the generated code had to be embedded in smart cards as it would be done if the application was directly written in C. Moreover, the chain should guarantee that the code is correct with respect to the high level specifications and it is runtime error free. At last, the translator should be adaptable to various target platforms and compilers.

In this paper, we focused the attention on the techniques introduced in the translation chain to achieve adaptability and embedding. Others results of the BOM project are the definition of an operational semantics of the B_0 language in order to establish the total correctness of the translation process and a generalization of the adaptability of the B_0 language for other languages or types. With respect to the purpose of software embedding, the (light) restrictions imposed to the B language were sufficient to implement a translator which generates a reasonably compact code. The optimization phase, although relatively simple, decreases significantly the code size. Comparisons of Section 5.4 show a promising result, since the overhead compared to manually translated C code is reduced to around 10% using the BOM translator. This overhead, although it cannot be neglected, still remains acceptable, especially if the benefits of using formally proved code are taken into account. With respect to adaptability, two techniques were considered useful, implemented and tested on the case study. The adaptation of the translation rules needs more complete experiments, specially for their impact on the execution time for some specific platforms. On the contrary, adaptation of the integer types to basic C types has been found very convenient for example, for the 8-bit AVR platform.

So, the project results are satisfactory and demonstrate the ability to generate automatically executable code which is comparable to a code written by hand with ordinary programming languages. The gains rely then on the guarantees provided by the use of a formal method and on the certification level which can be obtained by this way. As far as we know, only few formal methods support code generation which is as time/space efficient as handwritten code. The Coq proof assistant [20] allows the extraction of functional programs from proofs in constructive logic. This approach has not been chosen by Gemplus: writing specifications requires a high level of expertise; traceability between proofs and generated programs is not straightforward; generated programs are functional and there is no compiler specialized for smartcard platforms.

For synchronous languages, in [14] an alternative approach is developed: rather than proving in advance that the translator always produces a target code which correctly implements the source code (translator verification), each individual translation (i.e. run of the translator) is verified. A key feature of this validation is its full automation. Nevertheless, such an approach seems not possible in the B framework, due to the generality of the considered programs.

References

1. J.-R. Abrial. *The B Book - Assigning Programs to Meanings*. Cambridge University Press, August 1996.
2. P. Behm, P. Benoit, A. Faivre, and J.-M. Meynadier. Météor: A Successful Application of B in a Large Project. In *FM'99 - Formal Methods*, pages 369–388. LNCS 1708, Springer-Verlag, 1999.
3. P. Behm, L. Burdy, and J-M Meynadier. Well Defined B. In D. Bert, editor, *B'98: Recent Advances in the Development and Use of the B Method*. LNCS 1393, Springer-Verlag, 1998.
4. D. Bert. Étude de la traduction B0 vers C : Conventions de nommage. Technical Report D10, http://lifc.univ-fcomte.fr/~tatibouet/WEBBOM, 2003.
5. D. Bert, M.-L. Potet, and Y. Rouzaud. A Study on Components and Assembly Primitives in B. In H. Habrias, editor, *Proceedings of the 1st Conference on the B method*, pages 47–62. IRIN, Nantes, 1996.

6. L. Casset. Development of an Embedded Verifier for Java Card Byte Code using Formal Methods. In L.-H. Eriksson and P. A. Lindsay, editors, *Formal Methods Europe (FME)*, pages 290–309, Copenhagen, 2002. LNCS 2391, Springer-Verlag.
7. L. Casset, L. Burdy, and A. Requet. Formal Development of an embedded verifier for Java Card Byte Code. In *International Conference on Dependable Systems & Networks (DSN)*, pages 51–58, Washington, D.C., USA, June 2002. IEEE Computer Society.
8. L. Casset and J.-L. Lanet. How to Formally Specify the Java Bytecode Semantics using the B Method. pages 1–8, Lisbon, June 1999.
9. ClearSy. B Language Reference Manual, version 1.8.5. Technical report, ClearSy System Engineering, URL :http://www.clearsy.com/, 2001.
10. J.-L. Lanet and A. Requet. Formal Proof of Smart Card Applets Correctness. In J.-J. Quisquater and B. Schneier, editors, *CARDIS*, pages 85–97. LNCS 1820, Springer-Verlag, 2000.
11. C. Morgan. *On the Refinement Calculus*. Springer-Verlag, 1992.
12. S. Motré. A B automaton for Authentification Process. In *WITS: Workshop on Issues in the Theory of Security*, Genève, Suisse, 2000.
13. S. Motré and C. Téri. Using Formal and Semi-Formal Methods for a Common Criteria Evaluation. In *EUROSMART*, Marseille, France, 2000.
14. A. Pnueli, M. Siegel, and O. Shtrichman. Translation Validation for Synchronous Languages. In K. G. Larsen, S. Skyum, and G. Winskel, editors, *Proc. of the 25th Int. Colloquium on Automata, Languages and Programming (ICALP 1998)*, pages 235–246. LNCS 1443, Springer-Verlag, 1998.
15. M-L. Potet. *Spécifications et développements formels: Etude des aspects compositionnels dans la méthode B*. Habilitation à Diriger des Recherches, INPG, 2002.
16. M.-L. Potet and Y. Rouzaud. Composition and Refinement in the B method. In D. Bert, editor, *B'98 : Recent Advances in the Development and Use of the B Method*, pages 46–65. LNCS 1393, Springer-Verlag, 1998.
17. A. Requet. A B Model for Ensuring Soundness of the Java Card Virtual Machine (Extended Version). *Science of Computer Programming, Elsevier Science*, 46(3):283–306, 2003.
18. A. Requet. Évaluation du traducteur C. Technical Report D11, http://lifc.univ-fcomte.fr/~tatibouet/WEBBOM, 2003.
19. International Standard. Programming languages - C. ISO/IEC 9899:1999 (E).
20. Coq Development Team. *The Coq Proof Assistant -Reference Manual, Version 7.4*. INRIA, http://coq.inria.fr/doc-fra.html, February 2003.

Integrating Model-Checking Architectural Analysis and Validation in a Real Software Life-Cycle

Daniele Compare[1], Paola Inverardi[2],
Patrizio Pelliccione[2], and Alessandra Sebastiani[1]

[1] Lab. NMS C2, Marconi Selenia,
L'Aquila, Italy,
{daniele.compare,alessandra.sebastiani}@marconi.com
[2] University of L'Aquila, Computer Science Department,
Via Vetoio 1, 67010 L'Aquila, Italy,
{inverard,pellicci}@di.univaq.it

Abstract. In this paper we describe the use of a model-checking based tool, Charmy, in the Marconi Selenia software development environment. The goal of the project is to model and analyze the software architecture of a software system currently under development. We define and formally check its overall architecture. By zooming into relevant subsystems we are able to identify a set of incorrect behaviors. We use an iterative process, where both the architectural sub-systems models and the properties to be checked can be defined, checked and revised several times.

The results of the experience allow an evaluation of the effort to use the analysis framework in the considered industrial software development environment and an assessment of the efficacy and the role of the architectural analysis in the software development process. The main relevance of this experience is in the effort to smoothly integrate the use of model-checking techniques in a standard software life-cycle, in particular concerning the discovery and definition of architectural properties.

Keywords: Architectural analysis, model checking, software development process, models consistency.

1 Introduction

In the last years there has been a growing interest for the architectural level description of software systems.

The Software Architecture (SA) description represents the first, in the development life-cycle, complete system description. It provides at the high abstraction level of components and connectors both a description of the static structure of the system and a model of its dynamic behavior. The aim of SA descriptions is twofold: on one side they force the designer to separate architectural concerns from other design ones. On the other, they allow for analysis and validation of architectural choices, both behavioral and quantitative in order to obtain better software quality in an increasingly shorter time-to-market development scenario.

Despite the high level of abstraction very often SA can still be too complex to be managed. A way to tackle system complexity consists of representing the system through several view points [11, 10, 4]; as a direct consequence, different models are used to represent the different views.

In the current industrial practice *state-based machines* and *scenarios* are the most common used views to model behavioral aspects: state diagrams describe components' behavior while scenarios (message sequence charts or sequence diagrams) identify how they interact. Although very expressive, this approach has two drawbacks with respect to analysis and validation.

The first one deals with the *model incompleteness* of the system specification: in general these models are not completely specified. Typically we can rely only on a finite set of scenarios that complement (sub-)systems state models.

The second one is a problem of *views consistency*: the use of several views facilitates the growing of inconsistencies [13, 14]. Indeed, state diagrams and scenarios provide different views of the system that are not independent and can erroneously specify contradictory or inconsistent behaviors.

The approach proposed in Charmy (CHecking Architectural Model consistencY) [7, 9, 6] assumes a description of a system software architecture through state and sequence diagrams (scenarios) views. Charmy, starting from these (incomplete) dynamic views, synthesizes, through a suitable translation into Promela, the specification language of the SPIN [17] model checker, an actual SA complete model that can be executed and verified in SPIN. This model can be validated with respect to a set of properties, e.g. deadlock, correctness of properties, starvation, etc., expressed in Linear Temporal Logic (LTL) [12].

The model checker SPIN, is a widely distributed software package that supports the formal verification of concurrent systems allowing to analyze their logical consistency by on-the-fly checks, i.e. without the need of constructing a global state graph, thus reducing the complexity of the check. It is the core engine of Charmy and it is not directly accessible by a Charmy user.

In this paper we describe the use of Charmy in an industrial software development environment. The goal of the project is to model and analyze an industrial software system currently under development. We define and formally check its overall architecture. By zooming into relevant sub-systems we are able to identify a set of incorrect behaviors. We use an iterative process, where both the architectural sub-systems models and the properties to be checked can be defined, checked and revised several times.

The results of the experience allow an evaluation of the effort to use the analysis framework in the Marconi Selenia software development environment and an assessment of the efficacy and the role of the architectural analysis in the software development process. Marconi Selenia is a global communications and information technology company headquartered in Pomezia (Roma - Italy). We have a collaboration with the Lab. NMS C2, Marconi Selenia L'Aquila, Italy.

The main relevance of this experience is in the effort to smoothly integrate the use of model-checking techniques in a standard software life-cycle, in particular concerning the architectural properties discovery and definition.

In the literature much work has been directed to improve the model generation phase, little attention has been put in the properties to be proved. In general these are assumed to exist as part of the problem specification. Research efforts in system properties and in the corresponding (temporal) formulae mainly concern the ability to informally describe the properties and then translate them in the formal formulae [16, 5]. Little or no attention is devoted to the problem of properties *elicitation*, that is the ability to determine from the software artifacts at hand which are the relevant properties to check for. Similarly very little support can be found for model refinement. We can certainly assume that at the requirements level, explicitly stated behavioral requirements exist. These are "global" system requirements, that is they characterize the input-output behavior of the system. Once a software architecture is specified, it is possible to check if it guarantees the global functional requirements. However, this might not be enough to gain confidence on the specified design. Often, we need to be able to refine both the models and the global properties into sub-properties that focus on relevant portions of the system software architecture. This is exactly the process we followed.

The paper is organized as follows. In Section 2 we summarize the framework and the way it works. Sections 3, 4, 5 describe the framework applied on the case study. Section 3 describes the system specification of the case study and its main properties. Section 4 shows the system modelling and verification. Section 5 shows the refined process applied to significant portions of the system. Section 6 summarizes our experience and presents conclusions and future work.

2 Integrating Charmy in the Marconi Selenia Life-Cycle

The framework we used in the project aims at integrating several tools in order to correctly drive the software architect during the system modelling design phase. The framework involves the UML notation, and the Charmy tool.

2.1 UML

Nowadays industry is increasingly using the Unified Modelling Language (UML) [1] as Architecture Description Language (ADL). UML use for graphically depicting, specifying, constructing and documenting the artifacts of a software system has been recognized as a de facto standard.

Twelve types of diagrams can be defined, divided into three categories: four diagram types for the static application structure, five to represent dynamic behavior aspects and three to represent organization and managing of application modules. In the following we assume a basic knowledge of the UML notation.

Marconi Selenia uses UML as design support for all software development phases. The system requirements formalization is performed using use-case and sequence diagrams. The system software architecture is specified by means of state and sequence diagrams. They are used to describe internal component behaviors and components interactions, respectively.

2.2 Charmy

Formal methods and in particular model-checking techniques require specialized knowledge and skills that usually the industry does not have.

Other drawbacks in using model-checker techniques are the time efficiency and the state explosion problem. Experience shows that there is generally a big difference in efficiency and memory size between models developed by a "casual" user and models developed by an "expert" user.

Charmy tries to overcome these problems. It is a tool that helps the software architect to draw architectural state diagrams and scenarios and automatically translates these models in Promela code and in LTL formulae expressing suitable system behavioral properties. The Promela specification is obtained getting information about the internal behavior of components from the state diagrams and about components interaction from sequence diagrams, e.g. synchronous or asynchronous communication between two components. In order to help the designer to specify behavioral properties in LTL, Charmy provides facilities to obtain LTL formulae from system behaviors expressed as sequence diagrams.

The verification step starts in Charmy defining a sequence diagram, i.e. an intuitive and familiar formalism, representing desired behavioral properties. In an industrial context it is unfeasible to write by hand LTL formulae, as pointed out by Holzmann in [5], where the author proposes a tool to write temporal properties in a graphical notation. An alternative approach in this direction is presented in [3] where the user chooses a LTL formula from a library of predefined LTL formulae.

Charmy offers to the user an interface to specify scenarios and a set of options on how these scenarios can be interpreted as behavioral properties. For example, among these options, a user can say that a scenario has to be verified for all possible system behaviors, or that it represents just one possible behavior. Other options allow for more sophisticated verifications.

The set of properties that can be specified in this way is just a subset of LTL properties. This limitation is common also to the other approaches mentioned above. However, this does not appear to be a significant restriction since the subset of specifiable properties, as confirmed by several case studies we have considered so far, are sufficiently expressive for a software designer.

The actual verification step is finally carried on by SPIN. It checks whether the LTL formulae are verified on the obtained SA global model. Technical details on Charmy may be found in [7, 8].

The role of Charmy is to guide the system designer in the SA specification and validation phases. In this project we start from a first system SA high level abstraction, which identifies few main subsystems and a set of high level interaction scenarios. From this specifications we obtain a model that can already be validated with respect to significant high level behaviors. This first validation step allows us to gain confidence on the global design architectural choices and to identify portions of the SA that might need further and deeper investigation. The subsequent steps are to zoom into the potentially problematic subsystems by identifying implied sub-properties. The latter is not an easy task. In a simplistic approach we can think that the set of LTL formulae to prove can be easily extracted from the system specification. This is only true for high level global behavioral properties. In our case, the actual formulae that we prove at the architectural level must be more refined in order to point out critical architectural interactions. There is no automatic way to do this refinement step, which is connected with the identification of the most critical sub-systems that need a deeper modelling and verification. In the following we describe the process followed in the project, trying to highlight the motivations that allowed us to focus on significant sub-systems and to identify relevant properties.

2.3 Integration Process

The process we use starts from a set of available software artifacts that include use-case and sequence diagrams specifying system requirements, the requirement documents in natural language and a high level SA description in terms of state and sequence diagrams. From these artifacts we summarize below how we used the proposed framework:

1. by using state and sequence diagrams a SA model in Promela code is produced in Charmy. Sequence diagrams are also separately translated into LTL formulae and used to test the correctness of the SA Promela model. Note that the information taken out of the sequence diagrams to generate a Promela model is only related to the communication type (graphically indicated by the type of arrows);
2. the executable model is also extensively simulated to gain confidence on system behaviors and to get suggestions about potentially wrong behaviors;
3. the global behavioral properties (desired scenarios), stated in the requirements, are proved on the system model; we can also analyze the system with respect to undesired scenarios (wrong behaviors as suggested in the previous step);
4. identify critical sub-systems and their relevant properties which suitably derived from the global properties and the architectural structure;
5. refine the sub-systems architecture and iterate the process.

Our approach is based on the construction of an executable prototype of the system software architecture in order to understand its behaviors and its features. It is clear that we would not be able to catch all the potentially detectable behaviors in one verification step. For this reason we iterate the process; at each iteration we focus on a system part refining its specification and identifying other potentially critical sub-parts.

The process of focussing on a system part that we consider critical implies that we intentionally restrict our visibility of the system behaviors by removing "not interesting" behaviors from the original system. This abstraction step is an *under approximation*: if an error is found in the abstract model it is sure that the error also appears in the original model; the opposite does not hold.

To some extent, our approach is similar to extracting test cases. In eliciting test cases a tester focusses on the critical parts of the system in order to verify his intuitions. In the same way we elicit the properties that represent potential flaws and check them on the system model by using model checking techniques. Also the testing process can only show the presence of errors, not their absence.

3 The NICE Case Study: System Specification

The Naval Integrated Communication Environment (NICE), a project developed by Marconi Selenia, operates in a naval communication environment.

The purpose of the system is to fulfill the following main functionalities:

- provide voice, data and video communication modes;
- enable system aided message preparation, processing, storage, retrieval distribution and purging;
- implement radio frequency transmission and reception, variable power control and modulation;
- provision of remote control and monitoring including detection of equipment failures in the transmission/reception radio chain and the management system elements;
- provision of a data distribution service;
- implement communications security techniques to the required level of evaluation, accreditation and certification.

On a gross grain the SA is composed of the NICE Management Sub-system (NICE MS), CTS and EQUIPMENT components as highlighted in Figure 1. In the following we focus on the NICE MS, the more critical component. It controls both internal and external communications, defining the following class of requirements:

1. fault and damage management;
2. system configuration;
3. security management;
4. traffic accounting;
5. performance management.

Each requirements class groups a set of functionalities.

The NICE MS complexity and heterogeneity (different hardware and operating systems and relative applications) together with its real time context needs the definition of a precise software architecture to express its coordination structure. The system involves several operational consoles that manage the heterogeneous system equipment including the ATM based Communication Transfer System(CTS) through blind Proxy computers. For this reason the high level design is based on a manager-agent architecture that is summarized in Figure 1, where the Workstation (WS) component represents the management

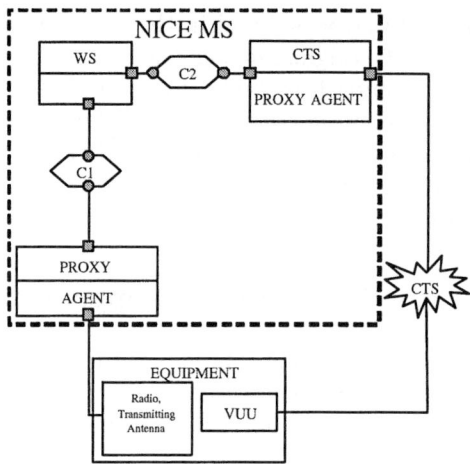

Fig. 1. NICE static software architecture

entity while the Proxy Agent and the CTS Proxy Agent component represent the interface to control the managed equipment and the CTS respectively. Subsystems are connected by connectors (C1 and C2) that allow the communication between them.

WS-CTS Proxy Agent communication is based on the SNMPv2 protocol [2] where WS is the manager entity while CTS Proxy Agent is the managed agent. The exchanged messages are the following:

- Set: the manager asks the agent to change a specified variable;
- Get: the manager asks the agent to report value of a specified variable;
- Notify: the agent acknowledges a received Set/Get message by the manager;
- Trap: the agent warns the manager about its own change of the state; note that a Trap message does not have an acknowledge message.

WS-Proxy Agent communication is based on a proprietary protocol over LAN. The Proxy Agent is directly connected to the managed equipment and simply converts messages coming from WS into a format that the equipment is able to understand and vice-versa. In doing such activity, it also monitors the equipment state through timer-based polling. In order to avoid useless network overload, it forwards to the WS only the variations of the equipment state.

Our work focusses on requirements 1 and 2 because more interesting analysis results are obtained for them. In the following two subsections we present the formalization of these requirements. For the sake of the presentation, only some functionalities related to these requirements are presented. We make use of use case and sequence diagrams.

3.1 Requirement 1: Fault and Damage Management

Starting from the NICE global model we consider two situations: the CTS Proxy Agent detects a CTS or VUU (Voice User Unit) failure; the CTS performs recovery actions. Note that a VUU is a ISDN voice terminal equipment to access the ship's operational internal and external communications, including the ship's telephone system.

This requirement is composed of the following two functionalities:

1.1. **Failure management:** when a fault occurs CTS/VUU alerts the CTS Proxy Agent that forwards it to the WS. The NICE Manager is alerted by the WS.
   Figure 2.a shows the use case diagram relative to the fault management while Figure 3.a describes two possible alert management interactions.

1.2. **Recovery management:** when the user requires a *Recovery* the CTS Proxy Agent performs the Recovery operations and update the WS. The connectivity restored message is showed to the NICE Manager.
   Figure 2.b shows the use case diagram relative to the recovery management while Figure 3.b describes the recovery management interactions.

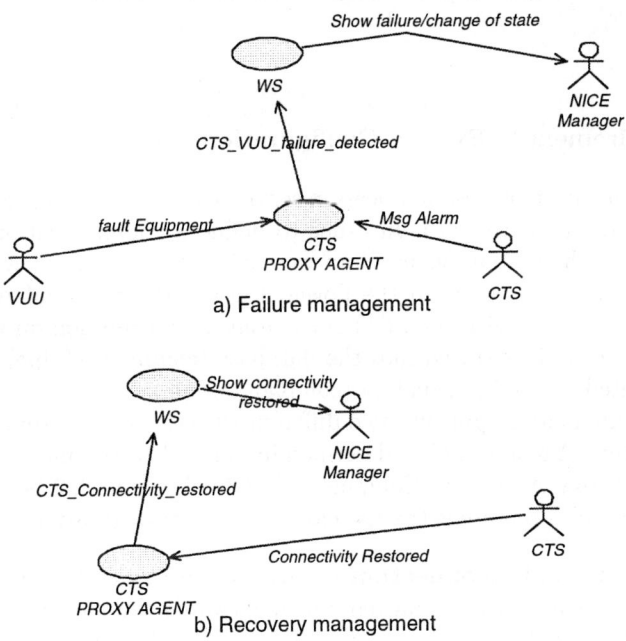

Fig. 2. Use-Case diagrams for the requirement 1

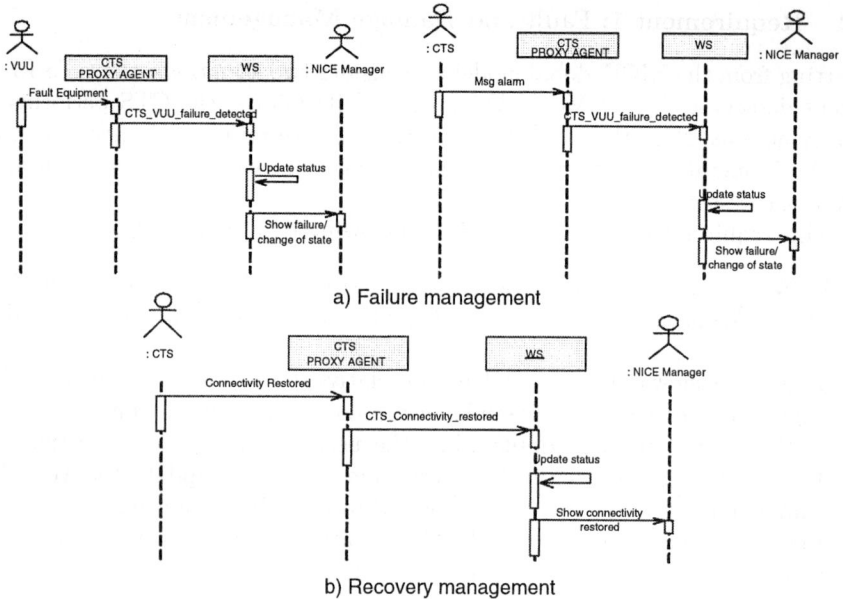

Fig. 3. Sequence diagrams for the requirement 1

3.2 Requirement 2: System Configuration

On board of a ship more communication services are defined through a complan (COMmunication PLANning). In order to define a communication service we must configure the system devices and we must define the naval ATM network paths. So we need to establish the power, the transmission and receiving frequency, etc... of the devices and define the routing information on the network. A complan can be just stored into the database (complan off-line) for a future use or activated to use immediately (complan on-line).

This requirement is split into two different situations: the interaction among WS, CTS Proxy Agent and CTS described in item 2.1 below and the interaction among WS, Proxy Agent and Equipment described in item 2.2 below.

Figures 4 and 5 represent the use cases of these two situations.

2.1. Connection/Disconnection configuration: when the WS component gets in input a configuration request, it forwards the path configuration to the CTS Proxy Agent. The configuration request is then sent to the CTS.

2.2. Equipment configuration: focusing on the components WS, Proxy Agent and Equipment after a configuration request the WS forwards the Equipment data (frequency, power, etc...) to the Proxy Agent. Finally the data are sent to the interested Equipment.

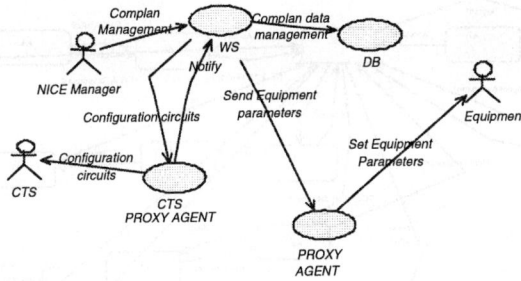

Fig. 4. Use case diagrams for the requirement 2

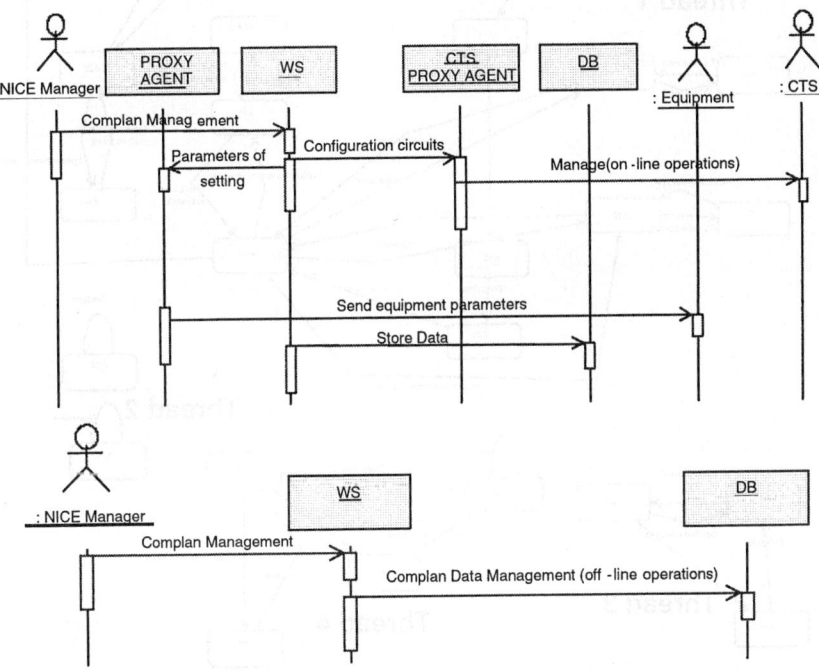

Fig. 5. Sequence diagram for the requirement 2

4 The NICE Case Study: System Modelling and Verification

In previous sections we have defined the static SA of the NICE system and we have formalized the requirements specification through use case and sequence diagrams. Now we extract from these artifacts the state diagrams for the components and the scenarios defining component interactions.

Figure 6 shows the state diagram for the WS component. This component has several different threads. The whole SA model is composed of 26 state diagrams

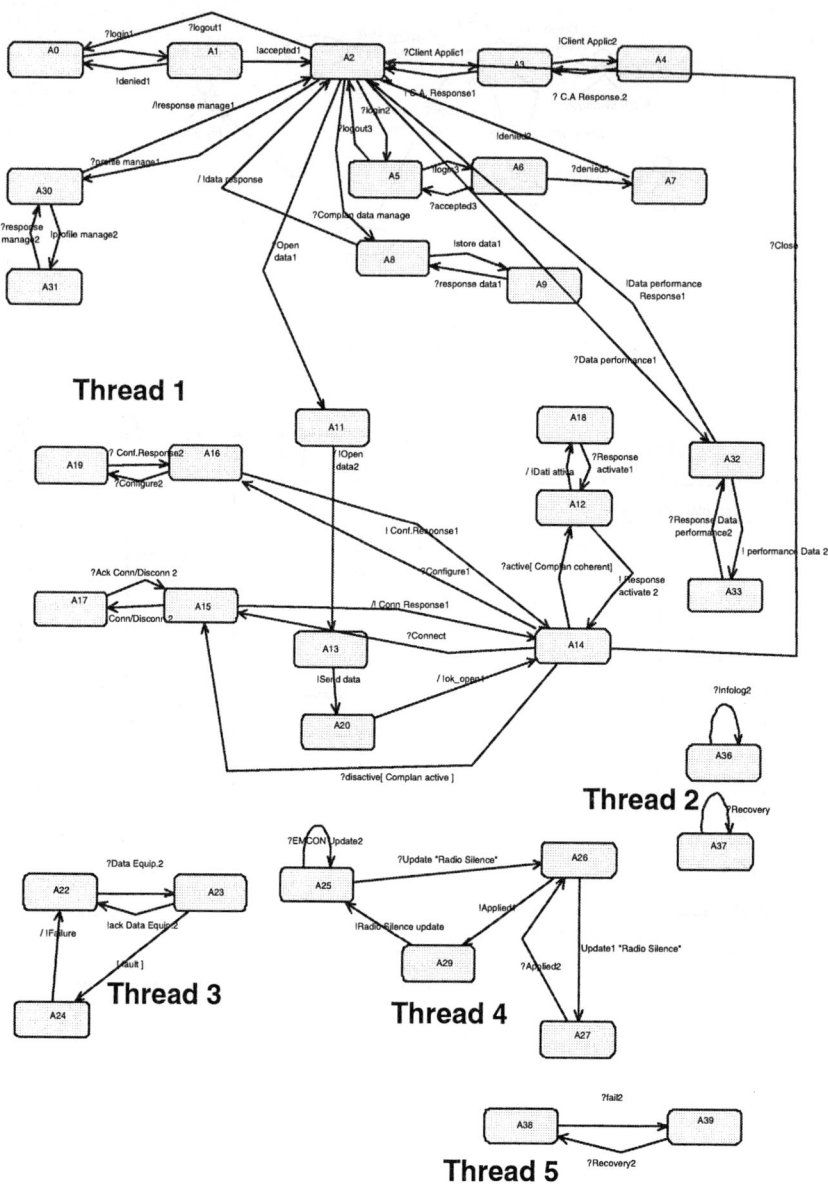

Fig. 6. Workstation component

and 85 messages and the size of a single state diagram is comparable to that in Figure 6. The actual size of the system does not permit to report in the paper details about the whole system. For this reason in the following we illustrate our approach only on significant excerpts of the system in order to give an idea of the modelling technique and of the analysis process followed. We consider for each component only the threads involved in the system behaviors we are illustrating. For example for the WS component in the following section we consider only thread 5 for the requirement 1 (see Figures 6 and 7.c) and part of thread 1 for the requirement 2 (see Figures 6 and 8.c). Interested readers can refer to [15] for a full treatment of the system. We recall that we use scenarios to represent the properties that must be checked.

In Subsections 4.1 and 4.2 we describe the system modelling and verification for two functionalities of requirements 1 and 2, respectively.

4.1 Requirement 1: Fault and Damage Management

In Figures 7.a, 7.b and 7.c the CTS, the CTS Proxy Agent and the WS state diagrams are shown.

Note that in the diagrams, the symbol ? denotes a message reception and the symbol ! denotes a message sending. When we have more transitions between the same pair of states we represent the set of transitions with only one transition whose label is composed of all transitions labels separated by the symbol '/'.

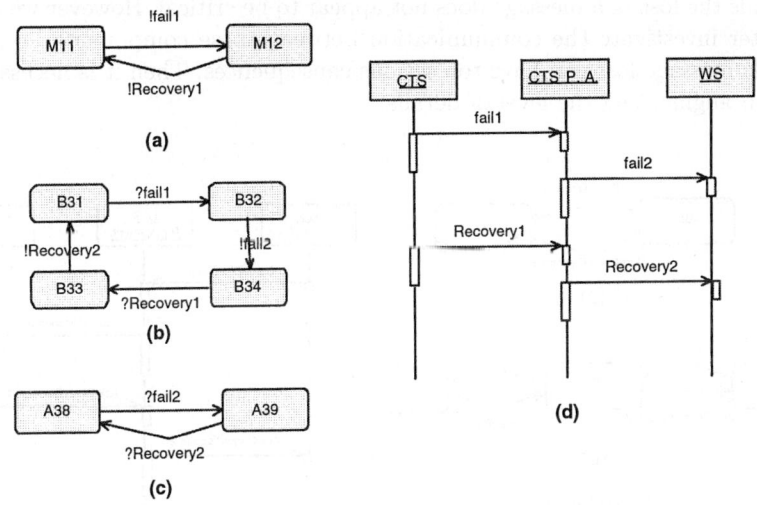

Fig. 7. State Diagrams and Sequence Diagram: requirement 1

In Figure 7.d the interaction among these components is represented.

When the CTS component raises a *fail1* then the CTS Proxy Agent component must send a *fail2* message to WS component. The consequence of this messages sequence must be a send of *Recovery1* and *Recovery2* messages. Therefore we want to verify the system with respect to this scenario. All system behaviors that issue the described sequence of fail actions must eventually exhibit a recovery action. The verification phase shows that there exist paths that falsify the sequence because the system can lose the messages i.e. it could lose the message *fail2*. Moreover since the messages exchanged in this scenario are Trap messages that do not require an acknowledgement there is no way to recognize the loss of a message. Therefore this requirement is not verified. To solve the problem we must manage the Trap messages in a different way. This is a case in which the existence of a problem immediately showed up and there is no need for further refining the modelling.

4.2 Requirement 2: System Configuration

The system configuration concerns the equipment configuration and path configuration on the CTS network.

Figures 8.a, 8.b and 8.c represent the interested parts for this requirement of CTS, CTS Proxy Agent and WS, respectively. The scenario in Figure 8.d represents the interactions of interest, i.e. the properties we want to verify.

In this case the components exchange configuration message, by means of Set messages, for the *Connection* and the *Disconnection*.

As reported in Figure 8 a possible message loss is managed through an ack message (notify) that assures that the message has been received. At this level of details the loss of a message does not appear to be critical. However we decide to better investigate the communication between these components because a possible message loss can have too serious consequences. Then it is necessary to zoom in augmenting the level of details.

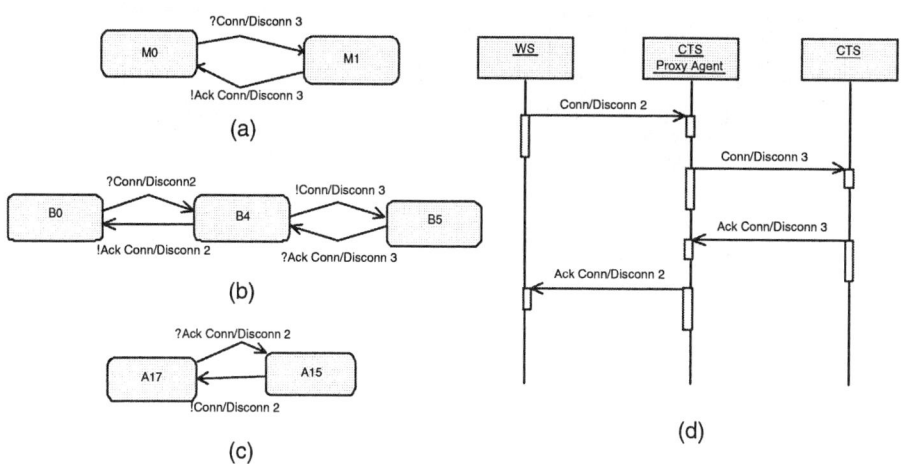

Fig. 8. State Diagrams and Sequence Diagram: requirement 2

5 The NICE Case Study: Refinement Step

This section reports on the refinement step concerning requirement 2.

Subsection 5.1 deals with the refinement step applied to the system part involved in the requirement 2.1: i.e. Connection/Disconnection management. We show the modelled subsystem, composed of 3 components (state diagrams) and 26 messages. It models the interaction between WS and the CTS Proxy Agent. In terms of properties here we focus on the possible loss of messages during the interactions between the WS and the CTS Proxy Agent. In this subsection we report also the results of the analysis. The modelled sub-system is limited to 3 components (state diagrams) and 26 messages.

Subsection 5.2 deals with the refinement step applied to the system part involved in the requirement 2.2: Equipment configuration. The considered subsystem is composed of 3 components exchanging 22 messages. It models the interactions between WS, Proxy Agent and Equipment. Here the focus is on the possible loss of messages during the interactions between the WS the Proxy Agent and the Equipment. However, since the modelling and verification process are the same of the previous subsection, we discuss only the results obtained.

Note that for both sub-systems models the refinement step is the result of an abstraction process. In particular we make an abstraction on the messages, considering generic Set and Get messages. Some components were left out, focusing only on interesting ones and refining the communication among them. For further details the interested reader can see [15]. In the following subsections we explain by means of sequence diagrams the obtained analysis results. This is the way we make the analysis output comprehensible to system designers.

5.1 Requirement 2.1: Connection/Disconnection Configuration

Figure 9 describes the components models while Figure 10 shows the components interaction relative to Set messages. We have analogous scenarios for Get messages. In Figures 9 and 10 two threads of the WS component: WS1_1 and WS1_2 are reported.

Note that in this refined modelling, the communication between the two entities WS and CTS Proxy Agent is based on a retry mechanism that sends at least N times (e.g. N=3) the same message when no acknowledge or "ErrS" (Set message corrupt; "ErrG" in Figure 9 is Get message corrupt) is received after a certain amount of time. Only after the failure of all the N sends the communication cannot occur and a "Nack" message is sent to the NICE MS Manager. In the scenario 10 after N attempts, WS signals the generated failure by sending the "Nack" message to the NICE MS Manager.

In terms of verification we want to prove that this communication protocol is robust with respect to a loss of messages. Therefore, the scenarios in Figure 10 were checked on the refined subsystem. The results of the verification, reported in terms of the scenario in Figure 11, allowed us to identify a system misbehavior. The scenario shows that it might happen that WS believes its request

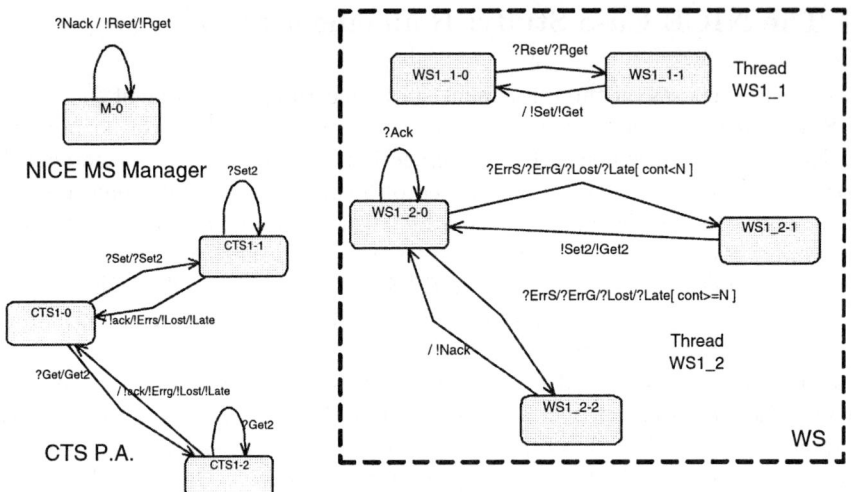

Fig. 9. WS-CTS Proxy Agent communication

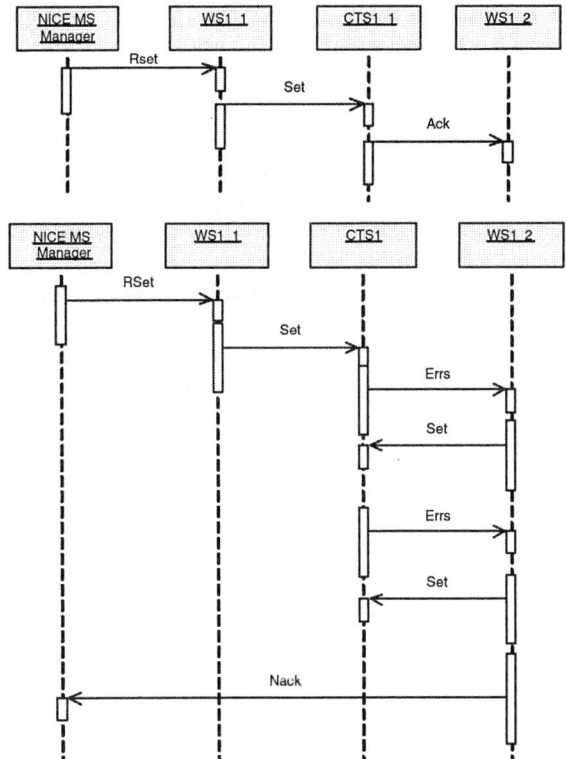

Fig. 10. WS-CTS Proxy Agent interactions

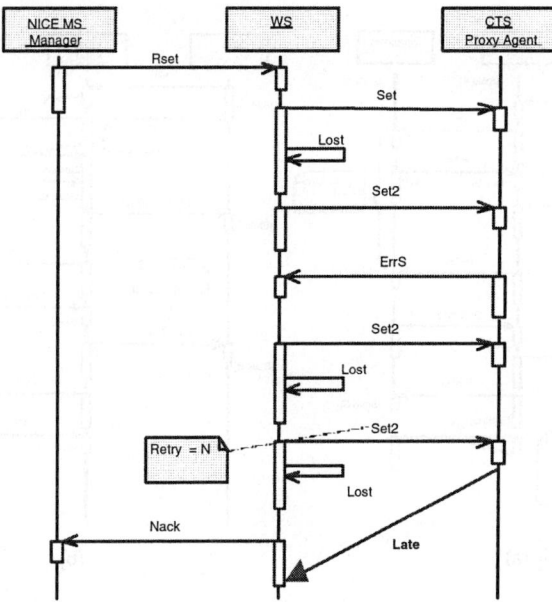

Fig. 11. WS CTS P.A. anomalous scenarios

is not accepted while CTS Proxy Agent already accepted it (CTS Proxy Agent responds too late and at the last set message sending attempt).

A possible solution to this problem is a right timer setting choice. This verification result indicated that the timer setting must be careful managed in the subsequent system development stages.

5.2 Requirement 2.2: Equipment Configuration

On this sub-model several different scenarios were verified. Here we show only an analysis of the results, in order to give an idea of the kind of information we obtained through the verification. Figure 12 represents anomalous behaviors obtained with the verification. Let us recall that also in this subsystem we focus on the effects of a possible loss of messages between the WS the Proxy Agent and the Equipment interactions.

In Figure 12 the [State X] labels on each lifeline component represent the local Equipment state view.

Referring to the scenario in Figure 12.a, a state inconsistency occurs between WS and the managed Equipment because of a loss of message between the Proxy agent and WS. After the reception of the "set2" message the Equipment changes its state to [STATE B]; then it applies the request, changing its state to [STATE C] while WS keeps knowing [STATE B].

In the sequence diagrams the lost messages are highlighted with a note.

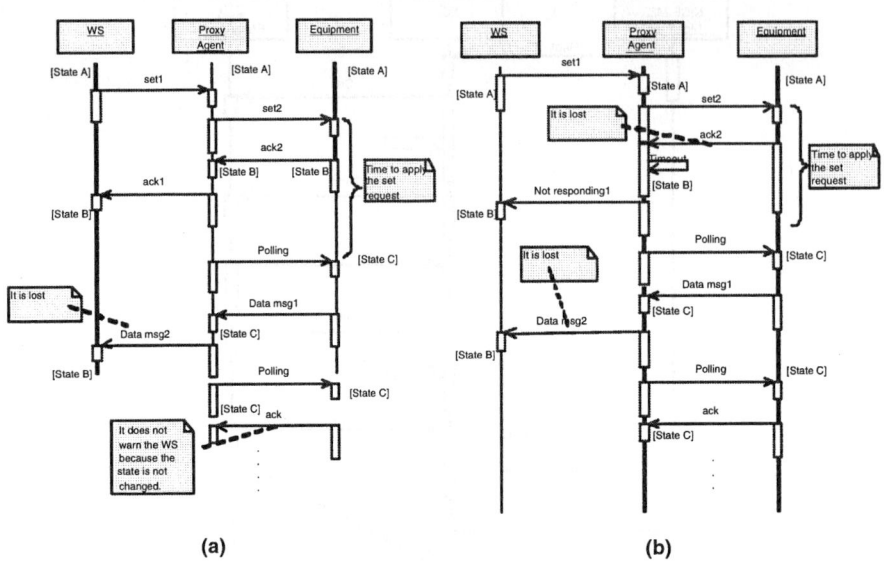

Fig. 12. WS P.A. anomalous scenarios

The misbehavior reported in Figure 12. shows that the highlighted problem is the loss of the "datamsg2" message; a possible solution is the introduction of a timer which allows the Proxy Agent to resend periodically the equipment state.

The sequence diagram in Figure 12.b shows the system behavior caused by the expiration of the Proxy Agent's timer due to the loss of the equipment "ack2" message. This implies that the Proxy Agent sends a "not_responding1" message to WS which signals an equipment malfunctioning. Note that the timer is set by the Proxy Agent every time it sends a message to the equipment. The loss of the message sent by the Proxy Agent and containing the new equipment state induces inconsistency. In fact WS continues to believe that the managed Equipment is in a not_responding state ([STATE B]), even if the managed Equipment is correctly working. This situation persists until a new equipment state change occurs.

6 Conclusions and Future Work

In this paper we presented our experience in integrating Charmy in the Marconi Selenia software development environment. Only few results about the NICE MS system are reported in this paper: details on the complete system model can be found in [15]. The goal of the experiment was twofold:

1. to evaluate the effort to use the analysis framework proposed;
2. to evaluate the efficacy and the role of the analysis itself.

Since state and sequence diagrams are commonly used in industry software development practice, it is easy and quick to use the framework, given that Charmy's inputs subsumes UML diagrams. In order to follow this process no specific skill on model checking is required since the framework feedback is easily comprehensible for a software designer acquainted with UML notation. The time required for the verification is strongly dependent on the size of the model. Considering the abstraction used in the case study, the verification time was always acceptable since it always was smaller than 10 minutes.

As far as the efficacy and the role of the proposed analysis is concerned, it must be noticed that the framework actually helps the software architect in reasoning about the system. The framework easies the definition of a right architecture and provides an executable prototype to perform analysis. As we discussed in the Introduction, it is not easy to define the properties to be investigated on a given model. In this experience, as one might expect, we saw that the process of properties elicitation and sub-systems identification proceeds incrementally and it is driven by the confidence and system knowledge that the software architect acquires along the modelling process. Properties were always described as set of sequence diagrams, characterizing either wanted or un-wanted behaviors and then automatically translated into LTL formulae. In the same way, output traces were offered to the software architect always as sequence diagrams. This allowed a rather straightforward integration with the standard software development process and allowed early identification of critical sub-systems behaviors whose design and implementation should be carefully carried out.

Summarizing the study carried out clearly indicated future work directions:

1. the Charmy tool should be integrated with existing case environment based on UML to eliminate input costs;
2. scenarios are a good way to express properties at the architectural level. A comprehensive set of interpretation options has to be provided and their translation to LTL formulae has to be completely hidden from the user.

Acknowledgments

The authors would like to acknowledge the Italian M.I.U.R. national project SAHARA that partly supported this work.

References

1. Rational Corporation. UML Resource Center. UML documentation, version1.3. On-line at: <http://www. rational.com/uml/index.jtmpl>.
2. R. community. RFC On-line at: <http://community.roxen.com/developers/idocs/rfc/rfc1901.html>.
3. M. Dwyer, G. Avrunin, and J. Corbett. Patterns in property specifications for finite-state verification. In *Proc. 21th International Conference on Software Engineering (ICSE1999)*, May 1999.
4. C. Hofmeister, R. Nord, and D. Soni. *Applied Software Architecture*. Addison Wesley, 1999.

5. J. G. Holzmann. The logic of bugs. *In Proc. Foundations of Software Engineering (SIGSOFT 2002/FSE-10)*, 2002.
6. P. Inverardi, F. Mancinelli, H. Muccini, and P. Pelliccione. An Experience in Architectural Extensions: Active Objects in J2EE. In *Proc. FIDJI'2002 International Workshop on scientiFic engIneering of Distributed Java appLIcations*. LNCS n.2604, February 2003, pp 87-98., November 28-29, 2002.
7. P. Inverardi, H. Muccini, and P. Pelliccione. Automated Check of Architectural Models Consistency using SPIN. In *the Automated Software Engineering Conference Proceedings (ASE 2001)*. San Diego, California, November 2001.
8. P. Inverardi, H. Muccini, and P. Pelliccione. Charmy: A framework for model based consistency checking. Technical report, Department of Computer Science, University of L'Aquila, January 2003.
9. P. Inverardi, H. Muccini, and P. Pelliccione. Checking Consistency Between Architectural Models Using SPIN. In *Proc. the First Int. Workshop From Software Requirements to Architectures (STRAW'01)*, year 2001.
10. P. Kruchten. The 4+1 View Model of Architecture. pages pp.42–50. IEEE Software, 12(6) November 1995.
11. J. Magee, J. Kramer, and D. Giannakopoulou. Behaviour analysis of software architectures. *In Proc. First Working IFIP Conference on Software Architecture (WICSA1)*, San Antonio, Texas, 1999.
12. A. Pnueli. The temporal logic of programs. In *In Proc. 18th IEEE Symposium on Foundation of Computer Science*, pages pp. 46–57, 1977.
13. C. Pons, R. Giandini, and G. Baum. Dependency Relations Between Models in the Unified Process. In *Proc. IWSSD 2000*, November 2000.
14. G. Reggio, M. Cerioli, and E. Astesiano. Towards a Rigorous Semantics of UML Supporting its Multiview Approach. In *Proc. FASE 2001, LNCS n. 2029*. Berlin, Springer Verlag, 2001.
15. A. Sebastiani. Specifica e verifica formale dell'architettura di gestione di un sistema integrato reale per le telecomunicazioni. *Tesi di Laurea in Informatica, Universitá di L'Aquila, Facoltá di Scienze Matematiche Fisiche e Naturali*, (On line at: http://www.di.univaq.it/pellicci/dissertations.html), October 2002.
16. R. L. Smith, G. S. Avrunin, L. A. Clarke, and L. J. Osterweil. PROPEL: An Approach Supporting Property Elucidation. In *Proc. 24th International Conference on Software Engineering (ICSE2002)*, pages pp.11–21, May 19-25 2002.
17. SPIN. Home page on line at: <http://cm.bell-labs.com/cm/cs/what/spin/index.html>.

Lessons Learned from a Successful Implementation of Formal Methods in an Industrial Project

Alan Wassyng* and Mark Lawford**

Dept. of Computing and Software, Faculty of Engineering, McMaster University,
Hamilton, Ontario, Canada L8S 4L7

Abstract. This paper describes the lessons we learned over a thirteen year period while helping to develop the shutdown systems for the nuclear generating station at Darlington, Ontario, Canada. We begin with a brief description of the project and then show how we modified processes and notations developed in the academic community so that they are acceptable for use in industry. We highlight some of the topics that proved to be particularly challenging and that would benefit from more in-depth study without the pressure of project deadlines.

Keywords: Industrial application, specification, verification, inspection, safety critical software, experience paper.

1 Introduction

Among the reasons researchers have cited for the slow adoption of formal methods by industry are insufficient tool support, cumbersome notation, and a lack of "real world" examples (see e.g. [1]). Referring to the work on the flight software for the U.S. Navy's A-7 aircraft, one of the first well known applications of semi-formal methods to safety critical software development [2] and related works (e.g. [3]), Parnas writes: *"Although that project is still alive (now known as SCR) more than two decades later, I still see a strong lack of good examples. Other such projects would be a worthwhile investment."* [4]

This paper describes an application of formal methods in the development of safety critical software in the nuclear industry over a thirteen year period. The work makes use of tabular specifications, building upon the ideas of [2], but whereas that earlier work dealt solely with the formal specification of requirements, this paper describes an attempt to apply formal methods "all the way down" from requirements, through design, implementation and verification. The methods have been refined over use on several projects involving the specification, implementation and verification of hundreds of functions. We discuss methods of addressing the applicability of formal methods in a production setting, provide examples of how formal methods were used, and very briefly discuss the work that remains to be done to improve the utility of formal methods.

---

* Consultant to Ontario Hydro/Ontario Power Generation Inc., May 1989–June 2002
** Consultant to Ontario Hydro/Ontario Power Generation Inc., Feb 1997–Dec 1998

In the remainder of the paper, Section 2 describes the application of the formal methods to the Darlington Nuclear Generating Station Shutdown Systems software. Section 3 details the lessons learned over the course of applying and refining the formal methods. Open questions for future research are discussed in Section 4. Related work is discussed in more detail in Section 5, and Section 6 draws some final conclusions.

2 The Project

2.1 Application Setting

The software application described in this paper relates to the computerised shutdown system for a nuclear powered generating station. In the Canadian Nuclear Industry there is a mandatory split between plant operation and safety systems. The shutdown application is implemented on redundant hardware and consists of two independent systems, Shutdown System One (SDS1) and Shutdown System Two (SDS2). Each of these systems, SDS1 and SDS2, consists of three "channels", each channel involving a Trip Computer and a Display/Test Computer. The Trip Computers are connected to the plant sensors and contain the software that makes the decisions as to whether the plant should be shut down or not, and actually invoke the shutdown mechanism. This arrangement enables the Trip Computers to be concerned with safety issues alone. This paper is specifically about the development of software for the Trip Computers. Following a general introduction to SDS1 and SDS2 Trip Computers, we will restrict our attention to SDS1 software.

For comparison with other projects, the code produced for SDS1 consisted of approximately 60 modules, containing a total of 280 access programs. There were about 40,000 lines of code (33,000 FORTRAN and 7,000 Assembler) including comments. SDS1 has 84 system inputs (monitored variables) and 27 system outputs (controlled variables).

2.2 A (Very) Brief History

The original version of the software was developed in the late 1980s by Ontario Hydro. The regulators were not sure how to judge whether the software would perform correctly and reliably, and would remain correct and reliable under maintenance. David Parnas, as a consultant to the regulator, suggested that a requirements/design document be constructed without reference to the existing code. After validating that document, a verification process was conducted. The entire process was documented in [5]. The verification results were presented in a guided walkthrough with the regulators. At the conclusion of the walkthrough, the regulators concluded that the software was safe for use, but that it should be redesigned to enhance its maintainability.

2.3 Preparing a Strategy for the Redesign

Following the successful but painful completion of the verification and walk-through of the Darlington shutdown systems in 1990, a series of studies were conducted by Ontario Hydro (now Ontario Power Generation Inc., - OPG). Two major conclusions were: i) The software would be redesigned using Parnas' information hiding principle [6] as the principal design heuristic. ii) As far as possible, we would include verification activities in the "forward going process". Before embarking on the Darlington Shutdown Systems Redesign, OPG set about defining a working standard for safety critical software, as well as procedures for the major steps in the software lifecycle. The Standard for Software Engineering of Safety Critical Software [7] defines the lifecycle stages, attributes of related documents, team responsibilities and team independence requirements. Procedures describing how to perform and document the Software Requirements Specification (SRS), the Software Design Description (SDD) [8], and the Systematic Design Verification (SDV) [9] were developed at that time. The procedures were tried on actual projects and have been continually refined as we have gained experience in their application.

SDS1 and SDS2 are developed independent of each other as much as is prudent. The two systems employ different shutdown technologies and run on different kinds of computers. This helps prevent common failure modes in the two systems. The system-level requirements in both SDS1 and SDS2 are known as the "Design Input Documentation" (DID), consisting of the Trip Computer Design Requirements (TCDR) [10] and the Trip Computer Design Description (TCDD) [11]. In SDS1, the TCDR and TCDD are described mathematically, and the SRS is contained within the TCDD. The SDS1 lifecycle phases and documents are shown in Fig. 1.

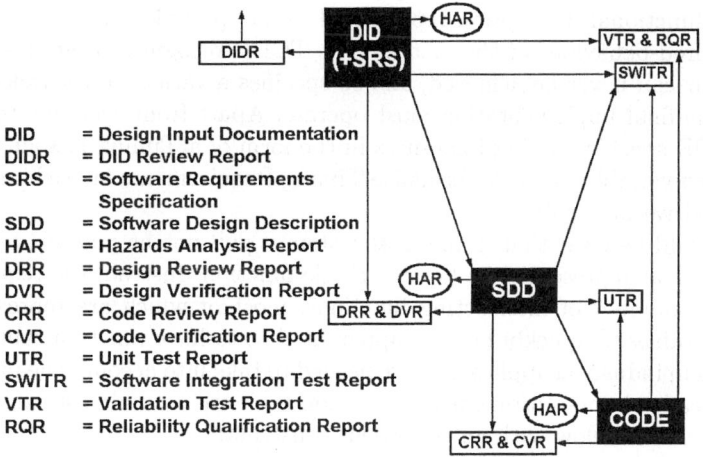

Fig. 1. SDS1 lifecycle phases and documents.

2.4 System-Level Requirements

The TCDR contains the externally visible requirements for the Trip Computer, while the TCDD augments those requirements by including requirements that are specifically computer related, and by providing detailed descriptions of all fail-safe requirements.

The Trip Computer Design Requirements (TCDR). The model chosen for the TCDR was a Mills-type black-box [12]. The system, which in this case is a Trip Computer, is represented by a "black box", which relates responses generated by the system, to stimuli received by the system. The relationship is described by a mathematical function. The functional descriptions are specified in Parnas-style "function tables" [13]. If S is the set of stimuli entering the black-box, R is the set of responses exiting the black-box, and S_h is the set of stimulus history, then

$$R = f(S, S_h) \tag{1}$$

describes the behaviour of the black-box. This model was chosen for the TCDR since it's level of abstraction is close to the way in which domain experts understand relevant system behaviour.

In all our documents, stimuli are referred to as monitored variables, and responses are controlled variables. We prefix identifiers by a suitable character followed by _ so as to help identify the role of the identifier, e.g. m_name is a monitored variable, c_name is a controlled variable, f_name is an internal function (produced as a result of decomposing the requirements), k_name is a numerical constant, and e_name is an enumerated token. In our model, time is an implicit stimulus and every monitored and controlled variable can be time-stamped. We use the notation m_name to represent the current value of the monitored variable m_name, and m_name_{-1} to represent the previous value of m_name.

The functional description represented by (1) provides an idealised view of the required behaviour of the system. The TCDR recognises that this idealised behaviour can never be achieved, and so specifies a variety of tolerances within which the final implementation must operate. Apart from accuracy tolerances, the TCDR specifies timing tolerances in the form of a Timing Resolution on all monitored variables, and Performance Timing Requirements on each monitored-controlled variable pair.

It should be clear that in any real system it will not be possible to describe the behaviour represented by (1) in a single function. Instead, the requirements include a number of inter-acting functions, most of which are represented by function tables. It quickly became apparent that to have function tables widely accepted in industrial applications we needed to take into account the preferences of non-academic practitioners. The function table we used almost exclusively in SDS1 is shown below with an equivalent construct:

Condition	Result
	name
Condition_1	res_1
⋮	⋮
Condition_n	res_n

if $Condition\_1$ **then** $name = res\_1$
elsif ...
elsif $Condition\_n$ **then** $name = res\_n$

where we insist that the following two properties hold:

Disjointness: $Condition\_i \land Condition\_j \Leftrightarrow FALSE, \forall i,j = 1..n, i \neq j$, and

Completeness: $Condition\_1 \lor ... \lor Condition\_n \Leftrightarrow TRUE.$

We also found that we can use the table structure to emphasize the logical relationships involved. For example, we extended the table structure to include tables of the form:

Condition		Result
		name
Condition_1	Sub_Condition_1	res_1.1
	Sub_Condition_2	res_1.2
Condition_2		res_2
⋮		⋮
Condition_n		res_n

in which adjoining cells are interpreted as being "anded".

One of the crucial challenges is to define heuristics for partitioning the system, and for finding notations that allow us to work with the partitioned system without losing intellectual control of the complete system behaviour as represented by the composition of (potentially) many function tables. One aid in this regard is the use of *natural language expressions* in the function tables. These are natural language phrases that have clear meaning to domain experts. Their use sometimes dramatically simplifies a function table. In order to retain complete mathematical rigour, all such natural language expressions are themselves defined in function tables in a separate section of the TCDR.

The following table illustrates an actual functional description in the TCDR. It evaluates the current value of the Neutron Overpower (NOP) setpoint, and clearly relies heavily on a number of natural language expressions.

Condition	Result f_NOPsp
NOP Low Power setpoint is requested	$k\_NOPLPsp$
NOP Low Power setpoint is cancelled & NOP Abnormal 2 setpoint is requested	$k\_NOPAbn2sp$
NOP Low Power setpoint is cancelled & NOP Abnormal 2 setpoint is cancelled & NOP Abnormal 1 setpoint is requested	$k\_NOPAbn1sp$
NOP Low Power setpoint is cancelled & NOP Abnormal 2 setpoint is cancelled & NOP Abnormal 1 setpoint is cancelled	$k\_NOPnormsp$

As an example "NOP Abnormal 1 setpoint is requested or cancelled" is defined by:

Condition	Result NOP Abnormal 1 setpoint is requested or cancelled
$(m\_NOPspAbn1ON = e\_NotPressed)$ & $(m\_NOPspAbn1OFF = e\_NotPressed)$	No Change
$(m\_NOPspAbn1ON = e\_NotPressed)$ & $(m\_NOPspAbn1OFF = e\_Pressed)$	cancelled
$(m\_NOPspAbn1ON = e\_Pressed)$ & $(m\_NOPspAbn1OFF = e\_NotPressed)$	requested
$(m\_NOPspAbn1ON = e\_Pressed)$ & $(m\_NOPspAbn1OFF = e\_Pressed)$	requested

Thus we can see that the natural language expressions effectively partition the system so that history-based requirements can be stated in much smaller tables. (Try, for example, to describe f_NOPsp without using the natural language expressions.) Actually, natural language expressions were developed for a different reason. They were a decisive factor in getting domain experts to buy-in to the idea of using tabular representations of requirements, since they enable those experts to read and understand the tables without undue effort, while still retaining the rigour and precision required by a formal approach. The positive effect on the decomposition of the requirements was a pleasant by-product.

The natural language expressions were carefully constructed so as to read as though they are simply text statements in a natural language, but are still reasonably easy to parse in associated software tools. Rather than "=", we use words like "is" and "are" to assign appropriate values. Clearly, in natural language expressions, the enumerated tokens representing the result values are not prefixed by "e_". The set of possible enumerated tokens is included in the natural language expression, elements being separated by "or".

The Trip Computer Design Description (TCDD). The model used in the TCDD is a Finite State Machine (FSM) with an arbitrarily small clock-tick. So, if $C(t)$ is the vector of values of all controlled variables at time t, $M(t)$ is the vector of values of all monitored variables at time t, $S(t)$ is the vector of values of all state variables at time t, and the time of initialisation is t_0, we have:

$$C(t_k) = REQ(M(t_k), S(t_k))$$
$$S(t_{k+1}) = NST(M(t_k), S(t_k)), \text{ for } k = 0, 1, 2, 3, \ldots \tag{2}$$

and the time between t_k and t_{k+1} is an arbitrarily small time, δt. Typically, state data in the TCDD has a very simple form, namely the previous values of functions and variables. We indicate elements of state data by f_name_{-1}, which is the value of f_name at the previous clock-tick, and similarly, m_name_{-1} and c_name_{-1}. We actually allow x_name_{-k}, x=c,f,m and k=1,2,3,..., but seldom use $k > 1$.

The description of required behaviour in the TCDD builds on the behaviour specified in the TCDR by converting all black-box representations into the FSM model, and by adding design specific behaviour that now recognises that the system will be implemented on a digital computer. This includes the introduction of fail-safe protection and self-checks.

As an example of how behaviour in the TCDD augments the behaviour in the TCDR, consider the case of momentary pushbuttons. In the TCDR, as we have already seen, the behaviour depends solely on the ON/OFF status of the pushbuttons. In the TCDD, that same behaviour takes into account that the pushbuttons have to be debounced. So the natural language expression "NOP Abnormal 1 setpoint is requested or cancelled" would be defined by:

	Result
Condition	NOP Abnormal 1 setpoint is requested or cancelled
f_NOPspAbn1ON = e_pbStuck OR f_NOPspAbn1OFF = e_pbStuck	requested
f_NOPspAbn1ON = e_pbNotDebounced & f_NOPspAbn1OFF = e_pbNotDebounced	No Change
f_NOPspAbn1ON = e_pbNotDebounced & f_NOPspAbn1OFF = e_pbDebounced	cancelled
f_NOPspAbn1ON = e_pbDebounced & f_NOPspAbn1OFF = e_pbNotDebounced	requested
f_NOPspAbn1ON = e_pbDebounced & f_NOPspAbn1OFF = e_pbDebounced	requested

and *f_NOPspAbn1ON* (for example) defined by

Condition	Results $f\_NOPspAbn1ON$
m_NOPspAbn1ON = e_NotPressed	e_pbNotDebounced
[m_NOPspAbn1ON = e_Pressed] & NOT [(m_NOPspAbn1ON = e_Pressed) Held for k_Debounce]	e_pbNotDebounced
[(m_NOPspAbn1ON = e_Pressed) Held for k_Debounce] & NOT [(m_NOPspAbn1ON = e_Pressed) Held for k_pbStuck]	e_pbDebounced
(m_NOPspAbn1ON = e_Pressed) Held for k_pbStuck	e_pbStuck

The above table illustrates the use of a generic function defined for use throughout the TCDD, namely "(condition) Held for duration", which evaluates to True when "condition" has been True for at least "duration" time. Such functions are defined precisely in the TCDD itself.

Not only does the TCDD define/redefine the behaviour specified in the TCDR, it also describes how the software will interface with the hardware. To achieve this we use Parnas' four-variable model [14]. This model relates the variables in the requirements domain to the variables in the software domain. Specifically, I and O represent the input and output variables in the software. SOF is the function that describes the software's behaviour as follows:

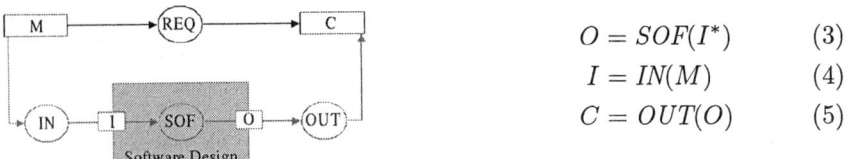

$$O = SOF(I^*) \qquad (3)$$
$$I = IN(M) \qquad (4)$$
$$C = OUT(O) \qquad (5)$$

where I^* indicates the variables in I as well as the state variables ultimately dependent on I. (We already saw in (2) that $C = REQ(M^*)$, where M^* indicates the variables in M as well as the state variables.)

All the required information relating to (4) and (5) is included in the TCDD. Another important element of the TCDD is the list of Anticipated Changes.

2.5 Software Design

The software design re-organises the way in which the behaviour in the TCDD is partitioned. This is done to achieve specific goals, two of which are: i) The software design should be robust under change; and ii) On the target platform, all timing requirements will be met.

Like all other stages in the lifecycle, the SDD process and documentation are described in detail in a Procedure. The quality of the design is tied closely to a number of quality attributes defined in the Procedure. The Procedure uses these attributes to drive the design process. It also describes what documentation is required.

Information hiding principles form the basis of the design philosophy. The list of anticipated changes in the TCDD is augmented by the software developers and is used to create a Module Guide that defines a tree-structure of modules, each module having a secret and responsibility. Leaf modules represent the eventual code, and the entries for those also list the TCDD functions to be implemented in that module.

The *module cover page* describes the responsibility of the module, and lists all exported constants and types as well as the access programs for the module. The role of each access program is described in natural language, and the black-box behaviour of the program is defined by referencing the TCDD functions implemented in the access program. (This will be explained in more detail when we discuss "supplementary function tables" later in this section.)

The *module internal declarations* describes all items that are private to the module, but not confined to a single program. The *detailed design* of each program is documented using either function tables or pseudo-code (sometimes both). Pseudo code is used when a sequence of operations is mandatory and cannot easily be described in tabular format, or when specific language constructs have to be used, for example when specific assembler instructions have to be used in transfer events. The function tables used in the software design are very similar to those used in the TCDD, but are arranged vertically rather than horizontally. Variables and constants in the SDD are restricted to 6 characters because the software design had to be implemented in FORTRAN 66, the only compiler available for the hardware platform.

As an example, we provide an extract from a typical module design. It consists of the module cover page shown in Fig. 2, and the module's internal declarations, and the specification of one of its programs, shown in Fig. 3. It is likely that just a portion of a TCDD function may be implemented in an access program, or that a composition of TCDD functions may be implemented in an access program. This poses a couple of important problems. i) We reference TCDD functions to specify the black-box behaviour of an access program, and so if the access program does not implement a single, complete TCDD function, this black-box behaviour is difficult to specify; and ii) It is difficult to verify the SDD behaviour against the TCDD behaviour when the data-flow topologies of the two are different.

The way we overcome these difficulties is by use of "supplementary function tables". Imagine a pseudo requirements specification in which the data-flow topology exactly matches that in the SDD. If such a pseudo requirements specification were to exist, then verifying the SDD against the TCDD could be performed in two steps: i) Verify the SDD against the pseudo requirements specification; and ii) Verify the pseudo requirement specification against the TCDD (we need to verify only those blocks that are different from the original TCDD). The way we create the pseudo requirements specification is by piece-wise "replacing" some composition of TCDD functions by a new set of functions that have the same behaviour as the TCDD functions, but the topology of the SDD.

n.m MODULE Watchdog (1.10)
Determines the watchdog system output.

	Name	Value	Type
Constants:	(None)		
	Name	Definition	
Types:	(None)		

Access Programs:

EWDOG
Updates the state of the watchdog timer Digital Output.
References: $c\_Watchdog$, 'Watchdog test active'.

IWDOG
Initializes all the Watchdog module internal states and sets the initial watchdog output.
References: Initial Value, Initialization Requirements.

SWDOG
NCPARM: `t_boolean` - in
Signals to Watchdog module that a valid watchdog test request is received if NCPARM = $TRUE. Note that NCPARM is a "Conditional Output Call Argument"; calling the program with NCPARM = $FALSE has no effects on the module.
References: 'Watchdog test active'.

Fig. 2. Example module cover page

These replacement functions are represented by what we called "supplementary function tables" (SFTs).

Thus, the SFTs are developed during the forward going process, by the software designers themselves, but are not considered "proved". They are then available to aid in the mathematical verification of the software design. Rather than show a series of function tables that demonstrates the use of SFTs, we present some simple data flow examples in Fig. 4 to illustrate these points.

The top left diagram in the figure shows an extract from the TCDD. If we assume that the software design includes programs that implement the behaviour starting with an input "a" and resulting in an output "e", but partitions the behaviour differently from the TCDD, we may have a situation as pictured in the top right diagram of Fig 4.

If this is the design, the designers must have had good reasons for partitioning the behaviour this way, and must also have good reason to believe it implements the original requirements. For instance, they may have split some of the functions in the TCDD, so that the requirements can be viewed as shown in the bottom left diagram.

Finally, we regroup the functions so that they match the topology of the design as shown in the bottom right portion of Fig. 4. We can now describe $f\_x, f\_y, f\_c', f\_d', f\_z$ and f_e' in tabular format, and these function tables "replace" the original f_c, f_d and f_e. The "replacement" tables are the SFTs, and they, as

n.m.1 MODULE Watchdog Internal Declaration

	Name	Value/Origin	Type
Constants:	KWDDLY	1000	t_integer
	Name	Definition/Origin	
Types:	t_boolean	Global	
	t_integer	Global	
	t_MsecTimerID	Timer	
	t_PBId	DigitalInput	
	t_PBStat	DigitalInput	
	t_PosInt	Global	
	t_TimerOp	Timer	
	t_WDogStat	DigitalOutput	
	Name	Type	
State Data:	WDGST	t_boolean	
	WDGTST	t_boolean	

n.m.1.1 ACCESS PROGRAM EWDOG

	Name	Ext_value	Type	Origin
Inputs:	l_CalEn	GPBKS($PBCAL)	t_PBStat	DigitalInput
	l_TREQD	GCMSEC($CWDG)	t_PosInt	Timer
	Name	Ext_value	Type	Origin
Updates:	WDGST	-	t_boolean	State
	WDGTST	-	t_boolean	State
	Name	Ext_value	Type	Origin
Output:	l_WdgClk	SCMSEC($CWDG, l_WdgClk)	t_TimerOp	Timer
	l_WdgDO	SDOWDG(l_WdgDO)	t_WDogStat	DigitalOutput

Range check assertion 1: (l_CalEn = $DBNC) OR (l_CalEn = $NDBNC)

Modes:

l_InTest	0 < l_TREQD < KWDDLY
l_NoTest	l_TREQD = 0
l_TstEnd	l_TREQD >= KWDDLY

VCT:EWDOG

		WDGTST = $FALSE		NOT(WDGTST = $FALSE)			
		WDGST= $FALSE	NOT(WDGST = $FALSE)	l_CalEn = $NDBNC	NOT(l_CalEn = $NDBNC)		
					l_NoTest	l_InTest	l_TstEnd
l_WdgClk	$CRSET	$CRSET	$CRSET	$CSTRT	$CNC	$CRSET
l_WdgDO	$WDON	$WDOFF	$WDNC	$WDNC	$WDNC	$WDNC
WDGST	$TRUE	$FALSE	NC	NC	NC	NC
WDGTST	NC	NC	$FALSE	NC	NC	$FALSE

Fig. 3. Example module internal declarations and program specification.

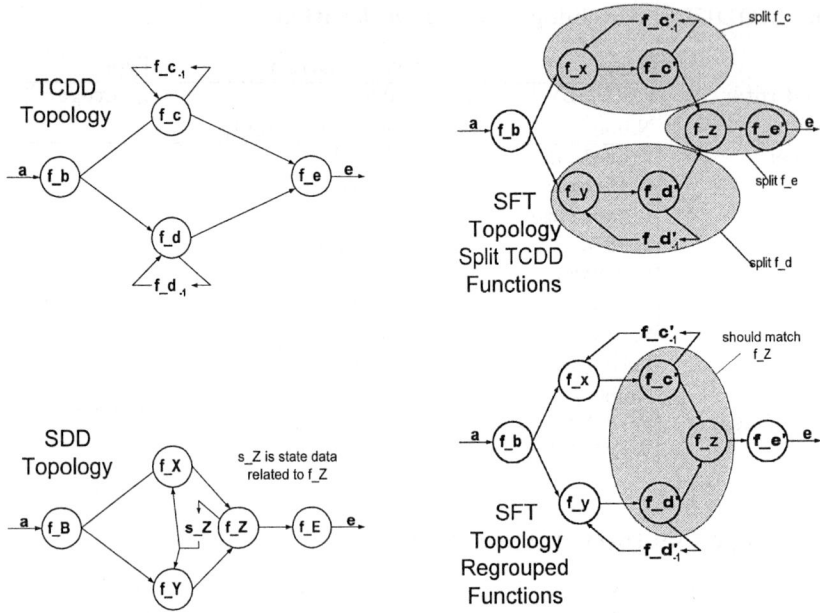

Fig. 4. Example use of supplementary function tables.

well as relevant TCDD functions, are used on module cover pages as references to the TCDD behaviour.

One final point regarding the SDD is that it is easy to "extend" the input and output mappings so that instead of I, and O, the transfer events work with M_p and C_p known as "pseudo M" and "pseudo C", constructed to be as close to M and C as possible. Then, instead of constructing SOF, the software design simply has to implement REQ, as described in the TCDD. This situation is shown graphically in Fig. 5. More details on this decomposition technique can be found in [15].

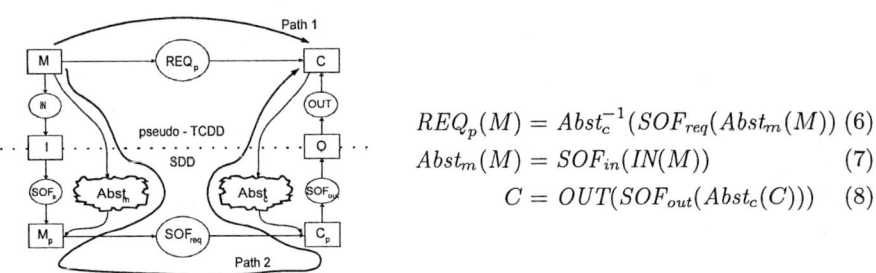

$$REQ_p(M) = Abst_c^{-1}(SOF_{req}(Abst_m(M))) \quad (6)$$
$$Abst_m(M) = SOF_{in}(IN(M)) \quad (7)$$
$$C = OUT(SOF_{out}(Abst_c(C))) \quad (8)$$

Fig. 5. Modified 4 variable model.

2.6 Software Design Verification (SDV)

There are two primary goals of the software design verification. i) Prove that the behaviour described in the SDD matches the behaviour described in the TCDD, within tolerance; and ii) Identify behaviour in the SDD that is outside the behaviour specified in the TCDD, and show that the behaviour is justified and that it cannot negatively affect TCDD specified behaviour. To accomplish the first goal, we conduct a mathematical comparison of behaviour in the SDD against the behaviour in the TCDD. This is by far the more time consuming of the two activities, since the SDD adds very little behaviour not already defined in the TCDD. To understand the verification process we need to start with the overall proof obligation. Fig. 5 shows the input and output mappings replaced by abstraction functions. Comparing Path 1 with Path 2 we see that our proof obligation is given by (6). The abstraction functions have to be verified through Equations (7) and (8).

We prove this in two steps. Firstly we prove the SDD complies with the pseudo-TCDD. Since the data-flow topology in the SDD is the same as in the pseudo-TCDD, we can show that verification can be performed block-by-block, as long as each block has equivalent inputs and outputs in the pseudo-TCDD and SDD. This piece-wise approach results in a feasible method. The second, smaller proof, pseudo-TCDD versus TCDD is dealt with on a case-by-case basis.

2.7 Automated SDD Verification

A report on manually applying tabular methods to the block-by-block SDD verification in [16], highlights the excessive effort required to perform the verification by hand. As a result, software tools were developed to extract the relevant behaviour specifications from the word processor documents that were used to describe the TCDD and SDD, into a format suitable for input to SRI International's PVS automated reasoning system [17]. In this way, a subset of all the verification blocks was proved by an automated system. Additional details on the reasons for choosing PVS, experience with the verification procedure, and the tooled tabular methods employed on the SDS Redesign project can be found in [18], [15].

2.8 Coding and Code Verification

One of the challenges we faced was to come up with a way of implementing information hiding modules in FORTRAN 66. Using labeled common statements we managed to define conceptual modules. The Coding Procedure defined quite specific rules for converting function tables into FORTRAN code. One of the decisions we made was that comments in the code usually just refer back to items in the SDD. This reinforced the concept that the SDD is a live document, and forced good traceability from code constructs to design constructs.

One of the really pleasant surprises we got, was how remarkably straightforward code verification is once the majority of the code is developed from function tables. We include comments in the code to indicate whether the code segment is based on a function table or "algorithm", i.e. pseudo-code. The basic strategy in the code verification is to create a function table or algorithm from the code, without reference to the SDD, and then to compare that function table or algorithm with its counterpart in the SDD.

3 Primary Lessons Learned

3.1 Pure Technology Lessons

Mathematical System-Level Requirements. The use of mathematical requirements at the TCDR and TCDD level in SDS1 was controversial. A full investigation of the benefits and drawbacks still has to be performed. On the plus side, some of us thought that the precision of the requirements prompted discussion with the domain experts at a very early stage, and in most situations the required behaviour was unambiguously interpreted by specifiers, software designers and verifiers. However, there were some cases in which details of the model had not been sufficiently understood or described, and just because the requirements seemed precise it did not mean that they were unambiguous. They turned out to be ambiguous because of differences in the interpretation of the model. For example, the Timing Resolution on a monitored-controlled variable pair effectively allows a tolerance on the frequency of evaluation of an internal function (say f_a) that depends on that monitored variable, and lies on the relevant data-flow path. What about an internal function (say f_b) that depends on f_a and previous values of f_a, but not directly on the current value of the specific monitored variable? In our project, one group decided that since no specific Timing Resolution seemed to apply, infinite tolerance was applicable. Another group argued that in the absence of a Timing Resolution, no tolerance was applicable. Since this is impossible to achieve, it was argued that the Timing Resolution for the relevant monitored-controlled variable pair applied to all internal functions on that data-flow path. This apparent ambiguity led to a design that was significantly different from that expected by the verifiers. Each group used the precision of the mathematical description to support its interpretation of the requirement.

A significant practical advantage of a mathematical TCDD, was that a separate SRS was not required, thus eliminating a source of potential errors as well as the review/verification step between an SRS and (a natural language) TCDD.

Coping with Accepted Discrepancies. It sometimes appears to be worthwhile to accept seemingly innocuous discrepancies between the SDD and TCDD in so-called "non-critical" functions (a historical report, for instance), when fixing them would strain resources or severely impact the schedule. However, although the discrepancies can be identified as mathematical mismatches between the two descriptions of behaviour, it can be difficult to identify all black-box visible effects of the discrepancy. Thus, domain experts may not be able to judge the full impact of the discrepancy. The time spent on justifying these accepted discrepancies, may be better spent in trying to "correct" them if at all possible.

The Effect of Older/Slower Hardware. The best scenario for the software scheduler is typically a single, infinite loop. However, one immediate effect of slower hardware is that specific functions may need to be scheduled more frequently within that infinite loop in order to meet timing requirements. This complicates the software scheduler. Since the systematic verification process is driven by the software schedule, a more complicated scheduler has a negative effect on the design verification. In general, difficulties related to meeting timing requirements often force us to make compromises we would not have to consider in other circumstances. This situation can stretch the design and verification teams to the limits of their capabilities - and has the potential to raise tensions between the two teams. Older hardware is sometimes not just slower than newer hardware. It is quite often less reliable as it ages. Thus, to develop a fail-safe solution may necessitate the inclusion of quite sophisticated self-checks that otherwise would not be necessary.

3.2 Soft Technology Lessons

Process. The shutdown systems projects we were involved in were successful, primarily due to two factors: i) The people working on the projects were highly motivated to succeed and were technically competent; and ii) The processes used were well researched, practical, and well documented. One of the major achievements of the developers of the processes was that the procedures were designed to work together. For example, the software design process was defined to use the mathematically precise requirements to advantage, and to produce mathematically precise specifications from which the code could be developed. In addition, the design process took into account the mathematical verification that would have to be performed, as well as design reviews and eventual unit testing. It is important to note that the mathematical aspects introduced into these processes were never an end unto themselves. They always served a practical purpose that would enable the teams to produce a software product that was demonstrably safe to use.

Technology/Research Transfer. The use of function tables throughout the development process was arguably the greatest single benefit we experienced. However, it was only through perseverance that we managed to get function tables accepted to the extent they are now. The convergence to a simplified notation allowed us to represent behaviour in a way that was readily understood by all readers/developers of the major system documents. An example of an original function table used in 1989 is shown in Fig. 6.

Special symbols were used to bracket identifiers to indicate the type of identifier, for example ##enumeration tokens##, #constants#, /inputs/, etc. In

	APPLY(OR, ((' |ai_tbl.pmp[d]| < 2745) OR ((2745 <= ' |ai_tbl.pmp[d]|<= 2795) & (' |lotrip.sgf.i[d]|<>##u##))), d=1..4) OR ((' |ai_tbl.pmp[5]|< ' |vsps.sgf|) OR ((' |vsps.sgf|<= ' |ai_tbl.pmp[5]|<= ' |vsps.sgf|+50) & (' |lotrip.sgf.i[5]|<>##u##)))	APPLY(&, ((' |ai_tbl.pmp[d]| > 2795) OR ((2745 <= ' |ai_tbl.pmp[d]| <= 2795) & (' |lotrip.sgf.i[d]|=##u##))), d=1..4) & ((' |ai_tbl.pmp[5]|>'|vsps.sgf|+50) OR ((' |vsps.sgf|<= ' |ai_tbl.pmp[5]|<= ' |vsps.sgf|+50) & (' |lotrip.sgf.i[5]|=##u##)))
|lotrip.sgf.n|'	1..5	0

Fig. 6. Example of original tabular notation

addition, $'x$ was used to indicate the value of x immediately prior to the evaluation of the table (pre-value of x), and x' indicated the post-value of x. Such tables were used successfully in the verification project in 1989, but when we tried to use these tables to present requirements behaviour, readers were quick to tell us that they probably would not use them. Domain experts especially found them close to unreadable.

So what did we do to function tables that made them suddenly acceptable to professional software developers and engineers responsible for determining system requirements?

One quite trivial change that worked wonders was - we simply turned the tables sideways. It was suggested by someone new to function tables who said something like "I would relate to the tables better if we read them left-to-right, just as we do normal text". We tried that and it worked. Not only did domain experts prefer them written that way, but it turned out that it was easier to format them on standard $8\frac{1}{2}'' \times 11''$ pages. At least this was true for the requirements documents, which tend to have single results, and seem to need more rows (disjoint primitives) than columns (nested conditions).

Another change we made was to remove all the bracketing symbols as well as the pre and post indicators. It turns out that in our simple tables it is quite obvious whether a variable is used as a pre-value or a post-value. The result/output of a table is a post-value, and we allow only pre-values of variables in any cells of the tables. Note that by pre- and post-values, we mean with respect to invocation of that particular table, not with respect to the clock-tick of the underlying model. We are always explicit with respect to the clock-tick.

Rather than bracket identifiers with special symbols, we decided to prefix identifiers with a character (occasionally two) followed by an underscore as outlined in Sec. 2.4. This arrangement is far easier to read, easier to remember, and still retains the effect that alphabetic sorting of identifiers also sorts identifiers into classification groups. After years of working with professional software engineers on these projects, we feel qualified to say that this aspect of formal methods, i.e. arriving at notation and presentation methods that industrial participants will accept, is about as important as the technology in the formal methods themselves. Without this effort, even the best of formal methods will probably not be used in practice.

A side benefit of using function tables was that we could easily identify conditions that lead to a safe-state. This is important in the software design, where we want to specify the behaviour in such a way that it can be coded into structures that produce safe behaviour even in the case of hardware malfunctions. By always having the safe-state in the right-most column, it was clear to designers and coders alike.

As we indicated earlier, one of the guiding principles for the redesign of the Darlington Shutdown Software, was Parnas' "Information Hiding" [6]. As usual, there is a world of difference between understanding and appreciating the principles versus putting those principles to work and implementing them in a software design process - it took us about two years through the first iteration. An important difference between what we put into practice compared with the original description was that most of the top level "secrets" that were to be encapsulated in a module, came from requirements that were likely to change, not from design decisions as described in [6]. It is important to note the enormous effort that had to be expended in order to use the ideas that came from academia, even though the ideas were well accepted (indeed, quite famous) within the academic community, twenty years after they were first introduced. Even today, it is not universally appreciated that information hiding is significantly more than data abstraction. The principles of information hiding can be used to develop a software design process that eventually results in the decomposition of the design into data abstractions. The importance of this process is that the resulting data abstractions are constructed in such a way that, if in the future we need to change the design to incorporate a "likely change", the changes will be confined to a single module, or, at most, a very small number of modules. This is a crucial selling point of the technology to senior management. Most people, quite rightly, would be skeptical of any claim to be able to cope "easily" with all future changes. What information hiding promises and delivers, is that future changes that are considered likely and are used to drive the decomposition of the software design, will be relatively easy to implement and verify.

Rationale. Most engineers already appreciate the importance of documenting rationale for design decisions. Even before the start of the redesign of the Darlington shutdown system software, the responsible group at Ontario Power Generation conducted a separate project to document the rationale for the existing software. Both the TCDR and TCDD contain appendices that record changes made from previous "in use" systems. In addition, rationale is documented for each function and natural language expression, whenever possible. However, rationale for some decisions that were made fifteen to twenty years ago has been lost. In at least one case, that lack of rationale led us to include a requirement that was later shown to be problematic.

Software Tools Limitations and Suggested Improvements. While the use of standard word processors created documents that were easily readable by a human, producing machine readable output from the documents was much more difficult. While particular projects may standardize on a given word processor (and version), maintenance and revision of software obviously becomes an issue when projects are tied to a specific vendor and revision of a product.

The utility and adoption of mathematically sound tools has been hampered by a lack of well defined (consistent) open standards and associated support tools. Significant resources are sometimes required to develop tools that are not directly related to a company's core competencies.

One lesson we learned was that developing tools to cope with mundane, but necessary and time-consuming tasks, can significantly reduce the effort required to perform those tasks, and thus reduce the schedule time that has to be allocated to those tasks. These tools may not present the same excitement and challenge to their developers as more sophisticated tools might, but their importance to the project can be even more substantial.

3.3 Political Lessons

People. Experienced project managers know that the success of their project is tied directly to the ability, knowledge and attitude of the people working on the project. Building reliable software applications of a non-trivial size requires team members to communicate with each other and with other teams. Often two teams are in an intentionally adversarial role - but both teams should be clear that they share the responsibility for achieving a high quality software application. "Scoring points" at the expense of an individual or team is counter-productive to the project. Since formal methods are not yet commonplace in industrial software projects, it is important that all project personnel buy-in to the specific methodology being used. It is healthy to argue over different approaches and processes, but compromises are often necessary, and continual second-guessing of such decisions, after the decision has been finalised, is usually destructive.

Don't Compromise Normal Best Practice. Ontario Power Generation wisely adopted a "defence-in-depth" policy for their safety critical software projects. Over the years, software professionals and researchers have developed heuristics for reducing defects at different stages of the software lifecycle. For example, at the coding stage, there are reasonably well accepted coding guidelines that take into account the strengths and weaknesses of the language, that help us to avoid situations that have been shown to be more error prone. It is sometimes tempting to argue that since we are applying so much more rigour to the entire lifecycle, we can relax these "best practice" heuristics. Our experience is that it is a mistake to follow this path. It is a good idea to remind ourselves periodically that mathematicians have been known to make mistakes.

4 Open Questions

Nothing is ever perfect. Software development is far from that ideal. Also, there are tremendous financial and schedule pressures on projects such as those described in this paper. It is always useful to examine what we did and try to determine what areas may be strengthened in future projects. We do not have the space to discuss this in detail, but wanted to mention them briefly, almost as a final lesson-learned.

Probably the most challenging issue throughout the projects has been to find ways to specify and verify functional and performance timing requirements. So far, our methods have dealt much better with the logic aspects of behaviour than with anything that involves timing. Nothing we have seen in the literature has stood out as clearly better than what we did. Another challenge is the way in which we should deal with selfchecks. In the case of hardware malfunction, it is important that the application be left in a safe-state if at all possible. The current software design achieves this at significant cost. More research in this area is warranted. Much progress has been made already on automating verification activities [3]. Extending these techniques to deal with more cases, especially those involving time-dependent behaviour, should be a high priority. In general, we should now be able to build significantly improved software tools. Finally, we are getting to the stage where we have sufficient experience with these processes to see how we can extend them to help with non safety critical software.

5 Related Work

Software practitioners have clearly indicated the need to automate routine tasks in order to effectively and reliably develop software. The application of formal methods similarly needs to become a largely automated process with tools of even better quality than those used for building and testing software. Knight *et al.* hypothesize that by incorporating formal methods tools into existing software packages such as off the shelf office suites and other software engineering tools, formal methods might be able to overcome their lack of "superstructure" and become more widely used in industry [19]. The experience described here and in [18] supports this conjecture.

While applications of tool supported formal methods to industrial examples have been previously described in e.g., [20], [21], such case studies typically focus on a specific aspect, such as requirements analysis. Our work differs from other successful industrial integrations of formal methods into the software engineering process such as [22] since in our case i) The formal methods were applied to the entire system, and ii) the formal methods documentation and the main project documentation are one and the same. It should be pointed out though that the application described here resulted in roughly one fifth the number of lines of code as the application in [22] and it was not distributed.

6 Conclusion

The use of formal methods in these projects was successful, primarily because of the quality of the personnel involved, and the fact that, by the nature of the problem, OPG was prepared to put sufficient resources into making it successful. It was successful also because it was practical. The level of rigour was commensurate with the task. The formal methods approach was pervasive, but was never allowed to develop beyond its usefulness. Tremendous progress was made in taking ideas from the formal methods research community, and making them practical. However, it is our opinion that the formal methods research community should be trying much harder to make their methods more practical in the first place. Even after thirteen years though, there are significant aspects that have not been completely solved - timing issues for example. We coped with them adequately, but to make these techniques more cost effective, we have to have much more general solutions. Finally, the methods are just too costly without reliable, comprehensive tool support.

Acknowledgements

The work presented in this paper represents the combined efforts of many current and former employees of Ontario Power Generation and AECL, including: Glenn Archinoff, Dominic Chan, Rick Hohendorf, Paul Joannou, Peter Froebel, David Lau, Elder Matias, Jeff McDougall, Greg Moum, Mike Viola, and Alanna Wong. The authors would like to thank Rick Hohendorf and Mike Viola for helping to obtain permission from OPG to publish this work. The FM 2003 reviewers provided invaluable feedback. Finally we would like to acknowledge David Parnas. This work represents the successful application of many of his ideas regarding software engineering.

References

[1] Saiedian H. (ed.): An invitation to formal methods. IEEE Computer **Apr** (1996) 16–30
[2] Heninger, K.L.: Specifying software requirements for complex systems: New techniques and their applications. IEEE Transactions on Software Engineering **6** (1980) 2–13
[3] Heitmeyer, C., Kirby, J., Labaw, B., Bharadwaj, R.: SCR*: A toolset for specifying and analyzing software requirements. In: Proc. 10th Int. Conf. Computer Aided Verification (CAV'98), Vancouver, BC, Canada, June-July 1998. Volume 1427 of LNCS, Springer (1998) 526–531
[4] Parnas, D.L.: Software design. In Hoffman, D., Weiss, D., eds.: Software Fundamentals: Collected Papers by David L. Parnas. Addison-Wesley (2001) 137–142
[5] Archinoff, G.H., Hohendorf, R.J., Wassyng, A., Quigley, B., Borsch, M.R.: Verification of the shutdown system software at the Darlington nuclear generating station. In: International Conference on Control and Instrumentation in Nuclear Installations, Glasgow, UK, The Institution of Nuclear Engineers (1990)

[6] Parnas, D.: On the criteria to be used in decomposing systems into modules. Communications of the ACM **15** (1972) 1053–1058
[7] Joannou, P., et al.: Standard for Software Engineering of Safety Critical Software. CANDU Computer Systems Engineering Centre of Excellence Standard CE-1001-STD Rev. 1 (1995)
[8] McDougall, J., Lee, J.: Procedure for the Software Design Description for Safety Critical Software. CANDU Computer Systems Engineering Centre of Excellence Procedure CE-1002-PROC Rev. 1 (1995)
[9] Moum, G.: Procedure for the Systematic Design Verification of Safety Critical Software. CANDU Computer Systems Engineering Centre of Excellence Procedure CE-1003-PROC Rev. 1 (1997)
[10] Wassyng, A.: Darlington NGD Shutdown System Trip Computer Software Redesign Project, SDS1, Trip Computer Design Requirements Procedure. Technical Report NK38-MAN-68200-003, Rev. 04, Ontario Hydro (2001)
[11] Wassyng, A.: Darlington NGD Shutdown System Trip Computer Software Redesign Project, SDS1, Trip Computer Design Description Procedure. Technical Report NK38-MAN-68200-001, Rev. 03, Ontario Hydro (2001)
[12] Mills, H.D.: Stepwise refinement and verification in box-structured systems. Computer **21** (1988) 23–36
[13] Janicki, R., Parnas, D.L., Zucker, J.: Tabular representations in relational documents. In Brink, C., Kahl, W., Schmidt, G., eds.: Relational Methods in Computer Science. Advances in Computing Science. Springer Wien New York (1997) 184–196
[14] Parnas, D.L., Madey, J.: Functional documents for computer systems. Science of Computer Programming **25** (1995) 41–61
[15] Lawford, M., McDougall, J., Froebel, P., Moum, G.: Practical application of functional and relational methods for the specification and verification of safety critical software. In Rus, T., ed.: Proceedings Algebraic Methodology and Software Technology, 8th International Conference, AMAST 2000, Iowa City, Iowa, USA, May 2000. Volume 1816 of LNCS, Springer (2000) 73–88
[16] Viola, M.: Ontario Hydro's experience with new methods for engineering safety critical software. In: SAFECOMP'95: The 14th International Conference on Computer Safety, Reliability and Security, Belgirate, Italy, Springer (1995) 283–298
[17] Owre, S., Rushby, J., Shankar, N., von Henke, F.: Formal verification for fault-tolerant architectures: Prolegomena to the design of PVS. IEEE Transactions on Software Engineering **21** (1995) 107–125
[18] Lawford, M., Froebel, P., Moum, G.: Application of tabular methods to the specification and verification of a nuclear reactor shutdown system. Accepted for publication in May 2002. http://www.cas.mcmaster.ca/~lawford/papers/ (To appear)
[19] Knight, J.C., Hanks, K.S., Travis, S.R.: Tool support for production use of formal techniques. In: 12th International Symposium on Software Reliability Engineering (ISSRE 2001), Hong Kong, China, IEEE Computer Society (2001)
[20] Heitmeyer, C., Kirby, Jr., J., Labaw, B., Archer, M., Bharadwaj, R.: Using abstraction and model checking to detect safety violations in requirements specifications. IEEE Transactions on Software Engineering **24** (1998) 927–948
[21] Crow, J., Di Vito, B.L.: Formalizing Space Shuttle software requirements: Four case studies. ACM Transactions on Software Engineering and Methodology **7** (1998) 296–332
[22] Hall, A., Chapman, R.: Correctness by construction: Developing a commercial secure system. IEEE Software **Jan/Feb** (2002) 18–25

Determining the Specification of a Control System from That of Its Environment

Ian J. Hayes[1], Michael A. Jackson[2], and Cliff B. Jones[3]

[1] School of Information Technology and Electrical Engineering,
The University of Queensland, Brisbane, 4072, Australia.
Ian.Hayes@itee.uq.edu.au
[2] 101 Hamilton Terrace, London NW8 9QY, England.
jacksonma@acm.org
[3] School of Computing Science,
The University of Newcastle-upon-Tyne, England.
cliff.jones@ncl.ac.uk

Abstract. Well understood methods exist for developing programs from given specifications. A formal method identifies proof obligations at each development step: if all such proof obligations are discharged, a precisely defined class of errors can be excluded from the final program. For a class of "closed" systems such methods offer a gold standard against which less formal approaches can be measured.

For "open" systems –those which interact with the physical world– the task of obtaining the program specification can be as challenging as the task of deriving the program. And, when a system of this class must tolerate certain kinds of unreliability in the physical world, it is still more challenging to reach confidence that the specification obtained is adequate. We argue that widening the notion of software development to include specifying the behaviour of the relevant parts of the physical world gives a way to derive the specification of a control system and also to record precisely the assumptions being made about the world outside the computer.

1 Introduction

A number of methods exist for developing sequential programs from formal specifications (e.g. [9, 1]). Although such methods are not universally practised, their existence provides a "gold standard" that encourages developers to believe that program design errors can be eliminated. A development method that can scale up to deal with realistic problems must be compositional in the sense that the specification of a sub-system is a complete statement of its required properties. For sequential programs, various forms of pre-/post-condition specifications are adequate. For concurrent programs, the task of finding tractable compositional methods proved more challenging [11]; but even here, techniques like rely and guarantee specifications (cf. [7, 8, 10, 2]) provide compositional methods.

If a distinction is made between "closed" and "open" systems –where the former are essentially algorithms in an understood computational domain– it could be said that adequate formal methods are available for closed systems. But the class of "open" systems, which interact with the physical world via sensors and actuators, is both large and very important. Such open systems are often deployed in safety-critical environments. For many of these systems, the task of obtaining a program specification is itself a major challenge. It is to the understanding of this task that the present paper is intended to contribute.

The approach proposed is first to specify the requirements and environment of the overall system; then to capture the assumptions on the physical components by recording rely-conditions; and only then to derive a specification of the computational part of the control system. The developer should resist the temptation to jump in and start specifying the control system from the beginning of a project.

Most open (control) systems must also be designed to tolerate failures in the physical components, both the sensors and actuators and others. Although this need does not change the problem of deriving a specification in any fundamental way, it poses a significant challenge: it is difficult to achieve perspicuity in a specification that addresses the possibility of failures. We address this concern in Section 4. Of course, we make no claim that such systems can be made perfectly safe; we claim only to offer a method that will make it easier to identify the assumptions about the physical components of the system and to ensure that they are formally documented.

Our emphasis on looking first at the external physical environment of a system is advocated in [6, 4, 5]. The original approach to rely/guarantee specifications was not rich enough to cope with continuously varying physical quantities like temperatures, and so we use the notation developed in [12, 13]. Earlier, partial, attacks using some of the ideas presented here include [14].

This paper presents an attack on a particular illustrative design problem. We do not claim that what follows is a universal method: indeed, it is not enough for some problems and too much for others. But the task of designing a *control system* for some part of physical reality is a common task, and achieving a dependable system is a challenging goal.

Essentially the idea is to insist that an initial specification be based on a wide view of a *system*, including both the *machine* and the *problem world*. The machine is the computer, executing the control program to be developed. The problem world is that part of physical reality in which the problem resides and in which the effects of the system, once installed and set in operation, will be evaluated. Drawing the boundaries of the problem world demands a judgement based on the responsibilities and the scope of authority of the customer for the system. The customer's responsibilities bound the effects to be evaluated in the problem world, while the scope of authority bounds the freedom of the developers in aiming to achieve those effects.

In general, execution of the control program can not bring about the desired effects directly. They must be brought about indirectly, relying on causal properties of the problem world. We therefore use rely conditions on the problem world in specifying the control system; with corresponding (or stronger) guarantee conditions one can then prove that the parallel composition of the machine with the problem world satisfies the specification of the whole system. The rely conditions remain in the specification as a reminder and a warning: they must be checked for safe deployment.[1]

A very simple illustration is a room heating system [12]. We should not jump at once into a specification of the control program, stating what corrective action should follow when the temperature sensor indicates that some limit value has been exceeded. Instead we should first specify the desired relationship between the actual room temperature and the target temperature set on the control knob: this is the *requirement*. Then we should record, in rely conditions, the properties of the environment: that is, the *assumptions* we make about the accuracy of the sensors and about the causal chain from activation of the heating equipment to changes in the actual room temperature. Only then are we ready to develop the specification of the control program.

Our ideas are presented using the example of a controller for an irrigation sluice gate. Section 2 begins with the overall requirement for an ideally reliable sluice gate. Section 3 introduces the sensors and motor used to control an ideal sluice gate and develops a specification for a controller for this ideal sluice gate. In Section 4 we consider faults in the problem world, and extend the controller to cope with those faults that it can detect.

2 The Sluice Gate Problem

The example considered below concerns a sluice gate [5] which controls the flow of water for irrigation purposes. The customer's requirement is that the time when the gate is fully open should be in a certain ratio to time when it is fully closed. This will lead us to a set of assumptions (expressed as rely-conditions) about the behaviour of the motor, sensors etc with which the gate is equipped. To clarify the earlier point about the customer's responsibility and authority, we mention some systems of wider scope that *could* be tackled. If the requirement were to deliver a certain flow of water, we would have to make assumptions about the available water flow. A yet wider system might be concerned with the growth of crops, leading to assumptions about the weather, plant physiology and the effects of irrigation. A requirement to maximise farm profits would lead to assumptions about a wide range of factors including prices and (in Europe) the Common Agricultural Policy. The example to be addressed here is a system with a far more restricted requirement. Our customer's responsibilities and authority are both bounded by the sluice gate itself and its stipulated operation. The effects of the irrigation schedule on the crops and and the farm profits are firmly outside our scope.

The requirement for our simple problem is that the sluice gate should be *open* for at least min_open in every hour and *closed* for at least min_closed; *open* and *closed* are *phenomena* of the physical gate. To formalise the requirement we introduce a variable denoting the position of the gate. The requirement is concerned only with whether the sluice gate is *open* or *closed*; however, we recognise that inevitably the gate will sometimes be in *neither* position:

$Height \widehat{=} open|closed|neither$
$pos : Height$

---

[1] There are strong reasons for thinking even more widely. The "Dependability IRC" project (see www.dirc.org.uk) considers computer-based systems whose dependability depends critically on the human (as well as the mechanical) components.

We are interested in the trace of *pos* values over time. Hence, in predicates, it will be treated as a function of time and it may be indexed by a time. An alternative representation for *pos* is as a real value giving the height of the sluice gate (for example, in metres). We reject this alternative because at this stage it complicates the development unnecessarily: the customer is interested only in whether the gate is *open* or *closed*, not in the different intermediate points in its vertical travel.[2]

The overall requirement can now be formalised, using two constants:

$min\_open \mathrel{\widehat{=}} 8\,min$
$min\_closed \mathrel{\widehat{=}} 48\,min$

the requirement will be that in every hour the sluice gate be fully open for at least min_open, and fully closed for at least min_closed. The remaining time in each hour allows for the travel times between the *open* and *closed* positions.

In the definition of *SluiceGateRequirement* below, the notation **interval** T stands for the set of all contiguous finite intervals that are subsets of the time interval T. The operator '#' gives the size of an interval. The integral of a predicate over an interval I, such as $\int_I (pos = open)$, treats the predicate, $pos = open$, as a function of time because *pos* is a function of time; it treats a true value as 1 and a false value as 0, as in the Duration Calculus [3]. In short, the two integrals in the formalisation give the total time in the interval I for which the variable *pos* is equal to *open* and *closed* respectively.

$SluiceGateRequirement \mathrel{\widehat{=}}$
$\forall I : \textbf{interval}\,T@$
$\quad \#I \geq 1\,\text{hr} \Rightarrow$
$\quad \int_I (pos = open) \geq min\_open \land \int_I (pos = closed) \geq min\_closed$

It might be that the customer prefers a looser constraint over each single hour and a constraint closer to "one sixth" over some longer period such as a week: this would allow the pattern of opening to be varied. Similarly, a further requirement might be added specifying that the gate should not be opened or closed more often than three times an hour. Since these possibilities add length to the specification without affecting the basic principles, we do not pursue them here.

The specification of the whole system is to achieve satisfaction of this requirement:

$SluiceGateSystem \mathrel{\widehat{=}}$
system
output $pos : Height$
guarantee $SluiceGateRequirement$

---

[2] It may also be argued that the alternative representation as a real value is pointless because (as we shall see) the gate sensors allow the control system to detect directly only the presence of the gate at the top or bottom of its travel. Although the conclusion may be correct, the argument is misconceived. In many systems the state of the problem world must be *inferred* from what can be sensed directly. The control system for the sluice gate, for example, might infer the gate's vertical position from assumptions about its rate of travel when the motor is on. Such assumptions would then appear in rely conditions in the development.

A system[3] specification explicitly lists the observed inputs and outputs of the system, any assumptions about its environment on which it relies, and the condition it guarantees to establish. In this case there are no assumptions and there are no inputs: the overall specification is concerned only with the gate position, which is an output.

3 Introducing the Controller

There is, of course, a question –even within the agreed boundaries– of which system is being designed here. In some applications the designer might have the luxury of starting from scratch and choosing the equipment, including the placing of sensors etc. Here we assume that all the equipment is already in place in the problem world, and must be treated as given. Figure 1 shows the *machine* (the computer executing the control program that we are developing), the *problem world* (the gate with its sensors and drive motor), and the requirement. The observable phenomena of the requirement are represented by the arrow marked a, and the interface of shared phenomena by which the Control machine monitors and controls the Gate-Sensor-Motor (GSM) problem world is represented by the line marked b.

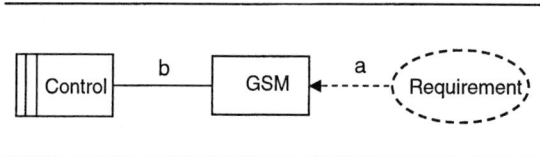

Fig. 1. The Machine, the Problem World and the Requirement

The requirement (which in the preceding section was called $SluiceGateRequirement$) is concerned only with *pos*

$a : \{pos : Height\}$

which is determined by the behaviour of GSM. At interface b, GSM also sets the sensors *top* and *bot*, but the $Control$ machine can set the direction control $dir = up$ or $dir = down$, and switch the motor by setting $motor = on$ or $motor = off$:

$b : Control\ !\ \{dir : up|down, motor : on|off\}$
$\quad\ GSM\ !\ \{top, bot : boolean\}$

We might have decomposed GSM into separate gate, sensor and motor components. We have not done so here because it is simpler, and adequate for our purposes, to describe the GSM subsystem as a whole.

---

[3] We will regard the subject of each specification of this kind as a *system*. Later we will write such a specification for the control machine, another for the sluice gate mechanism, and so on.

3.1 Specifying the Controller

The immediate objective is to arrive at a specification of the control system. It would obviously be possible to observe that $Control \| GSM$ must satisfy the specification of the Sluice Gate System and jump straight to an outline *algorithm* which indicated that the control system should open the sluice gate; pause 8 minutes; then move the gate down; pause for about 48 minutes; etc. Any temptation to specify the control system in this way should be resisted. The aim here is to derive an implicit specification of the control system from an understanding of the components. This identifies the assumptions clearly but the full payoff of this approach is apparent when faults are considered in Section 4.

The Control machine's inputs are the states of the sensors; its outputs are the motor controls. It relies on the sensors and the motor working correctly, and must guarantee that the required behaviour of the sluice gate is achieved, while not invalidating any assumptions about how the GSM subsystem must be operated.

The states of the two sensors, *top* and *bot*, can be formalised as boolean functions of time

top, bot : boolean

When functioning properly, they detect when the gate is fully open (*top*) or fully closed (*bot*). We formalise this notion in the following definition. A *timed predicate* of the form P over I states that the predicate P holds for every instant of time in the interval I. In the definition, T is the complete time interval over which the system operates.

$SensorProp \triangleq (((pos = open) \Leftrightarrow top) \wedge ((pos = closed) \Leftrightarrow bot))$ **over** T

This is equivalent to

$\forall t : T@((pos(t) = open) \Leftrightarrow top(t)) \wedge ((pos(t) = closed) \Leftrightarrow bot(t)).$

The sluice gate is driven by a motor that turns a screw thread that raises or lowers the gate. At the interface b the Control machine can switch the motor on or off, and can set the direction in which it drives the gate. If the motor has been on in the direction up for at least some constant *uptime*, the gate will have reached the open position and will remain there after the motor is turned off. A similar condition applies for the downward travel. First, we formalise the motor control and direction states, and define the constants *uptime* and *downtime*

$motor : on | off$
$direction : up | down$
$uptime \triangleq 1 \text{ min}$
$downtime \triangleq 1 \text{ min}$

Next, we formalise the definition of the motor's effect on the gate. In the definition, an interval I adjoins an interval J, written I **adjoins** J, if the supremum of I is equal to the infimum of J, i.e., $\sup I = \inf J$:

$MotorOperation \;\hat{=}$
$\forall I, J : \textbf{interval} \, T @ I \textbf{ adjoins } J \Rightarrow$
$\begin{pmatrix} \#I \geq uptime \land \\ ((motor = on \land dir = up) \textbf{ over } I) \land \\ ((motor = off) \textbf{ over } J) \end{pmatrix} \Rightarrow ((pos = open) \textbf{ over } J) \land$
$\begin{pmatrix} \#I \geq downtime \land \\ ((motor = on \land dir = down) \textbf{ over } I) \land \\ ((motor = off) \textbf{ over } J) \end{pmatrix} \Rightarrow ((pos = closed) \textbf{ over } J)$

The task of the controller is to achieve the *SluiceGateRequirement* on the assumption that it can rely on the properties of the sensor and the motor. Although *pos* is not a direct input or output of the controller (see Figure 1 and the accompanying descriptions of a and b), we allow the controller specification below to reference *pos* as an 'external' variable. This allows the specification to incorporate the original requirement directly.[4]

$Controller0 \;\hat{=}$
system
external $pos : Height$
input $top, bot :$ boolean
output $motor : on|off$
output $direction : up|down$
rely $SensorProp \land MotorOperation$
guarantee $SluiceGateRequirement$

3.2 The Breakage Concern

At first sight it seems that our specification, though unrefined, is complete so far as it goes. But it is not: we must first address several standard concerns. Here we will address only the *breakage concern* of [5]. In a control problem such as we are discussing here, it is necessary to ensure that the machine itself does not cause failure of any component of the problem domain by ignoring known restrictions on its use. For example, checking the motor equipment manual we learn that the motor will be damaged if it is switched between directions without being brought to rest in between. Between any two periods in which the motor is on and running in opposite directions there must therefore be a period in which it is switched off; and this period must not be less than the motor's shut down time, $motor\_shutdown$.

A second restriction applies when the motor has driven the gate to the open or shut position. It must then be switched off soon enough to avoid straining the motor and mechanism when the gate reaches the end of its vertical travel and further movement is impossible. $motor\_limit$ is the time within which the motor must be switched off once the gate has reached the open or closed position.

---

[4] Because *pos* is not in the interface b of phenomena shared by the Control machine and the GSM problem world, a program implementing the controller may not refer to it. Any reference to *pos* must be eliminated from the program text by a form of refinement in the problem domain. We discuss the removal of such external references in Section 3.3.

We formalise both restrictions in the definition $MotorRestrictions$. In this definition, an interval I precedes an interval J, written I **precedes** J, if the supremum of I is less than or equal to the infimum of J.

$MotorRestrictions \; \hat{=}$
$\forall I, J : \textbf{interval}\, T @$
$$\left(\begin{array}{l} I \textbf{ precedes } J \wedge (motor = on) \textbf{ over } I \wedge (motor = on) \textbf{ over } J \wedge \\ \left(\begin{array}{l} \exists dir : up|down @ \\ \quad (direction = dir) \textbf{ over } I \wedge (direction \neq dir) \textbf{ over } J \end{array} \right) \\ \left(\begin{array}{l} \exists K : Interval @ \# K \geq motor\_shutdown \wedge \\ \quad I \textbf{ precedes } K \textbf{ precedes } J \wedge (motor = off) \textbf{ over } K \end{array} \right) \end{array} \right) \Rightarrow$$
$\wedge$
$\forall I : \textbf{interval}\, T @$
$$\left(motor = on \wedge \left(\begin{array}{l} (pos = open \wedge direction = up) \vee \\ (pos = closed \wedge direction = down) \end{array} \right) \right) \textbf{ over } I \Rightarrow$$
$\# I \leq motor\_limit$

Only if it respects the $MotorRestrictions$ can the Control machine rely on the behaviour described in $MotorOperation$. Thus, the specification for the controller (still assuming fault-free sensors) is now

$Controller1 \; \hat{=}$
system
external $pos : Height$
input top, bot : boolean
output $motor : on|off$
output $direction : up|down$
rely $SensorProp \wedge MotorOperation$
guarantee $SluiceGateRequirement \wedge MotorRestrictions$

3.3 Removing the External Reference

References to the external variable pos must be eliminated from the controller specification before deriving an implementation. For our simple example this is straightforward because the assumption $SensorProp$ gives a way to rewrite the references to pos in terms of top and bot. For example, the revised sluice gate requirement becomes

$SluiceGateRequirement2 \; \hat{=}$
$\quad \forall I : \textbf{interval}\, T @ \# I \geq 1\,\text{hr} \Rightarrow \int_I top \geq min\_open \wedge \int_I bot \geq min\_closed$

$MotorRestrictions$ and $MotorOperation$ can be revised in the same manner to give $MotorRestrictions2$ and $MotorOperation2$ respectively. Because the controller specification can rely on $SensorProp$, rewriting it to use the revised predicates gives a specification that is formally equivalent[5].

---
[5] The equivalence is, of course, only formal: eliminating $SensorProp$ from the formulae can not eliminate our reliance on it in the physical problem world. We address this concern in the next section.

The assumption $SensorProp$ has now fulfilled its purpose, and can be removed to give a refined specification. Further, because pos is no longer referenced in the specification, its declaration can be removed. This gives the following refined specification.

$Controller2 \;\hat{=}\;$
system
input top, bot : boolean
output $motor : on|off$
output $direction : up|down$
rely $MotorOperation2$
guarantee $SluiceGateRequirement2 \wedge MotorRestrictions2$

4 Detecting Domain Faults

The specification $Controller2$ is idealised in the sense that all of the components in the problem world are assumed to function faultlessly. In a critical system –or any system in which it is important to limit the possible damage to the equipment– this assumption must be questioned. Potential faults must be identified and the software must deal with them appropriately. In [5] this obligation is called the *reliability concern*. If a faulty component is detected, the Control machine must switch off the motor and turn on an alarm to indicate that the system needs attention from the maintenance engineer and that the irrigation requirement is no longer being satisfied.

4.1 Domain Faults

In the present section we are concerned only with the analysis of domain faults and with formalising their detection. We address the composition of this requirement with the $SluiceGateRequirement$ in the next section. We start in the problem domain, and identify observable faults that can arise in the domain. Our analysis uncovers potential faults like these (but not only these):

- A log becomes jammed under the gate.
- A sensor develops an open circuit fault (fails $false$).
- A sensor develops a short circuit fault (fails $true$).
- The screw mechanism becomes rusty and the gate jams.
- The screw mechanism breaks, allowing the gate to slide freely.
- The direction control cable is cut.
- The motor efficiency is reduced by deterioration of the bearings.
- The motor overheats.

We then consider how these faults in the problem domain can be detected by the Control machine at its interface b with the domain (see Figure 1). Because this interface is very simple, and consists only of the states of the top and bot sensors and the motor settings, it is clear that the Control machine can not distinguish between different faults in the domain. For example, it can not distinguish between a log jammed under the gate and an open-circuit bot sensor: both manifest themselves by failure of the bot sensor to indicate arrival of the gate at the closed position in spite of the motor having been set *on* and *down* for at least *downtime*. In a safety-critical system we would consider improving the interface by adding new sensors. For example, we might add a sensor to detect motor temperature or motor speed; or we might provide a finer grain of sensing of the vertical position of the gate. For the purposes of this example, we add an additional Boolean sensor, *motor_too_hot*, that indicates the motor temperature is excessive. An interesting aspect of this fault is that the phenomena used to describe the fault are not part of the description of the ideal behaviour of the sluice gate.

The faulty state, *Faulty_GSM*, can be detected by the occurrence of any of these (informally expressed) conditions:

- The *top* sensor does not become *true* when it should.
- The *bot* sensor does not become *true* when it should.
- The *bot* sensor does not become *false* when it should (when the motor has been set *on* and *up* for a duration of at least *rise_start_time*).
- The *top* sensor does not become *false* when it should (when the motor has been set *on* and *down* for a duration of at least *fall_start_time*).
- The *top* sensor becomes *true* earlier than it should (when the motor has been set *on* and *up*).
- The *bot* sensor becomes *true* earlier than it should (when the motor has been set *on* and *down*).
- The *top* sensor changes value while the motor is set off.
- The *bot* sensor changes value while the motor is set off.
- *top* and *bot* are simultaneously *true* at any time.
- The *motor_too_hot* sensor becomes true.

For brevity we will not present the full formalisation of *Faulty_GSM*. Given suitable declarations of duration constants for the criteria of fault-free operation in the domain we obtain a definition of the faulty state. Recognition of the state is triggered by an interval J in which a fault condition is detected.

$Faulty\_GSM \triangleq \lambda J : \mathbf{interval}\, Time@$
$\exists I : \mathbf{interval}\, T@I\ \mathbf{adjoins}\ J \wedge$
$\begin{pmatrix} (motor = on)\ \mathbf{over}\ I \wedge (direction = up)\ \mathbf{over}\ (I \cup J) \wedge \\ \#I \geq healthy\_rise\_time \wedge (\neg top)\ \mathbf{over}\ J \end{pmatrix} \vee$
$\begin{pmatrix} (motor = on)\ \mathbf{over}\ I \wedge (direction = down)\ \mathbf{over}\ (I \cup J) \wedge \\ \#I > healthy\_fall\_time \wedge (\neg bot)\ \mathbf{over}\ J \end{pmatrix} \vee$
$\begin{pmatrix} (motor = on)\ \mathbf{over}\ I \wedge (direction = up)\ \mathbf{over}\ (I \cup J) \wedge \\ \#I > rise\_start\_time \wedge bot\ \mathbf{over}\ J \end{pmatrix} \vee$
$\vdots$

$((top \wedge bot)\ \mathbf{over}\ J) \vee$
$((motor\_too\_hot)\ \mathbf{over}\ J)$

We must now discharge the obligation to show that *Faulty_GSM* holds whenever a fault is present in the domain for which we require the Control machine to switch off the motor and turn on the alarm. We leave this as an exercise for the energetic reader who has completed the definition of *Faulty_GSM*.

4.2 Composing the Requirements

Our intention is to compose both requirements (irrigation and fault tolerance) in the one Control machine. We must therefore elaborate the interface b of Figure 1 to include the setting of the alarm and the temperature sensor. Modifying the annotation given in Section 3 we have:

$b: Control\ !\ \{dir : up|down, motor : on|off, alarm : on|off\}$
$GSM\ !\ \{top, bot : \text{boolean}, motor\_too\_hot : \text{boolean}\}$

First we must elaborate our existing Control machine, specifying that during its execution the alarm is off. The elaborated machine is $Controller3$:

$AlarmOff \triangleq$
system
output $alarm : on|off$
guarantee$(alarm = off)$ **over** T

$Controller3 \triangleq Controller2 \land AlarmOff.$

Two systems may be conjoined: the inputs and outputs of the conjoined system are the unions of the inputs and outputs respectively of the two systems (common inputs and outputs must have the same type), and the rely and guarantee conditions are the conjunctions of their rely and guarantee conditions respectively. So the specification

$Controller2 \land AlarmOff$

specifies a system that is the same as $Controller2$ but has an additional output $alarm$ that is always off.

The behaviour required when a domain fault has been detected is to switch the motor off and the alarm on within some permitted response time $fault\_response$:

$AlarmSet \triangleq$
$\quad \exists J, K : \textbf{interval}\, T@J\ \textbf{adjoins}\ K \land$
$\quad J \cup K = T \land \#J \leq fault\_response \land$
$\quad (alarm = on \land motor = off)\ \textbf{over}\ K$

The required behaviour for raising the alarm can be simply defined. Note that it requires the restrictions on controlling the motor to be maintained.

$Raise\_Alarm \triangleq$
system
input $top, bot : $ boolean
input $motor_too_hot : $ boolean
output $motor : on|off$
output $direction : up|down$
output $alarm : on|off$
guarantee $MotorRestrictions2 \land AlarmSet$

Finally, we must specify the combination of $Controller3$ and $Raise\_Alarm$ in response to faults. For this we need to consider two modes of fault detection:

- faults that persist over a long enough interval of time that we insist they are detected; and
- faults that exist for only a short period of time that may or may not be detected.

We introduce two separate (but similar) operators to allow these two different modes of fault detection to be specified. For systems $S1$ and $S2$ and a predicate C that takes a time interval as a parameter (like $Faulty\_GSM$)

- a hard fault obliges the system to take notice

$$S1 \textbf{ until } C \textbf{ requires } S2$$

and
- a "transient" fault allows the system to take notice

$$S1 \textbf{ until } C \textbf{ allows } S2$$

For example,

$$Controller4 \cong Controller3 \textbf{ until } Faulty\_GSM \textbf{ allows } Raise\_Alarm$$

describes a system that operates as an ideal controller, but *may* raise the alarm if there is a fault, and

$$Controller5 \cong Controller4 \textbf{ until } Hard\_Fault\_GSM \textbf{ requires } Raise\_Alarm$$

describes a system that must raise the alarm as soon as a hard fault appears, where

$$Hard\_Fault\_GSM \cong$$
$$(\lambda J : \textbf{interval} \, Time @ Faulty\_GSM(J) \wedge \#J \geq reaction\_time)$$

We describe the semantics of these two combinators, starting with the more liberal second combinator because it is slightly simpler. $S1$ **until** C **allows** $S2$ either behaves like $S1$, or if there exists an interval J over which $C(J)$ holds, it *may* (is allowed to) behave like $S1$ until the start of the interval J, and then behave like $S2$ from that time on. To describe the combinator more formally, we use the term *behaviour* to refer to a trace of the values of the variables over time, and the function $behaviours(S,T)$ gives the set of all possible behaviours of system S over the time interval T. The boolean term $C(J)(b)$ states that the predicate $C(J)$ holds for the behaviour b.

$b \in behaviours(S1 \textbf{ until } C \textbf{ allows } S2, T) \equiv$
$b \in behaviours(S1, T) \vee$
$\quad (\exists I, J, K : \textbf{interval} \, T @ I \textbf{ adjoins } J \textbf{ adjoins } K \wedge T = I \cup J \cup K \wedge C(J)(b) \wedge$
$\quad\quad (\exists b1 : behaviours(S1, T); b2 : behaviours(S2, J \cup K) @$
$\quad\quad\quad b = (I \triangleleft b1) \frown b2))$

The operator "$I \triangleleft b1$" takes a timed trace behaviour $b1$ and restricts it to a trace whose domain is contained in the interval I. The catenation of two traces, $b \frown c$ assumes that the domain of b has an end time equal to the start time of the domain of c and that the values of the variables at the end of trace b are equal to the values of the variables at the beginning of trace c; the resultant trace is then the union of the two traces.

The semantics of the obligatory exception mechanism is similar but it requires that there is no earlier occurrence of the condition C. The first alternative allows for the case where there is no interval over which C holds.

$b \in behaviours(S1 \text{ until } C \text{ requires } S2, T) \equiv$
$b \in behaviours(S1, T) \wedge \neg(\exists L : \text{interval} \, T@C(L)(b)) \vee$
$(\exists I, J, K : \text{interval} \, T@I \text{ adjoins } J \text{ adjoins } K \wedge T = I \cup J \cup K \wedge C(J)(b) \wedge$
$\quad (\neg \exists L : \text{interval} \, T@\inf L < \inf J \wedge C(L)(b))) \wedge$
$\quad (\exists b1 : behaviours(S1, T); b2 : behaviours(S2, J \cup K)@$
$\quad\quad b = (I \triangleleft b1) \frown b2))$

5 Further Work

This paper illustrates what the authors hope will become a method for handling a class of developments. However, much remains to be done to establish the scope of this method and to refine its details. In this section we consider some avenues for further work.

5.1 On the Sluice Gate Application

The Sluice Gate problem has proved very stimulating and we have tried to expose the issues it has thrown up rather than modify the problem to fit our evolving method. For example, the second author has on occasions played the role of our customer and has consistently refused requests to acquire new sensors to simplify formulations.

There are, of course, a variety of other (dependability) issues which could be considered; examples include:

- the power supply to the motor;
- the hardware signals levels used for *motor* and *dir*;
- the maximum load of the motor;
- the maximum start up time under any load less than the maximum;
- the running state revolutions per minute.

While we believe that such points do not bring in fundamentally different technical requirements, they should be categorised as an indication that nothing has been hidden.

5.2 More General Points

The aim to separate the treatment of errors from the behaviour required in an (unrealistically) ideal environment has caused us considerable difficulty. We have experimented with an asymmetric **otherwise** operator, ways of combining traces of descriptions which permit non-determinism, and only late on accepted the **allows/requires** distinction. The need to say that the presence of one condition overrides others appears to force an asymmetric operator and the (Deontic) distinction is at least plausible. Whether there is a smaller set of primitive concepts in terms of which these ideas can be expressed is the subject of further work.

Many open (real-time) systems appear to operate cyclicly. Indeed, even the sluice gate could be viewed as operating on an hourly cycle (possibly embedded in a larger cycle between, say, maintenance periods). The authors are not aware of any (temporal) notations that offer clear ways of indicating such cyclic behaviour.

It would be useful to have more systematic ways of looking for fault situations. If one followed [5] and constructed a *model* of the gate within the Control system, this would –for example– offer a notion within the Controller of the expected $height$ of the gate. This, in turn, would facilitate expression of a rely condition to show the degree of expected drift/conformance. We have only made tentative experiments with this idea so far.

One of the refrees raised the interesting point of the "evolvability" of a system. The authors agree that this is an important issue; evolution is in fact a major strand of work within the Dependability IRC. A study of the contribution of other research on "evolvability" to the issues of this paper will be undertaken in the future.

6 Conclusions

The starting point for the specification of a control system is a specification of the desired behaviour of the controlled system, e.g., the sluice gate position, given independently of the (physical) mechanisms used to implement the (physical) control. As indicated earlier, there are different possible models of the system that allow different aspects of the system to be specified. Choice of an appropriate model comes down to the customer's choice of requirements. The model must be rich enough to allow the requirements to be specified, but not so rich that the specification is unnecessarily complex.

Having specified the overall requirements, we must detail the properties of the given (physical) components (e.g., the sensors and motor). These are the properties the controller can rely on to achieve the desired goal. In addition, the components may have restrictions on the way in which they may be operated without risk of breakage. The controller must ensure that it conforms to these requirements too.

In specifying the requirements and the properties of the components it is in general necessary to make use of models of parts of the system that are not directly interfaced to the machine (for example, the external variable pos in the controller specification does not appear in the interface between the machine and the problem world). This necessity springs from two sources. First, the customer's interest is not, in general, restricted to phenomena at the interface: the Sluice Gate customer cares whether the gate is open or closed, not about the sensor states. Second, if we fail to distinguish phenomena at the interface from those that lie deeper in the problem world, we can not address the reliability concern: it arises precisely from that distinction. It is then a central goal of the process of refining the controller specification to rephrase its required behaviour solely in terms of its interface to the problem world.

A further technique we used to structure the controller specification is to separate the Control requirement when the problem domain is behaving faultlessly from the requirement in the presence of faults. It is first worthwhile to examine possible faults in the overall system. These may involve phenoma that are not part of the description of the idealised machine. Next one must consider the class of faults that can be phrased purely in terms of the system's interface to the environment. The utility of the machine's response to problem world failures is limited by the richness of the interface between them. A richer interface allows better diagnosis of faults and more specific responses. However, introducing richer interfaces has two consequences: first, they may be more prone to failure than the simple interface; and second, they make the control software itself more complicated and hence more prone to software error.

Our building blocks for specifications are *systems* specified in terms of their inputs, outputs and external variables as well as the assumptions about the inputs that they rely upon and the goals that they guarantee to achieve. To build more complex specifications one could continue to use systems specified in the same way, but with more complex rely and guarantee conditions. Alternatively, as we have done here, one can provide operators such as conjunction and **until-requires** to combine system specifications. Logically both approaches are equivalent; the choice between them is more one of ease of presentation and understandability of the resulting specification. A structured specification built from component systems can be flattened to a simple system specification with rely and guarantee conditions.

Acknowledgements

The first author acknowledges the support of Australian Research Council (ARC) Discovery Grant DP0345355, *Building dependability into complex, computer-based systems*. All three authors receive support from the (UK) EPSRC funding of the "Dependability IRC" (Interdisciplinary Research Collaboration): the third author is directly involved and the first two authors are Senior Visiting Fellows to DIRC. In addition, the third author's research has been partially supported by European IST DSoS Project (IST-1999-11585). The authors acknowledge the input from three anonymous referees.

References

[1] J.-R. Abrial. *The B-Book: Assigning programs to meanings*. Cambridge University Press, 1996.
[2] Manfred Broy and Ketil Stølen. *Specification and Development of Interactive Systems*. Springer-Verlag, 2001.
[3] Zhou Chaochen, C.A.R. Hoare, and A.P. Ravn. A calculus of durations. *Information Processing Letters*, 40:269–271, December 1991.
[4] M. A. Jackson. Problem analysis and structure. In Tony Hoare, Manfred Broy, and Ralf Steinbruggen, editors, *Engineering Theories of Software Construction (Proceedings of the NATO Summer School, Marktoberdorf, August 2000)*. IOS Press, 2000.
[5] M. A. Jackson. *Problem Frames: Analyzing and structuring software development problems*. Addison-Wesley, 2001.
[6] Michael Jackson. *Software Requirements & Specifications: a lexicon of practice, principles and prejudices*. Addison-Wesley, 1995.
[7] C. B. Jones. *Development Methods for Computer Programs including a Notion of Interference*. PhD thesis, Oxford University, June 1981. Printed as: Programming Research Group, Technical Monograph 25.
[8] C. B. Jones. Specification and design of (parallel) programs. In *Proceedings of IFIP'83*, pages 321–332. North-Holland, 1983.
[9] C. B. Jones. *Systematic Software Development using VDM*. Prentice Hall International, second edition, 1990. ISBN 0-13-880733-7.

[10] C. B. Jones. Accommodating interference in the formal design of concurrent object-based programs. *Formal Methods in System Design*, 8(2):105–122, March 1996.

[11] C. B. Jones. Compositionality, interference and concurrency. In Jim Davies, Bill Roscoe, and Jim Woodcock, editors, *Milennial Perspectives in Computer Science*, pages 175–186. Macmillian Press, 2000.

[12] B. P. Mahony and I. J. Hayes. A case study in timed refinement: A central heater. In *Proc. BCS/FACS Fourth Refinement Workshop*, Workshops in Computing, pages 138–149. Springer, January 1991.

[13] B. P. Mahony and I. J. Hayes. Using continuous real functions to model timed histories. In P. A. Bailes, editor, *Proc. 6th Australian Software Engineering Conf. (ASWEC91)*, pages 257–270. Australian Comp. Soc., 1991.

[14] B. P. Mahony and I. J. Hayes. A case-study in timed refinement: A mine pump. *IEEE Trans. on Software Engineering*, 18(9):817–826, 1992.

Managerial Issues for the Consideration and Use of Formal Methods

Donna C. Stidolph[1] and James Whitehead[2]

[1] Snaptrack Inc., Campbell, California,
donnas@qualcomm.com
[2] University of California, Santa Cruz,
ejw@cse.ucsc.edu

Abstract. The introduction of formal methods into the commercial community has been slow. This might, in part, be due to lack of guidance for program managers responsible for execution of a program, who must justify added expense or time to delivery. This paper first provides managers with guidance in deciding if a particular project is a good candidate for the use of formal methods. After the go/no go conditions are considered, the paper describes some of the management and reporting issues that may arise if the decision is made to use formal methods on a program.

Keywords: Program management, schedule, formal methods, specification, requirements, cost

1 Introduction

The formal methods community recognizes that formal methods are not often used in commercial software developments or well understood by most practicing software engineers [7, 24]. There appear to be a few commonly recognized reasons for this [33, 35, 2, 7, 12, 4].

- Application of formal methods requires the explicit use of discrete math skills.
- The effect of the use of formal methods on schedules is not well understood.
- The development tools are awkward and may not integrate with standard industry design tools.
- An expert is necessary to get started.

Each of the items above effectively add to program costs or risks. There are many concrete examples of this. British Aerospace reports a factor of seven decrease in programmer productivity going from a non-safety critical development project to a full formal methods development. Other surveys report that productivity is reduced by half [5, 3]. There are published cases where overall time to product delivery on a formal methods project is equivalent to that predicted for a traditional delivery. In these cases, though, the application of formal methods shifts the labor curve toward the end of the project. This potentially conflicts with a common business model in which costs are recovered based on customer identified milestones, which puts a premium on getting to actual code production. Many organizations that have tried formal methods, even in small research areas, seem to find the process too painful to repeat, so the work is abandoned and the small efforts are not scaled up to provide adequate real-world examples.

Other software methodologies have overcome introductory hurdles similar to those listed above and ultimately have been accepted in the production software world, so why not formal methods? There seem to be a number of reasons, but they all reduce to lack of return on investment. There have been very few instances where the use of formal methods has resulted in even the perception of cost savings [19]. It is enlightening to consider that one of the most accepted uses of formal methods in software is in the production of protocols and algorithms, where the cost of the formal methods can be amortized across all uses of the algorithm or protocol [24, 27]. Although formal methods can result in improved safety and reliability of software products, few organizations assign dollar values to improvements in those areas. If there is no measurement in place for the improvement, it is perceived as a cost with no resulting benefit.

However, the business environment is changing in ways that make formal methods more attractive:

- Use of formal methods are being mandated in some safety or security critical applications [32, 6].
- Litigation as a result of failed software is becoming more common [5]. Use of formal methods could demonstrate the developer's concern for reliability and safety.
- As e-commerce moves toward large scale business collaborations, it will become increasingly important to provide all participants with some proofs of integrity and formal methods may provide them.

In light of this, it is natural to ask if there are rules a software manager could follow to select appropriate uses for formal methods and to increase the chances of a successful application of formal methods.

This paper provides some guidelines for application of formal methods. A literature search was performed to find case studies involving use of formal methods in the software industry. Although very few formal methods projects were documented with the appropriate data and in sufficient detail for management comparisons, what information was available was used to start developing some rules of thumb to help on deciding when and how to use formal methods. As a result, our contributions are ones of synthesis, surveying the known literature with an eye towards managerial issues of adoption, and managerial guidelines for use of formal methods on projects. This paper does not introduce any new formal methods techniques or tools, instead focusing on certain of the managerial issues surrounding their use. Management of formal methods projects is one of a cluster of topics, including engineering curricula, in-practice training, and empirical validation, that are critical for crossing the gap between theory and practice in formal methods.

The management guidance provided by this paper is divided into two parts, deciding whether to use formal methods at all, and then, assuming they are used, rules of thumb for their application. The next section of this paper identifies conditions that must exist for formal methods use to succeed. Next, the paper provides a series of managerial issues to be considered in the event that formal methods are used on a project. The paper concludes with a brief summary of results.

2 Go–No Go Conditions for Application of Formal Methods

In order for a formal methods effort to succeed, the developing organization must have a compelling reason to use them, the effort should be structured so that the developing organization can control the amount invested in the effort, and management must be behind the effort. Each of these conditions is justified and discussed in more detail below.

2.1 You Have a Really Good Reason

A really good reason would be that your customer requires them. This isn't restricted to customers who explicitly require them, such as Great Britain's Ministry of Defense (MoD); you may be in a business that doesn't have a customer base that is sophisticated enough to realize the risks incurred by depending on software. If that's the case, you may decide to apply formal methods because it's the right thing to do. This might be the if your company develops heavy equipment assembly line control software or other types of manufacturing software; if there is a personal safety risk to employees, formal methods might be appropriate. Finally, there may be a competitive advantage if you do it first in security-aware sectors such as finance.

Another good reason would be that you expect this software to be around virtually forever. In the case of power plant control software [11] or an enterprise business product such as IBM's CICS [16], the expected life cycle of the software is decades, with continuous maintenance and upgrades. It is in your best interest to lock down every assumption and every corner case on every test because your experts won't be there to tell you what they were thinking in 25 years, particularly after 25 years of continuous maintenance. In the shorter term, having a fully proven test suite allows software maintenance to be approached with much greater confidence, since the likelihood of detecting unintended consequences is much higher. This results in lower design/analysis costs for the maintenance efforts and lower domain knowledge requirements for the maintenance programmers, both significant productivity enhancements.

2.2 The Development Is Internal, or on a Shared-Risk Contractual Vehicle

There are virtually no metrics for estimating cost or schedule for formal methods projects [15]. In the 66 cases studied, only 7 claimed equal or better cost numbers as compared to traditional developments [45, 35]. In the rest of the cases, the cost was not specifically addressed. For the cost/benefit analyses which would be required to justify incorporation of formal methods, cases where cost is not reported are not useful. It should also be noted that published case studies are probably not representative because they are usually domain specific and implemented by various All Star Teams. Finally, most of the projects are on "toy-sized" applications, not the millions of lines of code that is common in commercial software. Experienced formal methodologists insist that cost and schedule estimation techniques are unsatisfactory and will remain so until a large body of experience becomes available [4].

Since the cost/schedule impact of formal methods can't be predicted, it seems unwise to volunteer to use them unless you can control the amount you are willing to invest in them. If the proposed use is internal development or some type of contractual vehicle in which the customer shares risk (cost plus fixed fee, cost plus award fee, etc.), then formal methods can be considered. In these cases, the financial risk can be somewhat bounded. Interestingly, in one case study even though the acquirers needed help interpreting the formal system description, the use of formal methods was "important in the acceptability of the proposal" [13], meaning that the customer saw enough value to invest in being educated.

2.3 You Have Management Buy In

Use of formal methods might be expected to extend the initial phases of development (analysis, requirements and specification) and compress the design, code and test phases of a program schedule. Since this affects the investment profile for a program, your management must be aware of this and accept that initial investment will probably be higher on a formal methods program.

Figure 1 compares the time spent in each phase of development on a development program for a satellite control system and the (very successful) formal methods development for a rework of that software[1] [42].

Note that at the end of the specification phase, more than twice the hours were expended on the formal methods development as on the traditional development, but by the end of the test phase, the formal methods approach had proven much less expensive. Changes such as those shown in Fig. 1 are of serious concern for two reasons:

---

[1] An argument could be made that the effort on the rework should be lower because of the knowledge gained the first time. In this case, the task was designed as an experiment in applying formal methods, so the implementers selected had no previous domain knowledge or project-specific knowledge. However, they were formal methods practitioners.

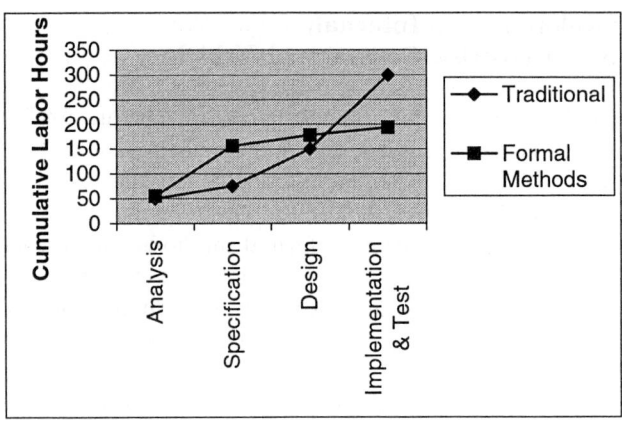

Fig. 1. Comparison of labor investment over time on a formal methods development versus a traditional investment

- The costing profile of the program is altered; that is, money is spent at different times in the program than in a traditional development.
- The drop dates of the interim deliverables are changed.

If an organization is working with a contract based on a traditional development model, these two factors may combine to make the developing organization's investment significantly higher for formal methods programs. Milestone payments, a common method of payment distribution in development contracts, are based on completion of various program phases, signified by the completion of a deliverable item, or by acceptance of some work product. Since the customer (internal or external) wants his investment to be proportional to the amount of useful "product" he currently holds, the payment schedule is usually back-loaded, so that the payments for requirements analysis and specification are small in comparison to those for design, code, and test.

In essence, the use of formal methods shifts the workload toward the beginning of the program. As can be seen, the investment by the developing organization is significantly higher for the formal methods development until completion of the design phase, even though total spending is decreased. As a result, the developing organization may find itself going into debt in the initial phases of a formal methods program, even a remarkably successful effort, rather than making an initial profit. If management is unaware of this, the program might be red-flagged early, getting saddled with the "costs of panic" that always accrue to a program that is thought to be in trouble, due to increased reporting requirements.

3 If You Still Think You Might Do It ...

If you have a project that cries out for formal verification, you have the power to cut your losses if the process isn't working, and you have management buy in to try [28, 46], here are some guidelines for proceeding:

3.1 Plan on Using Consultants

Most of the formal methods programs studied used expert formal methods teams, and all of them had expert consultants available. In the Formal Methods Europe (FME) database (www.fmeurope.org), 90% of the projects were done either by academic institutions, or in direct cooperation with one. If this is a one-time or few-time effort, like many formal methods projects are [44], you'll have a sharply limited opportunity to recover your training investment. Unless you believe that your organization is going to make a habit of using formal methods, the benefits accrued by training engineers to be experts in formal methods probably don't justify the cost of the training. In light of this, you might consider out-sourcing the entire effort [28, 17, 18].

Even if you decide to train your own staff, there is another reason you need consultants: to meet a commercial development schedule, you need instant expertise to quickly analyze the selected problem, identify the appropriate level of rigor and type of formal method to apply, and select the tool to match the problem. There are many method/tool/language combinations that have dedicated adherents, and each has different technical and cultural strengths, just as with programming languages. Just because a formal method has a large support base does not mean it is the right choice for your program. On the other hand, selecting the perfect tool may be a bad choice if the only expert is its author and her graduate student, who both live in time zones far, far away. The formal methods community isn't geared to provide general purpose tools, so you need an expert to select them, as well as to run them.

As always, there are disadvantages to outsourcing. First, your experts may come with a strong commitment to an existing formal method. Many of the formal methods were developed in research settings, and many experts became experts by developing new tools or by applying an academic tool to an industrial problem. As the saying goes "When you have a hammer, everything looks like a nail." The FME website has a current list of methods and a high level roadmap for the selection process. Use this website or something like it to inform yourself a little, so you can at least ask questions to ensure that your expert is open to considering multiple alternative solutions.

The major disadvantage of outsourcing is that the formal methods expert will probably not be a domain expert, and will require training about the domain. Communication between the formal methods experts and the domain experts was cited as a problem in several of the case studies [6, 15]. In some cases, the formal methods team was required to come up with an alternative method of presenting their specification in order to get it properly reviewed with respect to domain-specific technical content. Alternately, several of the participants cite misunderstanding of the domain by their formal methods team as a serious impediment to their progress. Viewing that from a different perspective, Easterbrook et al. [18] points out that the process of educating their formal methods experts resulted in detection and resolution of several requirements problems, as well as exposing areas that lacked clarity in the requirements, both valuable outcomes.

3.2 Formal Methods Leverage the Existing Software Process, Not Replace It

In most cases in which formal methods were successfully applied, the formal methods were used to augment an existing successful process to meet a new requirement[2]. Formal methods cannot be used to develop software, only to improve the chance of getting good software. For example, some formal methods tools support continuous refinement of design through code generation, but the requirements had to be identified before they could be formally specified, and the resulting code has to be tested and its configuration managed, all functions included in a mature software process. Another characteristic of organizations with successful software development processes is that there is a process for introduction of change, and recognition that different types of projects require different development models and tools [39]. Organizations such as these are likely to try new approaches, such as the addition of formal methods, in carefully selected pilot programs, with identified baselines for expected technical and schedule results. When change is planned for, it can be accommodated. As Fitzgerald and Larsen point out,

> In introducing such organisations to formal techniques, we are not in a position to require radical changes in development processes in the short term. This has to be done gradually as part of a process development plan.

The application of formal methods delays the beginning of the coding phase of a program. In light of this, formal methods will probably not be successful in an impatient organization, and patience is usually a characteristic of an organization with a mature process [28].

3.3 Expert Consultants Must Be Available

As mentioned previously, all the formal methods application programs reported on here were accomplished either by teams made up entirely of experts, or had

---

[2] One exception was a Tektronix oscilloscope development. In this case, formal methods were introduced to help bring clarity to the architectural design process. Although the use of formal methods was abandoned, this instance of use was judged to be a success based on the fact that the resulting product line was successful in a flat economy, and several generations of oscilloscopes have been built on the architectural base.

ready access to expert consultants. NASA has concluded that, at the least, expert consultants should be available to formal methods programs, and ideally, at least one team member should be an expert [25]. Surveys of participants in software projects that had used formal methods [44, 40] also included this as a lesson learned. So, even if you send your people to schools, expect them to need support and be prepared to provide it.

3.4 You Need "Early Adopters"

There must be a community of "early adopters"[3] on the program so their enthusiasm can be used to bridge through the training and initial frustration. Formal methods have to be introduced in the same way as any new technology. If you don't have someone eager to try the technology and support it when frustration sets in, the introduction won't be successful [46]. In the published cases, the implementers entered the project with confidence in the effectiveness of formal methods. For your formal methods project to be successful, you need to find someone to inculcate that confidence and enthusiasm in your own team and in the customer's - or do it yourself.

3.5 Know Exactly Where You Need the Extra Effort

Very few of the projects applied formal methods to the entire design, and those that did elected to start analysis several levels of detail down from the top [32] in order to avoid combinatorial explosion of proofs [24, 41].

Another reason to restrict the scope as much as possible is to keep the analysis timely and synchronized with development. Easterbrook [18] uses the term "lightweight formal methods" to "indicate that the methods can be used to perform partial analysis on partial specifications, without a commitment to developing and baselining complete, consistent formal specifications." Easterbrook describes the use of lightweight formal methods used selectively on identified problems with the results fed back into the existing process. NASA has used this process successfully in several cases, and a group at Nortel has concluded that selecting the right problem is critical to successful use of formal methods [48].

Scalability is another unknown in formal method developments. Most of the projects documented were relatively small, ranging from 1 KLOC to 200 KLOC, but many commercial and custom development projects run to millions of lines of code. Even if the formal methods tools and techniques worked superbly on the samples, there is no guarantee that they will work well on a large program. We all know that changes in size can cause changes in kind as well as quantity. With this in mind, risk can be bounded by carefully selecting the right, small portion of your program logic for formal methods application.

---

[3] Or "Early Majority-ers" as they are called in Geoffrey Moore's book Crossing the Chasm, which Craigen discusses in Craigen, D. (1999) Formal Methods Adoption: What's Working, What's Not., SPIN'99, Toulouse, France, Springer-Verlag.

3.6 Select an Appropriate Program Phase

Several of th projects that used formal methods for specification, design, and verification noted that the majority of the value came in using formal methods to develop a specification [23, 29]. The projects surveyed provide little evidence of value added by formally proving a program, either manually or with an automated theorem checker. There are probably a couple of reasons for this. One reason is that the formal methods tools for design don't appear to be as mature as the tools for specification. Another reason is requirement collection and specification are weak points in many processes. As a result, formal methods might provide the most value-added in the specification phase of the program by forcing rigor.

Using this as a guide, formal methods could be appropriate either in new development programs during the requirements/specification phase, or in the reverse engineering phase of re-engineering an existing system from its as-built configuration. In either case, the process of formally specifying the system can provide an unambiguous description of system requirements that can ensure the internal consistency of the requirements set and can be used for generating test cases. In the case of a greenfield system, it can be used to expose weaknesses in the natural language specification. In the reverse engineering application, creating a formal specification from the existing code allows the user to compare the as-built with the original specifications and also to verify what the code actually does, while forming a basis for a new requirements specification.

It should be realized that the formal methods should be applied after user requirements are relatively firm and the essential requirements are identified. It is difficult to express the concept of "desirable but not essential" in these languages [22].

If applied after the development is done, use of formal methods to reverse engineer the as-built specification can cost up to 50% of the original development [31]. If the system has been in the field for some time and the actual body of code has lost synchronization with the documentation, formal specification may be worth a look. If the alternative is maintaining the software with inaccurate documentation and resolving inconsistencies between the documentation and the code via testing, formal methods may actually represent a cost saving. "Specification Mining" is a new development that may help with this problem [1]. This approach assumes that a fielded program is mostly correct and infers the formal specification based on the behavior of the existing, running code.

There have also been successful pilot projects using code generation tools, in which the code was automatically generated from a formal specification and integrated with manually developed code [26]. This approach allows the formality developed in the specification stage to be "automatically" floated to the coding phase of a program.

3.7 You'll Probably "Lose" Your Domain Experts to the Development

Your domain experts may become absorbed in the formal methods effort and they may be lost as cross-organizational assets. Usually the domain experts who are most valuable to any single project are valuable to multiple projects, and using formal methods, even with consultants, will require them to learn enough formal methods to talk to the consultants. The learning process will cause more of the domain expert's time to be taken than a normal, intra-organization consultation does, since it involves, essentially, learning a new language [28]. Be prepared to defend your asset.

3.8 Select the Right Languages and/or Tools

Tool selection will be a critical decision, which should be based on suitability for your intended use [22, 10] and to match your existing process [20]. As mentioned above, it's probably best to have expert help making this decision. Just as in programming languages, it is important to match the formal method language to the problem. Also, again as in programming environments, the contents of formal methods tool suites are inconsistent, so you may be limited in your selection of tools by your application.

If you aren't driven to a single language or tool by your application, selection should be based on availability of experts and/or training and ease of learning. Furthermore, one project may require multiple notations for different aspects of the program [27, 22].

When assessing the formal methods tools, be aware that one of the major self-criticisms of the formal methods community is that the tools they produce are not usually robust, reliable, scalable or stable. The tool developers seem to try to extend the power of the tool, rather than making the present version more usable in a production environment [25, 22]. This is why access to an expert is so crucial. Your team needs to know quickly whether it's them, their theorem, or the tool that's misbehaving.

Finally, can the tool be qualified? "Qualification" is the process of meeting a guideline for development and maintenance to help ensure a given level of stability, reliability and performance. In certain application domains, all software, hardware, firmware and the tools to create each of them, such as compilers, have to be qualified. For example, in the US, FAA DO-178B is used as a qualification guideline for software for airborne systems. To be included on a US built aircraft, software developers must publish a plan that addresses essentially all phases and aspects of software development and maintenance. After the plan has been accepted, specific procedures must be written to implement the plan. Finally, the developer must create an audit trail to prove that the plan has been complied with [43, 14]. Guidelines such as DO-178B exist for many safety-critical domains.

If you're working in an environment that requires hardware and software qualification, it seems appropriate that you would want your formal methods tool or environment to be at least as trustworthy [2]. In fact, DO-178B requires that tools that automate a software task typically done by humans must be qualified. If a tool has not been qualified by its vendor, the user of the tool is responsible for qualifying it. Selecting a previously qualified tool, or one with extensive, accurate documentation, will make this process much less expensive.

A relatively new possibility in the area of tool selection is the translation of a formal specification from one notation to another, allowing use of the most appropriate tool/notation for the problem or the aspect of the problem that is currently under investigation [30]. The technical problem with this is that the translation or the translation tool needs to formally verified. The management problem is that there are relatively few people competent to help with the matching of problem aspect to formal approach.

3.9 Formal Methods Must Complement Other Techniques in Use

To be successful, formal methods need to be integrated into existing processes and support, and be supported by, other design notations and artifacts. Formal methods have been used successfully in combination with data flow diagrams, entity-relationship diagrams and various object modeling forms. The participants stated that the diagrams were useful for identifying system boundaries and providing a starting point when identifying interface relationships. There is ongoing work in formalizing UML and object oriented modeling techniques [9]. Andrew Butterfield, who has worked on a number of formal methods applications, says [10]

> "Do not rely on one model alone. Products of sufficient complexity give rise to different views. Checking for cross consistency will usually identify errors in understanding the requirements."

Good advice whether or not one of the models is a formal method.

Many formal methods practitioners feel that the output of the formal methods tool alone was not sufficient to communicate with either other developers or the customer [36, 47]. Since a formal methods specification does not provide an overview of the system [21], it is necessary to provide natural language expansions and explanations along with the formal methods product, particularly in the non-functional areas of discussion. A particularly bothersome aspect of this arises when your customer has to report on your project within her organization: in some cases [21], the customers had difficulty communicating about their system within their own organization, due to the use of formal notation. If your customer can't explain your project status to her boss, your program is in trouble.

In one of the most interesting developments, Heitmeyer has used domain specific front ends on simulators to allow validation of specifications by domain experts, combining the advantages of prototyping and formality [24]. The IBM team that developed the rehearsal scheduler, also developed a documentation style that embedded user interface information into the specification [45].

3.10 Estimating the Cost of Formal Methods

There is little or no history available for the cost and schedule impact of using formal methods. What history is available is of low value to most organizations due to differing processes, application domains, changes in tool suites, differing levels of in-house expertise, etc. The normal view of costing on formal methods projects is summed up by Koob [34] discussing the results of several short pilot programs using a formal methods framework called VSE-Tool:

> "Formal development, even using VSE, takes considerably more effort. The result might be a better product but it might also be too late and significantly more expensive than conventionally developed products. The solution to this still has to be worked out."

That said, one of the case studies used parallel development teams on the same task. The cost distribution was slightly different, but the two teams finished in nearly the same amount of time and spent nearly the same amount of money. And IBM's development of CICS actually resulted in an estimated 9% savings in development costs [8]. In a case where an Air Traffic Control (ATC) system was being built, the percent of engineer time spent in each phase was within 4% of the COCOMO prediction [21], thus highlighting that formal method use can result in schedules comparable to traditional development schedules. In the development of power plant control software, significant cost savings were achieved in comparison with the estimated cost of doing a traditional development [11]. All of these cases were developments where the teams had software processes in place and were already successful at working within a documentation structure.

An additional factor to consider is that there might be long term cost benefits not captured by current metrics. On the ATC system, although the number of defects found during system testing was similar, the number of post-delivery problems found was lower for the portions of the system that had been subjected to formal methods [22]. Since both types of code passed system test with the same number of defects, this implies that the code developed using the formal methods more closely matched the end user's expectations for characteristics that weren't documented by the requirements specification. Strengthening this argument, an IBM representative estimated that there is a 40% decrease in post-delivery failures on their software developed using formal methods when compared to their software developed using other methods [44]. Since the goal of all documentation and design is to enable us to meet or exceed customer expectations, this might be an extremely significant result.

Alternately, there are long term costs associated with the use of formal methods. For example, for formally specified and proved systems, the cost of change is may be large when compared to a traditionally specified system. If the investment has been made to formally specify and/or prove a system, to preserve formality, any change has to be inserted with the same level of formality. Furthermore, if the change affects interface properties of the module, the proofs that depend on those have to be reproven and little mention is made of this problem in the literature, except to note that it exists [37]. If the cost is excessive, this will result in fewer change proposals and less profit made on upgrades.

However, this may be a perceived problem, rather than a real problem: the life cycle cost may actually be less since the cost of maintaining an undocumented code base is uncertain. Parnas refers to a common software phenomena he calls "ignorant surgery", in which changes are made to a software baseline without deep understanding of the purpose and underlying design of the code base [38]. As a result, "repairs" and "enhancements" may result in the loss of key features or, possibly worse, an unexpected change in their behavior, resuling in large financial losses due to unintended and adverse effects on customers operations. Companies could avoid that risk by investing in rigorous and unambiguous specification - through use of formal methods. It is possible that the actual cost of performing maintenance could drop.

Another long term concern/cost that may be more applicable to formal methods than to other engineering approaches is that if tools were used in the development, the tools must be maintained in order to use the previous work as a starting point for changes. Since the formal methods tool market has hardly been established, much less wrung out, we cannot anticipate that the company that provided our tool will be around in 10 years, much less issuing updates on it for new hardware and software platforms. This puts the responsibility on the using organization to preserve the tool and its environment.

4 Conclusions

Use of formal methods in industry is still in the investigation stage and that fact must be recognized by any manager using them. The tools are not mature and a critical mass of users has not been created, much less an audience of informed consumers. As a result, education and resource management for both tools and people must have relatively larger allocations than in a normal development.

Formal methods appear to be most useful in the specification of systems, either during development or when re-specifying during a reverse engineering effort. The formal methods use should be deferred until there is a firm, intuitive understanding of the product and the user interface. The methods are designed to root out ambiguity, so they don't do well modeling "should" or "might" statements. Experts in the use of formal methods are essential on any effort; learning by doing is effective, but only when guidance is ultimately available. If experts aren't available, your people will get frustrated and your budget will get burned.

Formal methods are a tool to be used in an existing software process. If the organizational or project culture doesn't have a disciplined approach to software development, it is unlikely that formal methods will be successful.

The types of systems where formal methods appear to have the most success are in safety critical applications, such as large scale power management or flight and mission control systems. It is suspected that organizations that create the software for these tasks have the necessary supporting culture in place and have a requirement to prove the reliability of their products, a constraint that few other development teams labor under.

Although much of this paper has been dedicated to warnings about the difficulties of using formal methods, many factors are making them more attractive: tools are getting more robust, the community is working toward making their output more accessible, governments and standards bodies are recognizing the value of formal methods, and systems are getting unimaginably complex.

Finally, one of the studies [44] noted that post-delivery failures were decreased on a formal methods program. Post-delivery failures are those that are not detected during unit or system test, so they might be problems in areas that were unspecified or were thought to be of little concern. This a common problem when developing a system for a new purpose; neither the developer or the customer can visualize all the consequences of the use of the new system, so sometimes the wrong things are emphasized or ignored. If formal methods can be shown to help stretch the imaginations of the users and developers during analysis, this might be a huge step forward for software development.

References

1. Glenn Ammons, Rastislav Bodik, and James R Larus. Mining specifications. *ACM Sigplan Notices*, 37(1):4–16, 2002.
2. Mark R. Blackburn and Robert D. Busser. Requirements for industrial-strength formal methods tools. In *Workshop on Industrial Strength Formal Specification Techniques*, pages 137–8, Boca Raton, Fl., 1998. IEEE.
3. J. P. Bowen. Formal methods in safety-critical standards. In *1993 Software Engineering Standards Symposium*, pages 168–177. IEEE Computer Society Press, 1993.
4. J. P. Bowen. Ten commandments of formal methods. *IEEE Computer*, 28(4):56–63, 1995.
5. Jonathan Bowen and Victoria Stavridou. The industrial take-up of formal methods in safety critical and other areas: a perspective. In *FME'93: Industrial Strength Formla Methods*, volume First International Symposium of Formal Methods Europe Proceedings, pages 183–195. Springer-Verlag, 1993.
6. Jonathan Bowen and Victoria Stavridou. Safety-critical systems, formal methods and standards. *Software Engineering Journal*, 8:189–209, 1993.
7. J.P. Bowen and M.G. Hinchey. The use of industrial-strength formal methods. In *Twenty-First Annual International Computer Software and Applications Conference*, pages 332–7, Washington, DC, USA, 1997. IEEE Comput. Soc.
8. J.P Bowen and M. G. Hinchley. Seven more myths of formal methods. *IEEE Software*, 12(4):34–41, 1995.
9. Jean-Michel Bruel. Integrating formal and informal specification techniques. why? how? In *Proceedings of the 2nd IEEE Workshop on Industrial-Strength Formal Specification Techniques (WIFT'98)*, pages 50–57, Boca Raton, Florida, 1999. IEEE Computer Press.
10. A.. Butterfield. Introducing formal methods to existing processes. In *IEE Colloquium on Industrial Use of Formal Methods*, London, UK, 1997. IEE.
11. E Ciapessoni, E. Crivelli, and P Mirandola. From formal models to formally based methods: an industrial experience. *ACM Transactions on Software Engineering and Methodology*, 8(1):79–113, 1999.

12. G. Cleland and D. MacKenzie. Inhibiting factors, market structure and the industrial uptake of formal methods. In *Workshop on Industrial-Strength Formal Specification Techniques*, pages 46–60, Boca Raton, FL, USA, 1995. IEEE Comput. Soc. Press.
13. Tim Clement. Re dust expert. Private correspondence, 2002.
14. Software Productivity Consortium. Rtca do-178b, 2002.
15. Dan Craigen and Susan Gerhart. Formal methods reality check: Industrial usage. *IEEE Transactions on Software Engineering*, 21(2):90–98, 1995.
16. Dan Craigen, Susan Gerhart, and T. Ralston. An international survey of industrial applications of formal methods. Technical Report NIST GCR 93/626, US Dept of Commerce, 1993.
17. J. Dick and E. Woods. Lessons learned from rigorous system software development. *Information and Software Technology*, 39(8):551–60, 1997.
18. S. Easterbrook, R. Lutz, R. Covington, J. Kelly, Y. Ampo, and D. Hamilton. Experiences using lightweight formal methods for requirements modeling. *IEEE Transactions on Software Engineering*, 24(1):4–14, 1998.
19. K. Finney and N. Fenton. Evaluating the effectiveness of z: the claims made about cics and where we go from here. *Journal of Systems and Software*, 35(3):209–16, 1996.
20. P. Garbett, J.P. kes, M. Shackleton, and S Anderson. Secure synthesis of code: a process improvement experiment. In J.M. Wing, J. Woodcock, and J. Davies, editors, *FM'99 - World Congress on Formal Methods in the Development of Computing Systems*, volume II, pages 1816–1835, Toulouse, France, 1999. Springer-Verlag.
21. Anthony Hall. Using formal methods to develop an atc information system. *IEEE Software*, 13(2):66–76, 1996.
22. Anthony Hall. What does industry need from formal specification techniques? In *Second IEEE Workshop on Industrial Strength Formal Specification Techniques*, pages 2–7, Los Alamitos, Cal, 1999. IEEE.
23. Anthony Hall and Shari Lawrence Pleeger. Some metrics from a formal development. In *IEE Colloquium on 'Practical Application of Formal Methods'*, volume Digest No.1995/109, pages 6/1–4, London, UK, 1995. IEE.
24. C. Heitmeyer. On the need for practical formal methods. In A.P. Ravn and H. Rischel, editors, *Formal Techniques in Real-Time and Fault-Tolerant Systems*, FTRTFT'98, pages 18–26, Lygby, Denmark, 1998. Springer-Verlag.
25. C. Michael Holloway and Ricky Butler. Impediments to the industrial use of formal methods. *IEEE Computer*, 29(4):25–26, 1996.
26. Manuel J. Fernandez Iglesias, Fransisco J. Gonzalez-Castano, Jose M. Pousada Carballo, Martin Llamas Nistal, and Alberto Romero Feijoo. From complex specifications to a working prototype. a protocol engineering study. In J.N. Oliveira and P. Zave, editors, *FME 2001*, volume LNCS 2021, pages 436–448. Springer-Verlag, 2001.
27. Michael Jackson. Formal methods and traditional engineering. *Journal of Systems and Software*, 40:191–194, 1998.
28. L.J. Jagadeesan, P. Godefroid, J. Kelly, S. Miller, and Frank Weil. Transferring formal methods technology to industry. In *Second IEEE Workshop on Industrial Strength Formal Specification Techniques*, pages 128–131. IEEE, 1998.
29. Sara Jones, David Till, and Ann M. Wrightson. Formal methods and requirements engineering: Challenges and synergies. *Journal of Systems and Software*, 40(3):263–73, 1998.

30. Shmuel Katz. Faithful translations among models and specifications. In J.N. Oliveira and P. Zave, editors, *FME 2001*, volume LNCS 2021, pages 419–434. Verlag-Springer, 2001.
31. Richard Kemmerer. Integrating formal methods into the development process. *IEEE Software*, 7(5):37–50, 1990.
32. Steve King, Jonathan Hammond, Robd Chapman, and Andy Pryor. Is proof more cost-effective than testing? *IEEE Transactions on Software Engineering*, 26(8):675–685, 2000.
33. John Knight, Colleen DeJong, Matthew Gibble, and Luis Nakan. Why are formal methods not used more widely? In *Langley Formal Methods Workshop*. NASA, 1997.
34. F. Koob, M. Ullmann, and S. Wittmann. Industrial usage of formal development methods-the vse-tool applied in pilot projects. In *COMPASS '96. Proceedings of the Eleventh Annual Conference on Computer Assurance Systems Integrity. Software Safety. Process Security*, pages 56–64, Gaithersburg, MD, 1996. IEEE.
35. Peter Gorm Larsen. Applying formal specification in industry. *IEEE Software*, 13(3):48–56, 1996.
36. Baudouin Le Charlier and Pierre Flener. Specifications are necessarily informal or: Some more myths of formal methods. *Journal of Systems and Software*, (40):275–296, 1998.
37. J. McDermid, A. Galloway, S. Burton, J. Clark, I. Toyn, N. Tracey, and S. Valentine. Towards industrially applicable formal methods: Three small steps, and one giant leap. In J. Staples, M.G. Hinchey, and S. Liu, editors, *Conference on Formal Engineering Methods*, pages 76–88, Brisbane, Qld., Australia, 1998. IEEE Comput. Soc.
38. David Parnas. Software aging. In *Proceedings of the 16th International Conference on Software Engineering*, pages 279–287, Sorrento, Italy, 1994. IEEE Press.
39. M. C. Paulk, B. Curtis, E. Averill, J. Bamberger, T. Kasse, M. Konrad, J. Perdue, C. Wober, and J. Withey. Capability maturity model for software. Technical Report CMU/SEI-91-TR-24 ADA240603, Software Engineering Institute, 1991.
40. J.S. Pedersen. Introduction to formal methods and experiences from the lacos and orsted projects. In *IEE Colloquium on Industrial Use of Formal Methods*, volume Digest No: 1977/171, pages 2/1–2/3, London, UK, 1997.
41. Jakob Lyng Petersen. Automatic verification of railway interlocking systems: a case study. In *FMSP 98*, pages 1–6, Clearwater, Fl, USA, 1998. ACM.
42. A. Puccetti. Improving the software evolution process using mixed specification techniques. Technical Report 27492 ESSI - ISEPUMS, Esprit, 2000.
43. G. Romanski. The challenges of software certification. *CrossTalk*, Sep 2001 2001. Available at Software Technology Support Center website:.
44. C. Snook and R. Harrison. Practitioners' views on the use of formal methods: an industrial survey by structured interview. *Information and Software Technology*, 43(4):275–83, 2001.
45. Allen M Stavely. Integrating Z and cleanroom. In *Proceedings of the Fifth Annual Langley Formal Methods Workshop*, Langley, Va, 2000. NASA.
46. Frank Weil. Wift '98 working group report: Incorporating formal methods onto industrial process. In *Workshop on Industrial Strength Formal Methods '98*, pages 134-6, Boca Raton, Fla, USA, 1998. IEEE Computer Society.
47. R. Wieringa and E Dubois. Integrating semi-formal and formal software specification techniques. *Information Systems*, 23(3-4):159–78, 1998.

48. A. Wong and M. Chechik. Formal modeling in a commercial setting: a case study. In J.M. Wing, J. Woodcock, and J. Davies, editors, *FM'99 - World Congress on Formal Methods in the Development of Computing Systems.*, volume I of *Lecture Notes in Computer Science*, pages 590–607, Toulouse, France, 1999. Springer-Verlag.

Verifying Emulation of Legacy Mission Computer Systems

Colin J. Fidge

School of Information Technology and Electrical Engineering,
The University of Queensland, Australia.

Abstract. Processor obsolescence is a serious maintenance problem for long-lived embedded control systems. A practical solution is to interpose an emulator program between the 'legacy' software and a replacement processor, so that the old code can be reused on the new machine. Unfortunately, no verification techniques exist for proving that the resulting system preserves the original system's functional and timing behaviour. A particular challenge is that processor emulation mixes both legacy assembly code and new high-level language software patches. Nevertheless, we show that a formalism previously used for analysing program compilation, coupled with an understanding of the legacy software architecture, can be used to verify key aspects of an emulated control system.

1 Introduction

Military aircraft, and other safety and mission-critical systems, contain numerous embedded microcomputers. Aircraft remain in service for decades, while computer processors have a lifecycle measured in mere years. Processor obsolescence has therefore become a major technical [8] and economic [7] problem for long-lived embedded control systems.

Maintaining computer processors which are no longer mass produced is prohibitively expensive, and rewriting the original 'legacy' computer software for a modern processor can be unacceptably costly as well. Therefore, a number of ways have been proposed for replacing obsolete processors with new ones, while allowing legacy program code to be reused [8]. In particular, an approach currently being trialled for military Mission Computer Systems is to interpose a 'processor emulation' program between the legacy code and a new computer processor—the emulator interprets the legacy code on the new machine [24].

Trials of this technology to date have been highly successful [9]. Nevertheless, safety and mission-critical systems, where human life and national security are at stake, demand the strongest possible guarantees of correctness. In the field of computer software, such guarantees can be achieved via mathematically-based proofs. Unfortunately, existing proof methods do not allow for the mixture of old and new programming language code found in an emulated system.

Therefore, this paper aims to show how real-time program proof theories [16, 18, 30], especially those previously used for verifying compiler correctness [20, 29, 26], can be used to verify that an emulated Mission Computer Operational Flight

Program provides a behaviour 'equivalent' to that of the legacy system. This is done by modelling and analysing troubling aspects of the emulated system, guided by the structure of the legacy system's software architecture.

2 Legacy Mission Computer System Software

To illustrate important characteristics of legacy software, this section introduces an Operational Flight Program fragment. In particular, such programs are usually embedded within a larger system, so they interact directly with input and output devices; they are required to respond to multiple external inputs, so they involve concurrency; they must react in a timely manner, so they have imposed real-time constraints; and they have limited computing resources at their disposal, so there is no clear separation between 'system' and 'application' code.

To satisfy all these needs, Operational Flight Programs are designed using a well-understood and trusted architecture [12, 5], which consists of several *tasks*, to perform the necessary functions, and an *executive*, to control allocation of computing resources to tasks, especially processor time. The executive does this by following a predetermined task *schedule*.

For instance, Fig. 1 shows a possible schedule for an Operational Flight Program, as crafted by the programmer of the legacy system. It includes a 'Rate' task, which displays the aircraft's rate of ascent using readings from the altimeter. This task is required to be executed frequently, so it has been given a period of 50 milliseconds. There is also a 'Log' task, which writes data to a mission log. This task is less important and is executed only every 100 milliseconds. There are also many other tasks not shown here—actual Operational Flight Programs comprise dozens of tasks [12]. The schedule also contains shaded boxes which represent the overheads of executing the Mission Computer Executive, in between individual task invocations [12, Fig. 4-6]. The overall schedule is cyclic and is constructed as a sequence of 'frames', each of which is 50 milliseconds wide. In this case a complete 'major cycle' consists of two frames, after which the whole pattern repeats indefinitely. The idle time at the end of frames is a typical consequence of the tasks not fitting into the frames exactly.

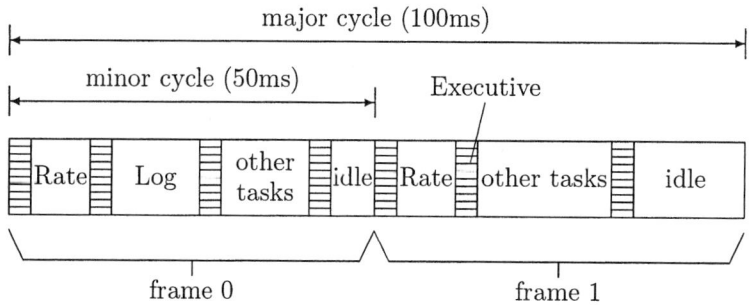

Fig. 1. Schedule for the example Operational Flight Program.

Label	Op.	Args.	Comment
TICK	LOAD	A, 500_{dir}	get current mode
	BRNE	OVERRUN	ensure current mode is 0 ('Exec')
	LOAD	A, 501_{dir}	get current frame number
	ADD	A, 1_{imm}	increment frame number
	MOD	A, 2_{imm}	2 minor cycles per major cycle
	STORE	A, 501_{dir}	save updated frame number
	RTRN		return to point of interruption
OVERRUN	...		error recovery action for task overrun

Fig. 2. Legacy assembly code for the Executive's timer interrupt handler.

To implement such a schedule, a 'timer-driven' executive [19] consists a loop which (a) waits for a periodic timer interrupt to occur, (b) increments a frame counter, and (c) performs one or more tasks, depending on the frame number, as per the schedule's allocation of tasks to frames [2]. Here we assume that timer interrupts occur with a frequency of 20 hertz on the legacy processor, thus corresponding with the 50 millisecond-wide frames in our schedule.

The interrupt handling component of a typical timer-driven Mission Computer Executive is shown in Fig. 2. When a timer interrupt occurs, we assume that control is transferred to label TICK. As an illustrative assembly language, we have used a two-address instruction set for a simple processor with eight general-purpose registers, A to H, and a comparison register which holds the results of explicit CMPR instructions, or the difference between the last register update and zero [14, Ch. 7]. Direct and immediate addressing modes for arguments are indicated by subscripts.

The current program 'mode' is maintained by the Executive in memory location 500. Let a value of 0 mean that the system is in 'Exec' mode, and 1 mean that the system is in 'Tasks' mode. The interrupt handler first checks that the current mode is 'Exec'. If this is *not* the case when a timer interrupt occurs then the tasks have overrun the current frame, and an appropriate error recovery action must be performed. (Unfortunately, it is difficult to know which task was responsible for the problem—the task that was executing when the interrupt occurred may have been delayed by the overrun of an earlier task.) Otherwise, the interrupt handler merely increments the frame number, which is stored at location 501. In this case it uses modulo 2 arithmetic, reflecting the fact that there are two minor cycles in each major one.

The Mission Computer Executive's main program is shown in Fig. 3. It is a classic 'cyclic executive' design [19] which interleaves executive functions with those of its subordinate tasks.

The executive first disables interrupts while data memory areas for itself and its tasks are initialised. The executive stores the mode, and the current and next frame numbers, in locations 500 to 502. Following this, data for the various tasks is initialised, including the Rate task's default altitude in location 600. (To avoid

Label	Op.	Args.	Comment
	DSBL		disable interrupts while initialising
	LOAD	A, 0_{imm}	initialise Executive's data
	STORE	A, 500_{dir}	set current mode to 0 ('Exec')
	STORE	A, 501_{dir}	set current frame number to 0
	LOAD	A, 1_{imm}	
	STORE	A, 502_{dir}	set next frame number to 1
	LOAD	A, 0_{imm}	initialise Rate task's data
	STORE	A, 600_{dir}	set initial altitude to 0
	...		initialise Log task's data
	...		initialise other tasks' data
	ENBL		enable timer interrupts after initialising
NEWFRM	LOAD	A, 0_{imm}	new frame starts here
	STORE	A, 500_{dir}	set current mode to 0 ('Exec')
	LOAD	B, 502_{dir}	get next frame number
WAIT	LOAD	A, 501_{dir}	get current frame number
	CMPR	A, B	compare current and next
	BRNE	WAIT	wait until current equals next
	ADD	B, 1_{imm}	increment next frame number
	MOD	B, 2_{imm}	2 minor cycles per major cycle
	STORE	B, 502_{dir}	save next frame number
	LOAD	A, 1_{imm}	tasks begin here
	STORE	A, 500_{dir}	set current mode to 1 ('Tasks')
	... (see Fig. 4)		code for Rate task, frames 0 and 1
	LOAD	A, 501_{dir}	get current frame number
	BRNE	OTHERS1	choose frame 0 or frame 1 tasks
	...		code for Log task, frame 0
	...		code for other frame 0 tasks
	BR	NEWFRM	end of frame 0
OTHERS1	...		code for other frame 1 tasks
	BR	NEWFRM	end of frame 1

Fig. 3. Legacy assembly code for the Mission Computer Executive.

conflicts, data memory usage is partitioned so that the Executive stores its data at 5XX locations, whereas the Rate task uses 6XX locations, and so on.)

The remaining code, from label NEWFRM onwards, represents a single frame, and is performed in each minor cycle. Firstly, the executive sets the current program mode to 'Exec' and then waits for the current frame counter to be incremented by the interrupt handler, signalling the start of the frame. It does this by iterating at label WAIT until the current frame number equals the next frame number—recall that the current frame number is incremented by the interrupt handler in Fig. 2. Once this occurs the executive increments the next frame number, and sets the program mode to 'Tasks'. The code for each task then follows. Since the Rate task occurs in every frame it is performed unconditionally. The

Log task and other tasks are preceded by a check to see if they are meant to occur in the current frame or not, as per the schedule in Fig. 1.

Although common, control programs like that in Fig. 3 have several disadvantages [23]. Such programs are notoriously *obscure*, because they arbitrarily mix system and application code fragments, regardless of their function. Also such programs are *fragile* with respect to changes that affect the execution times of the tasks or the executive—changing one task may cause another to overrun the frame.

We now turn our attention to the individual tasks. In an embedded system each task typically (a) reads inputs, (b) processes data, and (c) sends outputs. For instance, the legacy code for the Rate task, which displays the aircraft's rate of ascent, is shown in Fig. 4. It first fetches the altitude saved during its previous invocation from memory location 600. The next six instructions then read the altitude from the hardware altimeter through an Analog-to-Digital Converter. We assume the existence of a set of memory-mapped input/output ports, denoted P to W, to interface with hardware devices. The task writes '1' to the ADC's control register, via output port P, to start the conversion. It must then wait at least 30 microseconds for the conversion to be completed. Assuming an instruction execution time of 5 microseconds, the task does this by busy-waiting at label ADCDELAY (consuming 7 instruction cycles, including the initial LOAD). The task then reads the new altitude from the ADC's data register, via input port Q, and saves it.

The next two instructions use the previous and current altitude readings to calculate the ascent rate. The constant in the MULT instruction reflects the fact that the executive invokes this task at a frequency of 20 hertz. Finally, the two instructions at label DISPLAY send the result to the appropriate cockpit instrument via a Digital-to-Analog Converter (DAC) attached to ports R and S.

Label	Op.	Args.	Comment
	LOAD	A, 600_{dir}	get previous altitude
	LOAD	C, 1_{imm}	
READALT	OUT	C, P	start ADC conversion
	LOAD	B, 3_{imm}	initialise busy-wait counter
ADCDELAY	SUB	B, 1_{imm}	decrement busy-wait counter
	BRGT	ADCDELAY	iterate while counter exceeds zero
	IN	B, Q	read new altitude (in feet) from ADC
SAVEALT	STORE	B, 600_{dir}	save new altitude
	SUB	B, A	compute change in altitude (in feet)
	MULT	B, 20_{imm}	convert difference to feet per second
DISPLAY	OUT	B, S	load DAC data register with ascent rate
	OUT	C, R	start DAC conversion

Fig. 4. Legacy assembly code for the Rate task.

3 Processor Emulation

To illustrate the features of processor emulation which present a challenge for formal verification, this section shows how the Operational Flight Program described above may be emulated in a new hardware environment. In particular, emulated systems contain proprietary software components, whose correctness cannot be verified without the manufacturer's cooperation; they mix execution of assembly code and high-level language statements, and thus require a formalism that models both simultaneously; and although they typically preserve the legacy system's gross behaviour, they nonetheless introduce small changes, so a way of showing that such differences are unimportant is needed.

Consider the situation where the above program's obsolete processor must be replaced with a modern one executing a different instruction set. Accommodating this, without entirely rewriting the legacy code, involves introducing an emulator program to interpret the code from Figs. 2 to 4 on the new processor. Processor emulators are available as commercial, off-the-shelf products [24]. They are written for specific legacy instruction sets and execute on a standard Real-Time Operating System on a modern processor.

However, despite the desire to execute the legacy code without change, some alterations to its behaviour are inevitable if it is to work correctly in a new environment. To support this, emulator software packages allow programmers to associate software patches with particular instruction memory locations or input/output ports [34]. When the emulated program reaches such a point, the emulator transfers control to a corresponding subroutine written in the emulator's native high-level programming language, which uses operations provided by the emulation package to access the new hardware architecture, or modify the state of the *emulated* legacy processor.

Here, for instance, we assume that the outmoded altimeter and Analog-to-Digital Converter are replaced as part of the hardware upgrade. This invalidates the five instructions starting at label READALT in Fig. 4 which are all specific to the original altimeter and ADC. We assume the new ADC provides a 'busy' signal (with a known worst-case delay), as a more robust alternative to busy-waiting for the conversion to be completed [33], and further assume that the new altimeter is calibrated in metres, rather than feet.

To account for this, the parameterless C++ subroutine in Fig. 5 uses emulator operations to interface with the new altimeter and ADC. It starts the data conversion by writing to the new ADC's control register at output port T. It then waits while the ADC's busy signal at input port V equals 1 [22, p. 400]. Following this it reads the result from the ADC's data register via input port U. Since the new altitude is in metres, rather than feet as expected by the legacy code, this value is converted to the appropriate units. The altitude is then stored in (emulated) register B. The final step is to update the (emulated) processor's instruction counter, so that control bypasses the legacy instructions for accessing the ADC, and returns to label SAVEALT rather than READALT.

The need to introduce the software patch above is obvious. More worrying are necessary changes that may be overlooked when installing an emulator. For

```
void ReadAlt()      // patch linked to assembly label READALT
{ int Altitude, Busy;
    WriteIOPort(T, 1);              // start ADC conversion
    do { Busy = ReadIOPort(V);      // wait while ADC busy
        } while Busy == 1;
    Altitude = ReadIOPort(U);       // read ADC data
    Altitude = Altitude * 3.28;     // convert metres to feet
    WriteReg(B, Altitude);          // store altitude in register B
    UpdateIC(SAVEALT);              // bypass legacy ADC code
    return;
}
```

Fig. 5. New high-level language subroutine to read altimeter data.

```
void Display()    // patch linked to assembly label DISPLAY
{ int AscentRate;
    ReadReg(B, AscentRate);             // get skewed ascent rate
    AscentRate = AscentRate * 1.25;     // compensate for higher frame rate
    WriteReg(B, AscentRate);            // put corrected ascent rate
    return;
}
```

Fig. 6. New high-level language subroutine to correct displayed ascent rate.

instance, assume now that the new processor generates timer interrupts at a frequency of 25 hertz, rather than the legacy processor's 20 hertz. Because emulators can interpret instructions much faster than they could be executed on the old processor [24], the legacy program may still execute 'correctly' in this situation, in the sense that each task still completes all of its necessary computations within each frame. Indeed, the emulated system could be extensively tested without any problems being detected.

However, consider the purpose of the MULT instruction in Fig. 4. The legacy system's programmer used constant '20' in this instruction on the assumption that the Rate task is performed 20 times per second—any change to this frequency also requires the corresponding arithmetic to be updated. If this is not done in the situation described above, the displayed ascent rate will be inaccurate by 25%. Thus legacy code which is timing-sensitive, but not recognised as such, presents a significant danger. (To overcome this some emulation packages provide a 'speed matching' option [24], even though its use wastes available processor time.)

In this case a solution is to add another patch, associated with label DISPLAY, as shown in Fig. 6. (New subroutines are executed *before* the instruction at the corresponding label [34], so the patch is called between the MULT and OUT instructions.) The new code simply increases the calculated ascent rate by 25% to correct the distortion caused by the change in the interrupt frequency.

4 Verifying Emulated Mission Computer Software

Our technical challenge, therefore, is to prove that the legacy code, as emulated on the replacement processor, has the 'same' functional and timing behaviour as it did when executed on the original processor. In fact, we already know that this equivalence will *not* be exact. The emulator will interpret legacy instructions faster than the original processor [24], and the new code contains explicit patches to accommodate hardware changes. Thus the 'equivalence' to be proven between the two systems is an approximate one that accepts harmless differences.

Unfortunately, fully verifying the equivalence of the two systems is impossible with contemporary proof technology. The new system interposes both a proprietary processor emulator and a commercial Real-Time Operating System between the legacy code and the new processor. Verifying the correctness of these large-scale software components is well beyond the capabilities of current formalisms. As a compromise, we therefore *assume* that the manufacturer of the emulation package can provide evidence that the emulator has passed the original test suite for the legacy processor's instruction set, as is usually required in safety-critical applications [24]. We also *assume* that the underlying Real-Time Operating System is one intended for safety-critical applications and that its manufacturer can thus provide evidence that the RTOS's development met relevant standards [3]. Although neither of these requirements mean that the software has been verified correct in a formal sense, they give us sufficient confidence in the integrity of these system components that we need not attempt to verify them ourselves, and can instead concentrate on comparing the two versions of the Operational Flight Program.

Assuming that the emulator interprets legacy instructions correctly, our goal therefore is to prove an (approximate) equivalence between the legacy assembly code, and the legacy code augmented with high-level language patches. (Interestingly, we may also usually assume that the legacy code has a 'clean' in-service history—any serious problems with it will already have been detected and eliminated—so we do not need to prove the legacy code's 'correctness', merely our ability to duplicate its behaviour.) The closest analogy to this situation occurs in formalisms for modelling program compilation [29, 26, 32, 28] or decompilation [6], where relationships between high and assembly-level programs are proven. Below we build on a particular formalism for reasoning about compilation of real-time programs [20, 21, 13] since we need the ability to analyse time-sensitive code.

4.1 A Modelling Language

To perform the required proof we must first define its semantic basis. Below we use a partial-correctness semantics. Let the *weakest liberal precondition* of statement S with respect to postcondition R, denoted 'wlp.$S.R$', be a predicate characterising those initial states from which statement S will either terminate and achieve R [10, p. 21], will execute forever [10, p. 21], or cannot execute (is *infeasible*) [27, §5].

Table 1. Weakest liberal precondition semantics for basic modelling language statements. Let P, Q and R be predicates on state variables, where Q may include primed variables; v be a state variable, or list of variables; T be a type, or list of types; I be an indexing set; and S be a statement in our modelling language.

Statement S	Semantics wlp.$S.R$
skip	R
$\{P\}$	$P \Rightarrow R$
$v\colon[Q]$	$\forall v' \bullet (Q \Rightarrow R[v'/v])$
$S_1\,;\,S_2$	wlp.S_1.(wlp.$S_2.R$)
$\sqcap\, i:I \bullet S_i$	$\bigwedge_{i \in I}$ wlp.$S_i.R$
var $v:T \bullet S$	$\bigwedge_{v \in T}$ wlp.$S.R$, provided v is not free in R

Weakest liberal preconditions differ from the more well-known weakest preconditions in that the former cannot distinguish whether a statement terminates or not. Nevertheless, we prefer to use weakest liberal preconditions here because they have a simple conjunctive semantics for iteration, rather than the fixed-point definition needed for weakest preconditions [11, p. 185]. Their use can be justified provided that we are confident our partial-correctness proofs also imply total correctness. It is well known that total and partial-correctness proofs are the same for deterministic statements [1, p. 60]. In fact, it is sufficient for the statements of interest to be both *feasible* [17, p. 18] and *termination-determinate* [17, p. 110] only. The latter property means that, for any given initial state, the statement does not choose *nondeterministically* between a terminating behaviour and an endless computation.

Both of these properties hold for the program fragments in Figs. 4 to 6. The only potentially nonterminating statements are the loops in Figs. 4 and 5, neither of which can nondeterministically choose to terminate or not from a given state. (Importantly, we include 'time' in our state space below—termination of the loop in Fig. 5 depends on the passage of time.) Similarly, the only potentially infeasible statements in Figs. 4 to 6 are those that may attempt out-of-bounds memory accesses, but these can be considered safe here because the addresses are all constants. (Strictly speaking, the various arithmetic operations may be infeasible if they could cause register overflows, but we do not attempt to model machine-specific arithmetic in this short paper.)

A basic modelling language sufficient for this case study is shown in Table 1. The '**skip**' primitive does nothing other than terminate. To achieve postcondition R it must be started in a state where R already holds [11, p. 136]. The *assertion* '$\{P\}$' is used to state that predicate P is expected to hold; if P is not true then the statement does not terminate. Thus, postcondition R can be achieved provided that P held initially [17, p. 17].

The *specification statement*, '$v\colon[Q]$', achieves postcondition Q by changing those variables in list v only [25, §23.3.2]. Predicate Q can relate initial values, which appear undecorated as 'v', to final values, denoted by a prime 'v''.

To achieve postcondition R, R must be true for any values of the post-state variables v' that satisfy Q. Since predicate R refers to post-state variables in this definition, they must be primed for consistency with predicate Q's naming convention. Let $E[t/v]$ denote substitution of term(s) t for variable(s) v in expression E [25, §A.2.1].

The next two operators in Table 1 construct compound statements. Sequential composition 'S_1 ; S_2' is simply the semantics of the two statements, one after the other [11, p. 137]. The nondeterministic choice operator '$\sqcap$' denotes an arbitrary choice between statements, here over an arbitrary indexing set I. To achieve postcondition R, it must be the case that R is achieved by every alternative [17, p. 20].

Finally, the variable declaration '**var**' allows statement S's state space to be extended with a fresh variable v of type T. To achieve postcondition R, statement S must make R true for any initial value of v (since v is uninitialised). The proviso reminds us that 'v' must be a previously-unused name [25, §23.3.4].

4.2 Legacy Instruction Semantics

Using this modelling language, Table 2 defines the meaning of assembly instructions as executed on the legacy processor. This is done by describing the effect of

Table 2. Semantics of legacy assembly code instructions. Let S be a (compound) statement in our assembly language that does not contain branch instructions or labels that are the targets of branch instructions; r be a register; ℓ be a label; z be an integer (representable on the legacy processor); c be the comparison register; m be the data memory array; a be an address (in the range of m); X be a device-dependent external input value; and τ be the current time.

Instruction S	Equivalent modelling language statement
LOAD r, z_{imm}	$r, c, \tau : [r' = z \wedge c' = z \wedge \tau' = \tau + 5\mu s]$
LOAD r, a_{dir}	$r, c, \tau : [r' = m(a) \wedge c' = m(a) \wedge \tau' = \tau + 10\mu s]$
STORE r, a_{dir}	$m, \tau : [m' = m \oplus \{a \mapsto r\} \wedge \tau' = \tau + 10\mu s]$
SUB r_1, r_2	$r_1, c, \tau : [r'_1 = (r_1 - r_2) \wedge c' = (r_1 - r_2) \wedge \tau' = \tau + 5\mu s]$
SUB r, z_{imm}	$r, c, \tau : [r' = (r - z) \wedge c' = (r - z) \wedge \tau' = \tau + 5\mu s]$
MULT r, z_{imm}	$r, c, \tau : [r' = (r * z) \wedge c' = (r * z) \wedge \tau' = \tau + 10\mu s]$
'S_1 S_2'	$S_1 \, ; \, S_2$
'$\ell \ S$ BRGT ℓ'	$\sqcap \, n : \mathbb{N} \bullet ((S \, ; \tau : [c > 0 \wedge \tau' = \tau + 5\mu s])^n \, ; $ $S \, ; \tau : [c \leqslant 0 \wedge \tau' = \tau + 5\mu s])$
OUT r, P	$P^v, P^t, \tau : [P^{v'} = r \wedge \tau \leqslant P^{t'} \leqslant \tau' \wedge \tau' = \tau + 5\mu s]$
IN r, Q	$\{P^v = 1 \wedge P^t + 30\mu s \leqslant \tau\} \, ; $ $r, c, \tau : [r' = X \wedge c' = X \wedge \tau' = \tau + 5\mu s]$
OUT r, S	$S^v, S^t, \tau : [S^{v'} = r \wedge \tau \leqslant S^{t'} \leqslant \tau' \wedge \tau' = \tau + 5\mu s]$
OUT r, R	$\{r = 1\} \, ; \, R^v, R^t, \tau : [R^{v'} = S^v \wedge R^{t'} = \tau + 30\mu s \wedge \tau' = \tau + 5\mu s]$

each instruction on the legacy processor's state, which consists of registers r, data memory m, and the comparison register c. As in previous real-time formalisms [16, 18], we also explicitly model the current time by a special variable, τ.

The first group in Table 2 defines the effect of simple instructions. For instance, the 'LOAD' instruction with an immediate operand z changes the three variables r, c and τ. It sets both registers r and c equal to integer z, and adds 5 microseconds to current time τ, to account for the instruction's execution time. The other instructions follow similarly. Instructions that access memory or perform complex arithmetic are assumed to take 10 microseconds. Data memory m is represented as a function from addresses to values. In the 'STORE' definition let $m \oplus \{a \mapsto r\}$ denote function m with domain element a mapped to value r.

The next two groups in Table 2 define the behaviour of two commonly-occurring patterns of instructions. The first simply reminds us that vertically displayed sequences of assembly instructions are interpreted as being sequentially composed (provided that the sequence does not contain branches, or labels that are the targets of branch instructions, in which case sequential ordering may not be guaranteed). By giving a meaning to particular control-flow patterns in this way, we avoid the need to explicitly model the legacy processor's instruction counter [13].

The next pattern consists of a (possibly compound) statement S, labelled by ℓ, which is followed by a conditional branch 'BRGT' to ℓ. In effect this is a loop which performs one or more instances of statement S, terminating when the comparison register c is not positive. Modelling such patterns as a unit avoids the challenging problem of defining a separate semantics for branch instructions. (In the past this has been done by introducing an explicit interpreter of instruction sequences [28, 29, 26], or by adding **goto** statements to the modelling language [32, 4].) Let $\mathbb{N}$ be the natural numbers. The pattern's weakest liberal precondition semantics states that it performs zero or more instances of statement S, followed by a statement in which the comparison register c is positive, and then performs one more instance of S after which c is not positive. For a natural number n, let S^n abbreviate statement S sequentially composed with itself n times.

$$S^n \stackrel{\text{def}}{=} \begin{cases} \textbf{skip}, & n = 0 \\ \underbrace{S\,;\cdots;S}_{n \text{ times}}, & n > 0 \end{cases}$$

Specification statement '$\tau\colon [c > 0 \wedge \tau' = \tau + 5\mu s]$' models the effect of performing instruction 'BRGT ℓ' when register c is positive. It takes 5 microseconds to execute but can do so only if c has an appropriate value. Similarly, statement '$\tau\colon [c \leqslant 0 \wedge \tau' = \tau + 5\mu s]$' models the effect of performing instruction 'BRGT ℓ' when register c is not positive. The actual effect of the branching instruction on the program's control flow is captured by the whole modelling language construct. Similar definitions can be given for other common patterns [15, 13].

The final group in Table 2 defines the meaning of input/output instructions for specific memory-mapped i/o ports. Although we could model 'IN' and 'OUT' instructions in the same way as LOAD and STORE instructions, this would tell us nothing about the particular characteristics of the device attached to the port. Since knowledge of i/o device behaviour is essential for our correctness argument, we instead choose to explicitly model important device characteristics as part of the semantics of the instructions that access the ports. Inspired by the Temporal Agent Model [30], each output port X is modelled by two variables, X^v, which denotes the value currently stored in the port's location, and X^t, which is a timestamp denoting the last time the value changed. The latter variable is an auxiliary one—it cannot be accessed by the executable code, but is helpful in modelling time-sensitive behaviours. Thus, for example, instruction 'OUT r, P' writes the value in register r to the ADC's control register, and takes 5 microseconds to do so. The timestamp P^t associated with the update occurs somewhere between the starting time τ and finishing time τ' of the statement, but we cannot predict exactly when in this interval the update will be completed.

The 'IN r, Q' instruction reads from the ADC's data register. To account for the time required to perform the conversion, it is guarded by an assertion that the value '1' was written to control register P at least 30 microseconds ago. If so, the instruction sets registers r and c equal to some value X. Here 'X' represents an altitude reading produced by the altimeter. Since this is outside the control of the Mission Computer System, we cannot say what value it denotes.

The 'OUT r, S' instruction stores a value in the DAC's data register. The 'OUT r, R' instruction starts a data conversion using the value in the data register when '1' is written to the DAC's control register. The conversion takes 30 microseconds to complete, although the instruction takes only 5 microseconds to execute. This is modelled by assigning timestamp R^t a value in the *future*, marking the time when the conversion will be complete. Other statements accessing value R^v can use timestamp R^t to tell whether the value is ready yet or not.

4.3 Semantics of the Legacy Task

We now want to calculate the meaning of the legacy code fragment in Fig. 4 using the semantics in Section 4.2. Firstly, however, we must decide how to treat external inputs, i.e., value 'X' in Table 2. Since these values are sampled from the external environment, the Rate task makes no particular assumptions about them. Therefore, we merely denote the altitude sampled in the ith frame by symbolic constant A_i. Also, we must consider the state in which the code fragment of interest begins. Again, this is application-specific. The Rate task's only assumption about the initial system state is that the altitude sampled during its previous invocation must have been stored in memory location 600. Therefore, the legacy code fragment of interest consists of the sequence of instructions in Fig. 4 preceded by the following assertion.

$$\{m(600) = A_{i-1}\}$$

We can then calculate the semantics of the code fragment via the definitions in Tables 1 and 2. The calculations are lengthy but mechanical, so we merely note some key steps below. For two predicates P_1 and P_2, let equivalence

'$P_1 \equiv P_2$' mean that predicate equality $P_1 \Leftrightarrow P_2$ holds in every state [25, §2.8.1]. Two helpful simplifications of frequently-encountered specification statement semantics are as follows. When expression E does not contain primed variables, then wlp.$(v\colon [v' = E]).R \equiv R[E/v]$. Further, when predicate P does not contain primed variables, then wlp.$(v\colon [P \wedge v' = E]).R \equiv (P \Rightarrow R[E/v])$.

The calculation proceeds backwards up the sequence of instructions. For instance, the weakest liberal precondition semantics of the last two instructions in Fig. 4, with respect to an arbitrary postcondition R, can be found as follows.

$\quad$ wlp.(OUT B, S ; OUT C, R).R
$\equiv$ wlp.(OUT B, S).(wlp.(OUT C, R).R)
$\equiv$ wlp.(OUT B, S).(wlp.($\{\mathtt{C} = 1\}$;
$\qquad\qquad\qquad\qquad$ R^v, R^t, τ: [R$^{v'}$ = S$^v \wedge$ R$^{t'}$ = $\tau + 30\mu$s $\wedge \tau' = \tau + 5\mu$s]).$R$)
$\equiv$ wlp.(OUT B, S).($\mathtt{C} = 1 \Rightarrow R[\mathtt{S}^v/\mathtt{R}^v,\ \tau + 30\mu\mathrm{s}/\mathtt{R}^t,\ \tau + 5\mu\mathrm{s}/\tau]$)
$\equiv \bigwedge_{\tau \leqslant s \leqslant \tau+5\mu\mathrm{s}}(\mathtt{C} = 1 \Rightarrow$
$\qquad\qquad R[\mathtt{S}^v/\mathtt{R}^v,\ \tau+30\mu\mathrm{s}/\mathtt{R}^t,\ \tau+5\mu\mathrm{s}/\tau])[\mathtt{B}/\mathtt{S}^v,\ s/\mathtt{S}^t,\ \tau+5\mu\mathrm{s}/\tau]$
$\equiv \mathtt{C} = 1 \Rightarrow \bigwedge_{\tau \leqslant s \leqslant \tau+5\mu\mathrm{s}} R[\mathtt{B}/\mathtt{R}^v,\ \tau+35\mu\mathrm{s}/\mathtt{R}^t,\ \mathtt{B}/\mathtt{S}^v,\ s/\mathtt{S}^t,\ \tau+10\mu\mathrm{s}/\tau]$

Thus, necessary assumptions, such as the requirement that register C contains the value 1, accumulate in the antecedent of the implication; assignments to variables, such as the assignment of the value in register B to output port R, accumulate in the list of substitutions; and nondeterminism, such as the range of values that may be adopted by time s, which here represents the time at which output port S is written, accumulate in the conjunct (which models an arbitrary choice in weakest liberal precondition semantics).

Proceeding similarly back up the path yields the following semantics for the last six instructions in Fig. 4.

$\quad$ wlp.(IN B, Q ; $\cdots$; OUT C, R).R
$\equiv (\mathtt{P}^t + 30\mu\mathrm{s} \leqslant \tau \wedge \mathtt{P}^v = 1 \wedge \mathtt{C} = 1) \Rightarrow$
$\quad \bigwedge_{\tau+30\mu\mathrm{s} \leqslant s \leqslant \tau+35\mu\mathrm{s}} R[m \oplus \{600 \mapsto A_i\}/m,\ (A_i - \mathtt{A}) * 20/\mathtt{B},\ (A_i - \mathtt{A}) * 20/c,$
$\qquad\qquad (A_i - \mathtt{A}) * 20/\mathtt{R}^v,\ \tau + 65\mu\mathrm{s}/\mathtt{R}^t,\ (A_i - \mathtt{A}) * 20/\mathtt{S}^v,$
$\qquad\qquad s/\mathtt{S}^t,\ \tau + 40\mu\mathrm{s}/\tau]$

Again, the accumulated information can be read directly. For instance, the antecedent tells us that '1' must have been written to the ADC's control register at port P over 30 microseconds ago, while the substitutions tell us that memory location 600 has been updated with the sampled altitude A_i, and so on.

At this point we encounter the two instructions at label ADCDELAY that implement the busy-wait loop. With reference to the semantics in Table 2, the two statements that are repeated zero or more times have the following semantics.

$\quad$ wlp.(SUB B, 1_{imm} ; $\tau\colon [c > 0 \wedge \tau' = \tau + 5\mu\mathrm{s}]).R$
$\equiv \mathtt{B} > 1 \Rightarrow R[\mathtt{B} - 1/\mathtt{B},\ \mathtt{B} - 1/c,\ \tau + 10\mu\mathrm{s}/\tau]$

Zero or more sequentially composed copies of this behaviour, then yields the following semantics. The 0th case is special; let $\mathbb{N}_1$ denote the positive natural numbers (excluding zero).

$$\text{wlp.}(\sqcap n : \mathbb{N} \bullet (\text{SUB B}, 1_{\text{imm}} \,;\, \tau\!:\,[c > 0 \wedge \tau' = \tau + 5\mu s])^n).R$$
$$\equiv R \wedge \bigwedge\nolimits_{n \in \mathbb{N}_1}(\text{B} > n \Rightarrow R[\text{B} - n/\text{B},\ \text{B} - n/c,\ \tau + n * 10\mu s/\tau])$$

This is then composed before sequence 'SUB B, 1_{imm} ; $\tau\!:[c \leqslant 0 \wedge \tau' = \tau + 5\mu s]$' which represents the final compulsory iteration. To be performed, these two statements require that $\text{B} \leqslant 1$ initially (since comparison register c equals register B, and c must not be positive after B is decremented). When this predicate is used as part of R above, with $\text{B} - n$ substituting for B, we obtain constraint $\text{B} \leqslant n + 1$, as well as $\text{B} > n$ from the above antecedent. Thus $\text{B} = n + 1$, which expresses the number of iterations in terms of the initial value of register B. In the next backwards step up the path we encounter 'LOAD B, 3_{imm}'. Substituting 3 for B means that n must equal 2: the 'BRGT' instruction is executed successfully twice, and 'falls through' once. Application of the one-point law then eliminates all alternatives except one, thus providing the following semantics for the last nine instructions in Fig. 4.

$$\text{wlp.}(\text{LOAD B}, 3_{\text{imm}}\,;\,\cdots\,;\,\text{OUT C}, \text{R}).R$$
$$\equiv (\text{P}^t + 5\mu s \leqslant \tau \wedge \text{P}^v = 1 \wedge \text{C} = 1) \Rightarrow$$
$$\bigwedge\nolimits_{\tau+60\mu s \leqslant s \leqslant \tau+70\mu s} R[m \oplus \{600 \mapsto A_i\}/m,\ (A_i - \text{A}) * 20/\text{B},\ (A_i - \text{A}) * 20/c,$$
$$(A_i - \text{A}) * 20/\text{R}^v,\ \tau + 100\mu s/\text{R}^t,\ (A_i - \text{A}) * 20/\text{S}^v,$$
$$s/\text{S}^t,\ \tau + 75\mu s/\tau]$$

We then proceed backwards through the remaining three instructions, and the initial assumption described above, to produce the semantics of the whole code fragment in Fig. 4. In particular, these steps make the above antecedent 'true' by defining the values in port P and register C. An additional nondeterministically-chosen timestamp u is introduced by the update to port P.

$$\text{wlp.}(\{m(600) = A_{i-1}\}\,;\,\cdots\,;\,\text{OUT C}, \text{R}).R$$
$$\equiv \bigwedge\nolimits_{\tau+80\mu s \leqslant s \leqslant \tau+90\mu s,\ \tau+15\mu s \leqslant u \leqslant \tau+20\mu s}$$
$$R[m \oplus \{600 \mapsto A_i\}/m,\ m(600)/\text{A},\ (A_i - A_{i-1}) * 20/\text{B},\ 1/\text{C},$$
$$(A_i - A_{i-1}) * 20/c,\ (A_i - A_{i-1}) * 20/\text{R}^v,\ \tau + 120\mu s/\text{R}^t,$$
$$(A_i - A_{i-1}) * 20/\text{S}^v,\ s/\text{S}^t,\ 1/\text{P}^v,\ u/\text{P}^t,\ \tau + 95\mu s/\tau]$$

Most importantly, the overall effect of the Rate task can be read directly from the substitutions. The first tells us that it writes sampled altitude A_i to memory location 600. The ascent rate produced in the DAC's data register at port S is the difference between the current A_i and previous A_{i-1} altitudes multiplied by 20. Finally, the end-to-end execution time is 95 microseconds.

4.4 Emulated Statement Semantics

To define the meaning of emulated code we need to define a semantics for operations performed by the processor emulator. Since the emulator maintains its own representation of the legacy processor's state, these operations can be defined with respect to this state, together with locally-scoped high-level language variables.

We have assumed that the emulator works correctly, so interpreted legacy instructions have the same functional behaviour as they did on the original processor. The only difference is that emulated instructions will execute faster. Thus the emulated semantics for basic instructions is the same as that shown in Table 2, except that we assume all 5 microsecond execution times are replaced by 2 microseconds, and all 10 microsecond execution times are replaced by 4 microseconds.

The semantics for other emulator operations is shown in Table 3. The first group consists of C++ statements for assignment, declaring an integer, sequential composition and **do-while** iteration. Their semantics follows that of other real-time formalisms [16]. The assignment's execution time is denoted by a duration D^E whose value depends on the structure of expression E. (Ways of calculating Worst-Case Execution Times for high-level language statements and expressions have been well explored in the literature [31].) Similarly in the **do-while** semantics, duration D^B denotes the time required to evaluate expression B and branch to the appropriate location. The declaration block includes

Table 3. Semantics of emulator operations and statements. Let S be a (compound) statement in emulator's native programming language; i be the name of an integer-valued variable; v be a programming language variable; ℓ be an assembly language label; r be a legacy processor register; z be an integer; E be an expression in the emulator's native programming language; B be a boolean-valued expression; D^F be a non-negative duration (in microseconds) whose magnitude depends on expression F's structure; X be a device-dependent external input value; and τ be the current time.

Operation S	Equivalent modelling language statement
$v = E$	$v, \tau : [v' = E \land \tau' = \tau + D^E \mu s]$
{ int v; S; }	**var** $v : \mathbb{Z} \bullet (\tau : [\tau' = \tau + 2\mu s] \,;\, S \,;\, \tau : [\tau' = \tau + 2\mu s])$
$S_1; S_2$	$S_1 \,;\, S_2$
do { S } **while** B	$\sqcap n : \mathbb{N} \bullet ((S \,;\, \tau : [B \land \tau' = \tau + D^B \mu s])^n \,;\, $ $S \,;\, \tau : [\neg B \land \tau' = \tau + D^B \mu s])$
call	$\tau : [\tau' = \tau + 4\mu s]$
return	$\tau : [\tau' = \tau + 4\mu s]$
ReadReg(r, v)	$v, \tau : [v' = r \land \tau' = \tau + 1\mu s]$
WriteReg(r, v)	$r, c, \tau : [r' = v \land c' = v \land \tau' = \tau + 1\mu s]$
UpdateIC(ℓ)	$\tau : [\tau' = \tau + 1\mu s]$
WriteIOPort(T, z)	$T^v, T^t, \tau : [T^{v'} = z \land \tau \leqslant T^{t'} \leqslant \tau' \land \tau' = \tau + 2\mu s]$
v = ReadIOPort(V)	$\{T^v = 1\} \,;\, v, \tau : [(T^t + 10\mu s > \tau) \Rightarrow v' = 1 \land$ $(T^t + 10\mu s \leqslant \tau) \Rightarrow v' = 0 \land \tau' = \tau + 2\mu s]$
v = ReadIOPort(U)	$\{T^v = 1 \land T^t + 10\mu s \leqslant \tau\} \,;\, v, \tau : [v' = X \land \tau' = \tau + 2\mu s]$

2 microsecond overheads to respectively allocate and deallocate space for each newly-declared variable. Let $\mathbb{Z}$ denote the integers.

The '**call**' and '**return**' operations represent the actions taken by the emulator to respectively transfer control to and from a parameterless high-level language subroutine. These operations do not change the emulated legacy processor's state, so their only impact on our model is the 4 microsecond delay they introduce.

The third group in Table 3 includes emulator operations that can be used to modify the (emulated) legacy processor's state. The first two allow the value of a high-level language variable v to be read from and written to a legacy processor register r, respectively. The final operation updates the legacy processor's instruction counter but, since we have avoided introducing the instruction counter explicitly [13], the only effect of the operation is a 1 microsecond delay.

The final group of operations in Table 3 are specific to the new Analog-to-Digital Converter. The first writes an integer to its control register at port T. The operation simply stores the value, and takes 2 microseconds to do so; the effect on the device is modelled by other operations that subsequently access it. The next operation reads the ADC's busy signal, which is connected to port V. The statement is meaningful only if the control register at port T has previously been assigned value '1'. If so, then the statement's outcome is conditional on the time elapsed since port T was updated. Within 10 microseconds of this time the busy signal reads '1'. After this time it returns '0', indicating that it is now safe to read from the data register. The final operation reads from the ADC's data register at port U. It is well-defined only if at least 10 microseconds have elapsed since '1' was written to the control register at port T. If so, the operation reads an application-specific external input value X.

4.5 Semantics of the Emulated Task

In the emulated system, the Rate task consists of a sequence of (interpreted) legacy instructions, emulator actions, and statements in the emulator's native programming language, as shown in Fig. 7. Having defined the semantics of all of these operations above, we merely need to calculate the overall weakest liberal precondition by traversing this 'mixed language' code fragment backwards. As in Section 4.3, we model the external input values X in Table 3 symbolically. Let the altitude sampled in the ith 'emulated' frame be represented by symbolic constant $\overline{A}_i$. As we will see, the emulated system multiplies altitude samples by 3.28, to convert them from metres to feet, so the assumption in Fig. 7 says that memory location 600 should contain the previously sampled altitude A_{i-1} multiplied by this constant.

Calculating the semantics of the sequence in Fig. 7 begins with the two 'OUT' instructions at the end. They have the same semantics as calculated in Section 4.3 except that the emulator's higher instruction processing speed means that their execution time is 4 microseconds.

We then encounter the second of the software patches (Fig. 6). It is simple to calculate the semantics of the three statements in the subroutine's body. Let

```
{m(600) = A̅_{i-1} * 3.28} ;              SUB B, A ;
LOAD A, 600_dir ;                        MULT B, 20_imm ;
LOAD C, 1_imm ;                          call ;
call ;                                   { int AscentRate;
{ int Altitude, Busy;
                                           ⋮ (see Fig. 6)
  ⋮ (see Fig. 5)                          return;
  return;                                } ;
} ;                                      OUT B, S ;
STORE B, 600_dir ;                       OUT C, R

  ⋮ (continued in the next column)
```

Fig. 7. Behaviour of the emulated Rate task.

the execution time of the assignment in the middle be 2 microseconds.

$$\text{wlp.}(\text{ReadReg}(B, \text{AscentRate}); \cdots ; \text{WriteReg}(B, \text{AscentRate})).R$$
$$\equiv R[B * 1.25/B,\ B * 1.25/\text{AscentRate},\ \tau + 4\mu s/\tau]$$

The time required to allocate and deallocate space for variable 'AscentRate', and to call and return from the subroutine, adds another 8 microseconds to the execution time, and 'AscentRate' itself is eliminated from the predicate once we leave its scope, thus yielding $R[B * 1.25/B,\ \tau + 12\mu s/\tau]$ as the semantics of the whole patch.

This result can then be used to continue working backwards up the emulated path until the first patch is encountered.

$$\text{wlp.}(\text{STORE B}, 600_{\text{dir}} ; \cdots ; \text{OUT C}, R).R$$
$$\equiv C = 1 \Rightarrow$$
$$\bigwedge_{\tau+22\mu s \leqslant s \leqslant \tau+24\mu s} R[m \oplus \{600 \mapsto B\}/m,\ (B - A) * 20 * 1.25/R^v,$$
$$\tau + 57\mu s/R^t,\ (B - A) * 20 * 1.25/S^v,$$
$$s/S^t,\ \tau + 26\mu s/\tau]$$

To calculate the semantics of the first patch (Fig. 5), we work backwards through the final four statements.

$$\text{wlp.}(\text{Altitude} = \text{ReadIOPort}(U);\ \cdots;\ \text{UpdateIC}(\text{SAVEALT})).R$$
$$\equiv (T^v = 1 \wedge T^t + 10\mu s \leqslant \tau) \Rightarrow$$
$$R[\overline{A}_i * 3.28/\text{Altitude},\ \overline{A}_i * 3.28/B,\ \tau + 6\mu s/\tau]$$

To calculate the semantics of the **do-while** loop we first determine the semantics of the part that iterates while the condition is true. In this case let the time required to evaluate the C++ expression 'Busy == 1' and branch accordingly equal 2 microseconds.

$$\text{wlp.}(\sqcap n : \mathbb{N} \bullet (\text{Busy} = \text{ReadIOPort}(V) ; \tau: [\text{Busy} = 1 \wedge \tau' = \tau + 2\mu s])^n).R$$
$$\equiv R \wedge \bigwedge_{n \in \mathbb{N}_1}((T^v = 1 \wedge T^t + 10\mu s - (n-1) * 4\mu s > \tau) \Rightarrow$$
$$R[1/\text{Busy},\ \tau + n * 4\mu s/\tau])$$

We then combine this with the two following statements, representing the final, compulsory iteration, plus the semantics of the four statements calculated above. Finally, working back through the 'WriteIOPort(T, 1)' statement produces the constraints '$T^t + 10\mu s - n * 4\mu s \leqslant \tau + 2\mu s < T^t + 10\mu s - (n-1) * 4\mu s$' and '$\tau \leqslant T^t \leqslant \tau + 2\mu s$', linking the number of iterations n, the current time τ, and the timestamp T^t. Pleasingly, the only value of n that satisfies this is 3, thus establishing the number of iterations from the duration of the ADC's busy signal. (The statement in the loop is executed $n + 1 = 4$ times, since the last time is when the condition is false.)

The expression then simplifies considerably, and calculation continues by incorporating the timing overheads of declaring 'Altitude' and 'Busy', and calling and returning from the subroutine, giving the following overall semantics for the first software patch.

$$\text{wlp.}(\textbf{call}\,;\,\{\,\textbf{int}\,\text{Altitude, Busy};\,\cdots\,\textbf{return};\,\}).R$$
$$\equiv \bigwedge\nolimits_{\tau+8\mu s \leqslant u \leqslant \tau+10\mu s} R[\overline{A}_i * 3.28/\text{B},\ 1/\text{T}^v,\ u/\text{T}^t,\ \tau + 40\mu s/\tau]$$

We then combine this result with the calculation for the statements following the first subroutine, and continue working up the sequence to the initial assertion to complete the semantics for the emulated task.

$$\text{wlp.}(\{m(600) = \overline{A}_{i-1} * 3.28\}\,;\,\cdots\,;\,\texttt{OUT C, R}).R$$
$$\equiv \bigwedge\nolimits_{\tau+62\mu s \leqslant s \leqslant \tau+64\mu s,\ \tau+8\mu s \leqslant u \leqslant \tau+10\mu s}$$
$$R[m \oplus \{600 \mapsto \overline{A}_i * 3.28\}/m,\ m(600)/\text{A},$$
$$(\overline{A}_i - \overline{A}_{i-1}) * 3.28 * 20 * 1.25/\text{B},\ 1/\text{C},\ (\overline{A}_i - \overline{A}_{i-1}) * 3.28 * 20 * 1.25/c,$$
$$(\overline{A}_i - \overline{A}_{i-1}) * 3.28 * 20 * 1.25/\text{R}^v,\ \tau + 103\mu s/\text{R}^t,$$
$$(\overline{A}_i - \overline{A}_{i-1}) * 3.28 * 20 * 1.25/\text{S}^v,\ s/\text{S}^t,\ 1/\text{T}^v,\ u/\text{T}^t,\ \tau + 72\mu s/\tau]$$

Again, the substitutions include all the significant updates. The ascent rate produced in the DAC's data register at port S is the difference between the last two altitude samples multiplied by expression $3.28 * 20 * 1.25$. The overall execution time is 72 microseconds.

4.6 Comparison of the Legacy and Emulated Semantics

The semantics at the ends of Sections 4.3 and 4.5 show that the legacy and emulated Rate tasks do *not* have precisely the same behaviour. Therefore, it remains to justify the differences as acceptable in the light of the Mission Computer System's hardware upgrade. In a multi-tasking Operational Flight Program the issues to consider are: the task's functional behaviour; code that is dependent on instruction execution speeds; and code that depends on the frequency of task invocations.

Overall, the task's functional behaviour is preserved. The semantics show that both versions update memory location 600, general-purpose registers A, B and C, the comparison register c, and output ports R and S. However, the legacy task writes to port P, whereas the emulated one uses port T, but this is explained by the replacement of the Analog-to-Digital Converter. Also, recalling that the old altimeter was calibrated in feet, while the new one produces readings in metres, explains the way the emulated task scales all altimeter readings $\overline{A}_i$ by 3.28, to maintain consistency with the legacy code. (Notably, the value stored by the emulated task in location 600 is measured in feet, in case some other task accesses this value. For instance, the Log task may include this altitude reading in the mission log.)

With regard to instruction execution speeds, the most obvious difference is that the legacy Rate task takes 95 microseconds where the emulated one takes only 72. However, a *faster* task execution time is (usually) acceptable in cyclic-executive scheduling because it makes it easier for the task invocations to fit into their frame. (Curiously, this 'improvement' may change the behaviour of some systems by allowing tasks that previously always overran the frame to run to completion.) More importantly, we must beware of task code that relies for its correctness on instruction execution speeds. The busy-wait loop at label ADCDELAY in the legacy task has this characteristic but, in this case, the programmer has correctly patched the code while rewriting it to allow for the new input device. The semantics show that both versions of the task successfully sample altitudes from their respective ADCs, when the specific timing characteristics of the hardware interface are included. (The timestamps associated with output ports also reveal that the two versions of the task access these ports at different times, with respect to the task's starting time, but the *absolute* timing of i/o events within a frame is usually unimportant.)

Finally, we must consider code that depends on the frequency of task invocations. Typically, the programmer of a periodic task relies on the task being invoked regularly (with as little 'jitter', i.e., variation, between successive invocations as possible) but the *absolute* timing of frames is unimportant. Thus, expression '$A_i - A_{i-1}$' in the legacy task's semantics denotes the change in altitude in one minor cycle, i.e., 50 milliseconds. The corresponding expression in the emulated task's semantics, '$(\overline{A}_i - \overline{A}_{i-1}) * 1.25$', is meant to denote the same value. To allow for the fact that minor cycles are only 40 milliseconds long in the emulated system, it thus scales the measured change in altitude by $\frac{50}{40} = 1.25$. We have now accounted for all the differences between the legacy and emulated semantics and can thus conclude that the emulated system is indeed a satisfactory replacement for the legacy one.

5 Conclusion

Processor emulation is an important software maintenance technology which is now being deployed in safety-critical computer systems [9]. To be industrially relevant, formal methods must keep abreast of such developments. Here we have shown how an existing program compilation formalism can be used to verify part of an emulated flight program. However, although this result is encouraging, considerable simplification of the procedure is needed to make it routinely applicable by programmers who are not expert in formal methods.

Acknowledgements

I wish to thank Geoffrey Watson for his insights into processor emulation technology, Ian Hayes for feedback on the example, and the anonymous reviewers for suggesting improvements to the presentation. This work is funded by Australian Research Council Large Grant A00104650, *Verified Compilation Strategies for Critical Computer Programs*.

References

1. R. J. R. Back. On correct refinement of programs. *Journal of Computer and System Sciences*, 23:49–68, 1981.
2. T. P. Baker and A. Shaw. The cyclic executive model and Ada. *Journal of Real-Time Systems*, 1(1):7–26, June 1989.
3. L. Beus-Dukic. COTS real-time operating systems in space. *Safety Systems: The Safety-Critical Systems Club Newsletter*, 10(3):11–14, May 2001.
4. E. Börger and I. Durdanović. Correctness of compiling occam to transputer code. *The Computer Journal*, 39(1):52–92, 1996.
5. L. P. Briand and D. M. Roy. *Meeting Deadlines in Hard Real-Time Systems: The Rate Monotonic Approach*. IEEE Computer Society Press, 1999.
6. C. Cifuentes, D. Simon, and A. Fraboulet. Assembly to high-level language translation. In *Proceedings of the International Conference on Software Maintenance*, pages 228–237. IEEE Computer Society Press, 1998.
7. R. A. Comfort. The economics of microprocessor obsolescence. *COTS Journal*, pages 21–23, July/August 1998.
8. D. Corman, P. Goertzen, J. Luke, and M. Mills. Incremental Upgrade of Legacy Systems (IULS): A fundamental software technology for aging aircraft. In *Fourth Joint DOD/FAA/NASA Conference on Aging Aircraft*, 2000.
9. D. Culpin. Overcoming technology lag in mission computers. *Australian Defence Science*, 11(1):4–5, 2003.
10. E. W. Dijkstra. *A Discipline of Programming*. Prentice-Hall, 1976.
11. E. W. Dijkstra and C. S. Scholten. *Predicate Calculus and Program Semantics*. Springer-Verlag, 1990.
12. J. D. G. Falardeau. Schedulability analysis in rate monotonic based systems with application to the CF-188. Master's thesis, Department of Electrical and Computer Engineering, Royal Military College of Canada, May 1994.
13. C. J. Fidge. Timing analysis of assembler code control-flow paths. In L.-H. Eriksson and P. Lindsay, editors, *FME 2002: Formal Methods—Getting IT Right*, volume 2391 of *Lecture Notes in Computer Science*, pages 370–389. Springer-Verlag, 2002.
14. P. Gust. *Introduction to Machine and Assembly Language Programming*. Prentice-Hall, 1986.
15. I. J. Hayes, C. J. Fidge, and K. Lermer. Semantic characterisation of dead control-flow paths. *IEE Proceedings—Software*, 148(6):175–186, December 2001.
16. I. J. Hayes and M. Utting. A sequential real-time refinement calculus. *Acta Informatica*, 37(6):385–448, 2001.
17. W. H. Hesselink. *Programs, Recursion and Unbounded Choice: Predicate-Transformation Semantics and Transformation Rules*, volume 27 of *Cambridge Tracts in Theoretical Computer Science*. Cambridge University Press, 1992.

18. J. Hooman. Extending Hoare logic to real-time. *Formal Aspects of Computing*, 6(6A):801–825, 1994.
19. D. Kalinsky. Context switch. *Embedded Systems Programming*, 14(2):94–105, February 2001.
20. K. Lermer and C. J. Fidge. A formal model of real-time program compilation. *Theoretical Computer Science*, 282(1):151–190, July 2002.
21. K. Lermer, C. J. Fidge, and I. J. Hayes. Formal semantics for program paths. In J. Harland, editor, *Computing: The Australasian Theory Symposium (CATS 2003)*, volume 78 of *Electronic Notes in Theoretical Computer Science*. Elsevier, 2003.
22. L. A. Leventhal. *Introduction to Microprocessors: Software, Hardware and Programming*. Prentice-Hall, 1978.
23. C. D. Locke. Software architecture for hard real-time applications: Cyclic executives vs. fixed priority executives. *The Journal of Real-Time Systems*, 4:37–53, 1992.
24. J. A. Luke, D. G. Haldeman, and W. J. Cannon. A COTS-based replacement strategy for aging avionics computers. *CrossTalk—The Journal of Defense Software Engineering*, pages 14–17, December 2001.
25. C. Morgan. *Programming from Specifications*. Prentice-Hall, second edition, 1994.
26. M. Müller-Olm. *Modular Compiler Verification: A Refinement-Algebraic Approach Advocating Stepwise Abstraction*, volume 1283 of *Lecture Notes in Computer Science*. Springer-Verlag, 1997.
27. G. Nelson. A generalization of Dijkstra's calculus. *ACM Transactions on Programming Languages and Systems*, 11(4):517–561, October 1989.
28. T. S. Norvell. Machine code programs are predicates too. In D. Till, editor, *Sixth Refinement Workshop*, pages 188–204. Springer-Verlag, 1994.
29. A. Sampaio. *An Algebraic Approach to Compiler Design*, volume 4 of *AMAST Series in Computing*. World Scientific, 1997.
30. D. Scholefield. Real-time refinement in Manna and Pnueli's temporal logic. *Formal Aspects of Computing*, 8(4):408–427, 1996.
31. A. C. Shaw. Reasoning about time in higher-level language software. *IEEE Transactions on Software Engineering*, 15(7):875–889, July 1989.
32. S. Stepney. *High Integrity Compilation: A Case Study*. Prentice-Hall, 1993.
33. D. B. Stewart. 30 pitfalls for real-time software developers, part 1. *Embedded Systems Programming*, 12(1):32–41, October 1999.
34. TRW Inc. Emulator Application Programming Interface (API) for the 1750A Virtual Component Environment (VCE1750A). Technical Report HML-API-001, TRW Dayton Engineering Laboratory, March 2001. Revision D.

Improving Safety Assessment of Complex Systems: An Industrial Case Study*

Marco Bozzano[1], Antonella Cavallo[2], Massimo Cifaldi[3], Laura Valacca[3], and Adolfo Villafiorita[1]

[1] ITC-irst
bozzano@irst.itc.it
adolfo@irst.itc.it
[2] Alenia Aeronautica
acavallo@aeronautica.alenia.it
[3] Società Italiana Avionica
{cifaldi, valacca}@sia-av.it

Abstract. The complexity of embedded controllers is steadily increasing. This trend, stimulated by the continuous improvement of the computational power of hardware, demands for a corresponding increase in the capability of design and safety engineers to maintain adequate safety levels. The use of formal methods during system design has proved to be effective in several practical applications. However, the development of certain classes of applications, like, for instance, avionics systems, also requires the behaviour of a system to be analysed under certain degraded situations (e.g., when some components are not working as expected). The integration of system design activities with safety assessment and the use of formal methods, although not new, are still at an early stage. These goals are addressed by the ESACS project, a European-Union-sponsored project grouping several industrial companies from the aeronautic field. The ESACS project is developing a methodology and a platform – the ESACS platform – that helps safety engineers automating certain phases of their work. This paper reports on the application of the ESACS methodology and on the use of the ESACS platform to a case study, namely, the Secondary Power System of the Eurofighter Typhoon aircraft.

Keywords: Formal Verification and Safety Assessment of Complex Systems, Automated Fault Tree Computation, ESACS

1 Introduction

In the *development cycle* of a complex system, it is possible to identify a certain number of steps each involving different processes and tasks that the system development team has to carry out. In the classic *waterfall model*, the principal phases are: *requirements analysis* and *specification*, *design*, *implementation*, *testing*, *analyses* and *maintenance*. In the last decades, many variations of this model were proposed.

---

* This work has been and is being developed within ESACS, an European-sponsored project, Framework Programme 5 - Growth Contract no. G4RD-CT-2000-00361

Some of these are based on virtual prototyping and simulation, incremental development, reusable software and automated synthesis. As specification errors and misconceptions found in later phases of the system development cycle are extremely expensive to fix, it is evident that meticulous comprehension of the system and of its behaviour should be carried out as early as possible in the development cycle. Dedicated languages are therefore used in the requirements capturing phase to build a *model* of the system, and model checking techniques are used to analyse it in detail. The availability of a model is important for all participants in the system development; for example, if an unambiguous and executable model is available early on, customers and subcontractors can become aware with it, and can approve or improve the functionality and behaviour of the system before investing heavily in the implementation stages. Precise and detailed models are also in the best interest of the designers, analysers and testers of the system.

If the system under development is a *safety critical system,* in parallel to the standard development process described above, it is necessary to carry out a set of activities - *safety assessment activities* - whose goal is assessing the robustness of the system in degraded situations, that is, when some of the components are not working as expected. The phases, activities, and outputs of the safety assessment process are coded by various standards (e.g., ARP4754). The first step is defining the safety requirements of the system, that is, the minimum safety levels that the system must achieve. As an example, a safety requirement may be something like: *"no single failure shall yield to a loss of a given output".* The next step is assessing the safety of the architecture, by determining what are the combinations of failures of components that may cause a safety requirement to be violated. During this activity, safety engineers produce, e.g., fault trees, that are compact representations of the combination of failures leading to the violation of a given safety requirement [VGRH81]. System certification typically requires the probability of such combination of failures to be below a given threshold. The traditional safety verification process, that relies on the ability of the safety engineer to understand and to foresee the system's behaviour, is very difficult to carry out and error prone when dealing with highly complex systems. Moreover, even when formal methods are used during system development, the information passed to the safety engineer is still transmitted by means of informal specifications and the communication between system design and safety assessment activities can be seen as an "over the wall process" [FMPN94].

A solution to these issues is to perform the safety assessment analysis in some automated way, directly from the formal system model coming from the design engineer. This approach is being developed and investigated in ESACS (*Enhanced Safety Assessment for Complex Systems*), a European-Union-sponsored project in the area of safety analysis, involving several research institutions and leading avionics and aerospace industrial companies. The methodology developed within the ESACS project is supported by state-of-the-art and commercial tools for system modelling and safety analysis. Furthermore, the effectiveness of the ESACS methodology is being tested against a set of real-world industrial case studies. In this paper we report on the application of the ESACS methodology to one of such industrial case studies, namely the Secondary Power System (SPS, for short) of the Eurofighter Typhoon and we report on the obtained results.

Outline of the paper. The paper is structured as follows: in the next section we present the ESACS methodology and platform; in Section 3 we present the SPS case study and discuss our experience. In Section 4 we report on related work and in Section 5 we draw some conclusions and discuss future work.

2 The ESACS Methodology and the ESACS Platform

The main goal of the ESACS project is the definition of a methodology, that is compliant with the design and safety assessment processes of the industrial partners involved in the project. The methodology must also be supported by tools, that can be gently integrated with the other tools already in use by the industrial partners.

In order to achieve the above-mentioned goals, within ESACS we defined a methodology based on a set of key steps, that can be adapted by the various industrial partners according to their needs, and we set up a platform, called the *ESACS platform*, which is shipped in different configurations. The configurations of the ESACS platform are based on different tools, sharing the same architecture and providing the same basic functionalities. The use of different tools, although has lead to configurations that are not interoperable, has considerably eased the issue of integrating the platform within the development processes of the industrial partners.

The following two subsections describe in more details the methodology and the platform.

2.1 The ESACS Methodology

The main characteristic of the ESACS methodology is the capability of integrating the system design and the system safety assessment processes by providing an environment in which formal notations are the common and shared language to be used both during system design and safety assessment.

The methodology, sketched in Figure 1, is based on the following steps.

Model Capturing. The starting point of the ESACS methodology is a *formal model*, that is, a model written in some formal language. The formal model can be either written by the design engineer or by the safety engineer. This alternative gives rise to two different scenarios.

In the first scenario, that is, when the formal model is written by the design engineer, the model, that we call system model (SM), includes only the nominal behaviour of the system. The SM is used by the design engineer to verify the functional requirements and it is then passed to the safety engineer, to assess its safety. In order to validate the system with respect to the safety requirements, the safety engineers will enrich the behaviour of the SM by automatically *injecting* failure modes on the SM, according to what described in more details below.

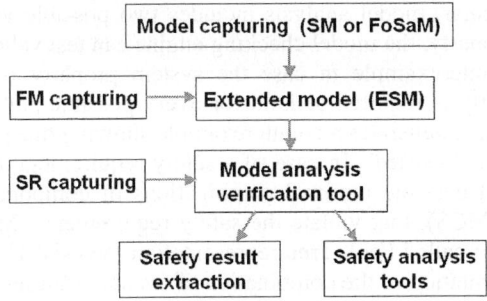

Fig. 1. ESACS methodology steps

In the second scenario, the formal model is built directly by the safety engineer and we call it FoSaM (Formal Safety Model). This model represents a formal view of the system highlighting its safety characteristics. To write a FoSaM, the safety engineer can browse a library of system components (that include both nominal and faulty behaviours) and a library of architectural safety patterns (containing typical structures of components to build a safety architecture, like, for instance, primary/backup of N-version systems). This second scenario is followed during the early phases of the system life cycle, when there are still no design models available, but only some system specification. In this second scenario, the main goal is assessing the system architecture.

Failure Mode Capturing, Model Extension. The second step of the methodology includes the failure modes (FMs) capturing, the model extension, and the safety requirements capturing phases. When the SM is written by the design engineer, in order to use it for safety analyses, the safety engineer must first extend it by *injecting* with failure modes, that is, with a specification of how the various components of the system can fail. This step yields to a model, that we call *extended system model* (ESM), in which all the components of the SM can fail according to the specified failure modes. The typologies of failure modes to inject into a SM can be stored and retrieved from a library of generic failure modes, the so-called Generic Failure Modes Library (GFML) and then automatically injected into the formal system model through an extension facility.

Safety Requirements Capturing. As long as a SM/ESM or a FoSaM is available, it is possible to verify its behaviour with respect to the desired functional (nominal behaviour) and safety requirements (degraded behaviour). During the safety requirements capturing phase, therefore, design and safety engineers define functional and safety requirements, that will be used at a later stage to assess the behaviour of the system. In particular the design engineer and/or the safety engineer will verify the system either by writing directly the system requirements using some formal notation (e.g., temporal logic [Eme90]) or by loading the basic safety requirements of a safety critical system from a so-called Generic Safety Requirement Library (GSRL).

Model Analysis. This is the phase in which the behaviour of a system is assessed against functional and safety requirements. The model analysis phase is performed by running formal verification tools (e.g., model checkers) on the given system properties. In particular, model analysis includes two possible verification tasks. In case of a system property, the model checking engine can test validity of the property, and generate a counterexample in case the system property is not verified (e.g., assuming the property is required to hold for every possible path of the system, the model checking engine generates a counterexample showing one particular path along which the property is falsified). In case of a safety requirement, the model checking engine generates all possible minimal combinations of components failures, called Minimal Cut Sets (MCS), that violate the safety requirements. Minimal cut sets can be arranged in the so-called Fault Tree representation [VGRH81]. Fault trees provide a convenient representation of the combination of events resulting in the violation of a given *top level event*, and are usually represented in a graphical way, as a parallel or sequential combination of AND/OR logical gates.

Result Extraction.. During this phase the results produced by the model analysis phase are processed to be presented in human-readable format. In particular, the result extraction phase is responsible for conveniently displaying all the outputs automatically generated by the model checking engine, e.g., simulation traces and minimal cut sets, and to present results of safety analyses in formats that are compatible with traditional fault tree analysis tools used by safety engineers.

2.2 The ESACS Platform

The ESACS platform supports and automates the application of the methodology described in the previous subsection.

The ESACS platform is shipped in four possible configurations, namely the Altarica configuration [AGPR00], based on the Cecilia-OCAS tool, the FSAP/NuSMV-SA configuration (http://sra.itc.it/tools/FSAP), based on the NuSMV2 model checker [CCG+02], the SCADE configuration, based on the SCADE tool (http://www.esterel-technologies.com) and on the PROVER plug-in [SS00], and the Statemate configuration, based on the Statemate tool (http://www.ilogix.com) and on the VIS model checker [BHS+96].

All the configurations of the ESACS platform share the same architectural principles and functional requirements. The delivery in four different configurations has guaranteed a more flexible integration of the platform within the industrial partners' processes, by allowing, for instance, choice on the formal notation to use for writing SM/FoSAM. The general architecture of the ESACS platform is shown in Figure 2.

The core of the ESACS platform is the so-called Safety Analysis Task (SAT). This block provides the core of the interaction with the system and allows users to access the libraries and to store and manage all the information relevant to the assessment of a system (SAT Repository). In particular, the SAT repository can store the following information: system models (i.e., SM, ESM or FoSaM), failure modes, system requirements (i.e., system properties and safety requirements), and the specifications and results of the analyses to perform.

The other blocks of the ESACS platform include facilities for system design, for automated system verification, and for automated safety assessment. The architecture is composed of both commercial off-the-shelf tools (i.e., for model capturing, for the verification of system properties, and for the presentation of safety analysis results)

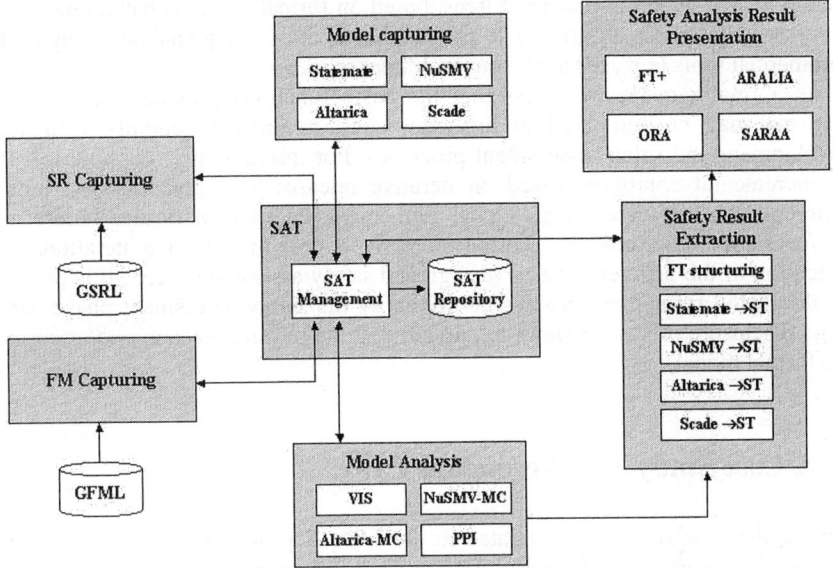

Fig. 2. ESACS Platform Architecture

and components (both libraries and algorithms) specifically developed for the ESACS project (e.g., for system requirements capturing, failure mode capturing and system model extension, model analysis – for the generation of MCS starting from a safety requirement, and safety result extraction).

The commercial tools provided for the different ESACS platform configurations are the following. For the *model capturing* block, which is used by the design engineer to define the system formal model, the following different modelling tools are used: Altarica, NuSMV, Statemate and Scade. The *model analysis* block, used to verify the SM/ESM or FoSaM with respect a specific system property, is based on one of the following model checking engines: VIS, Prover Plug-In, NuSMV-SA (an extension of NuSMV2, with safety analysis algorithms), and Altarica. Finally the *safety analysis result presentation* block is used to display the output of the automated fault tree generation in the traditional safety analysis tools, namely Isograph FT+, Aralia, ORA and SARAA.

The components specifically defined for ESACS include facilities for *failure mode capturing* and *model extension, system requirement capturing, model analysis* (in particular automated fault tree generation) and *result extraction*. The *failure mode capturing* block allows the user retrieve the specification of the failure modes from a specifically developed library of failure modes (GFML) and to instantiate them to a specific system model. When all the failure modes have been retrieved and instantiated, the *model extension* facility allows for the automatic extension of the SM into a ESM. The *safety requirements capturing* block allows to write functional and safety requirements; these can either be extracted from a library of generic properties (GSRL) or directly written using some standard logic formalism (e.g., temporal logic). Finally the *model analysis* and the *result extraction* blocks implement the most important facility of the ESACS approach, e.g., the computation algorithm for the automated generation of fault trees, based on formal methods techniques, and the necessary conversion algorithms to present the result of safety analysis using standard commercial tools (e.g., for analysing fault trees).

As a final remark, we stress that the basic functions provided by the ESACS platform may be combined in different ways, in order to comply with various development and safety assessment processes. For instance, it is possible to support an incremental approach, based on iterative releases of a given system model at different levels of detail (e.g., model refinement, addition of further failure modes and/or safety requirements). Furthermore, it is possible to have iterations in the execution of the different phases (design and safety assessment), e.g., it is possible to let the model refinement process be driven by the safety assessment phase outcome (e.g., disclosure of system flaws requires fixing the physical system and/or correcting the formal model).

3 A Case Study: The Secondary Power System

One of the case studies investigated in the ESACS project is the Secondary Power System (SPS hereafter) of the Eurofighter Typhoon aircraft. The case study has been chosen for the following reasons: it is of industrial interest, it is a heterogeneous system comprising various types of components like electromechanical components (e.g., control valves, relays), mechanical components (e.g., shafts, gearboxes, freewheels), electronic transducers (e.g., speed sensors, pressure sensors) and electronic controllers (SPS computers), and it has been judged of the right (medium/high) complexity to be analysed within the project. The case study has been conducted in collaboration among Alenia Aeronautica, Società Italiana Avionica, and ITC-IRST. The aims were twofold: on the one hand we wanted to investigate the behaviour of the SPS, on the other we wished to use the case study as a way to test two configurations of the ESACS platform.

The Secondary Power System drives the hydraulic and the electrical utilities of both the left and right hand side of the aircraft and therefore it can be considered as a "critical" system from the safety point of view. To satisfy the basic safety requirement, i.e. *"no single failures shall cause the total loss of the SPS utilities"*, the architecture of the system includes two basic redundancies: there are two independent and perfectly symmetric lines, whose purpose is to drive the left and the right hand side utilities, respectively; for each side, the mechanical drive of the relevant utilities (*normal mode*) is redounded by a pneumatic drive (*cross-bleed mode*) in case of failure of one of the components in the mechanical line.Figure 3 shows a schematic view of the SPS. The SPS normal operation consists in transmitting the mechanical power from the engines to the relevant hydraulic and electrical generators. In case of an engine failure, the SPS computers automatically initiate a *cross-bleed* procedure consisting in driving the hydraulic and electrical generators by means of an air turbine motor, using bled air from the opposite engine. Correct functioning of this procedure is an example of one safety requirement of the SPS system.

Improving Safety Assessment of Complex Systems: An Industrial Case Study 215

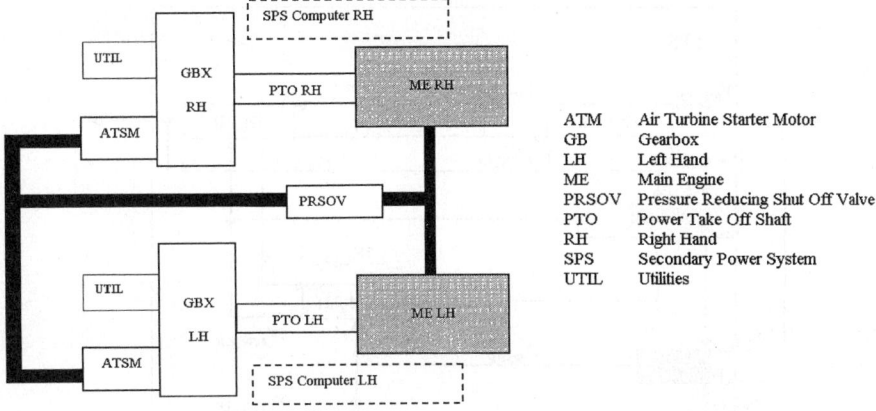

Fig. 3. SPS schematic view

In order to investigate the behaviour of the SPS, a set of formal models, described at different level of details, has been set up, using two configurations of the ESACS platform, namely the Statemate-based configuration and FSAP/NuSMV-SA. This hierarchy of models can be summarised as follows (in increasing order of complexity):

1. the simplest model, which – in the standard development process – is also representative of the first specification that the safety engineer receives from the design engineer - is a sort of block diagram. In our case, this simple model includes both the left and right hand side of the SPS and a very simplified model of the SPS computer. The variables used are all Boolean and the components are blocks which may be either working or not working; Figure 4 highlights the various components and the data flow among them;
2. in the second model, the behaviour of the components of the SPS is more realistic, even if the SPS computer is still very simplified. Using a *discretization* approach, variables representing physical quantities have been encoded by means of integer variables ranged between 0 and 20. Moreover, by exploiting the functional symmetry of the system, we removed some of the components, and we limited reasoning on just one side of the system;
3. the third model is as the previous one but with both sides of the system included;
4. the fourth model is derived from the previous one by enriching the SPS computer model; in the Statemate-based configuration we used real-valued variables, whereas in FSAP/NuSMV-SA we used discretized integer variables with ranges closer to the real values provided by the system;
5. finally, we realised two very detailed models in which both the nominal and the faulty behaviour of each component is modelled in detail. Variables are encoded like in the previous model. Graphs obtained by simulating these detailed models are in accordance with the graphs obtained from the telemetry on the real system.

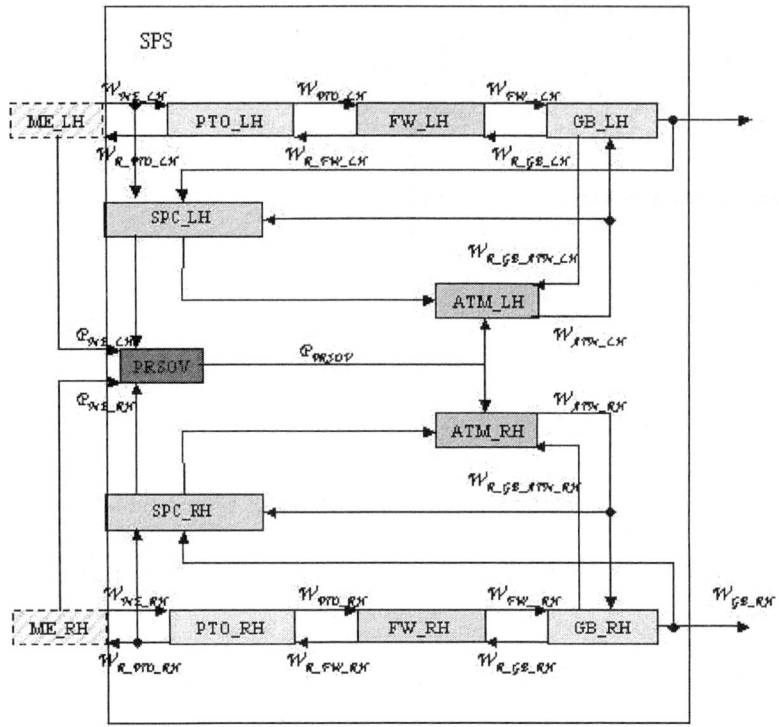

Fig. 4. SPS block diagram model

4 Results

The industrial partners involved in the SPS case study (Alenia Aeronautica and Società Italiana Avionica) performed a cycle of application, as end-users of the ESACS methodology and tool-set, in which the various SPS models were tested, in order to highlight *pros* and *cons* of the ESACS approach and to devise possible methodology and tool platform improvements. The main criteria of the evaluation were the following:

1. effectiveness of the methodology to improve the integration of the "design" and "safety" activities on the complex system;
2. effectiveness of the tool-set in the implementation of the different steps defined by the methodology (i.e., failure mode definition and injection in the system model, system property definition, system verification with respect to the functional and safety requirements, fault tree generation).

In the following we briefly summarise the results of our evaluation.

<u>Representational Issues</u>: one interesting aspect of the case study concerned the modelling of the various components of the SPS. In particular, one of the most

challenging modelling issue has been the modelling of hydraulic and mechanical components. For such systems, in fact, when reasoning about degraded situations, the standard input/output modelling with functional blocks may be particularly difficult. (For instance, a leakage in a pipe may cause loss of pressure in the whole pipe. As a second example, in certain situations, e.g. *grippage*, mechanical forces may need to be propagated in "reverse" - e.g., by affecting functional blocks that are further "up" in the functional chain). To address these issues, particular care had to be taken in modelling such kind of aspects. More in general, we think that the use of hybrid systems modelling tools may be extremely effective for such kind of models.

Integration of the "design" and "safety" activities: we experienced that the ESACS approach effectively improves and encourages the interaction between design and safety engineers as they, for instance, can "speak" the same unambiguous language, sharing the same formal system model. Moreover, the safety evaluation of the proposed system architecture, thanks to the possibility to simulate and verify the system model, can be performed in the very early phases of system design. However, an important issue concerns the possible "semantic gap" between the model provided and the actual design/system. In fact, while existing modelling and simulation tools (e.g., the ones provided by the Statemate-based configuration) support very rich input languages, often, in order to be able to formally verify properties it is necessary to scale the model down, e.g., by abstracting away certain characteristics of the design model. This leads to models whose accuracy with respect to the real models has to be agreed upon by specialists. On the other hand, future improvements of current model checking tools can help to ameliorate this problem. We will come back to this point in the next section.

Failure mode definition and injection: within the ESACS approach, as already discussed, there are two possibilities to include the failure modes of system components in the system model: the definition of user-defined failure modes as a particular class of variables included in the system model, and/or the injection of typical failure modes (such as *stuck-at*, *ramp-down*, *delay*, ...) to take into account all the possible faulty behaviours of system components. The facility for failure mode injection and system model extension experimented during the different test cycles of the ESACS platform works well but it is based on a library of generic failure modes specifically created for the ESACS purpose. As a consequence, the library needs to be enriched in the next future to include the failure modes typical of the main types of complex system components (e.g., electronic, electric, mechanical, pneumatic components and so on).

System property definition: the ESACS approach allows the definition of different types of verification tasks on system models, like, for instance, reachability of a given state (e.g., gearbox failure) or the fulfilment of a given condition (e.g., output from one utility a certain percentage under its nominal value). In any case, in order to write the system property, it is necessary to use some particular formalism (e.g., LTL or CTL temporal logics), that are often difficult to understand, especially by people who are not expert in formal verification. As a consequence, a future improvement of the ESACS platform concerns the inclusion of different classes of system properties to instantiate the main formalisms to be used for performing the different verification tasks.

<u>System property verification</u>: performing model checking of functional requirements on the system model often leads to the "*state explosion*" problem. In order to mitigate this problem, the definition of a set of different models has helped, as it has been possible to define "specialised" models to be used for certain properties.

From an industrial point of view, the possibility of using simulation and exhaustive techniques to "drive" the system into a state has been proven particularly useful, for example, to show that a safety critical state cannot be reachable when failure modes are disabled.

<u>Fault tree generation</u>: automatic generation of fault trees has been possible with satisfactory results only for the first two types of formal model, whereas with the more complex models we encountered difficulties due to the "*state explosion*" problem. Nonetheless, the generated fault trees can still be very informative for the safety engineers (see, for instance, the example of generated fault tree in Figure 5). The possibility for the safety engineer to have more complex system models, which, at least, can be used to perform simulations, remains also a valuable aspect.

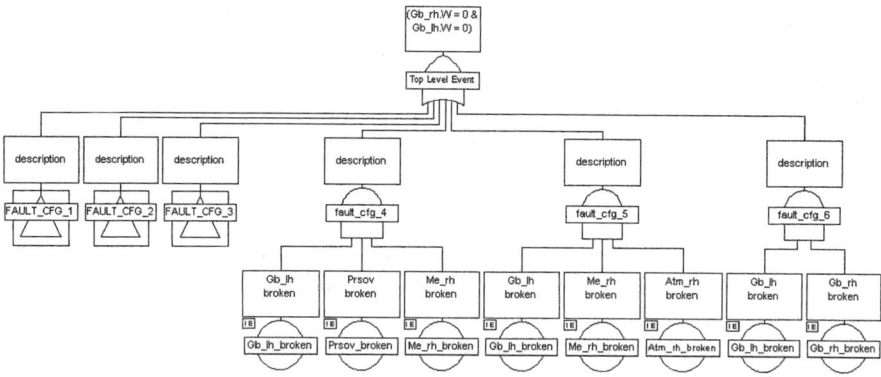

Fig. 5. An example of generated Fault Tree

5 Related Work

ESACS Project and Platform. The work described in this paper has been developed within the ESACS project. For more details about the project we refer the reader to the URL http://www.esacs.org/. The different configurations of the platform have been tested on various case studies, among which we would like to mention:

1. Air inlet control system APU (Auxiliary Power Unit) JAS39 Gripen, related to a critical subsystem of an airplane. The work has been carried out using the SCADE based configuration.
2. Wheel Steering System, related to a critical subsystem of a family of Airbus airplanes.
3. A controller of the Airbus A340 High Lift System.

4. Hydraulic System A320, related to the hydraulic system of the Airbus A320. The work carried out using the Altarica and (partly, FSAP-NuSMV-SA), is described in [BCS02].

FSAP/NuSMV-SA Configuration. Concerning the NuSMV-based configuration, the safety analysis capabilities provided by this platform include traditional fault tree generation [VGRH81] together with formal verification capabilities typical of model checking [CGP00, CCG+02]. The algorithms for cut set and prime implicant computation mentioned in Section 2.1 are based on classical procedures for minimization of boolean functions, specifically on the implicit-search procedure described in [CM92, CM93], which is based on Binary Decision Diagrams (BDDs) [Bry92]. This choice was quite natural, given that the NuSMV model checker [CCG+02] makes a pervasive use of BDD data structures. The ordering analysis procedure mentioned in Section 2.1 also makes use of these algorithms [BV03].

Fault Tree Computation. The ESACS Platform can compute fault trees using algorithms based on formal methods techniques. Related work includes, e.g., [LR98, Rae00]. The implemented algorithms support both *monotonic* and *non-monotonic* systems. We also mention [MDCS98, SDC99], which describe DIFTree, a methodology supporting (however, still at the manual level) fault tree construction and allowing for different kinds of analyses of sub-trees (e.g., Markovian or Monte Carlo simulation for dynamic ones, and BDD-based evaluation for static ones). The notation for non-logical (dynamic) gates of fault trees and the support for sample probabilistic distributions could be nice features to be integrated in our framework.

Probabilistic Safety Assessment. A large amount of work has been done in the area of probabilistic safety assessment (PSA) and in particular on dynamic reliability [Siu94]. Dynamic reliability is concerned with extending the classical event or fault tree approaches to PSA by taking into consideration the mutual interactions between the hardware components of a plant and the physical evolution of its process variables [MZDL98]. Examples of scenarios taken into consideration are, e.g., human intervention, expert judgment, the role of control/protection systems, the so-called failures on demand (i.e., failure of a component to intervene), and also the ordering of events during accident propagation. Different approaches to dynamic reliability include, e.g., state transitions or Markov models [Ald87, Pap94], the dynamic event tree methodology [CIMP92], and direct simulation via Monte Carlo analysis [SD92, MZDL98].

6 Conclusions and Future Work

In this paper we have presented the ESACS safety analysis platform and methodology. The ESACS platform can be used as a tool to assist the safety analysis process from the early phases of system design to the formal verification and safety assessment phases. The goal is to provide an environment that can be used both by design engineers to formally verify a system and by safety engineers to automate certain phases of safety assessments. To achieve these goals, the platform provides a set of basic functions which can be combined in arbitrary ways to realize different process development methodologies. The functionality includes traditional analysis methodologies like fault tree generation, together with exhaustive property verification capabilities typical of model checking, plus model construction facilities (e.g., automatic failure injection based on a library of predefined failure modes) and traceability capabilities, which improve exchange of information and make system maintenance easier. The major benefits provided by the use of the ESACS platform and methodology are a tight integration between the design and the safety teams, mechanisation of (some of) the activities related both to the verification and to the safety analysis of systems in a uniform environment, and support for the realization of different development methodologies (e.g., incremental development approach, based on iterative releases of a given system model at different levels of detail).

Concerning the works on dynamic reliability cited in Section 5, the most notable difference between our approach and the works mentioned there is that we present automatic techniques, based on model checking, for both fault tree generation and ordering analysis, whereas traditional works on dynamic reliability rely on manual analysis (e.g., Markovian analysis [Pap94]) or simulation (e.g., Monte Carlo simulation [MZDL98], the TRETA package of [CIMP92]). Current work is focusing on some improvements and extensions in order to make the methodology competitive with existing approaches. In particular, we need to extend our framework in order to deal with probabilistic assessment. Although not illustrated in this paper, associating probabilistic estimates to basic events and evaluating the resulting fault trees is straightforward. However, more work needs to be done in order to support more complex probabilistic dynamics (see, e.g., [DS94]). We also want to overcome the current limitation to permanent failures.

As far as FSAP/NuSMV-SA is concerned, the models used so far are discrete, finite-state transition models. In order to allow for more realistic models, we are considering an extension of NuSMV with hybrid dynamics, along the lines of [Hen96, HHW97]. This would allow both to model more complex variable dynamics, and also a more realistic modelling of time (which, currently, is modelled by an abstract transition step). Furthermore, this would ameliorate the problem of state explosion, which is partly due to the current use of discretized integer variables. Another direction of research that we are investigating is the use of SAT-based model-checking verification techniques [BCCZ99], which have been shown to be extremely efficient for model debugging and bug hunting [ABC+02, ACKS02]. In the near future, we plan to use these techniques both for interactive fault tree generation and for formal specification debugging.

Acknowledgements

Several other people contributed to the work presented in this paper. We wish in particular to thank: Ove Akerlund (Prover), Pierre Bieber (ONERA), Christian Bougnol (AIRBUS), E. Boede (OFFIS), Matthias Bretschneider (AIRBUS-D), Charles Castel (ONERA), Alain Griffault (LaBri, Universit´e de Bordeaux), C. Kehren (ONERA), Benita Lawrence (AIRBUS-UK), Andreas Luedtke (University of Oldenburg), Silvayn Metge (AIRBUS-F), Chris Papadopoulos (AIRBUS-UK), Renata Passarello (SIA), Thomas Peikenkamp (OFFIS), Per Persson (Saab), Christel Seguin (ONERA), and Luigi Trotta (Alenia Aeronautica).

Finally, FSAP/NuSMV-SA would have not been possible without the help of Paolo Traverso, Alessandro Cimatti, and Gabriele Zacco.

References

[ABC+02] Audemard, G. & Bertoli, P. & Cimatti, A. & Kornilowicz, A. & Sebastiani R. A SAT Based Approach for Solving Formulas over Boolean and Linear Mathematical Propositions. In *A. Voronkov (Ed.), Proc. Conference on Automated Deduction (CADE-18)*, volume 2392 of LNAI, pages 195-210, Springer-Verlag, 2002.

[ACKS02] Audemard, G. & Cimatti, A. & Kornilowicz, A. & Sebastiani R. Model Checking for Timed Systems. In *D. Peled, M.Y. Vardi (Eds.), Proc. Conference on Formal Techniques for Networked and Distributed Systems (FORTE 2002)*, volume 2529 of LNCS, pages 243-259, Springer-Verlag, 2002.

[AGPR00] Arnold, A. & Griffault, A. & Point, G. & Rauzy, A. The AltaRica formalism for describing concurrent systems. *Fundamenta Informaticae*, 40:109-124, 2000.

[Ald87] Aldemir, Y. Computer-assisted Markov Failure Modeling of Process Control Systems. *IEEE Transactions on Reliability*, R-36:133-144, 1987.

[BCCZ99] Biere, A. & Cimatti, A & Clarke, E.M. & Zhu, Y. Symbolic Model Checking without BDDs. In *R. Cleaveland (Ed.) Proc. 5th International Conference on Tools and Algorithms for Construction and Analysis of Systems (TACAS'99)*, volume 1579 of LNCS, pages 193-207, Springer-Verlag, 1999.

[BCS02] Bieber, P. & Castel, C. & Seguin, C. Combination of Fault Tree Analysis and Model Checking for Safety Assessment of Complex System. In *Proc. 4th European Dependable Computing Conference*, volume 2485 of LNCS, page 19-31, Springer-Verlag, 2002.

[BHS+96] Brayton R.K. & Hachtel G.D. & Sangiovanni-Vincentelli A.L. & Somenzi F. & Aziz, A. & Cheng S.-T. & Edwards S.A. & Khatri S.P. & Kukimoto Y. & Pardo A. & Qadeer A. & Ranjan R.K. & Sarwary S. & Shiple T.R. & Swamy G. & Villa T. VIS: A System for Verification and Synthesis. In *R. Alur and T.A. Henzinger (Eds.), Proc.8th International Conference on Computer Aided Verification (CAV'96)*, Volume 1102 of LNCS, pages 428-432, Springer-Verlag, 1996.

[Bry92] Bryant, R.E. Symbolic Boolean Manipulation with Ordered Binary Decision Diagrams. *ACM Computing Surveys*, 24(3):293-318, 1992.

[BV03] Bozzano, M. & Villafiorita, A. Integrating Fault Tree Analysis with Event Ordering Information. In *Proc. European Safety and Reliability Conference (ESREL 2003)*, Maastricht, The Netherlands, 2003.

[CCG+02] Cimatti A. & Clarke, E.M. & Giunchiglia, E. & Giunchiglia, F. & Pistore, M. & Roveri, M. & Sebastiani, R. & Tacchella, A. NuSMV2: An OpenSource Tool for Symbolic Model Checking. In *Proc. International Conference on Computer-Aided Verification (CAV 2002)*, Copenhagen, Denmark, 2002.

[CGP00] Clarke, E. & Grumberg, O. & Peled, D. *Model Checking*. MIT Press, 1999.

[CIMP92] Cojazzi, G. & Izquierdo, J.M. & Meléndez, E. & Perea, M.S. The Reliability and Safety Assessment of Protection Systems by the Use of Dynamic Event Trees. The DYLAM-TRETA Package. In *Proc. XVIII Annual Meeting Spanish Nucl. Soc.*, 1992.

[CM92] Coudert, O. & Madre, J. Implicit and Incremental Computation of Primes and Essential Primes of Boolean Functions. In *Proc. 29th Design Automation Conference (DAC'98)*, pages 36-39, IEEE Computer Society Press, 1992.

[CM93]   Coudert, O. & Madre, J. Fault Tree Analysis: 10^{20} Prime Implicants and Beyond. In *Proc. Annual Reliability and Maintainability Symposium*, 1993.
[DS94]   Devooght, J. & Smidts, C. Probabilistic Dynamics; The Mathematical and Computing Problems Ahead. In *T. Aldemir, N.O. Siu, A. Mosleh, P.C. Cacciabue and B.G. Göktepe (Eds.), Reliability and Safety Assessment of Dynamic Process Systems*, NATO ASI Series F, 120:85-100, Springer-Verlag, 1994.
[Eme90]   Emerson, E. Temporal and Modal Logic. In *J. van Leeuwen (Ed.), Handbook of Theoretical Computer Science*, Volume B, pp. 995-1072. Elsevier Science, 1990.
[FMPN94]   Fenelon, P. & McDermid, J.A. & Pumfrey D.J. & Nicholson. M. Towards Integrated Safety Analysis and Design. *ACM Applied Computing Review, 2(1):21-32*, ACM Press, 1994.
[Hen96]   Henzinger, T.A. The Theory of Hybrid Automata. In *Proc. 11th Annual International Symposium on Logic in Computer Science (LICS'96)*, pages 278-292, IEEE Computer Society Press, 1996.
[HHW97]   Henzinger, T.A. & Ho, P.-H. & Wong-Toi, H. Hytech: : A Model Checker for Hybrid Systems. *Software Tools for Technology Transfer*, 1:110-122, 1997.
[LR98]   Liggesmeyer, P. & Rothfelder, M. Improving System Reliability with Automatic Fault Tree Generation. In *Proc. 28th International Symposium on Fault Tolerant Computing (FTCS'98)*, Munich, Germany, pp. 90-99. IEEE Computer Society Press, 1998.
[MDCS98]   Manian, R. & Dugan, J.B., & Coppit, D. & Sullivan, K.J. Combining Various Solution Techniques for Dynamic Fault Tree Analysis of Computer Systems. In *Proc. 3rd International High-Assurance Systems Engineering Symposium (HASE'98)*, pages 21-28, IEEE Computer Society Press, 1998.
[MZDL98]   Marseguerra, M., & Zio, E. & Devooght, J. & Labeau, P.E. A concept paper on dynamic reliability via Monte Carlo simulation. *Mathematics and Computers in Simulation*, 47:371-382, 1998.
[Pap94]   Papazoglou, I.A. Markovian Reliability Analysis of Dynamic Systems. In *T. Aldemir, N.O. Siu, A. Mosleh, P.C. Cacciabue and B.G. Göktepe (Eds.), Reliability and Safety Assessment of Dynamic Process Systems*, NATO ASI Series F, 120:24-43, Springer-Verlag, 1994.
[Rae00]   Rae, A. 2000. Automatic Fault Tree Generation – Missile Defence System Case Study. *Technical Report 00-36*, Software Verification Research Centre, University of Queensland, 2000.
[SD92]   Smidts, C. & Devooght, J. Probabilistic Reactor Dynamics II. A Monte-Carlo Study of a Fast Reactor Transient. *Nuclear Science and Engineering*, 111(3):241-256, 1992.
[SDC99]   Sullivan, K.J., & Dugan, J.B., & Coppit, D. The Galileo Fault Tree Analysis Tool. In *Proc. 29th Annual International Symposium on Fault-Tolerant Computing (FTCS'99)*, pages 232-235, IEEE Computer Society Press, 1999.
[Siu94]   Siu, N.O. Risk Assessment for Dynamic Systems: An Overview. *Reliability Engineering ans System Safety*, 43:43-74, 1994.
[SS00]   Sheeran M. & and Stalmarck G. A tutorial on Stalmarck's proof procedure for propositional logic, *Formal Methods in System Design*, vol. 16(1):23–58, 2000.
[VGRH81]   Vesely, W. & Goldberg, F. & Roberts, N. & Haasl D. 1981. Fault Tree Handbook, *Technical Report NUREG-0492*, Systems and Reliability Research Office of Nuclear Regulatory Research U.S. Nuclear Regulatory Commission.

Compositional Verification of an ATM Protocol

Vlad Rusu

IRISA/INRIA Rennes, Campus de Beaulieu, Rennes, France,
rusu@irisa.fr, Fax: (+33) 2 99 84 71 71

Abstract. Compositionality and abstraction are key ingredients for the successful verification of complex infinite-state systems. In this paper we present an approach based on these ingredients and on theorem proving for verifying communication protocols. The approach is implemented in PVS. It is demonstrated here by verifying the data transfer function of the SSCOP protocol, an ATM protocol whose main requirement is to perform a reliable data transfer over an unreliable communication medium.

Keywords: Compositionality, abstraction, theorem proving, PVS, SSCOP protocol.

1 Introduction

Formal verification methods form a wide spectrum ranging from fully automatic *model checking* [7] to interactive *theorem proving* [22]. A recent trend in verification consists in combining model checking and theorem proving through *abstraction* [1, 14, 26]. In these approaches, a theorem prover [8, 12, 25] is used to simplify (to "abstract") the state space of the system under verification for a model checker [3, 10, 15] to explore. This has made it possible to automatically verify real-size systems [11, 17]. In other approaches based on *abstract interpretation* [6], the abstract system is automatically built and analyzed on the fly [19].

However, there are limits to what automatic methods can do. The main limitation of model checking is that it is restricted to (essentially) finite-state systems. Before a model checker is applied, e.g., for verifying a communication protocol, the user has to set the values of parameters (such as window and channel sizes) to small, usually unrealistic values. Abstraction allows in some cases to reduce an infinite-state system to a finite one; but there is no general recipe for finding adequate abstractions for complex data types such as those arising in specifications of real communication protocols. As a result, the abstract system may still contain infinite-state data and (except in some particular cases [1, 19]) still require interactive theorem proving rather than model checking to verify.

Another way to deal with the difficulty of verification is to perform *compositional* reasoning [9]. The system is broken down into components, and each component is verified individually, using only limited information about the environment (i.e., the remaining components). The correctness of the whole system is then inferred from that of the components. Compositional reasoning has also proved effective at dealing with large case studies [2, 20, 27].

In this paper we develop a verification method based on abstraction, compositional reasoning, and theorem proving, and illustrate it on a real system: the data transfer service of the SSCOP protocol, an ATM protocol defined by the International Telecommunications Union [21]. Among other uses, the protocol has been proposed as an alternative to TCP in datagram satellite networks [16].

The Service Specific Connection Oriented Protocol (SSCOP) is a member of the ATM adaptation layer, whose main role is to adapt the unreliable services provided by the lower (physical) layer, to reliable connections and data transfer between two ends. The SSCOP provides to its upper layers services such as connection establishment and release; error reporting; flow control, using a sliding-window mechanism; and secure data transfer, using selective retransmission of protocol data units (PDU). It is standardized in [21], a technical document consisting of an informal natural-language description and a formal specification written in SDL (Specification and Description Language).

The *data transfer* service is the core of the protocol. It consists of mechanisms for sending PDUs and detecting and retransmitting lost PDUs. It is the most complex and data-intensive service of the protocol; it occupies 12 of the 46 pages of the specification [21] and uses about twenty state variables of types ranging from the integers to complex types such as unbounded queues of records.

In this paper a formal verification of the data transfer service is presented. The *main property* verified concerns the reliable transmission of an arbitrary sequence of messages between the sender and the receiver. It says that when the last message has been acknowledged, the sequence of messages delivered to the receiver's client equals the sequence that the sender's client requested to send. The data transfer has been verified as a *unit*, and a natural question that arises is whether the property still holds when the data transfer service is connected to the rest of protocol. We formally prove a set of necessary and sufficient conditions on the behaviors of the upper and lower layers that surround the SSCOP, for the *main property* to hold on the whole protocol as well. The verification is based on abstraction, compositionality, and deductive reasoning.

Abstraction. An *atomicity abstraction* is employed, which consists in considering some sequences of actions (reading from or writing to channels, or internal actions such as assignments to local variables) as *atomic*. That is, a whole sequence of actions is executed by one entity (e.g., the sender) without being interrupted by actions of the other entity (e.g., the receiver). This semantics is implemented in SDL commercial tools [24] and used in verification case studies [13, 27].

While convenient for verification, this semantics is not realistic for modeling distant communicating entities, because one cannot reasonably assume that one entity, at one end of the protocol, performs a whole (potentially unbounded) sequence of actions, while the other entity at the other end does not move. Hence, we also prove as a meta-theorem that, under reasonable sufficient conditions, a property verified under this semantics also holds under the more realistic, full interleaving semantics of actions from both entities.

Compositional verification of invariants. An *invariant* is a state predicate which is true in every reachable state of the system. Invariants are the most common class of safety properties. For verifying invariants we use PVS [25], an interactive theorem prover based on typed higher-order logic, which contains enough automation to discharge the user of most tedious details of the proofs. A PVS strategy (that does not depend on the case study) is used, which attempts to prove that a predicate is inductive, i.e., it is true initially and is preserved by every transition. If this is the case, the predicate is an invariant, otherwise, the subgoals left unproved by PVS suggest auxiliary invariants that, if proved, would also help settling the initial invariants.

This systematic invariant strengthening is performed in a *compositional* manner: each entity (sender and receiver) requires its own set of auxiliary invariants, many of which are trivially preserved by the other entity; this saves many proof obligations, which otherwise would make the verification infeasible. A formally proved compositional rule guarantees the soundness of the approach.

Overall, we obtain a verification methodology for communication protocols, which is general enough to be applicable to systems of complexity similar to that of the SSCOP. The current case study took three months for a moderately experienced PVS user to complete. We believe this is a reasonable amount of time for verifying the core of a real protocol, which took several months and meetings for a normalization committee to define. Ideally, if the validation were done during the definition phase, this would lead to formally verified specifications without notably delaying their delivery date.

The rest of the paper is organized as follows. In Section 2 we describe the model of extended automata, to which a significant fragment of SDL can be translated, and the abstraction and compositional rules that we employ to verify specifications written in this model. In Section 3 we show how the compositional rule can be employed in conjunction with invariant strengthening to prove invariance properties of a very simple example. In Section 4 the SSCOP protocol and its verification using PVS are outlined. Section 5 presents conclusions and related work. The URL http://www.irisa.fr/vertecs/Equipe/Rusu/sscop contains PVS specifications and proofs for the case study, together with an Appendix with (manual) proofs for the compositional and abstraction rules employed.

2 Models

Extended Automata are a computational model for reactive programs. An extended automaton consists of a finite set of typed variables V, an initial condition Θ which is a predicate on the variables, a finite set of control locations L, a subset L_i of *initial* locations, and a finite set of transitions $\mathcal{T}$ that connect the locations. The locations are partitioned into a set of *stable* locations L_s, which include the initial locations L_i, and a set of *unstable* locations $L_u = L \setminus L_s$. The distinction between stable and unstable location will appear essential for verification purposes. Each transition is labelled with an input, an output, or an internal action, and consists of a guard and a set of assignments.

For example, the automaton represented in Figure 1 (left) has one stable location l_0, which is the initial location, two integer variables i and x, and one variable ch which is a FIFO queue, for which i plays the role of a "head" index. The initial condition sets i and x to 0; then, each time the output action **out**! occurs, the transition from l_0 to l_0 is taken, the value of x is stored into the head $ch[i]$ of the queue, and both variables i and x are increased by one.

Another example of extended automaton is depicted in Figure 1 (right). This automaton has two locations, l_1, l_2, three integer variables y, i, j, and one variable ch, a FIFO queue to which i is the head index and j the tail index. The initial location l_1 is the only stable location of the system. Starting with $y = 0$ and $j = 0$, the system waits for an input action **inp**?. Then, if the tail index j is less than the head index i (that is, if the queue ch is nonempty), the tail element $ch[j]$ is stored into y and j is simultaneously increased by one. Next, the control goes directly back to l_1 and the value of y is divided by 2. Here, the label τ denotes an internal action, which is not observable from the environment.

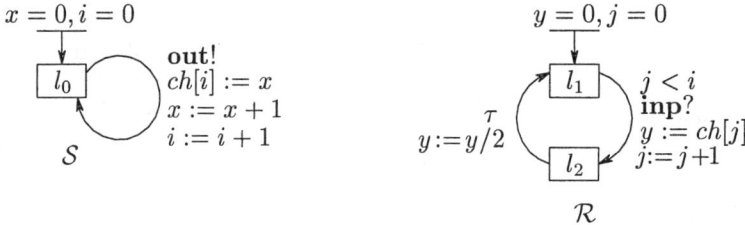

Fig. 1. Examples of Extended Automata

By composing these systems according to the usual shared-variable parallel composition we obtain a simple protocol in which the sender $\mathcal{S}$ places the sequence $0, 1, 2, \ldots$ on the channel, while the receiver $\mathcal{R}$ reads this sequence at the other end and memorizes its reading in variable y, which is immediately divided by 2. This example is used to demonstrate the verification method in Section 3.

Semantics. A *state* is a pair $\langle l, v \rangle$ where l is a location, and v a valuation of the variables. An *initial state* is a state whose location is initial and whose variables satisfy the initial condition Θ. For t a transition, the *transition relation* ρ_t is the set of pairs of states (s, s') such that, if $s = \langle l, v \rangle$ and $s' = \langle l', v' \rangle$, then the origin of t is l, the destination of t is l', the guard of t is satisfied by the values v of the variables in state s, and the values v' are obtained from v by the assignments of t, which are all executed in parallel. The transition relation of the automaton is $\rho = \bigcup_{t \in \mathcal{T}} \rho_t$. A *run fragment* of the automaton is a sequence of states such that each two consecutive states are in the transition relation ρ. A *run* is a run fragment that starts in an initial state. A state is *reachable* if it is the last state of some run. A state predicate P is an *invariant* of the automaton A, denoted $A \models \Box P$, if P holds in every reachable state of A.

Parallel Composition. We define two parallel composition operators. The first one, *micro-step* parallel composition, denoted by $\|$, is the usual asynchronous composition of programs with shared variables. The second one, *macro-step* parallel composition, denoted |, allows some particular sequences of steps (so called *macro-steps*) to be executed atomically.

The initial location of the *micro-step* parallel composition $A_1||A_2$ is the the set of pairs consisting of initial locations of A_1 and of A_2, and the initial condition is the conjunction of those of A_1, A_2. A state s of the composed system is a pair (s_1, s_2) of states of the components that agree on the values of the common variables. Formally, let $v^{\downarrow V'}$ denote the restriction of a valuation v to a subset $V' \subseteq V$ of variables. The states $s_1 = \langle l_1, v_1\rangle$ of A_1 and $s_2 = \langle l_2, v_2\rangle$ of A_2 constitute a state $s = (s_1, s_2)$ of $A_1||A_2$ if $v_1^{\downarrow V_1 \cap V_2} = v_2^{\downarrow V_1 \cap V_2}$, where V_1, V_2 denote the sets of variables of A_1, A_2. For a state $s = \langle l, v\rangle$, we denote by $s^{\downarrow V'}$ the pair $\langle l, v^{\downarrow V'}\rangle$. The transition relation ρ of the composed system $A_1||A_2$ holds for states $s = (s_1, s_2)$ and $s' = (s_1', s_2')$ of $A_1||A_2$ if either $s_1'^{\downarrow V_1 \backslash V_2} = s_1^{\downarrow V_1 \backslash V_2}$ and $\rho_2(s_2, s_2')$ holds, or $s_2'^{\downarrow V_2 \backslash V_1} = s_2^{\downarrow V_2 \backslash V_1}$ and $\rho_1(s_1, s_1')$ holds, where ρ_1 (resp. ρ_2) is the transition relation of A_1 (resp. A_2).

We now define the *macro-step* parallel composition. The initial location, initial condition, and states of the macro-step parallel composition $A_1|A_2$ are defined just like for $A_1||A_2$. For the transition relation, remember that the definition of Extended Automata says (cf. beginning of this section) that some locations are stable and some are unstable. A *macro-step* is a run fragment $s^1, \ldots, s^k$, where $s^i = \langle l^i, v^i\rangle$ for $i = 1, \ldots, k$ such that l^1 and l^k are stable and for $j = 2, \ldots k-1$, l^j is unstable. We define the *macro-step* relation ϱ_1 of A_1 (and similarly for A_2) as the set of pairs of states (s, s') for which there exists a macro-step between s and s'. The macro-step relation ϱ of the composed system $A_1|A_2$ holds for states $s = (s_1, s_2)$ and $s' = (s_1', s_2')$ if either $s_1'^{\downarrow V_1 \backslash V_2} = s_1^{\downarrow V_1 \backslash V_2}$ and $\varrho_2(s_2, s_2')$ holds, or $s_2'^{\downarrow V_2 \backslash V_1} = s_2^{\downarrow V_2 \backslash V_1}$ and $\varrho_1(s_1, s_1')$ holds, where ϱ_1 (resp. ϱ_2) is the macro-step relation of A_1 (resp. A_2).

Intuitively, the macro-step parallel composition allows one component to move by performing a whole macro-step, while the other component does not move. Thus, macro-step parallel composition has less behaviors than the micro-step version; consequently, it makes it easier to verify invariance properties.

On the other hand, the macro-step composition is not realistic for modeling communication protocols, because one cannot reasonably assume that one entity, which is at one end of a network, cannot move while the other entity at the other end performs a whole macro-step. For verification, this problem is solved by Proposition 2, defined below, which says that for a broad class of extended automata, it is enough to prove invariants on the macro-step parallel composition, for the invariants to hold in the "stable" states of the micro-step parallel composition as well. The macro-step semantics has another advantage: it allows a compositional verification of invariants. This is expressed by Proposition 1.

Definition 1. *Let A be an extended automaton, P a predicate on the variables of A, and L a set of locations of A. Then, $A\mathrm{init}\langle P, L\rangle$ is an extended automaton identical to A except that its initial condition is P and its set of initial locations is L.*

Proposition 1. *Let A_1, A_2 be extended automata over a set of variables V, and P a predicate on variables V such that P holds in the initial states of A_1, A_2. Assume that both A_1 **init** $\langle P, L_s^1 \rangle \models \Box P$, A_2 **init** $\langle P, L_s^2 \rangle \models \Box P$ hold, where L_s^1, L_s^2 denote the sets of stable locations of A_1, A_2. Then, $A_1 | A_2 \models \Box P$ holds.*

The proof is in the Appendix[1]. We show in Section 3 how to use Prop. 1 to prove invariants of |-composed systems. Under conditions expressed by the following definitions, these invariants carry over to the more realistic ||-composed systems.

Definition 2 (reading, writing access to variables).

♯1 *A transition t of an extended automaton has a writing access to a variable x if x appears in the left-hand side of an assignment of t. If x appears only in the guard or the right-hand side of an assignment, the access is a reading.*

♯2 *An automaton A has a (reading, resp. a writing) access to a variable x if at least one of the transitions of A has a (reading, resp. a writing) access to x.*

♯3 *A transition t has a (reading, resp. a writing) access to a set of variables V if t has a (reading, resp. a writing) access to at least one variable in V.*

Note that, according to Definition 2♯1, a transition may access a variable in either reading or writing, but not both; but by ♯3, for a *set* the access may be in both reading *and* writing. For example, the transition from l_1 to l_2 of the automaton $\mathcal{R}$ (Fig. 1) accesses variables ch, i in reading, and y, j in writing, hence, by Def. 2♯3 it accesses the *set* $\{ch, i, y, j\}$ in both reading and writing.

Definition 3 (syntactical macro-step). *A path in the graph of an extended automaton A is a syntactical macro-step of A if the path starts and ends in a stable location of A, and all the intermediary locations on the path are unstable.*

Definition 4 (single access). *Let A_1, A_2 be extended automata with sets of variables V_1, V_2. A_1, A_2 have single-access to their shared variables $V_1 \cap V_2$ if*

♯1 *no transition of A_1, A_2 accesses $V_1 \cap V_2$ in both reading and writing,*
♯2 *no variable in $V_1 \cap V_2$ is accessed in writing by both automata (cf. Def. 2♯2)*
♯3 *each syntactical macro-step of A_1, and each syntactical macro-step of A_2, contains at most one transition that accesses the variables $V_1 \cap V_2$, such that:*
  – *if the access is a reading then it is made by the* first *transition of the path;*
  – *if the access is a writing, then it is made by the* last *transition of the path.*

For example, the automata $\mathcal{S}$ and $\mathcal{R}$ depicted in Figure 1 have single-access to their common variables ch and i: $\mathcal{R}$ *reads* both variables on the *first* transition of the path $l_1 - l_2 - l_1$, and $\mathcal{S}$ writes *writes* to them on the *last* transition of the path $l_0 - l_0$ (which consists of only one transition). In the sequel, we employ a variable pc to encode the control, e.g., $pc = l$ holds when control is at location l.

---
[1] Available at http://www.irisa.fr/vertecs/Equipe/Rusu/sscop.

Proposition 2. *Let A_1, A_2 be extended automata with single access to their common variables $V_1 \cap V_2$, and P a predicate on $V_1 \cup V_2$. If P is an invariant of $A_1|A_2$ and l^1, l^2 are stable locations, then $A_1||A_2 \models \Box(pc_1 = l^1 \wedge pc_2 = l^2 \supset P)$.*

The proof can be found in the Appendix. Proposition 2 says that invariants that hold in stable locations of the |-parallel composition carry over to the ||-parallel composition. For example, the main property of the SSCOP protocol says that *when transmission ends*, the data delivered to destination equals the data received from source. The prequel "when transmission ends" denotes the presence in a stable state, thus, the property is in the class, and, by Proposition 2, it is only necessary to prove the property on the |-parallel composition.

3 Proving Invariants of Extended Automata Using PVS

In this section we show how to prove invariants of a parallel composition $A_1||A_2$ of extended automata. This process is first described for stand-alone components.

First, a transition t of an extended automaton A is said to *preserve* a predicate P if, by using only the hypothesis that P is true before the transition t, it can be inferred that P is still true after t is fired. The predicate P is *inductive* if P holds in the initial states of A and it is preserved by each transition of A. If P is inductive, then P is an invariant, but the converse is not true. This is because the basic hypothesis that P is true before a transition is usually not enough to prove its preservation. Typically, the hypothesis P has to be strengthened using *auxiliary invariants*; the definition of preservation becomes "by assuming that $P \wedge Q$ is true before a transition t, it can be inferred that P is still true after t is fired". Here the auxiliary predicate Q can always be chosen to be the *weakest precondition* of P by t, which is semantically defined by $wp(s) = \forall s'.\rho_t(s,s') \supset P(s')$. Alternatively, any predicate stronger than wp can be chosen. However, the previous definition does not provide a *syntactical* means for computing an adequate auxiliary predicate Q.

Our method implemented in PVS fills this gap. All invariance proofs are done using one single automated PVS proof strategy, which, if successful, proves that the predicate P under proof is inductive. If the strategy fails, PVS presents the user with pending subgoals, which suggest the auxiliary invariants Q required for proving P. To prove that Q is an invariant may necessitate yet another invariant R, etc. The process continues until all the invariants generated in this manner are proved, or until evidence is obtained that P is not an invariant.

We now show how to prove invariants of a parallel composition $A_1||A_2$. Of course, one could first build the parallel composition $A_1||A_2$ and use the above invariant-strengthening approach, but we want to do the verification in a compositional manner. First, Proposition 2 shows that, under reasonable restrictions, for proving that P is an invariant of $A_1||A_2$, it is enough to prove that P is invariant on the macro-step parallel composition $A_1|A_2$. Then, by Proposition 1, it is enough to prove that P holds initially in A_1, A_2, and that P is an invariant of A_1 init $\langle P, L_s^1 \rangle$ and of A_2 init $\langle P, L_s^2 \rangle$. The latter being stand-alone components, the basic invariant-strengthening technique can now be used. Again, the basic hypothesis that P is true before each transition is usually too weak, and the hypothesis has to be strengthened using auxiliary invariants suggested by PVS.

The difference here is that an auxiliary invariant Q used for proving P on one component may also have to be proved preserved by the other. Consider, for example, an attempt to prove $A_1 \text{ init } \langle P, L_s^1 \rangle \models \Box P$ for which PVS suggests the auxiliary invariant Q. Then, even if one proves that $A_1 \text{ init } \langle P \wedge Q, L_s^1 \rangle \models \Box(P \wedge Q)$ holds (and Q holds initially in A_1), in order to be able to use Proposition 1, one still has to prove that the second component preserves Q; that is, one has to prove that is Q holds initially in A_2 and that $A_2 \text{ init } \langle P \wedge Q, L_s^2 \rangle \models \Box(P \wedge Q)$ holds as well. Then, by Proposition 1 it can be deduced that $A_1|A_2 \models \Box(P \wedge Q)$; in particular, that P is an invariant of $A_1|A_2$. Finally, by Proposition 2, P is an invariant at all stable locations of $A_1||A_2$.

The benefit of the above compositional approach (over directly proving P by invariant strengthening over $A_1||A_2$) is that the compositional approach typically generates fewer proof obligations:

- Intuitively, a predicate Q describing properties at *unstable* locations of one component are trivially preserved by the other one, because when one component is in an unstable location, the other one does not move. Formally, if Q is an auxiliary invariant of the form $pc_1 = l \supset Q'$, where $l \in L_u^1$ is an *unstable* location of A_1, then Q trivially holds in the initial states of $A_1 \text{ init } \langle P, L_s^1 \rangle$. Thus, proving $A_1 \text{ init } \langle P \wedge Q, L_s^1 \rangle \models \Box(P \wedge Q)$ reduces to proving $A_1 \text{ init } \langle P, L_s^1 \rangle \models \Box(P \wedge Q)$. Hence, if one also prove $A_2 \text{ init } \langle P, L_s^2 \rangle \models \Box P$ then Proposition 1 can directly be used to deduce $A_1|A_2 \models \Box P$; that is, a proof that Q is preserved by A_2 has been saved;
- Intuitively, predicates that only involve variables to which a component has no writing access are trivially preserved by that component. Formally, if Q is an auxiliary invariant that involves only variables to which A_2 has no writing access, then $A_2 \text{ init } \langle P \wedge Q, L_s^2 \rangle \models \Box Q$ is trivially true, and the proof obligation $A_2 \text{ init } \langle P \wedge Q, L_s^2 \rangle \models \Box(P \wedge Q)$ reduces to $A_2 \text{ init } \langle P \wedge Q, L_s^2 \rangle \models \Box P$. Again, a proof that Q is preserved by A_2 has been saved.

In both cases, an invariance proof (that would have been required by a global verification) was eliminated by the compositional approach. Since proving an invariant usually requires proving a whole chain of auxiliary invariants, it is not just one proof that was saved, but many more; and the saved effort is multiplied by the number of components involved. For example, the data transfer of the SSCOP protocol is decomposed in five components (three for the sender, and two for the receiver, cf. Section 4). Its verification consisted in proving 252 invariants, out of which 47 needed to be proved only on one component out of five; and, among the remaining ones, many required a proof only on two or three components. In a global verification, each of these invariants would required a proof on the whole system, which would make the verification practically unfeasible.

Example 1. The method is illustrated on the system consisting of the parallel composition of the sender ($\mathcal{S}$) and receiver ($\mathcal{R}$) automata depicted in Figure 1.

We want to prove that the relation $x \geq y$ holds whenever $\mathcal{S}$ and $\mathcal{R}$ are in a stable location. That is, we have to prove $\mathcal{S}||\mathcal{R} \models \Box(pc_1 = l_0 \wedge pc_2 = l_1 \supset x \geq y)$.

For this, by Propositions 1 and 2, it is enough to prove (1) $\mathcal{S}\operatorname{init}\langle x \geq y, \{l_0\}\rangle \models \Box(x \geq y)$ and (2) $\mathcal{R}\operatorname{init}\langle x \geq y, \{l_1\}\rangle \models \Box(x \geq y)$. Now, (1) is trivial because the only transition of $\mathcal{S}$ increases x, thus, it preserves $x \geq y$. For (2), the transition from l_2 to l_1 preserves $x \geq y$ as y is divided by 2. The transition from l_1 to l_2 does not preserve $x \geq y$, as it assigns to y the value $ch[j]$ and we do not know anything about this value at this point. However, PVS suggests the following auxiliary invariant $Q: \quad pc_1 = l_1 \wedge 0 \leq j < i \supset x \geq ch[j]$, which is essentially the weakest precondition of $x \geq y$ by the transition. Thus, we prove (2') $\mathcal{R}\operatorname{init}\langle x \geq y \wedge Q, \{l_1\}\rangle \models \Box(x \geq y \wedge Q)$, which is trivial, because the auxiliary invariant was precisely chosen to settle it; and we still have to prove that Q is preserved by the sender, i.e., (3): $\mathcal{S}\operatorname{init}\langle x \geq y \wedge Q, \{l_0\}\rangle \models \Box(x \geq y \wedge Q)$. The latter amounts to proving that the only transition of $\mathcal{S}$ preserves the predicate $Q': \quad (0 \leq j < i \supset x \geq ch[j])$. This is not the case, and a few proof attempts with PVS suggest an auxiliary invariant stronger that Q', namely $R: \quad x = i \wedge \forall k.(0 \leq k < i \supset ch[k] = k)$.

Now, $\mathcal{S}$ preserves R, and R only refers to variables to which $\mathcal{R}$ does not have a writing access. Thus, $\mathcal{R}$ trivially preserves R, and the proof is done.

The remainder of the section shows how to encode the approach in PVS.

In PVS, specifications are structured into modules called *theories*. The sender theory in Figure 2 declares two enumerated types, Location and Action, with one element each, which correspond to the location and action sets of the sender automaton $\mathcal{S}$ from Figure 1. The state of the automaton is a record type State, which consists of a location, two integer variables i and x, and a function ch from integers to integers that encodes the channel. The fields of a record are accessed using the ' accessor, e.g., s'x is the field x of record s. The transition relation holds for a state, action, and next state as shown by the predicate trans. The WITH record modifier is used to encode assignments to the variables.

Figure 3 shows a part of the sender_invariants theory, which contains the initial condition init and invariants for the sender. Note that the initial condition is modified such as to include the invariants being proved (cf. Definition 1).

The comments (lines that start with %) next to the predicates in the initial condition are used to keep track of what has been proved and what remains to be proved, both in this theory and the corresponding theory for the receiver (if needed). For example, the predicate $x = i$ only refers to variables that cannot be modified by the receiver, thus, it is only proved by the sender (cf. lemma

```
sender : THEORY
BEGIN
Location: TYPE = {l0}
Action: TYPE = {out}
State: TYPE = [# pc : Location, i: int, x: int, ch: [int->int] #]
trans(s: State,a: Action,s_:   State): bool = s'pc =    l0 AND a = out AND
   s_ = s  WITH['pc := l0,'ch(s'i) := s'x,'x := s'x+1,'i := s'i+1]
END sender
```

Fig. 2. The Sender Automaton $\mathcal{S}$ (from Figure 1) in PVS

```
init(s:State) : bool = s'pc = 10 AND
    %x_ge_y, receiver_invariants.x_ge_y
  (s'x >= y) AND
    %channel_aux
  (s'x = s'i) AND
    %channel_aux_aux
  (FORALL (k:nat) : 0 <= k AND k < s'i IMPLIES s'ch(k) = k)
    %inductive
channel_aux : LEMMA invariant(LAMBDA(s:State) :s'i = s'x)
    %proved using channel_aux
channel_aux_aux : LEMMA invariant(LAMBDA(s:State) : FORALL (k:nat) : 0 <= k
                                  AND  k < s'i IMPLIES s'ch(k) = k)
    %inductive
x_ge_y: LEMMA invariant(LAMBDA(s:State) : s'x >= y)
```

Fig. 3. : A Fragment of the sender_invariants Theory

channel_aux), whereas $x \geq y$ also refers to variables to which the receiver has writing access, thus, it is proved both in lemma x_ge_z and in a lemma with the same name on the receiver side. The comments next to the lemmas show dependencies between invariants, e.g., channel_aux is a lemma describing an inductive invariant, which is used for proving lemma channel_aux_aux. By keeping track of what has been proved and what is still pending, we ensure that nothing is forgotten and eventually complete the proof of the original property.

4 Verifying the SSCOP Protocol

In this section the verification of the SSCOP protocol is described, using the approach presented in the previous section. Both the protocol and its verification are quite large, and cannot be described extensively. However, we try to give as much detail as possible, including a small part of the verification to illustrate how the method presented in the previous section scales up to a real case study.

The SSCOP protocol consists of a sender and a receiver that exchange Protocol Data Units (PDUs) through communication channels. Let SR designate the channel from the sender to the receiver, and RS the channel from receiver to sender (cf. Figure 4). The data transfer function involves four kinds of PDUs.

- SD (service data) PDUs transit on the SR channel. They convey the actual data from sender to receiver. Each SD PDU also carries a unique index number;
- POLL PDUs also transit on the SR channel. They are used by the sender to question the receiver on its status with regards to reception of SD PDUs;
- STAT (status) PDUs transit on the RS channel. The receiver replies with a STAT to a POLL of the sender, by reporting a list of SD PDU that are missing;
- USTAT (unsolicited status) PDUs also transit on the RS channel. They are similar to STAT, except that they are emitted spontaneously by the receiver, when a SD PDU with a higher index number than expected is received, which means some SD PDU were lost during the transmission.

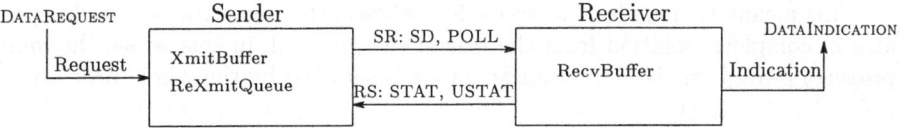

Fig. 4. The Data Transfer Function of the SSCOP Protocol

In addition, the data transfer function exchanges signals with its upper layer:

- the sender's client emits DATAREQUEST signals, carrying data encoded by the sender as SD PDU. This flow of data is modeled by the *Request* sequence;
- the receiver delivers correctly received SD PDUs by sending DATAINDICATION signals to its client. This flow is modeled by the *Indication* sequence.

There are other signals between the SSCOP and its upper layer (e.g., both clients may request disconnection while the data transfer is ongoing) but they are not included in the present specification. That is, the protocol is verified under the assumption that its clients do not disrupt an ongoing data transfer on purpose.

The *main property* verified concerns an arbitrary sequence of messages to be transmitted between the sender and the receiver's clients. The property says that when the last message has been acknowledged and the acknowledgment was received, the *Indication* and *Request* sequences are equal. As the channels are lossy, the protocol achieves this through selective retransmissions of SD PDUs, using a mechanism involving POLL, STAT and USTAT PDUs.

An important observation that can be made at this point is that the protocol is meant to operate under the hypothesis that channels may lose, but not create, duplicate, or reorder PDUs. This can be seen by simulating the SDL specification [21]. For example, if an SD PDU reaches the receiver with the same sequence number as one that was already received (duplication), then the protocol exits its data transfer mode and transmission is terminated. Similarly, if the order of arrival of two SD PDU is modified in the SR channel, the arrival of the first one triggers the retransmission of the second one, which eventually reaches the receiver, with the same consequence that the transmission is abruptly terminated. (The protocol does have a "recovery" service for these situations, which merely consists in waiting and restarting the transmission from the beginning.) Hence, the protocol is verified under the assumption that it may only *lose* PDUs.

The protocol cannot tolerate any amount of losses, either. A timer τ expires when no PDUs have arrived for a certain amount of time, which abruptly terminates the transmission and places the protocol back in disconnected mode.

We take advantage of these observations as follows. We isolate the data transfer mode of the SSCOP from the rest of the protocol, by replacing everything but the data transfer by an abstract state, and prove using PVS that, if the following conditions hold: (1) channels may only lose PDUs; (2) the timer τ never gets to expire while the transmission is ongoing; and (3) the clients do not request disconnection while transmission is ongoing, then: (a) the abstract state is not reachable, and (b) the data transfer mode satisfies the *main property*.

This means that under the above hypotheses, the data transfer mode operates in complete isolation from the rest of the protocol; in this sense, the *main property* proved on the data transfer mode is satisfied by the whole protocol as well. Conditions (1), (2) and (3) are also *necessary* for the property to hold, because in the recovery and disconnected modes (which are reachable from the data transfer mode if (1), (2) or (3) are violated) the receiver may retrieve the data it has received up to that point, which is typically an incomplete sequence.

Thus, if conditions (1), (2) or (3) are violated, the protocol does not satisfy the *main property* as it was stated. Of course, the property could be reformulated to include more behaviors, but this goes beyond the scope of this paper.

Formally modeling the protocol. To be consistent with the semantics of SDL, in which distant processes may interleave their actions, the protocol is described as SSCOP:= *Sender*||*Receiver*, where || is the *micro-step* parallel composition (cf. Section 2). A brief description of the sender and receiver processes follows. (The reader may consult [10, 21] for more details.) Both processes can be decomposed into several components, which correspond to SDL transitions in the specification [21].

4.1 The Sender

The sender process consists of one component for sending SD and POLL PDUs, another one for receiving USTAT, and a third one for receiving STAT PDUs. According to the semantics of SDL, only one of these components can be executing at one time, while the others are waiting in stable locations. This is because all three components belong to the same process, which is assumed to be executing on one single processor. When a component terminates its execution, it goes back to its initial location, and another one can take its turn. This behaviour is modeled by imposing that the extended automata of the components have only one stable location, which is their initial location, and by defining the sender as the *macro-step* parallel composition *Sender* := (SD&POLL *sender*|USTAT *receiver*|STAT *receiver*).

Sending SD and POLL. This component is in charge of sending new SD PDUs as well as old ones (retransmissions) and of interrogating the receiver by means of POLL PDUs. New SD PDUs are taken from the *Request* sequence (cf. Figure 4), whereas old ones are taken from the retransmission queue *ReXmitQueue*. Each new SD is given a unique index number and is sent on the SR channel, and its data and index are memorized in the sender's window *XmitBuffer*, together with the current poll sequence number *VTPS*. The latter is a variable whose initial value is zero and which is incremented each time a new POLL PDU is sent by the current component. This happens at least every $MaxPD \geq 1$ transmissions of new SD, and after every retransmission of an old SD PDU.

A POLL PDU carries, among other values, the current values of *VTPS* and of *VTS*, the highest index of an SD PDU that the sender has ever emitted.

Receiving USTAT. USTAT PDUs are sent by the receiver of the SSCOP upon reception of a SD PDU with an unexpectedly high index number. Technically, this happens when the index of the received SD PDU is higher than than the highest index the receiver knows about. For the sake of precision, let us name *VRH* the latter index. A USTAT PDU consists of a copy of the receiver's state variables, including *VRH* and the index of the message just received. The interval defined by these values constitutes a set of SD PDU the receiver assumes to be *lost*.

Upon reception of a USTAT PDU, the sender first checks that it is valid, i.e., that the values of its fields are consistent with the state variables of the sender. For example, *VTS*, the highest index of SD PDUs known to the sender, must be no less than the corresponding index of the receiver *VRH*. If this is the case, all SD PDUs defined as "lost" by the USTAT are added to the sender's retransmission queue *ReXmitQueue*. Otherwise, the sender concludes that the USTAT is invalid, and the protocol exits the data transfer mode and goes into recovery mode. In our model, we have abstracted everything but the data transfer mode by an abstract location *OutOfDtr*, which we will prove unreachable.

Receiving STAT. This is the third and last component of the sender and is somewhat similar to receiving USTAT. A STAT PDU is generated by the receiver of the SSCOP upon reception of a POLL PDU. It consists of copies of the state variables of the receiver, mainly, an abstract view of the receiver's window.

Upon reception of STAT PDU, the sender checks its validity just like for a USTAT, with the same outcome if it is found invalid, i.e., an (unreachable) exit from the data transfer mode. Then, the copy of the receiver's window is scanned, and the SD PDUs that it describes as missing are added to the retransmission queue of the sender. To avoid useless retransmission, an SD PDU will not be added to the retransmission queue if it is already there. The same happens if the *VTPS* value memorized together with the index of the SD in the sender's window *XmitBuffer* (cf. "*Sending* SD *and* POLL" paragraph) is above a certain threshold of acceptable values. This rather intricate mechanism is crucial for ensuring the property that no retransmissions occur unless really necessary, a property that the protocol consistently enforces for efficiency considerations.

4.2 The Receiver

The receiver can be described as *Receiver* := (SD *receiver*|POLL*receiver*), where | is the macro-step parallel composition, and the extended automata of the SD receiver and POLL receiver have their initial location as their only stable location.

Receiving SD. Upon reception of an SD PDU, the receiver checks if the SD was already received, i.e., if it is already memorized in the receiver's window *RecvBuffer*. If this is the case, the data transfer mode is terminated, which we model by the *OutOfDtr* location that we shall prove unreachable. Otherwise, if the index of the SD PDU is between the next expected index and the highest index ever received (called *VRH*, cf. "receiving USTAT" paragraph), the SD is stored in the receiver's window, and the lower bound of the window is advanced as long as the new reception has created a *contiguous* sequence of received SD. The latter are then delivered to the *Indication* channel (i.e., to the sender's client).

Otherwise, if the index of the SD is greater than VRH, the latter is updated, and a USTAT PDU is generated as described in the "receiving USTAT" paragraph.

Receiving POLL. This component and some of the invariants connected to it are described in the next section as an illustration of our verification methodology.

Verification: The Main Invariants

The system to be verified is the micro-step parallel composition *Sender*∥*Receiver*. To take advantage of the verification methodology presented in Section 3, the micro-step parallel composition ∥ has to be replaced by a *macro-step* one. For this, the single-access hypothesis to shared variables (cf. Proposition 2) has to be satisfied. Here, the shared variables are the communication channels; hence, the hypothesis translates to the fact that each *input* from a channel (i.e., a reading access) must occur in a stable location, each *output* (i.e., a writing access) must lead to a stable location, and each path from a stable location to another makes only one access to a channel. This is achieved by defining as *stable* some adequately chosen locations of the *Sender* and *Receiver* extended automata.

Note that this concerns locations of the *Sender* and *Receiver* automata, not of their components (SD and POLL sender, USTAT receiver, etc). The latter have only one stable location each (their initial location, cf. Sections 4.1 and 4.2). This is because unlike the actions of distant processes, the actions of components that belong to the same process are not interleaved. Ultimately, all these choices are required for making the verification methodology (presented in Section 3) consistent with the semantics of SDL.

The system to be verified is now (SD & POLL *sender* | USTAT *receiver* |STAT *receiver*) | (SD *receiver* | POLL *receiver*). This decomposes each proof in five independent parts. As shown in Section 3, this leads to significant savings in terms of the number of auxiliary invariants required to complete a proof. Moreover, we proceed incrementally, starting with three components only: the SD sender, the SD receiver, and the USTAT receiver. After having established a number of invariants of their composition, the two remaining components (POLL receiver and STAT receiver) are added, and we show that they preserve all the invariants previously established. The main invariants for the composition of the first three components is first briefly described. Then, to give a more concrete idea of the approach, we describe in more detail the verification of one of the main invariants that arise from adding the two remaining components in the protocol.

Verifying the composition (SD & POLL *sender* | USTAT *receiver*) | (SD *receiver*). Rather than starting with the main property of the protocol, the initial candidate invariants are the predicates stating that the *OutOfDtr* locations are unreachable; that is, under the hypothesis of reasonable lossy communication channels and noninterference from clients, the protocol remains in its data transfer mode. This, in turn, suggests to prove facts such as:

- all new SD that are currently in the SR channel have index numbers comprised between VRH and VTS, and form a strictly monotonic sequence;

- all old SD (i.e., retransmissions) that are currently in the SR channel have distinct sequence numbers, which are all less than VRH;
- the latter are all different from all the SD sequence numbers in the sender's retransmission queue, and also from all the sequence numbers comprised in the intervals carried by the USTAT that are currently in the RS channel;
- the latter are all distinct, and designate empty slots in the receiver's window.

Adding the POLL *and* STAT *receiver.* The two remaining components are added to the protocol, and we prove that they preserve the invariants established at the previous step. This part is probably the most intricate in the whole verification process, as now the two redundant mechanisms for requesting retransmissions: the USTAT and STAT PDUs, have to interact while preserving the property that SD PDUs are not retransmitted unless they were really lost, a property that the protocol consistently enforces. For example, one has to establish facts such as:

† *For each* STAT PDU *currently in the* RS *channel, every* SD PDU *that the* STAT *designates as* lost *is either not in the receiver's window, or it is memorized in the sender's window with a VTPS value greater than the one carried by the* STAT.[2]

In the following, we show how to formalize the property (†) and how to prove it.

The invariant is about STAT PDUs, which are generated by the POLL receiver component in response to a POLL PDU. The component (the smallest of all five in our system) is depicted, simplified for better understanding in Figure 5.

Execution starts in the *DataTransferReady* location by receiving a POLL input, which carries two numerical values: $mVTS$ and $mVTPS$. These values denote the values of the sender's VTS and $VTPS$ variables at the time the POLL was emitted. Remember (cf. "sending SD and POLL" paragraph) that VTS is the highest index of an SD PDU that the sender ever emitted.

The POLL is first checked for validity, which essentially means that its $mVTS$ field is not less than VRH (the highest index of an SD PDU that the receiver knows about). If the POLL is not valid, the receiver exits the data transfer mode, which is encoded here by going to the *OutOfDtr* location. An invariant of the system (not shown here) allows to prove that this location is unreachable.

Otherwise, VRH and the receiver's own copy of $VTPS$ are updated from the $mVTS$ and $mVTPS$ fields of the POLL PDU, respectively; and the system starts building a new STAT PDU, to be emitted as a response to the received POLL. The STAT will contain an abstract view of the receiver's window, namely, a list of indices that denote empty slots (SD not arrived, assumed to be lost) or full slots (containing an arrived SD) in the receiver's window. The rest of the component is essentially the process of building this list, encoded in Fig. 5 by variable *vList*.

The process is initiated by the transition from the *DataTransferReady* location to *DtrPollSkipArrived*, by initializing the length of the list to zero, and by initializing an index i to the bottom of the sender's window *RecvBuffer.Bottom*.

---

[2] An SD PDU that is memorized in the sender's window together with a too high $VTPS$ value will not be retransmitted; thus, the property (†) participates in enforcing the general property that SD PDUs are not retransmitted unless they were really lost.

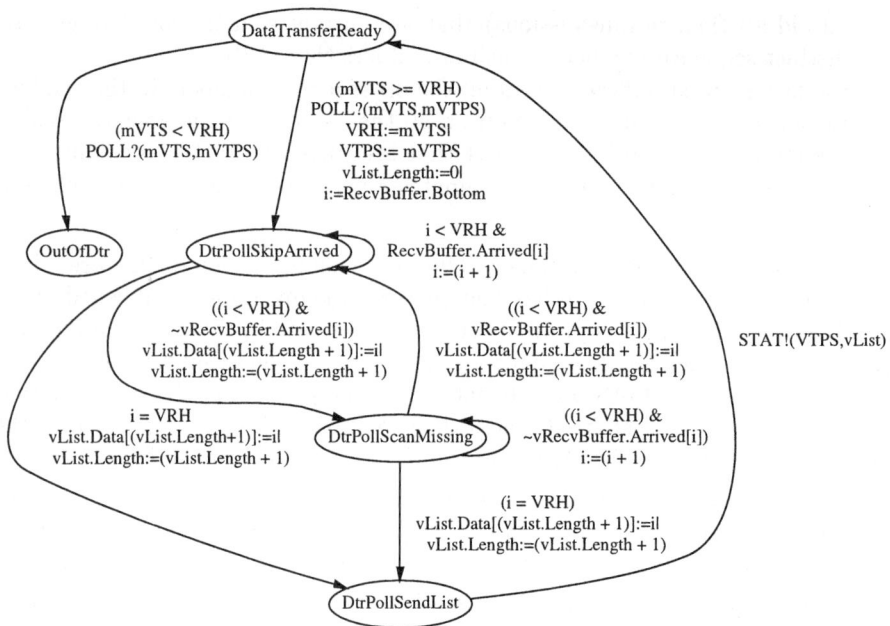

Fig. 5. The POLL receiver component.

In the *DtrPollSkipArrived* location, the index i is incremented until it meets an empty slot in the window. When this happens, the corresponding value of the index i is added to the list *vList*, and control goes to the *DtrPollScanMissing* location. Then, control stays in *DtrPollScanMissing* as long as the index i designates empty slots in the receiver's window, and goes back to *DtrPollSkipArrived* when a non-empty slot is found, by memorizing the index i of that slot.

This process continues while i is below the upper bound of the receiver's window *VRH*; when i reaches that bound, control goes to the *DtrPollSendList* location, where a STAT PDU carrying the list *vList* (together with the value of *VTPS* memorized at the beginning) is sent on the RS channel. Thus, the list *vList* is a strictly increasing sequence of integers $i_1, i_2, \ldots$ with the property:

‡ If j is even, then all indices in the interval $[i_{j+1}, i_{j+2})$ denote empty slots in the receiver's window RecvBuffer (the corresponding SD are assumed to be lost).

Hence, the statement (†) at the top of the previous page is written in PVS as

In the following, the formal proof that the POLL receiver component, depicted in Figure 5, preserves the invariant `retrans_inv1` depicted in Figure 6 is outlined. By applying the PVS strategy for proving invariants, we obtain that, in order to prove the `retrans_inv1` invariant, the following fact (Fig. 7) should be proved:

This is because at *DtrPollSendList*, a new STAT PDU will be added to the RS channel, with fields equal to *vList* and *VTPS* (cf. Figure 5); thus, the constraints on these fields expressed by `retrans_inv1` are translated to *vList* and *VTPS*.

```
retrans_inv1: LEMMA invariant(LAMBDA(s:State) :
FORALL (k: subrange(RS_sender_index, s'RS_receiver_index - 1)):
            LET pdu = s'RS_channel(k) IN
              STAT?(pdu) IMPLIES
                LET statlist = vList(pdu) IN
                  (FORALL (l: upto(statlist'Length - 2)):
                    even?(l) IMPLIES
                      LET elt1 = statlist'Data(l + 1),
                          elt2 = statlist'Data(l + 2)
                        IN FORALL (m: subrange(elt1,elt2-1)):
                             NOT RecvBuffer'Arrived(m) OR
                             XmitBuffer'VTPS(m) >= mVTPS(pdu)))
```

Fig. 6. PVS invariant to be enforced by the POLL receiver.

```
invariant(LAMBDA (s: State): s'pc = DtrPollSendList
           IMPLIES
             (FORALL (l: nat):
               even?(l) AND 1 <= s'vList'Length - 2 IMPLIES
                 (FORALL (m: subrange(s'vList'Data(l + 1),
                                      s'vList'Data(l + 2) - 1)):
                    NOT RecvBuffer'Arrived(m) OR
                    XmitBuffer'VTPS(m) >= s'VTPS)))
```

Fig. 7. potentially useful auxiliary invariant for proving retrans_inv1.

Now, when the POLL receiver component is in location *DtrPollSendList*, the two other components of the receiver are in their initial locations. This global location of the receiver has been defined as *stable*, because otherwise we would have an atomic execution that contains both the POLL input and the STAT output (cf. Figure 5), and this is forbidden by our verification methodology. According to the macro-step parallel composition, while the receiver is in a stable location, the *sender* of the SSCOP can move. Since the invariant in Figure 7 involves a variable of the sender (the sender's window XmitBuffer) this generates a proof obligation for the sender; namely, that the sender preserves the invariant depicted in Figure 7. This is recorded as a new proof obligation (not developed here), and we proceed with proving that the POLL receiver satisfies the invariant in Figure 7.

For this, note that the invariant that we are trying to prove is a disjunction of two properties; thus, establishing any of them is enough to prove it. We choose here to prove the disjunct that involves only variables local to the receiver of the SSCOP; i.e., we ignore the XmitBuffer'VTPS(m) >= s'VTPS disjunct:

Note that the invariant in Figure 8 is just the PVS encoding of the property (‡) from the previous page. The advantage with the latter invariant is that it only involves variables of which the sender of the protocol has no writing access; thus, we do not need to prove that the sender preserves it. To prove the invariant in Figure 8, the dedicated PVS strategy is applied, which suggests to strengthen it by imposing that it also holds in the locations *DtrPollSkipArrived* and *DtrPollScanMissing*; and furthermore, to prove the two following invariants:

```
retrans_inv1_aux1: LEMMA invariant(LAMBDA(s:State) :
  invariant(LAMBDA (s: State): s'pc = DtrPollSendList
              IMPLIES
              (FORALL (l: nat):
                  even?(l) AND l <= s'vList'Length - 2 IMPLIES
                    (FORALL (m: subrange(s'vList'Data(l + 1),
                                         s'vList'Data(l + 2) - 1)):
                        NOT RecvBuffer'Arrived(m))))
```

Fig. 8. actual auxiliary invariant used for proving `retrans_inv1`.

```
retrans1_inv1_aux1_aux1: LEMMA
  invariant(LAMBDA (s: State):
              (s'pc = DtrPollScanMissing AND s'vList'Length > 0) IMPLIES
                (FORALL (m: subrange(s'vList'Data(s'vList'Length), s'i - 1)):
                    NOT RecvBuffer'Arrived(m)))

retrans1_inv1_aux1_aux2:: LEMMA invariant(LAMBDA(s:State) :
              (s'pc = DtrPollSkipArrived IMPLIES even?(s'vList'Length))
              AND
              (s'pc = DtrPollScanMissing IMPLIES odd?(s'vList'Length)))
```

Fig. 9. inductive auxiliary invariants used for proving the invariant in Figure 8.

The invariants depicted in Figure 9 are inductive, and our PVS strategy automatically proves them. Finally, by using the corresponding lemmas in the proof of the `retrans_inv1_aux1` lemma depicted in Figure 8, all pending subgoals are settled and the proof succeeds; and by using the `retrans_inv1_aux1` lemma in the proof of the original goal (depicted in Figure 6) that proof succeeds as well.

This branch of the verification is terminated; however, it has generated a new branch, which (as we have seen) is to prove that the invariant depicted in Figure 7 is preserved by the sender of the SSCOP. That branch is treated in a similar manner and is eventually solved as well. We do not go further into details.

The composition of the first three components: SD sender, SD receiver, and USTAT receiver required to prove 140 invariants. Adding the POLL receiver and STAT receiver required to prove 111 more. The main property of the protocol then follows directly from these invariants. The total number of 252 theorems were proved in three months by a moderately experienced PVS user. An additional month was spent for understanding and translating of the protocol to PVS.

5 Conclusion and Related Work

We describe a methodology based on mechanized compositional and deductive reasoning, and illustrate it by verifying safety properties of the data transfer function of the SSCOP protocol. The methodology makes intensive use of the PVS theorem prover. Starting with a set of predicates that constitute the initial proof obligations, the user gradually discovers more properties of the protocol, which are indicated by the failed attempts of PVS at proving the protocol correct, given our current knowledge of it. The supplementary properties constitute new proof obligations. The protocol is decomposed into "components" that correspond to the transitions of its standard specification in the SDL language [21].

The method is compositional in that each component has to preserve only a subset of the properties, namely, those that involve variables that it can modify when it is executed. The user keeps track of obligations that have been proved and of those still pending, and eventually completes them all. Each PVS proof consists of applying essentially the same automatic strategy, where the user only has to provide adequate quantifier instantiations and, in case the proof fails, to interpret the pending subgoals generated by PVS as new proof obligations.

For the current case study, which is the core of a real communication protocol, the verification took three months. We believe this is reasonable, as the very definition of the protocol took several months as well. If the verification were done while the definition is ongoing, this would not significantly increase the duration of the process and may even save time. Typically, the people in charge of proving the protocol acquire a very good understanding of it (probably better than the protocol's designers!) and can point to errors early in the design phase.

Related Work. Abstraction-based verification methods are widely studied and applied [1, 2, 11, 17, 14, 26, 27]. In most cases, the abstractions used in the literature are *over*-approximations of the set of behaviors of the concrete system; by construction, this is sound for verifying safety properties. Our atomicity abstraction is an *under*-approximation. It is akin to partial-order reduction techniques, which are widely used in model checking [15]. The present work can be seen as an application of partial-order reduction to theorem-proving based verification.

Among the many existing compositional verification techniques, some deal like ours with shared-variable concurrent processes and properties (e.g., the classical method of Owicki and Gries. cf. [9], Chapter 3). The main advantage of our approach is that we provide a tool-supported, systematic method to obtain inductive invariants (which the hardest part of the verification process). By contrast, e.g., the Owicki-Gries method assumes that all invariants provided by the user are inductive right from the start. On the other hand, the Owicki-Gries method also handles with systems that do not satisfy the single-access hypothesis (cf. Section 2).

The automatic verification of protocols specified in SDL has received some attention recently; [4, 13, 18, 27] are some of the relevant works. These approaches are based on model checking, thus, they are subject to the usual limitations: some finite, usually "small" instances (in terms of the size of buffers and communication channels) of "large" case studies are verified. Compositionality and abstraction are also used to reduce a large state space to one amenable to model checking. In [5], the data transfer function of the SSCOP is model-checked for safety and liveness properties, but under more restrictive hypotheses than ours: the communication channels have a small fixed size and do not lose messages.

References

[1] P. Abdulla, A. Annichini, S. Bensalem, A. Bouajjani, P. Habermehl, Y. Lakhnech. Verification of infinite-state systems by combining abstraction and reachability analysis. *Computer Aided Verification*, LNCS 1633, 1999.

[2] R. Alur, T. Henzinger, F. Mang, S. Qadeer, S. Rajamani, S. Tasiran. Mocha: modularity in model checking. *Computer-Aided Verification*, LNCS 1427, 1998.

[3] J. Burch, E. Clarke, K. McMillan, D. Dill, J. Hwang. Symbolic model checking: 10^{20} states and beyond. *Information and Computation*, 98(2):142–170, 1992.

[4] D. Bosnacki, D. Dams, L. Holenderski, N. Sidorova. Model Checking SDL with Spin. *Tools and Algorithms for the Construction and Analysis of Systems*, LNCS 1785, 2000.

[5] M. Bozga, J.-C. Fernandez, L. Ghirvu, C. Jard, T. Jéron, A. Kerbrat, P. Morel, L. Mounier. Verification and test generation for the SSCOP protocol. *Science of Computer Programming* 36(1):27–52, 2000.

[6] P. Cousot, R. Cousot. Abstract intrepretation: a unified lattice model for static analysis of programs by construction or approximation of fixpoints. *4th ACM Symposium on Principles of Programming Languages*, 1977.

[7] E. Clarke, O. Grumberg, D. Peled. *Model checking*. MIT Press, 1999.

[8] C. Cornes, J. Courant, J.-C. Filliâtre, G. Huet, P. Manoury, C. Paulin-Mohring, C. Muñoz, C. Murthy, C. Parent, A. Saïbi, B. Werner. The Coq Proof Assistant Reference Manual Version 6.1. Technical Report RT-0203, INRIA, 1997.

[9] W-P. de Roever et. al. *Concurrency Verification: Introduction to Compositional and Noncompositional Methods*. Cambridge University Press, 2001.

[10] J-C. Fernandez, H. Garavel, A. Kerbrat, R. Mateescu, L. Mounier, M. Sighireanu. CADP: A protocol validation and verification toolbox. *Computer-Aided Verification*, LNCS 1102, 1996.

[11] C. Flanagan, S. Qadeer. Predicate abstraction for software verification. *Principles of Programming Languages*, 2002

[12] M. Gordon, T. Melham. *Introduction to the HOL system*. Cambridge University press, 1994.

[13] S. Graf, G. Jia. Verification experiments on the MASCARA protocol. *SPIN workshop on software model checking*, 2001.

[14] K. Havelund, N. Shankar. Experiments in theorem proving and model checking for protocol verification. *Formal Methods Europe*, LNCS 1051, 1996.

[15] G. Holzmann. The model checker Spin. *IEEE Transactions on Software Engineering*, 23(5): 279–295, 1997.

[16] T. Henderson, R. Katz. STP: a SSCOP-based transport protocol for Datagram Satellite Networks. *Intl. Workshop on Satellite-based Information Services*, 1997.

[17] T. Henzinger, R. Jhala, R. Majumdar, G. Sutre. Lazy abstraction. *Principles of Programming Languages*, 2002.

[18] N. Ioustinova, N. Sidorova, M. Steffen. Closing open SDL-systems for model checking with DTSpin. *Formal Methods Europe*. LNCS 2391, 2002.

[19] B. Jeannet. Representing and approximating transfer functions in abstract interpretation of heterogeneous datatypes, *Static Analysis Symposium*, LNCS 2477, 2002.

[20] R. Jhala, K. McMillan. Microarchitecture Verification by Compositional Model Checking. *Computer Aided Verification*, LNCS 2102, 2001.

[21] International Telecommunication Union. ATM Adaptation Layer - Service Specific Connection Oriented Protocol. *Recommendation Q.2110*, 1994.

[22] Z. Manna, A. Pnueli. *Temporal verification of reactive systems.* Vol. 1: Specification, Vol. 2: Safety. Springer-Verlag, 1991 and 1995.
[23] K. McMillan. A compositional rule for hardware design refinement. *Computer Aided Verification*, LNCS 1254, 1997.
[24] Telelogic SDL products. http://www.telelogic.com/products/sdl
[25] S. Owre, J. Rushby, N. Shankar, F. von Henke. Formal verification for fault-tolerant architectures: Prolegomena to the design of PVS. *IEEE Transactions on Software Engineering*, 21(2):107-125, 1995.
[26] H. Saïdi, N. Shankar. Abstract and model check while you prove. *Conference on Computer-Aided Verification*, LNCS 1633, 1999.
[27] N. Sidorova, M. Steffen. Verifying large SDL specifications using model checking *SDL Forum*, LNCS 2078, 2001.

Proving the Correctness of Simpson's 4-Slot ACM Using an Assertional Rely-Guarantee Proof Method

Neil Henderson

BAE SYSTEMS DCSC, University of Newcastle-Upon-Tyne, UK,
neil.henderson@ncl.ac.uk

Abstract. This paper describes a rely-guarantee proof to show that Simpson's 4-slot single-reader, single-writer ACM is Lamport atomic (as described fully in the paper). First an abstract ACM specification is proved Lamport atomic using an exhaustive assertional method. A formal model of Simpson's 4-slot is then given and this has been proved to be a refinement of the abstract specification using Nipkow's retrieve relation rule. Simpson's 4-slot is then shown to be Lamport atomic using an interleaved concurrency rely-guarantee proof method for shared variable concurrency.

Keyword: asynchronous communication, rely-guarantee, assertion networks.

1 Introduction

Inter-process communication is vital in any distributed system. One means of facilitating this communication is by using Asynchronous Communication Mechanisms (ACMs). ACMs are essentially shared variables that can be used to implement such inter-process communication without constraining the timing of the accesses of their reader(s) and writer(s). In this paper a particular implementation of an ACM is proved to be Lamport atomic (this term is fully defined in Section 3). Although, in general, ACMs can have multiple readers and/or writers the ACM considered in this paper only supports a single reader and a single writer. It is possible, however, for the reader of an ACM to end one read and start the next one while a single write is in progress and so multiple reads can overlap with a single write. Similarly multiple writes can overlap a single read. An item written to an ACM may be read by the reader a number of times and it is also possible that items written may not be read at all, because they are overwritten before the reader attempts to read them[1]. In the case of Simpson's 4-slot, as the name implies, there are 4 slots available to hold data. When a read

---

[1] The asynchronous communication that ACMs support is therefore to be distinguished from the model of "asynchronous communication" supported by (infinite) buffers, where all items written are read by the reader (normally in the order that they were written).

starts the reader is directed to the slot containing the latest complete item of data. If the writer starts to write a new item of data while the read is in progress it is directed to a different slot, to ensure that it does not overwrite part of the item that is being read. Similarly, if a read starts while a write is in progress, the reader is directed to a different slot to the one the writer is accessing. This ensures that the writer does not corrupt any data item while it is being read.

There are many interesting features of ACMs, for example they provide a means of decoupling the temporal interactions between communicating processes and they are robust against deadlock (for example if the writer is held up the reader can re-read the latest item written).

Simpson's 4-slot is an implementation of an ACM that is particularly efficient, which has been developed and used in the defence sector [23, 24, 26]. In [24], Simpson gave implementations of communication mechanisms that are implemented using 1, 2, 3, and 4-slots. The 1-slot mechanism can only be used where it is certain that the reader and writer will not access the shared memory at the same time. This *non interference* could happen accidentally, but can only be guaranteed if some type of synchronisation mechanism is used, for example a Hoare monitor [9]. The 2-slot mechanism similarly requires some form of synchronisation, otherwise the mechanism cannot guarantee data coherence or freshness, depending on the implementation (if the reader and writer processes access the shared variable at the same time either: the writer may partially overwrite the item that is being read, and coherence will be lost; or the reader may need to re-read the same item many times, even though newer items have been written, and will not get the *freshest* item). The 3-slot mechanism *almost* implements an ACM, but loses coherence and/or freshness if the reader and writer interleave in a particular manner. Simpson gives an additional timing constraint which, if it can be guaranteed, makes the 3-slot behave in the same way as an ACM. He then gave an implementation of an ACM [24], which uses 4-slots to communicate the data. This ACM is challenging to analyse, despite its deceptive brevity, because of the unconstrained manner in which the reader and writer can interact: it is this mechanism that is analysed in this paper.

A proof is given in [8] that the 4-slot is Lamport atomic [14, 15], using Nipkow's retrieve relation proof rules [16, 17, 13], subject to certain assumptions about the atomicity of the actions of the reader and writer. These assumptions mean that the reader and writer can only *interfere* with each other at certain points, by grouping a number of actions of the reader and writer into *atomic instructions*. This formal model of the 4-slot does not capture the fully asynchronous nature of the mechanism.

This paper gives a full correctness proof for the 4-slot that shows it is Lamport atomic, when these atomicity assumptions are relaxed and the read and write actions can interleave in an unconstrained manner, using the rely-guarantee method [10, 12, 11]. The formal model of the 4-slot used for the proofs is in the PVS logic [18], and is the same as that in [8]. The proofs have been completed using the PVS theorem prover [18] with the interleaved concurrency rely-guarantee proof method for shared variable concurrency from [6]. The proofs therefore still assume the individual actions of the reader and writer are atomic, whereas, for example in hardware implementations, the reader and writer can clash when they access control variables in the ACM.

The rest of the paper is organised as follows: Section 2 describes Simpson's 4-slot implementation; Section 3 gives a correctness proof for an abstract specification of atomicity; Section 4 gives details of a correctness proof for the 4-slot based on the rely-guarantee method from [6]; Section 5 describes related work (in particular correctness proofs for the 4-slot using different proof methods, for example CSP [21, 5, 4, 20], Petri-nets [28] and Role modelling [25]); and Section 6 gives the conclusions from this work.

The contribution of this paper is to show how an ACM implementation can be proved to be Lamport atomic: first by proving correctness to an abstract specification, which treats the ACM as a black box with start and end read and write actions, using Nipkow's retrieve relation rule [16, 17]; and then using an assertional rely-guarantee proof method [6] to show that it is still atomic when the individual actions of the reader and writer can interleave in an unconstrained manner. The particular ACM used as an example in the paper, i.e. Simpson's 4-slot, has been analysed using a number of model checking techniques, but the use of the rely-guarantee method, with PVS, has given greater insight into the operation of the ACM than is gained by using a model checker.

2 Simpson's 4-Slot ACM

In [23, 24] Simpson defined a fully asynchronous communication mechanism that maintained data-coherence and freshness, and which uses four *slots* for communicating data between the reader and writer.

In the 4-slot, bit control variables are used to ensure that the reader and writer are always directed to different slots, so the reader can never read values composed of partial items from more than one write. The 4-slot algorithm is deceptively simple, consisting of only five actions in the *write* operation and four actions in the *read* operation, and is shown in Table 1.

Simpson, in a later paper, gave a new algorithm for the 4-slot, which essentially reverses the order in which the reader and writer choose the pair and slot to read from or write to, [26]. That variant is not considered in this paper.

It is the intention of the design of the 4-slot mechanism that the reader and writer cannot access the same slot at the same time i.e. that it maintains coherence of the items communicated. It is also intended to support *data freshness* i.e. the reader should read the most recently written item.

The requirements for the 4-slot mechanism to maintain data coherence and freshness can be summarised by saying that the 4-slot should be Lamport atomic [8, 20] (the properties of a Lamport atomic ACM are described in the next section).

Table 1. The 4-slot mechanism

```
mechanism four slot;
  type PairIndex = (p0, p1);
       SlotIndex = (s0, s1);
  var data: array[PairIndex, SlotIndex] of Data;
      slot: array[PairIndex] of SlotIndex;
      latest, reading: PairIndex;

  procedure write (item: data);
  var writepair: PairIndex;
      writeindex: SlotIndex;
  begin
      writepair  := not reading;              (writerChoosesPair)
      writeindex := not slot[writepair];      (writerChoosesSlot)
      data[writepair, writeindex] := item;    (write)
      slot[writepair] := writeindex;          (writerIndicatesSlot)
      latest := writepair;                    (writerIndicatesPair)
  end;

  function read: Data;
  var readpair: PairIndex;
      readindex: SlotIndex;
  begin
      readpair  := latest;                    (readerChoosesPair)
      reading   := readpair;                  (readerIndicatesPair)
      readindex := slot[readpair];            (readerChoosesSlot)
      read := data[readpair, readindex];      (read)
  end;
end;
```

3 An Abstract Specification of Lamport Atomic ACMs

In [8] an abstract specification of Lamport atomic ACMs was given, which relied on an assumption about the relative speed of the reader and writer[2]. This section gives a revised specification which does not rely on this assumption. This specification assumes that the ACM has a single reader and single writer, which means that while multiple reads can overlap with a single write (because one read ends and a new read starts during the write), and vice versa, it is not possible for a read to overlap another read or a write to overlap another write.

The properties of Lamport atomic ACMs are:

1. The writer overwrites items in the ACM. This means that the reader may not read all of the items written if the writer is faster than the reader.
2. The reader may re-read items multiple times, if it is faster than the writer.
3. The reader must read items in the order they are written, so that, once it has read a particular item, it cannot subsequently read one that was written earlier.
4. The reader and writer can access the ACM in a totally asynchronous manner.
5. Reads and writes appear to have occurred in a particular order (as if the entire read and write operations were Hoare atomic [9] and interleaved with each other).

---

[2] It assumed that if the reader accessed the ACM more than once during a single write, it did not read the item written by the writer in that write access.

The last property is not characterised directly in the specification. The approach is taken of modelling the items that are written to the ACM as a sequence, which gives the order in which they were written. The presence of an item in the sequence models its availability to the reader[3]. The model has two booleans to record whether the reader and/or writer are accessing the mechanism, and uses the variables *nextIndex*, *indexRead* and *firstIndexAvailable* to record the indices of the next item to be written, the last item read and the first item available to a read. The specification has four operations, *start_read*, *end_read*, *start_write* and *end_write*, each of which is assumed to be atomic, which are given below[4]:

```
Val: NONEMPTY_TYPE

Data: TYPE = [# index: nat, val: Val #]

Val_Sequence: TYPE = {fin_seq: finite_sequence[Data] | fin_seq'length ≥ 1}

(seq : Val_Sequence ∪ {d : Data}): Val_Sequence =
    (# length := 1, seq := (λ (x : below[1]) : d) #) ∘ seq

Abs_State: TYPE = [# vals: Val_Sequence,
                    writerAccess: bool,
                    readerAccess: bool,
                    nextIndex: nat,
                    indexRead: nat,
                    firstIndexAvailable: nat #]
```

start_read: has a precondition that the reader is not already accessing the mechanism. The operation changes the *readerAccess* boolean to true to indicate that the reader is accessing the ACM, and removes items from the sequence of values that are not available to be read: if the sequence is of length one it is left unchanged, because there is always an item available to be read; and if the length of the sequence is greater than one and the writer is not currently accessing the mechanism the sequence is shortened to contain only the latest item, if the writer is accessing the mechanism the latest two items are available to be read. It also sets *firstIndexAvailable* equal to the index of the first item available to the reader.

```
pre_start_read(prot: Abs_State): bool = prot'readerAccess = FALSE

post_start_read(p: (pre_start_read))(prot: Abs_State): bool =
    IF p'vals'length = 1
        THEN prot = p WITH [readerAccess := TRUE, firstIndexAvailable :=
                                                  finseq_appl(p'vals)(0)'index]
    ELSE IF ¬ p'writerAccess
        THEN prot = p WITH [vals := p'vals ^ (0, 0),
                            readerAccess := TRUE,
                            firstIndexAvailable := finseq_appl(p'vals)(0)'index]
        ELSE prot = p WITH [vals := p'vals ^ (0, 1),
                            readerAccess := TRUE,
                            firstIndexAvailable := finseq_appl(p'vals)(1)'index]
        ENDIF
    ENDIF

start_read: [p: (pre_start_read) → (post_start_read(p))]
```

end_read: has a precondition that the reader is accessing the mechanism. The operation non-deterministically chooses one of the available items from the

---

[3] Each item is given a unique sequence number in the model, so that it is possible to reason about the order in which these items are written.

[4] This paper uses the encoding of VDM-SL operations developed in [2].

sequence to read and shortens the sequence to remove all earlier items to ensure they are not available for future reads. It also sets the *readerAccess* boolean to false to show that the read has ended, and *indexRead* to the index of the item read (which is the first item in the sequence after the read has finished).

```
pre_end_read(prot: Abs_State): bool = prot'readerAccess = TRUE

post_end_read(p: (pre_end_read))(prot: Abs_State, read_item: Val): bool =
    ∃ (i: nat): i < p'vals'length ∧
        read_item = p'vals'seq(i)'val ∧
        IF p'vals'length > 1
            THEN prot = p WITH [vals := p'vals ^ (0, i),
                                readerAccess := FALSE,
                                indexRead := p'vals'seq(i)'index]
            ELSE prot = p WITH [readerAccess := FALSE, indexRead :=
                                p'vals'seq(i)'index]
        ENDIF

end_read: [p: (pre_end_read) → (post_end_read(p))]
```

start_write: has a precondition that the writer is not already accessing the ACM. It adds the item being written to the sequence, increments *nextIndex*, and sets the *writerAccess* boolean to true to show that the writer is accessing the mechanism.

```
pre_start_write(prot: Abs_State): bool = prot'writerAccess = FALSE

write_parameter: TYPE = [# p_1: (pre_start_write), val: Val #]

post_start_write(p: write_parameter)(prot: Abs_State): bool =
    LET newItem: Data = (# index := p'p_1'nextIndex, val := p'val #) IN
        prot =
        p'p_1 WITH [vals := (p'p_1'vals ∪ {newItem}),
                    writerAccess := TRUE,
                    nextIndex := p'p_1'nextIndex + 1]

start_write: [p: write_parameter → (post_start_write(p))]
```

end_write: has a precondition that the writer is accessing the ACM. If the reader is accessing the mechanism it leaves the sequence unchanged, because there is no way of knowing which item the reader has chosen to read, otherwise it shortens the sequence to one item (because this is the only item available to the next read), and sets the *writerAccess* boolean to false to indicate that the write has finished.

```
pre_end_write(prot: Abs_State): bool = prot'writerAccess = TRUE

post_end_write(p: (pre_end_write))(prot: Abs_State): bool =
    (p'readerAccess = TRUE ⇒ prot = p WITH [writerAccess := FALSE]) ∧
    (p'readerAccess = FALSE ⇒
        prot = p WITH [vals := p'vals ^ (0, 0), writerAccess := FALSE])

end_write: [p: (pre_end_write) → (post_end_write(p))]
```

This relatively small specification has been proved Lamport atomic using an exhaustive assertional proof method [3] with PVS. The state space of the model is shown in Figure 1. Each of the states has an assertion associated with it (lambda expressions have been used here so that the same assertions can be used in multiple places in the PVS definitions and then expanded in-line when completing the proofs):

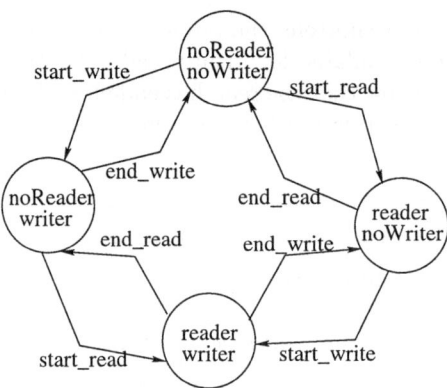

Fig. 1. State Model for the Abstract Specification of an Atomic ACM

noReader_noWriter_Assertion: [Abs_State → bool] =
  λ (abs: Abs_State):
    abs'indexRead ≤ abs'nextIndex − abs'vals'length ∧
    abs'firstIndexAvailable ≤ abs'nextIndex − abs'vals'length ∧
    finseq_appl(abs'vals)(0)'index = abs'nextIndex − 1

reader_noWriter_Assertion: [Abs_State → bool] =
  λ (abs: Abs_State):
    abs'indexRead ≤ abs'nextIndex − abs'vals'length ∧
    abs'firstIndexAvailable = abs'nextIndex − abs'vals'length ∧
    finseq_appl(abs'vals)(0)'index = abs'nextIndex − 1

noReader_writer_Assertion: [Abs_State → bool] =
  λ (abs: Abs_State):
    abs'indexRead ≤ abs'nextIndex − abs'vals'length ∧
    abs'firstIndexAvailable ≤ abs'nextIndex − abs'vals'length ∧
    finseq_appl(abs'vals)(0)'index = abs'nextIndex − 1

reader_writer_Assertion: [Abs_State → bool] =
  λ (abs: Abs_State):
    abs'indexRead ≤ abs'nextIndex − abs'vals'length ∧
    abs'firstIndexAvailable = abs'nextIndex − abs'vals'length ∧
    finseq_appl(abs'vals)(0)'index = abs'nextIndex − 1

The following proof has been discharged for each of the operations, from each of the states when they can be executed, to show that the operations do not invalidate the assertions in the respective target states of the transitions:

∀ (as1, as2: Abs_State): pre_op(as1) ∧ startState_Assertion(as1)
  ∧ as2 = op(as1) ⇒ targetState_Assertion(as2)

Finally the specification is proved Lamport atomic by showing that the following assertion always holds when the *end_read* operation is executed:

Lamport: [Abs_State, Abs_State → bool] =
  λ (as1, as2: Abs_State): as1'indexRead ≤ as2'indexRead ∧
    as2'firstIndexAvailable ≤ as2'indexRead ∧ as2'nextIndex − 1 ≥ as2'indexRead

This is equivalent to a guarantee condition, and is described as follows:

1. Each data item that is written to the mechanism is given an index number, starting at zero, and increasing each time a new item is written. New items are written to the head (index zero) of the sequence.

2. *firstIndexAvailable* gives the index number of the first item on the list when a read starts (the first item that is available to the reader for that read).
3. *indexRead* is the index number of the item that is read.
4. the above assertion guarantees that the item read has an index number greater than or equal to the number of the first item available at the start of the read, less than the index to be used for the next item written, and that it is the same or a later item than that read last time.

The remainder of the properties that are required to guarantee Lamport atomicity are encoded directly into the specification, for example: when a read takes place all items earlier than that read are removed from the sequence to ensure that an older item cannot be read the next time; and the atomicity of the operations ensure that it is not possible for the reader and writer to clash on accessing a particular item, so that coherence is guaranteed.

The specification in this section corrects that in [8]. The proofs described there, that used Nipkow's retrieve relation proof rule [16, 17] to show the 4-slot is a refinement of this specification, have been repeated for this revised specification. These proofs, however, are insufficient to show that the 4-slot implementation is Lamport atomic when the reader and writer can access the mechanism in a totally asynchronous manner. It is not clear how the implementation could be related directly to this specification using refinement. The exhaustive proof method used to show the specification is Lamport atomic could be used to prove the implementation is also Lamport atomic. This, however, would require an exploration of the entire state space of the 4-slot. This state space is not simply the cross product of the number of read and write operations, because, for example, the behaviour of the mechanism can change if a read occurs when the writer has changed pairs but has not indicated it has changed. Verification proofs for each of the states in the entire state space would then need to be discharged[5]. While it is anticipated that these proofs would be easier to discharge than those for the rely-guarantee method described in Section 4, it would be a non trivial task to ensure that the entire state space is explored correctly. For these reasons this is not considered to be a practical solution, so it was necessary to explore other proof methods to show that the 4-slot implementation is Lamport atomic. The next section describes such a method, using an assertional rely-guarantee proof method for shared variable concurrency.

4 A Rely-Guarantee Proof for Simpson's 4-Slot

This section presents a proof that Simpson's 4-slot ACM is Lamport atomic when the read and write actions can interleave in an unconstrained manner, using an interleaved concurrency assertional rely-guarantee method for shared variables from [6]. This involves producing *assertion networks* for the reader and

---

[5] It is anticipated that this would more than double the number of verification proofs that would need to be discharged to prove the 4-slot implementation is Lamport atomic compared to the proof method described in Section 4.

writer, as described in Section 4.1, and showing that the read operations do not interfere with the writer and that the write operations do not interfere with the reader (the Aczel semantics [1] described in [6]). The use of this proof method reduces the number of verification proofs that it is necessary to discharge to a manageable number: it is necessary to discharge three verification proofs for each of the states in the reader and writer networks, a total of 33 proofs. The correctness proof is split into two parts: the first part shows that the mechanism maintains coherence of the data items transmitted, and the second part proves that it is Lamport atomic. The proofs, which have all been discharged using the PVS theorem prover [18, 19], are based on the model of the 4-slot in the PVS logic given in Appendix A[6].

4.1 Assertion Networks for the Reader and Writer

The assertion networks for the reader and writer are shown in Figure 2 and Figure 3 respectively. The networks both contain a transition labelled *false*, which leads to their respective termination states. This is to indicate that the reader and writer algorithms do not terminate once they have started. Assertions are associated with the states in the network and these are described in Section 4.2.

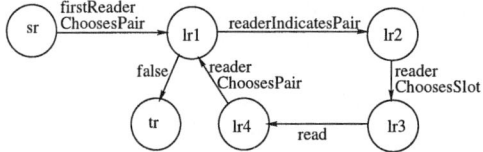

Fig. 2. Assertion Network for the Reader

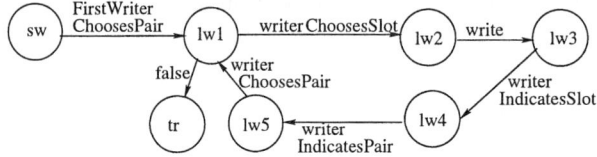

Fig. 3. Assertion Network for the Writer

4.2 Correctness Proofs

This section gives details of the proofs for coherence and Lamport atomicity. The proofs in both cases follow the same format:

– For each write operation it is necessary to show:

---

[6] The interested reader can download all of the PVS models and proof files described in this paper from http://homepages.cs.ncl.ac.uk/neil.henderson/fme2003.

```
∀ (cs1, cs2: Conc_State): pre_startState(cs1) ∧
    (startState_Assertion(cs1)) ∧ (readerChoosesPair_Assertion(cs1)) ∧
    (readerChoosesSlot_Assertion(cs1)) ∧
    (read_Assertion(cs1)) ∧ cs2 = writer_Op(cs1) ⇒
    (targetState_Assertion(cs2)) ∧ (readerChoosesPair_Assertion(cs2)) ∧
    (readerChoosesSlot_Assertion(cs2)) ∧ (read_Assertion(cs2))
```

i.e. that if the pre-condition of the operation and the assertion in the start state hold, then the assertion in the target state will hold after the operation has been executed; and furthermore that the operation does not interfere with any of the assertions in the states in the assertion network of the reader.

– Similarly for each read operation:

```
∀ (cs1, cs2: Conc_State): pre_startState(cs1) ∧
    (startState_Assertion(cs1)) ∧ (writerChoosesPair_Assertion(cs1)) ∧
    (writerChoosesSlot_Assertion(cs1)) ∧ (write_Assertion(cs1)) ∧
    (writerIndicatesSlot_Assertion(cs1)) ∧ (writerIndicatesPair_Assertion(cs1)) ∧
    cs2 = reader_Op(cs1) ⇒
    (targetState_Assertion(cs2)) ∧ (writerChoosesPair_Assertion(cs2)) ∧
    (writerChoosesSlot_Assertion(cs2)) ∧ (write_Assertion(cs2)) ∧
    (writerIndicatesSlot_Assertion(cs2)) ∧ (writerIndicatesPair_Assertion(cs2))
```

i.e. if the pre-condition and the assertion in the start state hold, the assertion of the target state will hold after the operation has been executed. In addition the reader will not interfere with any of the assertions in the assertion network of the writer.

– It is then necessary to show for each transition that the assertions in the source and target states of the assertion network are strong enough to meet the guarantee condition. In the case of the coherence proof the interesting proofs are when the reader and writer are both accessing the slots in the ACM, and for the Lamport atomic proof the interesting proof is for end read.

It is not necessary to make any assertions in the coherence proof for the reader network states sr, lr1 and lr4 (when the reader is about to execute firstReaderChoosesPair, readerIndicatesPair, and readerChoosesPair respectively) and the writer network state lw5 (when the writer is about to execute writerChoosesPair) other than the respective values of the auxiliary variables next read instruction (nri) and next write instruction (nwi). These values are, therefore, merely stated in line in the proofs.

The Proof of Coherence. The proofs of coherence rely on the following assertions in the respective states of the network:

```
readerChoosesSlot_Assertion: [Conc_State → bool] =
    λ (cs: Conc_State): cs'nri = rcs ⇒ cs'pairReading = cs'reader'readerPair

read_Assertion: [Conc_State → bool] =
    λ (cs: Conc_State): cs'nri = rd ⇒
        cs'pairReading = cs'reader'readerPair ∧
        (cs'reader'readerPair = cs'writer'writerPair ⇒
            (¬ cs'wisOccurred ⇒ cs'reader'readerSlot = cs'slotWritten(cs'reader'readerPair)) ∧
            (cs'wisOccurred ⇒
                (cs'rcsSinceWis ⇒ cs'reader'readerSlot =
                    cs'slotWritten(cs'reader'readerPair)) ∧
```

$$(\neg\ cs`rcsSinceWis \Rightarrow \neg\ cs`reader`readerSlot =$$
$$cs`slotWritten(cs`reader`readerPair))))$$

firstWriterChoosesPair_Assertion: [Conc_State → bool] =
  λ (cs: Conc_State): cs`nwi = firstWcp ⇒ ¬ cs`wisOccurred

writerChoosesSlot_Assertion: [Conc_State → bool] =
  λ (cs: Conc_State): cs`nwi = wcs ⇒ ¬ cs`wisOccurred ∧
    cs`writer`writerSlot = cs`slotWritten(cs`pairWritten)

write_Assertion: [Conc_State → bool] =
  λ (cs: Conc_State): cs`nwi = wr ⇒ ¬ cs`wisOccurred ∧
    ¬ cs`writer`writerSlot = cs`slotWritten(cs`writer`writerPair)

writerIndicatesSlot_Assertion: [Conc_State → bool] =
  λ (cs: Conc_State): cs`nwi = wis ⇒ ¬ cs`wisOccurred ∧
    ¬ cs`writer`writerSlot = cs`slotWritten(cs`writer`writerPair)

writerIndicatesPair_Assertion: [Conc_State → bool] =
  λ (cs: Conc_State): cs`nwi = wip ⇒ cs`wisOccurred ∧
    cs`writer`writerSlot = cs`slotWritten(cs`writer`writerPair)

These assertions give the relationship between the local copies of the control variables in the reader and writer and the values of those control variables in the mechanism itself. The interesting assertion is that for read, because the reader cannot rely on the local copy of the control variable for the slot it is accessing being the same as the value recorded in the mechanism. This is because only the writer has write access to the control variable in the mechanism and can change it after the reader has accessed it, but before the reader has used its local copy to access the relevant slot. Three different *cases* for this value therefore need to be considered when the reader is reading[7]:

1. The writer has not got as far as indicating the slot it is writing to in the pair it is accessing in the current write operation. In this case the reader's copy of the control variable will record the same value as the control variable itself.
2. The writer has indicated the slot it is writing to, in which case either:
   - The reader chose the slot to read from after the writer had indicated the new slot it had written to, in which case the readers local copy of the value will be the same as that in the control variable. The reader will access the same slot as the writer, but this is fine because the writer has finished writing the data. The reader may effectively get the latest data before it has been fully released.
   - The reader chose its slot before the writer indicated the new slot it had written to, in which case the reader will access the opposite slot in the pair to the writer. The reader will get the last item fully released.

Once the reader is reading from a slot, it has previously indicated the pair it is reading from (at *readerIndicatesPair*), so the writer will change pairs at the next start write, and cannot access the same pair in the next write.[8]

---

[7] The only cases of interest are when the reader and writer are in the same pair, otherwise they are by definition accessing different slots.

[8] The reader cannot subsequently follow the writer to the new pair until the writer has indicated it has changed to the new pair, which is last action in the next complete write access.

The guarantee condition that needs to be established is that the reader and writer do not access the same slot in the mechanism at the same time, in order to preserve coherence of data. This requires that the assertions in the networks are sufficient to prove the following:

$\forall\ (cs:\ \text{Conc\textasciigrave State}):$
$\quad cs\text{\textasciigrave nri} = rd \land cs\text{\textasciigrave nwi} = wr \Rightarrow$
$\quad\quad ((\neg\ cs\text{\textasciigrave reader\textasciigrave readerPair} = cs\text{\textasciigrave writer\textasciigrave writerPair}) \lor$
$\quad\quad (\neg\ cs\text{\textasciigrave reader\textasciigrave readerSlot} = cs\text{\textasciigrave writer\textasciigrave writerSlot}))$

This assertion guarantees that the reader and writer are in different pairs or different slots in the same pair in the mechanism when they are reading and writing data respectively. The reader and writer both rely on the other to only access the slot they have chosen.

The Proof of Atomicity. The proofs of Lamport atomicity use auxiliary variables to record extra information about the data items that are available to the reader in a similar method to the exhaustive proof for the abstract specification.

newMaxFresh: Incremented by the writer at start write, to indicate the index of the item to be written.

maxFresh: Used by the writer to indicate the index of the last item written.

minFresh: Used by the reader to record the index of the first item available at the start of a read.

indexRead: Used by the reader to record the index of the item read. It is compared with minFresh and newMaxFresh to ensure that the item is fresh, and with its previous value to ensure that the items are read in sequence.

lastIndexRead: Used by the reader to record the index of the last item read.

An example assertion from the assertion network for the reader, that is used to prove atomicity is:

$\text{readerChoosesPair\_Assertion}: [\text{Conc\_State} \rightarrow \text{bool}] =$
$\quad \lambda\ (cs:\ \text{Conc\_State}):$
$\quad\quad cs\text{\textasciigrave nri} = rcp \Rightarrow cs\text{\textasciigrave reader\textasciigrave readerPair} = cs\text{\textasciigrave pairReading} \land$
$\quad\quad (cs\text{\textasciigrave pairReading} = cs\text{\textasciigrave pairWritten} \land$
$\quad\quad\quad cs\text{\textasciigrave reader\textasciigrave readerPair} = cs\text{\textasciigrave writer\textasciigrave writerPair} \land$
$\quad\quad\quad cs\text{\textasciigrave reader\textasciigrave readerPair} = cs\text{\textasciigrave pairReading} \Rightarrow$
$\quad\quad\quad (\neg\ cs\text{\textasciigrave wisOccurred} \Rightarrow$
$\quad\quad\quad\quad cs\text{\textasciigrave minFresh} \leq cs\text{\textasciigrave maxFresh} \land$
$\quad\quad\quad\quad cs\text{\textasciigrave indexRead} \leq cs\text{\textasciigrave maxFresh} \land$
$\quad\quad\quad\quad cs\text{\textasciigrave indexRead} \geq cs\text{\textasciigrave minFresh} \land cs\text{\textasciigrave lastIndexRead} \leq cs\text{\textasciigrave indexRead}) \land$
$\quad\quad\quad (cs\text{\textasciigrave wisOccurred} \Rightarrow$
$\quad\quad\quad\quad (\neg\ cs\text{\textasciigrave rcsSinceWis} \Rightarrow$
$\quad\quad\quad\quad\quad cs\text{\textasciigrave minFresh} \leq cs\text{\textasciigrave maxFresh} \land$
$\quad\quad\quad\quad\quad cs\text{\textasciigrave indexRead} \leq cs\text{\textasciigrave maxFresh} \land$
$\quad\quad\quad\quad\quad cs\text{\textasciigrave indexRead} \geq cs\text{\textasciigrave minFresh} \land cs\text{\textasciigrave lastIndexRead} \leq cs\text{\textasciigrave indexRead}) \land$
$\quad\quad\quad\quad (cs\text{\textasciigrave rcsSinceWis} \Rightarrow$
$\quad\quad\quad\quad\quad cs\text{\textasciigrave minFresh} \leq cs\text{\textasciigrave newMaxFresh} \land$
$\quad\quad\quad\quad\quad cs\text{\textasciigrave indexRead} \leq cs\text{\textasciigrave newMaxFresh} \land$
$\quad\quad\quad\quad\quad\quad cs\text{\textasciigrave indexRead} \geq cs\text{\textasciigrave minFresh} \land cs\text{\textasciigrave lastIndexRead} \leq cs\text{\textasciigrave indexRead})) \land$
$\quad\quad\quad\quad\quad cs\text{\textasciigrave minFresh} \leq cs\text{\textasciigrave slots}(cs\text{\textasciigrave pairWritten},$
$\quad\quad\quad\quad\quad\quad\quad\quad\quad\quad\quad\quad cs\text{\textasciigrave slotWritten}(cs\text{\textasciigrave pairWritten}))\text{\textasciigrave index} \land$
$\quad\quad (cs\text{\textasciigrave pairReading} = cs\text{\textasciigrave pairWritten} \land$
$\quad\quad\quad \neg\ cs\text{\textasciigrave reader\textasciigrave readerPair} = cs\text{\textasciigrave writer\textasciigrave writerPair} \land$
$\quad\quad\quad cs\text{\textasciigrave reader\textasciigrave readerPair} = cs\text{\textasciigrave pairReading} \Rightarrow$

$$\begin{aligned}
&\text{cs'minFresh} \leq \text{cs'maxFresh} \land \\
&\text{cs'indexRead} \leq \text{cs'maxFresh} \land \\
&\text{cs'indexRead} \geq \text{cs'minFresh} \land \\
&\text{cs'lastIndexRead} \leq \text{cs'indexRead} \land \\
&\text{cs'minFresh} \leq \\
&\quad \text{cs'slots(cs'pairWritten, cs'slotWritten(cs'pairWritten))'index} \land \\
&(\neg\ \text{cs'pairReading} = \text{cs'pairWritten} \land \\
&\quad \neg\ \text{cs'reader'readerPair} = \text{cs'writer'writerPair} \land \\
&\quad \text{cs'reader'readerPair} = \text{cs'pairReading} \Rightarrow \\
&\text{cs'minFresh} \leq \text{cs'maxFresh} \land \\
&\text{cs'indexRead} \leq \text{cs'maxFresh} \land \\
&\text{cs'indexRead} \geq \text{cs'minFresh} \land \\
&\text{cs'lastIndexRead} \leq \text{cs'indexRead} \land \\
&\quad (\text{cs'pairWritten} = p_0 \Rightarrow \\
&\qquad \text{cs'minFresh} \leq \text{cs'slots}(p_1,\ \text{cs'slotWritten}(p_1))\text{'index} \land \\
&\quad (\text{cs'pairWritten} = p_1 \Rightarrow \\
&\qquad \text{cs'minFresh} \leq \text{cs'slots}(p_0,\ \text{cs'slotWritten}(p_0))\text{'index}))
\end{aligned}$$

This assertion describes the different relationships between the auxiliary variables, depending on the values of the control variables in the mechanism, that are used to prove atomicity of the 4-slot, when the reader is about to execute the *readerChoosesPair* operation.

An example of assertion for the writer, when it is about to execute the *writerIndicatesPair* operation, which gives the values of the indices of the data items in the slots, depending on whether the writer has changed pair for this write or not, is:

$$\begin{aligned}
&\text{writerIndicatesPair\_Assertion: [Conc\_State} \to \text{bool]} = \\
&\lambda\ (\text{cs: Conc\_State}): \\
&\quad \text{cs'nwi} = \text{wip} \Rightarrow \text{cs'wisOccurred} \land \\
&\quad \neg\ \text{cs'pairWritten} = \text{cs'pairReading} \Rightarrow \\
&\quad \text{cs'pairWritten} = \text{cs'writer'writerPair}) \land \\
&\quad \text{cs'writer'writerSlot} = \text{cs'slotWritten(cs'writer'writerPair)} \land \\
&\quad \text{cs'maxFresh} = \text{cs'newMaxFresh} - 1 \land \\
&\quad \text{cs'newMaxFresh} = \text{cs'slots(cs'writer'writerPair,} \\
&\qquad \text{cs'writer'writerSlot)'index} \land \\
&\quad (\text{cs'writer'writerPair} = \text{cs'pairWritten} \Rightarrow \\
&\qquad (\text{cs'slotWritten(cs'pairWritten)} = s_0 \Rightarrow \\
&\qquad\quad \text{cs'slots(cs'pairWritten, } s_1)\text{'index} \leq \text{cs'maxFresh}) \land \\
&\qquad (\text{cs'slotWritten(cs'pairWritten)} = s_1 \Rightarrow \\
&\qquad\quad \text{cs'slots(cs'pairWritten, } s_0)\text{'index} \leq \text{cs'maxFresh}) \land \\
&\qquad (\text{cs'pairWritten} = p_0 \Rightarrow \\
&\qquad\quad \text{cs'slots}(p_1,\ s_0)\text{'index} \leq \text{cs'maxFresh} - 1 \land \\
&\qquad\quad \text{cs'slots}(p_1,\ s_1)\text{'index} \leq \text{cs'maxFresh} - 1) \land \\
&\qquad (\text{cs'pairWritten} = p_1 \Rightarrow \\
&\qquad\quad \text{cs'slots}(p_0,\ s_0)\text{'index} \leq \text{cs'maxFresh} - 1 \land \\
&\qquad\quad \text{cs'slots}(p_0,\ s_1)\text{'index} \leq \text{cs'maxFresh} - 1)) \land \\
&\quad (\neg\ \text{cs'writer'writerPair} = \text{cs'pairWritten} \Rightarrow \\
&\qquad \text{cs'maxFresh} = \text{cs'slots(cs'pairWritten,} \\
&\qquad\qquad \text{cs'slotWritten(cs'pairWritten))'index} \land \\
&\qquad (\text{cs'slotWritten(cs'pairWritten)} = s_0 \Rightarrow \\
&\qquad\quad \text{cs'slots(cs'pairWritten, } s_1)\text{'index} \leq \text{cs'maxFresh} - 1) \land \\
&\qquad (\text{cs'slotWritten(cs'pairWritten)} = s_1 \Rightarrow \\
&\qquad\quad \text{cs'slots(cs'pairWritten, } s_0)\text{'index} \leq \text{cs'maxFresh} - 1) \land \\
&\qquad (\text{cs'writer'writerSlot} = s_0 \Rightarrow \\
&\qquad\quad \text{cs'slots(cs'writer'writerPair, } s_1)\text{'index} \leq \text{cs'maxFresh}) \land \\
&\qquad (\text{cs'writer'writerSlot} = s_1 \Rightarrow \\
&\qquad\quad \text{cs'slots(cs'writer'writerPair, } s_0)\text{'index} \leq \\
&\qquad\qquad \text{cs'maxFresh}))
\end{aligned}$$

This specifies, for example the slot that has been written to contains the item with the latest index, and, if the writer has changed pairs both of the slots in the opposite pair contain items with indices at least one less than the index of the latest item.

Lamport atomicity requires that the following guarantee condition must be implied by the assertions in the networks when the transitions are executed:

$$\forall(cs: \text{Conc\_State}): (cs\text{`nri} = rd \Rightarrow \\ cs\text{`minFresh} \leq cs\text{`newMaxFresh} \wedge cs\text{`indexRead} \leq cs\text{`newMaxFresh} \wedge \\ cs\text{`indexRead} \geq cs\text{`minFresh} \wedge cs\text{`lastIndexRead} \leq cs\text{`indexRead})$$

Where *minFresh* is the index of the first item available to the reader when it starts, *newMaxFresh* is the index of last possible item written when the read finishes, *indexRead* gives the index of the item read, and *lastIndexRead* gives the index of the item read the last time[9]. This requires two verification proofs for each transition, one to show that the guarantee condition holds before the operation associated with the transition is executed and the other to show that it still holds afterwards.

The use of the PVS theorem prover for discharging the verification proofs described in this section has been advantageous for a number of reasons. First PVS can be used to expose errors in the model. For example an error in the part of the model being verified may be indicated if part or all of a proof is unexpectedly discharged, or it is not possible to discharge all or part of a proof in the expected manner. For this reason it is advisable to work out the required tactics to discharge the proofs in advance (apart from saving time that may be wasted in following the incorrect tactics). Second PVS can be used to validate a *partial model* that does not describe all of the required behaviours of the required system. It is then easier to revise the proofs as the model is extended than it would be with hand written proofs. This helps to build confidence in the model as it evolves. The use of PVS has also increased confidence in the correctness of the final model and proofs.

5 Related Work

The proofs given in this paper are based the assumption that the actions of the reader and writer are Hoare atomic, although they can interleave in an unrestricted manner. It is recognised that this assumption does not hold in many implementations. When it does not hold it is possible for the reader and writer to clash on reading and writing a particular control variable, or to attempt to read a control variable in the mechanism when it is changing. The control variables are single bits, but there is no guarantee that the reader of the variable will get the value written in these situations. It is also possible that reading a changing value will cause the reader to become *metastable*, in other words it may take the reader an arbitrary length of time to decide whether it has read a zero or a one. The author has been involved in work which models the 4-slot that recognises that the reader and writer can clash on accesses to control variables. These models, in CSP, take account of metastability effects that arise in such circumstances. This work [20] has shown, using the FDR model checker [?], that the 4-slot mechanism still preserves coherence of data, and is Lamport atomic

---

[9] The reader must read data items in the order they are written and always reads a fresh item.

even when metastability occurs. This positive result is important because in [22] Rushby has shown that the 4-slot is not Lamport atomic if it is implemented with Lamport safe control variables.

Simpson's role model method [25, 27] has been used to prove correctness of the 4-slot, but this relies on an assumption about the behaviour of the read and write actions in the presence of metastability and clashes on control variables: that the reader of the variable gets the value either before or after the writer to the variable occurred. The 4-slot has also been proved correct using Petri-nets [29], and timed CSP [5, 4].

The method described in this paper has also been used with PVS to prove a 3-slot ACM implementation incorrect, because coherence of data is lost. The use of PVS helped to identify the sequence of actions of the reader and writer that would result in concurrent access by the reader and writer to the same data slot. It was then possible to show that if a timing constraint could be implemented to prevent this particular sequence of the actions the implementation would maintain coherence of the data transmitted[10].

6 Conclusions

This paper has presented a rely-guarantee proof of the correctness of Simpson's 4-slot ACM using the interleaved concurrency method for shared variable concurrency from [6]. The algorithm is deceptively simple, however the proofs are complex because of the unconstrained manner in which the read and write operations can interleave. The ACM has been proved correct using a number of different model checking methods, but the use of the rely-guarantee has provided much greater insight into how the algorithm operates than those methods. In addition the use of the interleaved concurrency method from [6] reduces the number of verification proofs to a manageable number (3 proofs for each of the states in the assertion networks in this case).

It was shown in [8] that the 4-slot implementation could be proved to be Lamport atomic with respect to an abstract implementation, subject to certain operations in the implementation being combined into *atomic operations*. A revised abstract specification is given in this paper with an exhaustive proof that this specification exhibits the desired Lamport atomic properties.

The paper then describes a proof using a rely-guarantee proof method for shared variable concurrency that shows that the implementation is Lamport atomic when the individual operations interleave in an unconstrained manner. The proofs described are sufficient to demonstrate correctness of the 4-slot when the control variables are Hoare atomic variables. In any implementation where this assumption does not hold it needs to be recognised that asynchronous accesses to control variables can result in an attempt to read such a variable when it is changing. In these circumstances it is possible that the reader will not return

---

[10] A revised 3-slot ACM implementation, from [?], that combines two of the actions of the original implementation into a single action to prevent the incorrect interleaving of actions has also been proved correct using PVS.

the value written, or that the reader may take an arbitrary length of time to decide whether it has read a zero or a one. It may be possible to extend the proofs to show correctness in these circumstances, but this would make the assertions significantly more complex, and the proofs will be daunting, if not intractable.

This paper shows that it is possible to to use the rely-guarantee method to prove properties of asynchronous networks of processes even when they are correct due to emergent properties of their asynchronous operation, rather than due to specific guarantees provided by their component processes. It may be easier to prove such properties by model checking, but the advantage of the proof method described here is that it gives much greater insight into the operation of the algorithm. The requirement to give assertions that hold in the states of the transitions of the reader and writer require an understanding of how the two processes interact, and this level of understanding could not be obtained simply by model checking the correctness of the mechanism. For example, in completing the proofs it was shown that the reader can read an item coherently before it has been *fully released* by the writer: after *writerIndicatesSlot* but before *writerIndicatesPair*, in certain circumstances when the reader and writer are accessing the same pair of slots. In addition the requirement to prove that the assertions hold in the target state of each transition, after executing the operation associated with the transition, provided the assertions hold in the source node of the transition gives increased confidence in the correctness of the model. A model checker will give counter examples for an incorrect implementation, however it will only give a positive result when the implementation is correct. This may lead to inefficient implementations being used, while more elegant implementations, that could be found with a better understanding of how the reader and writer interact, are overlooked.

The rely-guarantee method described in this paper has allowed a full proof of correctness of the 4-slot implementation with respect to an infinite state specification of atomicity (an unbounded number of reads can overlap with a single write and vice versa). Such a proof is not possible with a model checker without some form of data abstraction, and there is a danger that such an abstraction could leave out the very property that invalidates the proofs.

The use of PVS to validate the models and discharge the proof obligations has increased confidence in the correctness of the models and proof, and assisted in finding and correcting errors in the models. It was also easier to validate partial models and extend the proofs as the models evolved than would be the case if the proofs were discharged by hand. In addition, if a minor modification were made to the protocol the existing proofs could be modified more easily to check the correctness of the amended implementation, than with hand written proofs.

Acknowledgements

The BAE SYSTEMS Dependable Computing Systems Centre funded this research. This work has benefited from conversations with Profs. C.B. Jones and H.R. Simpson and Drs. J.M. Armstrong and S.E. Paynter.

References

1. P. Aczel. On an inference rule for parallel composition. Unpublished letter to Cliff Jones, March 1983.
2. S. Angerholm, J. Bicarregui, and S. Maharaj. On the Verification of VDM Specifications and Refinement with PVS. In J.C. Bicarregui, editor, *Proof in VDM: Case Studies*, FACIT. Springer, 1998.
3. E.A. Ashcroft. Proving assertions about parallel programs. *JCSS*, 10:110–135, February 1975.
4. Phillip Brooke, Jeremy L. Jacob, and James M. Armstrong. Analysis of the FourSlot Mechanism. In *Proceedings of the BCS-FACS Northern Formal Methods Workshop*, 1996.
5. P.J. Brooke. *A Timed Semantics for a Hierarchical Design Notation*. PhD thesis, Department of Computer Science, University of York, April 1999.
6. Willem-Paul de Roever et al. *Concurrency Verification: Introduction to Compositional and Noncompositional Methods*. Number 54 in Cambridge Tracts in Theoretical Computer Science. Cambridge University Press, 2001.
7. Formal Systems (Europe) Ltd. *Failures-Divergence Refinement: The FDR 2.0 User Manual*, August 1996.
8. N. Henderson and S.E. Paynter. The Formal Classification and Verification of Simpson's 4-Slot Asynchronous Communication Mechanism. In L.-H. Eriksson and P.A. Lindsay, editors, *Proceedings of FME'02*, number 2391 in Lecture Notes in Computer Science, pages 350–369. Springer, 2002.
9. C.A.R. Hoare. Monitors: An Operating System Structuring Concept. *Communications of the ACM*, 17(10):549–557, 1974.
10. C.B. Jones. *Development Methods for Computing Programs Including a Notion of Interference*. PhD thesis, Oxford University Computing Laboratory, 1981.
11. C.B. Jones. Specification and Design of (Parallel) Programs. *Information Processing Letters*, 83:321–331, 1983.
12. C.B. Jones. Tentative steps towards a development method for interfering programs. *ACM Transactions an Programming Languages and Systems*, 5(4):596–619, October 1983.
13. C.B. Jones. *Systematic Software Development Using VDM*. Second Edition. Prentice-Hall International Series in Computer Science, 1990.
14. L. Lamport. On Interprocess Communication – Part 1: Basic Formalism. *Distributed Computing*, 1:77–85, 1986.
15. L. Lamport. On Interprocess Communication – Part 2: Algorithms. *Distributed Computing*, 1:86–101, 1986.
16. T. Nipkow. Non-Deterministic Data Types: Models and Implementations. *Acta Informatica*, 22:629–661, 1986.
17. T. Nipkow. *Behavioural Implementation Concepts for Nondeterministic Data Types*. PhD thesis, University of Manchester, May 1987.
18. S. Owre, N. Shanker, J.M. Rushby, and D.W.J. Stringer-Calvert. PVS Language: Version 2.3. Technical report, Computer Science Laboratory – SRI International, September 1999.
19. S. Owre, N. Shanker, J.M. Rushby, and D.W.J. Stringer-Calvert. PVS System Guide: Version 2.3. Technical report, Computer Science Laboratory – SRI International, September 1999.
20. S.E. Paynter, N. Henderson, and J.M. Armstrong. Ramifications of metastability in bit variables explored via Simpson's 4-slot mechanism. Submitted to FACS, January 2003.

21. A.W. Roscoe. *The Theory and Practice of Concurrency.* Prentice Hall Series in Computer Science, 1998.
22. John Rushby. Model-Checking Simpson's Four-Slot Fully Asynchronous Communication Mechanism. Technical Report Issued, Computer Science Laboratory – SRI International, July 2002.
23. H.R. Simpson. Fully Asynchronous Communication. In *Proceedings of the IEE Colloquium an MASCOT in Real-Time Systems*, May 1987.
24. H.R. Simpson. Four-Slot Fully Asynchronous Communication Mechanism. *IEE Proceedings*, 137 Part E(1):17–30, January 1990.
25. H.R. Simpson. Correctness Analysis for Class of Asynchronous Communication Mechanism. *IEE Proceedings*, 139 Part E(1):35–49, January 1992.
26. H.R. Simpson. New Algorithms for Asynchronous Communication. IEE Proceedings of Computer Digital Technology, 144(4):227-231, July 1997.
27. H.R. Simpson. Role Model Analysis of an Asynchronous Communication Mechanism. IEE Proceedings of Computer Digital Technology, 144(4):232-240, July 1997.
28. F. Xia. Supporting the MASCOT method with Petri net techniques for real- time systems development. PhD thesis, London University, King's College, January 2000.
29. F. Xia and I. Clark. Complementing the role model method with petri-net techniques in studying issues of data freshness of the four slot mechanism. Technical Report CS-TR-654, Department of Computing Science, University of Newcastle, January 1999.
30. F. Xia, A.V. Yakovlev, I.G.Clark, and D. Shang. Data communication in systems with heterogeneous timing. IEEE Micro, 22(6), Nov-Dec 2002.

A Formal Model of the 4-Slot Implementation in PVS

This appendix contains the model of the 4-slot algorithm, in the PVS logic, that has been used in all of the proofs (apart from differences in auxiliary variables).

```
Val: NONEMPTY_TYPE

Data: TYPE = [# index: nat, val: Val #]

PairIndex: TYPE = {p_0, p_1}

SlotIndex: TYPE = {s_0, s_1}

NextReadInstruction: TYPE = {firstRcp, rcp, rip, rcs, rd}

NextWriteInstruction: TYPE = {firstWcp,wcp, wcs, wr, wis, wip}

WriterState: TYPE = [# writerPair: PairIndex,
                       writerSlot: SlotIndex,
                       currentState: WriterNetworkState #]

ReaderState: TYPE = [# readerPair: PairIndex,
                       readerSlot: SlotIndex,
                       currentState: ReaderNetworkState #]

Conc_State: TYPE = [# pairWritten: PairIndex,
                      slotWritten: [PairIndex → SlotIndex],
                      lastSlotWritten: [PairIndex → SlotIndex],
                      pairReading: PairIndex,
                      slots: [PairIndex, SlotIndex → Data],
                      nri: NextReadInstruction,
                      nwi: NextWriteInstruction,
                      writer: WriterState,
                      reader: ReaderState,
                      maxFresh: nat #]
```

The NextReadInstruction and NextWriteInstruction variables are used to model the progress of the reader and writer respectively through their algorithms. The operations of the reader and writer are encoded as follows[11]:

pre_readerChoosesPair(p: Conc_State): bool = p'nri = rcp

post_readerChoosesPair(p: (pre_readerChoosesPair))(prot: Conc_State): bool =
   prot = p WITH [nri := rip, reader := p'reader
               WITH [readerPair := p'pairWritten,
                    currentState := lr1]]

readerChoosesPair: [p: (pre_readerChoosesPair) → (post_readerChoosesPair(p))]

pre_readerIndicatesPair(p: Conc_State): bool = p'nri = rip

post_readerIndicatesPair(p: (pre_readerIndicatesPair))(prot: Conc_State): bool =
   prot = p WITH [nri := rcs,
             pairReading := p'reader'readerPair,
             reader := p'reader WITH [currentState := lr2]]

readerIndicatesPair: [p: (pre_readerIndicatesPair) → (post_readerIndicatesPair(p))]

pre_readerChoosesSlot(p: Conc_State): bool = p'nri = rcs

post_readerChoosesSlot(p: (pre_readerChoosesSlot))(prot: Conc_State): bool =
   prot = p WITH [nri := rd, reader := p'reader
              WITH [readerSlot :=
                    p'slotWritten(p'reader'readerPair), currentState := lr3]]

readerChoosesSlot: [p: (pre_readerChoosesSlot) → (post_readerChoosesSlot(p))]

pre_read(p: Conc_State): bool = p'nri = rd

post_read(p: (pre_read))(prot: Conc_State, v: Val): bool =
   v = p'slots(p'reader'readerPair, p'reader'readerSlot)'val ∧
   prot = p WITH [nri := rcp, reader := p'reader WITH [currentState := lr4]]

read: [p: (pre_read) → (post_read(p))]

pre_writerChoosesPair(p: Conc_State): bool = p'nwi = wcp

post_writerChoosesPair(p: (pre_writerChoosesPair))(prot: Conc_State): bool =
   (p'pairReading = p_0 ⇒ prot = p WITH [nwi := wcs,
               writer := p'writer WITH [writerPair := p_1, currentState := lw1]]) ∧
   (p'pairReading = p_1 ⇒ prot = p WITH [nwi := wcs,
               writer := p'writer WITH [writerPair := p_0, currentState := lw1]])

writerChoosesPair: [p: (pre_writerChoosesPair) → (post_writerChoosesPair(p))]

pre_writerChoosesSlot(p: Conc_State): bool = p'nwi = wcs

post_writerChoosesSlot(p: (pre_writerChoosesSlot))(prot: Conc_State): bool =
   (p'slotWritten(p'writer'writerPair) = s_0 ⇒
     prot = p WITH [nwi := wr, writer := p'writer
        WITH [writerSlot := s_1, currentState := lw2]]) ∧
   (p'slotWritten(p'writer'writerPair) = s_1 ⇒
     prot = p WITH [nwi := wr, writer := p'writer
        WITH [writerSlot := s_0, currentState := lw2]])

writerChoosesSlot: [p: (pre_writerChoosesSlot) → (post_writerChoosesSlot(p))]

pre_write(p: Conc_State): bool = p'nwi = wr

write_parameter: TYPE = [# p_1: (pre_write), v: Val #]

post_write(p: write_parameter)(prot: Conc_State): bool =
   prot = p'p_1 WITH [nwi := wis,
           (slots)(p'p_1'writer'writerPair, p'p_1'writer'writerSlot)
           := (# index := p'p_1'maxFresh, val := p'v #),

---

[11] The firstReaderChoosesPair and firstWriterChoosesPair operations are identical to the readerChoosesPair and writerChoosesPair operations, except for assignments to auxilliary variables, and are not shown here.

writer := $p`p_1`$writer WITH [currentState := lw3]]

write: [p: write_parameter → (post_write(p))]

pre_writerIndicatesSlot(p: Conc_State): bool = $p`$nwi = wis

post_writerIndicatesSlot(p: (pre_writerIndicatesSlot))(prot: Conc_State): bool =
   prot = p WITH [nwi := wip,
               (slotWritten)($p`$writer`writerPair) := ($p`$writer`writerSlot),
               writer := $p`$writer WITH [currentState := lw4]]

writerIndicatesSlot: [p: (pre_writerIndicatesSlot) → (post_writerIndicatesSlot(p))]

pre_writerIndicatesPair(p: Conc_State): bool = $p`$nwi = wip

post_writerIndicatesPair(p: (pre_writerIndicatesPair))(prot: Conc_State): bool =
   prot = p WITH [nwi := wcp,
               pairWritten := $p`$writer`writerPair,
               writer := $p`$writer WITH [currentState := lw5]]

writerIndicatesPair: [p: (pre_writerIndicatesPair) → (post_writerIndicatesPair(p))]

Synthesis and Verification of Constraints in the PGM Protocol*

Marc Boyer[1] and Mihaela Sighireanu[2]

[1] ENSEEIHT – IRIT/TéSA, 2, rue Camichel, 31071 Toulouse, France,
Marc.Boyer@enseeiht.fr
[2] LIAFA – University of Paris 7, 2 place Jussieu, 75251 Paris, France
Mihaela.Sighireanu@liafa.jussieu.fr

Abstract. Specifications of protocols usually involve several parameters, for example the number of retransmissions or the timeout delays. The properties satisfied by the protocol depend often on the relation between these parameters. Automatic synthesis of such relations becomes a difficult problem when the constraints are too complex, e.g., non-linear expressions between integer and/or real parameters. This paper reports about modeling and constraint synthesis in the Pragmatic General Multicast (PGM) protocol. The property that we aim to satisfy is the full reliability property for data transmission. The complexity of the PGM prevents us from doing automatic synthesis of this constraint. Instead, we propose a methodology to deal with this problem using classical model-checking tools for timed and finite systems. Our methodology consists of several steps. First, we identify the sources of complexity and, for each source, we propose several abstractions preserving the full reliability property. Then, we build an abstract parameterized model on which we test, after instantiation of parameters, that the basic properties of the protocol (deadlock freedom, liveness) are preserved. By analyzing the scenario which invalidate the full reliability property, we find a non-linear constraint between the parameters of the protocol. We check the relation found by instantiating the parameters with relevant values and applying model-checking.

Key words: PGM protocol, real-time multicast protocol, finite and timed model-checking, parameterized verification, constraint synthesis.

1 Introduction

In the last years, interesting results have been obtained in the verification of models using parameters (i.e., constants which values are not fixed) [AAB00, HRSV01, BCALS01, BCAS01]. The models considered are mainly parametric counter and timed automata, i.e., models with counters and/or clocks that can be compared with (expressions on) parameters in order to define lower and upper bounds on their possible values. On such models are studied two kind of

---

* This work was supported in part by the European Commission (FET project ADVANCE, contract No IST-1999-29082).

problems: *verify* that the model satisfies some property for *all* possible values of parameters (verification problem), or *find* constraints on parameters defining the set of all possible values for which the model satisfies a property (synthesis problem). These problems can be solved as reachability problems in parametric models. Since the reachability problem is undecidable for parametric timed [AHV93] and counter automata, semi-algorithmic approaches are used.

The interest of such a research is obvious, especially in the framework of compositional specification: components are parameterized and the system obtained would satisfy some property depending on the tuning of values for parameters. Unfortunately, this approach is strongly limited by the kind of relations between parameters, since only linear relations between integer parameters can be dealt. A possible solution [AAB00] is to use an over-approximation by considering that these integer parameters are reals. Another limitation is the size of the models that can be analyzed. While finite verification deals easily with models containing several tens of finite integer variables, the actual tools doing infinite model-checking (e.g., ALV [Bul98], LASH [Boi98], TREX [BCAS01]) can not manage the same number of infinite integer (counter) variables.

We show in this paper how it is possible to manage the current limits of the parameterized verification by using an accurate methodology and finite model-checking.

The example we consider is the Pragmatic General Multicast (PGM) protocol. PGM has been designed to support reliable multicast of small, real-time generated information to potentially millions of users, for example in video applications. The protocol was developed jointly by CISCO Systems and TIBCO, and presented to the IETF[1] as an open reference specification [SFC+01]. It is currently supported as a technology preview, usually over IP, with which users may experiment.

The main property that PGM intends to guarantee (stated in [SFC+01]) is the following: *a receiver either receives all data packets from transmissions and repairs or it is able to detect uncoverable data packet loss*. It means that the full reliability property of PGM is not mandatory. However, it is interesting to know under which conditions the full reliability is obtained, and our work focus on this concern.

The problem of reliable multicast protocols is that the classical solution of positive acknowledgments (ACKs) used for reliability in unicast protocols (like TCP) may produce excessive overhead for one-to-many communications. For this reason, the reliable multicast protocols often use negative acknowledgments (NAKs) sent by the receivers when some packets are not received. This solution does not work well during periods of congestion, when many receivers may be affected by losses. Multiple redundant NAKs can be issued by the group of receivers, adding to the congestion and causing the "NAK implosion" of the network or redundant retransmissions. PGM minimizes the probability of NAK implosion by using a NAK elimination mechanism in the intermediate nodes of the distribution tree.

---

[1] Internet Engineering Task Force

The protocol specification in [SFC+01] is too complex w.r.t. the full reliability property. Indeed, it includes a lot of mechanisms which are designed to minimize the loading of the network. In this paper, an important contribution is the design of a model for the protocol where the mechanisms which are not important for full reliability are abstracted. This abstract model uses twenties clocks, tens of counters, arrays, FIFO queues. None of the existing tools on infinite verification can deal with it. Moreover, we prove (manually) that the full reliability property is verified when some integers parameters satisfy a non-linear relation, so the parameterized reachability analysis can not be directly applied.

In order to check the constraint found, we instantiate systematically the six parameters of the protocol and apply the existing tools for real-time and finite model-checking. We work with the IF [BFG+00] and CADP [FGK+96] tool-boxes.

Moreover, since we have to do more than twenty thousand tests, we intensively use shell scripts to manage fully automatically the instantiation of parameters. This part shows us the interest of parameterized verification. Also, our work allows to find some abstractions for the PGM. They may be useful for verification by infinite model-checking.

In addition to these specific contributions for the PGM protocol, we highlight the current methodology for constraint synthesis using finite model-checking. We show (1) how to obtain a good model, (2) how constraints are obtained, and (3) how are chosen values for parameters in order to automatically verify the constraint by finite model-checking. The PGM is a good example to illustrate this methodology due to its complexity.

Related work. Recent work has been done in the verification of a simplified, timed version of the PGM protocol in [BBP02]. The model considered implements the same topology that our (linear one with three nodes). However, the model used for communication between automata corresponds to one-place buffers with delay. Our model is more general in this direction because it uses bounded FIFO queues with delays. They verify the reliability property of the protocol by instantiating the parameters and then calling the UPPAAL [PL00] tool for verification of timed systems. They didn't find the relation we synthesize, although they are interested by the same property.

The work done in [BL02] concerns the validation with LASH of the sliding window mechanism of the protocol for any number of data packets sent. A more theoretical work is done in [EM02] and consists of a mathematical framework for multicast protocol that allows to generalize the results obtained for linear topologies to tree topologies.

Outline. Section 2 gives an overview of the protocol. Section 3 presents the model we verified for the PGM protocol and describes the abstractions applied to this model. Section 4 contains the proof of the constraint we found for satisfaction of the full reliability property. Section 5 describes shortly the tools used and the methodology employed. Then, Section 6 gives the properties checked and the verification results. Section 7 summarizes the work done and gives some concluding remarks on this experience.

2 Overview of PGM

A "session" of the PGM protocol (a given data transfer from a source to a group of receivers) builds a tree: the source is the root of the tree, the receivers are the leaves, and the other network elements are intermediary nodes. This tree may change during the session by the dynamic join/leave of receivers. Figure 1 shows such a distribution tree and the direction (upstream or downstream) followed by the five basic packets of the protocol.

In the normal course of data transfer, a source multicasts sequenced data packets (ODATA) along a path of the distribution tree to the receivers. When a receiver detects missing data packets from the expected sequence, it unicasts repeatedly to the last network element of the path negative acknowledgments (NAKs) containing the sequence number of missing data. Network elements forward NAKs hop-by-hop to the source using the reverse path, and confirm each hop by multicasting a NAK confirmation (NCF) in response to the child from which the NAK was received. Receivers and network elements stop sending NAK at the reception of a corresponding NCF. Finally, the source itself receives and confirms the NAK by multicasting an NCF to the group. If the data missing is still in the memory, repairs (RDATA) may be provided by the source in response to the NAK.

To avoid NAK implosion, PGM specifies procedures for NAK elimination within network elements in order to propagate just one copy of a given NAK along the reverse of the distribution path.

The basic data transfer operation is augmented by SPMs (Source Path Messages) packets from a source, periodically interleaved with ODATA. SPMs have two functions. First, they carry routing informations used to maintain up-to-date PGM neighbor information and a fixed distribution tree. Second, they complement the role of data packets when there is no more data to send by holding the state of the sender window. In this way, the receiver may detect data losses and send further NAKs.

In the following, we describe the functions of each component of the protocol.

Source functions. The source executes five functions: multicast of ODATA packets, multicast of SPMs, multicast of NCFs in response to any NAKs received, multicast of RDATA packets, and maintain (update and advance) of the transmit window.

The transmit window plays an important role in the PGM operations. Any information produced by the application using PGM (upper level in the network layers) is put in the transmit window and split in several ODATA chunks,

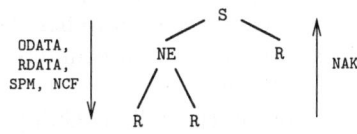

Fig. 1. Distribution tree of the PGM with packets involved (S = source, NE = network element, R = receiver).

numbered circularly from 0 to $2^{32} - 1$. This data is maintained in the window TXW_SECS time units for further repairs and sent with a maximum transmit rate of TXW_MAX_RTE (bytes/seconds). The left edge of this window, TXW_TRAIL, is defined as the sequence number of the oldest packet available for repairs. The right edge, TXW_LEAD, is defined as the sequence number of the most recent data packet the source has transmitted. To provide information about the sender window, TXW_TRAIL edge is sent with O/RDATA and SPM packets and the TXW_LEAD edge is included only in SPMs. If TXW_TRAIL = TXW_LEAD + 1, the window is considered empty. The maximum size of the window (TXW_SIZE = TXW_LEAD - TXW_TRAIL + 1) should be less than $2^{16} - 1$. The edge TXW_LEAD is advanced when data is produced by the application. The strategy of the source to advance the TXW_TRAIL edge is not fixed in [SFC$^+$01].

Two types of SPMs are sent by the source: *ambient* SPMs are sent "at least sufficient" [SFC$^+$01] rate to maintain routing information; *heartbeat* SPMs are transmitted in absence of data at a decaying rate, in order to assist detection of lost data before the advance of the transmit window.

Receiver functions. The receiver executes five functions: receive O/RDATA within the transmit window and eliminate duplicates, unicast NAKs repeatedly until it receives a matching NCF if it detects a loss, suppress NAKs sending after the reception of the NCF, maintain a local receive window.

The receive window is determined entirely by the packets from the source, since it evolves according to the information received from the source (data packets and SPMs). For each session, the receiver maintains the buffer and the two edges of the window: RXW_TRAIL is the sequence number of the oldest data packet available for repair from the source (known from data and SPMs) and RXW_LEAD is the greatest sequence number of any received data packet within the transmit window.

Network element functions. Network element forwards ODATA without intervention. They play an important role in routing, NAKs reliability, and avoiding NAKs implosion. Indeed, they forward only the first copy of a NAK and discard NAKs for which they have repair data. They also forward RDATA only to the child which signaled by a NAKs the loss of the corresponding data.

3 Modeling PGM

It is easy to see that modeling the full PGM protocol is out of the scope of existing model-cheking tools, because we need to handle dynamic topology with a lot of processes, dynamic routing, tens of counters and clocks per process, sequence numbers up to $2^{32} - 1$, etc.

In order to be able to look at the full reliability property, the first step consists of obtaining a "good" model. This model should be simple enough to be checked by the existing model-checking tools, but it has also to be realistic and to preserve the interesting behaviours for this property. To obtain such a model, we first analyze each dimension of complexity of PGM. For each dimension, we identify the abstractions that can be done and we specify those chosen for our model. This is the first step of our methodology.

3.1 Dimensions of Complexity

First dimension considered is the *topology*. The general topology is a dynamic graph, but we argue that we can focus our attention on static topologies.

Indeed, we can abstract the dynamic graph of a session by a maximal static graph where all the nodes belonging to the group at a moment in the session are present. When a node joins the group at a moment t during a session, it behaves like a node which loses all the data sent between the beginning of the session and t. When a node leaves the group, it can be abstracted into a node which receives all the data in time, i.e., it is silent w.r.t. reliability of data transfer. In this case, we may ignore all of the mechanisms proposed for joining/leaving for nodes and for sending routing (distribution path) information.

Moreover, the static distribution tree of a session may be abstracted into a linear topology. Indeed, if we consider that the loss rate does not depend on the number of receivers, adding more receivers to the tree does not change the advance of the transmit window. The loss of one data packet by several receivers may be abstracted by the loss detected in one receiver. More formal arguments in this direction are given in [EM02]. In conclusion, in order to study the full reliability property, we may consider linear topology with one source, one intermediate node, and one receiver, like in Figure 2.

Second dimension considered is the *policy of loss* for packets. In the general case, any number of any kind of packets could be loss. We can reduce the huge non determinism of such behaviour by noting that NAK, NCF, and SPM packets are small packets (they include one or two sequence numbers), for which the probability of loss using an IP network is small. Moreover, the loss of NAK and NCF packets is dealt by special mechanisms executed locally (for each link). Then, we may consider that the transmission of control packets is reliable. For data packets, we consider that at most MAX_NB_LOSS ODATA packets are lost, where MAX_NB_LOSS is a parameter of the model. The transmission of RDATA packets is abstracted to be reliable, as proposed in [SFC+01].

The third dimension considered is the *communication network*. Since PGM is designed to work on IP, the model for communication is unbounded, unordered, unreliable channels with no maximal transmission delay. However, the protocol

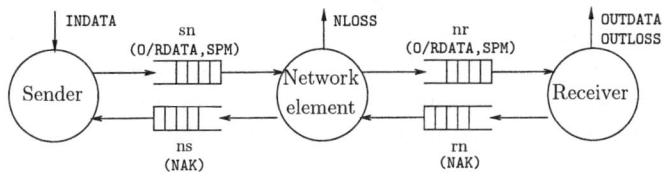

Fig. 2. Abstract model considered for topology and communication medium.

uses SPMs to carry routing informations in order to maintain a fixed distribution tree between sender and receivers. This allows us to abstract communication media to FIFO queues. The real-time feature of the protocol and the small sizes of PGM packets suggest us to put bounds on the size and the delays of communication channels. In conclusion, our communication media are reliable FIFO queues with bounded sizes and fixed delays of transmission (see Figure 2). Such a communication primitive is present in our modeling language, IF [BFG+00]. Losses of packets are simulated within the network element.

The next dimension concerns the *length of information to be transmitted* during the session w.r.t. the size of the transmit window. To cover most of the mechanisms of the protocol, this length should be greater than two transmit windows, and a transmit window should contain at least three data packets. This abstraction is implicitly used in [BBP02] since they consider that the maximal number of ODATA packets sent is ten. In our model, this length is a parameter, called MAX_NB_DATA.

Another dimension is the *shape of the traffic* from the application. In [SFC+01] is suggested that the source should implement a scheme for the traffic management and it should also bound the maximum rate of transmission. Moreover, a local absence of data should also be managed by sending heartbeat SPMs. A simple abstraction that avoids the heartbeat mechanisms (i.e., additional packets) and reduces the traffic shape is to consider a fixed rate of information generation. This rate is given by a parameter, DATA_PERIOD, specifying the time units between the generation of two data packets. The application sends the data at this rate until the end of the transmission. When this end is reached, the source signals it by a "closing SPM" [Boy02] packet containing the status of the window, which signals the absence of data and replaces the heartbeat mechanism.

The protocol also provides a lot of *mechanisms to ensure efficiency* of transmission. These mechanisms (e.g., filtering of NAKs in network elements, back-off timeouts for NAKs, filtering of RDATA) are not relevant to the reliability property that we aim to test.

Other mechanisms are introduced in order to obtain some properties for the transmission, mainly the reliability of the NAKs and NCFs. We abstract these mechanisms and consider that there are no loss of NAKs, so no need for NCFs.

The last dimension of complexity concern the *management of the transmit window*. In [SFC+01], no policy is fixed for the advance of the window and the sending of the ambient SPMs. In our model, we consider that the sender tries to keep in the window the maximum number of data packets in such a way that it can receive any time data from application, i.e. TXW_SIZE packets are always kept. When the application finishes the transmission, the packets are dropped out from the window each DATA_PERIOD time units. Concerning the sending of ambient SPMs, we choose to send an ambient SPM for every DATA_PER_SPM data packets generated by the application, with DATA_PER_SPM a parameter of the protocol.

3.2 Abstract Model Considered

The second step consists of applying the abstractions described above in order to obtain a formal model of the PGM protocol. The models obtained for the PGM source, receiver, and network element are given respectively on Figures 3, 5, and 4. We explain in this section the resulting model.

We use IF [BFG+00], which underlying model is a network of finite state, timed automata communicating by channels of different policies, rendez-vous,

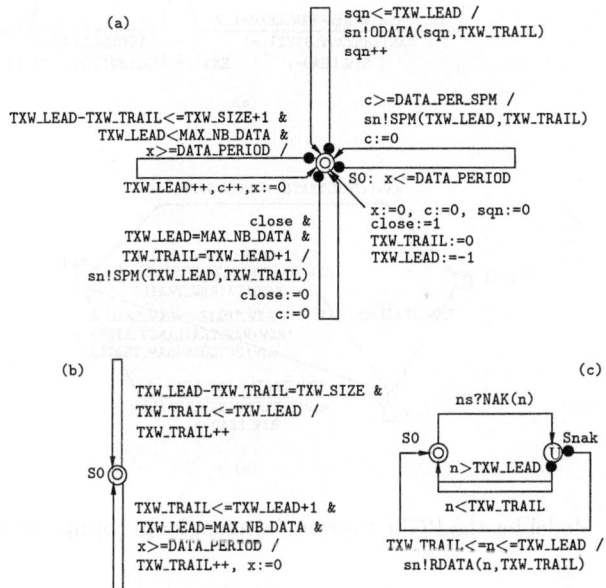

Fig. 3. Model for the PGM source: (a) sending ODATA and SPM, (b) window advance, (c) dealing with NAK and RDATA.

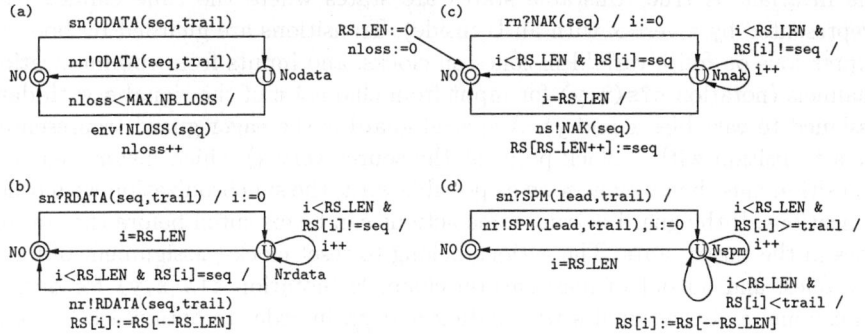

Fig. 4. Model for the PGM network element: (a) dealing ODATA, (b) dealing RDATA, (c) dealing NAKs, (d) dealing SPMs.

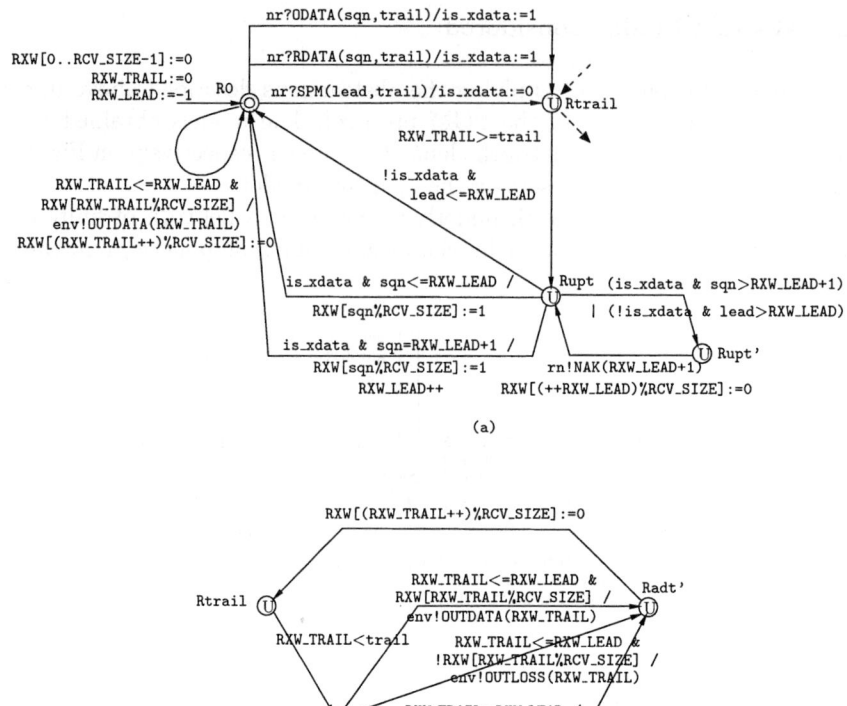

Fig. 5. Model for the PGM receiver: (a) main loop, (b) updating trail.

and shared variables. The finite types that can be used are boolean, bounded integer, user defined enumerated type, record and finite array of finite types. In IF, states can be decorated with invariants for time elapsing. By default, the invariant is true. Unstable states are states where the time cannot pass (represented by a vertex with an U inside). Transitions are guarded by boolean expressions on finite variables, zones on clocks, and inputs from communication channels (notation c?s(x,y) for input from channel c of the signal s with data assigned to variables x and y). A special guard is the eager guard (represented by a transition with a black point at the source vertex) which means that the transition must be taken as soon as possible w.r.t. the synchronization with other transitions. If the guard is true, some actions can be executed before the control goes in the target state. The actions belong to reset clocks, assignment of finite variables, and output of messages on channels (notation c!s(x,y) for output on channel c of the signal s with data x and y). In order to obtain easy to read automata, the automaton of each component is split in several parts, each part has like source a shared state and implements a specific function (see Section 2) of the component.

The source inputs data from the upper level (increments TXW_LEAD) each DATA_PERIOD time units until the limit of MAX_NB_DATA is reached (Figure 3, Part (a)). Interleaved with this activity, the source sends ODATA packets in the transmit window as soon as (eager transition) the data is available. For every[2] DATA_PER_SPM data packets generated by the application, the source sends an ambient SPM. When the MAX_NB_DATA limit is reached and all the data have been sent, a closing SPM packet is sent to inform the receiver about the absence of recovery. This solution has been proposed in [Boy02] to be able to give a correct status about the data packets sent in the last transmit window in absence of heartbeat SPMs. Part (b) specifies the policy of window advance. Part (c) specifies the treatment of NAK.

The network element forwards ODATA packets (Figure 4, part (a)) or non deterministically losses data (signaled to the environment by the NLOSS signal). The sequence numbers of data to be recovered are stored in a vector RS of maximal size RS_SIZE and of current size RS_LEN. This vector is updated at the arrival of RDATA, NAK, and SPM packets (parts (b), (c), and (d) respectively). It is used to avoid duplication of NAKs.

The receiver waits for any kind of packets (ODATA, RDATA, and SPM) and updates the receive window implemented by the array RXW (of maximal size RXW_SIZE). This array is used as a circular buffer (sequence numbers taken modulo the size of the array) and it stores booleans saying if the corresponding data packet has been received or not. Initially, all the entries are false. Based on RXW array, when the transmit window advance (the trail received is greater than RXW_TRAIL), the receiver sends either OUTDATA signal to the environment or it signals a loss (OUTLOSS signal).

The parameters of the model are summarized in Table 1. For each parameter we give either a value, if it has been fixed during experiments, or an interval of values otherwise. We discuss the choice of these value in Section 6.

4 Constraint for Recovering All Losses

In the third step of our methodology, we analyze the sequence of events needed to obtain the target property. In our case, the sequence allowing to recover a loss ensures the full reliability. It involves four steps:

1. one or more ODATA packets are lost (by the node, in our model);
2. the receiver receives a packet (ODATA, RDATA, or SPM) signaling that a previous data packets have been lost;
3. the NAK signaling the loss is received by the source before the corresponding data have been dropped from the transmit window;
4. the corresponding RDATA is sent and received.

---

[2] Although the guard for this transition is c>=DATA_PER_SPM, the transition is eager, so it will be taken immediately when the value DATA_PER_SPM is reached.

Table 1. Summary of parameters.

SIZE PARAMETERS		
TXW_SIZE	Transmit window size	1–6
MAX_NB_LOSS	Max. number of lost data at some point	0–5
MAX_NB_DATA	Max. number of data the source can send	3–18
DATA_PER_SPM	Nb. of data generated between two ambient SPM	1-3, ∞
RS_SIZE	Max. size of RS array	MAX_NB_LOSS
RXW_SIZE	Max. size of receiver window	TXW_SIZE
SN_SIZE, NS_SIZE	Max. size of sender-network element buffers	12, 4
NR_SIZE, RN_SIZE	Max. size of network element-receiver buffers	12, 4
TIME PARAMETERS		
DATA_PERIOD	Period of data sending TXW_MAX_RTE = 1/DATA_PERIOD, TXW_SECS = (TXW_SIZE − 1) × DATA_PERIOD	2–10,15
SN_DELAY, NS_DELAY	Max. delay for sender-network element buffers	2, 2
NR_DELAY, RN_DELAY	Max. delay for network element-receiver buffers	2, 2

These steps concern the following aspects of our model:

- the loss policy: in our model only MAX_NB_LOSS ODATA packets can be lost;
- the transit delay of packets (i.e., round trip time, RTT): is computed from the delays of communication buffers, RTT = SN_DELAY + NR_DELAY + RN_DELAY + NS_DELAY;
- the production rate of ODATA: given by DATA_PERIOD;
- the rate of ambient SPM: given by DATA_PER_SPM and DATA_PERIOD;
- the transmit window policy: fixed to maintain as long as possible data in the transmit window.

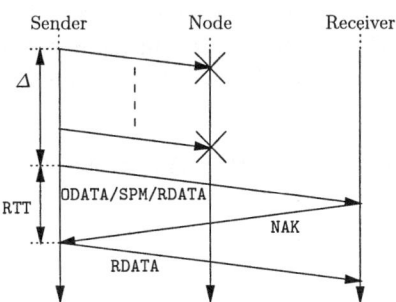

Fig. 6. Pattern of loss recovering.

Let Δ be the delay between the instant the first lost ODATA packet is sent and the instant that the first unlost packet is sent. The delay between the sending of the unlost packet and the reception of the matching NAK is the RTT, if we assume that a NAK is sent as soon as a loss is detected (it is the case in our model, but in a more realistic one, we should add a random back-off).

Then, the lost packets are recovered if $\Delta + \texttt{RTT}$ is less than[3] the lifetime of the data in the transmit window, i.e. $\texttt{DATA\_PERIOD} \times \texttt{TXW\_SIZE}$ in our model.

The value of Δ depends on the kind of the first non-lost packet: ODATA, RDATA, or SPM, i.e., $\Delta = \min(\Delta_{\texttt{ODATA}}, \Delta_{\texttt{RDATA}}, \Delta_{\texttt{SPM}})$. We cannot give an upper bound of $\Delta_{\texttt{RDATA}}$. Indeed, it could be ∞ if no packet has been lost before. For $\Delta_{\texttt{ODATA}}$, if we consider that no more than MAX_NB_LOSS packets are lost, its maximum value is $\texttt{MAX\_NB\_LOSS} \times \texttt{DATA\_PERIOD}$. This value is false for the last MAX_NB_LOSS packets since they can all be lost and not followed by any ODATA. For $\Delta_{\texttt{SPM}}$, the upper bound is $(\texttt{DATA\_PER\_SPM} - 1) \times \texttt{DATA\_PERIOD}$ (the -1 comes from the fact that the SPM is sent at the same time that the last ODATA of the DATA_PER_SPM set).

Then, we obtain the following property:

Property 1. If a data packet m does not belong to the last MAX_NB_LOSS packets, then m is always recovered if:

$$\texttt{TXW\_SIZE} - \min(\texttt{MAX\_NB\_LOSS}, \texttt{DATA\_PER\_SPM} - 1) > \frac{\texttt{RTT}}{\texttt{DATA\_PERIOD}} \quad (1)$$

5 Verification Methodology and Tools

The last step of our methodology is the verification of the constraint obtained using finite timed model-checking. It consists of the following actions:

1. We assign to parameters given in Table 1 relevant, concrete values (see Section 6).
2. Using these values, the parameterized model corresponding to the automata given on figures 3–5 is translated (by substitution) into a concrete model.
3. The concrete model is translated into a labeled transition system (LTS).
4. In order to check the model obtained, some basic, unparameterized properties like absence of deadlock, absence of overflows, etc. are checked on the LTS.
5. The parameterized property to be checked is also translated into a set of concrete properties, one property per sequence numbers from 0 to MAX_NB_DATA (which is a parameter).
6. The concrete properties are checked on the LTS.

In order to instantiate parameterized implementation and properties to concrete ones, we use shell scripts calling SED commands. The translation from the IF concrete implementation into the LTS is done using the GENERATOR tool of the IF toolbox. The LTS model is generated into the BCG [FGK+96] format. The temporal logic properties have been written using the regular alternation-free μ-calculus [Koz83, EL86] and checked using the EVALUATOR tool [MS00] of the CADP [FGK+96] toolbox. The tools used provide good performances: the time and memory spent for generating and checking the models are reasonable for the

---

[3] The inequality is strict because of the possible interleaving of actions dropping the data from the window and sending RDATA.

values of parameters reported here[4]. For example, the full series of experiments ($\approx$ three hundred cases) take 4 hours on a PC at 1GHz and 1Go of RAM.

6 Experiments

6.1 Choosing Relevant Values for Parameters

In searching relevant values for parameters, we follow three criteria:

C1: Cover all cases for both satisfaction values of Equation 1. This leads to a case analysis of Equation 1. When it is false, we may have two cases:
  C1.1: TXW_SIZE$-\min($MAX_NB_LOSS,DATA_PER_SPM$-1) \leq 0$
  C1.2: $0 <$ TXW_SIZE$- \min($MAX_NB_LOSS,DATA_PER_SPM$-1)$
    $\leq$ RTT/DATA_PERIOD
  which implies RTT $>$ DATA_PERIOD
  When Equation 1 is true, we may have also two cases:
  C1.3: TXW_SIZE$-\min($MAX_NB_LOSS,DATA_PER_SPM$-1) >$ RTT/DATA_PERIOD
    ≥ 1
  C1.4: TXW_SIZE$-\min($MAX_NB_LOSS,DATA_PER_SPM$-1) \geq 1$
    $>$ RTT/DATA_PERIOD

C2: Choose values preserving the ratio between the real life values of parameters. This criterion reduces the number of experiments selected with criterion **C1**. Indeed, we observe the following relation between the parameters:
  C2.1: The maximal number of losses MAX_NB_LOSS could be viewed like a fraction $1/p$ of the maximal number of data sent MAX_NB_DATA. Then, MAX_NB_DATA may be considered like a multiple n of the transmit window size, TXW_SIZE. If we suppose that the network has a low rate of losses (e.g., $p = 20$), the value of n/p may vary, for example, between 0.05 when the number of data is small (e.g., $n = 1$) and 100 when the number of data is great ($n \approx 10^3$).
  C2.2: The rate DATA_PER_SPM may belong to two classes of values. If DATA_PER_SPM is greater than MAX_NB_LOSS, it can be approximated to ∞ since the recover will not be done with SPMs packets. The second class of values is defined by the ratio between TXW_SIZE and DATA_PER_SPM. A great ration (a lot of SPMs sent by transmit window) implies an overload of the network but ensures quick data recovery. Then, we have to test values greater and less than 1 for this ration.
  C2.2: In real life, the RTT may vary considerably depending on the physical network. If the network is real-time oriented, the values taken by RTT may vary between 400ms to 40ms (ATM networks). For DATA_PERIOD, the value given as example in [SFC$^+$01] is $\approx$ 60ms. So, the interesting cases will concern values of RTT/DATA_PERIOD ≥ 1 or closer to 1 (video applications usually run faster than the network).

C3: Choose values allowing to generate the LTSs. For example, we abstract the real values of TXW_SIZE to values between 1–5. We do the same with RTT and DATA_PERIOD values.

---

[4] However, for values outside the set taken here, we obtain in some cases state explosion.

6.2 Properties Checked

On the LTS generated from the model we checked properties like deadlock freedom, absence of overflows for FIFOs, and a lost data packet is either signaled as lost or recovered. We used these properties only to check the correctness of our abstract model.

The temporal logic formulae ϕ used to prove Property 1 is: "ODATA packet number _SQN_ is sometimes signaled as lost". In the regular free μ-calculus, this formula is:

<true*.'.*sn_in,ODATA,{_SQN_},.*'.true*.'.*OUTLOSS,{_SQN_}.*'> true

which means that it is possible to have a sequence of transitions having an input of ODATA with number _SQN_ on queue sn (sub-string sn_in,ODATA,{_SQN_}) and then this packet is signaled as lost (sub-string OUTLOSS,{_SQN_}). The property is parameterized by the _SQN_ number which belongs to 0..MAX_NB_DATA.

If the result of model-checking ϕ *is false, then the packet is never signaled as lost* (i.e. it is either no lost or always recovered).

6.3 Results and Discussion

The results for a part of experiments done are presented on Tables 2–4. The experiments are looking to the truth value of checking ϕ while varying each parameter involved in the Equation 1. We report value $b \in \{t, f\}$ in the columns corresponding to a given sequence number if the result of checking ϕ for this sequence number is $\neg b$. The results in italic correspond to (unrelevant) cases when the sequence number does not satisfy the hypothesis of Property 1 or Equation 1 is not satisfied (see the last column of tables).

The tables 2 and 3 report about the recover of losses based on Δ_{ODATA} (assuming $\Delta_{SPM} = \infty$). Table 4 reports about the impact of ambient SPMs. In all these tables we limit our report to experiments with an RTT value fixed to 8. Instead, we vary the value of DATA_PERIOD in order to cover all the cases defined at the beginning of this section. The last paragraph below reports on the consequences of varying the RTT value.

Recovery based on ODATA This case corresponds to DATA_PER_SPM > MAX_NB_LOSS. The eight series of experiments done vary the three remaining parameters (MAX_NB_LOSS, TXW_SIZE, and DATA_PERIOD). Note that in all configurations tested in Tables 2 and 3, the MAX_NB_LOSS last packets may be definitively lost. So, the hypothesis of Property 1 is checked to be important. Another interesting result is the check of the necessity of Equation 1 since when it is false, all the packets (with numbers satisfying or not the hypothesis of Property 1) can be lost.

Recovery based on SPM To test this case, we consider only configurations where DATA_PER_SPM < MAX_NB_LOSS, except the first line of Table 4 which is used to show the difference between the recovering based on ODATA and on SPM. Indeed,

Table 2. Effect of the production rate DATA_PERIOD on the loss recovery.

MAX_NB_LOSS	MAX_NB_DATA	DATA_PER_SPM	TXW_SIZE	RTT	DATA_PERIOD	LTS States	LTS Trans.	0	1	2	3	4	5	6	7	8	9	Eq. 1
Increasing the size of the transmission, MAX_NB_DATA																		
1	4	∞	2	8	9	853	910	t	t	t	t	f	–	–	–	–	–	1 > 0.89
1	7	∞	2	8	9	1684	1795	t	t	t	t	t	t	t	f	–	–	1 > 0.89
1	9	∞	2	8	9	2353	2505	t	t	t	t	t	t	t	t	t	f	1 > 0.89
Varying the production rate, DATA_PERIOD																		
1	9	∞	2	8	15	2321	2473	t	t	t	t	t	t	t	t	t	f	1 > 0.53
1	9	∞	2	8	10	3607	4222	t	t	t	t	t	t	t	t	t	f	1 > 0.8
1	9	∞	2	8	9	2353	2505	t	t	t	t	t	t	t	t	t	f	1 > 0.89
1	9	∞	2	8	8	6390	7601	f	f	f	f	f	f	f	f	f	f	1 > 1
1	9	∞	2	8	7	2113	2238	f	f	f	f	f	f	f	f	f	f	1 > 1.1
1	9	∞	2	8	5	2347	2557	f	f	f	f	f	f	f	f	f	f	1 > 1.6
1	9	∞	2	8	3	4960	5941	f	f	f	f	f	f	f	f	f	f	1 > 2.7
Varying the production rate with wider window and same TXW_SIZE−MAX_NB_LOSS																		
2	9	∞	3	8	15	11420	13074	t	t	t	t	t	t	t	t	t	f	1 > 0.53
2	9	∞	3	8	10	19649	24575	t	t	t	t	t	t	t	t	f	f	1 > 0.8
2	9	∞	3	8	9	11829	13498	t	t	t	t	t	t	t	t	f	f	1 > 0.89
2	9	∞	3	8	8	60393	78011	f	f	f	f	f	f	f	f	f	f	1 > 1
2	9	∞	3	8	7	10853	12194	f	f	f	f	f	f	f	f	f	f	1 > 1.1
2	9	∞	3	8	5	17623	21324	f	f	f	f	f	f	f	f	f	f	1 > 1.6
2	9	∞	3	8	3	33717	42744	f	f	f	f	f	f	f	f	f	f	1 > 2.7
Varying the production rate with wider window and bigger TXW_SIZE−MAX_NB_LOSS																		
1	9	∞	4	8	15	2344	2489	t	t	t	t	t	t	t	t	t	f	3 > 0.53
1	9	∞	4	8	10	3532	4088	t	t	t	t	t	t	t	t	t	f	3 > 0.8
1	9	∞	4	8	5	3546	4106	t	t	t	t	t	t	t	t	t	f	3 > 1.6
1	9	∞	4	8	4	21180	28065	t	t	t	t	t	t	t	t	t	f	3 > 2
1	9	∞	4	8	3	6443	7848	t	t	t	t	t	t	t	t	t	f	3 > 2.7
1	9	∞	4	8	2	155587	225502	f	f	f	f	f	f	f	f	f	f	3 > 4

in the configuration corresponding to the first line, all packets are lost, but in the next configurations, all packets satisfying the hypothesis are recovered. An interesting point is that, even if the Equation 1 is not satisfied, some packets are always recovered (two per DATA_PER_SPM period). In fact, some packets sent before an SPM can always be recovered because the sum $\Delta_{\text{SPM}} + \text{RTT}$ is small enough to recover before the window advance.

In both cases, when DATA_PERIOD is increased, the number of packets lost increases.

Considerations on sizes of LTSs In some series of experiments, the size of the state space increases globally, but not locally. It is particularly visible on the second, third, and forth series of Table 2. This global increase seems "normal": there are more packets in the system when DATA_PERIOD increases so the system is more "complex".

Nevertheless, there are some local decreases: in the second series of Table 2, when DATA_PERIOD decreases from 10 to 9 or from 8 to 7, etc., and in the second series of Table 4 when DATA_PERIOD decreases from 10 to 9 and from 8 to 7. The explanation we found to this phenomenon involves the RTT and DATA_PERIOD. Indeed, when RTT and DATA_PERIOD are coprime, there are less events to inter-

Table 3. Effect of the number of losses MAX_NB_LOSS and of the window size TXW_SIZE on the loss recovery.

MAX_ NB_LOSS	MAX_ NB_DATA	DATA_ PER_SPM	TXW_ SIZE	RTT	DATA_ PERIOD	LTS States	Trans.	0	1	2	3	4	5	6	7	8	9	Eq. 1
Varying the window size, TXW_SIZE																			
1	9	∞	4	8	9	2376	2521	t	t	t	t	t	t	t	t	t	f	3 > 0.89
1	9	∞	3	8	9	2366	2515	t	t	t	t	t	t	t	t	t	f	2 > 0.89
1	9	∞	2	8	9	2353	2505	t	t	t	t	t	t	t	t	t	f	1 > 0.89
1	9	∞	1	8	9	2098	2225	f	f	f	f	f	f	f	f	f	f	0 > 0.89
Varying the window size and faster source, i.e. less DATA_PERIOD																			
1	9	∞	4	8	8	6088	7203	t	t	t	t	t	t	t	t	t	f	3 > 1
1	9	∞	3	8	8	6440	7641	t	t	t	t	t	t	t	t	t	f	2 > 1
1	9	∞	2	8	8	6390	7601	f	f	f	f	f	f	f	f	f	f	1 > 1
1	9	∞	1	8	8	4053	4929	f	f	f	f	f	f	f	f	f	f	0 > 1
Varying the window size and more losses																			
2	9	∞	5	8	9	11915	13566	t	t	t	t	t	t	t	t	f	f	3 > 0.89
2	9	∞	4	8	9	11878	13540	t	t	t	t	t	t	t	t	f	f	2 > 0.89
2	9	∞	3	8	9	11829	13498	t	t	t	t	t	t	t	t	f	f	1 > 0.89
2	9	∞	2	8	9	10597	11934	f	f	f	f	f	f	f	f	f	f	0 > 0.89
2	9	∞	1	8	9	7992	8536	f	f	f	f	f	f	f	f	f	f	−1 > 0.89
Varying the number of losses																			
0	9	∞	5	8	9	248	253	t	t	t	t	t	t	t	t	t	t	5 > 0.89
1	9	∞	5	8	9	2383	2523	t	t	t	t	t	t	t	t	t	f	4 > 0.89
2	9	∞	5	8	9	11915	13566	t	t	t	t	t	t	t	t	f	f	3 > 0.89
3	9	∞	5	8	9	46368	55966	t	t	t	t	t	t	t	f	f	f	2 > 0.89
4	9	∞	5	8	9	136148	170412	t	t	t	t	t	t	f	f	f	f	1 > 0.89
5	9	∞	5	8	9	307266	391888	f	f	f	f	f	f	f	f	f	f	0 > 0.89

Table 4. Effect of the ambient rate DATA_PER_SPM on the loss recovery.

MAX_ NB_LOSS	MAX_ NB_DATA	DATA_ PER_SPM	TXW_ SIZE	RTT	DATA_ PERIOD	LTS States	Trans.	0	1	2	3	4	5	6	7	8	9	Eq. 1
Varying the rate of ambiant SPM, DATA_PER_SPM																			
3	9	∞	3	8	6	186456	248566	f	f	f	f	f	f	f	f	f	f	0 > 1.3
3	9	4	3	8	6	610863	820882	f	f	t	f	t	f	t	f	f	f	0 > 1.3
3	9	3	3	8	6	483265	643931	f	t	t	f	t	f	t	f	t	t	1 > 1.3
3	9	2	3	8	6	283761	375570	t	t	t	t	t	t	t	t	t	t	2 > 1.3
3	9	1	3	8	6	702196	938857	t	t	t	t	t	t	t	t	t	t	3 > 1.3
Varying the production rate, DATA_PERIOD																			
3	9	3	3	8	10	138383	178656	t	t	t	t	t	t	t	t	t	f	1 > 0.8
3	9	3	3	8	9	76004	89939	t	t	t	t	t	t	t	t	t	f	1 > 0.89
3	9	3	3	8	8	683325	911658	f	t	t	f	t	t	f	t	t	f	1 > 1
3	9	3	3	8	7	75111	87847	f	t	t	f	t	f	t	t	t	f	1 > 1.1
3	9	3	3	8	6	483265	643931	f	t	t	f	t	f	t	t	t	t	1 > 1.3
3	9	3	3	8	5	115770	142441	f	t	t	f	t	f	t	t	t	f	1 > 1.6

leave than when they have a common divisor. So the sizes of LTSs are smaller in the first case than in the second. To check this explanation, we also did the experiments of in Table 2 with different values of RTT (more details presented in [Boy02]).

7 Conclusion

The verification and synthesis problems for parameterized system are difficult problems when the parameters are related by non-linear relations. In this paper we propose a methodology using finite and real-time model-checking to deal with the synthesis problem on such systems. Of course, the problem of synthesis is not completely managed. We obtain a relation by carefully modeling and analyzing the protocol.

Such a work gives some ideas about how the existing finite verification tools can be used to deal with parameterized verification. At the present time, the use of UNIX shell scripts seems to be unavoidable because there are no means to easily instantiate parameters in models and properties. It would be useful to have specification languages and verification scripts allowing to specify parameterized models and properties and then to instantiate these specifications with actual values in a functional style.

Another contribution is design of a (static but almost complete) formal model for the PGM protocol and the synthesis of the constraint between its parameters. The modeling process allows us to signal some lacks in the reference specification.

Finally, by doing the present work, we won the experience for obtaining simpler models for PGM such that they can be managed by the existing tools for infinite state systems. Indeed, the abstract model considered here is too complex for tools doing parameterized model-checking, e.g. TREX [BCAS01]. The sources of complexity are the great number of infinite domain variables (since finite integer variables are now considered as counters), and the non-linear relation between integer parameters. First experiments with TREX lead to memory explosion due to the size of symbolic representation used for parameterized configurations for clocks and counters. By looking at these representations, we obtain some hints about how to reduce their size. For example, the use of live analysis for counter variables may be useful due to the lack of communication by shared variables.

References

[AAB00] A. Annichini, E. Asarin, and A. Bouajjani. Symbolic techniques for parametric reasoning about counter and clock systems. In E.A. Emerson and A.P. Sistla, editors, *Proceedings of the 12th CAV*, volume 1855 of *LNCS*, pages 419–434. Springer Verlag, July 2000.

[AHV93] R. Alur, T.A. Henzinger, and M.Y. Vardi. Parametric real-time reasoning. In *ACM Symposium on Theory of Computing*, pages 592–601, 1993.

[BBP02] B. Bérard, P. Bouyer, and A. Petit. Analysing the pgm protocol with uppaal. In P. Pettersson and W. Yi, editors, *Proceedings of the 2nd Workshop RT-TOOLS, Copenhagen (Denmark)*, August 2002.

[BCALS01] A. Bouajjani, A. Collomb-Annichini, Y. Lacknech, and M. Sighireanu. Analysing fair parametric extended automata analysis. In *Proceedings of SAS'01*, LNCS. Springer Verlag, July 2001.

[BCAS01] A. Bouajjani, A. Collomb-Annichini, and M. Sighireanu. Trex: A tool for reachability analysis of complex systems. In *Proceedings of CAV'01*, LNCS. Springer Verlag, 2001.

[BFG+00] M. Bozga, J.-C. Fernandez, L. Girvu, S. Graf, J.-P. Krimm, and L. Mounier. If: A validation environment for times asynchronous systems. In E.A. Emerson and A.P. Sistla, editors, *Proceedings of the 12th CAV*, volume 1855 of *LNCS*, pages 543–547. Springer Verlag, July 2000.

[BL02] B. Boigelot and L. Latour. *ADVANCE Project Deliverable Report*, chapter Verifying PGM with infinitely many packets. LIAFA, 2002.

[Boi98] B. Boigelot. *Symbolic Methods for Exploring Infinite State Spaces*. PhD thesis, University of Liège, 1998.

[Boy02] M. Boyer. On modeling and verifying the pgm protocol. Technical report, LIAFA, 2002.

[Bul98] T. Bultan. *Automated symbolic analysis of reactive systems*. PhD thesis, University of Maryland, 1998.

[EL86] E. A. Emerson and C-L. Lei. Efficient model checking in fragments of the propositional mu-calculus. In *Proceedings of the 1st LICS*, pages 267–278, 1986.

[EM02] J. Esparza and M. Maidl. *ADVANCE Project Deliverable Report*, chapter Verifying PGM with infinitely many topologies. LIAFA, 2002.

[FGK+96] J.-C. Fernandez, H. Garavel, A. Kerbrat, R. Mateescu, L. Mounier, and M. Sighireanu. Cadp (cæsar/aldebaran development package): A protocol validation and verification toolbox. In R. Alur and T.A. Henzinger, editors, *Proceedings of the 8th CAV*, volume 1102 of *LNCS*, pages 437–440. Springer Verlag, August 1996.

[HRSV01] T. Hune, J. Romijn, M. Stoelinga, and F. Vaandrager. Linear parametric model checking of timed automata. In *Proceedings of TACAS'01*, 2001.

[Koz83] D. Kozen. Results on the propositional μ-calculus. *Theoretical Computer Science*, 27:333–354, 1983.

[MS00] R. Mateescu and M. Sighireanu. Efficient on-the-fly model-checking for regular alternation-free mu-calculus. In *Proceedings of the 5th International Workshop on Formal Methods for Industrial Critical Systems FMICS'2000 (Berlin, Germany)*, April 2000.

[PL00] P. Pettersson and K.G. Larsen. UPPAAL2k. *Bulletin of the European Association for Theoretical Computer Science*, 70:40–44, February 2000.

[SFC+01] Tony Speakman, Dino Farinacci, Jon Crowcroft, Jim Gemmell, Steven Lin, Dan Leshchiner, Michael Luby, Alex Tweedly, Nidhi Bhaskar, Richard Edmonstone, Todd Montgomery, Luigi Rizzo, Rajitha Sumanasekera, and Lorenzo Vicisano. PGM reliable transport protocol specification. RFC 3208, IETF, Decembre 2001. 111 pages.

Mapping Statecharts to Verilog
for Hardware/Software Co-specification

Shengchao Qin[1] and Wei-Ngan Chin[1,2]

[1] Singapore-MIT Alliance, National University of Singapore
[2] School of Computing, National University of Singapore,
{qinsc,chinwn}@comp.nus.edu.sg

Abstract. Hardware-Software co-specification is a critical phase in co-design. Our co-specification process starts with a high level graphical description in Statecharts and ends with an equivalent parallel composition of hardware and software descriptions in Verilog. In this paper, we investigate the Statecharts formalism by providing it a formal syntax and a compositional operational semantics. After that, we design a semantics-preserving mapping function to transform a Statecharts description into Verilog specification. We can combine this mapping with our previous formal partitioning process so as to form a more complete and automated co-specification process.

Keywords: Statecharts, Verilog, operational semantics, homomorphism

1 Introduction

The design of a complex control system is ideally decomposed into a progression of related phases. It starts with an investigation of properties and behaviours of the process evolving within its environment, and an analysis of the requirement for its safety performance. From these is derived a specification of the electronic or program-centred components of the system. The process then may go through a series of design phases, ending in a program expressed in a high level language. After translation into a machine code of a chosen computer, it can be executed at a high speed by electronic circuitry. In order to achieve time performance required by the customer, additional application-specific hardware devices may be needed to embed the computer into the system which it controls.

Classical circuit design methods resemble the low level machine language programming methods. These methods may be adequate for small circuit design, but not adequate for circuits that perform complicated algorithms. Industry interests in the formal verification of embedded systems are gaining ground since an error in a widely used hardware device can have adverse effect on profits of the enterprise concerned. A method with great potential is to develop a useful collection of proven equations and other theorems, to calculate, manipulate and transform a specification formulae to the product.

Hardware/software co-design is a design technique which delivers computer systems comprising hardware and software components. A critical phase of the co-design process is the hardware/software co-specification, which starts from a high level system specification and ends with a pair of sub-specifications representing resp. hardware and software. Our previous work ([17]) proposes a formal partitioning algorithm which splits a Verilog source program into hardware and software specifications. The partitioning correctness is verified using algebraic laws developed for the Verilog hardware description language. This algebraic approach has also been demonstrated in our earlier work [15, 16]. One of advantages of this approach is that it ensures the correctness of the partitioning process. Moreover, it optimises the underlying target architecture, and facilitates the reuse of hardware devices.

In this paper, we bridge the gap between the high level specification in Statecharts and the Verilog source program by defining a mapping function between the two formalisms. Through this work, the overall co-specification process can be automated, as illustrated in Fig.1. Two key contributions of the present paper are:

- we propose a formal operational semantics for a subset of Statecharts with data states, which adopts an asynchronous model and supports true concurrency;
- we define a formal mapping function which transforms a Statechart specification into a Verilog program. We show that the target program after mapping preserves the semantics of the source specification.

The mapping process can be integrated with our previous formal partitioning algorithm so as to form an automated hardware-software co-specification process for

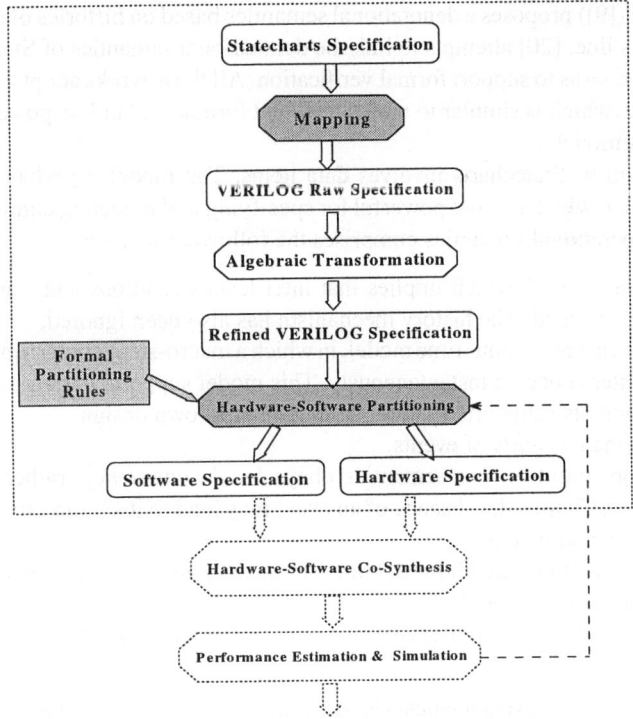

Fig. 1. HW-SW Co-Specification

hardware-software co-design, as summarised in Fig.1. The remainder of this paper is organised as follows. Section 2 first gives a formal (text-based) syntax for Statecharts with data states and proposes a compositional operational semantics for it afterwards. Section 3 introduces a subset of Verilog for behavioural specification. We build a mapping function from Statecharts into Verilog and prove that it is a homomorphism between the two formalisms in Section 4. Related works together with a simple discussion and conclusion follow afterwards.

2 Operational Semantics for Statecharts

The graphical language of Statecharts as proposed by David Harel ([4]) is suitable for the specification and modeling of reactive systems. While the (graphical) syntax of the language has been formulated quite early, the definition of its formal semantics proved to be more difficult than originally expected. As discussed in [14], these difficulties may be explained as resulting from several requirements that seem to be desirable in a specification language for reactive systems, but yet conflict with one another in some interpretations. This may be why there exist more than twenty variants of Statecharts ([21]), each of which can be regarded as a subset of the originally expected language. The version discussed in [6] for STATEMATE is rather large and powerful; however, their operational semantics is neither formal nor compositional. The work presented in [11] provides a compositional semantics for Statecharts, but does not contain data states. Hooman et.al ([9]) proposes a denotational semantics based on histories of computation. Following this line, [20] attempts to link the denotational semantics of Statecharts with temporal logic, so as to support formal verification. All these works adopt a synchronous model of time, which is simpler to understand and formalise, but less powerful than the asynchronous model.

Our version of Statecharts involves data items. The model we adopt is the asynchronous model, which is more powerful for specifying and modeling complex systems. Our formal operational semantics comprises the following features.

- It is *compositional*, which implies that inter-level transitions and state references have been dropped. The history mechanism has also been ignored.
- It adopts an asynchronous time model, in which a macro-step (comprising a sequence of micro-steps) occurs instantaneously. This model supports *perfect synchrony hypothesis* and also supports state refinement in top-down design.
- It reflects the *causality* of events.
- To be more intuitive, our semantics obeys *local consistency*, rather than *global consistency*. That is, the absence of an event may lead to itself directly or indirectly in the same macro-step.
- Instantaneous states are allowed, but each state cannot be entered twice or more at the same instant of time. [1]
- It covers the data-state issues of Statecharts, allowing assignments in state transitions.

---

[1] For simplicity, this checking is omitted in our semantics. We can include it by keeping records of the states that are passed so far in the current macro-step and prevent a former state from being re-entered in each macro-step.

- It supports true concurrency.

In this paper, timeout events are not included and this aspect is left as future work.

In what follows we give a formal syntax for Statecharts, and afterwards investigate its operational semantics thoroughly.

2.1 A Formal Syntax of Statecharts

Quoting from [5], *state charts = finite-state diagrams + depth + orthogonality + broadcast communication*. This equation indicates the typical features of the Statecharts formalism:

- It is an extension of conventional finite state machines (Mealy machine).
- It provides natural notion of depth. A state can either be a basic one, or of a hierarchical structure, inside which some other states are treated as its substates.
- It supports the modeling of concurrency. A state may contain several states as its concurrent components. This feature also helps to avoid state explosion.
- It provides the broadcast communication mechanism. Unlike CSP or CCS, its output events are asynchronous, and can be broadcast to any receiver without waiting. However, its input events are synchronous, and are blocked until the arrival of the corresponding output events. Such a communication mechanism is similar to Verilog.

In order to formalise the syntax of Statecharts, we introduce the following notations.

S: a set of names used to denote Statecharts which is large enough to prevent name conflicts.

Π_e: the set of all abstract events (signals). We also introduce another set $\overline{\Pi}_e$ to denote the set of negated counterparts of events in Π_e, i.e. $\overline{\Pi}_e =_{df} \{\overline{e} \mid e \in \Pi_e\}$, where $\overline{e}$ denotes the negated counterpart of event e, and we assume $\overline{\overline{e}} = e$.

Π_a: the set of all assignment actions of the form $v = exp$.

$\sigma : Var \to Val$ is the valuation function for variables, where Var is the set of all variables, Val is the set of all possible values for variables. A snapshot for variables $\bar{v}$ is $\sigma(\bar{v})$.

$\mathcal{T}$: the set of transitions, which is a subset of $S \times 2^{\Pi_e \cup \overline{\Pi}_e} \times 2^{\Pi_e \cup \Pi_a} \times \mathcal{B}_e \times S$, where $\mathcal{B}_e$ is the set of boolean expressions.

Similar to [12, 11], we give a term-based syntax for Statecharts. The set SC of Statecharts terms is constructed by the following inductively defined functions.

$\text{Basic} : S \to \text{SC}$
$\text{Basic}(s) =_{df} \|[s]\|$
$\text{Or} : S \times [\text{SC}] \times \text{SC} \times \mathcal{T} \to \text{SC}$
$\text{Or}(s, [p_1, \cdots, p_l, \cdots, p_n], p_l, T) =_{df} \|[s : [p_1, \cdots, p_n], p_l, T]\|$
$\text{And} : S \times 2^{\text{SC}} \to \text{SC}$
$\text{And}(s, \{p_1, \cdots, p_n\}) =_{df} \|[s : \{p_1, \cdots, p_n\}]\|$

Some informal explanations follow:

- $\text{Basic}(s)$ denotes a basic statechart named s.

- $\mathsf{Or}(s, [p_1, \cdots, p_l, \cdots, p_n], p_l, T)$ represents an Or-statechart with a set of substates $\{p_1, \cdots, p_n\}$, where p_1 is the default substate, p_l is the active substate, T is composed of all possible transitions among immediate substates of s.
- $\mathsf{And}(s, \{p_1, \cdots, p_n\})$ is an And-statechart named s, which contains a set of orthogonal (concurrent) substates $\{p_1, \cdots, p_n\}$.

2.2 Operational Transition Rules

The configuration of computation is defined by a triple $\langle p, \sigma, E_{in} \rangle$, where

- p is the syntax of the statechart of interest.
- σ gives the snapshot of data items.
- E_{in} denotes the current environment of active events.

The behaviour of a statechart is composed of a sequence of macro-steps, each of which comprises a sequence of micro-steps. A statechart may react to any stimulus from the environment at the beginning of each macro-step by performing some enabled transitions and generating some events. This may fire other state transitions and lead to a chain of micro-steps without advancing time. During this chain of micro-steps, the statechart does not respond to any potential external stimulus. When no more internal transitions are enabled, the clock tick transition will occur by emptying the set of active events and advancing time by one unit.

We explore a set of transition rules comprising state transitions and time advance transitions.

At any circumstance, what a basic statechart can do is to advance time by a clock tick.

1. $\langle |[s]|, \sigma, E \rangle \xrightarrow{\checkmark} \langle |[s]|, \sigma, \emptyset \rangle$

If a transition between two immediate substates of an Or-statechart is enabled and the transition condition is true in current circumstance, it can be performed.

2. $\dfrac{p = |[s : [p_1, \cdots, p_n], p_l, T]| \quad \tau \in En(p, E) \wedge \sigma(b)}{\langle p, \sigma, E \rangle \xrightarrow{\tau \& b} \left\langle p_{[l \to \mathbf{a2d}(tgt(\tau))]}, \sigma', (E - trig^+(\tau)) \cup a^e(\tau) \right\rangle}$

where

$src(\tau)$ and $tgt(\tau)$ denote, respectively, the source and target state of transition τ. $a^e(\tau) \subseteq \Pi$ represents all events generated by transition τ, whereas $a^a(\tau)$ denotes a single assignment action $v = ex$ generated by τ. No loss of general results since a sequence of instantaneous assignment statements can be transformed into a single one. This changes the data state from σ to $\sigma' = \sigma \oplus \{v \mapsto \sigma(ex)\}$.

$En(p, E)$ comprises all transitions among substates of p being enabled by events in E. It can be generated by the following definition.

$\tau \in En(|[s : [p_1, \cdots, p_n], p_l, T]|, E)$ **iff**
$\tau \in T \wedge src(\tau) = p_l \wedge trig^+(\tau) \subseteq E \wedge trig^-(\tau) \cap E = \emptyset$.

where $trig^+(\tau)$ and $trig^-(\tau)$ represent respectively the positive events and the negated events from τ.

The function $\mathbf{a2d}(p)$ changes the active substate of p into its default substate, and the same change is applied to its new active substate.

$$\mathbf{a2d}(\|[s]\|) =_{df} \|[s]\|$$
$$\mathbf{a2d}(\|[s:[p_1,\cdots,p_n],p_l,T]\|) =_{df} \|[s:[p_1,\cdots,p_n],\mathbf{a2d}(p_l),T]\|$$
$$\mathbf{a2d}(\|[s:\{p_1,\cdots,p_n\}]\|) =_{df} \|[s:\{\mathbf{a2d}(p_1),\cdots,\mathbf{a2d}(p_n)\}]\|$$

The substitution $p_{[l\mapsto p_m]}$ for an Or-statechart $p = \|[s:[p_1,\cdots,p_n],p_l,T]\|$ is defined by

$$p_{[l\mapsto p_m]} =_{df} \|[s:[p_1,\cdots,p_n],p_m,T]\|$$

Discussion: in rule 2, those events that are used to trigger τ are consumed by τ and will no longer exist. This mechanism looks intuitive and reasonable and can help to prevent incorrect looping. Consider an example given in Fig. 2 (a). When the first event e from the environment comes, the transition τ_1 is performed and the active substate is migrated from p_1 to p_2. This will not move back to p_1 until next event e occurs, as under normal expectation. Earlier work ([14]) suggests a different treatment, where active events are kept active during all micro-steps in a macro-step, where they may be reused many times. □

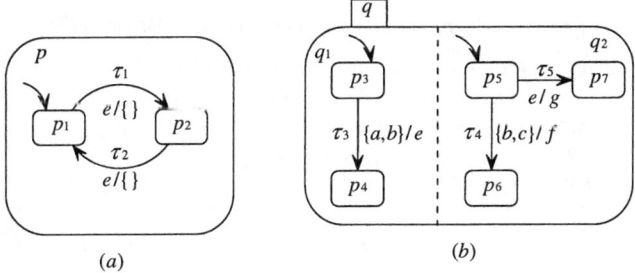

Fig. 2. Example Statecharts (a) and (b)

The transitions in Statecharts are considered hierarchically. If no transitions among immediate substates of an Or-statechart are enabled, an enabled (inner) transition for the active substate may be performed instead. This consideration is carried out inductively as highlighted in rule 3.

3. $$\dfrac{\begin{array}{c}p = \|[s:[p_1,\cdots,p_n],p_l,T]\|\\ En(p,E) = \emptyset\\ \langle p_l,\sigma,E\rangle \xrightarrow{\tau\&b} \langle p'_l,\sigma',E'\rangle\end{array}}{\langle p,\sigma,E\rangle \xrightarrow{\tau\&b} \left\langle p_{[l\mapsto p'_l]},\sigma',(E-trig^+(\tau))\cup a^e(\tau)\right\rangle}$$

If no transition is enabled for an OR-statechart, time advances, as shown below.

4. $$\dfrac{En^*(p, E) = \emptyset}{\langle p = \|[s : [p_1, \cdots, p_n], p_l, T]\|, \sigma, E\rangle \xrightarrow{\checkmark} \langle p, \sigma, \emptyset \rangle}$$

The premise indicates that no transitions in p can be triggered by E. The set of transitions that are enabled at multiple levels is defined as follows.

$En^*(\|[s]\|, E) =_{df} \emptyset$, for any basic state $\|[s]\|$;
$En^*(p = \|[s : [p_1, \cdots, p_n], p_l, T]\|, E) =_{df} En(p, E) \cup En^*(p_l, E)$;
$En^*(p = \|[s : \{p_1, \cdots, p_n\}]\|, E) =_{df} \bigcup_{1 \leq i \leq n} En^*(p_i, E)$.

For a parallel statechart, variables are shared by all orthogonal components. However, each variable can only be modified by one component. We use $WVar(p)$ to denote the set of variables that can be modified by a statechart p.

It is natural and intuitive to accept that several transitions allocated in orthogonal components may be fired simultaneously. This implies that they can be performed in a truly concurrent way. However, we have to write the transition rule for parallel statecharts carefully. Let us look at the statechart in Fig. 2 (b). Suppose the external stimulus is $E = \{a, b, c\}$, which will fire both τ_3 and τ_4 at the same moment. Under rule **2**, performing either of them will prevent another from happening since the common event b is consumed by the performed transition. This contradicts the above intuitive explanation.

We propose a more reasonable way in which simultaneously enabled transitions are allowed to occur concurrently within **And**-charts. In the following rule, we suppose $i_1, \cdots, i_n$ is a permutation of $1, \cdots, n$.

5. $$\dfrac{\begin{array}{c} p = \|[s : \{p_1, \cdots, p_n\}]\|,\ \text{all } p_i \text{ are constructed by } \textbf{Basic} \text{ or } \textbf{Or} \\ \langle p_{i_k}, \sigma, E \rangle \xrightarrow{\tau_{i_k} \& b_{i_k}} \langle p'_{i_k}, \sigma_{i_k}, E_{i_k} \rangle,\ \text{for all } 1 \leq k \leq m \\ En^*(p_{i_k}, E) = \emptyset,\ \text{for all } m < k \leq n \\ WVar(p_i) \cap WVar(p_j) = \emptyset,\ \text{for all } i, j,\ \text{where } i \neq j \\ \sigma' = \sigma_{i_1} \oplus \cdots \oplus \sigma_{i_m} \\ E' =_{df} (E - \bigcup_{1 \leq i \leq m} trig^+(\tau_{i_k})) \cup \bigcup_{1 \leq i \leq m} a^e(\tau_{i_k}) \end{array}}{\langle p, \sigma, E \rangle \xrightarrow{\& 1 \leq k \leq m (\tau_{i_k} \& b_{i_k})} \langle \|[s : \{p'_{i_1}, \cdots, p'_{i_m}, p_{i_{m+1}}, \cdots, p_{i_n}\}]\|, \sigma', E'\rangle}$$

In this rule, the overall transition that the **And**-chart p performs involves several simultaneously enabled transitions $\tau_{i_k} (1 \leq k \leq m)$ which are performed respectively by components $p_{i_k} (1 \leq k \leq m)$. Other components $p_{i_k} (m < k \leq n)$ are not involved in this transition.

A time advance transition will take place if all orthogonal components agree to do so.

6. $$\dfrac{En^*(p_i, E) = \emptyset,\ i = 1, \cdots, n}{\langle p = \|[s : \{p_1, \cdots, p_n\}]\|, \sigma, E \rangle \xrightarrow{\checkmark} \langle p, \sigma, \emptyset \rangle}$$

3 Verilog and Its Operational Semantics

Hardware description languages (HDLs) are widely used to express designs at various levels of abstraction in modern hardware design. A HDL typically contains a high level subset for behaviour description, with the usual programming constructs such as assignments, conditionals, guarded choices and iterations. It also has appropriate extensions for real-time, concurrency and data structures for modeling hardware. VHDL and Verilog ([10]) are two contemporary HDLs that have been widely used for years. Although the formal semantics of VHDL has been studied quite thoroughly, that of Verilog has been ignored until recently ([3, 7, 8, 22, 23]). However, it is reported that Verilog has been more widely used in industry (especially in US)([3]).

What we shall use is a simple version of Verilog with some notational extension (as discussed in [7]) which contains the following categories of syntactic elements.

1. A Verilog program can be a sequential process or a parallel program made up of a set of sequential processes.

$$P ::= S \mid P \parallel P$$

2. A sequential process in Verilog can be any of the following forms.

$$\begin{aligned} S ::= &\ PC\,(\text{primitive command}) \mid S;S\,(\text{sequential composition}) \\ &\mid S \triangleleft b \triangleright S\,(\text{conditional}) \mid b*S\,(\text{iteration}) \\ &\mid (b\&g\,S)[\!]\ldots[\!](b\&g\,S)\,(\text{guarded choice}) \mid \mu X \bullet S\,(\text{recursion}) \end{aligned}$$

where b is a boolean condition, and

$$\begin{aligned} PC ::= &\ skip \mid sink \mid \bot \mid \rightarrow \eta\,(\text{output event}) \mid v = ex\,(\text{assignment}) \\ g ::= &\ \rightarrow \eta \mid @(x = v)\,(\text{assignment guard}) \\ &\mid \#1\,(\text{time delay}) \mid eg\,(\text{event control}) \\ eg ::= &\ \eta \mid eg\,\&\,eg \mid eg\,\&\,\neg eg \\ \eta ::= &\ \uparrow v\,(\text{value rising}) \mid \downarrow v\,(\text{value falling}) \mid \underline{e}\,(\text{a set of abstract events}) \end{aligned}$$

Although Verilog has been standardised ([10]) and widely used in industry, its precise semantics is still lacking. Some recent work ([7, 8, 22, 23]) attempted to address its formal semantics issues from different points of views. The most recent work ([7]) discussed these distinct views, especially the algebraic and operational semantics for Verilog, and explored the underlying links between them.

The subset of Verilog we adopt is quite similar to that proposed by He ([7]). However, there are some different treatments between our version and He's version. We include explicitly the possible context environment of active events in our configuration, and change the operational rules for the parallel constructs. This facilitates our semantic mapping from Statecharts into Verilog, and does not change the observable behaviour of a program.

In our operational semantics of Verilog, transitions are of the form $S \xrightarrow{l} S'$. The configuration S describes the state of an executing mechanism of Verilog programs together with the environment of active events before an action l, whereas S' describes that immediately after. They are identified as triples $\langle P, \sigma, E \rangle$, where

- P is a program text, representing the rest of the program that remains to be executed.
- $\sigma : \textit{Var} \rightarrow \textit{Val}$ records the data state.
- E is the current set of active events.

A label l denotes a transition from state S to S'. It can be a clock tick event $\sqrt{}$, or a compositional event possibly with three conjunctive parts: $b\&g^i\&g^o$ representing the enabling condition, the set of events consumed, and the set of events generated, respectively.

Now we present a critical subset of transition rules which are relevant to our transformation from Statecharts into Verilog.

The primitive *sink* can do nothing but advance time by a clock tick.

$$\langle sink, \sigma, E \rangle \xrightarrow{\sqrt{}} \langle sink, \sigma, \emptyset \rangle$$

The guarded choice construct

$$P = (b_1 \& g_1^i \& g_1^o \ P_1) [\!] \ldots [\!] (b_n \& g_n^i \& g_n^o \ P_n)$$

can take a guarded transition if that guard is enabled.

$$\frac{\sigma(b_k) \wedge (E \vdash g_k^i), \text{ for some } k}{\langle P, \sigma, E \rangle \xrightarrow{b_k \& g_k^i \& g_k^o} \langle P_k, \sigma', E - e^c(g_k^i) \cup e^g(g_k^o) \rangle}$$

where $E \vdash g^i$ indicates that the input guard g^i is enabled by E. This is defined as:

$$E \vdash \underline{e_1} \& \cdots \& \underline{e_m} \& \neg \underline{e'_1} \& \cdots \& \neg \underline{e'_n} =_{df} \wedge_{1 \leq i \leq m}(\underline{e_i} \subseteq E) \wedge \wedge_{1 \leq i \leq n}(\underline{e'_i} \cap E = \emptyset)$$

Also, $e^c(g^i)$ extracts all "positive" events from the input guard g^i (to be consumed when enabling the guard), i.e.,

$$e^c(\underline{e_1} \& \cdots \& \underline{e_m} \& \neg \underline{e'_1} \& \cdots \& \neg \underline{e'_n}) =_{df} \bigcup_{1 \leq i \leq m} \underline{e_i}$$

and $e^g(g^o)$ records the set of events generated by the output guard g^o. Given an output guard $g^o = \rightarrow \underline{e} \& @(x = v)$, the generated events are

$$e^g(g^o) =_{df} \begin{cases} \underline{e} \cup \{\uparrow x\}, & \text{if } \sigma(x) < v, \\ \underline{e} \cup \{\downarrow x\}, & \text{if } \sigma(x) > v, \\ \underline{e}, & \text{otherwise.} \end{cases}$$

If no guard is enabled, the clock tick can be performed.

$$\frac{\forall k : 1 \leq k \leq n \bullet \neg(\sigma(b_k) \wedge (E \vdash g_k^i))}{\langle P, \sigma, E \rangle \xrightarrow{\sqrt{}} \langle P', \sigma, \emptyset \rangle}$$

where P' is the same as P if no time delay guards (#1) appear in P. Otherwise, it is the guarded choice obtained from P by eliminating all time delay guards.

A parallel construct of guarded choices P is of the form $G_1 \parallel \cdots \parallel G_n$ where

$$G_k = [\!]_{1 \leq j \leq r_k} b_{jk} \& g_{jk}^i \& g_{jk}^o \ P_{jk}, \ 1 \leq k \leq n$$

This can be transformed into a guarded choice construct by algebraic laws ([7]). Here, we give the transition rules for the parallel construct directly. It can perform a (compositional) guarded transition if some threads agree, where $i_1, \cdots, i_n$ denotes a permutation of $1, \cdots, n$.

$$\frac{\begin{array}{c}\langle G_{i_k}, \sigma, E\rangle \xrightarrow{l_{i_k}} \langle P_{i_k}, \sigma_{i_k}, E_{i_k}\rangle, \ 1 \leq k \leq m \\ \forall j : 1 \leq j \leq r_k \bullet \neg(\sigma(b_{ji_k}) \wedge (E \vdash g^i_{ji_k})), \ m < k \leq n \\ \sigma' = \sigma_{i_1} \oplus \cdots \oplus \sigma_{i_m} \\ E' = (E - \bigcup_{1 \leq k \leq m} e^c(g^i_{i_k})) \cup \bigcup_{1 \leq k \leq m} e^g(g^o_{i_k})\end{array}}{\langle P, \sigma, E\rangle \xrightarrow{\&_{1 \leq k \leq m} l_{i_k}} \langle P', \sigma', E'\rangle}$$

where $P' =_{df} Q_1 \parallel \cdots \parallel Q_n$, and $Q_{i_k} =_{df} \begin{cases} P_{i_k}, & 1 \leq k \leq m, \\ G_{i_k}, & m < k \leq n \end{cases}$

If no threads can take a guarded transition, then the clock tick event can take place, as follows:

$$\frac{\forall j : 1 \leq j \leq r_k \bullet \neg(\sigma(b_{ji_k}) \wedge (E \vdash g^i_{ji_k})), \ 1 \leq k \leq n}{\langle P, \sigma, E\rangle \xrightarrow{\checkmark} \langle P', \sigma, \emptyset\rangle}$$

Note that P' is the same as P if no time delay guards (#1) appear in P. Otherwise, it is the guarded choice obtained from P by eliminating all time delay guards.

A *sink* thread does not block the behaviour of its partners.

$$\frac{\langle P, \sigma, E\rangle \xrightarrow{l} \langle P', \sigma', E'\rangle}{\langle sink \parallel P, \sigma, E\rangle \xrightarrow{l} \langle sink \parallel P', \sigma', E'\rangle}$$

4 Mapping Statecharts into Verilog

In this section, we build a link between Statecharts and Verilog, by which a Statecharts description can be mapped to its corresponding Verilog program. We show such a mapping preserves the semantics and can be conducted in a compositional manner.

4.1 Mapping Function

Before constructing the mapping function called L, we address some subtle issues and introduce some notations. There exist two features which complicate the definition of L on an Or-chart, one is the hierarchical feature of Statecharts and the priority of transitions, whereas the other lies in that an And-chart can be a sub-chart of an Or-chart. This feature differentiates Statecharts from conventional programming languages. The former indicates that transitions in an outer level (rule 2) has higher priority than those in an inner level (rule 3). The possible transitions are considered hierarchically, starting from the current active state, and progressing into inner active substates where applicable. By enumerating these transitions in accordance with the hierarchy, we can cope with the different priorities for transitions occurring in distinct levels.

To deal with the above features, we prepare the following formal notations. We first give a function *or-depth* : $\mathsf{SC} \to \mathbb{N}$ to calculate the "or-depth" of a statechart, which is defined as follows:

- for a statechart $c = ||[s]||$ constructed by Basic, $\textit{or-depth}(c) =_{df} 0$;
- for a statechart $c = ||[s : [p_1, \cdots, p_n], p_l, T]||$ constructed by Or, $\textit{or-depth}(c) =_{df} \textit{or-depth}(p_l) + 1$;
- for a statechart $c = ||[s : \{p_1, \cdots, p_n\}]||$ constructed by And, $\textit{or-depth}(c) =_{df} 1$.

The *or-depth* of an Or-chart just records the deepness of the path transitively along its active Or-substates. We stop going further once an And-state is encountered. The *or-depth* of an And-chart is simply 1.

Secondly, we extend some notations from Or-charts to And-charts. As already known, for an Or-chart $c = ||[s : [p_1, \cdots, p_n], p_l, T]||$, $active(c) = p_l$ denotes its current active substate; for any transition $\tau \in T$, $src(\tau)$ and $tgt(\tau)$ respectively represent its source and target state. Given a parallel statechart $c = ||[s : \{p_1, \cdots, p_n\}]||$, where all p_i are Or-charts, we define its current active state as a vector of the active states of these constituents, i.e., $active(c) =_{df} (active(p_1), \cdots, active(p_n))$. We use $T(c)$ to denote all possible (perhaps compositional) transitions of the And-chart c. Given a transition $\tau = \&_{1 \leq k \leq m} \tau_{i_k} \in T(c)$, where $\tau_{i_k} \in T^*(p_{i_k})$, for $1 \leq k \leq m$, and $i_1, \cdots, i_n$ is a permutation of $1, \cdots, n$, we define its source state and target state respectively as follows:[2]

$src(\tau) =_{df} (q_1, \cdots, q_n)$, where $q_{i_k} = src(\tau_{i_k})$, for $1 \leq k \leq m$, and $q_{i_k} = active(p_{i_k})$, for $m < k \leq n$;

$tgt(\tau) =_{df} (r_1, \cdots, r_n)$, where $r_{i_k} = tgt(\tau_{i_k})$, for $1 \leq k \leq m$, and $r_{i_k} = active(p_{i_k})$, for $m < k \leq n$.

Thirdly, we need to know the resulting statechart after a transition is taken. When a transition τ occurs, any involved statechart can have changes in its (transitive) active substates. We use a function

$resc : \mathcal{T} \times \mathsf{SC} \to \mathsf{SC}$

to return the modified statechart after performing a transition in a statechart. It is defined inductively with regard to the type of the statechart.

- for a Basic-chart c, and any transition τ, $resc(\tau, c) =_{df} c$;
- for an Or-chart $c = ||[s : [p_1, \cdots, p_n], p_l, T]||$, and a transition τ,

$resc(\tau, c) =_{df} \begin{cases} c_{[l \mapsto \mathsf{a2d}(tgt(\tau))]}, & \text{if } \tau \in T \land src(\tau) = p_l, \\ c_{[l \mapsto resc(\tau, p_l)]}, & \text{if } \tau \in T^*(p_l), \\ c, & \text{otherwise}. \end{cases}$

- for an And-chart $c = ||[s : \{p_1, \cdots, p_n\}]||$, and a transition τ,

$resc(\tau, c) =_{df} \begin{cases} c_\tau, & \text{if } \tau = \&_{1 \leq k \leq m} \tau_{i_k} \in T(c), \\ c, & \text{otherwise}. \end{cases}$

where $c_\tau = c[q_1/p_1, \cdots, q_n/p_n]$ is the statechart obtained from c via replacing p_i by q_i, for $1 \leq i \leq n$, $q_{i_k} = resc(\tau_{i_k}, p_{i_k})$, for $1 \leq k \leq m$, and $q_{i_k} = p_{i_k}$, for $m < k \leq n$.

---

[2] For an Or-chart $p = ||[s : [p_1, \cdots, p_n], p_l, T]||$, $T^*(p)$ contains all possible transitions inside p along its transitive active substate chain, i.e., $T^*(p) =_{df} \{\tau \mid \tau \in T \land src(\tau) = p_l\} \cup T^*(p_l)$.

With the help of $T^*(p)$, we define the aforementioned possible transition set $T(c)$ for an And-chart $c = ||[s : \{p_1, p_2\}]||$ formally as $T(c) =_{df} \{\tau_i \& h_{3-i} \mid \tau_i \in T^*(p_i), i = 1, 2\} \cup \{\tau_1 \& \tau_2 \mid \tau_i \in T^*(p_i), i = 1, 2\}$, where $h_i =_{df} \& \{\neg \tau \mid \tau \in T^*(p_i)\}$. The transition set for the general And-chart with n components can be defined similarly.

The definition of L is split into three cases in accordance with the type of the source statechart.

Definition 1 (Mapping function L). *The function*

$$L : \mathsf{SC} \to \mathsf{Verilog}$$

maps any statechart description into a corresponding Verilog process. It keeps unchanged the set of variables employed by the source description, i.e.,

$$\forall c \in \mathsf{SC} \bullet \mathit{vars}(L(c)) = \mathit{vars}(c)$$

and it is inductively defined as follows.

- For a statechart $c = \|[s]\|$ constructed by **Basic**, L maps it into an idle program sink which can do nothing but let time advance, i.e.,

$$L(c) =_{df} \mathit{sink}$$

- For a statechart $c = \|[s : \{p_1, \cdots, p_n\}]\|$ constructed by **And**, L maps it into a parallel construct in Verilog.

$$L(c) =_{df} \|_{1 \le i \le n} L(p_i)$$

- For a statechart $c = \|[s : [p_1, \cdots, p_n], p_l, T]\|$ constructed by **Or**, we define L by exhaustively figuring out the first possible transitions of c if any, otherwise it sinks.

$$L(c) =_{df} \begin{cases} \mathit{sink}, & \text{if } T^*(c) = \emptyset \\ P, & \text{otherwise} \end{cases}$$

where

$$P =_{df} \|_{0 \le k < \mathit{or\text{-}depth}(c)} \| \{b_{\tau_k} \& g_{\tau_k}^i \& (\&_{1 \le j \le k} h_j) \& g_{\tau_k}^o \; L(\mathit{resc}(\tau_k, c)) \mid \\ \tau_k \in T(\mathit{active}^k(c)) \land \mathit{src}(\tau_k) = \mathit{active}^{k+1}(c) \land \\ h_j = \& \{\neg g_\tau^i \mid \tau \in T(\mathit{active}^{j-1}(c)) \land \mathit{src}(\tau) = \mathit{active}^j(c)\}\}$$

and

$$\mathit{active}^0(c) =_{df} c, \; \mathit{active}^1(c) =_{df} \mathit{active}(c)$$
$$\mathit{active}^{i+1}(c) =_{df} \mathit{active}(\mathit{active}^i(c))$$

The input guard $g_{\tau_k}^i$ comprises the overall trigger events of τ_k, which has the form $\underline{e_1} \& \neg \underline{e_2}$, where $\underline{e_1}$ are events from $\mathit{trig}^+(\tau_k)$, whereas $\underline{e_2}$ are events out of $\mathit{trig}^-(\tau_k)$. Due to the priority mechanism of Statecharts, an enabled transition τ_k in an inner level (k) can occur only when no transitions from any outer level $(0, \cdots, k\text{-}1)$ are enabled. The part $(\&_{1 \le j \le k} h_j)$ is used to denote this condition.

The output guard $g_{\tau_k}^o$ is the overall action performed by τ_k, which has the form $\to \underline{e} \& @(x = v)$, where $\underline{e}$ comprises all abstract events out of $a^e(\tau_k)$, and the assignment action $x = v$ is from $a^a(\tau_k)$.

For each statechart, we always assume each of its variables has bounded range, and the set of possible events is finite, which implies that the set of its configurations is finite. Therefore, the set of configurations (under transition relation) forms a well-founded quasi order, which indicates the mapping function L is *terminating*.

The following example deals with the transformation of statecharts in Fig. 2.

Example 1. The statechart (a) in Fig. 2 can be described as p:

$$p = \|[s : [p_1, p_2], p_1, \{\tau_1, \tau_2\}]\|$$

where $\tau_i =_{df} \langle p_i, \{e\}, \emptyset, true, p_{3-i}\rangle$, $i = 1, 2$.

After applying the mapping function L onto it, the statechart (a) becomes the following process

$$\mu X \bullet (e\,(e\,X))$$

which does nothing but just waits to be fired by an event e from the environment.

The statechart (b) can be described as q:

$$q = \|[s : \{q_1, q_2\}]\|$$
$$q_1 = \|[s_1 : [p_3, p_4], p_3, \{\tau_3\}]\|$$
$$q_2 = \|[s_2 : [p_5, p_6, p_7], p_5, \{\tau_4, \tau_5\}]\|$$

where

$$\tau_3 = \langle p_3, \{a, b\}, \{e\}, true, p_4\rangle$$
$$\tau_4 = \langle p_5, \{b, c\}, \{f\}, true, p_6\rangle$$
$$\tau_5 = \langle p_5, \{e\}, \{g\}, true, p_7\rangle$$

It is mapped into the following parallel construct

$$(a\&b\&(\to e)\,sink)\,\|\,((e\&(\to g)\,sink)\|((b\&c)\&(\to f)\,sink))$$

where the two parallel processes are mapped from q_1 and q_2, respectively. □

Example 2. The statechart in Fig. 3 is more complicated than those in Fig. 2. It is described by:

$$p = \|[s : [p_1, p_{10}], p_1, \{t_1\}]\|$$
$$p_1 = \|[s_1 : [p_2, p_9], p_2, \{t_2, t_3\}]\|$$
$$p_2 = \|[s_2 : \{p_3, p_4\}]\|$$
$$p_3 = \|[s_3 : [p_5, p_6], p_5, \{t_4\}]\|$$
$$p_4 = \|[s_4 : [p_7, p_8], p_7, \{t_5\}]\|$$
$$p_{10} = \|[s_{10} : [p_{11}, p_{12}], p_{11}, \{t_6, t_7\}]\|$$

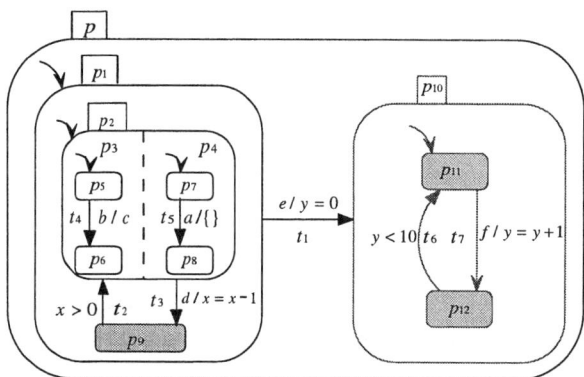

Fig. 3. A More Complicated Statechart

where
$$t_1 = \langle p_1, \{e\}, \{@(y = 0)\}, true, p_{10}\rangle$$
$$t_2 = \langle p_9, \emptyset, \emptyset, x > 0, p_2\rangle$$
$$t_3 = \langle p_2, \{d\}, \{@(x = x - 1)\}, true, p_9\rangle$$
$$t_4 = \langle p_5, \{b\}, \{c\}, true, p_6\rangle$$
$$t_5 = \langle p_7, \{a\}, \emptyset, true, p_8\rangle$$
$$t_6 = \langle p_{12}, \emptyset, \emptyset, y < 10, p_{11}\rangle$$
$$t_7 = \langle p_{11}, \{f\}, \{@(y = y + 1)\}, y < 10, p_{12}\rangle$$

After applying L onto it, we obtain the following recursive process.

$$\mu X \bullet \begin{pmatrix} Q \parallel P \parallel (b\&\neg a\&\neg d\&\neg e\& \to c)\,(Q \parallel P \parallel (a\&\neg d\&\neg e)\,(Q \parallel P)) \\ \parallel (a\&\neg b\&\neg d\&\neg e)\,(Q \parallel P \parallel (b\&\neg d\&\neg e\& \to c)\,(Q \parallel P)) \\ \parallel (b\&a\&\neg d\&\neg e\& \to c)\,(Q \parallel P) \end{pmatrix}$$

where $Q =_{df} e\&@(y = 0)\,\mu Y \bullet (f\&@(y = y+1)\,(y<10)\,Y)$
$P =_{df} (d\&\neg e\&@(x = x-1))\,((x>0)\&\neg e)\,X$

Let us illustrate a more practical example: a simple remote controller for an air-conditioner.

Example 3. Part of the specification for an air-conditioner remote controller is presented in Fig. 4. It is composed of five orthogonal components namely *Fan, Temperature, Timer, TempDisplay,* and *TimerDisplay*. They will be respectively mapped to Verilog programs *pFan, pTemperature, pTimer, pTempDisplay,* and *pTimerDisplay*.

After applying the mapping function L to the statechart in Fig.4, we obtain the following target program *pon*:

$$pon =_{df} pFan \parallel pTemperature \parallel pTimer \parallel pTempDisplay \parallel pTimerDisplay$$

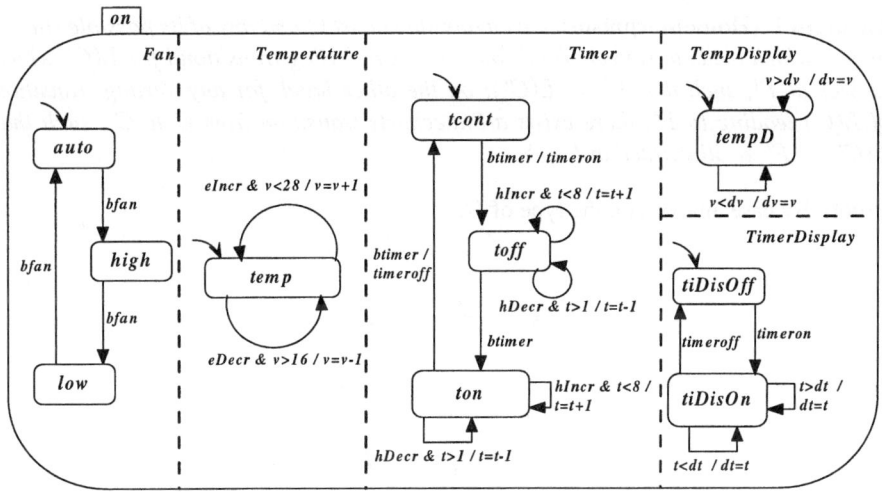

Fig. 4. An Air-Conditioner Remote Controller: the *on* state

The five component programs are respectively

$$pFan =_{df} \mu X \bullet (bfan\ (bfan\ (bfan\ X)))$$

$$pTemperature =_{df} \mu X \bullet \binom{((v<28)\&eIncr\&@(v=v+1)\ X)}{\|\ ((v>16)\&eDecr\&@(v=v-1)\ X)}$$

$$pTimer =_{df} \mu X \bullet ((btimer\&\rightarrow timeron)\ P)$$

where

$$P =_{df} \mu Y \bullet \begin{pmatrix} ((t<8)\&hIncr\&@(t=t+1)\ Y)\\ \|\ ((t>1)\&hDecr\&@(t=t-1)\ Y)\\ \|\ (btimer\ Q) \end{pmatrix}$$

$$Q =_{df} \mu Z \bullet \begin{pmatrix} ((t<8)\&hIncr\&@(t=t+1)\ Z)\\ \|\ ((t>1)\&hDecr\&@(t=t-1)\ Z)\\ \|\ ((btimer\&\rightarrow timeroff)\ X) \end{pmatrix}$$

$$pTempDisplay =_{df} \mu X \bullet \binom{((v>dv)\&@(dv=v)\ X)}{\|\ ((v<dv)\&@(dv=v)\ X)}$$

$$pTimerDisplay =_{df} \mu X \bullet timeron\ \mu Y \bullet \begin{pmatrix} ((t>dt)\&@(dt=t)\ Y)\\ \|\ ((t<dt)\&@(dt=t)\ Y)\\ \|\ (timeroff\ X) \end{pmatrix}$$

4.2 Correctness

The following theorem shows that the mapping function from Statecharts into Verilog is a homomorphism between the two formalisms.

Theorem 1 (Homomorphism). *Given any statechart C and any of its possible transitions τ which leads to statechart C', there exists a Verilog transition l for $L(C)$ which arrives at P', such that $P' = L(C')$; on the other hand, for any Verilog transition of $L(C)$ leading to P', there exists a Statecharts transition from C to C', such that $L(C') = P'$, as illustrated in Fig. 5.*

Proof. By case analysis on the type of C.

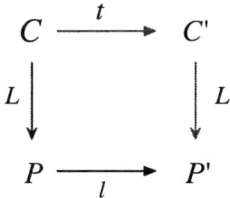

Fig. 5. Mapping function L

1. $C = \|[s]\|$ is constructed by Basic.
   What C can do is to perform the clock tick and remains as C after the transition. On the other hand, from Definition 1 we know $L(C) = sink$, which does nothing but performs the clock tick and remains as $sink$ after that.
2. $C = \|[s : [p_1, \cdots, p_n], p_l, T]\|$ is constructed by Or.
   In case that $T^*(C) = \emptyset$, it can be proved similar to the first case. Now suppose $T^*(C) \neq \emptyset$, C can (1) perform a transition $\tau \in T(active^k(C))$ for some $k \geq 0$ in case that all transitions of outer levels (if any) are not available, which changes the active substate of $active^k(C)$ from its source state to its target state and results in $resc(\tau, C)$; (2) otherwise, it can take a clock tick and remain its state. From Definition 1 of L, we know that $L(C)$ has the form $\|(g_\tau\ P_\tau)$. If (1) occurs, g_τ is fired, from the semantics of Verilog, such a program can perform the corresponding transition and become P_τ, otherwise it can perform the clock tick transition. From the definition of L, it is straightforward that $P_\tau = L(resc(\tau, C))$.
   The second part can be proved similarly from the definition of L.
3. $C = \|[s : \{p_1, \cdots, p_n\}]\|$ is constructed by And.
   From Definition 1, we know

$$L(C) = L(p_1) \| \cdots \| L(p_n).$$

Given any possible transition $\tau \in T(C)$, we assume $\tau = \&_{1 \leq k \leq m} \tau_k$, where $\tau_k \in T^*(p_k)$, without loss of generality. If τ can be performed at the current environment, from rule **5**, we know that τ_k, for $1 \leq k \leq m$, are ready to take place and orthogonal components other than $p_1, \cdots, p_m$ do not have available transitions. This implies all processes $L(p_1), \cdots, L(p_m)$ can take the transition corresponding to $\tau_1, \cdots, \tau_m$ respectively in the current environment, whereas others can not. From the operational semantics of parallel construct of Verilog, a parallel transition corresponding to τ can take place and after the transition the program becomes

$$P_1 \| \cdots \| P_n$$

where

$$P_i = \begin{cases} L(resc(\tau_i, p_i)), & \text{for } 1 \leq i \leq m, \\ L(p_i), & \text{otherwise.} \end{cases}$$

It exactly accords with $L(resc(\tau, C))$. The case for a clock tick transition is trivial. The second part is also straightforward, since any transition of the result parallel construct $L(C)$ in Verilog either involves several threads or a single thread. From the definition of L, we can conclude, in either case, there exists a corresponding Statecharts transition for C, which yields C' and $L(C') = P'$ holds. □

The following theorem shows the soundness of the mapping function.

Theorem 2 (Soundness). *The mapping function L in Definition 1 transforms any Statecharts specification into a Verilog program with the same observable behaviour as the original chart.*

Proof. In addition to the results from Theorem 1, we need to show that, given a statechart C and its image $L(C)$ in Verilog, any possible pair of their corresponding steps (a statechart transition and a Verilog transition), starting from the same context environment(the same σ and E in the corresponding configurations), consume the same set of events, generate the same set of events, and bring the updates of data state into accord. These follow directly from the construction of the mapping function L. □

5 Discussion and Related Work

In our co-specification process, we conduct the partitioning task after a Verilog behaviour specification has been generated from the higher level system description in Statecharts. We use this approach because the semantics of Verilog has been well investigated and a collection of algebraic laws ([7]) can be used as the fundamental support of the partitioning algorithm. In contrast, most work on Statecharts' semantics focuses on its operational rules since it has proved to be quite difficult to present a simple denotational model from which algebraic laws of Statecharts can be derived. Due to this difficulty, the partitioning problem is currently not addressed at the Statecharts level. Although it may seem unnatural to obtain a software specification in Verilog after partitioning, it is still reasonable in the sense that the behaviour subset of Verilog is very similar to C programming language and can be readily transformed into C code.

Due to the involvedness of formal semantics for Statecharts, there have been so many related works that we can hardly discuss all here. Some of them are presented in [6, 9, 11, 12, 14, 21]. Many of these works adopt the simpler synchronous model. The work in [6] takes into account a very large subset of Statecharts, but the semantics is neither compositional nor formal. In contrast, our operational semantics is formal, compositional and supports asynchronous model.

Although it is reported that Verilog has been widely used in industry (especially in United States) for years, its precise semantics has been ignored until recently. The results [8, 22, 23, 7] are all based on Gordon's interpretation on simulation cycles [3]. A simple operational semantics is given in [8]. Zhu, Bowen and He [22, 23] investigate the consistency between Verilog's operational and denotational semantics, while He [7] explores a program algebra for Verilog and its connection with both operational and denotational semantics.

Some of related works on connecting Statecharts with other formalisms are presented in [1, 2, 13, 19, 20, 18]. Beauvais et.al. [1] and Seshia et.al. [19] translate STATEMATE Statecharts to synchronous languages *Signal* and *Esterel* respectively, aiming to use supporting tools provided in the target formalisms for formal verification purposes. However, all these translations are based on the informal semantics [6] lacking correctness proofs. The authors of [2, 13] transform variants of Statecharts into hierarchical timed automata and use tools (UPPAAL, SPIN) to model check Statecharts properties. Also, [20] based on the denotational semantics [9] aims to connect a subset of Statecharts with temporal logic *FNLOG* for theoretically proving Statecharts' properties. More recently, a translation from Statecharts to B/AMN is reported in [18]. However, no correctness issue has been addressed. In comparison, the translation from Statecharts to Verilog in this paper aims at code generation for system design. Our mapping function is constructed based on formal semantics for both the source and target formalisms and has been proven to be semantics-preserving.

6 Conclusion

This paper proposes a mapping function which transforms a high level specification in visual formalism Statecharts into a behaviour description in Verilog HDL. We explore a compositional operational semantics to Statecharts which contains many powerful features that Statecharts owns, but proved to be difficult to be combined into a uniform formalism. Based on this semantics and an operational semantics for Verilog, we show our mapping function provides as a semantic link between the two formalisms. Moreover, we combine this transformation process with our previous formal partitioning approach yielding a hardware/software co-specification process that can be automated. However, the translation from Statecharts to Verilog can also be used in pure hardware design. After translating into a behavioural description in Verilog, existed Verilog synthesizer can be used to obtain low level descriptions, like netlists, for direct implementation in hardware (ASICs or FPGAs).

As an immediate future work, the obtained guarded choice specification should be transformed into simplified behavioural description in Verilog using algebraic laws [7]. An implementation for this mapping from graphical descriptions in Statecharts to Verilog specifications is also being considered.

Acknowledgement

We would like to thank Jifeng He for inspiration, thank Khoo Siau Cheng, P.S. Thiagarajan, Wang Yi and Zhu Huibiao for useful discussions. We are also grateful to anonymous referees for many helpful comments.

References

1. J.-R. Beauvais, et. al., "A Translation of Statecharts to Signal/DC+", Technical Report, IRISA, 1997.
2. Alexandre David, M. Oliver Möller and Wang Yi, "Formal Verification of UML Statecharts with Real-Time Extensions", in the *Proc. of Fundamental Approaches to Software Engineering (FASE 2002)*, LNCS 2306, pp. 218–232, Springer-Verlag, 2002.
3. M. Gordon, "The Semantic Challenge of Verilog HDL", In *the Proc. of Tenth Annual IEEE Symposium on Logic in Computer Science*, IEEE Computer Society Press, pp. 136–145, 1995.
4. D. Harel, "Statecharts: a Visual Formalism for Complex Systems", *Science of Computer Programming*, vol.8, no.3, pp. 231–274, 1987.
5. D. Harel, "On Visual Formalisms", *Communications of the ACM*, Vol. 31, No. 5, pp. 541–530, 1988.
6. D. Harel and A. Naamad, "The STATEMATE Semantics of Statecharts", *ACM Transactions on Software Engineering and Methodology*, Vol. 5, No. 4, pp. 293–333, October, 1996.
7. J. He, "An Algebraic Approach to the VERILOG Programming", in the *Proc. of 10th Anniversary Colloquium of the United Nations University / International Institute for Software Technology (UNU/IIST)*, Springer-Verlag, 2002.

8. J. He and Q. Xu, "An Operational Semantics of a Simulator Algorithm", in the *Proc. of the 2000 International Conference on Parallel and Distributed Processing Techniques and Applications (PDPTA'2000)*, Las Vegas, Nevada, USA, June 26-29, 2000.
9. J.J.M. Hooman, S. Ramesh, and W.P. de Roever, "A Compositional Axiomatization of Statecharts", *Theoretical Computer Science* 101, pp. 289–335, 1992.
10. IEEE Computer Society, *IEEE Standard Hardware Description Language Based on the Verilog Hardware Description Language (IEEE std 1364-1995)*, 1995.
11. G. Lüttgen, M. von der Beeck, and R. Cleaveland, "A Compositional Approach to Statecharts Semantics", NASA/CR-2000-210086, ICASE Report No.2000-12, March, 2000.
12. A. Maggiolo-Schettini, A. Peron, and S. Tini, "Equivalences of Statecharts", in *7th International Conference on Concurrency Theory (CONCUR'96)*, Pisa, Italy, Aug. 1996, LNCS 1119, pp.687–702, Springer-Verlag.
13. E. Mikk, Y. Lakhnech, M. Siegel and G. Holzmann, "Implementing Statecharts in Promela/SPIN", in the *Proc. of the 2nd IEEE Workshop on Industrial-Strength Formal Specification Techniques*, IEEE Computer Society, 1999.
14. A. Pnueli and M. Shalev, "What is in a Step: On the Semantics of Statecharts", in the *Proc. of the Symposium on Theoretical Aspects of Computer Software*, LNCS 526, pp. 244–264, Springer-Verlag, Berlin.
15. S. Qin and J. He, "An Algebraic Approach to Hardware/software Partitioning", in *the Proc of the 7th IEEE International Conference on Electronics, Circuits and Systems (ICECS'2k)*, IEEE Computer Society Press, pp 273–276, Lebanon, Dec., 2000.
16. S. Qin and J. He, "Partitioning Program into Hardware and Software", in *the Proc of APSEC 2001*, IEEE Computer Society Press, pp. 309–316, Macau, Dec., 2001.
17. S. Qin, J. He, Z. Qiu, and N. Zhang, "Hardware/Software Partitioning in Verilog", in the *4th International Conference for Formal Engineering Methods (ICFEM2002)*, LNCS 2495, pp. 168–179, Springer-Verlag.
18. E. Sekerinski and R. Zurob, "Translating Statecharts to B", in B. Butler, L. Petre, and K. Sere, eds.,*Proc. of the 3rd International Conference on Integrated Formal Methods*, Turku, Finland, LNCS 2335, pp. 128–144, Springer-Verlag, 2002.
19. S. Seshia, R. Shyamasundar, A. Bhattacharjee and S. Dhodapkar, "A Translation of Statecharts to Esterel", In J. Wing, J. Woodcock, and J. Davies, eds., *FM99: World Congress on Formal Methods*, LNCS 1709, pp. 983–1007, 1999.
20. A. Sowmya and S. Ramesh, "Extending Statecharts with Temporal Logic", *IEEE Transactions on Software Engineering*, Vol. 24, No. 3, March, 1998.
21. M. von der Beeck, "A Comparison of Statecharts Variants", in *Formal Techniques in Real-Time and Fault-Tolerant Systems*, L. de Roever and J. Vytopil, Eds. LNCS 863, pp. 128–148, Springer-Verlag, New York.
22. Zhu H., J. Bowen and He J., "From Operational Semantics to Denotational Semantics for Verilog", in *the Proc. of CHARME 2001*, *LNCS* 2144, pp. 449–464.
23. H. Zhu, J. Bowen and J. He, "Soundness, Completeness and Non-redundancy of Operational Semantics for Verilog Based on Denotational Semantics", in the *4th International Conference for Formal Engineering Methods (ICFEM2002)*, LNCS 2495, pp. 600–612, Springer-Verlag.

A Strategy for Compiling Classes, Inheritance, and Dynamic Binding

Adolfo Duran[1], Ana Cavalcanti[1], and Augusto Sampaio[2]

[1] Computing Laboratory, University of Kent,
Canterbury CT2 7NF, United Kingdom,
{aad2,A.L.C.Cavalcanti}@ukc.ac.uk
[2] Centro de Informática, Universidade Federal de Pernambuco,
Po Box 7851, 50740-540 Recife PE, Brazil,
acas@cin.ufpe.br

Abstract. This paper presents a refinement strategy for the compilation of a subset of Java that includes classes, inheritance, dynamic binding, visibility control, and recursion. We tackle the problem of compiler correctness by reducing the task of compilation to that of program refinement. More specifically, refinement laws are used as compilation rules to reduce the source program to a normal form that models an interpreter running the target code. The compilation process is formalized within a single and uniform semantic framework, where translations or comparisons between semantics are avoided. Each compilation rule can be proved correct with respect to the algebraic laws of the language.

1 Introduction

The concern with correctness of computer programs has increased due to their use in applications where failure could result in unacceptable losses. Correct compilers address the translation of source programs into a target language, with a guarantee that the semantics is preserved. Several approaches have been suggested; the majority focus on procedural languages [12, 14, 17].

Even though object-oriented programming has become very popular in recent years, most applications are developed using informal methods. Approaches to compiler correctness covering object-oriented features are rare in the literature. Recently, there have been works based on verification, focused on the translation between Java programs and the Java Virtual Machine (JVM) [3, 16].

Here, we describe an algebraic approach to construct a provably correct compiler for an object-oriented language called ROOL (for Refinement Object-oriented Language), which is based on a subset of sequential Java. This language includes classes, inheritance, dynamic binding, recursion, type casts and tests, and class-based visibility. It also includes specification constructors like those of Morgan's refinement calculus [13]. Our language was devised as a means to study refinement of object-oriented programs in general, not only compilation. Its weakest precondition and its algebraic semantics have been studied in [4, 2]. In [5], it is used to formalise refactoring as a refinement activity.

Our approach to compilation is inspired on that first described in [10], and further developed for imperative programs in [15]. Its main advantage is the characterisation of the compilation process within a uniform framework, where translations are avoided. Compilation is identified with the reduction of a source program, written in an executable subset of the language, to a normal form.

Our normal form is an interpreter-like program which emulates the behavior of the target machine. From this interpreter we capture the sequence of generated instructions. We define a ROOL Virtual Machine (RVM) as our target. It is based on the Java Virtual Machine (JVM)[11].

The purpose of this paper is to provide a description of the compilation process, and an example. We first presented our approach in [7]; there, however, we do not consider classes, inheritance, recursive method calls, and dynamic binding. In this paper, we consider the compilation of all these constructs; the rules that justify in detail all our reduction steps can be found in [8]. We also present an improved normal form, which provides the same functionality as that in [7], but is more amenable to proof.

The remainder of this paper is structured as follows. In Section 2 we describe ROOL and introduce our case study. In Section 3, we describe the target machine and our normal form. In Section 4, we describe and illustrate the compilation phases and the transformations they impose on our example. Finally, in Section 5, we outline our conclusions and discuss related and future work.

2 ROOL

A program in ROOL consists of a sequence *cds* of Java-like class declarations followed by a main command c, which may contain objects of classes declared in *cds*. A class declaration has the following form.

    class N_1 **extends** N_2
        {**pri** $x_1 : T_1$; }*{**prot** $x_2 : T_2$; }*{**pub** $x_3 : T_3$; }*   //*attributes*
        {**meth** $m \stackrel{\wedge}{=} (pds \bullet c)$ **end**}*   //*methods*
        {**new** $\stackrel{\wedge}{=} (pds \bullet c)$ **end**}*   //*Initialiser*
    end

First of all, the class name N_1 is introduced. The clause **extends** determines the immediate superclass of N_1; if it is omitted, the built-in empty class **object** is regarded as the superclass. A class can be recursive in that attributes and method parameters of a class N, can have type N itself. Attributes are declared with visibility modifiers similar to those of Java: **pri**, **prot**, and **pub** are used for private, protected, and public attributes.

The clauses **meth** declare methods, which are regarded as public. Methods are seen as parametrised commands in the style of Back [1]; the declaration *pds* of the parameters of a method is separated from its body c by the symbol '•'. The declaration of a parameter x of type T can take the form **val** $x : T$ or **res** $x : T$, corresponding to the traditional conventions of parameter passing known as call-by-value and call-by-result. The **new** clause declares initialisers: methods that are called after creating an object of the class.

```
class Step
    pri dir, len : int;
    meth setDirection ≜ (val d : Int;  • self.dir := d) end
    meth setLength ≜ (val l : Int;  • self.len := l) end
    meth getLength ≜ (res l : Int;  • l := self.len) end
end
class Path extends Step
    pri previous : Path;
    meth addStep ≜ (val d, l : Int •
        self.previous := self;  self.setDirection(d);  self.setLength(l);
    ) end
    meth getLength ≜ (res l : Int •
        var aux : Int •
            if (self.previous <> null) → self.previous.getLength(aux)
            [] (self.previous = null) → aux := 0
            fi;
            super.getLength(l);  l := l + aux;
        end
    ) end
    new ≜ (val d, l : Int •
        self.setDirection(d);  self.setLength(l);  self.previous := null
    ) end
end
•   var p : Path •
        p := new Path(north, l₀);  p.aadStep(north, l₁);  p.aadStep(east, l₂);
        p.aadStep(south, l₃);  p.aadStep(west, l₄);  p.getLength(out);
    end
```

Fig. 1. ROOL program for keeping tracking of a robot's path

In Figure 1, we give an example of an executable program in ROOL that will be used to illustrate our compilation strategy. It simulates a mechanism to keep track of a robot's path. The robot starts in the position $(0,0)$. Every time it moves, a step of length l is taken towards *north*, *south*, *east*, or *west*. The outcome of this program is the total length of the route described by the robot.

Two classes are declared in our example, *Step* and *Path*. The first one has two integer attributes: *dir* and *len*, corresponding to the direction and length of a step. The values of these attributes can be set using the methods *setDirection* and *setLength*, whereas the length of a step can be retrieved using the method *getLength*.

The class *Path* extends *Step*, introducing the attribute *previous* to hold the preceding steps that outline the robot's path; *Path* is a recursive class. The method *addStep* introduces a step in the path; it first assigns the current path (*self*) to *previous*, and then invokes the two methods *setDirection* and *setLength* to record the current step. The length of a path is calculated by the method *getLength*, a recursive redefinition of the method with same name declared in

Step. Each recursive invocation of *getLength* visits a step in the path; it traverses the list of steps accumulating the length. The sequence of nested invocations ends when the first step is reached: the value of *previous* is **null**. To get the length of the current step, we use a method call **super**.*getLength* to guarantee that the method declared in *Step*, which is *Path*'s superclass, is invoked.

A method call *le.m* is as a parametrised command; *m* refers to the method associated with the object that is the current value of the expression *le*. In addition to method calls, the main command, the body of methods, and initialisers are defined using imperative constructs similar to those of Morgan's refinement calculus [13]. They are described in the following grammar.

$$
\begin{array}{ll}
c \in Com ::= le := e \mid x : [pre, post] & \text{assignment, specification} \\
\quad \mid c_1; c_2 & \text{sequential composition} \\
\quad \mid pc(e) & \text{parametrised command application} \\
\quad \mid \textbf{if } []_i \bullet b_i \rightarrow c_i \textbf{ fi} & \text{alternation} \\
\quad \mid \textbf{rec } X \bullet c \textbf{ end} \mid X & \text{recursion, recursive call} \\
\quad \mid \textbf{var } x : T \bullet c \textbf{ end} & \text{local variable block} \\
\quad \mid \textbf{avar } x : T \bullet c \textbf{ end} & \text{angelic variable block}
\end{array}
$$

Left-expressions *le* are those that can appear as target of assignments and method calls, and as result and value-result arguments. An assignment has the form *le* := *e*, where *e* is an arbitrary expression; the semantics is of copy rather than reference. The specification statement $x : [pre, post]$ describes a program that, when executed in a state that satisfies the precondition *pre*, terminates in a state that satisfies the postcondition *post*, modifying only variables in *x*.

A parametrised command can have the form **val** $x : T \bullet c$ or **res** $x : T \bullet c$. The alternation is composed by a collection of guarded command $b_i \rightarrow c_i$, as in Dijkstra's language [6]. The block **rec** $X \bullet c$ **end** introduces a recursive command named X with body c; occurrences of X in c are recursive calls. The difference between the two kinds of variable blocks is the way in which the variables are initialised; in a **var** block, the initial value is arbitrary, whereas in a **avar** block, it is angelically chosen. The variables introduced in a **avar** block are angelic variables, also known as logical constants. ROOL does not include a **while** statement, but it can be defined in the standard way using recursion.

The following grammar describes the ROOL expressions, which are mainly those normally found in an object-oriented language.

$$
\begin{array}{ll}
e \in Exp ::= \textbf{self} \mid \textbf{super} \mid \textbf{null} & \\
\quad \mid \textbf{new } N & \text{object creation} \\
\quad \mid x \mid f(e) & \text{variable, built-in application} \\
\quad \mid e \textbf{ is } L \mid (N) & \text{type test and cast} \\
\quad \mid e.x \mid (e; x : e) & \text{attribute selection and update}
\end{array}
$$

The reference **self** corresponds to *this* of Java. The expression **new** N creates an object of class N. A type test allows to check the dynamic type of an object, like the *instanceof* in Java. An update expression $(e_1; x : e_2)$ denotes a fresh object copied from e_1, but with attribute x mapped to a copy of e_2.

3 Target Machine

In our approach to compilation, the behavior of the target machine is given by an interpreter written in ROOL itself. Each executable command is translated to a sequence of bytecode instructions encoded as ROOL commands. The ROOL interpreter models a cyclic mechanism which executes one instruction at a time.

The interpreter represents the target machine components using the variables PC (program counter), S (the operand stack), F (the frame stack), M (store for variables), Cls (symbol table for the classes declared in the source program), and CP (constant pool). The execution of an instruction changes these components, updating the machine state. The PC register contains the address of the bytecode instruction currently being executed. Because the virtual machine has no registers for storing temporary values, everything must be pushed onto the operand stack S before it can be used in a calculation. The frame stack F is composed by objects of a class *FrameInfo* that hold the state of execution of a method. When a method is invoked, a new frame is placed on the top of the frame stack; when the method completes, the frame is discarded.

The observable data space of our interpreter is a store for variables M: the concrete counterpart of the variables of the source program. It is a map from the address of the variables to their values; the model is a sequence of objects. Each method invocation frame possesses a store for variables, which records the values of the variables visible during the invocation.

The component Cls is a symbol table holding the essential information about the class declarations in the source program; it is represented by a sequence of objects of the class *ClassInfo*. Each of them has the following attributes: *name*, which records the class name; *super*, the superclass name; *subcls*, the sequence of immediate subclasses names; *mtds*, the sequence of methods (objects of a class of *MethodInfo*) declared in the class; and *attrib*, the sequence of attributes (objects of a class of *AttribInfo*) declared in the class. An object of *MethodInfo* holds the following attributes: *name*, which records the method name; and *descriptor*, the list of the type and mechanism used to pass each of the parameters. Attributes are recorded using objects of the class *AttribInfo*; their attributes are also *name* and *descriptor*; the latter contains the type and visibility of the attribute.

The constant pool is a heterogeneous list of references to classes, attributes, methods, and constants; these references are entries obtained through an index. Entries are objects of four different classes. A class entry is an object of a class *CpEntryClass*, which contains only a class name; from that class we can obtain the corresponding object of *ClassInfo* in Cls. An attribute entry contains an object of *CpEntryAttrib*, which holds an attribute name and the class where the attribute is defined. A method entry holds an object of *CpEntryMtd* containing the method name and the name of the class where the method is defined. Finally, an entry containing an integer constant is an object of a class *DataInfoInt*; integer values are encapsulated in objects.

3.1 Normal Form

Our normal form is an interpreter-like program modelling a cyclic mechanism that executes one instruction at a time. Every cycle fetches the next instruction to be executed and simulates its effect on the internal data structures of the interpreter. The normal form consists of a sequence of class declarations (cds_{RVM}) followed by a main command named I, as shown in Figure 2. The class declarations define the classes mentioned in the description of the RVM components. The main command describes the behavior of our target machine executing a compiled program: an iterated execution of a sequence of bytecodes represented by the set of guarded commands GCS.

The main command is a **var** block declaration that introduces three local variables, PC, S, and F: the program counter, the operand stack, and the frame stack. The first two commands in the variable block are assignments to create a new operand stack and a new frame stack.

$$cds_{RVM} \bullet \mathbf{var}\ PC, S, F : Int, Stack, FrameStack \bullet$$
$$S := \mathbf{new}\ Stack;\ \ F := \mathbf{new}\ FrameSTack;$$
$$PC := s;$$
$$\mathbf{while}\ PC \geq s \land PC < f \rightarrow \mathbf{if}\ GCS\ \mathbf{fi}\ \mathbf{end}$$
$$\mathbf{end}$$

Fig. 2. The ROOL Interpreter ($cds_{RVM} \bullet I$)

The variable PC is used for scheduling the selection and sequencing of instructions. The abbreviation GCS depicts the stored program as a set of guarded commands of the form $(PC = k) \rightarrow q$, where q is a machine instruction that is executed when PC is k. The initial value of PC is the address s of the first instruction to be executed; the final address is f. The **while** statement is executed until PC reaches a value beyond the interval determined by s and f. The body of the while tests the PC value and selects the instruction to be executed. All instructions modify PC. The set of guarded commands is an abstract representation of the target code. The design of a compiler in our approach is actually an abstract design of a code generator.

For convenience, we define some abbreviations.

Definition 1 (Abbreviations for the interpreter)

$Init \stackrel{def}{=} S := \mathbf{new}\ Stack;\ \ F := \mathbf{new}\ FrameStack;$
$v : [s, GCS, f] \stackrel{def}{=} PC := s;$
  $\mathbf{while}\ PC \geq s \land PC < f \rightarrow \mathbf{if}\ GCS\ \mathbf{fi}\ \mathbf{end}$
where v is the list $PC,\ S,\ F$.

Together, $Init$ and $v : [s, GCS, f]$ compose the body of variable block in the main command.

3.2 Machine Instructions

In this section, we give some examples of how the instructions of our virtual machine are defined. We assume that n stands for an address in M, and k for an address in the sequence of bytecodes.

Definition 2 (Instructions definition)
$$load(n) \stackrel{def}{=} S := \langle M[n] \rangle \frown S; \quad PC := PC + 2$$
$$bop \stackrel{def}{=} S := \langle head(tail(S)) \text{ bop } head(S) \rangle \frown tail(tail(S)); \quad PC := PC + 1$$
$$goto(k) \stackrel{def}{=} PC := k$$
$$new(j) \stackrel{def}{=} \textbf{var } o : ObjectInfo \bullet$$
$$\qquad o := \textbf{new } ObjectInfo; \quad o.create(Cls, CP, j);$$
$$\qquad S := \langle o \rangle \frown S; \; ; \; PC := PC + 2$$
$$\quad \textbf{end}$$

Pushing a local variable onto the operand stack is done by the instruction *load*, and involves moving a value from the store of variable M to the operand stack S. To deal with operators, we group them so that *bop* stand for binary operators. The instruction *goto* always branches: the integer argument k is assigned to PC. The instruction *new* builds an object of class *ObjectInfo* to hold the representation of an object whose type is indicated by the argument j. This is an index to a class entry in the constant pool. The call $o.create(Cls, CP, j)$ traverses Cls, the representation of the source program class hierarchy, determining and recording in o the attributes of the class indicated by j, and of its superclasses. The resulting object o is pushed into the operand stack S.

4 Strategy for Compilation

In this section we give an overview of our reduction strategy for compilation. There are five phases: class pre-compilation, redirection of method calls, simplification of expressions, data refinement, and control elimination. Class pre-compilation records the structure of the classes in the source program and introduces the class L, which includes just one method, *lookUp*, to resolve dynamic binding. The redirection of method calls consists of rewriting each method call to a call to *lookUp*. The simplification of expressions eliminates nested expressions in assignments and guards. In the data refinement phase, the abstract space of the source program is substituted by the the concrete space of the target machine. Finally, the purpose of control elimination is to reduce the nested control structure of the source program to the single flat iteration of the normal form. The idea is to progressively change the structure of the source program to get to the normal form.

The compilation process is justified by reduction theorems; for each phase, a theorem asserts the expected outcome, and a main theorem links the intermediate steps and establishes the outcome for the entire process. Since the reduction theorems are proved from the basic laws of ROOL, they corroborate the correctness of the compilation process. We anticipate the main theorem.

Theorem 1 (Compilation Process) *Let $cds \bullet c$ be an executable source program. Given the symbol tables Φ and Ψ, then there are s, GCS, and f such that*
$$\overline{\Psi}(cds \bullet c) \sqsubseteq cds_{RVM} \bullet Init; \; v : [s, GSC, f]$$

The symbol $\sqsubseteq$ represents the refinement relation; this theorem guarantees that the normal form embeds a correct implementation of the source program. Its constructive proof characterises the compilation process, discussed in the sequel.

Since the source program operates on a data space different from that of the normal form, it does not make sense to compare them directly. A function $\overline{\Psi}$ performs the necessary change of data representation. The symbol table Ψ maps the variables declared in the source program to addresses in the store M, in such a way that $M[\Psi_x]$ holds the value of x.

Before we describe our compilation strategy, we explicit the following restrictions, which we assume to hold for the source programs; there is no name clashing for attributes in the set of class declarations cds; name clashing for methods are allowed only in the case of redefinitions; and all references to an attribute have the form **self**.a. These conditions are necessary to ensure the applicability of the compilation rules and the convergence of the overall process. They do not impose any semantic restrictions, and can be satisfied with simple syntactic changes to an arbitrary source program. We further discuss the roles of these conditions during the detailed description of the reduction steps for compilation.

4.1 Class Pre-compilation

The outcome of this phase is summarised by the theorem below. It establishes that the compilation rules applied in this phase are sufficient to end up with a program in a form where all method declarations of the source program are copied to the *lookUp* method of a new class L.

Theorem 2 (Class Pre-compilation) *Let $cds \bullet c$ be an executable source program, then there is a program cds_{RVM}, cds', $L \bullet c'$ such that*
$$cds \bullet c \sqsubseteq cds_{RVM}, L, cds' \bullet c'$$
where the main command c' differs from c only by trivial casts; cds' has the same structure of cds, but all the attributes are public; and the class L has only a declaration of a method lookUp.

Initially, the source program does not refer to the set of class declarations cds_{RVM}. The commands that will be introduced in L and in the main command are built using methods, attributes, and types defined in cds_{RVM}. For that reason, when we start the process of restructuring the code, introducing the class L, the need to introduce cds_{RVM} arises. Throughout the compilation process, the class L plays a fundamental role in our strategy: it establishes the basic conditions that will allow the elimination of cds, and all source program references.

In order to define *lookUp*, we need to copy all method bodies declared in *cds*. The idea is to transform all method calls to a unique pattern, where the invoked method is always *lookUp*. Once *lookUp* is invoked, the method body associated with the original method call should be selected, and then executed. As a consequence of such transformations, the method declarations in *cds* become useless and can be eliminated. Since the association of a method call with its corresponding method body is affected by dynamic binding and by the use of **super**, it is necessary to address the treatment of these issues.

This compilation phase comprise three steps; the first two change the visibility of the attributes in *cds*, and introduce trivial casts. Both are necessary to avoid syntactic errors that can be originated by the introduction of *lookUp*. The last step in this phase deals with the *lookUp* creation.

Changing visibility of attributes. We need to guarantee that the bodies of the methods do not contain references to private and protected attributes; otherwise, an error can arise when we copy them to the *lookUp* method. Therefore, we change the declarations of the attributes to make them all public. Even though this is not a good idea from a software engineering point of view, this does not change the behaviour of a complete program.

To perform these transformations, we use the laws presented in [2]. Due to space restrictions, we omit most of the compilation rules; our objective in this paper is to present and illustrate the compilation strategy. In our example, we change the declarations of *dir* and *len* in *Step*, and *previous* in *Path*.

Introducing trivial casts. We introduce type casts to produce an uniform program text in which all targets are cast with its static type. The purpose of this step is to explicitly annotate in the program text the declared type of each target. The casts have no effect.

We need a data structure that maps the elements declared in the source program to indexes in the constant pool *CP*. From these indexes, the objects representing the classes, methods, or attributes can be obtained from *Cls*; the constants are represented by objects in *CP*. We assume that this data structure built as part of the syntactic analysis and type checking of the program.

***lookUp* creation.** Basically, *lookUp* consists of a sequence of two conditionals. The first conditional treats the dynamic binding and the use of **super**, whereas the second implements the method body selection. The general format of the *lookUp* declaration is as follows.

    meth $lookUp \triangleq$ (**val** $S : Stack$; **res** $Sres : Stack$•
      var $mtd : Int$; $o : Object$; $w : T$; •
        $S.Pop(db)$; $S.Pop(mtd)$; $S.Pop(o)$;
        $conditional_1$; $conditional_2$;
        $S.Push(o)$; $Sres := S$;
      end
) **end**

The formal parameters are the operand stacks S and $Sres$. When *lookUp* starts, it pops two values from S: mtd and o. The former indicates the method to be executed, and the latter, the target of the method call. When the dynamic binding is considered in the $conditional_1$, the value of mtd may be modified. The $conditional_2$ selects the method body denoted by mtd; arguments are handled through variables declared in the list w. The two last commands pushes a copy of o back onto S and assigns S to $Sout$.

Associated with each method m, we have three indexes, ι, σ and δ. The first, $\iota_{C.m}$, identifies the declaration of the method m occurring in the class C. In our robot example, we use the following values: $\iota_{Step.setDirection} \mapsto 1$, $\iota_{Step.setLength} \mapsto 2$, $\iota_{Step.getLength} \mapsto 3$, $\iota_{Path.addStep} \mapsto 4$, $\iota_{Path.getLength} \mapsto 5$, and $\iota_{Path.initialiser} \mapsto 6$. The initialiser declared in $Path$ is treated like an ordinary method, and is denoted by 6. There is no ι index for the $setDirection$ method of $Path$, because this class does not include a declaration for this method

The second index, $\sigma_{C.m}$, is used to identify references to the method m of the class C in calls of the form **super**.m, which do not require dynamic binding. If a declaration of a method m is shared (through inheritance) by two classes D and E, then $\sigma_{D.m}$ and $\sigma_{E.m}$ have the same value. In our example, we chose the following values for this index: $\sigma_{Step.setDirection} \mapsto 1$, $\sigma_{Path.setDirection} \mapsto 1$, $\sigma_{Step.setLength} \mapsto 2$, $\sigma_{Path.setLength} \mapsto 2$, $\sigma_{Step.getLength} \mapsto 3$, $\sigma_{Path.getLength} \mapsto 5$, $\sigma_{Path.addStep} \mapsto 4$, $\sigma_{Path.initializer} \mapsto 6$. It is important to observe that, since $Path$ inherits $setDirection$ from $Step$, this method is available in both classes, and so the values of $\sigma_{Step.setDirection}$ and $\sigma_{Path.setDirection}$ are both 1.

The last index, $\delta.m$, identifies references to m in calls that may require dynamic binding: those of the form $le.m$. When m has just one definition, the values of $\sigma_{C.m}$ and δ_m are identical for all classes C in which m is available. Otherwise, δ_m has a value that is not associated with any method declaration by ι and by σ. In our example, the values chosen are as follows: $\delta_{setDirection} \mapsto 1$, $\delta_{setLength} \mapsto 2$, $\delta_{setLength} \mapsto 2$, $\delta_{getLength} \mapsto 0$, $\delta_{addStep} \mapsto 4$, $\delta_{initializer_{Path}} \mapsto 6$. In the case of the method $getLength$, it is defined in $Step$ and redefined in $Path$; for this reason, it is associated with 0, an index not used by ι or by σ. This indicates that calls to $getLength$ require dynamic binding. For $setLength$, on the other hand, we use 2, which is the value of σ for $setLength$ in $Step$ and $Path$. This indicates that calls to $setLength$ do not require dynamic binding.

A function creates the $conditional_1$ based on the class hierarchy in Cls and the indexes above. Starting from the bottom of the hierarchy, for each redefined method m, a nest of conditionals is created. The outermost conditional addresses the class C at the bottom of the hierarchy of classes where m is available. In this conditional, one first guard tests if C is the dynamic type of the object o. If so, the command associated with this guard is an assignment of $\sigma_{C.m}$ to the variable mtd. One other guard tests if C is not the dynamic type of the o. In this case, the command associated with this guard is a similar conditional, addressing the immediate superclass of C. For instance, in our example, the only redefined method is $getLength$. We chose 0 as the value of $\delta_{getLength}$. When the $conditional_1$ is created, a test is introduced to check if the value in mtd is 0. In this case, the type of o is tested, and 3 or 5, corresponding to $\sigma_{Step.getLength}$ and

$\sigma_{Path.getLength}$, is assigned to mtd to indicate which version has to be executed. The resulting conditional is as follows.

$$\begin{array}{l}\textbf{if } mtd = \delta_{getLength} \;\rightarrow\\ \quad \textbf{if } o \textbf{ is } Path \;\rightarrow\; mtd := \sigma_{Path.getLength}\\ \quad []\neg(o \textbf{ is } Path) \;\rightarrow\; \textbf{if } o \textbf{ is } Step \;\rightarrow\; mtd := \Phi_{Step.getLength}\\ \qquad\qquad\qquad\qquad\qquad []\neg(o \textbf{ is } Step) \;\rightarrow\; \textbf{skip}\\ \qquad\qquad\qquad\qquad\quad \textbf{fi}\\ \quad \textbf{fi}\\ []\neg(mtd = \delta_{getLength}) \;\rightarrow\; \textbf{skip}\\ \textbf{fi}\end{array}$$

In summary, the first conditional tests the dynamic type of o. If C is the current type of o, an assignment of $\sigma_{C.m}$ to the variable mtd is done. The value of mtd is tested in $conditional_2$ to select the method body that has to be executed.

The creation of $conditional_2$ is based on the class hierarchy described in Cls. Each guard in the conditional tests the value in mtd to identify a method declaration. The general form of the $conditional_2$ is as follows.

$$\begin{array}{l}\textbf{if } []_{\langle 0 \le\ i\ \le\ k \rangle}(mtd = \iota_{C.m}) \;\rightarrow\; In(\iota_{C.m}, v);\\ \qquad\qquad\qquad\qquad\qquad\quad pc_{\iota_{C.m}}[o/\textbf{self}](w);\\ \qquad\qquad\qquad\qquad\qquad\quad Out(\iota_{C.m}, r)\\ \textbf{fi}\end{array}$$

The notation $pc_{\iota_{C.m}}[o/\textbf{self}]$ expresses the substitution of o for every occurrence of **self** in the parametrised command $pc_{\iota_{C.m}}$: the body of the method declaration identified by $\iota_{C.m}$. It is applied to the list of variables w, which is formed from two other lists v and r. The input arguments are popped from S and stored in v, whereas the result arguments are placed in r. The function $In(\iota_{C.m}, v)$ inspects the signature of m, and creates the list of commands that pop the input values from the operand stack S, initialising the list of variables v. Similarly, $Out(\iota_{C.m}, r)$ creates the list of commands that push the result values on S.

In our example, the $conditional_2$ is formed by six guards, one for each method declaration in the source program. To select the parametrised command corresponding to the method body that has to be executed, the value of mtd is used. For our example, the first guard in the $conditional_2$ is as follows.

$$\textbf{if } mtd = 1 \;\rightarrow\; S.Pop(x_1); (\textbf{val } d : Int;\; \bullet\; (Step)o.dir := d)(x_1)[]\;\ldots$$

It tests if the value in mtd is equal 1. If so, the body of the method $setDirection$ declared in $Step$ is executed, with the element at the top of the operand stack as argument.

4.2 Redirecting Method Calls

In this phase all method calls are redirected to $lookUp$, so that the method declarations in cds become useless and can, therefore, be eliminated. The outcome is summarised by the Theorem 3: the compilation rules applied in this phase are sufficient to end up with a program where all calls are to the $lookUp$ method.

Theorem 3 (Redirection of method calls) *Let $cds_{RVM}, cds, L \bullet c$ be an executable program where all attributes in cds are public, and the class L and its*

$lookUp$ method are as above, then there is a program cds_{RVM}, cds', $L' \bullet c'$ such that $cds_{RVM}, cds, L \bullet c \sqsubseteq cds_{RVM}, L', cds' \bullet c'$, where cds' contains only the attribute declarations of cds, the main command c' has the same functionality of c, but neither c' nor $lookUp$ refer to the methods declared in cds.

In order to transform each method call that appears in the program into a method call to $lookUp$, we need to simplify the targets. In calls $le.m(e)$ and **super**.$m(e)$, both le and e can have nested expressions. The idea is to reduce all possible method calls to a simpler form, suitable to be manipulated by the subsequent steps. The laws needed can be found in [7, 8].

We also use rules that rely on the type of parameter passing used to to determine which arguments have to be pushed onto and popped from S. To illustrate these transformations, we present the rule that addresses calls-by-result. We use the notation $cds_{RVM}, cds, N \triangleright c \sqsubseteq c'$ to mean that the refinement $c \sqsubseteq c'$ holds in the context of the sequence of class declarations of cds_{RVM}, cds, for a command c inside N, which denotes the main command or a class in cds_{RVM} or cds.

Rule 1 (Result parameter)
$cds_{RVM}, cds'', L' \triangleright$
$(C)le.m(x) \sqsubseteq$ **var** $o : Object;\ S : Stack;\ V : L \bullet$
$\quad\quad\quad\quad\quad\quad\quad\quad S := $ **new** $Stack;\ V := $ **new** $L;\ o := le;$
$\quad\quad\quad\quad\quad\quad\quad\quad S.Push(o);\ S.Push(\delta_{C.m});\ V.lookUp(S);$
$\quad\quad\quad\quad\quad\quad\quad\quad S.Pop(o);\ S.Pop(x);\ le := o;$
$\quad\quad\quad\quad\quad\quad$ **end**
provided the definition of m in C has one result parameter, and o, S and V are fresh names.

For the compilation of a call-by-result, a variable block is introduced, declaring an object o, the operand Stack S, and a variable V of class L. New objects are created to initialise S and V, whereas o receives a copy of the object denoted by le. Then, o and $\delta_{C.m}$ are pushed onto S. After the invocation of the $lookUp$ method, the value of the parameter is popped from S and assigned to x; the resulting object is assigned to le.

As an example, we consider the method call $p.getLength(out)$ in the main command of the robot program. This method has a result parameter. The result of applying Rule 1 is as follows.
$\quad$ **var** $o : Object;\ S : Stack;\ V : L \bullet$
$\quad\quad\quad S := $ **new** $Stack;\ V := $ **new** $L;$
$\quad\quad\quad o := p;\ S.Push(o);$
$\quad\quad\quad S.Push(0);\ V.lookUp(S);$
$\quad\quad\quad S.Pop(o);\ S.Pop(out);\ p := o;$
$\quad$ **end**

The indication that dynamic binding must be performed is done by $S.Push(0)$, where 0 is the value of $\delta_{getLength}$. In $lookUp$, the value associated to mtd is modified, based on the type of o. In this case, o is an instance of the class $Path$, thus, 5 is the value that is assigned to mtd, indicating that the method body declared in $Path$ is the one that has to be executed. When $lookUp$ completes, the value of *out* is popped from S. Finally, the returning value of o is also popped from S, and assigned to p.

Applying compilation rules like that above introduces several variable blocks. To accomplish the result in Theorem 3, we need to apply laws that expand the scope of variable blocks. These laws are standard [8].

When **super** appears as target in a method call, the check of dynamic binding is not necessary. Therefore, we use a slightly different version of the above rules. Instead of δ_m, $\sigma_{(C.super).m}$ is used. This modification prevents the value of mtd from being changed in $lookUp$, because $\sigma_{(C.super).m}$ denotes an specific method body, the one declared as m and associated with the immediate superclass of C.

The method *getLength* uses recursion to find the length of a robot's path. The redirection of a recursive method call does not imply in any overhead. Any recursion is automatically embedded in recursive calls to $lookUp$. For instance, the recursive call $(Path)o.previous.getLenth(aux)$ appears in $lookUp$, in the method body related to the *getLength* method of *Path*. When we rewrite this method call, we obtain the following.

    var o_1 : *Object*; S : *Stack*; V : L •
        $S :=$ **new** *Stack*; $V :=$ **new** L;
        $o_1 := o.previous$; $S.Push(o_1)$;
        $S.Push(0)$; $V.lookUp(S)$; $S.Pop(o_1)$;
        $S.Pop(out)$; $o.previous := o_1$;
    end

Recursion arises because we use 0 again to identify the method to be called.

In order to eliminate a parametrised commands, we use the standard definitions in the literature [1]. For each parametrised command, a variable block is introduced. We can combine them using standard laws of ROOL.

This phase considers method calls in $lookUp$ and in the main command. In Figure 3, we show the main command resulting from the compilation of our

    var p : *Path* o : *Object*; S : *Stack*; V : L •
        $p :=$ **new** *Path*; $S :=$ **new** *Stack*; $V :=$ **new** L;
        $o := p$; $S.Push(l_0)$; $S.Push(north)$; $S.Push(o)$;
        $S.Push(6)$; $V.lookUp(S)$; $S.Pop(o)$; $p := o$;
        $o := p$; $S.Push(l_1)$; $S.Push(north)$; $S.Push(o)$;
        $S.Push(4)$; $V.lookUp(S)$; $S.Pop(o)$; $p := o$;
        $o := p$; $S.Push(l_2)$; $S.Push(east)$; $S.Push(o)$;
        $S.Push(4)$; $V.lookUp(S)$; $S.Pop(o)$; $p := o$;
        $S.Pop(o)$; $p := o$; $o := p$; $S.Push(l_3)$;
        $S.Push(south)$; $S.Push(o)$; $S.Push(4)$; $V.lookUp(S)$;
        $S.Pop(o)$; $p := o$; $o := p$; $S.Push(l_4)$; $S.Push(west)$; $S.Push(o)$;
        $S.Push(4)$; $V.lookUp(S)$; $S.Pop(o)$; $p := o$; $o := p$; $S.Push(o)$;
        $S.Push(0)$; $V.lookUp(S)$; $S.Pop(o)$; $S.Pop(out)$; $p := o$;
    end

Fig. 3. Main command obtained after redirecting method calls

example. For each call in the main command, a variable block is introduced and further manipulated to expand its scope. The first call to *lookUp* has 6 as an argument, indicating that the body of the initialiser declared in *Path* has to be executed to give p its first value. Then, the next four *lookUp* invocations correspond to calls to *addStep*. Finally, the last one refers to a call to *getLength*.

4.3 Simplification of Expressions

This phase eliminates nested expressions that appear in assignments and guards. The expected outcome is stated by Theorem 4.

Theorem 4 (Simplification of Expressions) *Let cds_{RVM}, cds, $L \bullet c$ be an executable source program, then there is a program cds_{RVM}, cds', $L' \bullet c'$ such that cds_{RVM}, cds, $L \bullet c \sqsubseteq cds_{RVM}$, cds', $L' \bullet c'$ where each assignment in c', cds' and, L' operates through the operand stack, and each boolean expression is a variable.*

Variables that represent the components of RVM, and the auxiliary variable V used to invoke *lookUp* are not affected by the transformations of this phase. Basically, the task of eliminating nested expressions in a source program involves rewriting assignments and boolean expressions in the L and in main command. Since new variables are introduced, we apply extra laws to expand the scope of variable blocks.

Before we proceed to the Data Refinement phase, we need to change the parameters of the method *lookUp*. This change is due to the need to access the class hierarchy information and constants stored in the global variables Cls and CP. Then, the refactoring rule that allows us to add a parameter is applied twice to introduce the desired parameters in *lookUp*.

In Figure 4, we show the result of applying these laws to the class L of our example. The simplification of the conditionals required the introduction of 11 boolean variables. Every boolean expression is assigned to a boolean variable, and these variables replace the corresponding expression in the guards, so that, each guard now consists of a simple boolean variable. Each assignment is rewritten to operate exclusively through the operand stack S. Since the pair $(S.Pop(x), S.Push(x))$ is a simulation $(S.Pop(x); S.Push(x) \sqsubseteq \textbf{skip})$. Dispensable sequences of push and pops are eliminated.

4.4 Data Refinement

The data refinement phase replaces the abstract space of the source program with the concrete state of the target machine. This means that all references to variables, methods, attributes, and classes declared in the source program must be replaced with the corresponding ones in the target machine.

The following theorem summarizes the outcome of this phase of compilation.

Theorem 5 (Data Refinement) *Consider a program of the form cds_{RVM}, cds, $L \bullet$ (var $S, V, w : Stack, L, T \bullet r$ end), where in r there are no*

class L
  meth $lookUp \stackrel{\wedge}{=}$
    (val CP, Cls, S : $Seq\ Object, Seq\ ClassInfo, Stack$;   res $Sres$: $Stack\bullet$
    var x_1, x_2 : Int; mtd, aux : Int; o : $Object$
       $b_1, b_2, b_3, b_4, b_5, b_6, b_7, b_8, b_9, b_{10}, b_{11}$: $Boolean$ $\bullet$
       $S.Pop(mtd)$; $S.Pop(o)$; $S.Push(0)$; $S.Push(mtd)$; $S.Equal$;
       $S.Pop(b_1)$; $S.Push(o$ is $Path)$; $S.Pop(b_2)$;
       $S.Push(o$ is $Path)$; $S.Neg$; $S.Pop(b_3)$;
       if $b_1 \to$
         if $b_2 \to$ $S.Load(5)$; $S.Pop(mtd)$;
         $[]\, b_3 \to$ if o is $Step \to$ $S.Load(3)$; $S.Pop(mtd)$;   fi
         fi
       fi;
       $S.Push(1)$; $S.Push(mtd)$; $S.Equal$; $S.Pop(b_4)$;
       $S.Push(2)$; $S.Push(mtd)$; $S.Equal$; $S.Pop(b_5)$;
       $S.Push(3)$; $S.Push(mtd)$; $S.Equal$; $S.Pop(b_6)$;
       $S.Push(4)$; $S.Push(mtd)$; $S.Equal$; $S.Pop(b_7)$;
       $S.Push(5)$; $S.Push(mtd)$; $S.Equal$; $S.Pop(b_8)$;
       $S.Push(\mathbf{null})$; $S.Push(o.previous)$; $S.NEqual$; $S.Pop(b_9)$;
       $S.Push(\mathbf{null})$; $S.Push(o.previous)$; $S.Equal$; $S.Pop(b_{10})$;
       $S.Push(6)$; $S.Push(mtd)$; $S.Equal$; $S.Pop(b_{11})$;
       if $b_4 \to S.Pop(o.dir)$ $[]\, b_5 \to S.Pop(o.len)$; $[]\, b_6 \to Push(o.len)$;
       $[]\, b_7 \to S.Pop(x_1)$; $S.Pop(x_2)$; $S.Push(o)$; $S.Pop(o.previous)$;
              $S.Push(o)$; $S.Push(x_1)$; $S.Push(1)$; $V.lookUp(S, S)$;
              $S.Push(x_2)$; $S.Push(2)$; $V.lookUp(S, S)$; $S.Pop(o)$;
       $[]\, b_8 \to$ if $b_9 \to S.Push(o.previous)$; $S.Push(0)$;
                    $V.lookUp(S, S)$; $S.Pop(o.previous)$; $S.Pop(aux)$;
                $[]$ $b_{10} \to S.Push(0)$; $S.Pop(aux)$
              fi; $S.Push(o)$; $S.Push(3)$; $V.lookUp(S, S)$;
              $S.Pop(o)$; $S.Push(aux)$; $S.Add$
       $[]\, b_{11} \to S.Pop(x_1)$; $S.Pop(x_2)$; $S.Push(o)$; $S.Push(1)$;
              $V.lookUp(S, S)$; $S.Push(x_2)$; $S.Push(2)$;
              $V.lookUp(S, S)$; $S.Pop(o)$; $S.Push(\mathbf{null})$; $S.Pop(o.previous)$
       fi
       $S.Push(o)$; $S.Push(S)$; $S.Pop(Sres)$;
    end
) end
end

Fig. 4. Program generated by the simplification of expressions

local declarations, all assignments are through the operand stack, and all boolean conditions are boolean variables. In addition, the class L includes only a declaration of a method called $lookUp$, whose format is as follows

  meth $lookUp \stackrel{\wedge}{=}$
        (val CP, Cls, S : $Seq\ Object, Seq\ ClassInfo, Stack$;   res $Sres$: $Stack$ $\bullet$
         var o : $Object$; V : L; x : T $\bullet$ l end
)end

where l satisfies the same restrictions as r. Then, there are programs q and u such that

$\overline{\Psi}(\overline{\omega}(cds_{RVM}, cds, L \bullet (\textbf{var } S, V, w : Stack, L, T \bullet r \textbf{ end})))$
$\sqsubseteq cds_{RVM}, L' \bullet \textbf{var } S, V : Stack, L' \bullet q \textbf{ end}$

and the method lookUp declared in L' has the following form.

    meth $lookUp \stackrel{\wedge}{=}$
        (val $CP, Cls, S : Seq\ Object, Seq\ ClassInfo, Stack;$ res $Sres : Stack \bullet$
          var $V : L';\ M : Memory \bullet u$ end
)end

where q and u preserve the control structure of r and l, respectively, but operate mainly on the concrete space.

Only in the next phase, after introducing the stack of frames F, we can eliminate the local variables V and M, and join the code in the lookUp method with the code in the main command.

To carry out the change of data representation, we use the distributivity properties of the function $\overline{\Psi}$ as in [15, 7]. It is a polymorphic function that applies to programs and commands, and distributes over the commands in the class declarations and main command, applying a function with the same name. The function $\overline{\Psi}$ does not affect the classes used to define our interpreter (cds_{RVM}), the components of our target machine, and commands that have no reference to variables or classes of the source program.

For example, after the simplification of expressions, objects are created by $S.Push(\textbf{new } C)$, where the expression new C references a class C declared in the source program. The function $\overline{\Psi}$ eliminates this reference, introducing a method call whose parameter is an index in CP corresponding to C. When applied to constructors that deal with control, like the conditional and iteration commands, $\overline{\Psi}$ distributes over the components of these commands. For illustration, Figure 5 presents the initial segment of the class L. The classes and variables declared in the source program are eliminated. The program operates exclusively on the concrete space.

4.5 Control Elimination

In this phase, the nested control structure of the source program is reduced to a single flat iteration. The result is a program in the normal form described in Figure 2. The next theorem summarises the outcome of this phase of compilation.

Theorem 6 (Control Elimination) *Consider a program $cds_{RVM}, L \bullet q$, which operates mainly on the concrete space, with the method lookUp of L declared in the following form.*

    meth $lookUp \stackrel{\wedge}{=}$
        (val $CP, Cls, S : Seq\ Object, Seq\ ClassInfo, Stack;$ res $Sres : Stack \bullet$
          var $o : object;\ V : L;\ M : Memory \bullet u$ end
) end

Then, there is a normal form program such that $cds_{RVM}, L \bullet q \sqsubseteq cds_{RVM} \bullet I$.

class L
   meth $lookUp \;\hat{=}$
      val $Cls, CP, S\, :\, Seq\ ClassInfo, Seq\ Object, Stack;$ **res** $Sres : Stack\bullet$
      $S.Store(\Psi_{mtd});\quad S.Store(M[\Psi_o])$
      $S.Load(CP[\Phi_0]);\quad S.Load(M[\Psi_{mtd}]);\quad S.Equal;\quad S.Store(M[\Psi_{b_1}]);$
      $S.Load(M[\Psi_o]);\quad S.Instanceof(Cls, CP, \Phi_{Path});\quad S.Store(M[\Psi_{b_2}]);$
      $S.Load(M[\Psi_o]);\quad S.Instanceof(Cls, CP, \Phi_{Path});\quad S.Neg;\quad S.Store(M[\Psi_{b_3}]);$
      if $M[\Psi_{b_1}] \rightarrow$
         if $M[\Psi_{b_2}] \rightarrow\quad S.Load(CP[\Phi_5]);\quad S.Store(M[\Psi_{mtd}]);$
         $[]\, M[\Psi_{b_3}] \rightarrow\quad$ **if** o **is** $Step \rightarrow\quad S.Load(CP[\Phi_3]);\quad S.Store(M[\Psi_{mtd}]);\quad$ **fi**
         fi
      fi
      ...
end

Fig. 5. Class L after the the data refinement

To accomplish the goal established by this theorem, we apply to the commands in the main command and in the body of *lookUp* rules that create the corresponding series of guarded commands. Eventually, we produce a program $v : [s+1, GCS_m, i-1]$ in *lookUp*, and $v : [i+1, GCS_c, f]$ in the main command. In the program below, we present the general form our example at this stage.

class L
   meth $lookUp \;\hat{=}\; ($
      val $Cls, CP, S : Seq\ ClassInfo, Seq\ Object, Stack;$ **res** $Sres : Stack\,\bullet$
      var $A : N;\ M : Seq\ object;\; \bullet\; V := $ **new** $N;\ v : [s+1, GCS_m, i-1]$ **end**)
   end
end
   $\bullet$ **var** $A : N;\ S : Stack\,\bullet$
      $V := $ **new**$N;\ S := $ **new**$Stack;\ v : [i+1, GCS_c, f]$
   end

To reduce this program to our normal form, we need to eliminate the class L. The only obstacle resides in the method calls to *lookUp* that may exist in GCS_m and GCS_c. Both correspond to conditionals, in which the guarded commands are closely related to the definition of the behaviour of the machine. To produce the desired normal form, it is necessary to join them. To achieve this goal we need to expand GCS_c using the guards presented in GCS_m. Using basic laws of ROOL, we can extend a conditional by introducing new guarded commands. This leads to a refinement, because the resulting program is more deterministic.

We modify the program above, to obtain the program in the normal form, as shown below. The first action is to deviate the execution flow to the address $i+1$, where the instructions corresponding to the main command start. When a method invocation occurs, the execution flow is deviated to $s+1$. Executing the instructions in GCS_m, the PC eventually reaches the address i. Then, the saved values of PC and M are popped from F, and the execution flow is deviated to just after the invocation. The program ends when PC gets the value f.

 class L
  meth $lookUp \triangleq ($
   val $Cls, CP, S : Seq\ ClassInfo, Seq\ Object, Stack;$ **res** $Sres : Stack \bullet$
   var $A : N;\ M : Seq\ object;\ \bullet\ V := $ **new** $N;\ v : [s+1, GCS_c, i]$ **end** $)$
  end
 end
  $\bullet$ **var** $A : N;\ S : Stack \bullet$
   $V := $ **new** $N;\ S := $ **new** $Stack;$
   $v : [s, (PC = s) \rightarrow PC := i+1$
    $[]\ GCS_m$
    $[]\ (PC = i) \rightarrow F.Pop(PC);\ F.Pop(M)$
    $[]\ GCS_c, f]$
 end

Using the next rule we can eliminate method calls to $lookUp$, and afterwards, we can eliminate the auxiliary class L.

Rule 2 (Eliminating method calls)

$cds_{RVM}\ L \triangleright$
$V.lookUp(Cls, CP, S)\ \sqsubseteq\ F.Push(PC);\ F.Push(M);\ PC := s + 1;$

This rule compiles a call to $lookUp$ by pushing the value of the PC and M onto F, and the assigning of the value $s+1$ to PC. In this address, the code relative to $lookUp$ is stored. Once the frame stack F is introduced, we are able to eliminate all method calls, because F plays the same role of the implicit stack used when a method is called. Therefore, we can reduce the whole program to a flat iteration.

4.6 The Compilation Process

Here, we sketch the proof to the Theorem 1. Basically, we want to transform $\overline{\Psi}(cds \bullet c)$ into $cds_{RVM} \bullet Init;\ v : [s, GSC, f]$. From Theorem 2 (Class Precompilation), we can transform $cds \bullet c$, and obtain $cds_{RVM}, cds', L \bullet c'$. At this point, we can refer to the Theorem 3 (Redirection of method calls) which establishes that $cds_{RVM}, cds, L \bullet c\ \sqsubseteq\ cds_{RVM}, L, cds' \bullet c'$. Then Theorem 4 (Simplification of Expressions), states that we can obtain $cds_{RVM}, cds', L' \bullet c'$ from $cds_{RVM}, cds, L \bullet c$. Using monotonicity of $\overline{\Psi}$, we can conclude that $\overline{\Psi}(cds \bullet c)\ \sqsubseteq\ \overline{\Psi}(cds_{RVM}, cds', L' \bullet c')$. At this point, based on the Theorem 5 (Data Refinement), cds is eliminated and the outcome program operates over the concrete space. Finally, from Theorem 6 we achieve a program in our normal form, $cds_{RVM} \bullet Init;\ v : [s, GSC, f]$.

5 Final Considerations

As an attempt to address the correct implementation of object-oriented programs, we have proposed a refinement strategy for the compilation of ROOL, a language that includes classes, inheritance, dynamic binding, and recursion. This language is sufficiently similar to Java to be used in meaningful case studies; our result represents significant advance on previous work. In [7], we detail the compilation rules for the phases of simplification of expressions, data refinement, and control elimination. Here, we focus on the overall strategy for the compilation, illustrating the whole process through a case study.

The classes declared in the source program have to be eliminated during the compilation process. In order to remove them, we developed a strategy based on the introduction of an auxiliary class L that allows us to eliminate the references to methods of the source program. Inheritance is treated through the generation of a data structure Cls resembling the original class hierarchy. Dynamic binding is handled with the use of a function to construct a conditional to check the type of the target object at run time.

The main difference between our work and those in [3, 16] resides in the fact that their approach is based on verification, instead of on calculation. Recently, a case study in verified program compilation from imperative program to assembler code was presented in [17]. The compiled code is data refined by calculation. That case study, however, does not comprise object-oriented features.

In [2], a similar strategy for normal form reduction was adopted as a measure of completeness of the set of proposed laws for ROOL. Here, a similar set of laws, together with specific compilation rules, are used to carry out the design of a provably correct compiler. Obviously, due to the nature of our application, our normal form and our strategy need to be different.

We are currently working on the proof soundness of the compilation rules. Initial results are reported in [9]. The proofs are based on basic laws of rule, that are sound with respect to its weakest precondition semantics [2].

Further work is needed towards the mechanisation of this approach. Its algebraic nature makes the mechanisation easier, allowing the use of a term rewrite system as a tool for specification, verification, and prototype implementation. We already have initial results in this direction.

Acknowledgments

Adolfo Duran is supported by UFBA (Universidade Federal da Bahia, Brazil) and CAPES: grant BEX0786/02-0. The other authors are partially suported by CNPq: grants 520763/98-0 and 472204/01-7 (Ana Cavalcanti), 521039/95-9 (Augusto Sampaio), and 680032/99-1.

References

1. R. J. R. Back. Procedural abstraction in the refinement calculus. Technical Report Ser. A No. 55, Department of Computer Science, Abo - Finland, 1987.
2. P. Borba, A. Sampaio, and M. Cornélio. A refinement algebra for object-oriented programming. In *To Appear in the Proceedings of ECOOP 2003*, 2003.
3. E. Börger and W. Schulte. Defining the java virtual machine as platform for provably correct java compilation. In *MFCS'98.*, number 1450, pages 17–35. Springer LNCS, 1998.

4. A. Cavalcanti and D. Naumann. A weakest precondition semantics for refinement of object-oriented programs. *IEEE Transactions on Software Enginnering*, 26(08):713–728, 2000.
5. M. Cornélio, A. Cavalcanti, and Augusto Sampaio. Refactoring by transformation. In Proceedings of REFINE'2002, *Electronic Notes in Theoretical Computer Science*, 2002.
6. E. W. Dijkstra. *A Discipline of Programming*. Prentice-Hall, Engewood Cliffs, 1976.
7. A. Duran, A. Cavalcanti, and A. Sampaio. Refinement algebra for formal bytecode generation. In *ICFEM 2002 - 4th International Conference on Formal Engineering Methods*, pages 347–358, Shanghai, China, October 2002. Springer-Verlag.
8. A. Duran, A. Cavalcanti, and A. Sampaio. A refinement strategy for the compilation of classes, inheritance, and dynamic binding (extended version). Technical report, Computing Laboratory, University of Kent at Canterbury, 2003.
9. A. Duran, A. Sampaio, and A. Cavalcanti. Formal bytecode generation for rool virtual machine. In *IV WMF— Workshop on Formal Methods*. PUC—Rio de Janeiro/Brazil, October 2001.
10. C. A. R. Hoare, J. He, and A. Sampaio. Normal form approach to compiler design. *Acta Informatica*, 30:701–739, 1993.
11. Tim Lindholm and Frank Yellin. *The java Virtual Machine Specification*. Addison-Wesley, 1997.
12. J. McCarthy and J. Painter. Correctness of a compiler for arithmetic expressions. In *Symposium on Applied Mathematics*, pages 33–41. American Mathematical Society, 1967.
13. C. Morgan. *Programming from Specifications*. Prentice Hall, second edition, 1994.
14. M. Müller-Olm. *Modular Compiler Verification: A Refinement-Algebraic Approach Advocating Stepwise Abstraction*, volume 1283 of *LNCS*. Springer-Verlag, Heidelberg, Germany, 1997.
15. A. Sampaio. *An Algebraic Approach to Compiler Design*, volume 4 of *AMAST Series in Computing*. World Scientific, 1997.
16. R. Stärk, J. Schmid, and E. Börger. *Java and the Java Virtual Machine - Definition, Verification, Validation*. Springer-Verlag, 2001.
17. L. Wildman. A formal basis for a program compilation proof tool. In Lars-Henrik Eriksson and Peter Alexander Lindsay, editors, *FME2002: Formal Methods – Getting IT Right*, Copenhagen, Denmark, July 2002. International Symposium of Formal Methods Europe, Springer.

A Semantic Foundation for TCOZ in Unifying Theories of Programming

Shengchao Qin[1], Jin Song Dong[2], and Wei-Ngan Chin[1,2]

[1] Singapore-MIT Alliance, National University of Singapore
[2] School of Computing, National University o Singapore
{qinsc,dongjs,chinwn}@comp.nus.edu.sg

Abstract. Unifying Theories of Programming (UTP) can provide a formal semantic foundation not only for programming languages but also for more expressive specification languages. We believe UTP is particularly well suited for presenting the formal semantics for integrated specification languages which often have rich language constructs for state encapsulation, event communication and real-time modeling. This paper uses UTP to formalise the semantics of Timed Communicating Object Z (TCOZ) and captures some TCOZ new features for the first time. In particular, a novel unified semantic model of the channel based synchronisation and sensor/actuator based asynchronisation in TCOZ is presented. This semantic model will be used as a reference document for developing tools support for TCOZ and as a semantic foundation for proving soundness of those tools.

Keywords: UTP, semantics, integrated formal specifications

1 Introduction

Formal semantics of specification languages provide foundations for language understanding, reasoning and tools construction. Various formal specification languages are often integrated for modeling large and complex systems. The development of the formal semantics for those integrated formal specifications provides some challenges due to the richness of the language constructs that facilitate complex states encapsulation, communication and real-time modeling. Hoare and He's Unifying Theories of Programming (UTP) [6] can present formal semantics not only for programming languages but also for specification languages. We believe UTP is particularly well suited for giving formal semantics for the integrated specification languages. One integrated formal notation namely Timed Communicating Object Z (TCOZ) [8] builds on the strengths of Object-Z [4, 16] and Timed CSP [13, 2] notations in order to provide a single notation for modeling both the state and process aspects of complex systems. In addition to CSP's channel-based communication mechanism (where messages represent discrete synchronisations between processes), TCOZ has recently been extended with asynchronous interface inspired by process control theory, sensors and actuators [7]. Based on the infinite failure model of Timed CSP, an enhanced semantics for TCOZ has been proposed [9] where the process behavioural aspects are focused. However, other important aspects of TCOZ were left out. In particular, it does not cover the semantics of the asynchronous communication mechanism of sensors and actuators. It is difficult to extend that semantics to cover sensors and actuators because the meta framework used is based on events (channel), which is incompatible with the shared-variable nature of sensors and actuators.

This paper demonstrates how UTP can be used for constructing a formal observation-oriented model for TCOZ. In particular, a novel unified semantic model for both channel and sensors/actuators based communications is presented. This UTP model not only covers the TCOZ communication and process aspects, but also other features, such as class encapsulation, inheritance, dynamic binding and extended TCOZ timing constructs (deadline and waituntil commands), which have not been covered by the previous semantics. This semantic model will be used as a reference document and a semantic foundation for developing sound tools support for TCOZ. Our philosophy on tools support for integrated formal methods is to reuse/link existing tools especially graphical tools as much as possible. For example, one approach is to develop transformation rules from TCOZ to Timed Automata (TA) so that existing TA tools can be used to model check TCOZ timing properties, or to Message Sequence Chart (MSC) so that MSC tools can be used to analyse TCOZ's message passing and interaction behaviour. The proof of the soundness of those transformation rules can be based on this UTP semantic framework.

The remainder of the paper is organised as follows. Section 2 outlines the TCOZ syntax with a simple example. Section 3 starts with a brief introduction to UTP then presents the UTP observation model with meta variables. Section 4 develops the UTP semantics for TCOZ operations and processes. Section 5 presents the UTP semantics for TCOZ classes. Section 6 addresses related works with a conclusion and points out some future directions.

2 The TCOZ's Syntax and Example

The abstract syntax of TCOZ is given as follows.

```
Specification ::= CDecl; · · · ; CDecl
CDecl ::= ↾ VisibList; InheritC; StateSch; INIT; StaOp*; ProOp*; [MAIN]
VisibList ::= VisibAttr; VisibOp
VisibAttr ::= AttrName*
VisibOp ::= OpName*
InheritC ::= Inherits CName*
StateSch ::= VarDecl*; ChanDecl*; SenDecl*; ActDecl*
VarDecl ::= v : T
ChanDecl ::= ch : chan
SenDecl ::= sv : T sensor
ActDecl ::= sv : T actuator
StaOp ::= Δ(AttrName* | ActName*), VarDecl* • Pred(u,v')
ProOp ::= VarDecl* • Process
MAIN ::= Process
```

Process ::= Skip | Stop | Chaos (*primitives*)
  | StaOp (*state update*) | Comm → Process (*communication*)
  | b • Process (*state guard*) | Process ▷{t} Process (*timeout*)
  | WAIT t (*wait*) | Process • DEADLINE t (*deadline*)
  | Process • WAITUNTIL t (*waituntil*)
  | Process; Process (*sequential composition*)
  | Process☐Process (*external choice*)
  | Process ⊓ Process (*internal choice*)
  | Process |[E]| Process (*parallel composition*)
  | Process\E (*hiding*) | μX • Process (*recursion*)

Comm ::= ch!e (*chan. ouput*) | b • ch?x (*chan. input*) | b • sv?x (*sensor read*)

where b is a boolean condition, t is a time expression, E is a finite set of communication events, e is a message, and x is a variable.

Let us use a simple timed message queue system to illustrate the TCOZ notation. The behaviour of the following timed message queue system is that it can receive a new message (of type [*MSG*]) through an input channel '*in*' within a time duration 'T_j' or remove a message and send it through an output channel '*out*' within a time duration 'T_l'. If there is no interaction with environment within a certain time 'T_o', then a message will be removed from the current list but stored in a (window like) actuator list (*lost*) so that other objects (un-specified) with a sensor '*lost*' can read it at any time. The message queue has a FIFO property.

─── *TimedQueue* ──

items : seq *MSG* *in*, *out* : **chan** *lost* : seq *MSG* **actuator** T_l, T_j, T_o : $\mathbb{N}$	─ INIT ───────── *items* = *lost* = ⟨ ⟩
	─ *RecLost* ───── Δ(*lost*) *lost*′ = ⟨*head*(*items*)⟩⌢*lost*
─ *Add* ───── Δ(*items*) *i*? : *MSG* *items*′ = *items* ⌢ ⟨*i*?⟩	─ *Del* ───── Δ(*items*) *i*! : *MSG* *items* ≠ ⟨ ⟩ ⇒ *items* = ⟨*i*!⟩⌢*items*′ *items* = ⟨ ⟩ ⇒ *items*′ = ⟨ ⟩

Join ≙ [*i* : *MSG*] • *in*?*i* → *Add* • DEADLINE T_j
Leave ≙ [*items* ≠ ⟨ ⟩] • *out*!*head*(*items*) → *Del* • DEADLINE T_l
MAIN ≙ μQ • (*Join* ☐ *Leave*) ▷{T_o} (*RecLost*; *Del*) • DEADLINE T_l; Q

3 The UTP Observation Model

In the Unifying Theories of Programming (UTP), the relational/predicate calculus is adopted as a fundamental basis for unifying various programming theories across three dimensions: different computational paradigms, different levels of abstraction, and distinct mathematical representations. For each programming paradigm, specifications, designs, and programs are all interpreted as relations between an initial observation and a subsequent (intermediate stable or final) observation of the behaviour of their executions. Program correctness and refinement calculus can be represented by inclusion of relations. All the laws in a relational calculus are also valid in reasoning about correctness in all theories and languages.

Formal theories differ from one another by their alphabet, signature, and healthiness conditions. The *alphabet* of a theory is just a set of names used to record external observations of the behaviour. The names for initial observations are undecorated, whereas the names for subsequent observations are primed. The *signature* gives the way to represent the elements of the theory by taking primitives directly as elements and using operations to construct elements in an inductive manner. The *healthiness conditions* help filter out required elements for a sub-theory from those of a larger theory in which it is embedded. For example, in a top-down design process, programs are just a subset of intermediate designs, while designs are a subset of specifications.

To give a semantic model for the timed communicating language TCOZ, we need to choose an appropriate model of time. There are two typical models: a discrete model and a continuous one. The continuous model is very expressive and closer to the nature of real time. However, it is difficult to implement exactly for digital computer systems. On the other hand, the discrete model is implementable and closer to an untimed model. Timed CSP has a denotational semantics based on continuous time [2], and the existing semantics for TCOZ also adopts the continuous model [9]. However, to follow the objective of making our model simple and apt for exploration of algebraic refinement laws, we choose the discrete model. The discrete time model has also been adopted by the Sherif and He's work [14] on the semantics for timed Circus [17], which naturally extends Woodcock and Cavalcanti's semantics for Circus [18]. Although the general approach of the timed Circus semantics is adopted in our UTP semantic model for TCOZ processes, our semantic model contains many new aspects especially the formal treatment of both channel and sensor/actuator communication interfaces.

3.1 The Meta Process Model and Variables

TCOZ is mainly used to specify complex reactive systems. The behaviour of such a system can be modeled by observations of two kinds. The initial observation reflects the state of the system when the system starts to run. The follow-up observation records the state of the system when the system reaches a stable state. A stable state is either a termination state, in which the system terminates and the corresponding observation is called the final observation, or an intermediate waiting state, in which the system has no interaction with its environment and does not have infinite internal active events (not divergent) [6].

The process model starts with the above observations: at the initial and final (or intermediate stable) states of the system. Due to the timing feature of TCOZ, the observations on the interactions with the environment are enriched by adding time information. The existing model for Timed CSP and TCOZ attaches an explicit time stamp on each observation. The discrete model of time allows us to add time information implicitly. The interactions of a system with its environment are recorded as a sequence of tuples, each element of the sequence representing the observations over a single time unit. The first component of the tuple is a sequence of communication events or shared-variable updates which occur during a time unit. The second component represents a set of refused events (refusal) at the end of the time unit.

The following meta variables are introduced in the alphabet of the observations of the TCOZ process behaviour, some of them are similar to those in the previous UTP semantic frameworks [6, 14, 18]. The key difference is that timed trace has now been encoded with a set of shared-variable updates (due to sensors/actuators).

- ok, ok' : Boolean. In order to analyse explicitly the phenomena of process initiation and termination, these variables are introduced to denote these observations.
  ok records the observation that the process has started. When ok is *false*, the process has not started, so no observation can be made.
  ok' records the observation that the process has terminated or has reached an intermediate stable state. The process is divergent when ok' is *false*.
- $wait, wait'$: Boolean. Because of the requirement for synchronisation, an active process will usually engage in alternate periods of internal activity (computation) and periods of quiescence or stability, while it is waiting for a reaction or an acknowledgement from its environment. We therefore introduce a variable $wait'$, which is *true* just when a process is waiting in such quiescent periods. Its main purpose is to distinguish intermediate observations from the observations made on termination. $wait$ is used in the initial observation, which is *true* when the process starts in an intermediate state.
- $state, state'$: Var $\to$ Value. In order to record the state of data variables (class attributes/local variables) that occur in a process, these two variables are introduced to associate resp. every variable with its value in the corresponding observations.
- tr, tr' : seq(seq($Event \cup Update$) $\times \mathbb{P}\, Event$). Each of these two variables records a sequence of observations on the process's interactions with its environment. tr records the observations that occur before the process starts, and tr' records the observations that take place so far. Each element of the sequence denotes the observations over one time unit, which is specified by a tuple. The first component of the tuple is the sequence of communication events or updates on sensor-actuator variables that occur during the time unit, the second is an associated set of refusals at the end of the time unit.
  The set *Event* denotes all possible communicating events. The set *Update*, defined as $Update =_{df} ((SV \to Value) \times Tag)$, represents the set of all possible updates (states) of all sensor-actuator variables (SV). The binary set $Tag =_{df} \{0, 1\}$ shows which process is making the current update: 1 indicates that current update is made by the current process, whereas 0 indicates that current update is due to an environmental process.
- $trace$: seq($Event \cup Update$). This variable is used to record a sequence of events/updates that take place so far since the last observation. It can be derived from tr, tr' by taking their difference as follows:

    $flat(tr) \frown trace = flat(tr')$, where $\frown$ is the concatenation operator, and
    $flat$: seq(seq($Event \cup Update$) $\times \mathbb{P}\, Event$) $\to$ seq($Event \cup Update$)

$$flat(\langle\rangle) =_{df} \langle\rangle \qquad flat(\langle(es, ref)\rangle \frown tr) =_{df} es \frown flat(tr)$$

Two auxiliary functions $cs(trace), ds(trace)$ are adopted to extract resp. the subsequences of communication events and shared-variable states from the sequence $trace$. The function cs is defined as

$$cs(\langle\rangle) =_{df} \langle\rangle \qquad cs(\langle e\rangle \frown tail) =_{df} \begin{cases} \langle e\rangle \frown cs(tail), & \text{if } e \in Event, \\ cs(tail), & \text{otherwise.} \end{cases}$$

The function ds can be defined similarly.
- $gs : \text{SV} \to \text{Value}$. This variable is used to hold the latest updated state of all shared sensor-actuator variables.

In our semantics model, the observation-based semantics for a TCOZ process will be described by a predicate whose alphabet contains the above variables [6].

A binary relation $\stackrel{t}{\preceq}$ is defined over two sequences of observations as follows.

$$tr_1 \stackrel{t}{\preceq} tr_2 =_{df} (front(tr_1) \preceq tr_2) \wedge (\pi_1(last(tr_1)) \preceq \pi_1(tr_2(\#tr_1)))$$

where $\preceq$ is the ordinary subsequence relation between sequences of the same type. $front(tr)$ is the initial part of tr obtained by dropping those observations recorded in last time unit. $last(tr)$ gets the last element of the sequence tr. $\pi_1(tup)$ returns the first component of the tuple tup. $\#tr$ is the number of elements in tr, while $tr(n)$ returns the nth element.

This definition states that, given two timed traces, tr_1 and tr_2, tr_2 is an expansion of tr_1, if the initial part of tr_1 is a subsequence of tr_2, and the untimed traces recorded at the last time unit of tr_1 is a subsequence of the untimed traces at the same time in tr_2.

Since the execution of a process can never *undo* any action performed previously, each trace can only get longer. The current value of tr must therefore always be an expansion of its initial value. Hereby, the semantics predicate P for any process P should satisfy the healthiness condition **R** defined as follows:

$$\mathbf{R}(P) =_{df} P = (P \wedge tr \stackrel{t}{\preceq} tr')$$

3.2 The Class Model

TCOZ has two kinds of classes, active and passive ones. The behaviour of (an object of) an active class can be specified by a record of its continuous interactions with its environment via its MAIN process, whereby any update on its data state is hidden. Passive class does not have its own thread of control and its state and operations (processes) are available for use by its controlling object. We model an active class as a predicate with an assumption and a commitment (also known as design in [6]), and a passive class as a service provider, which provides a set of services to its environment.

In order to address issues like class encapsulation and dynamic typing that are essential for object-orientation, the following TCOZ features are considered in the UTP model.

1. An object-oriented specification contains not only variables of simple types but also objects. To ensure a legal access to a variable, the model is equipped with a set of visible attributes/operations.
2. Due to the subclass mechanism, an object can lie in a subclass of its originally declared one. Therefore, the behaviour of its operations will depend on its current type. To support such a dynamic binding mechanism for operation calls, our model keeps track of the dynamic type for each object. This enables us to validate operations in a framework where the type of each variable is properly recorded.
3. A value of an object variable is a finite tuple, which may record the current type of the object, and the values of its attributes. Since an object may contain attributes of object types, its value is often defined with nested recursions.

In order to address the above issues clearly, the following meta variables are introduced to keep track of the class information.

- *CN* and *super* are used to record the contextual information on classes and their relationships. *CN* is the set of classes already declared, *super* is a partial function which maps a class to the set of its direct superclasses. For example, $C_1 \in super(C_2)$ states that C_1 is a direct superclass of C_2. C is a *superclass* of C' if there exists a finite sequence of classes $C_0, \cdots, C_n$, such that $C = C_n$ and $C' = C_0$ and $C_{i+1} \in super(C_i)$ for all $0 \leqslant i < n$. We use the set $super^+(C)$ to denote all superclasses of C, and $super^*(C)$ to present all superclasses of C and itself. Note that $super^*(C) =_{df} super^+(C) \cup \{C\}$.
- For each class $C \in CN$, we use the following notations to denote its structure and record different variables involved in its specification.
  - The set of state attributes of class C, $attr(C) = \{\langle a_1 : T_1 \rangle, \cdots, \langle a_m : T_m \rangle\}$, comprises both the attributes declared in C and those that C inherits from its superclasses, where T_i stands for the type of attribute a_i of class C, and will be referred by $type(C.a_i)$. The set of channels declared in class C is denoted by $chan(C) = \{ch_1, \cdots, ch_n : \mathbf{chan}\}$.
  - The set of operations declared or inherited by C, $op(C) = op_s(C) \cup op_p(C)$. It is composed of a set of state operations ($op_s(C)$) and a set of process operations ($op_p(C)$).
  - *senvar, actvar*: the set of sensor and actuator variables declared in current class or inherited from its superclasses. They provide an interface between the control system and its controlled system.
  - *locvar*: the set of local definitions, $\{v_1 : T_1, \cdots, v_m : T_m\}$;
  - *visibattr, visibop*: the set of visible state attributes and visible operations.

For notational convenience, we assume the following four sets of names are pairwise disjoint: classes, attributes, operations and (local or shared) variables.

A state binds variables to their current values. A variable of a primitive data type can take any value of that type. The value of an object variable is composed of the values of its attributes together with its current type (as in [5]):

$$\{a \mapsto value \mid a \in attr(C)\} \cup \{myclass \mapsto C\}$$

In what follows, we investigate the observation-based semantics of TCOZ processes, and as well explore some associated algebraic laws. After that, we formalise the TCOZ class semantics. Following the notation style in UTP [6], we adopt the italic format to represent semantic notations (e.g., predicates), whereas we use the sans serif format to denote syntactic notations (e.g., specifications) in this paper. For instance, the semantics of a process P is simply represented by a predicate P, rather than $[\![P]\!]$.

4 Process Semantics

In this section, the observation model for TCOZ processes is developed. Some process models that are similar to [14] are moved to the Appendix.

4.1 Communication

This subsection is devoted to communications. Other primitives Chaos, Skip and Stop are presented in the Appendix.

A synchronisation ch.e can take place only if an output event ch!e is ready, an input event b • ch?x is also ready, and the message to be passed satisfies the condition b.

In order to describe the behaviour of these two primitives, we introduce two auxiliary predicates, $com\_blk(ch)$ and $com\_syn(ch)$, to represent the waiting behaviour for communication and the synchronised communication respectively.

$$com\_blk(ch) =_{df} ok' \land wait' \land no\_interact(trace) \land not\_ref(tr, tr', ch)$$
$$com\_syn(ch.e) =_{df} ok' \land \neg wait' \land trace = \langle ch.e \rangle \land \#tr' = \#tr$$

Note that predicate $not\_ref(tr, tr', ch)$ is true if any events with respect to channel ch do not occur in the refusals of the observations recorded from tr to tr'.

$$not\_ref(tr, tr', ch) =_{df} \forall n : \#tr \leq n \leq \#tr' \bullet ch \notin \pi_2(tr'(n))$$

The predicate $no\_interact(trace)$ denotes that there are no communication events recorded in $trace$, while the shared-variable updates recorded in $trace$ (if any) are due to the environmental process. That is, for any $s \in seq(Event \times Update)$,

$$no\_interact(s) =_{df} cs(s) = \langle\rangle \land \forall u \in ds(s) \bullet \pi_2(u) = 0$$

An output primitive ch!e stays in a waiting state before some other process becomes ready to receive a message via the channel ch, or finishes the communication instantaneously once the receiver is ready.

$$ch!e =_{df} com\_blk(ch) \lor (com\_blk(ch) \circ (com\_syn(ch.e) \land state' = state))$$

where the operator ∘ is the composition of two sequentially made observations. For two observation predicates $P(\underline{v}, \underline{v}'), Q(\underline{v}, \underline{v}')$, where $\underline{v}, \underline{v}'$ represent respectively the initial and final versions of all observation variables, the composition of them is

$$P(\underline{v}, \underline{v}') \circ Q(\underline{v}, \underline{v}') =_{df} \exists \underline{v}_0 \bullet P(\underline{v}, \underline{v}_0) \land Q(\underline{v}_0, \underline{v}')$$

Note that the final observation from P coincides with the initial observation from Q.

For the input primitive b • ch?x, if the message to be passed does not satisfy the condition b, it results in deadlock. Once this communication occurs, the value passed along the channel will be assigned to the variable x and recorded in the state.

$$b \bullet ch?x =_{df} com\_blk(ch) \lor (com\_blk(ch) \circ \\ (b[e/x] \land com\_syn(ch.e) \land state' = state \oplus \{x \mapsto e\} \lor \\ \neg b[e/x] \land Stop))$$

The guarded sensor read command b(x) • sv?x is defined in terms of the following recursive process. Intuitively, it consecutively reads values from the sensor (once per time unit) until the sensed value meets the guard.

$$b(x) \bullet sv?x =_{df} \mu X \bullet sv?x \to ((b(x) \bullet Skip) \Box (\neg b(x) \bullet (\text{WAIT } 1; X)))$$

where the simple read sv?x obtains the latest value of the sensor-actuator variable sv.

$$sv?x =_{df} ok' \land \neg wait' \land tr' = tr \land state' = state \oplus \{x \mapsto gs(sv)\}$$

The simple prefix process Comm→ P is explained as a sequential composition of the communication behaviour and the behaviour of the process that follows.

$$Comm \to P =_{df} Comm; P$$

Semantics for sequential composition is presented in the Appendix.

4.2 State Operation

There are two kind of state operations, one only updates the local state of the current class, whereas the other updates the global state, i.e., the sensor-actuator variables that it is in charge of.

Local State Update. A local state operation $\Delta(\underline{y}), \underline{x} : \underline{T} \bullet Pred(\underline{u}, \underline{v}')$ enlarges the state with its local definitions and updates the state afterwards.

$$\Delta(\underline{y}), \underline{x} : \underline{T} \bullet Pred(\underline{u}, \underline{v}') =_{df} ok' \land \neg wait' \land no\_interact(trace) \land \\ ((\exists \underline{val}_1 \bullet state' = state \oplus \{\underline{x} \mapsto \underline{val}_1\}) \circ \\ (\exists \underline{val} \bullet state' = state \oplus \{\underline{v} \mapsto \underline{val}\} \land Pred(state(\underline{u}), state'(\underline{v}))))$$

Actuator Update. An actuator update operation $\Delta(\underline{sv}), \underline{x} : \underline{T} \bullet Pred(\underline{u}, \underline{sv}, \underline{sv}')$ specifies that expected values can be assigned to the sensor-actuator variables $\underline{sv}$.

$$\Delta(\underline{sv}), \underline{x} : \underline{T} \bullet Pred(\underline{u}, \underline{sv}, \underline{sv}') =_{df} ok' \land \neg wait' \land \#tr' = \#tr \land \\ \exists \underline{val} \bullet gs' = gs \oplus \{\underline{sv} \mapsto \underline{val}\} \land ((\exists \underline{val}_1 \bullet state' = state \oplus \{\underline{x} \mapsto \underline{val}_1\}) \circ \\ Pred(state(\underline{u}), gs(\underline{sv}), gs'(\underline{sv}))) \land trace = \langle (gs', 1) \rangle$$

where gs and gs' indicate the value of the variable gs resp. before and after the update.

In our model, consecutive actuator update operations are combined into one atomic update operation. Therefore, the above update list can be a list of actuator variables.

4.3 Timeout Process

The timeout process P ▷{t} Q behaves as P if P has no interaction with the environment at all but terminates within time t, or it reacts to the environment within time t, otherwise it behaves as Q.

$P \triangleright \{t\} \; Q =_{df} (P \wedge \mathit{no\_interact}(\mathit{trace}) \wedge \#tr' - \#tr \leqslant t) \vee$
$(\exists k : \#tr < k \leqslant \#tr+t, \exists \tilde{tr} \bullet \pi_1(tr'(k)) \neq \langle\rangle \wedge tr \preceq \tilde{tr} \wedge \#\tilde{tr} - \#tr = k \wedge$
$(\forall i : \#tr < i < \#tr+k \bullet \mathit{no\_interact}(\pi_1(tr'(i))) \wedge \tilde{tr}(i) = tr'(i)) \wedge P[\tilde{tr}/tr]) \vee$
$(\exists \tilde{tr} \bullet tr \preceq \tilde{tr} \wedge \#\tilde{tr} - \#tr = t \wedge$
$(\forall i : \#tr < i < \#tr+t \bullet \mathit{no\_interact}(\pi_1(tr'(i))) \wedge \tilde{tr}(i) = tr'(i)) \wedge Q[\tilde{tr}/tr])$

If P is ready to react to the environment exactly when it has waited for time t, the timeout process chooses P or Q non-deterministically.

The following are some algebraic laws that can be derived from our semantic definition. For simplicity, the proofs are omitted.

T1. P ▷{t} P = P
T2. Skip ▷{t} P = Skip
T3. (a → P) ▷{t} (b → P) = ((a → Skip) ▷{t} (b → Skip)); P
T4. P ▷{t} (Q ⊓ R) = (P ▷{t} Q) ⊓ (P ▷{t} R)
T5. (P ⊓ Q) ▷{t} R = (P ▷{t} R) ⊓ (Q ▷{t} R)

4.4 Wait

The process WAIT t just waits for t time units to pass before terminating immediately. It can be defined as follows in terms of timeout construct defined in section 4.3.

$\mathit{Wait} \; t =_{df} \mathit{Stop} \triangleright \{t\} \; \mathit{Skip}$

It is subject to the following laws.

W1. WAIT t_1; WAIT t_2 = WAIT $(t_1 + t_2)$
W2. (WAIT t_1) ‖E‖ (WAIT t_2) = WAIT $(\max(t_1, t_2))$
W3. Stop ▷{t} P = WAIT t; P

4.5 Deadline

The *Deadline* construct P • DEADLINE t imposes a timing constraint on a specification P, which requires the computation of P to be finished within time t.

$P \bullet \mathit{Deadline} \; t =_{df} P \wedge (\#tr' - \#tr \leqslant t)$

It enjoys the following properties.

D1. P • DEADLINE t_1 • DEADLINE t_2 = P • DEADLINE $\min(t_1, t_2)$
D2. (P ⊓ Q) • DEADLINE t = (P • DEADLINE t) ⊓ (Q • DEADLINE t)

4.6 WaitUntil

In case that P terminates within time t, the *WaitUntil* construct P • WAITUNTIL t has to keep waiting after the termination of P until t time units have passed.

$$P \bullet \textit{WaitUntil } t =_{df} (\exists \tilde{tr}' \bullet tr \preceq \tilde{tr}' \preceq tr' \wedge (\#\tilde{tr}' - \#tr < t) \wedge \\ (P[\tilde{tr}'/tr', true/ok', false/wait'] \circ \\ (\textit{Wait } (t - (\#\tilde{tr}' - \#tr))[\tilde{tr}/tr]))) \vee P \wedge (\#tr' - \#tr \geqslant t)$$

It enjoys the following properties.

U1. P • WAITUNTIL t_1 • WAITUNTIL t_2 = P • WAITUNTIL $\max(t_1, t_2)$
U2. (P ⊓ Q) • WAITUNTIL t = (P • WAITUNTIL t) ⊓ (Q • WAITUNTIL t)

4.7 State-Guarded Process

The state-guarded process b • P behaves as P if the condition b is initially satisfied, otherwise it waits for ever (like the process Stop).

$$b \bullet P =_{df} b \wedge P \vee \neg b \wedge \textit{Stop}$$

It satisfies the following properties.

G1. *false* • P = Stop
G2. *true* • P = P
G3. b • Stop = Stop
G4. b • (c • P) = (b ∧ c) • P
G5. b • (P; Q) = (b • P); Q

4.8 Parallel Composition

The parallel composition of two processes represents all the possible behaviours of both processes which are not only synchronised on a specific set of events and on the time when these events occur, but also coincide with each other on the state of sensor-actuator variables at each update. The overall process will terminate when both component processes do.

The parallel composition is defined in terms of the general parallel merge operator $\|_M$ in UTP [6], where the predicate M denotes the way to merge two observations.

In the following definition, our new merge predicate $M(E)$ is in charge of both channel based communications and shared-variable updates, due to the existence of two distinct communication mechanisms (channel and sensor/actuator) in TCOZ.

$$P \, \|[E]\| \, Q =_{df} (((P; \textit{idle}) \, \|_{M(E)} \, Q) \vee (P \, \|_{M(E)} \, (Q; \textit{idle}))); \\ ((ok \Rightarrow \textit{Skip}) \wedge (\neg ok \Rightarrow tr \stackrel{t}{\preceq} tr'))$$

An *idle* process, which may either wait or terminate, follows after each of the two processes. This is to allow each of the processes to wait for its partner to terminate.

$$\textit{idle} =_{df} ok' \wedge \textit{no\_interact}(\textit{trace}) \wedge \textit{state}' = \textit{state}$$

The merge predicate $M(E)$ is defined as

$$M(E) =_{df} ok' = (0.ok \wedge 1.ok) \wedge wait' = (0.wait \vee 1.wait) \wedge \\ state' = (0.state \oplus 1.state) \wedge \\ tr' \in syn(0.tr, 1.tr, E) \wedge \#tr' = \#0.tr = \#1.tr \wedge \\ \forall i : \#tr..\#tr' \bullet consistent(ds(\pi_1(0.tr(i))), ds(\pi_1(1.tr(i))))$$

Given two timed traces tr_1, tr_2, and a set of events E, the set $syn(tr_1, tr_2, E)$ is defined inductively as follows.

$$syn(tr_1, tr_2, E) =_{df} syn(tr_2, tr_1, E)$$
$$syn(\langle\rangle, \langle\rangle, E) =_{df} \{\langle\rangle\}$$
$$syn(\langle(t,r)\rangle, \langle\rangle, E) =_{df} \{\langle(t',r)\rangle \mid t' \in (t \underset{E\ U}{\|} \langle\rangle)\}$$
$$syn(\langle(t_1,r_1)\rangle \frown tr_1, \langle(t_2,r_2)\rangle \frown tr_2, E) =_{df}$$
$$\{\langle(t',r')\rangle \frown u \mid t' \in (t_1 \underset{E\ U}{\|} t_2) \wedge r' = r_1 \cup r_2 \wedge u \in syn(tr_1, tr_2, E)\}$$

The predicate $consistent(s_1, s_2)$ specifies that two sequences of updates on shared variables are consistent. It is used in the above definition to ensure that two individual records of shared-variable updates coincide with each other in every time unit.

$$consistent(s_1, s_2) =_{df} \#s_1 = \#s_2 \wedge \forall i : 1..\#s_1 \bullet (\pi_1(s_1(i)) = \pi_1(s_2(i)) \wedge \\ \pi_2(s_1(i)) + \pi_2(s_2(i)) \neq 2)$$

$s \underset{E\ U}{\|} t$ is used to merge untimed traces s and t into one untimed trace, where E is the set of events to be synchronised, U is the set of possible shared-variable updates. In comparison to Roscoe's model for the parallel merge of untimed traces [12], the following definition is more sophisticated as it also captures the shared variable communications. In the following clauses, e, e_1, e_2 are representative elements of E (events), u, u_1, u_2 are representative elements of U (updates), whereas x, x_1, x_2 represent communication events not residing in E.

$$s \underset{E\ U}{\|} t =_{df} t \underset{E\ U}{\|} s \qquad \langle\rangle \underset{E\ U}{\|} \langle\rangle =_{df} \{\langle\rangle\} \qquad \langle e \rangle \underset{E\ U}{\|} \langle\rangle =_{df} \{\}$$
$$\langle u \rangle \underset{E\ U}{\|} \langle\rangle =_{df} \{\} \qquad \langle x \rangle \underset{E\ U}{\|} \langle\rangle =_{df} \{\langle x \rangle\}$$
$$\langle x \rangle \frown s \underset{E\ U}{\|} \langle e \rangle \frown t =_{df} \{\langle x \rangle \frown l \mid l \in (s \underset{E\ U}{\|} \langle e \rangle \frown t)\}$$
$$\langle e \rangle \frown s \underset{E\ U}{\|} \langle e \rangle \frown t =_{df} \{\langle e \rangle \frown l \mid l \in (s \underset{E\ U}{\|} t)\}$$
$$\langle e_1 \rangle \frown s \underset{E\ U}{\|} \langle e_2 \rangle \frown t =_{df} \{\}, \text{ where } e_1 \neq e_2$$
$$\langle u_1 \rangle \frown s \underset{E\ U}{\|} \langle u_2 \rangle \frown t =_{df} \begin{cases} \{\}, & \text{if } \neg consistent(\langle u_1 \rangle, \langle u_2 \rangle) \\ \{u \frown l \mid join(\langle u \rangle, \langle u_1 \rangle, \langle u_2 \rangle) \wedge l \in (s \underset{E\ U}{\|} t)\}, & \text{otherwise} \end{cases}$$
$$\langle x \rangle \frown s \underset{E\ U}{\|} \langle u \rangle \frown t =_{df} \{\langle x \rangle \frown l \mid l \in (s \underset{E\ U}{\|} \langle u \rangle \frown t)\}$$
$$\langle e \rangle \frown s \underset{E\ U}{\|} \langle u \rangle \frown t =_{df} \{\}$$
$$\langle x_1 \rangle \frown s \underset{E\ U}{\|} \langle x_2 \rangle \frown t =_{df} \{\langle x_1 \rangle \frown l \mid l \in (s \underset{E\ U}{\|} \langle x_2 \rangle \frown t)\} \cup \{\langle x_2 \rangle \frown l \mid l \in (\langle x_1 \rangle \frown s \underset{E\ U}{\|} t)\}$$

The predicate $join(s, s_1, s_2)$ merges two consistent sequences of updates (s_1 and s_2) into one overall sequence (s).

$$join(s, s_1, s_2) =_{df} consistent(s_1, s_2) \land \#s = \#s_1 \land$$
$$\forall i : 1..\#s_1 \bullet (\pi_1(s(i)) = \pi_1(s_1(i)) \land$$
$$\pi_2(s(i)) = \pi_2(s_1(i)) + \pi_2(s_2(i)))$$

The following are some properties that parallel composition owns.

P1. Chaos $\|[E]\|$ P = Chaos
P2. Stop $\|[E]\|$ P = Stop
P3. P $\|[E]\|$ Q = Q $\|[E]\|$ P
P4. P $\|[E_1]\|$ (Q $\|[E_2]\|$ R) = (P $\|[E_1]\|$ Q) $\|[E_2]\|$ R
P5. P $\|[E]\|$ (Q ⊓ R) = (P $\|[E]\|$ Q) ⊓ (P $\|[E]\|$ R)

Definitions for *sequential composition, internal/external choices, recursion*, and *hiding* are presented in the Appendix, which are similar to the definitions in [14].

5 Class Semantics

This section aims to deal with class declarations, their well-definedness and their composition.

Given a class declaration *cdecl* as follows.

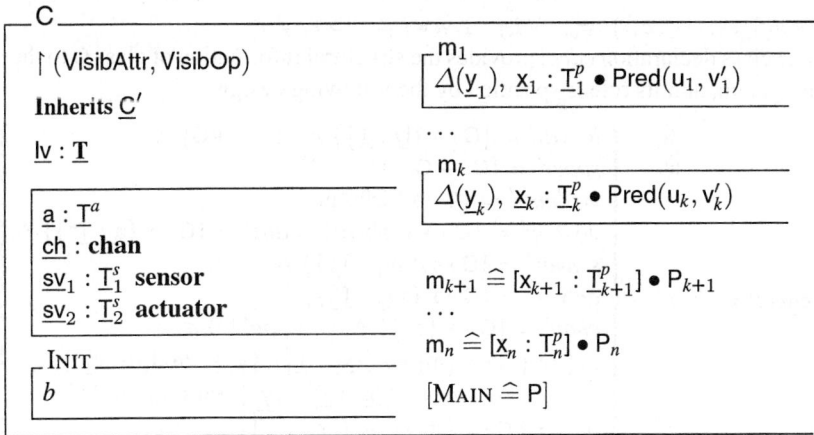

where

- C is the name of the class which is declared as a direct subclass of classes $\underline{C'}$.
- The names of visible attributes and operations are listed in VisibList(resp. in VisibAttr and VisibOp).
- $m_1, \cdots, m_n$ are operations declared in C. $\Delta(\underline{y_i})$ states that only attributes (or actuators) $\underline{y_i}$ can be modified by m_i. $\underline{x_i} : \underline{T_i^p}$ are the parameters of the operation m_i. The set of operations is divided into two parts, the first part, $m_1, \cdots, m_k$, called *state*

operations, represent operations in Object-Z style, where the body is specified by a predicate. The second part, $m_{k+1}, \cdots, m_n$, called *process operations*, are operations in process style, where the body is specified by a process.
- the MAIN operation is optional. If it is present in the definition, the class is called an *active* class. Otherwise, it is called a *passive* class.

We first discuss the passive class where the MAIN operation is absent. A passive class declaration *cdecl* is well-defined, denoted by $w\mathcal{D}(cdecl)$, if it satisfies the following conditions: (1) C is distinct from $\underline{C}'$, (2) the following names are distinct: local variables, state attributes, channels, sensors, actuators, operations, operation parameters, (3) each state operation can only modify the attributes or actuators in its Δ-list, (4) the VisibAttr and VisibOp are resp. subsets of the attributes and operations declared in the current class or inherited from its superclasses, (5) each Δ-list in state operations should be names of attributes or actuators (declared in current class or inherited from superclasses), (6) the set of sensors and the set of actuators should also include those inherited from superclasses. The last three conditions cannot be tested based on an individual class declaration, but can be checked at the end of all class declarations. Formally, the well-definedness of the above class declaration given for C is defined by the following predicate.

$$w\mathcal{D} =_{df} \left\{ \begin{array}{l} C \notin \{\underline{C}'\} \wedge type(\underline{a}) = \underline{T}^a \wedge \#\underline{a} = \#\underline{T}^a \wedge type(\underline{lv}) = \underline{T} \wedge \#\underline{lv} = \#\underline{T} \\ type(\underline{sv}_1) = \underline{T}_1^s \wedge \#\underline{sv}_1 = \#\underline{T}_1^s \wedge type(\underline{sv}_2) = \underline{T}_2^s \wedge \#\underline{sv}_2 = \#\underline{T}_2^s \wedge \\ \forall i \bullet (dif(\langle \underline{lv} \rangle \frown \langle \underline{a} \rangle \frown \langle \underline{ch} \rangle \frown \langle \underline{sv}_1 \rangle \frown \langle \underline{sv}_2 \rangle \frown \langle m_1, \cdots, m_n \rangle \frown \langle \underline{x}_i \rangle) \\ \wedge \#\underline{x}_i = \#\underline{T}_i^p) \wedge \forall i : 1..k \bullet \{v_i\} \subseteq \{\underline{y}_i\} \cup \{\underline{x}_i\} \end{array} \right\}$$

where $dif(\langle e_1, \cdots, e_n \rangle) =_{df} \forall i,j : 1..n \bullet i \neq j \Rightarrow e_i \neq e_j$.

The class declaration *cdecl* provides the structural information of class C to the state of the system, and its role is specified by the following design.

$$cdecl =_{df} w\mathcal{D} \vdash \left\{ \begin{array}{l} locvar' = \{C \mapsto \{\underline{lv} : \underline{T}\}\} \wedge CN' = \{C\} \wedge \\ super' = \{C \mapsto C_i \mid C_i \in \underline{C}'\} \wedge \\ visibattr' = \{C \mapsto \text{VisibAttr}\} \wedge \\ visibop' = \{C \mapsto \text{VisibOp}\} \wedge attr' = \{C \mapsto \{\underline{a} : \underline{T}^a\}\} \wedge \\ senvar' = \{C \mapsto \{\underline{sv}_1 : \underline{T}_1^s\}\} \wedge \\ actvar' = \{C \mapsto \{\underline{sv}_2 : \underline{T}_2^s\}\} \wedge \\ chan' = \{C \mapsto \{\underline{ch}\}\} \wedge op' = op'_s \cup op'_p \wedge \\ op'_s = \{C \mapsto \{m_1 \mapsto (\langle \underline{x}_1 : \underline{T}_1^p \rangle, \{\underline{y}_1\}, \text{Pred}(u_1, v'_1)), \\ \quad \cdots, m_k \mapsto (\langle \underline{x}_k : \underline{T}_k^p \rangle, \{\underline{y}_k\}, \text{Pred}(u_k, v'_k))\}\} \wedge \\ op'_p = \{C \mapsto \{m_{k+1} \mapsto (\langle \underline{x}_{k+1} : \underline{T}_{k+1}^p \rangle, P_{k+1}), \\ \quad \cdots, m_n \mapsto (\langle \underline{x}_n : \underline{T}_n^p \rangle, P_n)\}\} \end{array} \right\}$$

The design $P \vdash Q =_{df} ok \wedge P \Rightarrow ok' \wedge Q$ as in UTP [6].

The above environment generated by an individual class declaration *cdecl*, only records the names of those variables, attributes and operations. The complete information will be generated at the end of the class declaration section when class dependencies are also available.

The well-definedness of the operation bodies can not be determined by the *individual* class declaration itself, and it will be defined at the end of all class declarations. As a result, the logic variable $op(C)$ binds each operation m_i to its body rather than its meaning. The meaning of m_i will be calculated at the end of the declarations.

We now turn our attention to active classes. The MAIN operation is used to determine the behaviour of objects of an active class after initialisation. Objects of an active class have their own thread of control and their mutable state attributes and operation definitions are fully encapsulated. This condition should be reflected in the well-definedness of the definition of an active class.

Suppose the MAIN process is present in the above definition $cdecl$ for class C. The well-definedness is specified by

$$w\mathcal{D}(cdecl) =_{df} w\mathcal{D} \land \mathsf{VisibAttr} = \emptyset \land \mathsf{VisibOp} = \{\mathrm{MAIN}\}$$

where the predicate $w\mathcal{D}$ is defined as above.

The MAIN operation part: $\mathrm{MAIN} \mapsto (b \bullet \mathsf{P})$ should be added into the value of the logic variable $op_p(C)$ in the above definition of the design $cdecl$, where b is the condition declared in INIT schema. However, when we calculate the set of process operations for a class later, MAIN is implicitly removed from the set of process operations of any of its active superclass, since TCOZ does not allow MAIN process to be inherited.

5.1 Composing Class Declarations

All class definitions $cdecls$ for a specification is a composition of a number of class declarations

$$cdecls =_{df} cdecl_1; \cdots; cdecl_k$$

Based on these complete definitions, we derive the whole context information for the specification by composing all the class declarations. This is done by simply adding up the contents of the current environment generated by the component class declarations provided that there is no redefinition of a class in its scope. It is also defined by the parallel merge operator:

$$cdecl_1; cdecl_2 =_{df} cdecl_1 \|_M cdecl_2$$

where the merge predicate M is defined as the following design

$$M =_{df} (CN_1 \cap CN_2 = \emptyset) \vdash \left\{ \begin{array}{l} CN' = CN_1 \cup CN_2 \land \\ super' = super_1 \cup super_2 \land \\ visibattr' = visibattr_1 \cup visibattr_2 \land \\ visibop' = visibop_1 \cup visibop_2 \land \\ locvar' = locvar_1 \cup locvar_2 \land \\ senvar' = senvar_1 \cup senvar_2 \land \\ actvar' = actvar_1 \cup actvar_2 \land \\ attr' = attr_1 \cup attr_2 \land op' = op'_s \cup op'_p \land \\ op'_s = op_{s1} \cup op_{s2} \land op'_p = op_{p1} \cup op_{p2} \end{array} \right\}$$

5.2 Well-Definedness of the Class Declarations

A sequence of class declarations for a specification is well-defined if the contents of the environment it has generated meet the following well-definedness conditions:

- The visible attributes (resp. operations) declared in a class should be members of the state attributes (resp. operations) in the current class or in any of its superclasses.

$$WD_1 =_{df} \forall C \in CN \bullet \text{VisibAttr}(C) \subseteq attr(super^*(C)) \\ \wedge \text{VisibOp}(C) \subseteq op(super^*(C))$$

where $super^*(C)$ is composed of all superclasses of C and C itself as before, and

$$attr(\{C_1, \cdots, C_n\}) =_{df} \bigcup_{i:1..n} attr(C_i), \quad op(\{C_1, \cdots, C_n\}) =_{df} \bigcup_{i:1..n} op(C_i)$$

- Multiple inheritances are allowed in TCOZ. However, distinct direct superclasses of any class are not permitted to have any common process operations (i.e. process operations with the same name and signature).

$$WD_2 =_{df} \forall C \in CN \bullet \#super(C) > 1 \Rightarrow (\forall C_1, C_2 \in super(C) \bullet \\ (C_1 \neq C_2 \Rightarrow dom(op_p(super^*(C_1))) \cap dom(op_p(super^*(C_2))) = \emptyset \\ \wedge \pi_1(ran(op_p(super^*(C_1)))) \cap \pi_1(ran(op_p(super^*(C_2)))) = \emptyset))$$

- The Δ-list in each state operation can only comprise attributes or actuator variables declared in the current class or inherited from any superclass.

$$WD_3 =_{df} \forall C \in CN, m \in op_s(C) \bullet \pi_2(ran(m)) \subseteq attr(super^*(C)) \vee \\ \pi_2(ran(m)) \subseteq actvar(super^*(C))$$

- No parallel process operation is allowed to update any actuator variable in more than one component.

$$WD_4 =_{df} \forall C \in CN, (P_1 \,|[E_1]|\, \cdots \,|[E_{n-1}]|\, P_n) \in op_p(C) \bullet \\ \forall i, j : 1..n \bullet i \neq j \Rightarrow avar(P_i) \cap avar(P_j) = \emptyset$$

where $avar(P)$ is the set of actuators employed by P.
- In addition, other well-definedness conditions, such as the inheritance relation does not contain circularity, are omitted here, since similar conditions have been discussed in He, Liu and Li's work [5] for Java-like object-oriented languages.

5.3 Formalising the Behaviour of Class Operations

The dynamic behaviour of class operations is defined as the least fixed point of a set of recursive equations due to the inheritance (dependency) relation among the declared classes. We deal with the state operations and the process operations separately, since the former follow the inheritance rules of Object-Z, whereas the latter do not.

State Operations. For each class $C \in CN$ and every state operation $m \in \{op_s(C') \mid C' \in super^*(C)\}$, it contains an equation $D(C.m) = f(D)$, which is defined with respect to the following cases.

Case (1): m is newly introduced, i.e., it is declared in C, but not in any superclasses. Suppose the declaration of m is $\Delta(\underline{y})$, $\underline{x} : \underline{T} \bullet \text{Pred}(\underline{u}, \underline{v}')$.

$$D(C.m) =_{df} \Delta(\underline{y}), \underline{x} : \underline{T} \bullet \text{Pred}(\underline{u}, \underline{v}')$$

The right-hand side is the semantic predicate defined in section 4.2.

Case (2): m is not declared in C but in its "nearest" superclasses, $C_1, \cdots, C_r$, i.e.,

$$m \notin op_s(C) \land \forall i : 1..r \bullet (m \in op_s(C_i) \land C_i \in super^+(C))$$

We can always assume none of these classes is a superclass of others, i.e., $C_i \notin super^*(C_j)$, for any $i, j : 1..r$. Otherwise, we remove C_i from the list if $C_i \in super^*(C_j)$. We also assume that each C_i is the nearest one to C that defines m in the corresponding dependence path, i.e.,

$$\forall i : 1..r, \neg \exists C' \bullet C' \in super^+(C) \land C_i \in super^+(C') \land m \in op_s(C')$$

The equation for $D(C.m)$ is

$$D(C.m) = \bigwedge\nolimits_{i:1..r} D(C_i.m)$$

Case (3): m is defined in class C as $\Delta(\underline{y})$, $\underline{x} : \underline{T} \bullet \text{Pred}(\underline{u}, \underline{v}')$, but also defined in some "nearest" superclasses, $C_1, \cdots, C_r$, i.e.,

$$m \in op_s(C) \land \forall i : 1..r \bullet (m \in op_s(C_i) \land C_i \in super^+(C))$$

Using the same assumption as in case (2), the equation for $D(C.m)$ is

$$D(C.m) = (\Delta(\underline{y}), \underline{x} : \underline{T} \bullet \text{Pred}(\underline{u}, \underline{v}')) \land \bigwedge\nolimits_{i:1..r} D(C_i.m)$$

Process Operations. Given a class name C, and a process operation m, there are two cases to deal with.

Case (1). The process is not defined in C, but in a superclass C' of C. Then simply

$$D(C.m) = D(C'.m)$$

Case (2). The process operation is defined in C. Its dynamic behaviour is captured by its body and the environment in which it is executed. The design $D(C.m)$ is thus subject to the equation $D(C.m) = \varphi(body(C.m))$. φ is used to pass the actual parameters to their corresponding formal parameters, and generate the semantics predicate afterwards, as discussed in section 4.

The function φ distributes over operators and is inductively defined as:

$\varphi(P_1 \text{ op } P_2) =_{df} \varphi(P_1) \text{ op } \varphi(P_2)$, where $\text{op} \in \{;\ ,\ \Box,\ \sqcap,\ \|[E]\|\ ,\ \triangleright\{t\},\ \rightarrow,\ \bullet\}$
$\varphi(P \bullet \text{DEADLINE } t) =_{df} \varphi(P) \bullet \text{Deadline } t$
$\varphi(P \bullet \text{WAITUNTIL } t) =_{df} \varphi(P) \bullet \text{WaitUntil } t$
$\varphi(\mu X \bullet P) =_{df} \mu X \bullet \varphi(P), \quad \varphi(P \backslash E) =_{df} \varphi(P) \backslash E$
$\varphi(x) = x, \quad \varphi(f(\underline{e})) = f(\varphi(\underline{e})),$

where f can be any legal arithmetic operator $(+, -, *, /, \leqslant, \neq, \cdots)$, logical connector $(\wedge, \vee, \neg, \Rightarrow, \cdots)$, or set operator $(\in, \notin, \subseteq, \cdots)$.

An operation invocation o.m is mapped by φ to

$$\varphi(\text{o.m}(\underline{\text{val}})) =_{df} \Box\{\text{o}(\mathit{myclass}) = \text{C}' \wedge \text{m} \in \mathit{visibop}(\text{C}') \bullet D(\text{C}'.\text{m})[\underline{\mathit{val}}/\underline{x}]\}$$

where $\underline{x}$ is the parameters of the operation C'.m.

5.4 The Behaviour of Active Classes

This subsection is devoted to formalising the behaviour of active classes. The behaviour of a system specified in TCOZ is determined by the MAIN processes of active classes.

Given a sequence of class declarations $\text{cdecls} =_{df} \text{cdecl}_1, \cdots, \text{cdecl}_n$, where cdecl_n is an active class of interest which may depend on (inherit from) the other classes. The behaviour of (any objects of) this active class is defined as the following predicate:

$\mathit{cdecls};\ \mathit{initial};\ D(\mathit{cdecl}_n.\text{MAIN})$

The design *initial* performs the following tasks: (1) to check the well-definedness of the complete declaration section; (2) to derive the final values of the logical variables; (3) to define the dynamic behaviour of every operation.

$$\mathit{initial} =_{df} \bigwedge_i w\mathcal{D}_i \vdash \left(\begin{array}{l} \mathit{super}' = \mathit{super} \wedge CN' = CN \wedge \forall C \in CN\bullet \\ \mathit{locvar}'(C) = \mathit{locvar}(\mathit{super}^*(C)) \wedge \mathit{attr}'(C) = \mathit{attr}(\mathit{super}^*(C)) \wedge \\ \mathit{senvar}'(C) = \mathit{senvar}(\mathit{super}^*(C)) \wedge \mathit{actvar}'(C) = \mathit{actvar}(\mathit{super}^*(C)) \wedge \\ op'_s(C) = \{(\text{m} \mapsto (\langle \underline{x}:\underline{T}\rangle, \Delta(\underline{y}), D(C.\text{m}))) \mid \exists \text{Pred}\bullet \\ \quad (\text{m} \mapsto (\langle \underline{x}:\underline{T}\rangle, \Delta(\underline{y}), \text{Pred})) \in op_s(C') \wedge C' \in \mathit{super}^*(C)\} \wedge \\ op'_p(C) = \{(\text{m} \mapsto (\langle \underline{x}:\underline{T}\rangle, D(C.\text{m}))) \mid \exists P\bullet \\ \quad (\text{m} \mapsto (\langle \underline{x}:\underline{T}\rangle, P)) \in op_p(C') \wedge C' \in \mathit{super}^*(C)\} \wedge \\ \mathit{visibattr}' = \{C \mapsto (\mathit{attr}(\mathit{super}^*(C)) \upharpoonright \mathit{visibattr}(C)) \mid C \in CN\} \wedge \\ \mathit{visibop}' = \{C \mapsto (\mathit{op}(\mathit{super}^*(C)) \upharpoonright \mathit{visibop}(C)) \mid C \in CN\} \end{array}\right)$$

where $w\mathcal{D}_i$ is the well-definedness condition discussed in section 5.2. $D(C.\text{m})$ discussed in last section defines the dynamic behaviour of the operation m of class C.

6 Related Work, Conclusion and Future Work

The semantics of Object-Z has been investigated earlier. For example, Object-Z has a fully abstract semantics [3, 15]. Timed CSP's semantics has also been well studied [2, 10, 11]. The process model used by TCOZ [9] presented a conservative extension to the basic timed failures model [10]. The semantic model of TCOZ in this paper is based on the UTP framework. The most closely related works are the UTP timed [14] and untimed [18] semantic models of Circus and the UTP semantic model [5] of object-oriented programming languages. A significant contribution of this paper is the unified semantic model for both channel and sensor/actuators based communications in TCOZ. This new model is far more complete. It not only covers the communication and process aspects of TCOZ, but also other features, such as class encapsulation, inheritance, dynamic binding and extended TCOZ timing constructs (deadline and waituntil commands), which have not been covered by the previous result [9].

This paper also demonstrates that UTP can provide a formal semantic foundation not only for programming languages but also for much more expressive specification languages. In particular, UTP is well suited for capturing formal semantics for integrated specification languages (i.e., TCOZ) which often have rich language constructs for state encapsulation, event communication and real-time modeling. Our semantic model will be used as a reference document for developing tools support for TCOZ. For example, in the semantic model, the well formed rules can be used as precise requirements for developing a type checking system. Various laws for the language constructs can be encoded as theorems to support a reasoning system.

The semantic model presented in this paper is a discrete time model which can readily be connected to an untimed model, so that model checker like FDR [12] can also be used to check untimed properties of TCOZ. For checking timing properties, we have recently developed transformation rules from TCOZ to Timed Automata (TA) so that various TA tools, i.e. UPPAAL [1], can be applied to check timing properties. We plan to give a UTP semantic model for TA, and to prove the soundness of our transformation rules based on UTP semantics for both TCOZ and TA.

Another further research work would be to develop operational and data refinement techniques for TCOZ and to look into transforming TCOZ to object-oriented programming languages, e.g., Java. This work should be achievable given that UTP semantics for Java-like language has already been formulated in [5].

Acknowledgement

We would like to thank Jifeng He for helpful comments and inspiring related work. We are also grateful to anonymous referees for many helpful comments.

References

1. J. Bengtsson, K. Larsen, F. Larsson, P. Pettersson, and Y. Wang. UPPAAL - a Tool Suite for Automatic Verification of Real-Time Systems. *Hybrid Systems*, LNCS 1066, pages 232–243. Springer-Verlag, 1996.
2. J. Davies and S. Schneider. A brief history of Timed CSP. *Theoret. Comput. Sci.*, 138:243–271, 1995.
3. D. Duke and R. Duke. Towards a semantics for Object-Z. In D. Bjørner, C.A.R. Hoare, and H. Langmaack, eds., *VDM'90: VDM and Z!*, LNCS 428, pages 242–262. Springer-Verlag, 1990.
4. R. Duke and G. Rose. *Formal Object Oriented Specification Using Object-Z*. Cornerstones of Computing Series. Macmillan, March 2000.
5. J. He, Z. Liu, and X. Li. A relational model for specification of object-oriented systems. Technical Report 262, UNU/IIST, October 2002.
6. C.A.R. Hoare and J. He. *Unifying Theories of Programming*. Prentice-Hall, 1998.

7. B. Mahony and J. S. Dong. Sensors and Actuators in TCOZ. In J. Wing, J. Woodcock, and J. Davies, eds., *FM99: World Congress on Formal Methods*, LNCS 1709, pages 1166–1185, 1999.
8. B. Mahony and J. S. Dong. Timed Communicating Object Z. *IEEE Transactions on Software Engineering*, 26(2):150–177, February 2000.
9. B. Mahony and J. S. Dong. Overview of the semantics of TCOZ. In K. Araki, A. Galloway, and K. Taguchi, eds, *IFM'99: Integrated Formal Methods*, pages 66–85. Springer-Verlag, 1999.
10. M. Mislove, A. Roscoe, and S. Schneider. Fixed Points Without Completeness. *Theoret. Comput. Sci.*, 138:273–314, 1995.
11. G. Reed and A. Roscoe. A timed model for communicating sequential processes. *Theoret. Comput. Sci.*, 58:249–261, 1988.
12. A.W. Roscoe. *The Theory and Practice of Concurrency*. Prentice-Hall, 1998.
13. S. Schneider, J. Davies, D. Jackson, G. Reed, J. Reed, and A. Roscoe. Timed CSP: Theory and practice. *Real-Time: Theory in Practice*, LNCS 600, pages 640–675. Springer-Verlag, 1992.
14. A. Sherif and J. He. Towards a timed model for circus. In C. George and H. Miao, eds., *ICFEM'02 Formal Methods and Software Engineering*, LNCS 2495, pages 613–624. Springer-Verlag, 2002.
15. G. Smith. A fully abstract semantics of classes for Object-Z. *Formal Aspects of Computing*, 7(3):289–313, 1995.
16. G. Smith. *The Object-Z Specification Language*. Kluwer Academic Publishers, 2000.
17. J. Woodcock and A. Cavalcanti. Circus: a concurrent refinement language. Technical report, Oxford University Computing Laboratory, Oxford OX1 3QD, UK, July 2001.
18. J. Woodcock and A. Cavalcanti. The Semantics of Circus. In D. Bert, J. Bowen, M. Henson and K. Robinson, eds., *2nd International Conference on Z and B*, LNCS 2272, pages 184–203. Springer-Verlag, 2002.

Appendix

The semantics for the process constructs (e.g., primitives, internal/external choices, etc.) that are similar to Sherif and He's work[14] are listed here.

$$Skip =_{df} ok' \land \neg wait' \land tr' = tr \land state' = state$$
$$Stop =_{df} ok' \land wait' \land state' = state \land no\_interact(trace)$$
$$Chaos =_{df} \mathbf{R}(true)$$
$$P; Q =_{df} P[false/ok'] \lor P \land wait' \lor P[true, false/ok', wait'] \circ Q$$
$$P \sqcap Q =_{df} P \lor Q$$
$$P \Box Q =_{df} (P \land Q \land wait' \land trace = \langle\rangle) \lor$$
$$\qquad (((P \land Q \land ok' \land wait' \land trace = \langle\rangle \land state' = state) \lor Skip)$$
$$\qquad \circ (\neg wait' \lor (\neg(tr \preceq tr') \land trace \neq \langle\rangle))) \land (P \lor Q); Skip$$
$$\mu X \bullet F(X) =_{df} \sqcap \{X \mid X \sqsupseteq F(X)\}$$
$$P \backslash E =_{df} (\exists \tilde{tr} \bullet P[\tilde{tr}/tr'] \land \forall k : \#tr \leqslant k \leqslant \#tr' \bullet$$
$$\qquad \pi_1(tr'(k)) = \pi_1(\tilde{tr}) \upharpoonright (Event - E) \land$$
$$\qquad \pi_2(\tilde{tr}(k)) = \pi_2(tr'(k)) \cup E); Skip$$

Refinement and Verification of Synchronized Component-Based Systems

Olga Kouchnarenko* and Arnaud Lanoix

Laboratoire d'Informatique de l'Université de Franche-Comté, FRE CNRS 2661,
16, route de Gray, 25030 Besançon Cedex, France,
Ph:(33) 3 81 66 65 24, Fax:(33) 3 81 66 64 50,
{kouchna,lanoix}@lifc.univ-fcomte.fr, http://lifc.univ-fcomte.fr

Abstract. This article deals with specification, refinement and verification approaches for systems designed with synchronized components. First of all, we define a synchronized composition of components. Transition systems are used to specify or/and to model synchronized component-based systems. Second, we give refinement semantics for these component-based systems before proposing a method to verify the refinement of a whole system from the weak refinement of its components. We also present *SynCo*: a tool we are implementing using our method. Third, a compositional way to verify safety properties is proposed: the unreachability of a (set of) state(s) can be efficiently ensured for a synchronized component-based system.
The different aspects of our work are illustrated on an industrial example of a wind-screen wipers system composed of a control lever, a rain sensor and two (left and right) wind-screen wipers.

Keywords: composition, synchronization, refinement, algorithmic verification, compositional verification, reachability analysis

1 Introduction

Verification across abstraction and refinement steps is a central and important issue in formal system validation. It presents both practical and theoretical difficulties that have not yet been satisfactory solved.

In this paper, we deal with specification and verification of component-based finite state systems supporting a top-down refinement paradigm. We suppose a specification obtained by a refinement process. Several methods, like B [1, 4], $TLA+$ [20], $CSP2B$ [12], etc. propose a refinement based development. The system specification and modelling we consider in this paper, are inspired by the syntactic and semantic concepts of the B refinement method which has been successfully used to specify many reactive systems. On overview, the reader can refer to case studies such as an industrial automatism [2], as well as industrial

---
* This work was partially supported by the LIFC-LORIA/INRIA Research Group CASSIS

applications such as *MÉTÉOR* [5] by *Matra Transport International*, and the *SPECTRUM* project [28] by *GEC-Marconi Avionics Limited*.

In [16, 18], it has been proposed to enrich B specifications with dynamic properties formulated in the Propositional Linear Temporal Logic ($PLTL$). In [8], we express the refinement semantics as a relation between transition systems. In general, behavioural properties established for an abstract system model are not preserved when the system is refined to a richer level of detail. It is not the case for us: in [14], we show that our refinement relation preserves the abstract system $PLTL$ properties. This way, an algorithmic verification of the refinement by model exploration can be associated with the verification of the $PLTL$ properties, by model-checking.

However, it is well-known that the algorithmic verification quickly meets its limits when applied to huge systems. Therefore, we have to face the problem of combinatorial explosion during refinement since details introduced by the refinement tend to drastically increase the number of states of the systems. It is also the case while verifying properties by model-checking. Compositional approaches partially avoid this problem.

A way to have components in the B method is to decompose the application into separate machines. There are many works on structured development using decomposition into machines and refinement (see, for example [13, 11, 27]). Generaly, B event systems which are closed systems can be used to describe the components. So, the interactions between components have to be described independently. This is the idea used for example in [12] or in [29].

Unlike the Schneider and Treharne's approach [26], we propose in [9] to remain in the framework of the B event systems. We assume that components do not share variables and we propose to specify a synchronization as pairs of events belonging to two different components with feasibility conditions. These conditions achieve the synchronization by constraining the activation of events of a component by a predicate over the variables of another component. Moreover, during the refinement verification we take the external non-determinism into account.

In this paper, we go further to conciliate the synchronized component-based specification with the refinement verification. First, we propose to use transition systems both for specifying and for modelling synchronized component-based systems. Second, we define a refinement relation of component-based systems which is weaker than the refinement relation defined in [9]. Third, we give the conditions to ensure the refinement of the whole system from the weak refinements of its synchronized components, and vice versa. Furthermore, we propose to exploit the refinement to verify safety properties in a compositional way. The interest of this proposition is that the component-based refinement guarantees preservation of the abstract systems properties for the refined systems.

As a comparison, our goal for addressing the B event systems composition is different from the B *decomposition* one proposed by J.-R. Abrial. In [3], the event systems decomposition is based on extern shared variables and synchronized events. The main advantage of our technique is that it frees the user from the whole system design.

This paper is organised as follows. After giving preliminary notions, we define, in Section 2, the behavioural semantics of synchronized component-based systems. In Section 3, we define a refinement relation for these systems and explain our main compositionality result using for the compositional refinement verification. Then, in Section 4, we investigate how our approach is used in the context of a compositional safety property verification. Section 5 introduces a tool implementing the synchronized component refinement verification. Throughout this paper, we illustrate the use of our framework on an industrial example of a wind-screen wipers system. We end by some perspectives.

2 Synchronized Parallel Composition

In this section, we introduce interpreted labelled transition systems to specify and to model the behaviours of a component. We specify the synchronized behaviours of components by tuples of labels with feasibility conditions constraining activations of transitions with these labels. We provide a definition for a context-in component (i.e. a component in the context of the others). This definition is required to define the synchronized parallel composition of components under a synchronization.

Let $Var = \{X_1, \ldots, X_n\}$ be a finite set of variables with their respective domains $\mathbb{D}_1, \ldots, \mathbb{D}_n$. Let AP be a set of atomic propositions $ap \stackrel{\text{def}}{=} (X_i = v)$ with $X_i \in Var$ and $v \in \mathbb{D}_i$. Let SP be a set of state propositions sp defined by following grammar: $sp_1, sp_2 ::= ap \mid \neg sp_1 \mid sp_1 \vee sp_2$.

Definition 1 (Interpreted Labelled Transition System (LTS)). *A interpreted labelled transition system S over Var is a tuple $< Q, Q_0, E, T, l >$ where:*
- *Q is a set of states,*
- *$Q_0 \subseteq Q$ is a set of initial states,*
- *E is a finite set of transitions labels or actions,*
- *$T \subseteq Q \times E \times Q$ is a labelled transition relation, and*
- *$l : Q \to SP$ is an interpretation of each state on the system variables.*

We define the sum of two transition systems over the same set of variables Var. Furthermore, we will show how to compute a parallel composition of synchronized components using this operator.

Definition 2 (Sum of Two LTSs). *Let $S_1 =< Q_1, Q_{01}, E_1, T_1, l_1 >$ and $S_2 =< Q_2, Q_{02}, E_2, T_2, l_2 >$ be two transition systems over Var. The sum of S_1 and S_2, written $S_1 \uplus S_2$, is $< Q_1 \cup Q_2, Q_{01} \cup Q_{02}, E_1 \cup E_2, T_1 \cup T_2, l_{12} >$ where l_{12} is defined by:*

$$l_{12}(q) = \begin{cases} l_1(q) \text{ if } q \in Q_1, \\ l_2(q) \text{ if } q \in Q_2. \end{cases}$$

Moreover, $\forall q_1.\ q_1 \in Q_1,\ \forall q_2.\ q_2 \in Q_2.\ (l_1(q_1) = l_2(q_2) \Leftrightarrow q_1 = q_2)$.

In order to define our synchronized parallel composition, we give the definition of a *synchronization* of n components. For that, we introduced a new transition label '−' for the fictive action "skip".

Definition 3 (Synchronization of n Components). *Let $S_1,\ldots,S_n$ be n components. A synchronization Synch is a set of elements (α when p) where:*
- $\alpha = (e_1,\ldots,e_n) \in \prod_{i=1}^{n}(E_i \cup \{-\})$,
- p *is a state proposition on the components variables.*

To illustrate the previous definitions, we introduce the example of a car windscreen wipers system. Consider the wipers system WS_A composed by a control lever, a rain sensor and two (left and right) wind-screen wipers. The control lever CO_A can select the mode of the wiper system: *co=manual, co=auto* or *co=stop*. Its behaviour is shown in Fig. 1. The left and the right wipers have the same behaviour. The transition system in Fig. 2 shows two positions for the left wiper LW_A: *lw=leftUp* or *lw=leftDown*. It is the same thing for the right wiper RW_A. The rain sensor SE_A can detect the rain amount (*se=not, se=tiny* or *se=strong*). Moreover, it can be off (*se=off*) (see Fig. 3).

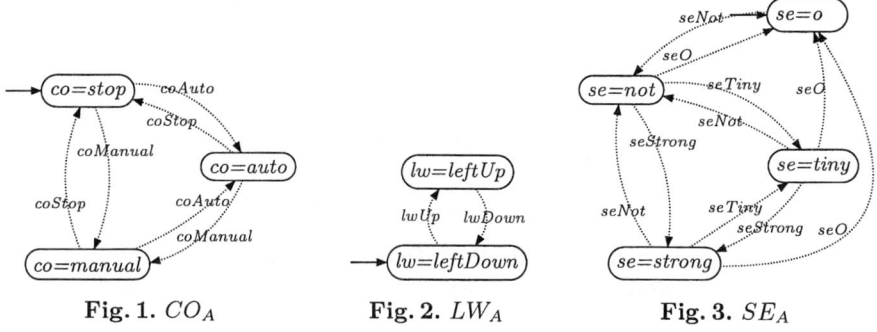

Fig. 1. CO_A Fig. 2. LW_A Fig. 3. SE_A

A synchronization csw_A is given to describe the authorized behaviours of the complete system WS_A. For example, the left and right wipers must move together (($lwDown,rwDown$) and ($lwUp,rwUp$)), the rain sensor sends information only if the control lever mode is *auto* (*seTiny*, (*seStrong* and *seNot*), the control lever mode or the rain sensor can change only if the wipers are down (($coManual,seOff$), ($coAuto,seNot$)), etc. csw_A is given in Fig. 4. For readability reason the fictive transition label '-' is not shown in csw_A.

($lwDown,rwDown$) **when** (($co=manual$) ∧ ($se=o$)) ∨ (($co=auto$) ∧ ($se=tiny$)) ∨ (($co=auto$) ∧ ($se=strong$)),
($lwUp,rwUp$) **when** (($co=manual$) ∧ ($se=o$)) ∨ (($co=auto$) ∧ ($se=tiny$)) ∨ (($co=auto$) ∧ ($se=strong$)),
$coManual$ **when** ($lw=leftDown$) ∧ ($rw=rightDown$) ∧ ($co=stop$) ∧ ($se=o$),
$coStop$ **when** ($lw=leftDown$) ∧ ($rw=rightDown$) ∧ ($co=manual$) ∧ ($se=o$),
$seTiny$ **when** ($co=auto$) ∧ ($lw=leftDown$) ∧ ($rw=rightDown$) ∧ ($se!=o$),
$seStrong$ **when** ($co=auto$) ∧ ($lw=leftDown$) ∧ ($rw=rightDown$) ∧ ($se!=o$),
$seNot$ **when** ($co=auto$) ∧ ($lw=leftDown$) ∧ ($rw=rightDown$) ∧ ($se!=o$),
($coManual, seO$) **when** ($co=auto$) ∧ ($lw=leftDown$) ∧ ($rw=rightDown$),
($coStop,seO$) **when** ($co=auto$) ∧ ($lw=leftDown$) ∧ ($rw=rightDown$),
($coAuto,seNot$) **when** ($se=o$) ∧ ($lw=leftDown$) ∧ ($rw=rightDown$)

Fig. 4. Synchronization csw_A

Each component $S_1, \ldots, S_n$ is a context-free component. However, to take synchronization into account, we need to define a context-in component, i.e. a component in the context of the others under a synchronization $Synch$.

Definition 4 (Context-in Component). *Let $S_1, \ldots, S_n$ be n components. Let $Synch$ be their synchronization. A context-in component S_i^c is defined by the tuple $< Q_i^c, Q_{0i}^c, E_i^c, T_i^c, l_i^c >$ where:*
- *$Q_i^c \subseteq Q_1 \times \ldots \times Q_n$ with $(q_1, \ldots, q_n) \in Q_i^c$,*
- *$Q_{0i}^c \subseteq Q_{01} \times \ldots \times Q_{0n}$,*
- *$E_i^c = \{(e_1, \ldots, e_i, \ldots, e_n) \mid (((e_1, \ldots, e_i, \ldots, e_n) \text{ when } p) \in Synch)$ $\wedge (e_i \in E_i)\}$,*
- *$l_i^c((q_1, \ldots, q_n)) = l_1(q_1) \wedge \ldots \wedge l_n(q_n)$,*
- *$T_i^c \subseteq Q_i^c \times E_i^c \times Q_i^c$ with*
  $((q_1, \ldots, q_n), (e_1, \ldots, e_n), (q_1', \ldots, q_n')) \in T_i^c$ iff:
  - *$((e_1, \ldots, e_n)$ when $p) \in Synch$,*
  - *$l_i^c((q_1, \ldots, q_n)) \Rightarrow p$, and*
  - *$\forall k.(k \in \{1, \ldots, n\} \Rightarrow ((e_k = - \wedge q_k = q_k') \vee (e_k \neq - \wedge (q_k, e_k, q_k') \in T_k)))$.*

All context-in components have the same set of variables $Var = \bigcup_{j=1}^n Var_j$. Note that the graph representing a context-in component may be unconnected.

Figure 5 shows a representation of the context-in component SE_A^c that presents all behaviours of SE_A under csw_A. It is either simple behaviours ($seNot$, $seTiny$, $seStrong$) or synchonized behaviours ($(seOff, coManual), (seNot, coAuto)$). We have similar figures for the context-in components CO_A^c, LW_A^c and RW_A^c. Remark that RW_A^c and LW_A^c are identical. Indeed, all behaviours of LW_A and RW_A are synchronized ($(lwDown, rwDown)$ and $(lwUp, rwUp)$).

The whole system is a rearrangement of its separate parts, i.e., the components and their interactions. This arrangement is specified by a synchronized composition between components. We define a synchronized composition of n

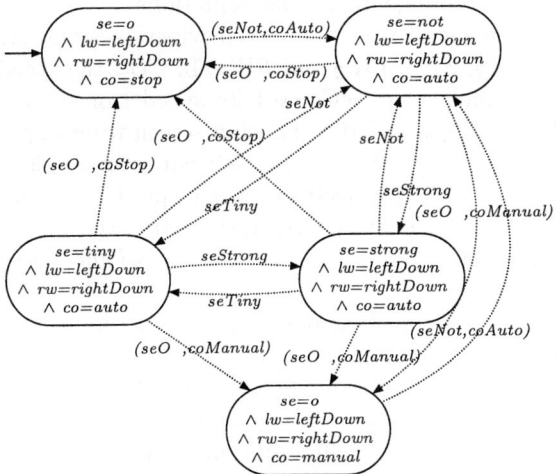

Fig. 5. SE_A^c

components $S_1, \ldots, S_n$ under a synchronization $Synch$ by the sum of the n context-in components $S_1^c, \ldots, S_n^c$.

Definition 5 (Synchronized Composition of n Components). *Let $S_1, \ldots, S_n$ be n components and $Synch$ their synchronization. Let $S_1^c, \ldots, S_n^c$ be their respective context-in components. The synchronized parallel composition of $S_1, \ldots, S_n$ under $Synch$ is defined by:*

$$\|_{Synch}(S_1, \ldots, S_n) \stackrel{def}{=} \biguplus_{i=1}^{n}(S_i^c)$$

Notice that our parallel composition is more expressive than the classical synchronized product of transition systems. This is due to feasibility conditions, i.e., predicates over variables of the n components that constrain the composition. It is not a designer's task to write the context-in components nor their sum. As they can be automatically generated (thanks to Definitions 2 and 4), the designer only specifies the components and the synchronization.

Recall that the four context-in components have the same set of variables $Var_A = \{co, lw, rw, se\}$. The wipers system $WS_A = \|_{csw_A}(CO_A, SE_A, LW_A, RW_A)$ equals to $CO_A^c \uplus SE_A^c \uplus LW_A^c \uplus RW_A^c$.

3 Synchronized Component-Based Systems Refinement

In this section, we first recall the refinement semantics given in [8,9] for classical one component transition systems. A refinement relation in the style of the Milner-Park simulation relation between abstract and concrete transition systems is given. Second, we want these semantics to fit with the synchronized component-based systems. For that we define a refinement relation between transition systems which is weaker than the refinement relation introduced in [8,9]. Nevertheless, this weak refinement allows us to ensure the refinement of the whole system in a compositional way, unlike the refinement defined in [8,9]. We begin by an example before giving formal definitions.

Consider a refinement of the wind-screen wipers system, still composed of four components: CO_R, SE_R, LW_R and RW_R. In CO_R the speed choice $seCo$ is performed in the manual mode: $seCo=se1$ for speed 1 or $seCo=se2$ for speed 2 (see Fig. 6). In both LW_R and RW_R the wind-screen wipers speed is taken into account. For LW_R a new variable lws (for left wiper speed) is introduced with $\mathbb{D}(lws) = \{ls0, ls1, ls2\}$ for respectively, no speed, speed 1 or speed 2 (see Fig. 7). Idem for RW_A. In the abstract system SE_A, there are two rain levels. We observe in SE_R both limits of the tiny-rain level ($se_R=maxTiny$) and the strong-rain level ($se_R=minStrong$).

The authorized behaviours of the refined wipers system WS_R are described in the synchronization csw_R. We still have the old synchronized behaviours, i.e. left and right wipers must move together (($lwDown, rwDown$) and (($lwUp, rwUp$)), the control lever and the rain sensor change only if the wipers are down (*coManual, coStop, seTiny, seStrong*), etc. In addition, some of the new transitions are also synchronized. For example, the speed selection in the control lever manual mode can happen only if the wipers are down (*coSelect*). The wipers change their

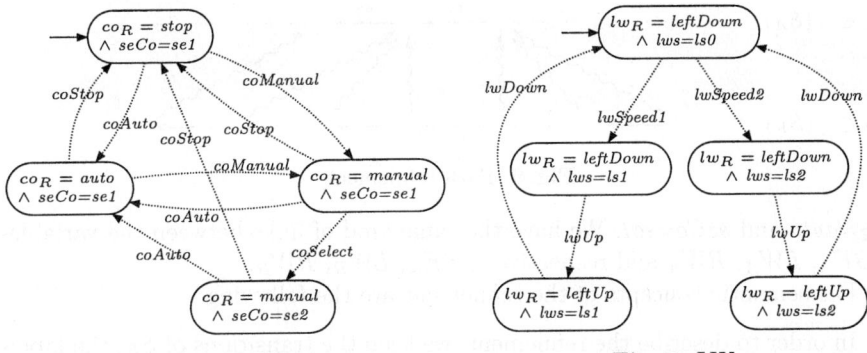

Fig. 6. CO_R **Fig. 7.** LW_R

speeds simultaneously ($(lwSpeed1, rwSpeed1)$ and $(lwSpeed2, rwSpeed2)$). In the control lever auto mode, the tiny-rain detection is synchronized with the level 1 of the wipers speeds (($seMaxTiny, lwSpeed1, rwSpeed1$)), and the strong-rain detection is synchronized with the level 2 of the wipers speeds (($seMinStrong$, $lwSpeed2, rwSpeed2$)).

3.1 Basic Transition Systems Refinement

Let $SA = <Q_A, Q_{0A}, E_A, T_A, l_A>$ be an abstract transition system over Var_A and $SR = <Q_R, Q_{0R}, E_R, T_R, l_R>$ a concrete transition system over Var_R. In this section, some basic definitions about transition systems refinement are given. The syntactic concepts of the refinement are the following. Refinement introduces new transition labels, so $E_A \subseteq E_R$. Refinement introduces new variables and renames abstract ones, so $Var_A \cap Var_R = \emptyset$.

Let GI be a formula over $SP_A \cup SP_R \cup SP'$ where SP_A is over Var_A, SP_R is over Var_R, and $SP' \stackrel{def}{=} \{X_A = X_R\}$ with $X_A \in Var_A$ and $X_R \in Var_R$ and $\mathbb{D}(X_A) = \mathbb{D}(X_R)$. GI is commonly known as a gluing invariant linking variables of the abstract and concrete systems. A binary relation $\mu \subseteq Q_R \times Q_A$ allows us to express this link between the states of two transition systems [8, 9].

Definition 6 (Gluing Relation). *Let GI be a gluing invariant between SR and SA. The states $q_R \in Q_R$ and $q_A \in Q_A$ are glued, written $q_R \mu q_A$, iff $l_R(q_R) \land GI \Rightarrow l_A(q_A)$.*

The gluing invariant GI_W linking variables of the refined system WS_R and the abstract system WS_A is given in Fig. 8. The abstract variable co from CO_A is linked with the concrete variables co_R and $seCo$. If $co=manual$ then $co_R=manual$, if $co=stop$ then $co_R=stop$ and $seCo=se1$, and if $co=auto$ then

$((co=manual) \Leftrightarrow (co_R=manual)) \land ((co=stop) \Leftrightarrow ((co_R=stop) \land (seCo=se1)))$
$\land ((co=auto) \Leftrightarrow ((co_R=auto) \land (seCo=se1))) \land ((se=o\ ) \Leftrightarrow (se_R=o\ ))$
$\land ((se=not) \Leftrightarrow (se_R=not)) \land ((se=strong) \Leftrightarrow ((se_R=strong) \lor (se_R=minStrong)))$
$\land ((se=tiny) \Leftrightarrow ((se_R=tiny) \lor (se_R=maxTiny))) \land ((lw=leftDown) \Leftrightarrow (lw_R=leftDown))$
$\land ((lw=leftUp) \Leftrightarrow ((lw_R=leftUp) \land (lws \neq ls0))) \land ((rw=rightDown) \Leftrightarrow (rw_R=rightDown))$
$\land ((rw=rightUp) \Leftrightarrow ((rw_R=rightUp) \land (rws \neq rs0)))$

Fig. 8. Gluing invariant GI_W

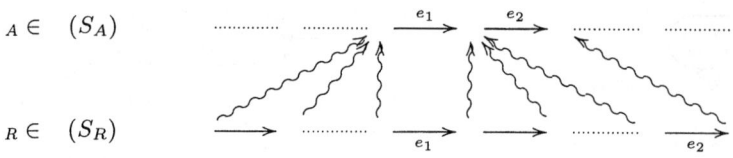

Fig. 9. Path refinement

$co_R=auto$ and $seCo=se1$. We have the same kind of links between the variables of SE_A, LW_A, RW_A and respectively, SE_R, LW_R, RW_R.

The semantic concepts of the refinement are the following.

1. In order to describe the refinement, we keep the transitions of S_R, the labels of which are in E_A (i.e. labelled by the "old" labels) and we consider the new transitions introduced during the refinement design (i.e. labelled in $E_R \setminus E_A$) as being non-observable; they are labelled by τ and called τ-transitions. Each portion of path containing τ-transitions must end by a transition labelled in E_A. Therefore, the transition refinement is either a strict refinement or a stuttering refinement (see Fig. 9).
2. In order to avoid livelocks, new transitions should not take control forever. So, the paths containing infinite sequences of τ-transitions are forbidden.
3. Moreover, new transitions should not introduce deadlocks.

The refinement relation η is defined in [8, 9] as a restriction of μ that verifies the previous concepts.

Definition 7 (Strict Refinement Relation [8,9]). *Let SA and SR be two transition systems, and e be a label from E_A. We define the refinement relation η as the greatest binary relation included into μ and satisfying the following conditions:*

1) strict transition refinement
$(q_R \ \eta \ q_A \ \wedge \ q_R \xrightarrow{e} q'_R \in T_R) \Rightarrow \exists q'_A.\ (q_A \xrightarrow{e} q'_A \in T_A \ \wedge \ q'_R \ \eta \ q'_A)$,
2) stuttering transition refinement
$(q_R \ \eta \ q_A \ \wedge \ q_R \xrightarrow{\tau} q'_R \in T_R) \Rightarrow (q'_R \ \eta \ q_A)$,
3) lack of new deadlocks
$(q_R \ \eta \ q_A \ \wedge \ q_R \not\to_R) \Rightarrow (q_A \not\to_A)^1$,
4) lack of τ-divergence
$q_R \ \eta \ q_A \Rightarrow \neg\ (q_R \xrightarrow{\tau} q'_R \xrightarrow{\tau} q''_R \xrightarrow{\tau} \ldots \xrightarrow{\tau} \ldots)$,
5) external non-determinism preservation
$(q_A \xrightarrow{e} q'_A \in T_A \ \wedge \ q_R \ \eta \ q_A) \Rightarrow \exists\ q'_R, q''_R, q''_A.(\ q'_R \ \eta \ q_A \ \wedge \ q'_R \xrightarrow{e} q''_R \in T_R \ \wedge \ q_A \xrightarrow{e} q''_A \in T_A \ \wedge \ q''_R \ \eta \ q''_A)$.

We say that SR refines SA, written $SR \sqsubseteq SA$, when the conditions above are verified between the states of SR and SA i.e. $SR \sqsubseteq SA \Leftrightarrow \forall q_R.\ (q_R \in Q_R \Rightarrow \exists q_A.\ (q_A \in Q_A \ \wedge \ q_R \ \eta \ q_A))$.

It has been shown in [8] that η is a kind of τ-simulation. It is well-known that a simulation can be computed iteratively for finite state systems. We have an

---
[1] We note $q \not\to$ when $\forall q', e.\ (q' \in Q \wedge e \in E \Rightarrow (q \xrightarrow{e} q') \notin T)$.

algorithm based on a depth-first search enumeration of the reachability graph of the refined system. Its order is $O(|SR|)$ where $|SR| = |Q_R| + |T_R|$.

3.2 Compositional Component-Based Systems Refinement

In this section, the refinement semantics is fitted with synchronized component-based systems. We define a refinement relation weaker than the refinement relation presented in Section 3.1, and we clarify how τ covers the new transition labels. Then we give a compositionality theorem allowing us to compositionally ensure the refinement of the whole system from the refinement of its components.

We have shown in [21] that η is too strong to verify a component-based systems refinement. The problem is that some new deadlocks in the context-in components, could cause the refinement verification of a context-in component to fail whereas the refinement of the whole system is verified. That is why, we introduce another relation, called the weak refinement relation and written η_f. This relation is fitted to ensure the refinement verification in this case. The relation η_f uses the set $D \subseteq Q_R$ of new deadlocks which is built during the refined system exploration.

Definition 8 (Weak Refinement Relation). *Let SA and SR be two transition systems, and e be a label from E_A. Let $D \subseteq Q_R$ (Initially $D = \emptyset$) be the set of new deadlocks. We define the weak refinement relation η_f as the greatest binary relation included into μ and satisfying the conditions 1), 2), 4) and 5) of Definition 7 and the following condition:*
3') old or new deadlocks
$(q_R \ \eta_f \ q_A \ \wedge \ q_R \not\rightarrow_R) \Rightarrow ((q_A \not\rightarrow_A) \vee ((q_A \xrightarrow{e} q'_A \in T_A) \Rightarrow (q_R \in D)))$.

We say that SR weakly refines SA, written $SR \sqsubseteq_D SA$, when the conditions above are verified between the states of SR and SA i.e. $SR \sqsubseteq_D SA \Leftrightarrow \forall q_R.(q_R \in Q_R \Rightarrow \exists q_A. \ (q_A \in Q_A \ \wedge \ q_R \ \eta_f \ q_A))$.

The relation η_f can be computed by an iterative algorithm with a complexity order in $O(|SR|)$ too. It is easy to see that the strict refinement relation η implies the weak refinement relation η_f when $D = \emptyset$, and vice versa. Indeed, condition *3')* of Definition 8 is verified for the old deadlocks, so D remains empty.

Property 1. Let SA and SR be two transition systems. Let $D \subseteq Q_R$ be the set of new deadlocks. We have $(SR \sqsubseteq SA) \Leftrightarrow (SR \sqsubseteq_D SA \ \wedge \ D = \emptyset)$.

We have to clarify how τ covers new transition labels when we deal with synchronized component-based systems. Indeed, we want to avoid the refinement verification failure when an old transition and a new one are synchronized. The problem is then to decide whether this synchronized transition has to be covered by τ or not.

Our approach is the following. On the one hand, the old transition label must be saved if it is a label of the component being considered. On the other hand, the transition must be kept out if its label is not a label of the considered component. We define a context-in τ-component to be a context-in component covered by τ. The first step of Definition 9 deletes some transitions and their labels, and the second step covers by τ the remaining transition labels.

Definition 9 (Context-in τ-component). *Let SA_1, SA_2, SR_1 and SR_2 be four components. Let SR_1^c be a context-in component. The context-in τ-component SR_1^τ is the tuple $< Q_{R1}^\tau, Q_{R01}^\tau, E_{R1}^\tau, T_{R1}^\tau, l_{R1}^\tau >$ where:*
- $Q_{R1}^\tau = Q_{R1}^c$,
- $Q_{R01}^\tau = Q_{R01}^c$,
- $l_{R1}^\tau((q_1, q_2)) = l_{R1}^c((q_1, q_2))$,
- $T_{R1}^\tau = T_{R1}^c \smallsetminus \{((q_1,q_2),(e_1,e_2),(q_1',q_2')) \mid ((q_1,q_2),(e_1,e_2),(q_1',q_2')) \in T_{R1}^c \wedge e_1 \in E_{R1} \smallsetminus E_{A1} \wedge e_2 \in E_{A2}\}$,
- $E_{R1}^\tau = E_{R1}^c \smallsetminus \{(e_1,e_2) \mid (e_1,e_2) \in E_{R1}^c \wedge e_1 \in E_{R1} \smallsetminus E_{A1} \wedge e_2 \in E_{A2}\}$.

Then, the elements of E_{R1}^τ are covered as follows[2]:
- *if $(e_1, -) \in E_{R1}^\tau$ and $e_1 \in E_{R1} \smallsetminus E_{A1}$ then $(e_1, -) \backslash \tau$,*
- *if $(e_1, e_2) \in E_{R1}^\tau$, $e_1 \in E_{R1} \smallsetminus E_{A1}$ and $e_2 \in E_{R2} \smallsetminus E_{A2}$ then $(e_1, e_2) \backslash \tau$,*
- *if $(e_1, e_2) \in E_{R1}^\tau$, $e_1 \in E_{A1}$ and $e_2 \in E_{R2} \smallsetminus E_{A2}$ then $(e_1, e_2) \backslash (e_1, -)$.*

Our first result is a compositional refinement verification theorem. This theorem links the separate context-in components weak refinements with the component-based system refinement. It is based on deadlocks reduction. A state inducing a new deadlock in a component does not induce a deadlock in the whole system if there exists another component in which this state is not a deadlock state.

Definition 10 (New Deadlocks Reduction). *Let SA_1, SA_2, SR_1 and SR_2 be four components such that $SR_1^\tau \sqsubseteq_{D_1} SA_1^c$ and $SR_2^\tau \sqsubseteq_{D_2} SA_2^c$. Let Synch and Synch' be two respective synchronizations. The set $D_{1,2} \subseteq Q_{R1}^\tau \cup Q_{R2}^\tau$ of states producing new deadlocks during the weak refinement of $SR_1 \|_{Synch'} SR_2$ is defined by:*

$$D_{1,2} \stackrel{def}{=} (D_1 \cap D_2) \cup (D_1 \smallsetminus Q_{R2}^\tau) \cup (D_2 \smallsetminus Q_{R1}^\tau)$$

We can compute the set $D_{1,...,n}$ containing the new deadlocks during the weak refinement verification of $\|_{Synch'}(SR_1,...,SR_n)$. It is an associative computation: $D_{1,...,n} = D_{(1,...,n-1),n} = D_{1,(2,...,n)}$. Then, *Property 1* allows us to decide the strict refinement of the whole system.

Theorem 1 (Refinement of a Synchronized Component-based System). *Let $SA_1,...,SA_n$, and $SR_1,...,SR_n$ be n abstract and refined components. Let Synch and Synch' be two respective synchronizations.*

$\|_{Synch'}(SR_1,...,SR_n) \sqsubseteq \|_{Synch}(SA_1,...,SA_n)$ *iff*
- $\forall i.\ 1 \leq i \leq n \Rightarrow SR_i^\tau \sqsubseteq_{D_i} SA_i^c$
- $D_{1,...,n} = \varnothing$

A proof is given in [19].

---
[2] We note $e_1 \backslash e_2$ the relabelling of e_1 by e_2.

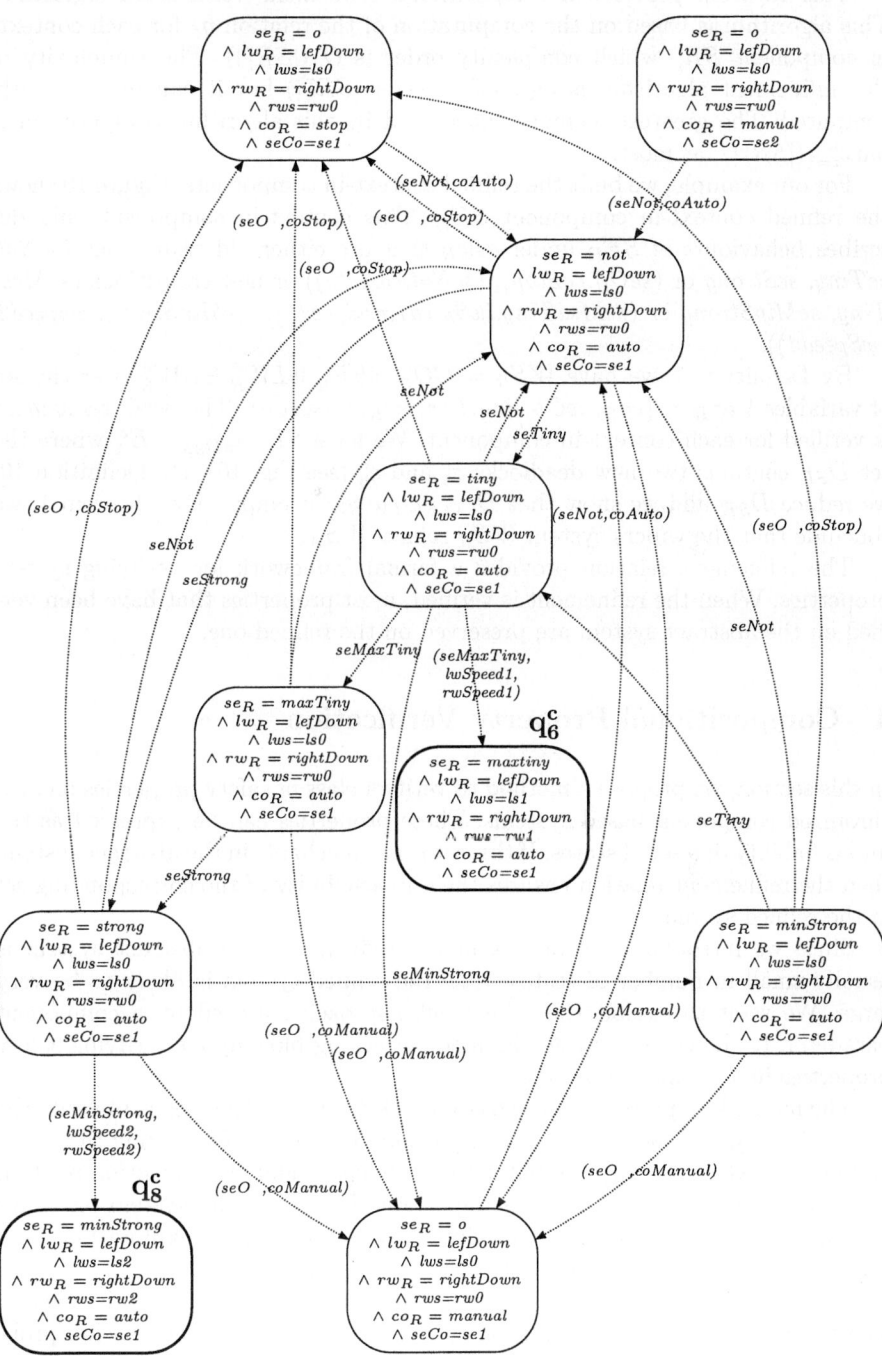

Fig. 10. SE_R^c

This theorem provides a compositional refinement verification algorithm. This algorithm is based on the computation of the relation η_f for each context-in component SR_i^τ which complexity order is $O\left(|SR_i^\tau|\right)$. The complexity of this refinement algorithm is $O(|SR_1^\tau| + \cdots + |SR_n^\tau|)$ but it can be iteratively computed. The greatest memory space used by this algorithm computation is $max_{i=1}^n(|SR_i^\tau|)$, at most.

For our example, we built the refined context-in components. Figure 10 shows the refined context-in component SE_R^c. This context-in component only describes behaviours of SE_R under csw_R that are either old transitions (*seNot*, *seTiny*, *seStrong* or (*seOff,coStop*), (*seNot,coAuto*)) or new transitions (*seMaxTiny*, *seMinStrong* or (*seMaxTiny,lwSpeed1,rwSpeed1*), (*seMinStrong,lwSpeed2, rwSpeed2*)).

By Definition 5, we have $WS_R = CO_R^c \uplus SE_R^c \uplus LW_R^c \uplus RW_R^c$ over the set of variables $Var_R = \{co_R, seCo, lw_R, lws, rw_R, rws, se_R\}$. The weak refinement is verified for each context-in component. We have $SE_R^c \sqsubseteq_{D_{SE}} SE_A^c$ where the set D_{SE} contains two new deadlocks q_6^c and q_8^c (see Fig. 10). By Definition 10, we reduce D_{SE} and we show that $D_{CO,SE,LW,RW}$ is empty. By Theorem 1, we conclude that the wipers system WS_R refines WS_A.

The refinement relation provides a formal framework for verifying system properties. When the refinement is verified, most properties that have been verified on the abstract system are preserved on the refined one.

4 Compositional Property Verification

In this section, we propose a method to verify a class of safety properties on synchronized component-based systems. These properties can be expressed as the unreachability of a set of states. If this set is not reachable in the abstract system, then the refinement relation ensures the unreachability of the corresponding set in the refined system.

Since we introduce new details in the refinement, the abstract system is usually small in number of states while the refined system is likely to be very large. We want to exploit the refinement approach enriched by a component paradigm. It allows us to avoid the model-checking blow-up by verifying safety properties in a compositional way.

The method we propose here is based on Definition 5. The idea is to verify the reachability among the context-in components S_i^c instead of exploring the whole system $\|_{Synch}(S_1, \ldots, S_n)$. Actually, the state space and the transition relation of a context-in component are less important than the entire system ones. We reduce the number of possible behaviours during the system exploration, and, consequently, we postpone the state space explosion problem.

Let $\|_{Synch}(S_1, \ldots, S_n)$ be a synchronized parallel composition under $Synch$. The reachability problem for $\|_{Synch}(S_1, \ldots, S_n)$ is the following decision problem.

Input: n context-in components $S_1^c, \ldots, S_n^c$ and a target state q_t^c s.t. $q_t^c \in \bigcup_{i=1}^n Q_i^c$.

Reachability problem (RP): Determine whether q_t^c is in $\{q^c \mid q^c \in \bigcup_{i=1}^n Q_i^c \land \exists q_0^c. (q_0^c \in \bigcup_{i=1}^n Q_{0i}^c \land \exists w. (w \in (\bigcup_{i=1}^n E_i^c)^* \land (q_0^c, w, q^c) \in (\bigcup_{i=1}^n T_i^c)^*))\}$, where $(\bigcup_{i=1}^n T_i^c)^*$ is the reflexive and transitive closure of the transition relation $\bigcup_{i=1}^n T_i^c$.

Theorem 2 (RP for a Synchronized Component-based System). *There exists an algorithm to decide the reachability problem for a synchronized component-based system $\|_{Synch}(S_1,\ldots,S_n)$ whose complexity order is in $O(|S_1^c| + \cdots + |S_n^c|)$.*

In practice, to verify the reachability of a target state q_t^c in a context-in component, we apply the backward-reachability analysis from q_t^c. During this exploration, the set Q_D of the deadlock states is built. If no initial state is reachable, we choose another context-in component, and, often, a new target state among the deadlock states (in Q_D), in order to continue the reachability analysis from this state. We can choose a new target, since the state q_t^c is reachable from this new state. We stop when either an initial state $q_0^c \in \bigcup_{i=1}^n Q_{0i}^c$ is reached or exploration of all possible choices is already done.

The verification algorithm below formally presents the compositional reachability analysis.

Algorithm 1 (Compositional Reachability)

```
1  Input
2    (Q₀ᶜ = ⋃ⁿᵢ₌₁ Q₀ᵢᶜ  (*Initial state space*)
3     qₜᶜ ∈ ⋃ⁿᵢ₌₁ Q₀ᵢᶜ  (*Target state*)
4     CI ⊆ {S₁ᶜ,...,Sₙᶜ} set of context-in compo-ts*)
5  Result
6     reach: boolean(*true if qₜᶜ is reachable*)
7  Variables
8     Q_Dᶜ, Q_NDᶜ, Q_sucᶜ, Q_preᶜ ⊆ ⋃ⁿᵢ₌₁ Q₀ᵢᶜ
9     Sᵢᶜ ∈ CI
10    (qᵢᶜ ∈ ⋃ⁿᵢ₌₁ Q₀ᵢᶜ
11    tested ⊆ ⋃ⁿᵢ₌₁ Q₀ᵢᶜ × {S₁ᶜ,...,Sₙᶜ}
12    end, possible, deadlock: booleen
13 Begin
14    Q_Dᶜ := {qₜᶜ}
15    end := false
16    reach := false
17    WHILE (end = false) DO
18       Choice (Q_Dᶜ, CI, tested, possible, qᵢᶜ, Sᵢᶜ)
19       IF (possible = false) DO
20          end := true
21       ELSE
22          tested := tested ∪ {(qᵢᶜ, Sᵢᶜ)}
23          deadlock := false
24          Q_sucᶜ := {qᵢᶜ}
25          Q_preᶜ := {}
26          WHILE (deadlock = false) DO
27             Predecessors (Q_sucᶜ, Sᵢᶜ, Q_preᶜ, Q_NDᶜ)
28             Q_Dᶜ := Q_Dᶜ ∪ Q_NDᶜ
29             IF (Q_preᶜ = {}) DO
30                deadlock := true
31             ELSE
32                IF (Q₀ᶜ ∩ Q_preᶜ ≠ {}) DO
33                   deadlock := true
34                   end := true
35                   reach := true
36                ELSE
37                   Q_sucᶜ := Q_preᶜ
38                FI
39             FI
40          ENDWHILE
41       FI
42    ENDWHILE
43 End
```

This algorithm uses the following procedures.
- Predecessors(Input: Q_{suc}^c, S_i^c, Output: Q_{pre}^c, Q_{ND}^c),
- Choice(Input: Q_D^c, CI, $tested$, Output: $possible$, q_i^c, S_i^c).

The first procedure computes Q_{pre}^c in S_i^c, i.e., the set of precessors of Q_{suc}^c. The states in Q_{suc} without predecessors are put in a set Q_{ND}^c of new deadlocks. Formally we have $Q_{pre}^c \stackrel{\text{def}}{=} \{q^c \mid (q^c, \alpha, q^{c\prime}) \in T_i^c \land q^{c\prime} \in Q_{suc}^c\}$. The second procedure chooses, among both states in Q_D^c and context-in components in CI, the most convenient and not tested yet pair (q_i^c, S_i^c). To be efficient, this choice has to be based on some heuristics. For example, the strong dependency analysis of [22] between components can be used for an efficient reachability analysis of their synchronized composition.

This compositional reachability algorithm becomes very interesting when combined with the refinement verification approach. Indeed, all the components in the context are computed during the refinement verification.

Theorem 3 (Correctness of Algorithm 1). *Algorithm 1 eventually terminates and indicates whether the target state is reachable (reach = true) or not (reach = false).*

Proof idea. The computation in the loop $WHILE$ ($deadlock = false$) (lines 26-42) stops. The predecessors computation stops either when an initial state is reached (line 33), or when there are no predecessors (line 30). The computation of the loop $WHILE$ ($end = false$) (lines 17-42) eventually terminates. The variable end becomes $true$ since either an initial state is reached (line 34), or there is no other choice for a pair of a context-in component and a deadlock state (line 20). The only possibility to have the variable $reach$ equal to $true$ (line 35) is to reach an initial state.

For our running wind-screen wipers example, we want some states to be forbidden. For instance, states where the wipers system can move only one of the wind-screen wipers, must be unreachable. Then we exploit the refinement to ensure this property for the refined system.

Consider q_t^c, a state such that $l(q_t^c) \stackrel{def}{=} (lw = leftDown \wedge rw = rightUp \wedge co = manual \wedge se = off)$. We want to ensure the unreachability of the state q_E^c, written $\Box(\neg q_t^c)$ in $PLTL$. By Algorithm 1, it is possible to show that q_t^c is not reachable in the abstract system WS_A. As the system WS_R refines the system WS_A (as explained in Section 3), the refined system states corresponding to q_t^c by the gluing invariant GI_W are unreachable too.

5 *SynCo*: A Tool Verifying the Synchronized Component-Based Systems Refinement

Theorem 1 in Section 3 gives the required conditions to ensure the strict refinement of a whole system from the weak refinements of its synchronized components, and vice versa. This way, we have an algorithm to verify the strict refinement of a synchronized component-based system. The most important advantage of this refinement verification is that it is not necessary to build the whole system to verify the refinement.

We are developing *SynCo (Synchronized Component-based System Analyser)*[3]; a tool implementing with Java the synchronized component refinement verification (Figure 11 show a capture of its interface). We specify the components as transition systems using the STeP's Fair Transition Systems syntax [23, 10]. Each transition is specified with its activation condition (`enable`) and its assignments (`assign`). Figure 12 gives the STeP specification of the component CO_R.

The context-in components are built automatically from both STeP and synchronization specifications. Each component or each context-in component can

---

[3] *SynCo* home page: `http://lifc.univ-fcomte.fr/~lanoix/synco.html`

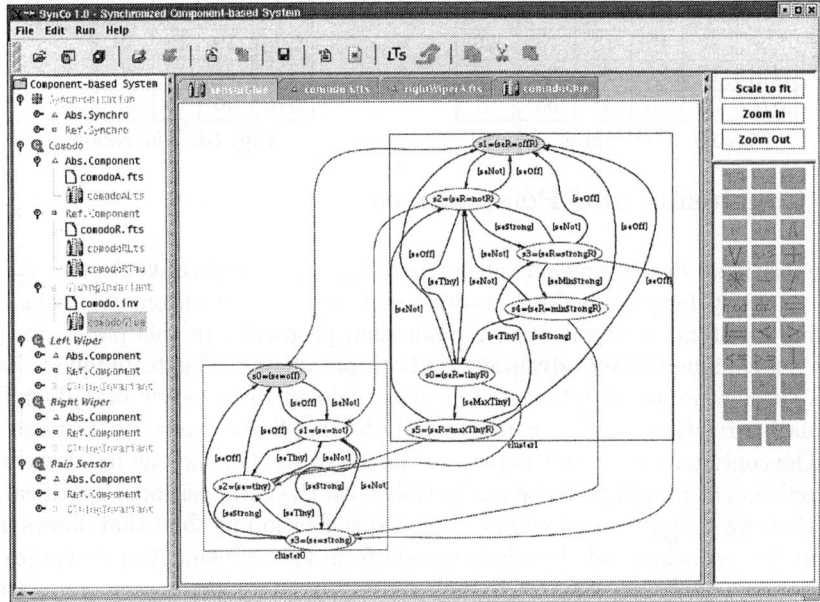

Fig. 11. The tool *SynCo*

be visualised as an automaton using the Java package *Grappa* from the toolkit *Graphviz*[4].

```
Transition System
type CONTROLR = {stopR, autoR, manualR}
type SELECTR = {se1, se2}
local coR : CONTROLR
local seCo : SELECT
Initially (coR = stopR) ∧ (seCo = se1)
Transition coStop :
  enable (coR != stopR) ;
  assign coR := stopR, seCo := se1
Transition coAuto :
  enable (coR != autoR) ;
  assign coR := autoR, seCo := se1
Transition coManual :
  enable (coR = stopR) ∨ (coR = autoR) ;
  assign coR := manualR, seCo := se1
Transition coSelect :
  enable (coR = manualR) ∧ (seCo = se1) ;
  assign seCo := se2
```

Fig. 12. CO_R in STeP

Theorem 1 is implemented in *SynCo* to verify the refinement of a synchronized component-based system. We compute the relation η_f for each context-in τ-component using a kind of depth-first search enumeration of the reachability graph of this context-in τ-component. Then, we conclude about the refinement of the whole system. Figure 11 shows the relation η_f between a refined component and an abstract component.

The refinement verification of a simple system can be done with *SynCo* too. We assume that the simple system is the one component of a synchronized component-based system. Obviously, the new deadlocks set is empty by Property 1.

With this tool the refinement verification of the wind-screen wipers system and of an industrial robot has been done. Thanks to *SynCo* we can measure the efficiency of our method. Tables 13 and 14 give the results of our tests. For the wind-screen wipers system WS_R both the states and the transitions are decreased by a third between the whole system and the greatest context-in component (see Fig. 13). We have similar results in Fig. 14 for the industrial robot RO_R moving pieces thanks to a clip CL_R, a handle HA_R and a lift LI_R. We plan to test *SynCo* on more complex examples.

---

[4] Graphviz official page: http://www.research.att.com/sw/tools/graphviz

	CO_R^c	SE_R^c	LW_R^c	RW_R^c	WS_R
$|Q_R|$	8	10	18	18	20
$|T_R|$	17	25	20	20	47
$|SR|$	25	35	38	38	67

Fig. 13. The wipers system

	CL_R^c	LI_R^c	HA_R^c	RO_R
$|Q_R|$	19	13	19	25
$|T_R|$	21	13	20	40
$|SR|$	40	26	39	65

Fig. 14. The robot

6 Conclusion and Perspectives

Compositional design and refinement paradigms are very convenient to specify and to verify large embedded reactive systems such as automatic trains, car driving assistance systems or communication protocols. In this paper, we propose a technique to take advantages of both paradigms. This technique is based on a specific notion of refinement relation defined in the style of Milner-Park simulation relation between concrete and abstract finite transition systems.

The contributions of this paper are the following. On the one hand, we want the refinement paradigm to be compatible with the compositional specification. For that, we propose a new compositional specification method that allows us to ensure the refinement of the whole system from the refinement of its context-in components, and vice versa. Although context-in components seem comparable with the whole system, they are generally smaller than the whole system. On the other hand, we want to avoid the model-checking blow-up by verifying a class of safety properties in a compositional way. For that, we give an algorithm to ensure the unreachability of a set of states of a synchronized component-based system. Moreover, this algorithm is very interesting when combined with the compositional refinement verification algorithm.

A tool that implements the compositional refinement verification has been implemented in Java. This tool, *SynCo*, allows us to measure the efficiency of our approach, and to test it to real industrial examples. We are currently working on extending this tool to incorporate the compositional reachability algorithm. In addition, we are going to use the strong dependency analysis of [22] as heuristics to efficiently choose a pair (q_i^c, S_i^c). As far as we know, other compositional tools also implement a reachability compositional verification (see for instance [15, 22]). However, they were designed for a very different purpose than *SynCo* and, thus, do not implement compositional refinement verification.

One of the consequences of the composition theorem in [25] is the limitation of the compositional verification. It has been shown that the composition theorem fails for very simple parallel operators if there is a property expressing that "there is a path such that all the nodes of the path have a property p". Moreover, we have established in [14] that the strict refinement relation preserves the abstract system $PLTL$ properties, i.e. safety and liveness properties because of Conditions *3)* and *4)* of Definition 7. This preservation partially avoids the combinatorial explosion problem. Indeed, a property proof on an abstract system can be reused as a hypothesis for its verification on the refined system. That is why we are interested in a compositional verification of $PLTL$ properties.

More generally, we are going to use the works on property preservation [14], modular verification [24, 17], and dynamic property refinement [6, 7] in the framework of the component-based system specification and refinement presented in this paper. We hope this will allow us to verify a large spectrum of properties in a compositional way.

Acknowledgement

We are very grateful to Steve Campos and Caroline Lasalle for their participation in the development of *SynCo*.

References

1. J.-R. Abrial. *The B Book*. Cambridge University Press - ISBN 0521-496195, 1996.
2. J.-R. Abrial. Constructions d'automatismes industriels avec B. In *Congrès AFADL*, ONERA-CERT - Toulouse, France, May 1997. Invited lecture.
3. J.-R. Abrial. Discrete system models. Version 1.1, February 2002.
4. J.-R. Abrial and L. Mussat. Introducing dynamic constraints in B. In *Second Conference on the B method, France*, volume 1393 of *LNCS*, pages 83–128. Springer Verlag, April 1998.
5. P. Behm, P. Desforges, and J.M. Meynadier. MÉTÉOR: An industrial success in formal development. In *Second conference on the B method*, volume 1393 of *Lecture Notes in Computer Science*, Montpellier, France, April 1998. Springer Verlag. Invited lecture.
6. F. Bellegarde, C. Darlot, J. Julliand, and O. Kouchnarenko. Reformulate dynamic properties during B refinement and forget variants and loop invariants. In *Proc. First Int. Conf. ZB'2000, York, Great Britain*, volume 1878 of *LNCS*, pages 230–249. Springer-Verlag, September 2000.
7. F. Bellegarde, C. Darlot, J. Julliand, and O. Kouchnarenko. Reformulation: a way to combine dynamic properties and B refinement. In *In Proc. Int. Conf. Formal Method Europe'01, Berlin, Germany*, volume 2021 of *LNCS*, pages 2–19. Springer Verlag, March 2001.
8. F. Bellegarde, J. Julliand, and O. Kouchnarenko. Ready-simulation is not ready to express a modular refinement relation. In *Proc. Int. Conf. on Fundamental Aspects of Software Engineering, FASE'2000*, volume 1783 of *LNCS*, pages 266–283. Springer-Verlag, April 2000.
9. F. Bellegarde, J. Julliand, and O. Kouchnarenko. Synchronized parallel composition of event systems in *B*. In D. Bert, J. P. Bowen, M. C. Henson, and K. Robinson, editors, *ZB 2002 : Formal specification and development in Z and B*, volume 2272 of LNCS, pages 436–457. Springer-Verlag, 2002.
10. N. Bjørner, A. Browne, M. Colón, B. Finkbeiner, Z. Manna, M. Pichora, H. B. Sipma, and T. E. Uribe. *STeP - The Stanford Temporal Prover - Educational Release - User's Manual*. Computer Science Department - Stanford University, Stanford, California 94305, july 1998.
11. P. Bontron and M.-L. Potet. Automatic construction of validated B components from structured developments. In *Proc. First Int. Conf. ZB'2000, York, Great Britain*, volume 1878 of *LNCS*, pages 127–147. Springer-Verlag, September 2000.
12. M. J. Butler. csp2B: A practical approach to combining CSP and B. *Formal Aspects of Computing*, 12:182–198, 2000.

13. M. J. Butler and M. Waldén. *Program Development by Refinement (Case Studies Using the B Method)*, chapter Parallel Programming with the B Method. Springer, 1999.
14. C. Darlot, J. Julliand, and O. Kouchnarenko. Refinement preserves PLTL properties. In D. Bert, J. P. Bowen, S. C. King, and M. Walden, editors, *ZB'2003: Formal Specification and Development in Z and B*, volume 2651 of *LNCS*, Turku, Finland, June 2003. Springer-Verlag.
15. Hubert Garavel, Frédéric Lang, and Radu Mateescu. An overview of CADP 2001. Technical Report RT-254, INRIA, December 2001.
16. J. Julliand, F. Bellegarde, and B. Parreaux. De l'expression des besoins à l'expression formelle des propriétés dynamiques. *Technique et Science Informatiques*, 18(7), 1999.
17. J. Julliand, P-A. Masson, and H. Mountassir. Vérification par model-checking modulaire des propriétés dynamiques introduites en B. *Technique et Science Informatiques*, 20(7):927–957, 2001.
18. J. Julliand, P.A. Masson, and H. Mountassir. Modular verification of dynamic properties for reactive systems. In *International Workshop on Integrated Formal Methods (IFM'99)*, York, Great Britain, 1999.
19. O. Kouchnarenko and A. Lanoix. Refinement and verification of synchronized component-based systems. INRIA Research Report, June 2003. To appear.
20. L. Lamport. Specifying concurrent systems with TLA+. In *Calculational System Design*, Amsterdam, 1999. IOS Press.
21. A. Lanoix. Raffinement de systèmes à composants synchronisés et leur vérification. Mémoire de DEA - UFR Sciences et Techniques - Université de Franche-Comté, Septembre 2002.
22. J. Lind-Nielsen, H. R. Andersen, H. Hulgaard, G. Behrmann, K. Kristoffersen, and K. G. Larsen. Verification of large state/event systems using compositionality and dependency analysis. *Formal Methods in System Design*, 18(1):5–23, January 2001.
23. Z. Manna, N. Bjørner, A. Browne, E. Chang, M. Colón, Luca de Alfaro, H. Devarajan, A. Kapur, J. Lee, H. B. Sipma, and T. E. Uribe. STeP - the stanford temporal prover. *Theory and Practice of Software Developpement*, 915 of LNCS:793–794, May 1995.
24. P.-A. Masson, H. Mountassir, and J. Julliand. Modular verification for a class of PLTL properties. In T. Santen W. Grieskamp and B. Stoddart, editors, *2nd international conference on Integrated Formal Methods, IFM 2000*, volume 1945 of *LNCS*, pages 398–419. Springer-Verlag, November 2000.
25. A. Rabinovich. On compositional method and its limitations. Technical report, University of Edinburgh, Research Report EDI-INF-RR-0035, 2001.
26. S. Schneider and H. Treharne. Communicating *B* machines. In D. Bert, J. P. Bowen, M. C. Henson, and K. Robinson, editors, *ZB 2002 : Formal specification and development in Z and B*, volume 2272 of LNCS, pages 416–435. Springer-Verlag, 2002.
27. E. Sekerinski. *Program Development by Refinement (Case Studies Using the B Method)*, chapter Production Cell. Springer, 1999.
28. H. Treharne, J. Draper, and S. Schneider. Test case preparation using a prototype. In *Second conference on the B method*, LNCS 1393, pages 293–312, Montpellier, France, April 1998. Springer Verlag.
29. H. Treharne and S. Schneider. Using a process algebra to control B OPERATIONS. In *IFM'99 1st International Conference on Integrated Formal Methods*, pages 437–457, York, 1999. Springer-Verlag.

Certifying and Synthesizing Membership Equational Proofs

Grigore Roşu[1], Steven Eker[2], Patrick Lincoln[2], and José Meseguer[1]

[1] Department of Computer Science, University of Illinois at Urbana-Champaign, USA
[2] Computer Science Laboratory, SRI International, USA

Abstract. As the systems we have to specify and verify become larger and more complex, there is a mounting need to combine different tools and decision procedures to accomplish large proof tasks. The problem, then, is how to be sure that we can *trust* heterogeneous proofs produced by different tools based on different formalisms. In this work we focus on certification and synthesis of *equational proofs*, that are pervasive in most proof tasks and for which many tools are poorly equipped. Fortunately, equational proof engines like ELAN and Maude can perform millions of equational proof steps per second which, if properly certified, can be trusted by other tools. We present a general method to certify and synthesize proofs in membership equational logic, where the synthesis may involve generating full proofs from proof traces *modulo* combinations of associativity, commutativity, and identity axioms. We propose a simple representation for proof objects and give algorithms that can synthesize space-efficient, machine-checkable proof objects from proof traces.

1 Introduction

As the systems we have to specify and verify become larger and more complex, there is a mounting need to use specialized high-performance proof engines and efficient decision procedures, because general-purpose single-formalism approaches typically do not scale up well to large tasks [1]. For this reason, in many tools (e.g., [18, 17, 9]) such general formalisms are combined or extended with a variety of decision procedures and specialized proof accelerators. More generally, there is a growing interest in supporting *heterogeneous proofs*, in which not a single tool, but a combination of tools, developed by different researchers and based on different formalisms, can cooperate to solve an overall proof task. The problem, however, is how to be sure that we can *trust* the correctness of a heterogeneous proof. We have called this problem the *formal interoperability problem* [14] (see also [22, 15]). It can be naturally decomposed into two subproblems: (1) relating the semantics of different formalisms by adequate *maps of logics* [11, 7, 22, 15] that are then proved correct; and (2) providing machine-checkable *proof objects* for the proof subtasks carried out within each formalism by each tool. For example, in [20, 21] subproblems (1) and (2) have been solved in a special case by proving the correctness of a mapping between the logics of HOL [8] and NuPRL [6], and by defining a mapping between HOL and NuPRL proof objects.

In this paper we focus on subproblem (2), that is, on how to *certify* in a system-independent and machine-checkable way *proofs* carried out in a given formalism. This means that *we do not have to trust the tool* proving the subtask in question: if a machine-checkable proof of the result is provided, then it can be certified using a trusted proof checker. More specifically, we focus on certification of *equality proofs*, which are typically represented as sequences of uses of the straightforward inference rules of equational logics. There is great practical interest in certified equality proofs not only because of the pervasive need for equational reasoning, but also because of the need to use fast equational engines within theorem proving tasks: on the one hand, some, otherwise quite powerful, theorem provers such as provers based on higher-order logics, need to carry out equality proofs step by step and do not scale up well to large equality proofs [1]; on the other hand, the wealth of results and techniques in equational reasoning and term rewriting, combined with advanced compilation technology, has made possible the recent development of very high performance *equational proof engines* such as ELAN [2] and Maude [5] that routinely carry out millions of equational proof steps per second. Furthermore, the equational proofs carried out by such engines are quite sophisticated: in ELAN they can be proofs *modulo* associativity and commutativity (AC), and in Maude they can be proofs *modulo* any combination of associativity (A), commutativity (C), and identity (U) axioms for different operators.

The power of equational deduction modulo such axioms brings about a corresponding *proof synthesis problem*: the tools must certify not only their *explicit* deduction steps, but also their *implicit* equational reasoning modulo axioms such as A, C, and U. For example, Maude provides a *trace* of equality steps that, in the simpler case of unconditional equations, looks roughly as follows:

$$t_0 \stackrel{e_1}{=} t_1 \stackrel{e_2}{=} t_2 \ldots t_{n-1} \stackrel{e_n}{=} t_n$$

with e_i the equation used in the ith step. However, since each such step is performed *modulo* axioms, say $\mathcal{AX}$, to have a full proof object certifying the task the implicit $\mathcal{AX}$-equality steps must be expanded out to:

$$t_0 \stackrel{\mathcal{AX}}{=} t'_0 \stackrel{e_1}{=} t_1 \stackrel{\mathcal{AX}}{=} t'_1 \stackrel{e_2}{=} t_2 \stackrel{\mathcal{AX}}{=} t'_2 \ldots t_{n-1} \stackrel{\mathcal{AX}}{=} t'_{n-1} \stackrel{e_n}{=} t_n$$

where each proof $t_i \stackrel{\mathcal{AX}}{=} t'_i$ is no longer a one-step equality replacement, but may involve repeated application of the axioms in $\mathcal{AX}$. The proof synthesis problem involves synthesizing *short proofs* to fill the above "$\mathcal{AX}$-gaps" $t_i \stackrel{\mathcal{AX}}{=} t'_i$. Since a typical trace may contain many millions of explicit equality steps, finding short proofs of the $\mathcal{AX}$-gaps is essential for scalability.

Our goals in this work are:

1. supporting the greatest possible generality in the kinds of equational proofs that can be certified and synthesized;
2. achieving the greatest possible simplicity, efficiency, and ease of check for the proof objects; and

3. synthesizing proofs that are as short as possible.

We address goal (1) by considering proofs in *membership equational logic*, a framework logic for equational reasoning [13] that contains many other logics (unsorted, many-sorted, order-sorted, etc.) as special cases, yet is efficiently implemented in Maude. Additional generality is gained by considering proofs *modulo* any combination of A, C, and U axioms. Our approach to goal (2) takes the form of extremely simple proof objects, that can be easily checked without any need for parsing, and where proof subtasks can be *shared* for greater space and time checking efficiency. Goal (3) is addressed by new synthesis algorithms for $\mathcal{AX}$-gap proofs $t_i \stackrel{\mathcal{AX}}{=} t'_i$, with $\mathcal{AX}$ any combination of A, C, and U axioms, that have length $\mathcal{O}(|t_i| \times log(|t_i|))$ in the worse case.

Our work has been stimulated by recent work of Q.H. Nguyen, C. Kirchner, and H. Kirchner [16] on proof objects for equality proofs that can be used to certify to the Coq prover equality proofs carried out in the ELAN engine. Besides using a different proof representation that we think has important advantages, the main differences between our work and theirs are: (1) the greater generality of the equational logic (many-sorted in their case, membership equational logic in ours) and of the proofs modulo (AC in their case, any combination of A, C, and U in ours); and (2) the shorter length of the synthesized proofs for $\mathcal{AX}$-gap proofs ($\mathcal{O}(|t_i|^2)$ in their case, $\mathcal{O}(|t_i| \times log(|t_i|))$ in ours).

2 Membership Equational Logic

In this section we recall membership equational logic (MEL) definitions and notations needed in the paper. The interested reader is referred to [13, 3] for a comprehensive exposition of MEL.

A *membership signature* Ω is a triple (K, Σ, π) where K is a set of *kinds*, Σ is a K-sorted (in this context called K-*kinded*) algebraic signature, and $\pi\colon S \to K$ is a function that assigns to each element in its domain, called a *sort*, a kind. Therefore, sorts are grouped according to kinds and operations are defined on kinds. For simplicity, we will call a "membership signature" just a "signature" whenever there is no confusion. For any given signature $\Omega = (K, \Sigma, \pi)$, an Ω-*(membership) algebra* A is a Σ-algebra together with a set $A_s \subseteq A_{\pi(s)}$ for each sort $s \in S$, and an Ω-*homomorphism* $h\colon A \to B$ is a Σ-homomorphism such that for each $s \in S$ we have $h_{\pi(s)}(A_s) \subseteq B_s$. Given a signature Ω and a K-indexed set of *variables*, an *atomic* (Ω, X)-*equation* has the form $t = t'$, where $t, t' \in T_{\Sigma,k}(X)$, and an *atomic* (Ω, X)-*membership* has the form $t : s$, where s is a sort and $t \in T_{\Sigma,\pi(s)}(X)$. An Ω-*sentence* in MEL has the form $(\forall X)$ a if $a_1 \wedge \ldots \wedge a_n$, where $a, a_1, \ldots, a_n$ are atomic (Ω, X)-equations or (Ω, X)-memberships, and $\{a_1, \ldots, a_n\}$ is a set (no duplications). If $n = 0$, then the Ω-sentence is called *unconditional* and written $(\forall X)$ a. Given an Ω-algebra A and a K-kinded map $\theta\colon X \to A$, then $A, \theta \models_\Omega t = t'$ iff $\theta(t) = \theta(t')$, and $A, \theta \models_\Omega t : s$ iff $\theta(t) \in A_s$. A *satisfies* $(\forall X)$ a if $a_1 \wedge \ldots \wedge a_n$, written $A \models_\Omega (\forall X)$ a if $a_1 \wedge \ldots \wedge a_n$, iff for each $\theta\colon X \to A$, if $A, \theta \models_\Omega a_1$ and ... and $A, \theta \models_\Omega a_n$, then $A, \theta \models_\Omega a$. An

Ω-specification (or Ω-theory) $T = (\Omega, E)$ in MEL consists of a signature Ω and a set E of Ω-sentences. An Ω-algebra A *satisfies* (or *is a model of*) $T = (\Omega, E)$, written $A \models T$, iff it satisfies each sentence in E. We let $\mathbf{MAlg}_T$ denote the full subcategory of $\mathbf{MAlg}_\Omega$ of membership Ω-algebras satisfying an Ω-theory T.

MEL admits complete deduction (see [13], where the rule of congruence is stated in a somewhat different but equivalent way; in the congruence rule below, $\sigma \in \Sigma_{k_1...k_i,k}$, W is a set of variables $w_1 : k_1, \ldots, w_{i-1} : k_{i-1}, w_{i+1} : k_{i+1}, \ldots, w_n : k_n$, and $\sigma(W, t)$ is a shorthand for the term $\sigma(w_1, \ldots, w_{i-1}, t, w_{i+1}, \ldots, w_n)$):

(1) Reflexivity : $\dfrac{}{E \vdash_\Omega (\forall X)\ t = t}$

(2) Symmetry : $\dfrac{E \vdash_\Omega (\forall X)\ t = t'}{E \vdash_\Omega (\forall X)\ t' = t}$

(3) Transitivity : $\dfrac{E \vdash_\Omega (\forall X)\ t = t',\ E \vdash_\Omega (\forall X)\ t' = t''}{E \vdash_\Omega (\forall X)\ t = t''}$

(4) Congruence : $\dfrac{E \vdash_\Omega (\forall X)\ t = t'}{E \vdash_\Omega (\forall X, W)\ \sigma(W, t) = \sigma(W, t'),\ \text{for each } \sigma \in \Sigma}$

(5) Membership : $\dfrac{E \vdash_\Omega (\forall X)\ t = t',\ E \vdash_\Omega (\forall X)\ t : s}{E \vdash_\Omega (\forall X)\ t' : s}$

(6) Modus Ponens : $\left\{ \begin{array}{l} \text{Given a sentence in } E \\ \quad (\forall Y)\ t = t'\ \text{if}\ t_1 = t'_1 \wedge ... \wedge t_n = t'_n \wedge w_1 : s_1 \wedge ... \wedge w_m : s_m \\ \quad (\text{resp. } (\forall Y)\ t : s\ \text{if}\ t_1 = t'_1 \wedge ... \wedge t_n = t'_n \wedge w_1 : s_1 \wedge ... \wedge w_m : s_m) \\ \text{and } \theta \colon Y \to T_\Sigma(X)\ \text{s.t. for all } i \in \{1,..,n\}\ \text{and } j \in \{1,..,m\} \\ \dfrac{E \vdash_\Omega (\forall X)\ \theta(t_i) = \theta(t'_i),\ E \vdash_\Omega (\forall X)\ \theta(w_j) : s_j}{E \vdash_\Omega (\forall X)\ \theta(t) = \theta(t')\quad (\text{resp. } E \vdash_\Omega (\forall X)\ \theta(t) : s)} \end{array} \right.$

The rules above can therefore prove any unconditional equation or membership that is true in all membership algebras satisfying E. [19] gives a four-rule categorical equational inference system which can handle directly conditional equations, but that proof system is not well explored yet and seems hard to formalize at the level of detail needed in this paper. In order to derive conditional statements, we will therefore consider the standard technique adapting the "deduction theorem" to equational logics, namely deriving the conclusion of the sentence after adding the condition as an axiom; in order for this procedure to be correct, the variables used in conclusion need to be first transformed into constants. All variables can be transformed into constants, so we only consider the following simplified rules:

(7) Theorem of Constants : $\dfrac{E \vdash_{\Omega \cup X} (\forall \emptyset)\ a\ \text{if}\ a_1 \wedge ... \wedge a_n}{E \vdash_\Omega (\forall X)\ a\ \text{if}\ a_1 \wedge ... \wedge a_n}$

(8) Implication Elimination : $\dfrac{E \cup \{a_1, \ldots, a_n\} \vdash_\Omega (\forall \emptyset)\ a}{E \vdash_\Omega (\forall \emptyset)\ a\ \text{if}\ a_1 \wedge ... \wedge a_n}$

Theorem 1. *(from [13]) With the notation above, $E \models_\Omega (\forall X)\ a\ \text{if}\ a_1 \wedge ... \wedge a_n$ if and only if $E \vdash_\Omega (\forall X)\ a\ \text{if}\ a_1 \wedge ... \wedge a_n$. Moreover, any statement can be proved by first applying rule (7), then (8), and then a series of rules (1) to (6).*

Maude [5] is an executable specification language supporting membership equational logic and also rewriting logic [12]. To make specifications easier to read, and to emphasize that order-sorted specifications are a special case of MEL ones, the following syntactic sugar conventions are supported by Maude:

Subsorts. Given sorts s, s' with $\pi(s) = \pi(s') = k$, the declaration $s < s'$ is syntactic sugar for the conditional membership $(\forall x : k)\ x : s'$ if $x : s$.

Operations. If $\sigma \in \Omega_{k_1 \ldots k_n, k}$ and $s_1, \ldots, s_n, s \in S$ with $\pi(s_1) = k_1, \ldots, \pi(s_n) = k_n$, $\pi(s) = k$, then the declaration $\sigma : s_1 \cdots s_n \to s$ is syntactic sugar for $(\forall x_1 : k_1, \ldots, x_n : k_n)\ \sigma(x_1, \ldots, x_n) : s$ if $x_1 : s_1 \wedge \ldots \wedge x_n : s_n$.

Variables. $(\forall x : s, X)\ a$ if $a_1 \wedge \ldots \wedge a_n$ is syntactic sugar for the Ω-sentence $(\forall x : \pi(s), X)\ a$ if $a_1 \wedge \ldots \wedge a_n \wedge x : s$. With this, the operation declaration $\sigma : s_1 \cdots s_n \to s$ is equivalent to $(\forall x_1 : s_1, \ldots, x_n : s_n)\ \sigma(x_1, \ldots, x_n) : s$.

We next give two examples of MEL specifications in Maude.

Example 1. This example is inspired by group theory. Suppose that a MEL specification defines a kind k, a constant $e :\to k$, a unary operation $\_^{-} : k \to k$, a binary operation $\_\star\_ : k \times k \to k$, and the three equations $(\forall A : k)\ e \star A = A$, $(\forall A : k)\ A^{-} \star A = e$, and $(\forall A, B, C : k)\ A \star (B \star C) = (A \star B) \star C$. The right-inverse and right-identity properties can then be proved.

In Maude, kinds are declared only implicitly, via declarations of sorts and subsorts. More precisely, a kind is automatically defined for every connected component in the partial order on sorts. Maude also implements efficient algorithms for rewriting modulo any combination of A, C, and U; however, in order to make proper use of them, the user needs to declare associativity, commutativity and/or identity as operator attributes rather than equations. The MEL specification of groups can then be implemented in Maude as follows:

```
fmod GROUP is sort S .
    op _*_ : S S -> S [assoc] .   op _- : S -> S .   op e : -> S .
    var A : S .   eq e * A = A .   eq (A -) * A = e .
endfm
```

The above specification is not confluent when regarded as a rewriting system. However, one can still use Maude to prove group properties, such as the right inverse law by giving two variants of a common expression modulo associativity, reduce ((A - -)*(A -))*(A * (A -)) and reduce (A - -)*(((A -) * A)*(A -)), which reduce to A * (A -) and e, respectively.

Example 2. Let us now consider a MEL specification of graphs with nodes, edges and paths, which additionally involves sorts and conditional statements. There are two kinds, k_n and k_p, for node and path elements, respectively. k_n contains a sort *Node*, and k_p contains *Edge* and *Path*. Any edge is a path, so we add the "subsort" membership (we label axioms to refer to them later):

[*EdgeIsPath*] $(\forall P : k_p)\ P : Path$ if $P : Edge$.

Source and target operators are also defined, $s, t : k_p \to k_n$, noticing that they return proper nodes only for proper paths:

[*SourceNode*] $(\forall P : k_p)\ s(P) : Node$ if $P : Path$,
[*TargetNode*] $(\forall P : k_p)\ t(P) : Node$ if $P : Path$.

Paths can be concatenated using the operator $\_;\_ : k_p \times k_p \to k_p$, but a correct path can be obtained only under appropriate conditions:

[*CorrectPath*] ($\forall E, P : k_p$) $E; P : Path$ if $E : Edge \wedge P : Path \wedge t(E) = s(P)$.

The source and target of a path are defined also under appropriate conditions:

[*PathSource*] ($\forall P, Q : k_p$) $s(P; Q) = s(P)$ if $P : Path \wedge Q : Path \wedge t(P) = s(Q)$,
[*PathTarget*] ($\forall P, Q : k_p$) $t(P; Q) = t(Q)$ if $P : Path \wedge Q : Path \wedge t(P) = s(Q)$.

Finally, we introduce the associativity of path composition:

[*Assoc*] ($\forall P, Q, R : k_p$) $(P; Q); R = P; (Q; R)$ if
$P : Path \wedge Q : Path \wedge R : Path \wedge t(P) = s(Q) \wedge t(Q) = s(R)$.

These axioms are all declared in the following (sugared) Maude specification:

```
fmod GRAPH is sorts Node Edge Path .        subsort Edge < Path .
  ops s t : Path -> Node .                  op _;_ : Path Path -> [Path] .
  vars P Q R : Path .  var E : Edge .
  cmb E ; P : Path if t(E) = s(P) .
  ceq s(P ; Q) = s(P) if t(P) = s(Q) .   ceq t(P ; Q) = t(Q) if t(P) = s(Q) .
  ceq (P ; Q) ; R = P ; (Q ; R) if t(P) = s(Q) /\ t(Q) = s(R) .
endfm
```

3 Formalizing Proofs

In order to be mechanically checked, MEL proofs have to be first formalized. In this section we present such a formalization, for which a proof certifier will be given in the next section. By Theorem 1, any MEL sentence can be proved by first applying the theorem of constants, followed by implication elimination, and then by a series of applications of rules (1)–(6). This is reflected in our formalization of proofs by considering that proof objects have the following structure:

⟨*Proof Object*⟩ ::= ⟨*Proof Goal: Desugared Specification and Sentence*⟩
⟨*Theorem of Constants*⟩ ⟨*Implication Elimination*⟩
⟨*Ground Proof*⟩

The proof goal, containing a specification and a sentence, both in desugared form, can be just a name referring to a file containing it. Keeping it isolated from proofs is a desirable feature for certifying authorities, who essentially want to consider proofs as nothing but mechanically checkable correctness certificates for well defined, often public, verification tasks. We do not enforce any specific syntax for defining and referring to the specification and the sentence to prove. The theorem of constants rule just adds constants to specification's signature:

⟨*Theorem of Constants*⟩ ::= (constants (⟨*Constant*⟩ : → ⟨*Kind*⟩)*)

⟨*Constant*⟩ and ⟨*Kind*⟩ are identifiers. The syntax of the implication elimination rule is similar, in the sense that one adds equations or memberships to the specification; these new axioms should have (unique) labels:

⟨*Implication Elimination*⟩ ::=
  (implication ([⟨*AxLabel*⟩] (eq ⟨*Term*⟩ = ⟨*Term*⟩ | mb ⟨*Term*⟩ : ⟨*Sort*⟩))*)

⟨*Sort*⟩ is an identifier. ⟨*Term*⟩ is a list of characters that the proof checker will ensure that is a well formed, disambiguated prefix term over the signature of the specification. A ground proof is a nonempty sequence of proof steps

⟨*Ground Proof*⟩ ::= (⟨*Proof Step*⟩)$^+$,

where a proof step applies one of the rules (1)–(6). Each proof step is supposed to have a unique label, which is an integer number; the proof checker will ensure that these labels are used in increasing order:

⟨*Proof Step*⟩ ::= (⟨*Label*⟩ ⟨*Rule*⟩)
⟨*Rule*⟩ ::= ⟨*Reflexivity*⟩ | ⟨*Symmetry*⟩ | ⟨*Transitivity*⟩ |
        ⟨*Congruence*⟩ | ⟨*Membership*⟩ | ⟨*Modus-Ponens*⟩
⟨*Reflexivity*⟩ ::= reflexivity eq ⟨*Term*⟩ = ⟨*Term*⟩
⟨*Symmetry*⟩ ::= symmetry eq ⟨*Term*⟩ = ⟨*Term*⟩ follows by ⟨*Label*⟩
⟨*Transitivity*⟩ ::= transitivity eq ⟨*Term*⟩ = ⟨*Term*⟩
        follows by ⟨*Label*⟩ ⟨*Label*⟩
⟨*Congruence*⟩ ::= congruence eq ⟨*Term*⟩ = ⟨*Term*⟩
        position ⟨*Integer*⟩ follows by ⟨*Label*⟩
⟨*Membership*⟩ ::= membership mb ⟨*Term*⟩ : ⟨*Sort*⟩
        follows by ⟨*Label*⟩ ⟨*Label*⟩
⟨*Modus-Ponens*⟩ ::= modus-ponens
        (eq ⟨*Term*⟩ = ⟨*Term*⟩ | mb ⟨*Term*⟩ : ⟨*Sort*⟩)
        axiom ⟨*AxLabel*⟩ map ((⟨*Var*⟩:⟨*Kind*⟩ <- ⟨*Term*⟩)*
        [follows by (⟨*Label*⟩)*]

Spaces and new lines should be read as white spaces in the formalized syntax of MEL rules above. The list of labels in a modus-ponens rule application represents the proofs of the instantiated conditions of the axiom ⟨*AxLabel*⟩; not needed if the axiom is unconditional. The keywords can be shortened and some other encoding conventions can be devised in practical implementations in order to reduce the size of proofs, but essentially the same amount of information is needed in order to simplify the proof checker as much as possible.

Example 3. Let the group axioms in Example 1 have the labels *leftId*, *leftInv*, and *assoc*, respectively. In fully disambiguated form, as our proof certifier defined in the next section expects its input, these equational axioms are written as

$(\forall A : k)$ $\_\star_{-kk,k}(e_{\lambda,k}, A) = A,$
$(\forall A : k)$ $\_\star_{-kk,k}(\bar{\_}_{-k,k}(A), A) = e_{\lambda,k},$
$(\forall A : k, B : k, C : k)$ $\_\star_{-kk,k}(A, \_\star_{-kk,k}(B,C)) = \_\star_{-kk,k}(\_\star_{-kk,k}(A,B),C).$

Suppose now that the goal is to prove the right identity property, namely the equation $(\forall A : k)$ $\_\star_{-kk,k}(A, e_{\lambda,k}) = A.$ Then the following is a proof according to the formalization described above: (constants $a_{\lambda,k} :\to k$) (implication)
(1   modus-ponens eq $\_\star_{-kk,k}(e, \_\star_{-kk,k}(a_{\lambda,k}, \bar{\_}_{-k,k}(a_{\lambda,k}))) = \_\star_{-kk,k}(a_{\lambda,k}, \bar{\_}_{-k,k}(a_{\lambda,k}))$
    axiom *leftId* map $A : k$ <- $\_\star_{-kk,k}(a_{\lambda,k}, \bar{\_}_{-k,k}(a_{\lambda,k}))$)

(2 modus-ponens eq $\_\ast_{-kk,k}(-\bar{{}_{k,k}}(-\bar{{}_{k,k}}(a_{\lambda,k})), -\bar{{}_{k,k}}(a_{\lambda,k})) = e$ axiom $leftInv$ map $A : k$ <- $-\bar{{}_{k,k}}(a_{\lambda,k}))$
(3 symmetry eq $e = \_\ast_{-kk,k}(-\bar{{}_{k,k}}(-\bar{{}_{k,k}}(a_{\lambda,k})), -\bar{{}_{k,k}}(a_{\lambda,k}))$ follows by 2)
(4 congruence eq $\_\ast_{-kk,k}(e, \_\ast_{-kk,k}(a_{\lambda,k}, -\bar{{}_{k,k}}(a_{\lambda,k}))) =$
    $\_\ast_{-kk,k}(\_\ast_{-kk,k}(-\bar{{}_{k,k}}(-\bar{{}_{k,k}}(a_{\lambda,k})), -\bar{{}_{k,k}}(a_{\lambda,k})), \_\ast_{-kk,k}(a_{\lambda,k}, -\bar{{}_{k,k}}(a_{\lambda,k})))$ position 1 follows by 3)
(5 symmetry eq $\_\ast_{-kk,k}(\_\ast_{-kk,k}(-\bar{{}_{k,k}}(-\bar{{}_{k,k}}(a_{\lambda,k})), -\bar{{}_{k,k}}(a_{\lambda,k})), \_\ast_{-kk,k}(a_{\lambda,k}, -\bar{{}_{k,k}}(a_{\lambda,k}))) =$
    $\_\ast_{-kk,k}(e, \_\ast_{-kk,k}(a_{\lambda,k}, -\bar{{}_{k,k}}(a_{\lambda,k})))$ follows by 4)
(6 transitivity eq $\_\ast_{-kk,k}(\_\ast_{-kk,k}(-\bar{{}_{k,k}}(-\bar{{}_{k,k}}(a_{\lambda,k})), -\bar{{}_{k,k}}(a_{\lambda,k})), \_\ast_{-kk,k}(a_{\lambda,k}, -\bar{{}_{k,k}}(a_{\lambda,k}))) =$
    $\_\ast_{-kk,k}(a_{\lambda,k}, -\bar{{}_{k,k}}(a_{\lambda,k}))$ follows by 5 1)
(7 modus-ponens eq $\_\ast_{-kk,k}(-\bar{{}_{k,k}}(a_{\lambda,k}), a_{\lambda,k}) = e$ axiom $leftInv$ map $A : k$ <- $a_{\lambda,k}$)
(8 congruence eq $\_\ast_{-kk,k}(\_\ast_{-kk,k}(-\bar{{}_{k,k}}(a_{\lambda,k}), a_{\lambda,k}), -\bar{{}_{k,k}}(a_{\lambda,k})) = \_\ast_{-kk,k}(e, -\bar{{}_{k,k}}(a_{\lambda,k}))$
    position 1 follows by 7)
(9 modus-ponens eq $\_\ast_{-kk,k}(e, -\bar{{}_{k,k}}(a_{\lambda,k})) = -\bar{{}_{k,k}}(a_{\lambda,k})$ axiom $leftId$ map $A : k$ <- $-\bar{{}_{k,k}}(a_{\lambda,k})$)
(10 transitivity eq $\_\ast_{-kk,k}(\_\ast_{-kk,k}(-\bar{{}_{k,k}}(a_{\lambda,k}), a_{\lambda,k}), -\bar{{}_{k,k}}(a_{\lambda,k})) = -\bar{{}_{k,k}}(a_{\lambda,k})$ follows by 8 9)
(11 modus-ponens eq $\_\ast_{-kk,k}(-\bar{{}_{k,k}}(a_{\lambda,k}), \_\ast_{-kk,k}(a_{\lambda,k}, -\bar{{}_{k,k}}(a_{\lambda,k}))) =$
    $\_\ast_{-kk,k}(\_\ast_{-kk,k}(-\bar{{}_{k,k}}(a_{\lambda,k}), a_{\lambda,k}), -\bar{{}_{k,k}}(a_{\lambda,k}))$
    axiom $assoc$ map $A : k$ <- $-\bar{{}_{k,k}}(a_{\lambda,k})$ $B : k$ <- $a_{\lambda,k}$ $C : k$ <- $-\bar{{}_{k,k}}(a_{\lambda,k})$)
(12 transitivity eq $\_\ast_{-kk,k}(-\bar{{}_{k,k}}(a_{\lambda,k}), \_\ast_{-kk,k}(a_{\lambda,k}, -\bar{{}_{k,k}}(a_{\lambda,k}))) = -\bar{{}_{k,k}}(a_{\lambda,k})$ follows by 11 10)
(13 congruence eq $\_\ast_{-kk,k}(-\bar{{}_{k,k}}(-\bar{{}_{k,k}}(a_{\lambda,k})), \_\ast_{-kk,k}(-\bar{{}_{k,k}}(a_{\lambda,k}), \_\ast_{-kk,k}(a_{\lambda,k}, -\bar{{}_{k,k}}(a_{\lambda,k})))) =$
    $\_\ast_{-kk,k}(-\bar{{}_{k,k}}(-\bar{{}_{k,k}}(a_{\lambda,k})), -\bar{{}_{k,k}}(a_{\lambda,k}))$ position 2 follows by 12)
(14 modus-ponens eq $\_\ast_{-kk,k}(-\bar{{}_{k,k}}(-\bar{{}_{k,k}}(a_{\lambda,k})), \_\ast_{-kk,k}(-\bar{{}_{k,k}}(a_{\lambda,k}), \_\ast_{-kk,k}(a_{\lambda,k}, -\bar{{}_{k,k}}(a_{\lambda,k})))) =$
    $\_\ast_{-kk,k}(\_\ast_{-kk,k}(-\bar{{}_{k,k}}(-\bar{{}_{k,k}}(a_{\lambda,k})), -\bar{{}_{k,k}}(a_{\lambda,k})), \_\ast_{-kk,k}(a_{\lambda,k}, -\bar{{}_{k,k}}(a_{\lambda,k})))$ axiom $assoc$ map
    $A : k$ <- $-\bar{{}_{k,k}}(-\bar{{}_{k,k}}(a_{\lambda,k}))$ $B : k$ <- $-\bar{{}_{k,k}}(a_{\lambda,k})$ $C : k$ <- $\_\ast_{-kk,k}(a_{\lambda,k}, -\bar{{}_{k,k}}(a_{\lambda,k}))$)
(15 symmetry eq $\_\ast_{-kk,k}(\_\ast_{-kk,k}(-\bar{{}_{k,k}}(-\bar{{}_{k,k}}(a_{\lambda,k})), -\bar{{}_{k,k}}(a_{\lambda,k})), \_\ast_{-kk,k}(a_{\lambda,k}, -\bar{{}_{k,k}}(a_{\lambda,k}))) =$
    $\_\ast_{-kk,k}(-\bar{{}_{k,k}}(-\bar{{}_{k,k}}(a_{\lambda,k})), \_\ast_{-kk,k}(-\bar{{}_{k,k}}(a_{\lambda,k}), \_\ast_{-kk,k}(a_{\lambda,k}, -\bar{{}_{k,k}}(a_{\lambda,k}))))$ follows by 14)
(16 transitivity eq $\_\ast_{-kk,k}(\_\ast_{-kk,k}(-\bar{{}_{k,k}}(-\bar{{}_{k,k}}(a_{\lambda,k})), -\bar{{}_{k,k}}(a_{\lambda,k})), \_\ast_{-kk,k}(a_{\lambda,k}, -\bar{{}_{k,k}}(a_{\lambda,k}))) =$
    $\_\ast_{-kk,k}(-\bar{{}_{k,k}}(-\bar{{}_{k,k}}(a_{\lambda,k})), -\bar{{}_{k,k}}(a_{\lambda,k}))$ follows by 15 13)
(17 symmetry eq $\_\ast_{-kk,k}(a_{\lambda,k}, -\bar{{}_{k,k}}(a_{\lambda,k})) =$
    $\_\ast_{-kk,k}(\_\ast_{-kk,k}(-\bar{{}_{k,k}}(-\bar{{}_{k,k}}(a_{\lambda,k})), -\bar{{}_{k,k}}(a_{\lambda,k})), \_\ast_{-kk,k}(a_{\lambda,k}, -\bar{{}_{k,k}}(a_{\lambda,k})))$ follows by 6)
(18 transitivity
    eq $\_\ast_{-kk,k}(a_{\lambda,k}, -\bar{{}_{k,k}}(a_{\lambda,k})) = \_\ast_{-kk,k}(-\bar{{}_{k,k}}(-\bar{{}_{k,k}}(a_{\lambda,k})), -\bar{{}_{k,k}}(a_{\lambda,k}))$ follows by 17 16)
(19 transitivity eq $\_\ast_{-kk,k}(a_{\lambda,k}, -\bar{{}_{k,k}}(a_{\lambda,k})) = e$ follows by 18 2)

Example 4. Let us now consider the MEL specification of graphs in Example 2. In order to keep the notation simple, in this example we do not write symbols in their disambiguated form, as we did in the previous example. However, our proof checker described in the next section requires each symbol to be disambiguated. We next give a formalized proof object for the following conditional equation: $(\forall N_1, N_1, N_3 : k_n; E_1, E_2, E_3 : k_p)$ $(E_1; E_2); (E_3; E_1) = E_1; ((E_2; E_3); E_1)$ if $N_1 : Node \wedge N_2 : Node \wedge N_3 : Node \wedge E_1 : Edge \wedge E_2 : Edge \wedge E_3 : Edge \wedge$ $s(E_1) = N_1 \wedge s(E_2) = N_2 \wedge s(E_3) = N_3 \wedge t(E_1) = N_2 \wedge t(E_2) = N_3 \wedge t(E_3) = N_1$. Despite its apparently intuitive simplicity, the proof of the above implication is quite tedious. This is because one actually has to prove *all* the conditions of a sentence before applying it via the modus-ponens rule. In a mechanically checkable proof this information is needed.

(constants $n_1 :\to k_n$ $n_2 :\to k_n$ $n_3 :\to k_n$ $e_1 :\to k_p$ $e_2 :\to k_p$ $e_3 :\to k_p$)
(implication [imp1] mb $n_1 : Node$ [imp2] mb $n_2 : Node$ [imp3] mb $n_3 : Node$ [imp4] mb $e_1 : Edge$
    [imp5] mb $e_2 : Edge$ [imp6] mb $e_3 : Edge$ [imp7] eq $s(e_1) = n_1$ [imp8] eq $s(e_2) = n_2$
    [imp9] eq $s(e_3) = n_3$ [imp10] eq $t(e_1) = n_2$ [imp11] eq $t(e_2) = n_3$ [imp12] eq $t(e_3) = n_1$)
(1 modus-ponens mb $e_1 : Edge$ axiom $imp4$ map)
(2 modus-ponens mb $e_1 : Path$ axiom $EdgeIsPath$ map $P : k_p$ <- e_1 follows by 1)
(3 modus-ponens mb $e_2 : Edge$ axiom $imp5$ map)
(4 modus-ponens mb $e_2 : Path$ axiom $EdgeIsPath$ map $P : k_p$ <- e_2 follows by 3)
(5 modus-ponens eq $s(e_1) = n_1$ axiom $imp7$ map)
(6 symmetry eq $n_1 = s(e_1)$ follows by 5)
(7 modus-ponens eq $t(e_3) = n_1$ axiom $imp12$ map)
(8 transitivity eq $t(e_3) = s(e_1)$ follows by 7 6)
(9 modus-ponens mb $e_3 : Edge$ axiom $imp6$ map)

(10 modus-ponens mb e_3 : $Path$ axiom $EdgeIsPath$ map $P : k_p$ <- e_3 follows by 1)
(11 modus-ponens mb $e_3; e_1$: $Path$ axiom $CorrectPath$ map $E : k_p$ <- e_3 $P : k_p$ <- e_1
      follows by 9 2 8)
(12 modus-ponens eq $s(e_2) = n_2$ axiom $imp8$ map)
(13 symmetry eq $n_2 = s(e_2)$ follows by 12)
(15 transitivity eq $t(e_1) = s(e_2)$ follows by 14 13)
(16 modus-ponens eq $t(e_2) = n_3$ axiom $imp11$ map)
(17 modus-ponens eq $s(e_3; e_1) = s(e_3)$ axiom $PathSource$ map $P : k_p$ <- e_3 $Q : k_p$ <- e_1
      follows by 10 2 8)
(18 modus-ponens eq $s(e_3) = n_3$ axiom $imp9$ map)
(19 transitivity eq $s(e_3; e_1) = n_3$ follows by 17 18)
(20 symmetry eq $n_3 = s(e_3; e_1)$ follows by 19)
(21 transitivity eq $t(e_2) = s(e_3; e_1)$ follows by 16 20)
(22 modus-ponens eq $(e_1; e_2); (e_3; e_1) = e_1; (e_2; (e_3; e_1))$ axiom $Assoc$
      map $P : k_p$ <- e_1 $Q : k_p$ <- e_2 $R : k_p$ <- $e_3; e_1$ follows by 2 4 11 15 21)
(23 transitivity eq $t(e_2) = s(e_3)$ follows by 21 17)
(24 modus-ponens eq $(e_2; e_3); e_1 = e_2; (e_3; e_1)$ axiom $Assoc$
      map $P : k_p$ <- e_2 $Q : k_p$ <- e_3 $R : k_p$ <- e_1 follows by 4 10 2 23 8)
(25 symmetry eq $e_2; (e_3; e_1) = (e_2; e_3); e_1$ follows by 24)
(26 congruence eq $e_1; (e_2; (e_3; e_1)) = e_1; ((e_2; e_3); e_1)$ position 2 follows by 25)
(27 transitivity eq $(e_1; e_2); (e_3; e_1) = e_1; ((e_2; e_3); e_1)$ follows by 22 26)

4 Certifying Proofs

The major reason why the proof objects formalized in the previous section are so low level is because a certifying authority will typically want to use a proof checker which is as simple as possible, in order to be easily validated and therefore trusted. A proof checker for generic logical frameworks, taking as input both a "logic", including its inference rules, and a proof within that logic, is a nice idea but in our view too complex to be easily trusted. Instead, we opt for logic specific proof checkers, having the inference rules of the logic, six in our case, hardwired. Interestingly, with the level of detail in proofs described above, the corresponding proof checker described in what follows does *not* even need parsing; it only needs to perform trivial checks in time linear on the size of the proofs. We expect its implementation to be quite trivial and short. For the rest of this section we assume a proof object satisfying the syntax in the previous section

(constants $c^1_{\lambda, k_1} :\to k_1$ ... $c^C_{\lambda, k_C} :\to k_C$)
(implication [$AxLabel1$] sentence1 ... [$AxLabelI$] sentenceI)
(1 proofStep1)
...
(N proofStepN)

where $C, I \geq 0$ and $N \geq 1$, and claiming to prove a goal $Spec \models \varphi$. Then a proof certifier algorithm works as follows:

Proof Goal. It first checks whether the specification and the sentence to prove satisfy the required format. This can be done by first collecting all the kinds and sorts declared in *Spec*, then all the operation declarations, checking whether each is correctly disambiguated, and finally checking each sentence in *Spec* as well as the sentence to be proved. For simplicity, we also require and check that each variable defined in a sentence is different from any other symbol in the signature of *Spec* and different from any other variable defined in the same sentence. A sentence $(\forall v_1 : k_1, ..., v_V : k_V)$ a if $a_1 \wedge ... \wedge a_m$ is then checked in three steps:

1. check that $k_1, ..., k_V$ are defined in *Spec*;
2. add $v_{\lambda,k_1}^1 :\mapsto k_1, ..., v_{\lambda,k_V}^V :\mapsto k_V$ as disambiguated constants to *Spec*, and let *Spec'* be the new specification; let also a', a'_1, ..., a'_m be the atoms a, a_1, ..., a_m with each occurrence of a variable v_i replaced by the constant v_{λ,k_i}^i, for each $1 \leq i \leq V$ (this can be simply and safely done by word/token substitution, because of the conventions on variable names).
3. check each atom $a', a'_1, ..., a'_m$ as follows: if it is a membership of the form $t : s$, then check that s is a sort of the kind k of t (k can be easily found by looking at the result of the topmost operator of t, because t is disambiguated), and then call the procedure $check(Spec', t)$, which is explained below; if the atom is an equality $t = t'$ then first check that the kinds of t and t' coincide and then call $check(Spec', t)$ and $check(Spec', t')$.

The procedure $check(Spec', t)$ ensures that t is a ground well-formed term under the syntax of *Spec'*. Since t is disambiguated, this is quite a trivial task: if t has the form $\sigma_{k_1 k_2 ... k_n, k}(t_1, t_2, ..., t_n)$ then we first check that the kind of each t_i is k_i (again, by just looking at the result kind of the topmost operator of t_i) and then recursively call $check(Spec', t_i)$ for each $1 \leq i \leq n$. The specification and the sentence to be proved are now checked, so we can start checking the proof.

Constants. Check that each constant $c_{\lambda,k_1}^1, ..., c_{\lambda,k_C}^C$ is different from any other symbol in *Spec* and from the other constants. Also check that C equals the number of variables in φ and that $k_1, ..., k_C$ are the kinds of those variables in this order, respectively, and that they are all defined in *Spec*. Add these constants to *Spec*. Let θ map variable $v_i : k_i$ in φ to constant c_{λ,k_i}^i, for each $1 \leq i \leq C$.

Implication. Check that φ has I conditions and that each of sentence1, ..., sentenceI is the instance by θ of the corresponding condition of φ; check also that [AxLabel1], ... [AxLabelI] are distinct and different from other labels in *Spec*. Add all the labeled sentences to *Spec*.

Proof Step. A proof step can have one of the following six types: reflexivity, symmetry, transitivity, congruence, membership and modus-ponens. Each type is analyzed separately. For simplicity of the checker, a common requirement, which needs to be checked, is that the proof step labels are given in increasing order. We next perform a case analysis on the type of the proof step:
(1) reflexivity eq $t = t'$. Check that t and t' are equal *as strings of characters* (to keep the checker simple) and also call the procedure $check(Spec, t)$.
(2) symmetry eq $t = t'$ follows by ⟨label⟩. Check that ⟨label⟩ is smaller than current label and that the (previous) proof step with label ⟨label⟩ was equational and proved equation $u = u'$, where u equals t' and u' equals t as strings.
(3) transitivity eq $t = t'$ follows by ⟨label$_1$⟩ ⟨label$_2$⟩. Check that ⟨label$_1$⟩ and ⟨label$_2$⟩ are smaller than the current label, that they refer to proof steps which are equational and prove the equations $u = u'$ and $v = v'$, respectively, where u equals t, u' equals v, and v' equals t' as strings of characters.

(4) `congruence eq` $t = t'$ `position` i `follows by` $\langle label \rangle$. First call the procedure $check(Spec, t)$. Check that t and t' have the forms $\sigma(t_1, ..., t_{i-1}, t_i, t_{i+1}, ..., t_m)$ and $\sigma(t_1, ..., t_{i-1}, t'_i, t_{i+1}, ..., t_m)$, respectively. This can be done by checking the topmost operators of t and t' which must be equal in their disambiguated form, then taking the two strings between the parentheses of σ in t and t', say α and α', and traversing them character by character from left to right in parallel, increasing a counter whenever a left parenthesis is encountered and decreasing it whenever a right one is encountered, and also counting the number of comma characters occurring when the parenthesis counter is 0; when the number of such commas becomes $i - 1$, then extract the terms t_i and t'_i (their ends can be found by also counting parentheses), and then continue the character level equality checks for the remaining substrings as before. Once t_i and t'_i are extracted, and everything else in t and t' being checked to be identical, we check that $\langle label \rangle$ is smaller than the current label and that proof step $\langle label \rangle$ proves an equality $u = u'$, where u equals t_i and u' equals t'_i as strings of characters.

(5) `membership mb` $t:s$ `follows by` $\langle label_1 \rangle$ $\langle label_2 \rangle$. We check that $\langle label_1 \rangle$ and $\langle label_2 \rangle$ are smaller than the current label, and that they refer to proofs of an equational and a membership proving $u = u'$ and $v : s'$, respectively, where u equals t, u' equals v, and s' equals s as strings of characters.

(6) `modus-ponens` *sentence* `axiom` $\langle AxLabel \rangle$ `map` $v_1 : k_1$ `<-` t_1 ... $v_V : k_V$ `<-` t_V `follows by` $\langle label_1 \rangle$ ... $\langle label_L \rangle$. Identify the sentence labeled $\langle AxLabel \rangle$ in *Spec* (including the sentences added by the implication proof step), and check that its variables are exactly $v_1 : k_1, ..., v_V : k_V$, in this order. Then for each $1 \leq i \leq V$, check that the kind of t_i is k_i and call the procedure $check(Spec, t_i)$. Then take all the atoms of the sentence labelled $\langle AxLabel \rangle$, say $a, a_1, ..., a_m$, and substitute in each $v_1, ..., v_V$ by $t_1, ..., t_V$, respectively (this is a simple word or token level substitution, because operations and symbols were always enforced to be distinct), obtaining new atoms $a', a'_1, ..., a'_m$, respectively. Then check that m equals L and that each $\langle label_i \rangle$ refers to a proof step for atom a'_i for each $1 \leq i \leq L$. Finally, show that a' is identical to *sentence*, as strings of characters.

Proofs can be quite large in practical applications. Rewriting-based equational systems can perform millions of rewrites per second involving several decision procedures, such as, for example, matching routines modulo associativity, commutativity and identity, which can easily transform into tens or hundreds of millions of proof steps per second of rewriting execution. Based on experience, we claim that there are many applications that need several minutes of rewriting to be executed, so we believe that, in order to be practical and thus accepted by certifying authorities, proof checkers should not only be linear in the size of the proof objects, but should also provide potential for parallel checking. The proof checker above involves a series of small and relatively independent tasks, which makes it attractive for parallelization. However, a parallel checker needs additional efforts in order to be itself validated.

5 Synthesizing Proofs

Even though the proof objects above are human readable, we think that it is highly undesirable for humans to produce such detailed proofs manually. We next propose several techniques to automatically generate detailed proof objects as above from not so detailed proof traces produced by other systems. The crucial aspect here is how to deal with *decision procedures*, that is, how to generate detailed proofs from decision procedure computations. Since the size of proofs can easily become a bottleneck in our low level proof checking algorithm, an important issue discussed in this section is how to generate *small* proof objects.

5.1 Replacement Proofs

Perhaps the most widely known representation of an equational proof is as a *replacement proof*, that is, as a series of applications of equational axioms, either forwards or backwards, at any position in a term.

Theorem 2. $E \models (\forall X) \, t = t'$ *iff* $t \, (\Rightarrow_R \cup \Leftarrow_R)^* \, t'$, *for any set of equations E and any terms t, t' over variables[1] in X, where R is the term rewriting system obtained from E regarding each equation as a (conditional) rewriting rule, and $\Rightarrow_R, \Leftarrow_R$ are the rewriting relation and its inverse, respectively, generated by R.*

Suppose that one has a replacement proof consisting of $n-1$ high level proof steps of the form $t_1 \, (\Rightarrow \cup \Leftarrow) \, t_2 \, (\Rightarrow \cup \Leftarrow) \, \ldots \, (\Rightarrow \cup \Leftarrow) \, t_n$. Each rewriting step i, for $1 \leq i \leq n-1$, is applied at a specific *position* p_i in t_i or in t_{i+1}, where a position is a path from the root of the term to the subterm to which an instance of the rewriting rule (or its inverse) is applied. A detailed proof object can be relatively easily generated from these higher-level replacement proofs as follows:

1. For each step $t_i \Rightarrow t_{i+1}$ involving a rewrite of l_i into r_i at position p_i in t_i of depth d_i, generate one modus-ponens step for $l_i = r_i$ followed by d_i congruences applied bottom-up along p_i, eventually proving $t_i = t_{i+1}$;
2. For each step $t_i \leftarrow t_{i+1}$ involving a rewrite of l_i into r_i at position p_i in t_{i+1} of depth d_i, generate one modus-ponens step proving $l_i = r_i$, then one symmetry proving $r_i = l_i$ followed by d_i congruences proving $t_i = t_{i+1}$;
3. $n-1$ transitivities can now generate a complete detailed proof of $t_1 = t_n$.

Therefore, for any high level replacement proof of $n-1$ steps we can generate a detailed proof object consisting of at most $(n-1) * (3 + \max\{depth(t_i) \mid 1 \leq i \leq n\})$ steps. The analysis above is for unconditional equations; the conditional case is more complex and we do not discuss it here.

5.2 Rewriting Proofs

Rewriting proofs are a special case of replacement proofs. More precisely, a rewriting proof of $E \models (\forall X) \, t = t'$ has the form $t \Rightarrow_R^*; \Leftarrow_R^* t'$, where the

---
[1] The variables in $t \, t'$ are regarded as constants during rewriting.

term to which both t and t' reduce is typically in normal form. We next argue that proof objects can be generated from rewriting proofs which are typically significantly smaller than those generated from general replacement proofs.

The idea is to speculate the fact that most rewritings are applied in depth-first order, by delaying the congruence steps until all the corresponding subterms are processed. More precisely, let us consider two consecutive steps in a depth-first rewriting sequence $t_1 \Rightarrow t_2 \Rightarrow t_3$, where $t_1 = t_p[\gamma[\alpha]]$, $t_2 = t_p[\gamma[\beta]]$, and $t_3 = t_p[\delta]$, with $\alpha \to_R \beta$ and $\gamma[\beta] \to_R \delta$ two instances of rewriting rules in R:

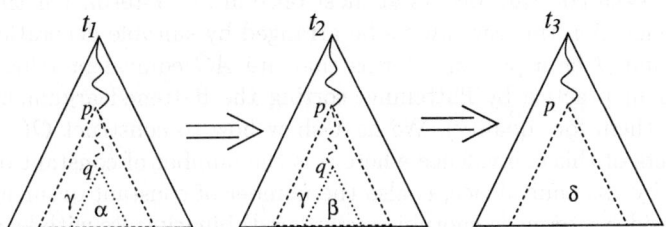

Following blindly the procedure to generate proof objects from replacement proofs would yield the following proof steps: (1) a modus-ponens step proving $\alpha = \beta$; (2) congruence steps for all the operators on the path to position q in t_1, in a bottom-up traversal of the path, eventually proving $t_1 = t_2$; (3) a modus-ponens step proving $\gamma[\beta] = \delta$; (4) congruence steps for the path to position p in t_2, eventually proving $t_2 = t_3$; (5) a transitivity step proving $t_1 = t_3$. Even though this proof object is correct, a much smaller proof can be generated by delaying the application of congruence rules corresponding to positions p and above:

1. a modus-ponens step proving $\alpha = \beta$;
2. congruence steps for all the operators on the path between positions q and p in t_1, in a bottom-up order, eventually proving $\gamma[\alpha] = \gamma[\beta]$;
3. a modus-ponens step proving $\gamma[\beta] = \delta$;
4. a transitivity step proving $\gamma[\alpha] = \delta$;
5. congruence steps for the path to position p in t_1, eventually proving $t_1 = t_3$.

Notice that as many congruence steps as the depth of p can be saved by using this alternative procedure. Moreover, one can extend it to multiple rewriting steps in depth-first order, minimizing the application of congruence steps.

5.3 AC Matching

Since the equations of associativity, commutativity and identity cannot be effectively interpreted as rewriting rules, any rewriting-based equational prover worth its salt implements efficient decision procedures for matching and rewriting modulo A, C, U and/or combinations of these. Even though rewriting engines can typically trace their applications of rewriting rules, the applications of matching decision procedures are typically opaque, thereby yielding proof gaps that need to be filled in order to generate proof objects that can be checked mechanically using external (trusted) proof checkers, such as the one described in Section 4. In this section we show how one can generate small proof objects from simplified terms which match modulo A and AC, respectively.

Let *Spec* declare a binary operator $\_\star\_$ together with corresponding axioms of associativity and commutativity, namely "$[Assoc]$ $(\forall A, B, C)$ $(A \star B) \star C = A \star (B \star C)$" and "$[Comm]$ $(\forall A, B)$ $A \star B = B \star A$". A $\star$-term can be regarded as a ground term constructed from $\star$ together with constants (alien subterms can be handled by constant abstraction). We will assume that these constants are unique; i.e. each constant occurs at most once in any $\star$-term. For the purposes of proof generation this can always be arranged by suitable decoration.

Let α and β be a pair of $\star$-terms that are *AC* equivalent (this can easily be checked in practice by flattening, sorting the flattened argument lists and comparing them for equality). We next show how to construct $\mathcal{O}(n \log n)$ step proof objects of this equivalence where n is the number of constant occurrences in α (and, by AC equivalence, is also the number of constant occurrences in β).

We consider $\star$-terms isomorphic to (ordered) binary trees with leaves labeled by constants, and we switch between term and tree nomenclature at will. The *height* of a $\star$-term is the largest number of $\star$-occurrences above a constant.

High Level Proof Plan. Let α_r and β_r be the right associative forms and of α and β respectively. Let α_b be a balanced form of α, such that each constant in α_b occurs beneath $\lfloor \log n \rfloor$ or $\lceil \log n \rceil$ occurrences of $\star$. Such a balanced form can be generated algorithmically by recursive subdivision of the flattened argument list. Notice that each subterm of a balanced term is also balanced. We generate a proof that consists of four subproofs.

1. We prove $\alpha \equiv_{AC} \alpha_r$ in $O(n)$ proof steps.
2. We prove $\alpha_b \equiv_{AC} \alpha_r$ in $O(n)$ proof steps.
3. We prove $\alpha_b \equiv_{AC} \beta_r$ using $O(n \log n)$ proof steps.
4. We prove $\beta \equiv_{AC} \beta_r$ in at most $O(n)$ proof steps.

This is illustrated in Figure 1. In the case of just A matching, only steps 1. and 4. are needed because the two right parenthesized forms must be identical.

These 4 subproofs can then be stitched together by 2 symmetry steps and 3 transitivity steps to give a proof of $\alpha = \beta$. Note that subproofs 1, 2, and 4 consist of generating the right associative form of a given term while subproof 3 requires generating the right associative form of a particular permutation, starting from a balanced form. This is the hardest subproof, and we give two distinct methods for generating it based on different sorting algorithms. We define a total ordering $\prec$ on the constants by the left-to-right order that the constants appear in β.

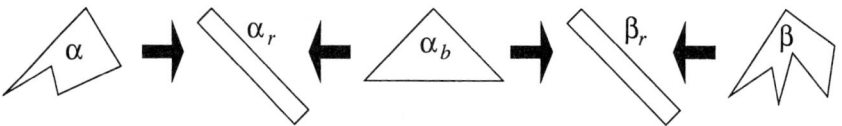

Fig. 1. Plan for proving $\alpha \equiv_{AC} \beta$.

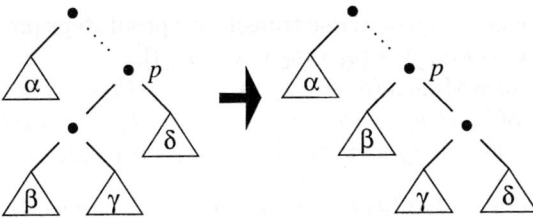

Fig. 2. Increasing the length of the rightmost path by a right rotation.

Right Associative Form. Given an $\star$-term t with n constant occurrences, we consider it as a binary tree. Let m be the number of $\star$-occurrences on its rightmost path. Clearly $m \geq 1$. If $m = n-1$ then t is already in right associative form. Otherwise there must exist some position p on the rightmost path such that $t|_{p.1}$ is headed by $\star$. We can perform a right associative proof step (a *right rotation* in the nomenclature of binary trees) at p to arrive at a new term t' whose rightmost path now contains $m + 1$ $\star$-occurrences, as illustrated in Figure 2.

By performing this transformation $n - 1 - m$ times we must eventually arrive at right associative form and will use at most $n - 2$ associative proof steps.

Notice that each associative step needs to be followed by several congruence and transitivity steps in order to generate detailed proof objects as needed by our proof checker, and that one can generate $\Omega(n^2)$ proof steps in total if one is not careful. However, if one executes the associative steps above using an outermost strategy, then one can minimize the total number of proof steps to at most 2(n-2). More precisely, one can devise a procedure RIGHTASSOC(t) which generates a proof for $t = t_r$, where t_r is the right associative form of t, as follows:

- if $t = (\alpha \star \beta) \star \gamma$ for some $\star$-terms α, β, γ, then generate a modus-ponens proof step of *Assoc* proving $(\alpha \star \beta) \star \gamma = \alpha \star (\beta \star \gamma)$, followed by a recursive call of RIGHTASSOC($\alpha \star (\beta \star \gamma)$) which generates a proof of $\alpha \star (\beta \star \gamma) = t_r$ (in case they are not already equal), followed by a transitivity step proving $(\alpha \star \beta) \star \gamma = t_r$ (if needed);
- if $t = a \star \alpha$, where a is some constant and α is a $\star$-term, then recursively call RIGHTASSOC(α) to prove $\alpha = \alpha_r$ (in case they are different), followed by a congruence step proving $a \star \alpha = a\alpha_r$ (if needed).

Then notice that one modus-ponens and one transitivity proof steps are needed $n - 1 - m$ times, and also that at most $n - 2$ congruence steps are needed; therefore, the generated proof object will have at most $3(n - 2)$ proof steps.

Permutation via Merge-Sort. Let t be a $\star$-term in balanced form. The idea of this AC proof generator is inspired from merge sorting. Suppose some arbitrary but fixed order $\prec$ on the constants occurring in t. Let MERGESORT(t) be the procedure defined below, which, for a given balanced $\star$-term $t = \alpha\beta$ generates an AC proof for $t = c_1 \star (c_2 \star (c_3 \star \cdots \star c_n))$, where $c_1 \prec c_2 \prec c_3 \prec \cdots \prec c_n$:

1. call MERGESORT(α) to generate proof for $\alpha = a_1 \star (a_2 \star \cdots \star a_{n_\alpha})$;
2. call MERGESORT(β), to generate proof for $\beta = b_1 \star (b_2 \star \cdots \star b_{n_\beta})$;

3. generate two congruence and one transitivity proof steps proving the equality
   $t = (a_1 \star (a_2 \star \cdots \star a_{n_\alpha})) \star (b_1 \star (b_2 \star \cdots \star b_{n_\beta}))$;
4. call the procedure MERGE($a_1 \star (a_2 \star \cdots \star a_{n_\alpha}), b_1 \star (b_2 \star \cdots \star b_{n_\beta})$) defined below, to get a proof of $(a_1 \star (a_2 \star \cdots \star a_{n_\alpha})) \star (b_1 \star (b_2 \star \cdots \star b_{n_\beta})) = c_1 \star (c_2 \star (c_3 \star \cdots \star c_n))$;
5. generate one transitivity step proving $t = c_1 \star (c_2 \star (c_3 \star \cdots \star c_n))$.

The procedure MERGE($a_1 \star (a_2 \star \cdots \star a_{n_\alpha}), b_1 \star (b_2 \star \cdots \star b_{n_\beta})$) assumes that its arguments are in right-associative sorted form, and then it generates a proof of the equality $(a_1 \star (a_2 \star \cdots \star a_{n_\alpha})) \star (b_1 \star (b_2 \star \cdots \star b_{n_\beta})) = c_1 \star (c_2 \star (c_3 \star \cdots \star c_n))$, where the right-hand term is also in right-associative sorted form:

1. if $a_1 \prec b_1$ then call MERGE($a_2 \star (a_3 \star \cdots \star a_{n_\alpha}), b_1 \star (b_2 \star \cdots \star b_{n_\beta})$) to generate a proof of $(a_2 \star (a_3 \star \cdots \star a_{n_\alpha})) \star (b_1 \star (b_2 \star \cdots \star b_{n_\beta})) = c_2 \star (c_3 \star \cdots \star c_n)$; then generate one modus-ponens of *Assoc*, one congruence and one transitivity proof steps that together prove that $(a_1 \star (a_2 \star \cdots \star a_{n_\alpha})) \star (b_1 \star (b_2 \star \cdots \star b_{n_\beta})) = c_1 \star (c_2 \star (c_3 \star \cdots \star c_n))$ (notice that $a_1 = c_1$);
2. if $b_1 \prec a_1$ then call MERGE($b_2 \star (b_3 \star \cdots \star b_{n_\beta}), a_1 \star (a_2 \star \cdots \star a_{n_\alpha})$) and proceed like in 1. to generate a proof for $(b_1 \star (b_2 \star \cdots \star b_{n_\beta})) \star (a_1 \star (a_2 \star \cdots \star a_{n_\alpha})) = c_1 \star (c_2 \star (c_3 \star \cdots \star c_n))$; one additional commutativity step followed by a transitivity prove the desired equality.

The analysis of this algorithm is straightforward: at most $5n$ proof steps are needed by MERGE, so the recurrence for MERGESORT is $T(n) = 2T(n/2) + 5n$. Therefore, the number of steps generated by MERGESORT is less than $5n \log n$.

Permutation via Selection Sort. We show how to reach the right associative form of an arbitrary permutation starting from a balanced form in $O(n \log n)$ proof steps. We perform $n - 1$ selection subproofs, each of which moves a chosen constant c to the next position in a growing right associative form.

These subproofs are generated by a procedure SELECT(t) that takes a term $t = \alpha \star \beta$ of height $h \geq 1$ and returns a proof that $t = c \star t'$ for some t' of height $\leq h$, where c is the least constant occurring in t. We consider two cases.

1. If c occurs in α then if $\alpha = c$ our input term already has the desired form and we are done. Otherwise α has height $h - 1 \geq 1$ and we call SELECT(α) to get a proof that $\alpha = c \star \alpha'$ for some α' of height $\leq h - 1$. We use a congruence step to show that $\alpha \star \beta = (c \star \alpha') \star \beta$. Substituting in the associative axiom we prove $(c \star \alpha') \star \beta = c \star (\alpha' \star \beta)$. Finally with a transitivity step we prove $\alpha \star \beta = c \star (\alpha' \star \beta)$. This is illustrated in Figure 3.
2. If c occurs in β then we use prove $\alpha \star \beta = \beta \star \alpha$ by substituting in the commutative axiom. We then follow the method of case 1 with the rôles of α and β reversed to prove that $\beta \star \alpha = c \star (\beta' \star \alpha)$ for some β' of height $h - 1$. Finally with a transitivity step we prove $\alpha \star \beta = c \star (\beta' \star \alpha)$.

Each subproof requires at most $5h$ steps however assembling to subproofs into the final proof must be done with some care to avoid a quadratic number of congruence steps. The key idea is to generate the subproofs top-down but stitch them together with congruence and transitivity steps bottom-up. This is done

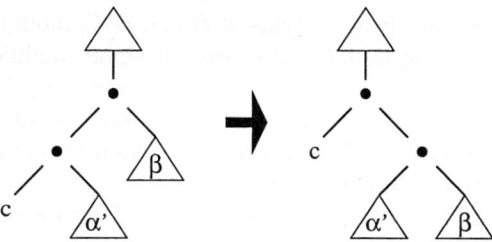

Fig. 3. Case 1 for SELECT

by a procedure SORT(t) which takes a term t of height h and returns its sorted right associative form. We consider two cases.

1. If t is a lone constant then we are done.
2. Otherwise we use SELECT(t) to get a proof that $t = c \star t'$ where c is the least constant in t. We then use SORT(t') to get a proof that $t' = t''$ where t'' is the sorted right associative form of t'. Using a congruence step we prove that $c \star t' = c \star t''$ and finally a transitivity step proves $t = c \star t''$.

SORT makes $n-1$ calls to SELECT and performs $n-1$ congruence steps and $n-1$ transitivity steps. Since $h \leq \lceil \log n \rceil$ we have an upper bound on the number of proof steps required of $5(n-1)\lceil \log n \rceil + 2(n-1)$.

5.4 Arbitrary Combinations of A, C and U Matching

We next assume that procedures generating proofs from A and AC matchings for ground terms constructed from a single binary operator together with unique constants are available (efficient such procedures were presented in the previous subsection), and informally describe a method by which these procedures can be combined to generate proof objects of size $\mathcal{O}(n \log n)$ for terms that match due to any combination of A, C and/or U at any positions and for any operators.

Suppose that t and t' are two ground terms involving several operators, each being potentially associative, commutative and/or have identity. We first associate to t and t' datastructures $d(t)$ and $d(t')$, respectively, which replace multiple consecutive occurrences of the same associative or associative and commutative operator by a list tagged with the operator name and containing all the corresponding subterms. Second, we eliminate all the constants (together with their immediately above binary operator) which are identities for operators, but only if they occur immediately under the operations for which they are identities; we need to store information regarding the places from which these identities have been removed, because appropriate identity proof steps have to be generated later. Finally, we *sort the subterms* of each commutative operator or list corresponding to an associative and commutative operator, storing information regarding the permutation of subterms that lead to the sorted order; notice that sorting must be performed in a bottom-up fashion on the datastructures, and use some conventions (arbitrary but fixed; for example, one can use lexicographic order) on how to compare lists of terms. $d(t)$ and $d(t')$ should be identical now; otherwise an error stating that t and t' are not equal modulo combinations of A, C and/or U axioms should be generated. By composing the permutations of each sorted list at each appropriate position in $d(t)$, one obtains a one-to-one map between subterms in t and subterms in t'; equality proof obligations will be generated for subterms in this relation.

We can now start generating the proof object. Traverse $d(t)$ bottom-up and for each node do the following: (1) if the node is a list corresponding to an associative or an associative and commutative operator then, then by calling the appropriate A or AC matching procedure on the subterms of t and t' from which the sorted list node in $d(t)$ has been formed, where all the alien subterms are replaced by some artificial distinct constants, we generate a proof of equality for those subterms of t and t'; (2) if the node is a commutative operator then we generate a commutativity proof step only if needed, i.e., if the two subterms occur in different order in t and t'. As the datastructure is traversed bottom-up, appropriate congruence proof steps need to be generated, as well as identity proofs for those nodes where an identity constant has been removed. Notice that only a linear number of proof steps is added to the ones already generated by the A and AC procedures. Therefore, the size of the proof is still $\mathcal{O}(n \log n)$ in the size n of t and t'.

5.5 System Dependent Aspects

The proof synthesis issues discussed so far are general to all equational provers. In this subsection we discuss some aspects which are more system dependent; our case study is Maude [5].

Disambiguation and Desugaring. As seen in Section 3, disambiguated specifications, sentences and proofs look ugly and unreadable. As a convenience to users, rewriting engines and theorem provers typically use a "sugared" and sometimes apparently ambiguous syntax. However, in order for the proof checker presented in Section 4 to be as simple as possible, all the symbols and statements are required to be completely disambiguated and desugared. We next discuss how this can be done in the case of Maude.

Kinds are not declared explicitly in Maude. Users only declare sorts and relate them via subsorts. Kinds are then generated automatically from the sort partial order, one kind per connected component. For s a given sort, $[s]$ refers to the kind to which s belongs. Therefore, a Maude desugarer needs to generate one kind per connected component and replace each occurrence of $[s]$ by the appropriate kind. Moreover, each subsort relation "$s < s'$" in kind k needs to be replaced by a conditional membership "$(\forall x : k)\ x : s'$ if $x : s$", and each operation declaration needs to be replaced by a disambiguated kind level operation declaration and an appropriate conditional membership (if needed). For example, $\sigma : s_1 \times \cdots \times s_n \to s$ needs to be replaced by $\sigma_{k_1...k_n,k} : k_1 \times \cdots \times k_n \to k$ and $(\forall x_1 : k_1, \ldots, x_n : k_n)\ \sigma_{k_1...k_n,k}(x_1, \ldots, x_n) : s$ if $x_1 : s_1, \ldots x_n : k_n$. Notice that some, or even all, of the arguments of an operation can be already declared as kinds (using the bracket notation). Only those arguments which are declared as sorts need a variable and an appropriate condition as above. A sentence is not needed for an operation only if all the arguments and the result of that operation are declared as kinds.

Another easy to desugar feature in Maude is the declaration of variables in sentences; these can also be declared as having sorts rather than kinds in Maude. Each sentence using variables in sort notation needs to be desugared by declaring those as kinded variables and by adding appropriate conditions to the sentence. For example, the sentence $(\forall x_1 : s_1, \ldots, x_n : s_n)$ a if $a_1, \ldots, a_n$ is replaced by the sentence $(\forall x_1 : k_1, \ldots, x_n : k_n)$ a if $a_1, \ldots, a_n, x_1 : s_1, \ldots, x_n : s_n$.

The harder part is to disambiguate operations occurring in terms in equations, memberships, or in high-level proofs given as Maude traces. A simple solution would, of course, be to implement the disambiguater as part of Maude and then provide an auxiliary Maude command or flag to disambiguate all operators. Even though this could probably be done, there is an alternative solution which would only require a small change in Maude, namely to tag each operation by its *result kind* only. Since variables also have a unique kind, one can easily devise an algorithm now that disambiguates any term.

Sharing and Memoization. A major reason for which we designed a low level proof representation and checker in Sections 3 and 4, besides generality and simplicity, was also to deal properly with sharing and memoization. An important optimization of rewriting engines, also supported by Maude, is to avoid redoing computations. A typical example occurs when the right-hand term of a rewriting rule contains multiple copies of the same subterm. Then, in any given instance of that rule, the shared subterm is reduced only once to its normal form, which is then copied multiple times in the resulting term. Another typical example involves memoization, or caching. In Maude, some operations can be declared with the attribute memo, meaning that the normal forms of terms having those operations at top are cached and never reduced again.

Even though sharing and/or memoization could probably be replaced in some complicated way by actual proof steps in a replacement or rewriting equational proof, we believe that such attempts would be not only artificial and error-prone, but also quite impractical because they would increase the size of proofs significantly. Our current formalization of proofs in Section 3 supports sharing and memoization naturally, because one can just refer to the appropriate (previous) proof step label when a shared sentence has been already derived. Sharing does not explicitly occurs in Maude's current execution traces; its existence can be inferred by just noticing gaps in traces. However, one can easily implement an independent algorithm which "fills the gaps" in Maude's traces and thus generate detailed proof objects as needed by our certifier: whenever a gap is noticed in a Maude trace (which is not given to an AC match - gap that can be filled using the algorithms in Subsection 5.3), search through the already generated proof object for a fitting sentence (such a sentence must exist, because otherwise Maude could not have generated the trace) and then refer to it by its label when generating the corresponding congruence rules.

Least Sort Calculation. Due to overloading operators, the same term can have multiple result sorts. For example, 3 + 5 can be a natural, an integer, or a rational number. Based on the partial order on sorts, Maude implements efficient decision procedures to calculate the least sort of any term. A term is substituted for a variable in a rewriting rule application only if the sort of the term is smaller or equal to the sort of the variable. These implicit applications of conditional membership rules need to be explicitly stated when generating the proof object. Again, this can be relatively easily done, without modifying Maude in any essential way, if Maude is slightly changed to report a resulting *sort* for each operation use in each term; this is a slightly stronger but more general requirement than the one needed for disambiguation and desugaring (where only the kind result of operations was needed).

6 Conclusion and Future Work

We have presented a general method to certify and synthesize proofs in membership equational logic, where the synthesis may involve generating full proofs from proof traces modulo combinations of A, C, and U axioms. We have proposed a simple representation of proof objects and have given algorithms that can synthesize short proofs for the $\mathcal{AX}$-gaps. Our proof representations and algorithms are quite close to an actual implementation of both a generic proof checker and of a synthesis tool to generate proof objects from Maude traces. We plan to develop both tools in the near future. This will provide certified proof objects for all equational computations in Maude. Since membership equational logic is a sublogic of rewriting logic [4], our work has a very natural extension to certification and synthesis of rewriting logic proofs. Therefore, a subsequent development will involve investigating such an extension. Since rewriting logic has good properties as a logical framework [10], the extension to rewriting logic is potentially interesting not only for interoperating Maude with other tools, but also to represent proof objects from different logics.

Acknowledgements

Grigore Roşu was supported in part by joint NSF/NASA grant CCR-0234524. Steven Eker was supported DARPA through Air Force Research Laboratory Contract F30602-02-C-0130. Patrick Lincoln was supported by ONR Grants N00014-01-1-0837, N00014-02-1-0109, and N00014-01-1-0795. José Meseguer was supported by ONR Grant N00014-02-1-0715.

References

1. H. Barendregt and E. Barendsen. Autarkik computations and formal proofs. *Journal of Automated Reasoning*, 28(3):321–336, 2002.
2. P. Borovanský, C. Kirchner, H. Kirchner, and P.-E. Moreau. ELAN from a rewriting logic point of view. *Theoretical Computer Science*, 285:155–185, 2002.

3. A. Bouhoula, J.-P. Jouannaud, and J. Meseguer. Specification and proof in membership equational logic. *Theoretical Computer Science*, 236:35–132, 2000.
4. R. Bruni and J. Meseguer. Generalized rewrite theories. Manuscript, January 2003, http://maude.cs.uiuc.edu.
5. M. Clavel, F. Durán, S. Eker, P. Lincoln, N. Martí-Oliet, J. Meseguer, and J. Quesada. Maude: specification and programming in rewriting logic. *Theoretical Computer Science*, 285:187–243, 2002.
6. R. Constable. *Implementing Mathematics with the Nuprl Proof Development System*. Prentice Hall, 1987.
7. J. Goguen and G. Roşu. Institution morphisms. *Formal Aspects of Computing*, 13(3–5):274–307, 2002.
8. M. Gordon and T. Melham, editors. *Introduction to HOL: A theorem proving environment for higher order logic*. Cambridge University Press, 1993.
9. M. Kaufmann, P. Manolios, and J. Moore. *Computer-Aided Reasoning: An Approach*. Kluwer, 2000.
10. N. Martí-Oliet and J. Meseguer. Rewriting logic as a logical and semantic framework. In D. Gabbay and F. Guenthner, editors, *Handbook of Philosophical Logic, 2nd. Edition*, pages 1–87. Kluwer Academic Publishers, 2002. First published as SRI Tech. Report SRI-CSL-93-05, August 1993.
11. J. Meseguer. General logics. In H.-D. E. et al., editor, *Logic Colloquium'87*, pages 275–329. North-Holland, 1989.
12. J. Meseguer. A logical theory of concurrent objects and its realization in the Maude language. In G. Agha, P. Wegner, and A. Yonezawa, editors, *Research Directions in Concurrent Object-Oriented Programming*, pages 314–390. MIT Press, 1993.
13. J. Meseguer. Membership algebra as a logical framework for equational specification. In F. Parisi-Presicce, editor, *Proc. WADT'97*, pages 18–61. Springer LNCS 1376, 1998.
14. J. Meseguer and N. Martí-Oliet. From abstract data types to logical frameworks. In E. Astesiano, G. Reggio, and A. Tarlecki, editors, *Recent Trends in Data Type Specification, May/June 1994*, pages 48–80. Springer LNCS 906, 1995.
15. T. Mossakowski. Heterogeneous development graphs and heterogeneous borrowing. In *Proceedings of FOSSACS'02: Foundations of Software Science and Computational Structures*, pages 326–341. Springer LNCS 2303, 2002.
16. Q. Nguyen, C. Kirchner, and H. Kirchner. External rewriting for skeptical proof assistants. *Journal of Automated Reasoning*, 29(3–4):309–336, 2002.
17. T. Nipkow, L. C. Paulson, and M. Wenzel. *Isabelle/HOL — A Proof Assistant for Higher-Order Logic*, volume 2283 of *LNCS*. Springer, 2002.
18. S. Owre, S. Rajan, J. Rushby, N. Shankar, and M. Srivas. PVS: Combining specification, proof checking, and model checking. In R. Alur and T. A. Henzinger, editors, *Computer-Aided Verification, CAV '96*, volume 1102 of *LNCS*, pages 411–414, New Brunswick, NJ, July/August 1996. Springer-Verlag.
19. G. Roşu. Complete categorical equational deduction. In L. Fribourg, editor, *Proceedings of Computer Science Logic (CSL'01)*, volume 2142 of *Lecture Notes in Computer Science*, pages 528–538. Springer, 2001.
20. M.-O. Stehr. Programming, Specification, and Interactive Theorem Proving — Towards a Unified Language based on Equational Logic, Rewriting Logic, and Type Theory. Doctoral Thesis, Universität Hamburg, Fachbereich Informatik, Germany, 2002. http://www.sub.uni-hamburg.de/disse/810/.

21. M.-O. Stehr, P. Naumov, and J. Meseguer. The HOL/NuPRl proof translator—A practical approach to formal interoperability. In *Proc. 14th Intl. Conf. on Theorem Proving In Higher Order Logics (TPHOL'2001) Edinburgh, Scotland, September 2001*, pages 329–345. Springer LNCS 2152, 2001.
22. A. Tarlecki. Towards heterogeneous specifications. In *Proc. Workshop on Frontiers of Combining Systems FroCoS'98, Amsterdam, October 1998*. Applied Logic Series, Kluwer Academic Publishers, 1998.

Team Automata Satisfying Compositionality

Maurice H. ter Beek[1,*] and Jetty Kleijn[2]

[1] Istituto di Scienza e Tecnologie dell'Informazione, CNR, Area della Ricerca di Pisa,
Via G. Moruzzi 1, 56124 Pisa, Italy,
maurice.terbeek@isti.cnr.it
[2] Leiden Institute of Advanced Computer Science, Universiteit Leiden,
P.O. Box 9512, 2300 RA Leiden, The Netherlands,
kleijn@liacs.nl

Abstract. A team automaton is said to satisfy compositionality if its behaviour can be described in terms of the behaviour of its constituting component automata. As an initial investigation of the conditions under which team automata satisfy compositionality, we study their computations and behaviour in relation to those of their constituting component automata. We show that the construction of team automata according to certain natural types of synchronization guarantees compositionality.

Keywords: team automata, compositionality, computations, behaviour, synchronizations, shuffles.

1 Introduction

Component-based system design is a complex task that benefits from stepwise development, i.e. an abstract high-level specification of a design is decomposed into a more concrete low-level specification by step-by-step refinement, at each step replacing components of the current specification by more detailed ones. To guarantee correct decompositions it is important that the specification model chosen is compositional, i.e. a specification of a composite system can be obtained from specifications of its components [16]. In case of automata-based specification models, compositionality requires that the relevant behaviour of a composite automaton can be obtained from the behaviour of its constituting automata.

Most automata-based specification models guarantee compositionality by choosing a single and very strict method of composing automata, in effect resulting in composite automata that are uniquely defined by their constituents. The choice prevalent in the literature is to allow the execution of an action in a composite automaton if and only if all of its constituting automata sharing this action simultaneously execute it. In [3] this type of synchronization of shared actions is coined *maximal-action-indispensable* (*maximal-ai* for short). Examples

---

[*] This author's research was supported by an ERCIM postdoctoral fellowship and was partly carried out during his stays at the Leiden Institute of Advanced Computer Science of Leiden University and at the Computer and Automation Research Institute of the Hungarian Academy of Sciences.

of automata-based specification models with composition based on *maximal-ai* synchronizations include I/O automata [20, 26], I/O systems [15, 16], Cooperating (Pushdown) Automata [8, 12], Timed Cooperating Automata [18], Reactive Transition Systems [5, 6], and Interacting State Machines [21, 22]. This *maximal-ai* type of synchronization also appears in disguise in non-automata-based specification models like CSP [13] and Statecharts [11].

Team automata were introduced for the specification of groupware systems and their interconnections and they were shown to provide a flexible framework for modelling collaboration between system components [1–3, 9]. Inspired by I/O automata, a team automaton is composed of component automata, which are automata with a partition of their sets of actions into input, output, and internal actions. Team automata model the logical architecture of a design, while abstracting from concrete data, configurations, and actions. They describe a system solely in terms of an automaton, the role of actions, and synchronizations.

The crux of composing a team automaton is to define the way its constituting components interact through synchronizations. While it is noted in [26] that a single notion of composition is rather restrictive and may hinder a realistic modelling of certain types of interactions, composition of I/O automata nevertheless is unique. Within a team automaton, however, a component automaton is not forced to participate in every synchronization of an action it shares. Hence there is no such thing as the unique team automaton. Rather, a whole range of team automata, distinguishable only by their synchronizations, can be composed over a set of component automata. A team automaton is determined on the basis of its components by choosing synchronizations reflecting the specific protocol of collaboration to be modelled. This freedom offers the flexibility to distinguish even the smallest nuances in the meaning of a design and thus sets this approach apart from most other automata-based specification models.

In [3] we introduced a variety of fixed strategies for choosing the synchronizations of a team automaton, thus leading to uniquely defined team automata. These strategies are based on the basic types of synchronization *maximal-ai*, *maximal-free*, *maximal-state-indispensable*, and on the more complex types of synchronization *maximal-peer-to-peer* and *maximal-master-slave* involving the role of actions [3]. This paper provides an initial investigation of the conditions under which these strategies lead to team automata satisfying compositionality. To this aim, we study the relation between the computations and behaviour of team automata defined according to the *maximal-ai* and *maximal-free* strategies and those of their constituting components. Since a team automaton's distinction of input, output, and internal actions is irrelevant for the results presented in this paper, it is ignored from now on. Moreover, we consider only finitary behaviour.

We begin this paper by fixing some notation, followed by some definitions and results concerning team automata. Subsequently we investigate the behavioural relation between team automata and their constituting components, only interrupted by some definitions and results concerning (synchronized) shuffles. We conclude this paper with a discussion of the obtained results.

2 Preliminaries

We assume familiarity with the basic notions from formal language theory [24].

We have the following conventions. Set inclusion is denoted by $\subseteq$, whereas $\subset$ denotes a strict inclusion. Set difference of sets V and W is denoted by $V \setminus W$. For a finite set V, its cardinality is denoted by $\#V$. For convenience we denote the set $\{1,2,\ldots,n\}$ by $[n]$. Then $[0] = \emptyset$, the empty set. The cartesian product of sets V_i, with $i \in [n]$, is denoted by $\prod_{i\in[n]} V_i$. For $j \in [n]$, $\text{proj}_j : \prod_{i\in[n]} V_i \to V_j$ is defined by $\text{proj}_j((a_1, a_2, \ldots, a_n)) = a_j$. The empty word is denoted by λ. The set of all finite words over an alphabet Σ (including λ) is denoted by Σ^*.

Let $f : A \to A'$ and $g : B \to B'$ be functions. Then $f \times g : A \times B \to A' \times B'$ is defined as $(f \times g)(a,b) = (f(a), g(b))$. We use $f^{[2]}$ as shorthand for $f \times f$ (not to be confused with iterated function application). Thus $f^{[2]}(a,b) = (f(a), f(b))$.

Let $h : \Sigma \to \Gamma^*$ be a function assigning to each symbol of Σ a finite word over the alphabet Γ. The homomorphic extension of h to Σ^*, also denoted by h, is defined in the usual way by $h(\lambda) = \lambda$ and $h(xy) = h(x)h(y)$ for all $x,y \in \Sigma^*$.

The function $\text{pres}_\Gamma : \Sigma \to \Gamma^*$, defined by $\text{pres}_\Gamma(a) = a$ if $a \in \Gamma$ and $\text{pres}_\Gamma(a) = \lambda$ otherwise, preserves the symbols from Γ and erases all other symbols.

3 Component Automata and Team Automata

In this section we recall some definitions and results concerning team automata from [3], while ignoring their distinction of input, output, and internal actions.

Definition 1. *A component automaton is a quadruple* $\mathcal{C} = (Q, \Sigma, \delta, I)$, *with Q its (possibly infinite) set of states, Σ its set of actions, $Q \cap \Sigma = \emptyset$, $\delta \subseteq Q \times \Sigma \times Q$ its set of labelled transitions, and $I \subseteq Q$ its set of initial states.* □

Let $a \in \Sigma$. Then the set δ_a of a-*transitions* of $\mathcal{C}$ is defined as $\delta_a = \{(q,q') \mid (q,a,q') \in \delta\}$. An a-transition $(q,q) \in \delta_a$ is called a *loop* (on a).

The dynamics of a component automaton is given through its computations, while focussing on (certain) actions leads to a notion of behaviour.

Definition 2. *Let $\mathcal{C} = (Q, \Sigma, \delta, I)$ be a component automaton.*
The set $\mathbf{C}_\mathcal{C}$ of its computations is defined as consisting of all finite sequences $\alpha = q_0 a_1 q_1 a_2 q_2 \cdots a_n q_n$, with $n \geq 0$, $q_i \in Q$ for $0 \leq i \leq n$, and $a_j \in \Sigma$ for $1 \leq j \leq n$ such that $q_0 \in I$ and $(q_i, a_{i+1}, q_{i+1}) \in \delta$ for all $0 \leq i < n$.
Let Θ be an alphabet disjoint from Q.
The Θ-behaviour $\mathbf{B}_\mathcal{C}^\Theta$ of $\mathcal{C}$ is defined as $\mathbf{B}_\mathcal{C}^\Theta = \text{pres}_\Theta(\mathbf{C}_\mathcal{C})$. □

The Σ-behaviour of $\mathcal{C}$ is also simply called its behaviour.

For the rest of this paper we consider an arbitrary but fixed set $\mathcal{S} = \{\mathcal{C}_i \mid i \in [n]\}$ of component automata, where $n \geq 0$ and each $\mathcal{C}_i$ is specified as $\mathcal{C}_i = (Q_i, \Sigma_i, \delta_i, I_i)$. A team automaton over $\mathcal{S}$ has the cartesian product $\prod_{i\in[n]} Q_i$ of the state spaces of its components as its state space, while its actions are the actions of its components. Its transition relation, however, is based on but not fixed by the transitions of its components. More precisely, the transition relation of a team automaton over $\mathcal{S}$ is defined by choosing certain synchronizations of actions of its components while excluding others.

Definition 3. *Let* $a \in \bigcup_{i \in [n]} \Sigma_i$. *The set* $\Delta_a(\mathcal{S})$ *of synchronizations of* a *in* $\mathcal{S}$ *is defined as* $\Delta_a(\mathcal{S}) = \{(q, q') \in \prod_{i \in [n]} Q_i \times \prod_{i \in [n]} Q_i \mid \exists j \in [n] : proj_j^{[2]}(q, q') \in \delta_{j,a}$ *and* $\forall i \in [n] : proj_i^{[2]}(q, q') \in \delta_{i,a}$ *or* $proj_i(q) = proj_i(q')\}$. □

Let $a \in \bigcup_{i \in [n]} \Sigma_i$. Then $\Delta_a(\mathcal{S})$ thus consists of all possible combinations of a-transitions of components from $\mathcal{S}$, with all non-participating components remaining idle. It is explicitly required that at least one component is *active*, i.e. executes an a-transition. The transformation of a state of a team automaton $\mathcal{T}$ over $\mathcal{S}$ is defined by the local state changes of the components from $\mathcal{S}$ participating in the action of $\mathcal{T}$ being executed. When defining $\mathcal{T}$, a specific subset δ_a of $\Delta_a(\mathcal{S})$ thus must be chosen for each action a. This enforces a certain kind of interaction between the components constituting the team automaton.

Definition 4. *A* team automaton *over* $\mathcal{S}$ *is a quadruple* $\mathcal{T} = (Q, \Sigma, \delta, I)$, *with* $Q = \prod_{i \in [n]} Q_i$, $\Sigma = \bigcup_{i \in [n]} \Sigma_i$, $\delta \subseteq \prod_{i \in [n]} Q_i \times \Sigma \times \prod_{i \in [n]} Q_i$ *such that* $\{(q, q') \mid (q, a, q') \in \delta\} \subseteq \Delta_a(\mathcal{S})$, *for all* $a \in \Sigma$, *and* $I = \prod_{i \in [n]} I_i$. □

Each choice of synchronizations thus defines a team automaton. Clearly every team automaton is again a component automaton, which in its turn can be used as a component in an iteratively composed hierarchical system.

Within the formalization of a team automaton, no explicit information on loops is provided. In general one thus cannot distinguish whether a component with a loop on an action a in its local state participates in a synchronization on a by the team: this component may have been idle or—after having participated in the execution of a starting from the global state—it may have returned to its original local state. In order to relate the computations of a team to those of its components we nevertheless resort to projections. The problem of loops is resolved by assuming that the presence of a component's loop in a transition of a team implies execution of that loop. This is a maximal interpretation of the components' participation in synchronizations.

Definition 5. *Let* $\mathcal{T} = (Q, \Sigma, \delta, I)$ *be a team automaton over* $\mathcal{S}$ *and let* $j \in [n]$. *The projection* $\pi_{\mathcal{C}_j}(\alpha)$ *on* $\mathcal{C}_j$ *of a computation* $\alpha \in \mathbf{C}_\mathcal{T}$ *is defined as* $\pi_{\mathcal{C}_j}(\alpha) = proj_j(q)$ *in case* $\alpha = q \in I$, *while in case* $\alpha = \beta q a q'$, *for some* $\beta q \in \mathbf{C}_\mathcal{T}$, $q, q' \in Q$, *and* $a \in \Sigma$, *then* $\pi_{\mathcal{C}_j}(\alpha) = \pi_{\mathcal{C}_j}(\beta q)$ *if* $a \notin \Sigma_j$ *or* $proj_j^{[2]}(q, q') \notin \delta_{j,a}$, *and* $\pi_{\mathcal{C}_j}(\alpha) = \pi_{\mathcal{C}_j}(\beta q) a proj_j(q')$ *if* $proj_j^{[2]}(q, q') \in \delta_{j,a}$. □

Computations of team automata correspond to sequences of synchronizations and the projection on the j-th component yields a computation of that component. However, since the transitions of a team automaton are only required to be subsets of all possible synchronizations, not every computation of a component of a team is part of a computation of that team.

Theorem 1. $\pi_{\mathcal{C}_j}(\mathbf{C}_\mathcal{T}) \subseteq \mathbf{C}_{\mathcal{C}_j}$ *for all* $j \in [n]$ *and all team automata* $\mathcal{T}$ *over* $\mathcal{S}$. □

In [3] we defined several strategies for choosing the synchronizations of a team automaton, each leading to a uniquely defined team automaton. These strategies fix the synchronizations of a team automaton by defining, per action a, certain conditions on the a-transitions to be chosen from $\Delta_a(\mathcal{S})$, thus defining a unique subset of $\Delta_a(\mathcal{S})$ as the set of a-transitions of the team automaton. We refer to such subsets as *predicates* for a. Once predicates have been chosen for all actions in $\bigcup_{i \in [n]} \Sigma_i$, the team automaton over $\mathcal{S}$ defined by these predicates is unique.

Definition 6. *Let $\mathcal{R}_a(\mathcal{S}) \subseteq \Delta_a(\mathcal{S})$, for all $a \in \Sigma$, and let $\mathcal{R} = \{\mathcal{R}_a(\mathcal{S}) \mid a \in \Sigma\}$. Then $\mathcal{T} = (Q, \Sigma, \delta, I)$ is the $\mathcal{R}$-team automaton over $\mathcal{S}$ if $\delta_a = \mathcal{R}_a(\mathcal{S})$, for all $a \in \Sigma$.* □

The predicates *is-free* and *is-ai* are based on those actions of $\mathcal{T}$ that are *free* and *ai*, respectively. An action a is *free* in $\mathcal{T}$ if none of its a-transitions is brought about by a synchronization of a by two or more components from $\mathcal{S}$, while a is *action-indispensable* (*ai* for short) in $\mathcal{T}$ if all its a-transitions are brought about by a synchronization of all components from $\mathcal{S}$ sharing a.

Definition 7. *Let $a \in \bigcup_{i \in [n]} \Sigma_i$. The predicate* is-free *in $\mathcal{S}$ for a is defined as*
$$\mathcal{R}_a^{free}(\mathcal{S}) = \{(q, q') \in \Delta_a(\mathcal{S}) \mid \#\{i \in [n] \mid a \in \Sigma_i \text{ and } proj_i^{[2]}(q, q') \in \delta_{i,a}\} = 1\}$$
and the predicate is-action-indispensable *(*is-ai *for short) in $\mathcal{S}$ for a is defined as*
$$\mathcal{R}_a^{ai}(\mathcal{S}) = \{(q, q') \in \Delta_a(\mathcal{S}) \mid \forall i \in [n] : \text{ if } a \in \Sigma_i, \text{ then } proj_i^{[2]}(q, q') \in \delta_{i,a}\}.$$
□

The predicate *is-free* thus contains *all* a-transitions from $\Delta_a(\mathcal{S})$ in which only one component participates (assuming the maximal interpretation) while the predicate *is-ai* contains *all* a-transitions from $\Delta_a(\mathcal{S})$ in which all components with a as an action participate.

The $\mathcal{R}^{free}$-team automaton ($\mathcal{R}^{ai}$-team automaton) over $\mathcal{S}$ is also called *the maximal-free* (*maximal-ai*) team automaton over $\mathcal{S}$ because it is the unique team automaton with the property that adding any synchronization yields a team automaton with an action that is not *free* (*ai*).

Note that whenever none of the components from $\mathcal{S}$ share an action, i.e. for all $i \in [n]$, $\Sigma_i \cap \bigcup_{k \in [n] \setminus \{i\}} \Sigma_k = \emptyset$, then the *maximal-free* team automaton over $\mathcal{S}$ and the *maximal-ai* team automaton over $\mathcal{S}$ are the same.

For the rest of this paper we fix $\mathcal{T} = (Q, \Sigma, \delta, I)$ as a team automaton over $\mathcal{S}$ and we fix an alphabet Θ disjoint from Q. We also fix an element $j \in [n]$.

4 From Team Automata to Component Automata

In this section we start out from the computations and behaviour of a team automaton which we want to relate to the computations and behaviour of its constituting component automata. We address this issue element-wise, i.e. given one particular computation (behaviour) of a team automaton we consider how to extract from it the underlying computation (behaviour) of one of its constituting component automata.

According to Theorem 1 we can apply projections on the computations of the team automaton in order to obtain computations of its components. By filtering

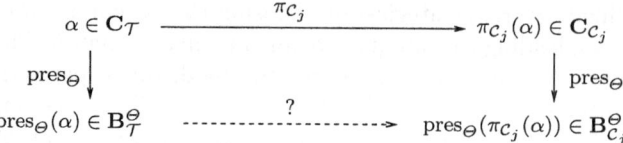

Fig. 1. Extracting behaviour from team automata to component automata.

out the state information from these computations we subsequently obtain their behaviour. We thus have the situation depicted by the diagram in Fig. 1.

In addition we are interested in an operation that yields the Θ-behaviour of C_j directly from the Θ-behaviour $\mathrm{pres}_\Theta(\alpha)$ of $\mathcal{T}$, i.e. an operation that makes the diagram depicted in Fig. 1 commute. A natural candidate is the homomorphism pres_{Σ_j} preserving only those actions from $\mathrm{pres}_\Theta(\alpha)$ that belong to C_j. However, $\mathrm{pres}_{\Sigma_j}(\mathrm{pres}_\Theta(\alpha)) = \mathrm{pres}_\Theta(\pi_{C_j}(\alpha))$ in general does not hold.

Example 1. Consider component automata C_1 and C_2 as depicted in Fig. 2 and team automaton $\mathcal{T}$ over $\{C_1, C_2\}$ as depicted in Fig. 3. We have $\Sigma_1 = \Sigma_2 = \{a, b\}$.

Now let $\Theta = \{a, b\}$ and let $\alpha = (q_1, q_2)b(q_1, q_2)a(q_1', q_2') \in \mathbf{C}_\mathcal{T}$. Then we have $\mathrm{pres}_{\Sigma_2}(\mathrm{pres}_\Theta(\alpha)) = ba \neq a = \mathrm{pres}_\Theta(q_2 a q_2') = \mathrm{pres}_\Theta(\pi_{C_2}(\alpha))$. □

This example shows that we cannot assume that a component participates in a synchronization *just* because it has the action that is being synchronized upon as one of its actions. There is thus no a priori relation between a component's set of actions and its participation in synchronizations of those actions. However, there exists a necessary and sufficient condition which guarantees that $\mathrm{pres}_{\Sigma_j}(\mathrm{pres}_\Theta(\alpha)) = \mathrm{pres}_\Theta(\pi_{C_j}(\alpha))$. This condition is based on the notion of *ai* actions and guarantees the participation of all components that share the action of a synchronization, but only for transitions that are actually used in team com-

Fig. 2. Component automata C_1 and C_2.

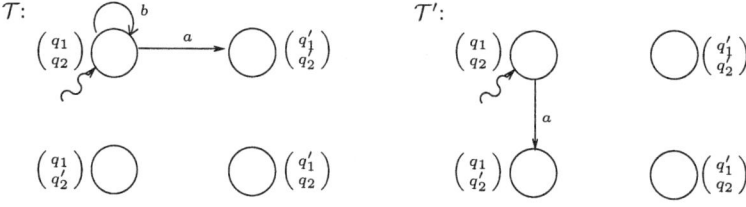

Fig. 3. Team automata $\mathcal{T}$ and $\mathcal{T}'$.

putations. A transition $(q,q') \in \delta_a$ is *useful* (*in* $\mathcal{T}$) if there exists a computation $\alpha \in \mathbf{C}_\mathcal{T}$ such that $\alpha = \beta q a q' \gamma$ for some $\beta \in (Q\Sigma)^*$ and $\gamma \in (\Sigma Q)^*$.

Definition 8. *The set* $uAI_j(\mathcal{T})$ *of useful j-ai actions is defined as* $uAI_j(\mathcal{T}) = \{a \in \Sigma_j \mid \forall q, q' \in Q: \text{ if } (q,q') \in \delta_a \text{ is useful, then } \text{proj}_j^{[2]}(q,q') \in \delta_{j,a}\}$. □

This leads to the following sufficient condition under which the preserving homomorphism pres_{Σ_j} makes the diagram of Fig. 1 commute.

Lemma 1. *If* $\Theta \cap \Sigma_j \subseteq uAI_j(\mathcal{T})$, *then for all* $\alpha \in \mathbf{C}_\mathcal{T}$, $\text{pres}_{\Sigma_j}(\text{pres}_\Theta(\alpha)) = \text{pres}_\Theta(\pi_{C_j}(\alpha))$.

Proof. Let $\Theta \cap \Sigma_j \subseteq uAI_j(\mathcal{T})$. We begin by considering $\alpha = q_0 a_1 q_1 a_2 q_2 \cdots a_n q_n \in \mathbf{C}_\mathcal{T}$. By induction on n we prove that $\text{pres}_{\Sigma_j}(\text{pres}_\Theta(\alpha)) = \text{pres}_\Theta(\pi_{C_j}(\alpha))$.

If $n = 0$, then $\alpha = q_0$ and thus $\text{pres}_{\Sigma_j}(\text{pres}_\Theta(q_0)) = \text{pres}_\Theta(\pi_{C_j}(q_0)) = \lambda$.

Next assume that $n = k+1$, for some $k \geq 0$, and that $\text{pres}_{\Sigma_j}(\text{pres}_\Theta(\beta)) = \text{pres}_\Theta(\pi_{C_j}(\beta))$, where $\beta = q_0 a_1 q_1 a_2 q_2 \cdots a_k q_k$. Hence $\alpha = \beta a_n q_n$. This implies $\text{pres}_{\Sigma_j}(\text{pres}_\Theta(\alpha)) = \text{pres}_{\Sigma_j}(\text{pres}_\Theta(\beta)) a_n$ if $a_n \in \Theta \cap \Sigma_j$ and $\text{pres}_{\Sigma_j}(\text{pres}_\Theta(\alpha)) = \text{pres}_{\Sigma_j}(\text{pres}_\Theta(\beta))$ if $a_n \notin \Theta \cap \Sigma_j$.

First let $a_n \in \Theta \cap \Sigma_j$. Then $\text{proj}_j^{[2]}(q_n, q_{n+1}) \in \delta_{j,a_n}$ since $\Theta \cap \Sigma_j \subseteq uAI_j(\mathcal{T})$ and thus $\text{pres}_\Theta(\pi_{C_j}(\alpha)) = \text{pres}_\Theta(\pi_{C_j}(\beta) a_n \text{proj}_j(q_{n+1})) = \text{pres}_\Theta(\pi_{C_j}(\beta)) a_n = \text{pres}_{\Sigma_j}(\text{pres}_\Theta(\beta a_n q_n))$ by the induction hypothesis. Hence $\text{pres}_{\Sigma_j}(\text{pres}_\Theta(\alpha)) = \text{pres}_\Theta(\pi_{C_j}(\alpha))$.

Next let $a_n \notin \Theta \cap \Sigma_j$. Then $a_n \notin \Theta$ or $a_n \notin \Sigma_j$.
If $a_n \notin \Sigma_j$, then $\pi_{C_j}(\alpha) = \pi_{C_j}(\beta)$ and thus, by the induction hypothesis, $\text{pres}_\Theta(\pi_{C_j}(\alpha)) = \text{pres}_\Theta(\pi_{C_j}(\beta)) = \text{pres}_{\Sigma_j}(\text{pres}_\Theta(\beta))$. Since $\text{pres}_{\Sigma_j}(\text{pres}_\Theta(\beta)) = \text{pres}_{\Sigma_j}(\text{pres}_\Theta(\beta a_n q_n))$ it follows that $\text{pres}_\Theta(\pi_{C_j}(\alpha)) = \text{pres}_{\Sigma_j}(\text{pres}_\Theta(\alpha))$.
If $a_n \notin \Theta$, then $\text{pres}_\Theta(\pi_{C_j}(\alpha)) = \text{pres}_\Theta(\pi_{C_j}(\beta))$ and thus, by the induction hypothesis, $\text{pres}_\Theta(\pi_{C_j}(\alpha)) = \text{pres}_{\Sigma_j}(\text{pres}_\Theta(\beta)) = \text{pres}_{\Sigma_j}(\text{pres}_\Theta(\alpha))$. □

This condition is also necessary.

Lemma 2. *If* $(\Theta \cap \Sigma_j) \setminus uAI_j(\mathcal{T}) \neq \emptyset$, *then there exists an* $\alpha \in \mathbf{C}_\mathcal{T}$ *such that* $\text{pres}_{\Sigma_j}(\text{pres}_\Theta(\alpha)) \neq \text{pres}_\Theta(\pi_{C_j}(\alpha))$.

Proof. Let $(\Theta \cap \Sigma_j) \setminus uAI_j(\mathcal{T}) \neq \emptyset$. Then the following situation must exist. Let $\alpha = q_0 a_1 q_1 a_2 q_2 \cdots a_n q_n \in \mathbf{C}_\mathcal{T}$ be such that for all $1 \leq i < n$, either $a_i \notin \Theta$, or $a_i \notin \Sigma_j$, or $\text{proj}_j^{[2]}(q_{i-1}, q_i) \in \delta_{j,a_i}$, while $\text{proj}_j^{[2]}(q_{n-1}, q_n) \notin \delta_{j,a_n}$, with $a_n \in \Theta \cap \Sigma_j$. Thus $\text{pres}_{\Sigma_j}(\text{pres}_\Theta(\alpha)) = \text{pres}_{\Sigma_j}(\text{pres}_\Theta(a_1 a_2 \cdots a_{n-1})) a_n$. As $\text{proj}_j^{[2]}(q_{n-1}, q_n) \notin \delta_{j,a_n}$ we however have $\text{pres}_\Theta(\pi_{C_j}(\alpha)) = \text{pres}_\Theta(\pi_{C_j}(q_0 a_1 q_1 a_2 q_2 \cdots a_{n-1} q_{n-1})) \neq \text{pres}_{\Sigma_j}(\text{pres}_\Theta(a_1 a_2 \cdots a_{n-1})) a_n = \text{pres}_{\Sigma_j}(\text{pres}_\Theta(\alpha))$. □

Theorem 2. *For all* $\alpha \in \mathbf{C}_\mathcal{T}$, $\text{pres}_{\Sigma_j}(\text{pres}_\Theta(\alpha)) = \text{pres}_\Theta(\pi_{C_j}(\alpha))$ *if and only if* $\Theta \cap \Sigma_j \subseteq uAI_j(\mathcal{T})$. □

Summarizing we thus have the following situation. Team automaton $\mathcal{T}$ is able to execute a computation α for which the diagram of Fig. 1 does not commute solely when C_j contains at least one action from Θ that is not useful j-ai in $\mathcal{T}$.

Until now we extracted the behaviour of the component automata of a team automaton from its computations. The above results however also provide us with a sufficient condition for obtaining the behaviour of components directly from the behaviour of the team automaton.

Theorem 3. *If $\Theta \cap \Sigma_j \subseteq uAI_j(\mathcal{T})$, then $\mathbf{B}_{\mathcal{T}}^{\Theta \cap \Sigma_j} \subseteq \mathbf{B}_{\mathcal{C}_j}^{\Theta}$.*

Proof. Let $\Theta \cap \Sigma_j \subseteq uAI_j(\mathcal{T})$ and let $v \in \mathbf{B}_{\mathcal{T}}^{\Theta \cap \Sigma_j}$. Then $v \in \mathrm{pres}_{\Theta \cap \Sigma_j}(\mathbf{C}_{\mathcal{T}})$. Now let $\alpha \in \mathbf{C}_{\mathcal{T}}$ be such that $\mathrm{pres}_{\Theta \cap \Sigma_j}(\alpha) = v$. By Theorem 1, $\pi_{\mathcal{C}_j}(\alpha) \in \mathbf{C}_{\mathcal{C}_j}$. Since $\Theta \cap \Sigma_j \subseteq uAI_j(\mathcal{T})$, Lemma 1 implies that $\mathrm{pres}_{\Sigma_j}(\mathrm{pres}_{\Theta}(\alpha)) = \mathrm{pres}_{\Theta}(\pi_{\mathcal{C}_j}(\alpha))$. Hence $v = \mathrm{pres}_{\Theta \cap \Sigma_j}(\alpha) = \mathrm{pres}_{\Sigma_j}(\mathrm{pres}_{\Theta}(\alpha)) = \mathrm{pres}_{\Theta}(\pi_{\mathcal{C}_j}(\alpha)) \in \mathbf{B}_{\mathcal{C}_j}^{\Theta}$. □

Contrary to what might be expected from Theorem 2, the statement of Theorem 3 cannot be reversed.

Example 2. (Ex. 1 cont.) Consider team automaton $\mathcal{T}'$ over $\{\mathcal{C}_1, \mathcal{C}_2\}$ as depicted in Fig. 3. Then $\Theta \cap \Sigma_1 = \{a, b\}$ and $uAI_1(\mathcal{T}') = \{b\}$. However, $\mathbf{B}_{\mathcal{T}'}^{\Theta \cap \Sigma_1} = \{\lambda, a\}$ is included in $\mathbf{B}_{\mathcal{C}_1}^{\Theta} = \{b^n, b^n a \mid n \geq 0\}$. □

Whereas a simple projection $\pi_{\mathcal{C}_j}$ applied to a computation of $\mathcal{T}$ suffices to obtain a computation of $\mathcal{C}_j$, a similarly simple preserving homomorphism pres_{Σ_j} applied to a behaviour of $\mathcal{T}$ need not always yield a behaviour of $\mathcal{C}_j$ unless all actions Σ_j of $\mathcal{C}_j$ are useful j-ai. The reason for this difference is as follows.

In a computation of $\mathcal{T}$ we still have available the information as to which components from $\mathcal{S}$ participated in each synchronization performed during this computation. When we deal with a behaviour of $\mathcal{T}$, however, only the sequence of executed actions is available, i.e. we have lost all information as to which components from $\mathcal{S}$ participated in which execution. This implies that whenever we can be sure of a component's participation in each execution of an action it has as an action itself, then we can simply apply our preserving homomorphism to a team behaviour in order to obtain the behaviour of that component.

Since every action of a component from $\mathcal{S}$ is useful j-ai in the *maximal-ai* team automaton $\mathcal{T}$ over $\mathcal{S}$, Theorem 3 implies the following result.

Corollary 1. *If $\mathcal{T}$ is the $\mathcal{R}^{ai}$-team automaton over $\mathcal{S}$, then $\mathbf{B}_{\mathcal{T}}^{\Theta \cap \Sigma_j} \subseteq \mathbf{B}_{\mathcal{C}_j}^{\Theta}$.* □

While this behavioural relation is well known for automata-based specification models with composition based on *maximal-ai* synchronizations, Theorems 2 and 3 show a more precise condition guaranteeing it and moreover exclude the existence of a similar relation in case composition is not *maximal-ai* based.

Thus far we studied how to obtain the computations (behaviour) of the components constituting $\mathcal{S}$ from the computations (behaviour) of team automata over $\mathcal{S}$. In the next section we consider the dual approach.

5 From Component Automata to Team Automata

In this section we start out from the computations and behaviour of the component automata constituting $\mathcal{S}$. Consequently we want to describe computations and behaviour of team automata over S. We begin by addressing this issue element-wise, i.e. given a computation (behaviour) of each component in a subset of S we want to know whether there exists a team automaton over S with a computation (behaviour) that uses this combination of computations.

Definition 9. *Let* $\alpha \in \prod_{i \in [n]} \mathbf{C}_{\mathcal{C}_i}$. *Then* α *is used in* $\mathcal{T}$ *if there exists a* $\beta \in \mathbf{C}_{\mathcal{T}}$ *such that for all* $i \in [n]$, $\pi_{\mathcal{C}_i}(\beta) = proj_i(\alpha)$. □

Note that any vector of initial states is used in $\mathcal{T}$ since $\prod_{i \in [n]} I_i \subseteq \mathbf{C}_{\mathcal{T}}$. If $K \subseteq [n]$ and $\alpha_k \in \mathbf{C}_{\mathcal{C}_k}$, for all $k \in K$, then we say that $\prod_{k \in K} \alpha_k$ is used in $\mathcal{T}$ whenever there exists a $\gamma \in \prod_{i \in [n]} \mathbf{C}_{\mathcal{C}_i}$ that is used in $\mathcal{T}$ and which is such that $proj_k(\gamma) = \alpha_k$, for all $k \in K$. Finally, as vectors over $\prod_j \mathbf{C}_{\mathcal{C}_j}$ have one element we identify the vector and its element in those cases.

In general not all vectors of computations of components from S are used in $\mathcal{T}$. As said before, it may be the case that a computation of a component from S never participates in a team computation. Moreover, it may happen that a vector over two or more computations of components from S is not used as such in $\mathcal{T}$, even when each entry of this vector *is* used in $\mathcal{T}$.

Example 3. (Ex. 1 cont.) Let $\alpha' = q_2 a q_2' b q_2' \in \mathbf{C}_{\mathcal{C}_2}$. Then α' is not used in $\mathcal{T}$ because there exists no $\beta \in \mathbf{C}_{\mathcal{T}}$ such that $\pi_{\mathcal{C}_2}(\beta) = \alpha'$. Now consider team automaton $\mathcal{T}''$ over $\{\mathcal{C}_1, \mathcal{C}_2\}$ as depicted in Fig. 4.

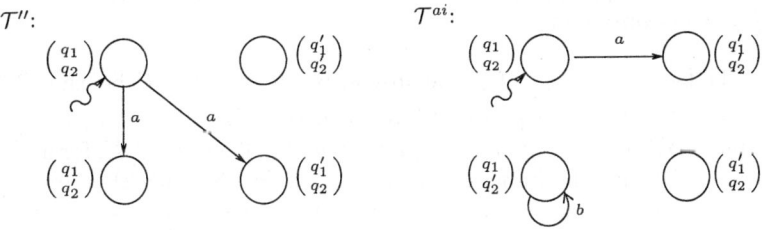

Fig. 4. Team automaton $\mathcal{T}''$ and *maximal-ai* team automaton $\mathcal{T}^{ai}$.

Now let $\alpha_1 = q_1 a q_1' \in \mathbf{C}_{\mathcal{C}_1}$ and let $\alpha_2 = q_2 a q_2' \in \mathbf{C}_{\mathcal{C}_2}$. Clearly both α_1 and α_2 are used in $\mathcal{T}''$ because $\beta_1 = (q_1, q_2) a (q_1', q_2) \in \mathbf{C}_{\mathcal{T}''}$ and $\beta_2 = (q_1, q_2) a (q_1, q_2') \in \mathbf{C}_{\mathcal{T}''}$. However, β_1 and β_2 are the only two nontrivial computations of $\mathcal{T}''$. Since $\pi_{\mathcal{C}_1}(\beta_2) = q_1$ and $\pi_{\mathcal{C}_2}(\beta_1) = q_2$ this means that there exists no $\beta \in \mathbf{C}_{\mathcal{T}''}$ such that $\pi_{\mathcal{C}_1}(\beta) = \alpha_1$ and $\pi_{\mathcal{C}_2}(\beta) = \alpha_2$. Hence (α_1, α_2) is not used in $\mathcal{T}''$.

Note that (α_1, α_2) *is* used in $\mathcal{T}$ because $\beta = (q_1, q_2) a (q_1', q_2') \in \mathbf{C}_{\mathcal{T}}$ is such that $\pi_{\mathcal{C}_1}(\beta) = proj_1((\alpha_1, \alpha_2)) = \alpha_1$ and $\pi_{\mathcal{C}_2}(\beta) = proj_2((\alpha_1, \alpha_2)) = \alpha_2$. □

While in general not every vector of computations of components from S is used in $\mathcal{T}$, we wonder if the situation improves when $\mathcal{T}$ is defined in a particular way.

In analogy with the previous section we first consider $\mathcal{T}$ to be the *maximal-ai* team automaton over S. However, not even in *maximal-ai* team automata over S need all vectors of computations of components from S be used.

Example 4. (Ex. 1, 3 cont.) The *maximal-ai* team automaton $\mathcal{T}^{ai}$ over $\{\mathcal{C}_1, \mathcal{C}_2\}$ is depicted in Fig. 4. Consider $q_1 \in \mathbf{C}_{\mathcal{C}_1}$ and recall that $\alpha_2 = q_2 a q_2' \in \mathbf{C}_{\mathcal{C}_2}$. Since $(q_1, q_2) a (q_1', q_2')$ is the only nontrivial computation of $\mathcal{T}^{ai}$ there exists no computation $\beta' \in \mathbf{C}_{\mathcal{T}^{ai}}$ such that $\pi_{\mathcal{C}_1}(\beta') = q_1$ and $\pi_{\mathcal{C}_2}(\beta') = \alpha_2$. Hence (q_1, α_2) is not used in $\mathcal{T}^{ai}$. □

The fact that the *maximal-ai* strategy forces components to synchronize on their shared actions provides us with enough information to formulate the conditions under which a vector of computations *is* used in a computation of the *maximal-ai* team automaton over $\mathcal{S}$. To this aim we define a vector α consisting of computations of the components from $\mathcal{S}$—one for each component—to be *ai-consistent* if there exists a word w over Σ with the following property: whenever we preserve from w only the actions of a component from $\mathcal{S}$, then we obtain exactly the behaviour resulting from the computation in α that originates from that component. In an *ai*-consistent vector the computations forming its entries thus "agree" with respect to the behaviour of their respective components.

Definition 10. *Let $\alpha \in \prod_{i \in [n]} \mathbf{C}_{\mathcal{C}_i}$. Then α is* ai-consistent *if there exists a $w \in \Sigma^*$ such that for all $i \in [n]$, $pres_{\Sigma_i}(w) = pres_{\Sigma_i}(proj_i(\alpha))$.* □

We now have a sufficient and necessary condition for a vector of computations of components from $\mathcal{S}$ to be used in the *maximal-ai* team automaton over $\mathcal{S}$.

Theorem 4. *$\alpha \in \prod_{i \in [n]} \mathbf{C}_{\mathcal{C}_i}$ is used in the $\mathcal{R}^{ai}$-team automaton over $\mathcal{S}$ if and only if α is ai-consistent.*

Proof. (If) Let $\alpha \in \prod_{i \in [n]} \mathbf{C}_{\mathcal{C}_i}$ be *ai*-consistent and let $\mathcal{T}$ be the $\mathcal{R}^{ai}$-team automaton over $\mathcal{S}$. Now let $w \in \Sigma^*$ be such that for all $i \in [n]$, $pres_{\Sigma_i}(w) = pres_{\Sigma_i}(proj_i(\alpha))$. Let $w = a_1 a_2 \cdots a_m$ for some $m \geq 0$ and $a_k \in \Sigma$, for all $k \in [m]$. For each $i \in [n]$, let the indices $i_1, i_2, \ldots, i_{m_i} \in [m]$ be such that $pres_{\Sigma_i}(w) = a_{i_1} a_{i_2} \cdots a_{i_{m_i}}$. Hence $m_i = 0$ if $pres_{\Sigma_i}(w) = \lambda$ and $1 \leq i_1 < i_2 < \cdots < i_{m_i} \leq m$ otherwise. Moreover, observe that $\bigcup_{i \in [n]} \{i_1, i_2, \ldots, i_{m_i}\} = [m]$. Since for all $i \in [n]$, $pres_{\Sigma_i}(w) = pres_{\Sigma_i}(proj_i(\alpha))$ and $proj_i(\alpha) \in \mathbf{C}_{\mathcal{C}_i}$, it follows that for all $i \in [n]$, $proj_i(\alpha) = q_0^i a_{i_1} q_1^i a_{i_2} \cdots a_{i_{m_i}} q_{m_i}^i$ with $q_0^i \in I_i$ and $q_1^i, q_2^i, \ldots, q_{m_i}^i \in Q_i$.

Now define $\beta = q_0 a_1 q_1 a_2 \cdots a_m q_m$, with $q_k \in \prod_{i \in [n]} Q_i$ for all $0 \leq k \leq m$, in such a way that for all $i \in [n]$ and for all $0 \leq k \leq m$, $proj_i(q_k) = q_\ell^i$ if $i_\ell \leq k < i_{\ell+1}$ with $\ell < m_i$ (by convention, $i_0 = 0$) and $proj_i(q_k) = q_{m_i}^i$ if $i_{m_i} \leq k \leq m$. Consequently we prove that $\beta \in \mathbf{C}_{\mathcal{T}}$ while—in one stroke—$\pi_{\mathcal{C}_i}(\beta) = proj_i(\alpha)$, for all $i \in [n]$, follows from an inductive argument.

By its definition, $q_0 = \prod_{i \in [n]} q_0^i \in \prod_{i \in [n]} I_i = I$. Next consider (q_{k-1}, a_k, q_k), for some $k \in [m]$. Let $i \in [n]$. We distinguish the following two cases.

If $a_k \in \Sigma_i$, then $k = i_\ell$ for some $\ell \in [m_i]$ and $i_{\ell-1} \leq k-1 < k = i_\ell$. The definitions of q_{k-1} and q_k then yield $proj_i(q_{k-1}) = q_{\ell-1}^i$ and $proj_i(q_k) = q_\ell^i$. Since $proj_i(\alpha) \in \mathbf{C}_{\mathcal{C}_i}$ it follows that $(q_{\ell-1}^i, q_\ell^i) \in \delta_{i, a_{i_\ell}} = \delta_{i, a_k}$.

If $a_k \notin \Sigma_i$, then $k \neq i_\ell$ for some $\ell \in [m_i]$. If $k < i_{m_i}$, then there exists an $\ell \geq 1$ such that $i_{\ell-1} \leq k-1 < k < i_\ell$. Thus $proj_i(q_{k-1}) = proj_i(q_k) = q_{\ell-1}^i$. Conversely, if $k \geq i_{m_i}$, then $i_{m_i} \leq k-1 < k \leq m$. Thus again $proj_i(q_{k-1}) = proj_i(q_k)$.

Since $\bigcup_{i\in[n]}\{i_1, i_2, \ldots, i_{m_i}\} = [m]$, it follows that $a_k \in \Sigma_i$ for at least one $i \in [n]$ and hence $(q_{k-1}, q_k) \in \mathcal{R}^{ai}_{a_k}(\mathcal{S}) = \delta_{a_k}$. This implies that for all $k \in [m]$, $q_0 a_1 q_1 a_2 \cdots a_k q_k \in \mathbf{C}_\mathcal{T}$ and for all $i \in [n]$, $\pi_{\mathcal{C}_i}(q_0 a_1 q_1 a_2 \cdots a_k q_k) \in \mathbf{C}_{\mathcal{C}_i}$. Hence for all $i \in [n]$, $\pi_{\mathcal{C}_i}(\beta) = \pi_{\mathcal{C}_i}(q_0 a_1 q_1 a_2 \cdots a_m q_m) = \text{proj}_i(\alpha)$ and α is thus used in the *maximal-ai* team automaton $\mathcal{T}$.

(Only if) Let $\alpha \in \prod_{i\in[n]} \mathbf{C}_{\mathcal{C}_i}$ be used in the $\mathcal{R}^{ai}$-team automaton $\mathcal{T}$ over $\mathcal{S}$. Then there exists a $\beta \in \mathbf{C}_\mathcal{T}$ such that $\pi_{\mathcal{C}_i}(\beta) = \text{proj}_i(\alpha)$, for all $i \in [n]$. Now let $w = \text{pres}_\Sigma(\beta) \in \Sigma^*$. Since $\mathcal{T}$ is the $\mathcal{R}^{ai}$-team automaton over $\mathcal{S}$, Lemma 1 implies that $\text{pres}_{\Sigma_i}(w) = \text{pres}_{\Sigma_i}(\text{pres}_\Sigma(\beta)) = \text{pres}_\Sigma(\pi_{\mathcal{C}_i}(\beta)) = \text{pres}_{\Sigma_i}(\pi_{\mathcal{C}_i}(\beta)) = \text{pres}_{\Sigma_i}(\text{proj}_i(\alpha))$, for all $i \in [n]$. Hence α is *ai*-consistent. □

In order to relate the computations of *maximal-ai* team automata to the computations of their constituting components, we define when $\mathcal{S}$ is *ai*-consistent.

Definition 11. $\mathcal{S}$ *is* ai-consistent *if for all $i \in [n]$ and for each $\gamma \in \mathbf{C}_{\mathcal{C}_i}$ there exists an ai-consistent vector $\alpha \in \prod_{i\in[n]} \mathbf{C}_{\mathcal{C}_i}$ such that $\text{proj}_i(\alpha) = \gamma$.* □

We have now defined *ai*-consistency both for vectors (of computations) and for $\mathcal{S}$. However, from the context it will always be clear whether we deal with an *ai*-consistent vector or rather with an *ai*-consistent $\mathcal{S}$.

If $\mathcal{S}$ is *ai*-consistent, then this guarantees that for all computations of its constituents there exists a vector of computations which is *ai*-consistent and thus each computation of a component from $\mathcal{S}$ is used in a computation of the *maximal-ai* team automaton $\mathcal{T}$ over $\mathcal{S}$. In that case the set of computations (behaviour) of a component from $\mathcal{S}$ thus equals the set of computations (behaviour) of the *maximal-ai* team automaton over $\mathcal{S}$ projected on that component.

Theorem 5. *Let $\mathcal{T}$ be the $\mathcal{R}^{ai}$-team automaton over $\mathcal{S}$. Then*

(1) $\mathbf{C}_{\mathcal{C}_i} = \pi_{\mathcal{C}_i}(\mathbf{C}_\mathcal{T})$, for all $i \in [n]$, if and only if $\mathcal{S}$ is ai-consistent, and
(2) if $\mathcal{S}$ is ai-consistent, then for all $i \in [n]$, $\mathbf{B}^{\Sigma_i}_{\mathcal{C}_i} = \mathbf{B}^{\Sigma_i}_\mathcal{T}$.

Proof. (1) (Only if) Let $\mathbf{C}_{\mathcal{C}_i} = \pi_{\mathcal{C}_i}(\mathbf{C}_\mathcal{T})$, for all $i \in [n]$. Let $\gamma \in \mathbf{C}_{\mathcal{C}_j}$. Since $\mathbf{C}_{\mathcal{C}_j} = \pi_{\mathcal{C}_j}(\mathbf{C}_\mathcal{T})$ there exists a $\beta \in \mathbf{C}_\mathcal{T}$ such that $\pi_{\mathcal{C}_j}(\beta) = \gamma$. Now let $\alpha \in \prod_{i\in[n]} \mathbf{C}_{\mathcal{C}_i}$ be such that for all $i \in [n]$, $\text{proj}_i(\alpha) = \pi_{\mathcal{C}_i}(\beta)$. Since $\mathbf{C}_{\mathcal{C}_i} = \pi_{\mathcal{C}_i}(\mathbf{C}_\mathcal{T})$, for all $i \in [n]$, this α exists. Furthermore, by Theorem 4, α is *ai*-consistent. Definition 11 then implies that $\mathcal{S}$ is *ai*-consistent.

(If) Let $\mathcal{S}$ be *ai*-consistent. Due to Theorem 1 we need to prove that for all $i \in [n]$, $\mathbf{C}_{\mathcal{C}_i} \subseteq \pi_{\mathcal{C}_i}(\mathbf{C}_\mathcal{T})$. Now let $\gamma \in \mathbf{C}_{\mathcal{C}_j}$. Since $\mathcal{S}$ is *ai*-consistent there exists an *ai*-consistent vector $\alpha \in \prod_{i\in[n]} \mathbf{C}_{\mathcal{C}_i}$ such that $\text{proj}_j(\alpha) = \gamma$. Then by Theorem 4 there exists a $\beta \in \mathbf{C}_\mathcal{T}$ such that $\pi_{\mathcal{C}_j}(\beta) = \text{proj}_j(\alpha) = \gamma$. Hence $\gamma \in \pi_{\mathcal{C}_j}(\mathbf{C}_\mathcal{T})$.

(2) Since $\mathcal{T}$ is the $\mathcal{R}^{ai}$-team automaton over $\mathcal{S}$, Corollary 1 implies that $\mathbf{B}^{\Sigma_i}_\mathcal{T} \subseteq \mathbf{B}^{\Sigma_i}_{\mathcal{C}_i}$. Moreover, by (1) and Lemma 1, $\mathbf{B}^{\Sigma_i}_{\mathcal{C}_i} \subseteq \mathbf{B}^{\Sigma_i}_\mathcal{T}$. □

We move on to the case that $\mathcal{T}$ is the *maximal-free* team automaton over $\mathcal{S}$.

Now $\mathcal{T}$ consists of completely independent, non-synchronizing components. Consequently, our first intuition might be to jump to the conclusion that in

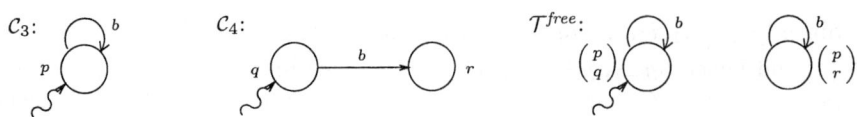

Fig. 5. Component automata C_1 and C_2, and *maximal-free* team automaton $\mathcal{T}^{free}$.

that case *every* single computation of a component from $\mathcal{S}$ is used in $\mathcal{T}$. In case the components from $\mathcal{S}$ contain loops, however, a computation of a component from $\mathcal{S}$ need not be used in $\mathcal{T}$. This is due to our maximal interpretation of the components' participation in synchronizations.

Example 5. Consider component automata C_3 and C_4, and the *maximal-free* team automaton $\mathcal{T}^{free}$ over $\{C_3, C_4\}$, as depicted in Fig. 5.

It is easy to see that $\alpha'' = qbr \in \mathbf{C}_{C_4}$ and that no computation $\beta \in \mathbf{C}_{\mathcal{T}^{free}}$ is such that $\pi_{C_4}(\beta) = \alpha''$. Hence α'' is not used in $\mathcal{T}^{free}$. □

By postulating that loops can never synchronize with transitions of other components, this problem can be avoided.

Definition 12. $\mathcal{S}$ *is* Θ-*loop limited if for all* $i \in [n]$ *and for all* $a \in \Theta \cap \Sigma_i$, *whenever* $(q,q) \in \delta_{i,a}$ *for some* $q \in Q_i$, *then for all* $k \in [n] \setminus \{i\}$, $\delta_{k,a} = \emptyset$. □

If $\mathcal{S}$ is Σ-loop limited, then we may also simply say that it is loop limited.

In the *maximal-free* team automaton $\mathcal{T}$ over a loop-limited $\mathcal{S}$, each action of C_j can be executed independently of the current local states that the other components from $\mathcal{S}$ are in, since none of these other components participates in such an execution. It thus comes as no surprise that in that case each computation of a component from $\mathcal{S}$ *is* used in a computation of $\mathcal{T}$.

Lemma 3. *If* $\mathcal{S}$ *is loop limited, then every* $\alpha \in \mathbf{C}_{C_j}$ *is used in the* $\mathcal{R}^{free}$-*team automaton over* $\mathcal{S}$.

Proof. Let $\mathcal{S}$ be loop limited and let $\mathcal{T}$ be the $\mathcal{R}^{free}$-team automaton over $\mathcal{S}$. Observe that together with Definitions 3 and 7 this implies that if $(p, p') \in \delta_{j,a}$, then for all $q \in Q$ such that $\text{proj}_j(q) = p$, $(q, q') \in \delta_a = \mathcal{R}_a^{free}(\mathcal{S})$ with $\text{proj}_j(q') = p'$, and for all $i \in [n] \setminus \{j\}$, $\text{proj}_i(q') = \text{proj}_i(q)$. Now let $\alpha = p_0 a_1 p_1 a_2 \cdots a_m p_m \in \mathbf{C}_{C_j}$, i.e. $(p_{k-1}, p_k) \in \delta_{j,a_k}$, for all $1 \leq k \leq m$. Since $Q = \prod_{i \in [n]} Q_i$ and $I = \prod_{i \in [n]} I_i$, the observation above implies that there exists a computation $\beta = q_0 a_1 q_1 a_2 \cdots a_m q_m \in \mathbf{C}_\mathcal{T}$ such that $\text{proj}_j^{[2]}(q_{k-1}, q_k) = (p_{k-1}, p_k) \in \delta_{j,a_k}$, for all $1 \leq k \leq m$. Hence $\pi_{C_j}(\beta) = \alpha$ and α is thus used in $\mathcal{T}$. □

From Theorem 1 we know that given a computation of a team automaton over $\mathcal{S}$, the projection on a component from $\mathcal{S}$ is included in the set of computations of that component. Together with Lemma 3 this implies that whenever $\mathcal{S}$ is loop limited, then the set of computations of a component from $\mathcal{S}$ equals the set of computations of the *maximal-free* team automaton $\mathcal{T}$ over $\mathcal{S}$ projected on that component. Moreover, the behaviour of that component is included in the behaviour of $\mathcal{T}$. Like the proof of Lemma 3, also the proof of this statement is based on the observation that in a *maximal-free* team automaton, each executed action has only one participating component. This implies that the team automaton can always execute any computation of any of its components while keeping all remaining components in an initial state.

Theorem 6. *Let $\mathcal{T}$ be the $\mathcal{R}^{free}$-team automaton over $\mathcal{S}$. Then if $\mathcal{S}$ is loop limited, then for all $i \in [n]$, $\mathbf{C}_{\mathcal{C}_i} = \pi_{\mathcal{C}_i}(\mathbf{C}_\mathcal{T})$ and $\mathbf{B}_{\mathcal{C}_i}^{\Sigma_i} \subseteq \mathbf{B}_\mathcal{T}^{\Sigma}$.*

Proof. Let $\mathcal{S}$ be loop limited and let $i \in [n]$. Then Lemma 3 implies that $\mathbf{C}_{\mathcal{C}_i} \subseteq \pi_{\mathcal{C}_i}(\mathbf{C}_\mathcal{T})$ and thus, by Theorem 1, $\mathbf{C}_{\mathcal{C}_i} = \pi_{\mathcal{C}_i}(\mathbf{C}_\mathcal{T})$. Now let $\alpha \in \mathbf{B}_{\mathcal{C}_i}^{\Sigma_i}$ and let $\beta \in \mathbf{C}_{\mathcal{C}_i}$ be such that $\mathrm{pres}_{\Sigma_i}(\beta) = \alpha$. Since $\mathbf{C}_{\mathcal{C}_i} = \pi_{\mathcal{C}_i}(\mathbf{C}_\mathcal{T})$, there must exist a $\gamma \in \mathbf{C}_\mathcal{T}$ such that $\beta = \pi_{\mathcal{C}_i}(\gamma)$. Moreover, since $\mathcal{T}$ is the $\mathcal{R}^{free}$-team automaton over $\mathcal{S}$, it follows that we may assume that $\pi_{\mathcal{C}_k}(\gamma) \in I_k$, for all $k \in [n] \setminus \{i\}$. Hence $\mathrm{pres}_\Sigma(\gamma) = \mathrm{pres}_\Sigma(\pi_{\mathcal{C}_i}(\gamma)) = \mathrm{pres}_{\Sigma_i}(\beta) = \alpha$ and thus $\alpha \in \mathbf{B}_\mathcal{T}^\Sigma$. □

The behaviour of the *maximal-free* team automaton $\mathcal{T}$ over $\mathcal{S}$ trivially is made up of the behaviour of not just one component from $\mathcal{S}$, but of the behaviour of all of the components from $\mathcal{S}$. Therefore, even if $\mathcal{S}$ is loop limited, $\mathbf{B}_{\mathcal{C}_j}^{\Sigma_j}$ may be strictly included in $\mathbf{B}_\mathcal{T}^\Sigma$. Furthermore, the fact that $\mathbf{C}_{\mathcal{C}_i} = \pi_{\mathcal{C}_i}(\mathbf{C}_\mathcal{T})$, for all $i \in [n]$, need not imply that $\mathcal{S}$ is loop limited.

Example 6. (Ex. 1 cont.) Consider the *maximal-free* team automaton $\mathcal{T}^{1,2}$ over $\{\mathcal{C}_1, \mathcal{C}_2\}$ as depicted in Fig. 6. We directly see that $\mathbf{B}_{\mathcal{C}_2}^{\Sigma_2} = \{\lambda, ab^n \mid n \geq 0\} \not\subseteq \{b^n, b^n a, b^n aa, b^n aab^n \mid n \geq 0\} = \mathbf{B}_{\mathcal{T}^{1,2}}^\Sigma$.

Recall that $\alpha' = q_2 a q_2' b q_2' \in \mathbf{C}_{\mathcal{C}_2}$. Since $\beta = (q_1, q_2) a (q_1, q_2') a (q_1', q_2') b (q_1', q_2') \in \mathbf{C}_{\mathcal{T}^{1,2}}$, α' is used in $\mathcal{T}^{1,2}$. It is moreover not difficult to see that for all $k \in [2]$, $\mathbf{C}_{\mathcal{C}_k} \subseteq \pi_{\mathcal{C}_k}(\mathbf{C}_{\mathcal{T}^{1,2}})$ and thus, by Theorem 1, $\mathbf{C}_{\mathcal{C}_k} = \pi_{\mathcal{C}_k}(\mathbf{C}_{\mathcal{T}^{1,2}})$. However, $\{\mathcal{C}_1, \mathcal{C}_2\}$ is not loop limited because $(q_1, q_1) \in \delta_{1,b}$ and $(q_2', q_2') \in \delta_{2,b}$. □

Both for *maximal-ai* and for *maximal-free* team automata over $\mathcal{S}$ we have formulated (in Theorems 5 and 6, respectively) a condition which guarantees that all component computations participate in at least one team computation. In fact, for *maximal-ai* team automata over $\mathcal{S}$ the *ai-consistency* of $\mathcal{S}$ was shown to be also a necessary condition. Given these conditions the relation between the behaviour of the components from $\mathcal{S}$ and that of the *maximal-ai* (*maximal-free*) team automaton over $\mathcal{S}$ could be precisely described. In the remainder of

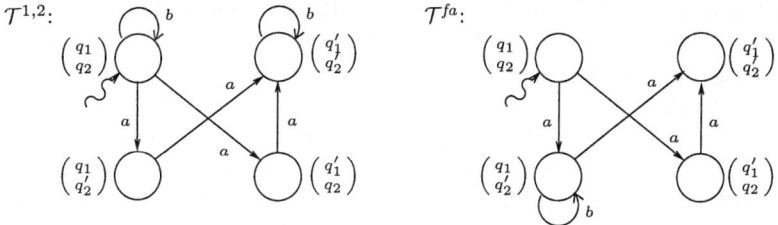

Fig. 6. Team automata $\mathcal{T}^{1,2}$ and $\mathcal{T}^{fa}$.

this paper we moreover define the behaviour of *maximal-ai* (*maximal-free*) team automata in terms of the behaviour of their constituting components. This requires establishing which combinations of words—if any—from the behaviour of components from $\mathcal{S}$ can be combined—and in particular how—such that a word from the behaviour of the *maximal-ai* (*maximal-free*) team automaton over $\mathcal{S}$ results. This leads us to the *shuffle* (a.k.a. *merge* or *weave*) operation from the theory of formal languages.

6 Shuffles and Synchronized Shuffles

In this section we give definitions and results concerning shuffles and synchronized shuffles. A shuffle of two words is an arbitrary interleaving of the symbol occurrences in the original words, like the shuffling of two decks of cards. This is a well-known language-theoretic operation with a long history in theoretical computer science, in particular within formal language theory [10, 14]. However, the underlying idea also appears in many other disguises throughout the computer science literature, e.g. in concurrency theory in the form of parallel operators modelling communication between processes [4, 23].

Definition 13. *Let Δ be an alphabet and let $u, v \in \Delta^*$. Then a word $w \in \Delta^*$ is a shuffle of u and v, denoted by $w \in u \parallel v$, if $w = u_1 v_1 u_2 v_2 \cdots u_n v_n$, with $n \geq 1$, $u_i, v_i \in \Delta^*$ for all $i \in [n]$, $u = u_1 u_2 \cdots u_n$, and $v = v_1 v_2 \cdots v_n$.
The shuffle of languages $K, L \subseteq \Delta^*$, denoted by $K \parallel L$, is defined as $K \parallel L = \bigcup_{u \in K, v \in L} (u \parallel v)$.* □

Example 7. Let $\Delta = \{a, b, c, d\}$. Let $u = abc \in \Delta^*$ and let $v = cd \in \Delta^*$. Then $u \parallel v = \{abccd, acbcd, cabcd, abcdc, acbdc, cabdc, acdbc, cadbc, cdabc\}$. □

The shuffle operation is both commutative and associative: for all $u, v, w \in \Delta^*$, $u \parallel v = v \parallel u$ and $(u \parallel v) \parallel w = u \parallel (v \parallel w)$, and likewise for languages. The shuffle of languages L_i, with $i \in [n]$, can thus be defined as $\parallel_{i \in [n]} L_i = L_1 \parallel L_2 \parallel \cdots \parallel L_n$.

We now generalize the basic shuffle by defining a synchronized shuffle. Rather than just interleaving the occurrences of the symbols in the words being shuffled, whenever a symbol is subject to synchronization the synchronized shuffle combines its occurrences in different words into one occurrence. Each thus synchronized occurrence of a symbol in the resulting words then corresponds to a synchronization. This means that the words in a synchronized shuffle have a common "backbone" consisting of occurrences of synchronized symbols. The idea underlying the various synchronized shuffles we define here appears in numerous disguises throughout the computer science literature, e.g. in concurrency theory as the concurrent composition or weave of synchronizing processes [17, 25] and in formal language theory as the 'produit de mixage' of languages [7, 19].

For the rest of this paper we use Γ to denote an arbitrary but fixed alphabet.

Definition 14. *Let Δ be an alphabet and let $u, v \in \Delta^*$. Then a word $w \in \Delta^*$ is a synchronized shuffle (S-shuffle for short) on Γ of u and v, denoted by $w \in u \parallel^\Gamma v$,*

if $w \in (u_1 \parallel v_1)x_1(u_2 \parallel v_2)x_2 \cdots x_{n-1}(u_n \parallel v_n)$, with $n \geq 1$, $u_i, v_i \in (\Delta \setminus \Gamma)^*$ for all $i \in [n]$, $x_i \in \Gamma$ for all $i \in [n-1]$, $u = u_1x_1u_2x_2\cdots x_{n-1}u_n$, and $v = v_1x_1v_2x_2\cdots x_{n-1}v_n$.
The S-shuffle on Γ of languages $K, L \subseteq \Delta^*$, denoted by $K \parallel^\Gamma L$, is defined as $K \parallel^\Gamma L = \bigcup_{u \in K, v \in L}(u \parallel^\Gamma v)$. □

Note that the S-shuffle is indeed a generalization of the shuffle: for all $u, v \in \Delta^*$, $u \parallel^\emptyset v = u \parallel v$, and likewise for languages.

Example 8. (Ex. 7 cont.) Now $u \parallel^{\{c\}} v = \{abcd\}$, whereas $u \parallel^{\{b,c\}} v = \emptyset$. □

We proceed by defining two special cases of the S-shuffle, each obtained by varying the set of symbols required to be synchronized. Given two words over two alphabets, the *full S-shuffle* requires all symbols in the intersection of these two alphabets to be synchronized, while the *relaxed S-shuffle* requires only a specified subset of the symbols in this intersection to be synchronized. Both operations are thus defined *with respect to* the alphabets of the words involved.

Definition 15. Let Δ_1 and Δ_2 be alphabets, let $u \in \Delta_1^*$, let $v \in \Delta_2^*$, and let $w \in (\Delta_1 \cup \Delta_2)^*$. Then

(1) w is a full S-shuffle (fS-shuffle for short) of u and v w.r.t. Δ_1 and Δ_2, denoted by $w \in u \;_{\Delta_1}\!\parallel_{\Delta_2} v$, if w is an S-shuffle on $\Delta_1 \cap \Delta_2$ of u and v, and

(2) w is a relaxed S-shuffle (rS-shuffle for short) on Γ of u and v w.r.t. Δ_1 and Δ_2, denoted by $w \in u \;_{\Delta_1}\!\parallel^\Gamma_{\Delta_2} v$, if w is an S-shuffle on $\Gamma \cap \Delta_1 \cap \Delta_2$ of u and v. □

Let $L_1 \subseteq \Delta_1^*$ and let $L_2 \subseteq \Delta_2^*$. Then the fS-shuffle of L_1 and L_2 w.r.t. Δ_1 and Δ_2, denoted by $L_1 \;_{\Delta_1}\!\parallel_{\Delta_2} L_2$, is defined as $L_1 \;_{\Delta_1}\!\parallel_{\Delta_2} L_2 = \bigcup_{u \in L_1, v \in L_2}(u \;_{\Delta_1}\!\parallel_{\Delta_2} v)$ and the rS-shuffle on Γ of L_1 and L_2 w.r.t. Δ_1 and Δ_2, denoted by $L_1 \;_{\Delta_1}\!\parallel^\Gamma_{\Delta_2} L_2$, is defined as $L_1 \;_{\Delta_1}\!\parallel^\Gamma_{\Delta_2} L_2 = \bigcup_{u \in L_1, v \in L_2}(u \;_{\Delta_1}\!\parallel^\Gamma_{\Delta_2} v)$. Note that for all $u \in \Delta_1^*$, $v \in \Delta_2^*$, and $\Gamma \supseteq \Delta_1 \cap \Delta_2$, $u \;_{\Delta_1}\!\parallel^\Gamma_{\Delta_2} v = u \;_{\Delta_1}\!\parallel_{\Delta_2} v$, and likewise for languages.

Example 9. (Ex. 8 cont.) Now $u \;_\Delta\!\parallel^{\{c\}}_\Delta v = \{abcd\}$, whereas $u \;_\Delta\!\parallel^{\{b,c\}}_\Delta v = u \;_\Delta\!\parallel_\Delta v = \emptyset$. Consequently, let $\Delta_1 = \{a,b,c\}$, $\Delta_2 = \{c,d\}$, $u = abc \in \Delta_1^*$, and $v = cd \in \Delta_2^*$. Then $u \;_{\Delta_1}\!\parallel^{\{c\}}_{\Delta_2} v = u \;_{\Delta_1}\!\parallel^{\{b,c\}}_{\Delta_2} v = u \;_{\Delta_1}\!\parallel_{\Delta_2} v = \{abcd\}$. □

Since the S-shuffle is defined in terms of the shuffle, its commutativity follows immediately: for all $u, v \in \Delta^*$, $u \parallel^\Gamma v = v \parallel^\Gamma u$, and likewise for languages. The fact that both the fS-shuffle and the rS-shuffle are defined in terms of the S-shuffle subsequently implies that also these operations are commutative in the following sense: for all $u \in \Delta_1^*$ and $v \in \Delta_2^*$, $u \;_{\Delta_1}\!\parallel_{\Delta_2} v = v \;_{\Delta_2}\!\parallel_{\Delta_1} u$ and $u \;_{\Delta_1}\!\parallel^\Gamma_{\Delta_2} v = v \;_{\Delta_2}\!\parallel^\Gamma_{\Delta_1} u$, and likewise for languages.

The S-shuffle is moreover associative: for all $u, v, w \in \Delta^*$, $\{u\} \parallel^\Gamma (v \parallel^\Gamma w) = (u \parallel^\Gamma v) \parallel^\Gamma \{w\}$, and likewise for languages. The S-shuffle on Γ of languages L_i, with $i \in [n]$, can thus be defined as $\parallel^\Gamma_{i \in [n]} L_i = L_1 \parallel^\Gamma L_2 \parallel^\Gamma \cdots \parallel^\Gamma L_n$.

Due to the importance of the alphabets w.r.t. which words are fS-shuffled or rS-shuffled, a notion of associativity for the rS-shuffle and fS-shuffle is intuitively not immediate. We do not provide proofs here, but for all $u \in \Delta_1^*$, $v \in \Delta_2^*$, and $w \in \Delta_3^*$, the fS-shuffle satisfies the property $\{u\}\ _{\Delta_1}\|\ _{\Delta_2 \cup \Delta_3}\ (v\ _{\Delta_2}\|\ _{\Delta_3}\ w) = (u\ _{\Delta_1}\|\ _{\Delta_2}\ v)\ _{\Delta_1 \cup \Delta_2}\|\ _{\Delta_3}\ \{w\}$, while the rS-shuffle satisfies the property that $\{u\}\ _{\Delta_1}\|^{\Gamma}_{\Delta_2 \cup \Delta_3}\ (v\ _{\Delta_2}\|^{\Gamma}_{\Delta_3}\ w) = (u\ _{\Delta_1}\|^{\Gamma}_{\Delta_2}\ v)\ _{\Delta_1 \cup \Delta_2}\|^{\Gamma}_{\Delta_3}\ \{w\}$, and likewise for languages. The fS-shuffle of languages $L_i \in \Delta_i^*$, with $i \in [n]$, can thus be defined as $\|_{\{\Delta_i | i \in [n]\}}\ L_i = (\cdots((L_1\ _{\Delta_1}\|_{\Delta_2}\ L_2)\ _{\Delta_1 \cup \Delta_2}\|_{\Delta_3}\ L_3) \cdots)\ _{\bigcup_{i \in [n-1]} \Delta_i}\|_{\Delta_n}\ L_n$, while the rS-shuffle on Γ of languages $L_i \in \Delta_i^*$, with $i \in [n]$, can thus be defined as $\|^{\Gamma}_{\{\Delta_i | i \in [n]\}}\ L_i = (\cdots((L_1\ _{\Delta_1}\|^{\Gamma}_{\Delta_2}\ L_2)\ _{\Delta_1 \cup \Delta_2}\|^{\Gamma}_{\Delta_3}\ L_3) \cdots)\ _{\bigcup_{i \in [n-1]} \Delta_i}\|^{\Gamma}_{\Delta_n}\ L_n$.

The following alternative definition of the fS-shuffle is used in the sequel.

Theorem 7. *If $w_i \in \Delta_i^*$, for all $i \in [n]$, then $\|_{\{\Delta_i | i \in [n]\}}\ w_i = \{w \in (\bigcup_{i \in [n]} \Delta_i)^*\ |\ \mathrm{pres}_{\Delta_i}(w) = w_i,\ \text{for all } i \in [n]\}$.* □

7 Team Automata Satisfying Compositionality

In this section we identify precisely some types of team automata that satisfy compositionality, i.e. whose behaviour can be obtained from that of their constituting components.

Since all synchronizations in a *maximal-ai* team automaton require the participation of all its components sharing the action being synchronized, it is not surprising that the behaviour of a *maximal-ai* team automaton equals the fS-shuffle of the behaviour of its constituting components. In fact, corresponding versions of this result have been formulated for other automata-based specification models with composition based on *maximal-ai* synchronizations [15, 26].

Theorem 8. *Let $\mathcal{T}$ be the $\mathcal{R}^{ai}$-team automaton over $\mathcal{S}$. Then*

$$\mathbf{B}_{\mathcal{T}}^{\Sigma} = \|_{\{\Sigma_i | i \in [n]\}}\ \mathbf{B}_{\mathcal{C}_i}^{\Sigma_i}.$$

Proof. ($\subseteq$) This follows immediately from Corollary 1 and Theorem 7.

($\supseteq$) Let $w \in \|_{\{\Sigma_i | i \in [n]\}}\ \mathbf{B}_{\mathcal{C}_i}^{\Sigma_i}$. Then, by Theorem 7, $\mathrm{pres}_{\Sigma_i}(w) \in \mathbf{B}_{\mathcal{C}_i}^{\Sigma_i}$, for all $i \in [n]$. Hence there exist $\alpha_i \in \mathbf{C}_{\mathcal{C}_i}$ such that $\mathrm{pres}_{\Sigma_i}(\alpha_i) = \mathrm{pres}_{\Sigma_i}(w)$, for all $i \in [n]$, and thus $\prod_{i \in [n]} \alpha_i$ is ai-consistent. As $w \in (\bigcup_{i \in [n]} \Sigma_i)^*$ is such that $\mathrm{pres}_{\Sigma_i}(w) = \mathrm{pres}_{\Sigma_i}(\alpha_i)$, for all $i \in [n]$, the proof of the (If)-direction of Theorem 4 implies there exists a $\beta \in \mathbf{C}_{\mathcal{T}}$ such that $\mathrm{pres}_{\bigcup_{i \in [n]} \Sigma_i}(\beta) = \mathrm{pres}_{\Sigma}(\beta) = w$. Hence $w \in \mathbf{B}_{\mathcal{T}}^{\Sigma}$. □

Example 10. (Ex. 1, 4 cont.) $\mathbf{B}_{\mathcal{T}^{ai}}^{\Sigma} = \{\lambda, a\} = \{b^n, b^n a\ |\ n \geq 0\}\ _{\Sigma_1}\|_{\Sigma_2}\ \{\lambda, ab^n\ |\ n \geq 0\} = \|_{\{\Sigma_i | i \in [2]\}}\ \mathbf{B}_{\mathcal{C}_i}^{\Sigma_i}$. Note that while $ba \notin \|_{\{\Sigma_i | i \in [2]\}}\ \mathbf{B}_{\mathcal{C}_i}^{\Sigma_i}$, clearly $ba \in \mathbf{B}_{\mathcal{T}}^{\Sigma}$. □

Each synchronization in a *maximal-free* team automaton is such that only one of its components participates—under the assumption that a loop on the action being synchronized is always executed. Hence, if we require $\mathcal{S}$ to be loop limited, then the behaviour of the *maximal-free* team automaton over $\mathcal{S}$ equals the shuffle of the behaviour of the components from $\mathcal{S}$. Actually we prove a more general result, viz. that the behaviour of a team automaton that is composed according to a mixture of the *maximal-free* and *maximal-ai* strategies equals the rS-shuffle of the behaviour of its constituting components.

Theorem 9. *Let $\bar{\varGamma} = \varSigma \setminus \varGamma$ and let $\mathcal{T}$ be the $\{\mathcal{R}_a^{ai} \mid a \in \varSigma \cap \varGamma\} \cup \{\mathcal{R}_a^{free} \mid a \in \bar{\varGamma}\}$-team automaton over $\mathcal{S}$. Then*

if $\mathcal{S}$ is $\bar{\varGamma}$-loop limited, then $\mathbf{B}_{\mathcal{T}}^{\varSigma} = \|_{\{\varSigma_i \mid i \in [n]\}}^{\varGamma} \mathbf{B}_{\mathcal{C}_i}^{\varSigma_i}$.

Proof. Let $\mathcal{T}'$ be the team automaton that is obtained from $\mathcal{T}$ by attaching a label to each action from $\bar{\varGamma}$ depending on the component executing that action, i.e. $\mathcal{T}' = (Q, \varSigma', \delta', I)$ with $\varSigma' = \{[a, i] \mid a \in \bar{\varGamma} \cap \varSigma_i, i \in [n]\} \cup (\varSigma \cap \varGamma)$ and $\delta' = \{(q, [a, i], q') \mid a \in \bar{\varGamma}, (q, a, q') \in \delta, \text{proj}_i^{[2]}(q, q') \in \delta_{i,a}, i \in [n]\} \cup (\delta \cap (Q \times \varGamma \times Q))$. Since all actions from $\bar{\varGamma}$ are *free* in $\mathcal{T}$, the behaviour of $\mathcal{T}$ is an encoding of the behaviour of $\mathcal{T}'$. Let $\psi : (\varSigma')^* \to \varSigma^*$ be the homomorphism defined by $\psi([a, i]) = a$ and $\psi(a) = a$. Then clearly $\mathbf{B}_{\mathcal{T}}^{\varSigma} = \psi(\mathbf{B}_{\mathcal{T}'}^{\varSigma'})$.

For all $i \in [n]$, let $\mathcal{C}_i'$ be the component automaton that is obtained from $\mathcal{C}_i$ by labelling each of its actions from $\bar{\varGamma}$ with i, i.e. $\mathcal{C}_i' = (Q_i, \varSigma_i', \delta_i', I_i)$ with $\varSigma_i' = \{[a, i] \mid a \in \bar{\varGamma} \cap \varSigma_i\} \cup (\varGamma \cap \varSigma_i)$ and $\delta_i' = \{(q, [a, i], q') \mid a \in \bar{\varGamma}, (q, a, q') \in \delta_i\} \cup (\delta_i \cap (Q_i \times \varGamma \times Q_i))$. Obviously, $\mathbf{B}_{\mathcal{C}_i}^{\varSigma_i} = \psi(\mathbf{B}_{\mathcal{C}_i'}^{\varSigma_i'})$, for all $i \in [n]$. Let $\mathcal{S}' = \{\mathcal{C}_i' \mid i \in [n]\}$. Since $\mathcal{S}$ is $\bar{\varGamma}$-loop limited it thus follows that $\delta_{[a,i]} = \mathcal{R}_{[a,i]}^{free}(\mathcal{S}')$, for all $a \in \bar{\varGamma}$ and $i \in [n]$. Hence $\mathcal{T}'$ is the $\{\mathcal{R}_a^{ai} \mid a \in \varSigma \cap \varGamma\} \cup \{\mathcal{R}_a^{free} \mid a \in \varSigma' \setminus \varGamma\}$-team automaton over $\mathcal{S}'$. Moreover, since the components from $\mathcal{S}'$ can share actions from $\varSigma \cap \varGamma$ but not from $\varSigma' \setminus \varGamma$, it follows that for all $K \subseteq [n]$, $\bigcap_{k \in K} \varSigma_k' = \bigcap_{k \in K} \varSigma_k \cap \varGamma$, i.e. the *free* actions of $\mathcal{T}'$ are *ai* and $\mathcal{T}'$ thus equals the *maximal-ai* team automaton over $\mathcal{S}'$. Consequently the relation between the fS-shuffle and the rS-shuffle stated immediately following Definition 15, together with Theorem 8, implies that $\mathbf{B}_{\mathcal{T}}^{\varSigma} = \psi(\mathbf{B}_{\mathcal{T}'}^{\varSigma'}) = \psi(\|_{\{\varSigma_i' \mid i \in [n]\}} \mathbf{B}_{\mathcal{C}_i'}^{\varSigma_i'}) = \psi(\|_{\{\varSigma_i' \mid i \in [n]\}}^{\varGamma} \mathbf{B}_{\mathcal{C}_i'}^{\varSigma_i'})$, which is equal to $\|_{\{\psi(\varSigma_i') \mid i \in [n]\}}^{\varGamma} \psi(\mathbf{B}_{\mathcal{C}_i'}^{\varSigma_i'}) = \|_{\{\varSigma_i \mid i \in [n]\}}^{\varGamma} \mathbf{B}_{\mathcal{C}_i}^{\varSigma_i}$ because $\psi(\varSigma' \setminus \varGamma) \cap \varGamma = \emptyset$. □

Theorem 10. *Let $\mathcal{T}$ be the $\mathcal{R}^{free}$-team automaton over $\mathcal{S}$. Then*

if $\mathcal{S}$ is loop limited, then $\mathbf{B}_{\mathcal{T}}^{\varSigma} = \|_{i \in [n]} \mathbf{B}_{\mathcal{C}_i}^{\varSigma_i}$.

Proof. This follows immediately from Theorem 9 with $\varSigma \cap \varGamma = \emptyset$. □

Example 11. (Ex. 1, 6 cont.) Since $\{\mathcal{C}_1, \mathcal{C}_2\}$ is not loop limited, it is no surprise that $ab \notin \mathbf{B}_{\mathcal{T}_{1,2}}^{\varSigma}$, whereas $ab \in \|_{i \in [2]} \mathbf{B}_{\mathcal{C}_i}^{\varSigma_i}$. Now consider the $\mathcal{R}_a^{free} \cup \mathcal{R}_b^{ai}$-team automaton $\mathcal{T}^{fa}$ over $\{\mathcal{C}_1, \mathcal{C}_2\}$, as depicted in Fig. 6. Clearly $\{\mathcal{C}_1, \mathcal{C}_2\}$ is $\{a\}$-loop limited and indeed $\mathbf{B}_{\mathcal{T}^{fa}}^{\varSigma} = \|_{\{\varSigma_i \mid i \in [2]\}}^{\{b\}} \mathbf{B}_{\mathcal{C}_i}^{\varSigma_i}$. □

8 Conclusion

In this paper we have shown that—under certain conditions—team automata defined according to the *maximal-ai* and *maximal-free* strategies exhibit a behaviour that equals a certain type of (synchronized) shuffles of the behaviour of their constituting component automata. We have thus identified for each of a few specific types of team automata an operation which proves compositionality. As is shown in [1], corresponding results hold when also infinitary behaviour is taken into account.

I/O automata fit in the framework of team automata as a special type of *maximal-ai* team automata [3]. This in fact holds for more automata-based specification models with composition based on the *maximal-ai* strategy [1]. For these models, most results of this paper on the relation between the computations and behaviour of team automata and those of their constituting components extend known results: we single out precisely which characteristics of the *maximal-ai* strategy—e.g. the fact that an action is ai, useful j-ai, or *maximal-ai*—are responsible for a particular behavioural relation. This often leads to less stringent conditions than those presented in the literature on these models.

Concerning the *maximal-free* strategy we present new results on the relation between the computations and behaviour of team automata and those of their constituting components. In this case, our maximal interpretation of the components' participation in synchronizations forced us to assume S to be loop limited in order to guarantee that all component computations participate in team computations. In [1, 2] we show how to circumvent this additional condition by using vectors to represent the actual participation of components in synchronizations.

To identify more types of team automata satisfying compositionality, it remains to determine the conditions under which the behaviour of team automata defined according to other strategies can be obtained from the behaviour of their constituting component automata.

While ignored in this paper, team automata distinguish input, output, and internal actions. In [3] we defined an operation that "hides" the input and output actions of a team automaton from other team automata by making them internal. This prohibits their further use in synchronizations on a higher level of an iteratively composed hierarchical system, which is important when using team automata for component-based design by means of a step-by-step refinement of specifications. As a case study we modelled the hierarchical design of a groupware architecture by means of a step-by-step refinement of specifications in terms of team automata. We furthermore showed—under certain very relaxed conditions—the order in which a team automaton is iteratively composed to be irrelevant.

Let team automata $\mathcal{T}$, $\mathcal{T}'$, and $\mathcal{T}''$ be iteratively composed over component automata $\mathcal{C}_1$, $\mathcal{C}_2$, and $\mathcal{C}_3$ in the way sketched in Fig. 7.

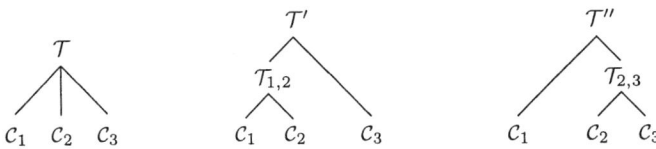

Fig. 7. Team automata $\mathcal{T}$, $\mathcal{T}'$, and $\mathcal{T}''$ composed iteratively over $\{\mathcal{C}_1, \mathcal{C}_2, \mathcal{C}_3\}$.

If all the depicted team automata are composed according to the same strategy, then $\mathcal{T}$, $\mathcal{T}'$, and $\mathcal{T}''$ have the same set of actions and—upto a reordering—the same set of (initial) states and the same transition relation. In that case they moreover exhibit the same behaviour. The results of this paper additionally show that if $\mathcal{T}$ is composed according to the *maximal-ai*, the *maximal-free* strategy, or a combination thereof, then its behaviour equals a certain type of (synchronized) shuffle of the behaviour of $\mathcal{C}_1$, $\mathcal{C}_2$, and $\mathcal{C}_3$. It remains to investigate how these results can be extended to the case of iteratively composed team automata such as $\mathcal{T}'$ and $\mathcal{T}''$.

Together with the syntactic hierarchical results of [3], the results presented in this paper thus show that the team automata framework is well suited for component-based system design by means of a stepwise development of specifications based on decomposition and refinement.

Acknowledgements

We thank Josep Carmona, Mieke Massink, and the three anonymous referees for their useful comments on a preliminary version of this paper.

References

1. M.H. ter Beek, *Team Automata—A Formal Approach to the Modeling of Collaboration Between System Components*. Ph.D. thesis, Leiden Institute of Advanced Computer Science, Universiteit Leiden, 2003.
2. M.H. ter Beek, C.A. Ellis, J. Kleijn, and G. Rozenberg, Team Automata for CSCW. In *Proc. 2nd Int. Coll. on Petri Net Technologies for Modelling Communication Based Systems* (H. Weber, H. Ehrig, and W. Reisig, eds.), Fraunhofer Institute for Software and Systems Engineering, 2001, 1-20.
3. M.H. ter Beek, C.A. Ellis, J. Kleijn, and G. Rozenberg, Synchronizations in team automata for groupware systems. *Computer Supported Cooperative Work—The Journal of Collaborative Computing* 12, 1 (2003), 21-69.
4. *Handbook of Process Algebra* (J.A. Bergstra, A. Ponse, and S.A. Smolka, eds.), Elsevier Science, 2001.
5. J. Carmona and J. Cortadella, Input/Output Compatibility of Reactive Systems. In *Proc. 4th Int. Conf. on Formal Methods in Computer-Aided Design* (M.D. Aagaard and J.W. O'Leary, eds.), LNCS 2517, Springer-Verlag, 2002, 360-377.
6. J. Carmona, J. Cortadella, and E. Pastor, Synthesis of Reactive Systems: Application to Asynchronous Circuit Design. In *Concurrency and Hardware Design—Advances in Petri Nets* (J. Cortadella, A. Yakovlev, and G. Rozenberg, eds.), Springer-Verlag, 2002, 107-151.
7. R. De Simone, Langages Infinitaires et Produit de Mixage. *Theoretical Computer Science* 31 (1984), 83-100.
8. D. Drusinsky and D. Harel, On the Power of Bounded Concurrency I: Finite Automata. *Journal of the ACM* 41, 3 (1994), 517-539.
9. C.A. Ellis, Team Automata for Groupware Systems. In *Proc. Int. Conf. on Supporting Group Work: The Integration Challenge* (S.C. Hayne and W. Prinz, eds.), ACM Press, 1997, 415-424.

10. S. Ginsburg and E.H. Spanier, Mappings of Languages by Two-Tape Devices. *Journal of the ACM* 12, 3 (1965), 423-434.
11. D. Harel, Statecharts: A Visual Formalism for Complex Systems. *Science of Computer Programming* 8 (1987), 231-274.
12. T. Hirst and D. Harel, On the Power of Bounded Concurrency II: Pushdown Automata. *Journal of the ACM* 41, 3 (1994), 540-554.
13. C.A.R. Hoare, *Communicating Sequential Processes*, Prentice Hall, 1985.
14. M. Jantzen, The Power of Synchronizing Operations on Strings. *Theoretical Computer Science* 14 (1981), 127-154.
15. B. Jonsson, Compositional Verification of Distributed Systems. Ph.D. thesis, Department of Computer Systems, Uppsala University, 1987.
16. B. Jonsson, Compositional Specification and Verification of Distributed Systems. *ACM Transactions on Programming Languages and Systems* 16, 2 (1994), 259-303.
17. T. Kimura, An Algebraic System for Process Structuring and Interprocess Communication. In *Proc. 8th Symp. on Theory of Computing*, ACM Press, 1976, 92-100.
18. R. Lanotte, A. Maggiolo-Schettini, and A. Peron, Timed Cooperating Automata. *Fundamenta Informaticae* 42 (2000), 1-21.
19. M. Latteux and Y. Roos, Synchronized Shuffle and Regular Languages. In *Jewels are Forever* (J. Karhumäki, H.A. Maurer, Gh. Păun, and G. Rozenberg, eds.), Springer-Verlag, 1999, 35-44.
20. N.A. Lynch and M.R. Tuttle, An Introduction to Input/Output Automata. *CWI Quarterly* 2,3 (1989), 219-246.
21. D. von Oheimb, Interacting State Machines: A Stateful Approach to Proving Security. To appear in *Proc. Int. Conf. on Formal Aspects of Security* (A. Abdallah, P. Ryan, and S. Schneider, eds.), *LNCS* 2629, Springer-Verlag, 2003.
22. D. von Oheimb and V. Lotz, Formal Security Analysis with Interacting State Machines. In *Proc. 7th European Symp. on Research in Computer Security* (D. Gollmann, G. Karjoth, and M. Waidner, eds.), *LNCS* 2502, Springer-Verlag, 2002, 212-228.
23. A.W. Roscoe, *The Theory and Practice of Concurrency*, Prentice Hall, 1997.
24. A. Salomaa, *Formal Languages*, Academic Press, 1973.
25. J.L.A. van de Snepscheut, *Trace Theory and VLSI Design*, *LNCS* 200, Springer-Verlag, 1985.
26. M.R. Tuttle, *Hierarchical Correctness Proofs for Distributed Algorithms*. Master's thesis, Department of Electrical Engineering and Computer Science, MIT, 1987.

Composing Invariants

Michel Charpentier

Department of Computer Science, University of New Hampshire, Durham, NH,
charpov@cs.unh.edu

Abstract. We explore the question of the composition of invariance specifications in a context of formal methods applied to concurrent and reactive systems. Depending on how compositionality is stated and how invariants are defined, invariance specifications may or may not be compositional. This paper examines three classic forms of invariants and their compositional properties. After pointing out what we see as deficiencies of these kinds of invariants, a new fourth form is defined and shown to have useful compositional properties that the more classic forms do not enjoy.

Keywords: formal specification, temporal logic, compositional verification, invariants.

1 Introduction

1.1 Motivation

Compositional reasoning, whether it is looked upon as a problem or as a solution, is receiving much attention in the Formal Methods community. As invariance properties are fundamental in the specification and verification of concurrent and reactive systems, it is natural to consider the question of compositional reasoning when invariants are involved. Are invariants *compositional*? The answer is not as straightforward as it may seem, because there are different definitions of what it means for a specification to be compositional and, maybe more surprisingly, there are different definitions of what it means for a specification to be an invariant.

In this paper, we focus our attention on two possible definitions of being compositional. One corresponds to a widespread intuition of what it means to compose invariants, namely that if all components of a system satisfy the same invariant, then this system also satisfies this invariant. The other form of composition, which might look more surprising at first but is indeed used in various formal notations, is to deduce that an invariant is satisfied by a system as long as it is satisfied by at least one component of that system.

Depending on how invariants are defined, they satisfy zero, one or both of these composition rules. We consider four possible definitions of invariants in this paper. Three of them are classic and are already used in various formalisms. One of them is introduced here (although it does have a close relative that appears in [30]). We explore the issue of compositional reasoning for each kind of invariant, and discuss what we see as the benefits of the new kind that is defined in this paper.

The context of this paper is one of reactive systems modeled as transition systems, as in UNITY or TLA$^+$. The question of invariants in an object-oriented context is briefly discussed in the conclusion. In this paper, we do not consider specifications other than invariance properties. In particular, we do not discuss the case of liveness and progress specifications. It has been argued that liveness specifications are inherently more difficult to compose than safety specifications. This question is also discussed in the conclusion.

The end of this introductory section is dedicated to presenting a basic set of notations that are used throughout this article. The remainder of the paper is organized as follows. Section 2 introduces two forms of invariants that are commonly defined on transition systems, independently from composition issues. Section 3 discusses the compositional properties of these two forms of invariants. The remaining two forms of invariance specifications (one less classic, one new) are defined in section 4, where their compositionality is also discussed. A simple example, initiated in section 2, is carried throughout the paper to illustrate the four kinds of invariants and their compositional properties. Proofs related to the new form of invariants are given in the full report [8]. Proofs related to classic invariants can be found in the literature [29, 27].

1.2 Notations and Terminology

Generic systems and components are denoted by capitals letters like F and G. In this paper, there are no fundamental differences between systems and components, and both words are used interchangeably, although, at an informal level, *component* conveys the idea that the system is used as a part of a larger system, and *system* conveys the idea that a component is itself composite. Parallel composition is denoted by $\|$.

Specifications are point-wise predicates on systems, i.e., functions from systems to booleans. Function application is denoted by a dot, which is assumed to be left associative and to have higher precedence than boolean connectives. For instance, $\text{inv}.p.F$ is $(\text{inv}.p).F$ and means that specification $\text{inv}.p$ is satisfied by system F.

Following [16], we rely on an *"everywhere"* operator denoted by square brackets. Given a predicate S, $[S]$ means that S is everywhere true, i.e., $S.x$ is true for all x (or $S.x.y$ is true for all x and y, or ..., depending on the type of S). $\neg[\neg S]$ means that S is not everywhere false or, equivalently, that S is satisfiable. We also use the usual quantifiers $\exists$ and $\forall$, which are assumed to have low precedence, as in TLA$^+$ [21]. For instance, $\forall x \in S : p \wedge \exists y : r \Rightarrow q$ is $(\forall x \in S : (p \wedge (\exists y : (r \Rightarrow q))))$.

2 Inductive and Operational Invariants

2.1 Transition Systems

We assume the systems that we reason about are modeled as *transition systems*. Typically, such transition systems are represented as tuples that include, at least, a definition of variables, states, transitions and fairness [23]. Fairness constraints (strong, weak, unconditional, ...) are required to reason about *liveness* (and progress) properties. In this paper, we are focusing our attention on invariance specifications, which belong to the class of *safety* properties. As a consequence, fairness issues do not play any role and can be ignored altogether in our discussion. Moreover, when fairness and liveness are not involved, any nonempty set of transitions can be assimilated to a unique (nondeterministic) transition that encompasses all the transitions from the set. Therefore, in this paper, we rely on (unfair) transition systems defined as 5-tuples. A system F is the tuple $(\mathcal{V}.F, \mathcal{L}.F, \Sigma.F, \mathcal{I}.F, \mathcal{W}.F)$ where:

- $\mathcal{V}$ is a finite set of variables, referred to as *state* variables. They are chosen from a universal vocabulary $\mathcal{D}$.
- $\mathcal{L}$ is a subset of $\mathcal{V}$ of *local* variables, which can be read but not written by other systems.
- Σ is a set of *states*. Each state assigns a value to each variable of $\mathcal{V}$.
- $\mathcal{I}$ is an initial condition that defines the possible initial states of the system. $\mathcal{I}$ is a state predicate (free variables in $\mathcal{V}$) which we assume to be satisfiable.
- $\mathcal{W}$ is a predicate transformer (function from state predicates to state predicates) which represents the transition[1] of the system using a *weakest precondition* semantics. In other words, if q is a state predicate, $\mathcal{W}.F.q$ is the (maximal) set of states that have a successor in q. A WP function, similar to our $\mathcal{W}$, is used in [29].
  We assume that the transition of a transition system allows for stuttering: it is always possible for the next state of a computation to be the same as the current state. Formally, this means that, for any system F and any state predicate q, $[\mathcal{W}.F.q \Rightarrow q]$: if the next state is guaranteed to satisfy q and stuttering is possible, the current state has to satisfy q as well. We also assume that the predicate transformer $\mathcal{W}.F$ is universally conjunctive for any system F, like any weakest (liberal) precondition transformer [16].

2.2 Inductive Invariants

A first kind of invariance specification can be defined directly in terms of a transition system. We call these invariants *transition-based* or *inductive* and denote them with $\mathsf{inv}_\mathcal{T}$. We define two types of specifications, next and inv[2]:

$$\mathsf{next}_\mathcal{T}.(p,q).F \triangleq [p \Rightarrow \mathcal{W}.F.q] \ ,$$
$$\mathsf{inv}_\mathcal{T}.p.F \triangleq \mathsf{next}_\mathcal{T}.(p,p).F \wedge [\mathcal{I}.F \Rightarrow p] \ .$$

Informally, $\mathsf{next}_\mathcal{T}.(p,q)$ means that whenever a transition is fired from a state that satisfies p, the resulting state satisfies q. Similarly, $\mathsf{inv}_\mathcal{T}.p$ specifies that p is

---

[1] If we were to mention individual transitions instead of a global transition, $\mathcal{W}$ would be defined as the conjunction of the weakest preconditions of all transitions. From this point on, we only refer to the system's transition(s) through $\mathcal{W}$.
[2] In [27], "next" is called "co" and "next.(p,p)" is called "stable p".

true in any initial state and is preserved by every atomic transition. Therefore, by induction, p is true in every state. It should be noted that, since $[\mathcal{W}.F.q \Rightarrow q]$ because of possible stuttering, $\text{next}_{\mathcal{T}}.(p,q).F \Rightarrow [p \Rightarrow q]$.

The approach chosen for this paper is to focus our attention on inv specifications. As we will see in section 3, the part $[\mathcal{I}.F \Rightarrow p]$ in the definition of inv does not involve any difficulty in terms of composition. The next part is where the core of compositional issues turns up. Therefore, although we state most results in terms of inv, our proofs are in terms of next, with inv simply being a special case.

2.3 Operational Invariants

Instead of relying on the definition of a transition system directly, a second kind of invariance specification can be defined in terms of the possible computations of such a system. A transition system F can be associated with a subset $\mathcal{O}.F$ of $(\Sigma.F)^\omega$ of infinite sequences of states defined as follows. An infinite computation $\sigma = \langle \sigma_0, \sigma_1, \ldots, \sigma_n, \ldots \rangle$ belongs to the set $\mathcal{O}.F$ if and only if:

1. $\mathcal{I}.F.\sigma_0$,
2. $\forall i \in \mathbb{N} : \mathcal{W}.F.\{\sigma_{i+1}\}.\sigma_i$, where $\{\sigma_{i+1}\}$ is the state predicate that evaluates to *true* for state σ_{i+1} and to *false* for any other state.

Informally, $\mathcal{O}$ consists of those sequences of states that begin with an initial state that satisfies $\mathcal{I}$ and in which each state has a successor in accordance with the transition $\mathcal{W}$. The set $\mathcal{O}$ is nonempty because $\mathcal{I}$ is satisfiable and $\mathcal{W}$ includes stuttering steps.

Once the computations of a transition system are built, next and inv specifications are defined as expected:

$$\text{next}_{\mathcal{O}}.(p,q).F \triangleq \forall \sigma \in \mathcal{O}.F : \forall i \in \mathbb{N} : p.\sigma_i \Rightarrow q.\sigma_{i+1} ,$$
$$\text{inv}_{\mathcal{O}}.p.F \triangleq \forall \sigma \in \mathcal{O}.F : \forall i \in \mathbb{N} : p.\sigma_i .$$

Informally, $\text{next}_{\mathcal{O}}.(p,q)$ means that, in any computation of the system, any state that satisfies p is immediately followed by a state that satisfies q. Although computations include stuttering steps, $\text{next}_{\mathcal{O}}.(p,q)$ does *not* imply that $[p \Rightarrow q]$. In the same way, $\text{inv}_{\mathcal{O}}.p$ means that any state of any computation of a system satisfies p. In linear time temporal logic, $\text{next}_{\mathcal{O}}$ corresponds to $\bigcirc$ and $\text{inv}_{\mathcal{O}}$ corresponds to $\square$ [23].

Naturally, $\text{next}_{\mathcal{O}}$ and $\text{inv}_{\mathcal{O}}$ are related in a way similar to the relationship between $\text{next}_{\mathcal{T}}$ and $\text{inv}_{\mathcal{T}}$, namely: $\text{inv}_{\mathcal{O}}.p.F \equiv \text{next}_{\mathcal{O}}.(p,p).F \wedge [\mathcal{I}.F \Rightarrow p]$.

2.4 Relationship between Inductive and Operational Invariants

Although they are related, inductive and operational invariants are not equivalent. The use of the word *invariant*, all by itself, without making clear whether inductive or operational invariants are discussed, has been a source of great confusion. A famous example is the case of the UNITY formalism, as it was introduced in [4], in which both $\text{inv}_\mathcal{T}$ and $\text{inv}_\mathcal{O}$ were used under the same name invariant. This led to inconsistencies that were heavily discussed at the time and solved in various ways, [29] being one of the earliest and cleanest solutions to the problem. Although the relationship between inductive and operational invariants is now well understood, the lack of an agreed upon terminology still makes it difficult to mention invariants without having to resort to stating definitions explicitly, as we have to do in this paper.

In this section, we examine the relationship between inductive and operational invariants in a context of closed systems. Section 3 investigates the question of their relationship when composition is involved.

First, inductive invariants are *stronger* than operational invariants or, equivalently, operational invariants are a consequence of inductive invariants. For any system F and any state predicates p and q:

$$\text{next}_\mathcal{T}(p,q).F \Rightarrow \text{next}_\mathcal{O}.(p,q).F ,$$
$$\text{inv}_\mathcal{T}.p.F \Rightarrow \text{inv}_\mathcal{O}.p.F . \qquad (1)$$

Along with the following weakening rule (which does not hold for inductive invariants):

$$\text{inv}_\mathcal{O}.(p \wedge q).F \Rightarrow \text{inv}_\mathcal{O}.p.F ,$$

it provides us with a technique to verify operational invariants on a given transition system. To prove $\text{inv}_\mathcal{O}.p.F$, one needs to find a state predicate q such that $\text{inv}_\mathcal{T}.(p \wedge q).F$, which itself can be proved directly from $\mathcal{J}.F$ and $\mathcal{W}.F$. From a practical point of view, the difficulty relies in the discovery of predicate q. This technique was known in UNITY as the *substitution axiom* (or in TLA [19] as INV2), but one must keep in mind that the invariant being deduced is operational only.

This proof rule is actually complete [29, 27] in the sense that, when $\text{inv}_\mathcal{O}.p.F$ holds, there always exists a predicate q such that $\text{inv}_\mathcal{T}.(p \wedge q).F$ is valid:

$$\text{inv}_\mathcal{O}.p.F \equiv \exists q : \text{inv}_\mathcal{T}.(p \wedge q).F . \qquad (2)$$

A similar relationship holds between $\text{next}_\mathcal{O}$ and $\text{next}_\mathcal{T}$:

$$\text{next}_\mathcal{O}.(p,q).F \equiv \exists r : \text{inv}_\mathcal{T}.r.F \wedge \text{next}_\mathcal{T}.(p \wedge r, q).F . \qquad (3)$$

From the definition of $\text{inv}_\mathcal{T}$ and the fact that $\mathcal{W}.F$ is universally conjunctive, (2) can be reformulated as:

$$\text{inv}_\mathcal{O}.p.F \equiv \text{inv}_\mathcal{T}.(p \wedge \forall q : \text{inv}_\mathcal{T}.q.F \Rightarrow q).F .$$

"$\forall q : \text{inv}_\mathcal{T}.q.F \Rightarrow q$" is the conjunction of all those state predicates q that are inductively invariant in F. It is itself an inductive invariant of F (conjunctions of inductive invariants are inductive invariants), known as the *strongest invariant* of F [29, 27]. We denote this state predicate by $\text{SI}.F$:

$$[\text{SI}.F \triangleq \forall q : \text{inv}_\mathcal{T}.q.F \Rightarrow q] . \qquad (4)$$

Therefore, (2) can still be rewritten as:

$$\text{inv}_\mathcal{O}.p.F \equiv \text{inv}_\mathcal{T}.(p \land \text{SI}.F) . \tag{5}$$

A similar relationship exists between $\text{next}_\mathcal{O}$, $\text{next}_\mathcal{T}$ and SI:

$$\text{next}_\mathcal{O}.(p,q).F \equiv \text{next}_\mathcal{T}.(p \land \text{SI}.F, q) . \tag{6}$$

Because $[\text{SI}.F \Rightarrow p] \equiv [p \land \text{SI}.F \equiv \text{SI}.F]$ and $\text{SI}.F$ is the strongest inductive invariant of F, it follows from (5) that:

$$\text{inv}_\mathcal{O}.p.F \equiv [\text{SI}.F \Rightarrow p] . \tag{7}$$

In other words, p is satisfied by every state of every computation of F if and only if p is a consequence of $\text{SI}.F$. Intuitively, it means that $\text{SI}.F$ characterizes those states that can appear in F's computations, also known as the *reachable states* of F. It should be emphasized that we are referring here to those states that system F can reach *in isolation*, not if F is to become a component of a larger system.

As a final remark, we can observe that, because of (7), $\text{SI}.F$ is also the conjunction of all the operational invariants of F:

$$[\text{SI}.F \equiv \forall q : \text{inv}_\mathcal{O}.q.F \Rightarrow q] .$$

In section 4.3, we show how the strongest invariant can be redefined to take into account the interaction of a system with its environment, thus leading to a variety of specifications with good compositional properties that are not enjoyed by $\text{inv}_\mathcal{O}$ and $\text{next}_\mathcal{O}$.

2.5 Example

To illustrate the relationship between inductive and operational invariants, this section introduces a simple example of a system. This system is reused in sections 3.3 and 4.4 when it becomes a component of a larger system.

At this point, we need a syntactic way of describing a transition system, particularly the transition $\mathcal{W}$. The syntax we rely on in this paper is inspired by UNITY. It is by no mean the best choice to represent transition systems. However, it is easy to read and should be directly accessible to a broad body of readers.

Figure 1 represents a transition system for a Door Manager. This system is responsible for opening the doors of an automatic train after the train has stopped, and for closing the doors before the train starts again. It can check the speed of the train but does not modify it. (The system might not open the doors at all, as we are not interested in progress properties here.)

$\mathcal{W}$ is represented by several state-changing statements separated by ||. This operator || represents a nondeterministic choice in which a successor to the current state can be obtained by applying any one of these statements. It corresponds to || in UNITY and $\lor$ in TLA. If a statement's guard is false, the next

```
𝒱 ≜ doors, checkStop, speed
ℒ ≜ doors, checkStop
Σ ≜ doors, checkStop ∈ 𝔹; speed ∈ ℕ
𝒥 ≜ ¬checkStop ∧ doors = closed
𝒲 ≜ checkStop := (speed = 0)
  ‖ if checkStop then doors := open
  ‖ doors, checkStop := closed, false
```

Fig. 1. System DoorManager

state is identical to the current state. Stuttering transitions are not represented explicitly and the assignment operator := only modifies those state variables that appear on its left-hand side. open and closed are aliases for *true* and *false*, respectively.

We consider the following invariant:

$$\text{inv}.(\text{doors} = \text{open} \Rightarrow \text{speed} = 0) \ .$$

Intuitively, this invariant says that, when the doors of a train are open, this train is stopped. If inv is $\text{inv}_\mathcal{T}$, this specification is *not* satisfied by DoorManager: from a state where checkStop = *true*, speed = 1 and doors = closed, $\mathcal{W}$ may lead to a state where speed = 1 and doors = open (by choosing the second statement), thus falsifying the requirement that $[q \Rightarrow \mathcal{W}.\text{DoorManager}.q]$ for inductive invariants q.

No such state, however, can be reached by this system in isolation: it is impossible to have checkStop = *true* and speed = 1 at the same time in a reachable state. In other words, $[\text{SI}.\text{DoorManager} \Rightarrow \neg(\text{checkStop} = true \land \text{speed} = 1)]$. Indeed, the following specification holds for this system:

$$\text{inv}_\mathcal{T}.(\ (\text{checkStop} = true \Rightarrow \text{speed} \neq 0) \land (\text{doors} = \text{open} \Rightarrow \text{speed} = 0)\ )$$

and, as a consequence, the following holds as well:

$$\text{inv}_\mathcal{O}.(\text{doors} = \text{open} \Rightarrow \text{speed} = 0).\text{DoorManager} \ . \qquad (8)$$

3 Composition of Invariants

3.1 Parallel Composition of Transition Systems

Parallel composition is defined in the usual way, similar to [4, 27, 2, 18]: set union of variables[3] and transitions and conjunction of initial predicates. More precisely, if F and G are two transition systems, $F\|G$ is defined by:

- $\mathcal{V}.(F\|G) \triangleq \mathcal{V}.F \cup \mathcal{V}.G.$

---
[3] We do not consider here the issue of variable renaming.

- $\mathcal{L}.(F\|G) \triangleq \mathcal{L}.F \cup \mathcal{L}.G$.
- $\Sigma.(F\|G)$ maps variables from $\mathcal{V}.F$ to values as in $\Sigma.F$, and variables from $\mathcal{V}.G$ to values as in $\Sigma.G$.
- $\mathcal{I}.(F\|G) \triangleq \mathcal{I}.F \wedge \mathcal{I}.G$.
- $\mathcal{W}.(F\|G) \triangleq \mathcal{W}.F \wedge \mathcal{W}.G$.

Some parallel compositions, however, are impossible and do not lead to transition systems, either because $\mathcal{L}.F$ (resp., $\mathcal{L}.G$) and $\mathcal{W}.G$ (resp., $\mathcal{W}.F$) are not compatible (a component would modify another component's local variable) or because $\mathcal{I}.F$ and $\mathcal{I}.G$ are not compatible (no initial state is suitable for both components). We denote by $F\sqrt{G}$ the fact that systems F and G can indeed be composed: $F\sqrt{G}$ is true exactly when:

1. $\mathcal{I}.F \wedge \mathcal{I}.G$ is satisfiable, i.e., $\neg[\neg(\mathcal{I}.F \wedge \mathcal{I}.G)]$,
2. For any state predicate q such that all free variables of q are in the set $\mathcal{L}.G$, $[q \Rightarrow \mathcal{W}.F.q]$; in other words, $\mathcal{W}.F$ does not involve modifying variables from $\mathcal{L}.G$,
3. For any state predicate q such that all free variables of q are in the set $\mathcal{L}.F$, $[q \Rightarrow \mathcal{W}.G.q]$.

It should be noted that, according to our definition, the local variables of a system can be read by other systems. A more standard definition would make a distinction between true local variables (which are invisible from outside the system) and "read-only" variables (which can be read but not written by other systems). As a consequence, our $\sqrt{}$ allows for composite systems that would otherwise be ruled out. The rationale for this choice is that, although it is important not to allow these compositions from a system design point-of-view, it does not influence our formal treatment of composition of specifications. More precisely, there is no specification in our discussion that would be satisfied if external systems were not allowed to read local variables but would not be satisfied if they were. Consequently, with respect to the results presented in this paper, true local variables and "read-only" variables are equivalent.

3.2 Composition of Inductive Invariants

Inductive invariants are compositional in the following way: If two systems F and G satisfy an inductive invariant $\mathsf{inv}_T.p$, their parallel composition $F\|G$ satisfies this inductive invariant as well. This rule also holds for transition-based next specifications. Formally, for any systems F and G such that $F\sqrt{G}$ and any state predicates p and q:

$$\mathsf{next}_T.(p,q).F \wedge \mathsf{next}_T.(p,q).G \Rightarrow \mathsf{next}_T.(p,q).(F\|G) , \qquad (9)$$

$$\mathsf{inv}_T.p.F \wedge \mathsf{inv}_T.p.G \Rightarrow \mathsf{inv}_T.p.(F\|G) . \qquad (10)$$

This is a direct consequence of the definition of inductive invariants and the definition of parallel composition of transition systems:

- From $[\mathcal{I}.(F\|G) \equiv \mathcal{I}.F \wedge \mathcal{I}.G]$, if $[\mathcal{I}.F \Rightarrow p]$ and $[\mathcal{I}.G \Rightarrow p]$, then $[\mathcal{I}.(F\|G) \Rightarrow p]$.
- From $[\mathcal{W}.(F\|G) \equiv \mathcal{W}.F \wedge \mathcal{W}.G]$, if $[p \Rightarrow \mathcal{W}.F.q]$ and $[p \Rightarrow \mathcal{W}.G.q]$, then $[p \Rightarrow \mathcal{W}.(F\|G).q]$.

$$
\begin{aligned}
\mathcal{V} &\triangleq \mathsf{doors}, \mathsf{speed} \\
\mathcal{L} &\triangleq \mathsf{speed} \\
\varSigma &\triangleq \mathsf{doors} \in \mathbb{B}; \mathsf{speed} \in \mathbb{N} \\
\mathcal{J} &\triangleq \mathsf{speed} = 0 \\
\mathcal{W} &\triangleq \mathsf{if}\ \mathsf{doors} = \mathsf{closed}\ \mathsf{then}\ \mathsf{speed} := \mathsf{speed} + 1 \\
&\mathrel{\|}\ \mathsf{if}\ \mathsf{speed} > 0\ \mathsf{then}\ \mathsf{speed} := \mathsf{speed} - 1
\end{aligned}
$$

Fig. 2. System Engine

3.3 Composition of Operational Invariants

Operational invariants, on the other hand, do *not* compose when they are not inductive. There is no equivalent to (9) and (10) for $\mathsf{next}_\mathcal{O}$ and $\mathsf{inv}_\mathcal{O}$ because these specifications are defined in terms of $\mathcal{O}$, the set of computations of a closed system, and interactions with a possible environment are not taken into account at all in the definition of $\mathcal{O}$.

As an example, let us consider the Engine system of Fig. 2. This component is responsible for starting and stopping a train. In this simple implementation, a train can accelerate (and, in particular, begin to move) only when its doors are closed. It can decelerate at any time, as long as it is not already stopped. This system satisfies the following specification:

$$\mathsf{inv}_\mathcal{T}.(\mathsf{doors} = \mathsf{open}\ \Rightarrow\ \mathsf{speed} = 0).\mathsf{Engine}\ . \tag{11}$$

If operational invariants were compositional, the system $\mathsf{DoorManager}\|\mathsf{Engine}$ would satisfy $\mathsf{inv}_\mathcal{O}.(\mathsf{doors} = \mathsf{open}\ \Rightarrow\ \mathsf{speed} = 0)$, since both components satisfy it. Obviously, this is not the case, as $\mathsf{DoorManager}\|\mathsf{Engine}$ admits computations in which a train starts to accelerate *after* variable $\mathsf{checkStop}$ is set to *true*, thus allowing the composed system to open the doors while the train is already in motion. So, $\mathsf{DoorManager}\|\mathsf{Engine}$ illustrates the case of a system in which all components satisfy a desirable safety specification (a train must be halted for its doors to be open) but the system as a whole does not satisfy this specification.

3.4 Discussion

One possible approach to deal with the difficulty that was illustrated in the previous section is to focus on inductive invariants and ignore operational specifications altogether as soon as composition issues are involved. One might think that, as long as inductive invariants can be composed, there is no need for another form of compositional invariants. Inductive invariants, however, are not well suited for specification. They are a reasonable tool in proofs, thanks to weakening rules such as (1), and they are indeed necessary to verify operational invariants. But they are not high-level enough to be used as logical specifications.

Component specifications have to be high-level enough to substantially abstract from component implementations. This constraint is what makes compositional reasoning such a difficult problem. If specifications are too low-level, there is not much benefit in using compositional techniques. There is an overhead cost in specifying independent components, because a component is always more difficult to verify than a closed system, including a closed systems made of several components [20]. That cost can be balanced by the fact that a verified component is reused in building different systems, and therefore that the effort that went into its verification is reused as well [17, 6]. If component specifications are too low-level, however, the part of the verification effort that is reused is minimal, and the main verification effort is to combine those low-level specifications to deduce a (presumably high-level) system specification. On the other hand, if specifications are too high-level, they hide too much of a component's implementation to guarantee the correctness fo a composed system.

Inductive invariants are too low-level. They do not hide much of a component's implementation, and it does not make sense to have to provide a component's implementation to specify it. Operational invariants, on the other hand, are very high-level. To force an operational invariant on a component still leaves much freedom regarding the ways this component can be implemented. The Engine' component of Fig. 5, for instance, relies on a very different implementation than Engine. One problem is that operational invariants are indeed too high-level. They hide so much of a component's implementation that they cease to enjoy reasonable compositional properties. In section 4, we present a form of invariants that are higher-level than inductive invariants (and lower-level than operational invariants) but still compose according to a rule identical to (10).

A different strategy has been proposed to deal with composition, which is used in particular in [13, 2, 18]. The idea is that the *system* DoorManager and the *component* DoorManager are two different things and should be specified using two different transition systems. The difference between these two systems lies in the way stuttering is implemented. When a closed system is considered, stuttering steps are defined to leave *all* variables unchanged. In our DoorManager system from Fig. 1 for instance, there is an implicit stuttering transition equivalent to doors, checkStop, speed := doors, checkStop, speed. If DoorManager is a *component* of a larger system instead, the stuttering transition becomes doors, checkStop, speed := doors, checkStop, $\langle?\rangle$: the shared variable speed is now free to take any value. DoorManager can be used as a component only if it is implemented using the second form. If the first form is used, it is a closed system and composition is not possible.

When such an approach is used, a component is associated with a transition system in such a way that the resulting computations are not computations of the component, but instead computations of any system that contains this component. An operational specification is not a specification of the component anymore. It is already a specification of a system that uses this component. Not too surprisingly, many difficulties related to composition then disappear naturally. One could even argue that there is no composition involved, as all component specifications are always referring to the global system that contains these components. In this case, even operational invariants are compositional, since they are defined in terms of the computations of a global system. In formalisms that follow this approach, any specification Spec is compositional in the following way. For any systems F and G such that $F\sqrt{G}$:

$$\text{Spec}.F \Rightarrow \text{Spec}.(F\|G) \ . \tag{12}$$

In particular, any operational invariant of F is an operational invariant of $F\|G$. It should be emphasized, though, that (12) is of a different form than (9) or (10). In section 4.1, we introduce a terminology that helps make a distinction between these two definitions of "being compositional".

Although there are many interesting specifications for which a composition rule such as (12) makes sense, including *assumption-commitment* specifications [5, 10, 12], there are also cases where they do not fit very well [9]. Even if operational invariants can be composed according to (12), specification (8) cannot be used to specify the desired safety property of DoorManager for instance. The reason is that it is impossible to implement a Door Manager that satisfies (8) in a formalism where (12) is valid without requiring that this component also has exclusive control over the speed of the train, which would break down compositionality. In a symmetric way, the Engine component cannot guarantee specification (8) as well, since it does not have control of the doors. There are ways of dealing with this problem within notations that rely on (12) for composition, but they involve using constructs that are more complicated than simple invariants ($\xrightarrow{+}$ in [2], $\Rightarrow$ combined with $\odot$ in [18]). In this paper, we advocate instead the use of a high-level form of invariants that compose according to rules similar to those of low-level inductive invariants.[4]

4 High-Level Compositional Invariants

4.1 Existential and Universal Specifications

In this section and in the remainder of the paper, we rely on a terminology that was introduced in [5] to help make a distinction between specifications that compose according to rules similar to (10) and those that compose according to (12). Specifications that follow (12) (for any systems F and G) are called *existential*: an existential specification holds in any system that contains at least one component that satisfies the specification. Specifications that follow rules such as (10) are called *universal*: a universal specification holds in any system in which all components satisfy the specification. Of course, any existential specification is also universal.

---

[4] The rule for composing invariants in [13], translated into this paper's notations, is:

$$\text{inv}.p.F \land \text{inv}.q.G \Rightarrow \text{inv}.(p \land q).(F\|G) \ .$$

Although it has the flavor of rule (10) for inductive invariants, it is actually a consequence of (12) (which holds for invariants in [13]) and a simple rule about conjunctions of invariants being invariants. It is as if one feels that invariants *should* compose according to (10), even in formalisms in which all specifications already compose according to (12).

According to this terminology, the discussion in the previous section can be summarized as follows:

- Inductive invariants are universal. However, they are not very high-level.
- Operational invariants are higher-level, but they are not universal in general.
- Some formalisms choose to tailor their semantics so that every operational specification becomes existential. In such formalisms, there is no simple way to express universal specifications that are not existential.

As mentioned earlier, it is the next part of the definition of invariants that is interesting with respect to composition. The part $[\exists.F \Rightarrow p]$ is existential and does not present any difficulty.

4.2 Specification Transformers

Many important component specifications are neither existential nor universal. A challenge for component and system designers is to derive compositional (existential or universal) specifications from non-compositional ones. To help study this fundamental question, we have defined a collection of predicate transformers that indeed transform a given specification into a corresponding compositional specification [11]. In this paper, we rely on one of these transformers, namely WE, defined in [12].

It can be shown that for any specification Spec, there exists a (unique) weakest existential specification stronger that Spec, which we denote by WE.Spec. WE.Spec characterizes those components that "bring" Spec into any system: if a component satisfies WE.Spec, then any system that uses this component will satisfy Spec. Conversely, if a component is such that any system that uses it satisfies Spec, this component satisfies WE.Spec. Given two specifications X and Y, WE.$(X \Rightarrow Y)$ provides us with a powerful form of *assumption-commitment* specifications [5, 10, 3, 12].

The fact that WE.Spec is defined to be the *weakest* existential specification stronger than Spec relates to the discussion of the previous section regarding low-level and high-level specifications. Let us suppose that we are interested in designing a component so that systems that use this component satisfy specification Spec. If Spec is existential, we simply design a component that satisfies Spec. But if Spec is not existential, it is not enough for a component to satisfy Spec. The component must be designed to satisfy a stronger specification, namely WE.Spec. However, we only want to force on this component what is necessary to make systems that use this component satisfy Spec. In particular, we do not want this specification to include too many details about the component's implementation. We want those details to be hidden to a user of this component, and much freedom given to the implementer of such a component.

For some specifications Spec, there does not exist a weakest universal specification stronger than Spec. As a consequence, there is no transformer WU for universal composition that achieves what WE does for existential composition.

4.3 Strongest Invariant for Composition

Operational invariants do not compose existentially or universally. However, the transformer WE can be applied to $\mathrm{inv}_\mathcal{O}$ to obtain a form of invariant that composes existentially:

$$[\mathrm{inv}_\mathcal{E}.p \triangleq \mathrm{WE}.(\mathrm{inv}_\mathcal{O}.p)] \ .$$

From the definition of WE, $\mathrm{inv}_\mathcal{E}$ is (existentially) compositional and stronger than $\mathrm{inv}_\mathcal{O}$. For any state predicate p and any systems F and G such that $F\sqrt{}G$:

$$\mathrm{inv}_\mathcal{E}.p.F \;\Rightarrow\; \mathrm{inv}_\mathcal{E}.p.(F\|G) \ ,$$
$$\mathrm{inv}_\mathcal{E}.p.F \;\Rightarrow\; \mathrm{inv}_\mathcal{O}.p.F \ .$$

Specifications $\mathrm{inv}_\mathcal{E}.p$ are actually equivalent to operational invariants in those formalisms where all specifications are existential.

In section 2.4, we defined the strongest invariant of a system to be the conjunction of all (inductive or operational) invariants of that system. In the same way, we define the *strongest invariant for composition* (SIC) of a system F to be the conjunction of all existential invariants of that system:

$$[\mathsf{SIC}.F \triangleq \forall q : \mathrm{inv}_\mathcal{E}.q.F \Rightarrow q] \ . \tag{4'}$$

Because conjunctions of invariants are invariants and the transformer WE is universally conjunctive [12], it follows that $\mathsf{SIC}.F$ is an existential invariant of F:

$$\mathrm{inv}_\mathcal{E}.(\mathsf{SIC}.F).F \ . \tag{13}$$

As a consequence, $\mathsf{SIC}.F$ is an operational[5] invariant of F and $[\mathsf{SI}.F \Rightarrow \mathsf{SIC}.F]$.

In the same way as the strongest invariant is used to characterize operational invariants using (7), SIC can be used to characterize existential invariants. It can be shown that, for any state predicate p and any system F:

$$\mathrm{inv}_\mathcal{E}.p.F \;\equiv\; [\mathsf{SIC}.F \Rightarrow p] \ . \tag{7'}$$

The following property shows that $\mathsf{SIC}.F$ is the union of all the predicates $\mathsf{SI}.(F\|G)$ for all the systems G that are compatible with F:

$$[\mathsf{SIC}.F \;\equiv\; \exists G : (F\sqrt{}G) \wedge \mathsf{SI}.(F\|G)] \ . \tag{14}$$

Since SI characterizes the reachable states of a system in isolation, it follows that $\mathsf{SIC}.F$ characterizes those states that can be reached by system F *when F interacts with some compatible environment G*. Equivalently, states outside of $\mathsf{SIC}.F$ *cannot* be reached by systems in which F is a component (Fig. 3).

Intuitively, if SIC replaces SI in proof rules (5) and (6) for inv and next, the composition problem illustrated in section 3.3 disappears: no new reachable state can interfere with the proof of an invariant when a system is composed.

---

[5] As it happens, $\mathsf{SIC}.F$ is actually an inductive invariant of F.

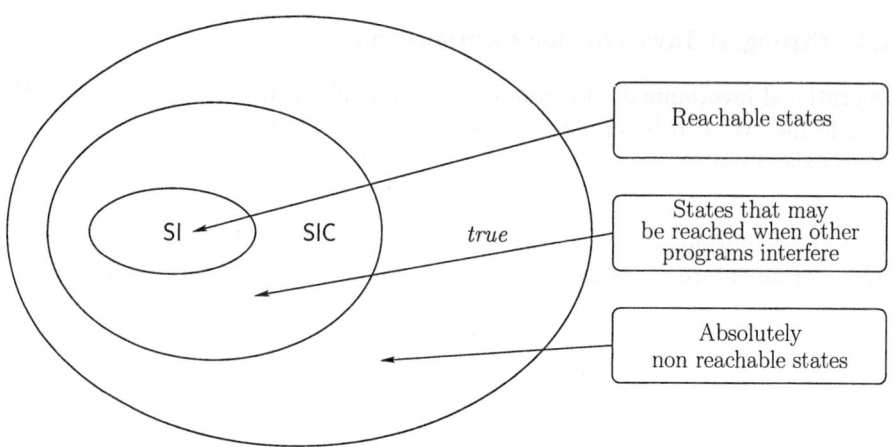

Fig. 3. State reachability

the following definitions of a new kind of next and inv specifications are based on this idea:

$$\text{next}_{\mathcal{U}}.(p,q).F \triangleq \text{next}_{\mathcal{T}}.(p \wedge \text{SIC}.F, q).F \,, \qquad (6')$$

$$\text{inv}_{\mathcal{U}}.p.F \triangleq \text{inv}_{\mathcal{T}}.(p \wedge \text{SIC}.F).F \,. \qquad (5')$$

Because SIC is defined to take the interaction of a system with its environment into account, contrary to SI, $\text{next}_{\mathcal{U}}$ and $\text{inv}_{\mathcal{U}}$ enjoy compositional properties that $\text{next}_{\mathcal{O}}$ and $\text{inv}_{\mathcal{O}}$ do not share. More precisely:

Proposition 1. *For any state predicates p and q, $\text{next}_{\mathcal{U}}.(p,q)$ and $\text{inv}_{\mathcal{U}}.p$ are universal specifications.*

Proposition 1 follows from the fact that $\text{SIC}.(F\|G)$ can be related to $\text{SIC}.F$ and $\text{SIC}.G$ in a simple way:[6]

$$[\text{SIC}.(F\|G) \Rightarrow \text{SIC}.F \wedge \text{SIC}.G] \,. \qquad (15)$$

No such simple relationship exist between $\text{SI}.(F\|G)$, $\text{SI}.F$ and $\text{SI}.G$. Intuitively, (15) means that any state reachable by a system in which $F\|G$ is a component is also reachable by a system in which F is a component (and a system in which G is a component), which is straightforward. It is not true of the reachable states of closed systems: a state can be reachable in $F\|G$ that was neither reachable in F nor in G.

Because SIC lies between SI and *true* (Fig. 3), $\text{inv}_{\mathcal{U}}$ lies between $\text{inv}_{\mathcal{O}}$ and $\text{inv}_{\mathcal{T}}$. If a system F does not have any local variables, then $\text{SIC}.F$ reduces to *true* (every state is reachable when F is composed) and $\text{inv}_{\mathcal{U}}$ is equivalent to $\text{inv}_{\mathcal{T}}$. But when systems have local variables, $\text{inv}_{\mathcal{U}}$ becomes strictly weaker than $\text{inv}_{\mathcal{T}}$,

---

[6] Implication from right to left does not hold.

while still being universal. This possibility, of course, is the interesting case: a component satisfies $\text{inv}_\mathcal{U}.p$ (and, therefore, is suitable for composition) but does not satisfy $\text{inv}_\mathcal{T}.p$ (and, therefore, would have to be ruled out if $\text{inv}_\mathcal{T}$ were used in its specification instead of $\text{inv}_\mathcal{U}$). This situation is illustrated in the following section.

We conclude this section with a discussion of how to prove $\text{next}_\mathcal{U}$ and $\text{inv}_\mathcal{U}$ specifications on a given system. $\text{next}_\mathcal{U}$ and $\text{inv}_\mathcal{U}$ specifications can be verified without computing SIC explicitly, as $\text{next}_\mathcal{O}$ and $\text{inv}_\mathcal{O}$ do not require the explicit knowledge of SI. For any system F and any predicates p and q:

$$\text{next}_\mathcal{U}.(p,q).F \equiv \exists r : \text{inv}_\mathcal{E}.r.F \;\wedge\; \text{next}_\mathcal{T}.(p \wedge r, q).F \;, \tag{3'}$$

$$\text{inv}_\mathcal{U}.p.F \equiv \exists q : \text{inv}_\mathcal{E}.q.F \;\wedge\; \text{inv}_\mathcal{T}.(p \wedge q).F \;. \tag{2'}$$

Equivalences (3') and (2') are direct consequences of the definitions of SIC, $\text{next}_\mathcal{U}$ and $\text{inv}_\mathcal{U}$. They correspond to (3) and (2) for operational specifications.

Consequently, all that is needed to prove $\text{next}_\mathcal{U}$ and $\text{inv}_\mathcal{U}$ specifications is a way to prove $\text{inv}_\mathcal{E}.p$ on a transition system, which is achieved through the following proposition:

Proposition 2. *Given a system F and a state predicate p, $\text{inv}_\mathcal{E}.p.F$ is true if there exists a state predicate q such that:*

1. *$\text{inv}_\mathcal{T}.q.F$,*
2. *$[q \Rightarrow p]$,*
3. *the free variables of q are a subset of $\mathcal{L}.F$.*

4.4 Example

The component DoorManager from Fig. 1, which is incorrect, is now replaced with DoorManager' from Fig. 4. This new component manages a set of lights in addition to opening and closing the doors of the train. More precisely, it turns the lights on as long as the doors are open and turns them off when the doors are closed. on and off are aliases for *true* and *false*, respectively.

This component does *not* satisfy:

$$\text{inv}_\mathcal{T}.(\text{doors} = \text{open} \Rightarrow \text{speed} = 0) \;. \tag{16}$$

$\mathcal{V} \triangleq \text{doors}, \text{speed}, \text{lights}$
$\mathcal{L} \triangleq \text{doors}, \text{lights}$
$\Sigma \triangleq \text{doors}, \text{lights} \in \mathbb{B}; \text{speed} \in \mathbb{N}$
$\mathcal{I} \triangleq \text{doors} = \text{closed} \wedge \text{lights} = \text{off}$
$\mathcal{W} \triangleq \textbf{if } \text{speed} = 0 \vee \text{lights} = \text{on } \textbf{then } \text{doors}, \text{lights} := \neg\text{doors}, \neg\text{lights}$

Fig. 4. System DoorManager'

However, it satisfies:

$$\text{inv}_\mathcal{T}.(\texttt{lights} = \texttt{on} \equiv \texttt{doors} = \texttt{open}) ,$$
$$\text{inv}_\mathcal{T}.(\ (\texttt{lights} = \texttt{on} \equiv \texttt{doors} = \texttt{open}) \wedge (\texttt{doors} = \texttt{open} \Rightarrow \texttt{speed} = 0)\ ) .$$

Because `lights` and `doors` are local to `DoorManager'`, from proposition 2 and (2'), it follows that:

$$\text{inv}_\mathcal{U}.(\texttt{doors} = \texttt{open} \Rightarrow \texttt{speed} = 0).\texttt{DoorManager'}$$

Since this specification is also satisfied by `Engine` (which satisfies it inductively as (11)), and it is universal from proposition 1, it holds for `DoorManager'`||`Engine` (and, therefore, the weaker operational specification holds as well in the global system).

To complete our train example, we consider the component `Engine'` as described in Fig. 5. In this new implementation of the Engine, the speed does not necessarily increase or decrease by one, but varies according to an integer variable `acceleration`. As a consequence, this new component does not satisfy the inductive specification (16). However, it satisfies:

$$\text{inv}_\mathcal{E}.(\texttt{acceleration} > 0 \Rightarrow \texttt{speed} > 0).\texttt{Engine'}$$

and, consequently,

$$\text{inv}_\mathcal{U}.(\texttt{doors} = \texttt{open} \Rightarrow \texttt{speed} = 0).\texttt{Engine'}$$

from which the correctness of the composed system can be deduced as before.

This example illustrates two important points concerning $\text{next}_\mathcal{U}$ and $\text{inv}_\mathcal{U}$ specifications:

- When a component is specified in terms of $\text{next}_\mathcal{U}$ and $\text{inv}_\mathcal{U}$, there is a freedom in the way this component can be implemented. This freedom is not available when a component is specified in terms of $\text{next}_\mathcal{T}$ and $\text{inv}_\mathcal{T}$, because $\text{next}_\mathcal{T}$ and $\text{inv}_\mathcal{T}$ are lower-level than $\text{next}_\mathcal{U}$ and $\text{inv}_\mathcal{U}$.

$\mathcal{V} \triangleq \texttt{doors}, \texttt{speed}, \texttt{acceleration}$
$\mathcal{L} \triangleq \texttt{speed}, \texttt{acceleration}$
$\Sigma \triangleq \texttt{doors} \in \mathbb{B}; \texttt{speed}, \texttt{acceleration} \in \mathbb{N}$
$\mathcal{J} \triangleq \texttt{speed} = 0 \wedge \texttt{acceleration} = 0$
$\mathcal{W} \triangleq$ if $\texttt{doors} = \texttt{closed}$ then $\texttt{speed} := 1$
   $\|$ $\texttt{speed} := \texttt{speed} + \texttt{acceleration}$
   $\|$ if $\texttt{speed} > \texttt{acceleration}$ then $\texttt{speed} := \texttt{speed} - \texttt{acceleration}$
   $\|$ if $\texttt{speed} > 0$ then $\texttt{acceleration} := \texttt{acceleration} + 1$
   $\|$ if $\texttt{acceleration} > 0$ then $\texttt{acceleration} := \texttt{acceleration} - 1$
   $\|$ if $\texttt{speed} = 1$ then $\texttt{speed}, \texttt{acceleration} := 0, 0$

Fig. 5. System `Engine'`

– To prove a $\text{next}_\mathcal{U}$ or an $\text{inv}_\mathcal{U}$ specification on a given system is not different in nature than to prove a $\text{next}_\mathcal{O}$ or an $\text{inv}_\mathcal{O}$ specification. It reduces to finding a suitable inductive invariant. The benefit is that, if some locality constraints hold for this inductive invariant, a universal specification can be claimed instead of a non-compositional specification.

5 Summary and Discussion

Compositional reasoning has been defined as the capacity to deduce the correctness of a system from the specifications (as opposed to implementations) of its components [14]. Although it can be argued that there is more to compositional reasoning than just this bottom-up deduction [11, 7], this question is indeed an important issue that must be dealt with. However, for the problem to be fully defined, one needs to add the important additional constraint, which too often is left implicit, that we expect specifications to be of a higher level than implementations. Without this constraint, the problem could be solved easily by choosing a low-level specification language close to implementation languages. After all, CSP processes, UNITY programs and TLA$^+$ formulas are formally defined and compose very naturally. The real issue, however, it to define *high-level* specifications such that the behavior of a system can be analyzed from the specifications of its components. Only in this case is compositional reasoning worthwhile, because substantial verification efforts are embedded in components and *reused* when components are reused.

A recent trend in compositional reasoning is to focus exclusively on existential specifications [1, 13, 30, 2, 18]. Although we acknowledge the importance of existential specifications and have indeed based entire case studies on them [10, 3], we also feel that other forms of composition can lead to better specifications in some cases. Universal specifications, in particular, seem to be especially important [9]. Universal composition is indeed what first comes to mind when composition of invariants is discussed.

In this paper, we have introduced a form of high-level invariant specifications, called $\text{inv}_\mathcal{U}$, that are compositional for universal composition. The definition of $\text{inv}_\mathcal{U}$ specifications is obtained through a simple modification of the notion of strongest invariant. Proof rules for $\text{inv}_\mathcal{U}$ and for the usual high-level (non-compositional) invariants are very similar. There are indeed a number of theorems related to $\text{next}_\mathcal{U}$ and $\text{inv}_\mathcal{U}$ that are identical to their counterparts for $\text{next}_\mathcal{O}$ and $\text{inv}_\mathcal{O}$ and that were not mentioned in this paper. To prove an $\text{inv}_\mathcal{U}$ specification is not different from proving an $\text{inv}_\mathcal{O}$ specification. Actually, one might say that high-level compositional invariants are proved routinely, but that their compositional nature is often lost for lack of a suitable name.

In [13], a form of strongest invariant similar to our SIC is defined. However, it is only used to define a variety of invariants that correspond to our $\text{inv}_\mathcal{E}$ (using a rule similar to (7')). There are no universal invariants. In [30], two forms of invariants are defined that correspond to our $\text{inv}_\mathcal{E}$ and $\text{inv}_\mathcal{U}$, but not in terms of a strongest invariant. Moreover, the universal form of invariant is defined only as a step in the construction of the existential form, which is the only form used to specify components. Both works are mixing these invariant specifications with complex assumption-commitment rules and, in the case of [30], with refinement rules. It is interesting to note that, in [13, 30], the starting point in the definition of compositional specifications is a transition system and its computations. Our method is different, as transitions and computations are completely absent from our definition of $inv_{\mathcal{U}}$ (although they are used, obviously, in the definition of $inv_{\mathcal{T}}$ and $inv_{\mathcal{O}}$). Our approach to making invariant specifications compositional is purely semantic and relies on a predicate transformer WE that is defined in a more general context (i.e., independent from transition systems and temporal logic).

The family of specifications $inv_{\mathcal{E}}$ is defined by direct application of WE to $inv_{\mathcal{O}}$. As a result, we know that $inv_{\mathcal{E}}.p$ is the weakest existential specification stronger than $inv_{\mathcal{O}}.p$. $inv_{\mathcal{U}}$, on the other hand, is not the result of applying a transformer WU to $inv_{\mathcal{O}}$. The reason is that we do not have such a transformer, because the weakest universal specification stronger than a given specification does not always exist. The absence of a transformer WU in the definition of $inv_{\mathcal{U}}$ raises an interesting question: Is $inv_{\mathcal{U}}.p$ the weakest universal specification stronger than $inv_{\mathcal{O}}.p$? This question is unanswered. Actually, we do not know whether a weakest universal specification stronger than $inv_{\mathcal{O}}$ exists at all.

As illustrated in Fig. 6, $inv_{\mathcal{U}}$ is indeed weaker than $inv_{\mathcal{T}}$[7], stronger than $inv_{\mathcal{O}}$, and encompasses enough information about a component to be universal. What we would like to know, is whether there is a better (weaker, higher-level) form of invariant that is also universal.

A key idea in compositional reasoning is the notion of non-interference in proofs, as found in the so called Owicki-Gries method [28] and applied to compositional reasoning [25, 31]. Intuitively, new components in the environment of a system should not interfere with the way a specification is proved on that system to ensure that this specification is not compromised. Non-interference with the specification itself is not enough in general. Our definition of $next_{\mathcal{U}}$ can be seen as a translation, at a semantic level, of this principle. A $next_{\mathcal{U}}$ specification is proved using an existential invariant $inv_{\mathcal{E}}$ which is not sensitive to interaction

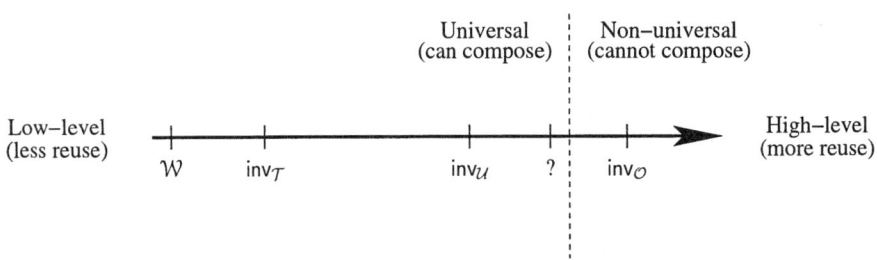

Fig. 6. Weakest universal invariant?

---

[7] It can be shown that it is also weaker than $inv_{\mathcal{E}}$.

with an external environment. Specifications $inv_\mathcal{O}$ are not compositional because their proof relies on an invariant that can be challenged by the environment.

The approach to building compositional specifications that is presented in this paper applies directly to inv and next specifications. A large class of useful safety specifications can be expressed in terms of next, including stability properties and *unless* (or weak until) specifications. Liveness and progress specifications, on the other hand, have not been considered at all. The argument has been made that liveness specifications are more difficult to compose than safety specifications. However, although leads-to specifications are notoriously difficult to compose [2, 24], a property like transient [26] composes very well (it is existential) and is the basis for the definition of liveness specifications in UNITY. However, transient is lower-level than leads-to. What makes leads-to difficult to compose may be that it is a high-level specification. For instance, the specification of a component responsible for resource allocation might include a property of fair access to resources (expressed as a leads-to). But it could also be specified in terms of a property of absence of deadlock (expressed as an invariant), from which fair access to resources can be derived after composition. The absence of deadlock specification is lower level than the fair access specification: The leads-to specification allows a resource allocator to be implemented through a mechanism that resolves deadlocks *a posteriori* while the invariant-based specification does not. Therefore, the main challenge might well be to compose high-level specifications, whether they are safety or liveness properties.

Our paper also focuses on invariants in the context of reactive systems and temporal logic. Another question is to consider the case of invariants in an object-oriented programming context (class invariants). Both notions of inductive invariants (true before and after each method call, considered individually and atomically) and operational invariants (true of the data fields of an object in between method calls at any point during its lifetime) still exist. They can still be related by a form of strongest invariant that characterizes the reachable states of an object. The argument has been made that the first kind of invariant is preferable because they can be composed more easily [22]. A counter argument is that they are too low-level to be a good specification tool. The laws of composition that are involved there, however, can be more complex than parallel composition (interleaving of atomic transitions). It would be interesting to investigate the generalization of the approach followed in this paper for this new context.

References

1. Martín Abadi and Leslie Lamport. Composing specifications. *ACM Transactions on Programming Languages and Systems*, 15(1):73–132, January 1993.
2. Martín Abadi and Leslie Lamport. Conjoining specifications. *ACM Transactions on Programming Languages and Systems*, 17(3):507–534, May 1995.
3. K. Mani Chandy and Michel Charpentier. An experiment in program composition and proof. *Formal Methods in System Design*, 20(1):7–21, January 2002.
4. K. Mani Chandy and Jayadev Misra. *Parallel Program Design: A Foundation*. Addison-Wesley, 1988.

5. K. Mani Chandy and Beverly Sanders. Reasoning about program composition. http://www.cise.ufl.edu/~sanders/pubs/composition.ps.
6. Michel Charpentier. Reasoning about composition: A predicate transformer approach. In *Specification and Verification of Component-Based Systems (SAVCBS'2001)*, pages 42–49. Workshop at OOPSLA'2001, October 2001.
7. Michel Charpentier. An approach to composition motivated by wp. In R.D. Kutsche and H. Weber, editors, *Fundamental Approaches to Software Engineering (FASE'2002)*, volume 2306 of *Lecture Notes in Computer Science*, pages 1–14. Springer-Verlag, April 2002.
8. Michel Charpentier. Composing invariants. Technical Report 03-10, University of New Hampshire, May 2003.
9. Michel Charpentier and K. Mani Chandy. Examples of program composition illustrating the use of universal properties. In J. Rolim, editor, *International workshop on Formal Methods for Parallel Programming: Theory and Applications (FMPPTA'99)*, volume 1586 of *Lecture Notes in Computer Science*, pages 1215–1227. Springer-Verlag, April 1999.
10. Michel Charpentier and K. Mani Chandy. Towards a compositional approach to the design and verification of distributed systems. In J. Wing, J. Woodcock, and J. Davies, editors, *World Congress on Formal Methods in the Development of Computing Systems (FM'99), (Vol. I)*, volume 1708 of *Lecture Notes in Computer Science*, pages 570–589. Springer-Verlag, September 1999.
11. Michel Charpentier and K. Mani Chandy. Reasoning about composition using property transformers and their conjugates. In J. van Leeuwen, O. Watanabe, M. Hagiya, P.D. Mosses, and T. Ito, editors, *Theoretical Computer Science: Exploring New Frontiers of Theoretical Informatics (IFIP-TCS'2000)*, volume 1872 of *Lecture Notes in Computer Science*, pages 580–595. Springer-Verlag, August 2000.
12. Michel Charpentier and K. Mani Chandy. Theorems about composition. In R. Backhouse and J. Nuno Oliveira, editors, *International Conference on Mathematics of Program Construction (MPC'2000)*, volume 1837 of *Lecture Notes in Computer Science*, pages 167–186. Springer-Verlag, July 2000.
13. Pierre Collette. *Design of Compositional Proof Systems Based on Assumption-Commitment Specifications. Application to UNITY*. Doctoral thesis, Faculté des Sciences Appliquées, Université Catholique de Louvain, June 1994.
14. Willem-Paul de Roever, Frank de Boer, Ulrich Hannemann, Jozef Hooman, Yassine Lakhnech, Mannes Poel, , and Job Zwiers. *Concurrency Verification: Introduction to Compositional and Noncompositional Methods*. Cambridge University Press, November 2001.
15. Willem-Paul de Roever, Hans Langmaack, and Amir Pnueli, editors. *Compositionality: The Significant Difference. International Symposium, COMPOS'97*, volume 1536 of *Lecture Notes in Computer Science*. Springer-Verlag, September 1997.
16. Edsger W. Dijkstra and Carel S. Scholten. *Predicate calculus and program semantics*. Texts and monographs in computer science. Springer-Verlag, 1990.
17. J.L. Fiadeiro and T. Maibaum. Verifying for reuse: foundations of object-oriented system verification. In I. Makie C. Hankin and R. Nagarajan, editors, *Theory and Formal Methods*, pages 235–257. World Scientific Publishing Company, 1995.
18. Bernd Finkbeiner, Zohar Manna, and Henry B. Sipma. Deductive verification of modular systems. In de Roever et al. [15], pages 239–275.
19. Leslie Lamport. The Temporal Logic of Actions. *ACM Transactions on Programming Languages and Systems*, 16(3):872–923, May 1994.
20. Leslie Lamport. Composition: A way to make proofs harder. In de Roever et al. [15], pages 402–423.

21. Leslie Lamport. *Specifying Systems: The TLA$^+$ Language and Tools for Hardware and Software Engineers*. Addison-Wesley, July 2002.
22. K. Rustan M. Leino, Greg Nelson, and James B. Saxe. *ESC/Java User's Manual*. Compaq Systems Research Center, October 200.
23. Zohar Manna and Amir Pnueli. *The Temporal Logic of Reactive and Concurrent Systems: Specification*. Springer-Verlag, 1992.
24. David Meier and Beverly Sanders. Composing leads-to properties. *Theoretical Computer Science*, 243(1–2):339–361, 2000.
25. Jayadev Misra. The importance of ensuring. In *Notes on Unity*. Department of Computer Science, University of Texas at Austin, 1990. Note 11.
26. Jayadev Misra. A logic for concurrent programming: Progress. *Journal of Computer and Software Engineering*, 3(2):273–300, 1995.
27. Jayadev Misra. A logic for concurrent programming: Safety. *Journal of Computer and Software Engineering*, 3(2):239–272, 1995.
28. Susan Owicki and David Gries. An axiomatic proof technique for parallel programs. *Acta Informatica*, 6:319–340, 1976.
29. Beverly A. Sanders. Eliminating the substitution axiom from UNITY logic. *Formal Aspects of Computing*, 3(2):189–205, April–June 1991.
30. Rob T. Udink. *Program Refinement in UNITY-like Environments*. PhD thesis, Utrecht University, September 1995.
31. Qiwen Xu, Willem-Paul de Roever, and Jifeng He. The rely-guarantee method for verifying shared variable concurrent programs. *Formal Aspects of Computing*, 9(2):149–174, 1997.

Java Applet Correctness: A Developer-Oriented Approach

Lilian Burdy, Antoine Requet, and Jean-Louis Lanet

Gemplus Research Labs,
La Vigie, Avenue du Jujubier – ZI Athelia IV, 13705 La Ciotat CEDEX, France,
{Lilian.Burdy,Antoine.Requet,Jean-Louis.Lanet}@gemplus.com

Abstract. This paper presents experiments on formal validation of Java applets. It describes a tool that has been developed at the Gemplus Research Labs. This tool allows to formally prove Java classes annotated with JML, an annotation language for Java that provides a framework for specifying class invariants and methods behaviours. The foundations and the main features of the tool are presented. The most innovative part of the tool is that it is tailored to be used by Java programmers, without any particular background in formal methods. To reduce the difficulty of using formal techniques, it aims to provide a user-friendly interface which hides to developers most of the formal features and provides a "Java style view" of lemmas.

Keywords: Java, Correctness Proof, Proof User Interface

1 Introduction

Providing high quality on applet development is becoming a crucial issue, especially when those applets are aimed to be loaded and executed in smart cards. Actually, the card remains a specific domain where post issuance corrections are very expensive due to the deployment process and the mass production. Currently, the quality is ensured by costly test campaigns, whenever tests are technically possible. We consider that using formal techniques is a solution that allows us to increase the quality, but also to reduce validation costs.

Formal validation of Java programs is a growing research field. As Java has become a reference language, many technologies are emerging to help Java program validation. Java can also be considered as a good support for formal techniques, as it has precise semantics [10].

Nevertheless, proving program correctness, and more generally using formal methods, is traditionally an activity reserved for experts. This restriction is usually caused by the mathematical nature of the concepts involved. This explains why formal techniques are difficult to introduce in industrial processes, even if they are now widely used in research and teaching activities. However, we believe that this restriction can be reduced by providing notations and tools hiding the mathematical formalisms. Therefore, formal tools should be developed to fit into classical developers environment. We strongly believe that efforts should be done to allow users to benefit from formal techniques without having to learn new formalisms and to become experts. Java developers should be able to validate their code, or at least to get a good assurance on its correctness.

This paper presents such a tool: the Java Applet Correctness Kit (or `JACK`). This tool, already briefly described in [2], is a formal tool that allows one to prove properties on Java programs using the Java Modeling Language [15] (JML). Its application domain is, at the moment, smart card applets, but one can consider that it can be useful in many development contexts. It generates proof obligations allowing to prove that the Java code conforms to its JML specification. The lemmas are translated into the B language [1], allowing to use the automatic prover developed within the B method.

But the tool is not yet another lemma generator for Java, since it also provides a lemma viewer integrated in the eclipse IDE[1]. This allows to hide the formalisms used behind a graphical interface. Lemmas are presented to users in a way they can understand them easier, by using the Java syntax and highlighting code portions to help the understanding. Using `JACK`, one does not have to learn a formal language to be convience on code correctness.

The remainder of the paper is organized as follow. Section 2 describes JML and the different tools supporting it. Section 3 presents the architecture and the main principles of the tool we have developed. Section 4 describes more precisely the innovative parts of the tool and explains why we consider it as accessible to any developers. Section 5 describes experiments on an applet and the metrics that have been collected. Section 6 presents research perspectives and Section 7 concludes.

2 Java Modeling Language

This section briefly presents JML and the tools that have been developed around it. JML [15] is a language that allows one to specify Java classes by formally expressing properties and requirements on those classes and their methods. Some keywords and logical constructions have been added to Java, but the core expression language is close to Java. JML benefits from Java's precise semantics. JML has also been defined so that specifications are easy to read and write by Java programmers. Taking those facts into account, many tools have been developed around JML annotations.

2.1 Specifying Java Applets

Figure 1 presents an example JML specification. The language provides keywords to specify:

- *Class invariants*: invariants correspond to properties on member and class variables that must always hold (from an external observer point of view, since invariants are not required to hold inside method implementations),

---
[1] http://www.eclipse.org

```
class C {
    short i;
    //@ invariant i >= 0;

    //@ requires c != null;
    //@ modifies i, c.i;
    //@ ensures i == 3 && c.i == 2;
    //@ exsures (Exception) false;
    void m(C c) {
        i = 3;
        c.i = 2;
    }
}
```

Fig. 1. JML example

and are introduced using the `invariant` keyword. In the example, the integer i is positive.

- *Preconditions*: preconditions are associated to methods, and correspond to properties that must hold in order to call the method. The `requires` keyword is used to define preconditions. In the example, the method parameter c is required to be non-null.
- *Postconditions*: as preconditions express the properties that must be true when calling a method, postconditions describes the behavior of the method by expressing the properties ensured by the method. They are expressed using the `ensures` keyword. In the example, the value of i will become 3 for the current instance and 2 for the parameter c. Special postconditions can also be used to describe exceptional behaviors, in particular, when the method throws an exception. JML uses the special `exsures` keyword to define those special postconditions. In the example, it is expressed that the method will not throw any exceptions.

Additionally, JML requires specifying which variables can be modified by a method. This is specified with the `modifies` keyword. In the example, it is specified that only the variables i will be modified for the instances this and c by the method m.

The language contains more complex constructions that allows one to model more complex behaviors. Some realistic examples have already been modeled using JML: the Java Card API [18], part of the Java Standard Edition API [13], or a banking applet for smart cards [5]. Those examples show that using JML is a realistic way to model Java programs, especially with the Java Card[2] restrictions.

---

[2] Java Card is a standard defined by Sun Microsystems tailored to smart card. It is a subset of Java. It does not support threads, multi-dimensional arrays, floating point types, etc.

2.2 Tools

Before presenting the tool that we have developed, we describe, in this section, the other existing tools that are supporting JML in order to compare them with our approach. An overview on tools supporting JML is presented in [16]. From this time, different new tools have been developed and existing tools have been improved. Three categories can be distinguished: runtime checkers, static validation tools and proof tools.

Runtime checker. A runtime checker is part of the JML release. The JML release consists of different tools:

- a type-checker, allowing to verify the syntax of the JML specifications,
- the jmldoc tool, that is similar to JavaDoc, but adds the JML specification to the generated html documentation and
- the jmlc tool [6], that uses the JML annotation in order to add runtime assertions in the generated code.

The assertion checking allows running the code with dynamic tests checking for the correctness of the preconditions, the postconditions and the invariants. Thus, problems can be found early, as a specification violation will generate false assertions, potentially before introducing a visible runtime error. jmlc is integrated with Junit[3] giving jmljunit [7]. This tool generates an oracle and skeletons used by Junit to run test cases.

Static validation tools. The main tool in this category is the ESC/Java [9] static checker for Java. It performs a static analysis of a Java source file in order to check for potential errors in the program. This tool does not aim to provide a formal assurance that the verified class is correct. The spirit of ESC/Java is to be a lightweight tool that aims to be used during development in order to identify and correct bugs early. For example, it is really efficient to warn about potential null pointer usage, and provides counter-examples when a property expressed could be erroneous. An experiment on ESC/Java is notably presented in [5].

Proof tools. This is the category that our tool, JACK, belongs to. The idea behind those tools is to convert the JML annotated source code into formal models. Such a conversion allows to reason mathematically on the program, and to achieve correctness proofs. Those proof tools are targeted to Java Card, which does not contain complex Java features which would be difficult to handle such as, for example, multi-threading.

- The LOOP tool [14, 12, 19] is a tool converting Java annotated sources to PVS models. It treats the complete Java Card language and now proposes an automated proof obligation generation using weakest precondition calculus.
- The Java Interactive Verification Environment (Jive) [17] aims to also translate JML annotated Java in PVS models. It proposes an interactive environment to deal with the proof obligation generation. Nevertheless, it does not handle all the Java Card language.

---

[3] JUnit is a regression testing framework, see http://www.junit.org

- The Krakatoa tool [8] is the more recent one. It aims to translate Java annotated sources into an internal language from which proof obligations are generated into Coq[4].

All those tools are actually developed within the VerifiCard[5] project. They all have the same goal but approaches are slightly different.

3 Foundations

The previous section presented several tools that exist to handle JML annotated Java programs. However, we feel that the aspects of user friendliness and automatization are not sufficiently addressed by these tools, therefore we decided to develop our own tool.

The main design goals were the following:

- it should provide an easy accessible user interface, that enables average Java programmers to use the tool without too much difficulties (in contrast to for example LOOP). This interface is described section 4;
- it should provide a high degree of automation, so that most proof obligations can be discharged without user interaction. Only in this way, the tool can be effectively used by non-expert users, which is necessary if we want that formal methods will ever be used in industry. This is in contrast with the LOOP and Jive approach, where users need in-depth PVS knowledge to be able to do verifications;
- it should provide high correctness assurance: at the moment the prover says that a certain proof obligation is satisfied, it should be possible to trust this without any reservation (in contrast to ESC/Java). Nevertheless the tool is not formally developed, as LOOP is. It implements, in Java, a weakest precondition calculus that generates lemmas without user interaction. We cannot prove that those lemmas are necessary and sufficient to ensure the correctness of the applet but the tool is designed in this way;
- it should be relatively independent of the particular prover used, so that if the use of another prover is required (for example by a certification institute) it is relatively easy to adapt the tool accordingly.

This section presents the tool architecture and its principles, concerning object-oriented concepts formalization and lemma generation.

3.1 Architecture

Figure 2 presents an overview of the JACK architecture. JACK consists of two parts: a converter (a lemma generator) from Java source annotated with JML into B lemmas, and a viewer that allows developers to understand the generated

---

[4] Coq is a proof assistant developed by the INRIA: http://coq.inria.fr
[5] European IST Project: http://www.verificard.org

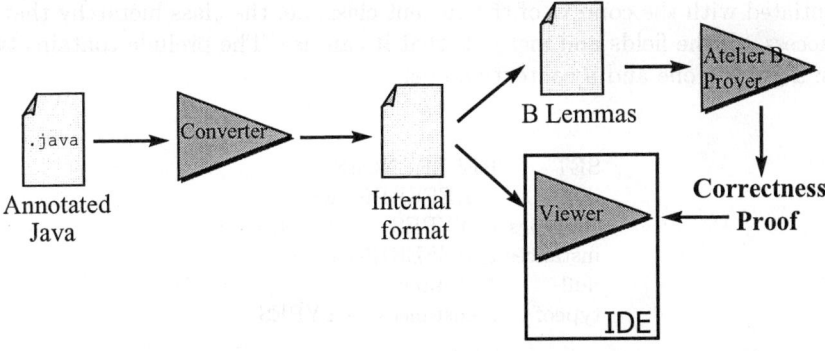

Fig. 2. JACK architecture

lemmas. The viewer is integrated in an IDE and is described more precisely in section 4.2. This part focuses on the converter.

The JACK converter converts a Java class into a B model and allows to prove properties. The B method [1] is a formal method with different features such as refinement schema, translation in C code, etc. We only use it as a framework that allows us to express lemmas and to prove them using a prover. This prover is part of the Atelier B[6] tool and provides two modules: an automatic one and an interactive one. The choice of the B method as the targeted prover is due to different reasons. The Atelier B prover is quite well automated with proof rate approaching 80%. It can also easily be customized to increase this rate by adding new proof tactics and theorems. Nevertheless, dealing with the interactive interface which allows to prove remaining lemmas is still an activity reserved to experts. Another more pragmatic reason is the good experience of our team in the Atelier B prover (see [3, 4]).

Our goal is to prove properties on source files written with the Java language. To reach this goal, one has to know how to "translate" a Java source file in B lemmas. The two main issues are:

1. How to formalize the object-oriented Java features in set theory (the B language is a first order language with set theory)?
2. How to generate lemmas from Java methods?

The following sections provide answers to those questions.

3.2 Object-Oriented Concepts Formalization

The adopted solution concerning the formalization of object-oriented concept is to generate lemmas with the point of view of one Java class. Each generated lemma for a class contains, as prelude, the formalization of the memory model

---

[6] Atelier B is a CASE tool developed by Clearsy (http://www.clearsy.com) that allows one to develop using the B method.

instantiated with the context of the current class, i.e. the class hierarchy that it can access, all the fields and methods that it can use. The prelude contains two parts: a generic one and a contextual one.

$$
\begin{array}{ll}
\text{SET} & \text{REFERENCES} \\
\text{null} & \in \text{REFERENCES} \\
\text{subtypes} & \in \text{TYPES} \leftrightarrow \text{TYPES} \\
\text{instances} & \subset \text{REFERENCES} \\
\text{null} & \notin \text{instances} \\
\text{typeof} & \in \text{instances} \to \text{TYPES}
\end{array}
$$

Fig. 3. Memory model representation

The generic prelude contains many definitions concerning built-in types with their operators. It contains also the memory model representation (see Figure 3). This model is defined by an infinite set of possible references, a particular reference corresponding to null, a subtyping relation, the set of currently allocated instances and a function associating a type to each instance. This model is completed with definitions allowing to handle arrays that are not given here. This set of constants and variables represents the memory state associated to each lemma, corresponding, for instance, to the state of the memory at the beginning of an operation. In this model, an object creation, for instance, will be defined as taking an arbitrary element from the set of references (different from the special constant null), adding this reference to the set of instances and assigning a type to it.

The set of types is defined by $\text{TYPES} = \text{NAMES} * \mathbb{N}$, where NAMES corresponds to the set of classes referenced by the program. This definition allows to handle the types corresponding to array types: a type corresponds to a class and a dimension represented by a natural number (for objects, this number is always 0). For instance the Java type Object will correspond to the type $c\_Object \mapsto 0$ and the Java type Object[][][] to $c\_Object \mapsto 3$.

The set NAMES is not generic since it depends on the reachable classes from the current one. It does not belong to the common prelude but to the contextual one. For instance, the valuation of NAMES in the case of the example in Figure 1 (where classes names are prefixed to avoid names conflict) is

$$
\text{NAMES} = \left\{ \begin{array}{l}
c\_int, c\_short, c\_char, c\_byte, c\_boolean, c\_Object, \\
c\_RuntimeException, c\_Exception, c\_Throwable, \\
c\_NullPointerException, c\_ArithmeticException, \\
c\_ArrayIndexOutOfBoundsException, \\
c\_NegativeArraySizeException, c\_ClassCastException, \\
c\_ArrayStoreException, c\_C
\end{array} \right\}
$$

One can notice that primitive types belongs to NAMES but they are only used to type arrays. For instance the Java type `short[]` will correspond to c_short ↦ 1, but the type short will correspond to a prelude-defined type t_short = −32768..32767.

The subtyping relation is also valuated depending on the class hierarchy. It assigns to a class itself and all its subclasses and to an interface itself and all its implementing classes and interfaces. This gives, for example,

$$\text{subtypes}[\{c\_RuntimeException \mapsto 0\}] = \left\{\begin{array}{l} c\_RuntimeException \mapsto 0, \\ c\_NullPointerException \mapsto 0, \\ c\_ArithmeticException \mapsto 0, \\ c\_ArrayIndexOutOfBoundsException \mapsto 0, \\ c\_NegativeArraySizeException \mapsto 0, \\ c\_ClassCastException \mapsto 0, \\ c\_ArrayStoreException \mapsto 0 \end{array}\right\}.$$

The fields are declared as variables, static fields are directly typed with their translated type, member fields are declared as functions from the set of instances of a type to the type of the field. For instance, the member field i (see Figure 1) is declared as follow:

$$f\_i \in \text{typeof}^{-1}[\text{subtypes}[\{c\_C \mapsto 0\}] \to t\_short.$$

The invariants are declared as properties quantified over the instances. For instance, the invariant of the class C (see Figure 1) is declared as follow:

$$\forall c.(c \in \text{instances} \land \text{typeof}(c) \in \text{subtypes}[\{c\_C \mapsto 0\}] \Rightarrow 0 \leq f\_i(c)).$$

The drawback of this approach is that one can not directly prove properties on the correctness of the formalization. But, proofs remain simpler as they remain centered on the specific case of a dedicated class.

3.3 Lemma Generation

The JML annotations are Java boolean expressions without side effects. Thus, they are easily translated in logical formulas: Java operators are translated into functions. For example, shift left (<<) is translated into a function associating an integer to a pair of integer. From those translated annotations and the methods code, lemmas can be generated automatically.

From the start, taking into account experiences in lemma generation for B machines, we have tried to implement a Weakest Precondition (WP) calculus to automate lemma generation. Huisman, in [11], presents how the classical Hoare logic can be completed to allow the generation of lemmas in the context of Java. The Java statements contain different features like control-flow breaks. So, the classical WP calculus should be completed to deal with them.

Moreover, JML should be lightly upgraded to allow fully automated proof obligation generation. Notably, to automate lemma generation for the loops, we have had to extend the JML language with new keywords: loop_modifies and `loop_exsures`. The `loop_modifies` keyword allows us to declare the variables modified in the body of the loop, as it is done for the methods. During the WP calculus, it is necessary to universally quantify the loop invariant with those variables, and since they cannot be automatically calculated, one has to specify them. The `loop_exsures` allows us to specify the exceptional behavior of a loop. It is not necessary to apply the WP calculus but it can improve the understandability of the specification.

The two main drawbacks of the WP calculus are the loss of information and potential exponentional explosion. After lemmas have been generated, it is often difficult to understand from which part of the code they are derived. To bypass this issue, program flow information is associated to each lemma. This information is used in the viewer to associate an execution path to each lemma. This feature is described in the next section.

Exponentional explosion remains a problem. Different solutions exist to avoid it. As the WP calculus can be considered as a brute force concept, trying to expand all the path of the methods, solutions are always based on interaction to reduce this brute force by introducing intelligence in the process.

A simple solution is to require users interaction during lemma generation in order to cut unsatisfiable branches. Rather than introducing interaction during generation, another solution is to allow to add special annotations in the source code to introduce formulas that are taken into account at generation to simplify the lemmas. The solution adopted in JACK is to allow to specify blocks. An exponentional explosion usually occurs in a method with many sequenced branched statement (`if`, `switch`, etc.) Such methods usually perform different distinct sequenced treatments. Figure 4 presents the skeleton of such a method. Specifying a block (here the second part of the method) allows to cut proof obligation generation. This corresponds, in fact, to the simulation of a method call.

```
m() {
    ⋮
    if () { ... }
    else { ... }
    ⋮
    /*@ modifies variables
      @ ensures property
      @*/ {
        ⋮
        if () { ... }
        else { ... }
        ⋮
    }
}
```

Fig. 4. Specified block

With those extensions to the JML language, we are able to obtain a fully automated proof obligation generation. That is the first step to reach user approval. The second one is to propose an access to those lemmas in a "Java style", this is described in the next section.

4 User Interface

JML has the advantage of being a language that can be rapidly and easily learned and used by developers. One can consider that using a prover is not so easy. Nevertheless formal activities like modeling and proving should not be reserved to experts. To demonstrate this concept, we provide a prover interface understandable to non-experts in formal methods.

In order to simplify the modeling activity with the JML language, our interface requirements are:

- to be integrated with other tools used by developers, and
- not to require the developer to use a mathematical formalism, but hide the mathematical formalism under a "Java" view.

Compared to other formal tools using the JML language, the efforts on the user interface and integration within the developement environment is probably the main strength of JACK, as is the fact that the underlying mathematical formalism is not exposed to the user.

4.1 Integration in Developers Environment

Java developers are used to develop using integrated development environments (IDE). Those IDEs provide many features useful during the development process. Integrating the tool in such IDEs allows the user to work in a familiar environment. This leads both to better acceptance of the tool, and to a reduced learning curve. Currently, JACK is integrated within the eclipse IDE. It could however be ported to other IDEs, and a standalone version that does not require an IDE also exists.

Another constraint has to be taken into account to obtain developer agreement: it is the tool's responsiveness. The tool has to be used interactively, with a debugger spirit: it should not require the developer to wait for a long time. Lemma generation takes, in realistic examples, less than one minute. Nevertheless, the automatic proof of lemmas is not such a reactive activity. Thus, the tool provides a feature that allows to schedule proof tasks in order to optimize proof time (see paragraph 4.3).

Several other minor features are available to integrate within the development cycle, for example, reports on the status of the project can be generated as Microsoft Excel files.

4.2 Lemma Viewer

One of the most important points of JACK is that it does not require developers to learn a mathematical language. Although lemmas are generated, those lemmas are not directly displayed to the user.

Instead, we provide the user with a graphical view (Figure 5) of the lemma. The viewer displays

- information concerning the current proof status;
- the class methods with their lemmas;
- the source code;
- and the currently selected lemma (goals and hypotheses with Java or B presentation).

Within a method, each execution path corresponds to a case. Possibly, several lemmas are associated to each case. When a case is selected, the corresponding execution path is highlighted. When a lemma is selected, its views are displayed.

Path highlighting. The source code of the program considered is displayed, and the path within the program that leads to the generated proof obligation is highlighted.

Different highlighting colors are used to represent this path:

- green indicates that the corresponding instruction has been executed normally;
- blue indicates that the corresponding instruction has been executed normally, and that additional information is available. For instance, the condition of an if construct will usually be displayed in blue with additional information indicating if the condition has been considered as true or false;
- red indicates that the corresponding instruction was supposed to raise an exception when it has been executed in the case considered. Additional information are also provided indicating the exception that has been raised.

The part of the specification (invariant or post-condition) that is involved in the current lemma is also highlighted. Highlighting the part of the source code involved in the proof obligation allows to quickly understand the proof obligation, and allows the user to treat the proof obligations as execution scenarios of the program.

Java presentation of lemmas. The hypothesis and goals of the current lemma are also displayed. As the conversion mechanism to B may be hard to follow, especially by non-experts, the internal representation used by the tool is used to present the hypothesis and goals in a Java representation. That is, all the variables are displayed using the Java dotted notation, and the Java operators are used instead of their corresponding function.

However, such a translation may be more complicated when operators that have no Java or Jml equivalent constructs are used. To emphasize this point, we present some lemmas that have been generated from the method of Figure 1

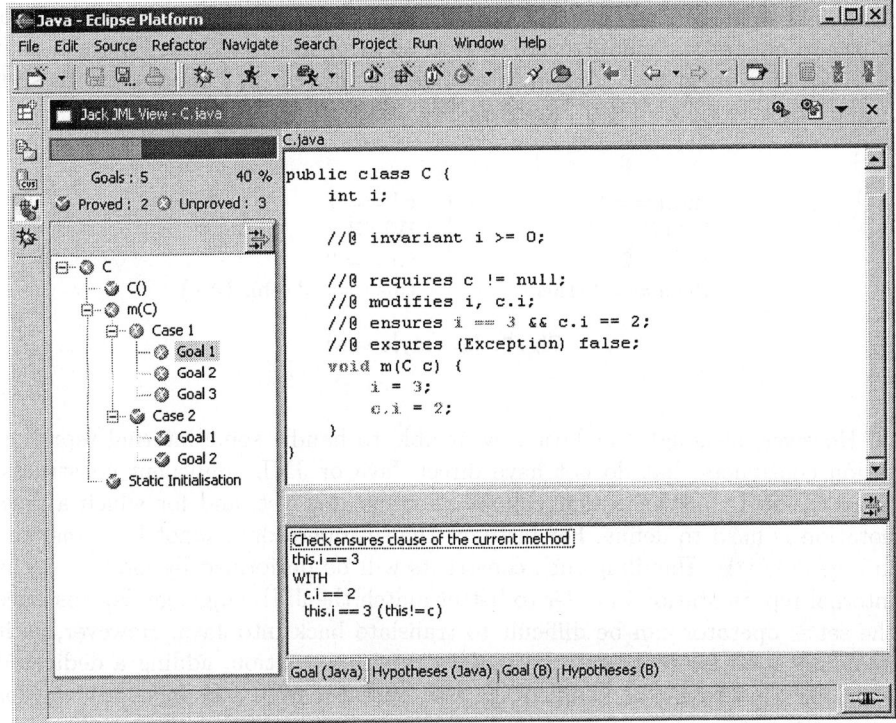

Fig. 5. Viewer integrated in eclipse

concerning the post-condition correction. The "B style view" (Figure 6) presents two lemmas concerning the fact that i becomes 3 for the instance this and becomes 2 for the instance c. The fact that i has changed during the method is denoted using the overriding operator ($\triangleleft$ in the B language) twice, replacing the value of i for the instances c and this.

$$(i \triangleleft \{this \mapsto 3\} \triangleleft \{c \mapsto 2\})(this) = 3$$
$$(i \triangleleft \{this \mapsto 3\} \triangleleft \{c \mapsto 2\})(c) = 2$$

Fig. 6. B style view

The "Java style view" (Figure 7) presents the same two lemmas. However, as Java has no operator equivalent to the B overriding operator, a special notation using the "WITH" keyword is used. This view allows to understand quickly which part of the specification is concerned by the lemma: the postcondition is presented as it appears in the code. Modifications concerning i are presented in a second part (under the WITH keyword) in a specific order, and possibly under constraints. In this example, the constraints express the fact that the value of this.i is equal to 3 under the assumption that this is different from c. This allows to understand rapidly that there is an error in the code in Figure 1, as it does not implement the requirements when c equals this. This can also be seen in the "B style view" but it requires more expertise.

this.i == 3 WITH c.i == 2 this.i == 3 (this != c)	c.i == 2 WITH c.i == 2 this.i == 3 (this != c)

Fig. 7. Java style view

However, although the Java view is able to handle some internal representation constructs that do not have direct Java or JML equivalent constructs, there are still constructs that cannot be translated yet, and for which a Java notation is hard to define. For instance the set operators cannot be translated in a generic way. Handling such constructs will be performed by modifying the internal representation in order to better match the JML language. For instance the set $\in$ operator can be difficult to translate back into Java. However, as it is mainly used for representing the Java type information, adding a dedicated operator (that would be handled like a *in* operator from a B point of view) for representing this type information would allow an easy translation.

Such changes to the internal representation would also be useful for generating lemmas to other proof language such as Coq or PVS, for which a translation using the set operators may not be the most appropriate translation.

4.3 Support for Verification

Apart from displaying the generated proof obligations, JACK also provides support for validating those proof, as detailed hereafter.

Support for automatic proof. A point that should not be taken lightly is the time taken by automatic proof: generating proof obligations for industrial size applications will generate thousands of proof obligations.

Typically, those proofs can be quite lengthy, and it is necessary that the user is not obliged to wait for proofs to finish.

To achieve this, JACK provides an independent proof view, where files can be queued in order to be submitted to the prover. Thus, the proofs are performed as soon as possible, possibly during the night, allowing the user to focus on cases inspection.

Support for interactive proof. Although the automatic prover allows discharging many proof obligations, it cannot discharge all the proof obligations. Thus, the remaining proof obligations have to be verified manually.

Currently, developers are not supposed to handle this task, but to delegate it to a team of experts that would perform the proofs using the interactive prover of the `Atelier B` tool.

However, it is expected that developers will be able to handle more and more of the interactive proofs. To achieve this, we provide limited support for interacting with the prover in order to allow users to prove common cases.

Currently, two interactions are provided:

- Identifying false hypothesis. In that case, the prover tries to prove the negation of the hypothesis, and if the proof succeeds, the goal is discharged.
- Showing "wrong pathes" in the source code. This is performed by clicking on a condition in the source code that "cannot happen". For instance, a condition within a `if` that is in contradiction with the preconditions.
  In that case, the corresponding hypothesis is retrieved and sent to the prover as a false hypothesis in a way similar to the previous case.

Those actions are still limited to one proof command that can either succeed or fail, and so cannot be used to perform full interactive proof yet. However, they still allow to discharge some classes of common proof obligations.

Checking proof obligations. Additionally to the *"proved"* and *"unproved"* states, JACK can also differentiate *"checked"* proof obligations. Checked proof obligations correspond to proof obligations that are not formally proved, but have been manually verified.

Checking a proof obligations is performed by the user to indicate that he has read and understood the proof obligation and has confidence that it is correct. Although the checked state provides no formal guarantee on the correctness of the proof obligations, it still provides valuable information on the state of a project.

The checked state of the proof obligations can be used in different ways:

- To flag cases as already seen in order to start an interactive proof only if we are pretty sure that the cases are correct, and
- In some cases, when a full correctness assurance of the program is not required, we may accept that not all the proof obligations are formally proved. In that case, it may however, be required that all the proof obligations have been checked.

5 Case Study

To test JACK, we have developed a little banking application. This section presents different metrics concerning the evaluation of the tool on this package. Different remarks can be made from Table 1, concerning the cost of adding JML annotations, the performance of the tool, as well as the cost associated to the proof.

Table 1. banking applet metrics

Classes	Java lines	JavaDoc lines	JML lines	Proof obligations	Automatic proof	Time to PO generate (s)	Time to prove (s)
Transfert_src	116	34	150	359	91%	22,5	238
AccountMan_src	105	51	236	269	82%	12,7	195
Currency_src	93	20	28	50	96%	7,6	17
Balance_src	64	38	58	335	95%	16,5	191
Spending_rule	40	33	62	42	67%	13,6	217

Cost of the annotations. A first remark concerns the cost of the annotations. The metrics given here only concern the number of lines but one can see that the documentation size (JavaDoc and JML) is one and half greater than the code size. So, writing the JML specification seems to be a costly activity. This remark can be moderated by two points: this development was the first that we made, and annotations were added to already existing code. So it suffers from its lack of abstraction, and the annotations are really verbose. Moreover the time to specify is to be compared to the time to develop test data.

Responsiveness. The automatic phases are quite responsive with some seconds to generate proof obligations. The automatic proof is not as cheap as the proof obligation generation and takes a few minutes. However, this still remains acceptable, since it is a non-blocking task that does not require users to wait for its completion.

For larger applets, it is however expected that the time required for the automatic proof will significantly increase.

Proof. The automatic proof rating is much good. It is quite greater than the usual value for a B development (around 80%). This is mainly due to the fact that we used this applet as a test applet for extending the prover. So, as a side effect, the automatic prover is customized for this special applet.

Nevertheless, after automatic proof step, there remain 111 lemmas to prove using the Atelier B interface. An expert needs between 4 and 5 days to prove them.

6 Perspectives

At the moment, we have developed a prototype that is becoming a usable tool. We are beginning experimentation outside the lab. But we are considering that there are still many points where the approach can be improved.

6.1 Interactive Proof Cost

Currently, the interactive proof support is rather limited. Thus, proving the remaining proof obligations requires users to directly use the `Atelier B` tool interactive prover. Such a task can be tedious, since the B representation of the generated proof obligations can be hard to follow. Different perspectives exist to reduce the interactive proof cost.

Java interface. Although full interactive proof will still be reserved to experts, providing an interface to the `Atelier B` interactive prover allowing to perform proofs by directly using the Java syntax would greatly improve the productivity of those experts. A first step would be to extend the Java view used to display the lemmas.

Test activity. Another way to reduce interactive proof activity is to balance it with testing activity. Methods where lemmas are not automatically proved could be tested. Using `JmlJunit` can be a good way to generate test skeleton on certain cases. A perspective is to integrate `JmlJunit` in our environment in manner to propose different validation level (full proof, proof mixed with test, etc).

Counter-example. Another idea to reduce the cost of false lemma detection is to provide counter-example when it is possible. `ESC/Java` already tempts to give such counter-examples. Studies on that subject could give results helpful for developers to understand errors on the code or on the specifications.

6.2 Allowing Expressions in the Target Formal Language

Currently, JACK can be seen as a proof-obligations generator from JML annotated Java programs to B lemmas. A possible extension would be to add different target languages for lemma generation, for instance Coq or PVS. Such extension would allow using different provers for different lemmas. On the other side, it is also possible to enrich the JML specification by adding inline expressions or variables in a target language of the lemma generator. Such an extension would have a role similar to Java "native methods" at a specification level. That is, allowing to describe in a lower-level language things that cannot be described in JML (or that cannot be described efficiently from a proof point of view).

We are currently investigating such extension mechanisms, that would allow adding different languages for such use without having to modify the weakest-precondition calculus core.

7 Conclusion

The presented work allows formal methods experts to prove Java applet correctness. Moreover, it allow Java programmers to obtain an high assurance on their code correctness. This leads to the most important point: it allows non-experts to venture into the formal world. This is a necessary starting point for such validation techniques to be widely used.

The tool has been developed following a main objective: let Java developers validate their own code. We claim that JML is well suited to express low level design and conception choices and that usage of JACK can replace effectively unitary tests, giving developers the means to furnish code with good quality and non ambiguous documentation.

Taking benefits from recent research on Java program validation, we have developed an automated tool that generates lemmas from Java classes annotated with JML. The JACK principles are not really different from the LOOP team choices. Nevertheless, one can highlight some important differences. The LOOP tool describes formally Java semantics and the WP-calculus rules are applied by the prover. The main advantage is that the rules have been proven sound with regards to the semantics in the theorem prover. Our point of view, is more pragmatic: lemma are generated automatically, using Java developed rules that can only be checked by usual validation: test, code-inspection. The soundness of the tool cannot be formally proved but on the other hand a big effort is done to present lemmas to users in a way that he can understand them and verify that they are valid.

The tool is fully integrated in the eclipse IDE and presents lemmas in a visual way that allows developers to form their opinion on the lemma validity. An automatic prover discharges an important part of the lemmas. The remaining lemmas have to be proved using the prover interface. Often, this task cannot be done by developers. Different ways are studied to bypass it: expert support, test case generation, counter-example detection, etc.

We are now experimenting on real industrial products. We are trying to collect metrics in order to prove that this kind of validation is cost-saving, especially when the cost of testing is taken into account.

Acknowlegdements

The authors would like to thank Marieke Huisman for its helpful comment on this paper.

References

[1] Jean-Raymond Abrial. *The B Book, Assigning Programs to Meanings.* Cambridge University Press, 1996.
[2] Lilian Burdy and Antoine Requet. Jack : Java Applet Correctness Kit. In *GDC 2002, Singapore*, November 2002.
[3] Ludovic Casset. Development of an embedded verifier for Java Card byte code using formal methods. In Lars-Henrik Eriksson and Peter Alexander Lindsay, editors, *Formal Methods – Getting IT Right*, volume 2391 of *Lecture Notes in Computer Science*, pages 290–309. Springer-Verlag, July 22-24 2002.
[4] Ludovic Casset, Lilian Burdy, and Antoine Requet. Formal development of an embedded verifier for Java Card byte code. In *DSN 2002, International Conference on Dependable Systems & Networks*, pages 51–56, Washington, D.C., USA, June 2002.
[5] Néstor Cataño and Marieke Huisman. Formal specification and static checking of Gemplus' electronic purse using ESC/Java. In Lars-Henrik Eriksson and Peter Alexander Lindsay, editors, *Formal Methods – Getting IT Right*, volume 2391 of *Lecture Notes in Computer Science*, pages 272–289. Springer-Verlag, July 22-24 2002.

[6] Yoonsik Cheon and Gary T. Leavens. A runtime assertion checker for the Java Modeling Language (JML). Technical Report 02–05, Department of Computer Science, Iowa State University, March 2002. In SERP 2002, pp. 322–328.

[7] Yoonsik Cheon and Gary T. Leavens. A simple and practical approach to unit testing: The JML and JUnit way. In Boris Magnusson, editor, *ECOOP 2002 — Object-Oriented Programming, 16th European Conference, Máalaga, Spain, Proceedings*, volume 2374 of *Lecture Notes in Computer Science*, pages 231–255, Berlin, June 2002. Springer-Verlag.

[8] Jean-Christophe Filliâtre, Claude Marché, Christine Paulin, and Xavier Urbain. Modeling of Java programs in Coq. in VeriSafe Workshop, Sept 2002.

[9] Cormac Flanagan, K. Rustan M. Leino, Mark Lillibridge, Greg Nelson, James B. Saxe, and Raymie Stata. Extended static checking for java. In Cindy Norris and James B. Fenwick Jr., editors, *Proceedings of the ACM SIGPLAN 2002 Conference on Programming Language Design and Implementation (PLDI-02)*, volume 37, 5 of *ACM SIGPLAN Notices*, pages 234–245, New York, June 17–19 2002. ACM Press.

[10] James Gosling, Bill Joy, and Guy Steele. *The Java Language Specification*. Addison Wesley, 1996.

[11] Marieke Huisman. *Java Program Verification in Higher-Order Logic with PVS and Isabelle*. PhD thesis, University of Nijmegen, The Netherlands, 2001.

[12] Marieke Huisman and Bart Jacobs. Java program verification via a Hoare logic with abrupt termination. In T. Maibaum, editor, *Fundamental Approaches to Software Engineering (FASE)*, volume 1783 of *Lecture Notes in Computer Science*, pages 284–303. Springer-Verlag, 2000.

[13] Marieke Huisman, Bart Jacobs, and Joachim van den Berg. A case study in class library verification: Java's vector class. CSI Report CSI-R0007, Computing Science Department, Nijmegen, March 2000. http://www.cs.kun.nl/csi//reports/full/CSI-R0007.ps.Z.

[14] Bart Jacobs and Erik Poll. A logic for the Java modeling language JML. In H. Hussmann, editor, *Fundamental Approaches to Software Engineering (FASE)*, volume 2029 of *Lecture Notes in Computer Science*, pages 284–299. Springer-Verlag, 2001.

[15] Gary T. Leavens, Albert L. Baker, and Clyde Ruby. Preliminary design of JML: A behavioral interface specification language for Java. Technical Report 98-06i, Iowa State University, Department of Computer Science, February 2000. ftp://ftp.cs.iastate.edu/pub/techreports/TR98-06/TR.ps.gz.

[16] Gary T. Leavens, K. Rustan M. Leino, Erik Poll, Clyde Ruby, and Bart Jacobs. JML: notations and tools supporting detailed design in Java. In *OOPSLA 2000 Companion, Minneapolis, Minnesota*, pages 105–106. ACM, October 2000.

[17] Jörg Meyer and Arnd Poetzsch-Heffter. An architecture for interactive program provers. In S. Graf and M. Schwartzbach, editors, *Tools and Algorithms for the Construction and Analysis of Systems (TACAS)*, volume 1785 of *Lecture Notes in Computer Science*, pages 63–77. Springer-Verlag, 2000.

[18] Erik Poll, Joachim van den Berg, and Bart Jacobs. Specification of the JavaCard API in JML. In *Fourth Smart Card Research and Advanced Application Conference (IFIP Cardis)*. Kluwer Academic Publishers, 2000.

[19] Joachim van den Berg and Bart Jacobs. The LOOP compiler for Java and JML. In T. Margaria and W. Yi, editors, *International Workshop on Tools and Algorithms for the Construction and Analysis of Systems (TACAS)*, volume 2031 of *Lecture Notes in Computer Science*, pages 299–312. Springer-Verlag, 2001.

Improving JML:
For a Safer and More Effective Language

Patrice Chalin

Computer Science Department, Concordia University, Canada
chalin@cs.concordia.ca
www.cs.concordia.ca/~faculty/chalin

Abstract. An unusually high number of published JML specifications are invalid or inconsistent, including cases from the security critical area of smart card applications. We claim that these specification errors are due to a mismatch between user expectations and the current JML semantics of expressions over numeric types. At the heart of the problem is JML's language design decision to assign to arithmetic operators the same semantics as in Java. Consequently, JML arithmetic is bounded in precision and more importantly loss of precision occurs stealthily. After a short discussion of JML language design goals and objectives, we introduce JMLa, an adaptation of JML supporting *primitive arbitrary precision* numeric types. To support our claim that the identified specification errors are due to JML's divergence from user expectations, we demonstrate that the invalidities and inconsistencies disappear under JMLa semantics with either no, or minor syntactic changes to the specifications. Other advantages of JMLa are illustrated including safety—how it allows an automated static checker like ESC/Java to detect more specification and implementation errors. We also briefly illustrate how these issues are applicable to other assertion-based languages like Eiffel.

Keywords: behavioral interface specification languages, Java Modeling Language, JML, specification language design and semantics, arbitrary precision numeric types, assertion-based languages, formal methods.

1 Introduction

The Java Modeling Language, JML, is a notation for specifying and describing the detailed design and implementation of Java modules. It is a model-based specification language offering, in particular, method specification by pre- and post-condition and class invariants to document required module behavior. JML is an open collaborative project. Gary Leavens of Iowa State University is coordinating JML language design efforts as well as the development of tools such as a JML type checker and run-time assertion-checker compiler. An Extended Static Checker, ESC/Java, developed at the Compaq Systems Research Center, uses a subset of JML to automatically carry out the (partial) verification of Java code based on its JML specifications. Also, the complete formal verification of Java modules can be achieved using the LOOP tool, from the University of Nijmegen. The LOOP tool can be used to automatically translate Java modules and their corresponding JML specifications into the language of the Prototype Verification System (PVS) [Owre96], an interactive theorem prover. PVS is then used to carry out the correctness proofs [Leavens+00]. Other tools that process JML specifications are described at JMLspecs.org.

JML is the product of over two decades of research in the area of Behavioral Interface Specification Language (BISL) design. The main goal driving its evolution has been to explore ways of creating a BISL that is both *practical* and *effective* [LBR02]. This paper focuses on an issue that is fundamental to most design specification languages: support for arbitrary precision integers and reals. This is in contrast to the programming language *approximations* to these numeric types. At the heart of the problem addressed in this paper is the JML design decision to assign to arithmetic operators the same semantics as in Java. Consequently, JML arithmetic is bounded in precision and more importantly, loss of precision occurs stealthily. As will be explained in Section 2, JML does offer support for arbitrary precision integers by means of the JMLInfiniteInteger model class, but use of such a class results in verbose specifications that rapidly become unclear and difficult to understand.

The main contributions of this paper are:
- A proposed refinement of the JML language design goals into specific objectives (Section 3).
- A proposed change to the language consisting of the added support for primitive arbitrary precision numeric types \bigint and \real (Section 4)[1]. In this paper, we will call this new version of the language JMLa.
- An illustration of how JML currently fails to meet its design goals and objectives. This is achieved by presenting a selection of recently published JML specifications that are invalid or inconsistent under the current JML semantics (Section 5).
- An illustration of how JMLa better meets the JML design goals and objectives (Section 5). In particular, we show how JMLa: better matches user expectations, allows simpler specifications to be written and, gives ESC/Java the opportunity to detect more errors.

1.1 Significance of the Research Results

All of the cases of invalid or inconsistent specifications reported in Section 5 are from conference proceedings, books, or the main JML reference document. Hence, the authors and reviewers of these specifications certainly had confidence in their accuracy. We claim that these are not simply cases of erroneous specifications, but rather that they are an indication of the mismatch between the current JML semantics and the meaning specification readers and writers expect. We believe that JMLa better matches user expectations. To support our claim, we demonstrate that the invalidity and inconsistency of the cases disappear under JMLa semantics with either no syntactic changes or minor syntactic changes to the specifications. We also illustrate other benefits of JMLa—including safety, i.e. how it allows ESC/Java to detect more errors.

---

[1] The need for slash characters in the names will also be explained in Section 0.

We believe it urgent to correct the JML language issues raised in this paper as the JML user base is increasing. Most importantly, it is being used in security-critical domains. For example, JML has been used for over two years as part of the VerifiCard project; this project's goal is to provide tools for the development of reliable Java Card based smart cards [BvdBJ02]. Of the cases discussed in Section 5, there are four published research results from the VerifiCard project—including one specification whose correctness is said to have been formally verified using the LOOP tool and PVS.

1.2 Overview

After a glance at JML's ancestry we take a closer look at its language design subgoals and the design decisions that ensued (Section 2). We then supplement these subgoals with a list of language design objectives inspired and partly adapted from those commonly used in the design of programming languages (Section 3). We introduce JMLa (Section 4) and the problematic JML specifications along with their resolution in JMLa (Sections 5). Finally, we discuss related work and conclusions (Sections 6 and 7).

2 JML Language Design Goals and Design Choices

In this section we will be examining the language design subgoals of JML. To help us better understand the motivation behind the creation of these subgoals, we will consider the BISL languages that preceded JML, but before doing so we briefly review the nature of a BISL.

By definition, a BISL is tightly coupled to a particular programming language since its purpose is to allow developers to specify modules written in that programming language. A behavioral interface specification is a description of a module consisting of two main parts [Wing87]:

- an *interface*, that captures language specific elements that are exported by the module, such as field and method signatures;
- a *behavior*—as well as other properties and constraints—of the elements described in the interface.

Prior to JML, the main BISLs were members of the Larch family of languages of which the two most notable members were Larch/C++ and LCL, the Larch/C interface specification language. A key characteristic of Larch is its two-tiered approach. The *shared* tier contains specifications written in the *Larch Shared Language* (LSL). These shared tier specifications, called traits, define multisorted first-order theories. The *interface* tier contains specifications written in a Larch interface language. Each interface language is specialized for use with a particular programming language, but all interface languages make use of LSL to express module behavior [GH93]. Unfortunately, the Larch languages were not widely adopted. One of the main reasons that has been cited is that the overhead of having to learn and use the Larch Shared Language is too large. Larch has nonetheless successfully given rise to *Splint*, an extended static checker for C currently in use by industry [EL02] and, a next generation of BISLs of which JML is a first instance.

JML inherits from Larch/C++ its general style of specification; the most important inherited language features are [LBR02]

- method specification through preconditions, postconditions and a frame axiom,
- model variables (fields) [Leino95].

As previously stated, JML's design has been guided by the overall goal that it be both practical and effective (**G0**). The JML Preliminary Design document further identifies these subgoals [LBR02]:

(**G1**) JML must be able to document the interfaces and behavior of existing Java software without change (regardless of the analysis and design methods used to create it).
(**G2**) JML should be readily understandable by Java programmers, including those with only standard mathematical training.
(**G3**) The language definition should be such that a formal semantics can be given and the language must be amenable to tool support.

While JML has directly inherited the most successful features of Larch, the following language design choice clearly demarcates it from its Larch predecessors [LBR02]:

(**D1**) Inspired by Eiffel [Meyer92], JML expressions are defined as an extension to side-effect free Java expressions[2]. Any expression that is valid in both languages is deemed to have the same meaning in both languages.

Hence, in JML the equivalent of the two Larch tiers have been merged. How then does one express in JML the mathematical theories that were codified in the Larch shared tier? By making use of the JML counterparts to Java interfaces and classes: *model* interfaces and *model* classes. These model interfaces and classes have essentially the same semantics as their Java counterparts but are used as an aide in writing specifications; i.e. they need not actually be implemented.

As a corollary to (**D1**), we note that

(**D2**) Support in JML for arbitrary precision integers is provided by means of the `JMLInfiniteInteger` model interface that documents methods somewhat like those of the standard Java `BigInteger` class.

We will illustrate use of `JMLInfiniteInteger` in Section 5.1. Note that currently there is no support for arbitrary precision floating-point numbers in JML.

3 Language Design Objectives

Designing a good computer language is a challenge. As a designer, one strives to achieve the right balance among often opposing design objectives. The challenge is

---

[2] Side-effect free expressions are called "pure" expressions in JML.

particularly great for a BISL designer because a BISL is at the junction of two kinds of languages with significantly different purposes: the BISL, a *specification* language, and its underlying *programming* language. We follow Parnas and others in making the important distinction between behavioral software *descriptions* and their *specifications*. A behavioral specification is a statement of *requirements*, i.e. it is an abstraction that captures the *essence* of an entity's behavior [Parnas01]. As BISL designers, we believe that it is particularly important to keep this distinction in mind.

We propose to evaluate JML and JMLa against the current JML design goals as well as the key language design objectives presented next. As an *overall objective* we believe that JML should be

- Effective for its intended purposes, i.e. it should:
  - Make it as easy as possible for developers to read and write *specifications* (in the sense of the term 'specification' previously given).
  - Be usable for run-time checking of assertions (including preconditions, postconditions and invariants).
  - Be usable for efficient extended static checking to detect as may errors as possible.
  - Be usable in the formal verification of Java modules.

(JML's run-time assertion checker compiler, ESC/Java and the LOOP tool currently support the last three bullets, respectively.) In support of Effectiveness, we define the following objectives—the first four have been excerpted and adapted from a text on programming language design [Finkel96]:

- Safe. Semantic errors should be detectable, preferably using (extended) static checking.
- Simple. There should be as few basic concepts as possible. JML building upon Java, it should introduce as few new concepts as possible.
- Clear. Specification statements should be easy to read and understand.
- Uniform. Basic concepts should be applied consistently and universally.
- Match User Expectations, or to state this in another way, it should not "violate user expectations" [MC96].

The design decision to keep the semantics of JML and Java expressions the same, i.e. (D1), certainly maximizes Simplicity. It also seems like the most obvious way to make the notation readily understandable to Java programmers (G2), but, as we shall illustrate in Section 5, (D1) has had some unanticipated consequences.

4 JMLa

4.1 Definition

Syntactically, JMLa is identical to JML except for the introduction of two keywords \bigint and \real. Use of slash characters at the start of JML keywords is necessary for the support of language design goal (G1). The absence of slash characters would prevent us from writing specifications for existing Java code that made use of identifiers with the names `bigint` or `real`.

JMLa semantics differ from JML semantics not only because of the addition of the two new primitive types, but also in the meaning assigned to arithmetic expressions. In summary, JMLa semantics ensure that by *default*, numeric *operations* that can result in overflow are performed over arbitrary precision types. As is typical in Java, cast expressions can be used to override this default (and thus identify that the JML semantics apply). For example, unary plus has the same semantics in JMLa, JML and Java. Unary minus, on the other hand, will first promote an integer operand to `\bigint`, negate the operand value, and yield a result of type `\bigint`. Given that `i` is an `int`, then `-i` will be of type `\bigint` whereas `-(int)i` will denote an application of the JML (Java) unary minus and thus will be of type `int`. Similarly, `i+i` will be of type `\bigint`, and `i+(int)i` or, `(int)i+i` will be of type `int`. To preserve JML and Java semantics to the maximum extent possible, JMLa allows constant expressions to retain their JML semantics (regardless of the operators used) provided that at no point in the evaluation an overflow occurs. Therefore `-1+3` will be of type `int`, but `-2147483648` would be of type `\bigint`.

The semantics of JMLa and JML differ for at most the following operators: unary `-`, binary `+`, `-`, `*`, `/` and `%`. Since bit operators treat their operands as bit vectors, they are excluded from the list. We explain the semantics of JMLa relative to the *differences* between it and JML (and hence Java) by following the organization and section numbering of the second edition of the Java Language Specification [GJSB00].

4.2 Primitive Types and Values

The type `\bigint` is a primitive arbitrary precision integral type and `\real` is a primitive arbitrary precision floating-point type.

5.1.2 Widening Primitive Conversion

Widening primitive conversions are also supported from any integral type to `\bigint` and from any numeric type to `\real`. Widening primitive conversions preserve values exactly.

5.1.3 Narrowing Primitive Conversion

Narrowing primitive conversion shall also be supported from `\bigint` to any other integral type as well as from `\real` to any other numeric type. Like in Java, "a narrowing conversion may lose information about the overall magnitude of a numeric value and may also lose precision."

Conversion from `\bigint`. For an integer i, find a natural number m greater than 64 for which $|i| < 2^m$, and let j be the m-bit signed two's-complement representation of i. In this case, a narrowing conversion of i to an integral type T simply discards all but the n lowest order bits of j, where n is the number of bits used to represent type T.

Conversion from `\real` *to* `\bigint`. In a narrowing conversion of a real r, r is rounded to the nearest *integer* value (by rounding toward zero).

Conversion from \real to a (primitive numeric) type other than \bigint. In a narrowing conversion of a real *r*, the value *r* is first rounded to the nearest double value *d*, unless *r* is beyond the range of values of doubles in which case *d* will be Double.NEGATIVE_INFINITY or Double.POSITIVE_INFINITY as appropriate. To complete the narrowing conversion of *r* one applies to *d* the Java rules for narrowing conversion of doubles.

5.6 Numeric Promotions

5.6.1a Unary Numeric Promotion

When an operator applies unary numeric promotion to its operand (which must denote a value of a numeric type) the following rules apply, in order, using widening conversion (§5.1.2) to convert the operand as necessary:
- If the operand is not a cast expression and it is of a floating-point type, then it is converted to \real.
- Otherwise, if the operand is not a cast expression, then it is converted to \bigint.
- Otherwise, if the operand is of compile-time type byte, short, or char, it is converted to int.
- Otherwise, the operand remains as is and is not converted.

In any case, value set conversion (§5.1.8) is then applied.

5.6.2a Binary Numeric Promotion

When an operator applies binary numeric promotion to a pair of operands, each of which must denote a value of a numeric type, the following rules apply, in order, using widening conversion (§5.1.2) to convert operands as necessary:
- If neither operand is a cast expression and either is of a floating-point type, then both are converted to \real.
- Otherwise, if neither operand is a cast expression, then both are converted to \bigint.
- Otherwise, if either operand is of type \bigint, the other is converted to \bigint.
- Otherwise, if either operand is of type \real, the other is converted to \real.
- Otherwise, if either operand is of type double, the other is converted to double.
- Otherwise, if either operand is of type float, the other is converted to float.
- Otherwise, if either operand is of type long, the other is converted to long.
- Otherwise, both operands are converted to type int.

After the type conversion, if any, value set conversion (§5.1.8) is applied to each operand.

15 Expressions

15.15.4 Unary Minus Operator -

If the operand is not a constant expression, or it is a constant expression whose value cannot be represented by a long, then unary promotion is to be performed according to §5.6.1a. (Otherwise, promotion is carried out as described in §5.6.1).

15.17 Multiplicative Operators

Binary promotion for *, / and % is to be performed according to §5.6.2a unless the multiplicative expression is a constant expression whose value can be represented by a long (in which case promotion is performed according to §5.6.2).

> **15.18.2 Additive Operators (+ and -) for Numeric Types**
> Binary promotion is to be performed according to §5.6.2a unless the additive expression is a constant expression whose value can be represented by a `long` (in which case promotion is performed according to §5.6.2).
>
> **15.10 Array Creation Expressions**
> Dimension *expressions* can be of type `int`, `long` or `\bigint`. Hence, it remains a proof obligation to demonstrate that a dimension expression value is in the range 0 to `Integer.MAX_VALUE`. *Arrays still contain at most* `Integer.MAX_VALUE` elements, and the type of `length` is `int`.
>
> **15.13 Array Access Expressions**
> Index expression can be of type `int`, `long` or `\bigint`.

Thus, in effect, JMLa offers implicit promotion to `\bigint` and `\real` (under the circumstances described above). Although JMLa looses out on **Simplicity** when compared to JML (due to the introduction of new primitive types), it more than makes up for this loss by better meeting the other design objectives as we shall demonstrate in the Section 5.

4.2 Supporting Class `JMLMath`

We also define a model class named `org.jmlspecs.lang.JMLMath` that, in particular, shall provide methods like those of `java.lang.Math` but that are defined over `\bigint`'s and `\real`'s.

5 Cases and Consequences

In the subsections that follow we present seven cases of recently published JML specifications. All specifications, but one, are invalid or inconsistent under the current JML semantics. The one case with valid specifications (Section 0) is used to reinforce the idea that JMLa semantics are **Safer** and more **Uniform**.

5.1 Integer Square Root

The example in this section also serves as a basic introduction to method specifications in JML.

5.1.1 Case Description (Invalid and Inconsistent Specification)
The JML Preliminary Design document was the first, and it remains the principal document describing JML. First published in June of 1998, the document's opening example is a specification of an integer square root method like the one given in Fig. 1 [LBR02]. The specification requires that a caller invoke the method with a nonnegative argument y, and in return, the method ensures that it will yield a

```
/*@ public normal_behavior
  @   requires y >= 0;
  @   ensures
  @     \result * \result <= y &&
  @     y < (Math.abs(\result)+1)
  @          * (Math.abs(\result)+1);
  @*/
public static int isqrt(int y)
```

```
/*@ public normal_behavior
  @   requires y >= 0;
  @   ensures Math.abs(\result) <= y
  @     && \result * \result <= y
  @     && y < (Math.abs(\result)+1)
  @          * (Math.abs(\result)+1);
  @*/
public static int isqrt(int y)
```

Fig. 1. JML specification of `isqrt`

Fig. 2. "Corrected" JML specification of `isqrt`

resulting value, r, such that $r^2 \le y < (|r|+1)^2$. The current definition of JML states that the expressions in the `requires` and `ensures` clauses are to be interpreted using the semantics of Java. At first sight, the specification may seem accurate but, under JML semantics, the specification allows `isqrt` to return (`Integer.MAX_VALUE` – 5) / 2, for example, when `y` is 1. This is due to Java's bounded integer arithmetic: e.g. the evaluation of `\result * \result` "overflows".

This unexpected situation is certainly not obvious on a first reading of the specification (violates Clarity[3]). Although rummaging through the Java language and API documentation *may* help clarify the issue, writing a small Java test program to print the value of the `ensures` clause expression is a quick and sure way to confirm it[4]. The anomaly having been identified, the `ensures` clause of the specification was strengthened, in a subsequent edition of the JML Preliminary Design document, by adding the following conjunct: `Math.abs(\result) <= y`, see Fig. 2. However, the "corrected" specification suffers from a similar anomaly in that it allows `Integer.MIN_VALUE` to be returned when `y` is 0. Surprisingly, these invalid specifications of `isqrt` remained uncontested for over four years even though they were published in the main JML reference document. After the author signaled this problem with the specification of Fig. 2 [Chalin03], it was again published in a revised form, but problems remain. We note that all of the published versions of the JML `isqrt` specification are actually inconsistent. For example, when `y` is `Integer.MAX_VALUE`, the `ensures` clause is unsatisfiable (even though a valid answer of type `int` exists, namely 46340). It should not be this difficult to get such a simple specification right. From all of this specification churn, we deduce that JML experts and non-experts alike "read" into the specifications a meaning other than that provided by the current JML semantics (violates User Expectations). We believe that JML users generally think in terms of arbitrary precision arithmetic.

Since the problems in the specifications of `isqrt` were due to the use of bounded integer arithmetic, it would seem reasonable to attempt to rewrite the specification using JML's current language mechanism for arbitrary precision integers, i.e. the `JMLInfiniteInteger` model interface. Fig. 3 is a version of the `isqrt` specification that makes use of `JMLInfiniteInteger`. The intent of the

---

[3] Points in the text that give evidence of the violation of a language design objective will be indicated like this.

[4] Having to write *code* to confirm the *meaning* of such a simple *specification* seems counter intuitive.

```
/*@ public normal_behavior
  @   requires y >= 0;
  @   ensures
  @     (new JMLInfiniteInteger(\result)).abs().compareTo(
  @             new JMLInfiniteInteger(y)) <= 0
  @     && (new JMLInfiniteInteger(\result)).multiply(
  @             new JMLInfiniteInteger(\result)).compareTo(
  @                 new JMLInfiniteInteger(y)) <= 0
  @     && (new JMLInfiniteInteger(y).compareTo(
  @             (new JMLInfiniteInteger(\result)).abs().
  @                 add(JMLInfiniteInteger.ONE).
  @                     multiply((new JMLInfiniteInteger(\result)).abs().
  @                         add(JMLInfiniteInteger.ONE))) < 0;
  @*/
public static int isqrt(int y)
```

Fig. 3. Specification of isqrt using JMLInfiniteInteger

```
/*@ public normal_behavior
  @   requires y >= 0;
  @   ensures JMLMath.abs(\result) == JMLMath.floor(JMLMath.sqrt(y));
  @*/
public static int isqrt(int y)
```

Fig. 4. JMLa specification of isqrt using jmlspecs.lang.JMLMath

specification is obviously lost due to its verbosity, and it becomes clear why JML developers avoid using JMLInfiniteInteger (violates **Effectiveness**).

5.1.2 JMLa: Matching User Expectations

Under the semantics of JMLa, the original specification of isqrt given in Fig. 1 and its revised forms (in Fig. 2 and [LBR02]) are valid and consistent (Matching User Expectations).

5.1.3 JMLa: Simpler, Clearer, More Effective

The integer square root method has been used as an opening example for presenting BISLs for over a decade. Invariably, the method has been described simply as: an integer approximation to the square root of y [GH93, LCPP, Leavens02a]. Being slightly more specific about the nature of the approximation, we can express our needed result with the mathematical formula: $\pm \lfloor \sqrt{y} \rfloor$. Using suitable methods from JMLMath we obtain the specification for isqrt given in Fig. 4, which we believe to be **Simple, Clear and Effective**.

Can we achieve the same degree of clarity with JML? At best, we can write the following JML ensures clause expression by assuming the existence of a model class, JMLInfiniteReal, which axiomatizes real numbers:

```
ensures (new JMLInfiniteInteger(\result)).abs().compareTo(
            JMLInfiniteReal.floor(JMLInfiniteReal.sqrt(y))) == 0;
```

This is less clear than the JMLa version, but more importantly, the axiomatization of reals numbers by means of JMLInfiniteReal would most likely require special provisions beyond the current JML semantics of model classes. (In JMLa, like in PVS, we can get around this difficulty by defining the semantics using a metalanguage rather than in the language of JMLa.)

5.2 Decimal Smart Card Class (Two Cases)

5.2.1 Description of Cases (Inconsistent Specifications)

Smart card applets[5] have been identified as ideal candidates for the application of formal methods [KP03]. Two of the main reasons are that smart card applets are relatively small (therefore tractable) and, security concerns justify the extra effort required in applying rigorous or formal methods. In this section we comment on two recently published case studies in the specification and verification of part of a commercial smart card applet. The subject of the studies was `Decimal`, a small but key class of the Java Card Electronic Purse applet by Gemplus [Gemplus]. Although the authors of both studies began from the same `Decimal` class source, they proceeded independently to annotate it with JML specifications based on the available informal documentation. The studies differ in their approach to verification.

In one case, Cataño and Huisman, performed verification using ESC/Java [CH02]. The main benefit of ESC/Java is that verification is fully automated, but as can be expected, its verification is both unsound and incomplete. Like other similar tools (e.g. Splint [EL02]), it has nonetheless proven to be quite useful in detecting program errors. In the other case study, Breunesse *et. al.* made use of the LOOP tool and the PVS theorem prover to perform a complete and formal verification of the correctness of the code relative to its specification [BvdBJ02]. The LOOP tool was used to automatically translate Java code and JML specifications into the language of PVS. Correctness proofs were then performed within PVS using specially developed proof rules and tactics. In light of the complementary strengths of these tools, it has been suggested that they be used together by first applying ESC/Java to identify easily detectable (and often common) errors, and then subjecting the most critical aspects of the code to formal verification using the LOOP tool and PVS [BvdBJ02].

Consider the `Decimal` specification excerpt given in Fig. 5. An instance of `Decimal` represents a fixed-point number with three digits of precision after the decimal point. Such a fixed-point number is implemented by two `short` fields: `intPart` for the integer part and `decPart` denoting the number of thousandths (e.g. 3 and 142, respectively, for the number 3.142). Note that the specification of `oppose` is inconsistent: i.e. there is a situation that satisfies its precondition (which is trivial since it is true) for which the postcondition is not satisfiable. This situation arises when `\old(intPart)`—the value of `intPart` in the pre-state, i.e. before `oppose` is called—is equal to `Short.MIN_VALUE`, in which case the first conjunct of the `ensures` clause would be evaluated as follows:

- `intPart == -\old(intPart)`
- `intPart == -(-32768`$_{\text{short}}$`)`   substitution of the value of `\old(intPart)`, `Short.MIN_VALUE`.
- `intPart == -(-32768`$_{\text{int}}$`)`   *numeric promotion* from `short` to `int` (due to unary minus semantics).
- `intPart == 32768`$_{\text{int}}$ application of unary minus (`int`).
- `(int)intPart == 32768`$_{\text{int}}$ *numeric promotion* of `intPart` from `short` to `int` (due to `==`).

There is no value that `intPart` can have that, after a widening primitive conversion to `int`, would make it equal to 32768 since `Short.MAX_VALUE` is 32767.

---

[5] A smart card application is called an applet.

```
class Decimal {
  /*@ spec_public @*/ private short intPart, decPart;
  ...
  /*@ invariant PRECISION == 1000 &&
    @   -PRECISION < decPart && decPart < PRECISION;
    @
    @ normal_behavior
    @   requires    true;
    @   modifiable  intPart, decPart;
    @   ensures     intPart == -\old(intPart) &&
    @               decPart == -\old(decPart) ...;
    @*/
  public Decimal oppose()
  ...
}
```

Fig. 5. `Decimal` class specification excerpt

Interestingly, ESC/Java reports the possibility that the post condition of `oppose` may fail to be satisfied when `intPart` is `Short.MIN_VALUE` in the pre-state, but Breunesse *et. al.* make no mention of the problem being identified during the formal verification processing using LOOP and PVS. This may indicate that the LOOP semantic embedding of JML and/or Java into PVS does not accurately reflect the current JML or Java semantics, respectively.

5.2.2 JMLa: Safer and More Uniform Semantics

Cataño and Huisman report that the use of ESC/Java allowed several errors to be detected. Of these errors, some[6] were detected only because `intPart` (and `decPart`) were declared to be of type `short`. As `int` is supported by the Java Card language [Sun02], it is conceivable that `intPart` could have been declared to be of type `int`. Consider, as we did previously, the evaluation in JML of the first conjunct of the `ensures` clause of `oppose` but assuming now that the type of `intPart` is `int`. In this situation:

- `intPart == -\old(intPart)`
- `intPart == -(-2147483648`$_{int}$`)`   value of `\old(intPart)`, namely `Integer.MIN_VALUE`.
- `intPart == -2147483648`$_{int}$ application of unary minus[7].

Note that there are no widening primitive conversions. It is actually the presence of widening conversions that allowed ESC/Java to detect an anomaly when `intPart` was of type `short`.

Under JMLa semantics, even with `intPart` declared to be of type `int` we have:

- `intPart == -\old(intPart)`
- `intPart == -(-2147483648`$_{int}$`)`   value of `\old(intPart)`.
- `intPart == -(-2147483648`$_{\backslash bigint}$`)`   *numeric promotion* from int to `\bigint`.
- `intPart == 2147483648`$_{\backslash bigint}$ application of unary minus.
- `(\bigint)intPart == 2147483648`$_{\backslash bigint}$ *numeric promotion*.

---

[6] For example, the specification of `oppose` given in Fig. 5 and that of `round` given in [CH02].

[7] Note that `-Integer.MIN_VALUE` is equal to `Integer.MIN_VALUE`.

```
class Decimal {
 private short intPart, decPart;
 ...
/*@ public model \real decimal;
  @ invariant decimal == round(decimal)
  @           decimal == intPart + decPart / (\real)PRECISION;
  @
  @  public normal_behavior
  @    ensures \result ==
  @        JMLMath.nearestInteger(r * PRECISION) / (\real)PRECISION;
  @ public static model pure \real round(\real r);
  @
  @  public normal_behavior
  @    ensures \result == Short.MIN_VALUE - 0.999 <= r &&
  @                       r <= Short.MAX_VALUE + 0.999
  @ public static model pure \real inRange(\real r);
 ...
  @ normal_behavior
  @   requires   d != null
  @              && inRange(round(decimal * d.decimal));
  @   modifiable decimal;
  @   ensures    decimal == round(\old(decimal) * d.decimal)
  @              && \result == this;
  @ also
  @ exceptional_behavior ...
  @*/
public Decimal mul(Decimal d) throws DecimalException
 ...
}
```

Fig. 6. Decimal class specification using a \real model field

As before, there is no value that intPart can have that, after a widening primitive conversion to \bigint, would make it equal to 2147483648 since Integer.MAX_VALUE is 2147483647. Hence, under JMLa semantics, ESC/Java would be as effective at detecting errors for expressions over int's (or any integral numeric type) as it is for short's or byte's. This is not the case for JML: there is a non-uniform semantics for expressions of type long or int vs. short or byte.

5.2.3 JMLa: Simpler, Clearer, More Effective

The availability of primitive arbitrary precision types allows us to write a specification for Decimal that is Simpler and Clearer than would otherwise be possible. In Fig. 6, we illustrate a version of the Decimal specification in which we have introduced a \real model field named decimal. For each Decimal instance representing a fixed-point number n, decimal will be equal to n. Hence, decimal is always rounded to the appropriate number of digits of precision (as expressed in the invariant). The model class method round makes use of the JMLMath.nearestInteger method[8]. Notice the conciseness and clarity of the specification of mul as compared to its original specification given in Fig. 7.

Although expressions such as those of the mul ensures clause of Fig. 7 may be useful as intermediate theorems to help checkers (like ESC/Java or the LOOP tool), they fail to server their purpose as *specifications* for human readers. This may

---

[8] Following the usual mathematical definition, nearestInteger(r) is easily specified as the integer nearest to its real argument r or, in the case that there are two such "nearest" integers, preference is given to the even one.

Improving JML: For a Safer and More Effective Language 453

indicate a need in JML for a language construct that would allow checker hints and/or theorems to be given. Such a construct should make it clear that these hints are not the specification.

5.3 Priority Queue

5.3.1 Case Description (Inconsistent Specification)

This section's example is taken from the main JML tutorial paper [LBR99b] cited on the JMLspecs.org documentation page—the sources for this example are also packaged with the JML distribution. Fig. 8 is an excerpt from the specification of the `PriorityQueue` class. The method of interest to our presentation is `addEntry` that will add a new `QueueEntry` to a queue. The specification of the model class `QueueEntry` is given in Fig. 9. JML model classes, like model fields and methods, need not be implemented; `QueueEntry` is used as an aid in specifying the behavior of methods like `addEntry` of the `PriorityQueue` class.

```
/*@ behavior
  @   requires d != null;
  @   modifiable intPart, decPart,
  @     DecimalException.instance, DecimalException.instance.ttype;
  @   ensures intPart >= 0 && intPart * PRECISION + decPart ==
  @     \old(intPart) * \old(d.intPart) * PRECISION +
  @     \old(intPart) * \old(d.decPart) + \old(decPart) * \old(d.intPart)
  @     /// difficult rest-part, consisting of:
  @     /// sign of product of decimal parts
  @     (( (\old(d.decPart) >= 0 && \old(decPart) >= 0) ||
  @        (\old(d.decPart) < 0 && \old(decPart) < 0) ) ? 1 : -1) *
  @     /// thousand part of product of rounded decimal parts
  @     (( ((-100 <= \old(d.decPart) && \old(d.decPart) <= 100)
  @            /// absolute value
  @            ? ( (\old(d.decPart) >= 0)
  @                ? \old(d.decPart) : -\old(d.decPart) )
  @            /// round last digit to 0 of absolute value
  @            : (\old(d.decPart) >= 0) ? 10 * (\old(d.decPart)/10)
  @              : 10 * (-\old(d.decPart)/10) ) *
  @        ((-100 <= \old(decPart) && \old(decPart) <= 100)
  @            /// absolute value
  @            ? ( (\old(decPart) >= 0) ? \old(decPart) : -\old(decPart) )
  @            /// round last digit to 0 of absolute value
  @            : (\old(decPart) >= 0) ? 10 * (\old(decPart)/10)
  @              : 10 * (-\old(decPart)/10) ) ) / 1000) &&
  @     DecimalException.instance
  @        == \old(DecimalException.instance) &&
  @     (DecimalException.instance != null ==>
  @        DecimalException.instance.ttype ==
  @        \old(DecimalException.instance.ttype));
  @   signals (DecimalException e) intPart < 0 && ...
  @*/
public Decimal mul(Decimal d) throws DecimalException
```

Fig. 7. Original specification of `mul(Decimal)`

Unfortunately, under JML semantics, the specification of `addEntry` is inconsistent since it is possible for it to attempt to add a new `QueueEntry` with a negative time stamp. This would violate the `QueueEntry` constructor precondition: a negative argument could arise if `largestTimeStamp()` returned `Integer.MAX_VALUE` (since `Integer.MAX_VALUE` + 1 == `Integer.MIN_VALUE` which is negative).

```
public class PriorityQueue implements ...
{ ...
/*@   public normal_behavior
  @     requires    entries.isEmpty();
  @     assignable  \nothing;
  @     ensures     \result == 0;
  @ also
  @   public normal_behavior
  @     requires    !(entries.isEmpty());
  @     assignable  \nothing;
  @     ensures(\forall QueueEntry e;
  @             entries.has(e);
  @             \result >= e.timeStamp);
  @ public pure
  @  model int largestTimeStamp();
  @*/
/*@   public normal_behavior
  @     requires argID != null
  @              && !contains(argID);
  @     assignable entries;
  @     ensures entries != null
  @     && entries.equals(
  @          \old(entries.insert(
  @             new QueueEntry(argID,
  @                argPriorityLevel,
  @                largestTimeStamp()+1))));
  @ also
  @   public exceptional_behavior ...
  @*/
public void addEntry(Object argID,
                    int argPriorityLevel)
```

Fig. 8. `PriorityQueue.jml-refined` from `org.jmlspecs.samples.jmlkluwer`[9]

```
/*@ public pure model
  @ class QueueEntry
  @    implements JMLType
  @ {
  @
  @ public Object iD;
  @ public int priorityLevel;
  @ public int timeStamp;
  @
  @ public invariant
  @   iD != null &&
  @   timeStamp >= 0;
  @
  @ public normal_behavior
  @   requires ... &&
  @     argTimeStamp >= 0;
  @   assignable ..., timeStamp;
  @   ensures ... &&
  @     timeStamp == argTimeStamp;
  @
  @ public QueueEntry(
  @   Object argID,
  @   int argLevel,
  @   int argTimeStamp);
  @ ...
  @ }
  @*/
```

Fig. 9. `QueueEntry` from `org.jmlspecs.samples.jmlkluwer`

5.3.2 JMLa: Matching User Expectation

There is no reason to place a bound on the values of time stamps as they are used solely in model classes. Therefore, changing the type of `timeStamp`, `argTimeStamp`, and `largestTimeStamp` from `int` to `\bigint` rids `PriorityQueue` of the inconsistency in the specification of `addEntry` without further modifications to the `PriorityQueue` and `QueueEntry` specifications.

---

[9] Note that the clause keywords `modifiable` and `assignable` are synonyms.

```
public /*@ pure @*/ interface Money extends JMLType
{
//@ public model instance long pennies;
...
}
```

Fig. 10. Money specification excerpt

5.4 MoneyOps Interface

5.4.1 Case Description (Invalid Specification)

This section highlights issues that arise in other specification taken from the JML Preliminary Design document [LBR02]. Fig. 10 contains a very short excerpt from the Money interface specification; the only specification feature that is relevant to our discussion is the `long pennies` model field. MoneyOps (Fig. 11) is a subinterface of Money that defines, among other methods, addition of Money's by means of the plus method. The precondition of plus is defined in terms of the can_add model method, which in turn, makes use of inRange. Clearly inRange is intended to be true when its argument can be represented by a long. Unfortunately, doubles have too few digits of precision to be able to represent all values of type long, thus, for example inRange(Long.MAX_VALUE - 100) is false when it should be true. Hence, under the current JML semantics, the specification of plus does not express the required behavior (failing to Match User Expectations).

5.4.2 JMLa: Matching User Expectations

The specification of plus can be easily made to match user expectations by changing the all occurrences of double, in the specifications of inRange, can_add and plus, to either \bigint or \real.

```
public /*@ pure @*/ interface MoneyOps extends ...
{
  /*@ public normal_behavior
    @    old double epsilon = 1.0;
    @    assignable \nothing;
    @    ensures \result <==> Long.MIN_VALUE + epsilon < d
    @                         && d < Long.MAX_VALUE - epsilon;
    @ public model boolean inRange(double d);
    @
    @ public normal_behavior
    @    requires m2!= null;
    @    assignable \nothing;
    @    ensures \result <==> inRange((double) pennies + m2.pennies);
    @ public model boolean can_add(Money m2);
    @
    @ public normal_behavior
    @    requires m2 != null && can_add(m2);
    @    assignable \nothing;
    @    ensures \result != null
    @            && \result.pennies == this.pennies + m2.pennies;
    @*/
  public MoneyOps plus(Money m2);
  ...
}
```

Fig. 11. MoneyOps specification excerpt

```
/*@ public behavior
  @   requires src != null &&  srcOff >= 0 &&   srcOff+length <= src.length
  @            && dest != null && destOff >= 0 && destOff+length <= dest.lengt
  @            && length >= 0;
  @   assignable dest[destOff..destOff+length-1], ...;
  @   ensures (\forall byte i; 0 <= i && i < length
  @                ==> dest[destOff+i] == \old(src[srcOff+i]));
  @   ...
  @ also ...
  @*/
  public static final short arrayCopy(
    byte[] src,  short   srcOff, byte[] dest, short destOff, short    length)
  throws ...;
```

Fig. 12. javacard.framework.Util class specification excerpt

5.5 Java Card API Specifications

5.5.1 Case Description ("Fragile" Validity and Consistency)

In this section we illustrate how the non-uniform semantics of JML numeric expressions leads to specifications that have precarious validity or consistency. Poll, van den Berg and Jacobs have contributed to improving the documentation of Java Card API classes by specifying them with JML [PvdBJ00, PvdBJ01]. Consider the specification given in Fig. 12 of the arrayCopy method from javacard.framework.Util class [HP02]. It would seem quite reasonable for this method to be adapted[10] to support the copying of segments of arrays that are larger than 32K bytes—i.e. concretely, to have source and destination array offsets as well as length be of type int rather than short. Unfortunately, under JML semantics, making this likely type change renders the specification inconsistent: for example, sufficiently large values of destOff and length will satisfy the precondition but will result in the ensures clause subexpression destOff+i being negative in dest[destOff+i]. Of course, it might be possible to rewrite the arrayCopy specification to avoid this inconsistency, but no such rewriting is necessary under JMLa.

5.5.2 JMLa: Simpler, More Uniform Semantics

Under JMLa semantics, the arrayCopy specification is valid regardless of the particular integral types used in the declaration of srcOff, destOff and length. This would seem reasonable since the essence of the behavior of this method is to copy array segments, and this should be independent of the particular integral type assigned to the method arguments.

---

[10] Either within the same class, at some point in the future when Java Card hardware limitations have been relaxed, or when copied to another class to be reused outside the context of Java Card applets.

5.6 Other Cases

There are other cases (e.g. from [RL00, PvdBJ01]) of invalid, inconsistent or "fragile" JML specifications with characteristics similar to those just presented. Likewise, JMLa semantics rids these other specifications of their invalidity or inconsistency with little or no syntactic changes to the specifications. We believe that the cases selected for detailed presentation in this paper provide a sufficient sampling.

6 Related Work

6.1 Languages Supporting Primitive Arbitrary Precision Numeric Types

Several computer languages and tools provide basic language support for arbitrary precision integers including:
- **Specification languages**. Support for the integers is fundamental to most design specification languages, including:
  - Model based and algebraic languages such as B, OBJ, VDM, and Z [Bowen03].
  - **BISLs** such as Larch, via the Larch Shared Language, and Extended ML (EML), via its underlying programming language, ML.
- **Functional programming languages**: e.g. ML , Haskell , and various flavors of Lisp.
- **Tools**: e.g. proof tools such as PVS, HOL and Isabelle as well as numeric and symbolic mathematics systems such as Mathematica and Maple.

Extended ML (EML), is a BISL for Standard ML that adopts an approach similar to JML in that, as the name implies, EML is defined as an extension to ML and hence it subsumes its semantics—with the exception of imperative features [KST97]. EML does not suffer from the difficulties of JML described in this paper since ML integers are of arbitrary precision. It is certainly an interesting prospect to consider adding the equivalent of \bigint to Java instead of JML. Basic support for real numbers is most common in general design specification languages (such as those mentioned above) and less common in other languages. Symbolic mathematics packages often provide arbitrary precision rational numbers.

Certainly the fact that several other specification languages and tools offer basic support for arbitrary precision integers does not, in itself, justify their addition to JML. But, in this paper we have presented evidence that this is what JML users generally expect and hence, JML should support primitive arbitrary precision numeric types.

6.2 Assertion Languages

The problem highlighted in this paper can be generalized to other assertion-based languages such as Eiffel. In Eiffel, we speak of contracts rather than specifications. An Eiffel class contract consists of method contracts (given by means of requires and ensures clauses) as well as class invariants. Eiffel contracts are generally less semantically "rich" than JML specifications since all expressions in contracts are

Eiffel expressions, and hence required to be executable. Consequently, it has been more difficult to find inconsistent or invalid Eiffel contracts, but they exist. As a simple example consider the contract for the abs functions from any one of the classes INTEGER_8, INTEGER_16, INTEGER, INTEGER_64, e.g.

```
abs: INTEGER_8 is
   ensure
      non_negative: Result >= 0
      same_absolute_value: (Result = item) or (Result = -item)
```

This contract is inconsistent since 'non_negative' cannot be satisfied when applied to INTEGER_8.Max_value. At this point, it is unclear to us how the solution presented here could be generalized to Eiffel.

6.3 Semantics

As previously mentioned, the LOOP tool translates JML specifications into the specification language of PVS by a "shallow" semantic embedding. Parts of the definition of this embedding have been published (e.g. [vdBJ01, JP01]) but they differ from the informal semantics of JML—as has been alluded to at the end of Section 5.2.1. It would seem that the semantics of JML expressions as treated in the LOOP tool more closely resembles the proposed semantics for JMLa. A more complete description of the semantic embedding is to be published soon as a Ph.D. thesis from the University of Nijmegen.

The work described in this paper has been inspired by our previous work on the semantics of LCL, the Larch/C interface specification language [CGR96]. In another report, we provide an exploration of language design alternatives for the JML support of arbitrary precision numeric types. In this same report, we provide a preliminary formal semantics of JMLa expressions as well as a comparison of the formal semantics of JML, JMLa, Larch/C++ and LCL [Chalin03].

7 Conclusions and Future Work

We believe that BISLs are one of the best ways of integrating formal methods into industrial practice [Chalin03]. Partial evidence of this is the increasing industrial use of Extended Static Checkers like Splint [EL02] and ESC/Java [Flanagan+02]. This paper focuses on the treatment of numeric types and the semantics of expressions over these types. This issue is fundamental to design specification languages since practically all specifications make use of numeric types. Although programming languages make the necessary compromise of providing support for bounded numeric types only, we have shown how a similar decision for a BISL like JML goes against user expectations. As a consequence we were able to illustrate several published JML specifications that were invalid or inconsistent. Seeking to better meet user expectations, we have defined a variant of JML called JMLa that has support for primitive arbitrary precision numeric types, and we have shown how

- JMLa semantics more closely match user expectations by demonstrating how invalid or inconsistent JML specifications recover their validity and consistency, when interpreted under JMLa with little or no changes to the specifications.
- JMLa can be used to write simpler, and clearer specifications.
- The meaning of JMLa specifications can be independent of the particular choice of numeric types of fields and variables (as it should be since, e.g. method specifications are meant to express *essential* method behavior which often is independent of field and variable types).
- ESC/Java will be able to detect more errors under JMLa semantics than it currently can for JML.

These points are particularly important as we witness the increased use of JML, particularly in security critical areas like smart cards. Of course these benefits come at the cost of a slightly more complex semantics and an increased departure from Java semantics. We believe though, that the benefits of JMLa outweigh its disadvantages.

In collaboration with other JML project partners we have begun transitioning ESC/Java and the JML tools to supporting JMLa. Preliminary results are encouraging since we have been able to use the tools to identify over a dozen other inconsistent method specifications in the JML model classes alone. The impact of supporting JMLa on the run-time assertion-checker compiler will be more significant. Although checking of \bigint expressions can be conveniently implemented using Java's BigInteger class we will still only be able to approximate \real's using, say, BigDecimal.

We will also pursue our analysis of JML as other issues related to bounded vs. unbounded "data types" (such as arrays, sets and sequences) need to be explored further to ensure that there are no unsuspected consequences as there have been for numeric types. Our work on the language analysis and formalization of the semantics of JML will be pursued so as to progressively include more language elements.

Acknowledgments

We thank the anonymous referees, as well as Gary Leavens, Erik Poll and Peter Grogono for helpful comments on earlier revisions of this work.

References

[Bowen03] Jonathan Bowen, WWW Virtual Library: Formal Methods, http://www.afm.sbu.ac.uk. February 2003.

[BvdBJ02] C.-B. Breunesse, J. van den Berg, and B. Jacobs. Specifying and verifying a decimal representation in Java for smart cards. In H. Kirchner and C. Ringeissen, editors, *AMAST'2002*, LNCS, pp. 304-318. Springer Verlag, 2002. Decimal class specification is available at www.cs.kun.nl/indexes/~ceesb/decimal/Decimal.java.

[CGR96] Patrice Chalin, Peter Grogono, and T. Radhakrishnan. "Identification of and solutions to shortcomings of LCL, a Larch/C interface specification language". In Marie-Claude Gaudel and James Woodcock, editors, *FME'96: Industrial Benefit and Advances in Formal Methods*, LNCS 1051, pages 385–404. Formal Methods Europe, Springer, March 1996.

[CH02] N. Cataño and M. Huisman. Formal specification of Gemplus' electronic purse case study. Proceedings of Formal Methods Europe (FME 2002). LNCS 2391, pages 272-289. Springer, 2002.

[Chalin03] Patrice Chalin. *Back to Basics: Language Support and Semantics of Basic Infinite Integer Types in JML and Larch*. Technical Report 2002-003.3, Computer Science Department, Concordia University, April 2003. (Previous revisions: March 2003, October 2002.)

[EL02] David Evans and David Larochelle. Improving Security Using Extensible Lightweight Static Analysis. IEEE Software, Jan/Feb 2002.

[Finkel96] Raphael A. Finkel. *Advanced Programming Language Design*. Addison-Wesley, 1996.

[Flanagan+02] Cormac Flanagan, K. Rustan M. Leino, Mark Lillibridge, Greg Nelson, James B. Saxe, and Raymie Stata. Extended static checking for Java. In Cindy Norris and James B. Fenwick, editors, *Proceedings of Conference on Programming Language Design and Implementation (PLDI-02)*, volume 37, 5 of ACM SIGPLAN, pages 234–245, June 17–19 2002.

[Gemplus] Gemplus Purse applet. http://www.gemplus.com/smart/r_d/publications/case-study.

[GH93] John V. Guttag and James J. Horning, editors. *Larch: Languages and Tools for Formal Specification*. Texts and Monographs in Computer Science. Springer-Verlag, 1993. With Stephen J. Garland, Kevin D. Jones, Andr´es Modet, and Jeannette M. Wing.

[GJSB00] James Gosling, Bill Joy, Guy Steele, Gilad Bracha. The Java™ Language Specification. Second Edition, Addison-Wesley, 2000. Also java.sun.com/docs/books/jls/second_edition/html.

[HP02] Engelbert Hubbers and Erik Poll. jml.javacard.framework.Util.jml. University of Nijmegen, 2002. (www.cs.kun.nl/indexes/~erikpoll/publications/jc211_specs/jml/javacard/framework/Util.jml).

[JP01] Bart Jacobs and Erik Poll. A Logic for the Java Modeling Language JML. In: H. Hussmann (ed.), *Fundamental Approaches to Software Engineering (FASE)*, LNCS 2029 pages284-299. Springer-Verlag 2001.

[KP03] Joseph Kiniry and Erik Poll. Opportunities and challenges for formal specification of Java programs. *Trusted Components Workshop*, Prato, Italy, January 2003.

[KST97] S. Kahrs, D. Sannella, and A. Tarlecki. The definition of Extended ML: A gentle introduction. *Theoretical Computer Science*, 173(2):445-484, 1997.

[LBR02] Gary T. Leavens, Albert L. Baker, and Clyde Ruby. Preliminary Design of JML: A Behavioral Interface Specification Language for Java. Department of Computer Science, Iowa State University, TR #98-06t, December 2002.

[LBR99b] Gary T. Leavens, Albert L. Baker and Clyde Ruby. JML: A Notation for Detailed Design. In Haim Kilov, Bernhard Rumpe, and Ian Simmonds (editors), *Behavioral Specifications of Businesses and Systems*, Chapter 12, pages 175-188. Kluwer, 1999.

[LCPP] Larch/C++ web page. www.cs.iastate.edu/~leavens/larchc++.html and www.cs.iastate.edu/~leavens/LarchC++.gif.

[Leavens+00] Gary T. Leavens, K. Rustan M. Leino, Erik Poll, Clyde Ruby, and Bart Jacobs. JML: notations and tools supporting detailed design in Java. In OOPSLA '00 Companion, Minneapolis, Minnesota, pages 105-106.

[Leavens02a] Gary T. Leavens. *A Java Modeling Language*, slides from presentation given at Clemson University. May 31, 2002

[Leavens99] Gary T. Leavens. *Larch/C++ Reference Manual*, Iowa State University, Version 5.41, April 1999.

[Leino95] K. Rustan M. Leino. Toward Reliable Modular Programs. PhD thesis, California Institute of Technology, 1995. Available as Technical Report Caltech-CSTR-95-03.

[MC96] L. McIver, and D. Conway. Seven Deadly Sins of Introductory Programming Language Design. *Proceedings, Software Engineering: Education & Practice 1996*, pages 309-316.

[Meyer92] Bertrand Meyer. *Eiffel: The Language*. Object-Oriented Series. Prentice Hall, New York, N.Y., 1992.

[Owre96] S. Owre, S. Rajan, J.M. Rushby, N. Shankar, and M. Srivas. PVS: Combining specification, proof checking, and model checking. In R. Alur and T.A. Henzinger editors, Computer Aided Verification, LNCS 1102, pages 411-414. Springer, 1996.

[Parnas01] David Lorge Parnas. Description and Specification. In Daniel M. Hoffman and David M. Weiss editors. *Software Fundamentals: Collected Papers by David L. Parnas*, pages 1-6. Addison-Wesley, 2001.

[PvdBJ00] Erik Poll, Joachim van den Berg, Bart Jacobs. Specification of the JavaCard API in JML. *Fourth Smart Card Research and Advanced Application IFIP Conference (CARDIS'2000)*, 2000.

[PvdBJ01] Erik Poll, Joachim van den Berg, Bart Jacobs. Formal Specification of the JavaCard API in JML: the APDU class. *Computer Networks*, Volume 36, Issue 4, pp. 407-421, Elsevier Science, 2001.

[RL00] Clyde Ruby and Gary T. Leavens. Safely Creating Correct Subclasses without Seeing Superclass Code. In *OOPSLA 2000 Conference Proceedings*, pages 208-228. Volume 35, number 10 of ACM SIGPLAN Notices, Oct. 2000.

[Sun02] Java Card 2.2 Virtual Machine Specification. Sun Microsystems. May 13, 2002.

[vdBJ01] Joachim van den Berg and Bart Jacobs. The LOOP compiler for Java and JML. In: T. Margaria and W. Yi editors, *Tools and Algorithms for the Construction and Analysis of Software (TACAS)*, LNCS 2031, pages 299-312. Springer, 2001.

[Wing87] Jeannette M. Wing. Writing Larch interface language specifications. ACM Transactions on Programming Languages and Systems, 9(1):1–24, January 1987.

Using Abstractions for Heuristic State Space Exploration of Reactive Object-Oriented Systems

Marc Lettrari

OFFIS, Escherweg 2, D-26111 Oldenburg, Germany
Marc.Lettrari@offis.de

Abstract. We present a novel framework for symbolically exploring very large or infinite state spaces of concurrent reactive object-oriented systems. In our framework we apply A* directed search algorithms for performing an efficient heuristic state space exploration towards user-defined search goals. The used heuristics exploit semantical knowledge about a system when searching for specific properties. The knowledge is extracted prior to the search process by computing abstractions of the considered systems. Based on an abstraction and a search goal we generate a heuristic function which can be used during state space exploration of the concrete system. The heuristics can be generated fully automatically and with different precision. Our approach to state space exploration has been implemented in a tool set called HORSE. The tool set can work in combination with an industrial UML case tool, and we show the applicability of our approach by applying the tool set to several sample models.

Keywords: heuristic search, symbolic execution, abstractions, UML

1 Introduction

Model checking [CGP99] is an automatic technique for verifying finite-state concurrent systems. The state space of a concurrent system can be seen as a directed graph that represents the combined behavior of all the concurrent components in the system. Model checking searches the state space of a system exhaustively to determine whether the system satisfies some property or not. The main practical limitation of model checking is dealing with the so-called *state explosion* problem: the number of states contained in the state space of complex systems can be huge or even infinite, therefore in many cases an exhaustive state-space exploration is impossible. Although many improvements to model checking were made (e.g. the use of binary decision diagrams [McM93], partial order reductions [GW91] or symmetry reductions [ES93]), combating state explosion for large designs is still very difficult.

Mainly two different applications in using model checking can be observed. On the one hand, model checking is used to certify that a system indeed satisfies a certain property. For this application an exhaustive state space exploration is inevitable. The second application, which also appears to be the more commonly used, is to employ model checking as a search tool to find errors or user-defined states in a system (e.g. [ABB+98]). In this case complete state space exploration is not necessary, since it suffices to partially explore the system's state space until the desired state is found. In our work, we will exploit the possibilities of incomplete state space exploration. More precisely, in this paper we explore the use of *heuristic search* for exploring large or infinite state spaces. In contrast to ordinary search algorithms like depth-first search (DFS) or breadth-first search (BFS) which searches the state space in a fixed order, a heuristic search computes dynamically which states to visit next. It does this by using a *heuristic function* h which computes an estimation of the distance to a given *search goal*. The term *distance* can be understood as a measure of how far the current state is away of a state which fulfills the given search goal.

With respect to previous approaches to heuristic search for state space exploration (see sect. 5 for a review of related work), we present extensions in different directions. Firstly, we present a framework which allows a symbolic state space exploration for concurrent reactive object-oriented systems, thus allowing heuristic state space exploration for a larger class of systems than previous approaches. Secondly, the question how to obtain efficient application specific heuristics for state space exploration has gained little attention so far. In existing approaches, the used heuristics are based either purely on the property to be searched for or on certain syntactical or structural elements of the considered system. Contrary to this, in our approach the applied heuristics exploit semantical knowledge of a system when searching for a specific property. The knowledge is extracted prior to the search process by computing abstractions of the considered system. Based on such an abstraction and a given search goal we generate a heuristic function which computes for each abstract state the minimal transition distance to an abstract state that fulfills the search goal. During the state space exploration of the concrete system we dynamically map concrete states to abstract ones and use the computed transition distance of the abstract state as the heuristic value for the corresponding concrete state. By varying the accuracy of the computed abstractions we can generate heuristics with different precision.

The state space exploration is performed on a special virtual machine that can execute multi-threaded object-oriented programs symbolically. Programs can be described in a symbolic variant of C++, called SymC++, which can be translated into the byte-code like language of the virtual machine. This tool set allows us to apply our state space exploration methods to systems whose semantics can be described by SymC++ programs. In this paper, we evaluate the methods we developed by applying them to Rhapsody[1] UML models. The case tool Rhapsody allows to build executable UML models for which C++ code can be generated. Together with a suitable set of predefined framework classes the generated code can easily be transformed into a SymC++ program, thus allowing state space exploration for such models. We provide an experimental evaluation of the developed methods by analyzing several sample UML models.

---

[1] Rhapsody by iLogix

1.1 Structure of the Paper

The rest of the paper is organized as follows. In sect. 2 we present the class of systems that can be analyzed with our symbolic state space exploration method, and we explain the symbolic exploration process and the tool set we developed in detail. In sect. 3 we introduce the abstractions we are using and show how we can generate and apply these abstractions for heuristic search. After that in sect. 4 we apply the methods developed in the previous sections to several sample models and present experimental results. In sect. 5 we give an overview about relevant related work and finally in sect. 6 we present concluding remarks.

2 Reactive Object-Oriented Systems

In our framework we want to be able to cope with large and complicated systems, which are often described in an object-oriented style, either directly as programs in object-oriented languages like *C++* and *Java*, or given as models in some other formalism like e.g. *UML*. To achieve this goal, we needed a suitable representation for the semantics of the systems we want to consider. Therefore we decided to build a virtual machine, similar to the *Java Virtual Machine*, which is able to express aspects like object-orientation (objects, polymorphism, ...), dynamic object creation (destruction) and concurrency. But our virtual machine should not be restricted to represent the semantics of general object-oriented programming languages only, it should also be capable of handling more abstract computational concepts as e.g. nondeterminism. Therefore, we added two concepts to our virtual machine, namely explicit nondeterminism and symbolic values.

Because nondeterminism is explicitly supported, every nondeterministic behavior present in the considered system can easily be represented on the level of the virtual machine. Furthermore, the behavior of the considered systems often depends on input values with large or even infinite domains. For state space exploration, an instantiation of these inputs with concrete values would be either impossible (for infinite domains) or very inefficient (for large finite domains). Therefore our virtual machine allows us to assign *symbolic values* to variables instead of concrete values. Since all instructions of the virtual machine can handle both concrete and symbolic values, our virtual machine allows *symbolic execution*. In symbolic execution, a (symbolic) state of the machine is characterized by the (concrete or symbolic) values of all variables and a so-called *path condition*, which represents constraints on the symbolic values caused by conditional statements on the current execution path. Therefore a symbolic state can represent a large or even infinite number of concrete states.

Although it is in principle possible to describe the semantics of the systems we want to consider directly as code of the virtual machine, it is not an adequate choice for presentation because it is too fine grained. Therefore we define an extension of C++, called SymC++, which can be used both as an intermediate format describing the semantics of other formalisms like i.e. UML and to illustrate the principles of symbolic execution. SymC++ extends C++ by providing

```
0  void main() {
1      int i=0;
2      int k=symInt();
3      while (true) {
4          i=nondet(2);
5          if (i==0)
6              k=k+i+1;
7          else if (k<(i-k))
8              k=2*k-i;
9      }
10 }
```

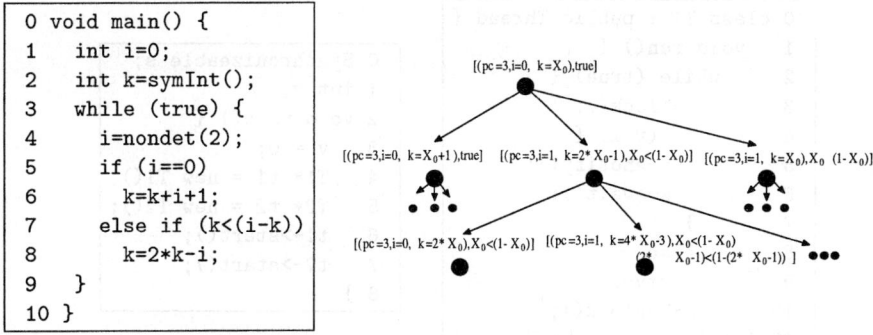

Fig. 1. Symbolic execution using SymC++

explicit nondeterminism by means of the global function `int nondet(int k)` which returns an integer i with $0 \leq i < k$. Furthermore SymC++ extends integral types like `int` or `float` to range not only over concrete values of that type but also to range over symbolic expressions. For all integral types there is a function (e.g. `symInt()` or `symFloat()`) which returns a new (fresh) symbolic variable representing an arbitrary value of that type. During execution more complex symbolic expressions are created due to computations using symbolic values. For example, Fig. 1 shows the execution of a (very simple) program. The execution tree (s. Fig. 1 right) shows different state configurations $[s, pcond]$ at program point pc=3 where s represents the current valuations of program variables (pc,i,k in our example) and $pcond$ contains the current path condition which constraints the possible valuations of symbolic variables.

Similar to Java, our virtual machine supports concurrency by providing interleaved execution of multiple threads together with synchronization mechanisms. The virtual machine supports a base class `Thread`, which is the base class for all threads in the system, that has methods to start, run, stop and resume a thread. For synchronization there is a base class `Synchronizeable` which supports exclusive access via `lock()` and `unlock()` like a semaphore and cooperative synchronization via `wait()` and `notify` (the waiting thread falls asleep until another thread calls notify). All threads are reentrant, i.e. when a thread falls asleep via `wait()` it implicitly releases all locks he owns so far and when a thread is awakened via `notify` it implicitly acquires all previously owned locks again. Additionally the virtual machine provides global functions `atomicbegin()` and `atomicend()` which can be used to mark atomic sections explicitly. Within atomic sections only the current thread is executable. Fig. 2 shows a sample program consisting of two threads `t1` and `t2` running concurrently. The run method of `t2` is the same as the one of `t1` (v. Fig. 2 left) except that the conditional of line 4 is changed to v > 9 and that t2 increments v (line 9). For synchronization the two threads use the global variable `s` which is on the one hand used to guarantee exclusive access when incrementing or decrementing the global variable `v` and on the other hand assures that `v` never becomes smaller than 0 (because when $v = 0$ thread `t1` falls asleep and t2 is awakened)

```
0  class T1 : public Thread {
1    void run() {
2      while (true) {
3        s->lock();
4        if (v<1) {
5          s->notify();
6          s->wait();
7        }
8        else
9          v=v-1;
10       s->unlock();
12 } } }
```

```
0  Synchronizeable s;
1  int v;
2  void main() {
3    v = 0;
4    T1* t1 = new T1();
5    T2* t2 = new T2();
6    t1->start();
7    t2->start();
8  }
```

Fig. 2. Concurrent execution of threads T1 and T2

resp. larger than 10 (because when $v = 10$ thread t2 falls asleep and t1 is awakened). It is important to note that with these synchronization mechanisms it is possible to model both synchronous communication (e.g. by synchronizing on a certain code area) as well as asynchronous communication (e.g. by introducing queues).

As stated in the introduction, to illustrate our approach to heuristic state space exploration we will consider Rhapsody UML models whose semantics can be expressed as SymC++ programs. The next section gives a short overview about UML in general and describes how certain UML concepts can be represented in SymC++.

2.1 UML Framework

The Unified Modelling Language (UML) has become accepted as the de facto standard notation for the design of object-oriented software systems. UML contains graphical languages that on the one hand can represent the static structure of a system, e.g. class diagrams, as well as languages that define the dynamic behavior of systems, e.g. state machine diagrams. In this paper, we concentrate on a subset of graphical notations which forms an executable part of UML, namely class diagrams, state machines and an object-oriented action language. The class diagrams are used to specify static aspects of a model, e.g. attributes of classes, inheritance relationships, associations and so on. State machines can be used to describe the *reactive* behavior of classes, i.e. how an instance of this class reacts to signal events or call events coming from the environment or from other objects. The object-oriented action language is used to describe all kinds of actions in the systems, e.g. the action part of state machine transitions or the effect of operations of classes.

Consider for example the UML model shown in Fig. 3, which consists of two classes A and B. Both class A and class B are so-called *active classes*, a notion which is defined in UML as a class which owns a thread of control. An instance of an active class, an *active object*, can act independently from other active objects

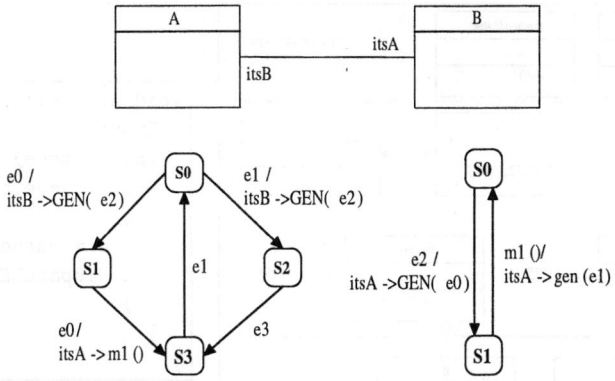

Fig. 3. UML model with classes A and B

in a system. In UML, there exists two kinds of communication between active objects. Either asynchronously via so-called *signal events*, or synchronously via so-called *call events*, which can be interpreted as if one object calls an operation of another object. Each active object is equipped with an event queue which stores all incoming events. The event processing is divided in so-called *run-to-completion* (RTC) steps. In one RTC step, an event is first dispatched from the queue. Dispatching this event enables some transitions in the statechart, depending on the current state configuration and values of attributes of the active object, and a maximal set of non-conflicting transitions will be taken, i.e. the state configuration changes and the actions associated to the taken transitions are executed. After that, so called *completion* events will be dispatched until the active object is in a stable configuration, i.e. the active object cannot take any transitions without dispatching a new event (not a completion event) from the event queue. For example, when an instance of class A is in state s0 and it dispatches an event e0 from the queue then it will change its state to s1 and when taking the transition it will send the event e2 (via the framework function GEN) along the association itsB (which is implemented as a reference to an object of type B). In contrast to asynchronous event sending an object of class A can also communicate synchronously with an object of class B, e.g. when A takes the transition from s1 to s3 by calling the method m1 of B.

Although there are many approaches that give different formal semantics to different subsets of UML, there is no official formal semantics for UML so far. Therefore we decided to take the simulation semantics of Rhapsody as a reference semantics for UML models, which is based on the model-specific C++ code generated by Rhapsody and several model-independent framework classes which encapsulate the semantics of certain UML concepts. We built our own version of these framework classes in SymC++ with slight extensions that were necessary to perform state space exploration. Figure 4 shows how we represent the semantics of UML models in our framework. For example, the class *Active* inherits from the virtual machine base class *Thread*, which represents the base

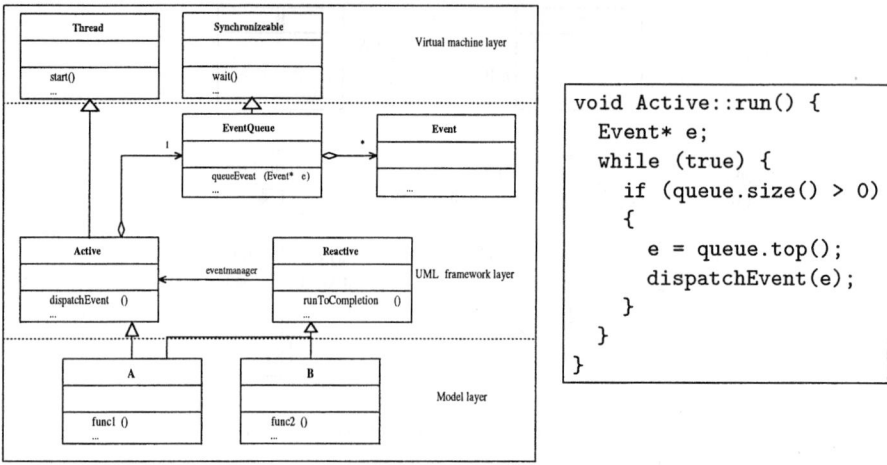

Fig. 4. Framework for UML models

class for all threads in the virtual machine. Each thread class has a method run which contains the main loop of the thread. *Active*'s implementation of the run method (v. Fig. 4 right) is a never ending loop which continuously checks the event queue associated to this object, and if there is an event in the queue, it is dispatched, i.e. a new RTC step with this event is initiated. To allow also reactive classes without an own thread of control there is the class *Reactive*. Every class which inherits from Reactive has to implement the method runToCompletion, which must perform the event processing together with possible completion events. An active class with a statechart can therefore be achieved by inheriting both from Active and Reactive, as it is shown in Fig. 4 for classes A and B.

2.2 The HORSE System

We have implemented the approach presented in this paper in a prototype called HORSE system. Figure 5 gives a schematic overview about the system. A core component is the symbolic virtual machine, which takes as input a byte-code like language representing object-oriented programs. As described in sect. 2 the virtual machine can handle both concrete and symbolic values. As a higher level language we support the SymC++ dialect. We have implemented a translator from SymC++ into the code of the virtual machine. Currently there are some minor restrictions of the C++ language features which can be translated, e.g. C++ exceptions and functions with varying number of arguments are currently not supported. The object system generator generates the object systems which serve as heuristic functions for heuristic state space exploration. The object system generator uses the virtual machine to symbolically execute methods of classes (s. sect. 3.1), and a linear constraint solver is used for performing the necessary proofs. The state explorer uses the virtual machine to execute programs

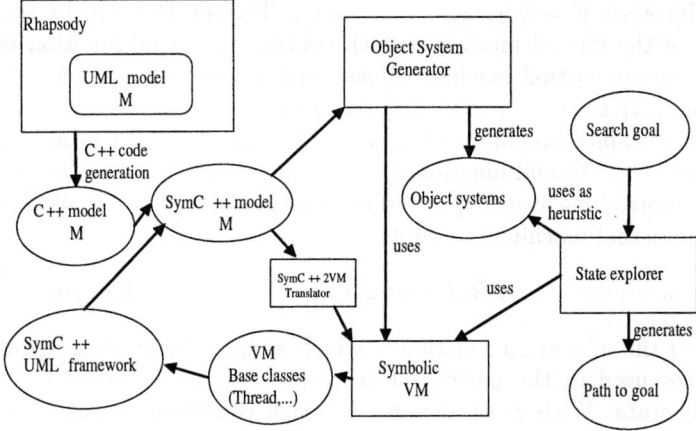

Fig. 5. Overview of HORSE system

and manages the storing and restoring of states. The state explorer can perform different kinds of explorations, e.g. breadth-first search or heuristic search. For heuristic search, the state space explorer uses the object systems generated by the object system generator as heuristic functions. When performing state space exploration, a search goal has to be defined. As search goals boolean expressions over the program variables can be defined, whereby navigation expression like o1->o2->v1 can be used to access member variables of objects. Furthermore quantifications over objects is allowed, e.g. the expression $\forall c : C \bullet c \rightarrow v = 0$ is true in a state s if all objects c of type C alive in state s fulfill $c \rightarrow v = 0$. With the UML case tool Rhaspody[2] we can translate UML models, which can, together with our UML framework based on the base classes of the virtual machine, be translated into code of the virtual machine.

2.3 Symbolic State Space Exploration

When performing a symbolic state space exploration of executions of the virtual machine, one has to take into account that the semantics of the virtual machine allows an infinite number of states for certain programs, therefore making a complete state space exploration impossible. As mentioned in the introduction, we are only interested in a partial state space exploration, because this is sufficient for many applications. More precisely, in this paper we are only considering the reachability problem, i.e., we want to find a path from the starting state to some state that has a certain property. By means of a (very abstract) formal model of the state of the virtual machine we want to illustrate some of the problems which has to be addressed for an efficient state space exploration. First of all, we assume a countable, infinite set $Ref = \{r_1, r_2, \ldots\}$ of so-called *references*

---

[2] Rhaspody by iLogix

and an infinite set $V = \{v_1, v_2, \ldots\}$ of values. The set Ref can be seen as the "memory" of the virtual machine, which contains every information belonging to it. Because our virtual machine allows symbolic values, we define the 3 sets $X = \{x_1, x_2, \ldots\}, Exp_X = \{e_1, e_2, \ldots\}, BExp_X = \{b_1, b_2, \ldots\}$, where X is a set of symbolic variables ranging over values of V, Exp_X is a set of arithmetic expressions over $(V \cup X)$ and functions $(+, -, *, /, div, mod)$, and $BExp_X$ is the set of boolean expressions over Exp_X and predicates $(<, \leq, >, \geq, =, \neq)$. A *symbolic state* of the virtual machine is a tuple

$$s = (\gamma, \pi), \quad \gamma : Ref \longrightarrow (Exp_X \cup \{\bot\}), \quad \pi \in BExp_X$$

consisting of the allocation function γ which assigns (symbolic) expressions to all references used in the current state resp. $\bot$ if the reference is unused in the current state. With π we denote the path condition, which is a boolean expression constraining the possible values for the symbolic variables. To describe the semantical effect of the path condition, we define the two functions

$$\sigma : X \longrightarrow V$$
$$\llbracket \cdot \rrbracket : (Exp_X \cup BExp_X) \times (X \times V) \longrightarrow V \cup \{\text{true}, \text{false}\}$$

whereby σ assigns values from V to the symbolic values, and $\llbracket \cdot \rrbracket$ computes, for a given assignment σ, a value from V for an expression $e \in Exp_X$ resp. $\{true, false\}$ for an expression $e \in BExp_X$ in the usual manner. For a boolean expression e the set $\llbracket e \rrbracket = \{\sigma : X \longrightarrow V \bullet \llbracket e \rrbracket(\sigma) = true\}$ denotes the set of assignments σ which fulfills e. For a given symbolic state $s = (\gamma, \pi)$ we say that

$$\pi_\gamma = \pi \wedge (\bigwedge_{\{i \in \mathbb{N} \bullet \gamma(r_i) \neq \bot\}} x_i = \gamma(r_i))$$

is the *constraint form* of s, whereby all prior occurrences of x_i in π and γ are replaced with fresh symbolic variables before building π_γ. With

$$\vec{\gamma} = \langle (i_1, \gamma(r_{i_1})), \cdots, (i_n, \gamma(r_{i_n})) \rangle$$
$$\wedge \forall r_i \bullet (i \in \{i_1, \cdots, i_n\}) \Leftrightarrow (\gamma(r_i) \neq \bot)$$
$$\wedge \forall k \in \{1, \cdots, n-1\} \bullet i_k < i_{k+1}$$

we denote the finite *state vector* for a symbolic state (γ, π). Due to space limitations we will not describe the transition relation between symbolic states formally here, but it should be clear that executing a statement in the program can cause a change to one or more symbolic successor states.

When performing a state space exploration, one has to decide in which order different states should be explored. However, because the state space we are considering can be infinite, we must take care of the search algorithm we are using, because otherwise we can descend along an infinite path not finding a goal state even if there is a finite path to a goal state. For example, consider a program which can nondeterministically increment or decrement a fixed variable by one, i.e. in our formal model for a state (γ, π) we have two successor states

$(\gamma'_i, \pi), i \in \{1, 2\}$ with $\gamma'_1(r_0) = \gamma(r_0) + 1$ and $\gamma'_2(r_0) = \gamma(r_0) - 1$. If the starting state fulfills $\gamma(r_0) = 0$, the search goal is $\gamma(r_0) = -2$, and we apply depth-first search (DFS) which always selects γ'_1 as the next state to consider, we either never find the path to the goal state (if the value referenced by r_0 is unbounded) or it would waste a lot of time on the wrong path (if the value referenced by r_0 belongs to a large domain). Using breadth-first search (BFS) would solve this problem, because BFS has the property that a state in depth d is visited only after all states up to depth $d-1$ has been visited before. But this property also implies that the number of visited states grows exponentially with the search depth, therefore due to limited computational resources (memory and time) BFS will not find goal states with a large path length to the start state.

The idea of heuristic search is that in contrast to DFS or BFS the next state to visit is determined dynamically during the search by applying a heuristic function h which estimates the distance to a state which fulfills the given search goal. A simple variant of heuristic search is best-first search (BF), which orders states by increasing h-values. However, if only the estimated distance h is used to determine the order in which states are visited, the same problem as in DFS occurs, namely that the search can descend an infinite path if the states on this path always yields the smallest h-values. To overcome this shortcoming, we decided to use a variant of the A* algorithm called weighted A* (WA), which can be seen in Fig. 6 (left). A* [HNR68] combines BF and BFS for a new evaluation function f by summing the path length g and the estimated distance h to a goal state (v. Fig. 6 right). Because f takes the actual path length into account, the search process will eventually find a path to a goal state if there exists one, and since the estimated distance h is also considered, the search process will expand less states than BFS, provided that h is accurate. WA generalizes A* by taking an additional weighting factor w into account, which controls the weighting between g and h. Using small w-values has the effect that the search proceeds similar to BFS ($w = 0$) or A* ($w = 1$) or something inbetween ($0 < w < 1$). Larger values for w ($w > 1$) will increase the influence of h thus allowing to find much longer

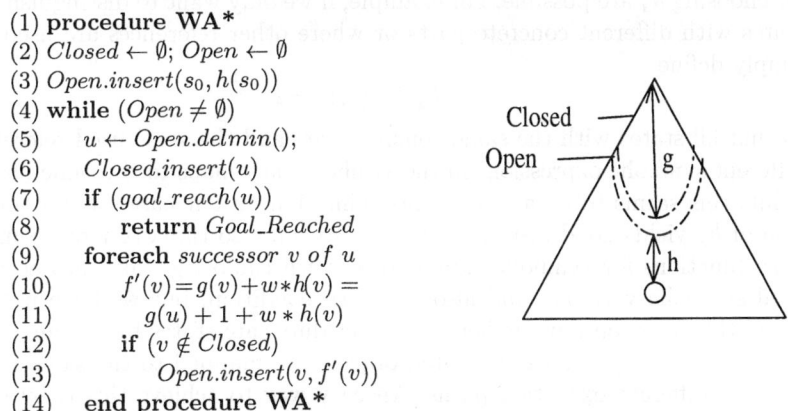

```
(1)  procedure WA*
(2)  Closed ← ∅; Open ← ∅
(3)  Open.insert(s₀, h(s₀))
(4)  while (Open ≠ ∅)
(5)      u ← Open.delmin();
(6)      Closed.insert(u)
(7)      if (goal_reach(u))
(8)          return Goal_Reached
(9)      foreach successor v of u
(10)         f'(v) = g(v) + w * h(v) =
(11)         g(u) + 1 + w * h(v)
(12)         if (v ∉ Closed)
(13)             Open.insert(v, f'(v))
(14) end procedure WA*
```

Fig. 6. Weighted A* algorithm

paths to goal states than BFS or A*. Crucial for the effectiveness of a heuristic search is that h provides a good approximation of the distance to a goal state. In sect. 3 we will discuss how to obtain such a good heuristic.

During state space exploration, to detect states which has been visited before, for each newly generated state it has to be checked if the state has been visited before (s. Fig. 6 line 12), which avoids unnecessary re-visiting of states. In our formal model, for a newly generated state $s' = (\gamma', \pi')$ we have to check if $s' \in \{s \bullet s \in Closed\}$. Since each symbolic states can represent a set of concrete states, in fact we have to check if

$$J\pi'_\gamma K \subseteq \bigcup_{(\gamma,\pi) \in Closed} J\pi_\gamma K \quad \text{or equivalent} \quad J\pi'_\gamma \wedge \bigwedge_{(\gamma,\pi) \in Closed} \neg \pi_\gamma K = \emptyset$$

holds. While this can be bone for limited subsets of constraints (e.g. linear arithmetic constraints), for general arithmetic constraints it is undecidable. Furthermore, even in the decidable cases, it is often a computationally expensive operation (e.g. if variables range over integers). Since we do not want to perform a complete state space exploration, we decided to use only the approximation

$$H(\vec{\gamma}) = h_n(\langle h_{sv}(i_1, r_{i_1}), \cdots, h_{sv}(i_n, r_{i_n}) \rangle) \in Closed_H$$

whereas H denotes a hash function which hashes a state vector to a natural number n with $0 \leq n \leq M$, and $Closed_H$ denotes the set of all hash values for all states visited so far. H works by first applying the function

$$h_{sv}(i, \gamma(r_i)) = \begin{cases} h_v(i, \gamma(r_i)) & \text{if} \gamma(r_i) \in V \\ h_s(i, \gamma(r_i)) & \text{otherwise} \end{cases}$$

to each element $(i, \gamma(r_i))$ of $\vec{\gamma}$ and then using the hash function h_n to hash the resulting vector to a natural number. We split h_{sv} into two cases to be able to handle concrete values and symbolic values differently by the two functions h_v and h_s. Whereas h_v and h_n can be simple hash functions which maps concrete values resp. sequences of concrete values to natural numbers, different solutions for choosing h_s are possible. For example, if we only want to distinguish between states with different concrete parts or where other references are used, we can simply define

$$h_s(i, \gamma(r_i)) = i$$

so that all states with the same concrete part and the same used references but different symbolic expressions in the symbolic part maps to the same hash value. While this seems to be a coarse approximation, in our case studies this definition of h_s yields good results. However, we can also think of more complicated hash functions for symbolic expressions which could e.g. take into account the used symbolic variables and also the path condition, but we have not investigated this question any further. To detect duplicate states by hashing, it is also necessary that dynamically created objects are mapped to the same references even on different execution paths. An easy way to achieve this is by recognizing which allocation statements allocated which references, and simply blocking once allocated references for other allocation statements.

3 Abstractions for Heuristic Search

As mentioned in sect. 2, to apply our approach to heuristic state space exploration we need a suitable heuristic function which estimates for a given state how far this state is away from a state which fulfills a given search goal. The basic idea how to obtain and apply such a heuristic function is simple: we build abstractions of the considered system which are small enough that we can analyze them statically before state space exploration, and during the on-the-fly state space exploration of the real system we dynamically map concrete states to abstract ones and use the statically computed information to obtain a heuristic estimate for the concrete state. For building the abstractions we apply predicate abstraction to parts of the system, namely to the classes of the system, and an analysis of these abstractions w.r.t. a given search goal computes the information which is relevant during the heuristic search.

The abstractions we want derive are so-called *object systems*, which are collections of several *object automatons*. An object automaton can be seen as an abstraction which reflects two central aspects of objects, namely the state of an object and the communications the object can perform when changing its state. An object system consists of several object automatons and describes the communication structure between the object automatons in the system, which can change dynamically. Formally, we assume a finite set $\Sigma = \Sigma_a \cup \Sigma_s$ consisting of synchronous (Σ_s) and asynchronous (Σ_a) events with $\Sigma_s \cap \Sigma_a = \emptyset$. Furthermore we assume a special event $\tau \notin \Sigma$, a set $\Sigma_E \subseteq \Sigma$ of external events and we define $\Sigma_\tau = \Sigma \cup \{\tau\}$. Communications are performed using so-called *links*. A communication $l \triangleright \sigma$ over a link l is a synchronous communication if $\sigma \in \Sigma_s$ and an asynchronous communication if $\sigma \in \Sigma_a$. For a set L of links and a set Σ of events the set

$$Act(L, \Sigma) = \{l \triangleright \sigma\} \bullet l \in L, \sigma \in \Sigma\} \cup \{\epsilon\}$$

denotes the set of communications which can be performed on links in L, whereas ϵ denotes the absence of communication. A valuation val assigns to each $l \in L$ a value $k \in \{1, \cdots, p, \top, \bot\}$ for some $p \in \mathbb{N}$. We use $\mathcal{L}(L)$ to denote the set of all valuations of L. To describe changes in the communication structure we use *link modifications* which are functions $\mathcal{L}(L) \to P(\mathcal{L}(L)) \setminus \emptyset$, i.e. the result of a link modification m for a given valuation val is a set of valuations $m(val)$ of L. This allows us to express nondeterministic link modifications. The set of all link modifications over L is denoted by $\mathcal{M}(L)$. We do not give a fixed syntax for link modifications, but we will use statements like $l = x$ to denote link modifications with the usual meaning. An object automaton o is a tuple $o = (Q, \to, L, q_1)$ such that

- $Q = \{q_1, \cdots, q_k\}$ is a set of control states
- $L = \{l_1, \cdots, l_j\}$ is a set of links
- $\to \subseteq Q \times \Sigma_\tau \times Act(L, \Sigma) \times \mathcal{M}(L) \times Q$ is the transition relation.
- $q_1 \in Q$ is the start state

An object system os is a tuple $os = (\vec{o}, OId, \mathcal{L})$ such that $\vec{o} = \langle o_1, \cdots, o_m \rangle$ is a vector of object automatons, $OId = \{1, \cdots, m, \top, \bot\}$ is a set of object identifiers, whereby $\top$ is used to represent an object identifier of any object which is not in $\{o_1, \cdots, o_m\}$, $\bot$ is used to represent an invalid object identifier and $\mathcal{L} = \bigcup_{i=1}^{m} L_i$. To describe the semantics of object systems, we first define *configurations* of object systems. A configuration of an object system os is a tuple $c = (\vec{q}, \vec{e}, val)$ such that

- $\vec{q} = \langle q_1, \cdots, q_m \rangle$ is a *control vector* s.t. $\forall j \in \{1, \cdots, m\} \bullet q_j \in Q_j$,
- $\vec{e} = \langle E_1, \cdots, E_m \rangle$ is a vector of event sets s.t. $\forall j \in \{1, \cdots, m\} \bullet E_i \subseteq \Sigma_A$,
- $val : \mathcal{L} \to OId$ is a valuation of links to object identifiers.

With $\mathcal{C}(os)$ we denote the set of all configurations of os. The event sets E_i are used for buffered asynchronous communication and can be seen as providing a queue of length one for each $\sigma \in \Sigma_A$. For a control vector $\vec{q}$ we denote with $\vec{q}[q_i'/q_i]$ a control vector in which the i-th component of $\vec{q}$ is changed to q_i'. For a vector of event sets $\vec{e}$ the function $ins(\vec{e}, i, \sigma)$ yields a vector of event sets in which σ is added to E_i, and $rm(\vec{e}, i, \sigma)$ yields a vector of event sets in which σ is removed from E_i. A configuration of an object system can change in three ways. Either an object automaton o_i can take a transition $t = (q, \{\sigma, \tau\}, a, m, q')$ by consuming an event $\sigma \in \Sigma_A$ or τ if $a = \epsilon$ or $a = l \triangleright \sigma \wedge \sigma \in \Sigma_A$, i.e. the communication over l needs no synchronization, or the objects $o_{i_1}, \cdots, o_{i_k}$ can synchronously take the transitions $t_1, \cdots, t_k$ if t_1 consumes an asynchronous event or τ, the action part of t_k is either ϵ or a sending of an asynchronous event, and the actions of $t_1, \cdots, t_{k-1}$ are sending of synchronous events σ_i s.t. each σ_i is the trigger of t_{i+1}. If neither of these transitions is possible, an object automaton can consume an external event. Formally we define the transition relation $\leadsto$ as follows:

((1) o_i consumes $\sigma \in \Sigma_A$ or τ):

$(\vec{q}, \vec{e}, val) \leadsto (\vec{q}[q_i'/q_i], \vec{e}', val' \in m(val))$ if
$\exists t = (q_i, \sigma, a, m, q_i') \in \to_i \bullet$
$(\sigma = \tau \vee \sigma \in E_i) \wedge \vec{e}'' = rm(\vec{e}, i, \sigma) \wedge$
$((a = \epsilon \wedge \vec{e}' = \vec{e}'') \vee (a = l \triangleright \sigma_a \wedge \sigma_a \in \Sigma_A \wedge \vec{e}' = ins(\vec{e}'', val(l), \sigma_a)))$

((2) synchronization of $o_{i_1}, \cdots, o_{i_k}$):

$(\vec{q}, \vec{e}, val) \leadsto (\vec{q}[q_{i_1}'/q_{i_1}, \cdots, q_{i_k}'/q_{i_k}], \vec{e}', val' \in \bigcup_{i_j \in \{i_1, \cdots, i_k\}} m_{i_j}(val))$ if
$\exists t_1 = (q_{i_1}, \sigma_{i_1}, a_{i_1}, m_{i_1}, q_{i_1}') \in \to_{i_1}, \cdots, t_k = (q_{i_k}, \sigma_{i_k}, a_{i_k}, m_{i_k}, q_{i_k}') \in \to_{i_k} \bullet$
$(\sigma_{i_1} = \tau \vee \sigma_{i_1} \in E_{i_1}) \wedge \vec{e}'' = rm(\vec{e}, i_1, \sigma_{i_1}) \wedge$
$((a_{i_k} = \epsilon \wedge \vec{e}' = \vec{e}'') \vee (a_{i_k} = l \triangleright \sigma_a \wedge \sigma_a \in \Sigma_A \wedge \vec{e}' = ins(\vec{e}'', val(l), \sigma_a)))$
$\wedge \forall j \in \{1, \cdots, k-1\} \bullet a_{i_j} = l \triangleright \sigma_{i_{j+1}} \wedge \sigma_{i_{j+1}} \in \Sigma_S \wedge val(l) = i_{j+1}$

((3) o_i consumes external event):

$(\vec{q}, \vec{e}, val) \leadsto (\vec{q}[q_i'/q_i], \vec{e}', val' \in m(val))$ if
$\neg(1) \wedge \neg(2) \wedge \exists t = (q_i, \sigma, a, m, q_i') \in \to_i \bullet$
$(\sigma \in \Sigma_E) \wedge$
$((a = \epsilon \wedge \vec{e}' = \vec{e}) \vee (a = l \triangleright \sigma_a \wedge \sigma_a \in \Sigma_A \wedge \vec{e}' = ins(\vec{e}, val(l), \sigma_a)))$

After defining the transition relation $\leadsto$ we can now define the semantics of an object system $os = (\langle o_1, \cdots, o_m \rangle, OId, \mathcal{L})$ as the tuple $JosK = (S, s_0, \leadsto)$ s.t.

- $s_0 \in \mathcal{C}(os) = (\langle q_1^1, \cdots, q_m^1 \rangle, \{1, \cdots, m, \top, \bot\}, val)$ is the starting configuration of os with $val(l) = \bot\ \forall l \in L$
- $S = \{s \in \mathcal{C}(os) \bullet s_o \leadsto^* s\}$ is the finite set of all configurations reachable from s_0 using $\leadsto$.
- $\leadsto$ is defined as above.

After introducing object systems formally we will now explain how we can generate an object system os for an UML model described as a program in SymC++ using the framework presented in sect. 2.1.

3.1 Generation of Object Systems

For generating object systems we firstly have to generate the object automatons as parts of the object system. We will compute one object automaton for every class in the system, and we will build object systems as instantiations using the object automatons. The first question we have to answer is what should be the states of an object automaton for an instance of class C. From an abstract point of view, a state of an object is given by a valuation of all its attributes. Since we want to generate object automatons which are small enough that we can analyze them statically we cannot represent each possible valuation as a single state. Therefore we abstract from single valuations of attributes and identify a valuation with a corresponding vector of boolean values $\vec{b} = \langle b_1, \cdots, b_n \rangle$ representing the values of predicates $\{p_1, \cdots, p_n\}$ over attributes of the object, a technique known as *predicate abstraction* [GS97]. Predicate abstraction is based on abstract interpretation [CC77,CC92] and requires an abstraction function relating concrete values to abstract ones. For example, although an object contains two integer attributes i_1 and i_2 which can take arbitrary values, in certain cases it is sufficient to know if $i_1 > i_2$, therefore we can replace i_1 and i_2 with a boolean variable b indicating that $i_1 > i_2$ holds or not, i.e. $b \iff (i_1 > i_2)$. If the state of an object automaton is given by a vector $\vec{b}$, then transitions of the automaton describe changes of $\vec{b}$, and the question is to what computational unit such a transition corresponds. Again, from an abstract point of view, state changes of an object are caused by invoking methods of the object, therefore it is natural to let transitions in the object automaton correspond to method invocations.

To be able to apply predicate abstraction, we have to determine the set $\{p_1, \cdots, p_n\}$ of predicates which should be used for abstraction. In our generation process we solve this step by creating an instance of class C, making all the member variables symbolic and then executing the methods m_i of the instance symbolically. If a certain path through a method depends on values of attributes of the instance, this dependency is reflected as a conditional in the path condition. Therefore after executing a method we simply collect all such conditionals contained in the path condition, and we use the collected conditionals as our predicates $\{p_1, \cdots, p_n\}$ for abstraction. To get reasonable small object automatons which can be analyzed statically, we limit the number of predicates we extract to a certain maximum, which is usually between 20 and 30 predicates. If there are more conditionals, then we just take the conditionals which occur most often in the path condition.

After the set $\{p_1, \cdots, p_n\}$ of predicates is extracted, the actual abstraction process begins with creating the set of possible abstract starting states S_A, which are determined through the possible values of $\{p_1, \cdots, p_n\}$ after executing any of the constructors of C. Because an object automaton can have only one starting state, we introduce a new state for the object automaton and add τ-transitions from this state to all possible abstract starting states. Then for each abstract state s_a in S_A the set of possible successor states is computed by executing each method m_i symbolically starting with a path condition describing s_a. Method calls to the same instance and loops are handled via a fixpoint computation on the set of abstract states, and method calls to other objects or global function calls are treated s.t. these calls always returns unconstrained symbolic values. A trigger of a transition of the object automaton is an element σ_m representing a call of the method m. Framework specific information is used to determine if the method m will be called as a result of receiving an asynchronous event, i.e. $\sigma_m \in \Sigma_A$, or if m is a method which will be called directly from another object, i.e. $\sigma_m \in \Sigma_S$. To assign communication actions and link modifications to transitions, we firstly add a link l_i to the object automaton for every attribute a_i of C which is a reference to an object of some other class C_i. After computing all paths through a method certain statements on these paths are mapped to communication actions resp. link modifications. For a normal method call $a_i \rightarrow m_k$ we add a σ_{m_k} to Σ_S and a communication action $l_i \triangleright \sigma_{m_k}$ to the corresponding transition resp. σ_{e_k} to Σ_A and $l_i \triangleright \sigma_{e_k}$ for sending an event (identifiable as the framework function $a_i \rightarrow gen(e_k)$). If there are more than one communication action on a path, then additional intermediate states are introduced and communication actions are performed on τ-transitions between these states. Additionally, for every assignment $a_i = e$ of an expression e to an attribute a_i which belongs to a link l_i we add a link modification $l_i = \bot$, if e denotes the constant $null$, $l_i = \top$ if e is the new-function, or otherwise $l_i = nd(range(l_i))$, whereby $nd(M)$ returns nondeterministically a value from the set M and $range(l)$ is a set of possible object identifiers for l which is determined when the object automaton is used in an object system. Figure 7 shows an object automaton for a class C created by the generation process described above.

Until now we have described how to obtain an object automaton for a class C only. Based on these object automatons we can now build object systems of different precision and complexity. For a class C_i the simplest object system we can construct contains only the object automaton of class C_i and it is defined as $os(C_i)_0 = (\langle o_i^1 \rangle, OId = \{n_i^1, \top, \bot\}, L_i^1)$. For each link modification of the form $l_k = nd(range(l_k))$ the set $range(l_k)$ is instantiated either with OId, if the corresponding attribute a_k is a reference to C_i, or with $\{\top, \bot\}$ if it is a reference to another class. The input interface Σ_E contains all $\sigma \in \Sigma$ which are not used in communication actions. Because we consider on object automaton

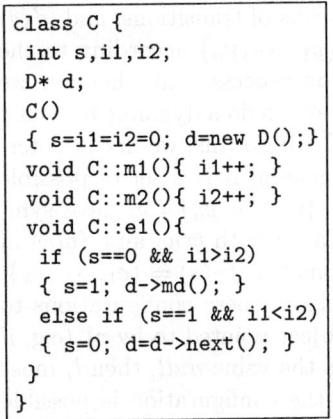
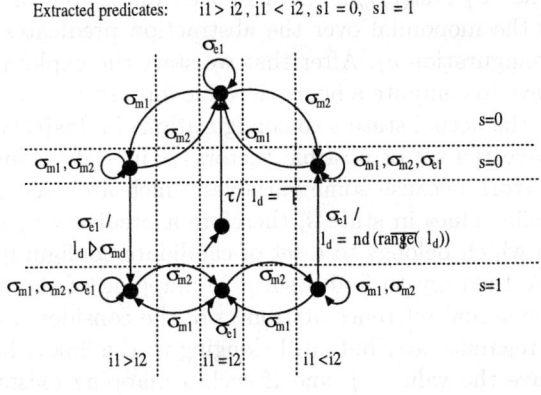

Fig. 7. Class C (left) and corresponding object automaton (right)

in isolation, the reachability graph $J\!os(C_i)_0 K$ of $os(C_i)_0$ is very similar to o_i^1 itself. A more complex object system for class C_i can be obtained if we consider not only o_i^1 but also the object automatons that can directly influence o_i^1. For example, consider class C from Fig. 7, and assume that besides class C there is also another class B which has an attribute c that is a reference to C. Then

$$os(C)_1 = (\langle o_c, o_b \rangle, OId = \{n_c, n_b, \top, \bot\}, L),$$

the link modifications are instantiated appropriately, e.g. a nondeterministic choice for l_c can return a value from $\{n_c, \top, \bot\}$, and Σ_E contains all events which do not occur in communication actions of o_c and o_b. Note that the set of objects which can influence an object of class C_i can sometimes also contain objects which are referenced by C_i itself, e.g. if C_i can perform a synchronous communication to another object which allows this synchronization only in some of its states. In this way we can iteratively build larger object systems, whose reachability graphs represent more global and therefore more precise descriptions of the behavior of objects. In the next section we will describe how the reachability graphs of the generated object systems can be applied as heuristic functions during state space exploration.

3.2 Using Object Systems as Heuristic Functions

When performing a heuristic state space exploration towards a specific search goal g as described in sect. 2.3, for each newly generated state s one has to estimate its distance to a state that fulfills g. For example, let $r1$ be a global variable pointing to an object of class C from Fig. 7, and the search goal is given as $g \equiv (r1 \to s = 1)$. Before starting the search, we create the reachability graph $J\!os(C)_0 K$ and compute for each configuration c_i in $J\!os(C)_0 K$ the distance function

$$d_C^g(i) = min\{dist(i,j) \bullet \overrightarrow{p}(j) \Rightarrow g\}$$

whereby $dist(i,j)$ is the distance from c_i to c_j in terms of transitions, and $\vec{p}(j)$ is the monomial over the abstraction predicates $\{p_1, \cdots, p_n\}$ according to the configuration c_j. After that we start the exploration process, and whenever we have to compute a heuristic value for a state s we have to do a dynamic mapping of the actual state s to configurations in $Jos(C)_0K$. To do this, we firstly determine the set of possible vectors $\vec{p}$ in state s (in general it is a set of possible vectors because some variables which are used in $\{p_1, \cdots, p_n\}$ can have symbolic values in state s, therefore a predicate p_j can be both $true$ and $false$ in s) which belongs to a set of candidate configurations $Conf_C(s) = \{c_1, \cdots, c_k\}$. We then try to find a suitable mapping of the links in these configurations to the actual reference attributes of the considered object pointed to by $r1$ (e.g. if a reference attribute a_i belonging to the link l_i has the value $null$, then l_i must have the value $\bot$), and if such a mapping exists, the configuration is possible in the actual state. For all possible configurations $PConf_C(s)$ we compute then the heuristic estimate $h(g,s) = min(\{d_C^g(i) \bullet c_i \in PConf_C(s)\})$. Figure 8 shows how we compute heuristic values for the class of formulas described in sect. 2.2 whereby F_1 denotes the subset of atomic formulas which contain attributes of one class only.

If we want a more precise heuristic function, we can compute a reachability graph $Jos(C)_k K$ with $k > 0$. For reachability graphs which represents the behavior of more than one object, our dynamic mapping works in a backward direction. Firstly, as described above, the set of possible configurations for the object used in the search goal is computed. Then this set is successively reduced by taking into account the possible instantiations for the other objects and their links in the object system according to the actual state. Crucial for this operation is the fact that in a certain state the HORSE system "knows" which objects exist and what the values of their attributes are. In the next section we will apply the methods presented in the previous sections to various sample models.

f	$h(f,s)$	$\bar{h}(f,s)$
$false$	∞	0
$true$	0	∞
atomic $f \in F_1$ with $class(f) = C$	if (f) then 0 else $min(\{d_c^f(i) \bullet c_i \in PConf_C(s)\})$	if $(\neg f)$ then 0 else $min(\{d_c^{\neg f}(i) \bullet c_i \in PConf_C(s)\})$
atomic $f \notin F_1$	if (f) then 0 else 1	if $(\neg f)$ then 0 else 1
$\neg f$	$\bar{h}(f,s)$	$h(f,s)$
$f \wedge g$	$\lceil (h(f,s) + h(g,s))/2 \rceil$	$min(\{\bar{h}(f,s), \bar{h}(g,s)\})$
$f \vee g$	$min(\{h(f,s), h(g,s)\})$	$\lceil (\bar{h}(f,s) + \bar{h}(g,s))/2 \rceil$
$\forall c : C \bullet f$	$\left\lceil \left(\sum_{c_i \in C} h(f[c_i/c], s)\right)/n \right\rceil$	$min(\{\bar{h}(f[c_i/c], s) \bullet c_i \in C\})$

Fig. 8. Heuristic values for state formulas

4 Experimental Evaluation

To assess the effect of using the approach described in the previous sections we have applied the HORSE system to several sample models. As described in sect. 2.2, we use UML models constructed for the UML case tool Rhapsody[3]. We use the C++ code generation capability of Rhapsody to translate the classes of the UML model, and together with our UML framework (s. sect. 2.1) we were able to perform state space exploration for these models with the Weighted A* algorithm described in sect. 2.3. The models we use are either part of the Rhapsody installation (PBX,Arcs,HHS) or self-made models (SMS,Watch). The number of UML classes in these models ranges from 6 (PBX,HHS) to 15 (ARCS), and the overall number of classes (UML classes + framework classes) reach up to 60 (ARCS).

The first set of experiments were made to evaluate the impact of heuristic search when using the reachability graph $Jos(C)_o K$ of an object system with only one object automaton. Figure 9 shows the number of generated states for search goals which are fulfilled in different depth of the search tree, both for BFS ($w = 0$) and heuristic search ($w = 10$). Although the use of heuristic search has different impact for different models, the results shown in Fig. 9 indicate that $Jos(C)_0 K$ is in general an effective heuristic because it significantly reduce the number of generated states for all tested models.

The second set of experiments were made to evaluate the impact of using a reachability graph $Jos(C)_k K$ with $k > 0$. Figure 10 shows the number of configurations in the reachability graphs $Jos(C)_k K$ for $k = \{0, 1, 2\}$ which is a measure of how expensive it is to generate $Jos(C)_k K$. We compute $Jos(C)_k K$ for two models (PBX,Watch) and compare the number of generated states of the reachability graphs with the number of states generated when using the reachability graphs for heuristic state space exploration. The results show that for increasing k the heuristic provided by $Jos(C)_k K$ is more precise because the number of generated states during state space exploration decreases. We can also observe that although the number of configurations in $Jos(C)_k K$ increases for $k = 2$ compared to $k = 1$, there is no more significant reduction in the number of generated states, but this can founded in the structure of the models.

Depth	PBX		ARCS		SMS		HHS		Watch	
	$w=0$	$w=10$	$w=0$	$w=10$	$w=0$	$w=10$	$w=0$	$w=10$	$w=0$	$w=10$
5	600	76	1300	112	900	320	230	24	1100	240
10	21500	1400	76000	11600	41000	17200	4900	620	62000	17000
15	-	5600	-	36000	-	105000	181000	4100	-	116000
20	-	18600	-	176000	-	-	-	19800	-	-
30	-	134000	-	-	-	-	-	129000	-	-

Fig. 9. Generated number of states with heuristic search ($Jos(C)_0 K, w = 10$) compared to BFS ($w = 0$)

---

[3] Rhapsody by iLogix

$Jos(C)_kK$	PBX		Watch	
	#c	#s	#c	#s
$Jos(C)_0K$	18	18600	12	17000
$Jos(C)_1K$	1200	4100	2300	2800
$Jos(C)_2K$	21000	4100	34000	2300

Fig. 10. Generated configurations (c) for $Jos(C)_kK$ compared to number of states (s) in state space exploration

5 Related Work

The work most closely related to our approach is presented in [ELL01b,ELL01a] and [GV02b,GV02a]. [ELL01b,ELL01a] apply heuristic search for the explicit state model checker SPIN. Similar to our approach they use a property specific heuristic to guide state space exploration with A* directed search algorithms. In contrast to our approach they do not incorporate application specific knowledge into their heuristics (with the exception of certain syntactical elements of an application, e.g. special *control states* in reactive processes). [GV02b,GV02a] apply heuristic search for model checking java programs. Additionally to heuristics for specific errors (like deadlocks etc.) they also propose to use structural heuristics like branch coverage. Contrary to our approach these structural heuristics do not exploit semantical knowledge of the model. [GK02] uses genetic algorithms for searching heuristically towards specific errors. Again, this approach does not take application specific knowledge into account. The technique of abstraction is most often used for verification of properties. For example, [DHJ+01] uses abstraction in the model checking framework Bandera to be able to generate finite state models from Java Source Code. In [CGJ+00] a counterexample-guided abstraction refinement scheme is presented, where an initial abstraction is subsequently refined to eliminate spurious counterexamples. Contrary to these approaches in our work the generated abstractions are only used as a heuristic and not directly for state space exploration, which avoids finding infeasible paths to the search goal.

6 Conclusion

In this paper we have exploited the usage of abstractions for heuristic state space exploration. We presented a new method that takes application specific semantical knowledge into account, which results in effective heuristics applicable for state space exploration. With the developed tool set we were able to perform heuristic state space exploration for several sample UML models. Although the experimental results were encouraging, we think further research is necessary in different directions. For example, it has to be explored how the abstractions can be used in combination with orthogonal heuristics, leading the search process into directions of specific error situations like deadlock etc, or if the approach presented in this paper can also be beneficial in other settings, e.g. when searching for violations of LTL properties.

Acknowledgements The author thanks Werner Damm and the other members of the working group for fruitful discussions on the subject of this paper, and Christian Mrugalla for implementing some parts of the tool set.

References

[ABB+98] R.J. Anderson, P. Beame, S. Burns, W. Chan, F. Modugno, D. Notkin, and J.D. Reese. Model Checking Large Software Specifications. *IEEE Transactions on Software Engineering*, 24(7):498–520, 1998.

[CC77] P. Cousot and R. Cousot. Abstract interpretation: A unified lattice model for static analysis of programs by construction or approximation of fixpoints. In *Conference Record of the Fourth Annual ACM Symposium on Principles of Programming Languages*, pages 238–252, 1977.

[CC92] P. Cousot and R. Cousot. Abstract Interpretation Framework. *Journal of Logic and Computation*, 4(2):511–547, August 1992.

[CGJ+00] E.M. Clarke, O. Grumberg, S. Jha, Y. Lu, and H. Veith. Counterexample-guided abstraction refinement. In *Computer Aided Verification*, pages 154–196, 2000.

[CGP99] E.M. Clarke, O. Grumberg, and D.A. Peled. *Model Checking*. MIT Press, 1999.

[DHJ+01] M. Dwyer, J. Hatcliff, R. Joehanes, S. Laubach, C. Pasareanu, W. Visser, and H. Zheng. Tool-supported Program Abstraction for Finite-state Verification. In *Proceedings ICSE 2001*, 2001.

[ELL01a] S. Edelkamp, A.L. Lafuente, and S. Leue. Directed explicit model checking with HSF-Spin. In *SPIN*, volume 2057 of *LNCS*, pages 57–79, 2001.

[ELL01b] S. Edelkamp, A.L. Lafuente, and S. Leue. Protocol verification with heuristic search. In *AAAI Symposium on Model-based Validation of Intelligence*, 2001.

[ES93] E.A. Emerson and A.P. Sistla. Symmetry and Model Checking. In *Proc. 5th Conference on Computer Aided Verification*, pages 463–478, 1993.

[GK02] P. Godefroid and S. Khurshid. Exploring very large state spaces using Genetic Algorithms. In *Proc. TACAS'02*, pages 1–10, 2002.

[GS97] S. Graf and H. Saidi. Construction of abstract state graphs with PVS. In *Proc. of the 9th International Conference on Computer Aided Verification*, number 1254 in Lecture Notes in Computer Science, pages 72–83. Springer, 1997.

[GV02a] A. Groce and W. Visser. Heuristic Model Checking for Java Programs. In *Proceedings of SPIN 2002*, Grenoble, France, 2002.

[GV02b] A. Groce and W. Visser. Model Checking Java Programs using Strucural Heuristics. In *Proceedings of ISSTA 2002*, Rome, Italy, 2002.

[GW91] P. Godefroid and P. Wolper. A partial approach to model checking. In *Proceedings of the 6th IEEE Symposium on Logic in Computer Science*, pages 406–415, Amsterdam, July 1991.

[HNR68] P.E. Hart, N.J. Nilsson, and B. Raphael. A formal basis for heuristic determination of minimum path cost. *IEEE Transactions on Systems Science and Cybernetics*, 4:100–107, 1968.

[McM93] K.L. McMillan. *Symbolic Model Checking*. Kluwer Academic Publishers, 1993.

A Formal Framework for Modular Synchronous System Design*

Maria-Cristina V. Marinescu and Martin C. Rinard

Laboratory for Computer Science, Massachusetts Institute of Technology,
Cambridge, MA 02139,
{cristina,rinard}@lcs.mit.edu

Abstract. We present the formal framework for a novel approach for specifying and automatically implementing systems such as digital circuits and network protocols. The goal is to reduce the design time and effort required to build correct, efficient, complex systems and to eliminate the need for the designer to deal directly with global synchronization and concurrency issues. Our compiler automatically transforms modular and asynchronous specifications of circuits written in our specification language, into tightly coupled, fully synchronous implementations in synthesizable Verilog. We formally state the correctness theorems and give an outline of the correctness proofs for two of the three main techniques that our compiler implements.

Keywords: formal, modular, asynchronous, system design

1 Introduction

We present the formal framework for our novel approach for specifying and automatically implementing efficient systems such as digital circuits and network protocols. We formally state our correctness theorems and give an outline of the correctness proofs for two of the three primary implementation techniques.

Our goal is to reduce the design time, effort, and expertise required to build correct and efficient systems. The key challenge is to reconcile the three goals of (1) shielding the developer from having to deal with difficult global issues such as coordinating the timing of events in widely separated parts of the system, (2) supporting a broad class of systems, and (3) enabling the automated synthesis of systems that are as efficient as the corresponding manually-developed versions. To meet this challenge, we have designed a specification language that is concise, expressive, and simple to use and implemented a compiler able to deliver efficient synchronous implementations of these specifications. Our language supports the following features:
- **Modular Specification via FIFO Queues:** The designer specifies a system as a set of modules connected by conceptually unbounded FIFO queues.

---
* This research was supported in part by NSF Grant CCR-9702297 and the Singapore-MIT Alliance.

These queues *temporally* separate the modules at the design level and enable meaningful local reasoning about the behavior of each module.
- **Atomic Updates:** The designer uses a set of atomic update rules to specify the behavior of each module. Atomic execution allows the developer to focus on one rule at a time when reasoning about the behavior of the system, without the need to consider the complex non-local interactions that occur with explicitly parallel models. This approach also facilitates the automated analysis and transformation of the specification.

The key implementation challenge is to construct the synchronization and scheduling details otherwise given explicitly by the designer. Three techniques together meet this challenge: (1) *relaxation*, which automatically extracts the concurrency from the specification, (2) *global scheduling*, which transforms the specification to implement each unbounded queue as a finite buffer, and (3) *pipelining*, which automatically transforms the base specification to obtain a more efficient pipelined implementation. Except for the last step of our synthesis algorithm, which generates Verilog from symbolic expressions, our compiler technology is not specially targeted to circuit design.

The primary contribution of this paper is the formalization of our design approach. Specifically, we provide a formal definition of our target class of systems and the algorithms that our compiler uses to implement these systems. We also sketch correctness proofs for two of our three primary compiler algorithms. This formal foundation gives the designer the guarantee that, if she starts from a correct initial specification, the resulting implementation is also correct (assuming the compiler is implemented correctly).

The remainder of the paper is organized as follows. Section 2 presents a simple example that illustrates our approach. Section 3 reviews our specification language and the basic idea behind the synthesis and pipelining algorithms. Section 4 presents the formal framework and the correctness proofs. Section 5 presents experimental results. Section 6 discusses related work; we conclude in Section 7.

2 Example

In general, a system consists of state and computation. Our language enables the designer to specify the computation as a set of *modules*. Each module performs local computation and interacts with other modules by reading and writing parts of the state. For circuits, the state holds values across clock cycles, is distributed throughout the circuit, and is implemented as hardware registers and memory. The computations are implemented as combinational logic that transforms data during each clock cycle.

We illustrate this approach by presenting a simple circuit example: a linear pipelined datapath with associated control, which implements a very reduced instruction set: an 'increment' instruction INC, and a 'jump if register value zero' instruction JRZ. We next present the specification for a three-stage pipelined implementation of this instruction set.

```
1 type reg = int(3), val = int(8), loc = int(8);
2 type ins = <INC reg> | <JRZ reg loc>;
3 type irf = <INC reg val> | <JRZ val loc>;
4 var pc : loc, im : ins[N], rf : val[8];
5 var iq = queue(ins), rq = queue(irf);
```

Fig. 1. State Variables and Type Declarations in Example

2.1 State

The state consists of all the state variables used to specify the system. Figure 1 presents the state declarations for our example. Line 1 declares three type names: a 3 bit integer value reg which is used to represent architecture register names, an 8 bit integer val which is used for the values in the register file, and an 8 bit integer loc, which represents the locations of the instructions in the instruction memory. To represent a data type with several different formats, introduce a tagged union type similar to those found in ML [23] and Haskell [16]. Line 2 declares a tagged union type ins which represents instructions. An ins type instruction can have of one of two data formats: the format <INC reg> has an INC tag and a register name field of type reg, while JRZ reg loc has the tag JRZ, a register name field of type reg, and a branch target field of type loc. Line 3 declares the type irf for instructions whose register operands the processor has already fetched from the register file. This type declaration is also of tagged union type and reads similarly to the type declaration on line 2.

Line 4 declares the following state variables: a program counter pc of type loc declared on line 1, an instruction memory im of type array of N instructions of type ins, and a register file rf of type array of 8 values of type val. The declarations on line 5 use a predefined data type: a queue is a conceptually unbounded first-in first-out (FIFO) queue that carries values between modules. Our language supports the following primitive operations on queues:
- head(q) : Retrieves the first element in the queue q.
- tail(q) : Returns the rest of q after the first element.
- insert(q,e) : Returns the queue after inserting element e at the end of q.
- replace(e1,e2,q) : Returns q after replacing all entries e1 by e2. This operation can involve a partial match if e1 contains don't care fields.
- notin(q,e) : Returns *true* if the element e is not in q; otherwise returns *false*. This operation can involve a partial match if e contains don't care fields.
- q = nil: Resets the queue to be empty.

We implement queues in the hardware as a number of registers equal to the length of the queue. Line 5 declares a queue iq of instructions of type ins, for fetched instructions, and a queue rq of instructions of type irf, for instructions whose register operands have been fetched.

2.2 Modules

Our circuit executes a sequence of instructions. To execute each instruction, the circuit performs the following steps:

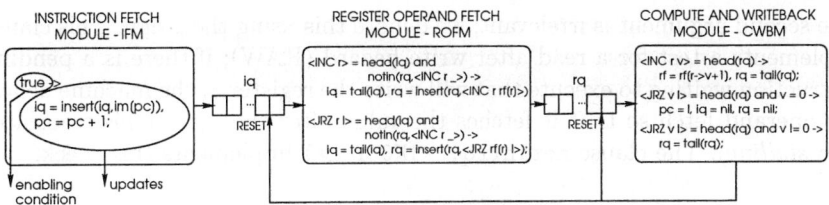

Fig. 2. Specification Example

- It reads the instruction from the instruction memory.
- If the instruction is an INC instruction, it reads a value from the register file, increments it and stores it back into the register file.
- If the instruction is a JRZ instruction with the value in its register argument zero, it jumps to the location argument and continues execution from there.
- If the instruction is a JRZ instruction with the value in its register argument different from zero, it does nothing.

As illustrated in Figure 2, there is one module per pipeline stage: an instruction fetch module IFM, a register operand fetch module ROFM and a compute and write back module CWBM. To keep the pipeline full, the circuit uses a speculative approach that starts the execution of the next instruction before it knows whether the instruction should execute or not. If the circuit starts executing an instruction but later determines that the instruction should not execute, it restores the state of the circuit to reflect the values before the instruction started executing, then restarts the execution. If the speculation was correct, the circuit performs useful computation for each clock cycle that otherwise would have been spent stalling. Pipelining combined with speculation can increase the parallelism in the system and therefore boost the throughput of the circuit.

Modules interact with other modules by reading and writing shared state. The rules in each module read values from input queues and other state variables, perform local computations, then write results to output queues and other state variables. Each rule has an enabling condition and a set of updates to the state, separated by an arrow. When the rules enabling condition evaluates to true, it is enabled and can atomically apply its updates to the current state to obtain the next state. We illustrate this conceptual model of execution by discussing the operation of the rules in ROFM.

The two rules in the module ROFM remove instructions from iq, fetch the register operands, and insert them into rq. The first rule processes INC instructions, and the second one processes JRZ instructions. Both rules use a form of pattern matching similar to that found in ML and Haskell. The enabling condition of the first rule is `<INC r> = head(iq) and notin(rq, <INC r _>)`.

- Its first clause, `<INC r> = head(iq)`, requires that the instruction at the head of iq be an increment instruction with register name r. If this is true, the clause matches and *binds* the variable r to the register name argument of the INC instruction, to be used later in the rule when referring to this operand.
- The second clause, `notin(rq, <INC r _>)`, uses the binding to test that the queue rq does not contain an increment instruction whose first argument is r.

The second argument is irrelevant; we denote this using the _ sign. This clause implements a test for a read after write hazard (RAW); if there is a pending instruction waiting to execute that will write the register r, the machine delays the operand fetch so that it fetches the value after the write (this translates into *stalling*). The clause notin(rq, <INC r _>) implements this check.

3 Background

Before presenting the formal framework and correctness proofs, we informally present the key elements of our approach and outline the algorithms in our compiler.

3.1 Specification Language

Timing issues such as synchronization, concurrency, and execution order are a primary source of complexity for circuit designers. For performance reasons, most languages for designing synchronous circuits are based on a synchronous model of execution. The advantage is that the developer can tightly control the specification to deliver an efficient circuit. The disadvantage is that the tight temporal coupling of this model makes local reasoning difficult, undercutting the advantages of modular design.

Our approach addresses this problem by presenting an asynchronous abstract model of execution. The designer specifies a circuit as a set of modules connected by conceptually unbounded FIFO queues; the update rules that model the computations of the modules execute atomically and asynchronously with regard to each other. This is a standard model of asynchronous execution found in systems such as Unity [8] and term rewriting systems [2]. Our synthesis algorithm eliminates the potential inefficiency associated with a direct asynchronous implementation by automatically generating a coordinated global schedule for all operations in the system. This schedule is used to generate an efficient synchronous implementation in synthesizable Verilog.

Advantages: Using conceptually unbounded queues to connect the modules has two benefits: (1) it enables the designer to reason about and develop each module in isolation, then compose the modules together into a complete system without the need to deal with complex global issues such as the coordinated assignment of operations to clock cycles, and (2) it enables the designer to reason about the correctness of the specifications without reasoning about the concurrent execution of the composed modules. In this sense, queues localize the temporal aspects of the design.

3.2 Implementation

A novelty of our approach is that it takes a modular specification with asynchronous execution semantics and converts it into a synchronous, parallel implementation. It is the compiler's job to efficiently bridge the gap between these models of execution. The key idea of the synthesis algorithm is to automatically compose the module specifications to derive, at the granularity of individual clock cycles, a global schedule for the operations of the entire system, including the removal and insertion of queue elements. The resulting implementation executes efficiently in a completely synchronous, pipelined manner [20].

To decrease the clock cycle of the generated circuit, our compiler implements a technique we call relaxation, which makes it possible to evaluate many or all of the enabling conditions immediately and in parallel rather than sequentially. The compiler also implements a set of techniques geared towards optimizing the generated combinational logic[1].

These algorithms are all based on the underlying assumption that each individual operation takes less time than the clock cycle time to complete. For the case in which this assumption does not hold, we have developed an automated technique that implements functional pipelining for sequential circuits [19]. The existing synthesis algorithm would need to be extended if certain individual basic operations are too expensive to implement in combinational logic.

Relaxation: The operation preceding relaxation in our synthesis algorithm orders all the rules of the specification for symbolic execution. The specification produced by this operation may suffer from an excessively long clock cycle, as the execution of the rules modifying shared state is completely sequentialized. Our implementation executes multiple rules at each clock cycle as follows. For each set that consists of rules with no data dependencies within the set, the compiler can execute all the rules in the set in parallel. If a set of rules has data dependencies, our compiler transforms the rules, when possible, so that their enabling conditions test the state of the system at the beginning of the clock cycle rather than the state created by the previously executing rule. For a rule R that updates state variables tested by a subsequent rule R', if we can prove that the execution of R will not disable the enabling condition of R', we can modify the precondition of R' to test the state before R executes. To preserve correctness, the updates still execute sequentially if they operate on the same state variable. This transformation ensures that each element of data traverses at most one module per clock cycle, producing an acceptable critical path for the circuit. By eliminating unnecessary serialization, we expose the additional parallelism in the specification and shorten the clock cycle of the circuit, and, indirectly, increase its throughput. Relaxation does not insert or remove delays in or from the circuit.

Global Scheduling: In the initial specification, queues have unbounded length. But the implementation must have a finite, specific number of entries allocated for each hardware buffer implementing a queue. The designer decides on the amount of memory elements he or she is willing to spend on each of these buffers,

---

[1] These optimizations include common subexpression elimination and mutual exclusion testing. The former avoids unnecessary replication of hardware, while the latter eliminates false paths in the implementation.

and the compiler generates an implementation based on this budget that, for any execution instance of the system, does not exceed that length.

The global scheduling algorithm can handle specifications whose rules can have both acyclic and cyclic queue insertion and removal dependencies. For cyclic specifications, the compiler looks at groups of rules that must execute together to maximize the concurrency and avoid both deadlock and overflow of the queues in the system; for acyclic specifications, it only needs to consider each rule in isolation. The scheduler augments each rule that inserts an element into a queue to ensure that it never causes any of the corresponding finite hardware buffers to overflow. The basic approach is to assume all queues are within length at the beginning of the clock cycle and schedule only those rules for firing that are 1) enabled and 2) whose combined execution leaves the queues within their length at the *end* of the clock cycle. As a result, the circuit can perform single or multiple reads or writes from and into each queue in the same clock cycle, even if the queues are initially full. The condition is that enough rules will execute that remove elements from queues, therefore making space for new elements to be inserted. Queues can get arbitrarily[2] large during the clock cycle as long as they are within the maximum specified length at the end of the cycle.

The generated global schedule enables the synchronous and concurrent execution of multiple rules per clock cycle. In hardware, global scheduling corresponds to generating the control signals for the combinational logic, and a given length of 1 for each queue translates into the synthesis of a standard pipeline. The global scheduling algorithm is the key to efficient pipelining; it also may reduce the area of the resulting circuit.

Pipelining: This transformation automatically generates a pipelined specification from a non-pipelined or insufficiently pipelined specification. The pipelining algorithm repeatedly shortens the clock cycle of the circuit by extracting a computation from the critical path and moving it into a new pipeline stage. The new stage precomputes the result of the selected expression, using a new queue to pass the result to the module from which the expression was removed. To keep the pipeline full, the new stage must produce the next value of the expression before the final values of the variables it accesses become available. The algorithm achieves this goal by speculating on these values, using state retention and recovery to respond to incorrect speculations.

Our algorithm uses several techniques to improve the quality of the pipelined circuit. If the amount of state necessary to recover from an incorrect speculation is excessive, our algorithm can generate stall logic that causes the pipeline stage to stall until the new values are available. This technique eliminates the need for retaining recovery state, as the execution of the pipeline stage will never need to roll back. Our algorithm can also generate circuits that forward the correct value to preceding pipeline stages. This technique increases the throughput of

---

[2] The maximum number of elements in a queue at any time is the maximum number of non-mutually exclusive rules that append elements into the queue plus the length of the buffer implementing the queue. We communicate these values within a clock cycle via wires.

the circuit by reducing the amount of time that the circuit spends recovering from incorrect speculations or waiting for correct values to become available. The pipelining transformation preserves the property that every register and memory variable in the circuit specification observes the same sequence of values after as before pipelining.

Our pipelining algorithm reduces the designer time and effort by automating complex techniques. The less obvious advantage, though equally important, is that it increases the confidence in the correctness of the resulting implementation. Pipelining starts from an easy specification with little or no concurrency, which is easy to verify for correctness; the resulting pipelined version needs to be highly concurrent, and therefore manually developed versions are a lot harder to verify.

4 Formalism

The first part of this section describes the general formal framework necessary for proving the correctness of the relaxation and global scheduling algorithms. We then define the specification of the system before and after applying each algorithm, as direct or extended instances of the general framework. The second part of the section states and gives a short outline of the proofs for theorems regarding the correctness properties of our algorithms.

4.1 Formal Definitions

We define a **system** to be a tuple $System\ G = \langle T, ex, f, g \rangle$.

A **transition system** is a set of **transitions** $T = \{t_i \equiv l_i : c_i \Rightarrow u_i\}$.

A **transition** $t \equiv l : c \Rightarrow u \in T$ has a label $l \in Label = \{1, ..., |T|\}$, a condition $c \in C$ and an update $u \in U$.

We have an **external** function $ex : t \to Bool$ s.t. $ex(t)$ is **true** if the transition t is observable from the exterior and **false** otherwise. We say that a transition $t \equiv l : c \Rightarrow u$ is **external** iff $ex(t)$ is **true** and **internal** otherwise.

The **set S of states** $s \in S$ is the set of functions $S = Vars \to Vals$, where $Vars$ is the set of all register, memory state variables and queues ($Queues$) in the circuit specification, and $Vals$ is the set of all values that the state variables in $Vars$ can take.

We define two functions f and g as follows:
- We assume a set of conditions C, a set of expressions E and a set of updates U. The evaluation of some $c \in C$ in some state returns a *Bool* value. The evaluation of some $e \in E$ in some state returns a value in $Vals$. To make the notation more concise, we extend $Vals$ to include *Bool*. The evaluation function $f : E \times S \to Vals$ returns the value of expression $e \in E$ in $s \in S$.
- An update function $g : U \times S \to S$. $g(u, s) = s'$ applies the updates in u to the state s and returns the modified state s'.

Each transition system T defines a **transition relation** $R \subseteq S \times T \times S$.

$$R = \{\langle s, t, s' \rangle.\ t \equiv l : c \to u \in T \wedge f(c, s) \wedge g(u, s) = s'\}$$

Assume there exists an **initial state** s_0 of T. In s_0 the following are true:
- $\forall v_k \in Vars - Queues$, $s_0(v_k) = initialVal_k$, where $initialVal_k \in Vals$ are the initial values of the registers and memories in the circuit.
- All the queues are empty: $\forall k$ s.t. $1 \leq k \leq maxQueue$, $s_0(queue_k) = \{\}$

An **execution fragment** is a finite alternating sequence of states and transitions $frag = \{s_1 t_1 s_2 t_2 s_3 ... s_n \mid s_i \in S \,.\, t_i \in T \,.\, \langle s_i, t_i, s_{i+1}\rangle \in R\}$.

An **execution** is an execution fragment starting in the initial state s_0.

A state s is **reachable** if s is the final state of some finite execution.

An **execution sequence** is the sequence of states in an execution obtained after dropping the intermediate transitions:

$$\tau = \{s_1, s_2, ..., s_n \mid s_1 t_1 s_2 t_2 ... s_n \text{ is an execution}\}$$

SPEC: is an instance of $System$ of the form $\langle T^S, ex^S, f^S, g^S \rangle$. T^S is a transition system that represents the nondeterministic specification of the circuit. We skip over the actual definitions for the set of expressions E^S, the set of updates U^S, and the functions f^S and g^S. For more details see [18].

RELAX: is an instance of $System$ of the form $\langle T^R, ex^R, f^R, g^R \rangle$. T^R is a transition system that represents the circuit implementation obtained as the result of relaxation.

We define a new **external** function ex^R that has the same values as $ex^S(t_i)$ for each transition $t_i \in T^R$ with the same label as the transition in T^S. We defer the definition of the external function for the newly introduced transitions to the construction of the new transition system.

The **set S^R of states** $s^R \in S^R$ is the set of functions $S^R = (Vars \times Versions) \cup \{\text{pc}\} \rightarrow Vals$, where $Versions$ is a set of integers and pc is a variable of type integer that represents the ordinal number of the transition in the relaxed implementation that is currently under evaluation. pc provides a way to express the deterministic execution of the transitions in the relaxed circuit, following the order used by the relaxation transformation.

The set of expressions E^R in RELAX is $e^R ::= c \mid (v, n, p) \mid \text{pc} \mid \rho(e^R{}_1, ..., e^R{}_n)$

The triple (v, n, p) stands for a variable $v \in Vars$, its version $n \in Versions$ and position $p \in Position$. $Position$ is a set of integers. Our transition system contains positions, while the state does not. A position and variable name pair uniquely denotes a state variable instance within the condition of a transition.

We also define the set of updates U^R in RELAX
$ur ::= \text{pc++} \mid \text{pc} = 1 \mid (v_1, nr_1, p_1) = e^R{}_1, ..., (v_n, nr_n, p_n) = e^R{}_n, \text{pc} = \text{pc++}$
$\mid (v_1, nr_1, p_1) = e^R{}_1, ..., (v_n, nr_n, p_n) = e^R{}_n, \text{pc} = 1$

We introduce a function **update:** $U^R \times S^R \rightarrow \mathcal{P}(Vars)$ which takes an update $u^R \in U^R$ and a state $s^R \in S^R$ and returns the set of variables in $Vars$ that get updated.

We define a numbering function as follows:
$RN: (E^S \cup U^S) \times Version \rightarrow E^R \cup U^R$
$RN(c)(n) = c$
$RN(v)(n) = (v, n, 0)$
$RN(\rho(e^S{}_1, ..., e^S{}_n))(n) = \rho(RN(e^S{}_1)(n), ..., RN(e^S{}_n)(n))$

$RN(\text{pc}++)(n) = \text{pc}++$
$RN(\text{pc} = 1)(n) = \text{pc} = 1$
$RN((v_1, nr_1, p_1) = e^R{}_1, ..., (v_n, nr_n, p_n) = e^R{}_n, \text{pc}++)(k) =$
$(v_1, k+1, 0) = RN(e^S{}_1)(k); ...; (v_n, k+1, 0) = RN(e^S{}_n)(k), \text{pc}++$
$RN((v_1, nr_1, p_1) = e^R{}_1, ..., (v_n, nr_n, p_n) = e^R{}_n, \text{pc} = 1)(k) = ((v_1, k+1, 0) =$
$RN(e^S{}_1)(k); ...; (v_n, k+1, 0) = RN(e^S{}_n)(k), \text{pc} = 1$

We define a **variable positioning** function as follows:
$VP : E^R \times Position \to E^R \times Position$
$VP(c, i) = (c, i)$
$VP((v, n, 0), i) = ((v, n, i), i+1)$
$VP(\text{pc}, i) = (\text{pc}, i)$
$VP(\rho(e^R{}_1, ..., e^R{}_n), i) = \text{let } (a_1, b_1) = VP(e^R{}_1, i), (a_2, b_2) = VP(e^R{}_2, b_1), ...,$
$(a_n, b_n) = VP(e^R{}_n, b_{n-1}) \text{ in } (\rho(a_1, a_2, ..., a_n), b_n)$

We can now define a relaxation function RE that replaces the current version of each variable $v \in Vars$ in position $p \in Position$ with its relaxed version. We obtain the relaxed version of a variable $v \in Vars$ with original version $n \in Versions$ in position $p \in Position$ by invoking a function $\sigma \in \Sigma : Vars \times Versions \times Position \to Versions$. The original version n is equal to $l \bmod |T^S|$, where l is the label of the transition that invokes $\sigma \in \Sigma$. From the construction of the new transition system we will see that the tuple (v, n, p) is unique within the set of all the external transitions in T^R.

$RE : E^R \times \Sigma \to E^R$
$RE(c, \sigma) = c$
$RE((v, n, p), \sigma) = (v, \sigma(v, n, p), p)$
$RE(\text{pc}, \sigma) = \text{pc}$
$RE(\rho(e^R{}_1, ..., e^R{}_n), \sigma) = \rho(RE(e^R{}_1, \sigma), ..., RE(e^R{}_n, \sigma))$

We define a new **transition system** $T^R = \{t_i \equiv l_i : c_i \Rightarrow u_i | i \in \{1, ..., n\}\}$ by modifying the previous transition system T^S as follows:

- For each transition $t \equiv l : c \Rightarrow u \in T^S$, construct two transitions in T^R, one external, one not external, as follows:
  $t_l \equiv l : (\text{pc} == l) \wedge RE(\pi_1(VP(RN(c^S)(l), 1)), \sigma) \Rightarrow RN(u^S)(l), \text{pc}++;$
  $t_{|T|+l} \equiv |T|+l : (\text{pc} == l) \wedge \overline{RE(\pi_1(VP(RN(c^S)(l), 1)), \sigma)} \Rightarrow \text{pc}++;$
  $|T|+l$ is a fresh label and $ex^R(t_{|T|+l}) = \text{false}$. We use π_1 for the projection of the first element of a tuple. For a pair (a, b) we have $\pi_1(a, b) = a$.

- Create a new transition $t_{2*|T|+1}$ to express the wrap-around after the relaxation algorithm tried all other transitions and either executed them or not. The new transition is not external.

$\forall v \in Vars \ t_{2*|T|+1} \equiv 2*|T|+1 : (\text{pc} == |T|+1) \Rightarrow s(v,1) = s(v, s(\text{pc})), \text{pc} = 1;$

$2 * |T| + 1$ is a fresh label and $ex^R(t_{2*|T|+1}) = \text{false}$.
Assume there exists an **initial state** $s^R{}_0$ of T^R. In $s^R{}_0$ the following are true:

- $\forall v_k \in Vars - Queues, \forall i \in \{1, ..., |T|+1\}, s^R{}_0(v_k, i) = initialVal_k$, where $initialVal_k \in Vals$ are the initial values of the registers and memories in the circuit.
- $s^R{}_0(\text{pc}) = 1$

- All the queues are empty: $\forall k$ s.t. $1 \leq k \leq maxQueue$, $s^R{}_0(queue_k) = \{\}$

We skip over the actual definitions for functions f^R and g^R. For details see [18].

RELAXQ: is a set of two inputs, a system $\langle T^R, ex^R, f^R, g^R \rangle$ of the same type with RELAX, and a user-defined length $maxLength(queue_k)$ for each queue $queue_k, k \in \{1, ..., maxQueue\}$. The semantics of a transition in this system is the same as the semantics of a transition in RELAX with one difference. If, for the given queue lengths, executing the update of the transition would overflow at least one of the queues, that transition is not enabled for execution, i.e:

$$[\![\langle c \Rightarrow u, T^R \rangle]\!] = \{\langle s, c \Rightarrow u, g^R(u,s) \rangle . f^R(c,s) \text{ and } u \Rightarrow \text{overflow}(s_i) \text{ is false}\}$$

where

$$\forall i \in \{s(\mathsf{pc})+1, ..., |T|\}, s_i = \begin{cases} g^R(u_{i-1}, s_{i-1}) & \text{if } f^R(c_{i-1}, s_{i-1}) \\ s_{i-1} & \text{otherwise} \end{cases} \quad (1)$$

and overflow(s) is only defined for the states in which $s(\mathsf{pc}) = |T| + 1$ as:

$$\text{overflow}(s) = \begin{cases} \exists queue_k \in Queues \, . \, length(queue_k, s) > maxLength(queue_k) \\ \qquad\qquad\qquad \text{if } s(\mathsf{pc}) = |T| + 1 \\ undefined \qquad \text{otherwise} \end{cases}$$

$length : Queues \times S^R \to Int$ is a function that returns the current length of the queue in the given state. We also define a function $room^R : Queues \times S^R \to Int$ that returns the number of empty slots of the given queue in the given state.

A transition system with this semantics defines a transition relation $R^R_q \subseteq S^R \times T^R \times S^R$. $R^R_q = \{\langle s^R, t^R, s^{R'} \rangle \, . \, t^R \equiv l_r : c^R \to u^R \in T^R \land f^R(c^R, s^R) \land g^R(u^R, s^R) = s^{R'} \land u^R \Rightarrow \text{overflow}(s^R{}_i) \text{ is false}\}$, where $s^R{}_i$ is defined as in (1).

FINIT: is an instance of $System$ of the form $\langle T^F, ex^F, f^F, g^F \rangle$. T^F is a transition system that represents the circuit implementation after global scheduling.

We define two functions, $tail : t \times Queues \to Bool$ and $append : t \times Queues \to Bool$ that take a transition and a queue and return true iff the transition contains a $tail$ or, correspondingly, an $append$ operation on the queue given as parameter. We also define a function $room^F : Queues \times S^F \to Int$ that returns the number of empty slots of the given queue in the given state.

We call a transition $t \equiv l : c \Rightarrow u \in T^F$ **appending** if $\exists queue_k \in Queues$. $append(t, queue_k) = \text{true}$.

We define a new **transition system** $T^F = \{t_i \equiv l_i : c_i \Rightarrow u_i | i \in \{1,...,n\}\}$ by modifying the previous transition system T^R such that for every appending transition $t \equiv l : c \Rightarrow u \in T^R$, we construct a transition in T^F of the form

$$t \equiv l : c \land finalLengthOK(s^F, T^F, \text{currentPath}) \Rightarrow u$$

where currentPath starts as $[](\text{nil})$.

Let a function $eval : Bool \to \{0,1\}$ return 1 for true and 0 for false. For some appending transition $t^F \equiv l^F : c^F \Rightarrow u^F \in R^F$ from state s^F, we define:

$finalLengthOKqueue(s^F, T^F, queue_k, \text{currentPath}) =$

$$\sum_i eval(tail(t_i, queue_k) \bigwedge$$

$$(f^F(c^F{}_i \wedge finalLengthOK(s^F{}_i, T^F, newPath), s^F{}_i) \vee (t_i \in \text{currentPath})))$$
$$+ \, room(queue_k, s^F) > 0, \; \forall i \in \{l^F+1, ..., |T|\} \; . \; tail(t_i, queue_k) = \text{true},$$

where $s^F{}_{l^F} = s^F$ and $s^F{}_i = \begin{cases} g^F(u^F{}_{i-1}, s^F{}_{i-1}) & \text{if } f^F(c^{F'}{}_{i-1}, s^F{}_{i-1}) \\ s^F{}_{i-1} & \text{otherwise} \end{cases}$

$$newPath = \begin{cases} \text{currentPath} & \text{if } t_i \in \text{currentPath} \\ \text{currentPath} \vee t_i & \text{otherwise} \end{cases}$$

$$finalLengthOK(s^F, T^F, \text{currentPath}) =$$
$$\bigwedge finalLengthOK queue(s^F, T^F, queue_k, \text{currentPath}),$$
$$\forall queue_k \in Queues \; . \; append(t^F, queue_k) = \text{true}$$

Here currentPath holds the set of currently explored transitions for each starting transition in the system. This set is necessary for cyclic specifications.

The semantics of a transition in T^F is the following. If, for the given queue lengths, executing the update of the transition does not ensure that all the queues are within their maximum lengths when $s^F(\text{pc}) = |T|+1$, then T^F goes into an ERROR state s_{ERROR}.

We will show that the condition $finalLengthOK(s^F, T^F, \text{currentPath})$ makes sure that FINIT never goes into an ERROR state provided that the designer specifies appropriate lengths for all the queues.

Assume there exists an **initial state** s^F_0 of T^F. In s^F_0 the following are true:
- $\forall v_k \in Vars - Queues, \forall i \in \{1, ..., |T|+1\}$, $s^F_0(v_k, i) = initialVal_k$, where $initialVal_k \in Vals$ are the initial values of the registers and memories in the circuit.
- $s^F_0(\text{pc}) = 1$
- All the queues are empty: $\forall k$ s.t. $1 \leq k \leq maxQueue$, $s^F_0(queue_k) = \{\}$

4.2 Correctness

We prove two properties for each algorithm: (1) simulation: the transformed and the original circuit are in a simulation relation, and (2) non-termination: the transformed circuit preserves the non-termination property of the original circuit. Relaxation takes as input a system of type SPEC, and outputs a system of type RELAX. Global scheduling takes a set of two inputs of the form described in RELAXQ, and outputs a system of type FINIT.

1. Relaxation – Simulation

We want to prove that the behavior of the resulting specification after relaxation never does anything that the specification before relaxation could not do. This

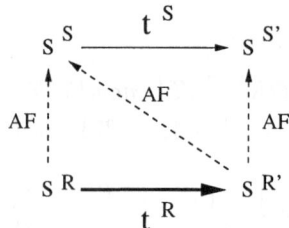

Fig. 3. Commutative Diagram for Simulation

means that we want to prove that for any execution in RELAX, we can find an execution in SPEC with the same execution sequence.

We first define the abstraction function AF that maps each state of RELAX to a state of SPEC: $AF(s^R) \to \{\forall v \in Vars \mid s^S(v) = s^R(v, s^R(\mathsf{pc}))\}$.

Theorem 1: (Simulation) $\forall s^R \in S^R, \forall s^S \in S^S, \forall t^R, \forall s^{R'} \in S^R$. $s^S = AF(s^R)$
if $\langle s^R, t^R, s^{R'} \rangle \in R^R$ then
$(\exists t^S, \exists s^{S'} \in S^S.\langle s^S, t^S, s^{S'} \rangle \in R^S$ and $s^{S'} = AF(s^{R'}))$ or $s^S = AF(s^{R'})$

The proof goes by induction on the length of the execution sequence. The induction step is a case analysis on the form of the transition t^R. It uses the definitions of the functions f^R, g^R, AF and the following property:

$\forall s^R \in S^R, \forall i$. ConsistentExecutionTrace(s^R, T^R) and
$f^R(RE(\pi_1(VP(RN(c^S{}_i)(l_i), 1)), \sigma), s^R) \wedge (\mathsf{pc} \geq l_i)$
$\to f^R(\pi_1(VP(RN(c^S)(l_i), 1)), s^R)$

where ConsistentExecutionTrace(s^R, T^R) is an invariant that ensures that the execution trace T^R is valid.

The intuition is that we can follow the constructive steps of the relaxation algorithm to prove that, if the enabling condition of some relaxed transition evaluates to true, than the enabling condition of the original transition also evaluates to true. Therefore, the transformed specification never takes any step that that the original specification cannot take.

2. Relaxation – Non-termination

We want to prove that relaxation cannot stop the progress in the execution of the system. Non-termination says that if from any state s of SPEC there exists an execution step that can be taken, there exists an execution step in RELAX that can be taken from some state in RELAX reachable only by internal transitions from any state that maps to s using AF.

Let $R_0 = \{\langle s_1, s_2 \rangle \mid \langle s_1, t, s_2 \rangle \in R^R$ and $ex^R(t) = \mathsf{false}\}$

Theorem 2: (Non-termination) $(\forall s^S \in S^S, \forall s^R \in S^R)$ such that
(ConsistentExecutionTrace(s^R, T^R) and $AF(s^R) = s^S$,

if $\exists t^S . \langle s^S, t^S, s^{S'}\rangle \in R^S$ then $\exists t^R \exists s^{R*}$.
$\langle s^R, s^{R*}\rangle \in R_0^{3*|T|+1}$ and $\langle s^{R*}, t^R, s^{R'}\rangle \in R^R$ and $ex^R(t^R) = \text{true}$

Lemma 1:
For any $k \geq 0$ and some state $s^R \in S^R$ s.t. $AF(s^R) = s^S$ and $l = s^R(\text{pc})$, there exists a sequence of states $s^{R0},...,s^{Rk}$ in RELAX starting from $s^{R0} = s^R$ s.t. the following hold: $\langle s^{R^{k-1}}, s^{R^k}\rangle \in R_0^1, \langle s^R, s^{R^k}\rangle \in R_0^k, s^S = AF(s^{R^k})$, and $\forall v\ s^{R^k}(v, l + d(k, l)) = s^R(v, l)$, where k is the number of transition executions in RELAX and

$$d(k, l) = \begin{cases} k & \text{if } k \leq |T| + 1 - l \\ k - (|T| + 1) & \text{otherwise} \end{cases}$$

The proof for *Lemma 1* goes by induction on the number of transition executions in RELAX. For k in *Lemma 1* s.t. $k = |T| + minI - l + 1$, where $minI$ is the smallest integer label of all the transitions in SPEC that can execute from s^S, we can prove the non-termination theorem by contradiction. The intuition behind the non-termination proof is that since a rule R in the transformed numbering tests a state previous to the current state, if R is enabled in the original numbering but not in the transformed one, *some* rule *does* execute in the transformed numbering and modifies the state originally tested by R.

3. Global Scheduling – Simulation

To prove that for any execution in FINIT, we can find an execution in RELAXQ with the same execution sequence, we first define an abstraction function AF^F that maps each state of FINIT to a state of RELAXQ.

$$FUNC\ AF^F(s^F) \rightarrow \{\forall v \in Vars | s^F(v, n) = s^R(v, n)\}$$

Theorem 3: (Simulation) $\forall s^F \in S^F, \forall s^R \in S^R, \forall t^F, \forall s^{F'} \in S^F$,
  if $s^R = AF(s^F)$ and $\langle s^F, t^F, s^{F'}\rangle \in R^F$, then
  $\exists t^R, \exists s^{R'} \in S^R . s^{R'} = AF(s^{F'})$ and $\langle s^R, t^R, s^{R'}\rangle \in R^R{}_q$.

The proof proceeds by induction on the length of the execution sequence. The induction step is a case analysis on the form of the transition t^F and it is similar (and less difficult) then the simulation proof for the relaxation algorithm. The idea is that if a transition in the transformed system executes, then it would have also executed in the original system. This is true because the enabling condition is strictly stronger after than before applying the scheduling transformation. Global scheduling will disable those rules whose execution would result in overflowing at least one queue in the system, but will never enable a rule that was not enabled when the queues were unbounded.

4. Global Scheduling – Non-termination

We want to prove that if from any state s of RELAXQ there exists an external execution step that can be taken, then there exists an external execution step in

FINIT that can be taken from any state that maps to s using AF s.t. the system does not go into an ERROR state. We also want to prove that FINIT goes into an ERROR state iff the only transition from the state s would overflow at least one of the queues. In other words, given enough buffer space such that executing the original specification on this budget does not exceed the given queue lengths, global scheduling does not introduce deadlock.

Theorem 4: (Non-termination) $\forall s^R \in S^R, \forall s^F \in S^F$,
  if $\exists t^R . AF(s^F) = s^R$ and $\langle s^R, t^R, s^{R'}\rangle \in R^R_q$ and $ex^R(t^R) = $ true then
  $\exists t^F, \exists s^{F'} \in S^F . \langle s^F, t^F, s^{F'}\rangle \in R^F$ and $ex^F(t^F)$ and $s^{F'} \neq s_{ERROR}$.
Also, $\forall s^R \in S^R, \forall s^F \in S^F, \forall t^R$,
  if $AF(s^F) = s^R$ and $\langle s^R, t^R, s^{R'}\rangle \in R^R$ and $ex^R(t^R))$ then
  $\langle s^R, t^R, s^{R'}\rangle \notin R^R_q$ iff $finalLengthOK(s^F, T^F, \text{currentPath}) = $ false.

Our global scheduling algorithm generates a correct transformed specification that correctly deadlocks if the designer specifies lengths for the queues that are not large enough for the particular application. It is the designer's responsability to know what queue length values are enough for the given circuit not to deadlock, we prove that, given such lengths, our scheduling algorithm does not introduce deadlock in the system.

The proof for (4.2) proceeds by contradiction to show that if an external transition t takes place in RELAXQ, we can infer that $room^F(q, s) > 0$, and therefore there is space in q for a transition t' in FINIT to execute. To prove (4.2), we start from the current states in RELAXQ and FINIT, in which we know that all corresponding queues have the same number of elements. We then only have to prove that corresponding rules in these two systems, following transitions t in RELAXQ and t' in FINIT, either both execute or neither does. This is sufficient because it proves strict equality between the lengths of corresponding queues in RELAXQ and FINIT, at the end of the cycle. Let r and r' be the corresponding rules immediately following t in RELAXQ and t' in FINIT. If r and r' are not appending rules, they both execute if their enabling conditions — which are identical — evaluate to true. Otherwise, none of them executes. If r and r' are appending rules, we reduced proving (4.2) for t and t' to proving (4.2) for r and r'. Because the number of rules following t and t', correspondingly, is finite, we will eventually reach the last rules in the two systems, where (4.2) holds, since there are no more following rules.

5. Global Scheduling – Correctness for Groups of Transitions

For cyclic specifications, the algorithm considers the coordinated execution of groups of transitions, rather than transitions in isolation. We call a **phase** a sequence of external transition executions, such that each transition executes at most once. The simulation theorem states that for any phase in FINIT, we can find a phase in RELAXQ with the same execution sequence. The proof is virtually identical to the simulation proof for one transition, and is based on the fact that the enabling condition of each of the transitions is strictly stronger in FINIT than in RELAXQ.

We can formulate a new non-termination theorem for groups of transitions which states that, if from any state s of RELAXQ there exists a phase that takes the system into a new state in which none of the queues overflows its designer-specified length, then from any state in FINIT, s', that maps to s using AF, there exists a phase in FINIT which does not take the new system into an ERROR state. The proof goes by contradiction and works on a phase instead of a single transition at a time. The idea is to infer that the transition from s' in the FINIT phase corresponding to the executing RELAXQ phase would have its enabling condition satisfied, and therefore execute.

5 Experimental Results

We have implemented a synthesis and pipelining system based on the algorithms presented in Sections 3.2 and 4. Our experiments are designed to investigate two aspects of using our system: (1) how natural and concise it is for the designer to write circuit specifications in our language, and (2) how well the resulting implementations perform. To evaluate our system, we developed a set of benchmarks in our specification language and used our system to produce synthesizable Verilog implementations at the RTL level. We then synthesized the resulting implementations using the Synopsys Design Compiler to an industry standard .25 micron standard cell process. We obtained manually written Verilog descriptions of the same or functionally equivalent circuits as the ones in our benchmark set, and we synthesized them in the same environment as the automatically generated versions. This is our reference point for performance evaluation.

Our benchmark set contains a processor and a few standard DSP applications: a bubblesort network, a butterfly network like the ones used in bitonic sort and FFTs, and a cascaded FIR filter. The processor is a 32-bit datapath, RISC-style, linearly pipelined processor with a complete instruction set. We obtained manually written versions of bubblesort and butterfly sort networks from the RAW benchmark suite at MIT. We were unable to obtain a free manually developed FIR application to match against our automatically generated FIR circuit. We obtained the processor benchmark off the web, from Santa Clara University; this is a standard 32-bit fixed point DSP that implements the same basic functionality as our processor. Figure 4 and Figure 5 show cycle time (MHz), total circuit area and and register area numbers for our four benchmarks and the corresponding manually written Verilog versions.

Benchmark	Cycle	Area	Register Area
Bubble Sort	324.67	1803.75	1371
Butterfly	204.08	1881.125	969
FIR filter	103.41	7384	3529
Pipelined Processor	88.89	28845	7533

Fig. 4. Clock Cycle and Area Estimates for Automatically Generated Versions

Benchmark	Cycle	Area	Register Area
Bubble Sort	308.64	1475.75	1192
Butterfly	120.34	2041.125	1348
FIR filter	—	—	—
SCU RTL 98 DSP	90.91	28359.75	7147

Fig. 5. Clock Cycle and Area Estimates for Manually Written Versions

5.1 Design Effort Evaluation

It took us less than 5 hours to develop the specification for the processor, and about 10 minutes for each of the other benchmarks. We believe this is significantly faster than developing the corresponding models by hand. Our processor specification contains 13 type and state declarations and 29 rule definitions for module specifications. The SCU RTL 98 DSP application, on the other hand, consists of approximately 885 lines of Verilog code. Our automatically generated implementation consists of about 1200 lines of synthesizable Verilog. The bubblesort benchmark has 2 multiple state declarations and 12 very simple rule definitions. The butterfly network has 3 multiple state declarations and 13 simple rule definitions. The FIR filter benchmark has 5 multiple state declarations and 4 rule definitions. The manually written specifications have 200 lines of Verilog code for bubblesort and 378 for butterfly.

The specification-to-Verilog synthesis time is roughly proportional to the complexity of the generated control. For all applications except the pipelined processor, our system required less than one minute to generate the Verilog output. For the processor, it took roughly half an hour. The synthesis times for the corresponding automatically generated Verilog versions, and manually written versions is comparable, and last roughly from 1 to 4 minutes for bubblesort and butterfly, while the automated version for the FIR filter takes about 15.00 minutes to synthesize. Our automatically generated RISC processor benchmark takes about 3:17 hours to synthesize; the functionally equivalent, manually developed SCU RTL 98 DSP application takes about 27.00 minutes to synthesize.

5.2 Performance Evaluation

For the bubblesort network, our compiler generates a circuit that is about 5 percent faster, and about 22 percent larger than the equivalent manually written version. The number of registers generated in the automatically synthesized version is about 15 percent larger than the equivalent number of registers in the manually written application. The extra register area comes from the counters and valid bits associated with each of the pipeline queues. Since the length of each such queue is given by the designer, the number of extra registers for the automatically generated application does not vary with the number of elements sorted by the bubblesort network. This means that the larger the number of elements sorted, the closer the gap in the total register area between the automatically generated and equivalent manually-written versions.

For our second benchmark, we took a manually written version of a bitonic sort network, and we introduced pipeline registers in the same places as in our high-level specification used as source for the automatically generated bitonic sort circuit. After synthesis, the manually written bitonic sort network application yields a circuit that is about 8.5 percent larger, and about 69.59 percent slower, than our automatically generated implementation. The circuit obtained after introducing the pipeline registers into the manually written application is only about 8.2 percent faster than the original manually written application. We stress here that we did not specify the same logic for this application in our language, as the one that is coded in the manually written version; rather, we designed and specified the bitonic sort network our own way, keeping the same number of numbers to be sorted, and the same width for the data paths.

In the case of our last, and biggest application, the RISC-style, linear pipelined processor, notice that the synthesized area is roughly the same, while the clock cycle of our processor is within 3 percent of the manually coded version.

6 Related Work

High-level synthesis approaches are based on a variety of languages such as concurrent languages, hardware description languages, software languages, data flow languages, and others. We can further distinguish different approaches within these categories. Concurrent languages consist of synchronous languages, protocol specification languages, and others like CSP, Occam, ADA, CCS, Unity, CRP, POLIS. Synchronous languages include Esterel [5], Lustre, Argos, Signal, RSML and Statecharts. Protocol specification languages include SDL, Lotos [26] and Estelle.

Software approaches are generally of one of three types: the library extension, the language extension, or the new language approach. The library extension approach includes systems like Scenic, work by Young et al. [27], SystemC, Lava and Hawk. The language extension approach includes Transmogrifier-C, Programmable Active Memory (PAM), Reactive-C, SpecCharts, ECL, SpecC, Data Parallel C. The new language approach includes the Olympus/Hercules system based on HardwareC, Superlog, V++, OpenJ, Rapide. There are also other systems like Compilogic, SpC, ADAS, RAW, and Fiper and Piper which use a specification language which is a subset of Standard Prolog. In industry, the hardware design languages that are heavily used are VHDL and Verilog.

Systems like Ptolemy, GRAPE, Warp at CMU, SPW from Cadence or COSSAP from Synopsys start from block diagram languages based on a dataflow semantics and are targeted to DSP design. Several specification and verification systems have taken an approach similar to ours, based on describing the behavior of a system by a state transition system [8, 14]. Closely related to our research, Hoe and Arvind develop a method for hardware description and synthesis based on an operation-centric approach. The hierarchical Production Based Specifications (PBS) model has similarities with our approach in that it enables temporal modularity when designing a circuit.

Traditionally, the correctness of a design was tested by simulation. Bryant's [7] introduction of reduced, ordered BDDs for circuit verification renewed interest in symbolic execution. Success in verification can be attributed to the development of formal methods like theorem provers and model checkers. Model checkers include EMC [9], Caesar [25], SMV [22], RuleBase [4], Spin [15], Murphi [10]. Theorem provers usually work using either the Boyer-Moore [6] system or the HOL [13] system. Other well-known theorem provers include LP [12], Nuprl [11], PVS [24], VERIFY [3], Esterel [5]. FoCs [1] (Formal Checkers) takes properties in CTL logic and automatically generates VHDL checkers from them, then integrates them into the simulation environment.

What is different about our approach is that we start from an initial specification in a high-level language, and generate a circuit implementation by applying algorithms that are formally correct. This ensures that, given a correct specification, the resulting implementation is also correct; no need for verification. In this way, our approach is closer to the formal synthesis work by Manohar [17] and Martin [21].

7 Conclusions

This paper presents the formal framework for our novel approach for specifying and automatically implementing efficient systems such as digital circuits and network protocols. Our goal is to reduce the design time, effort, and expertise required to build correct and efficient systems and to eliminate the need for the designer to deal directly with complex issues like global synchronization and explicit concurrency. Our approach uses a compiler to automatically transform modular, asynchronous specifications into efficient, tightly-coupled, synchronous implementations. Our results show that our specifications are roughly an order of magnitude shorter than corresponding synchronous specifications that deal directly with global timing issues, and that our compiler is capable of producing implementations that are of comparable efficiency.

We provide a formal definition of our target class of systems and the algorithms that our compiler uses to implement these systems. We also sketch correctness proofs for two of our three primary compiler algorithms. This formal foundation gives the designer the guarantee that, if a correct compiler starts from a correct initial specification, the resulting implementation is also correct.

References

1. Y. Abarbanel, I. Beer, L. Glushovsky, S. Keidar, and Y. Wolfsthal. Focs: Automatic generation of simulation checkers from formal specifications. In *CAV*, pages 538–542, 2000.
2. F. Baader and T. Nipkow. *Term rewriting and all that*. Cambridge University Press, 1998.
3. H. G. Barrow. Verify: A program for proving correctness of digital hardware designs. *Artificial Intelligence*, 24:437-91, 1984.

4. I. Beer, S. Ben-David, C. Eisner, and A. Landver. Rulebase: An industry-oriented formal verification tool. In *Proceedings of the 9th Design Automation Conference (DAC)*, pages 655–660. Association for Computing Machinery, Inc., June 1996.
5. F. Boussinot and R. de Simone. The ESTEREL language. In *Proceedings of the IEEE*, pages 79(9):1293–1304, Sept. 1991.
6. R. S. Boyer and J. S. Moore. *Computational Logic*. Academic Press, New York, 1979.
7. R. E. Bryant. A methodology for hardware verification based on logic simulation. *Journal of the ACM (JACM)*, 38(2):299–328, 1991.
8. K. M. Chandy and J. Misra. *Parallel program design: a foundation*. Addison-Wesley, Reading, Mass., 1988.
9. E. M. Clarke and E. A. Emerson. Synthesis of synchronization skeletons for branching time temporal logic. In *Logic of Programs: Workshop, Yorktown Heights, NY*, May 1981.
10. D. L. Dill, A. J. Drexler, A. J. Hu, and C. H. Yang. Protocol verification as a hardware design aid. In *IEEE International Conference on Computer Design: VLSI in Computers and Processors*, pages 522–525, 1992.
11. R. C. et al. *Implementing Mathematics with the NuPRL Proof Development Environment*. Prentice-Hall, 1986.
12. S. J. Garland and J. V. Guttag. Inductive methods for reasoning about abstract data types. In *Proceedings of the 15th Symposium on Principles of Programming Languages*, pages 219–228, 1988.
13. M. Gordon. Hol: A proof generating system for higher-order logic. In *VLSI Specification, Verification and Synthesis*. Kluwer, 1987.
14. C. A. R. Hoare. *Communicating Sequential Processes*. Prentice-Hall, Englewood Cliffs, N.J., 1985.
15. G. Holzmann. *Design and Validation of Computer Protocols*. Prentice-Hall, Englewood Cliffs, N.J., 1991.
16. P. Hudak et al. Report on the programming language Haskell: a non-strict, purely functional language (version 1.2). *SIGPLAN Notices*, 27(5), May 1992.
17. R. Manohar. A case for asynchronous computer architecture. In *Proceedings of the ISCA Workshop on Complexity-Effective Design*, June 2000.
18. M.-C. Marinescu. *Synthesis of Synchronous Pipelined Circuits from High-Level Modular Specifications*. PhD thesis, University of California, Santa Barbara, Dec. 2002.
19. M.-C. Marinescu and M. C. Rinard. High-level automatic pipelining for sequential circuits. In *Proceedings of the 14th International Symposium on System Synthesis*, Montreal, Canada, Oct. 2001.
20. M.-C. Marinescu and M. C. Rinard. High-level specification and efficient implementation of pipelined circuits. In *Proceedings of the ASP-DAC*, Yokohama, Japan, Jan. 2001.
21. A. J. Martin. Synthesis of asynchronous vlsi circuits. In *Formal Methods for CLSI Design*. North-Holland, 1990.
22. K. L. McMillan. *Symbolic Model Checking: An Approach to the State Explosion Problem*. Kluwer Academic Publishers, 1993.
23. R. Milner, M. Tofte, and R. Harper. *The Definition of Standard ML*. MIT Press, Cambridge, MA, 1990.
24. S. Owre, J. Rushby, and N. Shankar. Pvs: A prototype verification system. In *11th International Conference on Automated Deduction (CADE)*, number 607 in Lecture Notes in Artificial Intelligence, pages 748–752, 1992.

25. J. Quielle and J. Sifakis. Specification and verification of concurrent systems in caesar. In *Proceedings of 5th ISP*, 1982.
26. K. Turner and M. van Sinderen. *Lotos specification style for OSI, The LOTOSPHRE Project*. KLUWER, London, UK, 1995.
27. J. Young, J. MacDonald, M. Shilman, A. Tabbara, P. Hilfinger, and A. Newton. Design and specification of embedded systems in Java using succesive, formal refinement. In *Proceedings of the 35th ACM/IEEE Design Automation Conference*, June 1998.

Generating Counterexamples
for Multi-valued Model-Checking

Arie Gurfinkel and Marsha Chechik

Department of Computer Science, University of Toronto, Toronto ON M5S 3G4, Canada,
{arie,chechik}@cs.toronto.edu

Abstract. Counterexamples explain why a desired temporal logic property fails to hold, and as such are considered to be the most useful form of output from model-checkers. Multi-valued model-checking, introduced in [4] is an extension of classical model-checking. Instead of classical logic, it operates on elements of a given De Morgan algebra, e.g. the Kleene algebra [14]. Multi-valued model-checking has been used in a number of applications, primarily when reasoning about partial [2] and inconsistent [10] systems. In this paper we show how to generate counterexamples for multi-valued model-checking. We describe the proof system for a multi-valued variant of CTL, discuss how to use it to generate counterexamples. The techniques presented in this paper have been implemented as part of our symbolic multi-valued model-checker XChek [3].

Keywords: model-checking, De Morgan algebras, counterexamples, witnesses, CTL.

1 Introduction

A classical model-checker can tell the user not only whether a desired temporal property is violated, but also generate a counterexample, explaining the reasons behind the answer. Typically, counterexamples are fairly small, compared to the complexity of the model, and are given in terms of states and transitions of the model; thus, they are readily understood by engineers and can be effectively used for debugging the model. The counterexample generation ability has been one of the major advantages of model-checking in comparison with other verification methods.

Counterexamples are a form of a mathematical proof: to disprove that some property φ holds on all elements of some set S, it is sufficient to produce a single element $s \in S$ such that $\neg\varphi$ holds on s. For model-checking, counterexamples are restricted to universally-quantified formulas and can be viewed as infinite or finite trees starting from the initial state that illustrate failure of a given property [8]. A dual problem is that of computing witnesses to existential properties. A witness is a part of the model that is sufficient to prove that $[\![\varphi]\!](s) = \text{true}$, where φ is a temporal property and s is a state of the model.

In this paper, we study the generation of witnesses and counterexamples for multi-valued model-checking. Multi-valued model-checking, introduced in [4], is an extension of classical model-checking. A multi-valued model-checker operates on elements of a De Morgan (also known as quasi-boolean) algebra $(\mathcal{L}, \sqsubseteq, \neg)$ [6], where $(\mathcal{L}, \sqsubseteq)$ is a finite distributive lattice, $\sqcap$ and $\sqcup$ are meet and join of this lattice, respectively (i.e., $a \sqsubseteq b \equiv a \sqcap b = a$ and $a \sqcup b = b$), and $\neg$ preserves De Morgan laws and involution ($\neg\neg a = a$ for every $a \in \mathcal{L}$). Some examples include the classical logic (T = $\top$ and F = $\bot$ of the lattice, respectively) and Kleene algebra [14] with values T=$\top$, M, F=$\bot$ forming a total order ($\top \geq M \geq \bot$) with negation defined as $\neg$T = F, $\neg$F = T, $\neg$M = M. Multi-valued models, called $\mathcal{X}$Kripke structures, are extensions of classical Kripke structures, where values of variables and the transition relation are multi-valued. Temporal properties are expressed in $\mathcal{X}$CTL — a branching-time temporal logic with the same syntax as CTL but where atomic propositions can evaluate to any $\ell \in \mathcal{L}$. Multi-valued model-checking has been used in a number of applications, primarily when reasoning about partial [2] and inconsistent [10] systems.

Given a temporal property φ, a $\mathcal{X}$Kripke structure K, and a De Morgan algebra $\mathcal{L}$, a multi-valued model-checker (such as our model-checker $\mathcal{X}$Chek [3]) determines $[\![\varphi]\!]$ — a function mapping each state s of K to the value of φ on it. Thus, we are interested in giving the user an explanation why $[\![\varphi]\!](s) = \ell$, for $\ell \in \mathcal{L}$. To do so, we must explain both $[\![\varphi]\!](s) \sqsupseteq \ell$ and $[\![\varphi]\!](s) \sqsubseteq \ell$. When ℓ is $\top$, $[\![\varphi]\!](s) \sqsubseteq \top$ follows directly from the definition of $\top$ for any formula φ and thus requires no further explanation. Similarly, when ℓ is $\bot$, $[\![\varphi]\!](s) \sqsupseteq \bot$ requires no explanation. Thus, in classical model-checking, only one of the two explanations is given. We keep the same terminology in the multi-valued case, referring to $[\![\varphi]\!](s) \sqsupseteq \ell$ and $[\![\varphi]\!](s) \sqsubseteq \ell$ as witnesses and counterexamples, respectively.

In this paper, we show how to automatically generate witnesses and counterexamples for $\mathcal{X}$CTL. To do so, we describe witness and counterexample generation for $\mathcal{X}$ECTL (an existential fragment of $\mathcal{X}$CTL) and then give a treatment of negation. Often, counterexamples for existential properties are too large to be feasible. Yet, a partial exploration of such a counterexample may yield useful information. More importantly, this allows us to create a unified framework for giving witnesses and counterexamples for *arbitrary* $\mathcal{X}$CTL properties.

Note that our approach is quite different from the one used by Clarke et al. for classical model-checking [8]. Instead of developing an algorithm to construct witnesses and counterexamples from the model, we first develop a proof system for $\mathcal{X}$ECTL, show how to use it to automatically generate proofs, and finally how to extract witnesses and counterexamples from these proofs. Finally, we extend it to full $\mathcal{X}$CTL. A similar approach for classical model-checking was taken in [12, 13]. Due to space limitations, we do not consider proof generation from model-checking with fairness in this paper. For the treatment of this issue, please refer to [11]. The rest of this paper is organized as follows: Section 2 reviews the concept of multi-valued model-checking. Our approach to generating proofs for $\mathcal{X}$CTL is introduced in Section 3. We discuss how to use proof rules to construct witnesses and counterexamples in Section 4. The paper is concluded in Section 5 with discussion of related work and the outline of future research directions.

2 Background

In this section, we briefly review fundamentals of classical and multi-valued model-checking and fix some notation.

2.1 CTL Model-Checking

CTL model-checking [7] is an automated technique for verifying properties expressed in a propositional branching-time temporal logic called *Computation Tree Logic* (CTL). A *model* is a Kripke structure $K = (S, R, s_0, A, I)$ where S is a set of states; $R \subseteq S \times S$ is a (total) transition relation; $s_0 \in S$ is an initial state; A is a set of atomic propositions; and $I : S \times A \rightarrow \{\top, \bot\}$ is a (total) labeling function. Properties are evaluated on a tree of infinite computations produced by K.

The syntax of CTL is as follows. All atomic propositions are CTL formulas. In addition, if φ and ψ are CTL formulas, then so are $\neg \varphi, \varphi \vee \psi, \varphi \wedge \psi$. Temporal operators of CTL are: $EX\varphi$ ($AX\varphi$) — φ holds in one (all) of the next states; $EG\varphi$ ($AG\varphi$) — there is a path (for all paths), starting at the current state, where φ holds in every state; $E[\varphi\ U\ \psi](A[\varphi\ U\ \psi])$ — there is a path (for all paths) along which ψ eventually holds, and until that point, φ holds in every state; and $EF\varphi$ ($AF\varphi$) — there is a path (for all paths), along which φ eventually holds. We write $[\![\varphi]\!]^K(s)$ to indicate the value of φ in state s of K. If K is clear from the context, it is omitted from the notation. If a formula φ holds in the initial state, i.e. $[\![\varphi]\!](s_0) = \top$, it is considered to hold in the model.

EX, EG and EU form an adequate set for CTL [7]. These operators are defined as follows:

$$[\![EX\varphi]\!](s) \triangleq \exists t \in S \cdot R(s,t) \wedge [\![\varphi]\!](t)$$
$$[\![EG\varphi]\!](s) \triangleq [\![\nu Z \cdot \varphi \wedge EXZ]\!](s)$$
$$[\![E[\varphi\ U\ \psi]]\!](s) \triangleq [\![\mu Z \cdot \psi \vee (\varphi \wedge EXZ)]\!](s)$$

where $\mu Z \cdot f(Z)$ and $\nu Z \cdot f(Z)$ are the least and the greatest fixpoints of a function f, respectively.

The rest of the operators are defined using EX, EG and EU as follows:

$$[\![AX\varphi]\!](s) \triangleq \neg[\![EX(\neg\varphi)]\!](s)$$
$$[\![EF\varphi]\!](s) \triangleq [\![E[\top\ U\ \varphi]]\!](s)$$
$$[\![AG\varphi]\!](s) \triangleq \neg[\![EF(\neg\varphi)]\!](s)$$
$$[\![AF\varphi]\!](s) \triangleq \neg[\![EG(\neg\varphi)]\!](s)$$
$$[\![A[\varphi\ U\ \psi]]\!](s) \triangleq \neg[\![E[\neg\psi\ U\ \neg\varphi \wedge \neg\psi]]\!](s) \wedge \neg[\![EG\neg\psi]\!](s)$$

2.2 De Morgan Algebras

Here we give the basics of lattice theory and define De Morgan algebras.

Definition 1. *A* lattice *is a partial order* $(\mathcal{L}, \sqsubseteq)$, *where every finite subset* $B \subseteq \mathcal{L}$ *has a least upper bound (called "join" and written* $\sqcup B$*) and a greatest lower bound (called "meet" and written* $\sqcap B$*).* $\top$ *and* $\bot$ *are the maximal and the minimal elements of a lattice, respectively.*

In this paper, if $(\mathcal{L}, \sqsubseteq)$ is a lattice, and the ordering operation $\sqsubseteq$ is clear from context, we refer to it as $\mathcal{L}$.

Definition 2. *A lattice is* distributive *iff for all lattice elements* a, b, c,

$$a \sqcup (b \sqcap c) = (a \sqcup b) \sqcap (a \sqcup c)$$
$$a \sqcap (b \sqcup c) = (a \sqcap b) \sqcup (a \sqcap c)$$

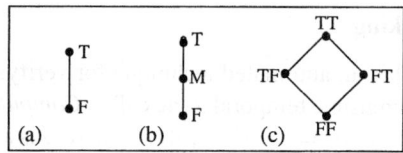

Fig. 1. Examples of a few distributive lattices.

A few examples of distributive lattices are given in Figure 1.

Definition 3. *Let a lattice $\mathcal{L}$ be given, and let $B \subseteq \mathcal{L}$ and $C \subseteq B$. Then, C is join-irredundant in B iff $\bigsqcup C = \bigsqcup B$, and $\forall D \subset C \cdot \bigsqcup D \neq \bigsqcup B$.*

For example, {TT} and {TF, FT} are join-irredundant subsets of a set {TT, TF, FT} defined over the lattice in Figure 1(c).

We now turn our attention to defining De Morgan algebras.

Definition 4. *A De Morgan algebra is a tuple $(\mathcal{L}, \sqsubseteq, \neg)$, where $(\mathcal{L}, \sqsubseteq)$ is a finite distributive lattice and $\neg$ is any operation that preserves involution ($\neg\neg\ell = \ell$) and De Morgan laws. Conjunction and disjunction are defined using meet and join operations of $(\mathcal{L}, \sqsubseteq)$, respectively.*

In De Morgan algebras, we get $\neg\top = \bot$ and $\neg\bot = \top$, but not necessarily the law of non-contradiction ($\ell \sqcap \neg\ell = \bot$) or excluded middle ($\ell \sqcup \neg\ell = \top$).

We can define several De Morgan algebras using the lattices given in Figure 1. The domain of logical values of the classical logic, referred to as **2**, is the lattice in Figure 1(a). The three-valued algebra **3** (Kleene logic [14]) is defined on the lattice in Figure 1(b), where ¬T = F, ¬F = T, ¬M = M. The four-valued algebra **2x2** is defined on the lattice in Figure 1(c), where ¬ TF = FT and ¬ FT = TF. This algebra can be used for reasoning about inconsistency. Note that $\top$ and $\bot$ of the lattice are interpreted as values true and false of the algebra, respectively.

When the negation and the ordering operators of an algebra $(\mathcal{L}, \sqsubseteq, \neg)$ are clear from the context, we refer to it simply as $\mathcal{L}$.

2.3 Multi-valued Model-Checking

Multi-Valued CTL model-checking [4] is a generalization of the CTL model-checking problem. A multi-valued model-checker receives a De Morgan algebra, a multi-valued model, and a temporal property and determines the value with which this property holds in the model. We define multi-valued models on χ*Kripke structures* — generalizations of Kripke structures, where each atomic proposition and each transition between a pair of states is labeled with values from the algebra [4]. Formally, $K = (S, s_0, \mathbb{R}, I, A, L)$ is a χKripke structure, where S is a set of states; $L = (\mathcal{L}, \sqsubseteq, \neg)$ is a De Morgan algebra; A is a (finite) set of atomic propositions; $s_0 \in S$ is the initial state; $\mathbb{R} : S \times S \to \mathcal{L}$ is the multi-valued transition relation; $I : S \times A \to \mathcal{L}$ is a (total) labeling function, such that for each atomic proposition $a \in A$, $I(s, a) = \ell$ means that the proposition a evaluates to ℓ in state s. Thus, any Kripke structure is also a χKripke structure over the algebra **2**.

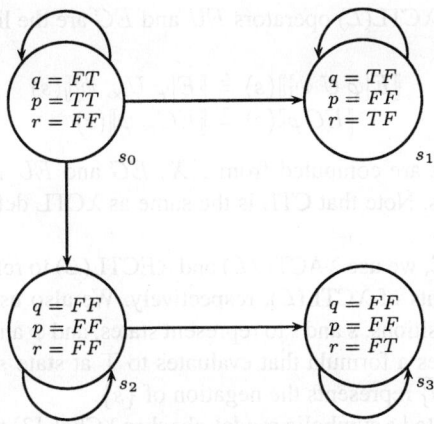

Fig. 2. An example $\mathcal{X}$Kripke structure.

An example $\mathcal{X}$Kripke structure for the algebra **2x2** is given in Figure 2. When presenting finite-state machines graphically, we follow the convention of not showing $\perp$ transitions and not labeling $\top$ transitions, to avoid clutter.

Properties are specified in a multiple-valued extension of CTL called $\mathcal{X}$CTL. Given a De Morgan algebra $\mathcal{L}$, $\mathcal{X}$CTL($\mathcal{L}$) has the same syntax as CTL, except that any $\ell \in \mathcal{L}$ is also a $\mathcal{X}$CTL($\mathcal{L}$) formula. The semantics follows:

$$[\![\ell]\!](s) \triangleq \ell, \text{ for } \ell \in \mathcal{L}$$
$$[\![a]\!](s) \triangleq I(s,a), \text{ for } a \in A$$
$$[\![\neg \varphi]\!](s) \triangleq \neg [\![\varphi]\!](s)$$
$$[\![\varphi \wedge \psi]\!](s) \triangleq [\![\varphi]\!](s) \sqcap [\![\psi]\!](s)$$
$$[\![\varphi \vee \psi]\!](s) \triangleq [\![\varphi]\!](s) \sqcup [\![\psi]\!](s)$$
$$[\![EX\varphi]\!](s) \triangleq \bigsqcup_{t \in S}(\mathbb{R}(s,t) \sqcap [\![\varphi]\!](t))$$

The semantics of the EX operator comes from extending the notion of existential quantification for multi-valued reasoning through the use of disjunction [1, 17]. The other operators are defined as their CTL counterparts (see Section 2.1), where $\vee$ and $\wedge$ are interpreted as lattice $\sqcup$ and $\sqcap$, respectively.

We also introduce bounded versions of EU and EG operators.

$$[\![E[\varphi\, U_i\, \psi]]\!](s) \triangleq \begin{cases} [\![\psi]\!](s) & \text{if } i = 0 \\ [\![\psi \vee \varphi \wedge EXE[\varphi\, U_{i-1}\, \psi]]\!](s) & \text{if } i > 0 \end{cases}$$

$$[\![EG_i \varphi]\!](s) \triangleq \begin{cases} [\![\varphi \wedge EX\top]\!](s) & \text{if } i = 0 \\ [\![\varphi \wedge EXEG_{i-1}\varphi]\!](s) & \text{if } i > 0 \end{cases}$$

Intuitively, the bound i corresponds to the restriction of the operators to finite paths of length at most i. Formally, they correspond to the ith approximation in their respective fixpoint computation. χCTL($\mathcal{L}$) operators EU and EG are the limits of EU_i and EG_i, respectively:

$$[\![E[\varphi\ U\ \psi]]\!](s) \triangleq [\![E[\varphi\ U_\infty\ \psi]]\!](s)$$
$$[\![EG\varphi]\!](s) \triangleq [\![EG_\infty\varphi]\!](s)$$

Other χCTL operators are computed from EX, EG and EU in the same manner as their CTL counterparts. Note that CTL is the same as χCTL defined over the classical logic **2**.

Given an algebra $\mathcal{L}$, we use χACTL($\mathcal{L}$) and χECTL($\mathcal{L}$) to refer to the universal and the existential fragments of χCTL($\mathcal{L}$), respectively. We also use p and q to stand for arbitrary atomic propositions, s and t to represent states, and φ and ψ to represent χCTL formulas. $\{s\}$ expresses a formula that evaluates to $\top$ at state s and $\bot$ otherwise, i.e. $[\![\{s\}]\!](t) \triangleq (s = t)$. $\overline{\{s\}}$ represents the negation of $\{s\}$.

We have implemented a symbolic model-checker χChek [3] that receives a χKripke structure K that uses some De Morgan algebra L, and a χCTL formula φ and returns an element of L corresponding to the value of φ in K. For example, if the algebra is **2**, χChek returns true if φ holds in K and false if it does not: this is the classical model-checking. For more information about multi-valued model-checking, please consult [3, 4].

3 Proof Rules for χCTL

In this section, we develop a proof system that allows us to generate proofs for χCTL properties over χKripke structures. We begin by giving proof rules and axioms for reasoning about χKripke structures and De Morgan algebras. We then proceed with proof rules for witnesses and counterexamples for χECTL and then extend our framework to deal with negation and χACTL, resulting in full χCTL.

3.1 Preliminaries

Since we are interested in proving statements about a particular χKripke structure K expressed in a particular De Morgan algebra $\mathcal{L}$, we assume that our proof system incorporates all axioms and proof rules of propositional logic and De Morgan algebras. Several of such proof rules are given in Figure 3. For example, in the one-point rule, f is a predicate and x is some element of D. Intuitively, the one-point rule of propositional logic states that to justify an existential statement $\exists x \in D \cdot f(x)$, one simply needs to exhibit an element $x' \in D$ for which $f(x')$ holds. Note that in what follows, we only consider quantification over finite domains. Thus, although we do use universal and existential quantification, the proof system remains propositional rather than first order.

In addition, we also assume that the axiomatization of a given algebra $\mathcal{L}$ is available. Such an axiomatization defines relations $\sqsupseteq$ and $\neg$. For example, some of the axioms describing the algebra **2x2** shown in Figure 1(c) are:

$$\text{TT} \sqsupseteq \text{TF} \qquad \text{TF} \sqsupseteq \text{FF}$$
$$\neg \text{TT} = \text{FF} \qquad \neg \text{TF} = \text{FT}$$

$$\frac{a}{a \vee b} \text{ ∨-intro}$$

$$\frac{b}{a \vee b} \text{ ∨-intro}$$

$$\frac{a \sqsupseteq \ell \quad b \sqsupseteq \ell}{a \sqcap b \sqsupseteq \ell} \text{ ⊓-intro}$$

$$\frac{a \sqsubseteq \neg \ell}{\neg a \sqsupseteq \ell} \text{ De Morgan-not}$$

$$\frac{a \quad b}{a \wedge b} \text{ ∧-intro}$$

$$\frac{f(x')}{\exists x \in D \cdot f(x)} \text{ one-point rule}$$

$$\frac{a \sqsubseteq \ell \quad b \sqsubseteq \ell}{a \sqcup b \sqsubseteq \ell} \text{ ⊔-intro}$$

$$\frac{a \sqsupseteq \neg \ell}{\neg a \sqsubseteq \ell} \text{ De Morgan-not}$$

$$\frac{f(d_1) \quad f(d_2) \quad \ldots \quad f(d_n)}{\forall d \in D \cdot f(d)} \text{ finite quantification, with } \bigcup_{i=1}^{n}\{d_i\} = D$$

Fig. 3. Some proof rules of propositional logic and De Morgan algebras.

In addition, we assume that all axioms of the theory of χKripke structures and the axiomatization of a particular χKripke structure K are also available. Such axioms define the transition relation $\mathbb{R}$ and the state labeling function I. For example, an axiom of χKripke structures is that $I(s, a)$ is defined for any atomic proposition a and any state $s \in S$. Some of the axioms of the χKripke structure in Figure 2, specified using an algebra **2x2**, are:

$$\mathbb{R}(s_0, s_1) = \text{TT} \quad \mathbb{R}(s_0, s_3) = \text{FF}$$
$$I(s_0, p) = \text{TT} \quad I(s_0, q) = \text{FT}$$

3.2 Proof Rules for Witnesses for χECTL

Our initial goal is to develop a sound and complete proof system that allows us to prove validity of sentences of the form $[\![\varphi]\!](s) \sqsupseteq \ell$, where φ is a χECTL formula, ℓ is a lattice value, and s is a state of a given χKripke structure K. We refer to these as *witnesses*.

The proof rules for non-temporal operators and EX are shown in Figure 4. They follow directly from the definitions of the corresponding operators. For example, the ∨-rule states that in order to prove $[\![\varphi \vee \psi]\!] \sqsupseteq \ell$, we need to find algebra values ℓ_1 and ℓ_2 such that $[\![\varphi]\!](s) \sqsupseteq \ell_1$, $[\![\psi]\!](s) \sqsupseteq \ell_2$, and their join is above ℓ. Thus, this rule introduces two existential quantifiers, which are typically eliminated by several applications of the one-point rule shown in Figure 3.

The proof rules for the bounded EU are given in Figure 5 and follow directly from the definition of this operator. To derive the rule for the unbounded EU, we start by noting the monotonicity of EU_i:

Proposition 1. *Let φ, ψ be ECTL formulas and $i, j \in \text{nat}$. Then,*

$$i \geq j \Rightarrow \forall s \in S \cdot ([\![E[\varphi \ U_i \ \psi]]\!](s) \sqsupseteq [\![E[\varphi \ U_j \ \psi]]\!](s))$$

The proof rule for unbounded EU (given in Figure 5) is obtained by combining Proposition 1 with the fact that the unbounded EU is an upper bound of the bounded EU_i:

$$\forall i \in \text{nat} \cdot [\![E[\varphi \ U \ \psi]]\!] \sqsupseteq [\![E[\varphi \ U_i \ \psi]]\!]$$

$$\frac{\ell_1 \sqsupseteq \ell}{[\![\ell_1]\!](s) \sqsupseteq \ell} \text{ value-rule} \qquad \frac{\neg \ell_1 \sqsupseteq \ell}{[\![\neg \ell_1]\!](s) \sqsupseteq \ell} \text{ neg-value-rule}$$

$$\frac{\exists \ell_1 \in \mathcal{L} \cdot (I(s,p) = \ell_1) \wedge (\ell_1 \sqsupseteq \ell)}{[\![p]\!](s) \sqsupseteq \ell} \text{ atomic-rule} \qquad \frac{\exists \ell_1 \in \mathcal{L} \cdot (\neg I(s,p) = \ell_1) \wedge (\ell_1 \sqsupseteq \ell)}{[\![\neg p]\!](s) \sqsupseteq \ell} \text{ neg-atomic-rule}$$

$$\frac{[\![\varphi]\!](s) \sqsupseteq \ell \wedge [\![\psi]\!](s) \sqsupseteq \ell}{[\![\varphi \wedge \psi]\!](s) \sqsupseteq \ell} \wedge\text{-rule} \qquad \frac{\exists \ell_1, \ell_2 \in \mathcal{L} \cdot ([\![\varphi]\!](s) \sqsupseteq \ell_1) \wedge ([\![\psi]\!](s) \sqsupseteq \ell_2) \wedge (\ell_1 \sqcup \ell_2 \sqsupseteq \ell)}{[\![\varphi \vee \psi]\!](s) \sqsupseteq \ell} \vee\text{-rule}$$

$$\frac{\exists t_1, \ldots, t_n \in S \cdot \exists \ell_1, \ldots, \ell_n \in \mathcal{L} \cdot ([\![\mathbb{R}(s, t_1) \wedge \varphi]\!](t_1) \sqsupseteq \ell_1) \wedge \cdots \wedge ([\![\mathbb{R}(s, t_n) \wedge \varphi]\!](t_n) \sqsupseteq \ell_n) \wedge (\bigsqcup_{i=1}^n \ell_i \sqsupseteq \ell)}{[\![EX\varphi]\!](s) \sqsupseteq \ell} EX$$

Fig. 4. Proof rules for non-temporal operators and EX.

$$\frac{[\![\psi]\!](s) \sqsupseteq \ell}{[\![E[\varphi U_0 \psi]]\!](s) \sqsupseteq \ell} EU_0 \qquad \frac{[\![\psi \vee \varphi \wedge EXE[\varphi U_{n-1}\psi]]\!](s) \sqsupseteq \ell}{[\![E[\varphi U_n \psi]]\!](s) \sqsupseteq \ell} EU_i$$

$$\frac{\exists n \in nat \cdot [\![E[\varphi U_n \psi]]\!](s) \sqsupseteq \ell}{[\![E[\varphi U \psi]]\!](s) \sqsupseteq \ell} EU$$

$$\frac{[\![\varphi \wedge EXE[\varphi U \varphi \wedge \overline{\{s\}}] \vee \varphi \wedge EXEG(\varphi \wedge \overline{\{s\}})]\!](s) \sqsupseteq \ell}{[\![EG\varphi]\!](s) \sqsupseteq \ell} EG$$

Fig. 5. Proof rules for EU and EG.

Note that since we assume that the state space is finite, the EU rule is actually bi-directional. That is, for a given Kripke structure K, there always exists a natural number n, which depends on the diameter of the directed graph induced by K, such that $E[\varphi \, U \, \psi] = E[\varphi \, U_n \, \psi]$.

To complete our proof system, we still need to find a proof rule for EG. Unfortunately, we cannot proceed as in the previous cases and use the χECTL equivalence $EG\varphi = \varphi \wedge EXEG\varphi$ to define the proof rule. Doing so would result in a proof system which is not complete, since this proof rule can be potentially applied an infinite number of times.

Instead, note that $[\![EG\varphi]\!](s)$ is the join of evaluating $G\varphi$ on all infinite paths emanating from the state s. Moreover, since we are dealing with finite state systems, every infinite path can be decomposed into a finite (possibly empty) prefix and a finite repeating suffix. Thus, we can decompose $[\![EG\varphi]\!](s)$ into the join of the EG restricted to all non-trivial cycles around s, and EG restricted to all infinite paths that do not contain s in the future.

First, we consider the restriction of $[\![EG\varphi]\!](s)$ to all non-trivial cycles around s. The set of non-trivial cycles around s is exactly the set of paths along which s occurs infinitely often[1]. Furthermore, since our starting state is s, any infinite path along which s occurs

---
[1] This is referred to as *fair-EG*, where the fairness condition is given by a single formula $\{s\}$ [7].

infinitely often is equivalent to a finite path from s to itself. Thus, to evaluate $[\![EG\varphi]\!](s)$ restricted to cycles around s, it is sufficient to consider only finite paths from s to s. This intuition is formalized in the following theorem, the proof of which is available in [11]:

Theorem 1. *Let φ be an ECTL formula and s be a state of a Kripke structure. Then,*

$$[\![EG\varphi]\!](s) = [\![(\varphi \wedge EXE[\varphi\ U\ \varphi \wedge \{s\}]) \vee (\varphi \wedge EXEG(\varphi \wedge \overline{\{s\}}))]\!](s)$$

A proof rule for a EG witness is given in Figure 5.

Theorem 2. *The proof system for witnesses for XECTL is sound and complete.*

Due to space limitations, we do not provide proofs of most theorems in this paper. They are available in [11].

3.3 Automatic Proof Generation for Witnesses for XECTL

Given a statement $[\![\varphi]\!](s) \sqsupseteq \ell$, we are interested in an automated proof of its validity. We can achieve this by embedding the proof system of Section 3.2 into an automated theorem prover, such as PVS [16], and using its facilities for proof generation. This is always possible, because we assume that the state space of XKripke structures is finite. We can also use a multi-valued theorem prover that already includes the encoding of a large class of multi-valued algebras [18]. A more efficient approach is to use the model-checker as a decision procedure for (a) deciding the validity of a given subformula (so that our proof generator avoids exploring irrelevant proof branches) and for (b) applying the one-point rule. We call this decision procedure modelCheck and assume that modelCheck(φ, s) computes $[\![\varphi]\!](s)$. We also assume the presence of qblat — a decision procedure for determining the validity of De Morgan lattice equalities and inequalities.

We start with a statement $[\![p]\!](s) \sqsupseteq \ell$, where p is an atomic proposition, and apply the atomic-rule (see Figure 4) to obtain

$$\exists \ell_1 \in \mathcal{L} \cdot (I(s,p) = \ell_1) \wedge (\ell_1 \sqsupseteq \ell)$$

We now need to decide whether it is possible to apply the one-point rule by instantiating ℓ_1.

Proposition 2. *Let p be an atomic proposition and let s be a state of a XKripke structure K. Then,*

$$I(s,p) = \ell \Leftrightarrow \text{modelCheck}(p,s) = \ell$$

Therefore, the one-point rule is applicable if and only if the statement

$$I(s,p) = \text{modelCheck}(p,s) \wedge \text{modelCheck}(p,s) \sqsupseteq \ell$$

is valid. Since it is a conjunction, to decide its validity we must show that both $I(s,p) = $ modelCheck(p,s) and modelCheck(p,s) $\sqsupseteq \ell$ are valid. The validity of the first conjunct follows from the definition of modelCheck(p,s); therefore, it is sufficient to just establish the validity of modelCheck(p,s) $\sqsupseteq \ell$. As the result, we obtain the algorithm given in Figure 6(a). The case of $[\![\neg p]\!](s) \sqsupseteq \ell$ is handled similarly.

Next, we consider the boolean connectives. Given a statement of the form $[\![\varphi \vee \psi]\!](s) \sqsupseteq \ell$, we apply the ∨-rule shown in Figure 4. Using the monotonicity of the ⊔ operator, we get the following proposition:

(a)
```
1: proc atomicOnePoint(p, s, ℓ)
2:     k := modelCheck(p, s)
3:     if qblat(k ⊒ ℓ)) then
4:         apply one-point rule substituting k
               for ℓ₁
5:     else
6:         terminate with invalid
7:     end if
8: end proc
```

(b)
```
1: proc orOnePoint(φ, ψ, s, ℓ)
2:     k_φ := modelCheck(φ, s)
3:     k_ψ := modelCheck(ψ, s)
4:     if qblat(k_φ ⊔ k_ψ ⊒ ℓ) then
5:         apply one-point rule substituting k_φ
               for ℓ₁, k_ψ for ℓ₂
6:     else
7:         terminate with invalid
8:     end if
9: end proc
```

(c)
```
1:  proc euOnePoint(φ, ψ, s, ℓ)
2:      i := 0
3:      eu = modelCheck(E[φUψ], s)
4:      eui = ⊥
5:      while eui ≠ eu and not qblat(eui ⊒ ℓ) do
6:          eui := modelCheck(E[φU_iψ], s)
7:          i := i + 1
8:      end while
9:      if qblat(eui ⊒ ℓ) then
10:         apply one-point rule substituting i
                for n
11:     else
12:         terminate with invalid
13:     end if
14: end proc
```

(d)
```
1: proc exOnePoint(φ, s, ℓ)
2:     k := modelCheck(EXφ, s)
3:     if not qblat(k ⊒ ℓ) then
4:         terminate with invalid
5:     end if
6:     (r₁, p₁)...(r_n, p_n) :=
               exWitness(φ, s)
7:     apply one-point rule substituting
               (r_i, p_i) for (t_i, ℓ_i)
8: end proc
```

Fig. 6. Algorithms for automatic proof generation.

Proposition 3. *Let φ and ψ be XECTL formulas, let s be a state of a XKripke structure, and let ℓ be a lattice element. Then,*

$$\exists \ell_1, \ell_2 \in \mathcal{L} \cdot [\![\varphi]\!](s) \sqsupseteq \ell_1 \wedge [\![\psi]\!](s) \sqsupseteq \ell_2 \wedge \ell_1 \sqcup \ell_2 \sqsupseteq \ell$$
$$\Leftrightarrow \exists \ell_3, \ell_4 \in \mathcal{L} \cdot [\![\varphi]\!](s) = \ell_3 \wedge [\![\psi]\!](s) = \ell_4 \wedge \ell_3 \sqcup \ell_4 \sqsupseteq \ell$$

Using the fact that $[\![\varphi]\!](s) = \text{modelCheck}(\varphi, s)$, we see that the one-point rule is applicable if and only if instantiating ℓ_1 to $\text{modelCheck}(\varphi, s)$ and ℓ_2 to $\text{modelCheck}(\psi, s)$ does not result in invalid statements. As in the previous case, this simplifies to requiring that $\ell_1 \sqcup \ell_2 \sqsupseteq \ell$ be valid for the instantiated values. The resulting algorithm is shown in Figure 6(b). The $\wedge$ operator is handled similarly.

We now examine the case of analyzing the unbounded EU operator. Given a statement $[\![E[\varphi \ U \ \psi]]\!](s) \sqsupseteq \ell$, we first apply the EU-rule, shown in Figure 5. The next step is to find an instantiation of n for the one-point rule. Recall that bounded EU_i is monotone when viewed as a function of i (by Proposition 1). Moreover, it is bounded above by the unbounded EU. Therefore, we can find the instantiation of n by a linear search, starting from $n = 0$. The algorithm for the application of the one-point rule is given in Figure 6(c). The intermediate computations performed by this algorithm are exactly those done by a symbolic multi-valued model-checking algorithm. Thus, if the results of the intermediate computations performed by modelCheck($E[\varphi \ U \ \psi], s$) are available, a more efficient binary search can replace the linear one.

For example, consider the χKripke structure in the Figure 2 and assume that we want to prove that $[\![E[p \ U \ q]]\!](s_0) \sqsupseteq$ TT. After the application of the EU-rule, we get

$$\exists n \in nat \cdot [\![E[p \ U_n \ q]]\!](s_0) \sqsupseteq \text{TT}$$

To apply the one-point rule, we first try $[\![E[p \ U_0 \ q]]\!](s_0) = [\![q]\!](s_0) = \text{FT} \not\sqsupseteq \text{TT}$. Increasing the bound, we get $[\![E[p \ U_1 \ q]]\!](s_0) = [\![q]\!](s_0) \vee [\![EXE[p \ U_0 \ q]]\!](s_0) = \text{FT} \vee \text{TF} = \text{TT}$, and therefore we can apply the one-point rule by instantiating n to 1.

Finally, given the statement $[\![EX\varphi]\!](s) \sqsupseteq \ell$, we first apply the EX-rule (see Figure 4) and then eliminate the existential quantifiers by applying the one-point rule. For example, suppose we want to prove that $[\![EXq]\!](s_0) \sqsupseteq$ TT in the χKripke structure in Figure 2. First, we apply the EX-rule, obtaining

$$\frac{\exists \ell_1, \ldots, \ell_n \in \mathcal{L} \cdot \exists t_1, \ldots, t_n \in S \cdot ([\![\mathbb{R}(s_0, t_1) \wedge q]\!](t_1) \sqsupseteq \ell_1) \\ \wedge \cdots \wedge ([\![\mathbb{R}(s_0, t_n) \wedge q]\!](t_n) \sqsupseteq \ell_n) \wedge (\bigsqcup_{1 \leq i \leq n} \ell_i) \sqsupseteq \text{TT}}{[\![EXq]\!](s_0) \sqsupseteq \text{TT}} \ EX$$

We now have to apply the one-point rule to instantiate the pairs $\{(\ell_i, t_i) \mid 1 \leq i \leq n\}$. For notational convenience, we introduce a function $img : S \to \mathcal{L}$, defined as

$$img(x) \triangleq [\![\mathbb{R}(s, x) \wedge \varphi]\!](x)$$

Note that $[\![EX\varphi]\!](s) = \bigsqcup_{t \in S} img(t)$.

Proposition 4. *Let $K = (S, s_0, I, \mathbb{R}, A, \mathcal{L})$ be a χKripke structure, $s \in S$ an arbitrary state of K, φ a $\chi CTL(\mathcal{L})$ formula, and img as defined above. Then,*

$$\exists \ell_1, \ldots, \ell_n \in \mathcal{L} \cdot \exists t_1, \ldots, t_n \in S \cdot \\ ([\![\mathbb{R}(s, t_1) \wedge \varphi]\!](t_1) \sqsupseteq \ell_1) \wedge \cdots \wedge ([\![\mathbb{R}(s, t_n) \wedge \varphi]\!](t_n) \sqsupseteq \ell_n) \\ \wedge ((\bigsqcup_{1 \leq i \leq n} \ell_i) \sqsupseteq \ell) \\ \Leftrightarrow \\ (\bigsqcup_{t \in S} img(t)) \sqsupseteq \ell$$

Thus, in order to apply the one-point rule, we must find a subset U of S such that $(\bigsqcup_{t \in U} img(t)) \sqsupseteq \ell$. If $U = \{u_1, \ldots, u_n\}$ is such a set, we can apply the one point rule by instantiating t_i to u_i, and ℓ_i to $img(u_i)$. Of course, we can always let $U = S$; however, this unnecessarily increases the size of the proof.

Alternatively, we can obtain U by considering the range of the function img. Let $U' = \{\ell_i \mid \exists t_i \in S \cdot img(t_i) = \ell_i\}$. Clearly, it is smaller than the size of the state space $|S|$ and the size of the De Morgan algebra $\mathcal{L}$, that is, $|U'| \leq \min\{|S|, |\mathcal{L}|\}$. Furthermore, given $U' = \{u'_1, \ldots, u'_n\}$, we can construct the set U by letting u_i be any element of $img^{-1}(u'_i)$. In our example, we take representatives from the inverse of $img(S) = \{\text{TF}, \text{FT}\}$: $s_0 \in img^{-1}(\text{FT})$, and $s_1 \in img^{-1}(\text{TF})$. Finally, we apply the one-point rule, obtaining

$$[\![\mathbb{R}(s_0, s_0) \wedge q]\!](s_0) \sqsupseteq \text{FT} \wedge [\![\mathbb{R}(s_0, s_1) \wedge q]\!](s_1) \sqsupseteq \text{TF} \wedge \text{FT} \sqcup \text{TF} \sqsupseteq \text{TT}$$

Note that in contrast to other XECTL operators, the procedure for generating a proof for $[\![EX\varphi]\!](s) \sqsupseteq \ell$ does not use the model-checker as a simple black-box. In fact, it can only be accomplished efficiently if the model-checker can produce the states comprising the witness.

The algorithm for the application of the one-point rule is given in Figure 6(d). The algorithm makes use of the function exWitness(φ, s) that computes the witness for $[\![EX\varphi]\!](s) = \text{modelCheck}(EX\varphi, s)$. The witness is returned as a set of pairs (t_i, ℓ_i), such that $img(t_i) = \ell_i$, and $\bigsqcup_{1 \leq i \leq n} \ell_i = \text{modelCheck}(EX\varphi, s)$.

3.4 Extending the Proof System to XCTL

Here we extend the results presented earlier in this section to counterexamples for XECTL, and finally to witnesses and counterexamples for full XCTL.

Extension to counterexamples for XECTL. Our goal is to extend the proof system to deal with statements of the form $[\![\varphi]\!](s) \sqsubseteq \ell$, where φ is in XECTL. We refer to these as *counterexamples*.

The proof rules for propositional operators are similar to their witness counterparts and are shown in Figure 7. Note that because of the duality of $\wedge$ and $\vee$, the witness proof rules for $\wedge$ and $\vee$ are similar to the counterexample proof rules of $\vee$ and $\wedge$, respectively.

The counterexample proof rule for EX is also shown in Figure 7. To prove that $[\![EX\varphi]\!](s) \sqsubseteq \ell$, we must prove that $[\![\mathbb{R}(s,t) \wedge \varphi]\!](t) \sqsubseteq \ell$ for every state t since EX is defined as a join over all states of the XKripke structure. Thus, even one application of the EX rule may increase the size of the proof tree dramatically.

Finally, the counterexample proof rules for EG and EU are given in Figure 8. Note that the counterexample rule for EG is similar to the witness rule for EU, and is based on the fact that bounded EG_i approximates the unbounded EG from above.

The counterexample proof rule for EU is the most complicated one. It is similar to the witness proof rule for EG in a sense that it decomposes the overall proof into (a) the proof about the current state, and (b) the proof about the rest of the system excluding the current state. It is formally justified by the following theorem.

$$\frac{\ell_1 \sqsubseteq \ell}{[\![\ell_1]\!](s) \sqsubseteq \ell} \text{ value-rule} \qquad \frac{\neg \ell_1 \sqsubseteq \ell}{[\![\neg \ell_1]\!](s) \sqsubseteq \ell} \text{ neg-value-rule}$$

$$\frac{\exists \ell_1 \in \mathcal{L} \cdot (I(s,p) = \ell_1) \wedge (\ell_1 \sqsubseteq \ell)}{[\![p]\!](s) \sqsubseteq \ell} \text{ atomic-rule} \qquad \frac{\exists \ell_1 \in \mathcal{L} \cdot (\neg I(s,p) = \ell_1) \wedge (\ell_1 \sqsubseteq \ell)}{[\![\neg p]\!](s) \sqsubseteq \ell} \text{ neg-atomic-rule}$$

$$\frac{\exists \ell_1, \ell_2 \in \mathcal{L} \cdot ([\![\varphi]\!](s) \sqsubseteq \ell_1) \wedge ([\![\psi]\!](s) \sqsubseteq \ell_2) \wedge (\ell_1 \sqcap \ell_2 \sqsubseteq \ell)}{[\![\varphi \wedge \psi]\!](s) \sqsubseteq \ell} \wedge \text{-rule} \qquad \frac{[\![\varphi]\!](s) \sqsubseteq \ell \wedge [\![\psi]\!](s) \sqsubseteq \ell}{[\![\varphi \vee \psi]\!](s) \sqsubseteq \ell} \vee \text{-rule}$$

$$\frac{\forall t \in S \cdot [\![\mathbb{R}(s,t) \wedge \varphi]\!](t) \sqsubseteq \ell}{[\![EX\varphi]\!](s) \sqsubseteq \ell} EX$$

Fig. 7. Proof rules for counterexamples for non-temporal operators and EX.

$$\frac{[\![\varphi \wedge EX\top]\!](s) \sqsubseteq \ell}{[\![EG_0\varphi]\!](s) \sqsubseteq \ell} EG_0 \qquad \frac{[\![\varphi \wedge EXEG_{n-1}\varphi]\!](s) \sqsubseteq \ell}{[\![EG_n\varphi]\!](s) \sqsubseteq \ell} EG_i$$

$$\frac{\exists n \in nat \cdot [\![EG_n\varphi]\!](s) \sqsubseteq \ell}{[\![EG\varphi]\!](s) \sqsubseteq \ell} EG$$

$$\frac{[\![\psi \vee \varphi \wedge EXE[\varphi \wedge \overline{\{s\}} \ U \ \psi \wedge \overline{\{s\}}]]\!](s) \sqsubseteq \ell}{[\![E[\varphi \ U \ \psi]]\!](s) \sqsubseteq \ell} EU$$

Fig. 8. Proof rules for counterexamples for EG and EU.

Theorem 3. *Let* φ, ψ *be* χ*CTL formulas, s be a state of a* χ*Kripke structure. Then,*

$$[\![E[\varphi \ U \ \psi]]\!](s) = [\![\psi \vee \varphi \wedge EXE[\varphi \wedge \overline{\{s\}} \ U \ \psi \wedge \overline{\{s\}}]]\!](s)$$

Theorem 4. *The proof system for counterexamples for* χ*ECTL is sound and complete.*

Extension to χCTL. To extend our proof system to witnesses and counterexamples for full χCTL, we must extend the not-rule of De Morgan algebras (see Figure 3) to χCTL, and provide proof rules for χACTL— the universal fragment χCTL. The extension of the not-rule of De Morgan algebras is trivial, and yields the witness and counterexample proof rules shown in Figure 9. The proof rules for χACTL can be obtained from the well-known dualities between χECTL and χACTL (see Section 2.1). For example, the duality $AX\varphi = \neg EX\neg\varphi$ yields the witness and counterexample proof rules for AX shown in Figure 9. The rest of χACTL rules are derived similarly.

Theorem 5. *The proof system for* χ*CTL is sound and complete.*

$$\frac{[\![\varphi]\!](s) \sqsubseteq \neg\ell}{[\![\neg\varphi]\!](s) \sqsupseteq \ell} \text{not-rule} \qquad \frac{[\![\varphi]\!](s) \sqsupseteq \neg\ell}{[\![\neg\varphi]\!](s) \sqsubseteq \ell} \text{not-rule}$$

$$\frac{[\![\neg EX\neg\varphi]\!](s) \sqsupseteq \ell}{[\![AX\varphi]\!](s) \sqsupseteq \ell} AX \qquad \frac{[\![\neg EX\neg\varphi]\!](s) \sqsubseteq \ell}{[\![AX\varphi]\!](s) \sqsubseteq \ell} AX$$

Fig. 9. Witness (left) and counterexample (right) proof rules for negation and AX.

4 Witness and Counterexample Generation

In this section, we describe how to use the proof system introduced in Section 3 to generate witnesses and counterexamples for multi-valued model-checking. We also discuss and illustrate the tool support for this approach.

4.1 From Proofs to Witnesses and Counterexamples

In this section we show how to extract a witness to $[\![\varphi]\!](s) = \ell$, where $\ell \in \mathcal{L}$, from a proof of $[\![\varphi]\!](s) \sqsupseteq \ell$. Counterexamples are extracted in a similar way.

The general form of the proof of validity of $[\![EX\varphi]\!](s) \sqsupseteq \ell$ is shown in Figure 10(a). This proof corresponds to a witness for EX, namely, a tree rooted at s, with children $t_1, \dots, t_n$, where an edge from s to t_i is labeled by the value of $\mathbb{R}(s, t_i)$. This correspondence between the proof and the witness suggests a simple procedure for extracting the witness from the proof:

1. remove all nodes from the proof tree except for (a) the root node, and (b) nodes that result from the application of the one-point rule (see Figure 10(b));
2. replace horizontal bars by directed edges, and label each edge incoming into a node $[\![\mathbb{R}(s, t_i) \wedge \varphi]\!](t_i)$ by the value of $\mathbb{R}(s, t_i)$ (see Figure 10(c));
3. relabel the top node by s, and each node of the form $[\![\mathbb{R}(s, t_i) \wedge \varphi]\!](t_i)$ by t_i (see Figure 10(d)).

The result is a tree rooted at s, with successor states $t'_1 ... t'_n$ — the witness for EX.

In general, the proof tree for a statement $[\![\varphi]\!](s) \sqsupseteq \ell$ can be partitioned into proof nodes that result from the application of the one-point rule to EX (and thus correspond directly to a step in the χKripke structure); and the "glue" that binds these steps into a complete witness. The witness can be extracted from the proof tree by the same procedure as in the EX case.

(a)

$$\dfrac{\dfrac{[\![\mathbb{R}(s,t'_1) \wedge \varphi]\!](t'_1) \sqsupseteq \ell_1 \quad \cdots \quad [\![\mathbb{R}(s,t'_n) \wedge \varphi]\!](t'_n) \sqsupseteq \ell_n \quad \bigsqcup_{1\leq i\leq n} \ell'_i \sqsupseteq \ell}{\begin{array}{l}\exists \ell_1, \dots, \ell_n \in \mathcal{L} \cdot \exists t_1, \dots, t_n \in S \cdot [\![\mathbb{R}(s,t_1) \wedge \varphi]\!](t_1) \sqsupseteq \ell_1 \wedge \cdots \wedge \\ [\![\mathbb{R}(s,t_n) \wedge \varphi]\!](t_n) \sqsupseteq \ell_n \wedge \bigsqcup_{1\leq i\leq n} \ell_i \sqsupseteq \ell\end{array}}\ \text{one-point rule}}{[\![EX\varphi]\!](s) \sqsupseteq \ell}\ EX$$

(b)

$$\dfrac{[\![\mathbb{R}(s,t'_1) \wedge \varphi]\!](t'_1) \sqsupseteq \ell_1 \quad \cdots \quad [\![\mathbb{R}(s,t'_n) \wedge \varphi]\!](t'_n) \sqsupseteq \ell_n}{[\![EX\varphi]\!](s) \sqsupseteq \ell}$$

(c)

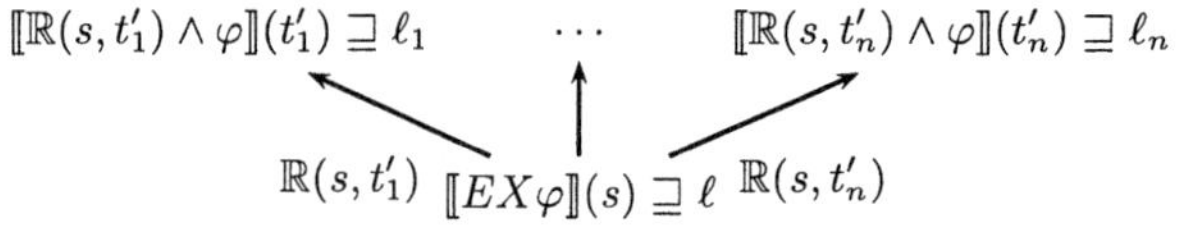

(d)

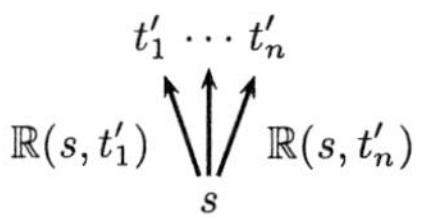

Fig. 10. From proofs to witnesses.

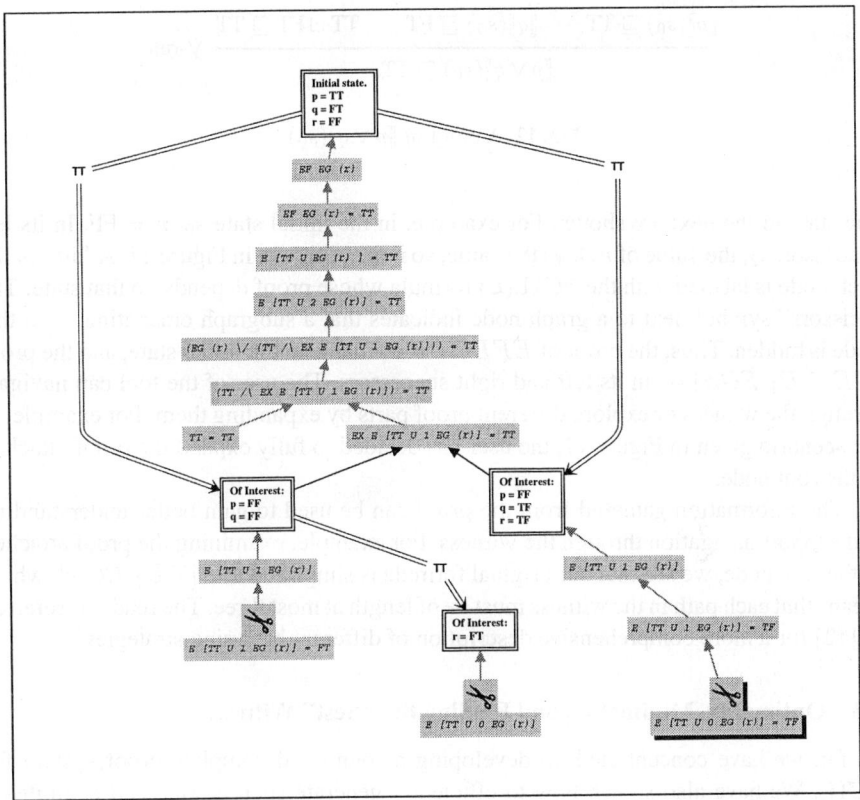

Fig. 11. Screenshot of KEGVis.

4.2 Tool Support

As discussed above, extracting witnesses from proofs effectively amounts to hiding certain proof steps, so proofs and witnesses are just two extremes in the presentation of the reasons behind the result of the model-checker to the user. The trade-off here is between size/complexity and ease of use. Proofs exhibit all of the reasoning steps explicitly, and make it easy for the user to follow each step. However, this excessive verbosity makes proofs much larger than corresponding witnesses and counterexamples. On the other hand, witnesses and counterexamples require the user to have a more detailed knowledge of the model-checking algorithm and the underlying De Morgan algebra.

To leverage the advantages of both presentations, we have developed an interactive witness browser tool — KEGVis [12]. Internally, the tool uses the proof view of the witness, while providing the user with the witness view.

A snapshot of KEGVis, showing the proof for $\varphi = ((EFEG\ r) \sqsupseteq TT)$ on the χKripke structure in Figure 2 using the algebra **2x2**, is given in Figure 11. Initially, the user is presented with the witness view of the proof, indicated by double-line nodes and arrows in the graph. Each state of the χKripke structure is represented by values of its atomic propositions, and for conciseness only the propositions that change from

$$\frac{[\![p]\!](s_0) \sqsupseteq \mathsf{TT} \quad [\![q]\!](s_0) \sqsupseteq \mathsf{FT} \quad \mathsf{TT} \sqcup \mathsf{FT} \sqsupseteq \mathsf{TT}}{[\![p \vee q]\!](s_0) \sqsupseteq \mathsf{TT}} \text{ V-rule}$$

Fig. 12. A proof of $[\![p \vee q]\!](s_0)$.

one state to the next are shown. For example, in the initial state s_0, $r = \mathsf{FF}$. In its left successor, s_2, the value of r stays the same, so it is not shown in Figure 11. Additionally, each node is labeled with the $\mathcal{X}\mathrm{CTL}(\mathcal{L})$ formula whose proof depends on that state. The "scissors" symbol next to a graph node indicates that a subgraph emanating from this node is hidden. Thus, the proof of $EFEG\ r$ is available in the initial state, and the proof of $E[\top\ U_1\ EG\ r]$ — in its left and right successors. The user of the tool can navigate through the witness or explore different proof parts by expanding them. For example, in the scenario given in Figure 11, the user has decided to fully expand the proof attached to the root node.

The information gathered from the proof can be used to gain better understanding and support navigation through the witness. For example, examining the proof attached to the root node, we see that our original formula is simplified to $E[\top\ U_2\ EG\ r]$, which means that each path in the witness must be of length at most three. The reader is referred to [12] for a more comprehensive description of different browsing strategies.

4.3 Optimality, Minimality, and Finding the "Best" Witness

So far, we have concentrated on developing a sound and complete proof system for $\mathcal{X}$CTL. We have also shown how to efficiently generate such proofs, and exhibited a one-to-one correspondence between proofs and witnesses. To simplify our reasoning, we have tried to use the simplest proof rules possible. The downside of this technique is that it treats all valid witnesses as equivalent.

In the rest of this section, we explore how a particular user objective, i.e. finding the smallest witness, can be met by introducing additional proof rules into our system. For brevity, we only concern ourselves with witnesses for $\mathcal{X}$ECTL.

We start by identifying the points in the proof where an improvement is possible. In general, such points correspond to branches in the proof tree, and in the case of witnesses for $\mathcal{X}$ECTL, they are identified by a disjunction: (a) a disjunction that occurs explicitly in a $\mathcal{X}$ECTL formula, and (b) a disjunction that is implicitly introduced by the EX operator.

Consider the proof of $P = [\![p \vee q]\!](s_0) \sqsupseteq \mathsf{TT}$ for the $\mathcal{X}$Kripke structure in Figure 2. The proof is shown in Figure 12. Clearly, since $[\![p]\!](s_0) = \mathsf{TT}$, it is sufficient to justify P; however, our current $\vee$-rule requires us to prove the fact that $[\![q]\!](s) \sqsupseteq \mathsf{FT}$ as well. We solve this problem by strengthening the $\vee$-rule as follows:

$$\frac{\exists \ell_1 \cdot [\![\varphi]\!](s) \sqsupseteq \ell_1 \wedge \ell_1 \sqsupseteq \ell}{[\![\varphi \vee \psi]\!](s) \sqsupseteq \ell} \text{ V-rule}$$

This ensures that the resulting proof does not contain any unnecessary branches.

Next, consider the proof for $[\![E[\top\ U\ r]]\!](s_0) \sqsupseteq \mathsf{TT}$ on the $\mathcal{X}$Kripke structure in Figure 2. A fragment of this proof is given in Figure 13. The problematic leaf is the one

$$\cfrac{\cfrac{[\![r]\!](s_1) \sqsupseteq \text{TF} \quad \cfrac{[\![r]\!](s_1) \sqsupseteq \text{TF}}{[\![E[\top\ U_0\ r]]\!](s_1) \sqsupseteq \text{TF}}\ EU_0}{\cfrac{[\![r]\!](s_1) \sqsupseteq \text{TF} \quad [\![EXE[\top\ U_0\ r]]\!](s_1) \sqsupseteq \text{TF}}{\cfrac{[\![r \vee EXE[\top\ U_0\ r]]\!](s_1) \sqsupseteq \text{TF}}{[\![E[\top\ U_1\ r]]\!](s_1) \sqsupseteq \text{TF}}\ EU_i}\ \vee\text{-rule}} \quad \cfrac{[\![r]\!](s_3) \sqsupseteq \text{FT} \quad \vdots}{\cfrac{\vdots}{[\![E[\top\ U_1\ r]]\!](s_2) \sqsupseteq \text{FT}}\ EX}}{\cfrac{[\![E[\top\ U_2\ r]]\!](s_0) \sqsupseteq \text{TT}}{[\![E[\top\ U\ r]]\!](s_0) \sqsupseteq \text{TT}}\ EU}$$

Fig. 13. Partial proof of $[\![E[\top\ U\ r]]\!](s_0)$.

labeled with

$$[\![r \vee EXE[\top\ U_0\ r]]\!](s_1) \sqsupseteq \text{TF}$$

Since $[\![r]\!](s_1) = \text{TF}$ and $[\![EXE[\top\ U_0\ r]]\!](s) = \text{TF}$, the proof generator non-deterministically chooses the subformula to expand. Thus, it can potentially decide to expand the EU formula, leading to a longer witness. This particular problem is solved by introducing an additional heuristic, telling the proof generator to always resolve non-deterministic choices by picking the smallest formula. However, in general, it is not possible to predict the size of the witness based solely on the syntax of the formula. A choice of a good heuristic typically depends on the additional domain and model knowledge. We leave the exploration and evaluation of various heuristics possible in this case for future work.

Finally, we consider the EX operator. In Section 3.3 we have shown that the breadth of the witness at the point where the one-point rule is applied to EX is determined by the size of the set $U' = \{\ell_i \mid \exists t \in S \cdot img(t) = \ell_i\}$. However, this solution is not optimal. For example, if $U' = \{\text{TT}, \text{TF}, \text{FT}\}$, then our witness for EX, given by the set U in Section 3.3, contains three states: t_1 with $img(t_1) = \text{TT}$, t_2 with $img(t_2) = \text{TF}$, and t_3 with $img(t_3) = \text{FT}$. However, it is sufficient to use either $\{t_1\}$ or $\{t_2, t_3\}$ since $img(t_1) = \text{TT}$ and $img(t_2) \sqcup img(t_3) = \text{TT}$. Thus, we can use one of the join-irredundant subsets of U' for the application of the one-point rule, instead of using U' directly.

5 Conclusion and Related Work

In this paper, we presented a technique for witness and counterexample generation for multi-valued model-checking. This technique is based on the concept of *proof-like* counterexamples, introduced in [12]. In fact, the automated proof-generation of Section 3.3 can be seen as simulating a run of a local tableau-based model-checker [19], where the information collected from a run of a global model-checker is used to guide the construction of the proof. However, unlike Stevens et al. [19], we restrict our attention to $\chi\text{CTL}(\mathcal{L})$ for the given algebra $\mathcal{L}$, and use the insights provided by the counterexample generation algorithm of Clarke et al. [8, 9] to derive a specialized EG-rule.

The automated proof-generation algorithm presented in Section 3.3 makes use of a model-checker as a decision procedure. Alternatively, the same information can be extracted from the support sets of Tan and Cleaveland [20], or deductive proofs of Namjoshi [15]. This makes it possible to use the technique presented here for interactive unrolling of deductive proofs (and support sets) into witnesses and counterexamples.

In this paper, we have concentrated on the technical issues surrounding the counterexample and witness generation for multi-valued model-checking. We have only briefly discussed the potential of introducing an ordering on witnesses and identifying the best or the most interesting witness. The proof-like representation of witnesses and counterexamples allows us to define a number of strategies for their navigation and exploration. For example, they allow the user to specify starting and stopping conditions so that he/she can navigate to the "interesting" part of the witness. Other examples include preferring the state with maximum/minimum number of successors, choosing step granularity, forward/ backward exploration, etc. We have also built a tool KEGVis [11] for visualization and interactive exploration of witnesses and counterexamples. A partial list of strategies together with the description of KEGVis appear in [12]. A more comprehensive treatment is in [5].

Acknowledgment

We thank the anonymous referees for helping improve the presentation of this paper. Financial support for this research has been provided by NSERC and CITO.

References

1. N.D. Belnap. "A Useful Four-Valued Logic". In Dunn and Epstein, editors, *Modern Uses of Multiple-Valued Logic*, pages 30–56. Reidel, 1977.
2. G. Bruns and P. Godefroid. "Temporal Logic Query-Checking". In *Proceedings of 16th Annual IEEE Symposium on Logic in Computer Science (LICS'01)*, pages 409–417, Boston, MA, USA, June 2001. IEEE Computer Society.
3. M. Chechik, B. Devereux, and A. Gurfinkel. "χChek: A Multi-Valued Model-Checker". In *Proceedings of 14th International Conference on Computer-Aided Verification (CAV'02)*, volume 2404 of *LNCS*, pages 505–509, Copenhagen, Denmark, July 2002. Springer.
4. M. Chechik, S. Easterbrook, and V. Petrovykh. "Model-Checking Over Multi-Valued Logics". In *Proceedings of Formal Methods Europe (FME'01)*, volume 2021 of *LNCS*, pages 72–98. Springer, March 2001.
5. M. Chechik and A. Gurfinkel. "Exploring Counterexamples". In preparation, June 2003.
6. M. Chechik and A. Gurfinkel. "TLQSolver: A Temporal Logic Query Checker". In *Proceedings of 15th International Conference on Computer-Aided Verification (CAV'03)*, July 2003.
7. E. Clarke, O. Grumberg, and D. Peled. *Model Checking*. MIT Press, 1999.
8. E.M. Clarke, O. Grumberg, K.L. McMillan, and X. Zhao. "Efficient Generation of Counterexamples and Witnesses in Symbolic Model Checking". In *Proceedings of 32nd Design Automation Conference (DAC 95)*, pages 427–432, San Francisco, CA, USA, 1995.
9. E.M. Clarke, Y. Lu, S. Jha, and H. Veith. "Tree-Like Counterexamples in Model Checking". In *Proceedings of the Seventeenth Annual IEEE Symposium on Logic in Computer Science (LICS'02)*, pages 19–29, Copenhagen, Denmark, July 2002. IEEE Computer Society.
10. S. Easterbrook and M. Chechik. "A Framework for Multi-Valued Reasoning over Inconsistent Viewpoints". In *Proceedings of International Conference on Software Engineering (ICSE'01)*, pages 411–420, Toronto, Canada, May 2001. IEEE Computer Society Press.

11. A. Gurfinkel. "Multi-Valued Symbolic Model-Checking: Fairness, Counterexamples, Running Time". Master's thesis, University of Toronto, Department of Computer Science, October 2002. Available from http://www.cs.toronto.edu/\char126chechik/pubs/gurfinkelMSThesis.ps.
12. A. Gurfinkel and M. Chechik. "Proof-like Counterexamples". In *Proceedings of 9th International Conference on Tools and Algorithms for the Construction and Analysis of Systems (TACAS'03)*, volume 2619 of *LNCS*, pages 160–175, April 2003.
13. Alexander Kick. "Tableaux and Witnesses for the μ-calculus". Technical Report iratr-1995-44, 1995.
14. S. C. Kleene. *Introduction to Metamathematics*. New York: Van Nostrand, 1952.
15. K. Namjoshi. "Certifying Model Checkers". In *Proceedings of 13th International Conference on Computer-Aided Verification (CAV'01)*, volume 2102 of *Lecture Notes in Computer Science*. Springer, 2001.
16. S. Owre, N. Shankar, and J. Rushby. "User Guide for the PVS Specification and Verification System (Draft)". Technical report, Computer Science Lab, SRI International, Menlo Park, CA, 1993.
17. H. Rasiowa. *An Algebraic Approach to Non-Classical Logics. Studies in Logic and the Foundations of Mathematics*. Amsterdam: North-Holland, 1978.
18. V. Sofronie-Stokkermans. "Automated Theorem Proving by Resolution for Finitely-Valued Logics Based on Distributive Lattices with Operators". *An International Journal of Multiple-Valued Logic*, 6(3-4):289–344, 2001.
19. P. Stevens and C. Stirling. "Practical Model-Checking using Games". In B. Steffen, editor, *Proceedings of 4th International Conference on Tools and Algorithms for the Construction and Analysis of Systems (TACAS'98)*, volume 1384 of *LNCS*, pages 85–101, New York, NY, USA, 1998. Springer.
20. L. Tan and R. Cleaveland. "Evidence-Based Model Checking". In *Proceedings of 14th Conference on Computer-Aided Verification (CAV'02)*, volume 2404 of *LNCS*, pages 455–470, Copenhagen, Denmark, July 2002. Springer.

Combining Real-Time Model-Checking and Fault Tree Analysis*

Andreas Schäfer

Department of Computing Science, University of Oldenburg,
26111 Oldenburg, Germany

Abstract. We present a semantics for fault tree analysis, a technique used for the analysis of safety critical systems, in the real-time interval logic Duration Calculus with Liveness and show how properties of fault trees can be checked automatically. We apply this technique in two examples and show how it can be connected to other verification techniques.

Keywords: Real-time systems, model-checking, fault tree analysis

1 Introduction

In this paper we bring together the two worlds of safety engineering on the one hand and real-time model-checking on the other hand. We present an approach of using model-checking to determine whether a fault tree is designed properly. Fault tree analysis [VGRH81] is a technique widely used by engineers to analyse safety of safety-critical systems. Originally, it did not have a formal semantics and relied on the expertise of safety engineers. Recently there have been several attempts to define a formal semantics for fault trees [RST00,Han96]. In this paper we go one step further and show how to combine the fault tree analysis with real-time model-checking.

Both parties benefit from this combination. From the point of view of the safety engineer formal models and proofs by model-checking raise the quality of safety analysis. The aim is to make implicit assumptions on the behaviour of the system explicit and to discover problems that have been overlooked. So we add extra redundancy to the safety analysis itself.

On the other hand, model-checking benefits because the formal model is compared with the fault tree that is created from the system independently. Additionally, the knowledge of the system which is present in the fault tree can be used to simplify the verification process. Instead of verifying one complex property of the whole system, we decompose the property into simpler properties of subsystems using fault tree analysis. Then we verify that the decomposition is correct and finally show that the simple properties hold.

As the underlying formalism we use Duration Calculus with Liveness (DCL) [Ska94], which is designed to describe and reason about real-time systems. As the operational formalism for model-checking we use Phase Automata [Tap01,DT03]

---

* This research was partially supported by the DFG under grant Ol/98-2.

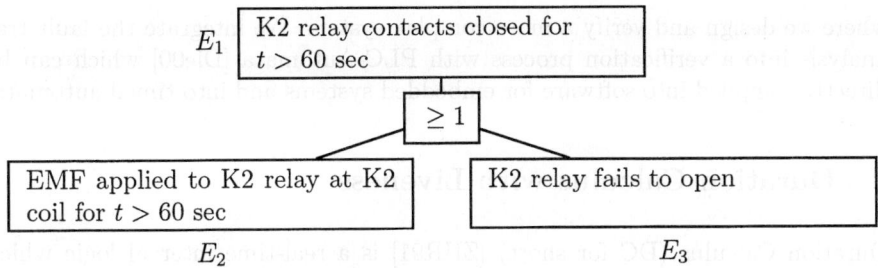

Fig. 1. Example of decomposition

because they have a semantics in Duration Calculus. Since we define the fault tree semantics in Duration Calculus with Liveness, too, we completely stay in this formal framework.

As an example consider the fault tree in Fig. 1. Let it be designed for a system in which a relay K2 controls a pump which pressurizes a tank. We assume that the tank will burst if the contacts of relay K2 are closed for more than 60 seconds. The fault tree decomposes this event and states that if it occurs then either an electromagnetic field (EMF) must have been applied to the coil for more than 60 seconds or erroneously the relay does not open. The aim is to verify that this is in fact true. To this end, we create an operational model of our relay to express our assumptions on its behaviour. We formalise each event given in the fault tree by a formula in Duration Calculus with Liveness. In this example let E_1, E_2 and E_3 be these formalisations. We can be sure that no cause of the event E_1 is forgotten if the implication $E_1 \Rightarrow (E_2 \vee E_3)$ holds with respect to our operational model $\mathcal{M}$ of the relay. So in fact we have to verify

$$(\mathcal{M} \wedge E_1) \Rightarrow (E_2 \vee E_3).$$

This is done by translating each formula and its complement into a Phase Automaton. Let these Phase Automata be called $\mathcal{A}_{E1}, \mathcal{A}_{E2}, \mathcal{A}_{E3}$ and $\mathcal{A}_{\neg E1}, \mathcal{A}_{\neg E2}, \mathcal{A}_{\neg E3}$. We check whether there is a run of the model $\mathcal{M}$ which is also possible for $\mathcal{A}_{E1}, \mathcal{A}_{\neg E2}$ and $\mathcal{A}_{\neg E3}$. If this is not the case, the implication is true. Thus no causes of the event E_1 have been overlooked.

In this paper we give precise semantics of fault trees to express that a fault tree is well designed. Apart from the or-connective considered in this example the other connectives that may appear in fault trees are also treated. For a subclass of DCL formulae which is relevant for fault trees we give algorithmic constructions of Phase Automata. And we show how they can be composed so we can use model-checking to establish that the fault tree is well designed for a given model of the system.

The rest of this paper is organised as follows. In section 2 and 3, we introduce Duration Calculus with Liveness and Phase Automata. In section 4 we give a semantics for fault trees in Duration Calculus with Liveness. In section 5 we show how properties can be model-checked automatically using Phase Automata. This approach is applied to one example in section 6 and one case study in section 7 where we design and verify a more complex system. We integrate the fault tree analysis into a verification process with PLC-Automata [Die00] which can be directly compiled into software for embedded systems and into timed automata.

2 Duration Calculus with Liveness

Duration Calculus (DC for short) [ZHR91] is a real-time interval logic which allows reasoning about durations of states. As the properties which will be important for fault trees will be liveness properties, we use the extension *Duration Calculus with Liveness* (DCL) [Ska94], which introduces special modalities to express real liveness properties.

Real-time systems are described by a finite number of *observables* (time-dependent variables) which are denoted by $X, Y, \ldots$ and interpreted by an interpretation $\mathcal{I}$ which assigns to each observable X a function $\mathcal{I}(X) : \mathsf{Time} \to D$. Here Time is the time domain – in this case the real numbers – and D is the finite domain of the observable. Additionally we use rigid variables denoted by $x, y, \ldots$ and valuations $\mathcal{V}$ which assign a real number to each rigid variable.

State assertions π are generated by the grammar

$$\pi ::= 0 \mid 1 \mid X = c \mid \neg \pi_1 \mid \pi_1 \land \pi_2$$

and describe the state of the real-time system at a certain point of time, with the semantics:

$$\mathcal{I}[\![0]\!](t) = 0, \quad \mathcal{I}[\![1]\!](t) = 1, \quad \mathcal{I}[\![X = k]\!](t) = \begin{cases} 1 & \text{if } \mathcal{I}(X)(t) = k \\ 0 & \text{otherwise} \end{cases}$$

and the usual definition for the propositional connectives. Duration terms θ are either rigid variables or derived from state assertions using the $\int$ operator; their semantics depends on an interpretation $\mathcal{I}$, a valuation $\mathcal{V}$, and an interval $[a, b]$, and is defined by

$$\mathcal{I}[\![x]\!](\mathcal{V}, [a,b]) = \mathcal{V}(x), \quad \mathcal{I}[\![\int P]\!](\mathcal{V}, [a,b]) = \int_a^b \mathcal{I}[\![P]\!](t) dt$$

Duration formulae F are generated by the grammar

$$F ::= p(\theta_1, \ldots, \theta_n) \mid F_1; F_2 \mid F_1 \triangleleft F_2 \mid F_1 \triangleright F_2 \mid \neg F_1 \mid F_1 \land F_2 \mid \exists x F \mid \exists X F$$

and are evaluated in a given interpretation $\mathcal{I}$, a valuation $\mathcal{V}$, and a time interval $[a, b]$. The symbol p denotes a predicate symbol like $=, \leq, \geq$. In general, the meaning of a predicate p is given by the interpretation and denoted by $p_\mathcal{I}$. A formula $F_1; F_2$ holds iff the given interval can be "chopped" into two parts such that F_1 holds on the left part and F_2 on the right part. The expanding modalities $\triangleleft$ and $\triangleright$ allow an expansion of the interval to the left respectively to the right. Additionally to negation and conjunction we allow quantification over rigid variables and observables. Other propositional connectives can be defined as abbreviations. Formally,

$\mathcal{I}, \mathcal{V}, [a,b] \models p(\theta_1, \ldots, \theta_n)$ iff $p_{\mathcal{I}}(\mathcal{I}[\![\theta_1]\!](\mathcal{V},[a,b]), \ldots, \mathcal{I}[\![\theta_n]\!](\mathcal{V},[a,b]))$
$\mathcal{I}, \mathcal{V}, [a,b] \models F_1; F_2$ iff $\exists k \in [a,b] : \mathcal{I}, \mathcal{V}, [a,k] \models F_1$ and $\mathcal{I}, \mathcal{V}, [k,b] \models F_2$
$\mathcal{I}, \mathcal{V}, [a,b] \models F_1 \triangleright F_2$ iff $\exists k \geq b : \mathcal{I}, \mathcal{V}, [a,k] \models F_1$ and $\mathcal{I}, \mathcal{V}, [b,k] \models F_2$
$\mathcal{I}, \mathcal{V}, [a,b] \models F_1 \triangleleft F_2$ iff $\exists k \leq a : \mathcal{I}, \mathcal{V}, [k,a] \models F_1$ and $\mathcal{I}, \mathcal{V}, [k,b] \models F_2$

The definitions of the remaining connectives and quantifications over rigid variables and observables are like in first-order logic. Additionally, the following abbreviations will be used:

$\ell \stackrel{df}{=} \int 1$ (length of the interval) $\lceil P \rceil \stackrel{df}{=} \int P = \ell \wedge \ell > 0$

$\Diamond F \stackrel{df}{=} (true; F; true)$ (somewhere) $\Box F \stackrel{df}{=} \neg \Diamond \neg F$

$\Diamond_L F \stackrel{df}{=} (true; F; true) \triangleright true$ (eventually) $\Box_L F \stackrel{df}{=} \neg \Diamond_L \neg F$ (always)

3 Phase Automata

As an operational model for real-time systems we use Phase Automata [Tap01], which possess a formal semantics in DC and allow model-checking using the tool Moby/DC [DT03]. The intuition is similar to Timed Automata [AD94].

A Phase Automaton $\mathcal{A} = (P, E, C, cl, s, d, P_0)$ consists of finite sets of states P, and clocks C, a transition relation $E \subseteq P \times P$, and a set P_0 of initial states. The function cl assigns a set of clocks to each state, the function s assigns a state assertion to each state, and the function d assigns to each clock a time interval.

A Phase Automaton can stay in the present state only if the state assertion holds. Additionally, for each clock c the amount of time the automaton stays in states in $cl^{-1}(c)$ must be within the interval given by $d(c)$.

In Fig. 2 we present an example of a Phase Automaton modelling the formula $\Diamond_L(\lceil P \rceil \wedge 4 < \ell; \lceil Q \rceil \wedge 3 < \ell)$. The open intervals $(0, \infty)$ and $(4, \infty)$ express that the automaton may stay in s_0 and s_1 arbitrarily long but has to leave these states eventually, whereas the interval $(3, \infty]$ allows the automaton to stay in s_2 forever.

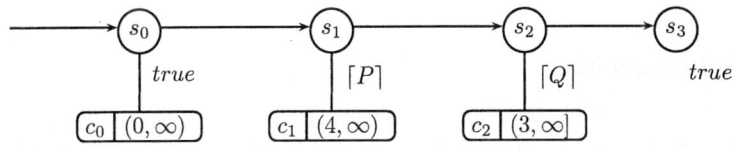

Fig. 2. Phase Automaton for $\Diamond_L(\lceil P \rceil \wedge 4 < \ell; \lceil Q \rceil \wedge 3 < \ell)$

3.1 Semantics

The semantics of a Phase Automaton $\mathcal{A}$ is defined in terms of one big DC formula. It encodes the behaviour using one fresh observable $\mathsf{ph}_\mathcal{A}$, which ranges over the state space of the automaton. The subformulae model the initial states, the successor state relation, and the clock constraints. To give a flavour of these formulae we just present one of them. It expresses that it is impossible to stay in a set of states which belong to the same clock c longer than the upper bound given in the clock interval $d(c)$. It encodes the progress of the automaton.

$$D_{pr}^c(\mathcal{A}) \stackrel{df}{=} \neg \Diamond (\lceil \bigvee_{p \in cl^{-1}(c)} \mathsf{ph}_\mathcal{A} = p \rceil \land \ell > d(c))$$

3.2 Model-Checking and Closure under Complementation

The model-checker Moby/DC [Tap01,DT03] checks whether a set of Phase Automata running in parallel have a common run. To exploit this, we use the following automata-theoretic approach to model-checking. We model the system to be checked by a set of Phase Automata. The property which is to be verified is negated. For this negated property we also construct a Phase Automaton and check whether there is a run which satisfies both the model of our system and the negated property. If this is not the case, the property holds. Unfortunately, Phase Automata are – like Timed Automata – not closed under complementation. Therefore we will have to restrict ourselves to a subset of Phase Automata that permits complementation.

4 Fault Tree Analysis

Fault tree analysis (FTA) [VGRH81] is an engineering technique to identify causes of system failures. Its main area of application are safety critical components in nuclear and aviation industries. Starting with an undesired event (called top-event) all possible causes (called sub-events) are identified. These causes are joined using and and or gates to the top-event depending on whether all events have to occur to yield the top-event or whether one event is sufficient. This procedure is iterated until a given granularity is reached. Events that are not developed further are called basic-events. In Fig. 1 we gave an example taken from the Fault Tree Handbook [VGRH81] in which for one event two possible causes are identified. We use the notation defined by the IEC 61025 standard [IEC93].

4.1 DCL Semantics

In order to use model-checking techniques to verify that a fault tree is constructed properly and to combine it with other formal techniques in one verification process we need a formal semantics. Originally, there was no formal semantics [VGRH81] but there have been several attempts [Han96,BA93,RST00] to define one in order to avoid ambiguities.

Events. Events are formalised by DCL formulae. Gorski [Gór94] divides the events occurring in fault trees into three groups. So we will restrict ourselves to DCL formulae for these groups and give a DCL formula pattern for each of them. We require the events to be formalized by such a DCL formula.

$$\diamond_L \lceil \pi \rceil \wedge a \sim \ell \qquad \text{(Reachable state)}$$
$$\diamond_L \square_L \lceil \pi \rceil \wedge \neg \diamond_L (\lceil \pi \rceil; \lceil \neg \pi \rceil) \qquad \text{(Final state/Deadlock)}$$
$$\diamond_L (\lceil \pi_1 \rceil \wedge a_1 \sim \ell; \lceil \pi_2 \rceil \wedge a_2 \sim \ell \sim b_2; \ldots; \quad \lceil \pi_{n-1} \rceil \wedge a_{n-1} \sim \ell \sim b_{n-1};$$
$$\lceil \pi_n \rceil \wedge a_n \sim \ell) \qquad \text{(State sequence)}$$

where $\sim \in \{<, \leq\}$, a and b are real numbers and π is a state assertion, describing the system state. Upper bounds for the duration are to be specified using the sequence pattern like $\diamond_L(\lceil \neg \pi \rceil; \lceil \pi \rceil \wedge \ell \leq b; \lceil \neg \pi \rceil)$. Examples for these type of pattern could be:

- Reachable state: The relay is eventually closed for more than 60 sec.
- Deadlock: Once the relay is closed, it will never open again.
- State sequence: Eventually the relay is closed for at least 60 sec and is open for at least 20 sec after that.

Gates. Events are joined by gates to express their dependence. We follow Reif et al.'s approach [RST00] and distinguish two kinds of gates:

- *decomposition gates* which do not impose any temporal relationship between the events joined by this gate, and
- *cause consequence gates* which express temporal dependencies.

We consider the two decomposition gates and ($\wedge$) and or ($\vee$) and three cause consequence gates. For the asynchronous or ($\vee$-acc) gate we require the event to happen after *one* of the causes have happened. For the asynchronous and gate ($\wedge$-acc) we require the event to happen after *all* of the causes have happened. And for the synchronous and gate ($\wedge$-scc) we require the event to happen after *all* events occurred *simultaneously*, which means that there is a time interval in which all formulae expressing the event hold.

After having given ideas what events and gates are, we can proceed to define syntax and semantics for fault trees.

4.2 Syntax

The set of *fault trees* is defined inductively as follows.

- Every basic event E formalized as a DCL formula is a fault tree with top event E.
- For a nonempty and finite set $\mathcal{T}$ of fault trees, a gate $G \in \{\wedge, \vee, \wedge\text{-scc}, \wedge\text{-acc}, \vee\text{-acc}\}$ and an event E, the term $(E, G, \mathcal{T})$ is a fault tree with top event E. As all gate conditions will be associative we do not have to impose an order on the fault trees in $\mathcal{T}$.

We continue to present fault trees graphically and not as a term structure. According to the IEC 61025 standard [IEC93] we use "&" and "≥ 1" in the graphical notation instead of "$\wedge$" and "$\vee$" and omit and gates with one child.

4.3 Semantics

For each gate we define two DCL proof obligations, one stating that the occurrence of sub-events is necessary for the event to occur and the other that they are sufficient. For fault tree T, we define in our semantics $[\![T]\!]_S$ to be the conjunction of all sufficient conditions and $[\![T]\!]_N$ as the conjunction of all necessary conditions. The proof obligations for the necessary conditions are especially important. They express that no cause has been overlooked. If all necessary conditions can be proved by model-checking, we call a fault tree *complete*. Additionally, if it can be proved that the sub-events cannot happen, it follows that the event itself cannot happen.

The precise semantics is defined inductively:

- For every basic event E we define $[\![E]\!]_N \stackrel{df}{=} [\![E]\!]_S \stackrel{df}{=}$ true
- Let $T = (E, G, \{T_1, \ldots, T_n\})$ be a fault tree and let $E_1, \ldots, E_n$ be the top events of $T_1, \ldots, T_n$. Then we define

$$[\![T]\!]_S \stackrel{df}{=} F_S^G \wedge \bigwedge_{i=1}^n [\![T_i]\!]_S$$

$$[\![T]\!]_N \stackrel{df}{=} F_N^G \wedge \bigwedge_{i=1}^n [\![T_i]\!]_N$$

where the proof obligations F_S^G and F_N^G are given by

$$F_S^\wedge \stackrel{df}{=} \left(\bigwedge_{i=1}^n E_i\right) \Rightarrow E \qquad (\wedge\text{-gate: sufficient condition})$$

$$F_N^\wedge \stackrel{df}{=} E \Rightarrow \left(\bigwedge_{i=1}^n E_i\right) \qquad (\wedge\text{-gate: necessary condition})$$

$$F_S^\vee \stackrel{df}{=} \left(\bigvee_{i=1}^n E_i\right) \Rightarrow E \qquad (\vee\text{-gate: sufficient condition})$$

$$F_N^\vee \stackrel{df}{=} E \Rightarrow \left(\bigvee_{i=1}^n E_i\right) \qquad (\vee\text{-gate: necessary condition})$$

For the cause consequence gates we have to express the notion of "after" in terms of DCL. So we have to get rid of the expanding modalities in $\Diamond_L$ and use the substitution $\{\Diamond_L/\}$ which removes the leading occurrence of a $\Diamond_L$ operator from a formula. After this substitution the formula is still a well-formed DCL formula.

$$F_S^{\wedge\text{-acc}} \stackrel{df}{=} \left(\bigwedge_{i=1}^n E_i\right) \Rightarrow E \qquad (\wedge\text{-acc-gate: sufficient condition})$$

$$F_N^{\wedge\text{-acc}} \stackrel{df}{=} \neg\left((\neg\bigwedge_{i=1}^n \Diamond E_i\{\Diamond_L/\}); E\{\Diamond_L/\}\right) \qquad (\wedge\text{-acc-gate necessary condition})$$

$$F_S^{\vee\text{-acc}} \stackrel{df}{=} \left(\bigvee_{i=1}^{n} E_i\right) \Rightarrow E \qquad (\vee\text{-acc-gate: sufficient condition})$$

$$F_N^{\vee\text{-acc}} \stackrel{df}{=} \neg\left((\neg \bigvee_{i=1}^{n} \Diamond E_i\{\Diamond_L/\}); E\{\Diamond_L/\}\right) \qquad (\vee\text{-acc-gate: necessary condition})$$

$$F_S^{\wedge\text{-scc}} \stackrel{df}{=} \Diamond_L \left(\bigwedge_{i=1}^{n} E_i\{\Diamond_L/\}\right) \Rightarrow E \qquad (\wedge\text{-scc-gate: sufficient condition})$$

$$F_N^{\wedge\text{-scc}} \stackrel{df}{=} \neg\left((\neg \Diamond \bigwedge_{i=1}^{n} E_i\{\Diamond_L/\}); E\{\Diamond_L/\}\right) \qquad (\wedge\text{-scc-gate: necessary condition})$$

If the consequence has already happened due to other causes the consequence does not need to happen again. So for the sufficient condition we do not require the consequence to happen after the causes.

5 Model-Checking

The proof obligations presented in the previous section should be verified automatically by model-checking. As one can only prove correctness propositions with respect to a given model, we assume that a formal model of the system is given in terms of Phase Automata.

So the model-checking problem for a given fault tree T is to check if a model $\mathcal{M}$ satisfies

$$\models \mathcal{M} \Rightarrow \llbracket T \rrbracket_N$$
$$\models \mathcal{M} \Rightarrow \llbracket T \rrbracket_S.$$

Zhou et al. [ZHS93] showed that the Duration Calculus is undecidable. As we can write every DC Formula F as $true \Rightarrow F$ and this is the necessary condition of the fault tree $(true, \wedge, (F))$ the model-checking problem for fault trees is undecidable in general. So a restriction to a subset of DCL is unavoidable. Therefore we only consider the three classes of events proposed by Gorsky [Gór94] and restrict the formulae to patterns given in section 4.1.

If we assume for the third pattern that two different state expressions occurring in a DCL formula of that type cannot hold at the same time, all formulae matching one of these patterns can be translated into Phase Automata. Therefore the fragment is decidable. The expressiveness can only be evaluated by considering case studies which we do in sections 6 and 7.

Idea. To verify the gate conditions arising from fault tree analysis they are translated into Phase Automata, too. Model-checking establishes whether or not the conditions hold for the given model. First we present constructions of Phase Automata for each event pattern of section 4.1 and its complement. After that we show how the proof obligations arising from different gates can be model-checked.

5.1 Constructing Phase Automata for Event Patterns

The construction of Phase Automata for most of the event patterns of section 4.1 is given in Figs. 3 to 5. Only the construction of the complement automaton for the sequence pattern requires extra attention. For all constructions given in this section, we assume that "$\leq$" is the only relation occurring in the DCL formula. If this is not the case, the corresponding open intervals have to become closed and vice versa.

Complement construction for Sequence Pattern. In general, Phase Automata are not closed under complementation and there are examples of Phase Automata for which no complement exists and which belong to the group of sequence formulae. To avoid these problems, we require that two state expressions within

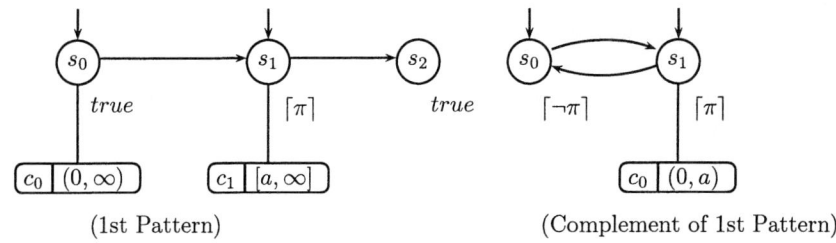

Fig. 3. Phase Automata for the first pattern of fault tree events and its complement.

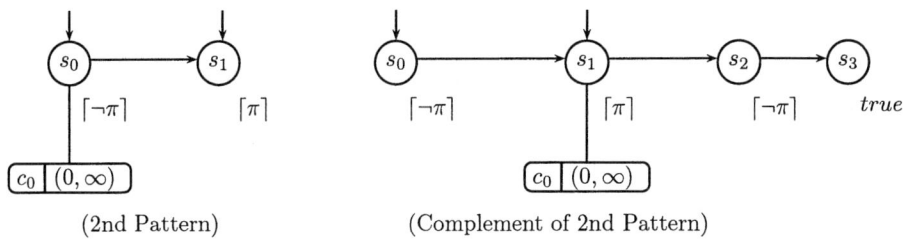

Fig. 4. Phase Automata for the second pattern of fault tree events and its complement.

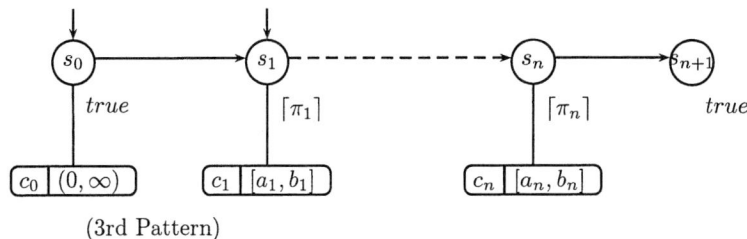

Fig. 5. Phase Automaton for the third pattern of fault tree events.

the pattern cannot be satisfied at the same time, that is

$$\pi_i \wedge \pi_j \equiv false \quad \text{for all } i \neq j. \tag{1}$$

A construction for this case is sufficient for our case studies. The detailed construction is given in the appendix. The restriction to this kind of formula unfortunately disallows formulae like

$$\Diamond_L \lceil \neg \pi \rceil; \lceil \pi \rceil \wedge \ell < t; \lceil \neg \pi \rceil$$

which describes that eventually π holds for less than t time units. This is the only way to describe upper bounds in DC. But this simple type of formula can still be translated although requirement (1) does not hold.

5.2 Decomposition Gates

Using the Phase Automata constructed in the previous subsection, we can express the *negation* of the different proof obligations by a set of Phase Automata as presented in Table 1. Then we check if this set of Phase Automata has a run together with the Phase Automata model $\mathcal{M}$ of our system. If this is not the case, the proof obligation is verified. In Table 1, $\overline{\mathcal{A}}$ denotes the complement of the Phase Automaton $\mathcal{A}$, $\|$ denotes the parallel composition, and $\vee$ the alternative. The alternative $\mathcal{A}_1 \vee \mathcal{A}_2$ is –like for finite automata– just the union of the two Phase Automata, where the name-spaces are disjoint.

Table 1. Model-checking gate conditions

Condition	Set of Phase Automata (Negation of Condition)
$F_S^{\wedge} = \left(\bigwedge_{i=1}^n E_i \right) \Rightarrow E$	$\overline{\mathcal{A}}_E \| \mathcal{A}_{E_1} \| \ldots \| \mathcal{A}_{E_m}$
$F_N^{\wedge} = E \Rightarrow \left(\bigwedge_{i=1}^n E_i \right)$	$\mathcal{A}_E \| (\overline{\mathcal{A}}_{E_1} \vee \ldots \vee \overline{\mathcal{A}}_{E_m})$
$F_S^{\vee} = \left(\bigvee_{i=1}^n E_i \right) \Rightarrow E$	$\overline{\mathcal{A}}_E \| (\mathcal{A}_{E_1} \vee \ldots \vee \mathcal{A}_{E_m})$
$F_N^{\vee} = E \Rightarrow \left(\bigvee_{i=1}^n E_i \right)$	$\mathcal{A}_E \| \overline{\mathcal{A}}_{E_1} \| \ldots \| \overline{\mathcal{A}}_{E_m}$

5.3 Cause-Consequence Gates

To perform model-checking for cause-consequence gates, we use the same automata constructed above, but impose a new oberservable Syn to synchronise the automata and express the temporal dependencies. Obviously the second pattern expressing a final state cannot be regarded as a cause for an event which takes place *after* this event, so we do not consider this type of pattern for cause-consequence gates.

Asynchronous Gates. The sufficient condition is the same for asynchronous cause-consequence gates and for the decomposition gates.

To check the necessary condition we construct a set of Phase Automata which allow all runs which violate the property. For the and-gate condition $F_N^{\wedge\text{-acc}} \stackrel{df}{=} \neg(\neg \bigwedge_{i=1}^{n} \Diamond E_i\{\Diamond_L/\}; E\{\Diamond_L/\})$ the construction is as follows:

1. Let Syn be a fresh boolean observable.
2. Construct the union of $\overline{\mathcal{A}_{E_1}}, \ldots, \overline{\mathcal{A}_{E_n}}$. The semantics of this automaton is the set of all runs in which at least one formula E_i is not *true*. Add the assertion Syn to every state. Add a new state p_{true} with the assertion $\neg Syn$ and transitions from all other states to this state. So Syn is *true* as long as at least one formula E_i is not satisfied.
3. Construct the automaton $\mathcal{A}_E$ and replace the condition *true* in the first state by Syn and add the assertion $\neg Syn$ to all other states. So E has to be *true* finally and Syn must hold before, so at least one formula E_i has not been true before.

The construction for or gates is similar, except that in step 2 instead of the union the parallel composition is used.

Synchronous Gates. Again, checking the sufficient condition is very easy and is skipped here. The necessary condition for synchronous and gate describes that an event occurs only if the sub-events occur at the same time, which means that several state assertions hold in the same interval. Therefore we only consider cases where the formulae E_i for the sub-events are of the first type $\Diamond_L \lceil \pi^{(i)} \rceil \wedge a^{(i)} \leq \ell$.

1. Let Syn be a fresh boolean observable.
2. Construct an automaton for the complement of the formula $\Diamond_L(\lceil \bigwedge_{i=1}^{n}(\pi^{(i)}) \rceil \wedge \bigwedge_{i=1}^{n}(a^{(i)} \leq \ell))$ using the construction in Fig. 3. The semantics of this automaton is the set of all runs in which not all state assertions are true simultaneously. Add the assertion Syn to every state. Add a new state p_{true} with the assertion $\neg Syn$ and transitions from all other states to this state. So Syn is *true* as long as not all state assertions are true on the same time interval.
3. Construct the automaton $\mathcal{A}_E$ and replace the condition *true* in the first state by Syn and add the assertion $\neg Syn$ to all other states. So E has to be *true* finally and Syn must hold before, which means that beforehand at no time interval all state assertions in $E_1, \ldots, E_n$ have been *true*.

6 Example – Pressure Tank

We apply our approach to the classical pressure tank example [VGRH81]. In the original work, the fault tree analysis is done completely manually; no formal techniques are considered. We present the scenario, a part of our formal model of the system, the first part of the fault tree, and explicitly check one gate condition.

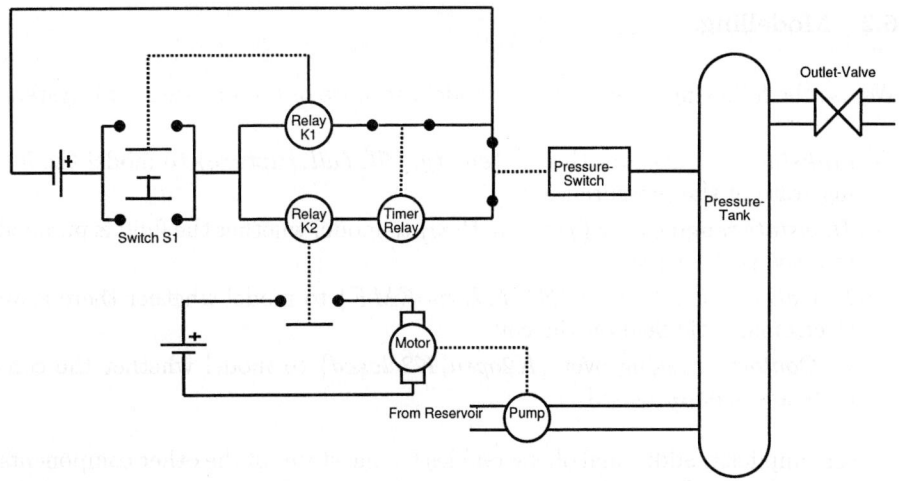

Fig. 6. Pressure Tank System

6.1 Scenario

The pressure tank system shown in Fig. 6 consists of three parts: a pressure tank, a pump-motor device and an associated control system to regulate the operation of the pump. We use the following assumptions of the system [VGRH81]:

- It takes 60 sec to pressurise the tank.
- The pressure switch contacts are closed until the threshold pressure is reached.
- The tank is fitted with an outlet valve which drains the entire tank in negligible time. The valve is not a pressure relief valve.

Then the operation of this system is as follows:

- Initially the system is dormant: the switch S1 contacts are open, the relay K1 contacts are open, the relay K2 contacts are open and the pressure switch is closed.
- Pressing switch S1 starts the system. Power is applied to the coil of relay K1, closing K1's contacts, so that relay K1 is electrically self-latched.
- The closure of relay K1 applies power to the coils of relay K2, causes relay K2's contacts to close and starts the pump.
- When the threshold pressure is reached, the pressure switch contacts open, deenergise the coil of relay K2, cause relay K2's contacts to open and stop the pump.
- The timer relay serves as a fall-back device if the pressure switch fails to open. After 60 sec of continuous power application to the timer relay, the contacts open, deenergise the coils of relay K1 and causes its contacts to open. Then the coil of relay K2 is deenergised, its contacts fall open and the pump is stopped.

6.2 Modelling

We use the following observables to model the state of the pressure tank system:

- *tankstate* ranging over the set $\{empty, fill, full, rupture\}$ to model the filling state of the pressure tank.
- *flowstate* ranging over $\{flow, noflow\}$ to model whether the fluid is pumped into the tank or not.
- *K2Coil* ranging over $\{K2EMF, K2noEMF\}$ to model whether there is an electromagnetic field on the coil.
- *K2Contacts* ranging over $\{K2open, K2closed\}$ to model whether the contacts are open or closed.

For simplicity, additional oberservables for the states of the other components are skipped here. Phase Automata are used to model our assumptions on the behaviour of the system. The ones presented in Fig. 7 to Fig. 9 model the operation of relay K2, the tank and the assumption that the tank will not withstand more than 60 sec of continuous flow. The possible failure of relay K2 is modelled by an extra failure state. The rest of our system model is again skipped.

Fig. 7. Phase Automaton $\mathcal{A}_{\mathsf{K2}}$ modelling Relay K2

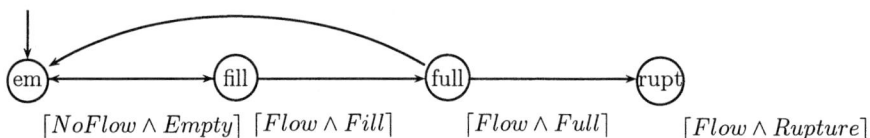

Fig. 8. Phase Automaton $\mathcal{A}_{\mathsf{tank}}$ modelling the behaviour of the tank.

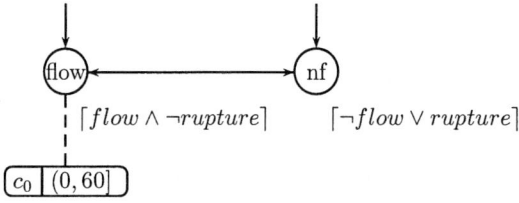

Fig. 9. Phase Automaton $\mathcal{A}_{\mathsf{ruptTime}}$ to model certain rupture after 60 sec of continuous flow.

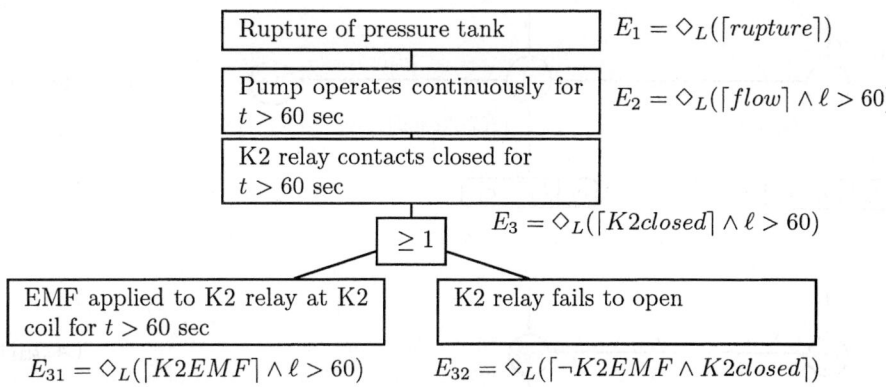

Fig. 10. First part of fault tree for pressure tank system and the event "Rupture of pressure tank"

6.3 Fault Tree Analysis

Figure 10 presents a simplified and shortened version of the fault tree developed by Veseley et al. [VGRH81]. Additionally, we have annotated every event with its DCL formula.

6.4 Verification

We are going to verify that the decomposition at the or gate is correct with respect to our model of the system. That means that the Events E_{31} and E_{32} are necessary for event E_3. To this end, we have to check the validity of

$$\mathcal{M} \Rightarrow (E_3 \Rightarrow (E_{31} \vee E_{32}))$$

where $\mathcal{M}$ is our model of the system in terms of Phase Automata. Therefore we use the construction given in section 5 for the first pattern to obtain Phase Automata $\mathcal{A}_{E3}, \mathcal{A}_{\neg E31}, \mathcal{A}_{\neg E32}$ representing E_3, $\neg E_{31}$ and $\neg E_{32}$ as given in Fig. 11 and check whether they have a common run together with the automata of our system model. In fact we only need $\mathcal{A}_{K2}$ of our model to prove this. The answer is obtained in 1.2 seconds using the tool Moby/DC.

This result holds only because we have neglected the time the relay K2 takes to open its contacts. If we considered this in our model, the implication would not hold any longer. Using this technique the engineer has to put all her assumptions on the behaviour of the system in the formal model which adds additional safety as implicit assumptions are discovered. On the other hand, the engineer can easily alter the model and check whether the fault tree remains correct under different assumptions.

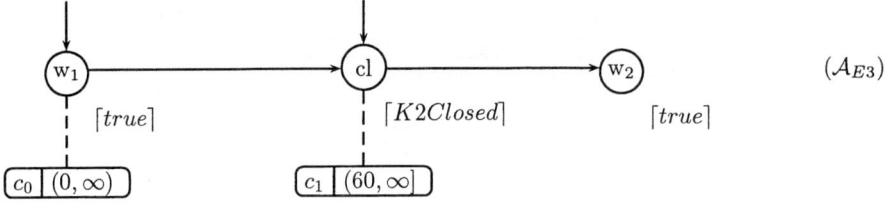
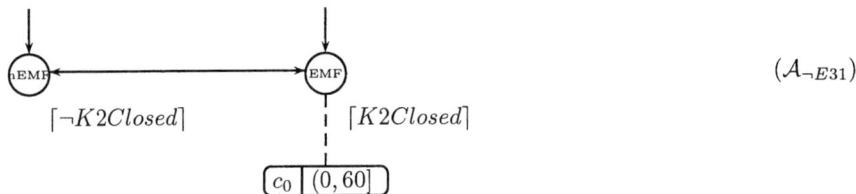
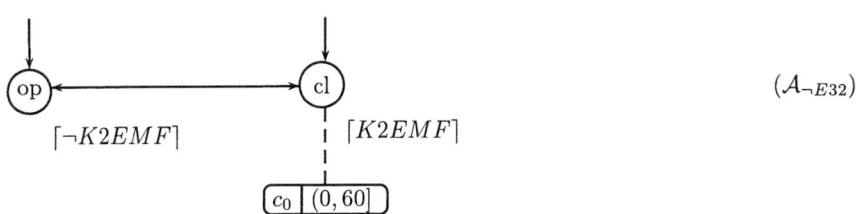

Fig. 11. Phase Automata corresponding to the events $E_3, \neg E_{31}$ and $\neg E_{32}$

7 Combination with Other Model-Checking Techniques

In the previous section we have shown how an engineer can benefit from the combination of fault tree analysis and real-time model-checking. In this section we look at the profit gained from the model-checking point of view. We demonstrate how fault tree analysis can be used as a decomposition method to allow model-checking of larger systems. The case study is the single track line segment [STL01].

7.1 Scenario

Two trains drive on the tracks shown in Fig. 12.

On the outermost track the trains may go clockwise and on the innermost track counterclockwise. In the critical section trains may go in both directions and may change their direction once. The task is to design a distributed controller ensuring that no collision may happen in the critical section. Each component of the controller has three sensors (S) attached and controls one light signal (L) and one point. This controller has to allow two trains to pass the critical section one directly after the other. In this case the first train may not change its direction.

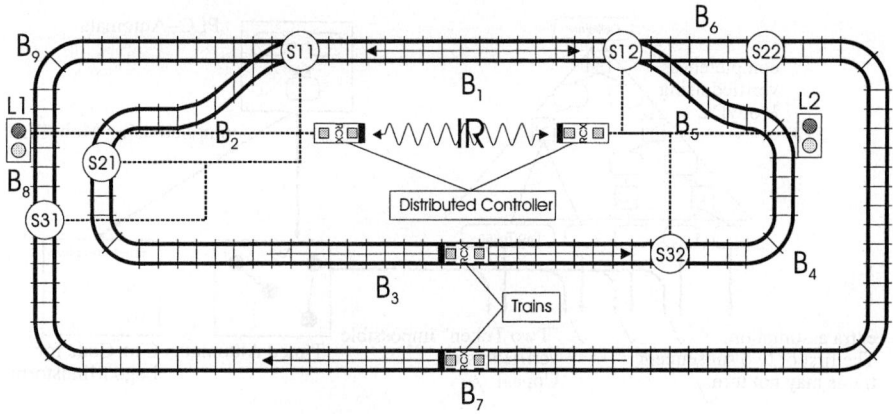

Fig. 12. Single Track Line Segment Scenario

7.2 Design

We built a real-life model of this case study using the Lego-Mindstorms and the open source operating system BrickOS We designed the controller using PLC-Automata [Die00], which also have a semantics in DC. Using the tool Moby/PLC [TD98] these automata can be compiled into ST-Code for Programmable Logic Controller, into C++ Code for BrickOS (Lego-Mindstorms), and into Timed Automata [AD94]. We used the compilation into C++ Code for BrickOS.

7.3 Verification

The goal is to verify that two trains do not collide in the critical section. The obvious idea would be to compile the PLC-Automata for the distributed controller into Timed Automata. Then one would model the environment using Timed Automata, and finally use the model-checker Uppaal [BBD+02] to verify that a collision in the critical section is impossible. But the model is too complex and hence direct model-checking failed. So instead we choose the following approach which is sketched in Fig. 13.

We perform a fault tree analysis with the top event "collision of two trains in critical section". In the fault tree this top-event is iteratively decomposed until we obtain a number of basic events. For each gate in the fault tree we apply the technique described in section 5, i.e. we translate the events into Phase Automata and verify, using Moby/DC, that for each decomposition the sub-events are necessary for the upper event. The fault tree for this example consists of 38 events and 27 gates. It turns out that due to symmetry only 14 gate conditions have to be checked.

For each basic event we verify that it cannot occur. First, all basic events in which the first of two subsequent trains turns around in the critical section may not occur, simply because this behaviour is forbidden by the specification.

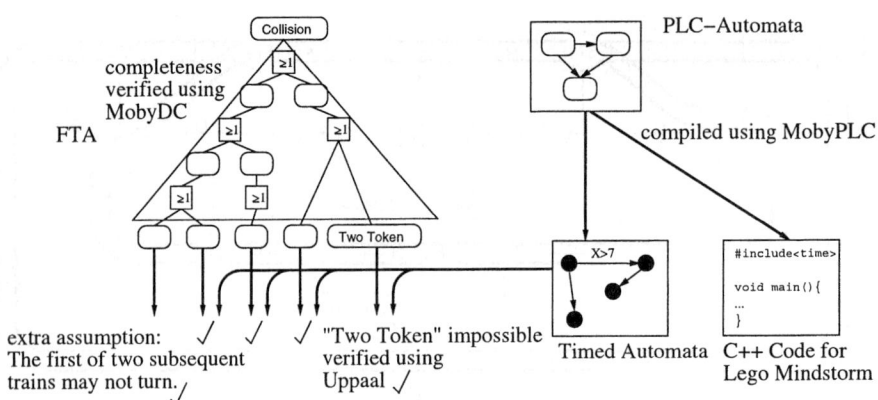

Fig. 13. Verification approach

Second, all other basic events are simple enough for automatic verification. We show that they cannot occur in the distributed controller modelled by PLC-Automata. To this end, we use MobyPLC to compile these automata into Timed Automata which are then checked by Uppaal against the basic events. Since none of the events is possible in the controller model, we conclude that the top-event, i.e. the collision, does not occur.

Modelling. Our formal model of the single track line segment system in terms of Phase Automata describes the topology of the tracks and the movement of the two trains.

Experimental Results. The verification that a basic event cannot occur took 1:04:37 h for the hardest one. We used Uppaal (Version 3.2.11) on a Dual-Pentium with 450 Mhz and 1 GB RAM. Checking each gate condition takes about 10 seconds on a Sun Ultra-1 with 384 MB RAM using Phase Automata and Moby/DC.

8 Related Work

There are several approaches to define formal semantics for fault tree analysis. Special timed transition systems and a first order logic with special predicates are introduced by Gorski [Gór94]. Dugan et al. [DBB93] introduced Markov Models to resolve ambiguities. Bruns and Anderson [BA93] use a modal μ-calculus semantics to check the validity of formal system models.

Hansen [Han96] gives a Duration Calculus semantics and uses fault tree analysis to derive safety requirements from a given fault tree. However, the work does not consider whether a fault tree is constructed properly.

In the FORMOSA project [RST00,STR02] semantics in Duration Calculus, CTL and ITL are considered. Discrete time model-checking, using Raven [Ruf01] and SMV, and fault tree analysis have been applied to several case studies but they are used rather independently and not tightly integrated; further integration is one aim of this project. Currently embedding fault tree analysis in the interactive theorem prover KIV is faced.

The ESACS project (http://www.cert.fr/esacs/) uses fault tree analysis and model-checking in different areas. It is used for test-case generation from fault trees and for compilation of mode automata into a boolean formula, which is presented as a fault tree. Furthermore a tool for the automatic generation of fault trees from a statemate model is developed. But neither order of events nor time is considered in current versions of this tool.

9 Conclusion and Future Work

We have shown how fault tree analysis can be turned into a formal method and how model-checking can be applied to prove necessary and sufficient conditions of this analysis. In the case study we integrated fault tree analysis with two other formal techniques, PLC-Automata and Timed Automata, to verify a larger system.

In our future work we would like to investigate whether we captured all usual cases of events which might occur in fault trees. We also would like to implement tool support. This tool should compile a given fault tree into Phase Automata and check which gate conditions hold and which do not. Translation into other operational models like Timed Automata may also be considered.

Acknowledgements

Our paper is inspired by the work of W. Reif, G. Schellhorn and A. Thums of Augsburg University. The author thanks E.-R. Olderog, H. Dierks, and M. Möller for draft-reading earlier versions and many helpful remarks and the members of the group "Correct System Design" at Oldenburg University for fruitful discussions and comments.

References

[AD94]   R. Alur and D. L. Dill. A theory of timed automata. *Theoretical Computer Science*, 126(2):183–235, 1994.

[BA93]   G. Bruns and S. Anderson. Validating safety models with fault trees. In *SAFECOMP '93: the 12th international Conference on Computer Safety*, pages 21–30. Springer, 1993.

[BBD+02] G. Behrmann, J. Bengtsson, A. David, K. G. Larsen, P. Pettersson, and Wang Yi. Uppaal implementation secrets. In W. Damm and E.-R. Olderog, editors, *Formal Techniques in Real-Time and Fault-Tolerant Systems 2002*, volume 2469 of *LNCS*, pages 3–22, 2002.

[DBB93] J. B. Dugan, S. J. Bavuso, and M. A. Boyd. Fault trees and markov models for reliablility analysis of fault-tolerant digital systems. *Reliability Engineering and System Safety*, 39:291–37, 1993.

[Die00]   H. Dierks. PLC-automata: A new class of implementable real-time automata. *Theoretical Computer Science*, 253(1):61–93, 2000.
[DT03]   H. Dierks and J. Tapken. Moby/DC – a tool for model-checking parametric real-time specifications. In H. Garavel and J. Hatcliff, editors, *Tools and Algorithms for the Construction and Analysis of Systems 2003*, volume 2619 of *LNCS*, pages 271–277, 2003.
[Gór94]   J. Górski. Extending safety analysis techniques with formal semantics. In F. Redmill, editor, *Technology and assessment of safety-critical systems: proceedings of the Second Safety-Critical Systems Symposium*, pages 147–163. Springer Verlag Berlin, 1994.
[Han96]   K. M. Hansen. *Linking Safety Analysis to Safety Requirements*. PhD thesis, Institut for Informationsteknologi, DTU Lyngby, 1996.
[IEC93]   IEC 61025: Fault tree analysis, 1993.
[RST00]   W. Reif, G. Schellhorn, and A. Thums. Safety analysis of a radio-based crossing control system using formal methods. In *Proceedings of the 9th IFAC Symposium Control in Transportation Systems 2000, June 13-15, Braunschweig, Germany*, 2000.
[Ruf01]   J. Ruf. RAVEN: Real-Time Analyzing and Verification Environment. *Journal of Universal Computer Science*, 7(1):89–104, January 2001.
[Sch02]   A. Schäfer. Fault tree analysis and real-time model-checking. Master's thesis, University of Oldenburg, 2002. in German.
[Ska94]   J. U. Skakkebæk. Liveness and fairness in duration calculus. In B. Jonsson and J. Parrow, editors, *CONCUR'94*, volume 836 of LNCS, pages 283–298. Springer-Verlag, 1994.
[STL01]   Practical course real-time systems: Final report. http://csd.informatik.uni-oldenburg.de/teaching/fp_realzeitsys_ws0001/result/eindex.html, 2001.
[STR02]   Gerhard Schellhorn, Andreas Thums, and Wolfgang Reif. Formal fault tree semantics. In *Proceedings of The Sixth World Conference on Integrated Design & Process Technology, Pasadena, CA*, 2002.
[Tap01]   J. Tapken. *Model-Checking of Duration Calculus Specifikations*. PhD thesis, Carl von Ossietzky Universität Oldenburg, 2001.
[TD98]   J. Tapken and H. Dierks. Moby/PLC – graphical development of PLC-automata. In A.P. Ravn and H. Rischel, editors, *Formal Techniques in Real-Time and Fault-Tolerant Systems 1998*, volume 1486 of *LNCS*, pages 311–314. Springer Verlag, 1998.
[VGRH81] W.E. Veseley, F.F. Goldberg, N.H. Roberts, and D.F. Haasl. *Fault Tree Handbook*. Washington DC: US Nuclear Regulatory Commission, NUREG-0492, 1981.
[ZHR91]   Zhou Chaochen, C.A.R. Hoare, and A.P. Ravn. A calculus of durations. *Information Processing Letters*, 40(5):269–276, 1991.
[ZHS93]   Zhou Chaochen, M. R. Hansen, and P. Sestoft. Decidability and undecidability results for duration calculus. In P. Enjalbert, A. Finkel, and K. W. Wagner, editors, *STACS 93, 10th Annual Symposium on Theoretical Aspects of Computer*, volume 665 of *LNCS*, pages 58–68, 1993.

A Complement-Construction for Sequence-Pattern

We give a construction for the complement of an automaton corresponding to the sequence pattern $\Diamond_L(\lceil \pi_1 \rceil \wedge a_1 \sim \ell; \lceil \pi_2 \rceil \wedge a_2 \sim \ell \sim b_2; \ldots; \lceil \pi_{n_1} \rceil \wedge a_{n-1} \sim$

$\ell \sim b_{n-1}; \lceil \pi_n \rceil \wedge a_n \sim \ell)$ and $\pi_i \wedge \pi_j \equiv false$ for all $i \neq j$. The cases where the relation $<$ occurs are analogous. This case is simpler than the more general one where only $\pi_i \wedge \pi_{i+1} \equiv false$ is required. But the sequences which occured in the case study presented in this paper were of this simpler type. For each state assertion π_i which occurs in the given sequence we create four states.

- p_i which is taken iff the assertion π_i holds and the sequence up to π_i has not yet been seen.
- p_i^* which is taken iff the assertion π_i holds and the sequence up to π_i has been seen.
- $p_{i<}$ iff π_i holds and the duration is too short.
- $p_{i>}$ iff π_i holds and the duration is too long.

Additionally we have a state p_{else} which is taken iff no state assertion in $\pi_1, \ldots, \pi_n$ holds. Let $\overline{\mathcal{A}_S} = (P, E, C, cl, s, d, P_0)$. The state space and transition relation is defined by

$$P \stackrel{df}{=} \{p_2, \ldots, p_n, p_1^*, \ldots, p_{n-1}^*, p_{1<}, \ldots, p_{n<}, p_{2>}, \ldots, p_{(n-1)>}, p_{else}\}$$

$$E \stackrel{df}{=} \{p_i \to p_j | i \neq j\} \cup \{p_i \to p_{j<} | i \neq j\} \cup \{p_i \to p_{j>} | i \neq j\} \cup \{p_i \to p_{else}\}$$
$$\cup \{p_i \to p_1^*\}$$
$$\cup \{p_{i<} \to p_j | i \neq j\} \cup \{p_{i<} \to p_{j<} | i \neq j\} \cup \{p_{i<} \to p_{j>} | i \neq j\}$$
$$\cup \{p_{i<} \to p_{else}\} \cup \{p_{i<} \to p_1^*\}$$
$$\cup \{p_{i>} \to p_j | i \neq j\} \cup \{p_{i>} \to p_{j<} | i \neq j\} \cup \{p_{i>} \to p_{j>} | i \neq j\}$$
$$\cup \{p_{i>} \to p_{else}\} \cup \{p_{i>} \to p_1^*\}$$
$$\cup \{p_i^* \to p_{i+1}^* | (i+1) < n\} \cup \{p_i^* \to p_j | i \neq j \wedge i+1 \neq j\} \cup \{p_i^* \to p_{j<} | i \neq j\}$$
$$\cup \{p_i^* \to p_{j>} | i \neq j\} \cup \{p_i^* \to p_1^*\} \cup \{p_i^* \to p_{else}\}$$
$$\cup \{p_{else} \to p_i\} \cup \{p_{else} \to p_{i<}\} \cup \{p_{else} \to p_{i>}\} \cup \{p_{else} \to p_1^*\}$$

We associate exactly one clock to each state. The state assertions for each state and the initial states and the assigned clock intervals are defined as follows.

$$s(p) \stackrel{df}{=} \begin{cases} \pi_i & \text{if } p = p_i \\ \pi_i & \text{if } p = p_i^* \\ \pi_i & \text{if } p = p_{i<} \\ \pi_i & \text{if } p = p_{i>} \\ \neg \bigvee_{i=1}^n \pi_i & \text{if } p = p_{else} \end{cases} \qquad d(p) \stackrel{df}{=} \begin{cases} [b_i, e_i] & \text{if } p = p_i \\ [b_i, e_i] & \text{if } p = p_i^* \\ (0, b_i) & \text{if } p = p_{i<} \\ (e_1, \infty] & \text{if } p = p_{i>} \end{cases}$$

$$P_0 \stackrel{df}{=} \{p_2, \ldots, p_n, p_1^*, p_{1<}, \ldots, p_{n<}, p_{2>}, \ldots, p_{(n-1)>}, p_{else}\}$$

Model-Checking TRIO Specifications in SPIN[*]

Angelo Morzenti[1], Matteo Pradella[2], Pierluigi San Pietro[1], and Paola Spoletini[1]

[1] Dipartimento di Elettronica e Informazione, Politecnico di Milano,
P.za Leonardo da Vinci 32,
20133 Milano, Italia
{morzenti, sanpietr, spoleti}@elet.polimi.it
[2] CNR Istituto di Elettronica e di Ingegneria dell'Informazione e delle Telecomunicazioni,
sez. Milano
Via Ponzio 34/5,
20133 Milano, Italia
pradella@elet.polimi.it

Abstract. We present a novel application on model checking through SPIN as a means for verifying purely descriptive specifications written in TRIO, a first order, linear-time temporal logic with both future and past operators and a quantitative metric on time. The approach is based on the translation of TRIO formulae into Promela programs guided by an equivalence between TRIO and 2-way alternating Büchi automata. An optimization technique based on the modularized TRIO specifications is also shown. The results of our experimentation are quite encouraging, as we are able to verify properties of the Railway Crossing Problem, a well-known benchmark used in the Formal Methods community, for values of the temporal constants that make the verification totally infeasible with traditional tools and approaches.

Keywords: temporal logic, model checking, modular specifications, Spin.

1 Introduction

TRIO is a first order, linear-time temporal logic with both future and past operators and a quantitative metric on time, that has been extensively applied to the specification, validation and verification of critical, real-time systems [7]. The logic TRIO has also been enriched with constructs, inspired by Object-Oriented Analysis and Design, for structuring specifications into a set of modules with clearly defined interfaces, thus providing a very useful support to the structuring and management of specification of highly complex systems, and at the same time building a bridge from requirements specification to high-level design. Over the years a variety of methods and tools have been defined to support typical V&V activities in TRIO. Validation of

---

[*] Work partially supported by the MIUR projects: "QUACK: Piattaforma per la qualità di sistemi embedded integrati di nuova generazione", by "FIRB: Applicazioni della Teoria degli Automi all'Analisi, alla Compilazione e alla Verifica di Sistemi Critici e in Tempo Reale." and by CNR project SP4 Società dell'Informazione: "Software Architectures for High Quality of Service for Global Computing onCooperative Wide Area Networks"

TRIO specification is obtained through generation of execution traces or checking of such simulations for consistency against the TRIO specification [4]. The execution traces derived from TRIO specifications, suitably classified and annotated, can be employed as functional test cases to support post-design verification [12]. A more systematic and general means of validation and verification can be pursued through proof of properties derivable from the TRIO axioms composing the specification. As TRIO is a first order logic that includes arithmetic on the temporal domain, it is undecidable in the general case, hence two basic approaches were devised to address the goal of providing mechanical support to the verification of TRIO specifications. One consists of adopting a deductive approach, based on the definition of a suitable axiomatization of the logic and on its encoding in the notation of a general purpose theorem prover, such as PVS [5]; this allows the construction of a tool supporting the semiautomatic (i.e., manual with assistance from the tool) derivation of system properties in the form of theorems. In this approach one maintains the generality and expressive power of the full language, at the price of sacrificing the construction of a completely automatic (so-called push-button) tool. Another, complementary approach to verification aims at the construction of tools that are fully automatic, or at least provides a quite strong support to the designer: it consists of defining a decidable approximation of a specification, upon which applying methods and algorithms for deciding satisfiability or, less generally but more efficiently, for checking satisfaction with respect to a given interpretation structure. In the past, the latter approach has been based on finitizing the domains of the variables that appear in the specifications [14], leading to the construction of tools built either on tableaux-based verification procedures [4, 12, 14] or on the encoding of TRIO into propositional languages and the use of sophisticated SAT-solvers [3]. This approach has the advantage of allowing the development of "pushbutton" tools, such as the cited [3], but the approximations introduced to make verification decidable (and feasible) may not assure the conservation of properties of the original specification. For instance, time must be finite rather than infinite for a SAT-solver to be used, making the verification of various fairness and liveness properties hard or even impossible.

In the present paper, we pursue a different approach for the mechanical verification of TRIO specifications, namely the definition of a decidable fragment of the logic that includes a suitable subset of its original operators, and the use of a well-known model checker such as SPIN [9] to perform proof of properties and simulation (in the form of generation of execution traces).

A TRIO specification consists of a set of temporal logic formulae that describe the desired properties of the system being designed; this kind of specification does not include any operational component (such as a state-transition system) that can *generate* values for the elements of the alphabet of the specification (predicates and variables representing the state of the various parts composing the system under design); on the contrary, and similarly to what occurs in any other purely descriptive specification notation, TRIO formulae define constraints on the values that the items appearing in the specification can assume in the "legal" (i.e., consistent with the specification) evolutions. Therefore, the problem of property proving in TRIO, when addressed in a model-checking approach, takes a form that is rather different from the one typically encountered in the literature on the subject. It is formulated in terms of the validity of a logic formula of the kind *specification* → *property*, where the premise *specification* is still a set of TRIO formulae describing properties that are assumed to hold for the analyzed system, and *property* is another TRIO formula describing the conjecture that we want to prove to be implied by the properties stated in the premise. As it happens in some other approaches based on model-checking, what we actually check might in fact be the negation of the above implication, i.e., ¬(*specification* → *property*) and the counterexamples generated by the model-checker in this case can be used as simulations or functional test cases for the desired property. Therefore, in our approach what we call *specification* has a role similar to the one played by the so-called *model* in the usual model checking scenery (e.g., a Promela program in SPIN) while what we call *property* in the above implication is usually called *specification* and takes the form of a formula in temporal logic (e.g., an LTL formula in SPIN).

Our approach to model checking TRIO specifications is based on the translation of the TRIO formulae into a set of Promela processes, derived from a well known correlation between temporal logic and alternating automata [20]. As opposed to previous approaches, however, the Promela code generated from TRIO formulae performs an actual simulation of an alternating automaton, rather than simulating a Büchi automaton equivalent to the alternating one, resulting in a Promela code whose size is essentially proportional to the length of the TRIO specification (although of course the state space may not be affected in either way). This is by itself a remarkable result since the TRIO logic, which contains metric and past operators, is quite concise compared with propositional, future-time temporal logics like LTL. Our approach can be naturally compared with recent works appeared in the literature (such as those on LTL2BA [6] and Wring [17]) that aim at the translation of LTL properties into Büchi automata and then Promela programs--such comparison will be provided in Section 4). We point out, however, that the result of those tools is usually the construction, as in the traditional model-checking scenario, of a so-called *never claim*, i.e., an automaton specifying the negation of a temporal logic property over an already available state-transition system. In our approach, instead, the Promela processes obtained from the translation of the TRIO specification act globally as an acceptor of a language defined over the alphabet of the specification, and therefore they must be coupled with some additional Promela program fragments generating the values, over time, for the logical variables that constitute the specification alphabet. This "generative" component of the Promela program can trivially be obtained by encoding a systematic, exhaustive enumeration of all possible variable values over time, but this can potentially lead to a combinatorial explosion of the search state space, thus making the proposed approach infeasible in practice. To address this issue we adopt two basic techniques, which can be roughly described as follows. First, we exploit the modular structure of TRIO specifications to obtain a maximum of encapsulation in the verification process, so that the execution of any Promela process verifying a TRIO subformula will be affected only by the values for the elements of the alphabet occurring in that subformula, and not by other ones. Second, we restrict the purely combinatorial generation of values to those variables that are truly independent from every other one; from a methodological standpoint, these variables can be easily recognized as the elements of the specification alphabet corresponding to components of the specified system that are a "pure input", thus ruling out any computed state or output value. These translation techniques, combined with other minor optimizations, related for example with the management of TRIO past-time operators, allowed us to perform efficiently the verification in SPIN of a system which is universally adopted as a benchmark in the verification of time-critical systems, namely the Railroad Crossing Example, fully described by a TRIO specification.

The remaining sections are organized as follows. To make the paper self-contained, Section 2 provides a brief introduction to the TRIO logic and outlines the decidable subset of the language on which we perform verification via model checking. Section 3 discusses the relation between TRIO and 2-way alternating automata (also introducing an extension of the classical model that explicitly deals with finite counters to account for TRIO's quantitative notion of time) and the translation schema from TRIO to Promela. Section 4 deals with specific issues related with verification via model-checking: it motivates the introduction of a network of processes, gives a rationale for the optimization performed, and discusses the results obtained on the case study, occasionally providing comparisons with related approaches. Finally, Section 5 draws conclusions and outlines directions of future research.

2 A Brief Introduction to TRIO

TRIO formulae are built much in the same way as in traditional mathematical logic, starting from variables, functions, predicates, predicate symbols, and quantifiers (a detailed and formal definition of TRIO can be found in [14]).

In TRIO, first-order variables and quantifiers are allowed over finite or infinite, dense or discrete, domains, including the time domain. Besides the usual propositional operators and the quantifiers, one may compose TRIO formulae by using a single basic modal operator, called *Dist*, that relates the *current time*, which is left implicit in the formula, with another time instant: the formula *Dist(F, t)*, where *F* is a formula and *t* a term indicating a time distance, specifies that *F* holds at a time instant at *t* time units from the current instant. Many *derived temporal operators* can be defined from the basic *Dist* operator through propositional composition and first order quantification on variables representing a time distance. The traditional operators of linear temporal logics can be easily obtained as TRIO derived operators. For instance, SomF (Sometimes in the Future) corresponds to the "Eventually" operator of temporal logic. Moreover, it can be easily shown that the operators of several versions of temporal logic (e.g., interval logic) can be defined as TRIO derived operators. This argues in favor of TRIO's generality since many different logic formalisms can be described as particular cases of TRIO.

For instance, the following TRIO formula specifies that every message *m* entering a channel is always delivered within 10 time instants. The meaning of the various symbols is obvious once the (bounded) derived temporal operator WithinF(A,t) is interpreted as "A will hold within t instants in the future":

AlwF($\forall$m (in(m) $\rightarrow$ WithinF(out(m),10))).

2.1 A Decidable Subset of TRIO

In general, TRIO formulae, adopting the full-fledged power of first-order logic are undecidable. In this paper, however, we consider a decidable subset of TRIO, where the time domain is the set of natural numbers, no time variable is allowed and every other domain is finite. This version of TRIO is basically a syntactically sugared, more concise version of PLTLB, Propositional Linear Time Temporal Logic with Both past and future operators (here we follow the terminology introduced by [1], while using the standard name "LTL" to denote the future fragment of PLTLB).

The syntax of TRIO formulae is described by the following grammar, where ϕ is the axiom, p stands for any element in a finite set Ap of atomic propositions, c stands for any element of a finite set of natural numbers, and {*Since, Until, Futr, Past, Lasts, Lasted,* (,)} is the set of terminal symbols:

$\phi ::= p \mid \phi \wedge \phi \mid \neg \phi \mid Until(\phi,\phi) \mid Since(\phi,\phi) \mid Futr(\phi,c) \mid Past(\phi,c) \mid Lasts(\phi,c) \mid Lasted(\phi,c)$

Table 1. A sample of derived temporal operators in TRIO.

Operator	Definition	Intuitive Meaning
SomF(F)	Until(true, F)	Sometimes F holds
SomP(F)	Since(true, F)	Sometimes F held
AlwP(F)	¬SomP(¬F)	F always held in the past
AlwF(F)	¬SomF(¬F)	F will always hold
$Since_{ii}(F_1, F_2)$	$F_1 \wedge Since(F_1, F_1 \wedge F_2)$	Since, both temporal extremes included
$UntilW_{ie}(F_1, F_2)$	$F_1 \wedge (Until(F_1,F_2) \vee AlwF(F_1))$	Weak until
WithinF(F,c)	¬Lasts(¬F,c)	F will hold within c instants in the future
WithinP(F,c)	¬Lasted(¬F,c)	F held within c instants in the past
$Lasts_{ie}(F,c)$	$F \wedge Lasts(F,c)$	Lasts(F,c) with the current instant included
$Lasted_{ie}(F,c)$	$F \wedge Lasted(F,c)$	Lasted(F,c) with the current instant included
$WithinF_{ii}(F,c)$	$F \wedge WithinF(F,c) \wedge Futr(F,c)$	WithinF, both temporal extremes included
$WithinP_{ii}(F,c)$	$F \wedge WithinP(F,c) \wedge Past(F,c)$	WithinP, both temporal extremes included
UpToNow(F)	Past(F,1)	F held (for at least one instant) until now

Usual shorthands for logical symbols such as *true, false,* $\vee$, $\rightarrow$, $\equiv$ are standard. Notice that, to rule out negative numbers, a pair of operators, namely *Futr* and *Past*, replace the basic TRIO Dist operator. Table 1 introduces a few derived temporal operators, with a short definition and explanation.

For instance, the formula *AlwF(push $\rightarrow$ Lasts(on, 6))* may specify the property that from now on the event of pushing a button causes a lamp to be on for the next 6 instants.

2.2 Semantics

The standard TRIO semantics is called *model parametric semantics* [14], and it is based on Kripke structures that can accommodate different time domains. However, since the version of TRIO used in this paper is equivalent to PLTLB, we simply define the semantics of basic TRIO formulae as a translation into the standard PLTLB.

A PLTLB formula has the following syntax:
$$\phi ::= p \mid \phi \wedge \phi \mid \neg \phi \mid \phi U \phi \mid \phi S \phi \mid X \phi \mid P \phi$$
where U and S are the Until and Since operators, respectively, and X and P are the Next and Previous operators. We also define, for every integer constant t≥0, $X^t \phi$ as X X...X ϕ (X repeated t times) if t>0, ϕ if t =0. $P^t \phi$ is its past conterpart and is defined analogously. Other standards operators, such as the eventually operator F (also denoted as <>) and the globally operator G (also denoted as []) can be defined as usual, e.g.: F ϕ = true U ϕ, G ϕ = ¬F¬ϕ.

The translation δ from TRIO formulae to PLTLB formulae is defined inductively as follows:

$\delta(\phi) = \phi$ if $\phi \in$ Ap
$\delta(\phi_1 \wedge \phi_2) = \delta(\phi_1) \wedge \delta(\phi_2)$
$\delta(\neg \phi) = \neg \delta(\phi)$
$\delta(Until(\phi_1, \phi_2)) = \delta(\phi_1)$ U $\delta(\phi_2)$
$\delta(Since(\phi_1, \phi_2)) = \delta(\phi_1)$ S $\delta(\phi_2)$
$\delta(Futr(\phi,t)) = X^t \delta(\phi)$
$\delta(Past(\phi,t)) = P^t \delta(\phi)$
$\delta(Lasts(\phi,t)) =$ true if t =0, $X \delta(\phi) \wedge X^2 \delta(\phi) \wedge \ldots \wedge X^{t-1} \delta(\phi)$ if t>0.
$\delta(Lasted(\phi,t)) =$ true if t =0, $P \delta(\phi) \wedge P^2 \delta(\phi) \wedge \ldots \wedge P^{t-1} \delta(\phi)$ if t>0.

Notice that the usage of both past and future operators is widely recognized [10] as making specifications simpler and more concise than using either only future or only past operators. TRIO adds another level of succinctness because of the metric operators Lasts and Lasted (and their duals WithinF and WithinP).

For instance, a simple TRIO formula such as:
  WithinF(Lasts(B,h), k)
for some h, k > 0, may be expressed only with a LTL formula, whose length is proportional to h·k.

2.3 Modular TRIO Specifications

The TRIO logic is augmented with object-oriented constructs for supporting modular specifications [15]. A modular TRIO (often called TRIO⁺) specification is built by defining suitable *classes*. Classes can be *simple* or *structured*. Simple classes contain a set of logic axioms along with the declaration of the elements of the alphabet (i.e., the predicate and function signatures) and a definition of those predicates, variables, and functions that belong to the class interface. Predicates, variables, and functions are collectively called *items*. Simple classes are graphically represented as boxes with arrows representing *input* and *output* items in the interface. Truly modular specifications are obtained by defining *structured classes*, i.e., classes whose instances have components –called *modules*– that are instances of other classes.

Items in the interface of the whole structured class and of the composing modules may be *connected* to denote an identity or equivalence that, for instance, may abstractly describe an information flow. A structured class may also include axioms, called global axioms, involving its own items and the interface items of its modules. Since the items of the component modules satisfy the axioms of their original class, the overall semantics of a structured class is given by the conjunction of the axioms of the class with those of the class of the component modules (if several instances of a class are included as modules of a structured class, then the axioms of the composing class are "duplicated" i.e., applied to duplicates of the class items (see [15]). From a strictly semantic viewpoint a structured class is thus equivalent to a TRIO formula obtained by flattening the modular structure and conjoining the axioms of the various modules. Figure 1 shows a structured class *KRC (Kernel Railroad Crossing)*, describing a TRIO version of the standard railroad crossing problem [8], with three modules specifying the *trainModel*, the *controller* and the *gate*. More details on this example will be provided in the presentation of the case study illustrated in Section 4.

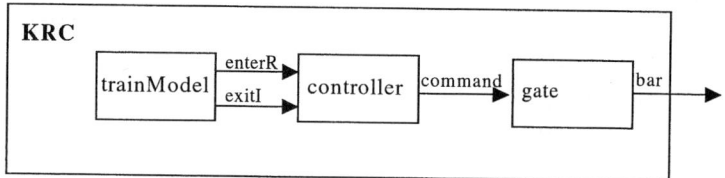

Fig. 1. An example of a TRIO structured class.

3 Translation

A TRIO specification can be translated into Promela, by introducing a network of communicating processes (*process network*), that may exchange truth values. When the process representing the whole specification returns false, the execution of the program is blocked. The translation is conceptually based on Alternating Automata and is presented in this section.

3.1 2-Way Alternating Modulo Counting Automata (2AMCA)

We introduce an intermediate notation useful to define our TRIO-to-Promela translation, namely 2-way Alternating Modulo Counting Automata (or *2AMCA* for short). Conceptually, a 2AMCA is a version of Büchi alternating automata (see for instance [2, 11]). A brief and intuitive description of alternating automata is the following. In a *deterministic* automaton, the transition function maps a ⟨*state, input symbol*⟩ pair to a *single* state, called the next state. The automaton accepts its input if either *state* is final and the input is finished, or from the next state the remaining suffix of the input word is accepted. On the other hand, in a nondeterministic automaton a ⟨state, input symbol⟩ pair is mapped to a *set* of states. Here we have two possible different interpretations of the transition function: either as an existential branching mode, or as a universal branching mode. In the existential mode, which is the standard interpretation of nondeterminism, the automaton accepts if at least *one* of the states of the set accepts the remaining input suffix; in the universal mode, it accepts if *all* the states of the set accept the remaining input suffix. An alternating automaton provides both existential and universal branching modes. Its transition function maps a ⟨state, input symbol⟩ pair into a (positive) boolean combination of states. Quite naturally, ∧ is used to denote universality, while ∨ denotes existentiality. Alternating automata are a very convenient tool since they may be exponentially more concise than nondeterministic automata and are very well suited for dealing with logic formulae.

To define properly TRIO's metric temporal operators, we use internal finite counters, associated with states. Moreover, we use *bidirectionality* for defining the past tense operators, following an approach presented in [10, 19].

Here are some preliminary definitions, following standard terminology (e.g., [18]). Let N be the set of natural numbers, and let $x \in N^*$ and $c \in N$. A *tree* is a set $T \subseteq N^*$ such that $x.c \in T \Rightarrow x \in T$ (c is called a *children* of x). The empty word ε is called the *root* of T. Elements of T are called *nodes*. A node is a *leaf* if it has no children. A *path* P of a tree T is a set $P \subseteq T$ which contains ε and such that for every $x \in P$, either x is a leaf or there exists a unique c such that $x.c \in P$.

An infinite word over Σ is a sequence $w = a_0 a_1 a_2 ...$, with $a_j \in \Sigma$. We will indicate an element a_j of w as w(j). Moreover, we will denote the set of all infinite word over Σ as Σ^ω.

A *2-way Alternating Modulo Counting Automata* (2AMCA) is a six-tuple $A = (\Sigma, Q, \mu, q_0, \tau, F)$, where Σ is the (finite) *alphabet*, Q is the set of *states*, μ is a positive integer, $q_0 \in Q$ is the *initial state*, τ is the *transition function*, $F \subseteq Q$ is the set of *final states*. Call Cnt = $[0..\mu]$ the *counter set*. The transition function is $\tau: Q \times Cnt \times \Sigma \to B^+(\{-1,+1\} \times Q \times Cnt)$, where, for every M, $B^+(M)$ indicates a positive boolean combination of elements in M, i.e. a boolean combination using ∧ and ∨ but not using ¬. The set {+1,-1} denotes the possible relative movements of the reading head. To improve readability, we will use the symbol '/' to separate Q from Cnt, and we will use +q or -q to denote (+1,q), (-1,q), respectively.

Consider a word $w \in \Sigma^\omega$. A *run* of A on w is a $Q \times Cnt \times N$-labeled tree (T, ρ), where ρ is the labeling function, such that $\rho(\varepsilon) = (q_0/0,0)$ and for all $x \in T$, with ρ(x) = (q/k,n), the set {(q'/h,d) | $c \in N$, x.c ∈ T, h ∈ Cnt, d ∈ {-1,+1}, ρ(x.c) = (q'/h,n+d)} satisfies the formula τ(q/k,w(n)).

For a path P, Inf(ρ, P) := {s | there are infinitely many $x \in P$ with ρ(x) ∈ {s}× N}. A run (T, ρ) of a 2AMCA is accepting if all infinite path P in T have Inf(ρ,P) ∩ F ≠ ∅.

3.2 From TRIO to 2AMCA

The translation of TRIO formulae into their equivalent 2AMCA follows the approach presented in [20].

Let Ap be a finite set of atomic propositions, and let φ be a TRIO formula on Ap and $Sf(\varphi)$ be the set of subformulae of φ.

The 2AMCA automaton for φ is $A_\varphi = (\Sigma, Q, \mu, q_0, \tau, F)$ where:
$\Sigma = \wp(Ap)$, $Q = \{\phi \mid \phi \in Sf(\varphi) \text{ or } \neg\phi \in Sf(\varphi)\}$, $q_0 = \varphi$,
μ is the greatest bounded temporal distance occurring in φ, and
$F = \{\phi \mid \phi \in Q \text{ and } \phi \mid \phi \text{ has the form } \neg Until(A,B) \}$

The *dual operation* dual(ϕ) is defined for every formula ϕ as the formula ϕ' obtained from ϕ, by switching true and false, $\vee$, $\wedge$, and by complementing all subformulae of ϕ.

The transition function is defined as follows:
$\tau(C/0, a) = +true/0$ for $C \in Ap$ and $C \in a$
$\tau(C/0, a) = +false/0$ for $C \in Ap$ and $C \notin a$
$\tau(A \wedge B/0, a) = \tau(A/0, a) \wedge \tau(B/0, a)$
$\tau(\neg A/0, a) = dual(\tau(A/0, a))$
$\tau(Futr(A,n)/n, a) = \tau(A/0, a)$
$\tau(Futr(A,n)/k, a) = +Futr(A,n)/k+1$, where $0 \leq k < n$
$\tau(Past(A,n)/n, a) = \tau(A/0, a)$
$\tau(Past(A,n)/k, a) = -Past(A,n)/k+1$, where $0 \leq k < n$
$\tau(Lasts(A,n)/n-1, a) = true/0$
$\tau(Lasts(A,n)/k, a) = A/0 \wedge +Lasts(A,n)/k+1$, where $0 \leq k < n-1$
$\tau(Lasted(A,n)/n-1, a) = true/0$
$\tau(Lasted(A,n)/k, a) = A/0 \wedge -Lasted(A,n)/k+1$, where $0 \leq k < n-1$
$\tau(Until(A,B)/0, a) = \tau(B/0, a) \vee (\tau(A/0, a) \wedge +Until(A,B)/0)$
$\tau(Since(A,B)/0, a) = \tau(B/0, a) \vee (\tau(A/0, a) \wedge -Since(A,B)/0)$
The transition function is undefined for every case not listed above.

3.3 From 2AMCA to Promela

The outcome of the previous step is a 2AMCA equivalent to the original TRIO specification. The expressive richness of the Promela language makes the 2AMCA-to-Promela translation a simple task, if we do not take into account optimizations. Indeed, we use the Promela code to directly simulate the alternating automaton equivalent to the original TRIO specification.

Conceptually, every state of the automaton will correspond to a single type of process (*proctype*). As in classical nondeterministic automata, an or-combination of states $(s_1 \vee s_2)$ in the transition function will correspond to a nondeterministic choice (*if* ::s_1; ::s_2; *fi*). Analogously, an and-combination $s_1 \wedge s_2$ will correspond to the starting of two new processes, having type s_1 and s_2, respectively.

As far as process synchronization is concerned, we have to proceed bottom-up: quite naturally, processes corresponding to simpler subformulae must be evaluated before more complex ones. The system does not require asynchronous communication among processes. In fact, it is possible to determine an arbitrary total evaluation order, starting from the original partial order defined by the relation "subformula of". Therefore, we used a single rendezvous channel.

Bounded temporal operators (Futr, Lasts and WithinF) use simple counting loops and variables to determine where to start and stop evaluating, and to store partial evaluations.

As an example, consider the formula: *AlwF(push → Lasts(on, 7))*.

The non-optimized Promela code contains two process types, one for *AlwF* and one for *Lasts*. In general, it is not necessary to define multiple process types for boolean operators applied to atomic propositions. For instance, in our example the implication '*push →*' can be handled directly within the AlwF process.

```
#define MAXP 6 /*maximum number of launched Lasts processes*/
proctype AlwF(chan environment; chan sync) {
bool push,on, ex[MAXP], dying, result;
byte n;
chan to_lasts = [0] of {bool, byte};
chan from_lasts = [0] of {bool, bool, byte};
do
:: environment?push,on; n = 0;
          do
          :: n < MAXP ->
             if
             :: ex[n] -> to_lasts!on,n;
                from_lasts?dying,result,eval(n);
                if
                :: dying -> ex[n] = 0;
                :: else;
                fi;
                if
                :: !result -> sync!0; goto stop; /* error */
                :: else;
                fi;
             :: else;
             fi;
             n++;
          :: n == MAXP -> break;
          od;
          if
          :: !push -> sync!1;
          :: push -> n = 0;
             do
             :: n < MAXP ->
                if
                :: !ex[n] -> break;
                :: else -> n++;
                fi
             :: n == MAXP -> sync!0; goto stop; /* overflow */
             od;
             ex[n] = 1;
             run Lasts(to_lasts,from_lasts,MAXP,n);
             sync!1;
          fi;
od;
stop: skip;
}
proctype Lasts(chan from_alw; chan to_alw; byte k; byte id) {
bool on;
```

```
do
:: from_alw?on,eval(id);
        if
        :: on && k == 1 -> to_alw!1,1,id; break;
        :: on && k  > 1 -> to_alw!0,1,id; k--;
        :: !on -> to_alw!1,0,id; break;
        fi;
od;
}
```

In this case, the AlwF process may launch at most six different instances of the Lasts process, since the boolean argument of Lasts must be checked in six different instants. This bound is dealt with by the constant definition of MAXP in the very first line of the Promela code

In the previous piece of code, we use two channels to manage the communication between the AlwF process and its children. First, AlwF sends to every alive instance of its children the value of *on* coming from the environment, then it reads the results of their evaluation. A Lasts process may send two boolean signals to AlwF: the first is about its immediate termination, while the second is the result of its evaluation. Both the AlwF process and the Lasts processes use an identifier (*n* and *id*, respectively) for synchronization purposes.

Past operators are treated a bit differently. The actual Promela code does not directly implement a back movement of the reading head of the automaton. On the contrary, it follows some of the ideas presented in [16, 19] for obtaining a 1-way automaton from a 2-way one, specifically tailored and optimized for the TRIO language. For instance, bounded past operators, instead of "going back in time" and evaluating subformulae, use arrays to store a bounded amount of previous subformula evaluations, so that they may directly access to them. Unbounded operators are implemented by means of processes which check, and properly store, past subformula evaluations.

3.4 A First Comparison with LTL2BA

LTL2BA (*LTL to Büchi Automata*) [6] is a tool that translates LTL formulae into Promela *never claims*. The formula of the previous example, *AlwF(push → Lasts(on, 7))*, can be written in LTL as follows: G(push → X(on ∧ X(on ∧ X(on ∧ X(on ∧ X(on ∧ X(on)))))))). LTL2BA uses alternating automata as an intermediate notation - the resulting Promela code is a direct representation of the equivalent (and simplified) Büchi automaton. In our example, we obtain the following code:

```
never {
accept_init:if
            :: (!push) -> goto accept_init
            :: (1) -> goto accept_S2
            fi;
accept_S2:if
            :: (!push && on) -> goto accept_S9
            :: (on) -> goto accept_S2
            fi;
```

```
accept_S9:if
         :: (!push && on) -> goto accept_S17
         :: (on) -> goto accept_S2
       fi;
accept_S17:if
         :: (!push && on) -> goto accept_S29
         :: (on) -> goto accept_S2
       fi;
accept_S29:if
         :: (!push && on) -> goto accept_S31
         :: (on) -> goto accept_S2
       fi;
accept_S31:if
         :: (!push && on) -> goto accept_S33
         :: (on) -> goto accept_S2
       fi;
accept_S33:if
         :: (!push && on) -> goto accept_init
         :: (on) -> goto accept_S2
       fi;
}
```

Another major difference is that LTL does not support metric operators; therefore both the formula and the resulting code size depend on the constants (only 7 in this case). With our technique, the Promela code for *AlwF(push → Lasts(on, k))*, for any given k, is not dependant on *k*, apart from the definition of MAXP. Hence, in general the size of the code does not depend on the values of the temporal constants, making the translation very concise. In this case, the size depends linearly on the size of the formula, because all the occurrences of bounded temporal operators (one in this case, namely Lasts) are not nested. Other techniques, such as LTL2BA, even though based on sophisticated optimizations to reduce the size of the resulting code, always enumerate explicitly all states of the Büchi automaton equivalent to the intermediate alternating automaton, which may have up to $n \cdot 2^n$ states, where n is the number of states of the alternating automaton (see [6] for details). Of course, SPIN is an exhaustive model checker, enumerating all reachable states, and the constants like MAXP do increase the state space. However, applying a translation process like LTL2BA to TRIO specifications may not be able to generate Promela code short enough to attempt verification, even in those cases, as shown below, where verification is actually feasible.

4 Verification

In traditional model checking, a property (e.g., a LTL formula) is verified against a model of the system (an automaton such as a Promela program). When translating a whole TRIO specification in order to check its satisfiability, however, no automaton model is already present. As a result, a special automaton, called a *generator*, is introduced and added to the process network. The generator exhaustively produces random input values, then it sends them to the Promela program; hence, the generator is able to generate any system behavior. These behaviors are verified by the process network. An event generator allows model checking of resulting Promela code, corresponding to satisfiability verification of the original TRIO specification. The event generator may however increase the number of reachable state of the resulting system. As shown below, modularity in the specification may be used to introduce *modular generators*, significantly reducing this increase.

The Promela representation of a 2AMCA may however be further optimized in order to obtain compact and easily verifiable code. Some optimizations are:

- Each occurrence of a bounded operator Lasts is translated using only one process that is updated whenever the temporal subformula has to be checked.
- Bounded operators nested in a Futr or Past operators are translated by shifting the starting point of the same constant amount used in the Futr (or Past) operator.
- A coordinator process is in charge of managing communication, to reduce the synchronization effort required by the potentially high number of processes produced by the translation of all subformulae.
- An additional component of each process manages error propagation to terminate immediately the whole process network when the specification is violated. More precisely, when a flag denoting an unacceptable behavior is activated, an error is propagated to kill each currently alive process. This actually reduces the number of reachable states, since in this way there is only one "error" state.

4.1 A Case Study

As a case study, the approach was applied to the KRC specification shown in Figure 1. The first version of the case study is not modularized, even though the original specification was, and later will be clear how the axioms are distributed among the modules. A "flat list" of the axioms is the following:

(K1) train = EnterR → Lasts($\neg$train = EnterR,μ)
(K2) train = EnterI → Lasts($\neg$train = EnterI,μ)
(K3) train = ExitI → Lasts($\neg$train = ExitI,μ)
(K4) train = EnterR → Futr(WithinF$_{ii}$(train = EnterI, d_M-d_m), d_m)
(K5) train = EnterI → Futr(WithinF$_{ii}$(train = ExitI, h_M-h_m), h_m)
(K6) train = EnterI → Past(WithinP$_{ii}$(train = EnterR, d_M-d_m), d_m)
(K7) train = ExitI → Past(WithinP$_{ii}$(train = EnterI, h_M-h_m), h_m)
(K8) $d_M \geq d_m > 0 \wedge h_M \geq h_m > 0 \wedge \mu > d_M + h_M \wedge d_m > \gamma$
(S1) InR ↔ WithinP$_{ii}$(train = EnterR,d_M) $\wedge$ Since$_{ii}$($\neg$train = EnterI, train = EnterR)
(S2) InI ↔ WithinP$_{ii}$(train = EnterI,h_M) $\wedge$ Since$_{ii}$($\neg$train = ExitI, train = EnterI)
(M1) UpToNow(bar = closed) $\wedge$ command = goUp → Lasts$_{ie}$(bar = mvUp,γ) $\wedge$ Futr(UntilW$_{ie}$(bar = open,command = goDown),γ)
(M2) UpToNow(bar = open) $\wedge$ command = goDown → Lasts$_{ie}$(bar = mvDown,γ) $\wedge$ Futr(UntilW$_{ie}$(bar = closed,command = goUp),γ)
(M3) AlwP$_i$($\neg$command = go(down)) → bar = open
(C1) command = goDown ↔ Past(train = EnterR,d_m-γ)
(C2) command = goUp ↔ train = ExitI

The goal of the original KRC specification in TRIO [13] was twofold: a formal definition of the KRC system, and the proof of the safety property that, whenever the train is inside the railway crossing, the bar is always down. Notice that KRC is a toy example per se, but in this case we are completely defining it with a temporal logic specification, thus obtaining a logic formula much bigger and more complex than those used in traditional model checking, where the KRC is defined with an automaton and short temporal logic formulae are used only for safety or utility properties.

We encoded the possible values of the *train* variable as: 1 (EnterR), 2 (EnterI), 3 (ExitI), and 0 for all the other situations. Likewise, *bar* may assume values: 0 (open), 1 (closed), 2 (mvUp), 3 (mvDown). *command* may be: 0 (no indications), 1 (goUp), 2 (goDown). Moreover variables train, command, bar may take the additional value 4 to signal an erroneous configuration.

For this unmodularized version of the specification, a unique generator for all events is defined, by means of the following Promela code:

```
proctype EventGenerator(chan in; chan out){
bool sync;
do
          ::in?sync,eval(1);
          if
          ::s==0 ->
              out!4,0,0,4,4,2; /* train,inR,inI,go,st to */
              break;            /* Process 2 (Coordinator) */
          ::else;
          fi;
          if
          ::train=0;
          ::train=1;
          ::train=2;
          ::train=3;
          fi;
          if
          ::inR=0; inI=0;
          ::inR=1; inI=0;    /*they are mutually exclusive*/
          ::inR=0; inI=1;
          fi;
          if
          ::command=0;
          ::command=1;
          ::command=2;
          fi;
          if
          ::bar=0;
          ::bar=1;
          ::bar=2;
          ::bar=3;
          fi;
          out!train,inR,inI,go,st,2;
od
}
```

As already explained, events are nondeterministically generated, then sent to the coordinator through the channel *out*. First, the generator waits for the synchronization

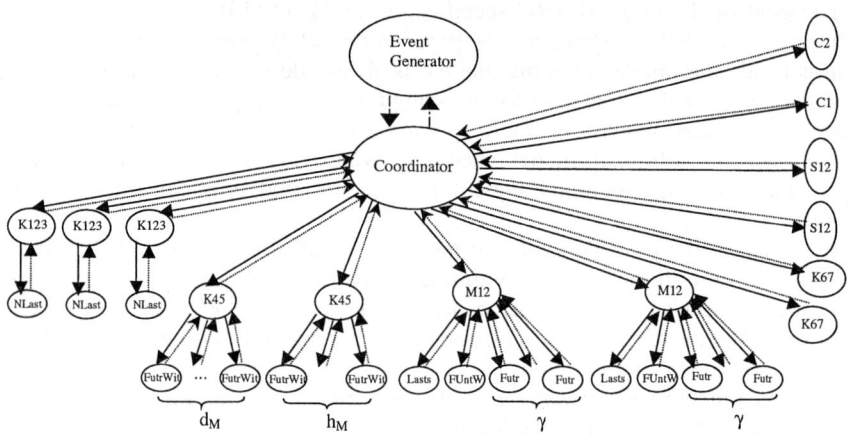

Fig. 2. The process network (nonmodular case)

signal *sync* from the coordinator. When a process signals an error to the coordinator, *sync* takes the value 0, halting the network (*train*, *command*, *bar* take the error value 4).

The resulting process network for the KRC, depicted in Figure 2, is composed by the following processes:

- the *coordinator*, which manages synchronization and checks validity of axiom M3,
- one event *generator*,
- 2 process instances each for K1, K2 and K3 (those based upon the Lasts operator), having process type K123 and NLast (a process type that defines Lasts($\neg$A,k), for some A and k),
- d_M-d_m and h_M-h_m process instances for K4 and K5 respectively (bounded eventualities), having process type K45 and FutrWit (composition of Futr and WithinF),
- a single process type (K67, S12) and two process instances each for the comparatively simpler K6, K7 and S1, S2 axioms, respectively;
- four process types each for M1 and M2 (M12, Lasts, FUntW, Futr), one instance for each of the first three types, and γ instances of the last.

Notice that in the picture we used different styles for different channels. For instance, signals are sent by coordinator to axiom processes through a single channel, denoted by a solid arrow.

Unfortunately, state explosion may be caused by both the exhaustive case enumeration carried on by the event generator, and by the high number of processes. For instance, consider Table 2, which contains a summary of our verification results (we used a PC equipped with a Pentium 4 processor @ 2GHz, 256 MB of RAM, and every computation took less than 2 minutes). When $\mu = 30$, values of h_M higher than 14 are not tractable (i.e., they cause a memory overflow).

Table 2. Verification - nonmodular case

μ	d_M	d_m	h_M	h_m	γ	Depth	Memory (KB)	States	Transitions
10	5	4	4	3	2	6039	40840	609787	611137
15	7	4	7	3	2	9379	156664	2190650	2194700
20	10	8	9	5	3	13639	194040	2442500	2446340
25	15	12	9	7	9	> 210 MB			
30	12	10	9	7	6	15517	197457	2420240	2423790

We also ran LTL2BA and Wring on the same specification with $\mu = 7$, $h_M = d_M = 3$, $h_m = d_m = 2$, and $\gamma = 1$. LTL2BA crashed after a memory overflow, while Wring was still running after three days and was therefore aborted.

4.2 Modular Approach

The results presented above clearly show that our approach is not well suited to large specifications. Hence, we decided to exploit the modular structure of a TRIO specification, computing, rather than randomly generating, some of the events.

First, we have to partition the set of atomic propositions into three subsets: *input*, *output*, and *state* propositions. After that, event generators are associated only with modules that directly deal with input predicates. On the other hand, output variables tend to be, by their very nature, deterministic, and therefore the TRIO modules using them do not need a generator.

To show how this approach works, consider the KRC case study, which consists of three modules: the first module (*trainModel*) describes the train position with respect to the critical regions R and I (axioms K1, K2, K3, K4, K5, K6 and K7); the second module (*globalAxioms*) contains the definition of *inR* and *inI* (axioms S1 and S2); the third module (*controller*) contains the bar control logic (C1 and C2); the last module (*gate*) is used to define the position of the bar (axioms M1 and M2).

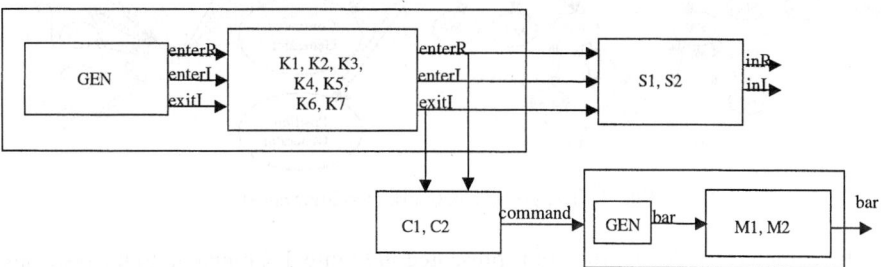

Fig. 3. Modular structure of KRC

In this case it is quite easy to identify the inputs: *enterR*, *enterI*, *exitI* (i.e., the variable *train*), and *bar*; while *inR*, *inI*, *command* and *bar* may be computed. In fact, we can identify *inR* and *inI* as state variables, defined by axioms S1 and S2 respectively. On the other hand, *command* is an output variable, defined by axioms C1 and C2.

As an example, let us consider the code that corresponds to C1, C2:

```
proctype CommandGenerator(chan ev; chan sync){ /*C1 and C2 */
byte t,n;
byte memo[Dm]; /*store the last significant values of train*/
command=0;
do
            ::ev?t,eval(3); /*receive 'train' from Process 3*/
            n=Dm-G;
            do
              ::n>0->memo[n]=memo[n-1];n--;
              ::n==0 -> memo[n]=t; break;
            od;
            if
              ::t==4 -> ev!4,5; goto stop;
              ::else ->
                if
                ::memo[Dm-G]==1 -> command=2;
                ::t==3 -> command=1;
                ::else -> command=0;
                fi;
                ev!command,5; /* send command to Process 5 */
            fi;
od;
stop:       skip;
}
```

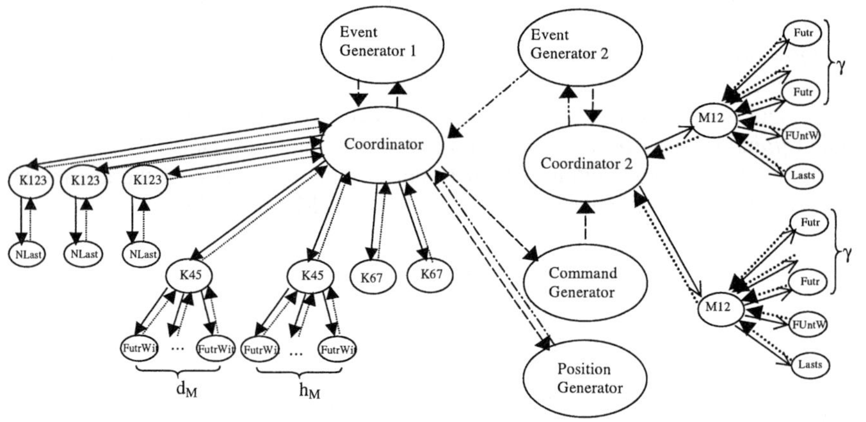

Fig. 4. The process network (modular case)

The complete modular structure is presented in Figure 3. Compared to the previous case, the number of processes is smaller, because axioms that are only used to compute variable values can always be translated into a single process. Moreover, we need one generator and one coordinator for each one of the two modules *trainModel* and *gate*.

Verification results, with the same system configuration for the results of Table 2, are shown in Table 3. Performance increases noticeably for the same constant values:

Table 3. Verification - modular case

μ	d_M	d_m	h_M	h_m	γ	Depth	Memory (KB)	States	Transitions
10	5	4	4	3	2	6791	12680	162727	164944
15	7	4	7	3	2	10606	39928	526592	531193
20	10	8	9	7	3	15371	48120	580929	585481
25	15	12	9	7	9	22532	105259	1097340	1102690
30	12	10	9	7	6	18167	62217	693635	698048
30	20	13	9	7	3	26343	130961	1462620	1471300
30	9	7	20	17	3	27001	92459	1025200	1031770
40	20	17	19	17	9	> 210 MB			
40	30	27	9	7	3	41117	115597	1138780	1145450

used memory is more than halved, and state number considerably decreased (running times are not reported, but always below two minutes).

5 Conclusions and Directions of Future Research

We presented a novel application of model checking through SPIN as a means for verifying purely descriptive specifications written in TRIO. The approach is based on the translation of TRIO formulae into Promela programs guided by an equivalence between TRIO and 2-way alternating modulo counting automata. The set of TRIO axioms is partitioned into the *specification* part, i.e., axioms describing assumptions on the systems being checked, and the *property* part, that must be proven to hold under such assumptions; then the SPIN model checker is employed to prove the validity of the implication *specification→property*. Since a TRIO specification does not include any operational model that accounts for the behavior to be checked against the property, an additional Promela component must be combined with the result of the translation of TRIO specification, to generate the values for variables occurring in the TRIO specification. This generative component of the Promela programs is the major source of complexity in the verification process, which is addressed at a linguistic level by exploiting the modular structure of TRIO specifications, and at an applicative/methodological level by limiting the combinatorial generation to the logical variables that are completely independent of any other value.

The results of our experimentation are quite encouraging, as we were able to verify properties of the Railway Crossing Problem for values of the temporal constants in the TRIO axioms that make the verification totally unfeasible with tools such as LTL2BA or Wring.

The translation of TRIO formulae into Promela programs was performed manually for the case study, but we are confident that it can be easily automated. This is apparent for what concerns the translation of the various TRIO constructs relying on their correspondence with 2-way alternating modulo counting automata; the optimizations based on the modular structure can also be automated if the TRIO specification is provided in modular form, while those based on restricting generation to input variables can be applied mechanically by taking into account the direction of the arrows representing items in the interface of specification modules (in any case the information on which are the input to the system under study is rather clear starting from the early phases of requirements analysis).

We have defined a verification procedure in a scenario where both the system under design and the desired property to be proven are expressed as TRIO axioms. *A fortiori*, our approach can be applied in the case when the system under design is described by means of an operational model such as a Promela program or any state-transition system that can be translated into Promela. In fact, in this case the verification procedure would be more efficient, as the principal source of complexity, namely the combinatorial generation of values for logical variables, would be avoided. From this viewpoint, our approach is more effective than other methods that construct a never claim from an LTL specification, because the Promela code produced from the TRIO formulae grows in size linearly with the size of the TRIO formula, while other approaches suffer from an "exponential blow up" of the state space: for instance, LTL2BA produces Promela code that coincides, in fact, with the Büchi automaton. Under this respect, we can therefore claim that our approach better exploits the potential of SPIN and Promela for verification.

Another application of the ideas presented here, that conceptually is a mere by-product of the verification method but has a relevant potential for construction of verification tools, is the generation of execution traces and of functional test cases starting from a purely descriptive specification given in TRIO. We expect the computational complexity of generating a simulation to be orders of magnitude smaller than the one of property proving, thus permitting the implementation of industrial-strength tools supporting validation of specifications and specification-based functional testing.

References

1. E. Allen Emerson. Temporal and Modal Logic. *Handbook of Theoretical Computer Science, Volume B: Formal Models and Sematics 1990*, J. van Leeuwen, ed., North-Holland Pub. Co./MIT Press, Pages 995-1072.
2. A. Chandra, D. Kozen, and L. Stockmeyer, Alternation. *Journal of the Association for Computing Machinery 28*, 1 (January 1981), 114-133.
3. FAST-ESPRIT Project No. 25581 – *Synthesis of the evaluation of the FAST toolset Experimentation*, FAST Report D7.5.1, The FAST Consortium, November 2000.
4. M.Felder, A.Morzenti, *Validating real-time systems by history-checking TRIO specifications*, ACM TOSEM-Transactions On Software Engineering and Methodologies, vol.3, n.4, October 1994.
5. A. Gargantini, A.Morzenti, *Automated Deductive Requirements Analysis of Critical Systems*, ACM TOSEM - Transactions On Software Engineering and Methodologies, Vol. 10, no. 3, July 2001, pp. 225-307.
6. P. Gastin, D. Oddoux, *Fast LTL to Büchi Automata Translation*, Proceedings of CAV'01, Lecture Notes in Computer Science 2102, p. 53-65, 2001.
7. C.Ghezzi, D.Mandrioli, A.Morzenti, *TRIO, a logic language for executable specifications of real time systems*, The Journal of Systems and Software, Elsevier Science Publishing, vol.12, no.2, pp. 107-123, May 1990.
8. C. Heitmeyer and D. Mandrioli, editors. *Formal Methods for Real-Time Computing*, volume 5 of Trends in Software. Wiley, 1996.

9. G. Holzmann, *The Model Checker SPIN*, IEEE Transactions on Software Engineering, Vol. 23, 5, May 1997.
10. O. Kupferman, N. Piterman, M. Vardi, *Extended Temporal Logic Revisited*, CONCUR'01, 2001.
11. O. Kupferman, M. Vardi, *Weak Alternating Automata Are Not That Weak*, Proceedings of the Fifth Israel Symposium on Theory of Computing and Systems, ISTCS'97, 1997
12. D.Mandrioli, S.Morasca, A.Morzenti, *Generating Test Cases for Real-Time Systems from Logic Specifications*, ACM TOCS-Transactions On Computer Systems, Vol. 13, No. 4, November 1995. pp.365-398.
13. Mandrioli D., Morzenti A., Pezzè M., San Pietro P. Silva S., *A Petri Net and Logic Approach to the Specification and Verification of Real Time Systems*, in [8].
14. A. Morzenti, D. Mandrioli, C. Ghezzi, *A Model Parametric Real-Time Logic*, ACM Trans. on Programming Languages and Systems 14, 4 (October 1992), 521-573.
15. A. Morzenti, P. San Pietro, *Object-Oriented Logic Specifications of Time Critical Systems*, ACM Trans. on Softw. Engin. and Meth., vol.3, n.1, Jan.1994, pp. 56-98.
16. N. Piterman, M. Vardi, *From Bidirectionality to Alternation*, MFCS'01, 2001.
17. F. Somenzi and R. Bloem, *Efficient Büchi automata from LTL Formulae*, CAV'00, pp.248-263, 2000
18. Wolfgang Thomas: *Automata Theory on Trees and Partial Orders.* TAPSOFT, 1997.
19. M. Vardi, *A Temporal Fixpoint Calculus*, POPL'88, 1988.
20. M. Vardi, *An automata-theoretic approach to linear temporal logic*, Banff'94, 1994.

Computing Meta-transitions for Linear Transition Systems with Polynomials

Julien Musset and Michaël Rusinowitch

Projet CASSIS, Inria-Lorraine, Nancy, France,
jmusset@loria.fr, rusi@loria.fr

Abstract. Transition systems have been intensively applied to the modeling of complex systems. Their safety properties can be verified using model-checking procedures based on an iterative computation of least or greatest fixed points. The approach has to face two main difficulties: the complexity of computations on the data domain and the termination of the iterative algorithm. In many cases an analysis of the transition system can be exploited in order to speed up the calculus. Meta-transitions are are over-approximations of transition relations that lead in one step to an superset of the set of the the states that can be reached by an infinite trajectory. Using polynomials, we compute meta-transitions for complex transition systems. Finally, we illustrate this method on a train controller.

Keywords: Infinite systems, model-checking, acceleration rules, complex systems

1 Introduction

Transition systems [1] have been applied to the modeling of complex systems, for example they have been used for giving semantics to synchronous languages such as LUSTRE [2], SIGNAL [3] or to hybrid automata [4]. Model-checking [5, 6] is a powerful technique for the automatic verification of systems: a model-checking algorithm determines whether a transition system meets a requirement specification that is given as a temporal formula. For discrete finite-state systems model-checking has been successful in validating communication protocols and hardware circuits. In recent years model-checking algorithms have been extended to infinite state systems. As the states cannot be enumerated they have to be represented symbolically. Moreover, proving that a model verifies a temporal formula is undecidable in general.

From the fixed point characterization of temporal properties [7], model-checking can be reduced to the successive computations of least or greatest fixed point of monotonic functions over sets of states. For instance, with the help of an observer [8], verifying a safety property is equivalent to verify a reachability property where backward or forward analysis can be used. To improve verification we need to overcome two main obstacles. Firstly, operations over symbolic representations of sets of states are expensive. Secondly, the computation of the fixed point may not terminate. Several tools allow for improving the fixed point computation: abstraction, that consists in substituting the domain of the concrete states by a simpler domain of abstract states [9], widening and narrowing operators that compute over- and under-approximation of unions and intersections of sets [10].

In this work we focus on reachability and safety properties. For infinite systems, there exists some classes of systems for which reachability problem is decidable but their restrictions are too strong to be efficient on real systems. To help the termination, acceleration rules help to compute in one step all the states that can be reached by an infinite trajectory. Andreas Podelski and Giorgio Delzanno introduce meta-transition with the following transition system [11].

Example 1. The set of states is Z^2, the transition relation $\rightarrow$ is the binary relation over Z^2 such that $(x,y) \rightarrow (x',y')$ is equivalent to $x' = x$ and $y' = y-1$, and the set of the initial states is $\{(x,y) \in Z^2 | x \leq y\}$. The reachability algorithm computes iteratively the set of states can be reached from the initial state in at most zero step, one step, two steps, three steps,... till it does not produce new state. For this example, we get the following sequence of sets:

$$\{(x,y) \in Z^2 | x \leq y\}, \{(x,y) \in Z^2 | x \leq y+1\}, \{(x,y) \in Z^2 | x \leq y+2\}, \ldots$$

This initial the computation leads us to believe that this sequence is infinite. Consequently, the reachability algorithm will not terminate. One technique that could help us consists in generalizing the transition relation $\rightarrow$. In the previous example, $(x,y) \xrightarrow{n \text{ times}} \ldots \rightarrow (x',y')$ is equivalent to $x' = x$ and $y' = y - n$. Applying reachability algorithm to the transition relation $\rightsquigarrow$ such that $(x,y) \rightsquigarrow (x',y')$ if and only if there exists $n \in N$ such that $x' = x$ and $y' = y - n$, we get the following finite sequence of sets:

$$\{(x,y) \in Z^2 | x \leq y\}, Z^2.$$

We can not reach new states from the set Z^2.

The aim of this work is to propose a method to compute such a generalized transition relation $\rightsquigarrow$ when $\rightarrow$ is described with complex polynomial functions. We will explain why we need to compute over-approximations. The generalized transition relations is called *meta-transition*.

Related works. Helping the termination of reachability and proof algorithms has been a topic study in different fields. Thomas Henzinger and Vlad Rusu propose to guess the set of reachable states from the first steps of the computation [12]. Andreas Podelski and Giorgio Delzanno improve this idea by using acceleration rules in their model-checking system based on constrained logic programming [11]. The notion of acceleration rules is equivalent to the notion of meta-transitions introduced by Bernard Boigelot in his PhD thesis [13]. Boigelot explain how they can be exploited to improve reachability algorithms. Then the author constructs meta-transitions for different kind of data-types.

These meta-transitions are used by Sébastien Bardin, Alain Finkel, Jérôme Leroux and Laure Petrucci in the tool FAST for accelerations of symbolic transtion systems [14]. With a similar approach, Ashih Tiwari in [15] computes supersets of transition relations defined by real linear differential equation and applied it to prove safety properties of hybrid automaton. Let us note that this approach can be seen in related research topic. For instance, Andrew Ireland and Alan Bundy use rippling, a syntaxic simplification heuristic, and information from failures to generalize the property to prove by induction [16].

Our work is directly related to these works. To begin with, we focus on systems with real variables instead of integer one. Moreover, we deal with the cases that can not be exactly handle corresponding to asymptotic behavior, cases that are not considered by Bernard Boigelot. Finally, compared to Ashih Tiwari, we are taking account of the behavior of the system in all the dimension and not only in the eigenspaces.

In Section 2, we define transition systems, safety properties, and introduce algorithm for computing reachability sets. Section 3 describes some previous works on integer linear systems and how our algorithm can be applied to these systems. Section 4 introduces our acceleration rules and in Section 5, we apply our algorithm to a train controller system.

We thank Ashish Tiwari for his comments on a first version of this paper.

2 Model-Checking Techniques

2.1 Notations for Sets

The complement of a set Q is denoted by $\overline{Q}$. The set of subsets of Q is denoted by $\mathcal{P}(Q)$. The least fixed point of a monotonic function f from $\mathcal{P}(Q)$ to $\mathcal{P}(Q)$ with the complete partial order $\subseteq$ is denoted by $\mu X.f(X)$. For all binary relations $\rightarrow$, the fact that $(x, y) \in \rightarrow$ is denoted by $x \rightarrow y$. Let Q and R be two sets and E be a subset of $Q \times R$. For all $x \in Q$, $E(x)$ is the set $\{y \in R | (x, y) \in E\}$. Let Q be a set, $\rightarrow$ and $\rightsquigarrow$ be two binary relations over Q. The binary relation $\rightarrow \circ \rightsquigarrow$ is the set $\{(x, z) \in Q^2 |$ there exists y such that $x \rightarrow y \rightsquigarrow z\}$. For all positive integer n, $\xrightarrow{n}$ is defined recursively by $\xrightarrow{0} = \{(x,y) \in Q^2 | x = y\}$ and for all n, $\xrightarrow{n+1} = \rightarrow \circ \xrightarrow{n}$. A binary relation $\rightarrow$ over a set Q is closed if $\rightarrow \circ \rightarrow \subseteq \rightarrow$.

2.2 Transition Systems and Safety Properties

Definition 1 (Transition system). *A transition systems is a triple $(Q, \rightarrow, I)$ in which:*

1. *Q is a set whose elements are called* **states**,
2. *$\rightarrow \subseteq Q \times Q$ is a binary relation over Q, called* **transition relation**, *and*
3. *$I \subseteq Q$ is a set whose elements are called* **initial states**.

A linear (resp. polynomial) transition systems is a system such that the transition relation can be describe using linear (resp. polynomial) formulas. An integer (resp. complex) transition systems is a system such that the set of state is Z^p (resp. C^p) with p a strictly positive integer number.

Definition 2 (Trajectory). *Let $(Q, \rightarrow, I)$ be a transition system. A trajectory of $(Q, \rightarrow, I)$ is a sequence of states $(q_i)_{0 \leq i \leq n}, n \in \mathbb{N} \cup \{+\infty\}$, such that $q_0 \in I$ and for all $0 \leq i < n$, $q_i \rightarrow q_{i+1}$.*

A state can be reached by a transition system if there exists a finite trajectory whose last element is this state.

Definition 3 (Safety problem). *The* **safety problem** *is the decision problem defined by:*

1. **instance:** *a tuple $(Q, \rightarrow, I, F)$ in which $(Q, \rightarrow, I)$ is a transition system and $F \subseteq Q$ is a set whose elements are called* **failure states***;*
2. **question:** *does some trajectory of $(Q, \rightarrow, I)$ reach a failure state ?*

If the answer to the safety problem is **yes** then the system is unsafe otherwise the system is safe.

Definition 4 (Post-condition operator). *Let Q be a set and $\rightarrow$ be a binary relation over Q. The* **post-condition** *operator $\text{post}_\rightarrow$ is the function from $\mathcal{P}(Q)$ to $\mathcal{P}(Q)$ defined by:*

$$\text{post}_\rightarrow(X) = \{q \in Q | \text{ there exists } q' \in X \text{ such that } q' \rightarrow q\}.$$

For solving the safety problem, model-checking algorithms compute the set of reachable states and check whether it contains a failure state. The set of reachable states is equal to $\bigcup_{i \in \mathbb{N}} \text{post}^i_\rightarrow(I)$. As the function $X \mapsto I \cup \text{post}_\rightarrow(X)$ is monotonic with respect to the order $\subseteq$, the set of reachable states is the least fixed point $\mu X. I \cup \text{post}_\rightarrow(X)$. The last equality leads to the Algorithm 1 generally used is model-checking tools.

Algorithm 1: Decision procedure for the safety problem
Input: A transition system $(Q, \rightarrow, I)$, a set $F \subseteq Q$
Output: Does some trajectory of $(Q, \rightarrow, I)$ reach a state of F
SAFETY$(Q, \rightarrow, I, F)$
(1) $X := \emptyset$
(2) $Y := I$
(3) while $Y \not\subseteq X$ do
(4) $X := Y$
(5) $Y := I \cup \text{post}_\rightarrow(X)$
(6) if $X \cap F = \emptyset$ then return no
(7)   else return yes

Remark 1 (Backward strategy). For an instance $(Q, \rightarrow, I, F)$ of the safety problem, backward strategy consist in applying Algorithm 1 to the instance $(Q, \leftarrow, F, I)$ where $x \leftarrow y$ if and only if $y \rightarrow x$. The algorithm computes the set of states that may reach a failure test and check whether an initial states is in this set.

Definition 5 (Meta-transition). *Let Q be a set and $\rightarrow$ be a binary relation over Q. A meta-transition for $\rightarrow$ is a closed binary relation $\rightsquigarrow$ over Q such that for all $n \in \mathbb{N}$, $\overset{n}{\rightarrow} \subseteq \rightsquigarrow$.*

2.3 Linear Algebra

Let p be a strictly positive integer. For all $i \in \{1, \ldots, m\}$, $j \in \{1, \ldots, n\}$, the coefficient in the position i, j of a $m \cdot n$ matrix M is denoted by $M_{i,j}$. Vectors are denoted by $\boldsymbol{x}$. For all $i \in \{1, \ldots, p\}$, the ith coordinate of a p vector $\boldsymbol{x}$ is denoted by $\boldsymbol{x}_i$. The identity (resp. zero) matrix of size p is denoted by Id_p (resp. 0_p). A matrix N is nilpotent of index n if $N^{n-1} \neq 0_p$ and $N^n = 0_p$.

Theorem 1 (Jordan decomposition). *Let A be a m square complex matrix. The matrix A is similar to a matrix $\mathrm{diag}(J_1, \ldots, J_n)$ where each J_i is a matrix of the form $\alpha Id_p + N$ where α is a complex number and N is a nilpotent p square complex matrix. Such a matrix $\mathrm{diag}(J_1, \ldots, J_n)$ is in Jordan form.*

For all couple of integers $(n, i) \in \mathbb{N}^2$, the binomial coefficient is denoted by $\binom{n}{i}$. For all complex number z, $|z|$ is the norm of z: $|z|^2 = \Re(z)^2 + \Im(z)^2$. We extend the operator $\leq$ for complex numbers as follows: $x \leq y$ if $\Re(x) \leq \Re(y)$ and $\Im(x) \leq \Im(y)$.

Definition 6 (Set algebra). *Given a set Q, an algebra on Q is a collection of subsets of Q which is closed under finite unions and complements.*

The set algebra $\mathcal{L}_p(\mathbb{Z})$ is generated by the sets $\{\boldsymbol{x} \in \mathbb{Z}^p | {}^t\boldsymbol{a}.\boldsymbol{x} \geq b\}$ where $\boldsymbol{a}$ is a p integer vector and b is an integer number. The set algebra $\mathcal{L}_p(\mathbb{C})$ is generated by the sets $\{\boldsymbol{x} \in \mathbb{C}^p | {}^t\boldsymbol{a}.\boldsymbol{x} \geq b\}$ where $\boldsymbol{a}$ is a p complex vector and b is a complex number. The set algebra $\mathcal{P}_p(\mathbb{C})$ is generated by the sets $\{\boldsymbol{x} \in \mathbb{C}^p | P(\boldsymbol{x}_1, \ldots, \boldsymbol{x}_p) \geq 0\}$ where $P(X_1, \ldots, X_p)$ is a complex polynomial.

3 From Integer Linear Systems to Complex Polynomial Systems

In this work, we focus on complex polynomial systems. To begin with, integer linear systems may be abstracted into a complex one. Then, solving integer formulas is more time expensive than solving complex ones. Finally, polynomial formulas allow to handle non-linear behaviors. We discuss here how this abstraction can be performed and we present the differences between our approach and the previous works on linear systems.

3.1 Meta-transition for Integer Linear Systems

Andreas Podelski and Giorgio Delzanno use meta-transitions for integer linear transition systems in their model-checking system based on constrained logic programming [11]. The authors describe four accelerations rules using the idea of Example 1. The authors note that these rules may be generalized to handle more complex sets and transition relations.

In his PhD thesis [13], Bernard Boigelot proposes such a generalization. The set of the states is Z^p. One of the main results is a characterization of the transition relations such that the set of the reachable states is in $\mathcal{L}_p(Z)$ if the sets of the initial states is in $\mathcal{L}_p(Z)$.

Theorem 2. *Let A be a p square integer matrix, b be a p integer vector and let $\rightarrow$ be the transition relation on Z^p such that $x \rightarrow y$ if and only if $y = Ax + b$. The two following properties are equivalent:*

(i) for all set I of $\mathcal{L}_p(Z)$, the set of the reachable states of the transition system $(Z^p, \rightarrow, I)$ is in $\mathcal{L}_p(Z)$;
(ii) there exists an integer m strictly positive such that the matrix A^m is similar to a matrix of the form $diag(Id_{p_1}, 0_{p_2})$.

The proof constructs the transitive closure of the transition relation $\rightarrow$. Commenting the cases that are not covered by the condition (ii) of Theorem 2, Boigelot remarks that:

> [note page 237] *Intuitively, the difficulty originates from the fact that, if a linear (transition relation $\rightarrow$) does not verify the hypothesis of Theorem 2 then the trajectory $(\bigcup_{n \in N} post^n_{\rightarrow}(\{x\}))$ of an individual vector value $x \in Z^p$ to which $\rightarrow$ is repeatedly applied is in general non linear. This makes a manageable description of $post^*_{\rightarrow}(S)$, for a subset S of Z^p, much more difficult to obtain.*

This is that problem we try to tackle in this paper.

3.2 Abstraction of Integer Systems

We define inductively the projection mapping $\gamma : \mathcal{L}_p(Z) \mapsto \mathcal{L}_p(C)$ by:

1. $\gamma(\{x \in Z^p |{}^t a \cdot x \geq b\}) = \{x \in C^p |{}^t a \cdot x) \geq b\}$ where a is a p integer vector and b is an integer number,
2. $\gamma(X \cup Y) = \gamma(X) \cup \gamma(Y)$ and $\gamma(\overline{X}) = \overline{\gamma(X)}$.

The mapping γ is extended to instances of the safety problem:

$$\gamma((Z^p, \rightarrow, I, F)) = (C^p, \gamma(\rightarrow), \gamma(I), \gamma(F)).$$

This abstraction is justified by the complexity of the satisfiability systems for integer formulas and complex formulas. [17]. Checking whether

$$\{x \in K^p |{}^t a \cdot x \geq b\} \subseteq \{x \in K^p |{}^t a' \cdot x \geq b'\}$$

where a, a' are p integer vector and b, b' are integer numbers is:

1. NP-complete in p if $K = Z$,
2. whereas it is polynomial in p if $K = C$

Checking whether

$$\{x \in K^p | P(x_1, \ldots, x_p) \geq 0\} \subseteq \{x \in K^p | P'(x_1, \ldots, x_p) \geq 0\}$$

where $P(X_1, \ldots, X_p), P'(X_1, \ldots, X_p)$ are integer polynomials and $b \in Z$ is undecidable if $K = Z$ whereas it is NP-hard in p if $K = C$.

This result leads designers of model-checking algorithms to weaken the test of comparison between sets of states by abstracting the integer sets into reals sets. In [11], Andreas Podelski and Giorgio Delzanno describe a class of sets for which the abstraction gives the same result. The following proposition is another correctness result that could be applied for backward strategies.

Proposition 1. *Let $(Q, \to, I, F)$ be an instance of the safety problem, let Q' and I' be two sets such that $Q \subseteq Q'$, $I \subseteq I' \subseteq Q'$ and $(I' \setminus I) \cap Q = \emptyset$. Let $\leadsto$ be a binary relation over Q' such that $\to \subseteq \leadsto$ and for all $x \in Q$, $y \leadsto x$ implies $y \in Q$ and $y \to x$. The two instances $(Q, \to, I, F)$ and $(Q', \leadsto, I', F)$ of the safety problem have the same answer.*

Proposition 1 can be applied easily in backward strategy when an integer transition system is abstracted into a complex one. In the abstracted system, the successive states of a integer state is always an integer state. The main condition of Proposition 1 is verified.

Example 2. The set of states is Z^p and the transition relation $\to$ is such that $x \to y$ is equivalent to $y = Ax$ where A is a p integer matrix. If I and F be subsets of Z then Proposition 1 implies that $I \cap \text{pre}_\to(F) = \emptyset$ is equivalent to $I \cap \text{pre}_{\gamma(\to)}(\gamma(F)) = \emptyset$.

3.3 Non-linear Trajectories

We adapt Theorem 2 of Bernard Boigelot for complex systems.

Theorem 3. *Let A be a p square complex matrix, b be a p vector and $\to$ be the transition relation on C^p such that $x \to y$ if and only if $y = Ax + b$. The two following properties are equivalent:*

(i) for all set I of $\mathcal{L}_p(C)$, there exists a set E of $\mathcal{L}_{p+1}(C)$ such that

$$\text{post}_\to(I) = \bigcup_{n \in \mathbb{N}} E(n),$$

(ii) there exists a strictly positive integer m such that A^m is similar to a matrix of the form $diag(Id_{p_1}, 0_{p_2})$.

This theorem has two main consequences. Firstly, as the sets of states are represented with complex variables, we won't be able to compute exactly the set of reachable states in general. Secondly, we will have to make different approximations according to the type of behavior of the systems, depending on the eigenvalues of the matrix A of the transition relation.

4 Computing Meta-transitions

4.1 General Method

The set of states is C^p, $p > 0$. We consider transition relations $\rightarrow$ on C^p of the form:

$x \rightarrow y$ if and only if there exists $z \in C^q$ such that
$$y = Ax + A'z + b \text{ and } (x, z) \in C$$

where q is a positive integer number, A is a complex p square matrix, A' is complex $p \cdot q$ square matrix, b is a complex p vector and C is a set in $\mathcal{P}_{p+q}(C)$. The set C is the *guard* and z is the *input*. We are looking for a meta-transition for $\rightarrow$. To compute such a binary relation, we add a variable n as suggested by Theorem 3.

Proposition 2. *Let Q be a set, let $\rightarrow$ be a binary relation over Q, and let E be a set of $\mathcal{P}_{2p+1}(C)$ such that $E(1)$ contains $\rightarrow$ and for all integer m and n greater than 0, $E(m) \circ E(n) \subseteq E(m+n)$. Then $\bigcup_{n \in R, n \geq 0} E(n)$ is a meta-transition for $\rightarrow$.*

In the following, we will say that E is an **approximation set for** $\rightarrow$. Once an approximation set has been computed, we will have to perform an elimination of existential quantifier over a polynomial formula. This operation can be expensive. It would be impossible with integer formulas.

Approximation sets will be represented by polynomial formulas, i.e. they will be member of $\mathcal{P}_{2p+1}(C)$. Compare to linear set, this representation allows to handle non-linear behaviors.

We construct approximation sets beginning from the simplest transition relations then we consider more and more general ones:

1. $q = 0$, $C = C^p$ and A is a nilpotent matrix and $b = 0$,
2. $q = 0$, $C = C^p$ and $A = Id_p + N$ where N is a p complex nilpotent matrix,
3. $q = 0$, $C = C^p$ and $A = \alpha Id_p + N$ and $b = 0$ where $\alpha \in C$, N is a p complex nilpotent matrix,
4. $q = 0$, $C = C^p$ and $A = \alpha Id_p + N$,
5. $q = 0$, $C = C^p$ and A in Jordan form,
6. $q = 0$, $C = C^p$,
7. $q = 0$.

Finally, we propose an heuristic to find an approximation set for the most general transition relation.

4.2 Simplest Cases

In this part, we consider the transition relation of the form:

$$x \rightarrow y \text{ if and only if } y = (\alpha Id_p + N)x + b$$

where α is a complex number, N is a nilpotent p square matrix and b is a p vector. There are three base cases: $\alpha = 0$ and $b = 0$, $\alpha = 1$, $\alpha \notin \{0, 1\}$ and $b = 0$.

Case $\alpha = 0$ and $b = 0$. When $\alpha = 0$, the function $x \mapsto Nx$ is nilpotent. If n is an integer number greater than p then N^n is the zero matrix. The set Z is not an element of $\mathcal{P}_1(C)$. Therefore the condition "n is an integer number greater than p" is replaced by "n is a real number greater than p".

Proposition 3. *Let p be an strictly positive integer and let $\to$ be the transition relation over C^p such that:*

$$x \to y \text{ if and only if } y = Nx$$

where N is a nilpotent p square matrix. The following set $E \in \mathcal{P}_{2p+1}(C)$ is an approximation set for $\to$:

$$E = \{(n, x, y) \in C \times C^p \times C^p \,|\, n \in \{0, \ldots, p-1\} \text{ and } y = N^n x\} \cup$$
$$\{(n, x, y) \in C^{2p+1} | n \in R \text{ and } n \geq p \text{ and } y = 0\}.$$

Case $\alpha = 1$. For all $n \in N$, we have the equality:

$$\text{post}^n_\to(\{x\}) = \left\{ \sum_{0 \leq i \leq max(p-1,n)} \binom{n}{i} N^i x + \sum_{0 \leq i \leq max(p-1,n-1)} \binom{n}{i+1} N^i b \right\}.$$

Our idea is to abstract the terms $max(p-1, n)$ and $max(p-1, n-1)$ into $p-1$ and to extend the binomial coefficients for real numbers.

We extend the binomial coefficient to complex number as follows. For all positive integer i and for all complex number z, $\binom{z}{i}$ is the polynomial defined by:

$$\binom{z}{i} = \frac{1}{(i)!} \prod_{0 \leq k \leq i-1} (z - k).$$

For each integer i, the function $z \mapsto \binom{z}{i}$ is a polynomial in z.

Fixing p, N, b, the function f is defined by:

$$f : \begin{array}{l} C \times C^p \to C^p \\ (n, x) \mapsto \sum_{0 \leq i \leq p-1} \binom{n}{i} N^i x + \binom{n}{i+1} N^i b \end{array}$$

For all positive integer n, $\text{post}^n_\to(x) = \{f(n, x)\}$ and for all complex numbers m, n, $f(n, f(m, x)) = f(m + n, x)$.

Proposition 4. *Let p be a strictly positive integer and let $\to$ be the transition relation over C^p such that :*

$$x \to y \text{ if and only if } y = (Id_p + N)x + b$$

where N is a nilpotent p square matrix and b is a p vector. The following set $E \in \mathcal{P}_{2p+1}(C)$ is an approximation set for $\to$:

$$E = \{(n, x, y) \in C \times C^p \times C^p | y = f(n, x)\}.$$

Case $\alpha \notin \{0,1\}$ and $b = 0$. Three kinds of asymptotic behaviors of $\xrightarrow{n}$ are possible when n goes to $+\infty$ according the value of $|\alpha|$:

1. if $0 < |\alpha| < 1$ then $\xrightarrow{n}(x)$ converges exponentially in n to $\{0\}$,
2. if $1 < |\alpha|$ then $\xrightarrow{n}(x)$ diverges in n,
3. if $|\alpha| = 1$ then $\xrightarrow{n}(x)$ diverges with a polynomial behavior in n.

For each of these cases, we are proposing an approximation set that will verify the asymptotic behavior. We use the following equality:

$$(\alpha Id_p + N)^n x = \alpha^n \sum_{0 \leq i \leq max(p-1,n)} \binom{n}{i} \alpha^{-i} N^i x.$$

If $\alpha \neq 1$ then the behavior of α^n can not be represented as a polynomial in n. Hence, α^n is replaced by a weaker polynomial constraint $\phi_\alpha(n)$ which degree will be chosen according to the asymptotic behavior. The function $\phi_\alpha(n)$ has to contain α^n and for the closure condition implies that if $c \in \phi_\alpha(m)$ and $c' \in \phi_\alpha(n)$ then $c \cdot c' \in \phi_\alpha(m+n)$.

For all $\alpha \notin \{0,1\}$, ϕ_α is the function from R into $\mathcal{P}_1(C)$ defined by:

1. $\phi_{-1}(n) = \{1, -1\}$,
2. if $|\alpha| = 1$ and $\alpha \notin \{1, -1\}$ then $\phi_\alpha(n) = \{c \in C | |c|^2 = 1\}$,
3. if $|\alpha| > 1$ then $\phi_\alpha(n) = \{c \in C | |c|^2 \geq ((|\alpha| - 1) \cdot n + 1)^2\}$,
4. if $0 < |\alpha| < 1$ then $\phi_\alpha(n) = \left\{c \in C \Big| |c|^2 \cdot ((|\alpha|^{-1/p} - 1) \cdot n + 1)^{2p} \leq 1\right\}$.

Fixing p, N, α, the function g is defined by:

$$g : \begin{array}{c} C \times C^p \to C^p \\ (n, x) \mapsto \sum_{0 \leq i \leq p-1} \binom{n}{i} \alpha^{-i} N^i x \end{array}$$

For all positive integer n, $post^n_{\to}(x) = \{\alpha^n \cdot g(n, x)\}$ and for all complex numbers m, n, $g(n, g(m, x)) = g(m + n, x)$. We can now describe the approximation set.

Proposition 5. *Let p be a strictly positive integer and let $\to$ be the transition relation such that:*

$$x \to y \text{ if and only if } y = (\alpha Id_p + N)x$$

where $\alpha \in C \setminus \{0, 1\}$ and N is a nilpotent p square matrix. The following set $E \in \mathcal{P}_{2p+1}(C)$ is an approximation set for $\to$:

$$E = \{(n, x, y) \in C \times C^p \times C^p |$$
$$\text{there exists } c \in C \text{ such that } c \in \phi_\alpha(n) \text{ and } y = c \cdot g(n, x)\}.$$

Remark 2. We evaluate these approximation sets by a qualitative analysis of their asymptotic behavior. The transition relation $E(n)$ is a close approximation of $\xrightarrow{n}$. We compare the states that can be reached using $\to$ and the approximated transition relation. The variable n is an integer and we study the approximated transition relation when n goes to $+\infty$:

(a) if $\alpha = -1$ then for all $x \in C^p$, for all positive integer n, $E(n, x) = \text{post}^n_{\rightarrow}(x) \cup \{y \in C^p | -y \in \text{post}^n_{\rightarrow}(\{x\})\}$;
(b) if $|\alpha| = 1$ and $\alpha \notin \{1, -1\}$ then for all $x \in C^p$, for all positive integer n, $E(n, x) = \{c \cdot y \in C^p | c \in C \text{ and } |c| = 1 \text{ and } y \in \text{post}^n_{\rightarrow}(\{x\})\}$;
(c) if $\alpha \in C \setminus \{0, 1\}$ then for all $x \in C^p$,

$$\lim_{n \to +\infty} \{|y| \in R | y \in E(n, x)\} = \lim_{n \to +\infty} \{|y| \in R | y \in \text{post}^n_{\rightarrow}(\{x\})\}.$$

4.3 Reduction

The case $\alpha \notin \{0, 1\}$ and $b \neq 0$ can be reduced to the case $\alpha \notin \{0, 1\}$ and $b = 0$ using the following remark. The equality $y = (\alpha I d_p + N)x + b$ is equivalent to $y + ((\alpha-1)Id_p + N)^{-1}b = (\alpha Id_p + N)(x + ((\alpha-1)Id_p + N)^{-1}b)$. We only need to make a translation of vector $-((\alpha-1)Id_p + N)^{-1}b$ to reduce the computation to one of the previous case.

Proposition 6. *Let p be a strictly positive integer and let $\rightarrow$ be the transition relation defined by:*

$$x \rightarrow y \text{ if and only if } y = (\alpha Id_p + N)x + b$$

where $\alpha \in C \setminus \{0\}$, N is a nilpotent p square matrix, b is a p vector and let $\rightsquigarrow$ be the transition relation defined by:

$$x \rightsquigarrow y \text{ if and only if } y = (\alpha Id_p + N)x.$$

If $E \in \mathcal{P}_{2p+1}(C)$ is an approximation set for $\rightsquigarrow$ then the following set $E' \in \mathcal{P}_{2p+1}(C)$ is an approximation set for $\rightarrow$:

$$E' = \{(n, x, y) \in C \times C^p \times C^p | \\ (n, x + ((\alpha-1)Id_p + N)^{-1}b, y + ((\alpha-1)Id_p + N)^{-1}b) \in E\}.$$

If the matrix A is a diagonal of matrices of the form $\alpha Id_p + N$ then our idea is to chose the product of the approximation sets in each characteristic space. Note that the variable n allows to synchronize the approximation sets instead of only computing the product of the transition relations.

Proposition 7. *Let $p_1, \ldots, p_q$ be strictly positive integers, let $\rightarrow_1, \ldots, \rightarrow_q$ be transition relations such that $\rightarrow_i$ is a transition relation over C^{p_i}, and let $E_1, \ldots, E_q$ be sets such that $E_i \in \mathcal{P}_{2p_i+1}(C)$ is an approximation set for $\rightarrow_i$. If $p = \sum_{1 \leq i \leq q} p_i$ and if $\rightarrow$ is the transition relation over C^p equal to $\bigotimes_{1 \leq i \leq q} \rightarrow_i$ then the following set E of $\mathcal{P}_{2p+1}(C)$ is an approximation set for $\rightarrow$:*

$$E = \left\{ (n, x, y) \in C \times C^p \times C^p \middle| (x, y) \in \bigotimes_{1 \leq i \leq q} E_i(n) \right\}.$$

Using Theorem 1, we can find a basis in which the matrix A is in form of Jordan.

Proposition 8. *Let p be a strictly positive integer and let $\to$ be the transition relation over C^p such that:*

$$x \to y \text{ if and only if } y = Ax + b$$

where A is a p square matrix and b a p vector. Let P and B be p square matrices such that B is in form of Jordan and P is reversible and $A = P^{-1}BP$. Let $\rightsquigarrow$ be the transition relation over C^p such that:

$$x \to y \text{ if and only if } y = Bx + Pb.$$

If $E \in \mathcal{P}_{2p+1}(C)$ is an approximation set for $\rightsquigarrow$ then the following set $E' \in \mathcal{P}_{2p+1}(C)$ is an approximation set for $\to$:

$$E' = \{(n, x, y) \in C \times C^p \times C^p | (n, Px, Py) \in E\}.$$

Let us consider the case where the transition relation $\to$ has a guard, i.e. of the form:

$$x \to y \text{ if and only if } x \in C \text{ and } y = Ax + b$$

et let $\rightsquigarrow$ be the transition relation without guard:

$$x \rightsquigarrow y \text{ if and only if } y = Ax + b.$$

For all vector x and for all integer n, the state y is in the set $\text{post}_{\to}^n(\{x\})$ if there exists a trajectory $x = q_0 \rightsquigarrow q_1 \rightsquigarrow \ldots \rightsquigarrow q_{n-1} \rightsquigarrow q_n = y$ verifying for all $i \in \{0, \ldots, n-1\}$ the condition of guard $q_i \subset C$. As all states have exactly one successive state by $\rightsquigarrow$, $\text{post}_{\rightsquigarrow}^n(\{x\})$ has exactly one element therefore $y \in \text{post}_{\to}^n(\{x\})$ is equivalent to

$$\text{for all } i \in \{0, \ldots, n-1\}, \text{post}_{\rightsquigarrow}^i(\{x\}) \subseteq C \text{ and } y \in \text{post}_{\rightsquigarrow}^n(\{x\}).$$

As we did before, we could replace the constraint "$i \in \mathbb{N}$" by "$i \in \mathbb{R}$ and $i \geq 0$" but the real constraint is stronger that the integer one, therefore we would get an under-approximation instead of an upper-approximation. Therefore, we can not use this approach to find an accurate approximation set. We can construct an approximation set using the following proposition.

Proposition 9. *Let p be a strictly positive integer and let $\to$ be the transition relation over C^p such that:*

$$x \to y \text{ if and only if } x \in C \text{ and } y = Ax + b$$

where A is a p square matrix, b is a p vector and C is a set of $\mathcal{P}_p(C)$. Let $\rightsquigarrow$ be the transition relation over C^p such that:

$$x \rightsquigarrow y \text{ if and only if } y = Ax + b.$$

If the set $E \in \mathcal{P}_{2p+1}(C)$ is an approximation set for $\rightsquigarrow$ then following set $E' \in \mathcal{P}_{2p+1}(C)$ is an approximation set for $\rightarrow$:

$$E' = \{(0, \boldsymbol{x}, \boldsymbol{y}) \in C \times C^p \times C^p | \boldsymbol{x} = \boldsymbol{y}\} \cup$$
$$\{(n, \boldsymbol{x}, \boldsymbol{y}) \in C^{2p+1} | n \in R \text{ and } n \geq 1 \text{ and } \boldsymbol{x} \in \rightarrow \circ E(n-1)\boldsymbol{y}\}.$$

Let us consider the case of a transition relation $\rightarrow$ input, i.e. of the form:

$\boldsymbol{x} \rightarrow \boldsymbol{y}$ if and only if there exists $\boldsymbol{z} \in C^q$ such that
$$(\boldsymbol{x}, \boldsymbol{z}) \in C \text{ and } \boldsymbol{y} = A\boldsymbol{x} + \boldsymbol{b} + A'\boldsymbol{z}$$

where q is a positive integer number, A is a complex p square matrix, A' is complex $p \cdot q$ square matrix, $\boldsymbol{b}$ is a complex p vector and C is a set in $\mathcal{P}_{p+q}(C)$. The transition relation $\rightarrow$ may be seen as the union of the transition relations $\rightarrow_{\boldsymbol{z}}$ where $\boldsymbol{z}$ is any vector of C^q:

$\boldsymbol{x} \rightarrow_{\boldsymbol{z}} \boldsymbol{y}$ if and only if $(\boldsymbol{x}, \boldsymbol{z}) \in C$ and $\boldsymbol{y} = A\boldsymbol{x} + \boldsymbol{b} + A'\boldsymbol{z}$.

There is not general solution to this problem. That is why we propose as a heuristic to compute an approximation set for each $\rightarrow_{\boldsymbol{z}}$ and to chose the union of these sets as approximation set for $\rightarrow$. The following heuristic construct a set of C^{2p+1} and we will have to check that this set is really an approximation set for $\rightarrow$. In practice, the closure condition may fail. In that case, we are not able to provide an approximation set.

Heuristic 1. *Let p be a strictly positive integer and let $\rightarrow$ be the transition relation over C^p such that:*

$\boldsymbol{x} \rightarrow \boldsymbol{y}$ if and only if there exists $\boldsymbol{z} \in C^q$ such that
$$(\boldsymbol{x}, \boldsymbol{z}) \in C \text{ and } \boldsymbol{y} = A\boldsymbol{x} + \boldsymbol{b} + A'\boldsymbol{z}$$

where q is a positive integer number, A is a complex p square matrix, A' is complex $p \cdot q$ square matrix, $\boldsymbol{b}$ is a complex p vector and C is a set in $\mathcal{P}_{p+q}(C)$. Let $\rightsquigarrow$ be the transition relation over C^{p+q} such that:

$(\boldsymbol{x}, \boldsymbol{z}) \rightsquigarrow (\boldsymbol{y}, \boldsymbol{t})$ *if and only if* $(\boldsymbol{x}, \boldsymbol{z}) \in C$ *and* $\boldsymbol{y} = A\boldsymbol{x} + \boldsymbol{b} + A'\boldsymbol{z}$ *and* $\boldsymbol{t} = \boldsymbol{z}$.

Let $E \in \mathcal{P}_{4p+1}(C)$ an approximation set for $\rightsquigarrow$. The following set $E' \in \mathcal{P}_{2p+1}(C)$ is a candidate as an approximation set for $\rightarrow$:

$$E' = \{(n, \boldsymbol{x}, \boldsymbol{y}) \in C \times C^p \times C^p |$$
$$\text{there exists } \boldsymbol{z} \in C^q \text{ such that } (n, (\boldsymbol{x}, \boldsymbol{z}), (\boldsymbol{y}, \boldsymbol{z})) \in E\}.$$

4.4 Backward Strategy

The previous can be apply also for backward strategies.

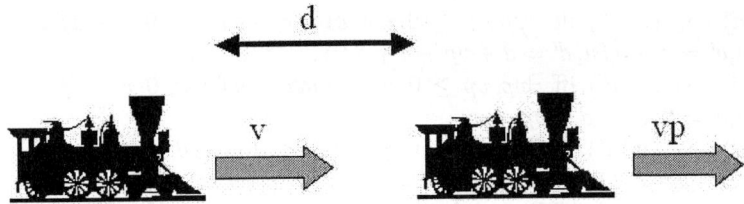

Fig. 1. The train controller problem

Proposition 10. *Let Q be a set, let $\rightarrow$ be a transition relation over Q and let $\leftarrow$ be the transition relation over Q such that $x \leftarrow y$ is equivalent to $y \rightarrow x$. If the set E is an approximation set for $\rightarrow$ then the following set E' is an approximation set for $\leftarrow$:*

$$E' = \{(n, x, y) \in C \times C^p \times C^p | (n, y, x) \in E\}.$$

5 Example: A Train Controller

A train controller is described using the synchronous reactive language LUSTRE [2] in [18] and [19]. One train is following another, the distance between the two trains is $d(t)$ and its initial value is $dinit$. The speed of the first train is $vp(t)$. The speed of the second train is $v(t)$ and its acceleration is $a(t)$. The acceleration depends from the mode fu of the train: the train may brake with the constant acceleration $-afu$, elsewhere the acceleration is less or equal than the constant $amax$. A controller $fu(t)$ decides when the second train has to brake. The goal is to check the correctness of the controller. This problem can be represented using synchronous reactive systems. The following program in LUSTRE describes the behavior of the second train:

```
const afu, amax, dinit;
a = 0 -> if fu then -afu else ap;
v = 0 -> (let vv = (0 -> (pre(v) + a))
          in if vv>=0 then vv else 0);
d = (dinit -> pre(d)) + vp - v;
assert((afu>0) and (ap<amax));
assert((dinit>0) and (vp>=0));
```

The semantics of LUSTRE leads to an instance of the safety problem. The set Q of the states is R^2, representing the speed of the second train and the distance between the two trains. The transition relation $\rightarrow$ is the union of the six transition relations $\rightarrow_1, \ldots, \rightarrow_6$ defined by:

1. $(v, d) \rightarrow_1 (v', d')$ iff $\exists vp\ vp \geq 0, d-v+amax < 0, v-afu \geq 0, a' = afu, v' = v - afu, d' = d + vp - v + afu$,
2. $(v, d) \rightarrow_2 (v', d')$ iff $\exists vp\ vp \geq 0, d - v + amax < 0, v - afu < 0, a' = afu, v' = 0, d' = d + vp$

3. $(v,d) \to_3 (v',d')$ iff $\exists vp\ vp \geq 0, v + amax - afu \geq 0, v - afu \geq 0, a' = afu, v' = v - afu, d' = d + vp - v + afu$
4. $(v,d) \to_4 (v',d')$ iff $\exists vp\ vp \geq 0, v + amax - afu \geq 0, v - afu < 0, a' = afu, v' = 0, d' = d + vp$
5. $(v,d) \to_5 (v',d')$ iff $\exists vp\ am\ vp \geq 0, am < amax, d - v + amax > 0, v + amax - afu < 0, v + am \geq 0, a' = am, v' = v + am, d' = d + vp - v - am$
6. $(v,d) \to_6 (v',d')$ iff $\exists vp\ am\ vp \geq 0, am < amax, d - v + amax > 0, v + amax - afu < 0, v + am < 0, a' = am, v' = 0, d' = d + vp$

The set I of the initial states is $\{(v,d) \in R^2 | v = 0, d > 0\}$. The set F of the failure states is $\{(v,d) \in R^2 | d \leq 0\}$. In [18] and [19], backward reachability does not terminate. The authors have to strengthen the property, i.e. use a greater set of failure states. Using the new set of failure states $\{(v,d) \in R^2 | d \leq 0$ or $afu \geq v\}$, backward reachability terminates and the safety of the controller is proved. How could we find this new set of failure states ?

Let us look more precisely the fixed point computation. It can be represented as a tree [20]. If $\to = \bigcup_{1 \leq i \leq m} \to_i$ then the proof tree corresponding to forward strategy applied to the safety problem $(Q, \to, I, F)$ is defined as follow. The root is associated to the set I. If the set X is associated to a node is included in the union of the sets associated to the nodes in the upper levels then the node is a leaf (square node). Elsewhere, the node has m children associated respectively to the sets $post_{\to_1}(X), \ldots, post_{\to_m}(X)$.

Figure 2 is the proof tree when we apply backward strategy. Remember that is that case, the computation begins with F instead of I. The tree of Figure 2 leads us to guess that the nontermination of the proof is related to the transition relations $\to_1$ and $\to_3$. Our method consists in substituting $\to_1$ and $\to_3$ by meta-transitions, expecting that it will not create new infinite branches.

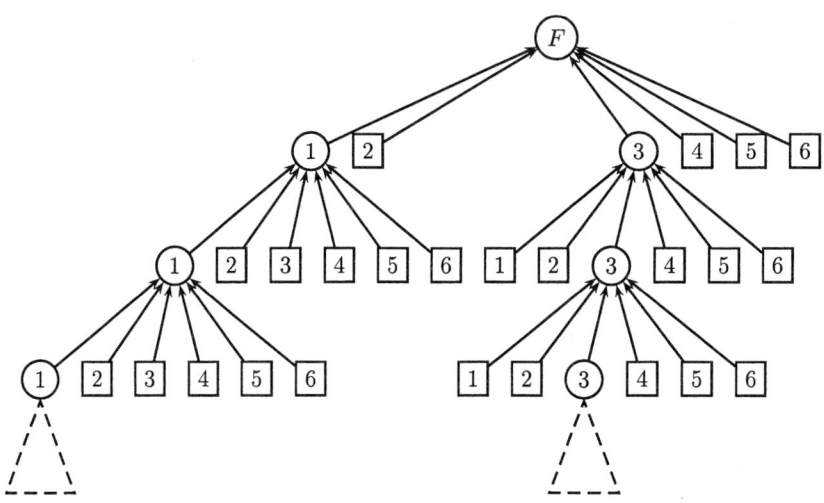

Fig. 2. Proof tree for the train controller

Computing Meta-transitions for Linear Transition Systems with Polynomials

Let us apply our technique to the transition relations $\rightarrow_1$. The relation $\rightarrow_1$ can be represented as follow:

there exists $vp \in \mathbb{R}$ such that
$(v,d) \in \{(x,y) \in \mathbb{R}^2 | vp \geq 0 \text{ and } y - x + amax < 0 \text{ and } x - afu \geq 0\}$

and $\begin{bmatrix} v' \\ d' \end{bmatrix} = \begin{bmatrix} 1 & 0 \\ -1 & 1 \end{bmatrix} \begin{bmatrix} v \\ d \end{bmatrix} + \begin{bmatrix} -afu \\ vp + afu \end{bmatrix}$.

The matrix $\begin{bmatrix} 1 & 0 \\ -1 & 1 \end{bmatrix}$ has only 1 as eigenvalue therefore to simplify the computation of the meta-transition, we can consider that all the variables are real. Proposition 10 implies that to compute an approximation set for backward strategy, we have to compute an approximation in forward strategy.

Step 1: input. To use Heuristic 1, we have to compute a meta-transition for the following transition relation $\leadsto_1$:

$(v, d, vp) \leadsto_1 (v', d', vp')$ id and only if
$(v, d, vp) \in \{(x, y, z) \in \mathbb{R}^3 | z \geq 0 \text{ and } y - x + amax < 0 \text{ and } x - afu \geq 0\}$ and

$\begin{bmatrix} v' \\ d' \\ vp' \end{bmatrix} = \begin{bmatrix} 1 & 0 & 0 \\ -1 & 1 & 1 \\ 0 & 0 & 1 \end{bmatrix} \begin{bmatrix} v \\ d \\ vp \end{bmatrix} + \begin{bmatrix} -afu \\ afu \\ 0 \end{bmatrix}$.

Step 2: guard. To use Proposition 9, we have to compute a meta-transition for the following transition relation $\leadsto_2$:

$(v, d, vp) \leadsto_2 (v', d', vp')$ if and only if

$\begin{bmatrix} v' \\ d' \\ vp' \end{bmatrix} = \begin{bmatrix} 1 & 0 & 0 \\ -1 & 1 & 1 \\ 0 & 0 & 1 \end{bmatrix} \begin{bmatrix} v \\ d \\ vp \end{bmatrix} + \begin{bmatrix} -afu \\ afu \\ 0 \end{bmatrix}$.

Step 3: Jordan form. Using the decomposition of Jordan, we have

$\begin{bmatrix} 1 & 0 & 0 \\ -1 & 1 & 1 \\ 0 & 0 & 1 \end{bmatrix} = \begin{bmatrix} 0 & -1 & 0 \\ 1 & 0 & -1 \\ -1 & 0 & 2 \end{bmatrix}^{-1} \begin{bmatrix} 1 & 1 & 0 \\ 0 & 1 & 0 \\ 0 & 0 & 1 \end{bmatrix} \begin{bmatrix} 0 & -1 & 0 \\ 1 & 0 & -1 \\ -1 & 0 & 2 \end{bmatrix}$.

Therefore, to use Proposition 8, we have to compute an approximation set for the following transition relation $\leadsto_3$:

$(x, y, z) \leadsto_2 (x', y', z')$ if and only if

$\begin{bmatrix} x' \\ y' \\ z' \end{bmatrix} = \begin{bmatrix} 1 & 1 & 0 \\ 0 & 1 & 0 \\ 0 & 0 & 1 \end{bmatrix} \begin{bmatrix} x \\ y \\ z \end{bmatrix} + \begin{bmatrix} 0 & -1 & 0 \\ 1 & 0 & -1 \\ -1 & 0 & 2 \end{bmatrix} \begin{bmatrix} -afu \\ afu \\ 0 \end{bmatrix}$.

Step 4: Jordan matrices. To use Proposition 7, we have to compute approximation sets for the transition relations $\leadsto_4$ and $\leadsto_5$ defined by :

$$(x,y) \leadsto_4 (x',y') \text{ if and only if } \begin{bmatrix} x' \\ y' \end{bmatrix} = \begin{bmatrix} 1 & 1 \\ 0 & 1 \end{bmatrix} \begin{bmatrix} x \\ y \end{bmatrix} + \begin{bmatrix} -afu \\ -afu \end{bmatrix},$$

$$z \leadsto_5 z' \text{ if and only if } z' = z + afu,$$

Step 5: basis cases. Using Proposition 4, an approximation set for $\leadsto_4$ is:

$$\{(n,x,y,x',y') \in \mathrm{R}^5 | x' = x + n \cdot y - \frac{n(n+1)}{2} afu \text{ and } y' = y - n \cdot afu\},$$

and an approximation set for $\leadsto_5$ is:

$$\{(n,z,z') \in \mathrm{R}^3 | z' = z + n \cdot afu\}.$$

Step 6: Jordan matrices. Using Proposition 7, an approximation set for $\leadsto_3$ is:

$$\{(n,x,y,z,x',y',z') \in \mathrm{R}^7 | x' = x + n \cdot y - \frac{n(n+1)}{2} afu \text{ and}$$
$$y' = y - n \cdot afu \text{ and } z' = z + n \cdot afu\}.$$

Step 7: Jordan form. Using Proposition 8, an approximation set for $\leadsto_2$ is:

$$\{(n,v,d,vp,v',d',vp') \in \mathrm{R}^7 | -d' = -d + n(v-vp) - \frac{n(n+1)}{2} afu \text{ and}$$
$$v' - vp' = v - vp - n \cdot afu \text{ and } -v' + 2vp' = -v + 2vp + n \cdot afu\}.$$

This set is equal to the set:

$$\{(n,v,d,vp,v',d',vp') \in \mathrm{R}^7 | d' = d - n \cdot v + n \cdot vp + \frac{n(n+1)}{2} afu \text{ and}$$
$$v' = v - n \cdot afu \text{ and } vp' = vp\}.$$

Step 8: guard. Using Proposition 9, an approximation set for $\leadsto_1$ is:

$$\{(n,v,d,vp,v',d',vp') \in \mathrm{R}^7 | d' = d \text{ and } v' = v \text{ and } vp' = vp\} \cup$$
$$\{(n,v,d,vp,v',d',vp') \in \mathrm{R}^7 | n \geq 1 \text{ and } vp \geq 0 \text{ and } d - v + amax < 0 \text{ and}$$
$$v - afu \geq 0 \text{ and } d' = d - n \cdot v + n \cdot vp + \frac{n(n+1)}{2} afu \text{ and}$$
$$v' = v - n \cdot afu \text{ and } vp' = vp\}.$$

Step 9: input. Using Heuristic 1, a candidate set as approximation set for $\to$ is :

$$\{(n, v, d, v', d') \in \mathbb{R}^5 | d' = d \text{ and } v' = v\} \cup$$
$$\{(n, v, d, v', d') \in \mathbb{R}^5 | \text{ there exists } vp \in \mathbb{R} \text{ such that }$$
$$n \geq 1 \land vp \geq 0 \text{ and } d - v + amax < 0 \text{ and } v - afu \geq 0 \text{ and }$$
$$d' = d - nv + nvp + \frac{n(n+1)}{2} afu \text{ and } v' = v - nafu \text{ and } vp' = vp\}.$$

Step 10: meta-transition. The meta-transition for the transition relation $\to_1$ is :

$$=_{\mathbb{R}^2} \cup \{(v, d, v', d') \in \mathbb{R}^4 | \text{ there exists } vp \in \mathbb{R} \text{ and } n \in \mathbb{R} \text{ such that }$$
$$n \geq 1 \land vp \geq 0 \text{ and } d - v + amax < 0 \text{ and } v - afu \geq 0 \text{ and }$$
$$d' = d - nv + nvp + \frac{n(n+1)}{2} afu \text{ and } v' = v - nafu \text{ and } vp' = vp\}.$$

Using quantifier elimination over real polynomial formulas, the meta-transition $\to_{1'}$ is:

$(v, d) \to_{1'} (v', d')$ if and only if
$$(v' = v \text{ and } d' = d)$$
or
$(d - v + amax < 0 \text{ and } v - afu \geq 0 \text{ and } afu' = afu \text{ and } amax' = amax)$.

Applying our algorithm to the transition relation $\to_3$, we get the following meta-transition $\to_{3'}$:

$(v, d) \to_{3'} (v', d')$ if and only if
$$(v' = v \text{ and } d' = d)$$
or
$(v + amax - afu < 0 \text{ and } v - afu \geq 0 \text{ and } afu' = afu \text{ and } amax' = amax)$.

We can now apply the backward reachability algorithm to the following input of the safety problem:

$$(\mathbb{R}^2, \to_{1'} \cup \to_2 \cup \to_{3'} \cup \to_4 \cup \to_5 \cup \to_6, I, F).$$

The corresponding proof tree is in Figure 3. The tree is finite and none of the states that can reach a failure state are initial states. Therefore the correctness of the controller is proved.

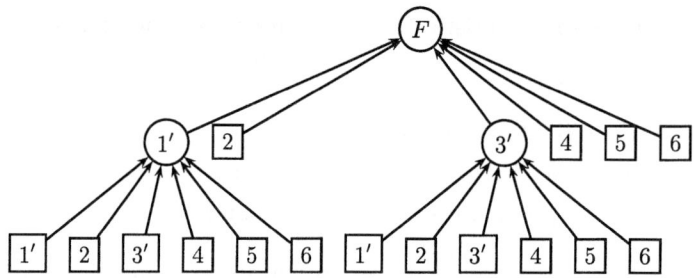

Fig. 3. Proof tree with meta-transitions

6 Conclusion

We have proposed a construction of meta-transitions for complex polynomial transition relations. Our approach takes into considerations of the asymptotic behavior of the dynamic system depending on the eigenvalues and the dimension of the characteristic space associated. Compared to previous works, we improve the class of transition relations for which we can construct a meta-transition. Finally, we use polynomials to represent these meta-transitions.

We are about to improve this work in two directions. Firstly, using a similar approach, we can construct linear meta-transitions that would be easier to use but will product less precise approximations. Secondly, we can handle also linear differential systems: the solution of the differential equation $\dot{x}(t) = Ax(t) + b$ is $x(t) = \exp^{At} x(0) + \int_0^t e^{(t-s)A} b \, ds$. It could be proved that the approximation set E associated to the transition relation $x \to y$ if and only if $y = \exp^A x(0) + \int_0^1 e^{(t-s)A} b ds$ verifies $x(t) \in E(t, x(0))$. Hence, our approach could be directly apply to continuous transition relations as those used in hybrid automaton.

References

1. Halbwachs, N.: Synchronous Programming of Reactive Systems. Kluwer Academic Press, Netherlands (1993)
2. Caspi, P., Pilaud, D., Halbwachs, N., Plaice, J.A.: LUSTRE: A declarative language for programming synchronous systems. In: Proceedings of the 14th ACM Symposium on Principles of Programming Languages, New York, NY, ACM (1987)
3. Benveniste, A., LeGuernic, P.: Hybrid dynamical systems theory and the SIGNAL language. IEEE Transactions on Automatic Control **35** (1990) 535–546
4. Henzinger, T.A.: The theory of hybrid automata. In: Proceedings, 11th Annual IEEE Symposium on Logic in Computer Science, New Brunswick, New Jersey, IEEE Computer Society Press (1996) 278–292
5. Clarke, E.M., Grumberg, O., Peled, D.A.: Model Checking. The MIT Press, Cambridge, Massachusetts (1999)
6. Queille, J.P.P., Sifakis, J.: Fairness and related properties in transition systems: a temporal logic to deal with fairness. Acta Informatica **19** (1983) 195–220

7. Emerson, E.A.: Temporal and modal logic. In van Leeuwen, J., ed.: Handbook of Theoretical Computer Science, Volume B: Formal Models and Semantics. Elsevier Science Publishers, Amsterdam, The Netherlands (1990) 995–1072
8. Halbwachs, N., Lagnier, F., Raymond., P.: Synchronous observers and the verification of reactive systems. In Univ. Twente; Enschede, N., ed.: Proceedings of Third International Conference on Algebraic Methodology and Software Technology, AMAST. (1993) 131–44
9. Bensalem, S., Lakhnech, Y., Owre, S.: Computing abstractions of infinite state systems compositionally and automatically. In: Proc. 10th International Computer Aided Verification Conference. (1998) 319–331
10. Cousot, P., Cousot, R.: Comparing the Galois Connection and Widening/ Narrowing Approaches to Abstract Interpretation. In: PLILP'92. Volume 631 of LNCS. Springer-Verlag (1992) 269–295
11. Delzanno, G., Podelski, A.: Model checking in CLP. Lecture Notes in Computer Science **1579** (1999) 223–239
12. Henzinger, T.A., Rusu, V.: Reachability verification for hybrid automata. In Henzinger, T.A., Sastry, S., eds.: Hybrid Systems: Computation and Control (First International Workshop, HSCC'98). Volume 1386 of Lecture Notes in Computer Science., Berkeley, CA, Springer-Verlag (1998) 190–204
13. Boigelot, B.: Symbolic Method for Exploring Infinite State Spaces. PhD thesis, Université de Liège (1997–1998)
14. Bardin, S., Finkel, A., Leroux, J., Petrucci, L.: FAST: Fast Acceleration of Symbolic Transition systems. In: Proc. 15th Int. Conf. Computer Aided Verification (CAV'2003), Boulder, CO, USA, July 2003. Volume 2725 of Lecture Notes in Computer Science., Springer (2003)
15. Tiwari, A.: Approximate reachability for linear systems. In Maler, O., Pnuelu, A., eds.: Hybrid Systems: Computation and Control HSCC. LNCS, Springer (2003)
16. Ireland, A., Bundy, A.: Extensions to a generalization critic for inductive proof. In McRobbie, M.A., Slaney, J.K., eds.: Proceedings of the Thirteenth International Conference on Automated Deduction (CADE-96). Volume 1104 of LNAI., Berlin, Springer (1996) 47–61
17. Schrijver, A.: Theory of Linear and Integer Programming. John Wiley and Sons, New York (1987)
18. Bensalem, S., Caspi, P., Parent-Vigouroux, C., Dumas, C.: A methodology for proving control systems with Lustre and PVS. In Weinstock, C.B., Rushby, J., eds.: Dependable Computing for Critical Applications—7. Volume 12 of Dependable Computing and Fault Tolerant Systems., San Jose, CA, IEEE Computer Society Press (1999) 89–107
19. Dumas, C.: Méthodes déductives pour la preuve de programmes LUSTRE. PhD thesis, Université Joseph Fourier – Grenoble 1 (2002)
20. Maidl, M.: A unifying model checking approach for safety properties of parameterized systems. In: CAV 2001. Volume 2102 of LNCS. (2001) 311–323

Translation-Based Compositional Reasoning for Software Systems*

Fei Xie[1], James C. Browne[1], and Robert P. Kurshan[2]

[1] Dept. of Computer Sciences, Univ. of Texas at Austin, Austin, TX 78712, USA
{feixie,browne}@cs.utexas.edu, Fax: +1 (512) 471-8885
[2] Cadence Design Systems, 35 Spring St., New Providence, NJ 07974, USA,
rkurshan@cadence.com, Fax: +1 (908) 898-1435

Abstract. Software systems are often model checked by translating them into a directly model-checkable formalism. Any serious software system requires application of compositional reasoning to overcome the computational complexity of model checking. This paper presents Translation-Based Compositional Reasoning (TBCR), an approach to application of compositional reasoning in the context of model checking software systems through model translation. In this approach, given a translation from a software semantics to a directly model-checkable formal semantics, a compositional reasoning rule is established in the software semantics and mapped to an equivalent rule in the formal semantics based on the translation. The correctness proof of the composition reasoning rule in the software semantics is established based on this mapping and the correctness proof of the equivalent rule in the formal semantics. The compositional reasoning rule in the software semantics is implemented and applied based on the translation from the software semantics to the formal semantics and reusing the implementation of the equivalent rule in the formal semantics. TBCR has been realized for a commonly used software semantics, the Asynchronous Interleaving Message-passing semantics. TBCR is illustrated by two applications of this realization.

Keywords. Translation-based compositional reasoning, model checking, compositional reasoning, model translation

1 Introduction and Overview

Model checking [1–3] has major potential for improving reliability of software systems. Model checking is often applied to software systems by translating them into a model-checkable formalism to avoid the difficulty and labor of developing special-purpose model checkers.

On account of the intrinsic computational complexity of model checking, we need to support compositional reasoning [4–9] where model checking a property on a system is accomplished by decomposing the system into components, checking component properties locally on the components, and deriving the property of the system from the component properties. Application of compositional reasoning to software systems requires establishing a compositional reasoning rule in the semantics of these systems,

---
* This research was partially supported by NSF grant 010-3725.

proving the correctness of the rule, and implementing the rule. A rule is implemented when methods have been provided for discharging its premises which are usually verification of component properties, validity check of possible circular dependencies among component properties, and derivation of a system property from component properties.

Directly proving the correctness of compositional reasoning rules for software systems is often difficult. Software systems are usually modeled in specification languages such as Executable UML [10] and SDL [11], or coded in programming languages such as Java and C/C++. These languages are sufficiently complicated in syntax and semantics so that it is very difficult (if not infeasible) to directly prove for these languages that a compositional reasoning rule is sound. Additionally, such a language often has varying operational semantics. A formal semantics is only formulated for software systems specified in this language when these systems are to be translated into a model-checkable formalism and verified. On the other hand, proof and implementation of compositional reasoning rules for directly model-checkable formal semantics such as the semantics of Promela [12], SMV [13], and S/R [14] is often easier due to the formality and simplicity of these semantics. It is often the case that a set of compositional reasoning rules have already been proven and implemented for these semantics.

This paper defines, describes, and illustrates Translation-Based Compositional Reasoning (TBCR), an approach to application of compositional reasoning in the context of model checking software systems through model translation. This approach has two phases: (i) establishment of compositional reasoning rules in the semantics of software systems and correctness proof of the rules; (ii) application of the proven rules in model checking software systems. Given a translation from a software semantics to a directly model-checkable formal semantics, a compositional reasoning rule in the software semantics is established and proven for correctness as follows:

- The compositional reasoning rule is defined in the software semantics.
- The rule in the software semantics is mapped to an equivalent rule in the formal semantics based on the translation.
- The correctness proof of the rule is established based on the above mapping and on the correctness proof of the equivalent rule in the formal semantics.

Given a software system and a property to be checked on the system, the proven compositional reasoning rule in the software semantics is then applied as follows:

- The system is decomposed into components on the software semantics level.
- Premises of the rule are formulated in the software semantics. These premises are discharged by translating them to their counterparts in the formal semantics and discharging their counterparts in the formal semantics through reusing the implementation of the equivalent rule in the formal semantics.
- If these premises are successfully discharged, then it can be concluded on the software semantics level that the system has the property to be checked.

There has been a large body of research [4–9] (surveyed in [9]) on compositional reasoning in the formal methods community, which mostly focuses on developing compositional reasoning rules and proving their correctness. Our research, instead, focuses on effective application of compositional reasoning to software systems in the context of model checking these systems via model translation. Rationales for our approach are:

- Software systems, to be model checked, usually have to be translated into a directly model-checkable formalism.
- Formulation of and reasoning about the properties of software systems and their components are more naturally accomplished in the software semantics.
- Compositional reasoning rules have already been established, proven, and implemented for several directly model-checkable formalisms.

We have realized TBCR for a commonly used software semantics, the Asynchronous Interleaving Message-passing (AIM) semantics. In this realization, compositional reasoning rules in the AIM semantics are proven, implemented, and applied in the context of a translation from the AIM semantics to the ω-automaton semantics [15] using the I/O-automaton semantics [16] as an intermediate semantics. (We choose I/O-automata as the intermediate semantics to reuse a translation from the I/O-automaton semantics to the ω-automaton semantics, established by Kurshan, Merritt, Orda, and Sachs [17].) This realization has been applied in an integrated state space reduction framework [18] and in model checking of component-based software systems [19].

The balance of this paper is organized as follows. In Section 2, we give the preliminaries of the I/O-automaton semantics and the ω-automaton semantics. A realization of TBCR for the AIM semantics is defined and described in detail in Section 3. Two applications of the realization of TBCR for the AIM semantics and their case studies are presented in Section 4. We conclude in Section 5.

2 Preliminaries

2.1 I/O-Automaton Semantics

The following definitions for I/O-automaton are from [17].

Definition 1. *An I/O automaton A is a quintuple $(\Sigma^A, S^A, I^A, \delta^A, R^A)$ where:*

- *the signature Σ^A is a triple $\Sigma^A = (\Sigma^A_{IN}, \Sigma^A_{OUT}, \Sigma^A_{INT})$, where Σ^A_{IN}, Σ^A_{OUT}, Σ^A_{INT} are pairwise disjoint finite sets of elements, called input, output, internal actions, respectively. We denote by $\Sigma^A_{EXT} = \Sigma^A_{IN} \cup \Sigma^A_{OUT}$ the set of external actions, by $\Sigma^A_{LOC} = \Sigma^A_{OUT} \cup \Sigma^A_{INT}$ the set of local actions, and we abuse notation, denoting by Σ^A also the set of all actions $\Sigma^A_{LOC} \cup \Sigma^A_{IN}$;*
- *S^A is a finite set of states;*
- *$I^A \subset S^A$ is a set of initial states;*
- *$\delta^A \subset S^A \times \Sigma^A \times S^A$ is a transition relation which is complete in the sense that for all $a \in \Sigma^A_{IN}$, $s \in S^A$ there exists $s' \in S^A$ with $(s, a, s') \in \delta^A$. For $a \in \Sigma^A_{LOC}$ and $s, s' \in S^A$ such that $(s, a, s') \in \delta^A$, we say that a is enabled at s and enables the transition (s, s'); Each element of δ^A is called a step of A;*
- *R^A is a partition of Σ^A_{LOC}, each element of which is termed a fairness constraint of A.*

Definition 2. *An execution of A is a finite string or infinite sequence of state-action pairs $((s_1, a_1), (s_2, a_2), \ldots)$, where $s_1 \in I^A$ and for all i, $s_i \in S^A$, $a_i \in \Sigma^A$ and $(s_i, a_i, s_{i+1}) \in \delta^A$.*

Definition 3. *An execution* $\mathbf{x}$ *of A is fair if, for all $C \in R^A$:*

- *if $\mathbf{x}$ is finite then no action in C is enabled in the final state in $\mathbf{x}$;*
- *if $\mathbf{x}$ is infinite then either some action in C occurs infinitely often in x or else infinitely many states in $\mathbf{x}$ have no enabled action which is in C.*

Definition 4. *Given a set $\triangle \subset \Sigma^A$, the projection of an execution $\mathbf{x}= ((s_i, a_i))$ of A onto $\triangle$, denoted by $\Pi_\triangle(\mathbf{x})$, is the subsequence of actions obtained by removing from the action sequence (a_i) all actions $a_i \notin \triangle$.*

Definition 5. *A behavior of A is the projection of a fair execution of A on the set Σ^A_{EXT} (i.e., the fair execution, with states and internal actions removed). The language $\mathcal{L}(A)$ of A is the set of all behaviors of A.*

Definition 6. *Of two I/O automata A and B, we say that A implements B (denoted by $A \leq B$) if, for $\triangle = \Sigma^A_{EXT} \cap \Sigma^B_{EXT}$, $\triangle \neq \emptyset$, $\Pi_\triangle(\mathcal{L}(A)) \subset \Pi_\triangle(\mathcal{L}(B))$.*

Definition 7. *For I/O automata $A_1, A_2, \ldots, A_k$, with respective pairwise disjoint sets of local actions, their parallel composition, denoted by $A_1 \| A_2 \| \ldots \| A_k$, is an I/O automaton A defined as follows. The set of internal actions of A is the union of the respective sets of internal actions of the component automata, and likewise for the output actions; the input actions of A are the remaining actions of the components not thus accounted for. The set of states of A, S^A, is the Cartesian product of the component state sets, likewise for the initial states I^A. The transition relation δ^A is defined as follows: for $s = (s_1, \ldots, s_k)$, $s' = (s'_1, \ldots, s'_k)$ and $a \in \Sigma^A$, $(s, a, s') \in \delta^A$ if and only if for all $i = 1, \ldots, k$, $(s_i, a, s'_i) \in \delta^{A^i}$ or $a \notin \Sigma^{A^i}$ and $s'_i = s_i$. R_A is the union of the fairness partitions of the respective components.*

2.2 ω-Automaton Semantics

We use the L-process model of ω-automaton semantics. Detailed specification of this model can be found in [15]. The concepts essential for understanding this paper are given below for the convenience of the reader.

Definition 8. *For an L-process, ω, its language, $\mathcal{L}(\omega)$, is the set of all infinite sequences accepted by ω.*

Definition 9. *For L-processes, $\omega_1, \ldots, \omega_n$, their synchronous parallel composition, $\omega = \omega_1 \otimes \ldots \otimes \omega_n$, is also an L-process and $\mathcal{L}(\omega) = \cap \mathcal{L}(\omega_i)$.*

Definition 10. *For L-processes, $\omega_1, \ldots, \omega_n$, their Cartesian sum, $\omega = \omega_1 \oplus \ldots \oplus \omega_n$, is also an L-process and $\mathcal{L}(\omega) = \cup \mathcal{L}(\omega_i)$.*

For a language, $\mathcal{L}$, let $\mathcal{CL}(\mathcal{L})$ denote the safety closure [20] of $\mathcal{L}$.[1]

---

[1] For a language $\mathcal{L}$ of sequences over a set of variables, V, the safety closure of $\mathcal{L}$, denoted by $\mathcal{CL}(\mathcal{L})$, is defined as the set of sequences over V where $x \in \mathcal{CL}(\mathcal{L})$ if and only if for all $j < |x|$ there exists y such that $x[0..j] : y$ belongs to $\mathcal{L}$ [8]. ($|x|$ denotes the length of x and $x : y$ denotes the concatenation of x and y where x and y are sequences over V.) In [15], $\mathcal{CL}(\mathcal{L})$ is termed as the smallest limit prefix-closed language that contains $\mathcal{L}$.

Definition 11. *The safety closure $CL^\omega(\omega)$ of an L-process ω is an L-process whose language is the safety closure of the language of ω, $\mathcal{L}(CL^\omega(\omega)) = \mathcal{CL}(\mathcal{L}(\omega))$.*

Given an L-process ω, $CL^\omega(\omega)$ can be derived from ω by computing the Strong Connected Components (SCCs) of the state graph of ω and for each SCC with an accepting state, marking every state of that SCC as accepting.

Under the ω-automaton semantics, model checking is reduced to checking L-process language containment. Suppose a system is modeled by the composition $\omega_1 \otimes \ldots \otimes \omega_n$ of L-processes, $\omega_1, \ldots, \omega_n$, and a property to be checked on the system is modeled by an L-processes, ω. The property holds on the system if and only if the language of $\omega_1 \otimes \ldots \otimes \omega_n$ is contained by the language of ω, $\mathcal{L}(\omega_1 \otimes \ldots \otimes \omega_n) \subset \mathcal{L}(\omega)$.

Definition 12. *Given two L-processes ω_1 and ω_2, ω_1 implements ω_2 (denoted by $\omega_1 \preceq \omega_2$) if $\mathcal{L}(\omega_1) \subset \mathcal{L}(\omega_2)$.*

3 Realization of TBCR for AIM Semantics

This section presents how TBCR is realized for the AIM semantics. First, we informally describe the AIM semantics. Then, we formalize the AIM semantics, which enables the establishment, correctness proof, implementation, and application of compositional reasoning rules. After that, we describe how a compositional reasoning rule for the AIM semantics is established. Then, we prove this rule based on a translation from the AIM semantics to the ω-automaton semantics using the I/O-automaton semantics as an intermediate semantics. Finally, we present the implementation of this rule through the translation from the AIM semantics to the ω-automaton semantics.

3.1 Informal Description of AIM Semantics

Under the AIM semantics, a system is a composition of processes that interact asynchronously via message-passing. Every process has a private message queue and locally defined variables. Behaviors of a process are captured by an extended Moore state model and each state in the state model may have an associated state action that is composed from executable statements such as an assignment statement, a messaging statement, and an "if" statement. At any given moment of a system execution, there is exactly one process that is executing either a state action or a state transition in a run-to-completion fashion.

3.2 Formalization of AIM Semantics

A state in the extended Moore state model of an AIM process represents a set of states in the state space of the process. A state action in the extended Moore state model represents multiple sequences of state transitions in the state transition structure of the process. To formally represent the extended Moore state model, we introduce a variable, *pc*, whose current value captures the current state in the Moore state model and the current position in the state action associated with the state. The message queue of the process is also formally represented by a variable, *queue*, whose domain includes all possible message permutations that may appear in the queue. Under this representation of message queues, the execution of a messaging statement in a process modifies the *queue* variable of the receiver process. With the above representations, we formally define an AIM process.

Definition 13. *An AIM process, P, is a six-tuple, (S, I, M, E, T, F), where:*

- *S, the state space of P, is the Cartesian product of the domains of the variables defined in the process and the two additional variables, pc and queue.*
- *I is a set of initial states.*
- *M is a messaging interface which is a pair, (M^i, M^o), where M^i is the set of messages that P inputs and M^o is the set of messages that P outputs.*
- *E is a set of events each of which is a state transition of the Moore state model, or an executable statement (such as an assignment statement, a messaging statement sending a message defined in M^o, or an "if" statement), or a reception of a message defined in M^i. E_{LOC} is a subset of E including all state transitions and executable statements in E. E_{EXT} is a subset of E including all messaging statements and message receptions in E.*
- *T is a set of state transitions defined on S and E, each of which is of the form, (s, e, s'), where s, s' ∈ S and e ∈ E.*
- *F is a partition of E_{LOC}. Each element of F is termed a fairness constraint.*

Definition 14. *An execution of P is a finite string or an infinite sequence of state-event pairs $((s_0, e_0), (s_1, e_1), \ldots)$ which conforms to the run-to-completion requirement (i.e., the action statements from a state action appear adjacently in the execution), where $s_0 \in I$ and for all i, $s_i \in S$, $e_i \in E$ and $(s_i, e_i, s_{i+1}) \in T$. Fair executions of P are defined analogously to fair executions of an I/O-automaton.*

Definition 15. *A behavior of P is the projection of a fair execution of P on E_{EXT} of P. The language of S, $\mathcal{L}(S)$, is the set of all behaviors of S.*

Definition 16. *Given two AIM processes P and Q, P implements Q (denoted by $P \models Q$) if for $\triangle = E_{EXT}(P) \cap E_{EXT}(Q)$ and $\triangle \neq \emptyset$, $\Pi_\triangle(\mathcal{L}(P)) \subset \Pi_\triangle(\mathcal{L}(Q))$.*

Definition 17. *The interleaving composition of a finite set of interacting AIM processes, $P_0, P_1, \ldots$, and P_n, denoted by $P_0[]P_1[]\ldots[]P_n$, is an AIM process, P, derived as follows. S is the Cartesian product of $S_0, S_1, \ldots$, and S_n. I is the Cartesian product of $I_0, I_1, \ldots$, and I_n. M^i includes the remaining messages in $M_0^i, M_1^i, \ldots$, and M_n^i that are not accounted for in the composition, and M^o is the union of $M_0^o, M_1^o, \ldots$, and M_n^o. E is the union of $E_0, E_1, \ldots$, and E_n. T is defined as follows: for $s = (s_0, s_1, \ldots, s_n)$, $s' = (s_0', s_1', \ldots, s_n')$, and $e \in E$, $(s, e, s') \in T$ if and only if for all $i \in [0, n]$, $e \in E_i$ and (s_i, e, s_i') or $e \notin E_i$ and $s_i' = s_i$. F is the union of the fairness partitions of the respective components.*

In this formalized AIM semantics, a system, components of the system, and properties of the system and the components are all represented by processes.

3.3 Establishment of Compositional Reasoning Rules

We establish compositional reasoning rules for the AIM semantics by porting existing rules in directly model-checkable formal semantics to the AIM semantics. We have ported to the AIM semantics two rules that have already been established, proven, and implemented in the ω-automaton semantics, the rule proposed by Amla, Emerson, Namjoshi, and Trefler in [8], *Rule 1*, and the rule proposed by McMillan in [7]. Below we show how *Rule 1* is ported to the AIM semantics.

Rule 1 *For AIM processes P_1, P_2, and Q, to show that $P_1[]P_2 \models Q$, find AIM processes Q_1 and Q_2 such that the following conditions are satisfied.*

C1: $P_1[]Q_2 \models Q_1$ and $P_2[]Q_1 \models Q_2$
C2: $Q_1[]Q_2 \models Q$
C3: *Either* $P_1[]CL^P(Q) \models (Q+Q_1+Q_2)$ *or* $P_2[]CL^P(Q) \models (Q+Q_1+Q_2)$

Let $P_1[]P_2$ denote a system composed from two components, P_1 and P_2. Q is a property to be checked on the system. Q_1 and Q_2 are properties of P_1 and P_2, respectively. Condition C1 checks if P_1 has the property, Q_1, assuming Q_2 holds on P_2, and if P_2 has the property, Q_2, assuming Q_1 holds on P_1. Condition C2 checks if Q can be derived from Q_1 and Q_2. Condition C3 conducts the validity check of circular dependencies between Q_1 and Q_2. (The counterpart of Rule 1 in the ω-automaton semantics, denoted by *Rule 1^ω*, is of the same form but with processes, $\models$, $[]$, CL^P, and + replaced by their ω-automaton counterparts.)

To port compositional reasoning rules to the AIM semantics, additional semantics concepts may need to be introduced for the AIM semantics. In the case of Rule 1, the concepts of safety closure of an AIM process and sum of AIM processes were defined:

Definition 18. *For an AIM process, Q, the safety closure of Q, $CL^P(Q)$, is an AIM process whose language is the safety closure [20] of the language of Q, $\mathcal{L}(CL^P(Q)) = \mathcal{CL}(\mathcal{L}(Q))$. ($CL^P(Q)$ can be derived from Q by removing the fairness constraints of Q.)*

Definition 19. *The Cartesian sum of AIM processes P and Q, denoted by $P+Q$, is the AIM process that behaves either as P or as Q and with the property of $\mathcal{L}(P+Q) = \mathcal{L}(P) \cup \mathcal{L}(Q)$.*

3.4 Proof via Semantics Translation

We first establish a translation from the AIM semantics to the ω-automaton semantics and then prove the soundness of Rule 1 based on the translation and the soundness proof of Rule 1^ω. To establish the translation from the AIM semantics to the ω-automaton semantics, we use the I/O-automaton semantics as an intermediate semantics.

Translation of AIM Processes to I/O-Automata. An AIM process, P, is translated to an I/O-automaton, A, through a two-step procedure. The first step maps semantic constructs of P to semantic constructs of A and the second step implements the run-to-completion requirement in A.

Step 1: Mapping semantic constructs

- The state space and the initial state set of P are mapped to the state space and the initial state set of A correspondingly, which is achieved by mapping the variables of P to the corresponding variables of A. (Note that the state space of an I/O automaton is also encoded by the domains of its variables.)
- Events of P are translated to actions of A as follows:
  - A state transition in the extended Moore state model of P is mapped to an internal action of A that simulates the state transition by modifying the variables, pc and $queue$, accordingly.
  - An assignment statement is mapped to an internal action that modifies the variable to be assigned by the assignment and the variable, pc.
  - An "if" statement is mapped to an internal action that modifies the variable, pc, to reflect the decision made in the "if" statement.
  - A messaging statement is mapped to an output action that is also an input action of the I/O-automaton corresponding to the receiver.
  - A message reception is mapped to an input action that modifies the variable, $queue$, and is also an output action of the sender I/O-automaton.
- Messages in the input (or output, respectively) interface of P are mapped to input (or output) actions of A.
- A state transition, (s_P, e_P, s'_P), of P is mapped to a state transition, (s_A, a_A, s'_A), of A where s_A, a_A, and s'_A are the corresponding translations of s_P, e_P, and s'_P as described above.

Step 2: Implementing run-to-completion requirement

- The I/O-automaton, A, resulting from Step 1 is extended with an additional boolean variable, RtC, and two output actions, $Enter$ and $Leave$. The $Enter$ action cannot be enabled unless the value of RtC is false.
- When A is composed with A', the I/O-automaton translation of another AIM process, P', the $Enter$ and $Leave$ actions of A are included by A' as input actions and vice versa.
- The transition relation of A is extended so that before A executes the first I/O-automaton action in the sequence of I/O-automaton actions corresponding to a state action of P, A executes the $Enter$ action and after A executes the last I/O-automaton action in the sequence of I/O-automaton actions corresponding to a state action of P, A executes the $Leave$ action. (A' is extended in the same way.)
- The transition relation of A' is extended so that as A executes the $Enter$ action, A' sets its RtC to true and as A executes the $Leave$ action, A' sets its RtC to false and vice versa.

Therefore, when a set of I/O-automata translated from AIM processes are ready to execute their $Enter$ actions, only one of them can proceed, execute its $Enter$ action, and get into the run-to-completion section. The automaton signals its leaving the run-to-completion section by executing its $Leave$ action. We refer to the translation from an AIM process to its corresponding I/O-automaton as T_A^P.

Theorem 1. *Given an AIM process, $P = P_1[] \ldots []P_n$, and its I/O automaton translation, $A = T_A^P(P_1)|| \ldots ||T_A^P(P_n)$, for $\triangle = \Sigma_P^A$ where Σ_P^A is the set of external actions of A excluding all Enter and Leave actions and $\triangle \neq \emptyset$, $\mathcal{L}(P) = \Pi_\triangle \mathcal{L}(A)$.*

Proof of Theorem 1: By the construction of A from P, $\mathcal{L}(P) = \Pi_\triangle \mathcal{L}(A)$. □

Translation of AIM Processes to ω-Automata. Kurshan, Merritt, Orda, and Sachs [17] have established a translation from I/O-automata to ω-automata, T_ω^A, and also proved that the translation is linear-monotone with respect to language containment (shown in Theorem 2).

Theorem 2. *For two I/O-automata, $A = A_1|| \ldots ||A_m$ and $B = B_1|| \ldots ||B_n$, $A \leq B \iff \mathcal{L}(T_\omega^A(A_1)) \otimes \ldots \otimes \mathcal{L}(T_\omega^A(A_m)) \subset \mathcal{L}(T_\omega^A(B_1)) \otimes \ldots \otimes \mathcal{L}(T_\omega^A(B_n))$.*

Based on the translation from AIM processes to I/O-automata, T_A^P, and the translation from I/O-automata to ω-automata, T_ω^A, we constructed a translation from AIM processes to ω-automata, T_ω^P. For a given AIM process, P,

- P is first translated to an I/O-automaton $T_A^P(P)$;
- $T_A^P(P)$ is then translated to an ω-automaton $T_\omega^A(T_A^P(P))$.

We demonstrate with Theorem 3 that T_ω^P is also linear-monotone with respect to language containment.

Theorem 3. *For two AIM processes, $P = P_1[] \ldots []P_m$ and $Q = Q_1[] \ldots []Q_n$, $P \models Q \iff \mathcal{L}(T_\omega^P(P_1) \otimes \ldots T_\omega^P(P_m)) \subset \mathcal{L}(T_\omega^P(Q_1) \otimes \ldots T_\omega^P(Q_n))$.*

Proof of Theorem 3: Follows directly from Theorem 1 and Theorem 2. □

Lemma 1. *For an AIM process P, $CL^\omega(T_\omega^P(P)) \preceq T_\omega^P(CL^P(P))$.*

Proof of Lemma 1:

$\Rightarrow$ {Definition 18, Definition 16}
$\quad P \models CL^P(P)$
$\Rightarrow$ {Theorem 3}
$\quad \mathcal{L}(T_\omega^P(P)) \subset \mathcal{L}(T_\omega^P(CL^P(P)))$
$\Rightarrow$ {Monotonicity of language closure}
$\quad \mathcal{CL}(\mathcal{L}(T_\omega^P(P))) \subset \mathcal{CL}(\mathcal{L}(T_\omega^P(CL^P(P))))$
$\Rightarrow$ {Definition 11}
$\quad \mathcal{L}(CL^\omega(T_\omega^P(P))) \subset \mathcal{CL}(\mathcal{L}(T_\omega^P(CL^P(P))))$
$\Rightarrow$ {A safety property is the safety closure of itself.}
$\quad \mathcal{L}(CL^\omega(T_\omega^P(P))) \subset \mathcal{L}(T_\omega^P(CL^P(P)))$
$\Rightarrow$ {Definition 12}
$\quad CL^\omega(T_\omega^P(P)) \preceq T_\omega^P(CL^P(P))$

□

Lemma 2. *For AIM processes* $P_1, \ldots, P_n$, $T_\omega^P(P_1 + \ldots + P_n) \preceq T_\omega^P(P_1) \oplus \ldots \oplus T_\omega^P(P_n)$.

Proof of Lemma 2: Follows directly from Definition 19, Theorem 3, Definition 10, and Definition 12. □

Theorem 4. *Rule 1 is sound for arbitrary AIM processes*, P_1, P_2, *and* Q.

Proof Sketch of Theorem 4: Suppose Conditions C1, C2, and C3 hold on P_1, P_2, and Q. Due to Theorem 3, Lemma 1, and Lemma 2, the counterparts of Conditions C1, C2, and C3 in the ω-automaton semantics hold on $T_\omega^P(P_1)$, $T_\omega^P(P_2)$, and $T_\omega^P(Q)$. Therefore, by Rule 1^ω (the counterpart of Rule 1 in the ω-automaton semantics), $T_\omega^P(P_1) \otimes T_\omega^P(P_2) \preceq T_\omega^P(Q)$. By Theorem 3, we conclude that $P_1 [] P_2 \models Q$. (Detailed proof of this theorem can be found in the appendix.) □

3.5 Implementation and Application of Rule 1 through Model Translation

TBCR suggests that a compositional reasoning rule in the AIM semantics be implemented based on the translation from the AIM semantics to the ω-automaton semantics and by reusing the implementation of its equivalent rule in the ω-automaton semantics. We first introduce an implementation of the AIM-to-ω-automaton translation and an implementation of Rule 1^ω (the ω-automaton semantics counterpart of Rule 1) in the ω-automaton semantics. We then discuss how Rule 1 is implemented and applied.

Translation from xUML to S/R. xUML [10] is an executable dialect of UML whose semantics conforms to the AIM semantics given in this paper. S/R [14] is an automaton language whose semantics conforms to the ω-automaton semantics. In previous research [18][21], we have implemented a translator from xUML to S/R. Given a system modeled in xUML and a property specified in an xUML level logic, the design and the property are translated to an S/R model and an S/R query. The S/R query is checked on the S/R model by the COSPAN [14] model checker. The property holds on the system if and only if the S/R query is successfully verified on the S/R model. As shown in Figure 1, the xUML-to-S/R translation syntactically translates an xUML model into S/R, which also implements the semantics mapping from the AIM semantics to the ω-automaton semantics.

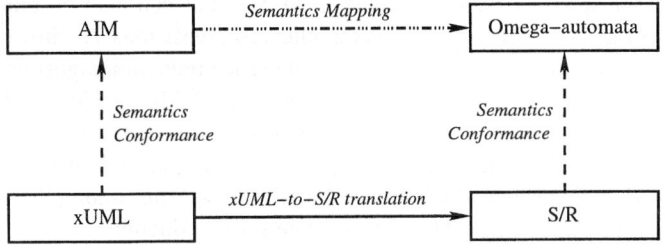

Fig. 1. xUML-to-S/R translation implements semantics mapping from AIM to ω-automata.

Existing Implementation of Rule 1^ω in S/R. Rule 1^ω has been implemented in S/R [8]. Since in S/R, systems, components, assumptions, and properties are all modeled as ω-automata which can be trivially composed, verification of component properties (Condition C1) and derivation of a system property from component properties (Condition C2) are discharged in the same way as a property is checked on a system. Validation of circular dependencies (Condition C3) additionally requires construction of the safety closure of an ω-automaton (which has been discussed in Section 2.2).

Implementation and Application of Rule 1 in xUML. The xUML-to-S/R translator requires that an xUML model to be translated specify a closed system. To support Rule 1, the translator is extended to allow a closed system formed by a component of a system and its assumptions on the rest of the system (i.e. properties that the component assumes the rest of the system to have). The extension is simplified by the fact that in S/R, systems, components, assumptions, and properties to be checked are all modeled as ω-automata which can be trivially composed. Based on the implementation of Rule 1^ω in S/R and the extended xUML-to-S/R translator, compositional reasoning using Rule 1 is applied in model checking software systems modeled in xUML as follows:

- Given a system modeled in xUML and a property to be checked, the system is decomposed on the xUML level and premises of Rule 1 are formulated in xUML.
- These premises are discharged by translating them to their counterparts in S/R using the extended xUML-to-S/R translator and discharging their counterparts using the implementation of Rule 1^ω in S/R.

Correct application of Rule 1 then depends on the correctness of the translation from xUML to S/R and the correctness of the implementation of Rule 1^ω in S/R.

4 Applications

We presents two major applications of the realization of TBCR for the AIM semantics.

4.1 Application in Integrated State Space Reduction Framework

In previous research [18], we presented an integrated state space reduction framework for model checking executable object-oriented software system designs. This framework is presented for system designs modeled in xUML, but can also be readily used to structure integrated state space reduction for other representations. As shown in Figure 2, the framework structures the application of state space reduction algorithms into three phases, the user-driven state space reduction phase, the xUML-to-S/R translation phase, and the S/R model checking phase. Different algorithms are applied in each phase and the application of an algorithm may span multiple phases. (In Figure 2, an algorithm is only associated with the phase in which it is initiated.) Interactions among these algorithms are utilized to maximize aggregate effect of state space reduction.

TBCR is one of the most powerful state space reduction algorithms applied in this framework. Its application spans across all the three phases:

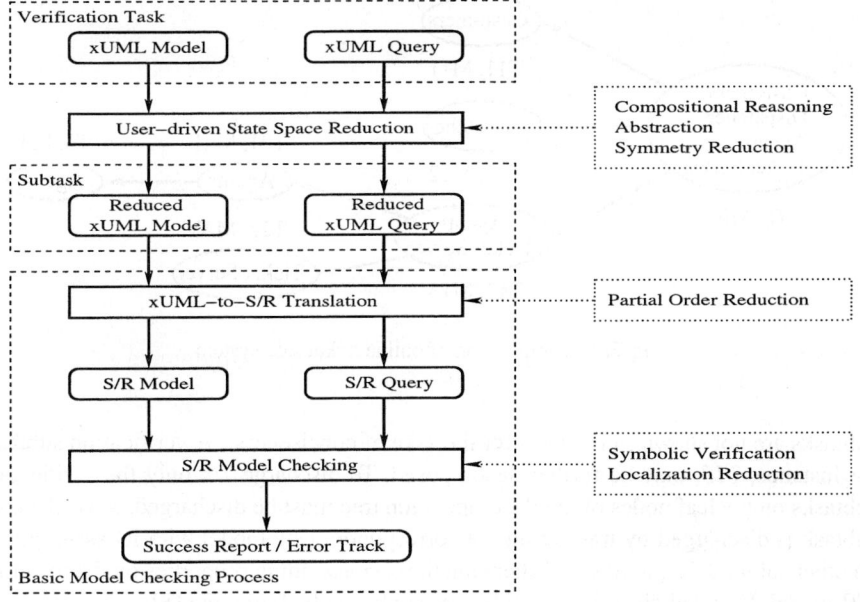

Fig. 2. Reduction hierarchy of integrated state space reduction framework

- In the user-driven state space reduction phase, a system (or a large component of the system) specified in xUML is decomposed into components and properties of the components are specified. Premises of Rule 1, verification of component properties, derivation of system properties from component properties, and validation of possible circular dependencies among component properties, are all formulated (on the AIM semantics level) as verification sub-tasks generated in the decomposition.
- These sub-tasks are either recursively reduced (on the AIM semantics level) with user-driven state space reduction into simpler sub-tasks, or translated into the S/R automaton language through the xUML-to-S/R translation phase and discharged (on the ω-automaton level) in the S/R model checking phase.

The general framework has been instantiated for the domain of distributed transaction systems by utilizing domain-specific design patterns. The instantiation has been applied in model checking an online ticket sale system. Figure 3 shows the decomposition of the system generated in checking an availability property, P: *After a request from a customer is received, a reply is eventually sent back to the customer.* In Figure 3, $M0$ denotes the complete model that consists of the *customers*, the *dispatcher*, the *agents*, and the *ticket server* while $M11, M12, M13, M21, M22$, and $M3$ denote the submodels of $M0$ derived in the decomposition. $T0$ is a verification task defined on $M0$: Checking the property, P, on the model, $M0$. $T0$ is decomposed into a set of verification subtasks, $T11$, $T12$, and $T13$, which check properties of $M11$, $M12$, and $M13$ locally. These properties of $M11$, $M12$, and $M13$ are specified according to the decomposition. (Derivation of P from these properties of $M11$, $M12$, and $M13$ and validation of possible circular dependencies between these properties are also verification sub-tasks, however, such

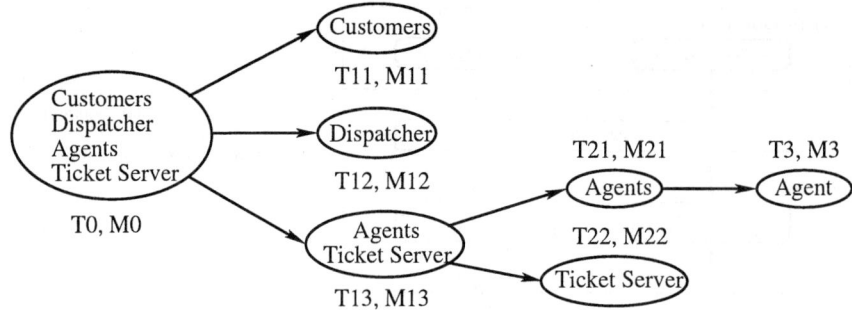

Fig. 3. Decomposition of online ticket sale system

subtasks are not shown in Figure 3 for the sake of conciseness.) A verification subtask, for instance, *T13*, may be further decomposed. To discharge *T0*, only the verification subtasks on the leaf nodes of the decomposition tree must be discharged. A verification subtask is discharged by translating the corresponding submodel with its assumptions on other submodels into S/R and checking the corresponding properties on the resulting S/R model. Detailed discussion of this case study can be found in [18].

4.2 Application in Integration of Model Checking into Component-Based Development of Software Systems

Overview. In [19], we defined, described, and applied an approach to integration of model checking into component-based development (CBD) of software systems, which is based on compositional reasoning and can be summarized as follows:

- As a software component is built, temporal properties of the component are formulated, verified, and then packaged with the component.
- Selecting a component for reuse considers not only its functionality but also its temporal properties.
- Verification of properties of a composed component reuses verified properties of its sub-components and is based on compositional reasoning.

Traditional applications of compositional reasoning take a top-down approach: To check properties of a system, the system is decomposed into modules recursively in a top-down fashion. (The application of TBCR in the integrated state space reduction framework, presented in Section 4.1, follows the top-down approach.) This integration of model checking into CBD combines the top-down application of TBCR with the bottom-up component composition process of CBD and discharge premises of a compositional reasoning rule by reusing previous component verification efforts as possible. Using Rule 1 as the compositional reasoning rule, the combination is conducted as follows:

- A property of a component is defined together with assumptions on the environment of the component and is verified on the component under these assumptions. When the component is reused in the composition of a larger component, the property

is *enabled* if the environment assumptions made in its verification hold on other components in the composition and/or the environment of the composed component.
- As a primitive component (a component built from "scratch" and not composed from other components) is verified, its properties are directly model checked on the executable representation of the component such as its executable design model.
- As a composed component is verified, premises of Rule 1 are discharged as follows:
  Condition C1: Verification of sub-component properties is reused from previous verification efforts.
  Condition C2: A property of the composed component is derived by being verified on an abstraction of the component, which is constructed from environment assumptions of the component and verified properties of its sub-components. A verified sub-component property is included in the abstraction if it is *enabled* in the composition and related to the property of the composed component according to the cone-of-influence analysis.
  Condition C3: Validation of circular dependencies among sub-component properties is executed to decide if a sub-component property is properly *enabled*.

In our implementation of this integration of model checking into CBD, the executable representations of components are specified in xUML. Therefore, formulation of and reasoning about the component properties are conducted in the AIM semantics. Following the TBCR approach, premises of Rule 1 are formulated in the AIM semantics and checked by translating them to their counterparts in S/R and then model checking their counterparts on the ω-automaton level.

Case Study. The integration of model checking into CBD has been applied to improve reliability of run-time images of TinyOS [22], a component-based run-time environment for networked sensors. In this case study, we discuss how the integration is applied in verifying a run-time image of TinyOS, the Sensor-to-Network component, which is composed from the Sensor component and the Network component. The Sensor (or Network, respectively) component outputs messages of the types, *Output* and *Done_Ack* (or *Data_Ack* and *Sent*), and inputs messages of the types, *OP_Ack* and *Done* (or *Data* and *Sent_Ack*). Figure 4 shows an abstracted communication diagram of the Sensor-to-Network component, where an annotation of the form of "Input message type (Output message type)" denotes that an output message type of a component is mapped to an input message type of the other component. In Figure 4, the arrows coming in and going out of the dashed box denote interrupts from the hardware platform and their corresponding replies. For the sake of conciseness, we omit the assumptions of the component on the hardware platform in the following discussion.

The goal of this case study is to check whether the Sensor-to-Network component has the following property (denoted by Q): *The component transmits sensor readings on physical network repeatedly*. The formal specification of Q is shown in Figure 5. *RFM.Pending* is a variable defined in the Network component. Setting and then clearing this variable indicate a transmission over the physical network. Q_1 and Q_2 are two properties formulated on the Sensor component. Q_1 asserts that the Sensor component outputs sensor readings repeatedly and Q_2 asserts that the Sensor component properly

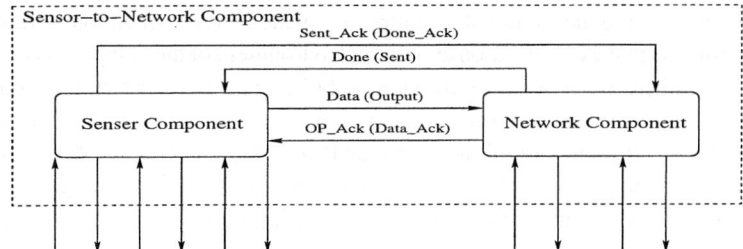

Fig. 4. Sensor-to-Network component

Properties of Sensor-to-Network Component:
Property Q
  Repeatedly (RFM.Pending);
  Repeatedly (Not RFM.Pending);

Properties of Sensor Component:
Property Q_1
  Repeatedly (Output);

Property Q_2
  After (Output) **Never** (Output) **UntilAfter** (OP_Ack);
  After (Done) **Eventually** (Done_Ack);
  Never (Done_Ack) **UntilAfter** (Done);
  After (Done_Ack) **Never** (Done_Ack) **UntilAfter**(Done);

Properties of Network Component:
Property Q_3
  IfRepeatedly (Data) **Repeatedly** (RFM.Pending);
  IfRepeatedly (Data) **Repeatedly** (Not RFM.Pending);

Property Q_4
  After (Data) **Eventually**(Data_Ack);
  Never (Data_Ack) **UntilAfter** (Data);
  After (Data_Ack) **Never** (Data_Ack) **UntilAfter** (Data);
  After (Sent) **Never** (Sent) **UntilAfter** (Sent_Ack);

Fig. 5. Properties of TinyOS components

handles its output hand-shakes. Q_3 and Q_4 are two properties formulated on the Network component. Q_3 asserts that the Network component transmits on physical network repeatedly if it inputs repeatedly and Q_4 asserts that the component properly handles its input hand-shakes.

Condition C1: Verification of sub-component properties In previous verification studies, Q_1 and Q_2 have been verified on the Sensor component by assuming Q_4 holds on its environment. (Q_4, when used as an assumption of Q_1 and Q_2, is formulated on input and output message types of the Sensor component.) Q_3 and Q_4 have been verified on the Network component by assuming Q_2 holds on its environment. Since the Sensor and Network components are both primitive components, the verification was conducted by translating the xUML design models of the two components into S/R and model checking on the S/R level.

Condition C3: Validation of circular dependencies An abstraction of the Sensor-to-Network component was constructed for verifying Q. Verification of Q on the abstraction failed since the abstraction cannot include Q_1, Q_2, Q_3, and Q_4 due to the circular dependency between Q_2 and Q_4. The circular dependency between Q_2 and Q_4 was validated by checking whether one of the following conditions holds:

- $Sensor \; [] \; CL^P(Q_2[]Q_4) \models (Q_2[]Q_4 + Q_2 + Q_4)$;
- $Network \; [] \; CL^P(Q_2[]Q_4) \models (Q_2[]Q_4 + Q_2 + Q_4)$.

These two verification tasks were discharged by translating them into S/R and model checking on the S/R level. Both conditions hold in this case.

Condition C2: Derivation of properties of composed component The abstraction was then refined by including Q_1 and Q_3 since the circular dependencies between Q_2 and Q_4 have been validated. Q was successfully verified on the refined abstraction by translating the abstraction into S/R and model checking on the S/R level.

Since conditions C1, C2, and C3 have been successfully discharged, it can then be concluded with Rule 1 that Q holds on the Sensor-to-Network component.

5 Conclusions

TBCR is a simple and effective approach to application of compositional reasoning in the context of model checking software systems via model translation. It simplifies the correctness proof of compositional reasoning rules in software semantics and reuses existing proofs and implementations of compositional reasoning rules in directly model-checkable semantics. The feasibility and effectiveness of TBCR has been demonstrated by its realization for the AIM semantics and by two applications of this realization.

Acknowledgment

We gratefully acknowledge Nina Amla and Nancy MacMahon for their generous help. We also thank the anonymous referees for their valuable suggestions.

References

1. Clarke, E.M., Emerson, E.A.: Design and synthesis of synchronization skeletons using branching time temporal logic. Logic of Programs Workshop (1981)
2. Quielle, J.P., Sifakis, J.: Specification and verification of concurrent systems in CESAR. 5th International Symposium on Programming (1982)
3. Clarke, E.M., Grumberg, O., Peled, D.: Model Checking. The MIT Press (1999)
4. Pnueli, A.: In transition from global to modular reasoning about programs. Logics and Models of Concurrent Systems (1985)
5. Alur, R., Henzinger, T.: Reactive modules. LICS (1996)

6. Abadi, M., Lamport, L.: Conjoining specifications. TOPLAS (1995)
7. McMillan, K.L.: A methodology for hardware verification using compositional model checking. Cadence TR (1999)
8. Amla, N., Emerson, E.A., Namjoshi, K.S., Trefler, R.: Assume-guarantee based compositional reasoning for synchronous timing diagrams. TACAS (2001)
9. de Rover, W.P., de Boer, F., Hannemann, U., Hooman, J., Lakhnech, Y., Poel, M., Zwiers, J.: Concurrency Verification: Introduction to Compositional and Non-compositional Proof Methods. Cambridge Univ. Press (2001)
10. Mellor, S.J., Balcer, M.J.: Executable UML: A Foundation for Model Driven Architecture. Addison Wesley (2002)
11. ITU: ITU-T Recommendation Z.100 (03/93) - Specification and Description Language (SDL). ITU (1993)
12. Holzmann, G.: Design and Validation of Computer Protocols. Prentice Hall (1991)
13. McMillan, K.L.: Symbolic Model Checking. Kluwer Academic Publishers (1993)
14. Hardin, R.H., Har'El, Z., Kurshan, R.P.: COSPAN. CAV (1996)
15. Kurshan, R.P.: Computer-Aided Verification of Coordinating Processes: The Automata-Theoretic Approach. Princeton University Press (1994)
16. Lynch, N.: Distributed Algorithms. Morgan Kaufmann Publishers (1996)
17. Kurshan, R.P., Merritt, M., Orda, A., Sachs, S.R.: Modeling asynchrony with a synchronous model. Formal Methods in System Design 15(3) (1999)
18. Xie, F., Browne, J.C.: Integrated state space reduction for model checking executable object-oriented software system designs. FASE (2002)
19. Xie, F., Browne, J.C.: Verified systems by composition from verified components. ESEC/FSE (2003)
20. Alpern, B., Schneider, F.: Defining liveness. Information Processing Letters **21** (1985)
21. Xie, F., Levin, V., Browne, J.C.: ObjectCheck: a model checking tool for executable object-oriented software system designs. FASE (2002)
22. Hill, J., Szewczyk, R., Woo, A., Hollar, S., Culler, D., Pister, K.: System architecture directions for networked sensors. ASPLOS-IX (2000)

Appendix: Detailed Proof of Theorem 4

Proof of Theorem 4:

$$P_1 [] Q_2 \models Q_1$$
$$\Rightarrow \{\text{Theorem 3}\}$$
$$T_\omega^P(P_1) \otimes T_\omega^P(Q_2) \preceq T_\omega^P(Q_1) \tag{1}$$

$$P_2 [] Q_1 \models Q_2$$
$$\Rightarrow \{\text{Theorem 3}\}$$
$$T_\omega^P(P_2) \otimes T_\omega^P(Q_1) \preceq T_\omega^P(Q_2) \tag{2}$$

$$Q_1 [] Q_2 \models Q$$
$$\Rightarrow \{\text{Theorem 3}\}$$
$$T_\omega^P(Q_1) \otimes T_\omega^P(Q_2) \preceq T_\omega^P(Q) \tag{3}$$

$$P_1 [] CL^P(Q) \models (Q + Q_1 + Q_2)$$
$\Rightarrow$ {Theorem 3}
$$T_\omega^P(P_1) \otimes T_\omega^P(CL^P(T)) \preceq (T_\omega^P(Q + Q_1 + Q_2))$$
$\Rightarrow$ {Lemma 1, Lemma 2}
$$T_\omega^P(P_1) \otimes CL^\omega(T_\omega^P(T)) \preceq (T_\omega^P(Q) \oplus T_\omega^P(Q_1) \oplus T_\omega^P(Q_2)) \quad (4)$$

$$P_2 [] CL^P(Q) \models (Q + Q_1 + Q_2)$$
$\Rightarrow$ {Theorem 3}
$$T_\omega^P(P_2) \otimes T_\omega^P(CL^P(Q)) \preceq (T_\omega^P(Q + Q_1 + Q_2))$$
$\Rightarrow$ {Lemma 1, Lemma 2}
$$T_\omega^P(P_2) \otimes CL^\omega(T_\omega^P(Q)) \preceq (T_\omega^P(Q) \oplus T_\omega^P(Q_1) \oplus T_\omega^P(Q_2)) \quad (5)$$

$\{(1),(2),(3),(4),(5)\}$
$\Rightarrow$ {Rule 1^ω}
$$T_\omega^P(P_1) \otimes T_\omega^P(P_2) \preceq T_\omega^P(Q)$$
$\Rightarrow$ {Theorem 3}
$$P_1 [] P_2 \models Q \quad (6)$$

□

Watchdog Transformations for Property-Oriented Model-Checking

Michael Goldsmith[1,4], Nick Moffat[2], Bill Roscoe[3], Tim Whitworth[1], and Irfan Zakiuddin[2]

[1] Formal Systems (Europe) Ltd.
{michael, tim}@fsel.com
[2] Systems Assurance Group, QinetiQ, Malvern, UK,
{N.Moffat,I.Zakiuddin}@eris.QinetiQ.com
[3] Computing Laboratory, University of Oxford, UK,
Bill.Roscoe@comlab.ox.ac.uk
[4] Worcester College, Oxford, UK

Abstract. We discuss how to transform a CSP refinement, $S \sqsubseteq I$, to enable all its events to be hidden; this is useful because many of the state space compression functions provided by the model-checker FDR are effective only when events are hidden [1]. In an earlier paper [2] we described a suitable transformation for the case where the refinement is in the traces semantics of CSP. This paper extends the approach to the more difficult case of the stable-failures semantics. In both cases, a watchdog transformation is applied to the specification S, resulting in a *watchdog process* WD_S, which is then composed in parallel with I, or with I in a simple context. The watchdog process monitors I and somehow indicates whether it can behave in a way that is incompatible with refinement of S. All events of the original assertion can be hidden in the transformed assertion. We also discuss the design of compression strategies that try to hide as many events as possible in the component processes of I and WD_S, and compress the composition as it is being built up. We describe our implementation of the watchdog transformations and some simple compression strategies.

Keywords: Compression, CSP, FDR, Model-Checking, State Explosion Problem, Watchdog Transformation.

1 Introduction

It is widely recognised that the state explosion problem limits the tractability of model-checking. There are several approaches to combating state explosion, perhaps the best known of which are compositional reasoning [3], abstraction [4], symmetry exploitation [5–7], and partial order reduction [8–10]. Symbolic model-checkers [11] use data structures, often BDDs, for efficiently representing the explored state space and the state transition function. An alternative approach is taken by the FDR [12] model-checker for CSP. FDR stores the set of explored states explicitly, but provides compression functions that approximate semantic minimisation, reducing the size of the (internal) state machine for a process, without changing its behaviour. Use of these compression functions can dramatically improve the tractability of CSP model-checking [13]. Property-oriented model-checking is a novel technique which uses the property – the specification process and the semantic model of refinement – to maximise the benefit of compression.

We discuss how to transform a CSP refinement, $S \sqsubseteq I$, to enable all its events to be hidden. This is useful because FDR's compression functions are most effective when events are hidden [1]. In an earlier paper [2] we described a suitable transform for the simple case where the refinement is in the traces semantics of CSP. This paper extends the approach to the more difficult case of the stable-failures semantics. In both cases, a watchdog transformation is applied to the specification process S, resulting in a watchdog process WD_S which is then composed in parallel with I, or with I in a simple context. In a suitable watchdog assertion, the watchdog process monitors I and somehow indicates whether it can behave in a way that is incompatible with refinement of S. We ensure that the truth or falsity of the assertion is preserved when all events of the original assertion are hidden in the watchdog assertion.

The traces watchdog process and watchdog assertion are summarised in Section 2. A common special case of the watchdog transformation for the more difficult case of the stable-failures semantics is presented in Section 3. This restriction is removed in Section 4, which presents the general transformation. These sections informally prove correctness (in a sense made precise later).

It is one thing to hide a given set of process events and then compress, and another to hide and compress efficiently. FDR operates on processes expressed in CSP_M [14], the machine-readable version of CSP. FDR's compression functions generally explore the full state space of a CSP_M process in order to derive a compressed state machine, so naively hiding all possible events and then compressing would cause FDR to traverse the full state space. Section 5 describes compression strategies that aim to achieve closer to optimal compression given a set of events to be hidden. These compression strategies try to reorganise the CSP_M process structure to allow events to be hidden as early as possible when combining component processes of I and WD_S, and thus compress the composition as it is being built up.

Section 6 discusses the implementation of the watchdog transformations and of some simple compression strategies. We end with a discussion in Section 7 of the relationship to other work.

Throughout, we use the notational convention that $\alpha(P)$ denotes the complete alphabet of a process P, and $\alpha(P, Q)$ denotes $\alpha(P) \cup \alpha(Q)$.

1.1 The Watchdog Approach

The basic technique consists of three distinct steps, the first of which is performed in a way that guarantees that the second is possible:

1. Transform $S \sqsubseteq I$ into an equivalent assertion $P(\alpha(S,I)) \sqsubseteq F(WD_S, I)$ in which P is a function from alphabets to processes, and watchdog process WD_S is composed with I using some composition function F.
2. Without affecting its truth, transform this assertion to one where $\alpha(S,I)$ is hidden on both sides: $P(\alpha(S,I)) \setminus \alpha(S,I) \sqsubseteq F(WD_S, I) \setminus \alpha(S,I)$.
3. Simplify the left-hand-side and apply a compression strategy to generate a compressed state machine for the right-hand-side $F(WD_S, I) \setminus \alpha(S,I)$.

2 Watchdog Transformations for the Traces Semantics

The watchdog (process) transformation described in [2] maps a specification process, S, to a watchdog process that monitors the traces of an implementation process, I, and indicates whether or not S is refined by I according to CSP's traces semantics.

The watchdog process, WD_S in Section 1.1, is defined so that it can perform a distinguished *fail_* event when I performs a trace not permitted by S. This transformation is most easily defined in terms of a normal form definition of S. This is unsurprising: the efficient checking of refinement within FDR relies upon normalisation of the specification – determinising the underlying state machine, while producing sufficient annotations to allow any interesting nondeterminism to be reconstru cted. Allowed behaviour of the implementation can then be verified by a local check. Also, a normal form generally has a simple structure (relying on a restricted set of process operators) which allows a simple definition of the watchdog process. We use the traces normal form defined in [1] since this is the one implemented within FDR. This allows the transformation to be implemented both directly and efficiently, as explained below.

In the remainder of this section, we describe the traces normal form, then the watchdog transformation for traces refinement, then the watchdog assertion, and finally we argue that the watchdog assertion holds iff the original assertion holds.

2.1 The Traces Normal Form

Any process P has a trace-equivalent expression as an entry into a mutual recursion of the following form (for some indexing set and functions A and *after*):

$$P'(i) = \Box\, a \in A(i) \bullet a \rightarrow P'(after(i, a)).$$

For example, we may take the indexing set to be the set of all traces of P; $A(s)$ to be $inits(P/s)$, the set of all events that P can perform after the trace s[1]; and $after(s, a)$ to be the extended trace $s\frown\langle a \rangle$. In general, though, that particular construction may give rise to an infinite mutual recursion even for very simple processes.

---

[1] The set returned by the function *inits* is often referred to as the *initials* of its argument. Thus, $inits(P/s)$ is the initials of P after it has performed trace s.

P is finite-state (in the traces model) precisely if there is such a representation with a finite indexing set, and this representation is a traces normal form if there is no non-trivial bisimilarity between terms in the recursion. Each set $A(i)$ is the union of the initial events of all operational states reachable on any trace that leads to $P'(i)$.

2.2 The Traces Watchdog Process

Given a specification $S = S'(i_0)$ as such a (finite) traces normal-form recursion, we can define a watchdog process, $WDT_S(i_0)$, in terms of a transform WDT_S defined by recursion over the same index set:

$$WDT_S(i) = (\Box \, a \in A(i) \bullet a \rightarrow WDT_S(after(i,a)))$$
$$\Box$$
$$(\Box \, b \in \alpha(I) - A(i) \bullet b \rightarrow fail\_ \rightarrow STOP)$$

Note that $A(i)$ is $inits(S/s_i)$ for any trace s_i that takes S to the state indexed by i, and $inits$ is a semantic function that is not expressible in the CSP$_M$ language; so $A(i)$ must be calculated (using FDR) as part of the transformation.

The intention is that $WDT_S(i_0)$ can perform any trace tr that S can perform, but it can also perform events from the alphabet of I not allowed by S/tr (after which it can only perform the $fail\_$ event).

Notice that this definition of WDT is expressed in terms of the alphabet, $\alpha(I)$, of the implementation process I. Similar formulations independent of $\alpha(I)$ are possible, but they require a slightly more complex composition function F. We use the formulation above for simplicity.

2.3 The Traces Watchdog Assertion

Having calculated the traces watchdog process $WDT_S(i_0)$, the transformed assertion is

$$RUN(\alpha(S,I)) \sqsubseteq_T I \underset{\alpha(S,I)}{\|} WDT_S(i_0) \qquad (1)$$

in which I synchronises with the watchdog process on $\alpha(S,I)$, the events of the original assertion. The process $RUN(\alpha(S,I))$ has a single state, in which it can perform any event of the original assertion (and return to the same state).

2.4 Correctness

We say that a watchdog assertion transformation for the traces semantics is correct if it preserves the truth of a traces assertion. In [2] it is proved that the transformation described in Section 2.3 (defined in terms of WDT) is correct in a stronger sense which, in addition, relates counterexamples of the watchdog assertion to corresponding counterexamples of the original assertion. We do not describe this stronger property here, due to lack of space.

Essentially, if I can only perform traces of S, then $WDT_S(i_0)$ is constrained by I to traces of S, so can never progress via its second branch. So the parallel composition of I and $WDT_S(i_0)$ can never perform the $fail_-$ event. Conversely, if this composition can perform $fail_-$, then it must be performed by $WDT_S(i_0)$ via its second branch, in particular after some event e outside $inits(S/s)$, where s is some trace of S – that is, there must be a trace $s \frown \langle e \rangle$ of I that is not a trace of S.

Notice that $RUN \sqsubseteq_\mathcal{T}$ is invariant under hiding on both sides when the set hidden is contained in the argument of RUN. Therefore the traces assertion transformation described allows events of $\alpha(S, I)$ to be hidden on both sides without affecting truth or falsity. Moreover, FDR's debugger can 'look inside' process operators, in particular the hiding operator; this allows the user to find a counterexample of the original assertion corresponding to any given counter-example of the watchdog assertion.

3 Watchdog Transformations for the Failures Semantics

In this section we introduce a stable-failures model watchdog transformation that is valid for a common special case of S and I. Section 4 describes the unrestricted form.

It is worth reviewing CSP's stable-failures model briefly. The *failures* of a process P, $failures(P)$, is the set of all possible observations (s, X) of a trace s of P leading to a stable state that can refuse to engage in any event in X, a so-called refusal (set) of P/s. (A *stable state* is one that cannot perform internal actions.) Then, a refinement $P \sqsubseteq_\mathcal{F} Q$ holds in the stable-failures model if $traces(Q) \subseteq traces(P)$ and $failures(Q) \subseteq failures(P)$. So failures refinement implies traces refinement[2]. Additionally, failures refinement requires that the implementation can never (stably) refuse more events after some trace than the specification might (stably) refuse after the same trace.

3.1 A First Look at the Failures Normal Form

In the case that there is no unbounded internal progress (such as would be divergence in the failures-divergences model), then each trace necessarily leads to a stable state and the normal form in the failures model can again be expressed as a minimal mutual recursion [1], shown below. Here the form of each clause is somewhat more complex than was the case for the traces normal form, reflecting the finer discrimination of the richer model.

$$P'(i) = (\Box\, a \in A(i) \bullet a \to P'(after(i, a)))$$
$$\triangleright$$
$$(\sqcap\, m \in M(i) \bullet \Box\, a \in m \bullet a \to P'(after(i, a)))$$

---

[2] when we say 'failures' without the prefix 'stable-' it is shorthand for 'stable-failures'

where $\triangleright$ is the *untimed timeout* operator[3], A and *after* play analogous roles to those in the traces normal form, and $M(i)$ is a (non-empty, finite) set of incomparable subsets of $A(i)$, the *minimal acceptances* of $P'(i)$. (The restriction that $M(i)$ is a non-empty set of minimal acceptances is dropped in Section 4.) While $A(i)$ represents the choice of events immediately possible for $P'(i)$, the set $M(i)$ encapsulates the range of nondeterminism within that choice. Each of the elements of $M(i)$ is a set of events that $P'(i)$ may nondeterministically choose to offer; it is not generally possible for an external observer to tell which minimal acceptance has been chosen by $P'(i)$, but one can rely on all events from at least one minimal acceptance being offered by the process. This fact is crucial in the construction of WDF_S below.

Note that a process $P'(i)$ that may immediately deadlock has $M(i) = \{\emptyset\}$, and the failures normal form of a deterministic process has $M(i) = \{A(i)\}$ for each i. A process $DF(X)$ – DF here stands for 'deadlock free' – that can do any sequence of events drawn from X and is the most nondeterministic such process that can never deadlock, has the single-state normal form with $A(i_0) = X$ and $M(i_0) = \{\{x\} \mid x \in X\}$ and singleton index set $\{i_0\}$.

3.2 The Restricted Failures Watchdog Assertion

There are now two conditions that the watchdog needs to be able to detect: an inadmissable event extending a trace, as before; but also any failure to fulfil the promises made by the specification as to the availability of events. The first we can trap much as before, but the second requires some examination of the failures of the implementation.

We remarked above that the minimal acceptances of the specification after any given trace capture its immediately visible nondeterminism, and that one can rely on all events from at least one of those sets being offered. This means that if we offer at least one event from each minimal acceptance, then we must be able to synchronise successfully on at least one of those events, namely the one we picked from the minimal acceptance it actually is offering. And so, under those circumstances, it should not be possible for the parallel composition of the specification with us as experimenter to immediately deadlock – unless the specification itself can deadlock, in which case it has the empty set as its only minimal acceptance. This leads us to the following use of a deadlock-freedom check (in the stable-failures model) for the stable-failures watchdog assertion. the stable-failures watchdog assertion is a deadlock freedom check (in the stable-failures model).

Given a watchdog process $WDF_S(i_0)$, the assertion $S \sqsubseteq_\mathcal{F} I$ is transformed to the watchdog assertion

$$I \underset{\alpha(S,I)}{\|} WDF_S(i_0) \quad \text{deadlock free } [\mathcal{F}] \tag{2}$$

---

[3] $P \triangleright Q$ may behave like P, but it will always offer the initial actions of Q. $P \triangleright Q = Q \square P \sqcap Q$ (which is independent of bracketing).

which asserts that the parallel composition of I and the watchdog process, synchronised on all events of the original assertion, is deadlock free in the failures semantics $\mathcal{F}$. (The test for deadlock freedom of a process P can be expressed as a failures refinement check against the process $DF(\alpha(P))$, but such checks are sufficiently common to have a special form of assertion in the FDR meta-language.)

3.3 The Restricted Failures Watchdog Process

In order to realise the strategy outlined in the previous section, we need to define a watchdog process which is capable of offering every possible "slice" through the minimal acceptances of the specification: if any leads to deadlock, then that will give rise to a counterexample to the original refinement query. In addition, we need to handle the case that the specification itself deadlocks (where any refusal behaviour of the implementation is permissible). Finally, for simplicity of the final check, we ensure that trace errors also lead to deadlock; although we continue to flag them with a distinguished event to facilitate debugging.

A suitable failures watchdog process is $WDF_S(i_0)$ where WDF_S is defined (relative to the stable-failures normal form of S) in CSP_M as follows:

```
1: channel trace_error_, spec_stopped_
2: sigma = Events − {trace_error_, spec_stopped_}
3:
4: WDF_S(i) =
5:    (□ a : A(i) • a → WDF_S(after(i, a)))
6:    □
7:    (□ a : sigma − A(i) • a → trace_error_ → STOP)
8:    ▷
9:    N(i) == 1 and empty(M_{i,1}) &
10:        − − spec state can stop (so has one minimal acceptance)
11:       spec_stopped_ → WDF_S(i)
12:    □
13:    N(i) > 0 and not empty(M_{i,1}) &
14:       − − spec state cannot stop (and has at least 1 min acceptance)
15:       (⊓ Y ∈ {{m_1, ..., m_{N(i)}} | m_1 ∈ M_{i,1}, ..., m_{N(i)} ∈ M_{i,N(i)}}
16:         • □ a ∈ Y • a → WDF_S(after(i, a)))
```

We have written $N(i)$ above as shorthand for $card(M(i))$, so we have that $M(i) = \{M_{i,1}, ..., M_{i,N(i)}\}$. Line 1 defines two distinguished events $trace\_error\_$ and $spec\_stopped\_$ (identifiers ending in an underscore are conventionally reserved for machine-generated text). Line 2 defines $sigma$ to be the set of all events $Events$ except these distinguished events. So $sigma$ contains (at least) all the events in $\alpha(S)$ and $\alpha(I)$.

3.4 Correctness

Recall that a refinement $P \sqsubseteq_\mathcal{F} Q$ holds in the stable-failures model if $traces(Q) \subseteq traces(P)$ and $failures(Q) \subseteq failures(P)$, where the latter are the sets of all possible observations (s, X) of a trace s of Q (or P) leading to a stable state that can refuse to engage in any event in X. Suppose we have normalised P to a mutual recursion of the form given in Section 3.1, and that i_s is the (unique) index such that $P'(i_s) = P/s$. Then a simple unwinding argument reduces the refinement check to a check that, for each trace s that both P and Q can perform, any operational state Q' that Q can reach on s (and so such that $Q/s \sqsubseteq_\mathcal{F} Q'$) has the following two properties:

1. $inits(Q') \subseteq A(i_s)$; and
2. if Q' is stable and can refuse X, then $\exists\, m \in M(i_s)$ such that $m \cap X = \emptyset$.

The first property says that Q' cannot offer more than P/s might, and the second says that Q' must fulfil at least one of the promises that P/s makes about what is offered.

We need to show that $S \sqsubseteq_\mathcal{F} I$ iff $I \underset{\alpha(S,I)}{\|} WDF_S(i_0)$ is deadlock free in $\mathcal{F}$. We argue both contrapositives.

Suppose that $S \sqsubseteq_\mathcal{F} I$ does not hold; then there are two generic possibilities, which we narrow by considering minimal counterexamples: either there is a trace $s^\frown\langle a\rangle \in traces(I)$ such that $s \in traces(S) \cap traces(I)$ but $s^\frown\langle a\rangle \notin traces(S)$; or there is a failure $(s, X) \in failures(I) - failures(S)$ where $s \in traces(S)$.

In the first case, since $s^\frown\langle a\rangle$ is a trace of I, it is possible for the left-hand-side of the parallel composition to perform s and reach a state that can do a; and, as s is a trace of S, a possible execution of the right-hand-side is always to take line 5 of the definition of WDF_S, and thus synchronise with the left-hand-side on trace s. So we reach a position where $i = i_s$ is by assumption such that $a \notin A(i)$, and so line 7 can contribute a. Thus the parallel composition can evolve by synchronising on a, after which the watchdog can do $trace\_error\_$ and prevent I doing any further events, by becoming $STOP$. So the system can deadlock on the trace $s^\frown\langle a, trace\_error\_\rangle$ and is therefore not deadlock free.

In the second case, again we can reach a state where the system has performed s and I has reached a state that can stably refuse X. The watchdog can then 'timeout' to the choice at lines 9–16. The boolean guard at line 9 cannot be true (as then S/s can refuse anything, in particular X), but the guard at line 13 is true, so the watchdog reduces to the last two lines. Property 2 above is not satisfied, since the refinement doesn't hold, and therefore for each $M_k \in M(i_s)$ there is a witness $m_k \in M_k \cap X$. Then $\{m_0, ..., m_{N(i_s)}\}$ is one of the possible nondeterministic choices for Y at line 15, and so the watchdog can offer only that Y (and we are only interested in the possibility of deadlock), while the left-hand-side of the parallel can refuse it (because $Y \subseteq X$, and refusals are closed under subset). So, again, the composition is not deadlock free.

Conversely, suppose the implementation in parallel with the watchdog deadlocks after some trace s_i, say; let us consider the state of the watchdog at that point. One possibility is that the watchdog is on line 7; but it cannot be before the $trace\_error\_$ event, since that can happen without the cooperation of its peer, and in any case the timeout operator could make internal progress and transfer control to the lower half of the process. So in this case it must have already done the *trace _error_* event; but that can only happen when I/s_i can do an event that S/s_i cannot, and so the refinement cannot hold. Similarly, if the guard at line 9 is true, the *spec_stopped_* event can happen autonomously, and repeatedly, and no deadlock is possible (this is, of course, the reason for the inclusion of this clause: if the specification is allowed to deadlock after some trace, we must ensure that this new composition does not deadlock at that point). So the guard at line 13 must be tru e, and it will have picked a particular Y with an element of each element of $M(i)$. Since there is a deadlock after trace s_i, I/s_i must be able to refuse all of Y, which implies that some operational state Q', reachable by I on s_i, refuses all of Y. But then I/s_i has a refusal X $(=Y)$ that does not satisfy property 2 above, and the refinement does not hold (as (s_i, X) is a failure of I but not S). This completes the proof.

In the stable-failures model, $P \setminus X$ is deadlock free iff P is deadlock free, for arbitrary process P and set of events X. So this transformed assertion is suitable for our overall game-plan.

4 General Watchdog Transformations for the Failures Semantics

We have explicitly assumed, in the previous section, that $M(i)$ is non-empty for all i, and we have implicitly made use of an analogous assumption about I, although it may not be immediately obvious where. But these assumptions do not hold, in general, for processes in the stable-failures model. The reason it is the *stable*-failures model is that we only record failures that are stable. The definition of refinement mentions traces as well as failures because a process might be able to perform some particular trace but never reach a stable state without subsequently doing a further event; and possibly not even then.

Such instability is analogous to divergence in the failures-divergences model, but the two denotational semantics (and, consequently, the two algebras) treat it rather differently. In particular, there are many different unstable processes, in contrast to the single and catastrophic divergence: in fact, any subsequent behaviour is possible in the stable-failures model. If the definition of distributed nondeterministic choice is extended so that (the usually illegal term) $\sqcap \emptyset$ is ident ified with the pure unstable process div $= P \setminus \{a\}$, where $P = a \rightarrow P$, then the definition of failures normal form in Section 3.1 continues to make sense even when some $M(i)$ are empty. Note that div, and more generally div $\square$ Q for any Q such that $inits(Q) \neq Events$, are rather miraculous in the stable-failures model: there are events that they can never do, but equally never refuse to do; this contradicts one of the (quite intuitive) axioms of the failures-divergences model. Also, not every divergence corresponds to an instability: because div is a unit of $\sqcap$, it is only when an operational divergence is unavoidable that it gives rise to instability; there are no refusals belonging to a trace only when there are no finite maximal τ-chains from any state that can be reached on that trace.

4.1 The General Failures Watchdog Process

The previously vacuous conjunct $N(i) > 0$ in the guard at line 13 now comes into play: if S/s is denotationally unstable (i.e., it has no minimal acceptances) then neither of the guards in the second half of the definition of $WDF_S(i_s)$ is true, and therefore the body of the definition degenerates to $\ldots \triangleright STOP$. Since the alphabet of I is a subset of the synchronisation set $\alpha(S, I)$, the parallel composition must be able to deadlock... unless I/s itself is unstable and so has no refusals. (The semantics of the parallel operator essentially make the refusals of the compound the pairwise unions of refusals of the components, and so if either side has none, then so does the whole.) the empty trace. But this is precisely what we want: if S has no refusals on s, we want I to have none, also, as otherwise that would be a failure too many.

Thus the existing definition of WDF_S will serve admirably in the general case.

4.2 The General Failures Watchdog Assertion

Unfortunately, the same feature of the semantics that gives us the correct behaviour when the specification is unstable admits the possibility that a trace error will be masked if the implementation can become unstable after performing some illegal event: the *trace_error_* event may happen, since the implementation cannot influence that, and thereafter no event in $\alpha(S, I)$ can happen. But, equally, they may not be refused by a miraculous state of the implementation: $(div \,\square\, ldots) \| \ldots \| STOP$ is deadlock free, provided the left-hand-side cannot make a transition to a stable state.

The full-abstraction results in [1] establish that we must be able to separate the test into one on traces, and another for immediate deadlock; but this would require two traversals of the complete state-space of I and, worse, two different transformations of S, including normalisation in two different models. We much prefer to find a modification to the transformed assertion that allows the test to be completed in a single check.

In fact, the change required is quite straightforward: we simply check

$$(I \vartriangle trace\_error\_ \to STOP) \;\underset{\alpha(S,I) \cup \{trace\_error\_\}}{\|}\; WDF_S(i_0) \quad \text{deadlock free } [\mathcal{F}] \qquad (3)$$

where $\vartriangle$ is the CSP *interrupt* operator, which effectively adds a deterministic choice of doing its second argument to every state of its first; it is not compositionally definable in terms of the other operators of the language, and we believe that this conflation of the checks into a single check could not be encoded without it.

4.3 Correctness

Essentially, the argument of Section 3.4 carries through unchanged, apart from the claim that the $STOP$ after the *trace_error_* event at line 7 introduces deadlock. This is not necessarily true in the presence of instability, as pointed out above.

Now, however, the *trace_error_* event cannot occur without the cooperation of the left-hand-side of the parallel; and since *trace_error_* $\notin \alpha(I)$, it must be the right-hand operand of the interrupt that does it. The left-hand-side of the parallel then becomes $STOP$, which (stably) deadlocks. So if *trace_error_* does occur, then both sides of the parallel are stable and deadlocked, so the whole parallel is also. It may be that I can make infinite internal progress instead of performing that event, but the interrupt operator ensures that it is always available, and the deadlock check will explore every possible execution, including those where it is eventually chosen.

5 Compression Strategies

As explained in Section 1, our motivation for the watchdog transformations presented above was the desire to improve the effectiveness of compressions. In this section we outline the approach we have taken to developing compression strategies that (attempt to) take full advantage of the increased amount of hiding that the watchdog transformations allow. This section is not intended to provide a full and final description of the compression strategies, which are still being developed. Our intention here is t o outline our approach in order to indicate how the watchdog transformations above can be exploited.

The original refinement assertion has now been transformed to a suitable watchdog assertion. In the traces case, the watchdog assertion is a traces refinement, and in the failures case it is a failures deadlock-freedom assertion (which can be expressed as a failures refinement). In both cases all events of the original assertion can be hidden without changing its truth or falsity, and we can construct an original counterexample from any watchdog counterexample.

Unfortunately, the naive approach of hiding all possible events and then compressing the whole process in one step is inefficient: FDR will traverse the full state space when calculating the compressed state machine.

Compression strategies generate a compressed state machine representation of a process. To explain how our compression strategies work, we begin by making four observations:

1. Compressing component processes before composing them can avoid the construction of large state machines that are later compressed.
2. Pushing hiding down through a process operator allows the composition to be compressed more effectively. Of course, events on which component processes synchronise with other processes cannot be hidden inside a parallel composition.
3. Rearranging the syntax tree of a process expression sometimes allows more hiding to be pushed down through process operators.
4. The syntax tree can be conveniently rearranged, without affecting semantics, when process operators are associative (perhaps allowing synchronization alphabets to change) and commutative.

These observations (in reverse order) motivate four principal compression activities: transform some or all parallel compositions to alphabetised parallel form, rearrange the order of alphabetised parallel compositions, push hiding down the syntax tree and, finally, apply one or more of FDR's compression functions at some places in the syntax tree. These activities are described in more detail in the following subsections.

5.1 Transforming Parallel Compositions to Alphabetised Form

CSP_M includes four parallel operators:

alphabetised parallel	$P \ _X\|_Y\ Q$
shared parallel	$P \ \|_X\ Q$
interleaving	$P \|\|\| Q$
linked parallel	$P\ [a_1 \leftrightarrow b_1, ..., a_n \leftrightarrow b_n]\ Q$

The alphabetised parallel operator synchronises processes on specified alphabets and constrains them to perform events within these alphabets. The shared parallel operator synchronises processes on the specified alphabet and interleaves them on other events. Linked parallel synchronises events of one process with corresponding (linked) events of the other; events that are not thus linked can occur independently of the other process.

Alphabetised parallel is the only associative parallel operator. We prefer to describe it as pseudo-associative, since there is an obligation to manage the synchronisation alphabets. By saying that alphabetised parallel is pseudo-associative we mean:

$$P\ _X\|_{Y \cup Z}\ (Q\ _Y\|_Z\ R) = (P\ _X\|_Y\ Q)\ _{X \cup Y}\|_Z\ R.$$

We wish to express all parallel compositions in terms of the alphabetised parallel operator.

Interleaving and linked parallel can be represented in terms of shared parallel, renaming and hiding:

$$P \|\|\| Q = P \ \|_\emptyset\ Q$$

and

$$P[a_1 \leftrightarrow b_1, ..., a_n \leftrightarrow b_n]Q = (rP \ \|_{\{c_1,...,c_n\}}\ rQ) \setminus \{c_1, ..., c_n\}$$

where $rP = P[[a_1 \leftarrow c_1, ..., a_n \leftarrow c_n]]$, $rQ = Q[[b_1 \leftarrow c_1, ..., b_n \leftarrow c_n]]$ and $c_1, ..., c_n$ are distinct new events.

To convert shared parallel into alphabetised parallel, we need two renamings:

$$P \ \|_X\ Q = (rP\ _{X \cup \alpha(rP)}\|_{X \cup \alpha(Q)}\ Q)\ [[b_1 \leftarrow a_1, ..., b_n \leftarrow a_n]]$$

where $rP = P[[a_1 \leftarrow b_1, ..., a_n \leftarrow b_n]]$, $a_1, ..., a_n$ are the events outside X that are in both $\alpha(P)$ and $\alpha(Q)$, and $b_1, ..., b_n$ are distinct new events. Essentially, if we simply put two processes P and Q from a shared parallel composition into alphabetised parallel over their respective alphabets, then synchronisation would occur on any event that both P and Q could perform. We want synchronisation to occur on only the set X (the set over which the processes synchronise in the shared parallel composition). So, before composing we rename those events of P on which undesired synchronisation would otherwise occur, and rename them back afterwards.

5.2 Reordering Alphabetised Parallel Compositions

We are working on several alternative heuristics for the reordering of parallel process composition. Space does not allow sufficiently detailed description of these heuristics, so we outline the approach here and discuss only the simplest heuristic in any detail.

Recall that we are trying to gain some advantage by pushing hiding down a syntax tree towards the leaves. In the traces case, the tree will initially look something like Figure 1, which depicts the case $I = Impl1 \;_{\alpha(Impl1)}\|_{\alpha(Impl2)} Impl2$.

Unfortunately, the watchdog process generated by transforming the specification synchronises with the implementation on all the events, $\alpha(S, I)$, of the original assertion, so hiding cannot be pushed far in. Therefore we want to transform the syntax tree, moving the watchdog process downwards; we need associativity and commutativity to do this.

Our simplest heuristic pushes the watchdog process as low in the syntax tree as possible. To illustrate this, consider again the syntax tree shown in Figure 1. Now, neither the implementation process nor any of its component processes can hide events that are (or are eventually renamed to) events in the alphabet of the implementation process. As already noted, this places a severe restriction on the effectiveness of compressions applied below this point in the syntax tree.

To make it possible to hide more events low in the syntax tree we can change the tree in Figure 1 to the one shown in Figure 2.

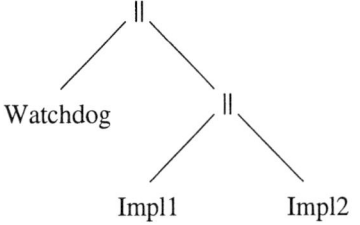

Fig. 1. Watchdog process at the top of the syntax tree.

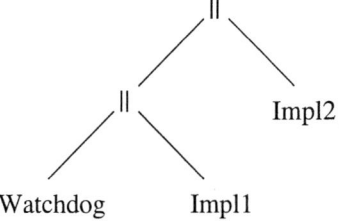

Fig. 2. Transformed syntax tree with the watchdog process moved down

That is, we can change

$$Watchdog\ _{sigma}\|_{\alpha(Impl1,Impl2)} (Impl1\ _{\alpha(Impl1)}\|_{\alpha(Impl2)} Impl2)$$

to

$$(Watchdog\ _{sigma}\|_{\alpha(Impl1)} Impl1)\ _{sigma}\|_{\alpha(Impl2)} Impl2$$

and so allow events on which *Impl2* does not synchronise to be hidden and then compressed from the composition of the watchdog process and *Impl1*. Once the watchdog process has been moved down the syntax tree, there is scope to re-arrange the components of the implementation, depending perhaps on the respective sizes of their interface alphabets. In the case described above, it might be worth composing *Impl2* with the watchdog and then composing the result with *Impl1*.

Clearly, the reordering heuristic described above is very simple, and we do not claim it is optimal. Nevertheless, it has the virtue of addressing an important limitation - outlined above - on the effectiveness of compressions: that one cannot 'compress away' transitions of a state machine that are needed for synchronisation. The framework we have developed allows us to experiment conveniently with a variety of heuristics and so compare them empirically; the emerging results, however, are postponed to a fol low-up paper due to lack of space.

5.3 Pushing Hiding down the Syntax Tree

It is easy to justify pushing hiding down any particular syntax tree. Once we have a syntax tree that composes processes in an optimal order, we are ready to push hiding down this tree, through the process operators.

Hiding can be pushed through alphabetised parallel compositions using the law:

$$(P\ _X\|_Y\ Q) \setminus H = (P \setminus H \cap X{-}Y\ _X\|_Y\ Q \setminus H \cap Y{-}X) \setminus H \cap X \cap Y$$

which exploits the fact that $\cap$ and $-$ associate. A corresponding law for shared parallel is:

$$(P\ \|_X\ Q) \setminus H = (P \setminus H{-}X\ \|_X\ Q \setminus H{-}X) \setminus H \cap X$$

These laws state that we can hide events from the set H at the level of P and Q, gaining efficiency, but only if P and Q cannot synchronise on these events when composed. There are similar laws, not presented here, that allow hiding to be pushed through other CSP_M operators.

5.4 Applying Compressions

There is some choice of which of FDR's compression functions to apply to which compositions (i.e., at which nodes of the syntax tree). For example, one might decide to apply a given compression operator at all leaf nodes, and another at all interior nodes. It is important not to compress too high up in the syntax tree because the full state space – traversed by FDR's compression functions – may become prohibitively large. There is considerable scope to choose the compression operator (if any) to apply at a node based on the nature of the composition and the processes that are being composed. We are currently experimenting with such heuristics.

Our simplest compression strategies are parameterised by a single compression function, which is applied at each interior node of the transformed syntax tree.

6 Implementation

Recall that normal form processes have their initials sets explicitly available. So, the watchdog process transformation can be performed in two parts: first normalise, then transform the normal-form process. FDR already has an efficient implementation of normalisation, and we make use of this to obtain the initials after any trace.

Before performing a refinement check, FDR *normalises* (the state machine for) the specification process – it transforms the specification state machine into a form where there is a unique operational state for each visible trace of the specification process. This operational normal form corresponds directly to the algebraic normal forms. Further, using the scripting interface to FDR it is possible to expose the normal-form of a specification and recurse over it to construct a state machine for the watchdog process. In this way, we have implemented the transforms WDT_S and WDF_S. Given the watchdog process, it is then straightforward to generate the watchdog assertion, and then hide the events of the original assertion (all at the level of state machines).

We have implemented a framework that interfaces with the FDR compiler and its normalisation functionality. This framework performs the watchdog transformations described in this paper and allows us to experiment with a range of compression strategies. The fruits of this experimentation will be reported in due course.

6.1 Complexity

A disappointing worst-case bound can be deduced for this strategy from Valmari and Kervinen's result [15] on the logarithmic complexity of refinement checking when the specification is a simple composition using alphabetised parallel, compared to when arbitrary parallel operators are allowed. Transforming general parallel compositions to alphabetised parallel must be EXPSPACE-hard, or be capable of producing output exponentially larger than its input, as otherwise one could transform any specification into that form and so reduce an EXPSPACE-complete problem to an NPSPACE one.

In practice, the pathological worst cases seem to arise infrequently: the normalisation procedure produces a state machine potentially exponentially larger than its argument, but it usually leaves it roughly the same size. It actually makes it significantly smaller often enough that it is a popular choice of compression function.

Here, the blow-up appears to arise mainly in the numerous large renamings that are required to implement nonsynchronising parallels in terms of the alphabetised form. One essentially needs to invent a new name for each way in which an event can arise at the top of the composition, from different combinations of leaf processes and pre-renaming events. But this cost is already paid once in the FDR "supercompiler" data structures, where it has rarely proven prohibitive. So there is hope that a fairly efficient coding of the transformation will perform satisfactorily in the majority of cases.

7 Related Work

The third author originally proposed the general approach in the course of discussion with Jay Yantchev.

Atanas Parashkevov, a student of Yantchev's, has recently and independently developed that original idea in a different direction, with a view to exploiting it for BDD-based tools. The intention is to hide events to improve the performance of BDD algorithms (rather than to improve the performance of compression algorithms). To this end, Parashkevov has formulated, though not yet published, an Observer process for the traces semantics; this is essentially the simple watchdog process in [2].

Acknowledgements

The third author wishes to thank Jay Yantchev for their conversations on these ideas in 1997. The second and fourth authors were partly funded by the EU Framework V project DSoS: Dependable Systems of Systems.

References

[1] Roscoe, A.W.: The Theory and Practice of Concurrency, Prentice Hall (1998).
[2] Zakiuddin, I., Moffat, N., Goldsmith, M., Whitworth, T.: Property Based Compression Strategies. In: *Proceedings of Second Workshop on Automated Verification of Critical Systems* (AVoCS 2002), University of Birmingham, 15-16 April 2002.
[3] de Roever, W. P., de Boer, F., Hannemann, U., Hooman, J., Lakhnech, Y., Poel, M., Zwiers, J.: Concurrency Verification: Introduction to Compositional and Noncompositional Proof Methods. Cambridge Tracts in Theoretical Computer Science, 54. (2001)
[4] Clarke, E.M., Grumberg, O.: Model Checking and Abstraction, In: *ACM Transactions on Programming Languages and Systems*, ACM Press (1992) 1512-1542
[5] Clarke, E., Filkorn, T., Jha, S: Exploiting symmetry in temporal logic model checking, In: *Proceedings of 5th International Conference on Computer Aided Verification*, (1993)

[6] Ip, C.N., Dill, D.L.: Better Verification Through Symmetry. Computer Hardware Description Languages and their Applications. Elsevier Science Publishers B.V., Amsterdam, Netherland (1996)
[7] Emerson, E.A., Sistla, A.P.: Symmetry and Model Checking. In: *Formal Methods in System Design: An International Journal*, Kluwer Academic Publishers (1994) 105-131
[8] Valmari, A.: A stubborn attack on state explosion, 2nd Workshop on Computer Aided Verification, New Brunswick, NJ, Lecture Notes in Computer Science 531, Springer-Verlag (1987) 156-165
[9] Peled, D., Pnueli, A.: Proving partial order properties, *Theoretical Computer Science*, 126. (1994) 143-182
[10] Godefroid, P.: Partial-order Methods for the Verification of Concurrent Systems, Springer-Verlag Berlin and Heidelberg (1996)
[11] McMillan, K.L.: Symbolic Model Checking. Kluver Academic Press. (1993)
[12] Formal Systems (Europe) Ltd.: FDR User Manual, 1992-99.
[13] Roscoe, A.W., Goldsmith, M., Gardiner, P.H.B., Jackson, D., Scattergood, B., Hulance, J.: Hierarchical Compression for Model-Checking CSP, or How to Check 10^{20} Dining Philosophers for Deadlock. In: *Proceedings of 1st TACAS*, BRICS Notes Series NS-95-1, Department of Computer Science, University of Aarhus, 1995; also Springer LNCS 1019.
[14] Scattergood, J.B.: Tools for CSP and Timed CSP. Oxford University D.Phil. thesis, 1998.
[15] Valmari, A., Kervinen, A.: Alphabet-Based Synchronisation is Exponentially Cheaper. In: Brim, L., Jancar, P., Kretinsky, M., Kucera, A. (eds.): *CONCUR 2002 – Concurrency Theory, 13th International Conference*, Brno, Czech Republic, August 20-23, 2002, Proceedings. Lecture Notes in Computer Science, Vol. 2421. Springer 2002.

A *Circus* Semantics for Ravenscar Protected Objects

Diyaa-Addein Atiya[1], Steve King[1], and Jim C.P. Woodcock[2]

[1] Department of Computer Science, University of York
[2] Computing Laboratory, University of Kent

Abstract. The Ravenscar profile is a subset of the Ada 95 tasking model: it is certifiable, deterministic, supports schedulability analysis, and meets tight memory constraints and performance requirements. A central feature of Ravenscar is the use of protected objects to ensure mutually exclusive access to shared data. We give a semantics to protected objects using *Circus*, a combination of Z and CSP, and prove several important properties; this is the first time that these properties have been verified. Interestingly, all the proofs are conducted in Z, even the ones concerning reactive behaviour.

Keywords: Ravenscar, Ada Protected Objects, Formal Semantics, Z, *Circus*.

1 Introduction

Ada [6, 3] is a high-level programming language designed specifically for large systems, where issues like reliability and safety are major concerns. The language has proved to be successful in the area of high-integrity industrial systems; for example, over 99% of the avionics software in the Boeing 777 is in Ada. Ada's model for concurrent programming is powerful and extensive, but it is also complex, making it difficult to reason about the properties of real-time systems. The Ravenscar profile has been proposed as a greatly simplified subset of the Ada tasking model [4, 5]. The profile has already been accepted [1] for inclusion in the next revision of the Ada language standard. It places an emphasis on predictability and verifiability, and is certifiable and deterministic, supports schedulability analysis, and meets tight memory constraints and performance requirements.

The Ravenscar profile does not allow Ada's rendezvous construct for communication between tasks. Instead, tasks in Ravenscar communicate through shared variables, usually encapsulated inside *protected objects*. This makes protected objects central and fundamental building blocks in Ravenscar programs, as they provide a safe mechanism for accessing the data shared between various tasks. We provide a formal semantics for Ravenscar protected objects, and prove that they enjoy several important properties. We are currently working on a cost-effective technique [2] for verifying Ravenscar programs and this formal semantics is a central part of our work.

The rest of this paper is organised as follows. Section 2 provides a brief, informal account of Ravenscar protected objects; Section 3 then gives a description of *Circus*, which is used to provide their formal model. Sections 4 and 5 contain the semantics and proofs of desired properties. Finally, Section 6 draws conclusions and discusses related work. We show that, although the motivation for providing a formal semantics for Ravenscar protected objects is a specialised one, the results are of general interest in the area of verifying concurrent programs.

2 Ravenscar Protected Objects

Ada protected objects [3, 6, 16] provide a mechanism for asynchronous communication between tasks over shared variables. The declaration of an Ada protected object comprises two main parts: the private data to be shared between the communicating tasks, and an interface of operations for accessing that data. The data encapsulated within a protected object can be accessed only through the interface provided by that object. It is guaranteed that the operations are executed in a manner that ensures mutual exclusion while the data is updated [6].

There are three kinds of interface operations: *protected functions*, *protected procedures*, and *protected entries*. Whilst protected functions provide concurrent read-only access, protected procedures and protected entries provide mutually exclusive read/write access to the data encapsulated in a protected object. Also, calls to protected functions are executed in mutual exclusion with calls to protected procedures/entries. Thus, at any moment, the protected object is in exactly one of the following states:

1. No calls are executing.
2. Only protected function calls are executing.
3. Only one call is executing, either a protected procedure or a protected entry.

An entry call is guarded by a boolean-valued *barrier*. If a protected entry call is made when the barrier is false, then the call is suspended, even if there are no function or procedure calls currently executing inside the protected object. The suspended task goes into the *entry queue*, to wait until the barrier is true and there are no calls are currently executing. All barriers get re-evaluated after the execution of any procedure or entry call [6, Chapter 7]. Thus, entry barriers can be used to provide conditional synchronisation between tasks accessing the protected object. For example, if the data encapsulated inside the protected object is an array, then one can use entry barriers to state that a read (write) cannot be performed when the array is empty (full).

To help provide a concrete view of the discussion above, Figure 1 presents an Ada protected object that encapsulates an integer variable. The encapsulated variable can be accessed only through the protected function *Read*, which returns the current value, and the protected procedure *Write*, which assigns a new value. Many tasks could be concurrently executing *Read* calls; however, if one task is actively executing a *Write* call, then no other task can concurrently execute either a *Read* or a *Write* call until the current task has finished.

```
-- A protected object containing an integer variable
protected pInteger is
    function Read return INTEGER;
    procedure Write (data : in INTEGER);
    private
        d : INTEGER;
end pInteger;

protected body pInteger is
    function Read return INTEGER is
    begin
        return d;
    end Read;

    procedure Write (data : in INTEGER) is
    begin
        d := data;
    end Write;
end pInteger;
```

Fig. 1. An example of a protected integer variable

The designers of the Ravenscar profile chose protected objects as the only mechanism for communication between tasks, in order to improve schedulability analysis [5]; they also imposed a number of other restrictions, in order to meet various design requirements, such as determinism. Many of these restrictions are syntactic; for example, Ravenscar does not permit declaration of protected objects local to subprograms, tasks, or other protected objects. The discussion of such restrictions is not relevant in this paper; rather, we are interested in the restrictions imposed on the functional aspects of protected objects, which can be summarised as follows:

- **R1:** A protected object can have at most one entry.
- **R2:** No more than one task may queue on an entry at any time.
- **R3:** The barrier must be either static or the value of a component.
- **R4:** Like in Ada, potentially blocking *operations* are not allowed.

An application could further restrict **R2** so that only one task is able to call each protected entry [5]. We adopt the strong version of **R2**, as a static check could be provided for it. Thus, at most one task can be associated with the protected entry of a protected object and this task can then be determined statically at compile time. In **R4**, the profile prohibits the presence of entry call statements inside the body of any protected operation, as the execution of that operation could then block.

Section 4 provides a formal model in *Circus* of Ravenscar protected objects; for those not familiar with the language, the next section describes *Circus*.

3 Circus

Circus is a unified programming language that combines Z [13, 25] and CSP [11, 19] constructs, together with specification statements [17] and guarded commands [9]. With Z and CSP integrated into the language, *Circus* can be used to describe both the state-oriented and the behavioural aspects of concurrent systems. Though there are several other examples of combining Z and CSP in the literature (see, for example, the survey in [10]), *Circus* distinguishes itself by a theory of refinement [7, 8, 21] for the derivation of programs from their specifications in a calculational style like Morgan's [18]. The formal semantics of *Circus* [24] is based on unifying theories of programming (UTP) [12], as well as various laws for refining [8] specifications into designs and code.

A *Circus* program is a sequence of:

- **Z paragraphs:** declaring the types, global constants, and other data structures used by the processes defined in the program.
- **Channel definitions:** declaring typed channels through which processes can communicate or synchronise.
- **Process definitions:** declaring encapsulated state and reactive behaviour.

In its simplest form, a process definition is a sequence of Z paragraphs describing the internal state, and a sequence of actions (defined in terms of Z schemas, CSP operators, and guarded commands) describing the possible interaction between the process and its environment. In more sophisticated forms, a process may be defined in terms of combinations of other processes using the operators of CSP.

Example: We use *Circus* to model a simple bank account that stores the account balance and provides four ways of interacting with the outside world:

- Initialise the balance and overdraft facility.
- Credit the account.
- Debit the account.
- Request the account balance and funds available.

Figure 2 contains the *Circus* program. Interaction with the outside world is through the four channels: *init*, *cred*, *deb*, and *bal*. The encapsulated state has three components: the account *balance* (which may be negative), the permitted overdraft (a non-negative value), and the funds available (invariantly, the sum of the balance and the overdraft). A further state invariant requires that the funds be non-negative too, so that the balance hasn't exceeded the overdraft facility. Thus, a legitimate state may have a *balance* of -£450, and an *overdraft* of £1,000; this implies that *funds* is set to £550, which satisfies the required constraint.

The external behaviour of this process is given by the *main action*

$init\,?\,(d, o) \rightarrow \mathit{InitAccountState};$
$\mu X \bullet (\mathit{Credit} \;\Box\; \mathit{Debit} \;\Box\; \mathit{CheckBalance}\,);\, X$

This depends on the definition of four auxiliary actions, each defined within the body of *BankAccount*. First the account is initialised with a communication of

channel $init, bal : \mathbb{Z} \times \mathbb{N};\ cred, deb : \mathbb{N}$

process $BankAccount \;\widehat{=}\;$ **begin**

$\quad AccountState \;\widehat{=}\; [\,balance, funds : \mathbb{Z};\ overdraft : \mathbb{N}\ |\ funds = overdraft + balance \geq 0\,]$

$\quad InitAccountState \;\widehat{=}\; [\,AccountState';\ d?, o? : \mathbb{N}\ |\ balance' = d \wedge overdraft' = o?\,]$

$\quad Credit \;\widehat{=}\; cred\,?\,value \rightarrow balance := balance + value$

$\quad Deduct \;\widehat{=}\; (\,amount : \mathbb{N} \bullet amount \leq funds\ \&\ balance := balance - amount\,)$

$\quad Debit \;\widehat{=}\; deb\,?\,value \rightarrow Deduct(value)$

$\quad CheckBalance \;\widehat{=}\; bal\,!\,(balance, funds) \rightarrow Skip$

$\quad \bullet\ (\,init\,?\,(d, o) \rightarrow InitAccountState;\ (\,\mu X \bullet (\,Credit\ \square\ Debit\ \square\ CheckBalance\,);\ X\,)\,)$

end

Fig. 2. A *Circus* BankAccount

the variables d and o through the channel *init*. Following the communication, the schema action *InitAccountState* is executed; this specifies that *balance* is assigned the value of d, and *overdraft* the value of o. This is followed by a non-terminating loop that repeatedly offers the external choice between three actions. The *Credit* action inputs a natural number *value* through the *cred* channel and then adds this to the *balance*. The *Debit* action inputs a natural number *value* through the *deb* channel and then behaves as specified by *Deduct(value)*. The parametrised action *Deduct* subtracts its argument from the *balance*, provided that there are enough *funds* to do this. Finally, *CheckBalance* outputs both the *balance* and *funds* available as a pair on the *bal* channel. □

4 Protected Objects: A *Circus* Model

4.1 Global Definitions

Protected objects are used for interaction between tasks in a Ravenscar program. Tasks are drawn from the given set *TaskId*; by convention, there is a distinguished identifier that is never used by any task.

$[\,TaskId\,]$

$\quad null\_task : TaskId;\ ValidTaskId : \mathbb{P}\,TaskId$

$\quad ValidTaskId = TaskId \setminus \{null\_task\}$

We model a protected object as a *Circus* process with nine channels, each corresponding to some interaction with its environment. The channel *read* (*write*) is used to communicate the events where a task issues a call to a protected function (procedure). If the entry task issues a call to the protected-object entry, and the barrier is true and no other task is accessing the object, then the entry task can gain access; this is modelled by a communication over the *enter* channel. Otherwise, the entry task must *wait*. If at some later point, the barrier becomes true and there are no tasks accessing the object, then the waiting entry task may *start*. An event on the channel *leave* corresponds to a task leaving the object. Changes in the state of the barrier are signalled through the *update_bar* channel, after the execution of a protected procedure or the protected entry. Finally, the channels *get* and *put* are used for accessing and updating the protected object's data.

channel *read*, *write*, *enter*, *wait*, *start*, *leave* : *ValidTaskId*
channel [*T*] *update_bar* : *T* × *Boolean*; *get*, *put* : *ValidTaskId* × *T*

Every communication between the protected object and a task requires the task's identity as part of the event; in each case, the *null_task* is excluded. Our model of the protected object is generic, in that we parametrise the type of the data being encapsulated. As a consequence, the channels *get* and *put* are also defined generically.

process $PO \mathrel{\widehat=} [\, T \,]$ **begin**

In the next section, we describe the state of a protected object.

4.2 Process State

There are six components in the state of a protected object.

- The data encapsulated, *data*, of type *T*.
- The entry task's identifier, *entry_task*. If this is the *null_task*, then no entry call is possible.
- The current value of the boolean entry barrier, *barrier*.
- A boolean flag that is true exactly when the entry task is *waiting*.
- The set of *readers*, those tasks currently actively executing a function call.
- The set of *writers*, those tasks currently actively executing a procedure or an entry call.

Both sets must be finite and contain only valid task identifiers. As usual, we use *Circus*'s boolean values as though they were predicates.

There are three further state invariants.

- Reading and writing are mutually exclusive.
- There must be no more than one writer.
- If the entry task is waiting, then it can neither be the *null_task* nor a reader or writer.

The declaration and invariants are collected into a schema describing the state of the process.

$\begin{array}{|l}\hline \_POState_____\\ data : T \\ entry\_task : TaskId \\ barrier, waiting : Boolean \\ readers, writers : \mathbb{F}\ ValidTaskId \\ \hline readers \neq \emptyset \Rightarrow writers = \emptyset \\ \#writers \leq 1 \\ waiting \Rightarrow entry\_task \neq null\_task \land entry\_task \notin readers \cup writers \\ \hline \end{array}$

The invariant that readers and writers be mutually exclusive is captured in our model by requiring that, if there are any *readers*, then there must be no *writers*. Note that this also requires as a consequence (its contrapositive), that, if there are any *writers*, then there must be no *readers*.

4.3 Process Actions

A protected object in its initial state has no waiting entry task and no readers or writers; its data, entry task identifier, and barrier must be given initial values.

$\begin{array}{|l}\hline \_InitPOState_____\\ POState' \\ d? : T \\ t? : TaskId \\ b? : Boolean \\ \hline data' = d? \land barrier' = b? \land entry\_task' = t? \\ \neg\ waiting' \land readers' = writers' = \emptyset \\ \hline \end{array}$

1. When a task issues a function call, it may become a reader within the protected object; this is signalled by the communication of the task's identifier over the *read* channel. This event is permitted if there are no writers, and no waiting entry task with an open barrier.

    $BecomeReader \,\widehat{=}\,$
      $writers = \emptyset \land \neg\ (barrier \land waiting)\ \&$
      $read\,?\,t : ValidTaskId \setminus (((\{entry\_task\} \lhd waiting \rhd \emptyset) \cup readers) \rightarrow$
        $readers := readers \cup \{t\}$

    Only valid task identifiers are candidates for becoming a reader; moreover, if the entry task is waiting, then it cannot also become a reader.

2. When a task issues a procedure call, it may become a writer within the protected object; this is signalled by the communication of the task's identifier over the *write* channel. This event is permitted if there are no readers or writers, and no waiting entry task with an open barrier.

    $BecomeWriter \,\widehat{=}\,$
      $readers \cup writers = \emptyset \land \neg\ (barrier \land waiting)\ \&$
      $write\,?\,t : ValidTaskId \setminus (\{entry\_task\} \lhd waiting \rhd \emptyset) \rightarrow$
        $writers := \{t\}$

Only valid task identifiers are candidates for becoming a writer; moreover, if the entry task is waiting, then it cannot also become a writer.

3. When the entry task issues the protected entry call, it may become a writer or it may have to wait, depending on the *barrier*. In both cases, there must be no readers or writers, and the entry task must not be already waiting.

   (a) If the barrier is open, then the entry task may enter the object; this is signalled by the event $enter.entry\_task$.

   $ETEnter \,\widehat{=}\,$
   $\quad readers \cup writers = \emptyset \wedge barrier \wedge \neg \, waiting \,\&$
   $\quad enter.entry\_task \rightarrow$
   $\quad\quad writers := \{entry\_task\}$

   The entry task becomes the sole writer.

   (b) If the barrier is closed, then the entry task must wait on the entry queue; this is signalled by the event $wait.entry\_task$.

   $ETWait \,\widehat{=}\,$
   $\quad readers \cup writers = \emptyset \wedge \neg \, barrier \wedge \neg \, waiting \,\&$
   $\quad wait.entry\_task \rightarrow$
   $\quad\quad waiting := \mathsf{True}$

   The next action describes how the waiting entry task can proceed.

4. If the barrier is open, there are no readers or writers, and there is a waiting entry task, then it may become a writer.

   $ETStart \,\widehat{=}\,$
   $\quad readers \cup writers = \emptyset \wedge barrier \wedge waiting \,\&$
   $\quad start.entry\_task \rightarrow$
   $\quad\quad writers, waiting := \{entry\_task\}, \mathsf{False}$

   When the waiting task starts, it leaves the entry queue.

5. When an actively reading task completes its function call, it leaves the protected object; this is signalled by the communication of the task's identifier over the *leave* channel.

   $ReaderLeave \,\widehat{=}\, leave \,?\, t : readers \rightarrow readers := readers \setminus \{t\}$

6. When an actively writing task completes its procedure or entry call, it also leaves the protected object; this is signalled by the communication of the task's identifier over the *leave* channel.

   $WriterLeave \,\widehat{=}\,$
   $\quad leave \,?\, t : writers \rightarrow update\_bar \,!\, data \,?\, b \rightarrow writers, barrier := \emptyset, b$

   The barrier may have changed as a result of the actions of the writer, so it must be updated.

7. Any of the tasks currently reading or writing may read the protected data; this is signalled by a communication on the *get* channel.

$$GetData \mathrel{\widehat{=}} get\,?\,t : (readers \cup writers)\,!\,data \rightarrow Skip$$

The state invariant ensures that, if there are tasks reading, then there are no tasks writing, and *vice versa*.

8. Any of the tasks currently writing may write to the protected object; this is signalled by a communication on the *put* channel.

$$PutData \mathrel{\widehat{=}} put\,?\,t : writers\,?\,d : T \rightarrow data := d$$

The state invariant ensures that, if a task is writing, then it is the sole writer.

The choice between actions (1–8) is offered repeatedly.

$$\begin{aligned}ReactiveBehaviour \mathrel{\widehat{=}} \mu X \bullet (\ &BecomeReader\\
\Box\ &BecomeWriter\\
\Box\ &ETEnter\\
\Box\ &ETWait\\
\Box\ &ETStart\\
\Box\ &ReaderLeave\\
\Box\ &WriterLeave\\
\Box\ &GetData\\
\Box\ &PutData\ );\ X\end{aligned}$$

The extensional behaviour of the process is given by its main action.

• *InitPOState*; *ReactiveBehaviour*

end

A useful check on the consistency of our model is that the initial state exists.

Theorem 1 (Consistency of protected object initial state).

$$\exists\, POState' \bullet InitPOState$$

Proof Each state component is fixed by an equality in *InitPOState*; these expression trivially satisfy *POState*'s invariant (by the one-point rule and properties of propositional calculus and set theory). □

5 The Model Exhibits the Expected Properties

In this section we prove that our *Circus* model of Ravenscar protected objects is free from the risk of deadlock or divergence, and that its state invariants are preserved by its actions. To do this, we define a deadlock-free, livelock-free abstraction that has the same structure, and then prove that our model refines the abstraction.

Our abstract model has the same structure as before. The abstract model has the same state components, with the same types and invariants. It uses the same channels. It has similar actions, except that there are no guards, and state changes are unconstrained, provided the state invariant is maintained. Its main action is the repeated nondeterministic choice between its actions, following the initialisation of the state.

process $APO \,\widehat{=}\, [\, T\,]$ **begin**

$\underline{\,APOState\,}$
$data : T$
$entry\_task : TaskId$
$barrier, waiting : Boolean$
$readers, writers : \mathbb{F}\, ValidTaskId$
$\rule{8cm}{0.4pt}$
$readers \neq \emptyset \Rightarrow writers = \emptyset$
$\#writers \leq 1$
$waiting \Rightarrow entry\_task \neq null\_task \wedge entry\_task \notin readers \cup writers$

$InitAPOState \,\widehat{=}\, [\, APOState';\ d? : T;\ t? : TaskId;\ b? : Boolean\,]$
$ABecomeReader \,\widehat{=}\, \sqcap\, t : ValidTaskId \bullet read.t \rightarrow \Delta APOState$
$ABecomeWriter \,\widehat{=}\, \sqcap\, t : ValidTaskId \bullet write.t \rightarrow \Delta APOState$
$AETEnter \,\widehat{=}\, \sqcap\, t : ValidTaskId \bullet enter.t \rightarrow \Delta APOState$
$AETWait \,\widehat{=}\, \sqcap\, t : ValidTaskId \bullet wait.t \rightarrow \Delta APOState$
$AETStart \,\widehat{=}\, \sqcap\, t : ValidTaskId \bullet start.t \rightarrow \Delta APOState$
$AReaderLeave \,\widehat{=}\, \sqcap\, t : ValidTaskId \bullet leave.t \rightarrow \Delta APOState$
$AWriterLeave \,\widehat{=}\, \sqcap\, t : ValidTaskId \bullet leave.t \rightarrow$
$\qquad (\sqcap\, d : T;\ b : Boolean \bullet update\_bar.d.b \rightarrow \Delta APOState\,)$
$AGetData \,\widehat{=}\, \sqcap\, t : ValidTaskId;\ d : T \bullet get.t.d \rightarrow \Delta APOState$
$APutData \,\widehat{=}\, \sqcap\, t : ValidTaskId;\ d : T \bullet put.t.d \rightarrow \Delta APOState$

$AReactiveBehaviour \,\widehat{=}\, \mu X \bullet (\ ABecomeReader$
$\qquad\qquad\qquad\qquad\qquad\sqcap\, ABecomeWriter$
$\qquad\qquad\qquad\qquad\qquad\sqcap\, AETEnter$
$\qquad\qquad\qquad\qquad\qquad\sqcap\, AETWait$
$\qquad\qquad\qquad\qquad\qquad\sqcap\, AETStart$
$\qquad\qquad\qquad\qquad\qquad\sqcap\, AReaderLeave$
$\qquad\qquad\qquad\qquad\qquad\sqcap\, AWriterLeave$
$\qquad\qquad\qquad\qquad\qquad\sqcap\, AGetData$
$\qquad\qquad\qquad\qquad\qquad\sqcap\, APutData\ );\ X$

- $InitAPOState;\ AReactiveBehaviour$

end

Theorem 2 (Abstraction total and non-stopping). *If both ValidTaskId and T are nonempty, then the abstraction APO is both deadlock and livelock-free.*

Proof There are eight conditions that are sufficient for a Circus process to be both deadlock and divergence-free:

1. It is sequential.
2. It is free from hiding.
3. It doesn't mention Stop or Chaos.
4. All internal and external choices are over non-empty sets.
5. Its channel types are non-empty.
6. It local definitions are satisfiable.
7. Its main action's initial state exists.
8. Its actions are all total on the state.

Conditions (1)–(3) are satisfied syntactically. Conditions (4) and (5) are guaranteed by the provisos of the theorem. Condition (6) is trivially satisfied, since there are no local definitions. Condition (7) may be stated as

$$\forall d? : T;\ t? : TaskId;\ b? : Boolean \bullet \exists APOState' \bullet InitAPOState$$

Expanding the schemas, we must prove that

$$\forall d? : T;\ t? : TaskId;\ b? : Boolean \bullet$$
$$\exists data' : T;\ entry\_task' : TaskId;\ barrier', waiting' : Boolean;$$
$$readers', writers' : \mathbb{F}\ ValidTaskId \bullet$$
$$(readers' \neq \emptyset \Rightarrow writers' = \emptyset) \land$$
$$\#writers' \leq 1 \land$$
$$(waiting' \Rightarrow entry\_task' \neq null\_task \land entry\_task' \notin readers' \cup writers')$$

which is true, since both T and $TaskId$ are non-empty. Condition (8) follows trivially from the construction of the actions from the total, but arbitrary state change $\Delta APOState$: all actions have true guards and never abort. □

Thus, if we can prove that PO is a refinement of APO, then we are sure that PO is also deadlock-free and divergence-free. Moreover, the main action of PO shall preserve the state invariants, otherwise the process would not be divergence-free. We state and prove that PO is a refinement of APO in Theorem 3, which will make use of the following three laws.

Law 1 is about the action refinement ($\sqsubseteq_\mathcal{A}$, see [7]) of internal choices over a number of prefixed actions. Using this law, the internal choice can be transformed to an external choice over a number of guarded actions.

Law 1 (Refine nondeterministic prefixed actions) *Suppose, for $i \in I$, that c_i is a channel, that S_i and T_i are subsets of the communicable values over c_i, that T_i is non-empty, that A_i and B_i are actions over a common state, that g_i is a boolean-valued expression over the state, and that pre is an assertion about the state.*

$$\{pre\}\ \sqcap i : I \bullet (\sqcap x : T_i \bullet c_i.x \to A_i)\ \sqsubseteq_\mathcal{A}\ \square i : I \bullet g_i\ \&\ c_i?x : S_i \to B_i$$

provided

1. $pre \Rightarrow \bigvee i : I \bullet g_i \wedge S_i \neq \emptyset$
2. $\forall i : I \bullet S_i \subseteq T_i$
3. $A_i \sqsubseteq_{\mathcal{A}} B_i$, for all $i : I$

There are two sources of nondeterminism in the abstract action: the choice between actions, and the choice between the value communicated; both of these become external choices, with certain alternatives excluded by the introduction of the guard and restricted range of input. The assertion $\{pre\}$ is used to record the abstract action's precondition. □

Law 2 applies to guarded prefixed actions. Simply, the law states that if the action does engage in a communication with its environment, then the guard (g) and the communicated value (x) are in scope for the that part of the action which follows the communication.

Law 2 (Guarded, prefixed action assumption) *Suppose that A is an action, g is a guard over A's state, c is a channel, and S is a subset of c's communicable values.*

$$g \;\&\; c\,?\,x : S \rightarrow A \quad = \quad g \;\&\; c\,?\,x : S \rightarrow \{g \wedge x \in S\}\; A$$

Although state is encapsulated in processes, it is not encapsulated in actions; however, if there are parallel actions, then partitioning the state ensures that the assumption is safe. □

Law 3 states the necessary conditions for the refinement of a schema operation into an assignment statement.

Law 3 (Refine schema action to assignment) *Suppose that Op is a schema action over a state with variables x and w, that e is an expression with the same type as x, and that pre is an assertion over the variables in scope.*

$$Op \quad \sqsubseteq_{\mathcal{A}} \quad \{pre\}\; x := e$$

provided

$pre \wedge \text{pre } Op \Rightarrow Op\,[\,x', w' := e, w\,]$

The notation $S\,[\,y := f\,]$ denotes the predicate S, with f systematically substituted for y. □

Now, we will show that our model of Ravenscar protected object PO is deadlock-free and divergence-free. To prove these properties for APO it was necessary to have $T \neq \emptyset$ and $ValidTaskId \neq \emptyset$, see Theorem 2 above. For PO, however, we will need a slightly stronger proviso: $T \neq \emptyset$, and $ValidTaskId \setminus \{entry\_task\} \neq \emptyset$. That is, T is not empty, and there exist at least one valid task which is not the entry task.

Theorem 3 (Protected object total and non-stopping). *Provided that TaskId \ {entry_task} has at least one element, and that PO is instantiated by a non-empty actual parameter, then PO is deadlock and livelock-free.*

Proof *It is sufficient to show that $APO \sqsubseteq_\mathcal{P} PO$. From [8], and since APO and PO have the same state, this refinement holds provided that*

(a) $InitAPOState \sqsubseteq_\mathcal{A} InitPOState$
(b) $AReactiveBehaviour \sqsubseteq_\mathcal{A} ReactiveBehaviour$

Proviso (a) follows from Theorem 1. We also know that $\sqsubseteq_\mathcal{A}$ distributes through recursion. Thus, to prove Proviso (b), it is sufficient to show that

$$(ABecomeReader \sqcap .. \sqcap APutData) \sqsubseteq_\mathcal{A} (BecomeReader \square .. \square PutData)$$

This, in turn, is a direct consequence of applying Law 1 to the nondeterministic choice over APO actions.
Thus, all we have to do now is prove that provisos 1–3, of Law 1, hold for APO and PO actions.
Provisos 1–2 are proven in Lemma 1, Appendix A
Proviso 3 follows from the following proof obligations:

1. *BecomeReader*

[$\Delta APOState; t : ValidTaskId$]
$\sqsubseteq_\mathcal{A}$ $\left\{ \begin{array}{l} writers = \emptyset \wedge \neg (barrier \wedge waiting) \\ t? \in ValidTaskId \setminus (((\{entry\_task\} \triangleleft waiting \triangleright \emptyset) \cup readers) \end{array} \right\}$
$readers := readers \cup \{t\}$

2. *BecomeWriter*

[$\Delta APOState; t? : ValidTaskId$]
$\sqsubseteq_\mathcal{A}$ $\left\{ \begin{array}{l} readers \cup writers = \emptyset \wedge \neg (barrier \wedge waiting) \\ t \in ValidTaskId \setminus (\{entry\_task\} \triangleleft waiting \triangleright \emptyset) \end{array} \right\}$ $writers := \{t\}$

3. *ETEnter*

[$\Delta APOState; t? : ValidTaskId$]
$\sqsubseteq_\mathcal{A}$ $\{readers \cup writers = \emptyset \wedge barrier \wedge \neg waiting\}$ $writers := \{entry\_task\}$

4. *ETWait*

[$\Delta APOState; t? : ValidTaskId$]
$\sqsubseteq_\mathcal{A}$ $\{readers \cup writers = \emptyset \wedge \neg barrier \wedge \neg waiting\}$ $waiting := \mathsf{True}$

5. *ETStart*

[$\Delta APOState; t? : ValidTaskId$]
$\sqsubseteq_\mathcal{A}$ $\{readers \cup writers = \emptyset \wedge barrier \wedge waiting\}$
$writers, waiting := \{entry\_task\}, \mathsf{False}$

6. *ReaderLeave*

$[\Delta APOState;\ t?: ValidTaskId\,] \sqsubseteq_A \quad \{t \in readers\}\ readers := readers \setminus \{t\}$

7. *WriterLeave*

$[\Delta APOState;\ t?: ValidTaskId\,]$
$\sqsubseteq_A \quad \{t \in writers\}\ update\_bar\,!\,data?\,b \to writers, barrier := \emptyset, b$

8. *GetData*

$[\Delta APOState;\ t?: ValidTaskId\,] \quad \sqsubseteq_A \quad \{t \in readers \cup writers\}\ Skip$

9. *PutData*

$[\Delta APOState;\ t?: ValidTaskId\,] \quad \sqsubseteq_A \quad \{t \in writers\}\ data := d$

Proof obligation (BecomeReader) follows directly from Lemma 2, Appendix A. The other obligations have similar proofs. □

As a direct consequence of Theorem 3, *PO* must preserve the state invariants; otherwise the process is cannot be divergence-free. Thus, like protected objects, *PO* provides concurrent read-only access to the encapsulated data, and ensures mutual exclusion when that data could be updated. Also, by definition, *PO* complies with restriction R1–R4 in Section 2. Therefore, *PO* satisfies the expected properties of Ravenscar protected objects.

One important remark before finishing that section is that although the statement of Theorem 3 is about reactive behaviour properties, the proof is conducted entirely in Z. This means that Z tools (e.g. [14, 20, 22]), usually used for verifying sequential systems, can be used to provide proofs about concurrent programs as well. Also, we now have one language in which we can reason about both the state-oriented and behavioural properties of a given system. In turn, this means less overhead in reasoning about different properties of the system in different notations.

6 Conclusions and Related Work

The Ravenscar profile is a restricted tasking model of Ada—designed for verifiability, certifiability, and predictability. The Ravenscar profile provides a shared-variable asynchronous tasking model for communications between tasks. This means that in Ravenscar, protected objects are important as the only mechanism for: encapsulating the data shared between the tasks, granting mutually exclusive access to that data, and providing condition synchronisation between the various tasks. In this report, we provided a formal model, in *Circus*, for Ravenscar protected objects. This is a novel contribution where the functional properties of Ravenscar protected objects have been completely formalised and verified.

Another formal model, presented in UPPAAL, of Ravenscar protected objects is provided in [15]. However, the UPPAAL model is mainly concerned with the timing of calls to protected objects. Also, being based on a model checking approach, the UPPAAL model of protected object was only verified for three tasks; no statement could be made by the authors about the validity of the model for a larger number of tasks. Unlike the work in [15] the proofs about our model are independent of the environment, i.e. the number of calling tasks and the details of which task is a reader and which task is a writer. Indeed, the proof technique presented in this report stand as an interesting result on its own. This is because, despite the fact that some of the properties verified are about the behavioural aspect of the model (e.g., freedom from deadlock), our proof-by-refinement approach enabled us to conduct all the proofs in Z—we believe that this approach can be easily adopted for reasoning about other *Circus* specifications.

The benefits of using Z to conduct proofs about concurrency are manifold. For example, we can hide the complicated details of the UTP semantics of *Circus* [24] away from the program verifier. Also, we can employ current tools for Z (e.g., CADiZ [22, 23], Z-Eves [20], or ProofPower [14]) and use them for reasoning about concurrent programs.

We are currently using the *Circus* model, presented here, as a basis for implementing CSP channels in Ravenscar. This is an essential part of a larger project [2] where we aim at a cost-effective technique for verifying Ravenscar programs against their *Circus* specifications.

Acknowledgements

This work is partially supported by the QinetiQ company. Thanks are also due to Alan Burns and Ana Cavalcanti for their insightful comments and useful discussions.

References

1. P. Amey and B. Dobbing. High Integrity Ravenscar. In *8th International Conference on Reliable Software Technologies — Ada-Europe 2003 (AE03)*, Toulouse, France, 2003. To appear.
2. D. M. Atiya and S. King. A compliance notation for verifying concurrent systems. In *ICSE02 – International Conference on Software Engineering*, pages 731–732, Orlando, USA, 2002.
3. J. Barnes. *Programming in Ada 95*. Addison-Wesley, 2nd edition, 1998.
4. A. Burns, B. Dobbing, and G. Romanski. The Ravenscar tasking profile for high integrity real-time programs. In L. Asplund, editor, *Ada-Europe 98*, volume 1411 of *Lecture Notes in Computer Science*, pages 263–275. Springer-Verlag, 1998.
5. A. Burns, B. Dobbing, and T. Vardanega. Guide for the use of the Ada Ravenscar Profile in high integrity systems. Technical Report YCS-2003-348, Department of Computer Science, University of York, January 2003.
6. A. Burns and A. Wellings. *Concurrency in Ada*. Cambridge University Press, 2nd edition, 1998.

7. A. L. C. Cavalcanti, A. C. A. Sampaio, and J. C. P. Woodcock. Refinement of actions in *Circus*. In *Proceedings of REFINE'2002*, Electronic Notes in Theoretical Computer Science, 2002.
8. A. L. C. Cavalcanti, A. C. A. Sampaio, and J. C. P. Woodcock. A refinement strategy for *Circus*. to appear in Formal Aspects of Computing, 2003.
9. E. W. Dijkstra. *A Discipline of Programming*. Prentice Hall, Englewood Cliffs, New Jersey, 1976.
10. C. Fischer. How to Combine Z with a Process Algebra. In J. P. Bowen, A. Fett, and M. G. Hinchey, editors, *Proceedings of the 11th International Conference of Z Users (ZUM'98)*, volume 1493 of *Lecture Notes in Computer Science*, pages 5–23, Germany, 1998. SpringerVerlag.
11. C. A. R. Hoare. *Communicating Sequential Processes*. Prentice-Hall, London, 1985.
12. C. A. R. Hoare and He Jifeng. *Unifying Theories of Programming*. Series in Computer Science. Prentice Hall, 1998.
13. ISO/IEC 13568:2002. Information technology—Z formal specification notation—syntax, type system and semantics. International Standard.
14. Lemma 1 Ltd. *ProofPower Compliance Tool: User Guide*. 2000.
15. K. Lundqvist, L. Asplund, and S. Michell. A Formal Model of the Ada Ravenscar Tasking Profile; Protected Objects. In M. G. Harbour and J. A. de la Puente, editors, *Reliable Software Technologies, Proceedings of the Ada Europe Conference.*, volume 1622 of *Lecture Notes in Computer Science*, pages 12–25, Santander, 1999. Springer-Verlag.
16. MITRE Corporation. Ada Reference Manual, ISO/IEC 8652:1995(E) with Technical Corrigendum 1, 2000.
17. Carroll Morgan. The specification statement. *ACM Transactions on Programming Languages and Systems*, 10(3):403–419, 1988.
18. Carroll Morgan. *Programming from Specifications*. Prentice Hall International, 2nd ed. edition, 1994.
19. A. W. Roscoe. *The Theory and Practice of Concurrency*. International Series in Computer Science. Prentice Hall, 1998.
20. M. Saaltink. The Z/EVES system. In J. P. Bowen, M. G. Hinchey, and D. Till, editors, *ZUM'97: The Z Formal Specification Notation, 10th International Conference of Z Users*, volume 1212 of *Lecture Notes in Computer Science*, pages 72–85. Springer-Verlag, 1997.
21. A. C. A. Sampaio, J. C. P. Woodcock, and A. L. C. Cavalcanti. Refinement in *Circus*. In L.-H. Eriksson and P. Lindsay, editors, *FME 2002 — Formal Methods Europe*, volume 2391 of *Lecture Notes in Computer Science*, pages 451–470. Springer-Verlag, 2002.
22. I. Toyn. Formal reasoning in the Z notation using CADiZ. In N. A. Merriam, editor, *2nd International Workshop on User Interface Design for Theorem Proving Systems*, 1996.
23. I. Toyn and J. A. McDermid. CADiZ: An architecture for Z tools and its implementation. *Software Practice and Experience*, 25(3):305–330, 1995.
24. J. C. P. Woodcock and A. L. C. Cavalcanti. The Semantics of Circus. In D. Bert, J. P. Bowen, M. C. Henson, and K. Robinson, editors, *ZB 2002: Formal Specification and Development in Z and B*, volume 2272 of *Lecture Notes in Computer Science*, pages 184–203. Springer-Verlag, 2002.
25. Jim Woodcock and Jim Davies. *Using Z—Specification, Refinement, and Proof*. Prentice Hall, 1996.

A Lemmas

This appendix presents the lemmas, used inside the proof of Theorem 3, and their proofs.

Lemma 1 (Protected object refinement, Law 1 provisos (1) and (2)). *In applying Law 1 in our proof that APO is refined by PO, provisos (1–2) hold.*

Proof. *Proviso (2) is trivially satisfied, since the abstract sets are all types. Proviso (1) requires that at least one branch in PO has a true guard and non-empty range of input. That is,*

$(\textit{readers} = \emptyset \land \neg\,(\textit{barrier} \land \textit{waiting}) \land$
$\quad \textit{ValidTaskId} \setminus (((\{\textit{entry\_task}\} \lhd \textit{waiting} \rhd \emptyset) \cup \textit{readers}) \neq \emptyset\,)$
$\lor$
$(\textit{readers} \cup \textit{writers} = \emptyset \land \neg\,(\textit{barrier} \land \textit{waiting}) \land$
$\quad \textit{ValidTaskId} \setminus (\{\textit{entry\_task}\} \lhd \textit{waiting} \rhd \emptyset) \neq \emptyset\,)$
$\lor$
$\textit{readers} \cup \textit{writers} = \emptyset \land \textit{barrier} \land \neg\,\textit{waiting} \land \{\textit{entry\_task}\} \neq \emptyset$
$\lor$
$\textit{readers} \cup \textit{writers} = \emptyset \land \neg\,\textit{barrier} \land \neg\,\textit{waiting} \land \{\textit{entry\_task}\} \neq \emptyset$
$\lor$
$\textit{readers} \cup \textit{writers} = \emptyset \land \textit{barrier} \land \textit{waiting} \land \{\textit{entry\_task}\} \neq \emptyset$
$\lor$
$\textit{readers} \neq \emptyset$
$\lor$
$\textit{writers} \neq \emptyset$
$\lor$
$\textit{readers} \cup \textit{writers} \neq \emptyset$
$\lor$
$\textit{writers} \neq \emptyset \land T \neq \emptyset$

This may be simplified in the propositional calculus to

$\textit{readers} \cup \textit{writers} = \emptyset \land \neg\,\textit{barrier} \land \textit{waiting} \Rightarrow \{\textit{entry\_task}\} \neq \textit{ValidTaskId}$

providing that the assumptions of Theorem 3 hold: that $\textit{ValidTaskId} \setminus \{\textit{entry\_task}\}$ *and T are non-empty. Thus, if no tasks are currently reading or writing, and the barrier is closed, and the entry task is waiting, then PO will deadlock if the entry task is the only valid task. In this case, the entry task can make progress only when the barrier opens; but this depends on another task completing its writing, and there is no other task. Deadlock is avoided if* $\textit{ValidTaskId} \setminus \{\textit{entry\_task}\} \neq \emptyset$. □

Lemma 2 (Correctness of action *BecomeReader*). *Applying Law 1 to prove that APO is refined by PO, then the correctness of BecomeReader requires us* to prove an instance of proviso (3):

$$[\Delta APOState;\ t?: ValidTaskId\ ] \quad \sqsubseteq_\mathcal{A} \quad readers := readers \cup \{t\}$$

Proof. Unfortunately, this is simply not true: we cannot prove it, because we have lost the guard and restrictions on t. Instead, we must first use Law 2 to preserve this information.

$BecomeReader$
$= \{$ by definition $\}$
$writers = \emptyset \wedge \neg\,(barrier \wedge waiting)\ \&$
$\quad read?\,t: ValidTaskId \setminus (((\{entry\_task\} \lhd waiting \rhd \emptyset) \cup readers) \rightarrow$
$\quad\quad readers := readers \cup \{t\}$
$= \{$ by Law 2 $\}$
$writers = \emptyset \wedge \neg\,(barrier \wedge waiting)\ \&$
$\quad read?\,t: ValidTaskId \setminus (((\{entry\_task\} \lhd waiting \rhd \emptyset) \cup readers) \rightarrow$
$\quad \left\{ \begin{array}{c} writers = \emptyset \wedge \neg\,(barrier \wedge waiting) \\ t \in ValidTaskId \setminus (((\{entry\_task\} \lhd waiting \rhd \emptyset) \cup readers) \end{array} \right\}$
$\quad readers := readers \cup \{t\}$

This means that we should prove that

$[\Delta APOState;\ t?: ValidTaskId\ ]$
$\sqsubseteq_\mathcal{A}$
$\left\{ \begin{array}{c} writers = \emptyset \wedge \neg\,(barrier \wedge waiting) \\ t \in ValidTaskId \setminus (((\{entry\_task\} \lhd waiting \rhd \emptyset) \cup readers) \end{array} \right\}$
$readers := readers \cup \{t\}$

Applying Law 3, and noting that $\theta APOState = \theta POState$, we should prove

$writers = \emptyset \wedge (\neg\,barrier \vee \neg\,waiting)\ \wedge$
$t \in ValidTaskId \setminus (((\{entry\_task\} \lhd waiting \rhd \emptyset) \cup readers)\ \wedge$
$POState \Rightarrow$
$\quad POState'\,[\,readers' := readers \cup \{t\};$
$\quad\quad\quad\quad\quad data', barrier', waiting', writers' := data, barrier, waiting, writers\,]$

$= \{$ by definition of $POState'$ $\}$

$writers = \emptyset \wedge (\neg\,barrier \vee \neg\,waiting)\ \wedge$
$t \in ValidTaskId \setminus (((\{entry\_task\} \lhd waiting \rhd \emptyset) \cup readers)\ \wedge$
$POState \Rightarrow$
$\quad (\ readers' \in \mathbb{F}\,ValidTaskId \wedge writers' \in \mathbb{F}\,ValidTaskId\ \wedge$
$\quad\ (readers' \neq \emptyset \Rightarrow writers' = \emptyset)\ \wedge$
$\quad\ \#writers' \leq 1\ \wedge$
$\quad\ (waiting' \Rightarrow entry\_task' \neq null\_task \wedge entry\_task' \notin readers' \cup writers')\ )$
$\quad [\,readers' := readers \cup \{t\};$
$\quad\ \ data', barrier', waiting', writers' := data, barrier, waiting, writers\,]$

= { by substitution }

$writers = \emptyset \land (\neg\, barrier \lor \neg\, waiting) \land$
$t \in ValidTaskId \setminus ((\{entry\_task\} \lhd waiting \rhd \emptyset) \cup readers) \land$
$POState \Rightarrow$
$\quad (readers \cup \{t\} \in \mathbb{F}\, ValidTaskId \land writers \in \mathbb{F}\, ValidTaskId \land$
$\quad (readers \cup \{t\} \neq \emptyset \Rightarrow writers = \emptyset) \land$
$\quad \#writers \leq 1 \land$
$\quad (waiting \Rightarrow entry\_task \neq null\_task \land entry\_task \notin readers \cup \{t\} \cup writers))$

= { by assumption and from $POState$, $readers \cup \{t\}$ and $writers \in ValidTaskId$ }

$writers = \emptyset \land (\neg\, barrier \lor \neg\, waiting) \land$
$t \in ValidTaskId \setminus ((\{entry\_task\} \lhd waiting \rhd \emptyset) \cup readers) \land$
$POState \Rightarrow$
$\quad ((readers \cup \{t\} \neq \emptyset \Rightarrow writers = \emptyset) \land$
$\quad \#writers \leq 1 \land$
$\quad (waiting \Rightarrow entry\_task \neq null\_task \land entry\_task \notin readers \cup \{t\} \cup writers))$

= { by the propositional calculus, and using $writers = \emptyset$ }

$writers = \emptyset \land \neg\, barrier \land waiting \land$
$t \in ValidTaskId \setminus (\{entry\_task\} \cup readers) \land$
$POState \Rightarrow$
$\quad entry\_task \neq null\_task \land entry\_task \notin readers \cup \{t\}$

= { by set theory }

$writers = \emptyset \land \neg\, barrier \land waiting \land$
$t \in ValidTaskId \land t \neq entry\_task \land t \notin readers \land$
$POState \Rightarrow$
$\quad entry\_task \neq null\_task \land entry\_task \notin readers \land entry\_task \neq t$

The first and second consequents follow from $POState$'s invariant and the antecedent that $waiting$ is true; the third consequent is also an antecedent. □

Constructing Deadlock Free Event-Based Applications: A Rely/Guarantee Approach*

Pascal Fenkam, Harald Gall, and Mehdi Jazayeri

Technical University of Vienna, Distributed Systems Group,
A-1040 Vienna, Argentinierstrasse 8/184-1,
{p.fenkam,h.gall,m.jazayeri}@infosys.tuwien.ac.at

Abstract. We have proposed a formal semantics for a programming language that supports the announcement of events. Based on this semantics, it is clear that event-based systems share some substantial properties with parallel systems. In particular, announcing an event results in the parallel execution of subscribers to this event with the remainder of the announcing program. In this paper, we show how usual concurrency concepts such as synchronization and mutual exclusion can be supported in the stepwise development of event-based applications. The approach in this paper is based on Jones's rely/guarantee method for the development of interfering programs. We also show how deadlock free event-based applications can be developed. Finally, the paper extends Stølen's technique of handling auxiliary variables to support the development of more complex event-based applications.

Keywords: event-based systems, parallel systems, rely/guarantee, deadlock, auxiliary variables.

1 Introduction

The event-based (EB) paradigm is recognized as a powerful technique for the development and the integration of large-scale and complex (distributed) software systems. It has, therefore, been rapidly incorporated in not only research prototypes but also commercial products, toolkits and even in software communication standards. Examples of such prototypes and products are programming environments (e.g. Smalltalk), communication middleware (e.g. Corba [16], Siena [5]), integration frameworks (e.g. JavaBeans [20], FIELD [19]), and message oriented middleware (e.g. TIB/Rendezvous[24]). Due to the lack of suitable specification and verification techniques, the development of applications based on this paradigm has mainly been performed in an ad hoc and informal manner.

We have recently proposed a framework, LECAP, for the development of correct event-based applications [10,9]. This framework includes 1) a core programming language for developing applications that announce events, 2) a set of rules for the stepwise

---
* This work was supported in part by the European Commission projects MOTION (MObile Teamwork Infrastructure for Organizations Networking) and EasyComp (Easy Composition in Future Generation Component Systems) and the Austrian Research Foundation (FWF) project OPELIX.

development of such programs, and 3) a rule for the composition of large specifications starting from smaller specifications. Let us assume that we want to build a software system that satisfies some requirements, say $\phi_1, \cdots, \phi_n$. The LECAP methodology consists of five steps:

1. Designing the architecture of the system (identification of components).
2. Developing the formal specifications $S_1, \cdots, S_m$ of these components and verifying some local properties.
3. Composing the specification S of the whole application starting with the specifications $S_1, \cdots, S_m$ of the components.
4. Verifying the global properties of the application.
5. Independent refinement of the specifications $S_1, \cdots, S_m$ to some implementations $I_1, \cdots, I_m$.

It is important to stress that the development of $I_1, \cdots, I_m$ can be performed by different teams that know nothing about each other. Each of them receives some specification S_i and is required to deliver some code that satisfies this specification. In other words, $I_1, \cdots, I_m$ might be off-the-shelf components that satisfy the specifications $S_1, \cdots, S_m$. Indeed, this is one of the expected benefits of the loose coupling of components in component-based software engineering.

The approach we propose is a combination of bottom-up and top-down approaches. It is bottom-up in the sense that we start from some components that we specify (or that exist), build the specification of the application starting from that of the components and verify the properties of the system. The approach is top-down in the sense that the specified components can be developed following the usual top-down development processes. This combination has shown to be suitable for the development of component based systems [3]. In particular, this is the way the EB paradigm is often applied, namely, for the integration of components [2].

Although the LECAP programming language is a while-parallel language extended with the announce construct, the issues of synchronization and mutual exclusion are not tackled in [10,9]. The aim of this paper is to extend the approach proposed in [9] to support the development of applications that depend on some kind of synchronization. Naive uses of the synchronization construct often lead to deadlocks where all processes of the system are waiting for some conditions to hold, an undesirable effect in many distributed systems. This paper also shows how deadlock-free event-based applications can be developed. More precisely, the contributions of the paper can be summarized as follows:

- We extend the semantics of the LECAP programming language to include the **await** construct used for synchronization and mutual exclusion.
- Similar to the wait-condition of Stølen [23] or the run-condition of Xu [25], we extend the specification technique for event-based applications to include a fifth component that specifies the states in which an event-based program is allowed to block.
- We propose a set of rules for the top-down development of programs that announce events.

- We give some rules for handling auxiliary variables that allow the development of more complex systems. These auxiliary variables are used in the style of Stølen: as a specification tool and as a verification tool.
- We provide a simple example whose intent is to give a flavor of the proposed development methodology.

The remainder of the paper is organized as follows. The next section presents related approaches. Section 3 provides the formal definition of the LECAP programming language. Section 4 shows how to specify event-based applications. The aim of section 5 is to present the rules for the stepwise development of event-based applications. Section 6 illustrates the use of auxilliary variables in the development of event-based applications. Section 7 presents an example for illustrating our approach and Section 8 concludes the paper.

2 Related Work

Although the EB paradigm is at the heart of countless software systems, not much work has been presented on building correct applications using this paradigm. There are four main research areas that are related to our work.

The first related area concerns event broadcasting. Broadcasting is an unbuffered communication paradigm where one process speaks at a time while all others are instantaneously listening [18]. Essentially, the issue in broadcasting systems is notification of all the components in the system. The requirements of such systems are, therefore, different from that of EB systems.

The second related area of research concerns construction of parallel programs. Jones's rely/guarantee [14] (extended e.g. by Stølen [23], Xu [25] and Dingel [6]) and the work of Owicki/Gries [17] are among the approaches that have influenced this area. Our work is strongly based on these two works.

The third area of work is about verifying the correctness of event based applications. The only work we are aware of is by Dingel et al. [8, 7]. A method for reasoning about EB applications is proposed. This approach, which we call Dingel's approach, is also based on Jones's rely/guarantee paradigm. We have shown in [10] that this approach cannot be applied to the development of large-scale and complex systems. In particular, it is intended for a-posteriori verification of systems (instead of stepwise construction of systems): components of the completed program are verified in isolation and then put together where general properties are attempted to be proved. Jones [14] argues that such approaches are unacceptable as program development methods: erroneous design decisions taken in early steps are propagated until the system is implemented and attempted to be proven correct. Finally, Dingel's approach assumes a static set of subscriptions; in this sense, it seems to miss a fundamental aspect of the event-based paradigm which is to ease the integration of components. In fact, we are not aware of the application of Dingel's approach to any real-life application.

Model checking EB applications is an intriguing alternative to the formal proof of software systems as a significant part of the process is carried out automatically. In [11], an attempt to apply model checking to the verification of EB applications is discussed. The authors try to provide a generic framework that can be reused by modelers in the process of defining the abstract structure related to their systems. Indeed, the authors succeeded in factoring the work such that, for instance, the event delivery policy is now a pluggable element with various packaged policies (prepared by the authors) that can be used off-the-shelf. They, however, concentrate on the run-time apparatus, i.e. the middleware. Not much is provided for tackling the correctness of the application (consumers and publishers) built on top of this middleware.

We propose an approach that overcomes these shortcomings. Similar to the work of Dingel et al. [8, 7], we restrict our work to partial correctness. That is, our proof system only provides rules for verifying that a terminated program satisfies its post-condition.

This paper extends the work in [9] to deal with synchronization and mutual exclusion. The work in [9] is, however, inspired by our early work [10] with which there are some substantial differences. First, the theory in [10] is based on the concept of announcement condition which is an assertion that conditions the announcement of an event while the work in this paper is based on structural specifications. The concept of announcement condition has some shortcomings such as the requirement that two programs that subscribe to the same event must announce disjoint sets of events. Second, in addition to the pre-, rely-, guar-, and post-conditions, the notion of announcement condition introduces a fifth component in the specification of systems called ann-condition; this is not necessary in this paper. Finally, [10] only presents a rule for the composition of event-based specifications; here, we introduce the rules for the top-down development of components.

3 The LECAP Language

This section introduces the LECAP programming language, a core language for the development of while-parallel programs that not only share some variables but also communicate through an EB system. We define the syntax of the language and its operational semantics. We also give a definition of the concept of an EB system.

3.1 Syntax

A LECAP program is a while-program augmented with parallel, synchronization, and event publication statements. The syntax of the language is following.

$$P ::= x := e \mid P_1; P_2 \mid \textbf{if } b \textbf{ then } P_1 \textbf{ else } P_2 \textbf{ fi} \mid \textbf{while } b \textbf{ do } P \textbf{ od}$$
$$\mid P_1 \| P_2 \mid \textbf{announce}(e) \mid \textbf{skip} \mid \textbf{await } b \textbf{ do } P \textbf{ od}.$$

The parallel construct models nondeterministic interleaving of the atomic actions of P_1 and P_2. Synchronization and mutual exclusion are achieved by means of the **await** construct. The **announce** construct allows announcement of events. It is intended for the notification of the EB system which in turn triggers some subscribers. We use the term application to denote a set of programs tied by means of some subscription-event announcement relation. The term component is also sometimes used instead of program; we do this when we want to emphasize that some programs are parts of an application. The concept of program in this paper may be compared to the Java notion of method.

To simplify the deduction rules, it is required that variables used in the boolean tests cannot be accessed by programs running in parallel. This constraint can be removed as discussed in [23].

We say that a program z_0 is a subprogram of another program z iff the latter can be written in one of the following forms: 1) $z_1;z_0;z_2$, 2) **if** b **then** z_1 **else** z_2 **fi**, with z_0 a subprogram of z_1 or z_2, 3) **while** b **do** z_1 **od**, with z_0 a subprogram of z_1, 4) $z_1\|z_2$, with z_0 a subprogram of z_1 or z_2, 5) **await** b **do** z_1 **od**, with z_0 a subprogram of z_1,

3.2 Event-Based System as Abstract Model

Although an EB system includes various paradigms in practice, not all of them are needed at the abstract level. We construct an abstract model based on a set of programs, a binding, and a set of shared variables. An event is a piece of data that may be published by a program; we assume a non-empty sort of events $\mathbb{E}$. Subscriptions are templates for allowing categorization of events. The set of programs is the set of handlers of events. Such programs are triggered (invoked) when an event is announced that matches one of their subscriptions. The programs in an EB system may not only communicate by announcing and consuming events, but also share some variables.

Definition 1. *An event-based system is a 3-tuple $(\mathcal{M}, \vartheta, \mathcal{B})$ composed of a set of programs $\mathcal{M}$, a set of global variables ϑ shared by programs in $\mathcal{M}$, and a binding $\mathcal{B}$ which maps each program in $\mathcal{M}$ to its set of subscriptions $\mathcal{B}(z)$.*

The process of determining which programs are interested in an event is called matching. A matching is performed between an event and a subscription. Formally, a subscription can be viewed as a unary relation over events.

Definition 2. *Assuming an EB system $(\mathcal{M}, \vartheta, \mathcal{B})$, a subscription s is a relation defined on the set of events $\mathbb{E}$. We define $\Gamma_\mathcal{B}(e) = \{z \in \mathcal{M} \mid \exists s \in \mathcal{B}(z), e \in s\}$ as the set of programs interested in the event e. Note that $\Gamma_\mathcal{B}$ indeed depends on the binding $\mathcal{B}$. We will simply write $\Gamma(e)$ when the binding is obvious from the context.*

Given an event e and a subscription s, we will also write $s(e)$ to say that e is in the relation s. An external event is an event that may be announced by programs not in $\mathcal{M}$. We denote the set of external events as $\mathcal{E}_x$ and the set of programs subscribed to some of these events as $\mathcal{M}_x$. Formally, $\mathcal{M}_x = \bigcup_{e \in \mathcal{E}_x} \Gamma_\mathcal{B}(e)$.

Definition 3. *An incomplete event-based system is EB system for which the binding is not defined. Such an event-based system is denoted $(\mathcal{M}, \vartheta)$.*

Note that an EB system with an undefined binding is different from an EB system where each program is mapped to the empty set. An EB system with adefined binding will be called a complete EB system.

3.3 Operational Semantics

We give the operational semantics of the LECAP programming language in the style of [1]. A state maps all programming variables to values and a configuration is a pair

$\langle p, s \rangle$ where p is a program and s is a state. The semantics of the LECAP programming language is given relative to an EB system $(\mathcal{M}, \vartheta, \mathcal{B})$.

An environment transition $\xrightarrow{v}$ is the least binary relation on configurations such that $\langle z, s_1 \rangle \xrightarrow{v} \langle z, s_2 \rangle$ holds; environment transitions are allowed to modify only the state of the EB system.

A program transition $\xrightarrow{i}$ is the least binary relation on configurations such that one of the following holds:

- $\langle \textbf{skip}, s \rangle \xrightarrow{i} \langle \epsilon, s \rangle$, the program does nothing but terminates.
- $\langle u := r, s \rangle \xrightarrow{i} \langle \epsilon, s[u/r] \rangle$, where $s[u/r]$ denotes the state obtained from s by mapping the variable u to the value of r and leaving all other state variables unchanged.
- $\langle \textbf{announce}(e), s \rangle \xrightarrow{i} \langle \|\Gamma(e), s\rangle$ if $\Gamma(e) \neq \{\}$. $\|\{z_1, \cdots, z_n\}$ is defined as $z_1\| \cdots \|z_n$, the parallel execution of programs in $\{z_1, \cdots, z_n\}$.
- $\langle \textbf{announce}(e), s \rangle \xrightarrow{i} \langle \epsilon, s \rangle$ if $\Gamma(e) = \{\}$.
- $\langle \textbf{announce}(e); z, s \rangle \xrightarrow{i} \langle \|\Gamma(e)\|z, s \rangle$ if $\Gamma(e) \neq \{\}$. The effect of announcing an event e is to trigger the set of programs that subscribed to e and execute them in parallel with the remainder of the announcing program. The programs triggered by an event announced by the running program are part of this program and their transitions are also internal transitions.
- $\langle z_1; z_2, s_1 \rangle \xrightarrow{i} \langle z_2, s_2 \rangle$ if $\langle z_1, s_1 \rangle \xrightarrow{i} \langle \epsilon, s_2 \rangle$,
- $\langle z_1; z_2, s_1 \rangle \xrightarrow{i} \langle z_3; z_2, s_2 \rangle$ if $\langle z_1, s_1 \rangle \xrightarrow{i} \langle z_3, s_2 \rangle$, $z_3 \neq \epsilon$ and $\textbf{announce}(e)$ is not a subprogram of z_1,
- $\langle \textbf{if } b \textbf{ then } z_1 \textbf{ else } z_2 \textbf{ fi}, s \rangle \xrightarrow{i} \langle z_1, s \rangle$ if $s \models b$ holds,
- $\langle \textbf{if } b \textbf{ then } z_1 \textbf{ else } z_2 \textbf{ fi}, s \rangle \xrightarrow{i} \langle z_2, s \rangle$ if $s \models \neg b$ holds,
- $\langle \textbf{while } b \textbf{ do } z \textbf{ od}, s \rangle \xrightarrow{i} \langle z; \textbf{while } b \textbf{ do } z \textbf{ od}, s \rangle$ if $s \models b$ holds,
- $\langle \textbf{while } b \textbf{ do } z \textbf{ od}, s \rangle \xrightarrow{i} \langle \epsilon, s \rangle$ if $s \models \neg b$ holds,
- $\langle \{z_1 \| z_2\}, s_1 \rangle \xrightarrow{i} \langle z_2, s_2 \rangle$ if $\langle z_1, s_1 \rangle \xrightarrow{i} \langle \epsilon, s_2 \rangle$,
- $\langle \{z_1 \| z_2\}, s_1 \rangle \xrightarrow{i} \langle z_1, s_2 \rangle$ if $\langle z_2, s_1 \rangle \xrightarrow{i} \langle \epsilon, s_2 \rangle$,
- $\langle \{z_1 \| z_2\}, s_1 \rangle \xrightarrow{i} \langle \{z_1' \| z_2\}, s_2 \rangle$ if $\langle z_1, s_1 \rangle \xrightarrow{i} \langle z_1', s_2 \rangle$, $z_1' \neq \epsilon$ and z_1 is not of the form $\textbf{announce}(e); z$.
- $\langle \{z_1 \| z_2\}, s_1 \rangle \xrightarrow{i} \langle \{z_1 \| z_2'\}, s_2 \rangle$ if $\langle z_2, s_1 \rangle \xrightarrow{i} \langle z_2', s_2 \rangle$, $z_2' \neq \epsilon$ and z_2 is not of the form $\textbf{announce}(e); z$.
- $\langle \{z_1 \| z_2\}, s_1 \rangle \xrightarrow{i} \langle \|\Gamma(e)\|\{z\|z_2\}, s_2 \rangle$, if z_1 is of the form $\textbf{announce}(e); z$ and $\Gamma(e) \neq \{\}$.
- $\langle \{z_1\|z_2\}, s_1 \rangle \xrightarrow{i} \langle \{z\|z_2\}, s_2 \rangle$, if z_1 is of the form $\textbf{announce}(e); z$ and $\Gamma(e) = \{\}$.
- $\langle \{z_1\|z_2\}, s_1 \rangle \xrightarrow{i} \langle \|\Gamma(e)\|\{z_1\|z\}, s_2 \rangle$, if z_2 is of the form $\textbf{announce}(e); z$ and $\Gamma(e) \neq \{\}$.
- $\langle \{z_1\|z_2\}, s_1 \rangle \xrightarrow{i} \langle \{z_1\|z\}, s_2 \rangle$, if z_2 is of the form $\textbf{announce}(e); z$ and $\Gamma(e) = \{\}$.
- $\langle \{z_1\|z_2\}; z_3, s_1 \rangle \xrightarrow{i} \langle \|\Gamma(e)\|\{\{z\|z_2\}; z_3\}, s_2 \rangle$, if z_1 is of the form $\textbf{announce}(e); z$ and $\Gamma(e) \neq \{\}$. The subscribers are executed in parallel with any other remaining part of the announcing program.

- $\langle \{z_1 \| z_2\}; z_3, s_1 \rangle \xrightarrow{i} \langle \| \Gamma(e) \| \{\{z_1 \| z\}; z_3\}, s_2 \rangle$, if z_2 is of the form **announce**$(e);z$ and $\Gamma(e) \neq \{\}$.
- $\langle$**await** b **do** z_1 **od**, $s_1\rangle \xrightarrow{i} \langle \epsilon, s_n \rangle$ if $s_1 \models b$, and there exists a finite list of configurations $\langle z_2, s_2 \rangle, \cdots, \langle z_n, s_n \rangle$, such that $z_n = \epsilon$ and for all $1 < k \le n$, $\langle z_{k-1}, s_{k-1} \rangle \xrightarrow{i} \langle z_k, s_k \rangle$.
- $\langle$**await** b **do** z_1 **od**, $s_1\rangle \xrightarrow{i} \langle$**await** b **do** z_1 **od**, $s_1\rangle$ if $s_1 \models b$, and there exists a finite list of configurations $\langle z_2, s_2\rangle, \cdots, \langle z_n, s_n\rangle$, such that:
  - For any $1 < k < n$, $\langle z_{k-1}, s_{k-1}\rangle \xrightarrow{i} \langle z_k, s_k\rangle$, and
  - $\langle z_n, s_n\rangle \xrightarrow{i} \langle z_{n+1}, s_{n+1}\rangle$ does not hold for any program z_{n+1}.

The meaning of an await statement is not very clear when its body does not terminate [25]. When it terminates, however, the final state is required to satisfy the post-condition. Given that we are not interested (in this work) in non-terminating programs we can stipulate that any computation of an await-statement has a finite length.

In addition to the state of the system that programs may read and update, they also have local variables that are hidden such that the environment is not allowed to access them. We do not model this concept since it has no impact on our rules.

Definition 4. *A configuration c_1 is disabled if there is no configuration c_2 such that $c_1 \xrightarrow{i} c_2$. A computation is a possibly infinite sequence of environment and program transitions: $\langle z_1, s_1\rangle \xrightarrow{l_1} \cdots \xrightarrow{l_{k-1}} \langle z_k, s_k\rangle \xrightarrow{l_k} \cdots$ such that the final configuration is disabled if the sequence is finite. A computation σ is blocked if it is finite and the program of the last computation is not ϵ. A computation terminates iff it is finite and the program of the last configuration is ϵ.*

Given a computation σ, then, $Z(\sigma)$, $S(\sigma)$ and $L(\sigma)$ are the projections to sequences of programs, states and transition labels, while $Z(\sigma_k)$, $S(\sigma_k)$ and $L(\sigma_k)$ and σ_k respectively denote the k'th program, the k'th state, the k'th transition label and the k'th configuration. The number of configurations in σ is denoted $len(\sigma)$. If σ is infinite, then $len(\sigma) = \infty$. The set of computations of the program z (denoted $cp[z]$) is the set of computations such that $Z(\sigma_1) = z$.

4 Specification of Programs

We show how rely- and guar- conditions can be extended and used for the specification of LECAP programs. In the style of Stølen [23], we extend specifications to include a new component called wait-condition which is a unary relation on states. A program is allowed either to terminate or to block in a state satisfying the wait-condition. Further, it is required that no program blocks within the body of an await-statement.

4.1 Specification

Hooked variables are used to denote an earlier state. For any variable v, there exists a corresponding hooked variable $\overleftarrow{v}$ of the same type that can appear neither in programs nor in states. An assertion is a predicate that may contain both hooked and unhooked variables.

A state is a map of all unhooked variables to values of corresponding sorts. If P is an assertion that contains no hooked variable, then the state s validates P iff P evaluates to true when each occurrence of a free variable v in P is assigned the value $s(v)$ given by s. This is denoted as $s \models P$ and P is said to be a unary assertion. If P also contains unhooked variables, then the tuple of states (s_i, s_j) validates P iff P evaluates to true when each hooked variable $\overleftarrow{v}$ in P is assigned the value $s_i(v)$ and each unhooked variable is assigned the value $s_j(v)$. This is denoted as $(s_i\ s_j) \models P$ and P is said to be a binary assertion.

We sometime also hook assertions such that $\overleftarrow{P}$ denotes the assertion P where any free occurrence of a variable v is replaced with its hooked version $\overleftarrow{v}$. If X is a set of variables and s_1 and s_2 are two states, then $s_1 \stackrel{X}{=} s_2$ means that for any variable $x \in X$, $s_1(x) = s_2(x)$ and $s_1 \stackrel{X}{\neq} s_2$ means that there exists $x \in X$ such that $s_1(x) \neq s_2(x)$.

We divide the set of specifications into complete and incomplete specifications on the one hand and into structural and behavioral specifications on the other hand.

Definition 5. *A behavioral specification is a formula* $\mathcal{S} :: (P, R, W, G, E)$, *where $\mathcal{S}$ is a an EB system, the* pre-condition P, *and the* wait-condition W *are unary assertions and the* rely-condition R, *the* guar-condition G *and the* post-condition E *are binary assertions. The behavioral specification is said to be complete (resp. incomplete) if the EB system is complete (resp. incomplete).*

Definition 6. *Given a complete EB system $\mathcal{S}$, a pre-condition P, and a rely-condition R, then* $ext[\mathcal{S}, P, R]$ *denotes the set of computations σ such that the following conditions hold:*
1) $\sigma_1 \models P$,
2) for all $1 \leq j < len(\sigma)$, if $L(\sigma_j) = v$ and $S(\sigma_j) \stackrel{\vartheta}{\neq} S(\sigma_{j+1})$ then $(\sigma_j, \sigma_{j+1}) \models R$.

The definition characterizes computations which are subject to environment transitions and whose first states satisfy the pre-condition. Informally, 1) the initial state must satisfy the pre-condition, and 2) any environment transition which changes the global state must satisfy the rely-condition.

Definition 7. *Assuming a complete EB system $\mathcal{S}$, a unary assertion W, and two binary assertions G, and E, then* $int[\mathcal{S}, W, G, E]$ *denotes the set of computations σ such that the following conditions hold:*
1) $len(\sigma) \neq \infty$,
2) if $Z(\sigma_{len(\sigma)}) = \epsilon$ then $(\sigma_1, \sigma_{len(\sigma)}) \models E$,
3) if $Z(\sigma_{len(\sigma)}) \neq \epsilon$ then $(\sigma_1, \sigma_{len(\sigma)}) \models W$,
4) for all $1 \leq j < len(\sigma)$, if $L(\sigma_j) = i$ and $S(\sigma_j) \stackrel{\vartheta}{\neq} S(\sigma_{j+1})$ then $(\sigma_j, \sigma_{j+1}) \models G$.

These definitions implicitly take into consideration the case of a program z_e triggered by an event e announced by z; z_e is part of the running program which becomes $z_e \| z_1$ where z_1 is the remainder of z. In the parallel composition $z_e \| z_1$, z_e and z_1 are in the environment of each other and are, therefore, required to coexist.

Similarly to process algebra specification languages such as CSP [4] and CCS [15], we allow specifications to take the the forms $S_1 \| S_2$, **if** b **then** S_1 **else** S_2 **fi**, $S_1; S_2$. This kind of specifications allows specifying not only the behaviors of the specified program, but also make obvious which components this program is composed of.

Definition 8. *If we assume that S_1 and S_2 are two complete or incomplete, behavioral or structural specifications on the same EB system S and that e is an event, then, the following formulas are structural specifications: $S::\mathbf{announce}(e)$, $S_1;S_2$, $S_1\|S_2$, and if b then S_1 else S_2 fi.*

We further adopt the following abbreviations.

$S::S_1;S_2$	stands for	$S::S_1 \,;S::S_2$
$S::S_1\|S_2$	stands for	$S::S_1 \,\|S::S_2$
$S::\text{if }b\text{ then }S_1\text{ else }S_2\text{ fi}$	stands for	if b then $S::S_1$ else $S::S_2$ fi
$S::\mathbf{await}\;b\;\mathbf{do}\;S_1\;\mathbf{od}$	stands for	await b do $S::S_1$ od

4.2 Satisfaction

Definition 9. *The program z satisfies the specification $S \stackrel{def}{=} (\mathcal{M},\vartheta,\mathcal{B})::(P,R,W,G,E)$ (denoted as $\models z\;\underline{sat}\;S$) iff $cp[z] \cap ext[\vartheta,P,R] \subseteq int[\vartheta,W,G,E]$ holds.*

Definition 10. *The program z satifies the specification $S \stackrel{def}{=} (\mathcal{M},\vartheta)::(P,R,W,G,E)$ iff for any binding $\mathcal{B}$, z satisfies the complete specification $(\mathcal{M},\vartheta,\mathcal{B})::(P,R,W,G,E)$.*

To show that $z\;\underline{sat}\;(\mathcal{M},\vartheta,\mathcal{B})::(P,R,W,G,E)$ is valid one proves that any computation of z started in a state satisfying P and is executed in an environment whose interference satisfies R has a final state satisfying E if it terminates and W if it blocks while any program transition changing the state variables satisfies G. A program z, in fact, satisfies an incomplete behavioral specification iff z satisfies this specification for some binding and announces no event.

Definition 11. *We say that $S::(P,R,W,G,E)$ is valid iff $z\;\underline{sat}\;S::(P,R,W,G,E)$ is valid for any program $z \in \mathcal{M}_x$.*

Definition 12. *A program z structurally satisfies $S \stackrel{def}{=} (\mathcal{M},\vartheta)::(P,R,G,E)$ (denoted as $z\;\underline{ssat}\;S$) iff $z\;\underline{sat}\;(\mathcal{M},\vartheta,\mathcal{B})::(P,R,G,E)$ is valid for any binding $\mathcal{B}$.*

The notion of structural satisfaction and behavioral satisfaction coincide on behavioral specifications. Other cases of structural specifications are given meanings as shown below.

Specification	*Semantics*
$z\;\underline{ssat}\;S::(P_1,R_1,W_1,G_1,E_1);(P_2,R_2,W_2,G_2,E_2)$	$\exists z_1,z_2 \cdot z = z_1;z_2$ and $z_1\;\underline{ssat}\;S::(P_1,R_1,W_1,G_1,E_1)$ $z_2\;\underline{ssat}\;S::(P_2,R_2,W_2,G_2,E_2)$
$z\;\underline{ssat}\;S::(P,R_1,W_1,G_1,E_1)\|(P,R_2,W_2,G_2,E_2)$	$\exists z_1,z_2 \cdot z = z_1\|z_2$ and $z_1\;\underline{ssat}\;S::(P,R_1,W_1,G_1,E_1)$, $z_2\;\underline{ssat}\;S::(P,R_2,W_2,G_2,E_2)$
$z\;\underline{ssat}\;S::\text{if}b\text{ then}(P \wedge b,R,W,G,E)\text{ else}(P \wedge \neg b,R,W,G,E)$	$z\;\underline{ssat}\;S::(P,R,W,G,E)$
$z\;\underline{ssat}\;S::\mathbf{await}\;b\;\mathbf{do}\;(P^R \wedge b, \textit{false}, \textit{true}, (G \vee I_\vartheta) \wedge E)$	$z\;\underline{ssat}\;S::(P,R,P^R \wedge \neg b, G, R^* \mid E \mid R^*)$
$z\;\underline{ssat}\;S::\mathbf{announce}(e)$	$z = \mathbf{announce}(e)$

These definitions justify that the satisfaction is indeed structural; not only the behavior of the specified program is constrained, but also its structure. For instance, a program that satisfies **if** b **then** S_1 **else** S_2 **fi** must be of the form **if** b **then** z_1 **else** z_2 **fi** where z_1 and z_2 respectively structurally satisfy S_1 and S_2.

5 Construction of Systems

We formulate the rules for the construction of LECAP programs. In the sequel, I_ϑ denotes the assertion $\bigwedge_{x \in \vartheta} x = \overleftarrow{x}$. The pair of states (s_i, s_k) satisfies $A \mid B$ (denoted as $(s_i, s_k) \models A \mid B$ where A and B are two binary assertions) iff there exists a state s_j such that $(s_i, s_j) \models A$ and $(s_j, s_k) \models B$. B^+ is defined as the transitive closure of B, the smallest relation that contains B and is transitive. B^+ is the limit of the series $B \vee B|B \vee B|B|B \cdots$. The reflexive transitive of B is denoted E^* and defined as $(I_\vartheta \vee E)^+$. A^B denotes an assertion that characterizes any state that can be reached from a state satisfying A by a finite number of B steps. Formally, $A^B \Leftrightarrow \overleftarrow{A} \wedge B^*$.

We denote the set of events that a program z possibly announces as $events(z)$ and the set of programs that are subscribed to events that z possibly announces as $\gamma(z) = \Gamma(events(z))$. The set of programs that will eventually be invoked following the announcement of an event by z is denoted $\gamma^+(z)$ and defined as $\gamma(z) \cup \bigcup_{s \in \gamma(z)} \gamma^+(s)$.

Definition 13. *The binding $\mathcal{B}$ of an EB system $(\mathcal{M}, \vartheta, \mathcal{B})$ is well founded iff for any program $z \in \mathcal{M}$, $z \notin \gamma^+(z)$.*

The intent of the definition is to avoid infinite computations. The simplest such case is when a program subscribes to events it announces. This restriction seems to be strong: a program may subscribe to events it announces without producing infinite computations. We doubt the necessity of such design decisions and exclude them as they may complicate the event composition rule. A similar restriction is imposed in [12, 13].

5.1 Construction of Programs

This section presents the rules for the top-down construction of programs (components). The rules are extensions of those investigated in [14, 22, 25] and show how a specification can successively be decomposed, hence are called decomposition rules. In the following rules, $\mathcal{S}$ represents the EB system $(\mathcal{M}, \vartheta, \mathcal{B})$.

Parallel Rule. Any state in which $z_1 \| z_2$ blocks is such that either both programs z_1 and z_2 are blocked or one of them is blocked and the other terminated. The rule is a generalization is that proposed in [23, 25]. Showing that the composition of z_1 and z_2 does not deadlock consists of proving that $z_1 \| z_2$ never blocks. That is, that $(W_1 \wedge W_2) \vee (W_2 \wedge E_1) \vee (W_1 \wedge E_2)$ is a contradiction.

$$\frac{\begin{array}{l} G_1 \Rightarrow R_2 \\ G_2 \Rightarrow R_1 \\ z_1 \underline{sat}\ \mathcal{S}::(P,R_1,W_1,G_1,E_1) \\ z_2 \underline{sat}\ \mathcal{S}::(P,R_2,W_2,G_2,E_2) \end{array}}{\{z_1 \| z_2\}\ \underline{sat}\ \mathcal{S}::(P,R_1 \wedge R_2, W, G_1 \vee G_2, E_1 \wedge E_2)} \quad \text{where } W \stackrel{def}{=} (W_1 \wedge W_2) \vee (W_2 \wedge E_1) \vee (W_1 \wedge E_2).$$

Announce Rule. The announce rule shows how to introduce the announce construct in a program. It results directly from the parallel rule and from the semantics of the announce construct. z_e represents the program $\|subscribers(e)$.

$$\frac{\begin{array}{l}G \Rightarrow R_e \\ G_e \Rightarrow R \\ z_e \underline{sat}\ S ::(P_e,R_e,W_e,G_e,E_e) \\ z_1 \underline{sat}\ S ::(P_1,R_1,W_1,G_1,E_1)\end{array}}{\textbf{announce}(e); z \underline{sat}\ S ::(P_1 \wedge P_e, R_1 \wedge R_e, W, G_1 \vee G_e, E_1 \wedge E_e)} \quad \text{where } W \stackrel{def}{=} (W_1 \wedge W_e) \vee (W_e \wedge E_1) \vee (W_1 \wedge E_e).$$

Await Rule. The await rule is intended for synchronization and mutual exclusion. The await statement blocks until b holds. During this blockage, the environment may interfere, hence, the construct's body will start in a state satisfying P^R. In addition to satisfying the post-condition, the final state of z must satisfy the guar-condition if the state is changed by the construct's body (expressed as $G \vee I_\vartheta$). Announcement of events between the body of an await construct is not forbidden.

$$\frac{z \underline{sat}\ S ::(P^R \wedge b, false, true, (G \vee I_\vartheta) \wedge E)}{\textbf{await}\ b\ \textbf{do}\ z\ \textbf{od}\ \underline{sat}\ S ::(P,R,P^R \wedge \neg b, G, R^* \mid E \mid R^*)}$$

Sequential Rule. The rule permits the sequential composition of programs. We consider two programs z_1 and z_2 such that z_1 announces no event, i.e. $events(z) = \{\}$. The sequential composition is possible iff the pre-condition of the second program follows from the post-condition of the first. The resulting program blocks if either of the composing programs blocks.

$$\frac{\begin{array}{l}events(z_1) = \{\} \\ E_1 \Rightarrow P_2 \\ z_1 \underline{sat}\ S_i ::(P_1,R_1,W_1,G_1,E_1) \\ z_2 \underline{sat}\ S_i ::(P_2,R_2,W_2,G_2,E_2)\end{array}}{z_1;z_2 \underline{sat}\ S_i ::(P_1,R_1 \wedge R_2,W_1 \vee W_2,G_1 \vee G_2,E_1 \mid E_2)}$$

Conditional Rule. The conditional rule is probably one of the simplest rule. The environment is not allowed to access variables used in the boolean test.

$$\frac{\begin{array}{l}z_1;z \underline{sat}\ S ::(P \wedge b, R, W, G, E) \\ z_2;z \underline{sat}\ S ::(P \wedge \neg b, R, W, G, E)\end{array}}{\textbf{if}\ b\ \textbf{then}\ z_1\ \textbf{else}\ z_2\ \textbf{fi}; z \underline{sat}\ S ::(P,R,W,G,E).}$$

Iteration Rule. In this rule, the pre-condition P is an invariant of the loop; each iteration must ensure that its post-condition implies the pre-condition of the next iteration. The rule is the same as that of Stølen [23]. We have not yet found an adequate expression for cases where the loop's body contains event announcements.

$$\frac{\begin{array}{l}events(z) = \{\} \\ E \Rightarrow P \\ z \underline{sat}\ S_i ::(P \wedge b, R, W, G, E)\end{array}}{\textbf{while}\ b\ \textbf{do}\ z\ \textbf{od}\ \underline{sat}\ S_i ::(P, R, W, G, (E^+ \vee R^*) \wedge \neg b)}$$

Consequence Rule. The consequence rule allows strengthening the assumptions while weakening the commitments. It is the basis for the refinement of specifications.

$$\frac{\begin{array}{l}E_1 \Rightarrow E_2, \\ G_1 \Rightarrow G_2, \\ R_2 \Rightarrow R_1 \\ W_1 \Rightarrow W_2, \\ P_2 \Rightarrow P_1 \\ z \underline{sat}\ S ::(P_1,R_1,W_1,G_1,E_1)\end{array}}{z \underline{sat}\ S ::(P_2,R_2,W_2,G_2,E_2)}$$

Assignment Rule. A single program transition is performed, namely the assignment of the value of r to the variable v while all other variables are kept unchanged. The assignment is done in a state satisfying P^R. If from these conditions we can derive that the guar- and the post-conditions will be satisfied, then the conclusion of the rule follows.

$$\frac{P^R \wedge v = \overleftarrow{r} \wedge I_{\vartheta \setminus \{v\}} \Rightarrow (G \vee I_\vartheta) \wedge E}{v := r \; \underline{sat} \; S :: (P, R, false, G, R^* \mid E \mid R^*)}$$

Global Rule. The rule allows introduction of new variables in specifications. Since the new variable is assumed not to occur in z, z does not change the value of v.

$$\frac{z \; \underline{sat} \; S :: (P, R, W, G, E)}{z \; \underline{sat} \; S :: (P, R, W, G \wedge v = \overleftarrow{v}, E)}$$

Pre and Post Rules. The pre- and post-rules are straightforward; they allow adding more information in the post-conditions.

$$\frac{z \; \underline{sat} \; S :: (P, R, W, G, E)}{z \; \underline{sat} \; S :: (P, R, W, G, \overleftarrow{P} \wedge E)} \text{ given.} \qquad \frac{z \; \underline{sat} \; S :: (P, R, W, G, E)}{z \; \underline{sat} \; S :: (P, R, W, G, E \wedge (R \vee G)^+)}.$$

Subscribers Rule. The rule determines the specification of subscribers to events and is a direct application of the parallel rule.

$$\frac{\mathcal{B} \text{ well-founded}, \quad \forall z \in \Gamma_{\mathcal{B}}(e), \quad G_z \Rightarrow \bigwedge_{t \in \Gamma(e) \setminus \{z\}} R_t}{z_e \; \underline{sat} \; S :: \left(\bigwedge_{z \in \Gamma_{\mathcal{B}}(e)} P_z, \bigwedge_{z \in \Gamma_{\mathcal{B}}(e)} R_z, W_e, \bigvee_{z \in \Gamma_{\mathcal{B}}(e)} G_z, \bigwedge_{z \in \Gamma_{\mathcal{B}}(e)} E_z \right)} \quad \text{where} \quad W_e = \left(\bigwedge_{z \in \Gamma_{\mathcal{B}}(e)} W_z \right) \vee \left(\bigvee_{z \in \Gamma_{\mathcal{B}}(e)} (W_z \wedge \bigwedge_{t \in \Gamma_{\mathcal{B}}(e) \setminus \{z\}} E_t) \right).$$

The program z_e may block in states where either all subscribers block or one of them blocks and all others are terminated. The specification of z_e depends on the specification of some program z that subscribed to e. On the other hand, the specification of these subscribers may depend on the specification of z, leading to a recursion in the definition. Such situations are excluded by the well-foundedness of the binding. It is assumed that $\bigwedge_{z \in \emptyset} P_z = \bigwedge_{z \in \emptyset} R_z = \bigwedge_{z \in \emptyset} E_z = \text{true}$ and $\bigvee_{z \in \emptyset} G_z = \bigvee_{z \in \emptyset} W_z = \text{false}$.

5.2 Instantiation of Incomplete Specifications

Incomplete structural specifications are structural specifications that are valid for any binding. On the other hand, incomplete behavioral specifications are valid for all bindings. For constructing a concrete application, however, a precise binding must be defined. Instantiation is the process of defining a binding and, therefore, transforming an incomplete specification into a complete specification.

$$\frac{\mathcal{B} \text{ is well-founded}}{z \; \underline{ssat} \; (\mathcal{M}, \vartheta) :: S} \qquad \frac{\mathcal{B} \text{ is well-founded}}{z \; \underline{sat} \; (\mathcal{M}, \vartheta) :: S}$$
$$\frac{}{z \; \underline{ssat} \; (\mathcal{M}, \vartheta, \mathcal{B}) :: S.} \qquad \frac{}{z \; \underline{sat} \; (\mathcal{M}, \vartheta, \mathcal{B}) :: S.}$$

There are two situations in which instantiation os specifications is required. First when verifying the local properties of a component and second, when verifying the global properties of an application. In the first case, the instantiation is done with a binding that maps each event to the unique program **skip**. Such a binding will be denoted $\mathcal{B}_0$ and called empty binding. In the second case, the binding is constructed depending on the application to be constructed. In general, after instantiation the specifications, the skolemization process must be applied to transform structural specifications to behavioral specifications.

5.3 Skolemization of Structural Specifications

Skolemization is the process of eliminating existential quantifiers in mathematical formulas. We defined the structural satisfaction as a relation based on such existential quantifiers. By removing these quantifiers, we allow transforming such specifications into behavioral specifications.

Let us consider the example $z \underline{ssat} \; \mathcal{S} :: (P_1, R_1, G_1, E_1); (P_2, R_2, G_2, E_2)$. By definition of a structural specification, there exists two programs z_1, and z_2 such that $z = z_1 \; \underline{ssat} \; \mathcal{S} :: (P_1, R_1, G_1, E_1), z_2 \; \underline{ssat} \; \mathcal{S} :: (P_2, R_2, G_2, E_2)$, and $z = z_1; z_2$. The skolemization operation allows us to directly write z as $z_1; z_2$. The following rules serve the purpose of skolemization of specifications. The double line in the rule means that the rule holds in both directions.

Sequential Skolemization Rule

$$\frac{z \; \underline{ssat} \; \mathcal{S} :: S_1; S_2}{\begin{array}{l} z_1 \; \underline{ssat} \; \mathcal{S} :: S_1 \\ z_2 \; \underline{ssat} \; \mathcal{S} :: S_2 \\ z = z_1; z_2 \end{array}}$$

Parallel Skolemization Rule

$$\frac{z \; \underline{ssat} \; \mathcal{S} :: S_1 \| S_2}{\begin{array}{l} z_1 \; \underline{ssat} \; \mathcal{S} :: S_1 \\ z_2 \; \underline{ssat} \; \mathcal{S} :: S_2 \\ z = z_1 \| z_2 \end{array}}$$

If Skolemization Rule

$$\frac{z \; \underline{ssat} \; \mathcal{S} :: \textbf{if } b \textbf{ then } S_1 \textbf{ else } S_2 \textbf{ fi}}{\begin{array}{l} z_1 \; \underline{ssat} \; \mathcal{S} :: S_1 \\ z_2 \; \underline{ssat} \; \mathcal{S} :: S_2 \\ z = \textbf{if } b \textbf{ then } z_1 \textbf{ else } z_2 \textbf{ fi} \end{array}}$$

The rules result from the application of the corresponding definition followed by a skolemization. The EB system may be either complete or incomplete.

5.4 Operations on Structural Specifications

We give some rules for manipulating structural specifications. The symbol $\diamond$ can be replaced indifferently with the parallel composition operator $\|$ or with the sequential composition operator ;. This replacement must, however, be the same in the same formula. That is, $\diamond$ can not be replaced with $\|$ at one place of a formula and with ; at another place of the same formula.

Structural Consequence Rule

$$P_2 \Rightarrow P_1$$
$$R_2 \Rightarrow R_1$$
$$G_1 \Rightarrow G_2$$
$$E_1 \Rightarrow E_2$$
$$\frac{z \; \underline{ssat} \; (\mathcal{M}, \vartheta) :: S_1 \diamond (P_1, R_1, G_1, E_1) \diamond S_2}{z \; \underline{ssat} \; (\mathcal{M}, \vartheta) :: S_1 \diamond (P_2, R_2, G_2, E_2) \diamond S_2.}$$

Structural Global Rule

$$\frac{z \; \underline{ssat} \; (\mathcal{M}, \vartheta \setminus \{v\}) :: S_1 \diamond (P, R, G, E) \diamond S_2}{z \; \underline{ssat} \; (\mathcal{M}, \vartheta \setminus \{v\}) :: S_1 \diamond (P, R, G \wedge v = \overleftarrow{v}, E) \diamond S_2.}$$

Structural Pre Rule

$$\frac{z \; \underline{ssat} \; (\mathcal{M}, \vartheta) :: S_1 \diamond (P, R, G, E) \diamond S_2}{z \; \underline{ssat} \; (\mathcal{M}, \vartheta) :: S_1 \diamond (P, R, G, \overleftarrow{P} \wedge E) \diamond S_2.}$$

Structural Post Rule

$$\frac{z \; \underline{ssat} \; (\mathcal{M}, \vartheta) :: S_1 \diamond (P, R, G, E) \diamond S_2}{z \; \underline{ssat} \; (\mathcal{M}, \vartheta) :: S_1 \diamond (P, R, G, (R \vee G)^+ \wedge E) \diamond S_2.}$$

These rules must be used with care. Let us illustrate the caveat in the light of the example $z \; \underline{ssat} \; \mathcal{S} :: (P_1, R, G, E_1); (P_2, R, G, E_2)$ where $E_1 \Rightarrow P_2$ is assumed. By skolemization and by application of the sequential rule, we deduce that $z \text{ } \underline{ssat} \text{ } \mathcal{S}::(P_1, R, G, E_1 \mid E_2)$ holds. On the other hand, by application of the structural consequence rule we deduce that $z \text{ } \underline{ssat} \text{ } \mathcal{S}::(P_1, R, G, E_1 \vee T); (P_2, R, G, E_2)$ holds. From this, since $E_1 \vee T \Rightarrow P_2$ does not necessarily follow from $E_1 \Rightarrow P_2$, we can not claim that $z \text{ } \underline{ssat} \text{ } \mathcal{S}::(P_1, R, G, (E_1 \vee T) \mid E_2)$ holds, unless we prove that $E_1 \vee T \Rightarrow P_2$ holds. In general, after applying one of these rules, the proof obligations need to be revised.

6 Auxiliary Variables

Auxiliary variables have been used as a tool not only for the verification of systems [25, 21], but also for their specification [23]. We extend Stolen's auxiliary variables rules [23] to leverage the event-based paradigm.

We extend the definition of an EB system to include a set of auxiliary variables α. The incomplete EB system $\mathcal{S}$ is now defined as $(\mathcal{M}, \vartheta, \alpha)$ where $\alpha \cap \vartheta = \emptyset$. An auxiliary variable is a variable that may be used for the specification of programs although it does not belong to ϑ. Correspondingly, the complete EB system $(\mathcal{M}, \vartheta, \mathcal{B})$ is extended to $(\mathcal{M}, \vartheta, \alpha, \mathcal{B})$.

There are some further restrictions on auxiliary variables:

– Auxiliary variables are not allowed to occur in tests of **if**, **while** and **await** statements. This restriction ensures that such variables have no influence on the implemented algorithm and correspondingly on the result of this implementation.
– Auxiliary variables are not allowed to appear on the left hand side of assignments unless the right hand side is also an auxiliary variable.
– Auxiliary variables should not depend on each other. In this way, it is possible to remove some auxiliary variables from the program without need of removing all auxiliary variables.
– Auxiliary variables should only be used in connection with the **await** statement.

6.1 Satisfaction

Based on these assumptions, any assignment $a := u$ where a is an auxiliary variable and u is an expression is such that any variable occurring in u is an element of $\vartheta \cup \{a\}$. Such an assignment is called a well defined assignment to an auxiliary variable. A sequence of well defined assignments to auxiliary variables is denoted $l_{(\vartheta,\alpha)}$. We define the concept of *program augmentation*.

Definition 14. *Given the EB system $(\mathcal{M}, \vartheta, \alpha, \mathcal{B})$, a program z_2 is an augmentation of the program z_1 (denoted $z_1 \hookrightarrow z_2$) iff z_2 can be obtained from z_1 by the following substitutions:*

– *any assignment $v := r$ with* **await** *true* **do** *$v := r; l_{(\vartheta,\alpha)}$* **od***, where $v := r$ does not occur in an await statement and $l_{(\vartheta,\alpha)}$ is a sequence of well defined assignments to auxiliary variables;*
– *any statement of the form* **await** *b* **do** *z* **od** *with* **await** *b* **do** *$z'; l_{(\vartheta,\alpha)}$* **od***, where $z \hookrightarrow z'$ holds and $l_{(\vartheta,\alpha)}$ is a sequence of well defined assignments to auxiliary variables.*

Definition 15. *The formula* z_1 *sat* $(\mathcal{M},\vartheta,\alpha,\mathcal{B})::(P,R,W,G,E)$ *is valid iff there exists a program* z_2 *such that* $z_1 \hookrightarrow z_2$ *and* $cp[z_2] \cap ext[\vartheta \cup \alpha, P, R] \subseteq int[\vartheta \cup \alpha, W, G, E]$.

To show that a program z_1 satisfies a specification, one constructs an augmentation of z_1 that satisfies this specification.

6.2 Deduction Rules

Assignment Rule. The rule expresses the ability to replace an assignment $v := r$ with the sequence of assignments $v := r; a := u$ without changing the results of the program. One can notice that the conclusion of the rule remains the same as for the assignment rule without auxiliary variables.

$$\frac{\overleftarrow{P^R} \wedge v = \overleftarrow{r} \wedge I_{(\vartheta \cup \alpha) \setminus \{v,a\}} \wedge a = \overleftarrow{u} \Rightarrow (G \vee I_{\vartheta \cup \alpha}) \wedge E}{v := r \; \underline{sat} \; (\mathcal{M},\vartheta,\alpha,\mathcal{B})::(P,R,false,G,R^* \mid E \mid R^*)}$$

Await Rule. The rule is obtained by a combination of the first await rule, the sequential rule, and the above assignment rule. By the sequential rule one deduces the validity of $\{z; a := u\}$ $\underline{sat}$ $(P^R \wedge b, false, false, true, E \mid (I_{\vartheta \cup \alpha \setminus \{a\}} \wedge a = \overleftarrow{u})$. By the wait-rule this program is embedded in an await-construct.

$$\frac{(E_1 \mid (I_{\vartheta \cup \alpha \setminus \{a\}} \wedge a = \overleftarrow{u}) \Rightarrow (G \vee I_{\vartheta \cup \alpha}) \wedge E_2}{z \; \underline{sat} \; (\mathcal{M},\vartheta,\alpha,\mathcal{B})::(P^R \wedge b, false, true, (G \vee I_\vartheta) \wedge E_1)}$$
$$\overline{\text{await } b \text{ do } z \text{ od } \underline{sat} \; (\mathcal{M},\vartheta,\alpha,\mathcal{B})::(P,R,P^R \wedge \neg b, G, R^* \mid E_2 \mid R^*)}$$

7 Example

We consider an example resembling that of Dingel et al. [8,7]. The goal is to develop a system including a stack and a counter. Whenever an element is pushed on the stack, the counter must be incremented. A version of this system is presented in [9] in which no interference is permitted. In this paper, we show how this restriction can be alleviated by using the await construct.

7.1 Component Specification

The first program, *push*, adds an element on the top of the stack and announces an event for notifying interested subscribers. The program *increment* increments the counter. On the other hand, *pop* removes the element on the top of the stack provided there is any and announces an event for notifying interested subscribers. The operation *decrement* decrements the counter. The specification of the data-structures is given below.

Element = token;   Stack=Element*;   Subscription = Event → $\mathbb{B}$;   Event::id : $\mathbb{N}$, elt : Element;
Prog = ⟨increment⟩ | ⟨push⟩ | ⟨decrement⟩ | ⟨pop⟩;   Binding = Prog ↦ Subscription-set;

An event is defined as a VDM composite type (record) which includes the identification number of the event and an element which is not further defined (declared as *token*). We introduce the enumeration type *Prog* for referring to operations defined in this specification and that are elements of the EB system's set of programs. Further, a subscription is a function that maps each event to a boolean. Finally, a binding associates each program (element of type *Prog*) to its set of subscriptions. The state of the EB system is composed of the global variables (*stack* and *count*), and the binding which initially maps each program to the empty set of subscriptions.

state *System* **of**
  stack : *Stack*, *count* : $\mathbb{N}$, *binding* : *Binding*
  inv mk-*System* (*stack*, *count*, *binding*) $\triangleq$ **len** (*stack*) = *count*
  init *ebs* $\triangleq$ *ebs.binding* = {⟨*increment*⟩ ↦ { }, ⟨*push*⟩ ↦ { }}
end

We propose the following structural specifications for the different programs:

simple-push : *Event* $\xrightarrow{o}$ ()

simple-push (*evt*)
pre true
rely I_ϑ
guar $stack = evt.elt \frown \overleftarrow{stack} \wedge I_{\vartheta \setminus \{stack\}}$
post $stack = evt.elt \frown \overleftarrow{stack}$

push : *Event* $\xrightarrow{o}$ ()

push (*evt*)
wait true **do**
  simple-push(*evt*);
  announce(mk-*Event*(1, *evt.elt*));
od

The specifications are easy to understand; any program that implements *push* performs *simple-push* and announces the event *mk-Event*(1, *evt.elt*), all in an atomic step. Any implementation of *simple-push* adds an element to the stack provided there is no interference. The specification of *pop* is also given below. Its pre-condition requires that the stack be non-empty.

simple-pop : *Event* $\xrightarrow{o}$ ()

simple-pop (*evt*)
pre $stack \neq []$
roly I_ϑ
guar $\overleftarrow{stack} = evt.elt \frown stack \wedge I_{\vartheta \setminus \{stack\}}$
post $\overleftarrow{stack} = evt.elt \frown stack \wedge I_{\vartheta \setminus \{count\}}$

pop : *Event* $\xrightarrow{o}$ ()

pop (*evt*)
wait true **do**
  simple-pop(*evt*);
  announce(mk-*Event*(2, *evt.elt*));
od

The specifications of *increment* and *decrement* are straightforward.

increment : *Event* $\xrightarrow{o}$ ()

increment (*evt*)
pre true
rely I_ϑ
guar $count = \overleftarrow{count} + 1 \wedge I_{\vartheta \setminus \{count\}}$
post $count = \overleftarrow{count} + 1 \wedge I_{\vartheta \setminus \{count\}}$

decrement : *Event* $\xrightarrow{o}$ ()

decrement (*evt*)
pre $count > 0$
rely I_ϑ
guar $count = \overleftarrow{count}\text{-}1 \wedge I_{\vartheta \setminus \{count\}}$
post $count = \overleftarrow{count}\text{-}1 \wedge I_{\vartheta \setminus \{count\}}$

Note that the rely-conditions of *simple-push*, *increment*, *simple-pop*, and *decrement* do not matter as we later embed these programs in the await construct. In the remainder, we omit pre and rely-conditions that are true.

7.2 Application Composition

The step consists of subscribing programs to events and verifying the global properties of the resulting specification.

Instantiation of the Specifications. We subscribe the programs *increment*, *decrement*, *push*, *pop*, to events with identifiers 1, 2, 3, and 4 respectively. This results in the following binding:

$$\{ \begin{array}{ll} \langle \text{increment} \rangle \mapsto \{\lambda e : Event \cdot e.id = 1\}, & \langle \text{decrement} \rangle \mapsto \{\lambda e : Event \cdot e.id = 2\}, \\ \langle \text{push} \rangle \mapsto \{\lambda e : Event \cdot e.id = 3\}, & \langle \text{pop} \rangle \mapsto \{\lambda e : Event \cdot e.id = 4\} \end{array} \}$$

Intuitively, the program *increment* is interested in events announced by *push* while *decrement* is interested in events announced by *pop*. The resulting behavior should be the incrementation of the counter whenever an element is added on the stack and its decrementation whenever an element is removed from the stack. The programs *push* and *pop* are interested in external events and are, therefore, accessible from outside the EB system. We abbreviate the event $mk\text{-}Event(a,b)$ as (a,b). The following equalities are straightforward:

$$\begin{array}{ll} subscribers(1,x) = \{\langle \text{increment} \rangle\} & subscribers(2,x) = \{\langle \text{decrement} \rangle\} \\ subscribers(3,x) = \{\langle \text{push} \rangle\} & subscribers(4,x) = \{\langle \text{pop} \rangle\} \end{array}$$

From these, we apply the subscribers rule and derive the specifications of the subscribers z_e.

$$\begin{array}{lll} pre_e(1,x) = \text{pre-increment} & pre_e(3,x) = \text{pre-push} & rely_e(1,x) = \text{rely-increment} \quad rely_e(3,x) = \text{rely-push} \\ guar_e(1,x) = \text{guar-increment} & guar_e(3,x) = \text{guar-push} & post_e(1,x) = \text{post-increment} \quad post_e(3,x) = \text{post-push} \\ wait_e(1,x) = \text{wait-increment} & wait_e(3,x) = \text{wait-push} \end{array}$$

Skolemization of the Specifications. A successive application of the sequence skolemization rule and of the sequential rule to *push* and *pop* leads to the requirement that $\overleftarrow{P_1} \wedge E_1 \Rightarrow P_e$ holds. Replacing (P_1, R_1, G_1, E_1) with *simple-push* and *simple-pop* respectively, we obtain the following proof obligations:

$$\begin{array}{l} po\text{-}push(1,x) = \forall s,s' : System, (s,s') \models \overleftarrow{pre\text{-}simple\text{-}push} \wedge post\text{-}simple\text{-}push \Rightarrow s' \models pre\text{-}increment \\ po\text{-}pop(2,x) = \forall s,s' : System, (s,s') \models \overleftarrow{pre\text{-}simple\text{-}pop} \wedge post\text{-}simple\text{-}pop \Rightarrow s' \end{array}$$

Discharging the Proof Obligations. We replace *post-simple-push*, *pre-simple-push*, *post-simple-pop*, *pre-simple-pop*, *pre-increment*, and *pre-decrement* with their respective definitions.

$$\begin{array}{l} po\text{-}push(1,x) = \forall s,s' : System, e : Event, s'.stack = e.elt \frown s.stack \wedge s.count = s'.count \Rightarrow \text{true} \\ po\text{-}pop(2,x) = \forall s,s' : System, e : Event, s.stack \neq [] \wedge s.stack = e.elt \frown s2.stack \wedge s.count = s'.count \Rightarrow s'.count > 0 \end{array}$$

The first proof obligation trivially holds since the right part of the implication is true. The second implication however is a contradiction. To see why, it is enough to consider the case where there is no interference and such that $s_1.count = -1$, $s_1.stack = [e_1]$, $s_2 = []$, $s_2.count = -1$. This may indicate that the proposed specification of *pop* is not sufficient for composing it with *decrement*. We refine the specification of *simple-pop* (and subsequently that of *pop*) by strengthening its pre-condition:

$$simple\text{-}pop : Event \xrightarrow{o} ()$$
$$simple\text{-}pop\ (evt)$$
pre $stack \neq [] \land count > 0$
rely I_ϑ
guar $\overleftarrow{stack} = evt.elt \frown stack \land I_{\vartheta \setminus \{stack\}}$
post $stack \neq [] \land \overleftarrow{stack} = e.elt \frown stack$

Re-applying the sequential conversion rule, we extract the new proof obligation. Next, observing that $I_{\vartheta \setminus \{stack\}}$ is defined as $count = \overleftarrow{count}$ this proof obligation becomes:

$$po\text{-}pop(evt) = \forall s,s' : System, (s,s') \models (\overleftarrow{stack} \neq [] \land \overleftarrow{count} > 0 \land stack \neq [] \land \overleftarrow{stack} = e.elt \frown stack \land count = \overleftarrow{count}) \Rightarrow s' \models count > 0$$

which holds if $\forall s,s' : System, (s,s') \models \overleftarrow{count} > 0 \land count = \overleftarrow{count} \Rightarrow s' \models count > 0$ holds; which is, however, obvious.

Verifying the Properties of the Application. Having completed the specification of our application, we can now verify some of its properties. In particular, we want to show that the counter will always indicate the size of the stack. We formulate the proof obligation for a program z as:

$$\forall s,s' : System, (s,s') \models (\overleftarrow{count} = \text{len}\ (\overleftarrow{stack}) \land \overleftarrow{pre\text{-}z} \land post\text{-}z) \Rightarrow s' \models count = \text{len}\ (stack).$$

Following Definition 11 we need to show that any subscriber of an external event satisfies the property of interest. The proof obligation is hence restricted to:

$$\forall s,s' : System, e \in Event_x, z \in subscribers(e) \cdot (s,s') \models (\overleftarrow{count} = \text{len}\ (\overleftarrow{stack}) \land \overleftarrow{pre\text{-}z} \land post\text{-}z) \Rightarrow s' \models count = \text{len}\ (stack).$$

where the set of external events E_x is the set of events with identifiers 3 or 4. The set of programs subscribed to these events is $\{push, pop\}$. We hence need to show that:

$$\forall s,s' : System, (s,s') \models \overleftarrow{count} = \text{len}\ (\overleftarrow{stack}) \land \overleftarrow{pre\text{-}push} \land post\text{-}push \Rightarrow s' \models count = \text{len}\ (stack) \text{ and}$$
$$\forall s,s' : System, (s,s') \models \overleftarrow{count} = \text{len}\ (\overleftarrow{stack}) \land \overleftarrow{pre\text{-}pop} \land post\text{-}pop \Rightarrow s' \models count = \text{len}\ (stack).$$

To discharge these POs, the behavioral specifications of *push* and *pop* must be extracted. We do this following the following steps. First, we expand the specification *simple-push*; **announce**(e) that we call *prelim-push*. Next, we add more information in the post-condition of *prelim-push* by means of the post-rule and weaken its guar-condition by the consequence rule. Finally, we embed the resulting specification in an await-construct by means of the await- rule. This leads to the following specification.

$$push : Event \xrightarrow{o} ()$$
$$push\ (evt)$$
guar $(stack = evt.elt \frown \overleftarrow{stack} \land I_{\vartheta \setminus \{stack\}} \lor \text{guar}_{e_1})^+$
post rely$^* \mid (stack = evt.elt \frown \overleftarrow{stack} \land I_{\vartheta \setminus \{stack\}} \mid \text{post}_{e_1}) \mid \text{rely}^*$

Despite this transformation, any attempt to directly discharge the PO of interest fails; the environment may interfere before and after the execution of *push*. To achieve the effect of counting the elements of the stack, we need to restrict the way the environment accesses the state variables. In particular, we require that any transition of the environment be such that $count = \operatorname{len}(stack)$. This is done by refining the specification of *push* by strengthening the pre- and rely-conditions.

$push : Event \xrightarrow{o} ()$
$push\ (evt)$
pre $\operatorname{len}(stack) = count$
rely $\operatorname{len}(stack) = count$
guar $(stack = evt.elt \frown \overleftarrow{stack} \wedge I_{\vartheta \setminus \{stack\}} \vee \operatorname{guar}_{e_1})^+$
post rely* $|\ (stack = evt.elt \frown \overleftarrow{stack} \wedge I_{\vartheta \setminus \{stack\}}\ |\ \operatorname{post}_{e_1})\ |\ \operatorname{rely}^*$

The first proof obligation is now formulated as:

$\forall s, s' : System,\ e : Event,\ (s,s') \models \operatorname{len}(\overleftarrow{stack}) = \overleftarrow{count} \wedge rely\text{-}push^* \ |\ (stack = e.elt \frown \overleftarrow{stack} \wedge count = \overleftarrow{count})\ |\ (count = \overleftarrow{count} + 1 \wedge stack = \overleftarrow{stack})\ |\ rely\text{-}push^* \Rightarrow (s,s') \models count = \operatorname{len}(stack).$

Considering the transitivity of *rely-push*, we transform this proof obligation to:

$\forall s, s' : System,\ e : Event,\ (s,s') \models \operatorname{len}(\overleftarrow{stack}) = \overleftarrow{count} \wedge (\operatorname{len}(stack) = count)\ |\ (stack = e.elt \frown \overleftarrow{stack} \wedge count = \overleftarrow{count})\ |\ (count = \overleftarrow{count} + 1 \wedge stack = \overleftarrow{stack})\ |\ (\operatorname{len}(stack) = count) \Rightarrow (s,s') \models count = \operatorname{len}(stack).$

We now expand this PO to:

$\forall s, s' : System,\ e : Event,\ (s,s') \models \operatorname{len}(\overleftarrow{stack}) = \overleftarrow{count} \wedge \exists s_2, s_3 : System, (s,s_2) \models \operatorname{len}(stack) = count \wedge (s_2,s_3) \models (\overleftarrow{stack} = e.elt \frown stack) \wedge count = \overleftarrow{count}) \wedge (s_3,s') \models count = \overleftarrow{count} + 1 \wedge stack = \overleftarrow{stack} \Rightarrow s' \models count = \operatorname{len}(stack).$

That we rewrite as:

$\forall s, s' : System,\ e : Event,\ \operatorname{len}(s.stack) = s.count \wedge \exists s_2, s_3 : System, \operatorname{len}(s_2.stack) = s_2.count \wedge s_2.stack = e.elt \frown s_3.stack \wedge s_2.count = s_3.count \wedge s'.count = s_3.count + 1 \wedge s'.stack = s_3.stack \Rightarrow s'.count = \operatorname{len}(s'.stack).$

Since, however, $s_2.stack = e.elt \frown s_3.stack$ implies $\operatorname{len}(s_2.stack) = \operatorname{len}(s_3.stack) + 1$, the PO holds if the following PO holds:

$\forall s, s' : System,\ e : Event,\ \operatorname{len}(s.stack) = s.count \wedge \exists s_2, s_3 : System, \operatorname{len}(s_2.stack) = s_2.count \wedge \operatorname{len}(s_2.stack) = \operatorname{len}(s_3.stack) + 1 \wedge s_2.count = s_3.count \wedge s'.count = s_3.count + 1 \wedge \operatorname{len}(s'.stack) = \operatorname{len}(s_3.stack) \Rightarrow s' \models count = \operatorname{len}(stack).$

From which the implication easily results. This proves that *push* conserves our invariant. A similar proof can be done for *pop*.

Components Implementation

We propose the following implementations for the above specifications.

$pop\text{-}impl : Event \xrightarrow{o} ()$

$pop\text{-}impl (evt) \triangleq$
wait true **do**
　　stack:= tl stack;
　　announce(mk-Event(2, evt.elt));
od

$push\text{-}impl : Event \xrightarrow{o} ()$

$push\text{-}impl (evt) \triangleq$
wait true **do**
　　stack:=evt.elt $\frown$ stack;
　　announce(mk-Event(1,evt.elt));
od

$increment\text{-}impl : Event \xrightarrow{o} ()$

$increment\text{-}impl (evt) \triangleq$
count:= count+1;

$decrement\text{-}impl : Event \xrightarrow{o} ()$

$decrement\text{-}impl (evt) \triangleq$
count:=count-1;

To prove that *push-impl* and *pop-impl* satisfy the specifications *push* and *pop* respectively, it is enough to show that $\models$ stack: $=$ evt.elt $\frown$ stack <u>sat</u> *simple-push* and $\models$ stack: $=$ tl stack <u>sat</u> *simple-pop* hold. We carry out the proof for the first case.

Let (R, P, G, E) denote the specification *simple-push*, i.e.:

1) $P \stackrel{def}{=} \mathsf{len}\ (stack) = count,$ 2) $R \stackrel{def}{=} \mathsf{len}\ (\overleftarrow{stack}) = \overleftarrow{count},$
3) $G \stackrel{def}{=} stack = evt.elt \frown \overleftarrow{stack} \wedge count = \overleftarrow{count},$ 4) $E \stackrel{def}{=} stack = evt.elt \frown \overleftarrow{stack}.$

The pre-condition requires that len $(stack) = count$ holds. Further, any transition performed by the environment is required to conserve this property. We, hence, deduce that any state which satisfies P^R (remember the definition of P^R, namely $\overleftarrow{P} \wedge R^*$) also satisfies P. The premise of the assignment rule ($\overleftarrow{P^R} \wedge v = \overleftarrow{r} \wedge I_{\vartheta \setminus \{v\}} \Rightarrow (G \vee I_\vartheta) \wedge E$) is expressed as (by replacing v with *stack* and $\overleftarrow{r}$ with $evt.elt \frown \overleftarrow{stack}$):

$(\mathsf{len}\ (\overleftarrow{stack}) = \overleftarrow{count} \wedge stack = evt.elt \frown \overleftarrow{stack} \wedge count = \overleftarrow{count}) \Rightarrow ((stack = evt.elt \frown \overleftarrow{stack} \wedge count = \overleftarrow{count})$
$\vee (stack = \overleftarrow{stack} \wedge count = \overleftarrow{count})) \wedge stack = evt.elt \frown \overleftarrow{stack}$, which in fact holds.

Applying the assignment rule (since we just showed that its premise is satisfied), we deduce that $\models stack: = evt.elt \frown \overleftarrow{stack}$ <u>sat</u> *simple-push* holds.

8 Conclusion

We have proposed an extension of the logic of events consumption and publication (LECAP) that allows the development of programs that depend on some kind of synchronization. We have also presented a way of using auxiliary variables for specifying and verifying more complex properties. We finally illustrated our ideas using a simple example.

The extension presented in this paper is part of a larger effort in establishing a methodology for the construction of reliable event-based applications. Such a methodology must allow developing applications that leverage the key concept of the event-based architectural style, namely, loose coupling of components. On the other hand, to support the development of emerging software systems, such a methodology must meet the requirements of component based software engineering as well as those of stepwise development of systems. We have, therefore, based our work on approaches that are well studied. In particular, we have proven that Jones's rely/guarantee technique is indeed well-suited for the stepwise development of event-based applications. Although the proposed approach is promising, the way to its application in industrial settings, our goal, remains fairly long. In particular, the soundness of the logic must be investigated, case studies have to be developed and tool support must be provided.

Acknowledgments

We would like to acknowledge the comments of Clemens Kerer, Gerald Reif, and Joe Oberleitner. We are also grateful to Ketil Stølen for the discussion with him.

References

1. P. Aczel. An inference rule for parallel composition. Technical report, University of Manchester, February 1983.
2. Daniel J. Barret, Lori A. Clarke, Peri L. Tarr, and Alexander E. Wise. A framework for event based software integration. *ACM Transactions on Software Engineering and Methodology*, 5(4):378–421, 1996.
3. Klaus Bergner, Andreas Rausch, and Marc Sihling. A componentware development methodology based on process patterns. In *Proceedings of 5th Annual Conference on Pattern Languages of Programs (PLOP98)*, 1998.
4. C.A.R Hoare. *Communicating Sequential Processes*. Prentice Hall, 1985.
5. A. Carzaniga, D.S. Rosenblum, and A.L. Wolf. Design and evaluation of a wide-area event notification service. *ACM Transactions on Computer Systems*, 3(19):332–383, August 2001.
6. J. Dingel. *Systematic parallel programming*. PhD thesis, School of Computer Science, Carnegie Mellon University, Pittsburgh, December 1999.
7. J. Dingel, D. Garlan, S. Jha, and D. Notkin. Reasonning about Implicit Invocation. In *Proceedings of the 6th International Symposium on the Foundations of Software Engineering, FSE-6*. ACM, 1998.
8. J. Dingel, D. Garlan, S. Jha, and D. Notkin. Towards a formal treatment of implicit invocation using rely/guarantee reasoning. *Formal Aspects of Computing*, 10, 1998.
9. Pascal Fenkam, Harald Gall, and Mehdi Jazayeri. A Systematic Approach to the Development of Event-Based Applications. In *Proceedings of the 22th IEEE Symposium on Reliable Distributed Systems (SRDS 2003), Florence, Italy*. IEEE Computer Press, October 2003.
10. Pascal Fenkam, Harald Gall, and Mehdi Jazayeri. Composing Specifications of Event Based Applications. In *Proceedings of FASE 2003 (Fundamental Approaches to Software Engineering 2003), Warsaw, Poland*, LNCS. Springer Verlag, April 2003.
11. David Garlan and Serge Khersonsky. Model checking implicit-invocation systems. In *Proceedings of the 10th International Workshop on Software Specification and Design, San Diego, CA*, November 2000.
12. David Garlan and David Notkin. Formalizing design spaces: Implicit invocation mechanisms. In *Proceedings of Fourth International Symposium of VDM Europe: Formal Software Development Methods*, Noordwijkerhout, Netherlands, October 1991. LNCS 551.
13. Daniel Jackson. Automatic analysis of architectural styles. Technical report, MIT Laboratory for Computer Sciences, Software Design Group, Unpublished Manuscript. Available at http://sdg.lcs.mit.edu/ dnj/publications.html.
14. C.B. Jones. Tentative steps towards a development method for interfering programs. *Transactions on Programming Languages and Systems*, 5(4), October 1983.
15. R. Milner. *The Calculus of Communicating Systems*. Prentice Hall, 1993.

16. Object Management Group. OMG Formal Documentation. Technical report, OMG, December 1999.
17. S. Owicki and D. Gries. Verifying properties of parallel programs: an axiomatic approach. *Communications of the ACM*, 19(5), May 1976.
18. K. Prasad. A calculus of broadcasting systems. In *Proceedings of TAPSOFT'91*, volume 493, 1991.
19. S.P. Reiss. Connecting tools using message passing in the field program development environment. *IEEE Software*, 19(5), July 1990.
20. Ed Roman, Scott W. Ambler, and Tyler Jewell. *Mastering Enterprise JavaBeans*. John Wiley & Sons, second edition, 2002.
21. N. Soundararajan. A proof technique for parallel programs. *Theoretical Computer Science*, 31:13–29, 1984.
22. Ketil Stølen. *Development of Parallel Programs on Shared Data-Structures*. PhD thesis, Department of Computer Science, University of Manchester, 1990.
23. Ketil Stølen. A Method for the Development of Totally Correct Shared-State Parallel Programs. In *Proceedings of CONCUR'91*, pages 510–525. Springer Verlag, 1991.
24. TIBCO Software Inc. TIB/Rendezvous TX Concepts Release 1.1. Technical report, TIBCO Software Inc.,Palo Alto, CA, November 2002. http://www.tibco.com.
25. Q. Xu and J. He. A theory of state-based parallel programming by refinement: part 1. In *Proceedings of the 4th BCS-FACS Refinement Workshop*. Springer Verlag, 1991.

A General Approach to Deadlock Freedom Verification for Software Architectures

Alessandro Aldini and Marco Bernardo

Università di Urbino "Carlo Bo", Istituto di Scienze e Tecnologie dell'Informazione,
Piazza della Repubblica 13, 61029 Urbino, Italy,
{aldini,bernardo}@sti.uniurb.it

Abstract. When building complex software systems, the designer is faced with the problem of detecting mismatches arising from the activity of assembling components. The adoption of formal methods becomes unavoidable in order to support a precise identification of such mismatches in the early design stages. As far as deadlock freedom is concerned, some techniques appeared in the literature, which apply to formal specifications of software architectures under some constraints. In this paper we develop a novel technique for deadlock freedom verification that can be applied to arbitrary software architectures, thus overcoming the limitations of the previous techniques.

Keywords: software architecture, deadlock, process algebra.

1 Introduction

The software architecture level of design enables us to cope with the increasing size and complexity of nowadays software systems during the early stages of their development [10, 11]. To achieve this, the focus is turned from algorithms and data structures to the overall architecture of a software system, where the architecture is meant to be a collection of computational components together with a description of their interactions. As software architecture emerges as a discipline within software engineering, it becomes increasingly important to support architectural development with languages and tools. It is widely recognized that suitable architectural description languages (ADLs) should be devised to formalize software architectures instead of using informal box-and-line diagrams, and companion tools should be implemented to support the automatic analysis of architectural properties in order to allow the designer to make principled choices. Among the formal method based ADLs appeared in the literature, we mention those relying on process algebras [2, 8, 3], Z [1], and the CHAM [6].

Complex software systems are typically made out of numerous components whose behavior is individually well known. The main problem faced by a software designer is that of understanding whether the components fit together well. If the architecture of a software system is given a formal description, then adequate techniques can hopefully be used to prove the well formedness of the system or to single out the components responsible for architectural mismatches. There are different kinds of architectural mismatches. A typical mismatch, which we address in this paper, is deadlock: starting from deadlock free components, the designer constructs a system that can deadlock. To adequately support the deadlock freedom verification at the architectural level of design, techniques must be developed that are scalable – because of the high number of components – and provide diagnostic information in case of mismatch – in order to know which part of the architecture must be modified.

In [2] a deadlock freedom verification technique has been developed, which exploits notions of equivalence defined for process algebra and considers single pairs of interactions of components communicating to each other. In [7] a more general technique has been proposed, which operates at the component level by taking into account the correlation among all the interactions of a component. In [3] an even more general technique has been presented, which considers not only the interactions between pairs of components, but also the interactions within sets of components forming a ring. The last technique has been proved to scale to families of software architectures, called architectural types, that admit a controlled variability of the component internal behavior and of the architectural topology [4, 5].

The current limitation of the technique of [3] is that it addresses only specific topologies: acyclic topologies and ring topologies. More precisely, two deadlock related architectural checks have been defined. The first one, called architectural compatibility check, is concerned with architectural types whose topology is acyclic. For an acyclic architectural type, if we take a component K and we consider all the components $C_1, \ldots, C_n$ attached to it, we can observe that they form a star topology whose center is K, as the absence of cycles prevents any two components among $C_1, \ldots, C_n$ from communicating via a component different from K. It can easily be recognized that an acyclic architectural type is just a composition of star topologies. By means of a weak bisimulation equivalence [9] based condition to be locally verified on each pair of components in the star topology, the architectural compatibility check ensures the absence of deadlock within a star topology whose center K is deadlock free, and this check scales to the whole acyclic architectural type. The second check, called architectural interoperability check, deals with ring topologies. Also in this case, a weak bisimulation equivalence based condition is employed, which can be verified in a rather efficient way and guarantees the absence of deadlock within a ring of components in case that at least one of them is deadlock free.

In this paper we overcome the limitation of [3] by proposing a general and scalable deadlock freedom verification technique for architectural types with an arbitrary topology. From a conceptual viewpoint, the idea underlying the new technique is that an acyclic topology is a special topology to which every topology can be reduced. Given an arbitrary topology that is not acyclic, we reduce every cyclic portion of the topology satisfying the interoperability check into a single equivalent component, until we obtain an architectural type not satisfying the check or we end up with an acyclic topology. From a practical viewpoint, the technique is implemented without actually having to reduce the topology. All we have to do is to apply a modified interoperability check, which is still based on the weak bisimulation equivalence, to some specific components of the topology.

This paper is organized as follows. In Sect. 2 we recall PADL, the process algebra based ADL of [3] that is used to formalize architectural types. In Sect. 3 we present our technique for detecting deadlock related architectural mismatches in arbitrary topologies. Finally, in Sect. 4 we report some concluding remarks.

2 Software Architecture Description

In this section we provide an overview of PADL, a process algebra based architectural description language for the representation of families of software systems, whose members share common component behaviors as well as common topologies. We start by recalling some notions about process algebra, then we present the syntax and the semantics for PADL. For more details, case studies, and comparisons with related work, the interested reader is referred to [3–5].

2.1 Process Algebra

The basic elements of any process algebra (see, e.g., [9]) are its actions, which represent activities carried out by the systems being modeled, and its operators – including a parallel composition operator – which are used to compose process algebraic descriptions.

The set of process terms of the process algebra PA that we consider in this paper is generated by the following syntax:

$$E ::= \underline{0} \mid a.E \mid E/L \mid E[\varphi] \mid E + E \mid E \parallel_S E \mid A$$

where a belongs to a set Act of actions including a distinguished action τ for unobservable activities, $L, S \subseteq Act - \{\tau\}$, φ belongs to a set of action relabeling functions preserving observability (i.e., $\varphi^{-1}(\tau) = \{\tau\}$), and A belongs to a set of constants each possessing a (possibly recursive) defining equation $A = E$.

In the syntax above, $\underline{0}$ is the term that cannot execute any action. Term $a.E$ can execute action a and then behaves as term E. Term E/L behaves as term E with each executed action a turned into τ whenever $a \in L$. Term $E[\varphi]$ behaves as term E with each executed action a turned into $\varphi(a)$. Term $E_1 + E_2$ behaves as either term E_1 or term E_2 depending on whether an action of E_1 or an action of E_2 is executed. Term $E_1 \parallel_S E_2$ asynchronously executes actions of E_1 or E_2 not belonging to S and synchronously executes equal actions of E_1 and E_2 belonging to S. The action prefix operator "." and the alternative composition operator "+" are called dynamic operators, whereas the hiding operator "/", the relabeling operator "[]", and the parallel composition operator "∥" are called static operators. A term is called sequential if it is composed of dynamic operators only.

The semantics for PA is defined in the standard operational style by means of a set of axioms and inference rules, which formalize the meaning of each operator.

The result of the application of the operational semantic rules to a term E is a state transition graph $\mathcal{I}[\![E]\!]$, where states are in correspondence with process terms and transitions are labeled with actions. In order to get finitely branching state transition graphs, as usual we restrict ourselves to closed and guarded terms, i.e. we require that every constant has exactly one defining equation and every constant occurrence is within the scope of an action prefix operator.

Due to their algebraic nature, process description languages like PA naturally lend themselves to the definition of equivalences. The notion of equivalence that we consider in this paper is the weak bisimulation equivalence [9], denoted $\approx_B$, which captures the ability of two terms to simulate each other behaviors up to τ actions. This equivalence has several useful properties that we shall exploit in the rest of the paper. First, $\approx_B$ is able to abstract from unobservable details, as witnessed by the following equational laws:
$$\tau.E \approx_B E$$
$$a.\tau.E \approx_B a.E$$
$$E + \tau.E \approx_B \tau.E$$
$$a.(E_1 + \tau.E_2) + a.E_2 \approx_B a.(E_1 + \tau.E_2)$$
Second, $\approx_B$ is a congruence with respect to the static operators: whenever $E_1 \approx_B E_2$, then
$$E_1/L \approx_B E_2/L$$
$$E_1[\varphi] \approx_B E_2[\varphi]$$
$$E_1 \parallel_S E \approx_B E_2 \parallel_S E$$
Finally, $\approx_B$ preserves deadlock freedom, i.e. it never equates a term whose semantic model has a state from which no other state can be reached by executing an observable action – possibly preceded by τ actions – to a term whose semantic model is deadlock free, i.e. a term that has not such a state.

2.2 PADL Syntax

PADL is an architectural description language, equipped with both a textual notation and a graphical notation, that makes explicit the inherent component orientation of process algebra. A PADL description represents an architectural type. As shown in Table 1, each architectural type is defined as a function of its architectural element types (AETs) and its architectural topology. An AET is defined as a function of its behavior, specified either as a family of sequential PA terms or through an invocation of a previously defined architectural type, and its interactions, specified as a set of PA actions occurring in the behavior that act as interfaces for the AET. The architectural topology is specified through the declaration of a set of architectural element instances (AEIs) representing the system components, a set of architectural (as opposed to local) interactions given by some interactions of the AEIs that act as interfaces for the whole architectural type, and a set of directed architectural attachments among the interactions of the AEIs. Graphically, the AEIs are depicted as boxes, the local interactions are depicted as black circles, the architectural interactions are depicted as white squares, and the attachments are depicted as directed edges between pairs of attachments.

Table 1. Structure of a PADL textual description

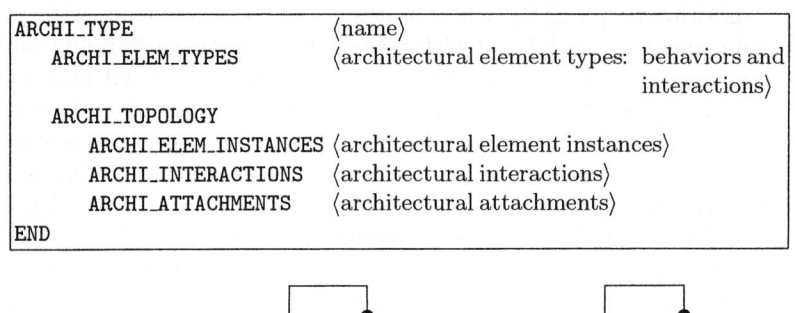

```
ARCHI_TYPE              ⟨name⟩
  ARCHI_ELEM_TYPES      ⟨architectural element types: behaviors and
                                                      interactions⟩
  ARCHI_TOPOLOGY
    ARCHI_ELEM_INSTANCES  ⟨architectural element instances⟩
    ARCHI_INTERACTIONS    ⟨architectural interactions⟩
    ARCHI_ATTACHMENTS     ⟨architectural attachments⟩
END
```

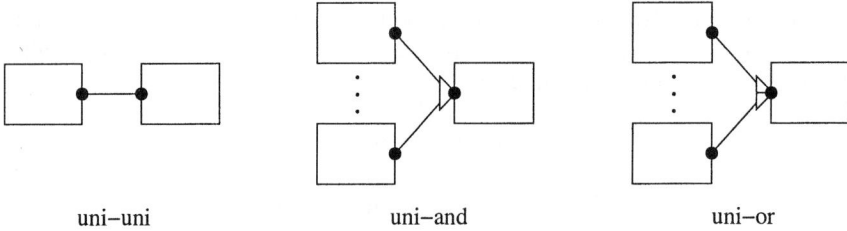

uni–uni   uni–and   uni–or

Fig. 1. Legal attachments

Every interaction is declared to be an input interaction or an output interaction and the attachments must respect such a classification: every attachment must involve an output interaction and an input interaction of two different AEIs. In addition, every interaction is declared to be a uni-interaction, an and-interaction, or an or-interaction. As shown in Fig. 1, the only legal attachments are those between two uni-interactions, an and-interaction and a uni-interaction, and an or-interaction and a uni-interaction. An and-interaction and an or-interaction can be attached to several uni-interactions. In the case of execution of an and-interaction, it synchronizes with all the uni-interactions attached to it. In the case of execution of an or-interaction, instead, it synchronizes with only one of the uni-interactions attached to it. An AEI can have different types of interactions (input/output, uni/and/or, local/architectural). Every local interaction must be involved in at least one attachment, while every architectural interaction must not be involved in any attachment. No isolated groups of AEIs are admitted in the architectural topology.

We now illustrate PADL by means of an example concerning a pipe-filter system. The system, which is depicted in Fig. 2 in accordance with the graphical notation, is composed of four identical filters and one pipe. Each filter acts as a service center of capacity two that is subject to failures and subsequent repairs. For each item processed by the upstream filter, the pipe forwards it to one of the three downstream filters according to the availability of free positions in their buffers. If all the downstream filters have free positions, the choice is resolved nondeterministically.

The pipe-filter system of Fig. 2 can be modeled with PADL as follows. First, we define the name of the architectural type:

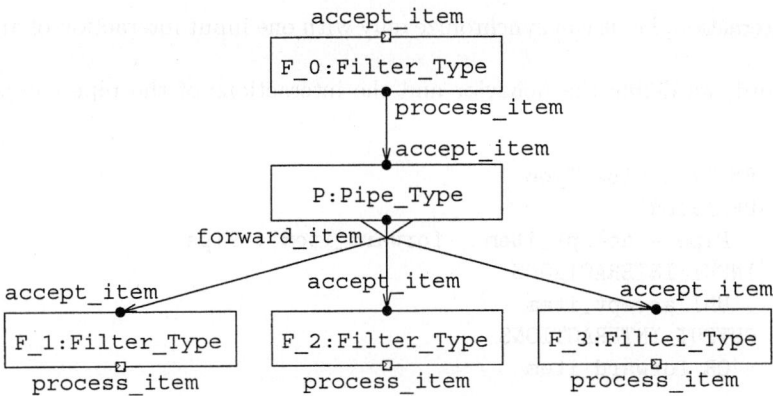

Fig. 2. Graphical description of Pipe_Filter

ARCHI_TYPE Pipe_Filter

Second, we start the AET definition section of the PADL description by specifying the behavior and the interactions of the filter component type:

ARCHI_ELEM_TYPES

```
    ELEM_TYPE Filter_Type
      BEHAVIOR
        Filter_0 = accept_item . Filter_1 +
                   fail . repair . Filter_0
        Filter_1 = accept_item . Filter_2 +
                   process_item . Filter_0 +
                   fail . repair . Filter_1
        Filter_2 = process_item . Filter_1 +
                   fail . repair . Filter_2
      INPUT_INTERACTIONS
        UNI accept_item
      OUTPUT_INTERACTIONS
        UNI process_item
```

Initially (Filter_0), the filter waits for an item to arrive. When an item is already in the filter buffer (Filter_1), there are two possibilities: either another item arrives at the filter, or a previously arrived item finishes to be processed and is sent out. Finally, when two items are already in the filter buffer (Filter_2), no more items can be accepted until one of the two previously arrived items finishes to be processed. In each of the three cases above, the filter can alternatively fail and be subsequently repaired. The action accept_item is declared to be an input uni-interaction, i.e. it can synchronize only with one output interaction of another AEI. The action process_item, instead, is declared to be an output uni-interaction, i.e. it can synchronize only with one input interaction of another AEI.

Third, we define the behavior and the interactions of the pipe component type:

```
ELEM_TYPE Pipe_Type
  BEHAVIOR
    Pipe = accept_item . forward_item . Pipe
  INPUT_INTERACTIONS
    UNI accept_item
  OUTPUT_INTERACTIONS
    OR forward_item
```

The pipe waits for an item, forwards it to one of several different destinations, then repeats this behavior. The fact that there may be several different destinations, and that the item is forwarded only to one of them, is witnessed by the declaration of forward_item as an or-interaction.

Fourth, we start the architectural topology section of the PADL description by declaring the instances of the previously defined AETs that compose the pipe-filter system of Fig. 2:

```
ARCHI_TOPOLOGY

  ARCHI_ELEM_INSTANCES
    F_0 : Filter_Type
    P   : Pipe_Type
    F_1 : Filter_Type
    F_2 : Filter_Type
    F_3 : Filter_Type
```

Fifth, we declare the architectural interactions, which can be used as global interfaces in the case in which the current architectural type is invoked in the definition of the behavior of a component type of a larger architectural type (hierarchical modeling):

```
ARCHI_INTERACTIONS
  F_0.accept_item
  F_1.process_item
  F_2.process_item
  F_3.process_item
```

Finally, we conclude the PADL description by specifying the attachments between the previously declared AEIs in order to reproduce the topology depicted in Fig. 2:

```
ARCHI_ATTACHMENTS
  FROM F_0.process_item TO P.accept_item
```

```
                FROM P.forward_item    TO F_1.accept_item
                FROM P.forward_item    TO F_2.accept_item
                FROM P.forward_item    TO F_3.accept_item

END
```

2.3 PADL Semantics

The semantics of a PADL specification is given by translation into PA. This translation is carried out in two steps. In the first step, the semantics of each AEI is defined to be the behavior of the corresponding AET projected onto its interactions. Such a projected behavior is obtained from the family of sequential PA terms representing the behavior of the AET by applying a hiding operator on all the actions that are not interactions. In this way, we abstract from all the internal details of the behavior of the AEI. In addition, the projected behavior must reflect the fact that an or-interaction can result in several distinct synchronizations. Therefore, every or-interaction is rewritten as a choice between as many indexed instances of uni-interactions as there are attachments involving the or-interaction.

Definition 1. *Let $\mathcal{A}$ be an architectural type and C be one of its AEIs with behavior E and interaction set $\mathcal{I}$. The semantics of C is defined by*
$$[\![C]\!] = \textit{or-rewrite}(E)/(Act - \{\tau\} - \mathcal{I})$$
where or-rewrite(E) is defined by structural induction as follows:

$$\textit{or-rewrite}(\underline{0}) = \underline{0}$$

$$\textit{or-rewrite}(a.G) = \begin{cases} a.\textit{or-rewrite}(G) & a \text{ not an or–interaction} \\ \sum_{i=1}^{n} a_i.\textit{or-rewrite}(G) & a \text{ or–interaction with } n \text{ attachs} \end{cases}$$

$$\textit{or-rewrite}(G_1 + G_2) = \textit{or-rewrite}(G_1) + \textit{or-rewrite}(G_2)$$

$$\textit{or-rewrite}(A) = A \qquad\blacksquare$$

For the pipe-filter system of Fig. 2 we have
$$[\![F\_0]\!] = \texttt{Filter\_0}/\{\texttt{fail},\texttt{repair}\}$$
$$[\![F\_1]\!] = \texttt{Filter\_0}/\{\texttt{fail},\texttt{repair}\}$$
$$[\![F\_2]\!] = \texttt{Filter\_0}/\{\texttt{fail},\texttt{repair}\}$$
$$[\![F\_3]\!] = \texttt{Filter\_0}/\{\texttt{fail},\texttt{repair}\}$$
$$[\![P]\!] = \textit{or-rewrite}(\texttt{Pipe})$$
where *or-rewrite*(Pipe) is a constant Pipe' such that

```
        Pipe' = accept_item . (forward_item_1 . Pipe' +
                                forward_item_2 . Pipe' +
                                forward_item_3 . Pipe')
```

It is worth observing that, in the semantics of the filters, the internal activities fail and repair have been abstracted away.

In the second step, the semantics of the architectural type is obtained by composing in parallel the semantics of its AEIs according to the specified attachments (the involved or-interactions need to be indexed). Recalled that the parallel composition operator is left associative, for the pipe-filter system of Fig. 2 we have

$[\![\text{Pipe\_Filter}]\!] = [\![\text{F\_0}]\!][\text{process\_item} \mapsto \text{a}] \|_{\{a\}}$
$\quad\quad [\![\text{P}]\!][\text{accept\_item} \mapsto \text{a},$
$\quad\quad\quad \text{forward\_item\_1} \mapsto \text{a\_1},$
$\quad\quad\quad \text{forward\_item\_2} \mapsto \text{a\_2},$
$\quad\quad\quad \text{forward\_item\_3} \mapsto \text{a\_3}] \|_{\{a\_1\}}$
$\quad\quad\quad\quad [\![\text{F\_1}]\!][\text{accept\_item} \mapsto \text{a\_1}] \|_{\{a\_2\}}$
$\quad\quad\quad\quad\quad [\![\text{F\_2}]\!][\text{accept\_item} \mapsto \text{a\_2}] \|_{\{a\_3\}}$
$\quad\quad\quad\quad\quad\quad [\![\text{F\_3}]\!][\text{accept\_item} \mapsto \text{a\_3}]$

The use of the relabeling operator is necessary to make the AEIs interact. As an example, F_0 and P must interact via process_item and accept_item, which have different names. Since the parallel composition operator allows only equal actions to synchronize, in $[\![\text{Pipe\_Filter}]\!]$ each process_item action executed by $[\![\text{F\_0}]\!]$ and each accept_item action executed by $[\![\text{P}]\!]$ is relabeled to the same action a. In order to avoid interferences, it is important that a be a fresh action, i.e. an action occurring neither in $[\![\text{F\_0}]\!]$ nor in $[\![\text{P}]\!]$. Then a synchronization on a is forced between the relabeled versions of $[\![\text{F\_0}]\!]$ and $[\![\text{P}]\!]$ by means of operator $\|_{\{a\}}$.

In general, when accomplishing the second step, first of all we have to determine the number of fresh actions that we need in order to make the AEIs interact according to the attachments. To achieve that, we have to single out all the maximal sets of synchronizing interactions, as all the members of a maximal set must be relabeled to the same fresh action. In the case of an attachment between two uni-interactions, the maximal set is composed of the two uni-interactions. In the case of an or-interaction, we have as many maximal sets of synchronizing interactions as there are attachments involving the or-interaction; each of such sets comprises the uni-interaction involved in the attachment and the uni-interaction obtained by indexing the or-interaction. In the case of an and-interaction, we have a single maximal set composed of the and-interaction and all the uni-interactions attached to it.

Given an architectural type $\mathcal{A}$, let $C_1, \ldots, C_n$ be some of its AEIs and let i, j, k range over $\{1, \ldots, n\}$. For each AEI C_i, let $\mathcal{I}_{C_i} = \mathcal{LI}_{C_i} \cup \mathcal{AI}_{C_i}$ be the set of its local and architectural interactions, and $\mathcal{LI}_{C_i; C_1, \ldots, C_n} \subseteq \mathcal{LI}_{C_i}$ be the set of its local interactions attached to local interactions of $C_1, \ldots, C_n$. Once we have identified the maximal sets of synchronizing interactions, we construct a set $\mathcal{S}(C_1, \ldots, C_n)$ composed of as many fresh actions as there are maximal sets of synchronizing interactions. Then we relabel all the local interactions in the same set to the same fresh action. This is achieved by defining a set of injective action relabeling functions of the form $\varphi_{C_i; C_1, \ldots, C_n} : \mathcal{LI}_{C_i; C_1, \ldots, C_n} \longrightarrow \mathcal{S}(C_1, \ldots, C_n)$ in such a way that $\varphi_{C_i; C_1, \ldots, C_n}(a_1) = \varphi_{C_j; C_1, \ldots, C_n}(a_2)$ iff $C_i.a_1$ and $C_j.a_2$ belong to the same set. Based on these relabeling functions that prepare the AEIs to interact, we now define two semantics for C_i restricted to its local interactions attached to local interactions of $C_1, \ldots, C_n$. The closed semantics will be used for deadlock freedom verification purposes. It abstracts from the architectural interactions of C_i as these must not come into play when checking for deadlock freedom. Since the open semantics will be used instead in the definition of the semantics of an architectural type, it does not abstract from the architectural interactions of C_i as these must be observable. If C_i has no architectural interactions, then the two semantics coincide.

Definition 2. *The closed and the open interacting semantics of C_i restricted to $C_1,\ldots,C_n$ are defined by*
$$[\![C_i]\!]^c_{C_1,\ldots,C_n} = [\![C_i]\!] / (Act - \{\tau\} - \mathcal{LI}_{C_i;C_1,\ldots,C_n}) \quad [\varphi_{C_i;C_1,\ldots,C_n}]$$
$$[\![C_i]\!]^o_{C_1,\ldots,C_n} = [\![C_i]\!] / (Act - \{\tau\} - (\mathcal{LI}_{C_i;C_1,\ldots,C_n} \cup \mathcal{AI}_{C_i})) \quad [\varphi_{C_i;C_1,\ldots,C_n}] \quad \blacksquare$$

Finally, we define the closed and the open interacting semantics of $C_1,\ldots,C_n$ by putting in parallel the closed and the open interacting semantics of each of the considered AEIs, respectively. To do that, we need to define the synchronization sets. Let us preliminarily define for each AEI and pair of AEIs in $C_1,\ldots,C_n$ the subset of fresh actions to which their local interactions are relabeled:
$$\mathcal{S}(C_i;C_1,\ldots,C_n) = \varphi_{C_i;C_1,\ldots,C_n}(\mathcal{LI}_{C_i;C_1,\ldots,C_n})$$
$$\mathcal{S}(C_i,C_j;C_1,\ldots,C_n) = \mathcal{S}(C_i;C_1,\ldots,C_n) \cap \mathcal{S}(C_j;C_1,\ldots,C_n)$$
Recalled that the parallel composition operator is left associative, the synchronization set between the interacting semantics of C_1 and C_2 is given by $\mathcal{S}(C_1,C_2;C_1,\ldots,C_n)$, the synchronization set between the interacting semantics of C_2 and C_3 is given by $\mathcal{S}(C_1,C_3;C_1,\ldots,C_n) \cup \mathcal{S}(C_2,C_3;C_1,\ldots,C_n)$, and so on.

Definition 3. *The closed and the open interacting semantics of $C_1,\ldots,C_n$ are defined by*
$$[\![C_1,\ldots,C_n]\!]^c = [\![C_1]\!]^c_{C_1,\ldots,C_n} \parallel_{\mathcal{S}(C_1,C_2;C_1,\ldots,C_n)}$$
$$[\![C_2]\!]^c_{C_1,\ldots,C_n} \parallel_{\mathcal{S}(C_1,C_3;C_1,\ldots,C_n)\cup\mathcal{S}(C_2,C_3;C_1,\ldots,C_n)} \cdots$$
$$\cdots \parallel_{\cup_{i=1}^{n-1}\mathcal{S}(C_i,C_n;C_1,\ldots,C_n)} [\![C_n]\!]^c_{C_1,\ldots,C_n}$$
$$[\![C_1,\ldots,C_n]\!]^o = [\![C_1]\!]^o_{C_1,\ldots,C_n} \parallel_{\mathcal{S}(C_1,C_2;C_1,\ldots,C_n)}$$
$$[\![C_2]\!]^o_{C_1,\ldots,C_n} \parallel_{\mathcal{S}(C_1,C_3;C_1,\ldots,C_n)\cup\mathcal{S}(C_2,C_3;C_1,\ldots,C_n)} \cdots$$
$$\cdots \parallel_{\cup_{i=1}^{n-1}\mathcal{S}(C_i,C_n;C_1,\ldots,C_n)} [\![C_n]\!]^o_{C_1,\ldots,C_n} \quad \blacksquare$$

Definition 4. *The semantics of an architectural type $\mathcal{A}$ whose AEIs are $C_1,\ldots,C_n$ is defined by $[\![\mathcal{A}]\!] = [\![C_1,\ldots,C_n]\!]^o$.* $\quad \blacksquare$

3 Deadlock Freedom Verification

The use of PADL for modeling large software systems represents a step towards bridging the gap between the rigorous view of difficult-to-use formal methods and the practical view of the software architect. However, if we want such an approach to be perceived as sufficiently appealing and profitable in practice, it must be accompanied by scalable and simple-to-use techniques both for the automatic detection of architectural mismatches and for the identification of their origins.

Among the several different architectural mismatches that can be encountered in the design process, in this paper we concentrate on deadlock. As mentioned in Sect. 1, two different architectural checks, called compatibility check and interoperability check, have been developed in [3] that deal with deadlock related architectural mismatches for two different topologies: acyclic architectural types and ring architectural types.

In this section, we present a general architectural check, which can be applied to any architectural type independently of its topology and provides a sufficient condition for deadlock freedom. To this purpose, we preliminarily recall from [3] the notion of reduced flow graph as well as the notion of compatibility check and we introduce a slight variant of the interoperability check. Based on these definitions, we then propose a novel technique for verifying deadlock freedom at the architectural level of design for systems with an arbitrary topology.

3.1 Reduced Flow Graph

When applying the deadlock related architectural checks to PADL descriptions of architectural types, as seen in [3] we can safely abstract from the direction of the information flow and from the multiplicity of the attachments between pairs of AEIs. As a consequence, an architectural type is classified as having an acyclic topology or a cyclic topology based on a modification of its graphical representation. The result of such a modification, called reduced flow graph, collapses all the directed edges between two boxes into a single, indirect edge.

3.2 Compatibility Check for Acyclic Topologies

The main principle underlying the compatibility check of [3] is based on the observation that an acyclic architectural type can be viewed as the composition of several star topologies, each one being formed by an AEI K, called the center of the star topology, and a set of AEIs $C_1, \ldots, C_n$ attached to K, called the border of the star topology and denoted by $\mathcal{B}_K$. The absence of cycles guarantees that $C_1, \ldots, C_n$ cannot directly communicate with each other. Therefore, the absence of deadlock can be investigated by analyzing the interactions between the center K of the star topology and the AEIs constituting the border of the star topology. The important result that can be derived is that verifying deadlock freedom for the whole architectural type reduces to checking the local interactions within each of the constituent star topologies.

The architectural compatibility check for a star topology with center AEI K attached to AEIs $C_1, \ldots, C_n$ works as follows. The intuition is that K is compatible with C_i if the potential interactions of K with the star topology components are not altered when attaching C_i to K. Formally, we verify whether the closed interacting semantics of K with respect to the star topology, namely $[\![K]\!]^c_{K,\mathcal{B}_K}$, is weakly bisimulation equivalent to the parallel composition of the closed interacting semantics of K and C_i. If this holds for any C_i of the star topology, then the interactions of K cannot be limited by the behavior of its neighbors.

Definition 5. *Given an architectural type $\mathcal{A}$, let $C_1, \ldots, C_n$ be the AEIs attached to an AEI K in $\mathcal{A}$. C_i is said to be compatible with K iff*

$$[\![K]\!]^c_{K,\mathcal{B}_K} \|_{\mathcal{S}(K;K,\mathcal{B}_K)} [\![C_i]\!]^c_{K,\mathcal{B}_K} \approx_B [\![K]\!]^c_{K,\mathcal{B}_K} \qquad \blacksquare$$

In a star topology, the compatibility between the center K and each C_i attached to K provides a sufficient condition for deadlock freedom in case K is deadlock free. Therefore, the deadlock freedom result for the whole star topology is obtained by simply applying peer-to-peer checks between its constituents. The main result saying that the absence of deadlock scales to the whole acyclic architectural type in case all the star topologies are deadlock free, is summarized by the following theorem [3].

Theorem 1. (Compatibility) *Let $\mathcal{A}$ be an acyclic architectural type. If the semantics of each AEI of $\mathcal{A}$ – with the architectural interactions being hidden – is deadlock free and every AEI of $\mathcal{A}$ is compatible with each AEI attached to it, then $[\![\mathcal{A}]\!]$ is deadlock free.* $\blacksquare$

3.3 Interoperability Check for Ring Topologies

Ensuring deadlock freedom for cyclic architectural types cannot be achieved by employing the peer-to-peer compatibility check described above, as there may be further causes of architectural mismatches due to the cyclic nature of the topology. To this aim, the interoperability condition presented in [3] is used to verify deadlock freedom in the presence of cycles. The intuition behind the interoperability check is almost the same as that of the compatibility check. Informally, given a cycle formed by the AEIs $C_1, \ldots, C_n$, if the potential local interactions of a given C_i are not altered when attaching C_i to the cycle, then the behavior of the cycle is the same as that expected by C_i and we say that C_i interoperates with the cycle. If there exists such a C_i within the cycle and C_i is deadlock free, then the cycle is deadlock free. Hence, with respect to the compatibility notion, here the minimal group of AEIs to be included in each check is given by all the AEIs $C_1, \ldots, C_n$ forming the cycle. This is because any AEI within the cycle could be responsible for limiting the local interactions of C_i with its neighbors.

In the following, given an architectural type $\mathcal{A}$ whose AEIs are $K_1, \ldots, K_m$, by abuse of notation we will use the abbreviation $\mathcal{A}$ to stand for $K_1, \ldots, K_m$. For instance, $[\![K]\!]^c_\mathcal{A}$ stands for $[\![K]\!]^c_{K_1,\ldots,K_m}$ and $\mathcal{S}(K;\mathcal{A})$ stands for $\mathcal{S}(K;K_1,\ldots,K_m)$.

Definition 6. *Let $\mathcal{A}$ be an architectural type and $C_1, \ldots, C_n$ be some of its AEIs. The closed interacting semantics of $C_1, \ldots, C_n$ with respect to $\mathcal{A}$ is defined by*

$$[\![C_1, \ldots, C_n]\!]^c_\mathcal{A} = [\![C_1]\!]^c_\mathcal{A} \|_{\mathcal{S}(C_1,C_2;\mathcal{A})}$$
$$[\![C_2]\!]^c_\mathcal{A} \|_{\mathcal{S}(C_1,C_3;\mathcal{A}) \cup \mathcal{S}(C_2,C_3;\mathcal{A})} \cdots$$
$$\cdots \|_{\cup_{i=1}^{n-1} \mathcal{S}(C_i,C_n;\mathcal{A})} [\![C_n]\!]^c_\mathcal{A} \qquad \blacksquare$$

The following definition formalizes the notion of interoperability as described above. Note that the behavior of a single AEI in the cycle is compared with the behavior of the whole cycle projected on the local interactions of that specific AEI.

Definition 7. *Given an architectural type $\mathcal{A}$, let $C_1, \ldots, C_n$ be AEIs forming a cycle in the reduced flow graph of $\mathcal{A}$. C_i is said to interoperate with $C_1, \ldots, C_{i-1}, C_{i+1}, \ldots, C_n$ iff*

$$[\![C_1, \ldots, C_n]\!]_{\mathcal{A}}^{c} / (Act - \{\tau\} - \mathcal{S}(C_i; \mathcal{A})) \approx_{\mathrm{B}} [\![C_i]\!]_{\mathcal{A}}^{c}$$

■

We point out that the interoperability notion of [3] is slightly different from that of Def. 7. The former compares the parallel composition of the closed interacting semantics of $C_1, \ldots, C_n$ projected on the interactions with C_i only and the closed interacting semantics of C_i projected on the interactions with $C_1, \ldots, C_n$. Instead, in Def. 7 all the local interactions of C_i are left visible. As we shall see in Sect. 3.4, this is needed if we want the results of the interoperability check to scale in the case of cyclic architectural types that are not rings. Obviously, the two notions of interoperability coincide in case the architectural type is a ring.

Before introducing the interoperability theorem, with respect to [3] we add the notion of frontier, which is useful to define a ring topology and also to prove the main result of this paper in Sect. 3.4.

Definition 8. *Given an architectural type $\mathcal{A}$, let $C_1, \ldots, C_n$ be some of its AEIs. The frontier of $C_1, \ldots, C_n$ is the unique subset $\mathcal{F}_{C_1, \ldots, C_n}$ of $\{C_1, \ldots, C_n\}$ such that $C_i \in \mathcal{F}_{C_1, \ldots, C_n}$ iff C_i is attached to AEI $K \notin \{C_1, \ldots, C_n\}$.* ■

Definition 9. *Let $\mathcal{A}$ be an architectural type. $\mathcal{A}$ is said to be a ring formed by the AEIs $C_1, \ldots, C_n$ iff $\mathcal{F}_{C_1, \ldots, C_n} = \emptyset$ and for each proper subset $\{C'_1, \ldots, C'_{n'}\}$ of $\{C_1, \ldots, C_n\}$, $C'_1, \ldots, C'_{n'}$ do not form a cycle in the reduced flow graph of $\mathcal{A}$.* ■

Theorem 2. *(Interoperability) Let the architectural type $\mathcal{A}$ be a ring formed by the AEIs $C_1, \ldots, C_n$. If there exists C_i such that $[\![C_i]\!]_{\mathcal{A}}^{c}$ is deadlock free and C_i interoperates with $C_1, \ldots, C_{i-1}, C_{i+1}, \ldots, C_n$, then $[\![\mathcal{A}]\!]$ is deadlock free.* ■

3.4 General Check for Arbitrary Topologies

While the architectural compatibility check scales from star topologies to arbitrary acyclic topologies, the architectural interoperability check does not scale from ring topologies to arbitrary cyclic topologies. This is because of subtle architectural mismatches that can arise from the interactions between intersecting cycles as well as between a cycle and an acyclic portion of the whole architectural topology. In particular, the architectural interoperability check applied to a cycle of AEIs $C_1, \ldots, C_n$ does not provide a sufficient condition for deadlock freedom if the cycle is such that some C_i interacts with some AEI K that is not in $C_1, \ldots, C_n$. In other words, if the frontier of the cycle is not empty, then the interoperability condition is not enough to decide the deadlock freedom. Assume, e.g., that it is possible to find a C_i in the cycle such that its interactions are not affected by the behavior of the other AEIs of the cycle. Even if C_i interoperates with the cycle, nothing can be deduced about the influence of other components

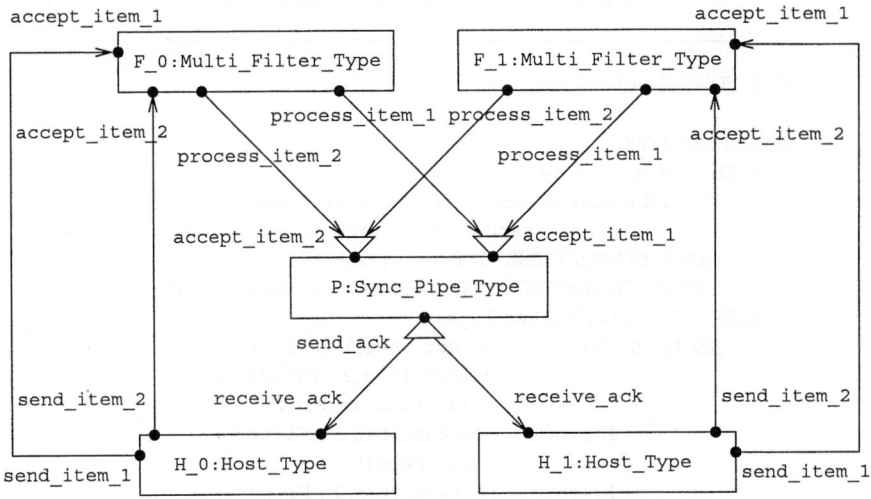

Fig. 3. Graphical description of Feedback_PF

of the architectural topology upon the cycle in case some AEIs of the cycle interact with some AEIs outside the cycle. This is because, when checking the interoperability condition for C_i, we abstract away from the interactions that attach the other components of the cycle to AEIs external to the cycle.

Let us consider, e.g., the system depicted in Fig. 3 and specified with PADL in Table 2. The system, called Feedback_PF, is composed of two hosts, two filters of capacity one, and a pipe with feedback. Each host forms a cycle with its dedicated filter and the pipe. In particular, host H_0 generates two types of items (called type 1 and type 2), which are sent to filter F_0, which in turn processes and passes the received items to the pipe (similarly for host H_1). Pipe P is willing to receive an item of type 1 from filter F_0 if and only if filter F_1 is ready to send an item of the same type too. The reception of these two items from both filters is synchronized (see the uni-and attachments between the two filters and the pipe in Fig. 3). Upon the synchronized reception of the two items of type 1, pipe P sends an acknowledgement to each host (see the uni-and attachments between the pipe and the two hosts in Fig. 3). We can argue similarly for items of type 2. Hence, pipe P can receive items if both filters (i) are ready to send an item and (ii) agree on the type of item to be processed. As we shall see, such a behavior of the pipe potentially causes a deadlock that cannot be detected through the interoperability check. Consider, e.g., the scenario where filter F_0 processes an item of type 1, while filter F_1 processes an item of type 2. The cycle composed of H_0, F_0, and P deadlocks since H_0 waits for an acknowledgement from P, F_0 waits for delivering the item of type 1 to the pipe, which instead waits for an item of the same type from F_1. On the other hand, filter F_1 is blocked since it is trying to send an item of type 2 to P and, as a consequence, host H_1 is blocked until the reception

Table 2. PADL description of Feedback_PF

ARCHI_TYPE Feedback_PF

ARCHI_ELEM_TYPES
   ELEM_TYPE Host_Type
      BEHAVIOR Host = send_item_1 . receive_ack . Host +
                            send_item_2 . receive_ack . Host
      INPUT_INTERACTIONS UNI receive_ack
      OUTPUT_INTERACTIONS UNI send_item_1, send_item_2
   ELEM_TYPE Multi_Filter_Type
      BEHAVIOR Filter = accept_item_1 . Filter$'$ +
                          accept_item_2 . Filter$''$ +
                          fail . repair . Filter
            Filter$'$ = process_item_1 . Filter +
                    fail . repair . Filter$'$
            Filter$''$ = process_item_2 . Filter +
                    fail . repair . Filter$''$
      INPUT_INTERACTIONS UNI accept_item_1, accept_item_2
      OUTPUT_INTERACTIONS UNI process_item_1, process_item_2
   ELEM_TYPE Sync_Pipe_Type
      BEHAVIOR Pipe = accept_item_1 . send_ack . Pipe +
                        accept_item_2 . send_ack . Pipe
      INPUT_INTERACTIONS AND accept_item_1, accept_item_2
      OUTPUT_INTERACTIONS AND send_ack

ARCHI_TOPOLOGY
   ARCHI_ELEM_INSTANCES H_0, H_1 : Host_Type
                             F_0, F_1 : Multi_Filter_Type
                             P   : Sync_Pipe_Type
   ARCHI_INTERACTIONS
   ARCHI_ATTACHMENTS FROM H_0.send_item_1   TO F_0.accept_item_1
                        FROM H_0.send_item_2   TO F_0.accept_item_2
                        FROM H_1.send_item_1   TO F_1.accept_item_1
                        FROM H_1.send_item_2   TO F_1.accept_item_2
                        FROM F_0.process_item_1 TO P.accept_item_1
                        FROM F_0.process_item_2 TO P.accept_item_2
                        FROM F_1.process_item_1 TO P.accept_item_1
                        FROM F_1.process_item_2 TO P.accept_item_2
                        FROM P.send_ack   TO H_0.receive_ack
                        FROM P.send_ack   TO H_1.receive_ack

END

---

of an acknowledgement that pipe P cannot send. However, it can be verified that H_0 interoperates with F_0 and P, and H_1 interoperates with F_1 and P. More formally, we have that, e.g., $[\![H_0]\!]^c_{\text{Feedback\_PF}}$ is weakly bisimulation equivalent to the closed interacting semantics of AEIs H_0, F_0, and P with respect to Feedback_PF. As can easily be seen, in both cases we abstract away from the local interactions of P with F_1, which is not in the cycle. Therefore, we cannot verify the influence of the cycle behavior upon the interaction between P and F_1 and, as a consequence, we cannot reveal the mismatch. Key to a successful detection of the deadlock is an interoperability check applied to P, whose interactions with both cycles cause the troublesome behavior described above.

We now show that, even in an arbitrary architectural topology like the one in Fig. 3, it is possible to verify the absence of deadlock by analyzing some specific local interactions of its AEIs. In the following theorem, deadlock freedom is guaranteed for an arbitrary architectural type under three assumptions. First, every AEI must be deadlock free. Second, every AEI must be compatible with each AEI attached to it. This ensures deadlock freedom for acyclic topologies. Third, if the architectural type has a cyclic topology, then there exists a cycle covering strategy (Def. 11) such that two constraints are satisfied, which are concerned with a set of intersecting cycles called a cyclic border (Def. 10). The first constraint requires that, if the architectural type is formed by a single cyclic border with empty frontier, then it must contain an AEI that interoperates with the other AEIs in the cyclic border (in analogy with the interoperability check for ring topologies). The second constraint requires that every AEI K in the frontier of any cyclic border must interoperate with all the other AEIs belonging to the cyclic border. This ensures a deadlock free combination of cyclic borders and acyclic portions of the topology.

Definition 10. *Given an architectural type $\mathcal{A}$, let K be one of its AEIs such that K is in (at least) one cycle in the reduced flow graph of $\mathcal{A}$. The set of all the AEIs involved with K in (at least) one cycle of the reduced flow graph of $\mathcal{A}$, called the cyclic border of K, is defined by $\mathcal{CB}_K^{\mathcal{A}} = \{K\} \cup \{H \mid \exists C_1, \ldots, C_n : K, H, C_1, \ldots, C_n \text{ form a cycle in the reduced flow graph of } \mathcal{A}\}$.* ∎

Definition 11. *Given a cyclic architectural type $\mathcal{A}$, a cycle covering strategy is defined by the following algorithm:*

1. *All the AEIs in the reduced flow graph of $\mathcal{A}$ are initially unmarked.*
2. *While there are unmarked AEIs in the cycles of the reduced flow graph of $\mathcal{A}$:*
   (a) Pick out one such AEI, say K.
   (b) Mark all the AEIs in $\mathcal{CB}_K^{\mathcal{A}}$. ∎

The application of a cycle covering strategy to a cyclic architectural type $\mathcal{A}$ generates a set involving all the AEIs in the cycles of the reduced flow graph of $\mathcal{A}$, which contains the cyclic borders considered by the algorithm.

Lemma 1. *Given a cyclic architectural type $\mathcal{A}$ and a cycle covering strategy that originates the set $\{\mathcal{CB}_{K_1}^{\mathcal{A}}, \ldots, \mathcal{CB}_{K_n}^{\mathcal{A}}\}$, then the two following conditions hold:*

1. *For any pair of different cyclic borders $\mathcal{CB}_{K_i}^{\mathcal{A}}, \mathcal{CB}_{K_j}^{\mathcal{A}} \in \{\mathcal{CB}_{K_1}^{\mathcal{A}}, \ldots, \mathcal{CB}_{K_n}^{\mathcal{A}}\}$, $\mathcal{CB}_{K_i}^{\mathcal{A}}$ can be directly attached to $\mathcal{CB}_{K_j}^{\mathcal{A}}$ in two different ways only:*
   I. They interact through a single, shared AEI K.

II. They do not share any AEI, but they interact through attachments between a single AEI H of $CB^A_{K_i}$ and a single AEI H' of $CB^A_{K_j}$.

2. If we replace each $CB^A_{K_i} = \{H_1, \ldots, H_l\}$ with an AEI that is isomorphic to
$$[\![H_1, \ldots, H_l]\!]^c_{\mathcal{A}} / (Act - \{\tau\} - \bigcup_{H_j \in \mathcal{F}_{H_1,\ldots,H_l}} S(H_j; \mathcal{A}))$$
then the obtained architectural topology is acyclic.

Proof. As far as condition 1.I is concerned, assume that $CB^A_{K_i}$ and $CB^A_{K_j}$ share another AEI H. Then the reduced flow graph of $\mathcal{A}$ would contain a cycle including K_i, K, K_j, H, thus contradicting the hypothesis that $CB^A_{K_i}$ is the cyclic border of K_i. Similarly, if there exists an attachment between an AEI H of $CB^A_{K_i}$ and an AEI H' of $CB^A_{K_j}$, then the reduced flow graph of $\mathcal{A}$ would contain a cycle including K_i, K, K_j, H', H, thus contradicting the hypothesis that $CB^A_{K_i}$ is the cyclic border of K_i.

As far as condition 1.II is concerned, assume that there exists another attachment between an AEI H'' of $CB^A_{K_i}$ and an AEI H''' of $CB^A_{K_j}$. Then the reduced flow graph of $\mathcal{A}$ would contain a cycle including $K_i, H, H', K_j, H''', H''$, thus contradicting the hypothesis that $CB^A_{K_i}$ is the cyclic border of K_i. On the other hand, if there exists another attachment between an AEI H'' of $CB^A_{K_i}$ and H', then the reduced flow graph of $\mathcal{A}$ would contain a cycle including K_i, H, H', H'', thus contradicting the hypothesis that $CB^A_{K_i}$ and $CB^A_{K_j}$ do not share any AEI. We can argue similarly in case of an attachment between an AEI H'' of $CB^A_{K_j}$ and H.

As far as condition 2 is concerned, the proof is a straightforward consequence of condition 1 and of the maximality of each cyclic border. ∎

Theorem 3. *Let $\mathcal{A}$ be an architectural type with an arbitrary topology. Suppose that the following conditions hold:*

1. *For every AEI K in $\mathcal{A}$, $[\![K]\!]^c_{\mathcal{A}}$ is deadlock free.*
2. *Every AEI of $\mathcal{A}$ is compatible with each AEI attached to it.*
3. *If $\mathcal{A}$ is cyclic, then there exists a set of cyclic borders generated by a cycle covering strategy such that:*
   I. *If the set has a single cyclic border $\{C_1, \ldots, C_n\}$ such that $\mathcal{F}_{C_1,\ldots,C_n} = \emptyset$, then there exists C_i that interoperates with $C_1, \ldots, C_{i-1}, C_{i+1}, \ldots, C_n$.*
   II. *Otherwise, for every cyclic border $\{C_1, \ldots, C_n\}$ in the set, we have that for each $C_i \in \mathcal{F}_{C_1,\ldots,C_n}$, C_i interoperates with $C_1, \ldots, C_{i-1}, C_{i+1}, \ldots, C_n$.*

Then $[\![\mathcal{A}]\!]$ is deadlock free.

Proof. We proceed by induction on the number m of cycles in the reduced flow graph of $\mathcal{A}$. As far as the induction base is concerned, if $m = 0$, then $\mathcal{A}$ is acyclic and the proof, by 1 and 2, is a straightforward consequence of the compatibility theorem.

Let the result hold for a certain $m \geq 0$ and consider an architectural type $\mathcal{A}$ satisfying 1, 2, and 3, whose reduced flow graph has $m+1$ cycles. Let $\{CB^A_K, CB^A_{K_1}, \ldots, CB^A_{K_n}\}$ be the set of cyclic borders originated by the cycle covering strategy of 3 and, by virtue of condition 2 of Lemma 1, let $CB_K^{\mathcal{A}} = \{C_1, \ldots, C_n\}$ be a cyclic border that directly interacts with at most one cyclic border in the set. Now we replace the AEIs $C_1, \ldots, C_n$ with a new AEI C such that its behavior is isomorphic to $[\![C_1, \ldots, C_n]\!]_{\mathcal{A}}^c / (Act - \{\tau\} - \bigcup_{C_j \in \mathcal{F}_{C_1,\ldots,C_n}} \mathcal{S}(C_j; \mathcal{A}))$, thus obtaining an architectural type $\mathcal{A}'$ such that:

- C preserves 1. In fact, by 3, there exists C_i such that
$$[\![C_1, \ldots, C_n]\!]_{\mathcal{A}}^c / (Act - \{\tau\} - \mathcal{S}(C_i; \mathcal{A})) \approx_B [\![C_i]\!]_{\mathcal{A}}^c$$
from which we derive that $[\![C_1, \ldots, C_n]\!]_{\mathcal{A}}^c / (Act - \{\tau\} - \mathcal{S}(C_i; \mathcal{A}))$ is deadlock free because so is $[\![C_i]\!]_{\mathcal{A}}^c$ due to 1. Therefore, we also have that $[\![C_1, \ldots, C_n]\!]_{\mathcal{A}}^c / (Act - \{\tau\} - \bigcup_{C_j \in \mathcal{F}_{C_1,\ldots,C_n}} \mathcal{S}(C_j; \mathcal{A}))$ is deadlock free.

- C preserves 2. In fact, let H be an AEI attached to C because it was previously attached to an AEI C_i of $\mathcal{F}_{C_1,\ldots,C_n}$. By 2 we have that
$$[\![C_i]\!]_{C_i,\mathcal{B}_{C_i}}^c \parallel_{\mathcal{S}(C_i; C_i, \mathcal{B}_{C_i})} [\![H]\!]_{C_i,\mathcal{B}_{C_i}}^c \approx_B [\![C_i]\!]_{C_i,\mathcal{B}_{C_i}}^c$$
from which it follows that
$$[\![C_i]\!]_{\mathcal{A}}^c \parallel_{\mathcal{S}(C_i; \mathcal{A})} [\![H]\!]_{C_i,\mathcal{B}_{C_i}}^c \approx_B [\![C_i]\!]_{\mathcal{A}}^c$$
Since $\approx_B$ is a congruence with respect to the parallel composition operator,
$$[\![C]\!]_{\mathcal{A}'}^c \parallel_{\mathcal{S}(C; \mathcal{A}')} [\![H]\!]_{C,\mathcal{B}_C}^c \approx_B [\![C]\!]_{\mathcal{A}'}^c$$
because we hide interactions that are not attached to H (only C_i can be attached to H otherwise $CB_K^{\mathcal{A}}$ would not be a cyclic border), from which it follows that
$$[\![C]\!]_{C,\mathcal{B}_C}^c \parallel_{\mathcal{S}(C; C, \mathcal{B}_C)} [\![H]\!]_{C,\mathcal{B}_C}^c \approx_B [\![C]\!]_{C,\mathcal{B}_C}^c$$
Similarly, it can be shown that
$$[\![H]\!]_{H,\mathcal{B}_H}^c \parallel_{\mathcal{S}(H; H, \mathcal{B}_H)} [\![C]\!]_{H,\mathcal{B}_H}^c \approx_B [\![H]\!]_{H,\mathcal{B}_H}^c$$

- If $\mathcal{A}'$ is cyclic, then 3 is preserved. In fact, let $\{\overline{CB}_{K_1}^{\mathcal{A}'}, \ldots, \overline{CB}_{K_n}^{\mathcal{A}'}\}$ be a new set of cyclic borders for $\mathcal{A}'$ obtained from the cyclic borders $CB_{K_1}^{\mathcal{A}}, \ldots, CB_{K_n}^{\mathcal{A}}$ of the old set for $\mathcal{A}$ by replacing every occurrence of $C_1, \ldots, C_n$ with C. Every cyclic border in the new set that does not include C has a corresponding isomorphic cyclic border in the old set. On the other hand, if we take in the new set a cyclic border formed by the AEIs $H_1, \ldots, H_l, C$, then the old set contains a cyclic border formed by the AEIs $H_1, \ldots, H_l, C_i$, where $C_i \in \mathcal{F}_{C_1,\ldots,C_n}$, because of condition 1 of Lemma 1. By virtue of 3.II,
$$[\![C_i]\!]_{\mathcal{A}}^c \approx_B [\![H_1, \ldots, H_l, C_i]\!]_{\mathcal{A}}^c / (Act - \{\tau\} - \mathcal{S}(C_i; \mathcal{A}))$$
Since $\approx_B$ is a congruence with respect to the parallel composition operator,
$$[\![C]\!]_{\mathcal{A}'}^c \approx_B [\![H_1, \ldots, H_l, C]\!]_{\mathcal{A}'}^c / (Act - \{\tau\} - \mathcal{S}(C; \mathcal{A}'))$$
because we hide interactions that do not occur in C. Thus, if $\mathcal{F}_{H_1,\ldots,H_l,C} = \emptyset$ then 3.I is preserved. On the other hand, if $C \in \mathcal{F}_{H_1,\ldots,H_l,C}$, then C preserves 3.II. Similarly, for each $H_j \in \mathcal{F}_{H_1,\ldots,H_l,C} - \{C\}$, by 3.II applied to $H_1, \ldots, H_l, C_i$, we have
$$[\![H_j]\!]_{\mathcal{A}}^c \approx_B [\![H_1, \ldots, H_l, C_i]\!]_{\mathcal{A}}^c / (Act - \{\tau\} - \mathcal{S}(H_j; \mathcal{A}))$$
From 3.II applied to $C_1, \ldots, C_n$ it follows

$$[\![C_i]\!]_{\mathcal{A}}^c \approx_B [\![C_1, \ldots, C_n]\!]_{\mathcal{A}}^c / (Act - \{\tau\} - \mathcal{S}(C_i; \mathcal{A}))$$

Since $\approx_B$ is a congruence with respect to the parallel composition operator,

$$[\![H_j]\!]_{\mathcal{A}'}^c \approx_B [\![H_1, \ldots, H_l, C]\!]_{\mathcal{A}'}^c / (Act - \{\tau\} - \mathcal{S}(H_j; \mathcal{A}'))$$

because we hide interactions that do not occur in H_j.
- *The reduced flow graph of $\mathcal{A}'$ has at most m cycles.*

Then, by the induction hypothesis it follows that $[\![\mathcal{A}']\!]$ is deadlock free, from which we derive that $[\![\mathcal{A}]\!]$ is deadlock free because

$$[\![\mathcal{A}']\!] = [\![\mathcal{A}]\!]/(\bigcup_{C_i \notin \mathcal{F}_{C_1,\ldots,C_n}} \mathcal{S}(C_i; \mathcal{A}) - \bigcup_{C_i \in \mathcal{F}_{C_1,\ldots,C_n}} \mathcal{S}(C_i; \mathcal{A}))$$

∎

We point out that a violation of one of the conditions of Thm. 3 does not imply that the architectural type can deadlock, but reveals the presence of some kind of mismatch in a specific portion of the topology. Diagnostic information can be inferred as explained in [3].

As far as the example of Table 2 is concerned, let us consider the set of cyclic borders $\{\mathcal{CB}_{H_0}^{\text{Feedback\_PF}}, \mathcal{CB}_{H_1}^{\text{Feedback\_PF}}\}$, obtained by applying a cycle covering strategy that does not pick up P. It can be verified that P, which represents the frontier for both cyclic borders $\{H_0, F_0, P\}$ and $\{H_1, F_1, P\}$, interoperates with neither H_0 and F_0, nor H_1 and F_1. For instance, the closed interacting semantics of H_1, F_1, P, computed with respect to Feedback_PF and projected on the local interactions of P, expresses the fact that the type of the item that the pipe can accept depends on the type chosen by F_1. Instead, the closed interacting semantics of P expresses the fact that the pipe is always ready to accept items of both types. Therefore, the two semantics cannot be weakly bisimulation equivalent and, as a consequence, the system has a potential mismatch that, as we have seen, in practice causes a deadlock.

4 Conclusion

In this paper we have presented a novel technique for deadlock freedom verification at the architectural level of design, which is independent of the architectural topology, thus overcoming the limitations of the techniques previously appeared in the literature. Applying such a technique is more convenient – for efficiency reasons and diagnostic purposes – than checking the whole system for deadlock freedom. On the efficiency side, the software architect is saved from generating the state space associated with the whole system, which could be composed of millions of states for large software architectures. Instead, two checks are applied. The former check is a compatibility check, which reduces to compare the semantics of any AEI C with the semantics of the parallel composition of C and any K attached to C. The latter check is a variant of the interoperability check applied to each AEI K belonging to the frontier of a specific cyclic border. Such a check reduces to compare the semantics of K with the semantics of the cyclic border that includes K. It is worth noting that, for each check, the projection on the local interactions of a single AEI, which are the only observable interactions, offers the possibility of a compositional construction of the considered state spaces in a minimized form with respect to $\approx_B$. This ensures a good degree of scalability in the average case. Concerning future research, we would like to investigate whether it is possible to further enhance the generality of the developed technique, passing from a specific property – deadlock freedom – to arbitrary properties expressed in some logic.

References

1. G.D. Abowd, R. Allen, and D. Garlan, *"Formalizing Style to Understand Descriptions of Software Architecture"*, in ACM Trans. on Software Engineering and Methodology 4:319-364, 1995.
2. R. Allen and D. Garlan, *"A Formal Basis for Architectural Connection"*, in ACM Trans. on Software Engineering and Methodology 6:213-249, 1997.
3. M. Bernardo, P. Ciancarini, and L. Donatiello, *"Architecting Families of Software Systems with Process Algebras"*, in ACM Trans. on Software Engineering and Methodology 11:386-426, 2002.
4. M. Bernardo and F. Franzè, *"Architectural Types Revisited: Extensible And/Or Connections"*, in Proc. of the 5th Int. Conf. on Fundamental Approaches to Software Engineering (FASE 2002), LNCS 2306:113-128, Grenoble (France), 2002.
5. M. Bernardo and F. Franzè, *"Exogenous and Endogenous Extensions of Architectural Types"*, in Proc. of the 5th Int. Conf. on Coordination Models and Languages (COORDINATION 2002), LNCS 2315:40-55, York (UK), 2002.
6. P. Inverardi and A.L. Wolf, *"Formal Specification and Analysis of Software Architectures Using the Chemical Abstract Machine Model"*, in IEEE Trans. on Software Engineering 21:373-386, 1995.
7. P. Inverardi, A.L. Wolf, and D. Yankelevich, *"Static Checking of System Behaviors Using Derived Component Assumptions"*, in ACM Trans. on Software Engineering and Methodology 9:239-272, 2000.
8. J. Magee, N. Dulay, S. Eisenbach, and J. Kramer, *"Specifying Distributed Software Architectures"*, in Proc. of the 5th European Software Engineering Conf. (ESEC 1995), LNCS 989:137-153, Barcelona (Spain), 1995.
9. R. Milner, *"Communication and Concurrency"*, Prentice Hall, 1989.
10. D.E. Perry and A.L. Wolf, *"Foundations for the Study of Software Architecture"*, in ACM SIGSOFT Software Engineering Notes 17:40-52, 1992.
11. M. Shaw and D. Garlan, *"Software Architecture: Perspectives on an Emerging Discipline"*, Prentice Hall, 1996.

Taking *Alloy* to the Movies

Marcelo F. Frias[1,*], Carlos G. López Pombo[2], Gabriel A. Baum[3],
Nazareno M. Aguirre[4,**], and Tom Maibaum[5]

[1] Department of Computer Science, School of Exact and Natural Sciences,
University of Buenos Aires, Argentina, and CONICET,
mfrias@dc.uba.ar
[2] Department of Computer Science, School of Exact and Natural Sciences,
University of Buenos Aires, Argentina,
clpombo@dc.uba.ar
[3] LIFIA, School of Informatics,
National University of La Plata, Argentina, and CONICET,
gbaum@sol.info.unlp.edu.ar
[4] Department of Computer Science,
King's College, United Kingdom,
aguirre@dcs.kcl.ac.uk
[5] Department of Computer Science,
King's College, United Kingdom,
tom@dcs.kcl.ac.uk

Abstract. We present a modified semantics and an extension of the *Alloy* specification language. The results presented in this paper are:
(a) We show how the modified semantics of *Alloy* allows us to avoid the higher-order quantification currently used both in the composition of operations and in specifications, keeping the language first-order.
(b) We show how the extended language, which includes features from dynamic logic, enables a cleaner (with respect to previous papers) treatment of properties of executions.
(c) We show that the automatic analysis currently available for *Alloy* specifications can be fully applied in the analysis of specifications under the new semantics.
(d) We present a calculus for the extended language that is complete with respect to the extended semantics. This allows us to complement the analysis currently provided in *Alloy* with theorem proving.
(e) Finally, we show how to use the theorem prover *PVS* in order to verify *Alloy* specifications.

1 Introduction

The specification of software systems is an activity considered worthwhile in most modern development processes. In non-formal settings, specification is usually

---
* Research partially funded by Antorchas foundation and project UBACYT X094.
** Currently on leave from Department of Computer Science, Universidad Nacional de Río Cuarto, Argentina.

referred to as *modelling*, since specifications allow us to build abstract models of the intended systems. Since these models are used as a means of communication with users and developers, as well as for analysis of the specified systems, it is generally considered important for modelling languages to possess a precise semantics.

Widely-used modelling languages, such as the *UML* [2] are being endowed with a formal semantics [3, 4]. Other languages, such as *VDM* [13], *Z* [23] and *Alloy* [12] were born formal, and their acceptance by software engineers greatly depends on their simplicity and usability. *Alloy* has its roots in the *Z* formal specification language. Its few constructs and simple semantics are the result of including some valuable features of *Z* and some constructs that are ubiquitous in less formal notations. This is done while avoiding to incorporate other features that would increase *Alloy*'s complexity more than necessary. *Alloy* is defined on top of what is called *relational logic*, a logic with a clear semantics based on relations. This logic provides a powerful yet simple formalism for interpreting *Alloy* modelling constructs. The simplicity of both the relational logic and the language as a whole makes *Alloy* suitable for automatic analysis. This automatic analysis is carried out using the *Alloy Analyzer* [11], a tool that incorporates state-of-the-art SAT solvers in order to search for counterexamples of specifications. *Alloy* has been used to model and analyze a number of problems of different domains, as for instance to simplify a model of the query interface mechanism of Microsoft's COM [10].

In this paper we present a modified version of *Alloy* that provides the following features:

1. The possibility of specifying functions that *formally* change the state, allowing one to describe the action that composite functions perform on models. This is possible due to the dynamic logic extension of relational logic that we will introduce. Note that, in the current version of *Alloy*, change of state is represented through the convention that some variables (e.g., primed variables) represent the final state (after execution) in function definitions. Therefore, specifications in *Alloy* provide "pictures" of a model. That is why we claim to be moving from static "pictures" to dynamic "movies".
2. The need for the second-order quantifiers in *Alloy* (see for instance [8, Section 2.4.4]) is eliminated, while keeping the expressive power and simplicity of the language. This is achieved by replacing *Alloy*'s relational logic by a similar but better-suited logic of binary relations. This logic can be automatically analyzed using the tools already available for *Alloy*.
3. An alternative technique for proving properties of executions is proposed. This technique does not make use of execution traces incorporated *within* model specifications as proposed in [12, Section 2.6], which is, to our understanding, an *ad-hoc* solution that confuses two clearly separated levels of description. Instead, our technique uses the fact that a first-order dynamic logic extending the (alternative) relational logic can be defined. This allows one to perform reasoning regarding execution traces in a simpler and more elegant way, which leads to a cleaner separation of concerns.

4. The modified version of *Alloy*'s semantics has a complete (and relatively small) proof calculus that we present here. This allows us to complement the techniques for finding counterexamples available in current *Alloy*, with theorem proving.
5. By encoding the newly defined semantics for *Alloy* in higher-order logic, we show how to verify *Alloy* specifications using the theorem prover *PVS*.

2   The *Alloy* Specification Language

We introduce the *Alloy* specification language by means of an example extracted from [12] that shows the standard features of the language. It will also help us to illustrate the shortcomings we wish to overcome.

We want to specify a memory system with cache. We start by indicating the existence of sets (of atoms) for data and addresses, which in *Alloy* are specified using signatures:

$$\text{sig } Addr \; \{ \; \} \qquad \text{sig } Data \; \{ \; \}$$

These are basic signatures, for which we do not assume any property of their structure. We can now say that a memory consists of set of addresses, and a (total) mapping from these addresses to data values:

```
sig Memory {
    addrs: set Addr
    map: addrs ->! Data
}
```

The "!" sign indicates that "map" is functional and total (i.e., for each element a of addrs, there exists exactly one element d in *Data* such that map(a) = d). Signatures defined as subsets of the set denoted by certain "parent" signature can be characterised using *signature extension*. The following signatures are defined as extensions of *Memory*:

$$\text{sig } MainMemory \text{ extends } Memory \; \{\}$$

```
sig Cache extends Memory {
    dirty: set addrs
}
```

MainMemory and *Cache* are special kinds of memories. In caches, a subset of addrs is recognized as *dirty*. We can express now that a system consists of a main memory and a cache:

```
sig System {
    cache: Cache
    main: MainMemory
}
```

```
problem ::= decl*form
decl ::= var : typexpr
typexpr ::=
  type
  | type → type
  | type ⇒ typexpr

form ::=
  expr in expr (subset)
  | !form (neg)
  | form && form (conj)
  | form || form (disj)
  | all v : type/form (univ)
  | some v : type/form (exist)

expr ::=
  expr + expr (union)
  | expr & expr (intersection)
  | expr − expr (difference)
  | ~ expr (transpose)
  | expr.expr (navigation)
  | +expr (closure)
  | {v : t/form} (set former)
  | Var

Var ::=
  var (variable)
  | Var[var] (application)
```

$M : \text{form} \to \text{env} \to \text{Boolean}$
$X : \text{expr} \to \text{env} \to \text{value}$
$\text{env} = (\text{var} + \text{type}) \to \text{value}$
$\text{value} = (\text{atom} \times \cdots \times \text{atom}) +$
$\quad (\text{atom} \to \text{value})$

$M[a \text{ in } b]e = X[a]e \subseteq X[b]e$
$M[!F]e = \neg M[F]e$
$M[F \&\& G]e = M[F]e \wedge M[G]e$
$M[F \parallel G]e = M[F]e \vee M[G]e$
$M[\text{all } v : t/F] =$
$\quad \bigwedge \{ M[F](e \oplus v \mapsto \{x\}) / x \in e(t) \}$
$M[\text{some } v : t/F] =$
$\quad \bigvee \{ M[F](e \oplus v \mapsto \{x\}) / x \in e(t) \}$

$X[a + b]e = X[a]e \cup X[b]e$
$X[a \& b]e = X[a]e \cap X[b]e$
$X[a - b]e = X[a]e \setminus X[b]e$
$X[\sim a]e = (X[a]e)^{\smile}$
$X[a.b]e = X[a]e ; X[b]e$
$X[+a]e = $ the smallest r such that $r;r \subseteq r$ and $X[a]e \subseteq r$
$X[\{v : t/F\}]e =$
$\quad \{x \in e(t) / M[F](e \oplus v \mapsto \{x\})\}$
$X[v]e = e(v)$
$X[a[v]]e = \{\langle \text{unit}, y \rangle /$
$\quad \exists x. \langle x, y \rangle \in e(a) \wedge \langle \text{unit}, x \rangle \in e(v)\}$

Fig. 1. Grammar and semantics of *Alloy*

As can be seen from the previous definitions, signatures define data domains and their structures. The attributes of a signature denote *relations*. For instance, the attribute "addrs" in *Memory* represents a relation from memory atoms to sets of atoms from *Addr*. Given a set (not necessarily a singleton) of *Memory* atoms m, m.addrs denotes the relational image of m under the relation denoted by addrs. This relational view of the dot notation leads to a simple and elegant semantics for dot, coherent with its intuitive navigational reading. In Fig. 1 we present the grammar and semantics of *Alloy*'s kernel. Notice that as an important difference with the previous version of *Alloy* presented in [9] where expressions range over binary relations, expressions now range over relations of arbitrary rank. Although composition of binary relations is well understood, we define composition of relations of higher rank by:

$$R;S = \{\langle a_1, \ldots, a_{i-1}, b_2, \ldots, b_j \rangle :$$
$$\exists b \, (\langle a_1, \ldots, a_{i-1}, b \rangle \in R \wedge \langle b, b_2, \ldots, b_j \rangle \in S)\} \ .$$

2.1 Operations in a Model

Following the style of Z specifications, operations can be defined as expressions relating states from the state space described by the signature definitions. Primed variables are used to denote the resulting values, although this is a convention that is not reflected in the semantics. Consider, for instance, an operation that specifies the writing of a value to an address in a memory:

> fun Write(m, m': *Memory*, d: *Data*, a: *Addr*) {
>   m'.map = m.map ++ (a -> d) }

This definition can be easily understood, having in mind that m' is meant to denote the memory (or memory state) resulting of the function application, that a -> d denotes the pair $\langle a, d \rangle$, and ++ denotes relational override.

Consider the following more complex function definition:

> fun SysWrite(s, s': *System*, d: *Data*, a: *Addr*) {
>   Write(s.cache, s'.cache, d, a)
>   s'.cache.dirty = s.cache.dirty + a
>   s'.main = s.main }

There are two important points that this function definition illustrates. First, function SysWrite is defined in terms of the more primitive Write. Second, the use of Write takes advantage of the *hierarchy* defined by signature extension: function Write was defined for memories, and in SysWrite it is being "applied" to cache memories.

As explained in [12], an operation that *flushes* lines from a cache to the corresponding memory is necessary, since usually caches are small. A nondeterministic operation that flushes information from the cache to main memory is specified in the following way:

> fun Flush(s, s': *System*) {
>   some x: set s.cache.addrs {
>   s'.cache.map = s.cache.map − { x->Data }
>   s'.cache.dirty = s.cache.dirty − x
>   s'.main.map = s.main.map ++
>   {a: x, d: Data | d = s.cache.map[a]} }
> }

Function Flush will serve us in Section 4.2 to illustrate one of the main problems that we try to solve. In the third line of the definition of function Flush, x->Data denotes all the pairs whose domain falls in the set x, and that range on the domain Data.

Functions can also be used to characterise *special* states. For instance, we can characterise those states in which the cache lines not marked as dirty are consistent with main memory:

> fun DirtyInv(s: *System*) {
>   all a : !s.cache.dirty | s.cache.map[a] = s.main.map[a] }

The "!" sign denotes negation, indicating in the above formula that "a" ranges over atoms that are non-dirty addresses.

2.2 Properties of a Model

As the reader might expect, a model can be enhanced by adding properties to it. These properties are written as logical formulae, much in the style of the Object

Constraint Language [16]. Properties or constraints are defined as *facts*. To give an idea of how constraints or properties are specified, we reproduce some here. We need to say that the sets of main memories and cache memories are disjoint:

fact {no (*MainMemory* & *Cache*)}

The expression "no x" indicates that x has no elements, and & denotes intersection. Another constraint, inherent to our specific model, states that in every system the addresses of its cache are a subset of the addresses of its main memory:

fact {all s: System | s.cache.addrs in s.main.addrs}

More complex facts can be expressed by using the significant expressive power of the relational logic.

2.3 Assertions

Assertions are the *intended* properties of a given model. Consider the following simple assertion in *Alloy*:

assert {
 all s: *System* | DirtyInv(s) && no s.cache.dirty
  => s.cache.map in s.main.map }

This assertion states that if "DirtyInv" holds in system "s", and there are no dirty addresses in the cache, then the cache agrees in all its addresses with the main memory. Assertions are used to test specifications. Using the *Alloy analyzer* it is possible to search for counterexamples of given assertions.

3 Features and Deficiencies of *Alloy*

Alloy is a formal specification language. What distinguishes *Alloy* from other specification languages, such as *Z* [23] or *VDM* [13], is that it has been designed with the goal of making specifications automatically analyzable. Some of its current features are:

- Fulfilling the goal of an analyzable language kept *Alloy* a simple language with an almost trivial semantics.
- *Alloy* incorporates some common idioms from object modelling. This makes *Alloy* a suitable replacement for the Object Constraint Language (OCL) [16]. The well-defined and concise syntax of *Alloy* is much easier to understand than the OCL grammar presented in [16]. A similar reasoning applies with respect to the OCL semantics. The attempt to describe all the various constructs of object modelling led to a cumbersome, incomplete, and sometimes even inconsistent semantics [1].

- The syntax of *Alloy*, which includes both a textual and graphical notation, is based on a small kernel with few constructs. Besides, the relational semantics of the kernel allows one to refer with the same simplicity to relations, sets and individual atoms.

Having described some of the features of *Alloy*, we will now describe the perceived deficiencies that will be addressed in this paper.

- Sequencing of operations, or even specifications as the one for function Flush (see Section 2.1), may require higher-order formulas. About this, Jackson says [9, Section 6.2]:

    "Sequencing of operations presents more of a language design challenge than a tractability problem. Following Z, one could take the formula $op1;op2$ to be short for

    $$some\ s : state/op1(pre, s)\ and\ op2(s, post)$$

    but this calls for a second-order quantifier."

    For composition of operations the problem was solved in [12] with the introduction of signatures. Signatures allow them to objectify the state and view objects containing relation attributes as atoms. However, higher-order quantifiers are used also in specifications. For instance, the definition of function Flush uses a higher-order quantifier over 1-ary relations (sets). In Section 4 we will endow the kernel of *Alloy* with a new semantics that will make higher-order quantifiers unnecessary.

- In [12], Jackson et al. present a methodology for proving properties of executions. The method consists of the introduction of a new sort of *finite traces*. Each element in a trace stands for a state in an execution. In this context, proving that a given assertion is invariant under the execution of some operations is reduced to proving the validity of the assertion in the last element of every finite trace. Even though from a formal point of view the technique is correct, from the modelling point of view it seems less appropriate. When a software engineer writes an assertion, verifying the assertion should not demand a modelling effort. In order to keep an adequate separation of concerns between the modelling stage and the verification stage, verifying the assertion should reduce to proving a property in a suitable logic. The logic extending *Alloy* that we propose in Section 5 will enable us to verify this kind of assertions (i.e., assertions regarding executions) in a simple and elegant way.

- *Alloy* was designed with the goal of being automatically analyzable, and thus theorem proving was not considered a critical issue. Nevertheless, having the possibility of combining model checking with theorem proving as in the STeP tool [15] is a definite improvement. Providing *Alloy* with theorem proving is not trivial, since *Alloy*'s relational logic does not admit a complete proof calculus. Despite this fact, in Section 6 we present a complete deductive system for an alternative logic *extending Alloy*'s kernel.

4 A New Semantics for *Alloy*

In most papers the semantics of *Alloy*'s kernel is defined in terms of binary relations. The current semantics [12] is given in terms of relations of arbitrary finite arity. The modified semantics for *Alloy* that we will present goes back to binary relations. This was our choice for the following three main reasons:

1. *Alloy*'s kernel operations such as transposition or transitive closure are only defined on binary relations.
2. There exists a complete calculus for reasoning about binary relations with certain operations (to be presented next).
3. It is possible (and we will show how) to deal with relations of rank higher than 2 within the framework of binary relations we will use.

4.1 Fork Algebras

Fork algebras [5] are described through few equational axioms. The intended models of these axioms are structures called *proper fork algebras*, in which the domain is a set of binary relations (on some base set, let us say B), closed under the following operations for sets:

- *union* of two binary relations, denoted by $\cup$,
- *intersection* of two binary relations, denoted by $\cap$,
- *complement* of a binary relation, denoted, for a binary relation r, by $\overline{r}$,
- the *empty* binary relation, which does not relate any pair of objects, and is denoted by $\emptyset$,
- the *universal* binary relation, namely, $B \times B$, that will be denoted by 1.

Besides the previous operations for sets, the domain has to be closed under the following operations for binary relations:

- *transposition* of a binary relation. This operation swaps elements in the pairs of a binary relation. Given a binary relation r, its transposition is denoted by $\breve{r}$,
- *composition* of two binary relations, which, for binary relations r and s is denoted by $r;s$,
- *reflexive–transitive closure*, which, for a binary relation r, is denoted by r^*,
- the *identity* relation, denoted by Id.

Finally, a binary operation called *fork* is included, which requires the base set B to be closed under an injective function $\star$. This means that there are elements x in B that are the result of applying the function $\star$ to elements y and z. Since $\star$ is injective, x can be seen as an encoding of the pair $\langle y, z\rangle$. The application of fork to binary relations R and S is denoted by $R\nabla S$, and its definition is given by: $R\nabla S = \{\,\langle a, b \star c\rangle : \langle a, b\rangle \in R \text{ and } \langle a, c\rangle \in S\,\}$.

Once the class of proper fork algebras has been presented, the class of fork algebras is axiomatized with the following formulas:

1. Your favorite set of equations axiomatizing Boolean algebras. These axioms define the meaning of union, intersection, complement, the empty set and the universal relation.
2. Formulas defining composition of binary relations, transposition, reflexive–transitive closure and the identity relation:
   $x;(y;z) = (x;y);z,$
   $x;Id = Id;x = x,$
   $(x;y) \cap z = \emptyset$ iff $(z;\breve{y}) \cap x = \emptyset$ iff $(\breve{x};z) \cap y = \emptyset,$
   $x^* = Id \cup (x;x^*),$
   $x^*;y;1 \leq (y;1) \cup \left(x^*;(\overline{y;1} \cap (x;y;1))\right).$
3. Formulas defining the operator ∇:
   $x \nabla y = (x;(Id\nabla 1)) \cap (y;(1\nabla Id)),$
   $(x \nabla y);(w \nabla z)^{\smile} = (x;\breve{w}) \cap (y;\breve{z}),$
   $(Id\nabla 1)^{\smile}\nabla(1\nabla Id)^{\smile} \leq Id.$

The axioms given above define a class of models. Proper fork algebras satisfy the axioms [6], and therefore belong to this class. It could be the case that there are models for the axioms that are not proper fork algebras. Fortunately, as was proved in [6], [5, Thm. 4.2], if a model is not a proper fork algebra then it is isomorphic to one. Notice also that binary relations are first-order citizens in fork algebras, and therefore quantification over binary relations is first-order.

4.2 Fork-Algebraic Semantics of *Alloy*

In order to give semantics to *Alloy*, we will give semantics to *Alloy*'s kernel. We provide the modified (in comparison to [12]) denotational semantics in Fig. 2. This semantics is given through two meaning functions. Function N gives meaning to formulas. It requires an environment in which types and variables with free occurrences take values, and yields a boolean as a result indicating wether the formula is true or not in the environment. Similarly, function Y gives meaning to expressions. Since expressions can also contain variables, the environment is again necessary. The general assumption is that variables in the environment get as values relations in an arbitrary fork algebra $\mathfrak{A}$ whose universe we will denote by U.

Representing Objects and Sets. We will represent sets by binary relations contained in the identity relation. Thus, for an arbitrary type t and an environment env, $env(t) \subseteq Id$ must hold. That is, for a given type t, its meaning in an environment env is a binary relation contained in the identity binary relation. Similarly, for an arbitrary variable v of type t, $env(v)$ must be a relation of the form $\{\langle x, x \rangle\}$, with $\langle x, x \rangle \in env(t)$. This is obtained by imposing the following conditions on $env(v)$[1]:

$$env(v) \subseteq env(t),$$
$$env(v);1;env(v) = env(v),$$
$$env(v) \neq \emptyset.$$

---
[1] The proof requires relation 1 to be of the form $B \times B$ for some nonempty set B.

$$N : \text{form} \to \text{env} \to Boolean$$
$$Y : \text{expr} \to \text{env} \to U$$
$$\text{env} = (\text{var} + \text{type}) \to U.$$

$$N[a \text{ in } b]e = Y[a]e \subseteq Y[b]e$$
$$N[!F]e = \neg N[F]e$$
$$N[F\&\&G]e = N[F]e \wedge N[G]e$$
$$N[F \;||\; G]e = N[F]e \vee N[G]e$$
$$N[\text{all } v : t/F] = \bigwedge \{N[F](e \oplus v \mapsto x)/x : e(t)\}$$
$$N[\text{some } v : t/F] = \bigvee \{N[F](e \oplus v \mapsto x)/x : e(t)\}$$

$$Y[a + b]e = Y[a]e \cup Y[b]e$$
$$Y[a\&b]e = Y[a]e \cap Y[b]e$$
$$Y[a - b]e = Y[a]e \cap \overline{Y[b]e}$$
$$Y[\sim a]e = (Y[a]e)^{\smile}$$
$$Y[a.b]e = Y[a]e \bullet Y[b]e$$
$$Y[+a]e = Y[a]e ; (Y[a]e)^*$$
$$Y[\{v : t/F\}]e = \bigcup \{x : e(t)/N[F](e \oplus v \mapsto x)\}$$
$$Y[v]e = e(v)$$
$$Y[a[v]]e = e(v) ; e(a)$$

Fig. 2. The new semantics of *Alloy*

Actually, given binary relations x and y satisfying the properties:

$$y \subseteq Id, \quad x \subseteq y, \quad x ; 1 ; x = x, \quad x \neq \emptyset, \qquad (1)$$

it is easy to show that x must be of the form $\{\langle a, a \rangle\}$ for some object a. Thus, given an object a, by a we will also denote the binary relation $\{\langle a, a \rangle\}$. Since y represents a set, by $x : y$ we assert the fact that x is an object of type y, which implies that x and y satisfy the formulas in (1).

Eliminating Higher-Order Quantification. We will show now that by giving semantics to *Alloy* in terms of fork algebras, higher-order quantifiers are not necessary. Recalling the specification of function Flush in Section 2.1, the specification has the shape

$$\text{some } x : \text{set } t \;/\; F. \qquad (2)$$

This is recognized within *Alloy* as a higher-order formula [8]. Let us analyze what happens in the modified semantics. Since t is a type (set), it stands for a subset of Id. Similarly, subsets of t are subsets of the identity, which are contained in t. Thus, formula (2) is an abbreviation for

$$\exists x \, (x \subseteq t \wedge F),$$

which is a first-order formula when x ranges over binary relations in a fork algebra.

Regarding the higher-order formulas that appear in the composition of operations, discussed in Section 3, no higher-order formulas are required in our setting. Formula

$$\text{some } s : state/op1(pre, s) \text{ and } op2(s, post) \qquad (3)$$

is first-order with the modified semantics. Operations $op1$ and $op2$ can be defined as binary predicates in a first-order language for fork algebras, and thus formula (3) is first-order.

Representing and Navigating Relations of Higher Rank in Fork Algebras. In a proper fork algebra the relations π and ρ defined by

$$\pi = (Id \nabla 1)^{\smile}, \quad \rho = (1 \nabla Id)^{\smile}$$

behave as projections with respect to the encoding of pairs induced by the injective function $\star$. Their semantics in a proper fork algebra $\mathfrak{A}$ whose binary relations range over a set B, is given by

$$\pi = \{\, \langle a \star b, a \rangle : a, b \in B \,\}, \quad \rho = \{\, \langle a \star b, b \rangle : a, b \in B \,\} \ .$$

Given a n-ary relation $R \subseteq A_1 \times \cdots \times A_n$, we will represent it by the binary relation $\{\, \langle a_1, a_2 \star \cdots \star a_n \rangle : \langle a_1, \ldots, a_n \rangle \in R \,\}$. This will be an invariant in the representation of n-ary relations by binary ones.

Recalling signature Memory, attribute map stands in *Alloy* for a ternary relation map $\subseteq$ Memory $\times$ addrs $\times$ Data. In our framework it becomes a binary relation map' whose elements are pairs of the form $\langle m, a \star d \rangle$ for m : Memory, a : Addr and d : Data. Given an object (in the relational sense — cf. 4.2) m : Memory, the navigation of the relation map' through m should result in a binary relation contained in Addr $\times$ Data. Given a relational object $a : t$ and a binary relation R encoding a relation of rank higher than 2, we define the navigation operation $\bullet$ by

$$a \bullet R = \breve{\pi} ; Ran\,(a;R) \,; \rho \ . \tag{4}$$

Operation Ran in (4) returns the range of a relation as a subset of the identity relation. It is defined by $Ran\,(x) = (x;1) \cap Id$. Its semantics in terms of binary relations is given by $Ran\,(R) = \{\, \langle a, a \rangle : \exists b\,(\langle b, a \rangle \in R) \,\}$.

For a binary relation R representing a relation of rank 2, navigation is easier. Given a relational object $a : t$, we define $a \bullet R = Ran\,(a;R)$.

Going back to our example about memories, it is easy to check that for a relational object $m' : Memory$ such that $m' = \{\, \langle m, m \rangle \,\}$,

$$m' \bullet map' = \{\langle a, d \rangle : a \in Addr, d \in Data \text{ and } \langle m, a \star d \rangle \in map'\} \ .$$

Analyzing the Modified *Alloy*. An essential feature of *Alloy* is its adequacy for automatic analysis. Thus, an immediate question is what is the impact of the modified semantics in the analysis of *Alloy* specifications. In the next paragraphs, we will argue that the new semantics can fully profit from the current analysis procedure. Notice that the *Alloy* tool is a refutation procedure. As such, if we want to check if an assertion α holds in a specification S, we must search for a model of $S \cup \{\, \neg \alpha \,\}$. If such a model exists, then we have found a counterexample that refutes the assertion α. Of course, since first-order logic is undecidable, this cannot be a decision procedure. Therefore, the *Alloy* tool searches for counterexamples of a bounded size, in which each set of atoms is bounded to a finite size or *"scope"*.

A counterexample is an environment, and as such it provides sets for each type of atom, and values (relations) for the constants and the variables. We will show now that whenever a counterexample exists according to *Alloy*'s standard semantics, the same is true for the fork algebraic semantics.

For the next theorem we assume that whenever the transpose operation or the transitive closure occur in a term, they affect a binary relation. Notice that this is the assumption in [12]. We also assume that whenever the navigation operation is applied, the argument on the left-hand side is a unary relation (set). This is because our representation of relations of arity greater than two makes defining the generalized composition more complicated than desirable. At the same time, the use of navigation in object-oriented settings usually falls in the situation modelled by us.

Given an environment e, we define the environment e' (according to the new semantics) by:

- Given a type T, $e'(T) = \{\langle a, a\rangle : a \in e(T)\}$.
- Given a variable v such that $e(v)$ is a n-ary relation,

$$e'(v) = \begin{cases} \{\langle a, a\rangle : a \in e(v)\} & \text{if } n = 1, \\ \{\langle a_1, a_2 \star \cdots \star a_n\rangle : \langle a_1, a_2, \ldots, a_n\rangle \in e(V)\} & \text{otherwise.} \end{cases}$$

Theorem 1. *Given a formula α, $M[\alpha]e = N[\alpha]e'$.*

The proof of Thm. 1 is by induction on the structure of formulas. Theorem 1 shows that all the work that has been done so far in the analysis of *Alloy* specifications can be fully profitted by the newly proposed semantics. The theorem proposes a method for analyzing *Alloy* specification (according to the new semantics), as follows:

1. Give the *Alloy* specification to the current *Alloy* analyzer.
2. Get a counterexample, if any exists within the given scopes.
3. Build a counterexample for the new semantics from the one provided by the tool, The new counterexample is defined in the same way environment e' is defined from environment e above. Notice that Thm. 1 implies that a counterexample exists with respect to the standard semantics if and only if one exists for the newly provided semantics.

5 Adding Dynamic Features to *Alloy*

In this section we extend *Alloy*'s kernel syntax and semantics in a way that is fully consistent with the extension we performed in Section 4. The reason for this extension is twofold. First, we want to provide a setting in which state transformations are not just simulated by distinguishing between primed and non-primed variables, but rather are identifiable in the semantics. Second, the framework allows one to reason about properties of executions in a simple and clean way. The section is structured as follows. In Section 5.1 we introduce the syntax and semantics of first-order dynamic logic. In Section 5.2 we present the formalism of dynamic logic over fork algebras. Finally, in Section 5.3 we show how to reason about executions.

5.1 Dynamic Logic

Dynamic logic is a formalism suitable for reasoning about programs. From a set of atomic actions (usually assignments of terms to variables), and using adequate combinators, it is possible to build complex actions. The logic then allows us to state properties of these actions, which may hold or not in a given structure. Actions can change (as usually programs do) the values of variables. We will assume that each action reads and/or modifies the value of finitely many variables. When compared with classical first-order logic, the essential difference is the dynamic content of dynamic logic, which is clear in the notion of satisfiability. While satisfiability in classical first–order logic depends on the values of variables in one valuation (state), in dynamic logic it may be necessary to consider two valuations in order to reflect the change of values of program variables; one valuation holds the values of variables *before* the action is performed, and another holds the values of variables *after* the action is executed.

Along the paper we will assume a fixed (but arbitrary) finite signature $\Sigma = \langle s, A, F, P \rangle$, where s is a sort, $A = \{a_1, \ldots, a_k\}$ is the set of atomic action symbols, F is the set of function symbols, and P is the set of atomic predicate symbols. Atomic actions contain input and output formal parameters. These parameters are later instantiated with actual variables when actions are used in a specification.

The sets of *programs* and *formulas* on Σ are mutually defined in Fig. 3.

As is standard in dynamic logic, states are valuations of the program variables (the actual parameters for actions). The environment env assigns a domain **s** to sort s in which program variables take values. The set of states is denoted by ST. For each action symbol $a \in A$, env yields a binary relation on the set of states, that is, a subset of $ST \times ST$. The environment maps function symbols to concrete functions, and predicate symbols to relations of the corresponding arity. The semantics of the logic is given in Fig. 3.

5.2 Dynamic Logic over Fork Algebras

In order to define first-order dynamic logic over fork algebras, we always include in the set of function symbols of signature Σ the constants 0, 1, Id; the unary symbols $^-$ and $^\smile$; and the binary symbols $+$, $\cdot$, ; and ∇. Since these signatures include all operation symbols from fork algebras, they will be called *fork signatures*.

We will call theories containing the identities specifying the class of fork algebras *fork theories*. By working with fork theories we intend to describe structures

```
action ::= a₁,...aₖ (atomic actions)
      | skip
      | action + action (nondeterministic choice)
      | action ; action (sequential composition)
      | action* (finite iteration)
      | dform? (test)

expr ::= var
      | f(expr₁,...,exprₖ) (f ∈ F with arity k)

dform ::= p(expr₁,...,exprₙ) (p ∈ P)
       | !dform (negation)
       | dform && dform (conjunction)
       | dform || dform (disjunction)
       | all v : type / dform (universal)
       | some v : type / dform (existential)
       | [action] dform (box)
```

$Q : \text{form} \to ST \to Boolean$
$P : \text{action} \to \mathcal{P}(ST \times ST)$
$Z : \text{expr} \to ST \to \mathbf{s}$

$Q[p(t_1,\ldots,t_n)]\mu = (Z[t_1]\mu,\ldots,Z[t_n]\mu) \in env(p)$
$Q[!F]\mu = \neg Q[F]\mu$
$Q[F\&\&G]\mu = Q[F]\mu \wedge Q[G]\mu$
$Q[F \;||\; G]\mu = Q[F]\mu \vee Q[G]\mu$
$Q[\text{all } v:t \;/\; F]\mu = \bigwedge \{Q[F](\mu \oplus v \mapsto x)/x \in env(t)\}$
$Q[\text{some } v:t \;/\; F]\mu = \bigvee \{Q[F](\mu \oplus v \mapsto x)/x \in env(t)\}$
$Q[\;[a]F\;]\mu = \bigwedge \{Q[F]\nu / \langle \mu, \nu \rangle \in P(a)\}$

$P[a] = env(a)$ (atomic action)
$P[skip] = \{\langle \mu, \mu \rangle : \mu \in ST\}$
$P[a+b] = P[a] \cup P[b]$
$P[a;b] = P[a] \circ P[b]$
$P[a^*] = (P[a])^*$
$P[\alpha?] = \{\langle \mu, \mu \rangle : Q[\alpha]\mu\}$

$Z[v]\mu = \mu(v)$
$Z[f(t_1,\ldots,t_k)]\mu = env(f)(Z[t_1]\mu,\ldots,Z[t_k]\mu)$

Fig. 3. Syntax and semantics of dynamic logic

for dynamic logic whose domains are sets of binary relations. This is indeed the case as shown in the following theorem whose proof will appear in an extended paper due to space limitations.

Theorem 2. *Let Σ be a fork signature, and Ψ be a fork theory. For each model $\mathfrak{A}$ for Ψ there exists a model $\mathfrak{B}$ for Ψ, isomorphic to $\mathfrak{A}$, in which the domain $\mathbf{s}$ is a set of binary relations.*

The previous theorem is essential, and its proof (which uses [5, Thm. 4.2]), heavily relies on the use of fork algebras rather than plain relation algebras [24]. A model for a fork theory Ψ is a structure satisfying all the formulas in Ψ. Such a structure can, or cannot, have binary relations in its domain. Theorem 2 shows that models whose domains are not a set of binary relations are isomorphic to models in which the domain is a set of binary relations. This allows us to look at specifications in first-order dynamic logic over fork algebras, and interpret them as properties predicating about binary relations.

Notice that fork signatures contain action symbols, function symbols (including at least the fork algebra operators), and predicate symbols. The relationship to *Alloy* is established as follows. We use actions to model *Alloy* functions. This is particularly adequate, since state modifications described by functions are better viewed as the result of performing an action on an input state. Thus, a definition of a function f of the form

$$\text{fun } f(s, s')\{\alpha(s, s')\} \tag{5}$$

has as counterpart a definition of an action f of the form

$$[s \; f \; s']\alpha(s, s') \;. \tag{6}$$

Although it may be hard to find out what are the differences between (5) and (6) just by looking at the formulas, the differences rely in the semantics, and in the fact that actions can be sequentially composed, iterated or nondeterministically chosen, while *Alloy* functions cannot.

5.3 Specifying and Proving Properties of Executions

Suppose we want to show that a given property P is invariant under sequences of applications of the operations "Flush", and "SysWrite" from an initial state. A technique useful for proving invariance of property P consists of proving P on the initial states, and proving for every non initial state and every operation O that $P(s) \wedge O(s, s') \Rightarrow P(s')$ holds. This proof method is sound but incomplete, since the invariance may be violated in non-reachable states. Of course it would be desirable to have a proof method in which the considered states were exactly the reachable ones. This motivated in [12] the introduction of *traces* in *Alloy*.

The following example, extracted from [12], shows signatures for clock ticks and for traces of states.

> sig Tick {}
>
> sig SystemTrace {
>   ticks: set Tick,
>   first, last: Tick,
>   next: (ticks - last) ! → ! (ticks - first),
>   state: ticks → ! System }

The following "fact" states that all ticks in a trace are reachable from the first tick, that a property called "Init" holds in the first state, and finally that the passage from one state to the next is through the application of one of the operations under consideration.

> fact {
>   first.next* = ticks
>   Init(first.state)
>   all t: ticks - last |
>   some s = t.state, s' = t.next.state |
>   Flush (s,s')
> || some d : Data, a : Addr | SysWrite(s,s',d,a) }

If we now want to prove that P is invariant, it suffices to show that P holds in the final state of every trace. Notice that non reachable states are no longer a burden because all the states in a trace are reachable from the states that occur before.

Even though from a formal point of view the use of traces is correct, from a modelling perspective it is less adequate. Traces are introduced in order to cope with the lack of real state change of *Alloy*. They allow us to port the primed variables used in single operations to sequences of applications of operations.

Dynamic logic [7], on the other hand, was created in the early 70s with the intention of faithfully reflecting state change. In the following paragraphs we will show how it can be used to specify properties of executions of *Alloy* operations. In order to increase the readability of formulas, rather than writing

$$\alpha \Rightarrow [a]\beta, \tag{7}$$

we will use the alternative notation $\{\alpha\}\ a\ \{\beta\}$. This notation is particularly adequate because a formula like formula (7) indeed asserts that action a is partially correct with respect to the pre-condition α and the post-condition β.

Going back to the example of cache systems, we will use an auxiliary predicate "Write", modelling the evolution of a memory state when main memory is written:

Write(m_0, m : *Memory*, d : *Data*, a : *Addr*)
$$\iff \quad \text{m.map} = m_0.\text{map} ++ (a \to d) .$$

Then, specification of functions SysWrite and Flush is done as follows:

$\{\ s = s_0\ \}$

SysWrite(s: *System*)

$\{$ some d: *Data*, a: *Addr* |
Write(s_0.cache, s.cache, d, a)
s.cache.dirty = s_0.cache.dirty + a
s.main = s_0.main $\}$

$\{\ s = s_0\ \}$

Flush(s: *System*)

$\{$ some x: set s_0.cache.addrs |
s.cache.map = s_0.cache.map - x→Data
s.cache.dirty = s_0.cache.dirty - x
s.main.map = s_0.main.map ++
$\{$a: x, d: Data | d = s_0.cache.map[a]$\}$ $\}$

Notice that the previous specifications are as understandable as the ones given in *Alloy*. Moreover, using dynamic logic for the specification of functions allows us to assert the invariance of a property P under finite applications of functions SysWrite and Flush as follows:

$$Init(s) \land P(s) \quad \Rightarrow \quad [(SysWrite(s) + Flush(s))^*]P(s) .$$

More generally, suppose now that we want to show that property Q is invariant under sequences of applications of arbitrary operations $O_1, \ldots, O_k$, starting from states s described by a formula *Init*. Specification of the problem in our setting is done through the formula $Init \land Q \Rightarrow [(O_1 \cup \cdots \cup O_k)^*]Q$.

As an instance of the properties of executions that can be proved in our formalism, let us consider a system whose cache agrees with main memory in all non-dirty addresses. A consistency criterion of the cache with main memory is that after finitely many executions of SysWrite or Flush, the resulting system must still satisfy invariant DirtyInv. In Section 7 we will prove this property, which is specified in the extended *Alloy* by:

$$\text{all } s : System\ /\ DirtyInv(s) => [(SysWrite(s) + Flush(s))^*]DirtyInv(s) . \tag{8}$$

Notice also that if after finitely many executions of SysWrite and Flush we flush all the dirty addresses in the cache to main memory, the resulting cache should fully agree with main memory. We will specify the property in this section, and leave its proof for Section 7. In order to specify this property we need to specify the function that flushes all the dirty cache addresses. The specification is as follows:

$\{ s = s_0 \}$

DSFlush(s : *System*)

$\{$ s.cache.dirty $= \emptyset$
s.cache.map $= s_0$.cache.map $- s_0$.cache.map$[s_0$.cache.dirty$]$
s.main.map $= s_0$.main.map $++ s_0$.cache.map$[s_0$.cache.dirty$]$ $\}$

We specify the property establishing the agreement of the cache with main memory by: FullyAgree(s : *System*) $\iff$ s.cache.map *in* s.main.map.

Once "DSFlush" and "FullyAgree" have been specified, the property is specified in the extended *Alloy* by:

all s : System / DirtyInv(s) =>
$$[(\text{SysWrite}(s) + \text{Flush}(s))^*; \text{DSFlush}(s)] \text{FullyAgree}(s). \quad (9)$$

Notice that there is no need to mention traces in the specification of the previous properties. This is because traces appear in the semantics of the Kleene star and not in the syntax, which shows an adequate separation of concerns.

6 A Complete Calculus

The set of axioms for the extended *Alloy* is the set of axioms for classical first-order logic, enriched with the axioms for fork algebras and the following formulas:

$\langle P \rangle \alpha \wedge [P] \beta \Rightarrow \langle P \rangle (\alpha \wedge \beta)$, $\langle P \rangle (\alpha \vee \beta) \iff \langle P \rangle \alpha \vee \langle P \rangle \beta$,
$\langle P_0 + P_1 \rangle \alpha \iff \langle P_0 \rangle \alpha \vee \langle P_1 \rangle \alpha$, $\langle P_0; P_1 \rangle \alpha \iff \langle P_0 \rangle \langle P_1 \rangle \alpha$,
$\langle \alpha? \rangle \beta \iff \alpha \wedge \beta$, $\alpha \vee \langle P \rangle \langle P^* \rangle \alpha \Rightarrow \langle P^* \rangle \alpha$,
$\langle P^* \rangle \alpha \Rightarrow \alpha \vee \langle P^* \rangle (\neg \alpha \wedge \langle P \rangle \alpha)$, $\langle x \leftarrow t \rangle \alpha \iff \alpha[x/t]$,
$\alpha \iff \widehat{\alpha}$,

where $\widehat{\alpha}$ is α in which some occurrence of program P has been replaced by the program $z \leftarrow x; P'; x \leftarrow z$, for z not appearing in α, and P' is P with all the occurrences of x replaced by z.

The inference rules are those for classical first-order logic plus generalization rule for necessity, and the infinitary convergence rule:

$$\frac{\alpha}{[P]\alpha} \qquad \frac{(\forall n : nat)(\alpha \Rightarrow [P^n]\beta)}{\alpha \Rightarrow [P^*]\beta}$$

A proof of the completeness of the calculus is presented in [7, Thm. 15.1.4]. Joining this theorem with the completeness of the axiomatization of fork algebras [5, Thm. 4.3], it follows that the above described calculus is complete with respect to the semantics of the extended *Alloy*.

7 Verifying *Alloy* Specifications with *PVS*

As has been shown in previous sections, the extended *Alloy* is a language suitable for the description of systems behavior. There are different options in order to reason about such descriptions. Techniques such as model checking, sat solving and theorem proving give the possibility to detect systems flaws in early stages of the design lifecycle.

Regarding the problem of theorem proving, there are several theorem provers that can be used to carry out this task. *PVS* (*Prototype Verification System*), is a powerful and widely used theorem prover that has shown very good results when applied to the specification and verification of real systems [19]. Thus, we will concentrate on the use of this particular theorem prover in order to prove assertions from *Alloy* specifications.

As it has been described in the basic *PVS* bibliography [21, 20, 22], *PVS* is a theorem prover built on classical higher-order logic. The main purpose of this tool is to provide formal support during the design of systems, in a way in which concepts are described in abstract terms to allow a better level of analysis. *PVS* provides very useful mechanisms for system specification such as an advanced data-type specification language [18], the notion of subtypes and dependent types [22], the possibility to define parametric theories [22], and a collection of powerful proof commands to carry out propositional, equality, and arithmetic reasoning [20]. These proof commands can be combined to form proof strategies. The last feature simplifies the process of developing, debugging, maintaining, and presenting proofs.

Using *PVS* to reason about *Alloy* specifications is not trivial because *Alloy* is not supported by the *PVS* tool. To bridge this gap, a proof checker was built by encoding the new semantics for *Alloy* in *PVS*' language [14].

Taking as a case-study the memories with cache (systems) presented in Section 5.3, in order to build the *PVS* specification we provided *PVS* with the definition of the symbols for the language of fork algebras, the definition of the semantics of the symbols of fork algebras, the definition of the atomic actions required in the model, and the assertion to be verified in the model. In Figs. 4 and 5 we show, as examples, the *PVS* translation of formulas (8) and (9).

```
Preservation_of_DirtyInv: LEMMA
    FORALL_(v(cs), DirtyInv(v(cs)) IMPLIES
                [](*(SysWrite(v(cs))+Flush(v(cs))), DirtyInv(v(cs))))
```

Fig. 4. *PVS* translation of Formula (8).

```
Consistency_criterion: THEOREM
  FORALL_(v(cs), DirtyInv(v(cs)) IMPLIES
                 [](*(SysWrite(v(cs))+Flush(v(cs)))//DSFlush(v(cs)),
                 FullyAgree(v(cs))))
```

Fig. 5. *PVS* translation of Formula (9).

We have proved in *PVS* the properties stated in Figs. 4 and 5. This required the implementation of new proof strategies in *PVS*.

8 Conclusions

We have presented an extension of *Alloy* that incorporates the following features:

1. Through the use of fork algebras in the semantics, quantifications that were higher-order in *Alloy* are first-order in the extension.
2. Through the extension of *Alloy* with dynamic logic, static models in which dynamic content was described using conventions such as primed variables, now have a real dynamic content.
3. The use of dynamic logic provides a clean and simple mechanism for the specification of properties of executions.
4. Combining the completeness of a calculus for dynamic logic and the complete calculus for fork algebras gives us a complete calculus for the extended *Alloy*. This enables theorem proving as an alternative to analysis by refutation.
5. Finally, we have also extended the theorem prover *PVS* in order to prove properties specified in the extended *Alloy*.

Acknowledgements

We wish to thank Daniel Jackson for reading preliminary versions of this paper and making valuable suggestions. We are also thankful to Sam Owre and Natarajan Shankar for their help in the verification of properties in *PVS*.

References

1. Bickford M. and Guaspari D., *Lightweight Analysis of UML*. TM-98-0036, Odyssey Research Associates, Ithaca, NY, November 1998.
2. Booch G., Jacobson I. and Rumbaugh J., *The Unified Modeling Language User Guide*, The Addison-Wesley Object Technology Series, 1998.
3. Evans A., Kent S. and Selic B. (eds.), *UML 2000 - The Unified Modeling Language. Advancing the Standard*, Proceedings of the Third International Conference in York, UK, October 2-6, 2000. Springer Verlag Berlin, LNCS 1939.
4. France R. and Rumpe B. (eds.), *UML '99 - The Unified Modeling Language. Beyond the Standard*, Proceedings of the Second International Conference in Fort Collins, Colorado, USA, October 28-30, 1999. Springer Verlag Berlin, LNCS 1723.

5. Frias M., *Fork Algebras in Algebra, Logic and Computer Science*, World Scientific Publishing Co., Series Advances on Logic, 2002.
6. Frias, M. F., Haeberer, A. M. and Veloso, P. A. S., *A Finite Axiomatization for Fork Algebras*, Logic Journal of the IGPL, Vol. 5, No. 3, 311–319, 1997.
7. Harel D., Kozen D. and Tiuryn J., *Dynamic Logic*, MIT Press, October 2000.
8. Jackson D., *Micromodels of Software: Lightweight Modelling and Analysis with Alloy*, 2002.
9. Jackson D., *Alloy: A Lightweight Object Modelling Notation*, ACM Transactions on Software Engineering and Methodology (TOSEM), Volume 11, Issue 2 (April 2002), pp. 256-290.
10. Jackson D. and Sullivan K., *COM Revisited: Tool Assisted Modelling and Analysis of Software Structures*, Proc. ACM SIGSOFT Conf. Foundations of Software Engineering. San Diego, November 2000.
11. Jackson D., Schechter I. and Shlyakhter I., *Alcoa: the Alloy Constraint Analyzer*, Proceedings of the International Conference on Software Engineering, Limerick, Ireland, June 2000.
12. Jackson, D., Shlyakhter, I., and Sridharan, M., A Micromodularity Mechanism. Proc. ACM SIGSOFT Conf. Foundations of Software Engineering/European Software Engineering Conference (FSE/ESEC '01), Vienna, September 2001.
13. Jones C.B., *Systematic Software Development Using VDM*, Prentice Hall, 1995.
14. Lopez Pombo C.G., Owre S. and Shankar N., *An A_g proof checker using PVS as a semantic framework*, Technical Report SRI-CSL-02-04, SRI International, June 2002.
15. Manna Z., Anuchitanukul A., Bjorner N., Browne A., Chang E., Colon M., de Alfaro L., Devarajan H., Sipma H. and Uribe T., *STeP: The Stanford Temporal Prover*, http://theory.stanford.edu/people/zm/papers/step.ps.Z. Technical report STAN-CS-TR-94-1518, Computer Science Department, Stanford University, July 1994.
16. *Object Constraint Language Specification"*. Version 1.1, 1 September 1997.
17. Owre S., Rushby J.M. and Shankar N., *PVS: A prototype verification system*, In Deepak Kapur, editor, 11th International Conference on Automated Deduction (CADE), volume 607 of Lecture Notes in Artificial Intelligence, pp. 748–752, Saratoga, NY, jun 1992. Springer-Verlag.
18. Owre S. and Shankar N., *Abstract datatypes in PVS*, Technical Report CSL-93-9R, SRI International, December 1993. Subtantially revised in June 1997.
19. Owre S., Shankar N., Rushby J,M, and Stringer-Calvert D.W.J., *PVS: An Experience Report*, in Proceedings of Applied Formal Methods—FM-Trends 98, Lecture Notes in Computer Science 1641, 1998, pp. 338–345.
20. Owre S., Shankar N., Rushby J,M, and Stringer-Calvert D.W.J., *PVS Prover Guide*, SRI International, version 2.4 edition, November 2001.
21. Owre S., Shankar N., Rushby J.M. and Stringer-Calvert D.W.J., *PVS System Guide*, SRI International, version 2.4 edition, December 2001.
22. Owre S., Shankar N., Rushby J.M. and Stringer-Calvert D.W.J., *PVS Language reference*, SRI International, version 2.4 edition, December 2001.
23. Spivey J.M., *Understanding Z: A Specification Language and Its Formal Semantics*, Cambridge Tracts in Theoretical Computer Science, 1988.
24. Tarski, A. and Givant, S.,*A Formalization of Set Theory without Variables*, A.M.S. Coll. Pub., vol. 41, 1987.

Interacting State Machines for Mobility

Thomas A. Kuhn and David von Oheimb

Siemens AG, Corporate Technology, D-81730 Munich,
{Thomas.Kuhn|David.von.Oheimb}@siemens.com

Abstract. We present two instantiations of generic Interactive State Machines (ISMs) with mobility features which are useful for modeling and verifying dynamically changing mobile systems.

ISMs are automata with local state exchanging messages simultaneously on multiple buffered ports. A system of generic ISMs also deals with global state used e.g. to describe their communication topology. We introduce Ambient ISMs (AmbISMs) whose features include hierarchical environments, migration, and locality constraints on communication. In this way we give an alternative operational semantics to the (boxed) ambient calculus. Moreover, we combine AmbISMs with dynamic ISMs which introduce dynamic communication structures and ISM activation and deactivation, as defined in an accompanying paper.

All ISM variants have been defined formally within the theorem prover Isabelle/HOL and provide an easy to learn description language for the development, documentation and verification of mobile systems. We motivate our development by a running example from the field of mobile agent systems, giving a reference specification using the boxed ambient calculus and comparing it with the formulation within our (dynamic) Ambient ISM approach, which we describe in detail.

Keywords: formal modeling, verification, mobility, dynamic communication, boxed ambients, mobile agents, Interacting State Machines.

1 Introduction

In the design and development of complex mobile systems, ensuring correctness, safety and security is an important and particularly difficult task. Formal modeling and verification can help to do that in a precise, systematic, error preventing, and reproduceable way. The standard techniques for modeling distributed systems, e.g. the process algebra CSP [Hoa80] and the π-calculus [MPW92], do not offer special constructs for expressing mobility, and thus locations (forming administrative domains) and movement between these have to be modeled explicitly without support by the calculus, which is particularly inconvenient when modeling complex systems. To overcome this deficit, Cardelli and Gordon have introduced mobile ambients [CG98] extending the π-calculus. Meanwhile there are several further enhancements, in particular, boxed ambients [BCC01] define more practical communication patterns. Other problems remain, in particular the integration with state and calculations performed within processes.

The approach presented in this paper combines the concepts of boxed ambients with the state-oriented modeling techniques of Interacting State Machines (ISMs) [Ohe02]. It supports expressing mobility properties (in particular hierarchies of environments, migration, and message passing restricted by locality) as well as describing classical functional and state-oriented features in a rather conventional and thus easily understandable way.

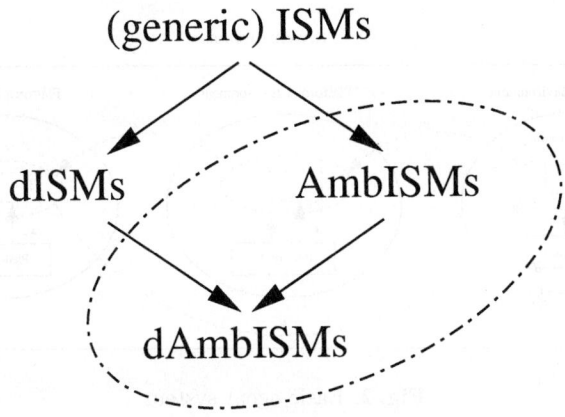

Fig. 1. ISM Hierarchy

This work has been motivated by ongoing industrial research for the security work package of project MAP [MAP] on the design, analysis and application of mobile agent systems. One of its visions is to be able to certify products according to the upper evaluation assurance levels of the so-called 'Common Criteria' [CC99] where formal description and analysis techniques are mandatory. To this end, we need a formal technique that is practical for modeling and verifying mobile systems, in particular for establishing security related properties. The ISM approach employed here has been first described in [OL02] and [Ohe02]. The accompanying paper [OL03] generalizes ISMs to generic ISMs, introduces the hierarchy of instantiations depicted by Figure 1, and describes dynamic ISMs (dISMs) in detail. The present paper focuses on AmbISMs, i.e. the extensions of ISMs with ambient features, and dAmbISMs, i.e. their combination with the dynamic port handling and ISM (de-)activation features of dISMs. For each of the two formalisms, we give a mathematical definition of the semantics and describe an illustrative application example in detail.

2 Motivation

In this section we introduce the reference example used for demonstrating the mobile extensions of the ISM approach. Furthermore, we present a basic definition of the boxed ambient calculus, express the basic reference example within

2.1 Reference Example: Distributed Accumulation

For demonstrating and comparing the approaches presented in this article, we introduce a basic and refined example of a mobile agent system.

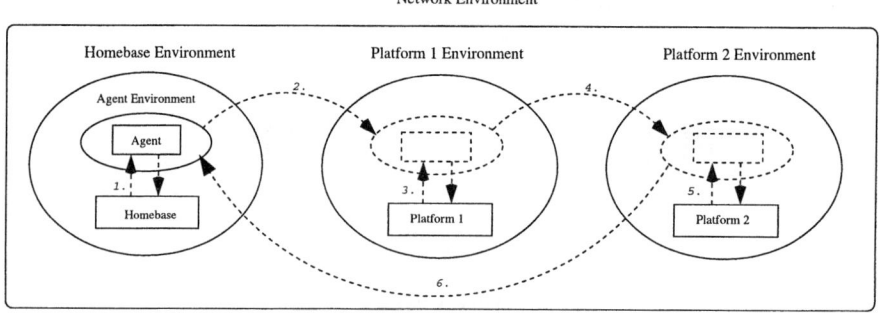

Fig. 2. Basic agent system

Basic Agent System. The mobile agent system consists of three agent platforms and a mobile agent (cf. Figure 2). One of the three agent platforms has a dominant position in that sense that it represents the homebase of the mobile agent. At the homebase platform the mobile agent is generated and parameterised, e.g. by a user. The homebase platform process is embedded in the homebase platform environment, the agent platform processes in their corresponding agent platform environments, the mobile agent process in the mobile agent environment, and all these environments are embedded in the network environment. The mobile agent with its environment departs from the homebase, migrates to each agent platform and finally returns to the homebase. The task of the mobile agent process is to collect values from the agent platform processes, to compute the sum of the values, and to give the result back to the homebase process.

Refined Platform Access. A variation of the above example is the following demonstration of agent delegation (cf. Figure 3): the mobile agent needs to collect values from an agent platform that has other communication interfaces and/or does only allow access by a privileged other mobile agent. This other agent knows the right communication interfaces, has the privilege to access the agent platform, and establishes the connection as a representative of the original agent. The representative agent transfers the data port where the platform offers the value to the mobile agent which can now collect the values from the platform via the data port.

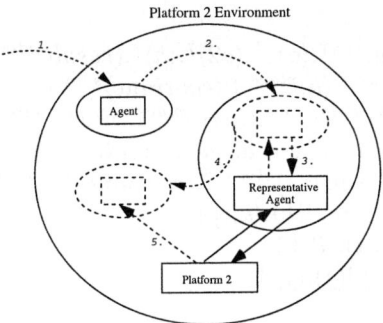

Fig. 3. Refined platform access

2.2 Boxed Ambient Approach

Concept. Process calculi like the ambient calculus form abstract (theoretical) modeling languages for specifying and analyzing distributed systems but are also used as a semantical basis in order to define programming languages. The operational semantics of a process calculus is expressed by reduction rules. Examples of process calculi are CSP [Hoa80], CCS [Mil80], and the π-calculus [MPW92]. The π-calculus is used as the basis of the ambient calculus [CG98] which has been introduced by L. Cardelli and A. D. Gordon investigating mobile systems. The ambient calculus includes particular elements called *capabilities* which allow to express mobile scenarios like mobile agent migration and agent systems. The ambient calculus has the following main features: hierarchical locations, migration, local communication, contextual equivalence, and reduction semantics.

The boxed ambient [BCC01] approach is a slight modification of the ambient calculus in the sense that communication is allowed also with the parent and children of the current ambient and dissemination of ambients is no more possible.

Let n express names, P and Q processes and M capabilities. The boxed ambient calculus offers the following elements: restriction $(\nu n)P$, empty process 0, composition $P \mid Q$, replication $!P$, ambient $n[P]$, exertion of capability $M.P$, input $(x)^a.P$ and output $\langle x \rangle^a$ where $a \in \{\star, \uparrow, n\}$ and $\star$ means local communication, $\uparrow$ means communication with the parent ambient, and n means communicaton with a subambient named n. The capabilities M are *in n* and *out n* for entering and exit the ambient n respectively.

Expressing the Distributed Accumulation Example. We use the boxed ambient calculus to model the basic agent system of the reference example. The top level ambient is the network ambient which encapsulates three subambients: the homebase ambient h as well as the two agent platform ambients $a1$ and $a2$. The mobile agent a is placed as subambient in the homebase ambient h at startup.

$network[$
$\quad h[\ (\nu a)\ (route[\ in\ a.\langle h\rangle^{\uparrow}.\langle a1\rangle^{\uparrow}.\langle a2\rangle^{\uparrow}.\langle h\rangle^{\uparrow}.(result)^{storage}.\ out\ a.\langle result\rangle^{\uparrow}\ ]\ |$
$\qquad a[\ \langle 0\rangle^{storage}\ |\ \langle h\rangle^{place}\ |\ \langle continue\rangle^{semaphore}\ |$
$\qquad\quad !((cont)^{semaphore}.(here)^{place}.(next)^{route}.\langle next\rangle^{place}.\ out\ here.$
$\qquad\quad in\ next.\ (r[\ out\ a.\ \langle a\rangle\ ]\ |\ (value)^{*}.\ (accu)^{storage}.$
$\qquad\quad \langle accu + value\rangle^{storage}.\langle continue\rangle^{semaphore}\ ))\ |$
$\qquad\quad semaphore[\ !(k).\langle k\rangle\ ]\ |$
$\qquad\quad place[\ !(i).\langle i\rangle\ ]\ |$
$\qquad\quad storage[\ !(j).\langle j\rangle\ ]$
$\qquad])$
$\quad]\ |$
$\quad a1[\ !(p)^{r}.\langle 1\rangle^{p}\ ]\ |$
$\quad a2[\ !(p)^{r}.\langle 2\rangle^{p}\ ]$
$]$

The homebase ambient houses an ambient with the name *route* which contains the route initialisation data and the result handler of the mobile agent ambient *a*. The *route* ambient transmits this information by moving (*in a* of the *route* ambient) into the agent ambient *a* while the agent ambient is in the homebase. The agent ambient *a* consists of several top level processes and several subambients which are used for storing data and tokens. The main top level process is a loop that receives the next place to be visited, migrates to that place, exchanges the reply ambient name *a* with the agent platform, receives the next value, and adds the new value to the accumulator. The replication is serialized by a token *continue* which triggers execution of exactly one process at a time. Some simplifications are used in order to make the term not too complicated. In particular the calculation of the sum is abbreviated by *accu+value* which can be coded as suggested in [CG98]. The subambient *semaphore* in the agent ambient *a* is used for handling the serializiation token *continue*, *place* is used to store the place not recent visited, and *storage* keeps the calculated sum. The agent platforms *a*1 and *a*2 have the same structure: they read the output ambient name and output the values 1 or 2. The output ambient name is communicated by an ambient *r* which migrates from the agent ambient *a* to the platform level and outputs the ambient name *a* to the agent platform. The agent *a* successively visits the places contained in *route*. After no more places are available in the ambient *route* the calculation stops and the result is returned to the homebase by a local output of the stored sum.

Problems with the Ambient Calculus. Specifying examples like the one above reveals several deficiencies of abstract process calculi like the (boxed) ambient calculus:

No direct handling state information. The ambient calculus does not have a built-in notion of state. State may be simulated by ambients containing special processes that use input operations to model write access and output for read access. The resulting artificial I/O operations have to be sequenced properly and distinguished from proper I/O.

Cumbersome expression of non-sequential control flow. The only way to impose a certain flow of control within the processes on the top level of an ambient is via synchronizing messages. As above, this adds unnecessary clutter to specifications.

No concept of named ports or channels. Even with proper message exchange, there is the risk of confusing data sent between processes because the messages are simply spilled into the local ether with no built-in addressing mechanism. Even in the presence of a type system, unwanted effects like corrupted computation and deadlocks may occur.

Cumbersome expression and verification of local computation. Even basic data types like numbers and the operations on them, which naturally occur within processes, have to be translated to ambient structures and related processes — an utterly inadequate representation that renders practical applications incomprehensible.

3 Generic and Dynamic Interacting State Machines

Interacting State Machines (ISMs) [Ohe02] are automata whose state transitions may involve multiple input and output simultaneously on any number of ports. The accompanying paper [OL03] generalizes their definition, introducing *generic ISMs* which feature global state and commands for changing this state.

3.1 Concepts of Dynamic ISMs

Dynamic ISMs (dISMs) are an instantiation of generic ISMs offering dynamic creation, transfer, enabling and disabling of ports as well as a basic form of dynamic ISM creation and deletion.

A system of dynamic ISMs uses the global state to keep track of the currently running dISMs, enabled ports, and port ownership. Changes to this state are made by members of the system issuing suitable commands: a dynamic ISM may request that a dISM not yet running is activated or a running dISM (including itself) is stopped. Moreover, a dynamic ISM may create a new port and become its initial owner. An owner of a port may receive input on the port, allow or forbid others to output to it, or convey it to any other dISM. The facility to enable or disable ports can be used to model e.g. flow control.

3.2 Semantics

The semantics definitions given in this paper are based on the definitions given for generic and dynamic ISMs in [OL03]. For lack of space, we cannot repeat all the relevant definitions here and thus ask the reader to refer to that companion paper for a detailed description. Here we just introduce in a semi-formal way the concepts directly referred to later in this paper.

All definitions and proofs within the ISM approach have been developed as a hierarchy of Isabelle/HOL [Pau94] theories and machine-checked using this theorem prover. Nevertheless, we give the semantics in the traditional "mathematical" style in order to enhance readability. We sometimes make use of λ-abstraction borrowed from the λ-calculus, but write (multi-argument) function application in the conventional form, e.g. $f(a,b,c)$. Occasionally we make use of partial application (also known as *currying*), such that, in the example just given, $f(a,b)$ is an intermediate function value that requires a third parameter to be given before yielding the actual function result.

A (generic) ISM a has type $ISM(\mathcal{C}, \Sigma)$ where $\mathcal{C}$ is the type of *commands* affecting the global state of an ISM system and Σ is the type of its *local state* with typical variable σ. The interface of an ISM gives two sets of the ports that it uses for sending and receiving messages, respectively. The *global state* has type Γ with typical variable γ. A *family* of ISMs $A = (A_i)_{i \in I}$ is an indexed collection of ISMs where the indices are of type $\mathfrak{I}$. Their parallel composition typically has the product type $\Pi_{i \in I} \Sigma_i$ as its local state type. An ISM *configuration* $CONF(X)$ is a pair of a family of its input buffers (used for internal communication and feedback) and the local state given by the type parameter X. The set of *composite runs*, $CRuns(As, \gamma_0, gtrans)$, contains all possible traces of a family of ISMs running in parallel. The ISM family As is parameterized by the global state such that it may evolve over time. The initial global state is γ_0 and the global transition relation $gtrans(j)$ takes as a parameter the index of the ISM whose transition is currently performed and yields a transition between the global pre-state γ, a command c, and a resulting global post-state γ'.

For dynamic ISMs, the global state type Γ gets instantiated to $dSTATE$, with typical variable δ. It specifies the set of dISMs currently active, the set of ports currently enabled, and the current (input) port ownership. The auxiliary function $init\_dSTATE(A,r)$ initializes this information according to the input interfaces of the ISMs in the ISM family A and the set r of initially running dISMs. The auxiliary function $set\_In\_Out(A, \delta)$ is used to transform A according to the current global dynamic state δ. The global transition relation $dTrans(js, i)$, where i is the current dISM and js is the set of dISMs that it is allowed to start or stop or convey ports to, specifies the transformation of the dynamic state δ to δ' induced by a sequence of dynamic commands $dcmds$.

4 Ambient Interacting State Machines

An instantiation of generic ISMs quite different from dynamic ISMs are *Ambient ISMs (AmbISMs)*. They give a novel form of operational semantics to the ambient calculus [CG98] where we extend the ability to communicate along the lines of boxed ambients [BCC01]. Most importantly, by combining ambient processes with ISMs, we introduce a concept of process state.

4.1 Concepts

Ambients are nested administrative domains that contain *processes* which (in our case) are ISMs. As usual, the ambient structure determines the ability of the processes to communicate with each other. In the original ambient calculus, only processes within the same ambient may exchange messages. We extend this rather strict notion of *local communication,* for the reasons given in [BCC01], to parent and child ambients of the ambient at hand. Ambients are *mobile* in the sense that an ISM may move the ambient it belongs to, together with all ISMs and subambients contained in it, out of the parent ambient or into a sibling. Moreover, an ambient may be deleted ("opened") such that its contents are poured into the surrounding ambient, or a new ambient may be created as a child of the current one, where for symmetry we give the ability to specify subsets of ISMs currently at the same level and other child ambients that shall immediately move into the new ambient. Finally, (new) ISMs may be assigned to ambients. In the ambient literature, ambient operations are called *capabilities* since their "possession" can be seen as a qualification to perform the respective action. Semantically speaking, the qualification simply boils down to knowing the name of the ambient involved.

4.2 Semantics

Ambient State and Commands. Let $\aleph$ be the type of ambient names. The hierarchical structure of ambients is given by a partial function of type $\aleph \rightsquigarrow \aleph$ mapping each ambient name n to the name of its parent m (if any) or the special value $\perp$ indicating that there is no parent, i.e. the ambient n is at the root of the tree. One may imagine the relation induced in this way as a forest of ambient trees[1]. Furthermore there is an assignment of ISMs to their home ambients, given by a partial function of type $\Im \rightsquigarrow \aleph$ where $\Im$ is the type of ISM identifiers. The *ambient state aSTATE,* instantiating the generic global state Γ, is the Cartesian product of the two partial functions, i.e. it has the form[2] $\alpha = (parent(\alpha), home(\alpha))$. Note that both $parent(\alpha)$ and $home(\alpha)$ are written in curried style, i.e. they may take a further argument besides the ambient state α.

The ISM type parameter C gets instantiated to Ambient ISM commands $aCMD^*$ where $aCMD = \{Assign(j,n) \mid j \in \Im \wedge n \in \aleph\} \cup \{In(n) \mid n \in \aleph\} \cup \{Out(n) \mid n \in \aleph\} \cup \{Del(n) \mid n \in \aleph\} \cup \{Ins(n, ns, is) \mid n \in \aleph \wedge ns \in \wp(\aleph) \wedge is \in \wp(\Im)\}$.

Ambient Transitions. The global transition relation $AmbTrans(i)$ is defined as $\{(\alpha, acmds, \alpha') \mid i \in dom(home(\alpha)) \wedge \alpha \xrightarrow{i:acmds}^* \alpha'\}$ where the single-step command execution relation $\alpha \xrightarrow{i:acmd} \alpha'$ means that the command $acmd$ issued by i transfers the ambient state α to α', as defined by the rules in Figure 4.

---
[1] assuming that the relation is acyclic, but actually this restriction is not required
[2] The definition pattern $x = (sel_1(x), sel_2(x), \ldots)$ should not be understood as a recursive definition of x but as a shorthand introducing a tuple with typical name x and with selectors (i.e., projection functions) sel_1, sel_2, ...

$$\frac{home(\alpha,i) = m \wedge (n = m \vee parent(\alpha,n) = m) \wedge home(\alpha,j) = \bot}{\alpha \xrightarrow{i:Assign(j,n)} \alpha(\!|home := home(\alpha)(j \mapsto n)|\!)}$$

$$\frac{home(\alpha,i) = m \wedge n \neq m \wedge parent(\alpha,m) = parent(\alpha,n)}{\alpha \xrightarrow{i:In(n)} \alpha(\!|parent := (parent(\alpha))(m \mapsto n)|\!)}$$

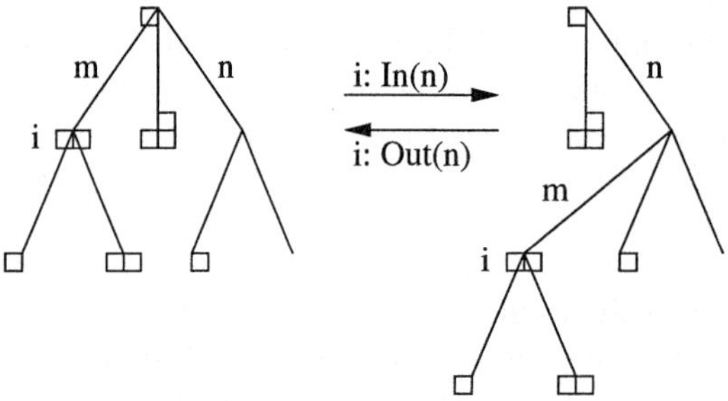

$$\frac{home(\alpha,i) = m \wedge n \neq m \wedge parent(\alpha,m) = n}{\alpha \xrightarrow{i:Out(n)} \alpha(\!|parent := (parent(\alpha))(m := parent(\alpha,n))|\!)}$$

$$\frac{home(\alpha,i) \in \{m,n\} \wedge n \neq m \wedge parent(\alpha,n) = m}{\alpha \xrightarrow{i:Del(n)} \alpha(\!|parent := (parent(\alpha))(n \rightsquigarrow m)(n := \bot), \ home := (\ home(\alpha))(n \rightsquigarrow m)|\!)}$$

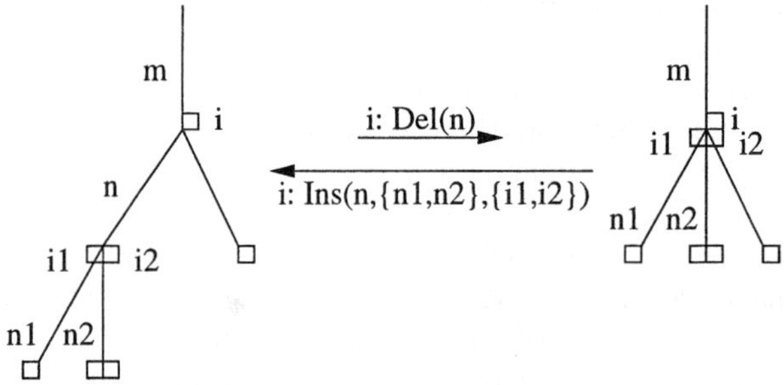

$$\frac{n \notin dom(parent(\alpha)) \cup ran(parent(\alpha)) \cup ran(home(\alpha)) \wedge home(\alpha,i) = m \wedge (\forall n \in ns.\ parent(\alpha,n) = m) \wedge (\forall i \in is.\ home(\alpha,i) = m)}{\alpha \xrightarrow{i:Ins(n,ns,is)} \alpha(\!|parent := (parent(\alpha))(ns\{\mapsto\}n)(n \mapsto m), \ home := (\ home(\alpha))(is\{\mapsto\}n)|\!)}$$

where

- $f(x \mapsto y)$ updates the partial function f at argument x to a value $y \neq \bot$
- $f(xs\{\mapsto\}y)$ updates f for all arguments in xs to a value $y \neq \bot$
- $f(y \rightsquigarrow y')$ substitutes all results y of the partial function f by y'
- $dom(f)$ abbreviates $\{x \mid f(x) \neq \bot\}$, i.e. the domain of f
- $ran(f)$ abbreviates $\{y \mid f(x) = y\}$, i.e. the range of f

Fig. 4. Ambient command semantics

The *Assign* command is typically used to populate a newly created ambient with AmbISMs. The operations $In(n)$ and $Out(n)$ are inverse to each other. $Ins(n, as, is)$ is inverse to $Del(n)$ if as is the set of subambients of n and is the set of AmbISMs originally inhabitating the ambient n just before deletion of n. $Del(n)$ is inverse to $Ins(n, as, is)$.

Composite Runs. The generic composite runs operator for ISMs is instantiated for Ambient ISMs in analogy to the instantiation for dynamic ISMs: for any family A of AmbISMs (of type $ISM(aCMD^*, aSTATE \times \Pi_{i \in I} \Sigma_i)$) and any initial ambient state α_0, $AmbCRuns(A, \alpha_0)$ gives the (set of traces of) composite runs of Ambient ISMs, of type $\wp((CONF(aSTATE \times \Pi_{i \in I} \Sigma_i))^*)$. It is defined as

$$AmbCRuns(A, \alpha_0) \equiv CRuns(local\_Out(A), \alpha_0, AmbTrans)$$

where

- $vicinity(\alpha, i)$ is the set of the home ambient of i and its parent (if any), defined as if $home(\alpha, i) = \bot$ then $\emptyset$ else $\{home(\alpha, i), parent(\alpha, home(\alpha, i))\} \setminus \{\bot\}$
- $local(\alpha, i) = \{j \mid vicinity(\alpha, i) \cap vicinity(\alpha, j) \neq \emptyset\}$ yields the set of all (names of) AmbISMs that belong to the same ambient as i or to its parent ambient (if any) or any child ambient
- $local\_Out(A, \alpha) = (A_i (\!| Out := Out(A_i) \cap \bigcup_{j \in local(\alpha, i)} In(A_j) |\!))_{i \in I}$ restricts the output interface of each member i of the ISM family A to the input ports of those AmbISMs which are currently local to i.[3]

Basic Properties. In contrast to dynamic ISMs, the set of AmbISMs running in a given system does not change, there is no change to the input interfaces (and thus port ownership) of AmbISMs, and ports are always enabled. As a consequence of parallel composition well-formedness is preserved trivially.

The function *local_Out* implements our (weakened) restrictions to message passing according to the ambient structure: output is possible only to local AmbISMs, i.e. those belonging to the same ambient as the sender or to the parent or any child ambient. AmbISMs may run in isolation but in this case cannot communicate with others. They may be assigned to ambients and then take part in communications. Furthermore, the ambient assignment can be changed by ambient insertion and deletion.

---

[3] where $(\!| \ldots |\!)$ expresses a record update

4.3 Expressing the Basic Distributed Accumulation Example

Here we express[4] the basic agent system example of §2.1 using the ambient ISM formalism[5] as an Isabelle theory[6]. Within the example we show the usage of the following ambient commands: insertion of new ambients to the ambient tree, assignment of ISMs to ambients, deletion of ambients, and movement of ambients within the ambient tree.

We call the theory 'Distributed Accumulation' and refer to the ISM package that defines generic ISMs and the ambient ISM extension:

theory `DistributedAccumulation = ISM_package:`

The ISMs of the agent, homebase, agent platform 1 and agent platform 2 use the following types:
The type `id` holds ISM identifiers where `AG` stands for agent, `HB` stands for homebase, and `AP` followed by a natural number n stands for the agent platform n.

datatype `id = AG | HB | AP nat`

The ISMs are or will be placed inside the corresponding ambient where the name is generated by the identifier followed by `_amb`. The top level network ambient is denoted by `NW_amb`.

datatype `ambient = AG_amb | HB_amb | AP_amb nat | NW_amb`

The ports used by the ISMs are the `AGData` port on which the agent receives its data, the `Request` port for getting into contact with the agent platform, and the `Reply` port to which the agent returns the result to its homebase.

datatype `port = AGData | Request | Reply`

The definition of the input and output message type is self-explanatory.

datatype `message = Route "ambient list" | Port port | Value nat`

The type `A_cmds` is an abbreviation for the instance of ambient ISM command type $aCMD$ (cf. §4.2) that we use in this example.

types `A_cmds = "(id, ambient) acmd list"`

Definition of All ISM States. For defining the system composed of all ISMs given below, we need to define all possible state types of the component

---

[4] we reproduce the complete Isabelle theory (emphasized text) and augment it with comments using the LaTeX documentation facility of Isabelle
[5] all sources are available from [ISM]
[6] for further information see [OL03, §2.4: Isabelle/HOL Representation]

ISMs. The agent ISM has a control state `AG_state` and data state `AG_data`. The homebase and the agent platforms ISMs have only control states `HB_state` and `AP_state`, respectively.

datatype `AG_state` = `Learn` | `Migrate` | `Decide` | `Read` | `Stop`

record `AG_data` =
    `accu`   :: `nat` — the accumulator
    `here` :: `ambient` — the current location
    `route` :: `"ambient list"` — the agent route

datatype `HB_state` = `Start` | `Instruct` | `Result` | `Sleep`

datatype `AP_state` = `Loop`

For technical reasons, namely the lack of dependent types in Isabelle/HOL, we have to construct the union type `state` of all different local ISM states which will be used in the **ism** setting and the definition of the overall `System` below.

datatype `state` = `AGs` `"AG_state × AG_data"`
                        | `HBs` `HB_state`
                        | `APs` `AP_state`

Definition of Agent. The ISM representing the agent has a single input port `AGData` and a single output port `Request`, used as described above. The agent starts in the initial control state `Learn` and has an data state referred to by `s`.
ism `Agent` =
  ports `"port"`
    inputs   `"{AGData}"`
    outputs `"{Request}"`
  messages `"message"`
  commands `"A_cmds"` **default** `"[]"`
  states `state`
    control `"AG_state"` **init** `"Learn"`
    data   `"AG_data"` **name** `s`
  transitions

In its first transition the agent receives the route from the homebase via its port `AGData`. The route is stored in the data state where the first element of the route list is initially stored to the local variable `here` and the tail of the route list is stored in the `route` variable.

    `learn:` — the agent receives its route from the homebase
      `Learn` → `Migrate`
    in `"AGData"` `"[Route (r#rs)]"`
    post `"(|accu=0, here=r, route=rs|)"`

The `migrate` transition is used to change the ambient tree structure. As specified by the local variables `here` and `route`, the agent migrates out of the ambient referred to by here and into the ambient named by the first element of the list route.

    migrate: — migrate to the next ambient on the route
      Migrate → Decide
      pre "route s = r#rs"
      cmd "[Out (here s), In r]"
      post here := "r", route := "rs"

When the agent reaches the last ambient in the route, e.g. the homebase ambient, it returns the accumulated value of the accumulator accu back via the Reply port and stops

    result: — return the result to the homebase
      Decide → Stop
      pre "route s = []"
      out "Reply" "[Value (accu s)]"

Otherwise, for reading the next value to be accumulated from a visited agent platform, the agent tells the platform via the standard port Request the input port name AGData to which the value will be sent:

    initread: — send the reply port to the platform
      Decide → Read
      pre "route s ≠ []"
      out "Request" "[Port AGData]"

The read transition reads the next accumulation value from the input port AGData and adds it to the accumulator. Then it returns to the Migrate state.

    read: — read the addend of the next platform
      Read → Migrate
      in "AGData" "[Value a]"
      post accu := "accu s + a"

Definition of Homebase. The homebase ISM reads from the Request and Reply port and outputs to the AGData port. It has no data state but control states where the initial control state is Start.

```
ism Homebase =
  ports "port"
    inputs "{Request, Reply}"
    outputs "{AGData}"
  messages "message"
  commands "A_cmds" default "[]"
  states state
    control "HB_state" init "Start"
  transitions
```

Initially the process located in the homebase ambient inserts the `AG_amb` ambient in the homebase ambient and assigns the agent ISM `AG` to the agent ambient.

    `start:` — the agent is placed in its ambient
      `Start → Instruct`
      `cmd "[Ins AG_amb {} {}, Assign AG AG_amb]"`

The homebase sends the list of ambients `Route` to the agent via the port `AGData`. The initial route consists of the homebase ambient, the agent platform 1 and 2 ambients, and the homebase ambient. The last one, the homebase ambient, is the final location of the agent where the result is delivered.

    `instruct:` — the agent gets the route imprinted
      `Instruct → Result`
      `out "AGData" "[Route [HB_amb, AP_amb 1, AP_amb 2, HB_amb]]"`

The homebase receives the result via the standard port `Reply`. Then it deletes the agent ambient from the ambient tree structure (withdrawing the terminated agent ISM from its ambient).

    `result:` — the homebase gets the value from the agent
      `Result → Sleep`
      `in "Reply" "[Value x]"`
      `cmd "[Del AG_amb]"`

Definition of Platform 1. The agent platform 1 has an input port `Request` where it receives the output port name of visiting agents. After receiving the output port from an agent it sends the value 1 to this port.

```
ism "AP1" =
  ports "port"
    inputs "{Request}"
    outputs "UNIV" — the universal set (of port names)
  messages "message"
  commands "A_cmds" default "[]"
  states state
    control "AP_state" init "Loop"
  transitions

    request: — the platform gets the reply channel and sends the value
      Loop → Loop
      in "Request" "[Port p]"
      out "p" "[Value 1]"
```

The definition of the platform 2 is analogous to the platform 1 with the difference that the value sent is 2.

Definition of the Overall System. The overall system maps the ambient ISM identifiers to the corresponding ambient ISMs. The definition of the composite runs of the system consists of the above mentioned system mapping and the initial mapping of the ambients to the network ambient `NW_amb` and the mapping of the ISMs identifiers to the corresponding ambients.

constdefs
```
 System :: "(id, (A_cmds, port, message, state) ism) family"
 "System ≡ (λi. case i of AG   ⇒ Agent.ism
                       | HB   ⇒ Homebase.ism
                       | AP n ⇒ if n = 1 then AP1.ism else AP2.ism,
          {AG, HB, AP 1, AP 2})"

 Runs :: "((port, message, (id, ambient) astate × (id ⇒ state))
           conf list) set"
 "Runs ≡ Amb_comp_runs System
 (|parent = empty(HB_amb↦NW_amb)(AP_amb 1↦NW_amb  )(AP_amb 2↦NW_amb ),
   home   = empty(HB     ↦HB_amb)(AP    1↦AP_amb 1)(AP    2↦AP_amb 2)|)"
```

Finally, one can show that the above model of the agent system enjoys the property that the agent returns the value 3 on the `Reply` port.

theorem `"∃r∈Runs. ∃(b,as,st) ∈ set r. b Reply = [Value 3]"`

Thus the theorem validates indirectly that the agent migrates and accumulates in a proper way. This ends the example and demonstrates that the AmbISM is an adequate mean to describe and verifiy mobile systems.

5 Dynamic Ambient Interacting State Machines

As the name suggests, *dynamic Ambient ISMs (dAmbISMs)* combine dynamic ISMs and Ambient ISMs.

5.1 Concepts

Dynamic Ambient ISMs inherit port handling and dAmbISM (de-)activation from dynamic ISMs and ambients from Ambient ISMs. The concepts are mostly orthogonal, except for one new feature: it is reasonable to offer the operations that affect other dAmbISMs (by activating or deactivating them or conveying ports to them) only to dAmbISMs that are in its vicinity. We call this property of dAmbISM manipulation *locality*.

5.2 Semantics

We have taken care in designing the semantics of dynamic ISMs and Ambient ISMs such that their combination can be described with minimal means, in particular avoiding redundancies.

Dynamic Ambient State and Commands. The *dynamic ambient state* type $daSTATE$ is simply the Cartesian product $dSTATE \times aSTATE$. Similarly, the type $daCMDs$ of sequences of *dynamic ambient commands* is $dCMD^* \times aCMD^*$. We may aggregate the dynamic commands and ambient commands in two separate command sequences (instead of defining a sequence where each element is of either kind) because the two kinds of commands operate on different parts of the global state.

Dynamic Ambient Transitions. The global transition relation $dAmbTrans(i)$ is defined essentially as the pointwise product of $dTrans$ and $dAmbTrans$:

$$dAmbTrans(i) \equiv \{((\delta,\alpha),(dcmds,acmds),(\delta',\alpha')) \mid \\ (\delta, dcmds, \delta') \in dTrans(\{j \mid home(\alpha,i) \in vicinity(\alpha,j)\}, i) \land \\ (\alpha, acmds, \alpha') \in AmbTrans(i)\}$$

Here the first parameter of $dTrans$ gets instantiated to the set of dAmbISMs belonging to the same ambient as i or its direct subambient, which implements the locality feature mentioned in §5.1.

Composite Runs. Composite runs of dAmbISMs inherit the elements of both dISMs and AmbISMs runs. This is reflected in their definition, which combines parameters and calls to auxiliary functions in the appropriate way.

For a family A of dAmbISMs (of type $ISM(daCMDs, daSTATE \times \Pi_{i \in I} \Sigma_i)$), a subset r of its members that shall be running initially, and an initial ambient state α_0, $dAmbCRuns(A, r, \alpha_0)$ gives the composite runs of dynamic Ambient ISMs, of type $\wp((CONF(daSTATE \times \Pi_{i \in I} \Sigma_i))^*)$. It is defined as

$$dAmbCRuns(A, r, \alpha_0) \equiv CRuns((\lambda(\delta,\alpha).\ local\_Out(set\_In\_Out(A,\delta),\alpha), \\ (init\_dSTATE(A,r), \alpha_0), dAmbTrans)$$

Note that since $local\_Out$ takes the input/output interfaces as set by set_In_Out, it further restricts the output interface (according to the ambient structure) taking into account also port ownership, enabledness, and running state.

Basic Properties. The properties of dAmbISMs are those of dISMs and AmbISMs in the sense that all constraints, plus the additional locality constraint, are combined by logical conjunction. In particular:

- locality of Ambient ISMs further restricts outputs of dynamic ISMs
- enabledness and the running state of dynamic ISMs restrict the transitions of Ambient ISMs, in particular their outputs
- locality restricts dynamic ISM manipulation
- composite runs preserve the well-formedness of parallel composition

5.3 Expressing the Refined Distributed Accumulation Example

The refined version of the distributed accumulation example of §2.1 presented here uses the dAmbISM formalism which is a combination of dynamic ISMs and ambient ISMs. Therefore the ISM commands in the following ISM theory section are expressed by a pair of two command lists where the first element represents dynamic and the second one ambient commands. In the refined example we demonstrate the additional usage of dynamic ISM commands: enabling and disabling ports, and conveying ports to other ISMs. In contrast to §4.3 here we list only the modified parts. Parts not mentioned do not change much[7].

theory DistributedAccumulation2 = ISM˙package:

The new definitions of types are extended by the corresponding elements for the new ISM theory section of the representative agent. The identifier type is extended by the RA identifier. The port type is extended by the new RAData port, the RAReq port, and the Request2 port. The ambient type is extended by the RA_amb ambient. The message types are extended by the possibility that an ISM identifier can be transmitted. The instance of dynamic ambients commands that we use here is:

types DA˙cmds = "(id, port, ambient) dacmds"

Definition of All ISM States. The agent control state gets extended by two new values Notify and Notify2 which handle the choice of looking for an representative agent if the agent platform does not support the standard communication interfaces. The data state of the agent is extended by a field named rp used by the agent for remembering a reply port.

Definition of Agent. The agent interface is extented by the additional output port RAReq which is used for communication with the representative agent if present. The transitions learn, migrate, and result do not change, initread and read change slightly and three new transitions are added. The transition initread is the same as before except for the new postcondition *post rp :=* "AGData" which assigns the port name AGData to the local data variable rp.

For the case that the agent platform has incompatible interfaces, the agent tries with transition initread2 to migrate into a representative agent ambient in order to use it for accessing the agent platform. After migration the agent tells the representative agent its port AGData and its identifier AG. The next transition waits for the name of the data port for the platform communication. Then the agent migrates back to the platform top level where it is able to receive the value.

    initread2: — try to go to representative agent environment, if present

---

[7] the complete theory sources are available from [ISM]

Decide → Notify
  pre "route s ≠ []"
  cmd "([],[In RA˙amb])"

init˙ra:
  Notify → Notify2
  out "RAReq" "[Port AGData, Ident AG]"

Note that `initread2` and `init_ra` cannot be combined into a single transition because output to the representative agent is possible only after migrating into it.

done˙ra: — the repres. agent delegates the agent to use the negotiated port
  Notify2 → Read
  in "AGData" "[Port p]"
  cmd "([], [Out RA˙amb])"
  post rp := "p"

After reading the value send by the platform via $rp\ s$, the agent disables the dynamic data port.

read: — read the addend of the next platform
  Read → Migrate
  in "rp s" "[Value a]"
  cmd "(if rp s = AGData then [] else [Disable (rp s)], [])"
  post accu := "accu s + a"

Definition of Representative Agent. Starting with the port `RAData 1`, the representative agent reads via the `RAReq` port the reply port and identifier of requesting agents. It tells the platform and the agent its dynamically generated data port name `RAData n` and conveys this data port to the agent ISM. Then the representative agent generates with `New` a new port `RAData n'` for any further requests.

ism RAgent =
  ports "port"
    inputs "-RAReq" ∪ -RAData n —n. True"" — all ports potentially owned

  outputs "-Request2""
  messages "message"
  commands "DA˙cmds" **default** "([],[])"
  states state
    data "port" **init** "RAData 1" **name** "np" — hold pre-allocated next port
  transitions

loop: — get reply port, tell platform port, convey port, create next port
   in "RAReq"   "[Port p, Ident pn]"
   out "Request2" "[Port np]",
      "p"   "[Port np]"
   cmd "([Convey np pn, New (RAData n')], [])"
   post "RAData n'"

Definition of Incompatible and Restrictive Platform 2. Platform 2 is now incompatible and restrictive: it accepts requests only via the non-standard port Request2 and transmits values only via (priviliged) dynamic ports RAData n.

request:
   Loop → Loop
   in "Request2" "[Port (RAData n)]"
   out "RAData n" "[Value 2]"

Definition of the Overall System. The System and Runs are extended by the representative agent identifer RA and the mapping of parent and home relations RA_amb ↦ AP_amb 2 and RA ↦ RA_amb.

Similarly to the basic agent system example of §2.1 it is possible to express and verify a theorem that proofs the final exchange of the value 3 with the homebase. Thus the enhancement of dynamic commands allows additionally easy expression and verification of delegation and (de)activation of ports in mobile scenarios.

6 Related Work

Depart from the process calculi [CG98,BCC01] mentioned before other work addressing the extension of state based approaches is available with particular aspects of dynamic and mobile behavior, e.g., [HS97,Zap02]. Also other approaches exist where the notion of location plays a major role. For instance, this is the case for Mobile Unity [RJH02] where location is modeled explicitly as a distinguished variable that belongs to the state of a mobile component and which provides an assertional-style proof logic. Other models start with different assumptions and impose a predefined structure on the space (typically hierachical). For instance, in the coordination model based specification language MobiS [Mas99a], an enhanced version of PoliS [Mas99b], a specification denotes a tree of nested spaces that dynamically evolves in time.

We believe that the generic ISM approach, in particular the dynamic and mobile extensions, have, in difference to above mentioned approaches, the advantage of combining the following properties: Expressiveness (from very abstract to very fine-grained), Flexibility (ease of further enhancements for special purpose system requirements), Simplicity (compositional state oriented view) and Availability of Tools (open-source editing and proving environment Isabelle).

7 Conclusion and Further Work

We have introduced Ambient Interactive State Machines (AmbISMs) featuring a variant of boxed ambients and their extension by dynamic communication (dAmbISMs), two formalisms for modeling and verifying (dynamic) mobile systems. We have demonstrated the practicability and benefits of using (dynamic) ambient ISMs in modeling a basic and refined mobile agent system example.

Both formalisms provide concepts for expressing mobility like locations, migration, and restricted input and output visibility easily. The possibility of expressing mobile systems in a stateful way gives the opportunity to refine a mobile system in detail and make the information flow clear. The ISM approach provides easy integration of states and calculations within processes, while Isabelle/HOL contributes an expressive specification metalanguage and powerful proof techniques. Our approach offers the designer the possibility of doing verification by expressing and proving theorems in Isabelle/HOL and thus checking in advance whether a system fulfils the desired properties. Furthermore the designer or user can combine the dynamic or mobile features (dISM, AmbISM, dAmbISM) as the application demands it and thus disburden from overloaded additional structure.

Further work concentrates on the usage of the AmbISMs and dAmbISM on designing and modeling security related protocols within mobile systems like mobile agent systems. Also the verification of security properties including further support for theorem proving is a major area of future investigations.

Acknowledgement

This work was supported in part by the German Federal Ministry of Economics and Labor (BMWA) under research grant no. 01MD931.

References

[BCC01] Michele Bugliesi, Giuseppe Castagna, and Silvia Crafa. Boxed ambients. In *TACS 2001, 4th. International Symposium on Theoretical Aspects of Computer Science*, number 2215 in LNCS. Springer-Verlag, 2001.
[CC99] Common Criteria for Information Technology Security Evaluation (CC), Version 2.1, 1999. ISO/IEC 15408.
[CG98] Luca Cardelli and Andrew D. Gordon. Mobile ambients. In Maurice Nivat, editor, *FOSSACS '98*, volume 1378 of *LNCS*. Springer-Verlag, 1998.
[Hoa80] C. A. R. Hoare. Communicating sequential processes. In R. M. McKeag and A. M. Macnaghten, editors, *On the construction of programs – an advanced course*, pages 229–254. Cambridge University Press, 1980.

[HS97]   Ursula Hinkel and Katharina Spies. Spezifikationsmethodik für mobile, dynamische FOCUS-Netze. In A. Wolisz, I. Schieferdecker, and A. Rennoch, editors, *Formale Beschreibungstechniken für verteilte Systeme, GI/ITG-Fachgespräch 1997*, 1997.
[ISM]   ISM homepage. http://ddvo.net/ISM/.
[MAP]   Project MAP homepage. http://www.map21.de/.
[Mas99a]   C. Mascolo. Mobis: A specification language for mobile systems. In *LNCS*. Springer-Verlag, 1999.
[Mas99b]   C. Mascolo. Specification, analysis, and prototyping of mobile systems. In *Doctoral Symposium of the 21st International Conference on Software Engineering. Los Angeles, CA*. IEEE, 1999.
[Mil80]   Robin Milner. *A Calculus of Communication Systems*, volume 92 of *LNCS*. Springer-Verlag, 1980.
[MPW92]   Robin Milner, Joachim Parrow, and David Walker. A calculus of mobile processes - parts i+ii. *Information and Computation*, 100(1):1–77, September 1992.
[Ohe02]   David von Oheimb. Interacting State Machines: *a stateful approach to proving security*. In Ali Abdallah, Peter Ryan, and Steve Schneider, editors, *Proceedings from the BCS-FACS International Conference on Formal Aspects of Security 2002*, volume 2629 of *LNCS*. Springer-Verlag, 2002. http://ddvo.net/papers/ISMs.html.
[OL02]   David von Oheimb and Volkmar Lotz. Formal Security Analysis with Interacting State Machines. In *Proc. of the 7th ESORICS*. Spinger, 2002. http://ddvo.net/papers/FSA_ISM.html. A more detailed journal version is submitted for publication.
[OL03]   David von Oheimb and Volkmar Lotz. Generic Interacting State Machines and their instantiation, 2003. Submitted for publication.
[Pau94]   Lawrence C. Paulson. *Isabelle: A Generic Theorem Prover*, volume 828 of *LNCS*. Springer-Verlag, 1994. For an up-to-date description, see http://isabelle.in.tum.de/.
[RJH02]   G.-C. Roman, C. Julien, and Q. Huang. Formal specification and design of mobile systems. In *Proceedings of the 7th International Workshop on Formal Methods for Parallel Programming: Theory and Applications*, 2002.
[Zap02]   Júlia Zappe. Towards a mobile TLA. In *Proceedings of the 7th ESSLLI Student Session, 14th European Summer School in Logic, Language and Information, Trento, Italy*, 2002.

Composing Temporal-Logic Specifications with Machine Assistance[*]

Jei-Wen Teng[1] and Yih-Kuen Tsay[2][**]

[1] Institute of Information Science, Academia Sinica, Taipei, Taiwan,
jackteng@iis.sinica.edu.tw
[2] Dept. of Information Management, National Taiwan University, Taipei, Taiwan,
tsay@im.ntu.edu.tw

Abstract. This paper presents an adaptation of a compositional verification framework based on linear-time temporal logic and its mechanization in PVS. We suggest an approach to avoiding the inconvenience of handling quantification over flexible variables in a general-purpose theorem prover. The use of the mechanized framework is illustrated by proving the mutual exclusion property of a token ring in a compositional manner.

Keywords: Assumption-Guarantee, Component-Based Software, Compositional Specification, Compositional Verification, Concurrent Systems, Formal Correctness, PVS, Temporal Logic, Theorem Proving.

1 Introduction

We consider compositional verification of concurrent systems and its mechanization in a general-purpose theorem prover. Our primary goal in this paper is to adapt a compositional framework based on linear-time temporal logic so as to make it more easily mechanizable and hence more practically useful. This is part of our continuous effort in extending the line of research on applications of temporal logic.

A concurrent system is normally the parallel composition of several modules. In the compositional verification of such a system, one seeks to deduce properties of the system from properties of its constituent modules. Though lately considered a promising alternative to harnessing the state-explosion problem [1,2], compositional approaches had come to existence primary for software methodological reasons. They are particularly indispensable when only the properties (or requirement specifications), not the code, of some modules are available. This situation has become more common with the growing prominence of component-based software [3].

---

[*] This work was supported in part by the National Science Council, Taiwan (R.O.C.) under grants NSC 87-2213-E-002-015 and NSC 88-2213-E-002-064 and by Center for Information and Electronics Technologies (CIET), National Taiwan University.

[**] Corresponding author. Contact him for a full version of this paper.

Temporal logic is one convenient formalism for specifying and reasoning about the behaviors of a concurrent system. The idea of representing concurrent systems and their specifications as temporal-logic formulas was first proposed by Pnueli [4]. Semantically, a concurrent system may be identified with a set of infinite computations or sequences of states, each of which represents a possible execution of the system (the last state is repeated indefinitely if the execution terminates). The system can thus be specified by a (linear-time) temporal logic formula in the sense that the executions of the system are exactly those satisfying the formula. Fundamental concepts in formal verification such as refinement (implementation), hiding, and parallel composition can all be conveniently treated with the logic [5–8].

Compositional verification requires an effective formulation for specifying the modules of a system and assumption-guarantee (A-G) specifications are one such formulation. Each module of a system interacts with other modules, referred to as its environment, and will behave properly only if its environment does. (Modules are open systems.) When specifying a module, one should therefore give (1) assumed properties about its environment and (2) guaranteed properties of the module if its environment obeys the assumption. This type of specification is essentially a generalization of pre and post-conditions for sequential programs [9]. The generalization was adopted in the early 1980's by Misra and Chandy [10], Jones [11], and Lamport [12] and became the so-called *assumption-guarantee* (also known as rely-guarantee or assumption-commitment) paradigm.

In [8, 13], Jonsson and Tsay proposed a compositional framework based on linear-time temporal logic (LTL) [14, 6] that follows the assumption-guarantee paradigm. One distinct feature of their work is that the formulation of A-G specifications as well as the derived composition rules are syntactic and entirely within LTL. This makes the framework amenable to mechanization in a general-purpose theorem prover once the LTL basis has been adequately formalized. We adapt the compositional framework so as to make it even more readily mechanizable.

One major change in the adaptation is that we impose more syntactic restriction on the formulas that specify the assumption and the guarantee, without losing much expressiveness. Another change is that we describe the transitions of a system from the current state to the next state rather than from the previous state to the current state. This change makes A-G specifications longer, but it does not really increase what needs to be proved when composing such specifications. We mechanize the adapted framework in PVS [15], a general-purpose theorem prover based on higher-order logic. Handling hiding (existential quantification over flexible variables of a temporal formula) in a general-purpose theorem prover is not as convenient as in hand proofs. We suggest an approach to avoiding this inconvenience.

The adapted and mechanized framework, like its origin, consists of a formulation of A-G specifications for specifying system modules and proof rules for composing such specifications. To illustrate its main usage, we formally prove in a compositional way the mutual exclusion property of a token ring that is composed of a servers module and a clients module. The servers module is responsible for circulating a unique token but is specified only as a "black box," i.e., the serves module is specified as an A-G temporal formula and its code is not disclosed.

2 Preliminaries

2.1 LTL

LTL, the linear-time temporal logic of Manna and Pnueli [14,6], is a logic for expressing and reasoning about properties of infinite sequences of states, where each state is an assignment to a predefined set of variables. The language of LTL assumes a set of constant, function, and predicate symbols with fixed interpretations. It classifies each variable as being *rigid*—having the same interpretation in all states of a sequence or *flexible*—with no restrictions on interpretation in different states; flexible variables are typically used for representing program or control variables, whose value may change over time. Primitive temporal formulas in LTL, called *state formulas*, are built from variables, constants, functions, and predicates using the usual first-order logical connectives. A state formula is interpreted over a state where each variable in the formula is assigned a value; this is analogous to first-order logic.

The expressive power of LTL mainly comes from *temporal operators*. In this paper, we will explicitly use only four temporal operators: $\bigcirc$, $\square$, $\ominus$, and $\boxminus$. A general *temporal formula* is constructed by applying temporal operators and first-order logical connectives to state formulas. An LTL temporal formula is interpreted over an infinite sequence of states, relative to a position in that sequence. We give below the semantics for temporal formulas involving a quantifier or one of the four temporal operators:

- $(\sigma, i) \models \bigcirc \varphi$ iff $(\sigma, i+1) \models \varphi$. In other words, $\bigcirc \varphi$ (read as "next φ") holds at a position (of some sequence) if φ holds at the next position (of that sequence).
- $(\sigma, i) \models \square \varphi$ iff $\forall k \geq i : (\sigma, k) \models \varphi$. In other words, $\square \varphi$ (read as "henceforth φ" or "always φ") holds at a position if φ holds at that current and all following positions.
- $(\sigma, i) \models \ominus \varphi$ iff $(i > 0) \to ((\sigma, i-1) \models \varphi)$. In other words, $\ominus \varphi$ (read as "before φ") holds at position i if either position i is the first position (i.e., $i=0$) of the sequence or φ holds at position $i-1$.
- *first* $\stackrel{\Delta}{=} \ominus \textit{false}$, which is true only at position 0.
- $(\sigma, i) \models \boxminus \varphi$ iff $\forall k : 0 \leq k \leq i : (\sigma, k) \models \varphi$. In other words, $\boxminus \varphi$ (read as "so-far φ") holds at a position if φ holds at that position and all preceding positions;

A sequence σ' is called a *u-variant* of σ if σ' differs from σ in at most the interpretation given to u in each state; note that the restrictions of rigid variables must be observed.

- $(\sigma, i) \models \exists u : \varphi$ iff $(\sigma', i) \models \varphi$ for some u-*variant* σ' of σ. Intuitively, this means that the truth of $\exists u : \varphi$ for a flexible variable u depends on the existence of an infinite sequence of u-values (one for each state), rather than just a single value, such that φ can be satisfied. Existentially quantified flexible variables are internal (local) to a system and their values are inaccessible from outside.

We say that a sequence σ satisfies a formula φ if $(\sigma, 0) \models \varphi$, often abbreviated as $\sigma \models \varphi$. A formula φ is *valid*, denoted $\models \varphi$, if φ is satisfied by every sequence.

When using LTL to specify a system, one very often would want to express constraints on the state changes that the system can make. This requires a means for specifying the values of an expression in any two consecutive states (a position and its preceding position or a position and its next position) of a sequence. As one possible solution, Manna and Pnueli introduced the notation u^- for denoting the value of u in the preceding state and the notation u^+ (written also as u' in this paper) for denoting the value of u in the next state. (By convention, the interpretation of u^- at position 0 is the same as the interpretation of u at position 0.) Note that the new notations do not increase the expressive power of LTL, as any formula with "$-$"-superscribed or "$+$"-superscribed variables can be translated into an equivalent formula without such variables.

A formula without temporal operators but possibly with "$-$"-superscribed variables is called a *transition formula* (this definition is slightly different from that in [6], where a transition formula always contains $\neg$*first* as a conjunct) and a formula without temporal operators but possibly with "$+$"-superscribed or primed ("$'$"-superscribed) variables is called an *action formula*. A formula without any future operator $\bigcirc$, $\square$, or $\diamond$ (which is omitted in this paper) is called a *past formula*; in particular, a transition formula is a past formula. A *safety formula* is one that specifies a safety property. Of particular importance, formulas of the form $\square H$, where H is a past formula, are for certain safety formulas; they will be referred to as *canonical safety formulas*. $\square H$ is still a safety formula when H additionally contains the $\bigcirc$ future operator but in a non-nested manner; formulas of this form will be referred to as *quasi canonical safety formulas*. (In general, $\square H'$ is a safety formula if the truth of H' depends only on the present and past states and up to a finite fixed number of future states.)

2.2 Concurrent Systems as Temporal Formulas

A concurrent system consists of a set of variables, an initial condition on the variables, and a set of actions that specify how the system may change the values of its variables in an execution step. Semantically, a concurrent system is associated with a set of computations or sequences of states, each of which represents a possible execution of the system. For our purpose, we distinguish two kinds of specification: system specification and requirement specification.

System specifications are basically programs in the form of a temporal formula. Consider Program KEEP-AHEAD in Fig. 1. The system specification of

$$
\boxed{\begin{array}{c}\text{local } a, b : \text{integer where } a = b = 0 \\ P_a :: \begin{bmatrix} \text{loop forever do} \\ [\, a := b + 1 \,] \end{bmatrix} \parallel P_b :: \begin{bmatrix} \text{loop forever do} \\ [\, b := a + 1 \,] \end{bmatrix}\end{array}}
$$

Fig. 1. Program KEEP-AHEAD.

KEEP-AHEAD is given by $\Phi_{\text{KEEP-AHEAD}}$ as defined below.

$$\Phi_{\text{KEEP-AHEAD}} \stackrel{\triangle}{=} (a = 0) \wedge (b = 0) \wedge \Box \begin{pmatrix} (a' = b + 1) \wedge (b' = b) \\ \vee\; (b' = a + 1) \wedge (a' = a) \\ \vee\; (a' = a) \wedge (b' = b) \end{pmatrix}$$

The formula $\Phi_{\text{KEEP-AHEAD}}$ states that the values of a and b are initially 0. It also states via the disjunction of three action formulas that, in each step of an execution, either the value of a becomes $b + 1$ (while the value of b is unchanged), the value of b becomes $a + 1$, or nothing is changed. The action formula $(a' = a) \wedge (b' = b)$ is called a stuttering step and is included to make the specification "invariant under stuttering."

We regard system specifications as formal definitions of concurrent systems so that we can do without a programming language and formal semantics of the programming language; programs in this paper are informal notations for readability. The (safety) formula in a system specification can be put in the quasi canonical form, specifically in the form of $\Box((\textit{first} \to \textit{Init}) \wedge N)$ ($\equiv \textit{Init} \wedge \Box N$), where $\textit{Init}$ is a state formula and N the disjunction of several action formulas.

Requirement specification is the usual type of temporal-logic specification. A property is represented by a temporal formula. A system (program) S is said to satisfy a formula φ if every computation of S satisfies φ. Let Φ_S denote the system specification of S. We will regard $\Phi_S \to \varphi$ as the formal definition of the fact that S satisfies φ, denoted as $S \models \varphi$. The safety formula in a requirement specification can usually be put in the canonical or quasi canonical form.

2.3 Parallel Composition as Conjunction

Program KEEP-AHEAD can be decomposed as the parallel composition of two modules as shown in Fig. 2. A module may read but not change the value of an **in** (input) variable. A *compatible* environment of a module may read but not change the value of an **own out** (owned output) variable of the module. In the system $M_a \parallel M_b$, M_b is the environment of M_a and M_a is the environment of M_b; both are clearly compatible with each other.

The system specifications Φ_{M_a} and Φ_{M_b} of modules M_a and M_b respectively are defined as follows:

$$\Phi_{M_a} \stackrel{\triangle}{=} (a = 0) \wedge \Box \begin{pmatrix} (a' = b + 1) \wedge (b' = b) \\ \vee\; (a' = a) \end{pmatrix}$$

```
┌─────────────────────────────────────┐     ┌─────────────────────────────────────┐
│ module  M_a                         │     │ module  M_b                         │
│ in       b  : integer               │     │ in       a  : integer               │
│ own out  a  : integer where a = 0   │  ║  │ own out  b  : integer where b = 0   │
│                                     │     │                                     │
│         loop forever do             │     │         loop forever do             │
│         [ a := b + 1 ]              │     │         [ b := a + 1 ]              │
└─────────────────────────────────────┘     └─────────────────────────────────────┘
```

Fig. 2. Program KEEP-AHEAD as the parallel composition of two modules.

$$\Phi_{M_b} \triangleq (b = 0) \wedge \Box \left(\begin{array}{l} (b' = a+1) \wedge (a' = a) \\ \vee\ (b' = b) \end{array} \right)$$

It is perhaps more accurate to say that Φ_{M_a} is the system specification of an imaginary system composed of M_a and an arbitrary but compatible environment; analogously, for Φ_{M_b}. A little calculation shows that

$$\models \Phi_{M_a} \wedge \Phi_{M_b} \leftrightarrow \Phi_{\text{KEEP-AHEAD}}.$$

This formally confirms that $M_a \parallel M_b$ is equivalent to Program KEEP-AHEAD.

A module M is said to satisfy a formula φ if every computation of M satisfies φ. Let Φ_M denote the system specification of M. Like in the case of specifying properties of a concurrent system, we will regard $\Phi_M \to \varphi$ as the formal definition of the fact that M satisfies φ, denoted as $M \models \varphi$. Since parallel composition is conjunction, it follows that, if M is a module of system S, then $M \models \varphi$ implies $S \models \varphi$.

3 Compositional Verification in LTL

We briefly review the temporal-logic framework developed by Jonsson and Tsay [8,13] for compositional specification and verification. Compositional verification hinges on an effective formulation for specifying the modules of a system. A key ingredient of their framework is the definition of assumption-guarantee (A-G) formulas for specifying properties of a module. Two types of A-G formulas had been defined. We consider only *strong* A-G formulas, referred to simply as A-G formulas. A-G formulas have a mutual induction mechanism built in and can be more readily composed.

Assuming that the assumption and the guarantee are canonical safety formulas respectively of the forms $\Box H_A$ and $\Box H_G$ (where H_A and H_G are past formulas), an A-G formula $\Box H_A \triangleright \Box H_G$ is defined as follows:

$$\Box H_A \triangleright \Box H_G \triangleq \Box(\ominus \boxminus H_A \to H_G).$$

The formula $\Box(\ominus \boxminus H_A \to H_G)$, which is equivalent to $\Box(\ominus \boxminus H_A \to \boxminus H_G)$, essentially says that $\boxminus H_G$ holds at least one step longer than $\boxminus H_A$ does; in particular, it asserts that H_G holds initially. Suppose that H_{G_1} and H_{G_2} are past formulas. Then,

$$\models (\Box H_{G_1} \triangleright \Box H_{G_2}) \wedge (\Box H_{G_2} \triangleright \Box H_{G_1}) \rightarrow \Box H_{G_1} \wedge \Box H_{G_2}.$$

The above result is essentially the composition principle formulated by Misra and Chandy [10]. It illustrates that A-G formulas have a mutual induction mechanism built in and hence permit "circular reasoning" (there is of course no real cycle if one looks at the semantic models and reasons state by state from the initial one), i.e., deducing new properties from mutually dependent properties. Below is a more general rule for composing A-G specifications:

Theorem 1. *Suppose that $\Box H_{A_i}$ and $\Box H_{G_i}$, for $1 \leq i \leq n$, $\Box H_A$, and $\Box H_G$ are canonical formulas. Then,*

1. $\models \Box \left(\boxminus H_A \wedge \boxminus \bigwedge_{i=1}^{n} H_{G_i} \rightarrow H_{A_j} \right)$, *for* $1 \leq j \leq n$
2. $\models \Box \left(\ominus \boxminus H_A \wedge \boxminus \bigwedge_{i=1}^{n} H_{G_i} \rightarrow H_G \right)$

$$\models \bigwedge_{i=1}^{n} (\Box H_{A_i} \triangleright \Box H_{G_i}) \rightarrow (\Box H_A \triangleright \Box H_G)$$

Intuitively, Premise 1 of the above composition rule says that the assumption about the environment of a module should follow from the guarantees of other modules and the assumption about the environment of the entire system (which may in turn be a larger module), while Premise 2 says that the guarantee of the entire system should follow from the guarantees of individual modules and the assumption about its environment.

We postpone the treatment of hidden local variables till Section 5. We will not consider liveness properties in this paper, as the built-in mutual induction mechanism (which is most characteristic of an A-G formula) really works for safety properties only.

4 Adaptation and Mechanization

Mechanization of Jonsson and Tsay's compositional framework in PVS is not as straightforward as it might appear. In the definition of an A-G formula, the assumption A and the guarantee G are assumed to be given respectively as $\Box H_A$ and $\Box H_G$, where H_A and H_G are past formulas. The assumption leads to a more succinct formulation of A-G specifications and rules for composing such specifications. Unfortunately, in a general-purpose theorem prover such as PVS it is inconvenient to enforce the restriction of a temporal formula being a past one. Even if we consider only a restricted form of past formula, there is still a nuisance of proving type checking conditions such as "$i > 0 \rightarrow i - 1 \geq 0$" that arise due to past temporal operators.

For the ease of mechanization, we restrict assumptions and guarantees to be of the quasi canonical form $\Box((\textit{first} \rightarrow \textit{Init}) \wedge N)$ ($\equiv \textit{Init} \wedge \Box N$), where

N is an action formula that relates the current state and the next state of the system. This restriction does lose much expressiveness, as quasi canonical safety formulas are typical for specifying safety properties of a system (see Section 2.2). As a result, $A \triangleright G$ (i.e., $\Box((\mathit{first} \to \mathit{Init}_A) \land N_A) \triangleright \Box((\mathit{first} \to \mathit{Init}_G) \land N_G))$ translates into

$$\mathit{Init}_G \land (\mathit{Init}_A \to N_G) \land \Box(\boxminus((\mathit{first} \to \mathit{Init}_A) \land N_A) \to \bigcirc N_G)$$

This new formulation of A-G specifications is longer, but it does not really increase what has to be proved when such specifications are composed. The formalization in PVS is as follows:

```
Init_A,Init_G: VAR sform
N_A,N_G: VAR aform

|>(Init_A,N_A,Init_G,N_G):tform =
            (s_t(Init_G) and a_t(s_a(Init_A) => N_G) and
            [](H(ia(Init_A,N_A)) => O(H(ia(Init_G,N_G)))))
```

where sform, aform, and tform (declared elsewhere) are respectively the types of state formula, action formula, and temporal formula, s_t is a function promoting a state formula to a temporal formula, a_t promotes an action formula to a temporal formula, s_a promotes a state formula to an action formula, and ia(Init,N) is a temporal formula representing $(\mathit{first} \to \mathit{Init}) \land N$. More details can be found in the full paper.

The composition rule is changed accordingly as follows; for readability, parentheses "(" and ")" are replaced by square brackets "[" and "]" in some places.

Theorem 2. *Suppose that* $A_i \equiv \mathit{Init}_{A_i} \land \Box N_{A_i}$, $G_i \equiv \mathit{Init}_{G_i} \land \Box N_{G_i}$, $A \equiv \mathit{Init}_A \land \Box N_A$, *and* $G \equiv \mathit{Init}_G \land \Box N_G$, *where* N_{A_i}, N_{G_i}, N_A, *and* N_G *are action formulas. Then,*

1. For $1 \leq j \leq n$,
$$\models [(\mathit{Init}_A \land \bigwedge_{i=1}^{n} \mathit{Init}_{G_i}) \to \mathit{Init}_{A_j}] \land$$
$$\Box[\boxminus((\mathit{first} \to \mathit{Init}_A) \land N_A) \land \boxminus \bigwedge_{i=1}^{n}((\mathit{first} \to \mathit{Init}_{G_i}) \land N_{G_i})$$
$$\to ((\mathit{first} \to \mathit{Init}_{A_j}) \land N_{A_j})]$$

2. $\models [\bigwedge_{i=1}^{n} \mathit{Init}_{G_i} \to \mathit{Init}_G] \land$
$$[\bigwedge_{i=1}^{n} (\mathit{Init}_{G_i} \land N_{G_i}) \to N_G] \land$$
$$\Box[\boxminus((\mathit{first} \to \mathit{Init}_A) \land N_A) \land \bigcirc\boxminus \bigwedge_{i=1}^{n}((\mathit{first} \to \mathit{Init}_{G_i}) \land N_{G_i})$$
$$\to \bigcirc((\mathit{first} \to \mathit{Init}_G) \land N_G)]$$

$$\overline{\models \bigwedge_{i=1}^{n}[\Box((\mathit{first} \to \mathit{Init}_{A_i}) \land N_{A_i}) \triangleright \Box((\mathit{first} \to \mathit{Init}_{G_i}) \land N_{G_i})]}$$
$$\to [\Box((\mathit{first} \to \mathit{Init}_A) \land N_A) \triangleright \Box((\mathit{first} \to \mathit{Init}_G) \land N_G)]$$

Below is the PVS formalization of the composition rule for two modules; more details can be found in the full paper.

```
composition_rule: THEOREM
   valid(s_t(Init_A and Init_G1 and Init_G2 => Init_A1) and
         [](H(ia(Init_A,N_A)) and
            H(ia(Init_G1 and Init_G2,N_G1 and N_G2))
            => H(ia(Init_A1,N_A1))))
   and
   valid(s_t(Init_A and Init_G1 and Init_G2 => Init_A2) and
         [](H(ia(Init_A,N_A)) and
            H(ia(Init_G1 and Init_G2,N_G1 and N_G2))
            => H(ia(Init_A2,N_A2))))
   and
   valid(s_t(Init_G1 and Init_G2 => Init_G) and
         a_t(s_a(Init_A and Init_G1 and Init_G2) and
            N_G1 and N_G2 => N_G) and
         [](H(ia(Init_A,N_A)) and
            O(H(ia(Init_G1 and Init_G2,N_G1 and N_G2)))
            => O(H(ia(Init_G,N_G)))))
   =>
   valid( |>(Init_A1,N_A1,Init_G1,N_G1) and
          |>(Init_A2,N_A2,Init_G2,N_G2) =>
          |>(Init_A,N_A,Init_G,N_G))
```

5 Hiding

Hiding is a common technique for making specifications more abstract and corresponds to existential quantification over flexible variables in LTL. Jonsson and Tsay [8] also considered A-G specifications where the assumption and the guarantee parts involve hiding. We will summarize the relevant part of their work below but with a slightly different style of presentation. In particular, we make the free variables of a formula explicit and we also incorporate a simplification to the definition of an A-G formula. A temporal formula φ may be written as $\varphi(z)$ or $\varphi(z,x)$ to indicate that the free (flexible) variables of φ are among the tuple z or the tuples z, x of variables. We write $\exists x \colon \varphi(z,x)$ to hide the x part of variables of a formula $\varphi(z,x)$.

An A-G formula with assumption $\Box(\exists x\colon \boxminus H_A(z,x))$ and guarantee $\Box(\exists y\colon \boxminus H_G(z,y))$ is defined below. The formula $\Box(\exists x \colon \boxminus H_A(z,x))$ represents the "safety part" (formally, safety closure) of $\exists x\colon \Box H_A(z,x)$ when H_A includes a stuttering step. The formula $\exists x\colon \Box H_A(z,x)$ may not be a safety formula, though $\Box H_A(z,x)$ is a safety one.[1]

---

[1] For example, $\exists a\colon \Box[(\mathit{first} \to (b=0)) \land (((a>0) \land (a'=a-1) \land (b'=b+1)) \lor ((a'=a) \land (b'=b)))]$ is not a safety formula. Because, a sequence σ in which b is incremented indefinitely does not satisfy the formula, while each prefix of σ is a prefix of some sequence that does.

$$\Box(\exists x\colon \boxminus H_A(z,x)) \triangleright \Box(\exists y\colon \boxminus H_G(z,y)) \triangleq \Box[\ominus(\exists x\colon \boxminus H_A(z,x)) \to (\exists y\colon H_G(z,y))]$$

Like in the case without hiding, the defining formula $\Box[\ominus(\exists x\colon \boxminus H_A(z,x)) \to (\exists y\colon H_G(z,y))]$ (which is shorter than but equivalent to $\Box[\ominus(\exists x\colon \boxminus H_A(z,x)) \to (\exists y\colon \boxminus H_G(z,y))]$, the original defining formula in [8]) says that $\exists y\colon \boxminus H_G(z,y)$ holds at least one step longer than $\exists x\colon \boxminus H_A(z,x)$ does. Below is a general rule for composing A-G specifications with safety assumptions and guarantees.

Theorem 3. *Assume that the tuples z, x, y, x_1, ..., x_n, y_1, ..., y_n of variables are pairwise disjoint. Then,*

1. *For $1 \le j \le n$,*

$$\models \Box\Big[(\exists x\colon \boxminus H_A(z,x)) \land (\exists y_1 \ldots y_n\colon \boxminus \bigwedge_{i=1}^{n} H_{G_i}(z,y_i)) \to (\exists x_j\colon H_{A_j}(z,x_j))\Big]$$

2. $\models \Box\Big[\ominus(\exists x\colon \boxminus H_A(z,x)) \land (\exists y_1 \ldots y_n\colon \boxminus \bigwedge_{i=1}^{n} H_{G_i}(z,y_i)) \to (\exists y\colon H_G(z,y))\Big]$

$$\frac{}{\models \bigwedge_{i=1}^{n} \Box[\ominus(\exists x_i\colon \boxminus H_{A_i}(z,x_i)) \to (\exists y_i\colon H_{G_i}(z,y_i))]}$$
$$\to \Box[\ominus(\exists x\colon \boxminus H_A(z,x)) \to (\exists y\colon H_G(z,y))]$$

The rule can be specialized for proving that an A-G specification refines another and that some module implements an A-G specification.

Introducing existential quantification over a flexible variable of a temporal formula in PVS (and in other general-purpose theorem provers such as HOL) is not as convenient as in hand proofs. The state of a system is typically represented in PVS as a tuple of named components, each corresponding to a flexible variable of the system. One is allowed to quantify over the entire tuple, but not its components individually. In particular, one may not universally quantify over some component while existentially quantify over another of the same tuple. It may be possible to divide the state of a system into the external and the internal parts represented as two separate tuples so that one can existentially quantify the internal part. However, as specifications are composed, it is common for an external variable to become internal in a different context.

We propose a way to avoid dividing the state of a system and yet be able to imitate the effect of hiding. The formulas in both premises of Theorem 3 are in a weaker form than the usual refinement relation between two canonical formulas with hidden variables, because the existential quantifications occur inside the $\Box$ operator. Like in the usual case, we may find appropriate state functions $f_1, \ldots, f_n, g$ that map from the free variables of $H_A, H_{G_1}, \ldots, H_{G_n}$, i.e., the tuples $z, x, y_1, \cdots, y_n$ of variables, to the domains of $x_1, \ldots, x_n, y$ and try to establish the validity of following formulas:

1. $\Box\Big[\boxminus H_A(z,x) \land \boxminus \bigwedge_{i=1}^{n} H_{G_i}(z,y_i) \to H_{A_j}(z, f_j/x_j)\Big]$, for $1 \le j \le n$.

2. $\Box\Big[\ominus \boxminus H_A(z,x) \land \boxminus \bigwedge_{i=1}^{n} H_{G_i}(z,y_i) \to H_G(z, g/y)\Big]$.

The above formulas respectively are in the same form as those in the premises of the following rule, which is obtained from Theorem 3 by removing all existential quantifications.

1. $\models \Box\Big[\boxminus H_A(z,x) \wedge \boxminus \bigwedge_{i=1}^{n} H_{G_i}(z,y_i) \to H_{A_j}(z,x_j)\Big]$, for $1 \leq j \leq n$

2. $\models \Box\Big[\ominus\boxminus H_A(z,x) \wedge \boxminus \bigwedge_{i=1}^{n} H_{G_i}(z,y_i) \to H_G(z,y)\Big]$

$\overline{\models \bigwedge_{i=1}^{n} \Box[\ominus\boxminus H_{A_i}(z,x_i) \to H_{G_i}(z,y_i)] \to \Box[\ominus\boxminus H_A(z,x) \to H_G(z,y)]}$

This rule is in fact identical to Theorem 1, which we have adapted as Theorem 2 (for two modules) and mechanized in PVS, except that the variables are made explicit and tuples of variables with different names are assumed to be disjoint. Our idea is to use Theorem 2 to bring out the proof obligations. The internal variables are declared as state functions separate from the tuple that represents the state of the system and the needed refinement mappings are introduced as axioms that relate those functions with appropriate free variables. Specifically, "$x_i = f_i$" is asserted for some f_i that is a state expression involving only free variables of $H_A, H_{G_1}, \ldots, H_{G_n}$, i.e., $z, x, y_1, \cdots, y_n$, and so on. Such refinement mappings should be easily checked by hand or by some external means for validity. As long as one follows the principles in defining a refinement mapping, there should be no inconsistency resulted from introducing the axioms.

6 Example: A Token Ring

The preceding compositional framework can be applied in various contexts. We consider an example that illustrates the following common situation in component-based software development:

> A developer designs an application module that is to be combined with an existing module to form a complete system. It is known that the existing module complies with certain specification, but its code is not disclosed. The developer nevertheless needs to verify that the complete system is correct.

The example concerns proper interaction between a group of servers, arranged as a ring, and a group of clients, each connected to a distinct server. By circulating a unique token around the ring, the servers module provides a mutual exclusion service to the clients module. When a client wants to enter the critical section, it sends a request to its server. The requested server, upon receiving the token from its predecessor server, will transmit the token (or any other equivalent representation) to the requesting client. Once the token is acquired, the client may proceed to the critical section. Upon exiting the critical section, the client sends the token back to its server, which will pass the token to the next server.

The safety property of the entire system, consisting of the servers and the clients modules, states that *at most one client is in the critical section at any time*. To apply the compositional framework, we envision that the servers module is specified by an A-G formula. We shall verify the safety property in a compositional way, given the A-G specification of the servers module and the code (system specification) of the clients module.

As illustrated in Fig. 3, $Server_i$ communicates with its client $Client_i$ via an input and an output channels: sin_i and $sout_i$. The input channel sin_i is for $Client_i$ to send a request or return the token to $Server_i$, while the output channel $sout_i$ is for $Server_i$ to send the token to $Client_i$. Both sin_i and $sout_i$ consist of three fields: sig, ack, and val of type boolean. A channel is clear and ready for sending when $sig = ack$. To send a message, the sender writes an appropriate value into val (*true* for a token and *false* for a request) and complements sig so that $sig = \neg ack$ to notify the receiver. The receiver reads the value of val and complements ack so that $sig = ack$ to clear the channel.

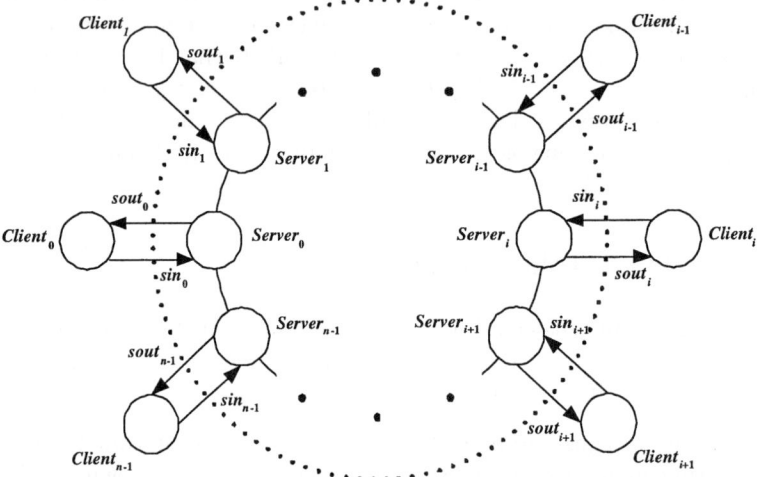

Fig. 3. A token ring with n servers and clients. The dotted full circle cutting through sin and $sout$ indicates the boundary of the $Servers$ and the $Clients$ modules.

Let M_s denote the ring of servers ($\|_{i=0}^{n-1} Server_i$) and M_c the collection of clients ($\|_{i=0}^{n-1} Client_i$). The entire system is therefore the parallel composition of the two modules: $M_s \| M_c$. The two modules interact with each other via the channel variables sin_0, ..., sin_{n-1} and $sout_0$, ..., $sout_{n-1}$. $Server_i$ controls the ack field of sin_i and the sig and val fields of $sout_i$, while $Client_i$ controls the sig and val fields of sin_i and the ack field of $sout_i$. Below are a few useful state and action formulas regarding a channel.

$$sinClear_i \triangleq sin_i.sig = sin_i.ack$$
$$sinToken_i \triangleq sin_i.sig \neq sin_i.ack \wedge sin_i.val = true$$
$$sinRequest_i \triangleq sin_i.sig \neq sin_i.ack \wedge sin_i.val = false$$
$$sinNotWritten_i \triangleq sin'_i.sig = sin_i.sig \wedge sin'_i.val = sin_i.val$$
$$sinNotRead_i \triangleq sin'_i.ack = sin_i.ack$$

Formulas $soutClear_i$, $soutToken_i$, $soutNotWritten_i$, and $soutNotRead_i$ are analogously defined, except that $soutToken_i$ is simplified as $sout_i.sig \neq sout_i.ack$.

6.1 A-G Specification of the Servers Module

What would be a reasonable specification for the servers module? For the servers module, the clients module is its environment. The servers module requires the cooperation of the clients module to provide the right service. Complying with the conventions of sending and receiving values through the channel variables, the servers' assumption about the clients should include the following:

1. Initially, no client has the token. To express this formally, we postulate an internal boolean variable $cliHasToken_i$ for each client i, whose truth value indicates whether client i is holding a token. Appropriate values for the channels incorporated, the initial condition should be:

$$Init_{A_s} \triangleq \bigwedge_{i=0}^{n-1} \neg cliHasToken_i \wedge \neg sin_i.sig \wedge \neg sout_i.ack \wedge sin_i.val$$

It is interesting to note that a single internal boolean variable for the entire clients module would not be adequate. The clients execute independently from one another, it is very well possible for two clients to hold a token at the same time if the servers behave incorrectly so as to generate an extra token in the system.

The stuttering step for each client should be:

$$cliUnchanged_i \triangleq (cliHasToken'_i = cliHasToken_i) \wedge sinNotWritten_i \wedge \\ soutNotRead_i$$

The stuttering step for the channel controlled by each server should be:

$$serChanUnchanged_i \triangleq sinNotRead_i \wedge soutNotWritten_i$$

The stuttering step for the channel controlled by the servers module should be:

$$serChanUnchanged \triangleq \bigwedge_{i=0}^{n-1} serChanUnchanged_i$$

2. In each step, the clients are assumed to do one of the following:

- Some client makes a request for the token by sending the request over the input channel of its server.

$$cliMakeRequest \triangleq [\bigvee_{i=0}^{n-1} \neg cliHasToken_i \wedge \neg cliHasToken'_i \wedge$$
$$sinClear_i \wedge sinRequest'_i \wedge soutNotRead_i \wedge$$
$$(\bigwedge_{j \neq i} cliUnchanged_j)] \wedge serChanUnchanged$$

- Some client with a token sitting in its input channel, i.e., the output channel of its server, grabs and keeps the token.

$$cliGrabToken \triangleq [\bigvee_{i=0}^{n-1} \neg cliHasToken_i \wedge cliHasToken'_i \wedge$$
$$soutToken_i \wedge soutClear'_i \wedge sinNotWritten_i \wedge$$
$$(\bigwedge_{j \neq i} cliUnchanged_j)] \wedge serChanUnchanged$$

- Some client holding a token sends the token back to its server, i.e., puts the token in the input channel of the server.

$$cliReleaseToken \triangleq [\bigvee_{i=0}^{n-1} cliHasToken_i \wedge \neg cliHasToken'_i \wedge$$
$$sinClear_i \wedge sinToken'_i \wedge soutNotRead_i \wedge$$
$$(\bigwedge_{j \neq i} cliUnchanged_j)] \wedge serChanUnchanged$$

- Do nothing, or more precisely, do not change the values of the interface variables controlled by the clients or the postulated internal variables $cliHasToken_0, \ldots, cliHasToken_{n-1}$.

$$cliUnchanged \triangleq \bigwedge_{i=0}^{n-1} cliUnchanged_i$$

The state transitions of the clients module should be:

$$\Box N_{A_s} \triangleq \Box(cliMakeRequest \vee cliGrabToken \vee cliReleaseToken \vee$$
$$cliUnchanged)$$

The assumption of the servers module should be:

$$A_s \triangleq Init_{A_s} \wedge \Box N_{A_s}$$

The formula A_s specifies the assumed behavior of the clients module. It involves not only the clients' interaction with the servers at the channels, but also the internal state of a client regarding whether the client holds the token via the postulated variables $cliHasToken_0, \ldots, cliHasToken_{n-1}$. We shall later try to relate $cliHasToken_0, \ldots, cliHasToken_{n-1}$ with the internal states of the clients when we compose the servers and the clients.

The guarantee of the servers module should state the following:

1. Initially, the servers module holds the token. Formally, we postulate an internal boolean variable $serHasToken_i$ for each server i, whose truth value indicates whether server i is holding a token. Appropriate values for the channels incorporated, the initial condition should be:

$$Init_{G_s} \triangleq [\bigvee_{i=0}^{n-1} serHasToken_i \land (\bigwedge_{j \neq i} \neg serHasToken_j)] \land$$
$$(\bigwedge_{i=0}^{n-1} \neg sin_i.ack \land \neg sout_i.sig)$$

The stuttering step for each server should be:

$$serUnchanged_i \triangleq (serHasToken'_i = serHasToken_i) \land sinNotRead_i \land soutNotWritten_i$$

The stuttering step for the channel controlled by each client should be:

$$cliChanUnchanged_i \triangleq sinNotWritten_i \land soutNotRead_i$$

The stuttering step for the channel controlled by the clients module should be:

$$cliChanUnchanged \triangleq \bigwedge_{i=0}^{n-1} cliChanUnchanged_i$$

2. In each step, the servers module will do one of the following:
   - Pass the token to the next server.

$$serPassToken \triangleq [\bigvee_{i=0}^{n-1} serHasToken_i \land \neg serHasToken'_i \land$$
$$\neg serHasToken_{(i+1)\%n} \land serHasToken'_{(i+1)\%n} \land$$
$$serChanUnchanged_i \land$$
$$serChanUnchanged_{(i+1)\%n} \land$$
$$(\bigwedge_{j=0}^{n-1} ((j \neq i) \land (j \neq ((i+1)\%n))) \to serUnchanged_j)]$$

   - Grant the token to one of the clients with an outstanding request.

$$serGrantToken \triangleq [\bigvee_{i=0}^{n-1} serHasToken_i \land \neg serHasToken'_i \land$$
$$sinRequest_i \land sinClear'_i \land soutToken'_i \land$$
$$(\bigwedge_{j \neq i} \neg serHasToken_j \land$$
$$(sinClear_j \lor sinRequest_j) \land serUnchanged_j)] \land$$
$$cliChanUnchanged$$

   - Reclaim the token that is sitting in the output channel of some client, or the input channel of some server.

$$serReclaimToken \triangleq [\bigvee_{i=0}^{n-1} \neg serHasToken_i \land serHasToken'_i \land$$
$$sinToken_i \land sinClear'_i \land soutNotWritten_i \land$$
$$(\bigwedge_{j \neq i} serUnchanged_j)] \land$$
$$cliChanUnchanged$$

- Do nothing, or more precisely, do not change the values of the interface variables controlled by the servers or the postulated internal variables $serHasToken_0, \ldots, serHasToken_{n-1}$.

$$serUnchanged \triangleq \bigwedge_{i=0}^{n-1} serUnchanged_i$$

The state transitions of the servers module should be:

$$\Box N_{G_s} \triangleq \Box(serPassToken \lor serGrantToken \lor serReclaimToken \lor serUnchanged)$$

The guarantee of the servers module G_s should be:

$$G_s \triangleq Init_{G_s} \land \Box N_{G_s}$$

The state of the system is represented in PVS as

```
state: TYPE = [# sin: [pid -> [# sig:bool, ack:bool, val:bool #]],
               sout: [pid -> [# sig:bool, ack:bool, val:bool #]],
               c_state: [pid -> nat] #]
```

Internal variables $serHasToken_0, \ldots, serHasToken_{n-1}, cliHasToken_0, \ldots, cliHasToken_{n-1}$ are declared separately (from the state variables of the system) as two functions:

```
serHasToken: [pid -> [state -> bool]]
cliHasToken: [pid -> [state -> bool]]
```

The A-G specification of the servers module in PVS can be found in the full paper.

6.2 Composing the Clients and the Servers

The code of the clients module may be given as a system specification in LTL, shown in Fig. 4. Its system specification in PVS can be found in the full paper.

Given the A-G specification $A_s \triangleright G_s$ of the servers module and the system specification (the code) M_c of the clients module, we apply the composition rule presented in Sect. 4 to prove the desired mutual exclusion property of the system as follows:

$$G \triangleq \Box(\bigwedge_{i \neq j} \neg atCrit_i \lor \neg atCrit_j)$$

$$\Phi_{mutex} \triangleq (A_s \triangleright G_s) \land (true \triangleright M_c) \to (true \triangleright G)$$

where $atCrit_i = (c\_state_i = 3)$ and $atCrit_j = (c\_state_j = 3)$. The required mapping is:

$$cliHasToken_i = ((c\_state_i = 3) \lor (c\_state_i = 4))$$

In the PVS mechanization, the mapping is postulated as an axiom:

```
mapping_clients: AXIOM cliHasToken(u)(s) = ((c_state(s)(u) = 3) or
                                            (c_state(s)(u) = 4))
```

More details can be found in the full paper.

$$Init_{M_c} \triangleq \bigwedge_{i=0}^{n-1} (c\_state_i = 0) \land \neg sin_i.sig \land \neg sin_i.ack \land$$
$$sin_i.val \land \neg sout_i.sig \land \neg sout_i.ack \land \neg sout_i.val$$

$Skip\_c_i \triangleq (c\_state'_i = c\_state_i) \land (sin'_i = sin_i) \land (sout'_i = sout_i)$

$Act\_c1_i \triangleq (c\_state_i = 0) \land (c\_state'_i = 1) \land (sin'_i = sin_i) \land (sout'_i = sout_i)$

$Act\_c2_i \triangleq (c\_state_i = 1) \land (sin_i.sig = sin_i.ack) \land sin_i.val \land (c\_state'_i = 2) \land$
$(sin'_i.sig = \neg sin_i.sig) \land \neg sin'_i.val \land (sin'_i.ack = sin_i.ack) \land$
$(sout'_i = sout_i)$

$Act\_c3_i \triangleq (c\_state_i = 2) \land (sout_i.sig \neq sout_i.ack) \land (c\_state'_i = 3)$
$\land (sout'_i.ack = sout_i.ack) \land (sout'_i.sig = sout_i.sig) \land$
$(sout'_i.val = sout_i.val) \land (sin'_i = sin_i)$

$Act\_c4_i \triangleq (c\_state_i = 3) \land (c\_state'_i = 4) \land (sin'_i = sin_i) \land (sout'_i = sout_i)$

$Act\_c5_i \triangleq (c\_state_i = 4) \land (sin_i.sig = sin_i.ack) \land \neg sin_i.val \land (c\_state'_i = 0) \land$
$(sin'_i.sig = \neg sin_i.sig) \land sin'_i.val \land (sin'_i.ack = sin_i.ack) \land$
$(sout'_i = sout_i)$

$Act\_skip\_c_i \triangleq (c\_state'_i = c\_state_i) \land (sin'_i.sig = sin_i.sig) \land$
$(sin'_i.val = sin_i.val) \land (sout'_i.ack = sout_i.ack)$

$Act\_c_i \triangleq Act\_c1_i \lor Act\_c2_i \lor Act\_c3_i \lor Act\_c4_i \lor Act\_c5_i \lor Act\_skip\_c_i$

$$N_{M_c} \triangleq \bigvee_{i=0}^{n-1} (Act\_c_i \land (\bigwedge_{j \neq i} Skip\_c_j))$$

$M_c \triangleq Init_{M_c} \land \Box N_{M_c}$

Fig. 4. System specification of the clients module

7 Related Work

We have chosen to adapt and mechanize Jonsson and Tsay's compositional framework because their formulation of A-G specifications as well as the derived composition rules are syntactic and entirely within LTL, which makes the framework amenable to mechanization in a general-purpose theorem prover once the LTL basis has been adequately formalized. Our adaptation has made the mechanization even easier. The simplicity of Jonsson and Tsay's framework and its adaptation that we presented can be attributed to the use of past temporal operators. Barringer and Kuiper [16] were probably the first to formulate A-G specifications in a temporal logic with past operators. However, they did not treat hiding.

Other frameworks that follow the assumption-guarantee paradigm, including [10–12, 17–19, 7, 20–22], typically reason about relevant properties at the semantic level or define a special-purpose logic. In [18], Abadi and Lamport gave a comprehensive treatment of compositionality in a general semantic setting. Their semantic composition rule used the notion of the "realizable part" of a specification (the behaviors that can possibly be produced by an implementation) which is quite a subtle concept to formalize. Heckman et al. [23] have attempted to translate Abadi and Lamport's composition method into HOL. However, their attempt was not very successful. They were not able to formally prove the composition rule, but chose to postulate it as an axiom. Moreover, they did not prove that, when applying the rule to verify an operating system microkernel, the specifications they wrote are actually realizable.

In [7], Abadi and Lamport proposed a compositional method using TLA, which is an improvement over earlier temporal logic-based works in handling hiding and liveness properties. Due to the absence of past operators in TLA, they extended the semantic model for TLA formulas to include *finite* sequences so that the assertion "a finite prefix of an execution satisfies a formula" (which plays a central role in A-G specifications) can be stated directly, which otherwise would require extensive usage of auxiliary variables that result in long and complicated formulas. Though also using temporal logic as a basis, their composition rules explicitly use the notion of safety closure, which makes mechanization less straightforward. Their method has been tested by the verification of a multiplier [2] using the TLP theorem prover [24] and the automata-theoretic model checker COSPAN [25].

In [26], Shankar proposed an alternative approach called *lazy composition*, where the properties of a module are verified under the parallel composition of the module and an abstract environment. He mechanized the lazy approach and tested by some examples using PVS [27].

There have been several works on mechanization of temporal logic reasoning. In [28], Andersen et al. embedded the UNITY logic [29] (a variant of linear-time temporal logic) in the theorem prover HOL [30]. In [24], TLA [5] specifications and proofs are translated by an ML program into LP (the Larch Prover) scripts and then processed by LP. Långbacka [31] embedded full TLA logic, including the rules dealing with data hiding and refinement mappings, in HOL. He did not encounter much difficulty in the treatment of hiding like we did, as he was not concerned with composition of specifications. In [32], a subset of TLA without hiding was formalized in PVS.

8 Conclusion

We have presented an adaptation of the compositional verification framework developed by Jonsson and Tsay [8, 13]. Compared to their original work, the adapted framework is more convenient for *mechanization*, though not as succinct for *hand* proofs. We have mechanized the adapted framework in PVS and experimented with it on the token ring example.

We suggested a convenient approach to dealing with data hiding and refinement mappings, which we believe is useful and leads to more succinct specification. As long as one follows the principles in defining a refinement mapping as we have explained in the paper, there should be no inconsistency resulted from introducing an axiom for the mapping. The formalized composition rules have been verified as theorems in PVS and can be integrated as a library of PVS. This would provide an alternative style of specification and verification in PVS and thus enhance the capabilities of PVS for modular design and verification.

References

1. Clarke, E., Long, D., McMillan, K.: Compositional model checking. In: Proceedings of the 4th IEEE Symposium on Logic in Computer Science. (1989) 353–362
2. Kurshan, R., Lamport, L.: Verification of a multiplier: 64 bits and beyond. In Courcoubetis, C., ed.: Computer-Aided Verification, CAV '93, LNCS 697, Springer-Verlag (1993) 166–179
3. Szyperski, C.: Component Software: Beyond Object-Oriented Programming. Addison-Wesley (1998)
4. Pnueli, A.: The temporal semantics of concurrent programs. Theoretical Computer Science **13** (1982) 45–60
5. Lamport, L.: The temporal logic of actions. ACM Transactions on Programming Languages and Systems **16** (1994) 872–923
6. Manna, Z., Pnueli, A.: Temporal Verification of Reactive Systems: Safety. Springer-Verlag (1995)
7. Abadi, M., Lamport, L.: Conjoining specifications. ACM Transactions on Programming Languages and Systems **17** (1995) 507–534
8. Jonsson, B., Tsay, Y.K.: Assumption/guarantee specifications in linear-time temporal logic. Theoretical Computer Science **167** (1996) 47–72 An extended abstract appeared earlier in TAPSOFT '95, LNCS 915.
9. Hoare, C.: An axiomatic basis for computer programs. Communications of the ACM **12** (1969) 576–580
10. Misra, J., Chandy, K.: Proofs of networks of processes. IEEE Transactions on Software Engineering **7** (1981) 417–426
11. Jones, C.: Tentative steps towards a development method for interfering programs. ACM Transactions on Programming Languages and Systems **5** (1983) 596–619
12. Lamport, L.: Specifying concurrent program modules. ACM Transactions on Programming Languages and Systems **5** (1983) 190–222
13. Tsay, Y.K.: Compositional verification in linear-time temporal logic. In Tiuryn, J., ed.: Proceedings of the Third International Conference on Foundations of Software Science and Computation Structures, LNCS 1784, Springer (2000) 344–358
14. Manna, Z., Pnueli, A.: The Temporal Logic of Reactive and Concurrent Systems: Specification. Springer-Verlag (1992)
15. Crow, J., Owre, S., Rushby, J., Shankar, N., Srivas, M.: A tutorial introduction to PVS. Technical report, Computer Science Laboratory, SRI International, Menlo Park, CA (1995)
16. Barringer, H., Kuiper, R.: Hierarchical development of concurrent systems in a temporal logic framework. In Brookes, S., Roscoe, A., Winskel, G., eds.: Seminar on Concurrency, LNCS 197, Springer-Verlag (1984) 35–61
17. Grønning, P., Nielsen, T., Løvengreen, H.: Refinement and composition of transition-based rely-guarantee specifications with auxiliary variables. In Nori, K., Veni Madhavan, C., eds.: Foundations of Software Technology and Theoretical Computer Science, LNCS 472, Springer-Verlag (1991) 332–348
18. Abadi, M., Lamport, L.: Composing specifications. ACM Transactions on Programming Languages and Systems **15** (1993) 73–132
19. Abadi, M., Plotkin, G.: A logical view of composition. Theoretical Computer Science **114** (1993) 3–30
20. Collette, P.: Application of the composition principle to Unity-like specifications. In: TAPSOFT '93: Theory and Practice of Software Development, LNCS 668, Springer-Verlag (1993) 230–242

21. Collette, P.: Design of Compositional Proof Systems Based on Assumption-Guarantee Specifications — Application to UNITY. PhD thesis, Université Catholique de Louvain (1994)
22. Xu, Q., Cau, A., Collette, P.: On unifying assumption-commitment style proof rules for concurrency. In Jonsson, B., Parrow, J., eds.: CONCUR '94: Concurrency Theory, LNCS 836, Springer-Verlag (1994) 267–282
23. Heckman, M., Zhang, C., Becker, B., Peticolas, D., Levitt, K., Olsson, R.: Towards applying the composition principle to verify a microkernel operating system. In: Proceedings of the 9th International Conference on Theorem Proving in Higher Order Logics (TPHOLs '96), LNCS 1125. (1996) 235–250
24. Engberg, U., Grønning, P., Lamport, L.: Mechanical verification of concurrent systems with TLA. In von Bochmann, G., Probst, D., eds.: Computer-Aided Verification, CAV '92, LNCS 663, Springer-Verlag (1992) 44–55
25. Har'El, Z., Kurshan, R.: Software for analytical development of communication protocols. AT&T Technical Journal **69** (1990) 45–59
26. Shankar, N.: Lazy compositional verification. In: Compositionality: The Significant Difference, LNCS 1536. (1999) 541–564
27. Shankar, N.: Machine-assisted verification using theorem proving and model checking. Computer and Systems Science **158** (1997) 499–528
28. Andersen, F., Petersen, K., Petterson, J.: Program verification using HOL-UNITY. In: LNCS 780. (1994) 1–16
29. Chandy, K., Misra, J.: Parallel Program Design: A Foundation. Addison-Wesley (1988)
30. Gordon, M.: HOL: A proof generating system for higher-order logic. In Birtwistle, G., Subrahmanyam, P., eds.: VLSI Specification, Verification and Synthesis, Kluwer (1988) 73–128
31. Långbacka, T.: A HOL formalization of the temporal logic of actions. In: Higher Order Logic Theorem Proving System and Its Applications, 7th International Workshop. (1994)
32. Kellomäki, P.: Verification of reactive systems using DisCo and PVS. In Fitzgerad, J., Jones, C., Lucas, P., eds.: FME '97: Industrial Applications and Strengthened Foundations of Formal Methods, LNCS 1313, Springer-Verlag (1997) 589–604

Model Checking FTA

Andreas Thums and Gerhard Schellhorn

Lehrstuhl für Softwaretechnik und Programmiersprachen,
Universität Augsburg, D-86135 Augsburg
{thums,schellhorn}@informatik.uni-augsburg.de

Abstract. Safety is increasingly important for software based, critical systems. Fault tree analysis (FTA) is a safety technique from engineering, developed for analyzing and assessing system safety by uncovering safety flaws and weaknesses of the system. The main drawback of this analysis technique is, that it is based on informal grounds, so safety flaws may be overlooked. This is an issue, where formal proofs can help. They are a safety techniques from software engineering, which are based on precise system descriptions and allow to prove consistency and other (safety) properties.
We present an approach which automatically proves the consistency of fault trees based on a formal model by model checking. Therefore, we define consistency conditions in Computational Tree Logic, a widely used input language for model checkers. In the second part, we exemplify our approach with a case study from the *Fault Tree Handbook*.

Keywords: model checking, safety analysis, fault tree analysis

1 Introduction

Safety is an important issue for software based, critical systems like aerospace, nuclear power plants, transportation, and medical control. In engineering, fault tree analysis (FTA, [23]) is commonly used to analyze system safety. It breaks down system level hazards to failures of components, called (failure) events. The events are connected through gates, indicating if all or only any sub-event is necessary to cause the failure. Each event is analyzed recursively, resulting in a tree of events. The leafs of a fault tree describe failures of basic components which in combination cause the system hazard.

FTA is based on an informal description of the underlying system. Therefore it is quite hard to check the consistency of the analysis. It is possible that causes are noted in the tree which do not lead to the hazard (in-correctness) and, more critical, that some causes for the hazard are overlooked during analysis (in-completeness).

This is an issue, where formal proofs can help. They are a formal method used in software engineering (although there are applications in hardware design, too) based on a specification of the system behavior in a precise and unambiguous notation. The specification is validated through proving required system properties. Verification guarantees safety properties and functional correctness. We will use model checking to automate these proofs.

The idea of the integration of FTA and formal methods is to formally specify the system model and to prove correctness and completeness of FTA. Therefore, the FTA has to be formalized. We define a semantics of fault trees which consists of proof conditions for every gate in the tree. We assign so called *correctness* and *completeness* conditions to the gates. The correctness condition guarantees, that the noted sub-events *actually* lead to the top event and the completeness condition, that *only* the sub-events lead top event, i.e. no cause was overlooked during the FTA. If every proof condition is verified, the correctness and completeness of the fault tree is guaranteed, i.e. the basic events are necessary for causing the system level hazard and only the basic events can cause the hazard. We call this integrated approach "formal FTA". For applying formal FTA we have to i) formally specify the system, ii) develop fault trees for the main system hazards, iii) formalize the fault tree events, and iv) verify the proof conditions for every gate.

Step iii) will formalize events by temporal logic formulae. Note, that first order formulae are not sufficient, since we do not use the term "event" as it is used in automata theory, where an event happens at a fixed point in time and has no duration. Events in safety engineering may also describe a system state or sequence of states and can last some time[1]. E.g. "10 sec flow of fluid" can describe a failure event. In the following, we use "event" with the more general meaning and distinguish between events with duration and events without duration by the terms *temporal* and *timeless* events, respectively.

We presented the approach of formal FTA in [20] and defined an ITL semantics for general system descriptions. But in industry, formal methods are accepted best, if verification can be automated. Model checkers can do this for finite state systems and additionally help to find failures by generating counterexamples. When validating fault trees, in most cases these counterexamples point to overlooked causes for the system hazard. Therefore, we develop a FTA semantics in Computational Tree Logic (CTL) in this paper. CTL is widely used as an input language for model checkers, e.g. in SMV [10], SVE [5], and RAVEN [14]. The drawback of CTL is, that its tree structure does not allow to treat temporal events directly in the logic. We introduce so called "observer automata" to cope with temporal events. They extend the system model and enter an acceptance state, if they observed the corresponding temporal event. Entering the acceptance state is a timeless event and can be treated correctly.

To exemplify our approach, we prove the correctness and completeness conditions for an example of the *Fault Tree Handbook* [23], the "pressure tank". This example extensively uses time intervals for its specification, which are supported by the model checker RAVEN. RAVEN uses timed automata [15, 18] for specifying the system model and an extended CTL, clocked CTL (CCTL, [17]), to specify the proof conditions. Using timed automata makes the specification of the example simpler and better understandable.

---

[1] As noted by Leveson [9], this is a common misunderstanding between safety engineers and (theoretical) computer scientists.

The paper is organized as follows. The "pressure tank" example is introduced in Sect. 2. In Sect. 3 we describe the informal FTA and present the fault tree of the pressure tank example from [23]. After this informal analysis, we consider the formal aspects. Logical foundations for formalizing FTA and specifying the pressure tank example are given in Sect. 4. We shortly introduce CTL, CCTL, and timed automata. Section 5 describes the formal CTL semantics of FTA. To cope with temporal events we introduce observer automata, which maps temporal to timeless events. After this theoretical part, we present the formal FTA of the pressure tank example in Sect. 6. Section 7 discusses differences and communities with other formalizations of FTA from literature and Sect. 8 concludes the paper.

2 Example: Pressure Tank

The pressure tank is an example from the *Fault Tree Handbook* [23, Chapter VIII]. It describes a control system regulating the operation of a pump, which fills fluid into a tank.

The control system is depicted in Fig. 1. It consists of a control part, powered by P_1, and an electrically isolated electrical circuit, powered by P_2, which energizes the motor of the pump. P_1 powers the electrical circuits c_1 and c_2. c_1 energizes the coil of relay K_1, if the push button S_1 or K_1 and the timer T are closed. The circuit c_2 energizes the coil of relay K_2 and the timer and is closed, if S_1 or K_1 and the pressure switch S are closed. P_2 powers c_3 which supplies power to the motor, if the relay K_2 is closed.

The control system starts operation when the push button S_1 is pressed. This closes the electrical circuit c_1 and applies power to relay K_1, which henceforth energizes the control system.

If the pressure tank is empty and, therefore, the pressure switch S is closed, the electrical circuit c_2 applies power to relay K_2, energizing electrical circuit c_3 and starting the motor of the pump. This situation is sketched in Fig. 1. We assume, that it takes 60 sec to pressurize the tank. When the tank is full, the pressure switch S is opening, de-energizing electrical circuit c_2, which in effect opens relay K_2 and electrical circuit c_3. The pump motor is switched off and the pump stops filling. Now the outlet valve may drain the tank and, if the tank is is empty, the cycle described above is repeated. So, in normal operation without failures, only the pressure switch S and the relay K_2 are opening and closing, depending on the liquid level of the tank.

If the pressure switch is defective, the timer is a fall-back to prevent tank rupture. If the pressure switch fails to open, although the tank is full, the timer sends a timeout. The timer registers, if the circuit c_2 is continuously energized for more than 60 sec and provides an emergency shutdown by de-energizing electrical circuit c_1. The timer T opens and de-energizes K_1. Then, neither S_1 nor K_1 are closed and the system has to be restarted by pressing S_1. In normal operation, when the pressure switch S de-energizes the electrical circuit c_2, the timer is reset.

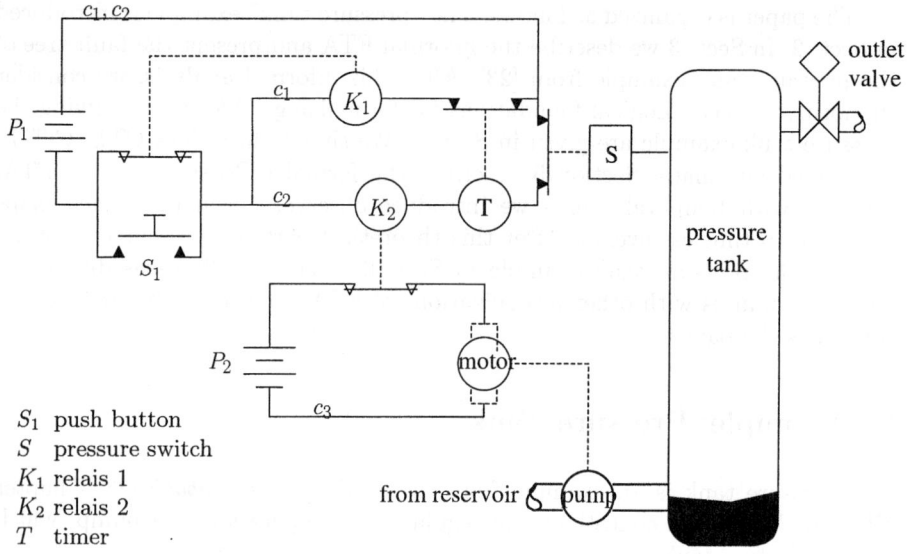

Fig. 1. Pressure Tank

3 Fault Tree Analysis (FTA)

Fault tree analysis (FTA) is a well known technique in engineering and was developed for technical systems to analyze, if they permit a hazard (top event). This event is noted at the root of the fault tree. Events, which cause the hazard (intermediate events), are given in the child nodes and analyzed recursively, resulting in a tree of events. Each analyzed event (main event, either top or intermediate) is connected to its causes (sub-events) by a gate in the fault tree (see Fig. 2). An AND-gate indicates that all sub-events are necessary to trigger the main event, for an OR-gate only one sub-event is necessary. An INHIBIT-gate states that in addition to the cause stated in the sub-event the condition (noted in the oval) has to be true to trigger the main event. The INHIBIT-gate is more or less an AND-gate with one cause and a condition, but the condition needs not to be a fault event.

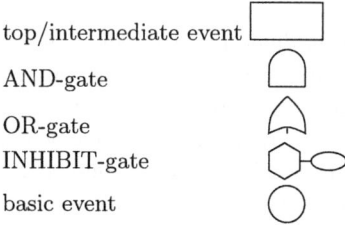

Fig. 2. Fault Tree Symbols

The leaves of the tree are the low level causes (basic events) for the top event, which have to occur in combination (corresponding to the gates in the tree) to trigger the top event. A set of basic events together leading to the hazard is called a *cut set*. A cut set is minimal, if it has no other cut set as a subset. I.e. a *minimal cut set* can not lead to the top level hazard, if at least one event of the set is prevented. Minimal cut sets can be computed from fault trees by combining the basic events with boolean operators as indicated by the gates. A minimal cut set then consists of the elements of one conjunction of the disjunctive normal form of the resulting formula.

Cut sets are used to identify failure events, which have a big impact on system safety. E.g., if one event occurs in different minimal cut sets, the probability of the top level hazard will strongly decrease, if this event can be excluded. Besides this *qualitative* analysis, FTA also allows *quantitative* analysis. If the failure probabilities of the basic events are known (failure probabilities of basic components can frequently be derived from statistical data) and the events occur only once in the fault tree, the probability of the occurrence of the hazard can be computed starting from the cut sets. For statistically independent failures, the failure probability of the main event is the sum of the probabilities of the minimal cut sets (for small values). These probabilities are the product of the failure probabilities of its events. For more sophisticated computations, we refer to the Fault Tree Handbook [23]. Therefore, FTA is a good starting point for the assessment of system safety.

Figure 3 describes the fault tree for the pressure tank example (see [23], page VIII-11). It analyses the hazard "rupture of pressure tank after the start of pumping". *Rupture* occurs, if the tank is *continuously filled for more than 60 sec*. The reason therefore is, that relay K_2 is *closed for more than 60 sec*. This could be the effect of *power at the coil of K_2 for more than 60 sec* or of a defective *relay K_2* (fails to open). Both causes are connected through an OR-gate to the effect. The rest of the fault tree is developed in the same manner and the resulting cut sets are

$$\{\{K_2,\},\{S,S_1\},\{S,K_1\},\{S,T\}\}.$$

The qualitative analysis of the cut sets shows, that relay K_2 is a single point of failure. With the failure probabilities for the basic events from [23] (see Fig. 3 on the right), we can quantify the system safety and compute the overall hazard probability to approximately $3*10^{-5}$.

4 Logical Foundations

We will formalize the semantics of FTA in CTL, because many model checkers use CTL as an input language for the properties to prove. We ourselves used the model checker RAVEN [14] for checking correctness and completeness of the pressure tank example. RAVEN uses timed automata for system specification and an extension of CTL, so called Clocked CTL (CCTL) for specifying the proof conditions. In the following we shortly introduce CTL and subsequently the extensions of RAVEN, CCTL and timed automata.

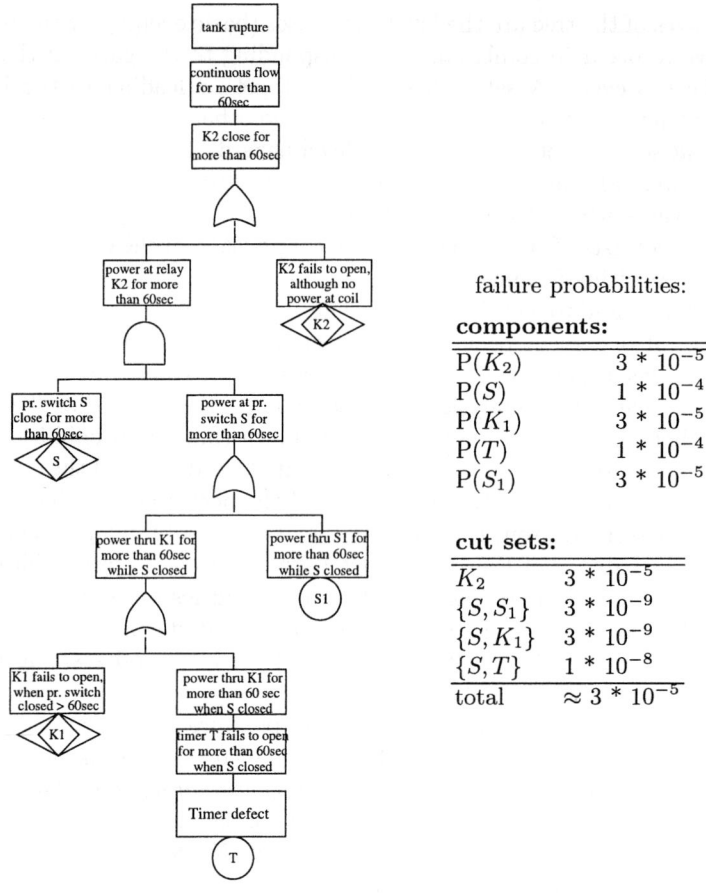

Fig. 3. FTA: Pressure Tank

4.1 CTL

The semantics of CTL [4] is based on state transition diagrams. A state transition diagram is a tuple $(\mathcal{P}, \mathcal{S}, \mathcal{T}, \mathcal{L})$ with $\mathcal{P}$ a set of atomic formulas, $\mathcal{S}$ a finites set of states, $\mathcal{T} \subseteq \mathcal{S} \times \mathcal{S}$ a finite set of transitions, and $\mathcal{L} : \mathcal{S} \to \wp(\mathcal{P})$ a label function. A state s is labeled with atomic formulas $\varphi \in \mathcal{P}$ and a formula holds in s ($s \models \varphi$), if and only if $\varphi \in \mathcal{L}(s)$.

Possible successors s' of a state s are described in the transition relation $\mathcal{T}$, i.e. $(s, s') \in \mathcal{T}$ and we require, that every state s has a successor s' with $(s, s') \in \mathcal{T}$. A path is an infinite sequence of states $\sigma = (s_0, s_1, \ldots)$ with $\sigma[i] = s_i$ and $(s_i, s_{i+1}) \in \mathcal{T}$ for every $i \in \mathbb{N}$. $\Pi(s)$ is the set of all possible paths starting in state s. CTL defines the following operators:

Definition 1 *CTL operators*

$s \models EX\varphi \quad :\Leftrightarrow \quad$ there exists a state $s' \in \mathcal{S}$
$\qquad\qquad\qquad\qquad$ with $(s, s') \in \mathcal{T}$ and $s' \models \varphi$
$s \models EG\varphi \quad :\Leftrightarrow \quad$ there exists a path $\sigma \in \Pi(s)$,
$\qquad\qquad\qquad\qquad$ s.t. for every $k \in I\!N: \sigma[k] \models \varphi$
$s \models E(\varphi \ U \ \psi) :\Leftrightarrow \quad$ there exists a path $\sigma \in \Pi(s)$,
$\qquad\qquad\qquad\qquad$ a $k \in I\!N : \sigma[k] \models \psi$, and for every $i < k : \sigma[i] \models \varphi$

Additional temporal operators can be derived:

Definition 2 *derived CTL operators*

$$\begin{aligned}
EF\varphi &= E(\text{true } U \ \varphi) \\
E(\varphi \ wB \ \psi) &= \neg A(\neg\varphi \ U \ \psi) \\
AX\varphi &= \neg EX\neg\varphi \\
AG\varphi &= \neg E(\text{true } U \ \neg\varphi) \\
A(\varphi \ U \ \psi) &= \neg E(\neg\psi \ U \ (\neg\varphi \wedge \neg\psi)) \wedge \neg EG\neg\psi \\
AF\psi &= \neg EG\neg\psi
\end{aligned}$$

One can distinguish between path operators E (there exists a path) and A (on every paths) and state operators X (next), F (eventually), G (generally), and U (until). In CTL, every state operator must be preceded by a path operator and every path operator must be followed by a state operator.

For the definition of the FTA semantics we define the precedes operator P.

Definition 3 *precedes*

$s \models A(\varphi \ P \ \psi) \quad \Leftrightarrow \quad$ for every path $\sigma \in \Pi(s)$:
$\qquad\qquad\qquad\qquad$ for every $k \in I\!N$ with $\sigma[k] \models \psi$,
$\qquad\qquad\qquad\qquad$ exists an $i \leq k$ with $\sigma[i] \models \varphi$

Informally, $A(\varphi \ P \ \psi)$ means for all paths, if ψ holds at some point in time, then φ must hold before or at the same point in time. If ψ never holds, φ need not hold either. The precedes operator $A(\varphi \ P \ \psi)$ is equivalent to $\neg E(\neg\varphi \ U \ (\psi \wedge \neg\varphi))$ and can therefore be specified by every CTL model checker.

4.2 Clocked CTL and Timed Automata

Clocked CTL (CCTL) [17] extends CTL with the possibility to annotate intervals to the state operators.

Definition 4 *CCTL state operators*

$X_{[a]}\varphi :\quad \varphi$ holds after a steps
$F_{[a,b]}\varphi :\quad \varphi$ holds somewhere between a and b steps
$G_{[a,b]}\varphi :\quad \varphi$ holds everywhere between a and b steps
$\varphi \ U_{[a,b]} \ \psi :\ \psi$ occurs at t, $a \leq t \leq b$, and φ holds until t

The path quantifiers keep their usual meaning. E.g. $A \varphi U_{[2,3]} \psi$ means, that on every path ψ must hold until ψ and ψ is true in the second or third step. If the lower bound of an interval $[a, b]$ is zero ($a = 0$), we simply write $[b]$. For $a = 0$ and $b = \infty$ we can omit the whole interval and get the usual CTL semantics.

CCTL formulas are interpreted over timed automata [15, 18] which are state transition diagrams with the possibility to annotate input events and interval expressions. We will explain the graphical notation only.

Definition 5 *timed automata*

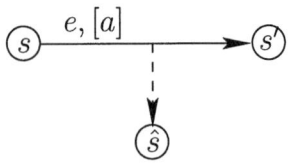

The input variable is e. If e holds for a time steps after entering s, state s' will be entered. If e holds, but less than a time steps, the error state $\hat{s}$ will be entered. If e doesn't hold at all, another transition leaving state s will be taken.

If $a = 0$, the error state $\hat{s}$ is irrelevant and we get the semantics of usual state transition diagrams.

If we want to state, that we leave state s if we can continuously watch the event e for a steps, we modify the automaton from definition 5: the dashed arrow will go back to state s, i.e. $s = \hat{s}$. By entering (the error state) s again, e "gets a second chance" to hold a time steps. Such automata are used in the specification of the pressure tank example. General timed automata can easily be translated into untimed ones [16].

5 FTA Semantics in CTL

For model checking the validity of fault trees we develop a CTL formalization for the conditions described by the fault tree gates. Unfortunately, this formalization is adequate only, if the events in the fault tree are timeless. But Górski [6] noticed three typical patterns for temporal events in fault trees.

1. event occurs (for a certain time), e.g. "(60 sec) pumping"
2. event occurs an continues to stay, e.g. "rupture" (can not be reversed)
3. a sequence of events (with duration) occurs with some state conditions, e.g. "S_1 pressed, then K_1 closed, ..., and finally pumping of fluid"

All three pattern (can) describe temporal events. To handle these events (e.g. "60 sec pumping") we introduce so called observer automata. They observe an event and accept its ending (60 sec pumping are over) by entering a corresponding state.

In the following, we present the FTA semantics in CTL and afterwards the extensions for handling temporal events. For better readability, we use CCTL and the timed automata notation for these extensions.

5.1 FTA Semantics

The aim is to develop a modular semantics for FTA. We assign proof obligations to each gate in the fault tree. They should guarantee, that if every proof obligation can be verified over the system model, the FTA is correct and complete, i.e. the causes in the cut sets actually lead to the system hazard and there exist no other causes for the system hazard. We develop proper poof obligations in the following.

The accepted informal semantics assigns the boolean semantics to each gate [23], i.e. the OR-gates are interpreted as disjunctions and the AND-gates as conjunctions. The correctness condition for a gate, which connects a cause φ with a consequence ψ, is $\varphi \to \psi$ (if the cause occurs, the consequence must occur). The cause is either $\varphi := \varphi_1 \land \varphi_2$ for an AND-gate or $\varphi := \varphi_1 \lor \varphi_2$ for an OR-gate. The completeness condition is $\psi \to \varphi$ (if the consequence occurs, cause must occur). In dynamic systems, these conditions have to be true for every system state, i.e. we formulate the correctness condition in CTL as $AG(\varphi \to \psi)$ and the completeness as $AG(\psi \to \varphi)$.

This boolean semantics seems adequate, but is not sufficient for dynamic systems. Consider the pressure tank example from Sect. 2. If the tank is full, but the pump continues pumping, this does not necessarily rupture the tank at once, but after a certain time. Therefore, we have to distinguish between *decomposition* gates (D-gates) with the boolean semantics and *cause consequence* gates (C-gates), where time may elapse between the causes and the consequence.

The cause consequence gates consider the case, where the causes *lead to* the consequence later on. We define correctness as $(EF\ \varphi) \to (EF\ \psi)$ and completeness as $A(\varphi\ P\ \psi)$. The correctness condition requires, that if the cause occurs eventually, the consequence has to occur as well. Unfortunately, we can formulate only a weak form of correctness which does not require that the cause φ occurs before the consequence ψ and not even that the cause occurs on the same path. But this property is guaranteed by the completeness condition. It requires, that if the consequence occurs, the cause has to occur before or at the same time. If completeness cannot be proven, there exists a run through the system, where the consequence occurs, but no mentioned cause has occurred before or at the same time. This means, there exists another cause which has been overlooked.

A distinction between decomposition and cause consequence gates is proposed in [2] as well. But we have to consider yet another case. For AND-gates we have to distinguish between so called synchronous and asynchronous AND-gates. For synchronous AND-gates, the causes have to occur together, for asynchronous AND-gates they may happen at different times. INHIBIT-gates are formalized like synchronous AND-gates. For correctness, the side-condition must happen together with the cause. Completeness is proven for the cause only, since the condition is no fault event. Note that specifying an exact condition χ, such that $\varphi \land \chi$ holds before the consequence, is often difficult and not necessary for the completeness. Therefore, we require only $A(\varphi\ P\ \psi)$ and not $A(\varphi \land \chi\ P\ \psi)$.

Summarizing, we get 7 types of gates: D-OR-, D-AND- and, D-INHIBIT-gates (⌂, ⌂, ⌂⊖), C-OR-gates (⌂), synchronous and asynchronous C-

AND-gates (⊂, ⊂_AC), and C-INHIBIT-gates (⊂—○). The correctness- and completeness conditions for each of these types of gates g are listed in Fig. 4. The case of two causes is shown, the generalization to any number $n \geq 1$ of causes should be obvious (for $n = 1$, AND- and OR-gates have the same meaning).

gate g	correctness CORR(g)	completeness COMPL(g)
AND-D ($\varphi_1, \varphi_2 \to \psi$)	AG $(\varphi_1 \wedge \varphi_2 \to \psi)$	AG $(\psi \to \varphi_1 \wedge \varphi_2)$
OR-D ($\varphi_1, \varphi_2 \to \psi$)	AG $(\varphi_1 \vee \varphi_2 \to \psi)$	AG $(\psi \to \varphi_1 \vee \varphi_2)$
INHIBIT-D ($\varphi, \chi \to \psi$)	AG $(\varphi \wedge \chi \to \psi)$	AG $(\psi \to \varphi)$
AND-C ($\varphi_1, \varphi_2 \to \psi$)	EX $(\varphi_1 \wedge \varphi_2) \to$ EX ψ	A $((\varphi_1 \wedge \varphi_2) \, P \, \psi)$
AND-AC ($\varphi_1, \varphi_2 \to \psi$)	(EX $\varphi_1 \wedge$ EX $\varphi_2) \to$ EX ψ	A $(\varphi_1 \, P \, \psi)$ $\wedge$ A $(\varphi_2 \, P \, \psi)$
OR-C ($\varphi_1, \varphi_2 \to \psi$)	EX $(\varphi_1 \vee \varphi_2) \to$ EX ψ	A $((\varphi_1 \vee \varphi_2) \, P \, \psi)$
C-INHIBIT ($\varphi, \chi \to \psi$)	EX $(\varphi \wedge \chi) \to$ EX ψ	A $(\varphi \, P \, \psi)$

Fig. 4. semantics of fault trees

Our explanatory statements above give some indication of the adequacy of the CTL semantics. The technical report [22] details a formal proof, that for timeless events this CTL semantics is equivalent to the more general ITL semantics presented in [20] and to other semantics from literature [7, 2]. As a corollary, the *minimal cut set theorem* proved in [20] is valid for the CTL semantics with timeless events. It guarantees, that if every event of one cut set occurs, the hazard occurs as well and if one event from every minimal cut set can be excluded, the hazard can not occur. A proven fault tree is a part of a formal safety statement (no cut set implies no hazard) for system models, which specified components failures or defects.

5.2 Events with Duration

To explain the problems of fault tree with temporal events, let us consider the topmost relation of the fault tree in Fig. 1. The cause φ is "60 sec pumping" and the consequence ψ is "tank rupture". Because 60 sec pumping must not immediately lead to tank rupture, the cause and consequence are related through a C-gate. If we want to prove the correctness condition $A\ (\varphi\ P\ \psi)$ we have to formalize the events φ and ψ.

A first try is to formalize "tank rupture" as $\psi := rupture$ and "60 sec pumping" as $AG_{[60]}pumping$ (if $rupture$ and $pumping$ are the suitable atomic formulae). But this formalization is not adequate, because it does not require that "60 sec pumping" is completed, before the consequence "rupture" occurs. Assume a system state s, wherein $rupture$ is true. The proof condition requires, that there exists a state s' before s, that fulfills the cause $AG_{[60]}pumping$. If $AG_{[60]}pumping$ holds for the predecessor of s, the cause and the consequence overlap, but the proof condition is fulfilled.

A second try is the formalization $A((G_{[60]}pumping)\ P\ X_{[60]}rupture)$. It ensures, that the consequence does not start until the cause has completed. But this is not a CTL formula. In CTL, every state operator must be prefixed with a path operator. So, we can formalize 60 sec pumping either as $\varphi := AG_{[60]}pumping$ or as $\varphi := EG_{[60]}pumping$. Again assuming a state s' before s, where $rupture$ holds, the first formula states, that on all paths, starting at s', pumping holds for 60 sec. This condition is too strong, because the cause must only occur on the path to s. The second formula states, that there exists a path starting from s', where pumping holds for 60 sec, but this need not be the path leading to s. So we cannot formulate, that 60 sec pumping holds on *exactly* the path, that leads to rupture.

To solve this problem, we introduce so called observer automata. Such an automaton runs in parallel to the system model. It observes the event "pumping" and enters an accepting end-state, when the 60 sec are over. This end-state flags, that 60 sec pumping have been occurred. Now, we can check, if this acceptance state was entered, before the corresponding consequence occurs. The entering of the acceptance state is a timeless event. Therefore we can prove, that it occurs on the path to and before the consequence.

We define a general observer automaton for accepting a temporal event as follows:

Definition 6 *observer automaton for temporal events*

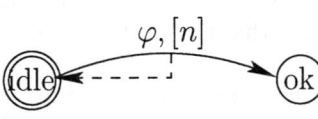

First, the automaton is in the idle state. If φ continuously holds for n time steps, the acceptance state ok with the label ok_φ is entered. To verify, that an event φ holds for n time steps before a consequence ψ occurs, we prove $A\ (ok_\varphi\ P\ rupture)$.

If we want to state "60 sec pumping", we set $\varphi := pumping$ and $n := 60$. To verify, that the only cause for rupture is 60 sec pumping, we prove:

$$A\ (ok_{pumping}\ P\ rupture)$$

Observing Typical Fault Tree Events: The automaton of definition 6 can observe the first fault tree event pattern of Górski (an event occurs for a certain time) and is the basis for the other two event patterns. For the second event pattern (event occurs and continuous to stay) we add an error state to the observer automaton which is entered, if the state ok is active, but the cause does no longer hold. Then we have to prove, that the ok state is active, when the consequence occurs, i.e. we get the proof condition $AG\ (\psi \to ok_\varphi)$.

Definition 7 *observer automaton for "event continues to stay"*

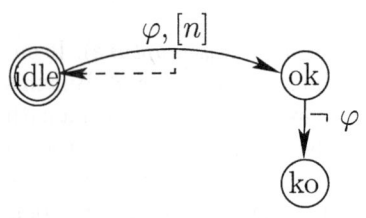

First, the automaton is in the idle state. If φ continuously holds for n time steps, the acceptance state ok with the label ok_φ is entered. The automaton stays in ok_φ as long as φ holds, otherwise it enters the state ko. To verify, that an event φ holds for n time steps and still holds, if the consequence ψ occurs, we prove $AG\ (\psi \to ok_\varphi)$.

Finally, we can observe the third event pattern (sequence of temporal events) by sequentially composing different instances of the observer automaton of definition 6, corresponding to the sequence of events, and observe the acceptance state for the last event of this sequence.

Definition 8 *composing observer automata*

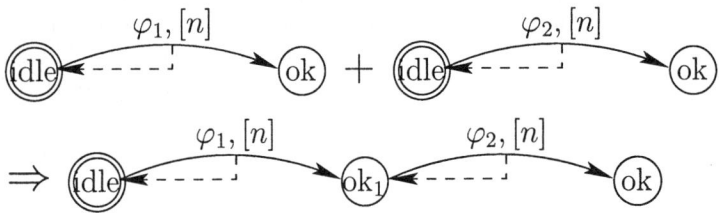

On the basis of observer automata for temporal events we can express every event pattern from Górski. These observer automata are run in parallel to the system automata. Entering the acceptance state marks, that the entire temporal event occurred.

For formal arguments showing the correctness of this construction we refer to [12]. This paper presents an approach to extend CTL* and its subset CTL with the ability to specify quantitative timing properties using formulae of the Quantified Discrete-time Duration Calculus (QDDC) [13]. For the extended CTL, the resulting CTL[DC] formulae can be automatically proven by usual CTL model checkers. This approach also uses observer automata to describe the quantitative timing properties in QDDC formulae and checks, if the accepting end-state is reached. Correctness of this construction was proven in [12].

We derive the correctness of our approach by stating that the FTA event patterns can be formulated as QDDC formulae and the construction in [12] results in the described observer automata of definitions 6-8.

6 Validating the Pressure Tank FTA

In this section, we exemplify the approach of formal FTA with the pressure tank example from Sect. 2. After describing the formal model, we formalize the corresponding fault tree from Fig. 3, generate the proof conditions according to Fig. 4, and verify them with the model checker RAVEN [14]. The specification language of RAVEN are timed automata and it is able to check CCTL formulae. Therefore, the formal model are timed automata and the proof conditions are formulated in CCTL.

6.1 The Formal Model

The model depicted in Fig. 5 consists of eight single modules, representing the components of the pressure tank. The boolean variables c_1 and c_2 correspond to the electrical circuit c_1 and c_2 from Fig. 1 and show, if they are energized or not. The constants *timeout*, *fill_t*, *drain_t*, and *full_t* abbreviate the corresponding time intervals for the timeout, filling and draining time, and how long the pressure sensor can detect "full" before the tank ruptures. Within this time span the control system has to react and to stop filling.

The module *env* describes the environment of the system, which indeterministically can press the push button s_1 (in state *env.c* the condition *env.press* holds). If pressed, the push button s_1 closes by entering state $s_1.c$ and stays therein as long as *press* holds. If *press* does no longer hold, the push button can indeterministically open by entering $s_1.o$ or stay in $s_1.c$ because of a defect. This behavior models the failure mode "fails to open" of the push button s_1.

The modules relay k_1, relay k_2, pressure switch s, and the pump *pump* are modeled analogously. The timer has similar behavior too, but stays closed for a maximum of *timeout* steps. Following the Fault Tree Handbook [23], we modeled the failure mode "fails to open" for the relay k_2, the push button s_1, the timer *timer*, and the pressure switch s.

The *tank* itself is either empty, *f*illing, *f*ull, or *r*uptured. When *flow* (*flow* := *pump.pumping*) holds the state filling is entered. If the pump continues filling for *fill_t* time units, the tank is full. The pressure switch detects if the tank is full and is fixed to the tank such, that the control system has enough time to stop filling, i.e. the tank ruptures not before *full_t* time units *flow* in state full. If filling the tank is interrupted, the tank reaches state drain and empties in *drain_t* time units.

We measure the time in seconds and set on time unit of the model to one second. The time values originate from the *Fault Tree Handbook* and we assign

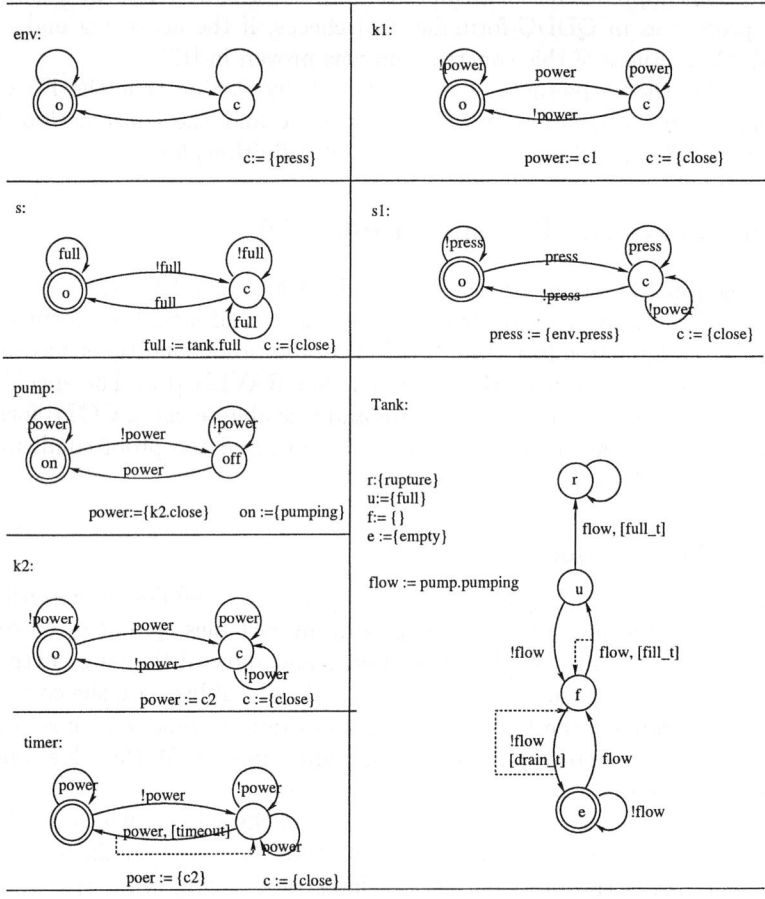

Fig. 5. Model of the pressure tank

the value 60 to *fill_t* and *drain_t*, the value 6 to *full_t*, and the value 65 to *timeout* (see top of Fig. 5).

6.2 Formalizing the Fault Tree

For formal FTA, we have to formalize the fault tree from Fig. 3, i.e. the events have to be described in terms of the formal model and we have to decide, whether the gates from the informal analysis are decomposition or cause consequence gates.

The top event "rupture" can easily be formalized as *tank.rupture*. The only cause for rupture is the continuous filling for more than 60 sec, which is formally $G_{[61]}$ *pump.pumping*. Now, we have to decide, if a decomposition or a cause consequence relation is described between the cause and the consequence. Because

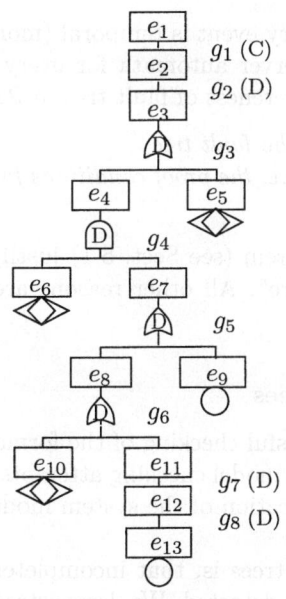

e_1: tank.rupture
e_2: $G_{[61]}$ pump.pumping
e_3: $G_{[61]}$ $k_2.close$
e_4: $G_{[61]}$ c_2
e_5: $\neg c_2 \rightarrow EX\ K_2.close$
e_6: $\neg tank.full \rightarrow EX\ S.close$
e_7: $G_{[61]}$ c_{in}
e_8: $G_{[61]}$ $K_1.close$
e_9: $G_{[61]}$ $S_1.close$
e_{10}: $\neg c_1 \rightarrow EX\ K_2.close$
e_{11}: $G_{[61]}$ c_1
e_{12}: $G_{[61]}timer.power \land timer.close$
e_{13}: as above

Fig. 6. Formalized Fault Tree

60 sec pumping must not immediately lead to rupture the two events are connected through a cause consequence gate. The other gates in the fault tree are decomposition gates. The formalization of the whole fault tree is depicted in Fig. 6.

6.3 Checking Correctness and Completeness

Because *more than 60 sec pumping* is a temporal event, we have to add an observer automaton to the formal system model, which accepts this event. Therefore, we instantiate the automaton of definition 6 with $idle := idle_{\text{pumping}}$, $ok := ok_{\text{pumping}}$, $\varphi := pump.pumping$, and $n := 61$. The pattern of the completeness condition for a cause consequence gate is, according to Fig. 4, $A(\varphi\ P\ \psi)$. This pattern is instantiated with $\varphi := ok_{\text{pumping}}$ for the cause and $\psi := tank.rupture$ for the consequence, resulting in

$$A\ (ok_{\text{pumping}}\ P\ tank.rupture)$$

the first verification condition for the completeness of the fault tree of Fig. 3. Analogous, we can derive the correctness condition

$$EX\ ok_{\text{pumping}} \rightarrow EX\ tank.rupture.$$

Both conditions are verified with the model checker RAVEN over the presented formal model.

The remaining gates are decomposition gates. The correctness condition is an implication from the cause to the consequence, the completeness an implication from the consequence to the cause. Because every event is temporal (more than 60 sec ...), we have to add corresponding observer automata for every event. Finally, we can prove the correctness and completeness of fault tree in RAVEN.

Theorem 1 *Correctness and completeness of the fault tree*
The fault tree of Fig. 6 is correct and complete, i.e. the proof conditions for every gate can be proven.

This theorem and the minimal cut set theorem (see Sect. 5.1) justify, that only the cut sets can cause the hazard "rupture". All other reasons are ruled out.

6.4 Benefit of Model Checking Fault Trees

In the previous section, we presented the successful checking of the formal fault tree for the pressure tank example. But, the first model checking attempts failed. We had to fix syntax errors, flaws in the specification of the system model, and the formalizations of events.

The big advantage of model checking fault trees is, that incompleteness of fault trees by an omitted cause for the hazard is detected. We demonstrate this, by, hypothetically, "forgetting" the cause "K_2 fails to open", the sub-event e_5 at gate g_3 in the fault tree of Fig. 6. When we try to prove completeness of gate g_3, RAVEN generates the counterexample depicted in Fig. 7.

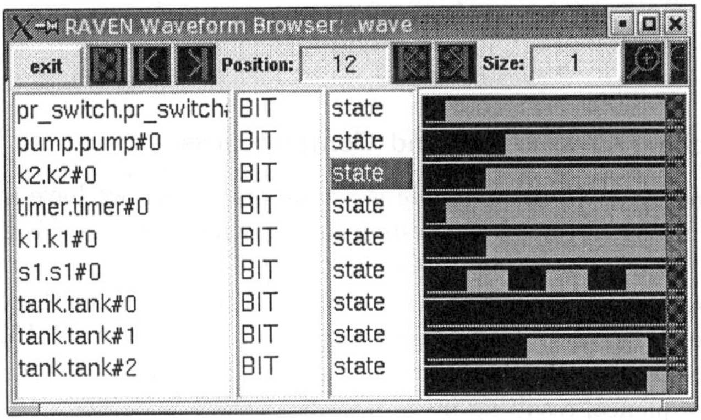

Fig. 7. Counterexample

The system states are noted on the left and the horizontal lines on the right show, when the state is active (fat line) or not (thin line). The failure state is marked with the vertical line at the right. It states, that the relay K_2 is closed ($K_2.K_2\#0$) although S is open ($pr\_switch.pr\_switch\#0$) and therefore K_2 is de-energized. This situation describes that K_2 fails to open. This cause has to be added to the fault tree. So, the counterexample directly points to the forgotten cause.

7 Related Work

Hansen et al. [7] proposed a formalization of FTA in Duration Calculus (DC, [3]). She used FTA to derive formal specifications from safety requirements. The formalization required, that the causes have to occur before (or at least at the same time as) the consequence. But, if causes and consequences are temporal events, the formalization allows an overlap, i.e. the (temporal) consequence can start before the (temporal) causes have finished. Furthermore, no minimal cut set theorem (see Sect. 5.1) was proven to justify the formalization.

Bruns and Anderson [2] presented a formalization for timeless events in the μ-calculus [8]. They distinguish between decomposition and cause consequence gates, as we do, but proved the minimal cut set theorem for decomposition gates only. If this formalization is used for temporal events, causes and consequences can overlap as well.

In [20] we discussed in detail the weaknesses of the two formalizations from above and presented an improved formalization in Interval Temporal Logic (ITL, [11]). We formalized decomposition and cause consequence gates and distinguished between synchronous and asynchronous AND-gates. The minimal cut set theorem was formally proven for this formalization for both, timeless and temporal events. Based on these results, we developed the CTL semantics for model checking FTA. The foundations of model checking FTA with the extension to timeless events by introducing observer automata and an example case study is the scope of this paper. In [22] we formally compared the three previous mentioned semantics with the CTL semantics. We proved in the specification and verification environment KIV [1], that if the fault tree consists of timeless events only, all four semantics are equivalent. The big advantage of the FTA semantics in CTL is, however, that it allows model checking the correctness and completeness of FTA.

A model checking approach is proposed in [19], as well. It uses the Duration Calculus model checker Moby/DC [21], which is based on phase automata and our ITL semantics from [20]. To prove correctness and completeness of the fault tree, the (negated) proof conditions for the gates have to be translated into phase automata and model checking excludes a common path with the system model. This verifies, that the proof conditions hold. Because phase automata are not closed against negation, not every event can be translated into a corresponding phase automata, but patterns are given for the typical fault tree events from Górski [6].

8 Conclusion

We presented an approach for the tight integration of FTA with model checking, for analyzing high assurance software based systems like aerospace, nuclear power plants, transportation and, medical control. This approach combines a typical engineering safety analysis technique with a safety technique from software engineering. The benefit of of this combination is twofold. It provides the possibility of formally validating FTA by proving correctness and completeness of the fault tree. Second, defects and failures of components can be treated within the formal system model and, nevertheless, safety properties (no cut set implies no hazard) can be proven. This is the basis of qualitative and quantitative system assessment of formal models.

To automating the formal proofs by model checkers, we presented a FTA semantics in CTL. Automated proof support is a necessary precondition for the acceptance of new approaches in industry. This CTL semantics is adequate for timeless events, justified by the minimal cut set theorem. A reduction of temporal to timeless events by using observer automata allows to treat temporal events as well. The pressure tank case study exemplified the approach.

References

[1] M. Balser, W. Reif, G. Schellhorn, K. Stenzel, and A. Thums. Formal system development with KIV. In T. Maibaum, editor, *Fundamental Approaches to Software Engineering*, number 1783 in LNCS. Springer, 2000.

[2] G. Bruns and S. Anderson. Validating safety models with fault trees. In J. Górski, editor, *SafeComp'93: 12th International Conference on Computer Safety, Reliability, and Security*, pages 21–30. Springer-Verlag, 1993.

[3] Zhou Chaochen, C. A. R. Hoare, and Anders P. Ravn. A calculus of durations. *Information Processing Letters*, 40(5):269–276, December 1991.

[4] E. M. Clarke and E. A. Emerson. Design and synthesis of synchronization skeletons using branching time temporal logic. In *Workshop on Logics of Programs*, number 131 in LNCS. Springer, 1981.

[5] Th. Filkorn, H.A. Schneider, A. Scholz, A. Strasser, and P. Warkentin. SVE user's guide. Technical Report ZFE BT SE 1-SVE-1, Siemens AG, Corporate Research and Development, Munich, 1994.

[6] J. Górski. Extending safety analysis techniques with formal semantics. In F. J. Redmill and T. Anderson, editors, *Technology and Assessment of Safety Critical Systems*, pages 147–163, London, 1994. Springer Verlag.

[7] K. M. Hansen, A. P. Ravn, and V. Stavridou. From safety analysis to formal specification. ProCoS II document [ID/DTH KMH 1/1], Technical University of Denmark, 1994.

[8] D. Kozen. Results on the propositional mu-calculus. *Theoretical Computer Science*, 17(3):333–354, December 1983.

[9] N. Leveson. *Safeware: System Safety and Computers*. Addison Wesley, 1995.

[10] K. L. McMillan. *Symbolic Model Checking*. Kluwer Academic Publishers, 1990.

[11] B. Moszkowski. A temporal logic for multilevel reasoning about hardware. *IEEE Computer*, 18(2):10–19, 1985.

[12] P. K. Pandya. Model checking CTL*[DC]. In T. Margaria and W. Yi, editors, *Prodeedings of TACAS 2001*, LNCS 2031, Genova, Italy, 2001. Springer-Verlag Berlin Heidelberg.

[13] P. K. Pandya. Specifying and deciding qauntified discrete-time duration calculus formulae using DCVALID. In *Proceedings of Workshop on Real-Time Tools RT-TOOL 2001*, Aalborg, Denmark, August 2001.

[14] J. Ruf. RAVEN: Real-time analyzing and verification environment. Technical Report WSI 2000-3, University of Tübingen, Wilhelm-Schickard-Institute, January 2000.

[15] J. Ruf and T. Kropf. Modeling real-time systems with I/O-interval structures. In *Methoden und Beschreibungssprachen zur Modellierung und Verifikation von Schaltungen ud Systemen.* Shaker Verlag, 1999.

[16] J. Ruf and T. Kropf. Modeling real-time systems with I/O-interval structures. In *Methoden und Beschreibungssprachen zur Modellierung und Verifikation von Schaltungen und Systemen*, pages 91–100. Shaker Verlag, March 1999.

[17] Jürgen Ruf and Thomas Kropf. Symbolic Model Checking for a Discrete Clocked Temporal Logic with Intervals. In E. Cerny and D.K. Probst, editors, *Conference on Correct Hardware Design and Verification Methods (CHARME)*, pages 146–166, Montreal, 1997. IFIP WG 10.5, Chapman and Hall.

[18] Jürgen Ruf and Thomas Kropf. Using MTBDDs for Composition and Model Checking of Real-Time Systems. In *FMCAD 1998*. Springer, November 1998.

[19] Andreas Schäfer. Fehlerbaumanalyse und Model-Checking. Master's thesis, Universität Oldenburg, 2001. in German.

[20] G. Schellhorn, A. Thums, and W. Reif. Formal fault tree semantics. In *Proceedings of The Sixth World Conference on Integrated Design & Process Technology*, Pasadena, CA, 2002.

[21] J. Tapken. Model-checking of duration calculus specifications. Master's thesis, University of Oldenburg, June 2001. http://semantik.informatik.uni-oldenburg.de/projects/.

[22] A. Thums, G. Schellhorn, and W. Reif. Comparing fault tree semantics. In D. Haneberg, G. Schellhorn, and W. Reif, editors, *FM-TOOLS 2002*, Technical Report 2002-11, pages 25–32. Universität Augsburg, 2002.

[23] W. E. Vesely, F. F. Goldberg, N. H. Roberts, and D. F. Haasl. *Fault Tree Handbook*. Washington, D.C., 1981. NUREG-0492.

Program Checking with Certificates: Separating Correctness-Critical Code

Sabine Glesner

Institut für Programmstrukturen und Datenorganisation,
Universität Karlsruhe, 76128 Karlsruhe, Germany,
http://www.info.uni-karlsruhe.de/~glesner

Abstract. We introduce program checking with certificates by extending the traditional notion of black-box program checking. Moreover, we establish program checking with certificates as a safety-scalable and practical method to ensure the correctness of real-scale applications. We motivate our extension of program checking with concepts of computational complexity theory and show its practical implication on the implementation and verification of checkers. Furthermore, we present an iterative method to construct checkers which is able to deal with the practically relevant problem of incomplete or missing specifications of software. In our case study, we have considered compilers and their generators, in particular code generators based on rewrite systems.

Keywords: program checking, certificates, correctness, validation, verification, safety-scalability, real-scale applications.

1 Just Let Me Double-Check!

Formal correctness of software is a desirable, yet expensive property. Program checking aims at reducing this cost. Instead of verifying a piece of software, one only verifies its result. In this paper, we present the notion of program checking with certificates which extends the established version of black-box program checking. Furthermore, we show that program checking with certificates is a practical and safety-scalable method which has proved itself in real-scale applications. To be practical and safety-scalable, we require a method to fulfill the following criteria: Its reliability should be scalable wrt. safety, ranging from "only" validated up to formally verified software. In safety-critical applications, one needs formally verified software. Hence, on its top level of reliability, the desired method should formally ensure the correctness of the computed results. But in many situations, one can already be satisfied with a sufficiently increased confidence that the software does indeed exactly what is defined in its specification. Furthermore, we require the method to have a manageable effort in practice. In particular, we want to avoid to verify the software in its entirety. This is an important requirement as many parts of a given piece of software do not influence the correctness of its results. E.g. optimizations are intended not only to compute a correct but also an optimal result. In many cases, its correctness can be established independently of its quality. Hence, we do not want to spend verification effort for the quality but only for the correctness of the result. There are even more parts of software which do not influence the correctness of the result. Nearly all software evolved over a certain amount of time and maintained by several programmers contains code which is not used any more. Programmers tend to leave over old code instead of deleting it. A practical method for ensuring the correctness of software should be able to deal with such scenarios. Moreover, it should be applicable for generated software. Consequently, the involved generators should be extendable to generate not only the desired software pieces but also the proofs for their correctness. As a sacrifice, we do not require total but only partial correctness. It is sufficient if the method proves the correctness of each result individually. If it cannot verify the correctness of a result, it simply says 'no', giving us only partial formal correctness.

With our investigations we show that program checking with certificates can cope with these requirements. Originally, program checking [BK95] assumes that an implementation P computing a function f is used as a black box. An independent program result checker for f checks for a particular input x if $P(x) = f(x)$. We extend the notion of a program result checker such that it is allowed to observe the implementation program P during its computation of the result. In particular, the program P might pass a certificate to the checker, telling the checker how P has computed the solution. This extension is natural as in many cases one has access to the implementation code. Moreover, it fits to the nature of search and optimization problems, in particular to **NP**-complete problems. Such problems are characterized by the fact that proofs for the correctness of a solution can be checked easily while the computation of solutions is believed to be significantly harder. We argue that a certificate is such a correctness proof. This gives us evidence that for many problems, checkers are significantly simpler than the actual implementations. In theoretical considerations (e.g. the checkers for numerical problems in [BLR93]), the specification of the checker is clear. It is supposed to check if a certain function f has been computed correctly for one specific argument x. Hence, the precondition of the checker states that x and $P(x)$ are admissible inputs. Its postcondition states that the output is 'yes' iff $P(x) = f(x)$. In practical situations, the specification of a complex system is not that obvious, making subsequent correctness proofs more difficult. Since software evolves over time, its specification might also change. We show that program checking can be deployed to determine pre- and postconditions in an iterative process. Therefore we start with a preliminary specification, implement a checker checking this specification, and use the checker for typical pairs of input and output values. Whenever the checker cannot establish the correctness of the result, we either have found a mistake in the implementation or the checker specification needs to be revised. This proceeding is continued until we are sufficiently assured that the specification of the checker reflects the connection between input and output values. In contrast to pure testing, the checker will say 'no' for all cases not included in the specification, instead of allowing the implementation to do something unpredictable. On the highest level of reliability, we require a formal proof for the correctness of the checker with an automated theorem prover. If this level of security is not necessary, we can still use the checker without a formal proof, giving us a safety-scalable method. In our experiments, we found that program checking emerges as a novel combination of existing validation and verification techniques.

As a real-scale test case, we have chosen compiler backend generators and the thereby generated compiler backends. In particular, we have focused on designing and implementing a checker for the CGGG system [Boe98]. This system generates compiler backends which transform intermediate SSA (static single assignment) representations into native machine code based on BURS (bottom-up rewrite systems). CGGG has been utilized to generate a compiler in the AJACS (Applying Java to Automotive Control Systems) project with industrial partners [Gau02,GKC01]. Compiler backend generators are well-suited as a test case due to several reasons. Typically, compiler generators are maintained for a long period of time. Several developers with changing design objectives and optimization goals modify the generators by adapting them to the constantly changing concepts in source programming languages or target machine architectures. This results in "naturally grown software" with a large variety of functionality, much of which is not used in the generation of one particular backend. Possibly, there are even combinations of different functionalities which are never chosen and which, if used together, may even be incorrect. A formal verification aiming for total correctness could fail due to such scenarios. Nevertheless, each actually generated backend could still be correct. Hence, a notion of partial correctness and, in turn, program checking is adequate for the correctness of compiler backends.

This paper is organized as follows. In section 2, we introduce our approach of program checking with certificates. In section 3, we discuss the nature of program checking in practice and derive a general safety-scalable validation and verification method. In section 4, we describe our case study regarding compiler generators. Our experimental results are explained in section 5. We discuss related work in section 6 and conclude in section 7.

2 Program Checking: Trust Is Good, Control Is Better!

In this section, we introduce the notion of program checking with certificates. It modifies the classical concept of black-box program checking [BK95] which is summarized in subsection 2.1. In subsection 2.2, we show how it can be extended to check the correctness of solutions for optimization problems by using certificates. Moreover, in subsection 2.3, we argue why it is unlikely that we might be able to construct efficient checkers for the optimality of solutions.

2.1 Classical Black-Box Program Checking

Program checking [BK95] has been introduced as a method to improve the reliability of programs. It assumes that there exists a black box implementation P computing a function f. A *program result checker* for f checks for a particular input x if $P(x) = f(x)$. Assume that $f : X \to Y$ maps from X to Y. Then the checker *checker* has two inputs, x and y, whereby x is the same input as the input of the implementation P and y is its result on input x. The checker has an auxiliary function f_ok that takes x and y as inputs and checks if $y = f(x)$ holds.

proc *checker*$(x : X, y : Y) : BOOL$
  if $f\_ok(x, y)$ **then return** True
  else return False
end proc

Note that the checker does not depend on the implementation P. Hence, it can be used for any program P' implementing f. Thereby the checker should be simpler than the implementation of f itself and, a stronger requirement, simpler than any implementation P' computing f. Simple checkers would have the advantage of potentially having fewer bugs than the implementation P. Since there is no reasonable way to define the notion of being simpler formally, [BK95] states a definition for being *quantifiably different*. The intention is to force the checker to do something different than the implementation P. A checker is forced to do something different if it has fewer resources than the implementation. This would imply that bugs in the implementation and in the checker are independent and unlikely to interact so that bugs in the program will be caught more likely. Formally, a checker is quantifiably different than the implementation if its running time is asymptotically smaller than the running time of the fastest known algorithm. However, for many interesting problems, the fastest algorithm is not known. As a weaker requirement, one can consider *efficient* checkers whose running time is linear in the running time of the checked implementation and linear in the input size. [BLR93] presents checking methods for a variety of numerical problems.

2.2 Program Checking with Certificates

We introduce the method of program checking with certificates by extending the notion of black-box program checking: We allow the checker to observe the implementation program P during its computation of the result. In our setting, the program P might tell the checker how it has computed its solution.

To motivate our idea theoretically, let us take a look at the common definition for problems in **NP**. **NP** is the union of all problems that can be solved by a nondeterministic polynomial time Turing machine. An alternative equivalent definition for **NP** states the following: Assume that a language L is in **NP**. Then there exists a polynomial time Turing machine M such that for all $x \in L$, there exists y, $|y| \leq poly(x)$ such that M accepts (x, y). Hence, for any language L in **NP**, there is a simple proof checker (the polynomial time Turing machine M) and a short proof (y) for every string $x \in L$. Given the proof y and the string x, the proof checker M can decide if the proof is valid. Clearly, the two definitions are equivalent: Com-

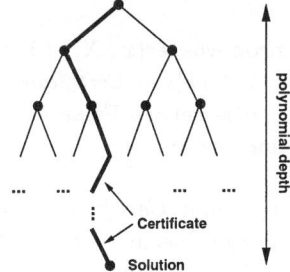

Fig. 1. Computation Spaces in **NP**

putations within nondeterministic polynomial time can be thought of as a search tree with polynomial depth. Each node represents the choice which the nondeterministic Turing machine has at any one time during computation. A proof for membership in the language L is a path to a solution through this search tree. Since the tree has polynomial depth, there always exists a proof of polynomial length. Such a proof is also called a *certificate*, cf. [Pap94]. **NP**-complete problems have the tendency to have very natural certificates.

When solving optimization problems, huge search spaces need to be searched for an optimal or at least acceptable solution. When we want to check its correctness, we do not care about its optimality. Hence, we can use the certificate to recompute the result. In particular for the optimization variants of **NP**-complete problems, we have the well-founded hope that the checker code is much easier to implement, and in turn to verify, than the implementation itself. Our checking scenario with certificates is summarized in Fig. 2.

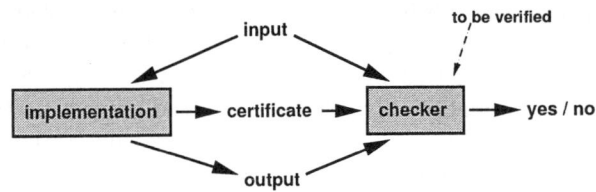

Fig. 2. Checker Scenario with Certificates

But what if the implementation is malicious and gives us a buggy certificate? The answer is simple: If the checker manages to compute a correct solution with this erroneous certificate and if, furthermore, this correct solution is identical with the solution of the implementation, then the checker has managed to verify the correctness of the computed solution. It does not matter how the implementation has computed the solution or the certificate as long as the checker is able to reconstruct the solution via its verified implementation.

proc $checker(x : X, y : Y, Certificate) : BOOL$
   if $f\_ok(x, y, Certificate)$ **then return True**
   else return False
end proc

We describe the checker functionality as follows. Let P be the implementation of a function f with input $x \in X$ and the two output values $y \in Y$ and $Certificate$ such that y is supposed to be equal to $f(x)$ and $Certificate$ a description how the solution has been computed. The checker has an auxiliary function f_ok that takes x, y, and $Certificate$ as inputs and checks whether $y = f(x)$ holds.

2.3 Can We Check the Optimality of Solutions?

Our notion of checking with certificates makes sure that a solution is correct but does not consider checking its quality. In this subsection, we argue that due to certain widely-accepted assumptions in complexity theory, we cannot hope to construct efficient checkers which check if a solution is optimal.

Problems in **NP** are always decision problems, asking if a certain instance belongs to a given language (e.g.: Is there a Hamiltonian path? Does the travelling salesman have a tour of at most length n?). These problems are characterized by their property that each positive instance has a proof of polynomial length, a *certificate*. E.g. the Hamiltonian path itself or a tour for the travelling salesman of length n or smaller would be such certificates. Conversely, the class **coNP** is defined as containing all those languages whose negative instances have a proof of non-membership, a *disqualification*, of polynomial length. E.g. the language containing all valid propositional formulas is such a language. A non-satisfying assignment for a formula proves that this formula does not belong to the language of valid formulas. Hence, this non-satisfying assignment is a disqualification. To prove that a solution is not only correct but also optimal, one would need a positive proof in the spirit of **NP**-proofs and a negative proof as in the case of **coNP**-proofs. The positive proof states that there is a solution at least as good as the specified one. The negative proof would state that there is no better solution. Complexity theory [Pap94] has studied this situation and defined the class **DP**. **DP** is the set of all languages that are the intersection of a language in **NP** and a language in **coNP**. One can think of **DP** as the class of all languages that can be decided by a Turing machine allowed to ask a satisfiability oracle twice. This machine accepts iff the first answer was 'yes' (e.g. stating that the optimal solution is at least as good as the specified one) and the second 'no' (stating that the optimal solution is at most as good as the specified one). It is a very hard question to decide whether an optimization problem lies in **DP**. The current belief in complexity theory is that **NP**-complete problems are not contained in **coNP**, implying that conceivably they do not have polynomial disqualifications. So if we design a checker for a problem being at least **NP**-complete, it does not surprise that we are not able to announce a polynomial checker also for the optimality of a solution, since such an announcement would solve a few very interesting questions in complexity theory.

3 Program Checking in Practice

In practical applications, program checking poses problems which do not appear in the theoretical setting discussed in the previous section. We discuss these problems in subsection 3.1. In subsection 3.2, we propose an iterative method to cope with them.

3.1 Problems in Practice

No Explicit Input-Output-Mapping: In many software systems, there is not one single function to be computed but rather a (finite) sequence of functions. Even though their concatenation could theoretically be expressed within one single function, this is not practical. It would result in a clumsy formulation.

A typical example for this problem are compilers which transform a source program by applying a sequence of compilation steps. The transformation is split up for efficiency reasons. Hence, the checker approach must be able to deal with such situations as they are typical for many software systems. In consequence, one needs to check a sequence of results. Some of these results are only available in main memory (otherwise the implementation would be too inefficient). This implies that the checker needs to run together with the implementation program so that the necessary checks can be done on the fly. A tight interlocking between checker and implementation program is necessary. Therefore it is absolutely necessary to have access to the implementation code.

Incomplete or Nonexistent Specifications: As a major practical problem, complete specifications do only rarely exist. As software has evolved over time, the most prominent functionality is known. But a complete specification defining results for special cases does not exist and might be very hard to set up. E.g. in our case study of compiler generation tools, we have the typical situation that specification and implementation of compiler passes are not fully separated. It is a common situation that the specification for a compiler generator might contain implementation code. As well-known examples, consider the Unix tools Lex and Yacc for the generation of the lexical and syntactic analysis. Input specifications for them can contain C code which will become part of the generated compiler pass. This observation holds for basically all compiler generators, in particular for the CGGG system considered in our case study.

3.2 Iterative Checking Method

We propose an iterative method to deal with the problem of non-existing specifications. Therefore, we postulate a preliminary specification which is revised iteratively. To deal with the existence of intermediate results and the necessity to check them, we use a multistage process, cf. also Fig. 3. We assume that we are given a hand-written or generated program without a formal specification. The first step is to guess the specification by assuming postulates, consisting of a pre- and a postcondition and of assertions describing intermediate states or results reached during the run of the program. This is the truly creative part of program checking in practice and requires code inspection. In the second step, checkers are to be implemented that check whether the postulates hold. Then we need to make sure that our assumed specification meets reality. Therefore we need to make tests which ensure that the specification covers the relevant pairs of input and output values. If such tests fail, we need to revise the specification (or correct bugs in the implementation), adapt the checkers, and start again with tests. We are done whenever we are confident that the specification and the respective checkers cover all practically interesting pairs of input and output values. In contrast to pure testing, the checker will say 'no' for all cases not included in the specification.

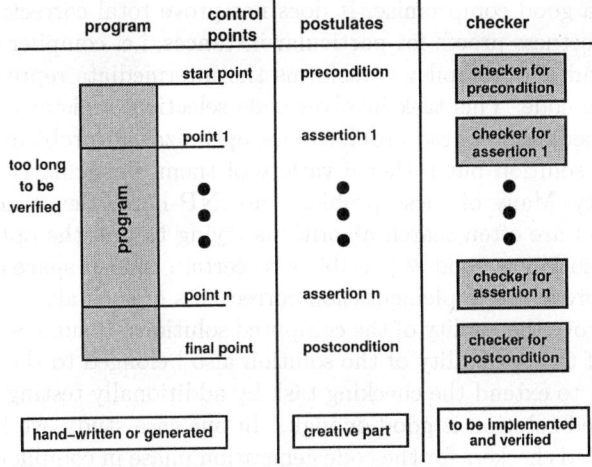

Fig. 3. Program Checking as a Validation and Verification Method

4 Case Study: Compilers and Compiler Generators

Compilers and their generators are good candidates for investigating the benefits of program checking in practical applications as they show the two major problems discussed in subsection 3.1. In our case study, we have considered compiler backend generators and the corresponding generated compiler backends.

The two major practical problems are the nonexistence of explicit input-output mappings and the absence of complete specifications. Both problems arise in the area of compiler construction. Compilers transform input programs consisting of a sequence of characters into target machine code. This translation consists of several steps, separated by explicit interfaces. The overall translation function as a concatenation of these individual steps is never stated explicitly as it would be much too unwieldy. Hence, we do not have an explicit input-output mapping for compilers, not even for their individual steps. As we argue below, for the code generation phase in a compiler backend, we could theoretically state the overall transformation function but simplify the translation and the checking task significantly if we regard the sequence of single transformations. In this context, we also have the problem that intermediate results of the translation are only available in main memory. Hence, we need a tight interlocking between compiler and checker. The second problem, namely incomplete specifications, also appears when using compiler generators. Typically, compiler generators are maintained over a long period of time. Many functionalities are implemented but the generation of one particular compiler backend needs only a few of them. It would be much too expensive to verify compiler backend generators. This verification task could even be impossible if there existed different functionalities whose combination would result in incorrect compilers, even though such a combination was never chosen in practice. Here program checking as a cheaper alternative is a good compromise. It does not prove total correctness but gives us formal correctness proofs for particular instances, i.e. compiler runs.

The backend of a compiler transforms the intermediate representation into target machine code. This task involves code selection, register allocation, and instruction scheduling. These problems are optimization problems that do not have a unique solution but rather a variety of them, particularly distinguished by their quality. Many of these problems are **NP**-hard. Hence, algorithms for code generation are often search algorithms trying to find the optimal solution or at least a solution as good as possible wrt. certain time or space constraints. If one wants to prove the implementation correctness of such algorithms, it is not necessary to prove the quality of the computed solutions. It suffices to prove their correctness. (If the optimality of the solution also belonged to the specification, we would need to extend the checking task by additionally testing if the quality of the computed solution is good enough.) In our case study, we have designed and implemented checkers for the code generation phase in compiler backends. In subsection 4.1, we describe code generation based on bottom-up rewrite systems (BURS) and the CGGG system [Boe98] (compiler generator generator based on graphs). In subsection 4.2, we present a generic checking algorithm for BURS code generation and the necessary modifications of the CGGG system.

4.1 BURS and the CGGG System

Bottom-up rewrite systems (BURS) are a powerful method to generate target machine code from intermediate program representations. Conventional BURS systems allow for the specification of transformations between terms which are represented as trees. Rules associate tree patterns with a result pattern, a target-machine instruction, and a cost. If the tree pattern matches a subtree of the intermediate program representation, then this subtree can be replaced with the corresponding result pattern while simultaneously emitting the associated target-machine instruction. The code generation algorithm determines a sequence of rule applications which reduces the intermediate program tree into a single node by applying rules in a bottom-up order.

Traditionally, BURS has been implemented by code generation algorithms which compute the costs of all possible rewrite sequences. This enormous computation effort has been improved by employing dynamic programming. The work by Nymeyer and Katoen [NK97] enhances efficiency further on by coupling BURS with the heuristic search algorithm A*. This search algorithm is directed by a cost heuristic. It considers the already encountered part of costs for selected code as well as the estimated part of costs for code which has still to be generated. A* is an optimally efficient search algorithm. No other optimal algorithm is guaranteed to expand fewer nodes than A*, cf. [DP85]. Using such an informed search algorithm offers the advantage that only those costs need to be computed that might contribute to an optimal rewrite sequence. [NK97] propose a two-pass algorithm to compute an optimal rewrite sequence for a given expression tree. The first bottom-up pass computes, for each node, the set of all possible local rewrite sequences, i.e. those rewrite sequences which might be applicable at that node. This pass is called *decoration* and the result is referred to as *decorated tree*. The second top-down pass trims these rewrite sequences by removing all those local rewrite sequences that do not contribute for the reduction of the term.

Static single assignment (SSA) form [CFR+91,CF95] has become the preferred internal program representation for handling all kinds of program analyses and optimizing program transformations prior to code generation. Its main merits comprise the explicit representation of def-use-chains and, based on them, the ease by which further dataflow information can be derived. By definition SSA-form requires that a program be represented as a directed graph of elementary operations (jump, memory read/write, unary or binary operation) such that each "variable" is assigned exactly once in the program text. Only references to such variables may appear as operands in operations. Thus, an operand explicitly indicates the data dependency to its point of origin. The directed graph of an SSA-representation is an overlay of the control flow and the data flow graph of the program. If a variable x has several static predecessors $x_1, \ldots, x_n$, one of which defines the value of x at runtime, this is expressed by $x := \phi(x_1, \ldots, x_n)$. This value is a selection amongst the values $x_1, \ldots, x_n$ and represents the unique value assigned to variable x at runtime.

BURS theory in an extended form [Boe98] can handle SSA representations by a two-stage process [Boe98]. The first stage concerns the extension from terms, i.e. trees, to terms with common subexpressions, i.e. DAGs. This modification involves mostly technical details in the specification and implementation of the rewrite rules. The second stage deals with the extension from DAGs to potentially cyclic SSA graphs. SSA graphs might contain data and control flow cycles. There are only two kinds of nodes which might have backward edges, ϕ nodes and nodes guiding the control flow at the end of a basic block to the succeeding basic block. For these nodes, one can specify general rewrite rules which do not depend on the specific translation, i.e., which are independent from the target machine language. In a precalculation phase, rewrite sequences are computed for these nodes with backward edges. These rewrite sequences contain only the general rewrite rules. In the next step, the standard computation of the rewrite sequences for all nodes in the SSA graph is performed. Thereby, for each node with backward edges, the precalculated rewrite sequences are used.

The BURS code generation algorithm has been implemented in the code generator generator system CGGG (code generator generator based on graphs) [Boe98]. CGGG takes a specification consisting of BURS rewrite rules as input and generates a code generator which uses the BURS mechanism for rewriting SSA graphs, cf. Fig. 4. The produced code generators consist of three major parts. First the SSA graph is decorated by assigning each node the set of its local alternative rewrite sequences. Then the A^*-search looks for the optimal solution, namely the cheapest rewrite sequence. This search starts at the final node of the SSA graph marking the end of computation, by working up through the SSA graph until the start node is reached. Finally, the target machine code is generated by applying the computed rewrite sequence.

An example for a rule from a code generator specification is:

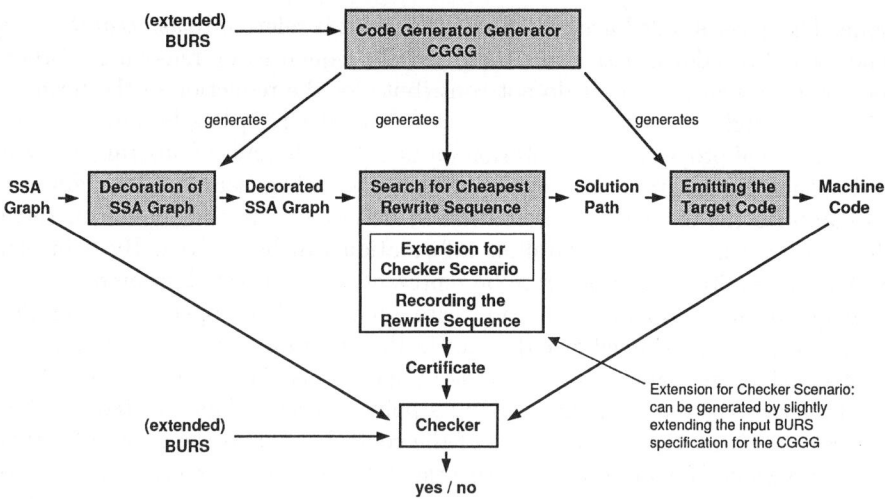

Fig. 4. Extended CGGG Architecture

```
RULE a:Add (b:Register b) -> s:Shl (d:Register c:Const);
RESULT d := b;
EVAL { ATTR(c, value) = 1; }
EMIT {}
```

This rule describes an addition of two operands. On the left hand side of the rule, the first operand is a register with short name b. The second operand is the first operand again, identified by the short name. Note that the left-hand side of this rule is a directed acyclic graph. If the code generator finds this pattern in the graph, it rewrites it with the right-hand side of the rule. In general, this could be a DAG again. Thereby the EVAL code is executed. This code places the constant 1 in the attribute field value of the Const node. The RESULT instruction informs the register allocator that the register d equals register b.

Optimal BURS code generation for SSA graphs is an **NP**-complete problem: In [AJU77], it is shown that code generation for expressions with common subexpressions is **NP**-complete. Each instance of such a code generation problem is also a BURS code generation problem for SSA graphs. Thus it follows directly that BURS code generation for SSA graphs is **NP**-complete.

4.2 A Generic Checker for Code Generators

The CGGG architecture can easily be extended for the program checking approach. Therefore we record which sequence of rewrite rules has been selected during the A^*-search for the cheapest solution. This sequence of rewrite rules is the certificate. The checker takes it and recomputes the result. This result is compared with the result of the code generator. Only if it is equal to that of the checker, the checker will output 'yes'. If the checker outputs 'no', then it has not been able to recompute the same result. Such a checker is generic in the sense that the respective BURS system is one of the checker inputs. Hence, the same generic checker can be used for all code generators generated by the CGGG system.

It is particularly easy to extend the CGGG architecture such that it outputs the certificate necessary to check the results of the generated code generators. We can extend the BURS specification such that not only the machine code is output but also, in a separate file, the applied rules. Therefore, we only need to extend the EMIT part of each rule. This part contains instructions which will be executed on application of the rule. We can place one more instruction there, namely a protocol function. This protocol function writes a tuple to the certificate file. This tuple contains the applied rule as well as the node identifier of the node where it has been applied. We have decided to take the address in main memory of each node as its unique identifier.

One might ask why it is not sufficient to check only the local decorations of the nodes on the solution path found during the A^*-search to ensure the correctness of the computed result. The answer concerns the sorts of the nodes in the SSA graph. Each node has a specific sort which might be changed on application of a rule. Hence, the correctness of a rule sequence can only be decided if one makes sure that the sorts of the nodes and the sorts required by the rules fit together in each rule application. Moreover, one needs to check that the rules are applied according to the bottom-up strategy of BURS. We do not know of any other checking method assuring well-sorting and bottom-up rewriting other than recomputing the solution. This problem is also an example for the first practical problem discussed in subsection 3.1. The transformation of an intermediate representation into its target code is not specified by a single input-output mapping but rather by a sequence of rule applications. For all theoretical as well as practical purposes, it would be much too complicated to express such rule-based transformations by a single function.

The exact checking algorithm is summarized in Fig. 5. The certificate *Certificate* is a list of tuples, each containing a rule and the node identifier *node_no*. This node identifier characterizes uniquely the node at which the rule has been applied. *BURS* is the extended rewrite system which the CGGG has taken as input. *SSA_Graph* is the intermediate representation or the intermediate results obtained during the rewrite process, resp. Finally, *Target_Code* is the result of the rewrite process, the machine instruction sequence. To keep the presentation of the checking algorithm as simple as possible, we did not give all details of the auxiliary procedures but only described them colloquially. Clearly, this checker is generic because the respective BURS system is not hardwired into its code but one of the input parameters.

Theorem 1 (Correctness of Checker). *If the checker outputs 'yes' (True) on input (BURS, SSA_Graph, Target_Code, Certificate), then the target code Target_Code has been produced correctly by transforming the intermediate representation SSA_Graph according to the rules of the BURS system BURS.* ⋄

```
proc CGGG_Checker(BURS, SSA_Graph, Target_Code, Certificate) : Bool;
  var Checker_Code : list of strings;
  Checker_Code := [];
  while Certificate ≠ [] do
    (rule, node_no) := head(Certificate);
    Certificate := tail(Certificate);
    if rule ∉ BURS then return False;
    SSA_Graph := apply_and_check(rule, SSA_Graph, node_no);
    insert(code(rule), Checker_Code); od;
  return compare(Checker_Code, Target_Code) end
proc apply_and_check(rule, SSA_Graph, node_no) : Bool;
  node := find_node(SSA_Graph, node_no);
  if node = Nil then return False;
  if BURS_successors(SSA_Graph, node_no) ≠ ∅ then return False;
  if not match(lhs(rule), node, SSA_Graph) then return False;
  apply(rule, SSA_Graph, node_no); end;
proc find_node(SSA_Graph, node_no) :
  returns node in SSA_Graph with number node_no;
  if node does not exist, it returns Nil; end
proc BURS_successors(SSA_Graph, node_no) :
  returns set of nodes in SSA_Graph that have to be rewritten before node
  node_no if bottom-up rewrite strategy is used;
  control and data flow cycles are disconnected as in the A*−search; end
proc lhs(rule) : returns left-hand side of the rewrite rule rule; end
proc match(pattern, node, SSA_Graph) :
  checks if pattern pattern matches subgraph located at node node; end
proc apply(rule, SSA_Graph, node_no) : does the rewrite step; end
proc compare(Checker_Code, Target_Code) :
  checks if Checker_Code and Target_Code are identical; end
proc code(rule) : returns code associated with rule rule; end
```

Fig. 5. Generic Checker for Code Generation

Proof. The CGGG system is supposed to generate code generators implementing the respective input rewrite system BURS. To check if a code sequence produced by such a code generator is correct, we need to make sure that there is a sequence of rule applications conforming to the BURS rewrite method. Instead of testing if there is any such sequence, we check the weaker proposition if the certificate produced by the code generator is a BURS rewrite sequence. This is done successively by repeating each rule application, starting with the same SSA intermediate representation. In each step, it is tested that the node exists at which the rewrite step is supposed to take place. Then it is tested that the rewrite step conforms to the bottom-up strategy of BURS. Finally, the left-hand side of the rule must match the graph located at the respective node. If all three requirements are fulfilled, then the rewrite step is performed by the checker. If this recomputation of the target machine code results in exactly the same code sequence, then the result of the code generator has been validated. If we verify the checker wrt. the requirements listed in this proof, then we have a formally verified correct result of the code generation phase. ∎

5 Experimental Results

The computations performed in the checker for the CGGG do the same rewrite steps as the backend itself and return 'False' if an error occurs. The only difference between checker and backend lies in the search for the optimal solution. The checker gets it as input for granted while the backend needs to compute it by an extensive search. In this section, we explain why this observation seems to be general for a variety of optimization problems and how we have exploited it in our checker implementation. Then we state our experimental results. Thereby we also explain how we have dealt with the practical problems of only implicitly stated input-output mappings and incomplete or nonexistent specifications (cf. section 3) by the proposed iterative method of assuming, testing, extending and eventually verifying a specification.

5.1 The Nature of NP-Problem Checkers

Problems in **NP** are characterized by the fact that a proof for the correctness of a solution has polynomial length. This holds in particular for the decision variant of many optimization problems. In general, it is unknown how such a proof looks like. For many practical problems such proofs are natural, cf. section 2. This observation has direct implications concerning the implementation of checkers for such optimization problems with natural proofs. The actual implementation keeps track of its decisions and collects them in its certificate. This certificate is the proof for the correctness of the computed solution. Based on it, the checker recomputes the solution and compares it with the solution of the implementation. Only if both solutions are identical, the checker outputs 'yes'. Speaking in the language of Turing machines, the problem implementation is a nondeterministic Turing machine that needs good random guesses to find a solution. The checker is a deterministic Turing machine that knows the good guesses (the certificate as its input) and just needs to recompute the solution. Hence, we can expect that the checker implementation is a part of the overall implementation of the optimization problem.

5.2 Experimental Results

For BURS code generation, this expectation has come true. We could extract most of the code for the checker implementation from the code generator implementation directly. This is an advantage since CGGG has been tested extensively, making sure that many obvious bugs have been eliminated from the (implementation and checker) code already in the forefront of our experiment. CGGG has been used during the last four years by many graduate students who tend to be very critical software testers. Moreover, the CGGG system has been utilized to generate a compiler in the AJACS project (Applying Java to Automotive Control Systems) with industrial partners [Gau02,GKC01]. This compiler transforms restricted Java programs into low-level C code.

We can distinguish three different kinds of code in the CGGG system:

1. Code that does not have any influence on the correctness of the results at all. This comprises in particular all debugging functionalities. This code does not need to be verified.
2. Code that implements the search for the optimal solution. This code needs to be extended by the protocol function which sets up the certificate. This code does not need to be verified.
3. Code that computes the rewrite steps. In a slightly extended form, this code becomes part of the checker and needs to be verified in order to get formally correct results of code generation.

	Code Generator	Checker
lines of code in .h-Files	949	789
lines of code in .c-Files	20887	10572
total lines of code	21836	11361

Fig. 6. Size of Code Generator and Checker

In our case study, we implemented a checker for the AJACS compiler described above. The table in Fig. 6 compares the overall size of the AJACS code generator generated by the CGGG system with the size of its checker. Both implementations, CGGG and the code generator, are written in C.

If one wants to obtain formally verified solutions for the code generation phase, one needs to verify only the checker code. A first comparison between the size of the code generator and its checker shows that the verification effort for the checker seems to be half of that of the code generator. This comparison is only half the truth as the verification effort is even smaller. Much of the checker code is generated from the code generator specification. This is very simple code which just applies the rewrite rules. The verification conditions for the various rewrite rules are basically the same, simplifying the verification task considerably. In contrast, the code for the A^*-search is very complicated and would need much more verification effort. Luckily it does not belong to the checker. Up to now we have not formally verified the checker code. For this task it seems helpful to parameterize the rewrite routines with the respective rewrite rules. In doing so, it would suffice to only formally verify the parameterized rewrite routine.

We designed and implemented the checker iteratively, as described in section 3. We started with the assumption that it takes SSA representations and transforms them directly by applying the graph rewrite rules of the compiler backend specification. It turned out that this assumption was not detailed enough. Instead, the compiler first transforms the SSA form into a slightly different representation which removes some of the data flow freedom of the SSA form in order to simplify the graph rewrite process. This is a typical example for the practical problem that the input-output mapping is not stated explicitly, cf. subsection 3.1. So we stated an intermediate assertion (cf. subsection 3.2 and in particular Fig. 3) about the result of this first auxiliary transformation. Then we proceeded by stating the next assertion that the result of the graph rewrite process, i.e. the target program, has been received by exclusively applying the rewrite rules of the specification. It turned out that this assumption was false. The CGGG system additionally uses two general rewrite rules to handle the data and control flow cycles in the SSA representations. These rules are not stated in the specification but hard-coded into the generated compiler backends because they are independent of the target language and needed in every backend. This is a classical example of an incomplete specification, the second major practical problem discussed in subsection 3.1. We extended the specification of our checker with these general rewrite rules and did not find any more inconsistencies.

6 Related Work

The original notion of program checking [BK95] assumes that an implementation is used as a black box and that an independent program result checker checks the correctness of each individual result. Black-box program checking has been applied to numerical problems [BLR93]. In our extended setting, we allow the checker to explicitly access the implementation code and to receive a certificate as input which records the run-time decisions of the implementation. Our checkers can use the certificate to recompute the solution. By employing concepts from computational complexity theory, we show that for many search and optimization problems, it is natural that the computations of the checker are a part of the computations of the implementation. So program checking with certificates becomes a method of separating the correctness-critical part of a given implementation. Our case study raises hope that the checker computations are those that can be verified more easily, cf. section 5.

Safety-scalable program checking is a good middle course between formal program verification and pure testing. Program verification is often too expensive since proofs are often longer than the program itself. Small changes in the program code require the proof to be redone. In contrast, testing does not give full reliability as it does not say anything about special inputs not included in the test suites. It is very difficult to decide if a test sample distribution is sufficient to predict that no errors will occur at run time. In our approach of safety-scalable program checking, we do not lose the advantages of program testing, which help in understanding existing software and in finding early mistakes.

In our case study, we have experienced safety-scalable program checking as a novel combination of existing methods. It combines code inspection, design by contract, testing, and formal program verification, cf. section 3.2. Code inspection is necessary to create the postulates. We employ design by contract [Mey97] by postulating assertions for certain points during program execution, cf. the assertions in Eiffel programs to be checked during runtime. To ensure the formal correctness of the implemented checkers, we need formal program verification.

Program checking has been used in the construction of correct compilers, most prominently in the Verifix project [GDG+96]. It has proposed program checking to ensure the correctness of compiler implementations. Program checking has been successfully applied in the context of frontend verification [HGG+99]. [GHZG99,GZG00] propose program checking to ensure the correctness of backend implementations but do not have a checking algorithm. The program checking approach has also been used in further projects aiming to implement correct compilers. [Nec00] shows how some backend optimizations of the GCC can be checked. Proof-carrying code [NL97,NL98,CLN+00] is another weaker approach to the construction of correct compilers which guarantees that the generated code fulfills certain necessary correctness conditions. During the translation, a correctness proof for these conditions is constructed and delivered together with the generated code. A user may reconstruct the correctness proof by using a simple proof checking method. In recent work [NR01], a variant of proof-carrying code has been proposed which is related to our notion of program checking with certificates. In this setting, trusted inference rules are represented as a higher-order logic program, the proof checker is replaced by a nondeterministic higher-order logic interpreter and the proof by an oracle implemented as a stream of bits that resolve the nondeterministic choices. This proof directly corresponds to our notion of certificate as it helps in resolving the nondeterminism in the same way as in our setting. Nevertheless, this work does not draw the same conclusion as we do, namely that checking with certificates isolates the correctness-critical part of an implementation. In [PSS98b,PSS98a], the problem of constructing correct compilers is also addressed, but only for very limited applications. Only those programs consisting of a single loop with loop-free body are considered and translated without the usual optimizations of compiler construction. Those programs are translated correctly such that certain safety and liveness properties of reactive systems are sustained. In more recent work [ZPL01], a theory for validating optimizing compilers is proposed similar to the method developed in the Verifix project. The main difference to our work is that these approaches do not assume to have access to the implementation of the compiler or its generator. This access gives us the freedom to modify the implementation to get a certificate used in the checker.

7 Conclusions

We have shown that program checking with certificates is a safety-scalable method for real-scale practical applications, i.e., its reliability is scalable wrt. safety. We deal with the practically relevant problem of incomplete or missing specifications of software with an iterative process. We postulate a specification, implement checkers for it, and iteratively improve it by testing it with typical input and output values. Since the checkers always reject results not fitting to the specification, we never get incorrect results. This gives us a significant advantage over pure testing and an increased confidence in the correctness of a given piece of software. If we need reliability on the highest possible level, we need to verify the checker implementation with an automated theorem prover. Such a verification ensures the formally proved correctness of the results.

We have extended the classical notion of black-box program checking to program checking with certificates which allows the checker to access the implementation code. The checker might observe the implementation and might receive a certificate recording the computation steps of the implementation. The checker might use this certificate to check the computed solution, typically by recomputing it. This scenario is especially suited for search and optimization problems, in particular for **NP**-complete problems. Thereby we use the property of these problems that results can be checked in polynomial time whereas the computation of results is believed to take much more time. As a practical consequence, the checker code is nearly identical with some parts of the implementation code: Many search and optimization problems can be solved by algorithms looking for an optimal solution. These algorithms have typically a fraction searching for an optimum and a fraction computing the respective solution. The checker is not concerned with the quality of the solution and only needs to recompute it via a trusted (i.e. validated or verified) implementation. Hence, program checking with certificates arises as a method to separate the correctness-critical part of a given implementation. We have tested our method with a system consisting of approximately 20.000 lines of code. The size of our checker is about half as much. It remains an open question how this ratio scales up for larger software.

In our case study, we have considered compilers and their generators, in particular code generators based on rewrite systems. For this problem, we could separate the search and the computation part. The computation part becomes the major part of the checker and eventually needs to be formally verified. We are convinced that the implementations for most optimization problems can be partitioned in the same way. In our experiments, safety-scalable program checking has appeared as a novel combination of well-known techniques as e.g. code inspection, design by contract, testing, and program verification. It is applicable also in many other software engineering areas. Compiler technology is a core methodology for automatically handling all kinds of program and data transformations. Hence, there are many practical problems which can be treated with compiler technology, e.g. XML processing, in general the adaptation of data formats, design patterns in software engineering, software maintenance, software components, component adaptation, meta programming, etc. In future work we want to apply safety-scalable program checking to these areas.

Acknowledgment

The author would like to thank Gerhard Goos, Wolf Zimmermann, Boris Boesler, Götz Lindenmaier, and Florian Liekweg for many helpful discussions. Moreover, thanks to Jan Olaf Blech for implementing the checker for the AJACS compiler. Finally, thanks to the anonymous reviewers for many helpful comments.

References

[AJU77] A. V. Aho, S. C. Johnson, and J. D. Ullman. Code Generation for Expressions with Common Subexpressions. *Journal of the ACM*, 24(1):146–160, January 1977.

[BK95] Manuel Blum and Sampath Kannan. Designing Programs that Check Their Work. *Journal of the ACM*, 42(1):269–291, 1995. Preliminary version: *Proceedings of the 21st ACM Symposium on Theory of Computing (1989)*, pp. 86-97.

[BLR93] Manuel Blum, Michael Luby, and Ronitt Rubinfeld. Self-Testing/Correcting with Applications to Numerical Problems. *Journal of Computer and System Sciences*, 47(3):549–595, 1993. Preliminary version: *Proceedings 22nd ACM Symposium on Theory of Computing (1990)*, pp. 73-83.

[Boe98] Boris Boesler. Codeerzeugung aus Abhängigkeitsgraphen. Diplomarbeit, Universität Karlsruhe, June 1998.

[CF95] R. Cytron and J. Ferrante. Efficiently Computing Φ-Nodes On-The-Fly. *ACM Transactions on Programming Languages and Systems*, 17(3):487–506, 1995.

[CFR$^+$91] R. Cytron, J. Ferrante, B. K. Rosen, M. N. Wegman, and F. K. Zadeck. Efficiently Computing Static Single Assignment Form and the Control Dependence Graph. *ACM Transactions on Programming Languages and Systems*, 13(4):451–490, October 1991.

[CLN$^+$00] Christopher Colby, Peter Lee, George C. Necula, Fred Blau, Mark Plesko, and Kenneth Cline. A Certifying Compiler for Java. In *Proceedings of the ACM SIGPLAN Conference on Programming Language Design and Implementation (PLDI'00)*, pages 95–107, Vancouver, British Columbia, Canada, May 2000.

[DP85] Rina Dechter and Judea Pearl. Generalized Best-First Search Strategies and the Optimality of A*. *Journal of the ACM*, 32(3):505–536, July 1985.

[Gau02] Thilo Gaul. AJACS: Applying Java to Automotive Control Systems. *Automotive Engineering Partners*, 4, August 2002.

[GDG$^+$96] W. Goerigk, A. Dold, T. Gaul, G. Goos, A. Heberle, F.W. von Henke, U. Hoffmann, H. Langmaack, H. Pfeifer, H. Ruess, and W. Zimmermann. Compiler Correctness and Implementation Verification: The Verifix Approach. In P. Fritzson, editor, *Poster Session of CC'96*. IDA Technical Report LiTH-IDA-R-96-12, Linkoeping, Sweden, 1996.

[GHZG99] Thilo Gaul, Andreas Heberle, Wolf Zimmermann, and Wolfgang Goerigk. Construction of Verified Software Systems with Program-Checking: An Application to Compiler Back-Ends. In *Proceedings of the Workshop on Runtime Result Verification (RTRV'99)*, 1999.

[GKC01] Thilo Gaul, Antonio Kung, and Jerome Charousset. AJACS: Applying Java to Automotive Control Systems. In Caspar Grote and Renate Ester, editors, *Conference Proceedings of Embedded Intelligence 2001, Nürnberg*, pages 425–434. Design & Elektronik, February 2001.

[GZG00] Thilo Gaul, Wolf Zimmermann, and Wolfgang Goerigk. Practical Construction of Correct Compiler Implementations by Runtime Result Verification. In *Proc. SCI'2000, International Conference on Information Systems Analysis and Synthesis*, Orlando, Florida, USA, 2000.

[HGG+99]   Andreas Heberle, Thilo Gaul, Wolfgang Goerigk, Gerhard Goos, and Wolf Zimmermann. Construction of Verified Compiler Front-Ends with Program-Checking. In D. Bjrner, M. Broy, and A.V. Zamulin, editors, *Perspectives of System Informatics, Third International Andrei Ershov Memorial Conference, PSI'99*, pages 493–502, Akademgorodok, Novosibirsk, Russia, July 1999. Springer Verlag, Lecture Notes in Computer Science, Vol. 1755.

[Mey97]   Bertrand Meyer. *Object-Oriented Software Construction, Second Edition*. Prentice Hall, 1997.

[Nec00]   George C. Necula. Translation Validation for an Optimizing Compiler. In *Proceedings of the ACM SIGPLAN Conference on Programming Language Design and Implementation (PLDI'00)*, pages 83–94, Vancouver, British Columbia, Canada, May 2000.

[NK97]   A. Nymeyer and J.-P. Katoen. Code generation based on formal BURS theory and heuristic search. *Acta Informatica 34*, pages 597–635, 1997.

[NL97]   George C. Necula and Peter Lee. Proof-Carrying Code. In *Proceedings of the 24th ACM SIGPLAN-SIGACT Symposium on Principles of Programming Languages (POPL'97)*, pages 106–119, Paris, France, January 1997.

[NL98]   George C. Necula and Peter Lee. The Design and Implementation of a Certifying Compiler. In *Proceedings of the ACM SIGPLAN Conference on Programming Language Design and Implementation (PLDI'98)*, pages 333–344, Montreal, Quebec, Canada, May 1998.

[NR01]   George C. Necula and S. P. Rahul. Oracle-Based Checking of Untrusted Software. In *Proceedings of the 28th ACM SIGPLAN-SIGACT Symposium on Principles of Programming Languages (POPL'01)*, pages 142–154, London, UK, January 2001.

[Pap94]   Christos H. Papadimitriou. *Computational Complexity*. Addison-Wesley Publishing Company, 1994.

[PSS98a]   A. Pnueli, O. Shtrichman, and M. Siegel. The code validation tool (cvt.). *International Journal on Software Tools for Technology Transfer*, 2(2):192–201, 1998.

[PSS98b]   A. Pnueli, M. Siegel, and E. Singermann. Translation validation. In B. Steffen, editor, *Proceedings of Tools and Algorithms for the Construction and Analysis of Systems*, pages 151–166, Lisbon, Portugal, April 1998. Springer Verlag, Lecture Notes in Computer Science, Vol. 1384.

[ZPL01]   L. Zuck, A. Pnueli, and R. Leviathan. Validation of Optimizing Compilers. Technical Report MCS01-12, Faculty of Mathematics and Computer Science, The Weizmann Institute of Science, August 2001.

Reification of Executable Test Scripts in Formal Specification-Based Test Generation: The Java Card Transaction Mechanism Case Study*

Fabrice Bouquet and Bruno Legeard

Laboratoire d'Informatique (LIFC)
Université de Franche-Comté
CNRS – INRIA projet CASSIS
16, route de Gray – 25030 Besançon cedex, France
Tel.: (33) 381 666 664
{bouquet,legeard}@lifc.univ-fcomte.fr

Abstract. Automatic generation of test cases from formal specification is a very promising way both to give a rationale for deciding the scope of testing and to reduce the time for test design and coding. In order to achieve this purpose, formal specification-based methods must solve the problem of executable test script generation from abstract test cases and automatic verdict assignment. This question requires calculating oracles, mapping between the abstract and concrete representations and monitoring test execution. In this paper, we present an effective use in the testing process of automatically generated test suites on an industrial application of Java Card Transaction Mechanism. Abstract test cases are synthesized from a B formal specification using a boundary value approach. From the abstract test cases, executable scripts are generated using execution context pattern and representation mappings. This is fully supported by a tool-set, called BZ-Testing-Tools. On the basis of this Java Card case study, we describe the difficulties that arose and present some generic solutions embedded in the BZ-Testing-Tools environment.

Keywords: B abstract machine, Formal methods, Java Card, Oracle synthesis, Representation mapping, Specification-Based test generation.

Type of contribution: Experience paper.

1 Introduction

During the past decade, test generation from formal specification has been a very intensive and productive research area. All the formal specification paradigms have been investigated for testing purpose. Algebraic specification has given rise

---

* This research was sponsored in part by the Smart Card Division of Schlumberger-Sema – Montrouge Research & Development center (Paris, France).

to very seminal work [3], defining uniformity and regularity hypotheses, and presenting a form of partition analysis by unfolding equations in the specification. Transition-based specification, like Input-Output Transition Systems, associated with on-the-fly model checking techniques, give rise to different proposals for test generation on reactive systems [20, 8]. More particularly, model-based specification notations, such as Z [18], B [1] and VDM [12] were the basis of various proposals [7, 10, 5] for the partition analysis of the individual operations and system state and the construction of a Finite State Automaton for test case generation. Although, it is easy to obtain big suites of abstract test cases from the formal specification and even to evaluate it on the basis of test data adequacy criteria [15]. In practice, the most difficult task is to put the tests to work. That is, to be useful, these test suites must be automatically converted into executable test scripts, including the oracle with automated test result checking. In other words, one key issue for technology transfer in the field of formal specification-based test generation is to be able to take the generated test cases and oracles, and to derive a test harness that conducts both the execution and the verdict assignment of the test scripts.

In [14, 13], we present an original method for boundary-value test case generation from B or Z formal specifications. This method is fully supported by a tool-set, called BZ-Testing-Tools – BZ-TT –, and was used for test case generation for an industrial application in the Smart Card area – the Java Card Transaction Mechanism validation. This method can be summed up as follows: from the formal model, the BZ-Testing-Tool computes boundary values to create boundary states. Then, test cases are generated by traversal of the state space (compute on-the-fly) with a preamble part (sequences of operations from the initial state to a boundary state), a body part (critical invocations), an identification part (observation and oracle state computation) and a postamble part (return path to initial or boundary state).

On the basis of this case study, this paper describes how generated test cases from the formal model are translated into executable test scripts and how this makes the monitoring of the test execution and automatic assignment possible. The next section introduces the BZ-Testing-Tools test generation method. Section 3 presents the Java Card Transaction Mechanism application and the B formal model. Section 4 gives the test generation results and Section 5 presents a framework for translating abstract test cases into executable test scripts. The final sections discuss this approach, future work and conclusions.

In the remainder of this paper, we use the acronym BZ-TT both for BZ-Testing-Tools method and environment.

2 Overview of the Tests Case Generation Method

BZ-TT is a method and a tool-set used to automate functional black box test generation. For a more detailed presentation of the method and tool presentation see [14] and [2] respectively.

2.1 Test Case Generation From a Formal Model of the System

The starting point of the BZ-TT method is to have an available formal model of the system under test either a B abstract machine [1] or a Z [18] specification. The formal model should be validated against the requirements and also be proved regarding its internal correctness (invariant property verification).

This formal model characterizes a system that has the implicit states (consisting of several state variables) and a number of operations in order to modify the state of the system. The behavior of such a system can be described in terms of a sequence of operations where the first operation is activated from the initial state of the B abstract machine. The initial state is given in the specification. Such a sequence of operations is called a trace. However, if the pre-condition of an operation is false, substitution cannot establish a post-condition. The traces in this case are of no interest, since it is impossible to determine the state of the machine. Thus, we define a test case to be any legal trace, i.e. trace where all pre-conditions are true. A test case corresponds to a sequence of system states, which present the value of each state variable after each operation invocation. The submission of a legal trace is a success if all the output values returned by the concrete implementation during the trace are equivalent (through a function of abstraction) to the output values returned by its specifications during the simulation of the same trace (or included in the possible values if the specification is non-deterministic).

2.2 Principles of the Method

In order to select the traces to be submitted, the BZ-TT approach consists in testing the operations when the system is in a *boundary state*. A boundary state is a state where at least one state variable has a value at an extremum – minimum or maximum – of its sub-domains. The trace constituting the test case is divided into four parts. According to the ISO9646 standard [11], the four successive parts are defined as follows (see Figure 1) :

1. **Preamble:** the part of a test case that takes the system from its initial state to a state in which the test purpose can be achieved (i.e. from initial state to boundary state).
2. **Body:** the part of a test case containing all the events essential to achieve some test purpose can be achieved (i.e. invocation of one operation with boundary values for its input variables).
3. **Identification:** the part of a test case consisting of invocations whose aim is to determine certain observable aspects of the system at the end of the test body. In addition to the possible output data returned by the operation of the body, the output values returned by the operations that compose the identification part give further information for assigning a verdict to the test.
4. **Postamble:** the part of a test case that takes the system from the final state of the identification part to the final state of the test case. This last part is used to reach a specific state in order to link several test cases together.

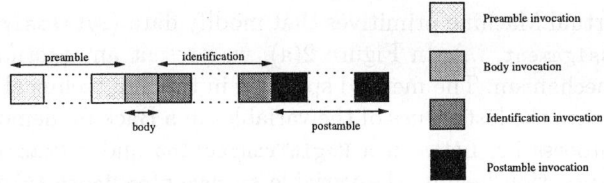

Fig. 1. Test case constitution

The body part is the critical test invocation of the test case and is constructed with operations that affect the system's state. Thus, the test engineer is required to partition the operations into update and observation operations. An update operation is an operation that modifies state variables. An observation operation is an operation that returns information on state variables without modifying them. Update observations are used in the preamble, body and postamble and the observation operations are used in the identification part. The test purpose is to test each update operation with all its boundary values for input variables from each boundary state of the B abstract model. Boundary values for input variables of an operation are defined as the extremum – minimum or maximum – of all sub-domains of the input variables of the operation.

To generate the test cases, BZ-TT uses a customized set-oriented constraint solver [4] which makes it possible to simulate the execution of the formal model.

Therefore, the BZ-TT generation method makes it possible to test an implementation in four main stages:

1. produce the formal model of the system and verify it using proof and validate it using animation;
2. compute boundary goals from the formal model;
3. generate a preamble for each boundary goal, followed by one for the body, identification and postamble parts;
4. translate abstract test cases into executable test scripts.

This paper focusses on this last step of the BZ-TT method on the basis of the Java Card Transaction Mechanism application.

3 Formalization of the Java Card Transaction Mechanism

The goal of this work was to evaluate the BZ-TT test cases generation method within a real industrial validation process: from the formalization of the technical requirements to the execution of generated test scripts and automatic verdict assignment on an implementation under test. In partnership with the SchlumbergerSema company, we chose the Java Card Transaction Mechanism as an industrial trial. The Java Card Transaction Mechanism is part of the Java Card *Run-Time Environment* [19]. It makes it possible to protect the data during the update process. It consists essentially of three following procedures: BeginTransaction, AbortTransaction or CommitTransaction, plus several other

Java Card Virtual Machine primitives that modify data (ByteAssignment, Array-Copy, ShortAssignment, ...). In Figure 2(a), we present an external view of the transaction mechanism. The method specified in the Sun technical requirements allows one to save the last values of the variables in a Backup memory during the transaction process i.e. between a BeginTransaction and a CommitTransaction. When the transaction begins, the variable transaction_depth takes the value 1 otherwise it is 0. All modification of the variables are saved in backup buffer. The end of transaction is given by CommitTransaction or AbortTransaction. In the first case, the modifications of the variables have done. In the second case, the modifications of the variables have reset. Several exceptions are directly linked to the Transaction Mechanism. For example: the *Backup_Full* exception and the *Transaction_Not_In_Progress* exception. In the remainder of this section, we will introduce the Java Card Transaction Mechanism technical specification and then the B formal model. In Figure 2(b), we present the exception management. We decide to limit the number of simultaneous exception to one. In fact, when an exception is raised and a second is raised too, we decide to stop the system (*out of system*). Each operation can raise an exception. When the exception is throw, we call BeginCatch to explain the begin of the instructions block associated to exception treatment. We call EndCatch to explain the end of the instructions block associated to exception treatment. We know the state of the system with the model state variable PROCESS. The state of exception management is known with the model state variable CATCH.

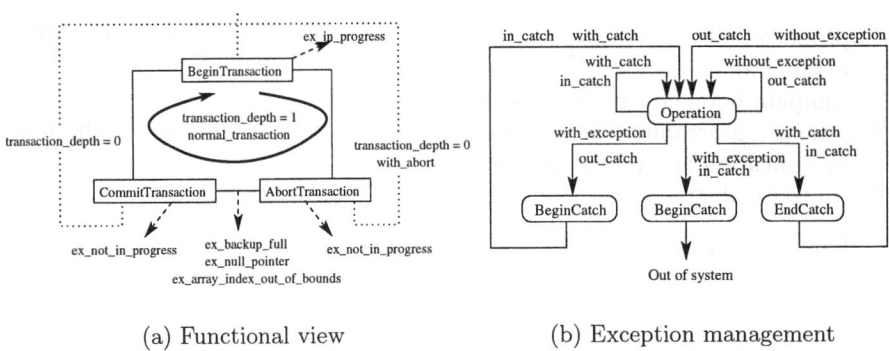

(a) Functional view   (b) Exception management

Fig. 2. Transaction mechanism

3.1 Java Card – Technical Specification

A Java Card uses two types of memory: an EEPROM and a RAM. Each memory is byte-addressed, but the memory address is coded by a short (two bytes). The variables used in the Java applets have three different types: *Boolean*, *Byte* and

Short. For the array, there are only two types: *Byte* and *Short*. These variables belong to two different categories: *normal* and *transient*. In both cases, arrays are considered as an object. An object is defined by an address and a size. An address contains two bytes (adr1, adr2) and size (size1, size2). The difference between *normal* and *transient* array is in the storage area of the elements (in EEPROM for *normal* and in RAM for *transient*). We identified the several components and their characteristics (type, category, object) to manage into the Java Card Transaction Mechanism.

3.2 The B Model – Overview

The Java Card Transaction Mechanism is formalized through a single B abstract machine.

The given sets introduce the different data types:

- BOOLVAR = {bo1, bo2}
- BYTEVAR = {b1, b2, b3, b4}
- SHORTVAR = {sh1, sh2, sh3, sh4}
- BYTE_ARRAY_SET = BYTE_ARRAY ∪ BYTE_ARRAY_TRANSIENT
  - BYTE_ARRAY = {ba1, ba2, ba3, banull}
  - BYTE_ARRAY_TRANSIENT = {bat1, bat2, batnull}
- SHORT_ARRAY_SET = SHORT_ARRAY ∪ SHORT_ARRAY_TRANSIENT
  - SHORT_ARRAY = {sha1, sha2, sha3, shanull}
  - SHORT_ARRAY_TRANSIENT = {shat1, shat2, shatnull}

The enumerated values give the variables' names, which will be used for executable test script generation.

The formal model introduces some constants:

- BACKUP_CAPACITY, indicates the maximum allowed memory for backup (usually 256 bytes).
- MAX_EEPROM, indicates the size of the EEPROM (usually 32kb).
- MAX_RAM, indicates the size of the RAM (usually 512 bytes).
- MAX_ARRAY, indicates the maximal size of array (coded with a short).
- NULL, used to identify the objects that have no elements (usually equals to 0).

The operations of the B abstract machine represent the modelled procedures and byte-code primitives. They are used to do 3 things:

- Managing transactions:
  BeginTransaction, CommitTransaction and AbortTransaction;
- Monitoring the system variables: GetTransactionDepth, GetMaxCommitCapacity and GetUnusedCommitCapacity;
- Manipulating the data: BooleanAssignment, ByteAssignment, ShortAssignment, ByteArrayAssignment, ObjectAssignment, ObjectAssignment2, ArrayCompare, ShortArrayAssignment, ArrayCopy, MakeShort, SetShort, ArrayFillNonAtomic.

Exceptions can occur during the execution of an operation. For example, when we start a transaction while another one is in progress or if data is written outside of the allowed memory space of an array. So, we add an exception manager to the model to obtain a good representation of the system.

The state of the abstract machine is described by three variables: PROCESS, EXCEPTION_TYPE, CATCH. Figure 2(b) gives the activated operations of the transaction according to the values of the three variables. Interlinked exception is not allowed. PROCESS represents process execution with the different events during activation of the operations (in transaction mode or not). EXCEPTION_TYPE gives the exception name in progress, and the invariant assures that when an exception is raised PROCESS takes the value of the exception mode. CATCH points out the processing of the raised exception. We define these variables as following:

- EXCEPTION_TYPE = {without_exception, ex_in_progress, ex_not_in_progress, ex_backup_full, ex_null_pointer, ex_array_index_out_of_bounds}
- PROCESS = {with_abort, with_exception, with_catch, normal_transaction}
- CATCH = {in_catch, out_catch}

Due to space limitation, this short presentation excludes some parts of the formal model (1200 lines in B notation) like the invariant predicate, variable initialization and operation definitions.

4 Test Case Generation

The test cases generation process starts by boundary goals computation, and then for each boundary goal generates preamble, body, identification and postamble parts. From the Java Card Transaction Mechanism B abstract machine, the BZ-TT environment computes 58 Boundary goals and generates 3700 test cases, in 12 hours on a Pentium 1.2GHZ with 1 GB RAM.

4.1 Boundary Goals

The boundary goals are extracted from the formal model by a partition analysis of the operations (cf. [14]) and the computation of extremum values by maximization/minimization. An example of a boundary goal is given in Example 1 with the name and the values of the variables and a description to explain them.

Example 1

Variable	Value	Description
backup_size	256	Max backup size buffer
exception_type	ex_null_pointer	An undefined pointer was used
transaction_depth	1	Transaction is in progress
transaction_process	with_catch	An exception was caught

This boundary goal corresponds to the exception that was caught from an array that was not allowed under the transaction mode.

4.2 Test Ccases

At this step, the system can compute the boundary goals. The boundary goals drive the animation of the specification to produce the preambule of the test cases. In the example 2, we give a test case.

Example 2 *Test case generation with this boundary goal: the system is in the transaction mode. These test cases allow one to evaluate the exception raised for backup capacity exceeded.*

1. **Limit value to reach:**

Variables	Values
transaction_depth	1
backup_size	249

2. **Preamble part:**

Operation	Input	Out	Modified data
BeginTransaction	[]	[]	[[transaction_depth,1]]
ByteAssignment	[b1,25]	[]	[[eeprom,[...,c(3,25)]], [backup_size,7]]
...	...	...	...
ByteAssignment	[b2,12]	[]	[[eeprom,[...,c(4,12)]], [backup_size,249]]

    This preamble part makes it possible to set the system into an almost full backup-memory (249 bytes) position minus one byte.

3. **Body part:**

    a)

Operation	Input	Out	Modified data
ByteAssignment	[b1,50]	[]	[[eeprom,[...,c(3,50)]], [backup_size,256]]

    b)

Operation	Input	Out	Modified data
ShortAssignment	[sh1,78523]	[]	[[exception_type, ex_backup_full], [transaction_process,with_exception]]

There are two bodies 3.a) and 3.b). The first one is a normal execution because only one byte with it header (5 bytes) are saved. The second simulates a problem (saturation of the backup buffer) because two bytes are saved(one short) with 5 bytes of header.

A test case includes the following information:

- a list of the operations invoked in the test case.
- for each operation:
    - the values of the input variables,
    - the values of the output variables (part of the oracle)
    - the values of the modified state variables (part of the oracle)

In Section 5.1, we will present the translation schema between abstract and concrete values.

4.3 Oracle Synthesis

The oracle of the test case is computed for each operation invocation in terms of the output values and state variables. Moreover, the identification part of the test case makes it possible to obtain more oracle information. For the Java card example, the monitoring operations are: `GetTransactionDepth`,`GetUnusedCommitCapacity` and `GetMaxCommitCapacity`. With Example 2, for the first body, the *identification* is:

Operation	Input	Output	Modified data
GetTransactionDepth	[]	[1]	None
GetUnusedCommitCapacity	[]	[0]	None
GetMaxCommitCapacity	[]	[256]	None

Solver of the constraints of BZ-TT gives the oracle by evaluation of the specification. The oracle is translated in reification process and it is compared with the concrete values into the executable test script. The result of comparaison gives the verdict.

5 Generating Executable Test Scripts

Generated test cases define sequences of operation invocations at an abstract level. More precisely, each operation invocation appears with the signature of the formal model and the input values are the same as those from the abstract data model. In the Java Card case study, we defined and implemented a solution for translating the generated test cases into executable scripts. This solution is as follows. The test engineer defines two inputs: a test script pattern and a mapping table. The test script pattern is a source code file in the target language with some tags indicating where to insert sequences of operation invocations. The mapping table contains three classes of information:

1. The operations and the substituted variables on the abstract model operations.
2. The monitoring of the variables and the associated operations.
3. The source equivalence instructions to the operations and the variables.

The first class of information is extracted automatically from the model. The two others must be given by the test engineer. This table is similar to the representation mappings defined in [17].

Figure 3 shows the different steps of executable test script generation. The dashed boxes are produced by or with the help of the test engineer. The square boxes define a file and the circle boxes define a program.

5.1 Mapping Table

The operations and the variables proposed by the mapping table are extracted from the formal model. The test engineer must add up the information in order to do the reification. The following data are identified for each element:

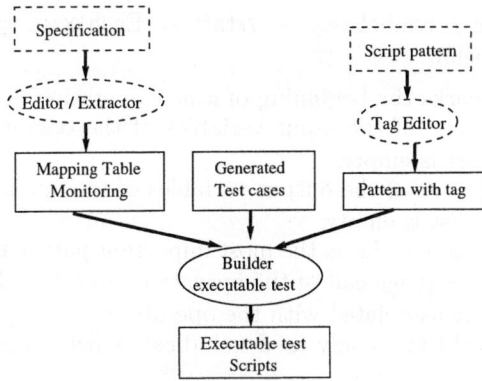

Fig. 3. The steps of test script generation

- For the *Operation*, there is the concrete call of the operation. It is the Application Programming Interface or system function call in the script source code.
- For the *Variable*, only the variables substituted into the operation are considered. There are three kinds of variables:
  - *input* is the input of the operation. Its value is given by a test case. We authorize the test engineer to manipulate the variable identifier into adding a dollar character to explain the mapping in the test reconstruction. Thus, the test engineer can use the variable with dollar character into the concrete instructions associated with the reification of the variable.
  - *output*, when available, is the oracle of the operation.
  - *state* is classified in to two kinds: monitored and unmonitored. The monitoring question must be omnipresent in the development of the formal model. For example, there is a variable associated to the backup buffer in the model, but it is not possible for the system under test to know the value of this variable. Therefore, the backup buffer is unmonitored. We only used it to verify the invariant properties of the system and there was no code associated to the variable for the reification because it is unmonitored.

The verdict assignment was achieved by comparing both operation output values and observable state variables using *observability expressions* from test cases with test script passing results. Observability expressions are procedure calls, which allows to compare the state variable values (after an operation invocation) with some results of an observation procedure on the system under test.

In Example 3, we present an operation in B notation and the associated part of mapping table associated with it (we used a XML representation for the table). For the record, each XML tag has two forms: a start form (e.g. <start>) and a close form with the / symbol (e.g. < /start>). Each XML tag of the mapping table is presented below:

- <operation>: marks the beginning of a new operation description.
- <input>: the name of the input variables of the operation. If there is no input then the list is empty.
- <output>: the name of the output variables of the operation. If there is no output then the list is empty.
- <concreteOperation>: this is the most important part of the mapping table. It is the source language call of the operation, and it is able to perform the test for the oracle associated with the operation.
- <modifyVariableList> is only used to indicate a list of the variables used by the operation.
- <modifyVariable> marks the beginning of the variable description used by the operation.
- <name> name of the variable in the model.
- <value> value of the variable. Static analysis of model gives the type of the variable. This type is used with the dollar character, to explain the mapping in the test reconstruction, as the value.
- <concrete> this is the second most important part of the mapping table. It is the source language instruction used to validate the oracle value. If it is an unmonitoring variable, there is no value: none.

Example 3 *B operation and the mapping table associate:*

```
depth <-- Operation(valeur) =
   PRE
      (valeur ∈ {0,1,2} )
   THEN
      If (valeur == 0) THEN
         depth := 0 ||
         backup := {}
      ELSE
         depth := card(backup)
      END
   END;
```

```
<operation>
   <name> Operation </name>
   <input> [$valeur] </input>
   <output> [$depth] </output>
   <concreteOperation> if ($depth !=
      JCSystem.operation($valeur))
      { // Verdict : ko}
      else { // Verdict : ok}
   </concreteOperation>
   <modifyVariableList>
      <modifyVariable>
         <name> $depth </name>
         <value> $integer </value>
         <concrete> if($depth!=$integer)
            { // Verdict : ko}
            else { // Verdict : ok}
         </concrete>
      </modifyVariable>
      <modifyVariable>
         <name> backup </name>
         <value> {} </value>
         <concrete> none </concrete>
      </modifyVariable>
   </modifyVariableList>
</operation>
```

For eac operation of the abstract model, the mapping table gives the expression that can be called by the system under test. Moreover, it gives procedures to compute the value of the state variables when this is possible. If necessary, this table is completed by a table that gives the equivalences between the abstract input and output values and concrete values (for example, correspondence between symbolic and hexadecimal values). A module computes the executable test scripts by inserting concrete expressions into the script pattern following the generated test cases and the equivalence and observability expression. This process is deterministic.

The results given by the substitutions defined in the mapping table (replacing the elements of the test sequences by the instructions of the concrete language) are added to the script pattern.

5.2 Script Pattern

The script pattern is a source file in the target language. This source file includes all the declaration and code prerequisites for testing. It contains some tags indicating where to insert each part of a test case: *preamble*, *body*, *identification* and *postamble*. For example, in the Java Card case study, the script pattern is a Java Card source file and the operation sequences to be inserted are API or Java instructions [19]. The tags used in the pattern source file are:

- INSERT INFORMATION: indicates the properties or the information of the sequences (version, date, parameters). It is an optional tag.
- INSERT PREAMBLE: indicates the operations of the *preamble*. It is an obligatory tag.
- INSERT BODY (CASE): indicates the operation of the *body*. It is used when the same preamble is used for many bodies. It is an obligatory tag.
- INSERT POSTAMBLE(INIT): indicates the operations of the *postamble* for coming back to its initial state. If there is a return to the Boundary state, the *postamble* is inserted after the *body*. It is an optional tag.

An example of the script pattern given in input of the reification process (cf. Figure 3) is presented in the Appendix (the tags are inserted in the pattern in comment form //).

6 Discussion

Our experience with the Java Card case study shows that automatic verdict assignment is one of the main difficult points. This is, on the one hand, due to well-known theoretical problems [9] such as the possibility of the non-determinism of the specification. On the other hand, there are also practical problems in comparing generated oracle values (values of abstract state variables) and concrete execution results [16]. Automatic verdict assignment is still an important research area for specification-based test generation. In this section, we will discuss several practical issues for formal specification-based test generation learned from the experiences. These issues include modelling for testing, observability and exception management.

6.1 Modelling for Testing

Specially developing the formal model (or also to adapt it) for testing purposes is a key element to success in formal specification-based software testing. This customized formal models have several advantages. Firstly, for the generation of executable test scripts from abstract test cases, the signature of the model's operations could have exactly the same form as the corresponding API to be tested, particularly for input and output parameters. This makes it much easier to construct the mapping table. Secondly, the development of the formal model should consider the control and observation points of the system under test. Thirdly, the development of the formal model depends on the test objectives. This means that the abstraction level of the formal model depends on which behaviors must be tested. All these considerations make it possible to simplify the formal model and to better focus it to the purpose of the test generation. This also helps to reduce the formalizing cost. Thus, for this Java Card Transaction Mechanism application, the domain comprehension costs 18 people/day and the formal modelling costs 20 people/day for 1200 lines of a B abstract machine, including validation using animation techniques (with the BZ-TT environment) and partial proof using Atelier B [6]. Such a focused formal model simplifies the test generation because it avoids useless inference or constraint propagation at the solver level (cf. Figure 4).

6.2 Observability

Observability is a key issue to ensure the automatic verdict assignment. In the Java Card application, some information is not always given directly: additional information is saved with the data during backup in transaction mode. For example, on the Java card transaction mechanism application, there are three kinds of observability:

- The transaction depth is given directly by the operation GetTransactionDepth.
- The backup buffer size is not given directly but it is a subtraction between the GetUnusedCommitCapacity and GetMaxCommitCapacity operations.
- The values saved in backup are not accessible, meaning there is no primitive to read the backup buffer.

The mapping table allows the test engineer to define how these variable should be observed. For the first and second cases, there are APIs to access the data (directly or using calculus). In the third case, the data are reduced to an abstraction in the model. This problem relies on the question of testability and on the design for testing. As the Java Card is a secure system, access to data is only allowed through standardized commands.

6.3 Exception Management

The exception mechanism of Java poses specific problems for the verdict assignment. Indeed, in Java, an error can cause an exception at any time. The exception terminates the execution of the applet and returns a code. Thus, we must protect all instructions from revealing about an exception in an untimely way. For example, in a sequence of operations, the exception capture information could be given just after it is thrown. Thus, in Java, we must indicate the protected block by the reserved instruction `try` and use the `catch` instruction to indicate the expected exception and which process is associated to this exception. This is done in the translation using the mapping table: every time that a `BeginCatch` / `EndCatch` invocation appears, the instruction is protected from an untimely exception. In Example 4, we show the translation of the sequence and the protected Java applet.

Example 4

Sequence	Java
	$try\{$
$Operation\_1$	$JavaOp\_1$
$BeginCatch$	$\}$ $catch(expectedException)$ $\{$
$Operation\_2$	$JavaOp\_2$
...	...
$EndCatch$	$\}$
	$catch(unexpectedException)\{$
	$Error\ message$ $\}$

7 Conclusion and Future Work

We have presented an approach to automatic boundary-value testing from set-oriented formal specification notations. Generated test cases are sequences of operations where, after placing the system at a boundary state, we tested all the update operations with boundary input values. From these sequences of operations, executable test scripts are generated on the basis of an executable source code pattern, a representation mapping from abstract names (procedure names, input and output names) to concrete ones, and a definition of observability procedures for certain state variables. This technique was described within the context of an industrial application: the Java Card Transaction Mechanism. This application shows the feasibility and the effectiveness of automated formal specification-based test case generation in a real industrial validation process for critical software. In this approach, the test engineer acquires another role. Instead of spending a lot of time writing repetitive test scripts in the target language, the test engineer can concentrate on more conceptual work.

The first part of this conceptual work involves formalizing the specification. This procedures makes it possible to really understand and disambiguate the requirements using both proof techniques (to prove the internal correctness of the formal model) and animation techniques (to execute user scenarios to validate the behavior defined by the technical requirements). This phase is costly, but this application shows that the effort of formalization is strongly recouped by the

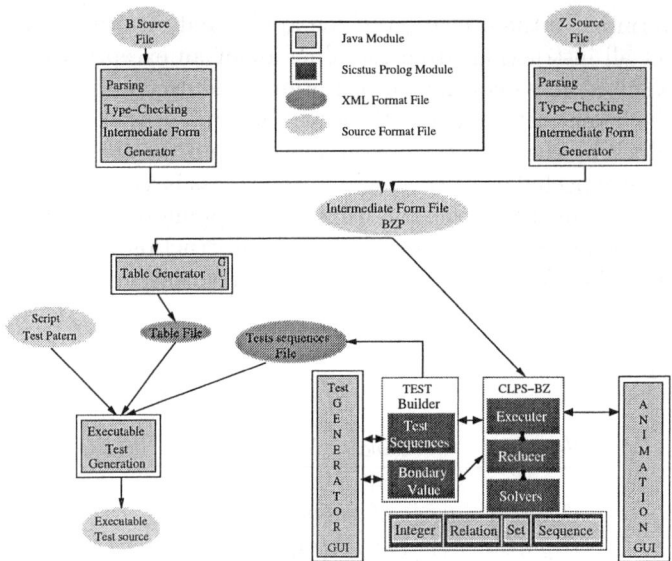

Fig. 4. BZ-Testing-Tools environment

saving obtained by the test case generation. Moreover, whether for manual or automated test generation, the initial phase of understanding the requirements is crucial for the quality of the test suites. Using formalization techniques forces the test engineer to fully master the technical requirements. In another light, the formal model can be seen as the test objective for the validation process. We believe that the test engineer must choose the part of the specification to be formalized, the level of abstraction, and the formalizing place of the point of view depending of the test objective. For example, in the Java Card Transaction Mechanism, the objective was to test the transaction mechanism procedures, so we decided that the test engineer to not model the memory management.

Moreover, the test engineer drives the generation process at several points: validating boundary goals and eventually supplementing the generated ones, overriding the default *preamble* computation (for example by defining some state in the state space to be reached during the graph traversal), defining update operations for the *body*-part computation, and defining the reification mapping and the pattern source file for executable test script generation. Doing this, the test engineer really uses his/her know-how to further the generation of accurate test suites.

This process is fully supported by a tool-set: the BZ-Testing-Tools environment. This environment is currently being consolidated for delivery to the scientific community. Its functional architecture is given in Figure 4. The kernel module is the CLPS/BZ solver [4] which transforms the formal model into a constraint system by computing the next state from the current state (represented by a constraint system) and an operation. This kernel is completed by a boundary goal computational procedure that uses maximization-minimization, and a preamble computational procedure that uses a best-first heuristic during the traversal of the constrained reachability graph. All these modules are developed in SICStus Prolog and the GUI is developed in Java.

8 Acknowledgements

We would like to thank Mark Utting from the university of Waikato – New-Zealand and Tim Muller from the University of Queensland – Australia, for their many helpful comments, and their insightful reading of our first draft.

References

[1] J.-R. Abrial. *The B-Book: Assigning Programs to Meaning.* Cambridge University Press, 1996.
[2] F. Ambert, F. Bouquet, S. Chemin, S. Guenaud, B. Legeard, F. Peureux, N. Vacelet, and M. Utting. BZ-TT: A tool-set for test generation from Z and B using constraint logic programming. In R. Hierons and T. Jerron, editors, *Formal Approaches to Testing of Software, FATES 2002 workshop of CONCUR'02*, pages 105–120. INRIA Report, August 2002.
[3] G. Bernot, M.-C. Gaudel, and B. Marre. Software testing based on formal specifications: a theory and a tool. *Software Engineering Journal*, 6(6):387–405, November 1991.
[4] F. Bouquet, B. Legeard, and F. Peureux. CLPS-B – A Constraint Solver for B. In *International Conference on Tools and Algorithms for Construction and Analysis of Systems, TACAS2002*, volume LNCS 2280, pages 188–204, Grenoble, France, April 2002. Springer-Verlag.
[5] D. Carrington, I. MacColl, J. McDonald, L. Murray, and P. Strooper. From object-Z specifications to classbench test suites. Technical Report 98-22, SVRC – University of Queensland, 1998.
[6] Clearsy, http://www.atelierb.societe.com. *Atelier B V3*, 10/2001.
[7] J. Dick and A. Faivre. Automating the generation and sequencing of test cases from model-based specifications. *FME'93: Industrial-Strength Formal Methods*, LNCS 670 Springer-Verlag:268–284, April 1993.
[8] J.-C. Fernandez, C. Jard, T. Jeron, and C. Viho. Using on-the-fly verification techniques for the generation of test suites. In *Computer Aided Verification*, volume LNCS 1102, pages 348–359. Springer-Verlag, 1996.
[9] M.-C. Gaudel. Testing can be formal too. In *TAPSoft'95: Theory and Practice of Software Developpement*, volume LNCS 915, pages 82–96. Springer-Verlag, 1995.
[10] R. Hierons. Testing from a Z specification. *The Journal of Software Testing, Verification and Reliability*, 7:19–33, 1997.
[11] ISO. *OSI Conformance Testing Methodology and Framework – ISO 9646*, 1999.
[12] C. Jones. *Systematic Software Development Using VDM.* Prentice-Hall, 2nd edition, 1990.
[13] B. Legeard and F. Peureux. Generation of functional test sequences from B formal specifications – presentation and industrial case-study. In 16th *IEEE International conference on Automated Software Engineering (ASE'2001)*, pages 377–381, San Diego, USA, 2001. IEEE press.

[14] B. Legeard, F. Peureux, and M. Utting. Automated boundary testing from Z and B. In L.-H. Eriksson and P. Lindsay, editors, *Formal Methods Europe, FME 2002*, volume LNCS 2391, pages 21–40. Springer-Verlag, July 2002.
[15] A. Offutt, Z. Jin, and J. Pan. The dynamic domain reduction procedure for test data generation. *The Journal of Software Practice and Experience*, 29(2):167–193, 1999.
[16] D. K. Peters and D. L. Parnas. Using test oracles generated from program documentation. *Software Engineering*, 24(3):161–173, 1998.
[17] D. Richardson and S. A. T. O'Malley. Specification-based test oracles for reactive systems. In *Proceedings of the 14th International Conference on Software Engineering (ICSE'92)*, pages 105–118, Melbourne, Australia, May 1992. ACM Press.
[18] J. Spivey. *The Z notation: A Reference Manual*. Prentice-Hall, 2nd edition, 1993.
[19] Sun microsystems. *Java Card 2.1.1 Virtual Machine Specification*. http://java.sun.com/products/javacard/javacard21.html#specification, 2000.
[20] J. Tretmans. Test generation with inputs, outputs and repetitive quiescence. *Software-Concepts and Tools*, 17(3):103–120, 1996.

A   Applet Example

```
// INSERT INFORMATIONS
import javacard.framework.APDU;
import javacard.framework.Applet;
import javacard.framework.Util;
import javacard.framework.JCSystem;
import javacard.framework.ISOException;
import javacard.framework.TransactionException;

public class Standard extends Applet
{
    final static byte P1_SETUP = (byte)0x00;
    final static byte P1_TEST  = (byte)0x01;

    // JCRE transaction tests specific
    // variables.
        // Booleans pool.
    private boolean bo1, bo2;
        // Bytes pool.
    private byte b1, b2, b3, b4;
        // Short pool.
    private short sh1, sh2, sh3, sh4;
        // Byte arrays pool.
    private byte[] ba1 = new byte[1];
    private byte[] ba2 = new byte[17];
    private byte[] ba3 = new byte[257];
        // Transient byte arrays.
    private byte[] bat1, bat2;
        // Short arrays pool.
    private short[] sha1 = new short[1];
    private short[] sha2 = new short[17];
    private short[] sha3 = new byte[257];
        // Transient short arrays.
    private short[] shat1, shat2;

    private short max_commit;
    private short unused;
    private short dsh;
    private short end_dest_index;
    private short end_index;

    private byte result;
    private byte depth;

    protected Standard(){
        bat1 = JCSystem.makeTransientByteArray(
            (short)1, JCSystem.CLEAR_ON_DESELECT);
        bat2 = JCSystem.makeTransientByteArray(
            (short)17, JCSystem.CLEAR_ON_DESELECT);
        shat1 = JCSystem.makeTransientShortArray(
            (short)1, JCSystem.CLEAR_ON_DESELECT);
        shat2 = JCSystem.makeTransientShortArray(
            (short)17, JCSystem.CLEAR_ON_DESELECT);
    }

    public static void install(byte[] buffer,
            short offset, byte length){
        // Creating one instance of the applet.
        Standard anInstance = new Standard();
        // Reg. instance into the JCRE
        // (mandatory).
        anInstance.register();
    }

    public boolean select(){
        return true;
    }

    public void deselect(){
        return;
    }

    public void process(APDU apdu){
        byte[] apduBuffer = apdu.getBuffer();
        byte p1 = apduBuffer[2];
        byte p2 = apduBuffer[3];

        if(selectingApplet()) return;

        switch (p1)
```

```
{                                           // INSERT BODY (CASE)
    case P1_SETUP : // Preparing the test environment.    default :
        // Default initializations.                 ISOException.throwIt(
        bo1 = false;                                    (short)0x6a86);
        bo2 = false;                                break;
        ...                                     }
        break;                                  break;
    case P1_TEST : // Performing real test      default :
        // sequence.                                ISOException.throwIt((short)0x6a86);
        // INSERT PREAMBULE                         break;
        switch (p2) // Switching between test   }
        // cases
        {                                   }
```

Checking and Reasoning about Semantic Web through Alloy

Jin Song Dong, Jing Sun, and Hai Wang

School of Computing,
National University of Singapore,
dongjs,sunjing,wangh@comp.nus.edu.sg

Abstract. Semantic Web (SW), commonly regarded as the next generation of the Web, is an emerging vision of the new Web from the Knowledge Representation and the Web communities. The Formal Methods community can also play an important role to contribute to SW development. Reasoning and consistency checking can be useful at many stages during the design, maintenance and deployment of SW ontology. However the existing reasoning and consistency checking tools for SW are primitive. We believe that formal techniques and tools, such as Alloy, can provide automatic reasoning and consistency checking services for SW. In this paper, we firstly construct semantic models for the SW language (DAML+OIL) in Alloy, and these models form the semantic domain for interpreting DAML+OIL in Alloy. Then we develop the translation techniques and tools which can automatically map the SW ontology into the DAML+OIL semantic domain in Alloy. Furthermore, with the assistance of Alloy Analyzer (AA) we demonstrate that the consistency of the SW ontology can be checked automatically and different kinds of reasoning tasks can be supported.

keywords: Semantic Web, Alloy

1 Introduction

In recent years, researchers have begun to explore the potential of associating web content with explicit meaning so that the web content becomes more machine-readable and intelligent agents can retrieve and manipulate pertinent information readily. The Semantic Web (SW) [1] proposed by W3C is one of the most promising and accepted approaches. It has been regarded as the next generation of the Web. SW not only emerges from the Knowledge Representation and the Web Communities, but also brings the two communities closer together. We believe in the SW development process, there is a role for formal techniques and tools to play and make important contributions.

In the development of Semantic Web there is a pivotal role for ontology, since it provides a representation of a shared conceptualization of a particular domain that can be communicated between people and applications. Reasoning can be useful at many stages during the design, maintenance and deployment of ontology. Because autonomous software agents may perform their reasoning and come to conclusions without human supervision, it is essential that the shared ontology is consistent. However, since the Semantic Web technology is still in the early stage, the reasoning and consistency checking tools are very primitive.

The software modeling language Alloy [9] is suitable for specifying structural properties of software. SW is a well suited application domain for Alloy because relationships between web resources are the focus points in SW and Alloy is a first order declarative language based on relations. Furthermore, Alloy specifications can be analyzed automatically using the Alloy Analyzer (AA) [10]. Given a finite scope for a specification, AA translates it into a propositional formula and uses SAT solving technology to generate instances that satisfy the properties expressed in the specification. We believe that if the semantics of the SW languages can be encoded into Alloy, then Alloy can be used to provide automatic reasoning and consistency checking services for SW. Various reasoning tasks can be supported effectively by AA.

The remainder of the paper is organized as follows. Section 2 briefly introduces the Semantic Web and Alloy. In section 3 semantic domain and functions for the DARPA Agent Markup Language (DAML+OIL) [14] constructs are defined in Alloy. Section 4 presents the transformation from DAML+OIL documents to an Alloy program. In section 5 different reasoning tasks are demonstrated. Section 6 concludes the paper.

2 Semantic Web and Alloy Overview

2.1 Semantic Web Overview

The Semantic Web is a vision for a new kind of Web with enhanced functionality which will require semantic-based representation and processing of Web information. W3C has proposed a series of technologies that can be applied to achieve this vision. The Semantic Web extends the current Web by giving the web content a well-defined meaning, better enabling computers and people to work in cooperation. XML is aimed at delivering data to systems that can understand and interpret the information. XML is focused on the syntax (defined by the XML schema or DTD) of a document and it provides essentially a mechanism to declare and use simple data structures. However there is no way for a program to actually understand the knowledge contained in the XML documents.

Resource Description Framework (RDF) [11] is a foundation for processing metadata; it provides interoperability between applications that exchange machine-understandable information on the Web. RDF uses XML to exchange descriptions of Web resources and emphasizes facilities to enable automated processing. The RDF descriptions provide a simple ontology system to support the exchange of knowledge and semantic information on the Web. RDF Schema [2] provides the basic vocabulary to describe RDF documents. RDF Schema can be used to define properties and types of the web resources. Similar to XML Schema which gives specific constraints on the structure of an XML document,

Table 1. DAML+OIL constructs (partial)

DAML+OIL constructs	Description
$DAML\_class$	classes
$DAML\_property$	properties
$DAML\_subclass[C]$	subclasses of C
$DAML\_subproperty[P]$	sub properties of P
$instanceof[C]$	instances of the DAML+OIL class C

RDF Schema provides information about the interpretation of the RDF statements. The DARPA Agent Markup Language (DAML) [14] is an AI-inspired description logic-based language for describing taxonomic information. DAML currently combines Ontology Interchange Language (OIL) [3] and features from other ontology systems. It is now called DAML+OIL and contains richer modelling primitives than RDF. The DAML+OIL language builds on top of XML and RDF(S) to provide a language with both a well-defined semantics and a set of language constructs including classes, subclasses and properties with domains and ranges, for describing a Web domain. DAML+OIL can further express restriction on membership in classes and restrictions on certain domains and ranges values.

Semantic Web is highly distributed, and different parties may have different understanding of the same concept. Ideally, the program must have a way to discover the common meanings from the different understandings. It is central to another important concept in Semantic Web service – ontology. The ontology for a Semantic Web service is a document or file that formally defines the relations among terms. The most typical kind of ontology for the Web has taxonomy and a set of inference rules. Ontology can enhance the functioning of the Web in many ways, and RDFS and DAML+OIL supply the language to define the ontology.

We summarize some essential DAML+OIL constructs in Table 1.

2.2 Alloy Overview

Alloy [9] is a structural modelling language based on first-order logic, for expressing complex structural constraints and behavior. Alloy treats relations as first class citizens and uses relational composition as a powerful operator to combine various structured entities. The essential constructs of Alloy are as follows:

Signature: A signature (sig) paragraph introduces a basic type and a collection of relation (called field) in it along with the types of the fields and constraints on their value. A signature may inherit fields and constraints from another signature.
Function: A function (fun) captures behaviour constraints. It is a parameterized formula that can be "applied" elsewhere,
Fact: Fact (fact) constrains the relations and objects. A *fact* is a formula that takes no arguments and need not to be invoked explicitly; it is always true.

Assertion: An assertion (`assert`) specifies an intended property. It is a formula whose correctness needs to be checked, assuming the facts in the model.

The Alloy Analyzer (AA) is a tool for analyzing models written in Alloy. Given a formula and a scope – a bound on the number of atoms in the universe – AA determines whether there exists a model of the formula that uses no more atoms than the scope permits, and if so, return it. It supports two kinds of automatic analysis: simulation, in which the consistency of an invariant or operation is demonstrated by generating a state or transition, and checking, in which a consequence of the specification is tested by attempting to generate a counterexample.

3 DAML+OIL Semantic Encoding

DAML+OIL has a well-defined semantics which has been described in a set of axioms [7]. In this section based on the semantics of DAML+OIL, we define the semantic functions for some important DAML+OIL primitives in Alloy. The complete DAML+OIL semantic encoding can be found in the appendix.

3.1 Basic Concepts

The semantic models for DAML+OIL are encoded in the module `DAMLOIL`. Users only need to import this module to reason DAML+OIL ontology in Alloy.

```
module DAMLOIL
```

All the things described in Semantic web context are called resources. A basic type `Resource` is defined as:

```
sig Resource {}
```

All other concepts defined later are extended from the `Resource`. `Property`, which is a kind of `Resource` itself, relates `Resource` to `Resource`.

```
disj sig Property extends Resource
    {sub_val: Resource -> Resource}
```

Each `Property` has a relation `sub_val` from set <Property, Resource, Resource> with type <Resource, Resource, Resource> (since in Alloy sub-signature does not introduce a new type). This relation can be regarded as a RDF statement, i.e., a triple of the form
<property(or predicate), subject, value(or object)>.
The class corresponds to the generic concept of type or category of resource. Each `Class` maps a set of resources via the relation `instances`, which contains all the instance resources. The keyword `disj` is used to indicate the `Class` and `Property` are disjoint.

```
disj sig Class extends Resource {instances: set Resource}
```

The DAML+OIL also allows the use of XML Schema datatypes to describe (or define) part of the datatype domain. However there are no predefined types in Alloy, so we treat Datatype as a special Class, which contains all the possible datatype values in the instances relation.

```
disj sig Datatype extends Class {}
```

3.2 Class Elements

The `subClassOf` is a relation between classes. The instances in a subclass are also in the superclasses. A parameterized formula (a function in Alloy) is used to represent this concept.

```
fun subClassOf(csup, csub: Class)
  {csub.instances in csup.instances}
```

The `disjointWith` is a relation between classes. It asserts that there are no instances common with each other.

```
fun disjointWith (c1, c2: Class) {no c1.instances & c2.instances}
```

3.3 Property Restrictions

A `toClass` function states that all instances of the class c1 have the values of property P all belonging to the class c2.

```
fun toClass (p: Property, c1: Class, c2: Class)
  {all r1, r2: Resource | r1 in c1.instances <=> r2 in r1.(p.sub_val) =>
                                                 r2 in c2.instances}
```

A `hasValue` function states that all instances of the class c1 have the values of property P as resource r. The r could be an individual object or a datatype value.

```
fun hasValue (p: Property, c1: Class, r: Resource)
  {all r1: Resource | r1 in c1.instances => r1.(p.sub_val) = r}
```

A `cardinality` function states that all instances of the class c1 have exactly N distinct values for the property P. The new version of Alloy supports some integer operations.

```
fun cardinality (p: Property, c1: Class, N: Int)
  {all r1: Resource| r1 in c1.instances <=> # r1.(p.sub_val) = int N}
```

3.4 Boolean Combination of Class Expressions

The `intersectionOf` function defines a relation between a class c1 and a list of classes clist. The List is defined in the Alloy library. The class c1 consists of exactly all the objects that are common to all class expressions from the list clist.

```
fun intersectionOf (clist: List, c1: Class)
    {all r: Resource| r in c1.instances <=>
        all ca: clist.*next.val | r in ca.instances}
```

The unionOf function defines a relation between a class c1 and a list of classes clist. The class c1 consists of exactly all the objects that belong to at least one of the class expressions from the list clist. It is analogous to logical disjunction;

```
fun unionOf (clist: List, c1: Class)
    {all r: Resource| r in c1.instances <=>
        some ca: clist.*next.val| r in ca.instances}
```

3.5 Property Elements

The subPropertyOf function states that psub is a subproperty of the property psup. This means that every pair (subject,value) that is in psup is in the psub.

```
fun subPropertyOf (psup, psub: Property) {psub.sub_val in psup.sub_val}
```

The domain function asserts that the property P only applies to instances of the class c.

```
fun domain (p: Property, c: Class) {(p.sub_val).Resource in c.instances}
```

The inverseOf function shows two properties are inverse.

```
fun inverseOf (p1, p2: Property) {p1.sub_val = ~(p2.sub_val)}
```

4 DAML+OIL to Alloy Transformation

In the previous section we defined the semantic model for the DAML+OIL constructs, so that analyzing DAML+OIL ontology in Alloy can be easily and effectively achieved. We also constructed a XSLT [15] stylesheet for the automatic transformation from DAML+OIL file to into Alloy program. [1]

A set of transformation rules transforming from DAML+OIL ontology to Alloy program are developed in the following presentation.

4.1 DAML+OIL Class Transformation

$$\frac{C \in DAML\_class}{static\ disj\ sig\ C\ extends\ Class\{\}}$$

A DAML_class C will be transferred into a scalar C, constrained to be an elements of the signature Class.

---

[1] The details of the XSLT program and other information on this project can be found at:
http://nt-appn.comp.nus.edu.sg/fm/alloy/

4.2 DAML+OIL Property Transformation

$$\frac{P \in DAML\_property}{static\ disj\ sig\ P\ extends\ Property\{\}}$$

A DAML_property p will be transferred into a scalar P, constrained to be an elements of the signature `Property`.

4.3 Instance Transformation

$$\frac{x \in instancesof[Y]}{static\ disj\ sig\ x\ extends\ Resource\{\}\\ fact\{\ x\ in\ Y.instances\}}$$

A DAML instance x of class Y will be transferred into a scalar x, constrained to be an element of the signature `Resource`. x is a subset of `Y.instances`.

4.4 Other Transformation

Other DAML+OIL constructs can be easily transferred into the Alloy function we defined in the previous section. For example the following rule shows how to transfer the DAML+OIL subclass relation into Alloy code.

$$\frac{subclass[X, Y], X \in DAML\_class, Y \in daml\_class}{fact\{subClassOf(X, Y)\}}$$

4.5 Case Study

A classical DAML+OIL ontology, "animal relation" is used to illustrate how the transformation and analysis could be achieved. The following DAML+OIL ontology defines two class `animal` and `plant` which are disjoint. The `eats` and `eaten_by` are two properties, which are inverse to each other. The domain of `eats` is `animal`. The `carnivore` is a subclass of animal which can only eat animals.

```
<daml:Class rdf:ID="animal">
  <rdfs:label>animal</rdfs:label> </daml:Class>
<daml:Class rdf:ID="plant">
  <rdfs:label>plant</rdfs:label>
  <daml:disjointWith rdf:resource="#animal"/></daml:Class>
<daml:ObjectProperty rdf:about="eaten_by">
  <rdfs:label>eaten_by</rdfs:label>
</daml:ObjectProperty>
<daml:ObjectProperty rdf:about="eats">
  <rdfs:label>eats</rdfs:label>
```

```
      <daml:inverseOf rdf:resource="#eaten_by"/>
      <rdfs:domain><daml:Class rdf:about="#animal"/>
      </rdfs:domain></daml:ObjectProperty>
   <daml:Class rdf:ID="carnivore">
      <rdfs:label>carnivore</rdfs:label>
      <rdfs:subClassOf rdf:resource="#animal"/>
      <rdfs:subClassOf>
         <daml:Restriction> <daml:onProperty rdf:resource="#eats"/>
            <daml:toClass rdf:resource="#animal"/>
         </daml:Restriction>
      </rdfs:subClassOf></daml:Class>
```

This DAML+OIL ontology will be transferred into Alloy as follow,

```
module animal
/*import the library module we defined*/
open DMALOIL
/* plant and animal are translated to two class instances, the key
 word static is used to a signature contains exactly one element.*/
static disj sig plant, animal extends Class {}

/* The disjoin element was transferred into fact in Alloy */
fact {disjointWith(plant, animal)}

/* eats, eaten_by are translated to two property instances */
static disj sig eats, eaten_by extends Property {}
fact {inverseOf(eats, eaten_by)}
fact {domain(eats, animal)}

static disj sig carnivore extends Class{}
fact{subClass(animal, carnivore)}
fact{toClass(eats, carnivore, animal)}
```

We can check the consistency of the DAML+OIL ontology and do some reasoning readily.

5 Analysing DAML+OIL Ontology

Reasoning is one of the key tasks for the semantic web. It can be useful at many stages during the design, maintenance and deployment of ontology.

There are two different levels of checking and reasoning, the conceptual level and the instance level. At the conceptual level, we can reason about class properties and subclass relationships. At the instance level, we can do the membership checking (instantiation) and instance property reasoning. The DAML+OIL reasoning tool, i.e. FaCT [8], can only provide conceptual level reasoning, while AA can perform both. The FaCt system originally is designed to be a terminological classifer (TBox) which concerns only about the concepts, roles and attributes, not instances. The semantic web reasoner based on the FaCT, like OILED, does not support instance level reasoning well.

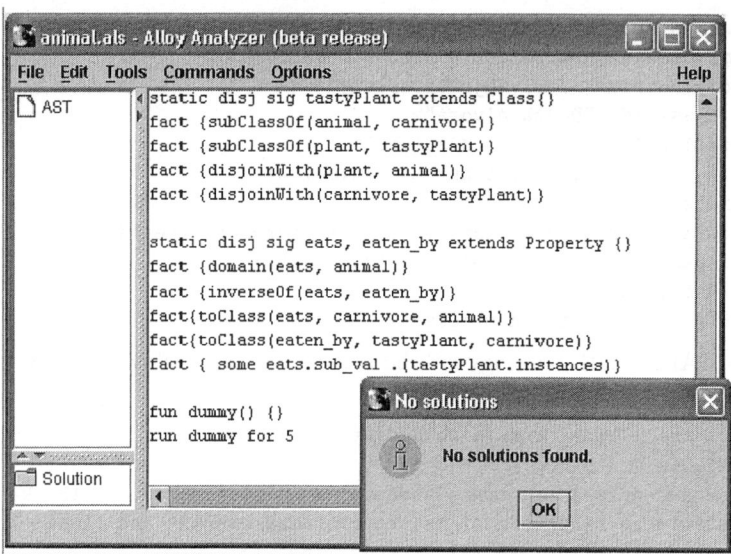

Fig. 1. Inconsistence example

5.1 Class Property Checking

It is essential that the ontology shared among autonomous software agents is conceptually consistent. Reasoning with inconsistent ontology may lead to erroneous conclusions. In this section we give some examples of inconsistent ontology that can arise in ontology development, and demonstrate how these inconsistencies can be detected by the Alloy analyzer. For example, we define another class tastyPlant which is a subclass of plant and eaten by the carnivore. There is an inconsistency since by the ontology definition carnivores can only eat animals. Animals and plants are disjoint.

```
<daml:Class rdf:ID="tastyPlant">
 <rdfs:label>tastyPlant</rdfs:label>
 <rdfs:subClassOf rdf:resource="#plant"/>
 <rdfs:subClassOf>
   <daml:Restriction>
     <daml:onProperty rdf:resource="#eat_by"/>
     <daml:toClass rdf:resource="#carnivore"/>
   </daml:Restriction></rdfs:subClassOf>
</daml:Class>
```

We transform the ontology into an Alloy program, add some facts to remove the trivial models (like everything type is empty set) and load the program into the Alloy Analyzer. The Alloy Analyzer will automatically check the consistency. We conclude that there is an inconsistency in the animal ontology since Alloy can not find any solutions satisfying all facts within the scope (Figure 1). Note that when Alloy can not find a solution, it may also be due to the scope being too small. By picking a large enough scope, "no solution found' is very likely to mean that an inconsistency has occurred.

Let us take another example. Suppose we define that the `polyphagic_animal` eats at least two kind of things i.e `polyphagic_animal` objects have at least two distinct values for the property `eats`. There is also one kind of animal called `picky_animal` which only eats one other kind of animal. The ontology will be defined as follows:

```
<daml:Class rdf:ID="polyphagic_animal">
 <rdfs:label>polyphagic_animal</rdfs:label>
 <rdfs:subClassOf rdf:resource="#animal"/>
 <rdfs:subClassOf>
   <daml:Restriction>
     <daml:onProperty rdf:resource="#eats"/>
     <daml:minCardinality> 2 </daml:minCardinality>
   </daml:Restriction></rdfs:subClassOf></daml:Class>
<daml:Class rdf:ID="#picky_animal">
 <rdfs:label>picky_animal</rdfs:label>
 <rdfs:subClassOf rdf:resource="#animal"/>
 <rdfs:subClassOf>
   <daml:Restriction>
     <daml:onProperty rdf:resource="#eats"/>
     <daml:Cardinality> 1 </daml:Cardinality>
   </daml:Restriction></rdfs:subClassOf></daml:Class>
```

From the above ontology we can infer that the `picky_animal` is not a kind of `polyphagic_animal`, otherwise it would be an inconsistency that AA can easily pick up.

5.2 Subsumption Reasoning

The task of subsumption reasoning is to infer a DAML+OIL class is the subclass of another DAML+OIL class. We use the relationship between the fish, shark and dolphin as a example to demonstrate this kind of reasoning task. In the animal ontology a property `breathe_by` is defined. A `fish` class is a subclass of the `animal` which `breathe_by` the `gill`. Since the purpose of this paper is to demonstrate ideas, we keep the ontology simple. In reality there are some animals such as frogs and toads, which can respire by use of gills when they are young and by lungs when they reach adult stage. Also we do not consider the animals which respire by use of the pharyngeal lining or skin, like newborn Julia Creek dunnarts.

```
<daml:ObjectProperty rdf:ID="breathe_by"/>
<daml:Class rdf:ID="gill">
   <rdfs:label>gill</rdfs:label></daml:Class>
<daml:Class rdf:ID="fish">
 <rdfs:label>fish</rdfs:label>
 <rdfs:subClassOf rdf:resource="#animal"/>
 <rdfs:subClassOf>
  <daml:Restriction>
    <daml:onProperty rdf:resource="#breathe_by"/>
    <daml:toClass rdf:resource="#gill"/>
  </daml:Restriction></rdfs:subClassOf></daml:Class>
```

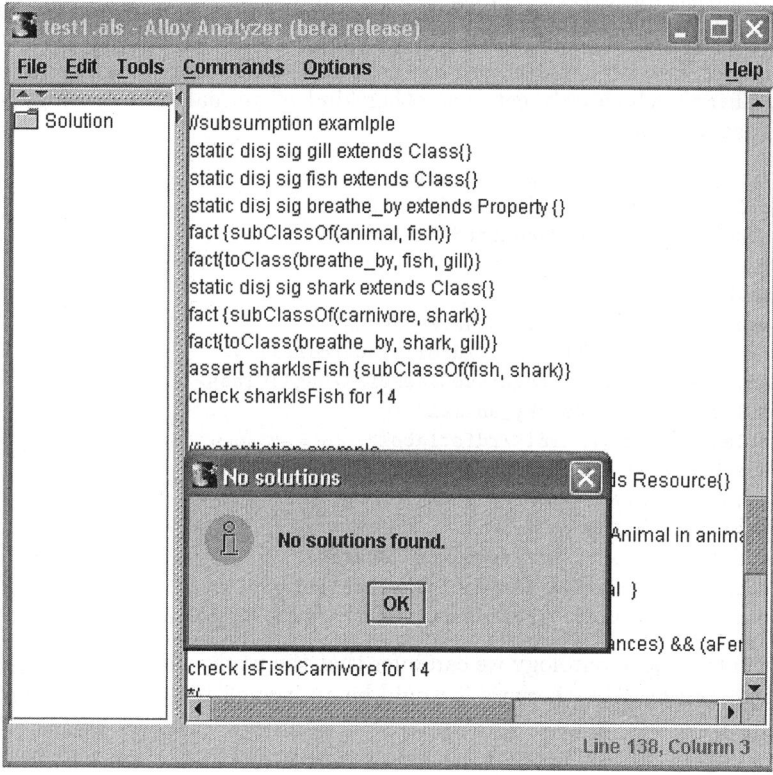

Fig. 2. Subsumption example

We also define a class shark, a subclass of carnivore which breathe by the gill.

```
<daml:Class rdf:ID="shark">
 <rdfs:label>shark</rdfs:label>
 <rdfs:subClassOf rdf:resource="#carnivore"/>
 <rdfs:subClassOf>
  <daml:Restriction>
   <daml:onProperty rdf:resource="#breathe_by"/>
   <daml:toClass rdf:resource="#gill"/>
  </daml:Restriction></rdfs:subClassOf></daml:Class>
```

Several of the classes were upgraded to being defined when their definitions constituted both necessary and sufficient conditions for class membership, e.g., a animal is a fish if and only if it breathes by the gill. Additional subclass relationships can be inferred i.e. the shark is also a subclass of fish. We transfer this ontology into an Alloy program and make an assertion that the shark is the subclass of fish. The Alloy analyzer will check the correctness of this assertion automatically (Figure 2). The Alloy Analyzer checks whether an assertion holds by trying to find a counterexample. Note that "no solution" means no

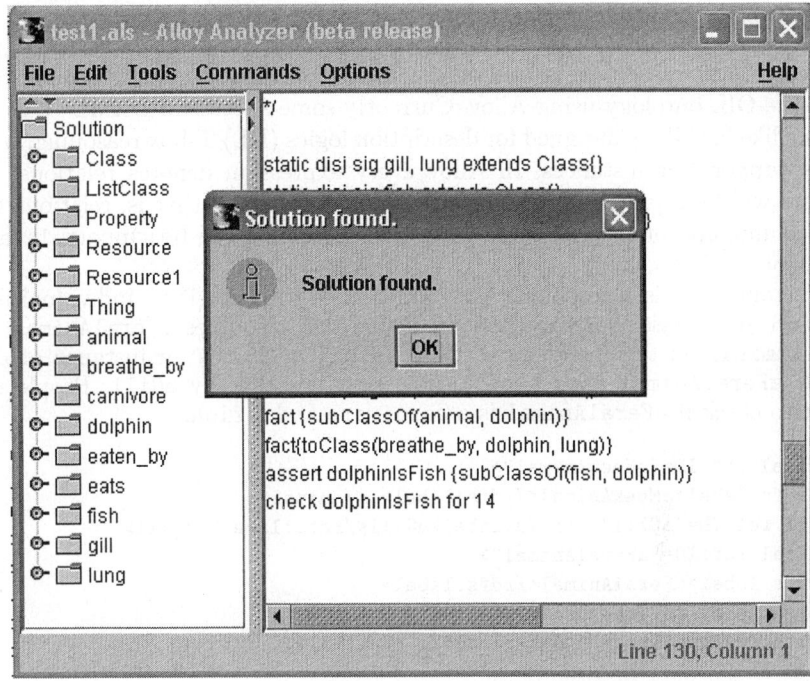

Fig. 3. Dolphin is not a fish

counterexample found, in this case, it indicates that the assertion is sound. To make it more interesting, we define classes dolphin and lung. The Dolphin is a kind of animal which breathe by lungs. The classes gill and lung are disjoint. Furthermore the breathe_by is a unique property.

```
<daml:Class rdf:ID="lung">
 <rdfs:label>lung</rdfs:label>
 <daml:disjointWith rdf:resource="#gill"/></daml:Class>
<daml:Class rdf:ID="dolphin">
 <rdfs:label>dolphin</rdfs:label>
 <rdfs:subClassOf rdf:resource="#animal"/> <rdfs:subClassOf>
  <daml:Restriction>
   <daml:onProperty rdf:resource="#breathe_by"/>
   <daml:toClass rdf:resource="#lung"/>
  </daml:Restriction></rdfs:subClassOf></daml:Class>
```

Suppose we make an assertion that the dolphin is a kind of fish, the Alloy Analyzer will refute it since some counterexample was found (Figure 3). If we add that dolphin is a fish as a fact in the module, the AA will conclude that an inconsistency has arisen.

5.3 Instantiation

Instance level reasoning is one of the main contributions for reasoning over DAML+OIL ontology using Alloy. Currently some successful DAML+OIL reasoners like FaCT are designed for description logics (DL) T-box reasoning, which lacks support for instances. In Alloy every expression denotes relations. The scalars will be represented by singleton unary relations - that is, relations with one column and one row. The instance level reasoning can be supported readily in Alloy.

Instantiation is a reasoning task which tries to check if an individual is an instance of a class. For example, we define two resources aFeralAnimal and aMeekAminal as the instances of class animal. aGill is an instance of class gill. aFeralAnimal eats aMeekAnimal and breathes by aGill. People may want to check if aFeralAnimal is a carnivore and a fish.

```
<animal rdf:ID="aMeekAnimal">
  <rdfs:label>aMeekAnimal</rdfs:label> </animal>
<gill rdf:ID="aGill"> <rdfs:label>aGill</rdfs:label></gill>
<animal rdf:ID="aFeralAnimal">
 <rdfs:label>aFeralAnimal</rdfs:label>
 <breathe_by rdf:resource="aGill"/>
 <eats rdf:resource="aMeekAnimal"/> </animal>
```

We transfer the ontology into an Alloy program and make an assertion as following:

```
static disj sig aFeralAnimal, aMeekAnimal extends Resource{}
static disj sig aGill extends Resource{}
fact {aFeralAnimal in animal.instances &&
      aMeekAnimal in animal.instances}
fact {aGill in gill.instances}
fact {(aFeralAnimal->aMeekAnimal) in eats.sub_val}
fact {(aFeralAnimal->aGill) in breathe_by.sub_val}
assert isFishCarnivore
  {(aFeralAnimal in fish.instances) &&
   (aFeralAnimal in carnivore.instances)}
check isFishCarnivore for 15
```

AA concludes that this assertion is correct.

5.4 Instance Property Reasoning

Instance property reasoning (often regarded as knowledge querying) is important in Semantic Web applications. Since one of the promising strengths of Semantic Web technology is that it gives the agents the capability to do more accurate and more meaningful searches. The agent can answer some questions for which the answer is not explicitly stored in the knowledge base.

For example, the emerge_early and emerge_later are two properties, which are inverse to each other. Animal A emerged early then B if the species of A emerges earlier than the species of B on the earth. emerge_early is transitive. Three animal instances firstDinosaur, firstApe and firstHuman are defined. firstDinosaur emerge_early firstApe and firstApe emerge_early firstHuman. One possible question people may ask is that whether firstHuman is emerge_later firstDinosaur. With the assistance of Alloy reasoner, such questions can be answered.

```
fact{TransitiveProperty(emerge_early)}
static disj sig firstDinosaur, firstApe, firstHuman extends Resource{}
fact { firstDinosaur in animal.instances
    && firstApe in animal.instances
    && firstHuman in animal.instances}
fact {(firstDinosaur->firstApe) in emerge_early.sub_val}
fact {(firstApe->firstHuman) in emerge_early.sub_val}
assert hum {(firstHuman->firstDinosaur) in emerge_later.sub_val}
check hum for 14
```

AA concludes that this assertion is correct.

6 Related Work and Conclusion

The main contribution of this paper is that it develops the semantic models for DAML+OIL language constructs in Alloy and the systematic transformation rules and (XSLT) program which can translate DAML+OIL ontology to Alloy automatically. With the assistance of Alloy Analyzer (AA), we also demonstrated that the consistency of the SW ontology can be checked automatically and different kinds of reasoning tasks can be supported. Alloy is chosen over other modeling techniques because

– Alloy is based on relations, where relations between web resources are the focus issues in SW.
– Alloy has an impressive automatic tool support.

We believe SW is a new novel application domain for Alloy. Recently, the technique/tool developed in this paper was successfully applied to a military case study [6]. Alloy was used to check and reason a *plan ontology* [12] developed by a research team at DSO National Laboratories in Singapore.

Recently, some researchers have begun to explore the potential of combining Web technologies and SE technologies together, e,g. [13]. However there has not been much work done on the application of formal techniques for semantic-web. In our previous work [5] we tried to extract web ontology from Z requirement models, which is a very different approach from the techniques demonstrated in this paper – checking and reasoning web ontology by encoding the semantics of DAML+OIL into the Alloy system.

From a completely different direction, i.e., applying SW to build software modeling environment, we recently investigated how RDF and DAML+OIL can be used to construct a Semantic Web environment for supporting, extending and integrating various specification languages [4]. We believe SW can contribute to the new developments for the software modeling environment.

In summary, there is a clear synergy between SW languages and software modeling techniques. The investigation of the links between those two paradigms will lead to great benefits for both areas.

Acknowledgements

We would like to thank Hugh Anderson, DSTA staffs and anonymous referees for many helpful comments. We also would thank Daniel Jackson and Ilya Shlyakhter for providing useful info and demo on Alloy. This work is supported by the Defence Innovative Research grant *Formal Design Methods and DAML* from Defence Science & Technology Agency (DSTA) Singapore.

References

1. T. Berners-Lee, J. Hendler, and O. Lassila. The semantic web. Scientific American, May 2001.
2. D. Brickley and R.V. Guha (editors). Resource description framework (rdf) schema specification 1.0. http://www.w3.org/TR/2000/CR-rdf-schema-20000327/, March, 2000.
3. J. Broekstra, M. Klein, S. Decker, D. Fensel, and I. Horrocks. Adding formal semantics to the web: building on top of rdf schema. In *ECDL Workshop on the Semantic Web: Models, Architectures and Management*, 2000.
4. J. S. Dong, J. Sun, and H. Wang. Semantic Web for Extending and Linking Formalisms. In L.-H. Eriksson and P. A. Lindsay, editors, *Proceedings of Formal Methods Europe: FME'02*, Copenhagen, Denmark, July 2002. Springer-Verlag.
5. J. S. Dong, J. Sun, and H. Wang. Z Approach to Semantic Web Services. In C. George and H. Miao, editors, *International Conference on Formal Engineering Methods (ICFEM'02)*. LNCS, Springer-Verlag, October 2002.
6. J. S. Dong, J. Sun, H. Wang, C. H. Lee, and H. B. Lee. Analysing web ontology in alloy: A military case study. In *Proc. 15th International Conference on Software Engineering and Knowledge Engineering: SEKE'03*, San Francisco, USA, July 2003.
7. Richard Fikes and Deborah L. McGuinness. An axiomatic semantics for rdf, rdf schema, and daml+oil. Technical Report KSL-01-01, Knowledge Systems Laboratory, 2001.
8. I. Horrocks. The FaCT system. *Tableaux'98, Lecture Notes in Computer Science*, 1397:307–312, 1998.
9. D. Jackson. Micromodels of software: Lightweight modelling and analysis with alloy. Available: http://sdg.lcs.mit.edu/alloy/book.pdf, 2002.
10. D. Jackson, I. Schechter, and I. Shlyakhter. Alcoa: the alloy constraint analyzer. In *Proc. 22nd International Conference on Software Engineering: ICSE'2000*, pages 730–733, Limerick, Ireland, June 2000. ACM Press.
11. O. Lassila and R. R. Swick (editors). Resource description framework (rdf) model and syntax specification. http://www.w3.org/TR/1999/REC-rdf-syntax-19990222/, Feb, 1999.

12. C. H. Lee. Phase I Report for Plan Ontology. DSO National Labs, Singapore, 2002.
13. Cecilia Mascolo, Wolfgang Emmerich, and Anthony Finkelstein. XML technologies and software engineering. In *International Conference on Software Engineering*, pages 775–776, 2001.
14. F. van Harmelen, P. F. Patel-Schneider, and I. Horrocks (editors). Reference description of the daml+oil ontology markup language. Contributors: T. Berners-Lee, D. Brickley, D. Connolly, M. Dean, S. Decker, P. Hayes, J. Heflin, J. Hendler, O. Lassila, D. McGuinness, L. A. Stein, ..., March, 2001.
15. World Wide Web Consortium (W3C). Xsl transformations (xslt) version 1.0. http://www.w3.org/TR/xslt, 1999.

A Completed DAML+OIL Semantic Encoding

A.1 Basic concepts

The semantic models for DAML+OIL are encoded in the module `DAMLOIL`. The semantic encoding for the basic concepts was summarized in the table 2.

`module DAMLOIL`

Table 2. DAML+OIL Semantic encoding (basic concepts)

DAML+OIL primitive	Alloy semantic function
Resource	sig Resource {}
$DAML\_Property$	disj sig Property extends Resource {sub_val: Resource → Resource}
$DAML\_Class$	disj sig Class extends Resource {instances: set Resource}
Datatype	disj sig Datatype extends Class {}

All the things described in Semantic web context are called resources. All other concepts defined later like `Property` and `Class` are extended from the `Resource`.

A.2 Class Elements

The semantic encoding for the class elements was summarized in the table 3. It includes constructs like `subClassOf`, `disjointWith`, `disjointUnionOf` and `sameClassAs`.

A.3 Property Restrictions

The semantic encoding for the property restrictions was summarized in the table 4. A property restriction defines the class of all objects that satisfy the restriction. For example the `toClass` function states that all instances of the class `c1` have the values of property P all belonging to the class `c2`. The other constructs include `hasValue`, `hasClass`, `cardinality` etc..

Table 3. DAML+OIL Semantic encoding (class elements)

DAML+OIL primitive	Alloy semantic function
$subClassOf$	fun subClassOf(csup, csub: Class) {csub.instances in csup.instances}
$disjointWith$	fun disjointWith (c1, c2: Class) { no c1.instances & c2.instances}
$disjointUnionOf$	fun disjointUnionOf(clist: List, c1: Class) {c1.instances = clist.*next.val.instances all disj ca1, ca2: clist.*next.val | no ca1.instances & ca2.instances }
$sameClassAs$	fun sameClassAs(c1, c2: Class) {c1.instances = c2.instances}

Table 4. DAML+OIL Semantic encoding (Property restrictions)

DAML+OIL primitive	Alloy semantic function
$toClass$	fun toClass (p: Property, c1: Class, c2: Class) {all r1, r2: Resource | r1 in c1.instances <=> r2 in r1.($p.sub\_val$) => r2 in c2.instances}
$hasValue$	fun hasValue (p: Property, c1: Class, r: Resource) {all r1: Resource | r1 in c1.instances => r1.($p.sub\_val$)=r }
$hasClass$	fun hasClass (p: Property, c1: Class, c2: Class) {all r1: Resource | r1 in c1.instances => some r1.($p.sub\_val$) & c2.instances}
$cardinality$	fun cardinality (p: Property, c1: Class, N: Int) {all r1: Resource | r1 in c1.instances <=> # r1.($p.sub\_val$) = int N }
$maxCardinality$	fun maxCardinality (p: Property, c1: Class, N: Int) {all r1: Resource | r1 in c1.instances <=> # r1.($p.sub\_val$) =< int N }
$minCardinality$	fun minCardinality (p: Property, c1: Class, N: Int) {all r1: Resource | r1 in c1.instances <=> # r1.($p.sub\_val$) >= int N }
$cardinalityQ$	fun cardinalityQ (p: Property, c1: Class, N: Int, c2: Class) {all r1: Resource | r1 in c1.instances <=> # r1.($p.sub\_val$) & c2.instances = int N }
$maxCardinalityQ$	fun maxCardinalityQ (p: Property, c1: Class, N: Int, c2: Class) {all r1: Resource | r1 in c1.instances <=> # r1.($p.sub\_val$) & c2.instances =< int N }
$minCardinalityQ$	fun minCardinalityQ(p: Property, c1: Class, N: Int, c2: Class) {all r1: Resource | r1 in c1.instances <=> # r1.($p.sub\_val$) & c2.instances >= int N}

A.4 Boolean Combination of Class Expressions

The semantic encoding for the boolean combination of class expression was summarized in the table 5.

Table 5. DAML+OIL Semantic encoding (Boolean combination)

DAML+OIL primitive	Alloy semantic function
$intersectionOf$	fun intersectionOf (clist: List, c1: Class) {all r: Resource| r in c1.instances <=> all ca: clist.*next.val | r in ca.instances}
$unionOf$	fun unionOf (clist: List, c1: Class) {all r: Resource| r in c1.instances <=> some ca: clist.*next.val| r in ca.instances}

A.5 Property Elements

The semantic encoding for the property elements was summarized in the table 6. It includes subPropertyOf, samePropertyAs etc..

Table 6. DAML+OIL Semantic encoding (Property elements)

DAML+OIL primitive	Alloy semantic function
$subPropertyOf$	fun subPropertyOf (psup, psub: Property) {psub.sub_val in psup.sub_val }
$domain$	fun domain (p: Property, c: Class) {(p.sub_val).Resource in c.instances }
$range$	fun range (p: Property, c: Class) {Resource.(p.sub_val) in c.instances }
$samePropertyAs$	fun samePropertyAs(p1, p2: Property) {p1.sub_val=p2.sub_val }
$inverseOf$	fun inverseOf (p1, p2: Property) {p1.sub_val = ~(p2.sub_val)}
$TransitiveProperty$	fun TransitiveProperty(p: Property) {all x, y, z: Resource | y in (p.sub_val).x && z in (p.sub_val).y => z in (p.sub_val).x }
$UniqueProperty$	fun UniqueProperty (p: Property) {all x : Resource | sole x.(p.sub_val) }
$UnambigousProperty$	fun UnambigousProperty(p: Property) {all x : Resource | sole (p.sub_val).x}

Structuring Retrenchments in B by Decomposition

Michael Poppleton[1] and Richard Banach[2]

[1] Department of Electronics and Computer Science,
University of Southampton, Highfield,
Southampton SO17 1BJ, UK,
mrp@ecs.soton.ac.uk

[2] Department of Computer Science, Manchester University,
Manchester M13 9PL, UK,
banach@cs.man.ac.uk

Abstract. Simple retrenchment is briefly reviewed in the B language of J.-R. Abrial [1] as a liberalization of classical refinement, for the formal description of application developments too demanding for refinement. This work initiates the study of the structuring of retrenchment-based developments in B by decomposition. A given coarse-grained retrenchment relation between specifications is decomposed into a family of more fine-grained retrenchments. The resulting family may distinguish more incisively between refining, approximately refining, and non-refining behaviours. Two decomposition results are given, each sharpening a coarse-grained retrenchment within a particular syntactic structure for operations at concrete and abstract levels. A third result decomposes a retrenchment exploiting structure latent in both levels. The theory is illustrated by a simple example based on an abstract model of distributed computing, and methodological aspects are considered.

Keywords decomposition, formal methods, refinement, retrenchment, structuring.

1 Introduction

From early concerns about proving correctness of programs such as Hoare's [15] and Dijkstra's [14], a mature refinement calculus of specifications to programs has developed. Thorough contemporary discussion can be found in [13, 2]. For model-based specifications the term "refinement" has a very precise meaning; according to Back and Butler [3] it is a "...correctness-preserving transformation...between (possibly abstract, non-executable) programs which is transitive, thus supporting stepwise refinement, and is monotonic with respect to program constructors, thus supporting piecewise refinement". A succinct characterisation of refinement is a relation between models where the precondition is weakened and the postcondition strengthened.

This work develops the *retrenchment* method, a liberalization of refinement. Early work [7, 8] motivated such a liberalization in terms of the problems applying refinement to "difficult" applications such as radiation dosimetry and magnetohydrodynamics. Such problem domains include infinite sets or properties, or models in continuous mathematics or classical physics, which do not relate in a simple way to the finite, discrete computer. A simple example is the impossibility of refining element addition/subtraction on an infinite set to a finite one. Classical refinement also prohibits I/O type change between what are conventionally known as the *abstract* and *concrete* models. By weakening the abstraction relation over the operation step, retrenchment allows concrete non-simulating behaviour to be described in, and related back to corresponding abstract behaviour. Concrete I/O may have different type to the abstract counterpart, and moreover the retrenchment relation may accomodate fluidity between state and I/O components across the development step from abstract to concrete model. [17, 20] developed a calculus of retrenchment in B, proved transitivity, and showed all primitive operators of the B generalized Substitution Language (GSL) to be monotonic with respect to retrenchment. [8, 9] explored the landscape between refinement, simulation and retrenchment. [5] addressed the integration of refinement and retrenchment from a methodological perspective. [18, 6] present two generalizations, evolving and output retrenchment respectively. The latter of these is used in this paper.

To provide application motivation for this liberalizing enterprise, a number of more substantial case studies of retrenchment have been presented. [19] gives a retrenchment model of the conventional approximating design step from an analogue linear control system to its discrete-time zero-order hold counterpart. Telephony feature interaction is a major application area characterised by requirements features which are in general mutually inconsistent and not simply composable; the utility of retrenchment was shown in a simple feature interaction case study [10]. This case study was developed to show how application domain knowledge could strengthen a retrenchment description [12].

Various methodological issues need to be addressed to support the effective use of retrenchment in practice: the choice of abstractions and designs for understandable and mechanisable retrenchment proof obligations, how best to integrate with refinement methods, how to compose atomic retrenchment steps up to the scale of realistic specifications, how to decompose coarse-grained "first-cut" retrenchments to improve descriptiveness. [11] makes some commentary on the first issue, and the second is becoming better understood [5]. [20] gave the monotonicity results on which to base a study of composability. This paper is concerned with the fourth issue, the decomposition of a given retrenchment.

A typical style of operational specification partitions the state/input domain in order to process each part of the partition appropriately; in B this case analysis approach is structured using a bounded choice over guarded GSL commands. This paper will concentrate on this style. A retrenchment relation covering the whole domain of such an operation and its concrete counterpart will in general document the processing choices in terms of a disjunctive choice of outcomes in the postcondition. Since there will usually be case structure at both levels, this disjunctive weakening effect is exacerbated. Describing such a given retrenchment as "coarse-grained", in this work we seek a decomposition into a family of retrenchments, each of which is restricted to one branch of the case structure (at abstract or concrete levels separately, or both levels simultaneously). Each such decomposed retrenchment should be "finer-grained" (i.e. have stronger postcondition on a restricted domain) in the sense of including only one or some of the disjunctive possibilities in the postcondition of the coarse-grained retrenchment. In this work we employ the output form of retrenchment [Op. cit.], which provides equipment for certain algebraic issues that arise.

The paper proceeds as follows. Section 2 briefly recalls the B GSL. Section 3 recaps syntactic and semantic definitions for retrenchment in GSL, extending them for output retrenchment. We extend the transitivity theorem of [20, 17] to provide the composition of two output retrenchments [Op. cit.]. Section 4 presents a running example to motivate the discussion, and demonstrates how the disjunctive shape of the retrenchment obligation is coarser and less descriptive than may desirable for certain purposes. Section 5 gives a number of retrenchment decomposition results. Three syntactic patterns are given for decomposing a single retrenchment into a finer-grained family of retrenchments. Each pattern is shown to be a valid decomposition in general. Section 6 applies the decomposition to the example to show its utility, and section 7 concludes.

2 The B Language of Generalized Substitutions

The B language was defined by [1] and is disseminated by textbooks such as [21]. B has as its central construct the *generalized substitution*: $[S]R$ (more conventionally written $wp(S, R)$) describes the weakest precondition under which program S is guaranteed to terminate satisfying postcondition R. generalized substitution distributes over conjunction and is monotonic w.r.t. implication. Programs (in general nondeterministic) are written using constructors inspired by Dijkstra's Guarded Command Language, called the generalized Substitution Language (GSL). The basic operation is the *simple substitution* (assignment, in procedural programming terms). For replacement of free variable x in formula R by expression E we write $[x := E]R$. The remaining simple constructors of B are axiomatised (for unbounded choice z is nonfree in R; this is written $z \setminus R$):

$$
\begin{aligned}
&[\text{skip}]R \equiv R &&\text{skip}\\
&[P \mid S]R \equiv P \wedge [S]R &&\text{precondition}\\
&[S[]T]R \equiv [S]R \wedge [T]R &&\text{bounded choice}\\
&[P \Longrightarrow S]R \equiv P \Rightarrow [S]R &&\text{guard}\\
&[@z \bullet S]R \equiv \forall z \bullet [S]R \; z \setminus R &&\text{unbounded choice}
\end{aligned}
\qquad (1)
$$

The precondition constructor explicitly strengthens the termination set, guard strengthens the feasibility set, bounded choice gives demonic nondeterministic choice between two operations, and unbounded choice a universally quantified demonic choice over all operations indexed on some (external) variable.

```
MACHINE          M(a)        REFINEMENT      N
                             REFINES         M
VARIABLES        u           VARIABLES       v
INVARIANT        I(u)        INVARIANT       J(u,v)
INITIALISATION   X(u)        INITIALISATION  Y(v)
OPERATIONS                   OPERATIONS
     S(u,i,o) ≘ ···              T(v,i,o) ≘ ···
END                          END
```

Fig. 1. B machine and refinement syntax

The action of an operation S, with state variable (list) x, on predicate $R(x)$ can be expressed in the following *normalised* form, where P is a predicate in variable x, Q is a predicate in variables x and x' (x' distinct from x):

$$[S]R \equiv P \wedge \forall x' \bullet (Q \Rightarrow [x := x']R) \qquad (2)$$

This decomposition into predicates P and Q is unique (modulo logical equivalence of predicates), and these are called $\mathsf{trm}(S)$ (termination: before-states from which S is guaranteed to terminate) and $\mathsf{prd}_x(S)$ (before-after transition) respectively. Theorem (2) interprets S as a predicate transformer: from initial state x, S establishes R precisely when S terminates at x and every x' reachable from x under S satisfies R. These predicates can be explicitly defined:

$$\mathsf{trm}(S) \equiv [S]\mathsf{true} \qquad \mathsf{prd}_x(S) \mathrel{\widehat{=}} \neg\, [S](x' \neq x)$$

The abstract syntax of the GSL is complemented by the concrete syntax of the Abstract Machine Notation (AMN), which includes constructs for modular structuring. The unit of modularity is the *machine*, which contains inter alia a state *variable* (list), an *invariant* predicate expressing type and other required state constraints, an *initialisation*, and a set of *operations*, which are expressed in terms of state, input and output variables. Fig. 1 shows an abstract machine and a refinement. The latter is a derivative construct: invariant clause $J(u,v)$ provides local variable type and constraint information, and the retrieve relation from concrete to abstract state variable.

The basic machine consistency proof obligations are *initialisation* (the initialisation establishes the invariant) and *operation consistency* (given invariant and operation termination, then the operation establishes the invariant):

$$[X]I \qquad I \wedge \mathsf{trm}(S) \Rightarrow [S]I \qquad (3)$$

The refinement proof obligations in B are equivalent to the classical forward simulation rules and are expressed as follows. Two abstract machines M and N are defined on state spaces u and v respectively, with a total relation J from v to u. There is a bijection between the operations of M and N (say, every operation S of machine M corresponds to exactly one operation T of N). If for every such pair (S,T) the following proof obligations (POBs) hold, then M is refined by N

(written $M \sqsubseteq N$): *initialisation refinement* (for every concrete initial step, there is an abstract initial step that establishes the retrieve relation) and *operation refinement* (for any concrete step of T, there is some abstract step of S that establishes the retrieve relation):

$$[Y]\neg\,[X]\neg\,J$$
$$I \wedge J \wedge \mathsf{trm}(S) \Rightarrow [T]\neg\,[S]\neg\,J \qquad (4)$$

3 Retrenchment

In its simple form, retrenchment weakens the refinement relation between two levels of abstraction: loosely speaking, it strengthens the precondition, weakens the postcondition, and introduces mutability between state and I/O at the two levels. The postcondition comprises a disjunction between a retrieve relation between abstract and concrete state, where refining behaviour is described, and a concession relation between abstract and concrete state and output. This concession (where non-refining concrete behaviour is related back to abstract behaviour) is the vehicle in the postcondition for describing I/O mutability. Use of the simple retrieve relation, however, precludes I/O mutability being described effectively in the case of refining behaviour.

Output retrenchment [6] improves matters by having an additional output conjunct specifically to cover this case. The ensuing tradeoff between additional syntactic complexity in the retrenchment and ease of use in discussing structural and algebraic aspects of retrenchment proves to be a big win technically. This paper will work with output retrenchment.

3.1 Retrenchment Defined

Figure 2 defines the syntax of output retrenchment in B, based on Fig. 1; it differs only from the simple form in the addition of the OUTPUT clause. Unlike a REFINEMENT, which in B is a construct derived from the refined machine, a retrenchment is an independent MACHINE. Thus N is a machine with parameter b (not necessarily related to a), state variable v, local invariant $J(v)$, initialisation $Y(v)$, and operation $OpNameC$ as wrapper for $T(v, j, p)$, a substitution with input j and output p. The RETRENCHES clause (replacing REFINES) makes visible the lexical environment of the retrenched construct. The RETRIEVES clause names the retrieve relation, from which the local invariant conjunct $J(v)$ has been separated syntactically into the INVARIANT clause. The name spaces of the retrenched and retrenching constructs are disjoint, but admit an injection of (retrenched to retrenching) operation names, allowing extra independent dynamic structure in the retrenching machine. This is reasonable in the light of the likelihood of machine N having a lower level and more detailed structure, possibly incorporating aspects that have no place in a cleaner, higher level model.

The relationship between concrete and abstract state is fundamentally different *before* and *after* the operation. We model this by distinguishing between a

```
MACHINE         M(a)           MACHINE              N(b)
                               RETRENCHES           M
VARIABLES       u              VARIABLES            v
INVARIANT       I(u)           INVARIANT            J(v)
                               RETRIEVES            G(u,v)
INITIALISATION  X(u)           INITIALISATION       Y(v)
OPERATIONS                     OPERATIONS
  o ⟵ OpName(i) ≘                p ⟵ OpNameC(j) ≘
    S(u,i,o)                       BEGIN
END                                  T(v,j,p)
                                   WITHIN
                                     P(i,j,u,v)
                                   OUTPUT
                                     E(u,v,o,p)
                                   CONCEDES
                                     C(u,v,o,p)
                                   END
                               END
```

Fig. 2. Syntax of output retrenchment

strengthened before-relation between abstract and concrete states, and a weakened after-relation. Thus the syntax of the concrete operation $OpNameC$ in N is precisely as in B, with the addition of the *ramification*, a syntactic enclosure of the operation. The precondition is strengthened by the WITHIN condition $P(i,j,u,v)$ which may change the balance of components between input and state. In the postcondition, the RETRIEVES clause $G(u,v)$ is weakened by the CONCEDES clause (the *concession*) $C(u,v,o,p)$, which specifies what the operation guarantees to achieve (in terms of after-state and output) if it cannot maintain the retrieve relation G, where the latter expresses the global relationship between abstract and concrete state variables. Since in simple retrenchment, the RETRIEVES clause gives no information about the relationship between concrete and abstract output, we conjoin to that clause an OUTPUT clause $E(u,v,o,p)$ in the postcondition. This means that, should any change occur in the balance of components between abstract and concrete state and output, the change is fully described both for refining and non-refining behaviour. We will see how the need for the OUTPUT clause arises in calculating certain compositions.

Retrenchment has the same initialisation requirements as refinement, i.e. that the retrieve relation be established:

$$[Y(v)] \neg [X(u)] \neg G(u,v) \tag{5}$$

Output retrenchment is defined[1] by all of the above together with the following operation proof obligation:

$$I(u) \wedge G(u,v) \wedge J(v) \wedge P(i,j,u,v) \wedge \mathsf{trm}(T(v,j,p))$$

---
[1] For simple retrenchment, simply remove the E clause.

$$\Rightarrow \text{trm}(S(u,i,o)) \wedge [T(v,j,p)]\neg [S(u,i,o)]\neg$$
$$((G(u,v) \wedge E(u,v,o,p)) \vee C(u,v,o,p)) \quad (6)$$

It is easy to see that retrenchment generalizes refinement[2]: choose $P \cong \text{trm}(S)$, $E \cong \text{true}$ and $C \cong \text{false}$ in (6). From this point we will refer to "retrenchment" where we actually mean "output retrenchment", and will use the following shorthand for (6): $S \lesssim_{G,P,E,C} T$.

3.2 Composing Output Retrenchments

It is straightforward to generalize the composition theorem for simple retrenchments [8, 20]. We assume as in section 3.1 that machine N RETRENCHES M, and further that machine O RETRENCHES N. Define machine O syntactically as a "lexicographic increment" on N, schematically replacing occurrences of $N,b,M,v,J,G,Y,p,j,T,P,E,C$ in N by $O,c,N,w,K,H,Z,q,k,U,Q,F,D$, respectively. Thus operation S in machine M is retrenched by operation T in machine N (w.r.t. G, P, E, C), which is in turn retrenched by operation U in machine O (w.r.t. H, Q, F, D).

Theorem If $S \lesssim_{G,P,E,C} T$ and $T \lesssim_{H,Q,F,D} U$ then $S \lesssim_{GJH,PQ,EF,CD} U$

where $GJH = \exists v \bullet (G(u,v) \wedge J(v) \wedge H(v,w))$
$PQ = \exists v,j \bullet (G(u,v) \wedge J(v) \wedge H(v,w) \wedge P(i,j,u,v) \wedge Q(j,k,v,w))$
$EF = \exists v,p \bullet (E(u,v,o,p) \wedge F(v,w,p,q))$
$CD = \exists v,p \bullet (G(u,v) \wedge E(u,v,o,p) \wedge D(v,w,p,q))$
$\vee \exists v,p \bullet (C(u,v,o,p) \wedge H(v,w) \wedge F(v,w,p,q))$
$\vee \exists v,p \bullet (C(u,v,o,p) \wedge D(v,w,p,q))$ (7)

The result is intuitively satisfying. The RETRIEVES clause GJH combines component RETRIEVES clauses and intermediate invariant. The WITHIN clause PQ combines all component before-state RETRIEVES and WITHIN constraints to ensure common v,j witnesses can be found for all the constituent terms. The OUTPUT clause EF combines the component OUTPUT clauses. The concession comes from a distribution of the disjunctions in the conjunction of the two postconditions $((G \wedge E) \vee C) \wedge ((H \wedge F) \vee D)$ over the conjunction, with the term corresponding to the combined RETRIEVES clause removed. It can be shown that the above definition of composition of retrenchments is associative.

4 Example: Resource Allocation

For brevity we use the abstract syntax of B GSL for operation bodies rather than the more verbose concrete B AMN syntax. We adopt the shorthand of an 'ELSE'

---
[2] In its I/O modulated form [8], which permits I/O type change.

clause in a choice of guarded commands, where ELSE denotes the complement of disjoined guards $\neg \exists z \bullet (P \vee Q \vee \cdots)$ in the following expression:

$$@z \bullet (P \Longrightarrow S) \, [] \, @z \bullet (Q \Longrightarrow T) \cdots [] \, \text{ELSE} \Longrightarrow W$$

Our example is a partial abstract model of a resource allocation and management system in a distributed environment: resources must be acquired, scheduled for processing, and released. In a centralised environment, functional requirements such as resource acquisition can be viewed as atomic until we descend to a fairly low level of abstraction, because the centralised scheduler in effect has all the aspects involved under its direct control. In a distributed environment, this is much less the case because of ignorance about what is going on at remote locations. Methodologically, we seek to separate concerns of functionality from those of distribution. Thus the abstract description models instantaneous allocation or not of a specified resource on the basis of a simple test.

In the concrete world, a number of lower level issues intrude to influence the success or otherwise of allocation. We could mention timeliness, contractual issues, quality of service – these relating to the requesting system's knowledge of the providing system's capabilities at that time – as well as the simple availability of what is requested. The situation is simplified here by modelling even the distributed allocation as an atomic process (i.e. described within a single syntactic entity), but entertaining nonetheless the possibility of outcomes displaying different degrees of success, in line with what can happen in real distributed systems.

We separate specification concerns by restricting consideration of such issues to the concrete level. This raises the question of how the abstract and concrete levels relate to each other – ideally, by refinement. But whether this is true or not depends strongly on how the extra concrete features fit together with the concrete description of the purely abstract model. If all goes well then the situation can be elegantly captured within a superposition refinement [16, 4]. But all is by no means guaranteed to go well. To address these less convenient situations, which are nevertheless prone to occur in practice, the authors introduced retrenchment, with its more forgiving operation proof obligation.

The example provides a simple vehicle for the contribution of this work – we restrict ourselves to little more than the distinct case splits in the two operation models to illustrate our contribution – and further motivates the utility of retrenchment.

Figure 3 specifies part of an abstract resource management machine *RsAlloc*, with allocation operation *Alloc*. *SPEC* is the set[3] of all resource specifications, and $spec_u$ is a static function returning the specification for any given resource from the universe of allocatable resources *RSS*. The state variable u records all resources already allocated. Operation *Alloc* allocates any resource not yet allocated in the set *RSS* whose specification meets the requirement *rqt* of the

---

[3] In this model resource specifications are unstructured, abstract entities, elements of the set *SPEC*, which in a real specification would be defined elsewhere.

MACHINE $RsAlloc$
SETS $RSS, SPEC$
CONSTANTS $spec_u$
PROPERTIES $spec_u : RSS \to SPEC$
VARIABLES u
INVARIANT $u \subseteq RSS$
INITIALISATION $u := \varnothing$
OPERATIONS
    $Alloc(rqt) \triangleq$
      $rqt \in SPEC \mid$
      $@x \bullet (x \in RSS - u \wedge spec_u(x) = rqt \Longrightarrow u := u \cup \{x\})$
      [] ELSE skip
    ...

END

Fig. 3. Resource allocation: specification

Alloc call. The operation tests only for availability of the resource, abstracting over the real-world constraints already mentioned.

Concrete machine *CRsAlloc* in Fig. 4 is the concrete counterpart of machine *RsAlloc*. In particular it contains the simple distributed resource allocation operation *CAlloc* (distributed only to the extent that the atomic operation exhibits some characterisitics normally associated with genuinely distributed allocation operations, in line with the remarks above).

Thus *CRSS* is the set of concrete distributed resources and $spec_v$ returns the specification of any given concrete resource in *CRSS*, with values in *SPEC*. There is also a trust function tr, defined over *CRSS*. This yields an abstract measure of the quality of the resource acquired in the case of successful allocation. v is the concrete state variable, recording resources allocated.

CAlloc retrenches *Alloc* by adding some of the "real-world constraints". We assume (for simplicity) that trust ratings of 0, 1 or 2 can be assigned to each candidate resource available for allocation. Trust level 2 indicates that requirements are fully met, level 1 that they are partially met, and level 0 indicates that an appropriate resource is available, but that the degree to which it meets requirements is unknown. Thus the concrete operation allocates level 2 and 1 resources from *CRSS* to v under separate guards, and skips for level 0 or no resource available[4]. Output *res* from *Calloc* reports the degree of success in matching an abstract allocation *Alloc*. There is no matching output from *Alloc*; this shows the I/O mutability possible in retrenchment. For simplicity we choose not to exploit such mutability further in this discussion.

Trust level 0 resources are strictly redundant here since we never do anything with them. However, the utility of trust level 0 is clear if we consider an

---

[4] We assume these guards are mutually disjoint and exhaustive. Formally, this would require the conjunction of each guard with the negation of each other guard, and so on, but we do not write this explicitly since to do so adds nothing to the discussion at this point. For the example application, this is admittedly simplistic.

MACHINE	$CRsAlloc$
RETRENCHES	$RsAlloc$
SETS	$CRSS, RESULT$
CONSTANTS	$spec_v, tr$
PROPERTIES	$spec_v : CRSS \to SPEC \land tr : CRSS \to \{0,1,2\} \land$
	$RESULT = \{Succ, Partial, Fail\}$
VARIABLES	v
INVARIANT	$v \subseteq CRSS$
RETRIEVES	$G_{\delta,n}(u,v)$
INITIALISATION	$v := \emptyset$
OPERATIONS	

$\quad res \longleftarrow CAlloc(rqt) \;\widehat{=}\;$
$\quad$ BEGIN
$\quad rqt \in SPEC \;|$
$\quad\quad @y \bullet (y \in CRSS - v \land spec_v(y) = rqt \land tr(y) = 2$
$\quad\quad\quad\quad\quad\quad\quad \Longrightarrow v := v \cup \{y\}) \;\|\; res := Succ \quad\quad\quad\quad\text{(i)}$
$\quad\quad [] \;@y \bullet (y \in CRSS - v \land spec_v(y) = rqt \land tr(y) = 1$
$\quad\quad\quad\quad\quad\quad\quad \Longrightarrow v := v \cup \{y\}) \;\|\; res := Partial \quad\quad\quad\text{(ii)}$
$\quad\quad [] \;$ ELSE $res := Fail \quad\quad\quad\quad\quad\quad\quad\quad\quad\quad\quad\quad\quad\quad\text{(i,iii)}$
$\quad$ WITHIN true
$\quad$ OUTPUT true
$\quad$ CONCEDES $G_{\delta,n+1}(u,v) \lor G_{\delta+1,n}(u,v)$
$\quad$ END

$\ldots$

END

Fig. 4. Resource allocation: retrenchment

additional concrete operation *CModifyTrust*, which can dynamically change the trust level of a resource in the environment in response to information received. Such an operation would have no abstract counterpart in line with the possibility admitted by the retrenchment formalism. We retain trust level 0 but do not discuss *CModifyTrust* further.

Retrieve relation $G_{\delta,n}$, defined by (8) below, relates concrete states to abstract ones. It is parameterised by δ, quantifying the maximum acceptable difference in numbers of resources allocated at the two levels, and n, the maximum number of partially-trusted resources that can be concretely allocated.

$$G_{\delta,n}(u,v) \;\widehat{=}\; \exists f \in v \rightarrowtail u \bullet spec_u \circ f = v \vartriangleleft spec_v$$
$$\land \#(u - v) \leq \delta \land \#(v \vartriangleleft tr \vartriangleright \{1\}) \leq n \quad\quad\quad (8)$$

To understand the RETRIEVES clause $G_{\delta,n}$, consider the pattern of resource allocation by the two operations. Abstractly, *Alloc* allocates if a resource is available, or otherwise skips. Concretely, *CAlloc* allocates a fully trusted resource if one is available, or allocates a partially trusted resource if one is available, and otherwise skips. That is, *CAlloc* may (i)[5] exactly simulate the behaviour of *Alloc*

---

[5] (i-iii) are annotations in Fig. 4

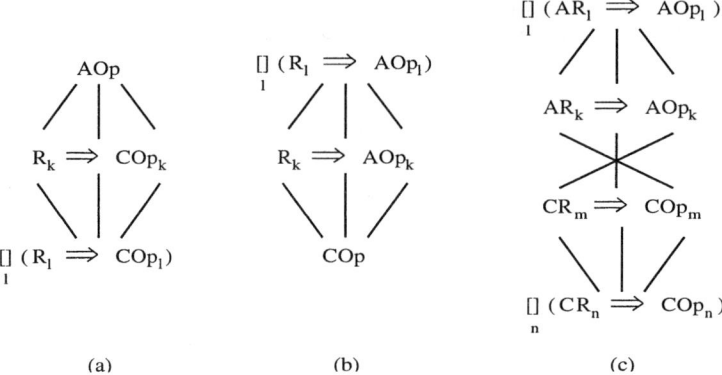

Fig. 5. Three patterns for decomposing a retrenchment

(either in allocating a trusted resource, or not allocating), may (ii) approximate it in allocating a partially trusted resource, or may (iii) more coarsely approximate it by simply doing nothing. This approximating behaviour is recorded by parameters δ, the maximum number of times allocation may fail, and n, the maximum number of partially trusted resources that may be allocated.

$G_{\delta,n}$ thus states that (a) there is a total injection from v to u which uniquely identifies corresponding resource pairs, (b) each resource pair shares a specification, (c) u has at most δ more elements than v, and (d) that the number of partially trusted concrete resources is at most n. The operation retrenchment POB formalises a varying representation: each allocation either (i) maintains precision of representation in retrieve relation $G_{\delta,n}$, or weakens it by establishing as concession either (ii) $G_{\delta,n+1}$ or (iii) $G_{\delta+1,n}$.

5 Decomposing Retrenchment

The retrenchment of Fig. 4 represents a first-cut design view of the problem, relating the abstract to the concrete allocation operation without exploiting the case structure at either level. It is thus a coarse-grained retrenchment picture, with a number of disjuncts in the postcondition, and no *a priori* guarantee as to which might be established. A systematic way is required to decompose this single retrenchment into a family of stronger-concession, thus finer-grained retrenchments. These will more sharply describe the partition (i-iii) of Fig. 4 of distinct relationships between the models.

Three approaches, shown schematically in Fig. 5, will be needed to decompose (a) w.r.t. given concrete structure, (b) w.r.t. given abstract structure, and (c) w.r.t. given structure at both abstract and concrete levels together. Approach (a), for example, in theorem 12 needs a k-indexed family of "component" retrenchments $AOp \lesssim R_k \Longrightarrow COp_k$ to be read from the specification (and proved). Each such retrenchment is composed as per (7) with the corresponding retrenchment $R_k \implies COp_k \lesssim [\!]_l (R_l \implies COp_l)$ given by lemma 11. Approach (b) is the converse of (a), and for (c) a three-step composition is required. To simplify matters, in each case the retrenchments linking a guarded command to a bounded choice of guarded commands are in fact I/O modulated refinements [Op.Cit.]. We will also see the algebraic necessity for the output, rather than simple, form of retrenchment in the proof of theorem (12).

For each of three decomposition results, a corresponding result enriched with nondeterministic choice will be given. This is both for generality as well as to support the example of section 4. Each of these six results is followed by a corollary which re-composes the retrenchment decomposition of that result.

5.1 Decomposition – The Concrete Level

We seek a retrenchment decomposition as per Fig. 5(a), where the abstract operation is atomic, and the concrete operation is one of guarded choice over an l-indexed collection of nested substitutions COp_l. We seek to decompose the single coarse-grained retrenchment

$$AOp \lesssim_{G,P,O,C} [\!]_l (R_l \implies COp_l) \tag{9}$$

into a finer-grained family of retrenchments between the same two operations. For each choice branch in turn, given guard R_k, we seek a retrenchment:

$$AOp \lesssim_{G, P \wedge R_k, O_k, C_k} [\!]_l (R_l \implies COp_l) \tag{10}$$

Each retrenchment in the family is intended to describe partition part k of the abstract/concrete frame (the case concretely guarded by R_k) by strengthening the WITHIN and CONCEDES clauses to $P \wedge R_k$ and C_k respectively. For each k we expect that $C_k \implies C$. The specifier will be free to choose C_k and O_k, which are expected to arise naturally from the specification.

We show that the single retrenchment (9) can be decomposed into the family (10) in two steps, by showing that, for each k, (10) is the composition as per (7) of two retrenchments. The second of these is given by a lemma to show that a guarded command is retrenched[6] by an indexed choice of guarded commands. The apparent increase in nondeterminism in this retrenchment is avoided by the assumption of mutual exclusivity of the guards. This is a strong assumption; the question of nondeterministically overlapping guards is addressed in section 5.2.

Lemma For each k in turn, given Q_k (where k and l independently index the same family of substitutions), we have

$$R_k(\tilde{v},\tilde{j}) \implies COp_k(\tilde{v},\tilde{j},\tilde{p}) \lesssim_{\tilde{v}=v, Q_k, \tilde{v}=v \wedge \atop \tilde{p}=p, false} [\!]_l (R_l(v,j) \implies COp_l(v,j,p))$$

$$\text{where } Q_k \hat{=} \tilde{j} = j \wedge R_k(\tilde{v},\tilde{j}) \wedge \bigwedge_{l \neq k} \neg R_l(\tilde{v},\tilde{j}) \tag{11}$$

---

[6] Lemma (11) is in fact an I/O-modulated refinement, as mentioned in section 3.1.

Proof is by writing out and manipulating the retrenchment POB (6):

$$J(\tilde{v}) \wedge \tilde{v} = v \wedge J(v) \wedge \tilde{j} = j \wedge R_k(\tilde{v},\tilde{j}) \wedge \bigwedge_{l \neq k} \neg R_l(\tilde{v},\tilde{j}) \wedge \mathsf{trm}([]R_l \Longrightarrow COp_l)$$
$$\Rightarrow \mathsf{trm}(R_k \Longrightarrow COp_k) \wedge [[]R_l \Longrightarrow COp_l] \neg [R_k \Longrightarrow COp_k] \neg (\tilde{v} = v \wedge \tilde{p} = p)$$

The RETRIEVES and WITHIN assumptions identify state and input respectively in the two models. The mutual exclusivity of the guards ensures that this retrenchment is effectively an identity refinement. By the algebra of the GSL we have $\mathsf{trm}([]R_l \Longrightarrow COp_l) \equiv \bigwedge_l (R_l \Rightarrow \mathsf{trm}(COp_l))$, and the consequent termination clause follows. The consequent simulation clause reduces to

$$\bigwedge_l (R_l \Rightarrow [COp_l] \neg (R_k \Rightarrow [COp_k] \neg (\tilde{v} = v \wedge \tilde{p} = p)))$$
$$\equiv \bigwedge_l (R_l \Rightarrow (R_k \wedge [COp_l] \neg [COp_k] \neg (\tilde{v} = v \wedge \tilde{p} = p)))$$

Syntactically, $R_k(\tilde{v},\tilde{j})$ distributes through $COp_l(v,j,p)$ since they are over disjoint variable spaces. The mutual exclusivity premise Q_k ensures that R_l only holds for $l = k$, and the clause follows by identity refinement. **QED**

Theorem (12) decomposes a retrenchment in terms of given concrete case structure:

Theorem Each retrenchment of index k may be transformed as follows:

$$AOp \lesssim_{G,P_k,O_k,C_k} R_k \Longrightarrow COp_k \vdash$$
$$AOp(u,i,o) \lesssim_{G,P'_k,O_k,C_k} [](R_l \Longrightarrow COp_l(v,j,p))$$
$$\text{where } P'_k \mathrel{\widehat{=}} P_k \wedge R_k \wedge \bigwedge_{l \neq k} \neg R_l \tag{12}$$

Proof Here the abstract model is in variables u, i, o and the intermediate and lower models have variables as per lemma (11). Proof is by transitive composition of the left-hand retrenchment in (12) with that in the lemma, as per (7). This is straightforward; as again per (7) we have the composed postcondition clause in the form $(G \wedge O) \vee C$. Note that two of the three C disjuncts collapse to **false** because the second-step concession is **false**:

$$(\exists \tilde{v}, \tilde{p} \bullet (G(u,\tilde{v}) \wedge J(\tilde{v}) \wedge \tilde{v} = v) \wedge \exists \tilde{v}, \tilde{p} \bullet (O_k(u,\tilde{v},o,\tilde{p}) \wedge \tilde{v} = v \wedge \tilde{p} = p))$$
$$\vee \exists \tilde{v}, \tilde{p} \bullet (C_k(u,\tilde{v},o,\tilde{p}) \wedge \tilde{v} = v \wedge \tilde{p} = p)$$

This gives composite WITHIN $\equiv G$, OUTPUT $\equiv O_k$, and CONCEDES $\equiv C_k$. We see here the need for output retrenchment: without the second-step OUTPUT clause $\tilde{p} = p$, the concrete p output would be completely unconstrained in the composite concession, which would be $\exists \tilde{p} \bullet C_k$. **QED**

The corollary recomposes the original coarse-grained retrenchment (9):

Corollary Given a decomposition of retrenchments (12), the following holds:

$$AOp \lesssim_{G, \bigvee_k P'_k, \bigvee_k O_k, \bigvee_k C_k} [](R_l \implies COp_l) \qquad (13)$$

Proof We use the facts that (i) if $A \Rightarrow B$ and $C \Rightarrow D$ then $A \vee C \Rightarrow B \vee D$ and (ii) the modal operator $[\ ]\neg[\ ]\neg$ is semidistributive over disjunction[7]. Take the disjunction over all k sets of hypotheses, infer the disjunction of the k consequents, and thus the composite consequent. **QED**

The example of section 4 includes nondeterministic choice, so the results of this section all need to be modified accordingly. Thus we have

Lemma For each k in turn, given Q_k, we have

$$@z \bullet (R_k \implies COp_k(\tilde{v}, \tilde{j}, z, \tilde{p})) \lesssim_{\tilde{v}=v, Q'_k, \tilde{\tilde{p}=p}^{v=v\wedge}, \text{false}} []@z \bullet (R_l \implies COp_l(v, j, z, p))$$

where $Q'_k \cong \tilde{j} = j \wedge \exists z \bullet R_k(\tilde{v}, \tilde{j}, z) \wedge \bigwedge_{l \neq k} \neg \exists z \bullet R_l(\tilde{v}, \tilde{j}, z) \qquad (14)$

Proof is as for lemma (11), with guard mutual exclusivity strengthened to include the choice variable z: given $\tilde{v}, \tilde{j}$, if any z satisfies R_k then *no* z satisfies any other guard R_l at $\tilde{v}, \tilde{j}$. The termination consequent follows as before. The simulation consequent reduces to

$$\bigwedge_l \forall z \bullet (R_l(v, j, z) \Rightarrow (\exists \tilde{z} \bullet R_k(\tilde{v}, \tilde{j}, \tilde{z})$$
$$\wedge [COp_l(v, j, z, p)] \neg [COp_k(\tilde{v}, \tilde{j}, \tilde{z}, \tilde{p})] \neg (\tilde{v} = v \wedge \tilde{p} = p)))$$

The WITHIN clause ensures that the $\forall$-quantified expression is vacuously **true** for guards other than R_k, and any z satisfying $R_k(v, j, z)$ can be used as the existential witness $\tilde{z}$. **QED**

The decomposition and recomposition results (15 - 16) with nondeterministic choice are proved as before.

Theorem Each retrenchment of index k may be transformed as follows:

$$AOp \lesssim_{G, P_k, O_k, C_k} @z \bullet (R_k \implies COp_k)$$
$$\vdash AOp(u, i, o) \lesssim_{G, P_k^{\forall}, O_k, C_k} []@z \bullet (R_l \implies COp_l(v, j, z, p))$$

where $P_k^{\forall} \cong P_k \wedge \exists z \bullet R_k \wedge \bigwedge_{l \neq k} \neg \exists z \bullet R_l \qquad (15)$

Corollary Given a decomposition of retrenchments (15), the following holds:

$$AOp \lesssim_{G, \bigvee_k P_k^{\forall}, \bigvee_k O_k, \bigvee_k C_k} []@z \bullet (R_l \implies COp_l) \qquad (16)$$

---
[7] That is, $[T(v)] \neg [S(u)] \neg C(u, v) \vee [T] \neg [S] \neg D(u, v) \Rightarrow [T] \neg [S] \neg (C \vee D)$

5.2 Mutual Exclusivity Considered Harmful?

The mutual exclusivity restriction of the above results is at first sight very constraining. Particularly so, considering that retrenchment is an early-specification activity, intended to separate out concerns of architecture and information loss in the reification of a rich model down to a discrete, finite computer program. Nondeterminism is an intrinsic feature of abstract descriptions.

It is possible to make retrenchment (11) more expressive by allowing nondeterministically overlapping guards in the WITHIN clause, and weakening the concession from false. However, a rather baroque picture results which we choose not to pusue here, not least for reasons of space.

Methodologically, the assumption of mutual exclusivity will not prove to be a serious restriction. A nondeterministic guarded choice operation is always refinable to a deterministic one, by removing excess transitions. This amounts to refinement to an IF-THEN-ELSIF nesting, with precedence ordering of guards a design decision. A refinement is always expressible as a false-concession retrenchment, as shown in section 3.1. It is thus trivial to see that the following retrenchments compose, where $R'_k \Rightarrow R_k$:

$$AOp \lesssim_{G,P,O_k,C_k} R_k \Longrightarrow COp_k \quad ,$$
$$R_k \Longrightarrow COp_k \lesssim_{\tilde{v}=v,\tilde{j}=j \wedge R'_k, \tilde{p}=p, \text{false}} R'_k \Longrightarrow COp_k$$
$$\vdash AOp \lesssim_{G,P \wedge R'_k, O_k, C_k} R'_k \Longrightarrow COp_k \tag{17}$$

Thus guard-strengthening retrenchments compose seamlessly. We simply retrench away the nondeterminism until mutual exclusivity obtains, and then apply the relevant decomposition theorem. Since guard strengthening should be designed to eliminate nondeterminism, the overall operation guard ought not to strengthen; it should remain exhaustive, if the original overall guard is.

5.3 Decomposition – The Abstract Level

Here we seek a retrenchment decomposition as per Fig. 5(b), where the abstract operation is one of guarded choice over an l-indexed collection of nested substitutions AOp_l, and the concrete operation is atomic. This is the complementary decomposition to that of section 5.1; i.e. to decompose the single retrenchment $[]_l (R_l \Longrightarrow AOp_l) \lesssim_{G,P,O,C} COp$ into a finer-grained family. Proofs are omitted in this section; the first proof straightforwardly rewrites a refinement as a retrenchment, and the rest are as before.

Lemma For each k in turn, given Q_k, we have

$$[]_l (R_l \Longrightarrow AOp_l(u,i,o)) \lesssim_{u=\tilde{u},P,o=\tilde{o},\text{false}} R_k \Longrightarrow AOp_k(\tilde{u},\tilde{i},\tilde{o})$$
$$\text{where } P \mathrel{\widehat{=}} i = \tilde{i} \wedge \bigwedge_l (R_l \Rightarrow \text{trm}(AOp_l)) \tag{18}$$

Theorem Each retrenchment of index k may be transformed as follows:

$$R_k \Longrightarrow AOp_k \lesssim_{G,P_k,O_k,C_k} COp_k$$
$$\vdash []_l (R_l \Longrightarrow AOp_l(u,i,o)) \lesssim_{G,P'_k,O_k,C_k} COp(v,j,p)$$

where $P'_k \stackrel{\frown}{=} P_k \wedge \bigwedge_l (R_l \Rightarrow \text{trm}(AOp_l))$ \hfill (19)

Corollary Given a decomposition of retrenchments (19), the following holds:

$$[]_l (R_l \Longrightarrow AOp_l) \lesssim_{G, \bigvee_k P'_k, \bigvee_k O_k, \bigvee_k C_k} COp \qquad (20)$$

Via the appropriate lemma, the analogue of (19) with nondeterministic choice is

Theorem Each retrenchment of index k may be transformed as follows:

$$@z \bullet (R_k \Longrightarrow AOp_k) \lesssim_{G,P_k,O_k,C_k} COp_k$$
$$\vdash []_l @z \bullet (R_l \Longrightarrow AOp_l(u,i,o,z)) \lesssim_{G,P_k^\forall,O_k,C_k} COp(v,j,p)$$

where $P_k^\forall \stackrel{\frown}{=} P_k \wedge \bigwedge_l \forall z \bullet (R_l \Rightarrow \text{trm}(AOp_l))$ \hfill (21)

Corollary Given a decomposition of retrenchments (21), the following holds:

$$[]_l @z \bullet (R_l \Longrightarrow AOp_l) \lesssim_{G, \bigvee_k P_k^\forall, \bigvee_k O_k, \bigvee_k C_k} COp \qquad (22)$$

5.4 Decomposition – Both Levels Together

The two sections above show how to decompose a coarse-grained retrenchment by exploiting concrete and abstract model structure respectively. An even more finely grained picture should be obtainable by considering all such structure simultaneously, as per Fig. 5(c). That is, given an abstractly decomposed retrenchment family (19) achieving $(G \wedge O) \vee C_k$ under assumptions H_k, and a concretely decomposed retrenchment family (12) between the same operations achieving $(G \wedge O) \vee D_l$ under assumptions H_l, we seek a retrenchment family (indexed on k and l) achieving $(G \wedge O) \vee (C_k \wedge D_l)$ under assumptions $H_k \wedge H_l$[8]. Unfortunately, the modal simulation operator $[\,]\neg[\,]\neg$ is not conjunctive. It is necessary to perform the full decomposition from first principles, as the application of three transitive composition steps (7) combining those of theorems (12), (19). We omit proofs in this section because of their similarity with previous proofs.

---

[8] Note that here the two retrenchment families share the OUTPUT clause O.

Theorem Each of a family of retrenchments indexed on k, m, where abstract guards are k-indexed and concrete guards m-indexed, can be transformed as follows:

$$AR_k \Longrightarrow AOp_k \lesssim_{G, P_{km}, O_{km}, C_{km}} CR_m \Longrightarrow COp_m$$
$$\vdash [\,]_l (AR_l \Longrightarrow AOp_l(u, i, o)) \lesssim_{G, P'_{km}, O_{km}, C_{km}} [\,]_n (CR_n \Longrightarrow COp_n(v, j, p))$$

where $P'_{km} \triangleq P_{km} \wedge \bigwedge_l (AR_l \Rightarrow \mathsf{trm}(AOp_l)) \wedge CR_m \wedge \bigwedge_{n \neq m} \neg CR_n$ (23)

We note the following points about this result. This fine-grained family of retrenchments fully exploits the structure in both models, meeting the goal discussed at the beginning of this section. Usually we will have $P_{km} \Rightarrow AR_k \wedge CR_m$, i.e. each retrenchment layer will be defined within the subdomain where both abstract and concrete guards hold. Guards may overlap nondeterministically in the abstract model, and, should they do so in the concrete model, the latter can be "retrenched down" seamlessly to the required mutual exclusivity of guards, as indicated in section 5.2.

Corollary Given a decomposition of retrenchments (23), the following holds:

$$[\,]_l (AR_l \Longrightarrow AOp_l) \lesssim_{G, \bigvee_k P'_{km}, \bigvee_k O_{km}, \bigvee_k C_{km}} [\,]_n (CR_n \Longrightarrow COp_n) \quad (24)$$

Note that where the corollary is indexed over k (all abstract guards), it is of course applicable over m (all concrete guards), and indeed over k, m (all guards at both levels).

Finally, the analogue of (23) and (24) including nondeterministic choice is

Theorem Each of a family of retrenchments, with abstract and concrete models indexed separately by k and m, can be transformed as follows:

$$@z \bullet (AR_k \Longrightarrow AOp_k) \lesssim_{G, P_{km}, O_{km}, C_{km}} @z \bullet (CR_m \Longrightarrow COp_m)$$
$$\vdash [\,]_l @z \bullet (AR_l \Longrightarrow AOp_l(u, i, o)) \lesssim_{G, P^{\forall}_{km}, O_{km}, C_{km}} [\,]_n @z \bullet (CR_n \Longrightarrow COp_n(v, j, p))$$

where $P^{\forall}_{km} \triangleq P_{km} \wedge \bigwedge_l \forall z \bullet (AR_l \Rightarrow \mathsf{trm}(AOp_l)) \wedge$

$$\exists z \bullet CR_m \wedge \bigwedge_{n \neq m} \neg \exists z \bullet CR_n \quad (25)$$

Corollary Given a decomposition of retrenchments (25), the following holds:

$$[\,]_l @z \bullet (AR_l \Longrightarrow AOp_l) \lesssim_{G, \bigvee_k P^{\forall}_{km}, \bigvee_k O_{km}, \bigvee_k C_{km}} [\,]_n @z \bullet (CR_n \Longrightarrow COp_n) \quad (26)$$

6 Decomposing The Example

We apply (25), (26) to the example retrenchment in order to extract a finer-grained family. Modulo comments in section 5.2 and footnote 4 about mutual exclusivity, from Figures 3, 4 we have guards

$AR_1 \triangleq x \in RSS - u \wedge spec_u(x) = rqt$ abstract, alloc
$AR_2 \triangleq \neg\, AR_1$ abstract, no-alloc
$CR_1 \triangleq y \in CRSS - v \wedge spec_v(y) = rqt \wedge tr(y) = 2$ (i) concrete, alloc-tr=2
$CR_2 \triangleq y \in CRSS - v \wedge spec_v(y) = rqt \wedge tr(y) = 1$ (ii) concrete, alloc-tr=1
$CR_3 \triangleq \neg\, (CR_1 \vee CR_2)$ (i,iii) concrete, no-alloc

We employ the annotations (i - iii) from Fig. 4. We have $P_{1m} \triangleq AR_1 \wedge CR_m$ for $m = 1 \ldots 3$, for the retrenchment of abstract allocation by cases (i, ii, iii) respectively. We have $P_{23} \triangleq AR_2 \wedge CR_3$ for case (i) with no allocation at either level. There are no retrenchments for $k = 2, m = 1 \ldots 2$ in this model since we cannot relate abstract non-allocation to concrete allocation. All simple guarded substitutions here of form $R \implies Op$ always terminate. Finally, we have $G \equiv G_{\delta,n}$ and for all indices $O_{km} \triangleq$ true.

Thus for input to theorem (25) we have four component retrenchments between single-guarded commands, say r_{km} with WITHIN clauses P_{km} etc., for $k = 1 \ldots 2$ and $m = 1 \ldots 3$. r_{11} represents the refining case (i) of allocation at both levels, and thus achieves G with concession $C_{11} \triangleq$ false. r_{12} achieves either G or concession $C_{12} \triangleq G_{\delta,n+1}$, in the approximating case (ii) of trust 2 concrete allocation. r_{13} achieves either G or concession $C_{13} \triangleq G_{\delta+1,n}$, in the case (iii) of no concrete allocation approximating abstract allocation. r_{23} achieves G with concession $C_{23} \triangleq$ false, in the (i) case where both models fail to allocate.

Applying (25) produces four fine-grained retrenchments r_{km} of *Alloc* to *Dalloc*, each qualified by RETRIEVES G, WITHIN P'_{km} combining relevant abstract and concrete guard predicates, OUTPUT true and CONCEDES C_{km}. Corollary (26) combines these retrenchments to recover the original coarse-grained retrenchment of Fig. 4. We see that two of the four retrenchments produced are in fact refinements, and the other two are each finer (have stronger concessions) than the original.

It is worth noting that there are further, finer decompositions possible of the example. By strengthening the guards with state information about approximation levels (e.g. how close $\#(u - v)$ is to δ), it is possible to tease out more retrenchments with stronger postconditions (e.g. $\neg\, G \wedge G_{\delta+1,n}$ when $\#(u-v) = \delta$ in WITHIN).

7 Conclusion

We have considered the problem of a first cut "coarse-grained" design of the abstract-to-concrete operation transformation $AOp \lesssim COp$ as a retrenchment r, say, and its decomposition into a finer-grained family of retrenchments $\{r_i\}$.

An approach of "decomposition by composition" was taken: using a general syntactic form for each of for the two operations, each member of the family was constructed as the transitive composition per theorem (7) of retrenchments via suitable intermediate operation fragments. Each component retrenchment in the family is stronger than the composite retrenchment in the sense that it delivers a stronger concession, i.e. guarantees more in the postcondition. Each component is also more restrictive in having a stronger WITHIN clause; moreover the WITHIN clauses of the family effectively partition the joint before-state/I/O frame of the composite retrenchment.

The general syntactic form used inductively covers all operations that may be specified using the primitive abstract syntax of B. We have not mentioned the precondition constructor, which factors through the theory trivially; in practice it is only used at the top level of an operation specification to type input parameters. Thus the results "cover most of the bases" required by practical specification work. We merely claim "most" since we have yet to address the parallel substitution || of B: this is the means by which multiple variables (and nontrivial transformations of such through retrenchment) and their dynamics are described.

Methodologically speaking, this work supports a natural (and traditional) approach to design. That is, one model at one abstraction level is developed, including choice, case-split and other structure. The next, more concrete model is then developed, bearing in mind the refinement or retrenchment abstraction to be used. Only then is the relation between the models examined; the retrenchment case, as we have seen, affording the option of further decomposition to a suitable granularity.

Finally, we briefly consider the theoretical decomposition question in its full generality: "given a retrenchment r from abstract AOp to concrete COp, can we find two retrenchments r_1 from AOp to some intermediate IOp and r_2 from IOp to COp such that $r_1 \mathbin{\raisebox{0.5ex}{\scriptsize$\circ$}} r_2 \Rightarrow r$?". Transitivity of retrenchment (7) gives some guidance: for the composite retrenchment r to be a logical consequence of the decomposition $r_1 \mathbin{\raisebox{0.5ex}{\scriptsize$\circ$}} r_2$ we must have

$$RETRIEVES(r) \equiv RETRIEVES(r_1 \mathbin{;} r_2) \land WITHIN(r) \Rightarrow WITHIN(r_1 \mathbin{;} r_2) \quad (27)$$
$$\land\ OUTPUT(r) \equiv OUTPUT(r_1 \mathbin{;} r_2) \land CONCEDES(r_1 \mathbin{;} r_2) \Rightarrow CONCEDES(r)$$

The obvious universality problem related to the full decomposition question above arises: "What are the 'best', i.e. weakest-WITHIN and strongest-concession component retrenchments r_1 and r_2?". Further work in the categorical style of the integration of refinement and retrenchment [5] is indicated here. The suggestion of [20] of a lattice theory of retrenchment (over the collection of all WITHIN clauses that satisfy a given retrenchment, similarly all CONCEDES clauses) also needs pursuing to this end.

References

[1] J.-R. Abrial. *The B-Book: Assigning Programs to Meanings.* Cambridge University Press, 1996.

[2] R. J. R. Back and J. von Wright. *Refinement Calculus: A Systematic Introduction.* Springer, 1998.
[3] R.J.R. Back and M. Butler. Fusion and simultaneous execution in the refinement calculus. *Acta Informatica*, 35:921–949, 1998.
[4] R.J.R. Back and K. Sere. Superposition refinement of reactive systems. *Formal Aspects of Computing*, 8(3):324–346, 1996.
[5] R. Banach. Maximally abstract retrenchments. In *Proc. IEEE ICFEM2000*, pages 133–142, York, August 2000. IEEE Computer Society Press.
[6] R. Banach and C. Jeske. Output retrenchments, defaults, stronger compositions, feature engineering. 2002. submitted, http://www.cs.man.ac.uk/~banach/some.pubs/Retrench.Def.Out.pdf.
[7] R. Banach and M. Poppleton. Retrenchment: An engineering variation on refinement. In D. Bert, editor, *2nd International B Conference*, volume 1393 of *LNCS*, pages 129–147, Montpellier, France, April 1998. Springer.
[8] R. Banach and M. Poppleton. Sharp retrenchment, modulated refinement and simulation. *Formal Aspects of Computing*, 11:498–540, 1999.
[9] R. Banach and M. Poppleton. Retrenchment, refinement and simulation. In J. Bowen, S. King, S. Dunne, and A. Galloway, editors, *Proc. ZB2000*, volume 1878 of *LNCS*, York, September 2000. Springer.
[10] R. Banach and M. Poppleton. Model based engineering of specifications by retrenching partial requirements. In *Proc. MBRE-01: IEEE Workshop on Model-Based Requirements Engineering*, University of California, San Diego, November 2001. IEEE Press.
[11] R. Banach and M. Poppleton. Engineering and theoretical underpinnings of retrenchment. submitted, http://www.cs.man.ac.uk/~banach/some.pubs/Retrench.Underpin.pdf, 2002.
[12] R. Banach and M. Poppleton. Retrenching partial requirements into system definitions: A simple feature interaction case study. *Requirements Engineering Journal*, 8(2), 2003. 22pp.
[13] W.-P. de Roever and K. Engelhardt. *Data Refinement: Model-Oriented Proof Methods and their Comparison.* Cambridge University Press, 1998.
[14] E.W. Dijkstra. *A Discipline of Programming.* Prentice-Hall, 1976.
[15] C.A.R. Hoare. An axiomatic basis for computer programming. *Communications of the ACM*, 12(10):576–583, October 1969.
[16] S. Katz. A superimposition control construct for distributed systems. *ACM TPLAN*, 15(2):337–356, April 1993.
[17] M. Poppleton and R. Banach. Retrenchment: extending the reach of refinement. In *ASE'99: 14th IEEE International Conference on Automated Software Engineering*, pages 158–165, Florida, October 1999. IEEE Computer Society Press.
[18] M. Poppleton and R. Banach. Retrenchment: Extending refinement for continuous and control systems. In *Proc. IWFM'00*, Springer Electronic Workshop in Computer Science Series, NUI Maynooth, July 2000. Springer.
[19] M. Poppleton and R. Banach. Controlling control systems: An application of evolving retrenchment. In D. Bert, J.P. Bowen, M.C. Henson, and K. Robinson, editors, *Proc. ZB2002: Formal Specification and Development in Z and B*, volume 2272 of *LNCS*, Grenoble, France, January 2002. Springer.
[20] M.R. Poppleton. *Formal Methods for Continuous Systems: Liberalising Refinement in B.* PhD thesis, Department of Computer Science, University of Manchester, 2001.
[21] S. Schneider. *The B-Method.* Palgrave Press, 2001.

Design of an Automatic Prover Dedicated to the Refinement of Database Applications

Amel Mammar and Régine Laleau

CEDRIC-IIE(CNAM) 18 allée Jean Rostand, 91025 Evry, France
{mammar,laleau}@iie.cnam.fr

Abstract. The paper presents an approach that enables the elaboration of an automatic prover dedicated to the refinement of database applications. The approach is based on a strategy of proof reuse and on the specific characteristics of such applications. The problem can be stated as follows. Having established a set of basic refinement proofs associated to a set of refinement rules, the issue is to study how these basic proofs can be reused to establish more elaborate refinements. Elaborate refinements denote refinements that require the application of more than one refinement rule. We consider the B refinement process. In B, substitutions are inductively built using constructors. For each B constructor, we have formally defined the necessary and sufficient conditions that enable the reuse of the basic proofs. An application of our approach to data-intensive applications is presented.

Keywords: Refinement process, Proof reuse, B method, Data-intensive applications

1 Introduction

The last decade has seen a growing use of databases in several different domains: e-business, financial systems, smart cards, etc. Although these areas are not critical (no human risk), economic interests are involved and a certain degree of safety is required. Our project aims at providing users with a complete formal environment for the specification and the development of database applications [13]. For this, we use the B formal method, developed by Jean-Raymond Abrial [1]. It is a complete method that supports a large segment of the development life cycle: specification, refinement and implementation. It ensures, thanks to refinement steps and proofs, that the code satisfies its specification. It has been used in significant industrial projects and commercial case tools [2, 3] are available in order to help the specifier during the development process.

The specification of a database application is composed of two parts: specification of the data structure by using an Entity/Relationship model and specification of user transactions which describe the functionalities of the system. These transactions are built on a set of generic basic operations (insert, delete or update elements). We have proposed a method that allows this specification to be described using the B specification language [9]. The obtained specification is then refined up to an implementation using the relational database model. In the database area, data refinement is usually achieved by the application of a well-known algorithm that generates a relational schema from an Entity/Relationship schema [8, 6]. In the B method, refinement process is generally manual, since target implementation languages can be various. We have defined a specific refinement process, dedicated to our application domain, that is automated [17]. A set of elementary rules refining the data structure and the basic operations have been elaborated [10]. It is based on the above-mentioned algorithm. An elementary refinement proof is associated to each rule, that ensures the correctness of the transformation.

Software engineers are resistant to use approaches based on formal methods mainly because of the proof phase that requires significant skills. In order to assist them, we have considered the automation of the refinement proof. In other words, we have studied the automation of transaction refinement. The problem addressed in the paper can be stated in this way. The B refinement process being monotonous, the refinement of a transaction comes down to the refinement of the basic operations which it is built on and the refinement of the B constructors used to combine the basic operations. Thus, is it possible to reuse the elementary refinement proofs to establish the proof of the refinement of a transaction ? For each B constructor, we have defined a set of reuse constraints, independently of any application domain. Then we have demonstrated that, in the database area, most of these constraints are always satisfied. This allows a great number of refinement proofs to be automatically discharged. This is a very interesting result. Indeed, if we want to extend the use of formal methods in other domains than those where they are usually applied (i.e. critical systems) we absolutely need to provide assistant tools with a lot of things which are automatically achieved or produced.

Improvement of proof processes by reusing already computed proofs is an active research area. Several techniques have been developed. Most of them are developed for the proof by induction of mathematical theorems. Among them, we can mention: *reusing by transformation* [15, 16], *reusing by type isomorphism* [5], *reusing by generalization* [18, 19] and *reusing by sub-typing* [14]. In [16], two different representations of natural numbers are considered: a binary representation and the usual representation using the two constructors 0 and successor. The authors have developed a tool that transforms each proof computed within one of the two representations into the other. In [14], if the type A is a subtype of B, a coercion function that transforms each term of type A into a term of type B is defined. This function permits to replay for A all the proofs already computed for B. This technique is largely used within the *Coq* prover which is a strongly typed language [4]. In [5], a theoretical foundation for proof reuse, based on type isomorphisms in dependent type theory is presented. Our work can be compared with the works of [18] and [19]. These works are based on the analysis of already established proofs, by producing an explanation or a justification of why it is successful. In order to reuse it, both the formula and its proof are generalized. To our knowledge, reuse of proofs in a refinement proof process remains an unexplored problem.

In the following, we briefly give an overview of the B refinement process (Section 2). In section 3, we present the framework of our work and explain why we can consider to define a reuse proof strategy in the refinement process of data-intensive applications. A formal definition of reuse constraints is presented in Section 4. Section 5 describes how they behave for database applications and enable the implementation of an automatic prover within Atelier B. The benefits expected from such reuse strategy and future works are discussed in Section 6.

2 Overview of B and Its Refinement Process

The B language is based on first order logic extended to set constructors and relations. The operations are specified in the generalized substitution language, which is a generalization of the Dijkstra's guarded command notations. The B method is a model-based method. A system is described in terms of abstract machines that contain state variables, invariant properties expressed on the variables and operations described in terms of preconditions and substitutions.

Refinement is the process that transforms an abstract specification into a less abstract one. These transformations operate on data and/or operations. Data are refined by adding new variables or replacing the existing ones by others which are supposed to be more concrete (closer to a target implementation language). Operation refinement consists in eliminating non-determinism. The last step of the refinement process produces an implementation component which is to be used as the basis for translation into executable code. Both specification and refinement give rise to proof obligations. Specification proofs ensure that operations preserve the invariant, whereas refinement proofs ensure the correctness of a refined component with respect to its initial component.

In order to prove the correctness of refinements, we use the relational semantics of substitutions based on the definition of the two predicates $Trm(S)$ and $Prd(S)$ associated to any substitution S. These predicates are defined in the B-Book [1] by:

$$Trm(S) \triangleq [S](x = x) \ . \tag{1}$$

$$Prd_{x,x'}(S) \triangleq \neg[S](x' \neq x) \ . \tag{2}$$

Intuitively: $Trm(S)$: gives the necessary and sufficient condition for the termination of S, $Prd_{x,x'}(S)$: gives the link between the values of variables x before (denoted x) and after (denoted x') the execution of S.

Notations: In the remainder of the paper, we need the following notations:

- Each substitution S is indexed by the set x of all the variables of the specification where S is defined : S_x
- $Prd_{y,y'}(S_x)$ where $y \subseteq x$ means that we consider the restriction of $Prd_{x,x'}(S_x)$ to the set of variables y. In general, y represents the set of the variables modified by S_x.

- In order to simplify expressions, $Prd_{x,x'}(S_x)$ is denoted $Prd(S_x)$.

Correctness of Refinements: With the previous definitions, correctness of refinements is expressed as follows.

Let S_a and T_b be two substitutions. Let $J(a,b)$ be the predicate, called the gluing invariant, that states the relation existing between a and b. T_b refines S_a according to $J(a,b)$, denoted $S_a \sqsubseteq_{J(a,b)} T_b$, iff:

$$\exists u, v.\ J(u, v) \qquad (3)$$
$$\forall a, b \cdot (Trm(S_a) \wedge J(a, b)) \rightarrow$$
$$[Trm(T_b) \wedge \forall b' \cdot (Prd(T_b) \rightarrow \exists a' \cdot (Prd(S_a) \wedge J(a', b')))] \qquad (4)$$

Let us explain each condition: (3) means that the gluing invariant must be satisfiable(it isn't a contradiction), (4) means firstly that for each possible interpretation of a that ensures the termination of S_a, the corresponding set b (that satisfies the gluing invariant) ensures the execution of T_b, and secondly that, for each possible result b' of T_b, there must exist a corresponding result a' of S_a such that a' and b' satisfy the gluing invariant J.

Simplification of Refinement Proofs: For some types of substitutions (e.g. assignment), the proof of its termination doesn't raise any difficulty : $Trm(T_b)$ is trivially true. Thus the proof of correctness of a refinement consists in exhibiting a value of a', associated to a given value b' satisfying $Prd(T_b)$, that satisfies the two predicates $Prd(S_a)$ and $J(a', b')$. So we have to prove that:

$$\exists a' \cdot (Prd(S_a) \wedge J(a', b'))$$

for given values of a, b, b' satisfying:

$$Trm(S_a) \wedge J(a, b) \wedge Prd(T_b)$$

We will use this simplified proof obligation to prove refinements in Section 3 because $Trm(T_b)$ is always trivially true in the examples we are considering.

3 Reuse of Proofs During the Refinement Process: an Illustrative Example

Our project aims at providing software engineers with a formal method for the specification and the development of safety data-intensive applications. The global framework of our project, represented by Figure 1, includes two main phases: *Specification* and *Refinement*. Both phases use a formal method (B in our case) and thus can be validated by proofs. Nevertheless, establishing proofs, and specially refinement proofs, is a long, hard and tedious task. A solution to assist engineers is to build tools in order to automate parts of the proofs. Of course, this is not possible in general but only for specific areas where a generic

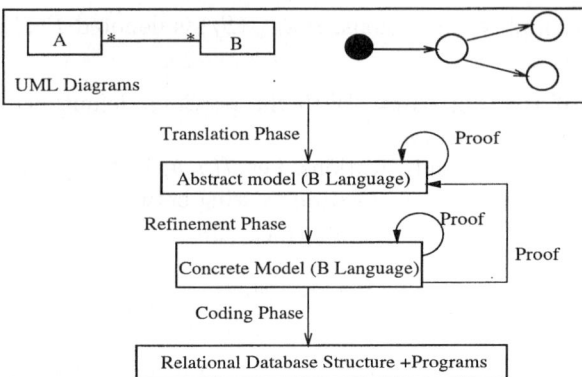

Fig. 1. Formal mapping of a UML conceptual model into a relational implementation using the B method

strategy of refinement may be defined. This is what we propose for data-intensive applications.

Firstly, we describe the characteristics of the abstract specifications of such applications. Then we illustrate, through an example, the refinement process and how it can be automated.

3.1 Elaboration of the Abstract Model of an Application

The first step of our development is to construct a B abstract model. It is derived from UML diagrams (class diagram, state/ collaboration diagrams) by using a set of translation rules. A description of this translation and a comparison with other work are already described in [9, 11] and are out of the scope of this paper. Which is important to have in mind in order to understand our approach is that the different UML diagrams are dedicated to data-intensive applications, with precise semantics defined in [12]. In particular, a class diagram is defined with the semantics of an E/R diagram. A consequence is that the specification we generate has always the same characteristics. It is composed of two layers:

a) The internal layer contains all the variables that define the state of the application and a set of basic operations that act upon them. The variables represent the classes, associations and attributes of the class diagram. The basic operations comprise insert and delete operations for each class and association and update operations that change the value of the attributes.

Let us consider the example of a simplified video club. A cassette is either loaned by a customer or available in a shop. Each customer and each shop are identified by an attribute, called a key, respectively *NumCu* and *NumSh*. They are natural numbers. Figure 2 presents the corresponding UML class diagram which gives a synthetic view of the data of the application.

The derived B specifications are as follows (just the relevant parts are given):

$$Loan \in Cassette \nrightarrow Customer \land Available \in Cassette \nrightarrow Shop \land$$

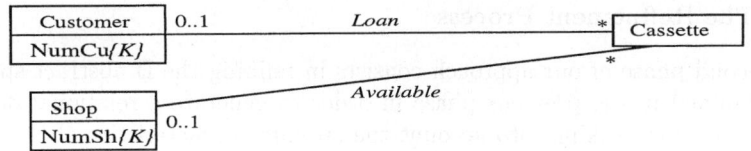

Fig. 2. Class diagram of a video club

$$NumCu \in Customer \rightarrowtail NAT \wedge NumSh \in Shop \rightarrowtail NAT$$

Cassette, *Customer* and *Shop* are variables representing the existing instances of the corresponding classes; the *Loan* and *Available* variables represent the corresponding monovalued[1] associations.

Basic operations are automatically generated from the class diagram. For example, *AddLoan*(*ca*, *cu*) creates a new link in the association *Loan* that relates a cassette *ca* to a customer *cu*; *DeleteAvailable*({*ca*}) deletes the links, related to a given set of cassette (here {*ca*})), from the association *Available*. In B, these operations are expressed by the two substitutions [2]:

$$Loan := Loan \cup \{ca \mapsto cu\} \text{ and } Available := \{ca\} \triangleleft Available$$

b) In the external layer, user transactions are specified. A transaction is specified by a B operation that calls the basic operations of the internal layer using different B constructors (test, parallel substitution, ...). No additional variables are defined in this layer. Moreover, variables of the internal level can be modified only by using basic operations. For example, let us consider the transaction *LoanCassette*(*ca*, *cu*, *sh*) that loans a cassette *ca* to a given customer *cu* from a shop *sh*. This transaction is constructed by calling the two basic operations *DeleteAvailable* and *AddLoan* using *Parallel* and *IF* constructors as follows[3]:

    IF *Available*(*ca*) = *sh* **THEN**
        AddLoan(*ca*, *cu*) ∥
        DeleteAvailable({*ca*})
    END

Note that in reality a class diagram may contain a great number of classes and associations, whereas a transaction involves few classes and associations and has a low algorithmic complexity. The transaction *LoanCassette* has been defined in order to facilitate an intuitive presentation of our approach. A more realistic transaction would be a little bit more complex, which would just require more steps of refinement.

---

[1] An association is called monovalued if one of its maximum multiplicities is 1
[2] The complete operations include preconditions that we omit here because they haven't any influence on our refinement process
[3] Such a transaction can be also described using state/collaboration diagrams, more detail can be found in [9, 11].

3.2 The Refinement Process

The second phase of our approach consists in refining the B abstract specification obtained in the previous phase in order to generate a relational database implementation. Taking into account the specific characteristics of the specification, the global refinement can be achieved in two successive steps: the first step concerns the refinement of the internal layer (i.e. variables and basic operations), the second one concerns the refinement of the external layer (i.e. user transactions).

a) Variables and Basic Operations Refinement

The refinement is based on the algorithm used in database design [6], thus we exactly know how the data are refined. This allows us to define a set of elementary generic refinement rules that act both on variables and basic operations [10].

Let us take the example of the refinement rules related to a monovalued asociation. Let C and D be two classes linked by a monovalued association f. In B, f is specified by a function from the variable C to the variable D. Let v be the key of the class D, of type T. In B, v is specified by an injective total function from D to T. The data refinement of the association f consists in replacing f by a new attribute, called f_1, in class C which is a reference to the key of D (in a relational database, it will be defined by a foreign key). In B, f_1 is specified by a function from C to T and the gluing invariant is $f_1 = (v \circ f)$. The refinement of a basic operation related to an association is just a rewriting of the operation in order to take into account the association refinement. The following table sums up the refinement of the *add* and *delete* operations, which *AddLoan* and *DeleteAvailable* are instantiation of:

RULE	Abstract_Subst.	Concrete_Subst.	Gluing invariant
Rule_Add	$f := f \cup \{c \mapsto d\}$	$f_1 := f_1 \cup \{c \mapsto v(d)\}$	$f_1 = (v \circ f)$
Rule_Del	$f := C_1 \triangleleft f$	$f_1 := C_1 \triangleleft f_1$	$f_1 = (v \circ f)$

where:

- c and d are elements of C and D respectively.
- C_1 is a subset of C.

To establish the correctness of *Rule_Add* and *Rule_Del*, we have to carried out the two following proofs:

- Proof of *Rule_Add* (P_{Add}): $\exists f'.(Prd(f := f \cup \{c \mapsto d\}) \wedge (f_1' = v \circ f'))$ for values of f, v, f_1, f_1' satisfying: $(f_1 = v \circ f) \wedge Prd(f_1 := f_1 \cup \{c \mapsto v(d)\})$
- Proof of *Rule_Del* (P_{Del}): $\exists f'.(Prd(f := C_1 \triangleleft f) \wedge (f_1' = v \circ f'))$ for values of f, v, f_1, f_1' satisfying: $(f_1 = v \circ f) \wedge Prd(f_1 := C_1 \triangleleft f_1))$

The proofs of these two rules are discussed in Section 5.

We have defined about 120 rules. With Atelier B (version 3.5), 70% of the proofs of these rules have been automatically discharged. However, just the easier proofs are concerned: the proofs related to the *Trm* predicates. The remaining proofs were rather hard and sometimes very tedious to achieve. Nevertheless, due to the generic feature of the rules, it is possible to define proof tactics that enable the automation of the refinement proofs. It means that, once the proof of a generic refinement rule has been achieved, it is possible to reuse it in all the instantiations of the rule.

Let us apply this strategy on our example. *AddLoan* and *DeleteAvailable* are refined by the refinement rules *Rule_Add* and *Rule_Del*. This gives the two concrete substitutions:

$$Available_1 := \{ca\} \triangleleft Available_1 \text{ and } Loan_1 := Loan_1 \cup \{ca \mapsto NumCu(cu)\}$$

To establish the correctness of these refinements, we just need to instantiate the generic proofs (P_{Add}) and (P_{Del}). This instantiation is achieved by taking: $(f = Loan, v = NumCu, c = ca, d = cu)$ and $(f = Available, v = NumSh, C_1 = \{ca\})$ respectively.

b) Transactions Refinement

The basic operations being refined, the following step deals with the refinement of user transactions. Recall that transactions act only upon variables defined in the internal layer. Thus the refinement of a transaction is an algorithmic refinement. As the specification of a transaction is based on the specification of basic operations, the refinement of a transaction uses the refinement of these latter. More precisely, the B refinement process being monotonous, the refinement of each transaction comes down to the refinement of the operations that it calls and the refinement (or rewriting) of the different B constructors that relate these operation calls.

For example, let us take the refinement of the transaction *LoanCassette*. The refinement step that corresponds to the refinement of the associations *Loan* and *Available* reuses the refinement of the basic operations *AddLoan* and *DelAvailable*. In addition, the predicate of the *IF* constructor is rewritten according to the concrete variables $Loan_1$ and $Available_1$. So, the transaction *LoanCassette* is refined by [4, 5]:

$$\begin{aligned}
&\textbf{IF } (NumSh^{-1} \circ Available_1)(ca) = sh \textbf{ THEN}\\
&\qquad Available_1 := \{ca\} \triangleleft Available_1 \parallel\\
&\qquad Loan_1 := Loan_1 \cup \{ca \mapsto NumCu(cu)\}\\
&\textbf{END}
\end{aligned}$$

As the variables *Loan* and *Available* are refined separately, the gluing invariant is equal to the conjunction of the gluing invariants associated to the refinement of

---

[4] The parallel constructor will be refined by the sequence constructor during one of the next steps
[5] The exact specification would be two calls to the operations that correspond to the refinement of *AddLoan* and *DelAvailable*.

the associations *Available* and *Loan*: $(Available_1 = NumSh \circ Available) \wedge (Loan_1 = NumCu \circ Loan)$.

To simplify expressions, we use the following notations:

- $S_1 \triangleq (Available := \{ca\} \triangleleft Available)$ and $S_2 \triangleq (Loan := Loan \cup \{ca \mapsto cu\})$
- $T_1 \triangleq (Available_1 := \{ca\} \triangleleft Available_1)$ and $T_2 \triangleq (Loan_1 := Loan_1 \cup \{ca \mapsto NumCu(cu)\})$
- $a_1 \triangleq \{Available\}$ and $a_2 \triangleq \{Loan\}$
- $b_1 \triangleq \{Available_1\}$ and $b_2 \triangleq \{Loan_1\}$
- $a = a_1 \cup a_2$ and $b = b_1 \cup b_2$
- $J(a, b) \triangleq (J(a_1, b_1) \wedge J(a_2, b_2)) \triangleq (Available_1 = NumSh \circ Available) \wedge (Loan_1 = NumCu \circ Loan)$
- $C_1 \triangleq (Available(ca) = sh)$ and $C_2 \triangleq (NumSh^{-1} \circ Available_1(ca) = sh)$

To check the correctness of the refinement, we must prove:

$$\exists a'.[Prd(\textbf{IF } C_1 \textbf{ THEN}(S_1 \| S_2)\textbf{END}) \wedge J(a', b')] \quad (G_1)$$

for given values of a, b, b' satisfying the following hypotheses:

$$Trm(\textbf{IF } C_1 \textbf{ THEN}(S_1 \| S_2)\textbf{END}) \wedge$$
$$Prd(\textbf{IF } C_2 \textbf{ THEN}(T_1 \| T_2)\textbf{END}) \wedge$$
$$J(a, b)$$

Not surprisingly, this proof is not automatically discharged by Atelier B. However, at a certain step of the elaboration of the interactive proof, the prover comes down to the proofs (P_{Add}) and (P_{Del}) (instantiated on *AddLoan* and *DelAvailable*). It is very interesting because it means that it is possible to reuse the basic proofs established for the refinement of the basic operations. In the following, we explain how the interactive proof is elaborated.

By applying the definition of *Prd* and *Trm* of a IF-THEN-ELSE substitution, G_1 becomes:

$$\exists a'.[(C_1 \rightarrow Prd(S_1 \| S_2)) \wedge (\neg C_1 \rightarrow (a'_1 = a_1 \wedge a'_2 = a_2)) \wedge J(a', b')] \quad (G_2)$$

for given values of a, b, b' satisfying the following hypotheses:

$$True \wedge$$
$$(C_2 \rightarrow Prd(T_1 \| T_2) \wedge (\neg C_2 \rightarrow (b'_1 = b_1 \wedge b'_2 = b_2))) \wedge$$
$$J(a, b)$$

To prove the goal G_2, the prover generates four sub-proofs given in the following table:

	Goal	Hypotheses
(1)	$\exists a'.(Prd(S_1 \| S_2) \wedge J(a', b'))$	$C_1 \wedge C_2 \wedge Prd(T_1 \| T_2) \wedge J(a, b)$
(2)	$\exists a'.(Prd(S_1 \| S_2) \wedge J(a', b'))$	$C_1 \wedge \neg C_2 \wedge b'_1 = b_1 \wedge b'_2 = b_2 \wedge J(a, b)$
(3)	$\exists a'.(a'_1 = a_1 \wedge a'_2 = a_2 \wedge J(a', b'))$	$\neg C_1 \wedge C_2 \wedge Prd(T_1 \| T_2) \wedge J(a, b)$
(4)	$\exists a'.(a'_1 = a_1 \wedge a'_2 = a_2 \wedge J(a', b'))$	$\neg C_1 \wedge \neg C_2 \wedge b'_1 = b_1 \wedge b'_2 = b_2 \wedge J(a, b)$

The last proof is automatically discharged by the prover. Indeed, it is trivially true for $a'_1 = a_1$ and $a'_2 = a_2$ because of the hypotheses $b'_1 = b_1$, $b'_2 = b_2$ and the invariant $J(a, b)$. The second and the third are proved interactively by reductio ad absurdum. Indeed the predicate C_2 being a rewriting of the predicate C_1, the two predicates are equivalent. So, both the conjunctions $(C_1 \wedge \neg C_2)$ and $(\neg C_1 \wedge C_2)$ are contradictory. It remains to interactively achieve the first proof (1).

As the set of variables modified by S_1 (resp. S_2) and the set of variables not modified by S_2 (resp. S_1) are disjoint, $Prd(S_1 \| S_2)$ is rewritten into $Prd(S_1) \wedge Prd(S_2)$. For the same reasons, the hypothesis $Prd(T_1 \| T_2)$ is rewritten into $Prd(T_1) \wedge Prd(T_2)$. Moreover, the sets of variables a_1 and a_2 are disjoint. So, the goal and the hypotheses of the proof (1) are rewritten into:

$$\exists a'_1.(Prd(S_1) \wedge J(a'_1, b'_1)) \tag{G_3}$$

under the hypotheses: $Prd(T1) \wedge J(a_1, b_1) \wedge C_1 \wedge C_2$, and

$$\exists a'_2.(Prd(S_2) \wedge J(a'_2, b'_2)) \tag{G_4}$$

under the hypotheses: $Prd(T2) \wedge J(a_2, b_2) \wedge C_1 \wedge C_2$.

Note that the hypotheses C_1 and C_2 are not relevant to prove G_3 and G_4. It is easy to remark that these two proofs are exactly the same that have been already established when we have proved the correctness of the basic operations *AddLoan* and *DeleteAvailable* refinements. Thus, they are discharged.

This example shows that *under some conditions* (above, conditions on sets of variables), it is possible to reuse the proofs of the refinement of the basic operations which a transaction is constructed on, in order to prove the refinement of the transaction. The different case studies we have carried out have confirmed this fact: most of the proofs to be achieved for proving the refinement of a transaction come down to the proofs of the refinement of its basic operations, whatever the B constructors used to combine these basic operations. The other proofs concern the refinement of the constructors themselves and are generally automatically discharged. This has led us to examine in more detail the formal definition of conditions that make the reuse of elementary refinement proofs possible. The objective of such a study is to provide a formal basis to the development of an automatic prover.

4 Defining Reuse Constraints

In B, substitutions are inductively constructed using B constructors (precondition, parallel, sequence, ...). For each B constructor, we have defined the necessary and sufficient conditions for reusing proofs. The complete results are detailed in [17]. Hereafter, we present the case of the parallel constructor.

Assume that we have already computed the proofs for the two elementary refinement rules:

$$S_{a_1} \sqsubseteq_{J_{ST}(a_1, a_2)} T_{a_2} \tag{H_1}$$
$$U_{b_1} \sqsubseteq_{J_{UV}(b_1, b_2)} V_{b_2} \tag{H_2}$$

Let $J(a_1 \cup b_1, a_2 \cup b_2)$ be a new predicate such that:

$$(S_{a_1} \| U_{b_1}) \sqsubseteq_{J(a_1 \cup b_1, a_2 \cup b_2)} (T_{a_2} \| V_{b_2}) \tag{G_5}$$

By definition of refinement, (H_1) and (H_2) give the following hypotheses:

$$\forall a_1, a_2.(Trm(S_{a_1}) \wedge J_{ST}(a_1, a_2)) \rightarrow$$
$$[Trm(T_{a_2}) \wedge \forall a_2'.(Prd(T_{a_2}) \rightarrow \exists a_1'.(Prd(S_{a_1}) \wedge J_{ST}(a_1', a_2')))] \tag{H_3}$$
$$\forall b_1, b_2.(Trm(U_{b_1}) \wedge J_{UV}(b_1, b_2)) \rightarrow$$
$$[Trm(V_{b_2}) \wedge \forall b_2'.(Prd(V_{b_2}) \rightarrow \exists b_1'.(Prd(U_{b_1}) \wedge J_{UV}(b_1', b_2')))] \tag{H_4}$$

And the goal (G_5) gives:

$$\forall c_1, c_2.(Trm(S_{a_1} \| U_{b_1}) \wedge J(c_1, c_2)) \rightarrow [Trm(T_{a_2} \| V_{b_2}) \wedge$$
$$\forall c_2'.(Prd(T_{a_2} \| V_{b_2}) \rightarrow \exists c_1'.(Prd(S_{a_1} \| U_{b_1}) \wedge J(c_1', c_2')))] \tag{G_6}$$

where c_1 (resp. c_2) denotes the union of a_1 and b_1 (resp a_2 and b_2).

The aim of the section is to present the reasoning that leads to, on one hand, the determination of the conditions under that the already computed proofs (H_3) and (H_4) can be reused to prove (G_6) and, on the other hand, the actual reuse of these proofs.

4.1 A Relevant Rewriting of the Goal (G_6)

The first issue is to rewrite (G_6) in order to exhibit parts of (H_3) and (H_4). In order to express the different predicates, we partition each set of variables (a_i and b_i) into the set of the modified variables (a_i^m and b_i^m) and the set of the unchanged ones (a_i^f and b_i^f). Using these new variables, the four predicates $Trm(S_{a_1} \| U_{b_1})$, $Trm(T_{a_2} \| V_{b_2})$, $Prd(S_{a_1} \| U_{b_1})$ and $Prd(T_{a_2} \| V_{b_2})$ are defined as follows[6]:

$$Trm(S_{a_1} \| U_{b_1}) = Trm(S_{a_1}) \wedge Trm(U_{b_1})$$
$$Trm(T_{a_2} \| V_{b_2}) = Trm(T_{a_2}) \wedge Trm(V_{b_2})$$
$$Prd(S_{a_1} \| U_{b_1}) = Prd_{a_1^m, a_1^{m'}}(S_{a_1}) \wedge Prd_{b_1^m, b_1^{m'}}(U_{b_1}) \wedge d_1' = d_1$$
$$Prd(T_{a_2} \| V_{b_2}) = Prd_{a_2^m, a_2^{m'}}(T_{a_2}) \wedge Prd_{b_2^m, b_2^{m'}}(V_{b_2}) \wedge d_2' = d_2$$

where d_1 (resp. d_2) denotes the sub-set of variables of $a_1 \cup b_1$ (resp. $a_2 \cup b_2$) that the substitution $S_{a_1} \| U_{b_1}$ (resp. $T_{a_2} \| V_{b_2}$) doesn't modify. So, we have:

$$d_i = (a_i^f \cup b_i^f) - (a_i^m \cup b_i^m) \tag{H_5}$$

By substituting these definitions in (G_6), eliminating of the universal quantifier

---
[6] $d_i' = d_i$ denotes a conjunction of a set of equalities. Each equality, of the form $x' = x$, is related to one variable x of d_i.

on the variables c_1 and c_2, and applying the deduction theorem, we obtain the following three goals:

$$Trm(T_{a_2}) \tag{G_7}$$

$$Trm(V_{b_2}) \tag{G_8}$$

$$\forall c_2'.(Prd_{a_2^m,a_2^{m'}}(T_{a_2}) \wedge Prd_{b_2^m,b_2^{m'}}(V_{b_2}) \wedge d_2' = d_2$$
$$\rightarrow \exists c_1'.(Prd_{a_1^m,a_1^{m'}}(S_{a_1}) \wedge Prd_{b_1^m,b_1^{m'}}(U_{b_1}) \wedge d_1' = d_1 \wedge J(c_1', c_2'))) \tag{G_9}$$

under the additional hypothesis:

$$Trm(S_{a_1}) \tag{H_6}$$

$$Trm(U_{b_1}) \tag{H_7}$$

$$J(c_1, c_2) \tag{H_8}$$

4.2 Identification of the Reuse Conditions

Proof of (G_7) by Reuse. In order to prove (G_7) by reusing (H_3), we must be able to deduce from our current environment the two hypotheses $Trm(S_{a_1})$ and $J_{ST}(a_1, a_2)$. $Trm(S_{a_1})$ being the hypothesis (H_6), it remains to derive from the hypothesis (H_6), (H_7) and (H_8), the predicate $J_{ST}(a_1, a_2)$. So, the first condition of reuse is:

$$\boxed{(Trm(S_{a_1}) \wedge Trm(U_{b_1}) \wedge J(c_1, c_2)) \rightarrow J_{ST}(a_1, a_2)} \tag{H_9}$$

(H_6), (H_7), (H_8), (H_9) and the instantiation of the variables a_1 and a_2 by themselves in (H_3) prove therefore (G_7) and give an additional hypothesis:

$$\forall a_2'.(Prd(T_{a_2}) \rightarrow \exists a_1'.(Prd(S_{a_1}) \wedge J_{ST}(a_1', a_2'))) \tag{H_{10}}$$

Proof of (G_8) by Reuse. This proof is similar to the previous one. It requires the following condition:

$$\boxed{(Trm(S_{a_1}) \wedge Trm(U_{b_1}) \wedge J(c_1, c_2)) \rightarrow J_{UV}(b_1, b_2)}$$

and gives the following new hypothesis:

$$\forall b_2'.(Prd(V_{b_2}) \rightarrow \exists b_1'.(Prd(U_{b_1}) \wedge J_{UV}(b_1', b_2'))) \tag{H_{11}}$$

Proof of (G_9) by Reuse. By eliminating of the universal quantifier and applying of the deduction theorem, the goal becomes :

$$\exists c_1'.(Prd_{a_1^m,a_1^{m'}}(S_{a_1}) \wedge Prd_{b_1^m,b_1^{m'}}(U_{b_1}) \wedge d_1' = d_1 \wedge J(c_1', c_2')) \tag{G_{9.1}}$$

under the additional hypothesis :

$$Prd_{a_2^m,a_2^{m'}}(T_{a_2}) \tag{H_{12}}$$

$$Prd_{b_2^m,b_2^{m'}}(V_{b_2}) \tag{H_{13}}$$

$$d_2' = d_2 \tag{H_{14}}$$

The instantiation of the universally quantified variables a_2' and b_2' by themselves in (H$_{10}$) and (H$_{11}$) and the substitution of a_2 and b_2 by $(a_2^m \cup a_2^f)$ and $(b_2^m \cup b_2^f)$ respectively give:

$$(Prd_{a_2^m, a_2^{m'}}(T_{a_2}) \wedge a_2^{f'} = a_2^f) \to \exists a_1'.(Prd(S_{a_1}) \wedge J_{ST}(a_1', a_2^{m'} \cup a_2^{f'})) \quad (H_{15})$$

$$(Prd_{b_2^m, b_2^{m'}}(V_{b_2}) \wedge b_2^{f'} = b_2^f) \to \exists b_1'.(Prd(U_{b_1}) \wedge J_{UV}(b_1', b_2^{m'} \cup b_2^{f'})) \quad (H_{16})$$

In order to be able to reuse these hypotheses to prove (G$_{9.1}$), the two hypotheses:

$$a_2^{f'} = a_2^f \quad (H_{17})$$

$$b_2^{f'} = b_2^f \quad (H_{18})$$

must appear in (H$_{14}$). This means that each unchanged variable of T_{a_2} (resp. V_{b_2}) must remain unchanged by $(T_{a_2} \| V_{b_2})$. So:

$$\boxed{a_2^f \cap b_2^m = \emptyset \quad \text{and} \quad b_2^f \cap a_2^m = \emptyset}$$

(H$_{12}$), (H$_{17}$) and (H$_{15}$); (H$_{13}$), (H$_{18}$) and (H$_{16}$) give:

$$\exists a_1'.(Prd_{a_1, a_1'}(S_{a_1}) \wedge J_{ST}(a_1', a_2^{m'} \cup a_2^f)) \quad (H_{19})$$

$$\exists b_1'.(Prd_{b_1, b_1'}(U_{b_1}) \wedge J_{UV}(b_1', b_2^{m'} \cup b_2^f)) \quad (H_{20})$$

4.3 Actual Reuse of the Proofs

Let $sol_{a_1'}$ and $sol_{b_1'}$ be one of the already computed values of a_1' and b_1' that satisfy the hypotheses (H$_{19}$) and (H$_{20}$) respectively. So:

$$[a_1' := sol_{a_1'}]^7 Prd_{a_1, a_1'}(S_{a_1}) \wedge [a_1' := sol_{a_1'}] J_{ST}(a_1', a_2^{m'} \cup a_2^f)$$

$$[b_1' := sol_{b_1'}] Prd_{b_1, b_1'}(U_{b_1}) \wedge [b_1' := sol_{b_1'}] J_{UV}(b_1', b_2^{m'} \cup b_2^f)$$

Partitioning the variables a_1 (resp. b_1) into a_1^m and a_1^f (resp. b_1^m and b_1^f) allows us to rewrite these last hypotheses as:

$$[a_1^{m'} := sol_{a_1'}] Prd_{a_1^m, a_1^{m'}}(S_{a_1}) \wedge [a_1' := sol_{a_1'}] J_{ST}(a_1', a_2^{m'} \cup a_2^f) \quad (H_{21})$$

$$[b_1^{m'} := sol_{b_1'}] Prd_{b_1^m, b_1^{m'}}(U_{b_1}) \wedge [b_1' := sol_{b_1'}] J_{UV}(b_1', b_2^{m'} \cup b_2^f) \quad (H_{22})$$

Reusing the proofs of $S_{a_1} \sqsubseteq_{J(a_1, a_2)} T_{a_2}$ and $U_{b_1} \sqsubseteq_{J(b_1, b_2)} V_{b_2}$ consists in checking that the solutions $sol_{a_1'}$ and $sol_{b_1'}$ are also a solution for the goal to prove. This means that the tuple $(sol_{a_1'}, sol_{b_1'})$ has to satisfy (G$_{9.1}$). By definition of the

---

[7] $[x := y]P$ denotes the substitution of each free variable x of P by y.

parallel substitution, we know that: $a_1^m \cap b_1^m = \emptyset$. So, the substitution of the values $sol_{a_1'}$ and $sol_{b_1'}$ in ($G_{9.1}$) gives:

$$[a_1' := sol_{a_1'} \| b_1^{f'} := sol_{b_1^{f'}}] Prd_{a_1^m, a_1^{m'}}(S_{a_1}) \qquad (G_{9.2})$$

$$[a_1^{f'} := sol_{a_1^{f'}} \| b_1' := sol_{b_1'}] Prd_{b_1^m, b_1^{m'}}(U_{b_1}) \qquad (G_{9.3})$$

$$[a_1' := sol_{a_1'} \| b_1' := sol_{b_1'}](d_1' = d_1) \qquad (G_{9.4})$$

$$[a_1' := sol_{a_1'} \| b_1' := sol_{b_1'}] J(a_1^{m'} \cup b_1^{m'} \cup d_1', a_2^{m'} \cup b_2^{m'} \cup d_2) \qquad (G_{9.5})$$

One condition to prove ($G_{9.2}$) (resp. ($G_{9.3}$)) by reuse of (H_{21}) (resp. (H_{22})) is that the modified variables a_1^m and b_1^f (resp. a_1^f and b_1^m) must be disjoint. i.e:

$$\boxed{a_1^f \cap b_1^m = \emptyset \quad \text{and} \quad b_1^f \cap a_1^m = \emptyset}$$

The goal ($G_{9.4}$) is obvious because the variables d_1 denote the common unchanged variables of a_1 and b_1. Finally, we must be able to deduce the goal ($G_{9.5}$) from the current hypothesis environment, that is, to prove that:

$$\boxed{\begin{array}{c}(Trm(S_{a_1}) \wedge Trm(U_{b_1}) \wedge J(c_1, c_2) \wedge Prd_{a_2^m, a_2^{m'}}(T_{a_2}) \wedge \\ Prd_{b_2^m, b_2^{m'}}(V_{b_2}) \wedge [a_1' := sol_{a_1'}] Prd_{a_1^m, a_1^{m'}}(S_{a_1}) \wedge \\ [b_1' := sol_{a_1'}] Prd_{b_1^m, b_1^{m'}}(U_{b_1}) \wedge [a_1' := sol_{a_1'}] J_{ST}(a_1', a_2^{m'} \cup a_2^f) \wedge \\ [b_1' := sol_{b_1'}] J_{UV}(b_1', b_2^{m'} \cup b_2^f)) \to \\ [a_1' := sol_{a_1'} \| b_1' := sol_{b_1'}] J(a_1^{m'} \cup b_1^{m'} \cup d_1, a_2^{m'} \cup b_2^{m'} \cup d_2)\end{array}}$$

Conclusion: let $S_{a_1} \sqsubseteq_{J_{ST}(a_1, a_2)} T_{a_2}$ and $U_{b_1} \sqsubseteq_{J_{UV}(b_1, b_2)} V_{b_2}$ be two already proved refinements. Let $J(a_1 \cup b_1, a_2 \cup b_2)$ a predicate such that:

  i. $(Trm(S_{a_1}) \wedge Trm(U_{b_1}) \wedge J(a_1 \cup b_1, a_2 \cup b_2)) \to J_{ST}(a_1, a_2)$
 ii. $(Trm(S_{a_1}) \wedge Trm(U_{b_1}) \wedge J(a_1 \cup b_1, a_2 \cup b_2)) \to J_{UV}(b_1, b_2)$
iii. $a_1^f \cap b_1^m = \emptyset$
 iv. $b_1^f \cap a_1^m = \emptyset$
  v. $a_2^f \cap b_2^m = \emptyset$
 vi. $b_2^f \cap a_2^m = \emptyset$
vii. Let a_1' and b_1' be solutions of the refinements $(S_{a_1} \sqsubseteq_{J_{ST}(a_1, a_2)} T_{a_2})$ and $(U_{b_1} \sqsubseteq_{J_{UV}(b_1, b_2)} V_{b_2})$ for given values of a_2' and b_2' respectively. If the values a_1' and b_1' satisfy :

$$(Trm(S_{a_1}) \wedge Trm(U_{b_1}) \wedge J(a_1 \cup b_1, a_2 \cup b_2) \wedge Prd(T_{a_2}) \wedge Prd(V_{b_2})$$
$$Prd(S_{a_1}) \wedge Prd(U_{b_1}) \wedge J_{ST}(a_1', a_2') \wedge J_{UV}(b_1', b_2'))$$
$$\to J(a_1' \cup b_1', a_2' \cup b_2')$$

then the tuple (a_1', b_1') can be reused to prove: $(S_{a_1} \| U_{b_1}) \sqsubseteq_{J(a_1 \cup b_1, a_2 \cup b_2)} (T_{a_2} \| V_{b_2})$ for the same values of a_2' and b_2'.

4.4 Analysis of the Results

1. Conditions (i) and (ii) are the first two necessary conditions of reuse. Indeed, if we want to adopt a reuse strategy in our proof process, then we must exhibit the gluing invariants of the refinements we would like to reuse in the refinement we are proving.
2. Conditions (iii, iv, v, vi) are related to the refinement of the parallel substitution. Indeed, if a proof is established in the case where a variable x is unchanged then it is obvious that this proof can only be reused in the same conditions (x must remain unchanged). This means that the set of variables modified by one substitution and the set of variables not changed by the other one must be disjoint.
3. Condition (vii) is the third necessary condition of reuse. It states that only the solutions a'_1 and b'_1, of $(S_{a_1} \sqsubseteq T_{a_2})$ and $(U_{b_1} \sqsubseteq V_{b_2})$ respectively, satisfying the global invariant can be reused.
4. If the two substitutions S_{a_1} and U_{b_1} are deterministic, then the condition (vii) always holds. Indeed, there exists only one value of (a_1', b_1') that satisfies the two basic refinements. This value is defined by $(Prd(S_{a_1}), Prd(U_{b_1}))$. Each possible solution of the refinement $(S_{a_1} \| U_{b_1}) \sqsubseteq_{J(a_1 \cup b_1, a_2 \cup b_2)} (T_{a_2} \| V_{b_2})$ must satisfy the two predicates $Prd(S_{a_1})$ and $Prd(U_{b_1})$ which have only one solution. So, the unique solutions of the basic refinements are also solutions for the parallel refinement.
5. If the predicates $J(a_1, a_2)$ and $J(b_1, b_2)$ are functional[8] on a_1 and b_1 respectively, then the condition (vii) holds. Indeed, each possible solution of the refinement $(S_{a_1} \| U_{b_1}) \sqsubseteq_{J(a_1 \cup b_1, a_2 \cup b_2)} (T_{a_2} \| V_{b_2})$ must satisfy $J(a_1 \cup b_1, a_2 \cup b_2)$. According to ($v$) and ($vi$) this solution satisfies $J(a_1, a_2)$ and $J(b_1, b_2)$. But, these two predicates have one unique solution. So, the unique solutions of the basic refinements are also solutions for the parallel refinement.
6. One may argue that it would be easier to directly establish the refinement proof than to check if some reuse conditions are satisfied. We don't think so. Indeed checking if a given value satisfies a formula is always easier than exhibiting the values themselves. Moreover, this verification can be automatically achieved. This implies that the refinement proof can be automatically discharged. It is an important benefit since provers generally fail to automatically prove existential formulae.

Whatever the B constructor, the reuse conditions are similar. We have also considered the case of operations whose refinement requires more than two basic refinement rules [17]. In conclusion, we have demonstrated that to reuse the proof of the refinement $S_{a_1} \sqsubseteq_{J(a_1, b_1)} T_{b_1}$, three conditions are required:

a. the gluing invariant of the refinement $S_{a_1} \sqsubseteq_{J(a_1, b_1)} T_{b_1}$ must be deduced from the proof environment.
b. the value, satisfying the refinement $S_{a_1} \sqsubseteq_{J(a_1, b_1)} T_{b_1}$, must satisfy the gluing invariant of the refinement to be proved.

---
[8] A predicate $P(a, b)$, depending on two set of variables a and b, is functional on a iff for each value of b, there is a unique value of a that satisfies the predicate $P(a, b)$

c. for the parallel constructor, the set of variables modified by one substitution and the set of variables not changed by the other one must be disjoint.

An interesting consequence of this result is that it is possible to develop an automatic prover for a domain of applications where the reuse conditions are always satisfied. This is the subject of the next section.

5 An Automatic Prover Dedicated to the Refinement of Data-Intensive Applications

In this section, we describe our approach for the development of an automatic prover dedicated to the refinement of data-intensive applications. Recall that our goal is to provide software engineers with a formal approach, based on the B refinement process, for the development of reliable data-intensive applications. Such an approach may be difficult to use if the users have to achieve by hand all the proofs necessary to establish the correctness of the code generated at the last step. Moreover, it is recognized that the proof phase requires significant skills. For this, we have consider the construction of a dedicated prover that makes this proof phase a push-button activity.

In the first subsection, we show that, within the database domain we are considering, all the gluing invariants of our refinement rules have the required characteristics to satisfy the conditions (a) and (b). Then, the construction of an automatic prover comprises two phases: the automation of the proof of the basic substitutions refinement and the automation of the proof of the B constructors refinement.

5.1 Satisfaction of the Reuse Conditions

As we can remark, the three conditions stated in the previous section depend closely on the substitutions and the gluing invariant features. As our refinement system is closed, only the rules defined in the base can be used. Let us examine why the conditions (a) and (b) are satisfied by the set of refinement rules we have defined.

The condition (a) is satisfied by construction of the global gluing invariant. Indeed this invariant is equal to the conjunction of the gluing invariants of the different elementary refinement rules which are applied.

The condition (b) is also satisfied. Indeed, each rule of our refinement process is characterised by a deterministic gluing invariant. In section 4, we have pointed out that this condition is sufficient to satisfy the second reuse condition.

Of course, the condition (c) depends on the way the user has specified the abstract substitution. For instance, the condition is not satisfied if he/she specifies a transaction that simultaneously modifies an attribute and uses its value in the update of another attribute. In this case, the proof must be achieved without reuse. Nevertheless, this is not a frequent case.

These results have a double interest. Indeed, the fact that the reuse conditions are fulfilled ensures that the solutions exhibited for the proof of the correctness of elementary refinements can be reused to prove the correctness of refinements built on the elementary refinements. This means that one are discharged from the search of the values of abstract variables to achieve the proof. In practice, this task may be rather difficult. Moreover, as the global invariant is the conjunct of the elementary invariants, establishing the global proof comes down to establishing the elementary proofs. This means that the proof trees of the elementary proofs can be reused as is in the proof tree of the global proof.

5.2 Refinement Proof of Basic Substitutions

We have defined for each refinement rule a proof tactic that enables the automation of its correctness. The tactics are implemented using the prover of Atelier B. Recall that the proof of correctness of a refinement consists in exhibiting a value of a', associated to a given value b' satisfying $Prd(T_b)$, that satisfies the two predicates $Prd(S_a)$ and $J(a', b')$ (see page 837). However, all the abstract and concrete substitutions of the basic operations we consider are deterministic assignments of the form $(a := E)$. So, the searched value a' is given directly by the term $Prd(S_a)$ $(a' = E)$. In the same way, the value of b' is given by the term $Prd(T_b)$. Then, to prove the correctness of the refinement, we just need to check that the term $J(a', b')$ is true for these values of a' and b'. For example, to prove the goal of Rule_Add, page 840, we have to check that:

$$(f_1 \cup \{c \mapsto v(d)\}) = (v \circ (f \cup \{c \mapsto d\}))$$

Using Atelier B, we have defined a tactic that achieves the proof of this last formula. A tactic is an application of an ordered set of deduction rules. To prove the Rule_Add rule, we defined the following B tactic[9]:

$$tac\_Add \,\hat{=}\, o\_dist\_\cup;\ equal\_union;\ (comp\_ima;\ axio)^+$$

where:

- $o\_dist\_\cup$ states the distributivity property of the composition operator on the union one:

$$\overline{a \circ (b \cup c) = (a \circ b) \cup (a \circ c)}$$

- $equal\_union$ is a simplification rule. It gives a sufficient condition to demonstrate that $a \cup c = b \cup d$

$$\frac{a=b \qquad c=d}{a \cup c = b \cup d}$$

- $comp\_ima$ expresses the property of the composition operator on a function:

$$\frac{binhyp(f \in c \to d) \qquad e \in c}{(f \circ \{g \mapsto e\}) = \{g \mapsto f(e)\}}$$

---

[9] $(r_1; r_2)$ means that the rule r_1 is applied first, then the rule r_2 is applied. r^+ means that the rule (or an ordered set of rules) is applied as many times as possible.

$binhyp(H)$ specifies a guard (condition) for the application of the considered rule. It enables the identification of the symbols used in the hypotheses and that don't appear in the goal (the symbols c and d in our case).
- $axio$ enables to discharge the goals that are in the hypotheses:

$$\frac{binhyp(H)}{H}$$

Using the B tactic tac_Add, the proof tree associated to the correctness of $Rule\_Add$ is constructed as follows:

$$\cfrac{\cfrac{\overline{f_1=(v \circ f)}\,axio \quad \cfrac{\overline{d \in C}\,axio}{\{c \mapsto v(d)\}=(v \circ \{c \mapsto d\})}\,comp\_ima, v \in C \to T}{(f_1 \cup \{c \mapsto v(d)\})=(v \circ f) \cup (v \circ \{c \mapsto d\})}\,equal\_union}{(f_1 \cup \{c \mapsto v(d)\})=(v \circ (f \cup \{c \mapsto d\}))}\,o\_dist\_\cup$$

In the same way, we have defined another B tactic for the proof of the $Rule\_Del$ refinement rule.

5.3 Refinement Proof of B Constructors

As we have already noted, the correctness proof of a transaction refinement comprises the correctness proof of the basic operations that compose it and the refinement proof of the B substitutions constructors that relate these basic operations. In the previous subsection, we have shown, through the running example, how the correctness of the first category of proofs is automated by defining B tactics. In this subsection, we illustrate the automation of the second category.

At the abstract level, a database transaction is constructed on basic substitutions using a combination of **IF** constructors, parallel constructors (∥) and non-deterministic constructors (**ANY**). In the following, we discuss the refinement and the correctness of the **IF** constructor, the reasoning is similar for the other constructors.

Using our refinement process, the conditional substitution (**IF** P **THEN** S **END**) is refined by rewriting the predicate P with respect to concrete variables, and by refining the substitution S by a substitution T. So, we obtain a concrete substitution of the form (**IF** Q **THEN** T **END**). According to the boolean values of P and Q, four proofs are raised by the proof obligations generator (GOP) of Atelier B:

- the first two proofs correspond to the cases where P and Q have opposite boolean values. These proofs are achieved by exhibiting that Q is a rewriting of P. In this case, the proof becomes trivially true because we have two contradictory hypotheses. For example, to achieve the proofs (2) and (3) of page 842, we have defined the following tactic:

$$tac\_abs \triangleq (replace;\ axio\_cont;\ axio^+)$$

where the rules *replace* and *axio_contradictory* are defined by[10]:

$$\frac{b=(a\circ c)}{c=(a^{-1}\circ b)}\ replace \qquad \frac{band(binhyp(H),binhyp(\neg H))}{G}\ axio\_contradictory$$

- the two other proofs concern the cases where the predicates P and Q have the same boolean value. In these two cases, we have to prove the correctness of the refinement of the abstract substitution by the corresponding concrete one. It is here that the reuse of the basic proofs previously elaborated take effect. Theses cases corresponds to the proofs (1) and (4) of the example of page 842.

¿From a practical point of view, the specialized prover have been implemented within Atelier B as follows. We have created a *PatchProver* file in which different tactics are defined. When a *PatchProver* file is executed, the tactics are applied, one after the other, on each unproven proof obligation. As this process may be very time consuming, we relate each tactic to a particular kind of proof goal.

6 Conclusion and Future Works

In this paper, we have presented the approach that enables the development of an automatic prover dedicated to the refinement of database applications. The approach is based on a proof reuse strategy. In practice, it is frequent that a prover fails to achieve a proof without user interventions. However, if a proof reuse strategy is applied, what has been learned from previously computed proofs may guide the solver to automatically prove a larger amount of proofs. Another important benefit of reuse is resources (memory for example) and time saving. In the B refinement, for example, the gluing invariant may be very complex, and retrieving the value that satisfies it is not an obvious task. It is especially crucial in case of provers operating with limited resources or time as it is the case of the prover of the Atelier B [2] witch breaks down automatically after a given time.

We consider proof reuse within the context of refinement reuse. Firstly, necessary and sufficient conditions of proof reuse have been defined for the refinement of each B constructor. We store elementary refinements as quadruplets of abstract/concrete substitutions, gluing invariant and the refinement solution. Then, the resolution of a new elaborated refinement consists in retrieving, in our refinement base, the quadruplets whose abstract and concrete substitutions appear in the new refinement. It remains to select which basic solutions satisfy the current gluing invariant, and to check if the proof reuse conditions hold, which is not difficult to achieve.

As all reuse strategies, the usefulness of such proposition depends on the properties of the underlying solver but also on the domain which is considered. In general, a reuse strategy is successful if it is applied to a domain where its

---

[10] $band(A, B)$ means that the prover searches for each possible hypothesis that matches A the corresponding hypothesis that matches B. The search stops when two hypotheses that match A and B respectively are found.

applicability conditions are often verified. In this paper, we have pointed out that, in data-intensive applications, these conditions most often hold. This result has allowed us to construct an automatic prover within the Atelier B prover.

The approach is developed in the framework of the B method and Atelier B. However it may be adapted to either another formal method or a different application domain, provided the following elements are defined: a systematic development strategy that provides a set of basic proofs for the considered application domain and a set of conditions to satisfy under which proof reuse is possible.

From a theoretical perspective, we have now to mechanically check that the demonstrations we have carried out to exhibit the reuse constraints are correct. This work requires a significant reflection about the prover to be used.

References

[1] Abrial, J.R.: The B-Book, Cambridge University Press, 1996.
[2] Clearsy. Atelier B, manuel de référence. available at http://www.atelierb.societe.com.
[3] B-Core. B-Toolkit, on-line manual. Oxford, UK, available at http://www.b-core.com.
[4] Barras, B., et al., The Coq Proof Assistant, Reference Manual (7.1), INRIA Rocquencourt, 2001.
[5] Barthe, G., Pons, O.: Type Isomorphisms and Proof Reuse in Dependent Type Theory, Proceedings of FOSSACS'01, volume 2030, pages 57-71, Springer, 2001.
[6] M. Blaha and W. Premerlani. *Object-Oriented Modeling and Design for Database Applications*. Prentice Hall, 1998.
[7] Burdy, L., Meynadier, J-M.. Automatic Refinement, BUG Meeting, FM'99, Toulouse, France, September 1999.
[8] S. Ceri. *Methodologies and Tools for Database Design*. Elsevier Science, 1983.
[9] R. Laleau. On the interest of combining UML with the B formal method for the specification of database applications. In *ICEIS2000: 2nd International Conference on Enterprise Information Systems, Stafford, UK*, July 2000.
[10] Laleau, R., Mammar, A.: A Generic Process to Refine a B Specification into a Relational Database Implementation, Int. Conf. ZB2000, Springer-Verlag, LNCS 1878, York, 2000. Extended version in the CEDRIC research report N 86.
[11] R. Laleau and A. Mammar. An overview of a method and its support tool for generating B specifications from UML notations. In *ASE: 15th IEEE Conference on Automated Software Engineering, Grenoble, France*. IEEE Computer Society Press, September 2000.
[12] R. Laleau and F. Polack. Specification of integrity-preserving operations in information systems by using a formal UML- based language. *Information and Software Technology*, 43:693–704, 2001.
[13] R. Laleau: Conception et développement formels d'applications bases de données. Habilitation Thesis, CEDRIC Laboratory, Évry, France, 2002. Available at http://cedric.cnam.fr/PUBLIS/RC424.ps.gz
[14] Luo, Z.: Coercive Subtyping in Type Theory, In CSL book,276-296, 1996. Also available from "citeseer.nj.nec.com/luo96coercive.html".

[15] Magaud, N., Bertot, Y.: Changement de Représentation de Données dans le Calcul des Constructions Inductives. Research report, RR-4039, INRIA, France, October 2000.
[16] Magaud, N., Bertot, Y.: Changement de Représentation de Structures de Données dans Coq: le cas des entiers naturels, In Proceedings of JFLA'2001.
[17] Mammar, A.: Un environnement formel pour le développement d'applications bases de données. PhD thesis, CEDRIC Laboratory, CNAM, Evry, France, November 2002. Available at http://cedric.cnam.fr/PUBLIS/RC392.ps.gz
[18] Pons, O.: Generalization in Type Theory Based Proof Assistants, In Proceedings of TYPES'00. Durham, United Kingdom December 2000.
[19] Walther, C., Kolbe, T.: Proving Theorem by Reuse, Artificial Intelligence, 116:17-66, 2000.

ProB: A Model Checker for B

Michael Leuschel and Michael Butler

Department of Electronics and Computer Science
University of Southampton
Highfield, Southampton, SO17 1BJ, UK
{mal,mjb}@ecs.soton.ac.uk

Abstract. We present PROB, an animation and model checking tool for the B method. PROB's animation facilities allow users to gain confidence in their specifications, and unlike the animator provided by the B-Toolkit, the user does not have to guess the right values for the operation arguments or choice variables. PROB contains a model checker and a constraint-based checker, both of which can be used to detect various errors in B specifications. We present our first experiences in using PROB on several case studies, highlighting that PROB enables users to uncover errors that are not easily discovered by existing tools.

Keywords: B-Method, Tool Support, Model Checking, Animation, Logic Programming, Constraints.

1 Introduction

The B-method, originally devised by J.-R. Abrial [1], is a theory and methodology for formal development of computer systems. It is used by industries in a range of critical domains, most notably railway control.

B is based on the notion of *abstract machine* and the notion of *refinement*. The variables of an abstract machine are typed using set theoretic constructs such as sets, relations and functions. Typically these are constructed from basic types such as integers and given types from the problem domain (e.g., *Name, User, Session,* etc). The invariant of a machine is specified using predicate logic. Operations of a machine are specified as *generalised substitutions*, which allow deterministic and nondeterministic assignments to be specified. In B refinement, a machine may be refined by another machine in which the state is represented by data structures that are more concrete and/or in which operations are more deterministic and imperative.

There are two main proof activities in B: *consistency checking*, which is used to show that the operations of a machine preserve the invariant, and *refinement checking*, which is used to show that one machine is a valid refinement of another. A refinement that is at a sufficiently low level can be translated into code. These activities are supported by industrial strength tools, such as Atelier-B [33] and the B-toolkit [4]. A B-tool generates a list of predicate logic proof obligations (POs). If each of these POs is proved, then the machine is consistent (or a correct refinement in the case of refinement checking). The B-tools have an automatic prover and an interactive prover. Typically the more complex POs are not proved automatically and need to be proved interactively. The tools also provide automatic translation of low level B specifications into executable code.

The PROB tool introduced in this paper currently supports automated consistency checking of B machines via *model checking* [12]. For exhaustive model checking, the given sets must be restricted to small finite sets, and integer variables must be restricted to small numeric ranges. This allows the checking to traverse all the reachable states of the machine. PROB can also be used non-exhaustively to explore the state space and find potential problems. The user can set an upper bound on the number of states to be traversed or can interrupt the checking at any stage. PROB will generate and graphically display counter-examples when it discovers a violation of the invariant. PROB detects attempts to evaluate undefined expressions, such as the application of a partial function to arguments outside its domain. PROB can also be used as an animator of B specifications. So, the model checking facilities are still useful for infinite state machines, not for verification, but for sophisticated debugging and testing.

PROB also offers an alternative checking method, inspired by the ALLOY [18, 19] analyzer. In this mode of operation, PROB does not explore the reachable states starting from the initial state(s), but checks whether applying an individual operation can result in an invariant violation, independently of the particular initialization of the B machine. This is done by symbolic constraint solving, and we call this approach *constraint-based checking* (another sensible name would be *model finding*).

Possible Applications of PROB: For finite state B machines it may be possible to use PROB for proving consistency without user intervention (cf. our case study in Sect. 8). However, we believe that PROB will be more useful as a complement to the current tools. Indeed, the interactive proof process with Atelier-B or the B-Toolkit can be quite time consuming: a typical development involves going through several levels of refinement to code generation *before* attempting any interactive proof [22]. This is to avoid the expense of reproving POs as the specification and refinements change in order to arrive at a satisfactory implementation. We therefore see one of the main uses of PROB as a complement to interactive proof, in that some errors will be discovered earlier in the development cycle and also that there will be less effort wasted by users trying to prove incorrect POs. We also believe that PROB will be very useful in teaching B, and making B more accessible to new users. Finally, even for experienced B users PROB may unveil problems in a specification that are not easily discovered by existing tools.

We proceed with an illustration of the use of PROB before continuing to describe its design.

2   Using ProB

PROB provides two ways of discovering whether a machine violates its invariant:

1. it can find a sequence of operations that, starting from a valid initial state of the machine, navigates the machine into a state in which the invariant is violated. Trying to find such a sequence of operations is the task of the PROB *(temporal) model checker*.
2. it can construct a state of the machine which satisfies the invariant, but from which we can apply a *single* operation to reach a state which violates the invariant. Finding such states is the task of the PROB *constraint-based checker*.

Let us examine how these approaches work on a simple example. Figure 1 presents a very simple B specification of a lift, which has an operation inc to go up one floor, and an operation dec to go down one floor.

```
MACHINE Lift
VARIABLES  floor
INVARIANT  floor : 0..99
INITIALISATION floor := 4
OPERATIONS
     inc = PRE floor<99 THEN floor := floor + 1 END ;
     dec = BEGIN floor := floor - 1 END
END
```

Fig. 1. Lift example in B

This B machine does not preserve its invariant and Fig. 2 presents two counter-examples found by PROB. The left one (a) is produced by the model checker and shows that it is possible to reach a state where the invariant is violated, i.e., the floor variable becomes negative. (Usually PROB will only display the sequence of operations and states that lead to an invariant violation, but for Fig. 2 we have used PROB to display all the states that were explored until the invariant violation was found.) The right one (b) is produced by the constraint-based checker, which has constructed a before state floor = 0 and found the operation dec which applied to that state yields an invariant violation in the after state. Note that in this case there is no guarantee that the constructed before state is actually reachable from the initial state(s), although in this particular example it is. Also note that the constraint-based checker can determine that the inc operation will never introduce an invariant violation on its own. Finally, the constraint-based checker can also be used to find abort conditions, and the model checker can be used to both detect abort conditions and deadlocks.

3 Brief Overview of the System

The PROB system has been developed mainly in SICStus Prolog, with a graphical user interface implemented in Tcl/Tk. An overview of PROB's main components can be found in Fig. 3.

The first implementation problem to be overcome is the translation of specifications written in B abstract machine notation (AMN) [1] into a notation

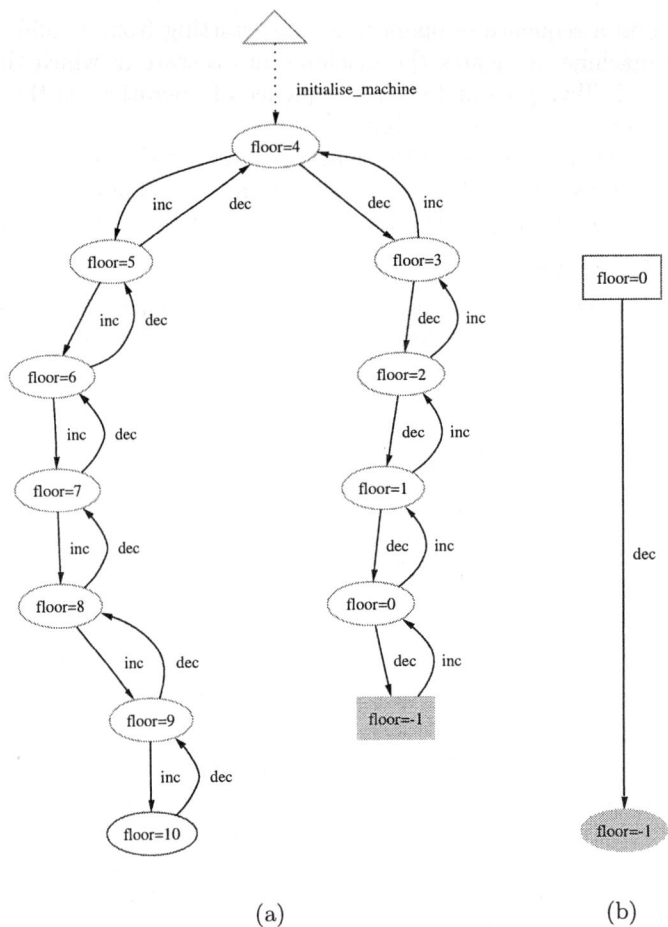

Fig. 2. Counter-examples for the Lift Machine

convenient for interpretation within Prolog. PROB uses the JBTools package developed by Tatibouet [34] and the Pillow package [10] to that effect. The JBTools package permits translation of AMN specifications into XML, while the Pillow package allows the conversion of XML files into a Prolog term representation. The PROB front end then postprocesses the general Prolog term tree representation of the Pillow library output into a more structured representation which will serve as the input to the interpreter. The PROB *interpreter* recurses through this structured representation of B machines and makes call to the PROB *kernel*, which provides support for the basic datatypes and operations of the B-language. The PROB kernel itself is written in SICStus Prolog with co-routining and constraints. The PROB animator and the two model checkers all make use of the PROB interpreter in various ways, as will be explained later in the paper.

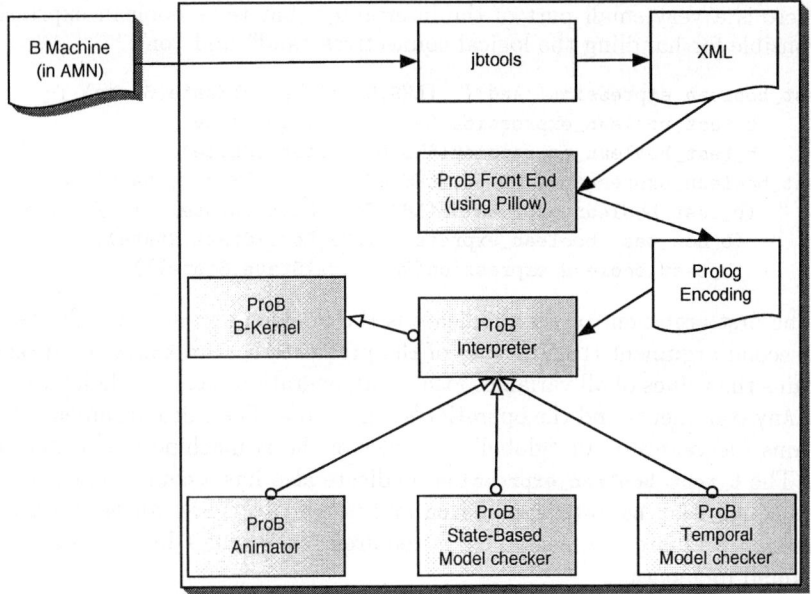

Fig. 3. Overview of the ProB System

4 The PROB Kernel and Interpreter

The PROB Interpreter: The PROB interpreter is written in a structured operational semantics [28] (SOS) style. More precisely, given a description σ_1 of the state of a B machine, we describe which operations (and with which argument values) can be applied in σ_1 and which new states can be reached by performing those operations. For this, the constructs of B were divided into three main classes:

1. *statements* which modify the variables of a B machine,
2. *expressions* which do not modify the variables but return values, and
3. *boolean expressions*, called predicates in B, which are expressions which return either true or false.

To manipulate these constructs the PROB interpreter provides Prolog predicates[1] to execute statements, compute expressions, and test boolean expressions. Each one of these predicate has access to the global state of the machine (the state of the variables of a machine) and a local state which contains the values for local variables and parameters of operations. In order to manipulate B's basic datastructures and operators, the PROB interpreter calls the PROB kernel, which we discuss later.

---
[1] Note that there is a potential confusion concerning the use of the word "predicate" in B and in Prolog. From now on, when we use the term predicate, we mean a predicate in our Prolog implementation and not a boolean expression in a B machine.

Here is a very small part of the interpreter that tests boolean expressions, responsible for handling the logical connectives "and" and "or":

```
b_test_boolean_expression('And'(_,[LHS,RHS]), LocalState,State) :-
      b_test_boolean_expression(LHS,LocalState,State),
      b_test_boolean_expression(RHS,LocalState,State).
b_test_boolean_expression('Or'(_,[LHS,RHS]), LocalState,State) :-
      (b_test_boolean_expression(LHS,LocalState,State)   ;   /* or */
      (b_not_test_boolean_expression(LHS,LocalState,State),
      b_test_boolean_expression(RHS,LocalState,State))).
```

The first argument of the predicate is the boolean expression to be tested.[2] The second argument (LocalState) of the predicate b_test_boolean_expression contains the values of all variables local to an operation, i.e., the choice variables from Any statements and the operation's arguments. The third argument (State) contains the values of all "global" variables of the B machine under consideration. The b_test_boolean_expression predicate also has a counterpart, which is called b_not_test_boolean_expression and is used to check whether a boolean expression evaluates to false. This is required, as Prolog's built-in negation is not sound in general.

While it is clearly difficult to cover the vast syntax of B, the code of the PROB interpreter is relatively simple. The reason is that the PROB kernel is very flexible and "hides" a lot of the complexities of B from the PROB interpreter. In fact, while the PROB interpreter is written in classical Prolog the PROB kernel uses advanced features of Prolog, such as co-routining and constraints. We discuss the PROB kernel in more detail below. Also, because of Prolog's support for non-determinism it was not too difficult to support non-deterministic operations.

The PROB Kernel: First, let us see how some of B's datastructures are actually encoded by the PROB Kernel:

B Type	B value	Prolog encoding
number	5	int(5)
boolean	true	term(true)
element of a finite set S	C	fd(3,'S')
pair	(2,5)	(int(2),int(5))
sequence	[2,5]	cons(int(2),cons(int(5),nil))
set	{2,5}	[int(2), int(5)]

As you can see, sets are represented by Prolog lists.[3] The Prolog term fd(3,'S') means that we are dealing with the third constant of the given set S. So if S is defined within the B machine by $S = \{A, B, C, D\}$ then fd(3,'S') denotes the constant C. There is also a special symbol abort reserved to indicate that an abort condition occurred while trying to compute this value. Also note

---

[2] This expression also contains some XML layout information, e.g., in the first argument of the 'And' symbol, which is ignored by the interpreter.

[3] To be able to detect typing errors, B lists are not represented as standard Prolog lists but use the special cons symbol instead.

that the above types can in principle be arbitrarily nested, e.g., we may have sets of sets of sequences of pairs.

There is nothing special about this mapping from B to Prolog, and one may wonder where the difficulties in writing an interpreter lie. To highlight these difficulties, let us examine the following non-deterministic B operation, that finds a symmetric partial function on a finite set Name:

```
cc <-- symmetric = ANY nn WHERE nn = nn~ & nn: Name +-> Name
                  THEN cc := nn      END;
```

Now, when the PROB interpreter reaches the construct nn = nn~ it does not yet have any information about nn. This will only be provided "later" when interpreting the construct nn: Name +> Name. When writing an interpreter for a "classical" programming language things are much simpler: within a statement we typically would know the type and value of any variable. But in B this is not the case, and the value of a variable might depend on many constraints, some of which may not yet have been encountered by the PROB interpreter. We have overcome this problem by using the co-routining facilities of SICStus Prolog, which allow one to suspend goals until sufficient information is available to evaluate them. For example, the inversion operator ~ is implemented by a binary Prolog predicate invert_relation, which will automatically suspend until enough information is available. This is done as follows:

```
invert_relation(R,IR) :- when((nonvar(R);nonvar(IR)),inv_rel2(R,IR)).
inv_rel2([],[]).
inv_rel2([(X,Y)|T],[(Y,X)|IT]) :-
              when((nonvar(T);nonvar(IT)),inv_rel2(T,IT)).
```

The when co-routining predicate will suspend until its first argument becomes true, in which case it will then call its second argument. From a logical point of view, the when declarations can be ignored, as they are just annotations guiding the Prolog execution engine; they do not change the logical meaning of a Prolog program.

The co-routining has made the invert_relation much more robust and usable. As the following two queries show, it can now handle information that is incrementally provided about its arguments (both of these queries would have looped without the when declarations):

```
| ?- invert_relation(R,R), R=[(int(1),int(2))].
no
| ?- findall(R,(invert_relation(R,R), R=[(X,int(2))]),Answers).
Answers = [[(int(2),int(2))]] ?
yes
```

When the PROB interpreter encounters the expression nn = nn~ in the above B operation symmetric, it would basically call the PROB kernel as follows: invert_relation(NN,InvN),equal_object(NN,InvN).[4] Now, the PROB kernel will not compute any value for the variable NN, it will simply suspend and wait for

---
[4] One has to use PROB's equal_object predicate instead of Prolog unification because the same B set can be represented by different Prolog lists.

NN to be further instantiated. So, how does PROB get concrete values for the ANY statement?

To understand this, we have to examine how the kernel treats the expression nn: Name +> Name. In fact, any global set of the B machine, such as Name, will be mapped to a finite domain within SICStus Prolog's CLP(FD) constraint solver [11]. A finite domain within CLP(FD) is a finite set of integers, typically an interval. CLP(FD) provides a wide variety of constraints that can be expressed on such domains, and it provides a way of enumerating all concrete solutions (called *labeling*).

For example, supposing that Name is mapped to the finite domain $\{1,2\}$, the expression n: Name will be mapped to the SICStus Prolog code N = fd(C,'Name'), C in 1..2, where C in 1..2 is a CLP(FD) constraint.

To force the enumeration of concrete values and thus force the execution of suspended goals we use CLP(FD)'s labeling operation.[5] Note that this enumeration is only used as a last resort: sometimes operations can be fully evaluated without having to enumerate at all.

Note, for our approach to work we have to be sure that we will not generate infinitely many solutions or candidate solutions for an ANY statement. This is achieved by requiring that every choice variable of an ANY statement is given a finite type. For example, ANY x WHERE x:NAT THEN is not supported by PROB. However, the above operation symmetric is supported by PROB, and all possible symmetric partial functions over Name will be generated by the interpreter.

5 The PROB Animator

The PROB animator was developed using the Tcl/Tk library of SICStus Prolog 3.10. The user interface was inspired by the ARC tool [17] for system level architecture modelling and builds upon our earlier animator for CSP [23].

Our animator supports (backtrackable) step-by-step animation of B-machines, and supports non-deterministic operations. As can be seen in Fig. 4 it presents the user with a description of the current state of the machine, the history that has led the user to reach the current state, and a list of all the enabled operations, along with proper argument instantiations. Thus, unlike the animator provided by the B-Toolkit, the user does *not* have to guess the right values for the operation arguments. The same holds for choice variables in ANY statements, the user does not have to find values which satisfy the ANY statement. If the number of enabled operations becomes larger, one could envisage a more refined interface were not all options are immediately displayed to the user.

To extract all possible values for operation inputs and choice variables from the PROB interpreter, the PROB animator uses Prolog's findall construct together with the CLP(FD) labelling operation. For this to work properly, we require that all operation arguments are mapped finite types. For example, while it is admissible to have an operation:

---
[5] For more complicated types we may actually have to use the *hypercall* primitive discussed later in Sect. 6.

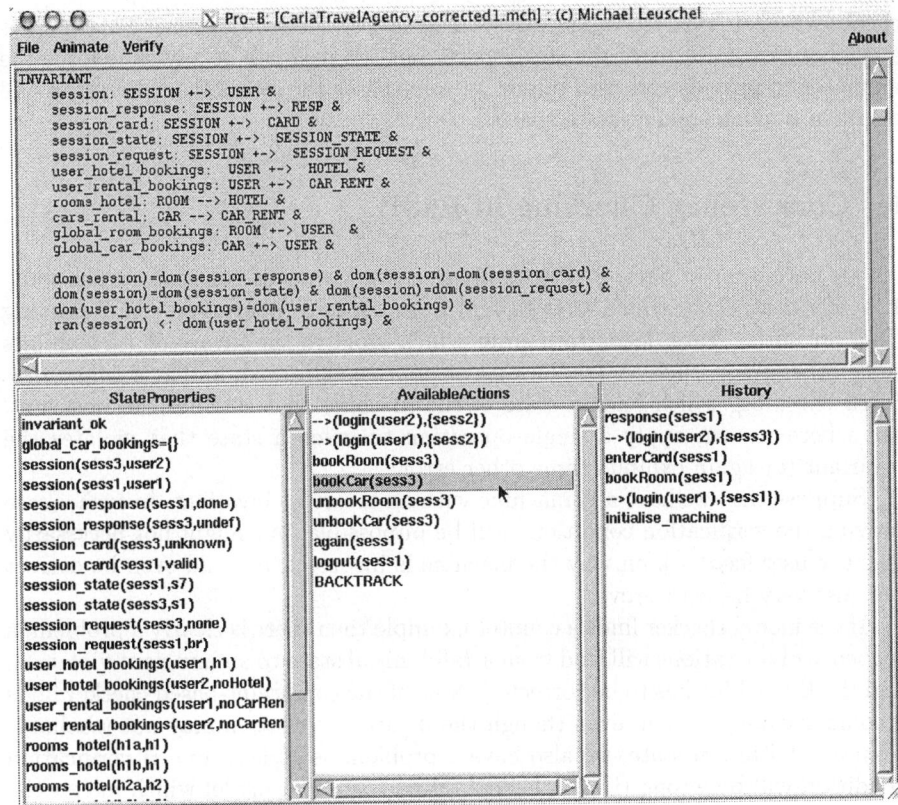

Fig. 4. Animation of the E-Travel Agency Case Study (c.f., Sect. 8)

```
add(nn) = PRE nn:0..10 THEN n := n +nn END
```

it is not allowed to have untyped or unbounded operation arguments, such as:

```
addinf(nn) = PRE nn:NAT THEN n := n +nn END
```

The same holds for set assignments, i.e., it is allowed to use x:: BOOL but it is not allowed to use x::NAT. However, it would be possible to extend the animator so that it allowed such constructs, but only provided values up to a certain limit.

The PROB animator also provides visualization of the state space that has been explored so far, and provides visual feedback on which states have been fully explored and which ones are still "open." One can also find the shortest trace (given the state space explored so far) to the current state. For the visualization we make use of the dot tool of the graphviz package [3].

Another noteworthy feature of the animator is its ability to perform *symbolic animation* as well as concrete, ordinary animation. This allows a user to trace a B-machine symbolically, without providing actual values for the parameters; the animator will set up constraints which the parameters have to satisfy (and checks whether concrete values exist which satisfy the constraints). This enables a symbolic exploration of the state space, but the user can at any time force the animator to provide concrete values. In some cases the symbolic exploration will result in a much smaller state space.

6   Consistency Checking in PROB

As we have seen in Sect. 2, PROB provides two ways of consistency checking: 1. a *model checking* which tries to find a sequence of operations that, starting from an initial state, leads to a state which violates the invariant (or exhibits some other error, such as deadlocking or abort conditions); and 2. a *constraint-based* checking, which finds a state of the machine that satisfies the invariant, but where we can apply a single operation to reach a state that violates the invariant (or again exhibits some other error).

Suppose that we have a B-machine with an incorrect invariant. In such a case proving the verification conditions will be impossible, but might not necessarily give the user feedback on why the machine is incorrect; it could even be correct but just very hard to prove.

If the model checker finds a counter-example then there is clearly a problem: a sequence of operations will lead from a valid initial state to an invariant violation, and the B machine has to be corrected. Now, if the constraint-based checker finds a counter-example then, even though the invariant violation may not reachable from a valid initial state, we also have a problem as at least one B verification condition will be wrong (i.e., in logical terms there is a model which makes the formula false), and we will never be able to prove the machine correct using the B proof rules. Take a look at the machine in Fig. 5. There is no sequence of operations that will lead to $n = 2$, but we can find the state $n = 1$ which satisfies the invariant and after applying *inc* we obtain the state $n = 2$ which violates the invariant.

From an implementation point of view, the model checking approach is simpler as every single state is clearly determined, and we can use our PROB interpreter to compute all possible successor states of any given state, and then perform a search on the right sequence of operations.

For the constraint-based approach things are more complicated. Indeed, even though we know there is only a single operation to apply, we initially have little information about the state of the B machine under consideration. One could of course try to enumerate all possible states of a B-machine, and then call the PROB interpreter to check whether any given state satisfies the invariant, and if it does call the PROB interpreter to compute and check the successor states. However, this will be highly inefficient and even very small machines will not be checkable in this way. To overcome this problem we have developed a symbolic approach, which makes use of Prolog's co-routining and constraint facilities.

Below, we present these two components of PROB in more detail. In Sect. 8, we will then show how we have successfully applied these components to verify various non-trivial machines.

Temporal Model Checking: By manually exploring a B-machine it is possible to discover problems with a machine, such as invariant violations or even deadlocks (states where no operation is applicable). We have implemented a model checker which will do this exploration systematically and automatically. It will alert the user as soon as a problem has been found, and will then present the shortest trace (within currently explored states) that leads from an initial state to the error. The model checker will also detect when all states have been explored, and can thus also be used to formally guarantee the absence of errors. This will obviously only happen if the state space is finite, but the model checker can also be applied to B machines with infinite state spaces and will then explore the state space until it finds an error or runs out of memory.

To detect whether a given state has already been explored, we implemented a normalisation procedure for states. Because the temporal property we need to check (i.e., all reachable states satisfy the invariant) is a safety property [12] a relatively simple, but liberal exploration algorithm can be used. Our exploration is an adaptation of the A* algorithm with cycle detection, and can be tuned to perform in the extreme cases as either a depth-first or breadth-first exploration. In the default setting of PROB, every new node has a 25% chance of being treated in a depth-first manner, which turned out to be a good compromise in our experiments: pure depth-first search employed by many model checkers is often very bad at finding even very short counter-examples (and is not guaranteed to find counter-examples present in infinite state systems), whereas pure breadth-first is bad at finding long counter-examples.

The visited states are stored in Prolog's clause database. While this is not as efficient as for example tabling[6], it allows the model checking state to be easily queried (e.g., for visualization) and saved to file. Anyway, for a formalism as involved as B, most of the model checking time will be spent computing new states and the time needed to look up whether a given state has already been encountered is probably insignificant.

Constraint-Based Checking: We achieved the constraint-based checking by delaying the state enumeration as long as possible. The idea is to first set up constraints which assert that the first state of the B-machine under consideration satisfies the invariant. We then apply an operation and set up constraints which assert that the invariant is no longer satisfied in the after state. In PROB this is done by the following code:[7]

```
constraint_check(OpName,State,Operation,NewState) :-
    b_extract_types_and_invariant(Variables,VarTypes,Invariant),
    b_set_up_variable_types(Variables,VarTypes,State),
```

---

[6] A tabled logic programming systems such as XSB [31] provides very efficient datastructures and algorithms to tabulate calls, i.e., it remembers which calls it has already encountered. This can be used to write very efficient model checkers [29, 26].

[7] Observe that the variables in the after state NewState are given correct types by b_set_up_variable_types, ensuring a finite search space. We suppose that invariant violations due to type errors will be caught by a standard B type checker.

```
              MACHINE counter
              VARIABLES n
              INVARIANT n : 0..10 & n /= 2
              INITIALISATION  n := 3
              OPERATIONS
                      inc = PRE n<10 THEN n := n + 1 END
              END
```

Fig. 5. A simple counter machine with an error

```
b_set_up_variable_types(Variables,VarTypes,NewState),
b_test_boolean_expression(Invariant,[],State),
b_not_test_boolean_expression(Invariant,[],NewState),
b_execute_operation(OpName,Operation,State,NewState,_Abort).
```

Calling `constraint_check` will involve no enumeration and thus no search, and may still discard a big part of the search space by partially instantiating variables and arguments. However, calling `constraint_check` on its own will not yet give us any counter-example, as many of the predicates it calls will suspend.

To extract solutions from `constraint_check`, we have developed a new Prolog built-in, the so-called `hypercall` primitive. This primitive takes its argument, executes it until only suspended goals remain, applies the CLP(FD) labeling operation, and then selects one of the suspended goals for a single expansion step. It then repeats the same procedure until there are no more suspended goals. For example, while calling `invert_relation(R,R)` from Sect. 4 will suspend and not give any information about R, `hypercall(invert_relation(R,R))` will enumerate all possible solutions for R. The PROB constraint-based checking is then simply achieved by calling `hypercall(constraint_check(opname,S,Op,NS))`. If we manage to find a solution for this query, we have uncovered a counter-example to the B machine's invariant.

Which Checker to Use? A user could run either or both of our model checkers before attempting to prove a certain B-machine correct using existing B-tools. If our model checking tool uncovers a counter-example it is clear that proving it will be in vain. Not only have we spared the user a lot of effort, the user also has a counter-example at his or her disposal which will hopefully make it easier to correct the B-machine's specification.

An obvious question is, when would one prefer using one approach over the other. In general, the temporal model checking approach will be more efficient, simply due to the fact that the underlying machinery is simpler and the induced overhead is smaller. However, constraint-based checking can still be more efficient for some applications, especially as we can focus on checking a single operation. This can be especially useful in circumstances where one has modified or added a single operation of a (previously verified) big machine. Also, constraint-based checking can proceed even if the initialisation operation is too restrictive or too expensive to perform exhaustively (e.g., if the initialisation chooses any state that satisfies the invariant). Finally, we believe that the constraint-based checking is easier to parallelise; something which we intend to exploit in future research.

7 Relationship with the Classical B Proof Method

In this section we outline how exhaustive temporal checking of a (finite) B machine entails standard B consistency. Consistency in B is defined by treating statements as predicate transformers. For statement S, and postcondition P, $[S]P$ represents the weakest precondition under which S, if it is enabled, is guaranteed to terminate in a state satisfying postcondition P. A machine is said to be consistent wrt an invariant I provided for each operation S_i of the machine[8]:

$$I \implies [S_i]I$$

Often an invariant I' which is stronger than I needs to be found (by adding conjuncts to I) so that

$$I' \implies I \quad \text{and} \quad I' \implies [S_i]I'$$

A successful exhaustive temporal model check computes the set of reachable states R and will have checked that all of those states satisfy the invariant I. This set of reachable states R corresponds to a stronger invariant I' above.

To show the formal correspondence between the consistency checking and exhaustive temporal checking, we make use of the set theoretic model of B which is defined in [1]. In this model, the state space of a machine is defined as the cartesian product of the types of each of the machine variables. Given a statement S, $pre(S)$ represents the set of states satisfying the precondition of S, while $rel(S)$ is the binary relation corresponding to the statement relating before states to after states. The *set transformer model* of a statement, $str(S)$, is a function from sets of after states to sets of before states, modelling the way in which a predicate transformer maps postconditions to preconditions. Given a set of after states q, we have [1]:

$$str(S)(q) = pre(S) \cap \overline{rel(S)^{-1}[\overline{q}]}$$

Here $R[s]$ is the relation image of set s under relation R, and $\overline{s}$ is the complement of set s. Writing I to represent the set of states satisfying the invariant, the proof obligation for consistency is characterised in the set transformer model as

$$I \subseteq str(S)(I)$$

It is relatively straightforward to show, by structural induction over the statement constructs, that the Prolog interpretation of a statement S used in PROB corresponds to $rel(S)$. A successful exhaustive temporal model check on a machine with invariant (set) I computes a set of reachable states R which is a subset of I, satisfying the following properties for each operation S_i:

$$R \subseteq pre(S_i)$$
$$rel(S_i)[R] \subseteq R$$

---

[8] The initialisation of a machine must also establish the invariant. Also, in standard B, the outermost precondition of an operation also appears as an antecedent to the proof obligation. This is equivalent to treating it as a guard rather than a precondition. Here we assume that the outermost precondition is included in S_i as a guard. PROB also treats the outermost precondition as a guard.

From this, it is straightforward to prove that the machine is consistent wrt invariant set R, i.e., that for each operation i:

$$R \subseteq str(S_i)(R)$$

8 Applications and Case Studies

Volvo Vehicle Function: We have tried our tool on a case study performed at Volvo on a typical vehicle function. The largest B machine had 15 variables, 550 lines of B specification, and 26 operations. This B specification was developed by Volvo as part of the European Commission IST Project PUSSEE (IST-2000-30103, http://www.keesda.com/pussee/).

We have first used PROB to animate the B machine, which worked very well. The machine was already finite state (apart from an auxiliary natural number variable which was used to make proofs possible). We have then used PROB to verify the B-machine using the temporal model checker. PROB managed to explore the entire state space of the B-machine in a few minutes, covering 1360 states and 25696 transitions, thereby proving the absence of invariant violations and deadlocks. However, PROB managed to identify a slight anomaly in the B machines behaviour: a crucial operation was only enabled in 8 of the 1360 states. This shows that PROB might be used to identify problems that would otherwise only emerge at implementation time.

To better test the model checkers, we have also injected a subtle fault into the specification, which both the temporal and the constraint-based checker managed to unveil fully automatically within a couple of minutes.

Discussion on Efficiency: Exploring 1360 states and 25696 transitions within a few minutes on a 1Ghz Powerbook G4 might seem slow compared to "classical" model checking using tools such as SMV or SPIN. Note, however, that PROB has not yet been tuned for speed. More importantly, the input language (B) is here of a much higher level, that every state contains information about 15 variables and that computing successor states for B is a quite expensive operation in itself (especially when ANY statements are involved, as they were for this example). Indeed, recent experiences show that a model checker in Prolog need not be much slower than tools such as SPIN, while being able to handle problems of similar size and allowing one to more easily check high-level languages [27].

E-TravelAgency: Within our ABCD[9] project we have developed various B models for a distributed online travel agency, through which users can make hotel and car rental bookings. The models were developed jointly with a Java/JSP implementation. The B model contains about 6 pages of B and, as can be seen in Fig. 4, has 11 variables with non-trivial types. Attempting to check consistency

---

[9] "Automated validation of Business Critical systems using Component-based Design," EPSRC grant GR/M91013.

of the *ETravelAgency* using Atelier-B resulted in a total of 206 POs. 156 of these were proved automatically by the Aterlier-B autoprover (75%), leaving 50 POs to be proved interactively.

PROB was very useful in the development of the specification, and was able to animate all of our models (see Fig. 4). The PROB model checker also discovered several invariant violations, e.g., related to incorrect responses or illegal multiple bookings. It was also able to discover a deadlock in one of the models, which was due to the fact that "session identifiers" were not properly recycled, meaning that after a while no new customers could log into the system. Such an error would have been more difficult to uncover within Atelier-B or the B-Toolkit.

9 Discussions

Scaling: We have already applied PROB on reasonably sized, industrial examples. Still, a big question is: how well will PROB scale for even larger specifications. First, concerning the *animation*, we do not believe that the size of the B machine and the number of the B machine's variables are an important factor. We conjecture that PROB should be able to handle B machines with hundreds of operations and thousands of variables. Of course, there will be a user interface issue on how to display a large number of variables and options (e.g., a hierarchical view of enabled operations and of the state space could be added to Fig. 4), but there should not be an intrinsic computational problem. Indeed, to prove this point we have constructed several artificial specifications (the largest one having 240 operations, 80 variables of type partial function, 80 conditions in the invariant) and have been able to successfully animate them.

The limiting factor of animating B, will be more the complexity of the ANY statements and the complexity of the datastructures that are passed as operation arguments. The latter will probably be less of a problem, as arguments typically have to be "B0 typed" in order for machines to be implementable (as arguments cannot be refined). However, a single ANY statement with a very large domain (e.g., Fermat's last theorem on a large domain) could break the animator. The same would be an ANY statement involving say a search over a function satisfying a certain property: ANY fun WHERE fun = ~fun & fun: 0..100 +-> 0.100 THEN.

It is well known that due to the state space explosion problem, *model checking* does not scale easily to large systems. Manual abstractions are still the key in many successful applications of model checking to larger examples. The same will be true here, at least if one wants to exhaustively explore the state space. PROB can still be used non-exhaustively to explore the state space and find potential problems. So, the model checking operations can still be useful for very large machines, not as a verification tool but as a sophisticated debugging tool.

Related Work: We are not the first to realise the potential of logic programming for animation and/or verification of specifications. See for example [7], where an animator for VERILOG is developed in Prolog, or [5] where Petri nets are mapped to CLP. Also, the model checking system XMC contains an interpreter for value-passing CCS [29, 13]. A logic programming approach to encode denotational semantics specifications was applied in [21] to verify an Ada implementation of the "Bay Area Rapid Transit" controller.

Probably the most strongly related work is [6, 2], which uses a special purpose constraint solver over sets (CLPS) to animate B and Z specifications using the so-called BZ-Testing-Tools. Unfortunately we were not able to get hold of either CLPS or of the B-tool built on top of it, hence we cannot perform a detailed comparison of the animation facilities of PROB and the BZ-Testing-Tools. Indeed, our own B-Kernel, can be viewed as constraint solver over finite sets and sequences (it seems that sequences are not yet supported by [2]). At a higher level, [6, 2] put a lot of stress on animation and test-case generation, but do not seem to cater for model checking nor constraint-based checking. Indeed, to our knowledge we developed the first temporal model checker and the first constraint-based checker for consistency checking in B. Bellegarde et al [15] describes the use of SPIN to verify that finite B machines satisfy LTL properties (though the translation from B to SPIN does not appear to be automatic). This differs from the PROB approach in that it does not check for standard B invariant violation, rather it checks for satisfaction of LTL properties, which are not part of standard B. Finally, while [6, 2] can handle Z as well as B specifications, we have interpreters for process languages such as CSP [23, 24] and StAC [16]. These can now be easily coupled with PROB to achieve an integration like [8], where B describes the state and operations of a system and where the process language describes the sequencing of the individual operations.

Another constraint solver over sets is CLP($\mathcal{SET}$) [14].[10] While it does not cater for sequences or relations, we plan to investigate whether CLP($\mathcal{SET}$) can be used to simplify the implementation of PROB. Still, it is far from certain whether CLP($\mathcal{SET}$) will be flexible enough for constraint-based checking.

Another related work is [35], which presents an animator for Z implemented in Mercury. Mercury lacks the (dynamic) co-routining facilities of SICStus Prolog, and [35] uses a preliminary mode inference analysis to figure out the proper order in which B-Kernel predicates should be put. It is unclear to us whether such an approach will work for more involved B machines, and we believe that such an approach will not be able to cope with constraint-based checking. Another, recent animator for Z is ZANS [20]. It has been developed in C++ and unlike PROB only supports deterministic operations (called explicit in [20]).

Our constraint-based checker is strongly related to the ALLOY analyzer developed by Jackson [18, 19]. ALLOY is a special purpose lightweight object language which does not have the same penetration as B, but is well suited to constraint checking. The tool uses SAT solvers to find counter-examples in which an operation relates a consistent before state to an inconsistent after state. The PROB constraint-based checker has been heavily inspired by ALLOY and it would be interesting to compare the performance of ALLOY's SAT solving approach with PROB's constraint solving technique.

---

[10] There are many more constraint solvers over sets; but most of them require sets to be fully instantiated or at least have fixed, pre-determined sizes, c.f., [14].

Future Work: A lot of avenues can be pinpointed for further work. There are still a few features of B left that we need to support, so as to cover the whole language. For example, currently PROB does not yet support multiple machines or abstract constants of complex type (such as functions). An example of such an abstract function may be found in [9] where a constant *net* is used to model the connectivity between track sections in a railway network: *net* ∈ *SECTION* ↔ *SECTION*. The specification includes properties restricting the number of sections that can be directly connected. The relation is not given explicitly, so there will be many models for *net*, depending on the size of the given type *SECTION*.

Another obvious step is, in addition to supporting invariant and abort condition model checking, to allow *refinement* checking. Both the temporal and constraint-based checker can in principle be extended to check whether a refinement machine is a proper refinement of a specification machine, much like FDR checks refinement between CSP processes [30].

Also, it is possible to apply the constraint-based checker on B's proof obligations. If one could extract from say Atelier-B, the unproved proof obligations of a B machine, then one could apply PROB to try to find counter-examples for those proof obligations. This would be of great help in assisting the user, and could prevent him from spending a lot of time trying to prove an unprovable proof obligation.

We are also currently working to extract test cases for boundary conditions from within PROB. PROB is already capable of driving a Java implementation in synchrony with the animator. The hope is to develop a system that can generate test cases and verify them directly on an implementation. Another plan for further work is to link PROB with our U2B converter [32] which is a tool that converts UML models to B specifications.

We would also like to extend PROB so that it can check more complicated temporal properties. Indeed, consistency checking basically amounts to checking the temporal logic formula *AlwaysGlobally*($\neg invariant\_violated$), but it may be interesting to check more involved properties, e.g., that whenever one executes an operation *Request* eventually the *Acknowledge* operation will become enabled. Ideally one could also try to port the PROB system to XSB-Prolog, so as to obtain efficient model checking via tabling in the style of [29, 26]. Unfortunately, XSB Prolog does neither support finite domain constraints nor sophisticated co-routining; hence this will be a major undertaking. However, for those cases where PROB can construct the full state space of a B machine it is already possible to use our model checker [26] to verify CTL [12] formulas.

Finally, now that PROB has acquired sufficient functionality to be practically useful, we can focus some of our efforts on improving the performance of PROB. To that end we plan to compile B machines before animation or model checking, using our partial evaluation system LOGEN [25]. We hope that this will yield a substantial performance improvement.

Conclusion: We have presented the PROB animation and model checking tool for the B method. We believe that this tool will be of high value to people developing B specifications, and our first case studies confirm this. PROB's animation facilities have allowed our users to gain confidence in their specifications, and has allowed them to uncover errors that were not easily discovered by Atelier-B. PROB's model checking capabilities have been even more useful, finding non-trivial counter-examples and allowing one to quickly converge on a correct specification.

In one case, the Volvo vehicle function machine, PROB was actually able to prove the absence of errors (no counter-example exists and model checking was performed on the original unsimplified machine) fully automatically. (Note that it was a non-trivial task to prove this machine correct using Atelier-B.) So, one could argue that we have made it possible to use B without proof. In general, however, it will still be necessary to manually prove the B machine using Atelier-B or the B-Toolkit. Nonetheless, after the model checking a lot of errors should have already been found and corrected, and hopefully proof should be successful.

While it still remains to be seen how PROB will scale for very large B machines, we have demonstrated its usefulness on medium sized specifications. We also believe that PROB could be a valuable tool to teach beginners the B method, allowing them to play with and debug their first specifications.

We plan to release the tool later this year, and make it available at the following URL: http://www.ecs.soton.ac.uk/~mal/systems/prob.html.

Acknowledgements

We would like to thank Laksono Adhianto, Stefan Gruner, Leonid Mikhailov, and especially Carla Ferreira for their help in implementing and testing PROB. We are very grateful to Andy Gravell, Daniel Jackson, Cliff Jones, Steve Schneider, and to anonymous referees of FM'03 for their valuable feedback.

References

1. J.-R. Abrial. *The B-Book*. Cambridge University Press, 1996.
2. F. Ambert, F. Bouquet, S. Chemin, S. Guenaud, B. Legeard, F. Peureux, M. Utting, and N. Vacelet. BZ-testing-tools: A tool-set for test generation from Z and B using constraint logic programming. In *Proceedings of FATES'02, Formal Approaches to Testing of Software*, pages 105–120, August 2002. Technical Report, INRIA.
3. AT&T Labs-Research. Graphviz - open source graph drawing software. Obtainable at http://www.research.att.com/sw/tools/graphviz/.
4. B-Core (UK) Limited, Oxon, UK. *B-Toolkit, On-line manual.*, 1999. Available at http://www.b-core.com/ONLINEDOC/Contents.html.
5. B. Bérard and L. Fribourg. Reachability analysis of (timed) petri nets using real arithmetic. In *Proceedings of Concur'99*, LNCS 1664, pages 178–193. Springer-Verlag, 1999.

6. F. Bouquet, B. Legeard, and F. Peureux. CLPS-B - a constraint solver for B. In J.-P. Katoen and P. Stevens, editors, *Tools and Algorithms for the Construction and Analysis of Systems*, LNCS 2280, pages 188–204. Springer-Verlag, 2002.
7. J. Bowen. Animating the semantics of VERILOG using Prolog. Technical Report UNU/IIST Technical Report no. 176, United Nations University, Macau, 1999.
8. M. Butler. csp2B: A practical approach to combining CSP and B. *Formal Aspects of Computing*, 12:182–198, 2000.
9. M. Butler. A system-based approach to the formal development of embedded controllers for a railway. *Design Automation for Embedded Systems*, 6(4):355–366, 2002,.
10. D. Cabeza and M. Hermenegildo. *The PiLLoW Web Programming Library*. The CLIP Group, School of Computer Science, Technical University of Madrid, 2001. Available at http://www.clip.dia.fi.upm.es/.
11. M. Carlsson and G. Ottosson. An open-ended finite domain constraint solver. In H. G. Glaser, P. H. Hartel, and H. Kuchen, editors, *Proc. Programming Languages: Implementations, Logics, and Programs*, LNCS 1292, pages 191–206. Springer-Verlag, 1997.
12. E. M. Clarke, O. Grumberg, and D. Peled. *Model Checking*. MIT Press, 1999.
13. B. Cui, Y. Dong, X. Du, N. Kumar, C. R. Ramakrishnan, I. V. Ramakrishnan, A. Roychoudhury, S. A. Smolka, and D. S. Warren. Logic programming and model checking. In C. Palamidessi, H. Glaser, and K. Meinke, editors, *Proceedings of ALP/PLILP'98*, LNCS 1490, pages 1–20. Springer-Verlag, 1998.
14. A. Dovier, C. Piazza, E. Pontelli, and G. Rossi. Sets and constraint logic programming. *ACM Transactions on Programming Languages and Systems (TOPLAS)*, 22(5):861–931, 2000.
15. F.Bellegarde, J. Julliand, and H. Mountassir. Model-Based Verification through Refinement of Finite B Event Systems. In *Formal Methods B Users Group Meeting (FM'99 B UGM Meeting)*, September 1999.
16. C. Ferreira and M. Butler. A process compensation language. In T. Santen and B. Stoddart, editors, *Proceedings Integrated Formal Methods (IFM 2000)*, LNCS 1945, pages 424–435. Springer-Verlag, November 2000.
17. P. Henderson. Modelling architectures for dynamic systems. In A. McIver and C. Morgan, editors, *Programming Methodology*. Springer-Verlag, 2003.
18. D. Jackson. Alloy: A lightweight object modelling notation. *ACM Transactions on Software Engineering and Methodology (TOSEM)*, 11:256–290, 2002.
19. D. Jackson, I. Shlyakhter, and M. Sridharan. A micromodularity mechanism. In *ACM SIGSOFT Conference on the Foundations of Software Engineering / European Software Engineering Conference (FSE / ESEC '01)*, pages 256–290, September 2001.
20. X. Jia. An approach to animating Z specifications. Available at http://venus.cs.depaul.edu/fm/zans.html.
21. L. King, G. Gupta, and E. Pontelli. Verification of a controller for BART. In V. L. Winter and S. Bhattacharya, editors, *High Integrity Software*, pages 265–299. Kluwer Academic Publishers, 2001.
22. J.-L. Lanet. The use of B for Smart Card. In *Forum on Design Languages (FDL02)*, September 2002.
23. M. Leuschel. Design and implementation of the high-level specification language CSP(LP) in Prolog. In I. V. Ramakrishnan, editor, *Proceedings of PADL'01*, LNCS 1990, pages 14–28. Springer-Verlag, March 2001.

24. M. Leuschel, L. Adhianto, M. Butler, C. Ferreira, and L. Mikhailov. Animation and model checking of CSP and B using Prolog technology. In *Proceedings of VCL'2001*, pages 97–109, Florence, Italy, September 2001.
25. M. Leuschel, J. Jørgensen, W. Vanhoof, and M. Bruynooghe. Offline specialisation in Prolog using a hand-written compiler generator. *Theory and Practice of Logic Programming*, 2004. To appear.
26. M. Leuschel and T. Massart. Infinite state model checking by abstract interpretation and program specialisation. In A. Bossi, editor, Logic-Based Program Synthesis and Transformation. *Proceedings of LOPSTR'99*, LNCS 1817, pages 63–82, Venice, Italy, 2000.
27. M. Leuschel and T. Massart. Logic programming and partial deduction for the verification of reactive systems: An experimental evaluation. In G. Norman, M. Kwiatkowska, and D. Guelev, editors, *Proceedings of AVoCS 2002, Second Workshop on Automated Verification of Critical Systems*, pages 143–149, 2002. Available as Technical Report CSR-02-6, University of Birmingham.
28. G. D. Plotkin. A structural approach to operational semantics. Technical Report DAIMI FN-19, Aarhus University, 1981.
29. Y. S. Ramakrishna, C. R. Ramakrishnan, I. V. Ramakrishnan, S. A. Smolka, T. Swift, and D. S. Warren. Efficient model checking using tabled resolution. In O. Grumberg, editor, *Proceedings of the International Conference on Computer-Aided Verification (CAV'97)*, LNCS 1254, pages 143–154. Springer-Verlag, 1997.
30. A. W. Roscoe. *The Theory and Practice of Concurrency*. Prentice-Hall, 1999.
31. K. Sagonas, T. Swift, and D. S. Warren. XSB as an efficient deductive database engine. In *Proceedings of the ACM SIGMOD International Conference on the Management of Data*, pages 442–453, Minneapolis, Minnesota, May 1994. ACM.
32. C. Snook and M. Butler. Verifying Dynamic Properties of UML Models by Translation to the B Language and Toolkit. In *UML 2000 WORKSHOP Dynamic Behaviour in UML Models: Semantic Questions*, October 2000.
33. Steria, Aix-en-Provence, France. *Atelier B, User and Reference Manuals*, 1996. Available at http://www.atelierb.societe.com/index_uk.html.
34. Tatibouet, Bruno. *The JBTools Package*, 2001. Available at http://lifc.univ-fcomte.fr/PEOPLE/tatibouet/JBTOOLS/BParser_en.html.
35. M. Winikoff, P. Dart, and E. Kazmierczak. Rapid prototyping using formal specifications. In *Proceedings of the 21st Australasian Computer Science Conference*, pages 279–294, Perth, Australia, February 1998.

SAT-Based Model-Checking of Security Protocols Using Planning Graph Analysis*

Alessandro Armando, Luca Compagna, and Pierre Ganty

DIST – Università degli Studi di Genova, Viale Causa 13 – 16145 Genova, Italy,
{armando,compa,pierre}@mrg.dist.unige.it

Abstract. In previous work we showed that automatic SAT-based model-checking techniques based on a reduction of protocol insecurity problems to satisfiability problems in propositional logic (SAT) can be used effectively to find attacks on security protocols. The approach results from the combination of a reduction of protocol insecurity problems to planning problems and well-known SAT-reduction techniques, called linear encodings, developed for planning. Experimental results confirmed the effectiveness of the approach but also showed that the time spent to generate the SAT formula largely dominates the time spent by the SAT solver to check its satisfiability. Moreover, the SAT instances generated by the tool get of unmanageable size on the most complex protocols. In this paper we explore the application of the Graphplan-based encoding technique to the analysis of security protocols and present experimental data showing that Graphplan-based encodings are considerably (i.e. up to 2 orders of magnitude) smaller than linear encodings. These results confirm the effectiveness of the SAT-based approach to the analysis of security protocols and pave the way to its application to large protocols arising in practical applications.

Keywords: bounded model-checking, security protocols, SAT-solvers, SAT encodings.

1 Introduction

Security (or cryptographic) protocols are communication protocols that aim at providing security guarantees (such as authentication of principals or secrecy of some piece of information) through the application of cryptographic primitives. Since these protocols are at the core of security-sensitive applications in a variety of domains (e.g. health-care, e-commerce, and e-government), their proper functioning is crucial as a failure may undermine the customer and, more in general, the public trust in these applications.

---

* This work was partially funded by the IHP-RTN EC project CALCULEMUS (HPRN-CT-2000-00102), by the FET Open EC Project AVISPA (IST-2001-39252), and by the project "Convenzione per lo svolgimento di tesi di dottorato in una Network di istituzioni europee e mutuo riconoscimento del titolo di dottore di ricerca. (Dottorato in Ingegneria Elettronica e Informatica)" of MIUR.

The problem is that – in spite of their apparent simplicity – security protocols are notoriously error-prone. Many published protocols have been implemented and deployed in real applications only to be found flawed years later. For instance, the Needham-Schroeder authentication protocol [23] was found vulnerable to a serious attack 17 years after its publication [20]. Quite interestingly, many attacks can be carried out without breaking cryptography. These attacks exploit weaknesses in the protocol that are due to the complex and unexpected interleavings of different protocol sessions as well as to the possible interference of malicious agents. Since these weaknesses are very difficult to spot by simple inspection of the protocol specification, security protocols have received growing attention by the formal methods community as a new, very promising and challenging application domain.

In previous work [3] we showed that automatic SAT-based model-checking techniques based on a reduction of protocol insecurity problems to satisfiability problems in propositional logic (SAT) can be used effectively to find attacks on security protocols. The approach results from the combination of a reduction of protocol insecurity problems to planning problems and well-known SAT-reduction techniques, called *linear encodings*, developed for planning (see [18] for a survey on the topic). A model-checker, SATMC, based on our ideas has been developed and experimental results obtained by running SATMC against security protocols drawn from the Clark-Jacob's library [10] confirm the effectiveness of the approach but also show that the time spent to generate the SAT formula largely dominates the time spent by the SAT solver to check its satisfiability. Moreover, the SAT instances generated by the tool get of unmanageable size on the most complex protocols. To cope with the problem in [4] we propose a new model-checking procedure based on an abstraction/refinement loop which interleaves the encoding and the solving phases. In this paper we follow a different route and explore the application of a sophisticated SAT-reduction technique, *Graphplan-based encoding* [18], which has been used with success in AI planning.

Even though linear and Graphplan-based encoding techniques have the same worst case (time and space) complexity, experimental data obtained by running SATMC on protocols drawn from the Clark-Jacob's library clearly indicate that Graphplan-based encodings are considerably (i.e. up to 2 orders of magnitude) smaller than linear encodings. These results confirm the effectiveness of the SAT-based approach to the analysis of security protocols and pave the way to its application to large protocols arising in practical applications. To the best of our knowledge our work is the first (successful) application of Graphplan-based encodings in bounded model-checking [6].

Structure of the paper. We start in Section 2 by introducing security protocol via a very simple (flawed) authentication protocol. In Section 3 we define the notion of protocol insecurity problem and show that it can be seen as a planning problem. Section 4 is devoted to the formal description of the linear and the Graphplan-based encodings together with the presentation of the experimental results. The related work is discussed in Section 5. We conclude in Section 6 with some final remarks and a discussion of the future work.

2 A Simple Example

As mentioned in Section 1 even small and convincing protocols are often wrong. To illustrate, consider the following one-way authentication protocol:

$$(1) \quad A \rightarrow B : \{N\}_K$$
$$(2) \quad B \rightarrow A : \{f(N)\}_K$$

where N is a nonce[1] generated by Alice, K is a symmetric key, f is a function known to Alice and Bob, and $\{X\}_K$ denotes the result of encrypting text X with key K. Successful execution of the protocol should convince Alice that she has been talking with Bob, since only Bob could have formed the appropriate response to the message issued in (1). In fact, Ivory can deceit Alice into believing that she is talking with Bob whereas she is talking with her. This is achieved by executing concurrently two sessions of the protocol and using messages from one session to form messages in the other as illustrated by the following protocol trace:

$$(1.1) \quad A \rightarrow I(B) : \{N\}_K$$
$$(2.1) \quad I(B) \rightarrow A : \{N\}_K$$
$$(2.2) \quad A \rightarrow I(B) : \{f(N)\}_K$$
$$(1.2) \quad I(B) \rightarrow A : \{f(N)\}_K$$

Alice starts the protocol with message (1.1).[2] Ivory intercepts the message and (pretending to be Bob) starts a second session with Alice by replaying the received message – cf. step (2.1). Alice replies to this message with message (2.2). But this is exactly the message Alice is waiting to receive in the first protocol session. This allows Ivory to finish the first session by using it – cf. (1.2). At the end of the above steps Alice believes she has been talking with Bob, but this is obviously not the case.

3 Protocol Insecurity Problems and Planning Problems

We model the concurrent execution of a protocol by means of a state transition system. Following [8, 17], we represent states by sets of variables-free atomic formulae and transitions by means of rewrite rules over sets of facts.

3.1 Protocol Insecurity Problems

A *protocol insecurity problem* is a tuple $\Xi = \langle \mathcal{S}, \mathcal{L}, \mathcal{R}, \mathcal{I}, \mathcal{B} \rangle$ where $\mathcal{S}$ is a set of atomic formulae of a sorted first-order language called *facts*, $\mathcal{L}$ is a set of function symbols called *rule labels*, and $\mathcal{R}$ is a set of rewrite rules of the form $L \xrightarrow{\ell} R$, where L and R are finite subsets of $\mathcal{S}$ such that the variables occurring

---
[1] *Nonces* are numbers generated by principals that are intended to be used *only once*.
[2] Notice that with $(i.j)$ we indicate that the message has been sent at protocol step j of session i.

in R occur also in L, and ℓ is an expression of the form $l(x)$ where $l \in \mathcal{L}$ and x is the vector of variables obtained by ordering lexicographically the variables occurring in L. Let S be a state and $(L \xrightarrow{\ell} R) \in \mathcal{R}$, if σ is a substitution such that $L\sigma \subseteq S$, then one possible next state of S is $S' = (S \setminus L\sigma) \cup R\sigma$ and we indicate this with $S \xrightarrow{\ell\sigma} S'$. We assume the rewrite rules are *deterministic* i.e. if $S \xrightarrow{\ell\sigma} S'$ and $S \xrightarrow{\ell\sigma} S''$, then $S' = S''$. The components $\mathcal{I}$ and $\mathcal{B}$ of a protocol insecurity problem are the initial state and a set of the bad states of the protocol respectively. A *solution to a protocol insecurity problem* Ξ (i.e. an attack to the protocol) is a sequence of rewrite rules $l_1\sigma_1, \ldots, l_n\sigma_n$ such that $S_i \xrightarrow{\ell_i\sigma_i} S_{i+1}$ for $i = 1, \ldots, n$ with $S_1 = \mathcal{I}$ and $S_n \in \mathcal{B}$.

A protocol insecurity problem specifies the runs allowed by the protocol when embedded in a hostile environment together with an initial state and a set of bad states (i.e. states whose reachability implies the violation of the desired security properties). The states of the transition system model the state of the honest principals, the knowledge of the intruder, as well as the messages sent over the channel but not yet processed by the intended recipients (or diverted by the intruder). Rewrite rules model the legal transitions that can be performed by honest participants as well as the abilities of the intruder. For the simple protocol presented in Section 2, facts are of the form:

- $i(t)$, meaning that the intruder knows the term t;
- $c(t)$, meaning that the fresh terms counter is equal to t;
- $m(j, s, r, t)$, meaning that a message t has been sent (supposedly) from principal s to principal r at protocol step j, and
- $w(j, s, r, [t_1, \ldots, t_k])$, representing the state of execution of principal r at step j; it means that r knows the terms $t_1, \ldots, t_k$ at step j, and (if $j = 1, 2$) that r is waiting for a message from s for step j to be executed.

The initial state of the system is:[3]

$$c(0) \cdot w(0, a, a, []) \cdot w(1, a, b, []) \cdot w(0, b, b, []) \cdot w(1, b, a, []) \cdot i(a) \cdot i(b)$$

Facts $w(0, a, a, [])$, $w(1, a, b, [])$, $w(0, b, b, [])$, and $w(1, b, a, [])$ state that principals a and b are ready to play both the role of the initiator and of the responder. Fact $c(0)$ states that the fresh terms counter is initialized with the value 0. Finally $i(a)$ and $i(b)$ state that the identities of a and b are known to the intruder.

The behavior of the honest principals and of the intruder is specified by means of rewrite rules. The activity of sending the first message is modeled by:[4]

$$c(T) \cdot w(0, A, A, []) \xrightarrow{step_1(A,B,T)} c(s(T)) \cdot m(1, A, B, \{n(T)\}_k)$$
$$\cdot w(2, B, A, [f(n(T))])$$

---

[3] To improve readability we use the "." operator as set constructor. For instance, we write "$x \cdot y \cdot z$" to denote the set $\{x, y, z\}$.
[4] Here and in sequel we use capital letters to denote variables.

Notice that in the above rule a nonce is generated thus the counter of fresh terms is incremented. Notice also that term $f(n(T))$ is added to the acquired knowledge of A for subsequent use. The receipt of the message and the reply of the responder is modeled by:

$$m(1, A, B, \{n(T)\}_k) \cdot w(1, A, B, []) \xrightarrow{step_2(A,B,T)} m(2, B, A, \{f(n(T))\}_k)$$
$$\cdot w(3, B, B, [])$$

The final step of the protocol is modeled by:

$$m(2, B, A, \{f(n(T))\}_k) \cdot w(2, B, A, [f(n(T))]) \xrightarrow{step_3(A,B,T)} w(4, A, A, [])$$

where steps 3 and 4 occurring as first parameter in w-fact are used to denote the final state of the responder and of the initiator, respectively.

The following rule models the ability of the intruder of diverting the information exchanged by the honest participants:

$$m(J, S, R, T) \xrightarrow{divert(J,R,S,T)} i(R) \cdot i(S) \cdot i(T) \qquad (1)$$

The ability of encrypting and decrypting messages is modeled by:

$$i(T) \cdot i(K) \xrightarrow{encrypt(K,T)} i(\{T\}_K) \qquad (2)$$
$$i(\{T\}_K) \cdot i(K) \xrightarrow{decrypt(K,T)} i(T) \qquad (3)$$

Finally, the intruder can send arbitrary messages possibly faking somebody-else's identity in doing so:

$$i(T) \cdot i(S) \cdot i(R) \xrightarrow{fake(J,R,S,T)} m(J, S, R, T)$$

Notice that with the above rules we represent the most general intruder based on the Dolev-Yao model [12]. In this model the intruder has the abilities to eavesdrop, divert and memorize messages as well as to compose, decompose, encrypt and decrypt – when he has the decryption key i.e. *perfect cryptography* – messages. Finally, he can send those messages to other participants with a false identity. It is worth pointing out that the rewrite rule formalism allows us to represent others intruders models. For instance, suppose honest agents belong to a local network, while the intruder does not. In this case the intruder cannot overhear and/or divert messages exchanged between honest agents. This can be simply modelled by removing the rewrite rule (1).

A security protocol is intended to enjoy a specific security property. In our example this property is the ability of authenticating Bob to Alice. A security property can be specified by providing a set of "bad" states, i.e. states whose reachability implies a violation of the property. For instance, any state containing a subset of facts of the form $w(4, A, A, []) \cdot w(1, A, B, [])$ (i.e. A has finished a run of the protocol as initiator and B is still at the beginning of the protocol run as responder) witnesses a violation of the expected authentication property and therefore it should be considered as a bad state. It is easy to build a propositional formula G such that each model of G represents a bad state. For the above example $G \equiv (w(4,a,a,[\,]) \wedge w(1,a,b,[\,])) \vee (w(4,b,b,[\,]) \wedge w(1,b,a,[\,]))$.

3.2 Planning Problem

A *planning problem* is a tuple $\Pi = \langle \mathcal{F}, \mathcal{A}, Ops, I, G \rangle$, where $\mathcal{F}$ and $\mathcal{A}$ are disjoint sets of variable-free atomic formulae of a sorted first-order language called *fluents* and *actions* respectively; Ops is a set of expressions of the form $(Pre \xrightarrow{Act} Add ; Del)$ where $Act \in \mathcal{A}$ and Pre, Add, and Del are finite sets of fluents such that $Add \cap Del = \emptyset$; I is a set of fluents representing the initial state and G is a boolean combination of fluents representing the final states. A state is represented by a set S of fluents meaning that all the fluents in S hold in the state, while all the fluents in $\mathcal{F} \setminus S$ do not hold in the state (close-world-assumption). An action is applicable in a state S iff the action preconditions (fluents in Pre) occur in S and the application of the action leads to a new state obtained from S by removing the fluents in Del and adding those in Add. A *solution to a planning problem* Π, called *plan*, is a sequence of actions whose execution leads from the initial state to a final state and the preconditions of each action appears in the state to which it applies. The *length* of a plan is the number of actions occurring in it. Plans can be represented in a compact way by means of a partial-order plan. A *partial-order plan* is a pair $\langle \Lambda, \leq \rangle$ where Λ is a set of pairs $\langle \alpha, i \rangle$ such that $\alpha \in \mathcal{A}$ and $i \in \{0, 1, \ldots\}$, and $\leq$ is a partial order[5] on $\{0, 1, \ldots\}$. A plan $\mathcal{P}$ is in the set of the plans denoted by the partial-order plan $\langle \Lambda, \leq \rangle$ iff (i) there exists a bijection between $\mathcal{P}$ and Λ and (ii) for each $\langle \alpha, i \rangle, \langle \beta, j \rangle \in \Lambda$ such that $j \not\leq i$ there is a subsequence of $\mathcal{P}$ in which α precedes β. The *length* of the partial-order plan $\langle \Lambda, \leq \rangle$ is the cardinality of the set $\{i \mid \langle \alpha, i \rangle \in \Lambda\}$. For instance, the partial-order plan $\langle \{\langle a, 0 \rangle, \langle b, 0 \rangle, \langle c, 3 \rangle, \langle d, 5 \rangle, \langle a, 5 \rangle\}, \{0 \leq 0, 0 \leq 3, 0 \leq 5, 3 \leq 3, 3 \leq 5, 5 \leq 5\} \rangle$ has length 3 and represents the set of plans $\{\langle a, b, c, d, a \rangle, \langle b, a, c, d, a \rangle, \langle a, b, c, a, d \rangle, \langle b, a, c, a, d \rangle\}$.

3.3 Protocol Insecurity Problems as Planning Problems

Given a protocol insecurity problem $\varXi = \langle \mathcal{S}, \mathcal{L}, \mathcal{R}, \mathcal{I}, \mathcal{B} \rangle$, it is possible to build a planning problem $\Pi_\varXi = \langle \mathcal{F}_\varXi, \mathcal{A}_\varXi, Ops_\varXi, I_\varXi, G_\varXi \rangle$ such that each solution to $\Pi_\varXi$ can be translated back to a solution to $\varXi$: $\mathcal{F}_\varXi$ is the set of facts $\mathcal{S}$; $\mathcal{A}_\varXi$ and $Ops_\varXi$ are the smallest sets such that $l\sigma \in \mathcal{A}_\varXi$ and $L\sigma \xrightarrow{l\sigma} R\sigma \setminus L\sigma; L\sigma \setminus R\sigma \in Ops$ for all $(L \xrightarrow{\ell} R) \in \mathcal{R}$ and all ground substitutions σ; finally $I_\varXi \equiv \mathcal{I}$ and $G_\varXi = \bigvee_{S_B \in \mathcal{B}} (\bigwedge S_B \wedge \mathcal{S} \setminus S_B)$.

---

[5] A reflexive, antisymmetric, and transitive binary relation.

4 Automatic SAT-Compilation of Planning Problems

Let $\Pi = \langle \mathcal{F}, \mathcal{A}, Ops, I, G \rangle$ be a planning problem with finite $\mathcal{F}$ and $\mathcal{A}$ and let n be a positive integer, then it is possible to build a propositional formula Φ_Π^n such that any model of Φ_Π^n corresponds to a partial-order plan of length n representing solutions of Π. The encoding of a planning problem into a set of SAT formulae can be done in a variety of ways (see [18, 14] for a survey). The basic idea is to add an additional time-index to the actions and fluents to indicate the state at which the action begins or the fluent holds. Fluents are thus indexed by 0 through n and actions by 0 through $n - 1$. If p is a fluent or an action and i is an index in the appropriate range, then p^i is the corresponding time-indexed propositional variable.

In the rest of this section we will formally describe the linear and the Graphplan-based encodings. These encoding techniques have been implemented in SATMC [3]. In order to compare them in the domain of security protocols, we have run SATMC against a selection of (flawed) security protocols drawn from [10]. For each protocol we have built a corresponding protocol insecurity problem modeling a scenario with a bounded number of principals which exchange messages on a channel controlled by the most general intruder based on the Dolev-Yao model. Moreover, we assume perfect cryptography (see Section 2) and that all atoms are typed i.e. we do not allow for type confusion (*strong typing assumption*).[6]

It is worth pointing out that SATMC is one of the back-ends of the AVISS tool [2]. Using the tool, the user can specify a protocol and the security properties to be checked using a high-level specification language similar to the Alice&Bob notation we used in Section 2 to present our simple authentication protocol. The AVISS tool translates the specification into a rewrite-based declarative Intermediate Format (IF) based on multiset rewriting which is amenable to formal analysis. SATMC can optionally accept protocol specifications in the IF language which are then automatically translated into equivalent planning problems.

4.1 The Linear Encoding

By using linear encoding techniques, Φ_Π^n is defined by

$$\Phi_\Pi^n = \iota(\boldsymbol{f}^0) \wedge \bigwedge_{i=0}^{n-1} \tau(\boldsymbol{f}^i, \boldsymbol{\alpha}^i, \boldsymbol{f}^{i+1}) \wedge \gamma(\boldsymbol{f}^n) \tag{4}$$

where $\boldsymbol{f}$ and $\boldsymbol{\alpha}$ are vectors of the fluents and actions in $\mathcal{F}$ and $\mathcal{A}$ respectively and

- $\iota(\boldsymbol{f}^0)$ is a formula encoding the initial state and is a conjunction of the formulae f^0 if $f \in I$ and $\neg f^0$ if $f \notin I$;

---

[6] As pointed out in [16] type-flaw attacks can be prevented by tagging the fields of a message with information indicating its intended type.

- $\gamma(\boldsymbol{f^n})$ is a formula encoding the final states and is obtained from G by replacing each fluent f with f^n;
- $\tau(\boldsymbol{f^i}, \boldsymbol{\alpha^i}, \boldsymbol{f^{i+1}})$ is a formula encoding the transition relation and is a conjunction of the *Universal Axioms*:

$$\alpha^i \supset \bigwedge \{f^i \mid f \in Pre\}$$
$$\alpha^i \supset \bigwedge \{f^{i+1} \mid f \in Add\}$$
$$\alpha^i \supset \bigwedge \{\neg f^{i+1} \mid f \in Del\}$$

for each $(Pre \xrightarrow{\alpha} Add\,;Del) \in Ops$, the *Explanatory Frame Axioms*:

$$(f^i \wedge \neg f^{i+1}) \supset \bigvee \left\{\alpha^i \mid (Pre \xrightarrow{\alpha} Add\,;Del) \in Ops, f \in Del\right\}$$
$$(\neg f^i \wedge f^{i+1}) \supset \bigvee \left\{\alpha^i \mid (Pre \xrightarrow{\alpha} Add\,;Del) \in Ops, f \in Add\right\}$$

for all fluents f, and the *Conflict Exclusion Axioms (CEA)*: $\neg(\alpha_1^i \wedge \alpha_2^i)$ for all $\alpha_1 \neq \alpha_2$ such that $(Pre_1 \xrightarrow{\alpha_1} Add_1\,;Del_1) \in Ops$, $(Pre_2 \xrightarrow{\alpha_2} Add_2\,;Del_2) \in Ops$, and $Pre_1 \cap Del_2 \neq \emptyset$ or $Pre_2 \cap Del_1 \neq \emptyset$.

It is immediate to see that the number of literals in Φ_Π^n is in $O(n|\mathcal{F}|+n|\mathcal{A}|)$. Moreover the number of clauses generated by the Universal Axioms is in $O(nP_0|\mathcal{A}|)$ where P_0 is the maximal number of fluents mentioned in an operator (usually a small number); the number of clauses generated by the Explanatory Frame Axioms is in $O(n|\mathcal{F}|)$; finally, the number of clauses generated by the CEA is in $O(n|\mathcal{A}|^2)$.

Computer experiments obtained by using linear encodings with increasing values of n and feeding the propositional formula generated at each step to a state-of-the-art SAT solver[7] soon showed that solving time is largely dominated by encoding time and that the latter is strictly related to the size of the SAT instances generated. We thus found it convenient to apply an *Abstraction Refinement Loop* [4] based on the idea of disabling the generation of the CEA and checking if the "pseudo" partial-order plan[8] found can be linearized (and hence executed). SATMC therefore looks for conflicting actions in the pseudo partial-order plan found and extends the previously generated formula with clauses negating the conflicts (if any). The resulting formula is then fed back to the SAT-solver and the whole procedure is iterated until a solution without conflicts is met or the formula becomes unsatisfiable. The results of our experiments are reported in Table 1 with the generation of the CEA enabled (**CEA=on**) and disabled (**CEA=off**).[9] For each protocol we give the smallest value of n at which the attack is found (**N**), the number of propositional variables (**A**) and clauses (**CL**) in the SAT formula (in thousands), the time spent to generate the SAT

---

[7] Currently Chaff [22], SIM [15], and SATO [26] are supported.
[8] A "pseudo" partial-order plan corresponds to a set of sequences of actions such that each sequence in the set is not guaranteed to be executable.
[9] Experiments have been carried out on a PC with a 1.4 GHz Processor and 1 GB of RAM.

formula (**EncT**), the time spent by Chaff to solve the last SAT formula (**Last**), and the total time spent by Chaff to solve all the SAT formulae generated for that protocol (**Tot**).[10] If the generation of the CEA is disabled, then the number of iterations of the Abstraction Refinement Loop is also given (#).

As anticipated, the data show that solving time is largely dominated by encoding time. However the size of the SAT formulae and the time to generate them drop significantly if CEA are disabled and the Abstraction Refinement Loop is activated. Notice that by applying the Abstraction Refinement strategy we are able to discover attacks to security protocols such as *Andrew*, *KaoChow 3* and *Woo-Lam M* that could not be analyzed with CEA enabled.

4.2 The Graphplan-Based Encoding[11]

By using the linear encoding thechnique, the encoding of the transition relation $- \tau(\boldsymbol{f}^i, \boldsymbol{\alpha}^i, \boldsymbol{f}^{i+1}) -$ is independent from the time step and this means that important simplifications are possible on the resulting formula. For instance, not all the actions are applicable at time step 0 but the formula

$$\tau(\boldsymbol{f}^0, \boldsymbol{\alpha}^0, \boldsymbol{f}^1) \tag{5}$$

encodes the effects of all possible actions. By looking at the initial state it is possible to build a simple but equivalent version of (5), say

$$\tau_0(\boldsymbol{f}^0, \boldsymbol{\alpha}^0, \boldsymbol{f}^1).$$

The same line of reasoning can be applied at the subsequent steps: by computing an over-approximation of the reachable steps at time step i we can then determine a simplified encoding of the transition relation at time step i, say $\tau_i(\boldsymbol{f}^i, \boldsymbol{\alpha}^i, \boldsymbol{f}^{i+1})$, for $i = 0, \ldots, n-1$.

Graphplan-based encoding[12] is based on this idea and preliminary to the generation of the encoding is the construction of a data structure (called planning graph) used to determine (among other things) an over-approximation of the reachable states at each time step i.

Let $k \geq 0$, then a *k-planning graph* for a planning problem $\langle \mathcal{F}, \mathcal{A}, Ops, I, G \rangle$ is a directed acyclic graph $G = \langle N_f, N_a, \xrightarrow[pre]{}, \xrightarrow[add]{}, \xrightarrow[del]{}, \oplus \rangle$ where N_f is a time-indexed family of sets of *fluent nodes*, i.e. $N_f = N_f^0 \cup \cdots \cup N_f^k$ where N_f^i is the set of fluent nodes of *layer* i; N_a is a time-indexed family of sets of *action nodes*, i.e. $N_a = N_a^0 \cup \cdots \cup N_a^{k-1}$ where N_a^i is the set of action nodes of *layer* i; $\xrightarrow[pre]{}$ is a time-indexed relation between fluent nodes and action nodes, i.e.

---

[10] Times are measured in seconds.
[11] Graphplan was the first planner due to Blum and Furst that uses the planning graph data structure. So when we talk about Graphplan we mean the algorithm defined in [7] that works on the planning graph data structure following a paradigm called Planning Graph Analysis.
[12] See [25] for a survey.

Table 1. Experimental data using the linear encoding

Protocol	N	A	CEA = on				CEA = off				
			CL	EncT	SolvingT		CL	EncT	SolvingT		
					Last	Tot			Last	Tot	#
Andrew	9	145	-	-	-	-	2,256	111.4	2.0	12.1	1
EKE	5	62	13,949	7,100	7.6	19.7	783	74.1	0.7	3.7	2
ISO-CCF-1 U	4	<1	<1	0.1	0.0	0.0	<1	0.1	0.0	0.0	0
ISO-CCF-2 M	4	<1	6	0.3	0.0	0.1	4	0.2	0.0	0.1	0
ISO-PK-1 U	4	<1	2	0.1	0.0	0.0	2	0.1	0.0	0.0	0
ISO-PK-2 M	4	2	17	0.9	0.0	0.0	10	0.6	0.1	0.1	0
ISO-SK-1 U	4	<1	<1	0.1	0.0	0.0	<1	0.1	0.0	0.0	1
ISO-SK-2 M	4	<1	3	0.4	0.0	0.0	3	0.4	0.0	0.0	0
KaoChow 1	7	36	355	18.4	0.1	0.7	131	8.0	0.1	0.7	4
KaoChow 2	9	586	35,178	1,494	-	-	1,804	140.4	1.6	15.6	5
KaoChow 3	9	995	-	-	-	-	5,737	585.5	7.5	41.6	1
KLS rep.	-	-	-	-	-	-	-	-	-	-	-
NSCK	9	115	787	41.3	0.4	1.6	334	17.1	0.3	1.3	0
NSPK	7	7	51	2.3	0.1	0.1	33	1.5	0.1	0.1	0
NSPK-server	8	9	212	8.0	0.1	0.2	54	2.8	0.1	0.1	0
SPLICE	9	14	91	4.6	0.1	0.2	62	3.6	0.1	0.2	0
Swick 1	5	4	17	1.0	0.1	0.1	13	0.8	0.0	0.1	1
Swick 2	6	8	59	3.2	0.1	0.1	29	1.7	0.1	0.1	0
Swick 3	4	5	12	0.8	0.1	0.1	11	0.7	0.0	0.1	1
Swick 4	5	15	64	11.0	0.1	0.2	57	10.2	0.1	0.3	1
Stubblebine rep	3	13	2,048	82.9	0.3	0.6	95	6.3	0.1	0.1	1
Woo-Lam M	6	481	-	-	-	-	2,498	304.4	1.8	7.7	1

- means that this data information is not available, because a memory out has been reached during the protocol analysis;
< 1 means that the number of atoms or clauses is less than 1 thousand.

$\xrightarrow[pre]{i} \subseteq N_a^i \times N_f^i$, whose instances are called *preconditions* edges; $\xrightarrow[add]{}$ and $\xrightarrow[del]{}$ are time-indexed binary relations between action nodes and fluent nodes, i.e. $\xrightarrow[add]{i} \subseteq N_a^i \times N_f^{i+1}$ and $\xrightarrow[del]{i} \subseteq N_a^i \times N_f^{i+1}$, whose instances are called *add edges* and *delete edges* respectively; finally $\oplus = \bigcup_{0 \leq i \leq k} \oplus_f^i \cup \bigcup_{0 \leq j \leq k-1} \oplus_a^j$ is a time-indexed (commutative) relation of mutual exclusion (mutex for short) between nodes, i.e. $\oplus_f^i \subseteq N_f^i \times N_f^i$ and $\oplus_a^j \subseteq N_a^j \times N_a^j$.

More in detail, the k-planning graph associated to a planning problem $\Pi = \langle \mathcal{F}, \mathcal{A}, Ops, I, G \rangle$ is inductively defined as follows:

1. $f \in N_f^0$ iff $f \in I$ and $f \in N_f^i$ iff there exists $a \in N_a^{i-1}$ such that $a \xrightarrow[add]{i-1} f$ for $i = 1, \ldots, k$;
2. $a \in N_a^i$ iff $(Pre \xrightarrow{a} Add ; Del) \in Ops$, $Pre \subseteq N_f^i$, and for all fluents $f, f' \in Pre$ not $f \oplus^i f'$ for $i = 0, \ldots, k-1$;
3. $a \xrightarrow[pre]{i} f$ iff $(Pre \cup \{f\} \xrightarrow{a} Add ; Del) \in Ops$ for $i = 0, \ldots, k-1$;

4. $a \xrightarrow[add]{}^i f$ iff $(Pre \xrightarrow{a} Add \cup \{f\}; Del) \in Ops$ for $i = 0, \ldots, k-1$;
5. $a \xrightarrow[del]{}^i f$ iff $(Pre \xrightarrow{a} Add ; Del \cup \{f\}) \in Ops$ for $i = 0, \ldots, k-1$;
6. $a \oplus_a^i a'$ iff $a \neq a'$ and (i) either there exists $f \in \mathcal{F}$ s.t. $a \xrightarrow[del]{}^i f$, and $a' \xrightarrow[add]{}^i f$ or $a' \xrightarrow[pre]{}^i f$, (ii) or there exist $f, f' \in \mathcal{F}$ s.t. $a \xrightarrow[pre]{}^i f, a' \xrightarrow[pre]{}^i f'$, and $f \oplus_f^i f'$ for $i = 0, \ldots, k-1$;
7. $f \oplus_f^i f'$ iff $f \neq f'$ and for all $a \in \mathcal{A}$ such that $a \xrightarrow[add]{}^{i-1} f$ and for all $a' \in \mathcal{A}$ such that $a' \xrightarrow[add]{}^{i-1} f'$ we have $a \oplus_a^{i-1} a'$ for $i = 1, \ldots, k$.

Our Graphplan-based algorithm alternates two phases: *graph expansion* and *solution extraction* which are iterated until a necessary (but not sufficient) condition for plan existence is achieved: there exists a subset S of N_f^k that corresponds to a state represented by G and there are no pairs $f_1, f_2 \in S$ such that $f_1 \oplus_f^k f_2$. During the graph expansion phase, the planning graph is extended by appending one action layer, which contains all actions that are applicable, and a fluent layer which is the union of the effects of the newly added action layer and the last fluent layer. The algorithm also calculates the mutex constraints for each newly added *action* and *fluent* layers.

Notice that, we also introduces "nop" actions, which provide the links between the identical fluents appearing in consecutive layers. The resulting planning graph is a compact way to represent an over-approximation of the forward search tree (i.e. the tree representing the forward reachable state space starting from the initial state). This planning graph is built in polynomial time with respect to the size of the corresponding planning problem. (See [7] for details.)

Once the planning graph expansion phase is completed, the algorithm carries out the solution extraction phase. This phase produces the equivalent SAT encoding of planning graph. This translation from the planning graph to SAT is due to Kautz and Selman in [18]. By equivalent we mean that the propositional formula Φ_Π^n is such that any model of Φ_Π^n corresponds to a partial-order plan of length n.

The encoding of a planning problem into SAT via the planning graph analysis of the planning problem is of the form :

$$\Phi_\Pi^n = \iota(\boldsymbol{f}^0) \wedge \bigwedge_{i=0}^{n-1} \tau_i(\boldsymbol{f}^i, \boldsymbol{\alpha}^i, \boldsymbol{f}^{i+1}) \wedge \gamma(\boldsymbol{f}^n)$$

where $\boldsymbol{f}$ and $\boldsymbol{\alpha}$ are vectors of the fluents and actions in $\mathcal{F}$ and $\mathcal{A}$ respectively and

- $\iota(\boldsymbol{f}^0)$ is a formula encoding the initial state and is a conjunction of the formulae f^0 if $f \in N_f^0$;
- $\gamma(\boldsymbol{f}^n)$ is a formula encoding the final states built out of G. Without loss of generality we assume that the formula G is in disjunctive normal form. The formula $\gamma(\boldsymbol{f}^n)$ is built from G by removing the disjunctions containing fluents not occuring in N_f^n.

Table 2. Experimental data using the Graphplan-based encoding

Protocol	N	$\oplus = \oplus_a \cup \oplus_f$				$\oplus = \widehat{\oplus}$			
		A	CL	EncT	SolT	A	CL	EncT	SolT
Andrew	9	699	4,459	17.0	0.0	701	1,811	1.5	0.0
EKE	5	545	3,584	10.9	0.0	553	1,648	1.5	0.0
ISO-CCF-1 U	4	154	621	0.2	0.0	154	398	0.1	0.0
ISO-CCF-2 M	4	169	600	0.3	0.0	169	402	0.2	0.0
ISO-PK-1 U	4	202	794	0.5	0.0	202	494	0.2	0.0
ISO-PK-2 M	4	196	707	0.6	0.0	196	468	0.2	0.0
ISO-SK-1 U	4	142	561	0.2	0.0	142	367	0.1	0.0
ISO-SK-2 M	4	234	747	0.5	0.0	234	511	0.2	0.0
KaoChow 1	7	526	4,055	14.6	0.0	583	2,230	1.5	0.01
KaoChow 2	9	1,020	10,325	108.1	0.02	1,136	4,507	4.2	0.03
KaoChow 3	9	1,229	18,532	419.1	0.01	1,467	7,927	8.8	0.05
KLS rep.	7	2,018	62,836	3,557.4	0.03	2,092	31,510	23.5	0.07
NSCK	9	622	3,823	9.5	0.01	627	1,710	1.3	0.01
NSPK	7	559	3,129	6.7	0.0	572	1,555	1.0	0.0
NSPK-server	8	1,077	6,043	24.5	0.0	1,079	2,951	3.9	0.0
SPLICE	9	972	7,545	52.2	0.01	1,008	2,953	3.8	0.0
Swick 1	5	329	1,300	1.1	0.0	329	783	0.4	0.01
Swick 2	6	438	1,937	2.6	0.0	438	1,143	0.1	0.0
Swick 3	4	231	889	0.7	0.0	231	594	0.3	0.0
Swick 4	5	405	1,469	2.7	0.0	405	939	0.6	0.0
Stubblebine rep	3	220	791	0.7	0.0	222	608	0.3	0.0
Woo-Lam M	6	665	3,806	17.3	0.0	687	1,813	2.9	0.0

- $\mathcal{T}_i(\boldsymbol{f}^i, \boldsymbol{\alpha}^i, \boldsymbol{f}^{i+1})$ is a formula encoding the transition relation at step i and is a conjunction of the *Action Preconditions Add-Effects Axioms*:

$$\alpha^i \supset \bigwedge \{f^i \mid \alpha \xrightarrow[pre]{i} f\} \qquad \alpha^i \supset \bigwedge \{f^{i+1} \mid \alpha \xrightarrow[add]{i} f\}$$

for all α in N_a^i, the *Backward Chaining Axioms*:

$$f^{i+1} \supset \bigvee \{\alpha^i \mid \alpha \xrightarrow[add]{i} f\}$$

for all f in N_f^{i+1}, and the *Mutex Axioms*: $\neg(a^i \wedge b^i)$ for all a and b such that $a \oplus b$.

The results of our experiments are reported in Table 2. For each protocol we give the smallest value of n at which the attack is found (**N**), the number of propositional variables (**A**) and clauses (**CL**) in the SAT formula, the time spent to generate the SAT formulae (**EncT**) and the total time spent by the SAT solver to solve the SAT formulae (**SolT**).

The columns of the table headed by $\oplus = \oplus_a \cup \oplus_f$ contain the results of experiments that we carried out with our implementation of the Graphplan algorithm.

Results show that the algorithm performs well on a large set of examples, however, for bigger ones (see, e.g., *KLS rep.* protocol) the time spent at generating the formula (**EncT**) gets high. This observation led us at investigating a new direction based on the computation of a weaker version of the mutex relation.

An interesting point shown in [11] is that, on average, the computation of the mutex relation between fluent nodes is time consuming. In our first implementation of the Graphplan algorithm mutexes were computed following clauses 6 and 7. We implemented a second version in which we restrict the computation on action nodes only (i.e. $\oplus = \oplus_a$). If we examine the inductive definition of $\oplus_a$ (clause 6) we see that only case *(i)* is relevant since $\oplus_f = \emptyset$. We call this particular subset of the mutex relation between nodes *static mutexes* (as in [11]) noted $\widehat{\oplus}$ and we call *dynamic mutexes* the set $\widetilde{\oplus} = \oplus \setminus \widehat{\oplus}$. This latter set is made of the mutexes between fluent node (clause 7) and mutexes between actions nodes defined by the case *(ii)* in clause 6.

Table 2 shows that when we restrict the computation of $\oplus$ to $\widehat{\oplus}$ (columns headed by $\oplus = \widehat{\oplus}$) we have a gain up to two orders of magnitude in the time of the planning graph analysis. See for instance the *KLS rep.* protocol.

By considering a weaker version of the mutex relation, we obtain a rougher over-approximation of the forward search tree since the more mutexes we have, the more accurate is the over-approximation. On the other side, when we compute all mutexes, we get either a less or equal number of atoms and a greater or equal number of clauses. This means that the over-approximation is more accurate. However experimental results show that this gain in accuracy on the over-approximation does not pay off (see, e.g., the *KaoChow 3* protocol).

We have also considered a third implementation of the algorithm characterized by the fact that we do not build the mutex relation and hence we do not generate any "Mutex Axioms" during the solution extraction phase. Similarly to the linear encoding, we apply an *Abstraction Refinement Loop* that checks if the pseudo partial-order plan found can be linearized (and hence executed). SATMC therefore looks for conflicting actions[13] in the pseudo partial-order plan found and extends the previously generated formula with clauses negating the conflicts (if any). The resulting formula is then fed back to the SAT-solver and the whole procedure is iterated until a solution without conflicts is met or the formula becomes unsatisfiable. However applying the Abstraction Refinement Loop to the Graphplan encoding, we do not have the same gain as in the linear encoding case. Also, there are no significant improvement in performance when compared to the second version of the algorithm.

The comparison between the linear and the Graphplan-based encoding techniques is summarized in Figures 1 and 2. For each encoding techniques and for each protocol those figures show (in logarithmic scale) the size of the SAT formulae (number of atoms and clauses), and the encoding time, respectively. Notice that, concerning the linear encoding technique we plot the results obtained by applying the Abstraction Refinement Loop (see Section 4.1), while concerning

---

[13] Differently from the linear encoding, two distinct actions α_1, α_2 are said to be in conflict iff $\alpha_1 \widehat{\oplus} \alpha_2$

the Graphplan-based encoding technique we report the results obtained by generating only the weaker version of the mutex relation. The comparison shows that, by using the Graphplan-based encoding technique, we obtain (i) SAT instances whose size is up to 2 orders of magnitude smaller and, in most of the cases, (ii) better encoding and solving times. This enables SATMC to analyze protocols (e.g., the KLS rep. protocol), that were not feasible using the linear approach. However, there are situations in which the use of the linear encoding technique is preferable to the use of the Graphplan-based encoding. For instance, in the domain of security protocols we are interested in analyzing scenarios in which a bounded number of concurrent sessions is specified without any constraint on which agent will play a particular role in a session. Therefore, instead of a single initial state, in these situations we have to deal with a set of possible initial states. By using the linear encoding it is sufficient to define $\iota(\boldsymbol{f}^0)$ to be a formula whose models are all the possible initial states. The application of the Graphplan-based encoding to the above scenario requires the analysis of a sequence of different problems (one for each possible initial state) and thus much of the efficiency of the approach is lost.

5 Related Work

The idea of regarding security protocols as planning problems is not new. In [1], it has been proposed an executable planning specification language $\mathcal{ALSP}$ for representing security protocols and checking the possibility of attacks via a model finder for logic programs with stable model semantics. Compared to this approach SATMC performs better (on the available results) and can readily exploit improvements of state-of-the-art SAT solvers.

Preliminary results obtained by running the SAT technology planning system blackbox [19] against our benchmark of protocols, indicate that even if the performance of the tools are comparable, the PDDL language used by blackbox (and by state-of-the-art planners) to specify planning problems is not appropriate to express in a compact way security protocols. This is due to the fact that PDDL is unable to specify complex term structure (only individual constants are allowed). Hence, in order to translate our compact protocol specifications into PDDL, time consuming operations such as flattening and grounding of fluents and operators must be executed.

Gavin Lowe and his group at the University of Leicester (UK) have analyzed problems from the Clark/Jacob library [10] using Casper/FDR2 [13]. This approach has been very successful for discovering new flaws in protocols. However, first experiments on the search time indicate that SATMC is more effective than Casper/FDR2. Besides that Casper/FDR2 limits the size of messages that are sent in the network and is not able to handle non-atomic keys.

The Murphi model-checker has been used in [21] for analyzing some cryptographic protocols such as the Needham-Schroeder Public-Key (NSPK). Experimental results indicate that Murphi suffers from state-space explosion. To

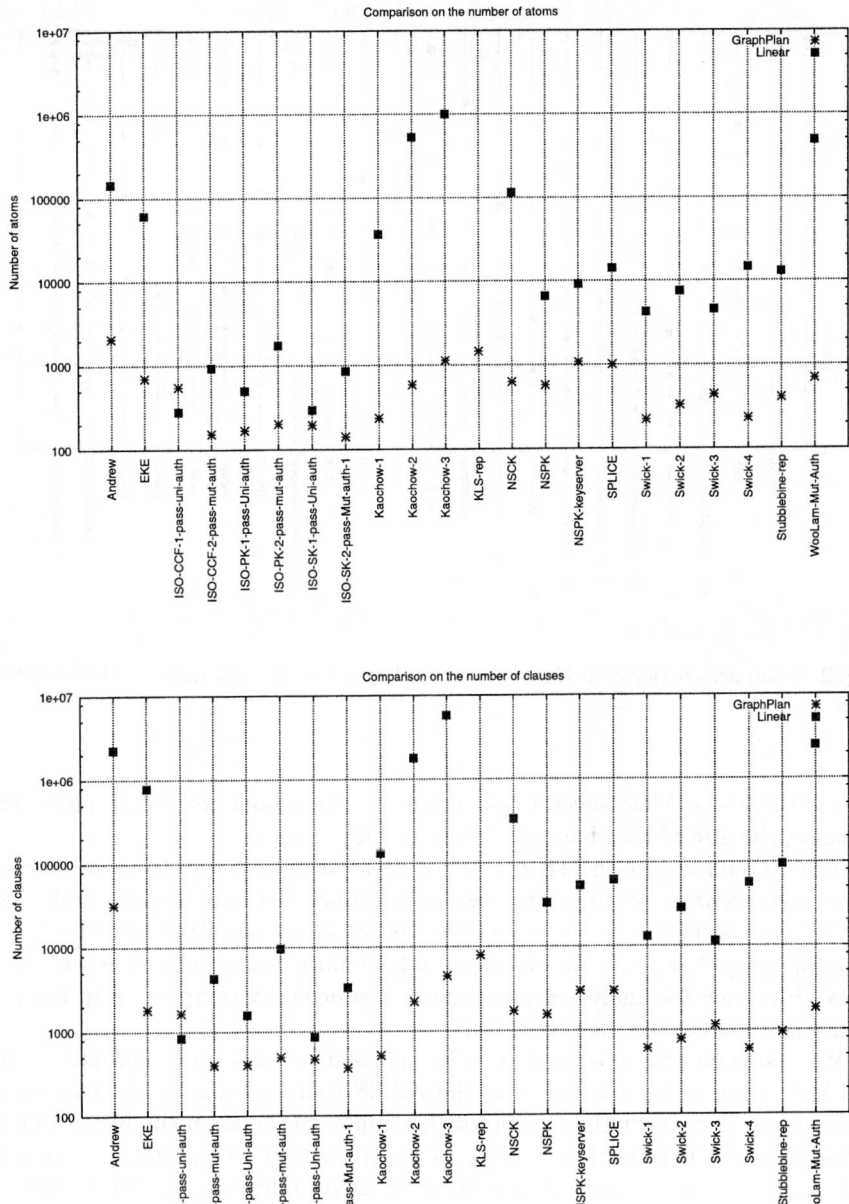

Fig. 1. Comparison between Graphplan-based and linear encodings on the number of atoms and clauses

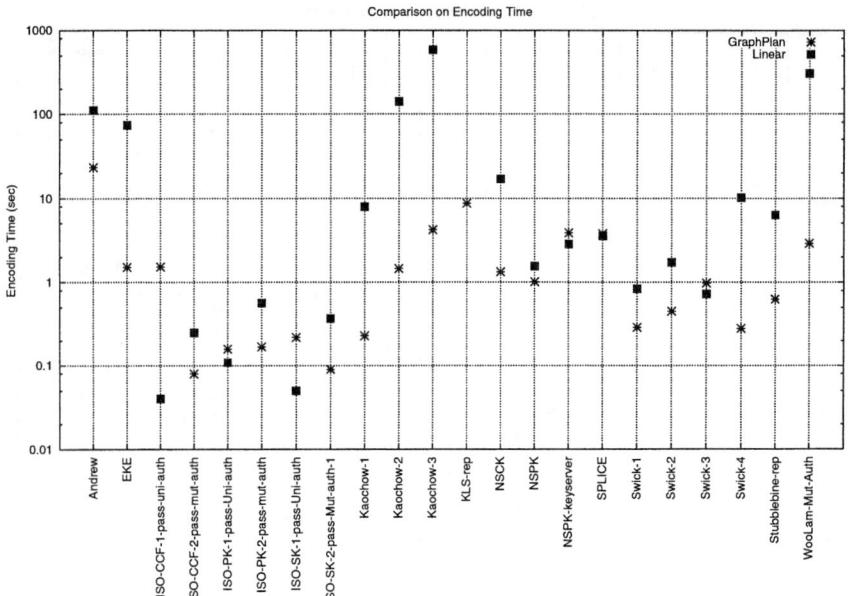

Fig. 2. Comparison between Graphplan-based and linear encodings on the encoding time

cope with this problem several restrictions on the model are put in place. For instance, the size of the channel is fixed a priori.

The Athena approach [24] combines model checking and theorem proving techniques with the strand space model to reduce the search space and automatically prove the correctness of or find an attack on security protocols (when it terminates). However, Athena does not support non-atomic keys, which is a real drawback for analyzing e-commerce protocols. A comparison in term of performance is left for the future work.

We conclude this overview of relevant related work by mentioning that SATMC is one of the back-ends of the AVISS tool and that in the context of that work we have performed a thorough comparison between the back-ends integrated in it.[14] The On-the-Fly Model-Checker (OFMC) [5] performs uniformly well on all the Clark/Jacob library. However, it is interesting to observe that in many cases the time spent by the SAT solver is equal to or smaller than the time spent by OFMC for the same protocol. The Constraint-Logic-based model-checker (CL) [9] is able to find type-flaw attacks (as well as OFMC). However, the overall timing of SATMC is better than that of CL. Detailed results about these experiments can be found in [2].

---

[14] Notice that the results shown in this comparison and concerning SATMC have been obtained by applying only the linear encoding technique.

6 Conclusions and Perspectives

We have enhanced our SAT-based Model-Checker, SATMC, with a sophisticated SAT reduction based on the Graphplan-based encoding technique. Experimental results obtained by running SATMC against a selection of security protocols drawn from the Clark-Jacob's library clearly show that the Graphplan-based encoding is superior to the linear encoding. This is due to the fact that the Graphplan-based encoding reduces dramatically both the size of the SAT instances and the time spent to generate them. As a consequence SATMC can now solve problems that can not be tackled with the linear encoding (e.g. the KLS rep. protocol). However, as pointed out in Section 4, when applied to protocol insecurity problems with multiple initial states the linear encoding can be preferable to the Graphplan-based encoding. This kind of scenarios will be subject of further investigations.

The results obtained confirm the effectiveness of the SAT-based approach for the analysis of security protocols and pave the way to its application to large protocols which arise in practical applications.

References

1. L. Carlucci Aiello and F. Massacci. Verifying security protocols as planning in logic programming. *ACM Trans. on Computational Logic*, 2(4):542–580, October 2001.
2. A. Armando, D. Basin, M. Bouallagui, Y. Chevalier, L. Compagna, S. Moedersheim, M. Rusinowitch, M. Turuani, L. Viganò, and L. Vigneron. The AVISS Security Protocols Analysis Tool. In *14th International Conference on Computer-Aided Verification (CAV'02)*. 2002.
3. A. Armando and L. Compagna. Automatic SAT-Compilation of Protocol Insecurity Problems via Reduction to Planning. In *22nd IFIP WG 6.1 International Conference on Formal Techniques for Networked and Distributed Systems (FORTE)*, Houston, Texas, November 2002. Also presented at the FCS & Verify Workshops, Copenhagen, Denmark, July 2002.
4. A. Armando and L. Compagna. Abstraction-driven SAT-based Analysis of Security Protocols. In *Proceedings of the Sixth International Conference on Theory and Applications of Satisfiability Testing (SAT 2003)*, S. Margherita Ligure, Italy, May 2003.
5. David Basin, Sebastian Moedersheim, and Luca Viganò. An On-the-Fly Model-Checker for security protocol analysis. Forthcoming, 2003.
6. Armin Biere, Alessandro Cimatti, Edmund Clarke, and Yunshan Zhu. Symbolic model checking without BDDs. In W. R. Cleaveland, editor, *Tools and Algorithms for the Construction and Analysis of Systems. Part of European Conferences on Theory and Practice of Software, ETAPS'99, Amsterdam*, volume 1579 of *LNCS*, pages 193–207. Springer-Verlag, 1999.
7. Avrim Blum and Merrick Furst. Fast planning through planning graph analysis. In *Proceedings of the 14th International Joint Conference on Artificial Intelligence (IJCAI 95)*, pages 1636–1642, 1995.

8. Iliano Cervesato, N. A. Durgin, Patrick Lincoln, John C. Mitchell, and Andre Scedrov. A meta-notation for protocol analysis. In *CSFW*, pages 55–69, 1999.
9. Y. Chevalier and L. Vigneron. A Tool for Lazy Verification of Security Protocols. In *Proceedings of the Automated Software Engineering Conference (ASE'01)*. IEEE Computer Society Press, 2001. Long version available as Technical Report A01-R-140, LORIA, Nancy (France).
10. John Clark and Jeremy Jacob. A Survey of Authentication Protocol Literature: Version 1.0, 17. Nov. 1997. URL http://www.cs.york.ac.uk/~jac/papers/drareview.ps.gz.
11. Minh Binh Do, Biplav Srivastava, and Subbarao Kambhampati. Investigating the effect of relevance and reachability constraints on SAT encodings of planning. In *Artificial Intelligence Planning Systems*, pages 308–314, 2000.
12. Danny Dolev and Andrew Yao. On the security of public-key protocols. *IEEE Transactions on Information Theory*, 2(29), 1983.
13. B. Donovan, P. Norris, and G. Lowe. Analyzing a library of security protocols using Casper and FDR. In *Proceedings of the Workshop on Formal Methods and Security Protocols*. 1999.
14. Michael D. Ernst, Todd D. Millstein, and Daniel S. Weld. Automatic SAT-compilation of planning problems. In *Proceedings of the 15th International Joint Conference on Artificial Intelligence (IJCAI-97)*, pages 1169–1177. Morgan Kaufmann Publishers, San Francisco, 1997.
15. E. Giunchiglia, M. Maratea, A. Tacchella, and D. Zambonin. Evaluating search heuristics and optimization techniques in propositional satisfiability. In *Proceedings of IJCAR'2001*, LNAI 2083, pages 347–363. Springer-Verlag, Heidelberg, 2001.
16. Heather, Lowe, and Schneider. How to prevent type flaw attacks on security protocols. In *PCSFW: Proceedings of The 13th Computer Security Foundations Workshop*. IEEE Computer Society Press, 2000.
17. Florent Jacquemard, Michael Rusinowitch, and Laurent Vigneron. Compiling and Verifying Security Protocols. In M. Parigot and A. Voronkov, editors, *Proceedings of LPAR 2000*, LNCS 1955, pages 131–160. Springer-Verlag, Heidelberg, 2000.
18. Henry Kautz, David McAllester, and Bart Selman. Encoding plans in propositional logic. In *KR'96: Principles of Knowledge Representation and Reasoning*, pages 374–384. Morgan Kaufmann, San Francisco, California, 1996.
19. Henry A. Kautz and Bart Selman. Unifying SAT-based and graph-based planning. In *Proceedings of the Sixteenth International Joint Conference on Artificial Intelligence (IJCAI'99)*, pages 318–325, Stockholm, Sweden, July 31-August 6 1999. Morgan Kaufmann.
20. G. Lowe. Breaking and fixing the Needham-Shroeder public-key protocol using FDR. In *Proceedings of TACAS'96*, pages 147–166. Springer-Verlag, 1996.
21. J.C. Mitchell, M. Mitchell, and U. Stern. Automated analysis of cryptographic protocols using murphi. In *Proceedings of IEEE Symposium on Security and Privacy*, pages 141–153. 1997.
22. Matthew W. Moskewicz, Conor F. Madigan, Ying Zhao, Lintao Zhang, and Sharad Malik. Chaff: Engineering an Efficient SAT Solver. In *Proceedings of the 38th Design Automation Conference (DAC'01)*. 2001.
23. R. M. (Roger Michael) Needham and Michael D. Schroeder. Using encryption for authentication in large networks of computers. Technical Report CSL-78-4, Xerox Palo Alto Research Center, Palo Alto, CA, USA, 1978. Reprinted June 1982.

24. D. Song. Athena: A new efficient automatic checker for security protocol analysis. In *Proceedings of the 12th IEEE Computer Security Foundations Workshop (CSFW '99)*, pages 192–202. IEEE Computer Society Press, 1999.
25. Daniel S. Weld. Recent advances in AI planning. *AI Magazine*, 20(2):93–123, 1999.
26. H. Zhang. SATO: An efficient propositional prover. In William McCune, editor, *Proceedings of CADE 14*, LNAI 1249, pages 272–275. Springer-Verlag, Heidelberg, 1997.

Correctness of Source-Level Safety Policies

Ewen Denney[1] and Bernd Fischer[2]

[1] QSS / [2] RIACS
NASA Ames Research Center, Moffett Field, CA 94035, USA
{edenney,fisch}@email.arc.nasa.gov

Abstract. Program certification techniques formally show that programs satisfy certain safety policies. They rely on the correctness of the safety policy which has to be established externally. In this paper we investigate an approach to show the correctness of safety policies which are formulated as a set of Hoare-style inference rules on the source code level. We develop a framework which is generic with respect to safety policies and which allows us to establish that proving the safety of a program statically guarantees dynamic safety, i.e., that the program never violates the safety property during its execution. We demonstrate our framework by proving safety policies for memory access safety and memory read/write limitations to be sound and complete. Finally, we formulate a set of generic safety inference rules which serve as the blueprint for the implementation of a verification condition generator which can be parameterized with different safety policies, and identify conditions on appropriate safety policies.

Keywords. Program verification, Hoare logic, program safety, code certification, proof-carrying code

1 Introduction

Program certification techniques like proof-carrying code (PCC) [12] use formal reasoning techniques to show that programs satisfy certain *safety policies* as for example memory safety (i.e., that they do not access out-of-bounds memory), rather than full functional correctness.

In effect, these techniques shift the trust burden from the original program to the certification system: instead of having to trust an arbitrary program to be safe, users have to trust the certifier to be correct. However, this still requires a lot of trust since a certifier is itself a complex system involving many different components and steps. In the original PCC approach [12], a compiler first translates an untrusted source program into an annotated machine program, to which a verification condition generator (VCG) then applies a safety policy, formulated as a set of Hoare rules. This produces a set of proof obligations, which are processed by a theorem prover; the resulting proofs are finally scrutinized by a proof checker (cf. Figure 1). Fortunately, not all of these components have to be trusted – here, trust is required only in the safety policy, the VCG, and the proof checker but not in the much larger prover or the compiler itself.

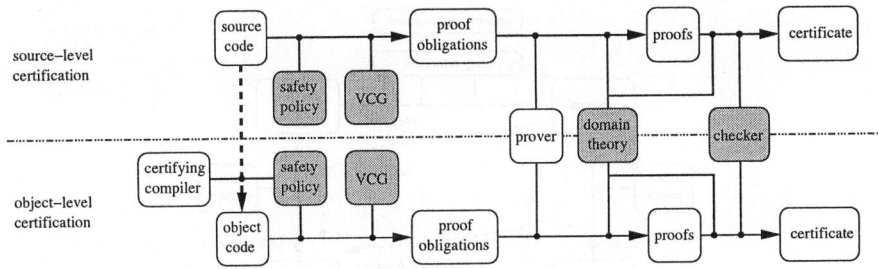

Fig. 1. System architecture for source-level certification and object-level certification; trusted components are shaded.

However, the fact that the safety policy still has to be trusted turns out to be the Achilles heel of the approach, both for theoretical and practical reasons. On the theoretical side, if the rules are unsound or do not exactly formalize the intuitive notion of safety, "all bets are off" [10], i.e., even a safety proof does not guarantee that the program is actually safe. On the practical side, since a safety policy can consist of a collection of fairly complex Hoare rules, it is as liable to error as any other component of the certifier. Moreover, the VCG and the proof checker can be reused essentially unchanged for different safety policies and can thus be hardened over time, but the Hoare rules change with each new safety policy. Recent work has thus concentrated on ways to guarantee the correctness of safety policies, using approaches like type-preserving compilation [10], foundational PCC [2,6], and reduction to core safety policies [13].

However, all these approaches work on the object code level, and cannot directly be extended to safety policies which are formulated on the source code level. Here, we investigate an approach to showing the correctness of source-level safety policies. Our goal is to develop a generic framework (cf. Figure 2) which lets us establish that proving the safety of a source program using a safety policy formulated as a set of Hoare rules guarantees safe execution, i.e., the program never violates the safety property.[1] In other words, we want to establish that the static and dynamic notions of safety coincide. We thus explicitly distinguish between the static safety *policies* (which are logical characterizations) and the dynamic safety *properties* (which are operational characterizations). We also explicitly separate the formalization of the safety properties from the operational semantics: a program can be unsafe even if its execution does not raise an exception. We restrict ourselves to the analysis of individual programs only, and do not consider system-level safety aspects. However, our techniques could be used with system-level analysis techniques, e.g., to decide whether a system is still safe even if an exception can occur in one of the system components.

Our interest in source-level policies has a number of reasons. (*i*) Programmers make errors on the source code level, so showing safety on the source code

---

[1] Provided that the compiler preserves the property, of course. See below for a more detailed discussion of this.

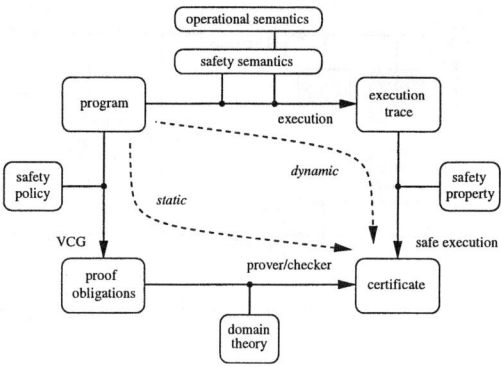

Fig. 2. Establishing correctness of source-level certification – general framework.

level seems not only to be more natural, it also makes it easier to pinpoint the errors. (*ii*) Some safety policies can be formulated more naturally (e.g., initialization-before-use) or only (e.g., loop variable restrictions) on the source code level.[2] In particular, high-level domain-specific policies such as *frame safety* [9] are inherently source level. (*iii*) Source-level certification is complementary to object-level approaches like PCC. In fact, to ensure that compilation does not compromise the demonstrated safety policy, source-level certification should be followed by object-level certification. However, explicit source-level certification provides a separation of concerns as different safety policies can be applied at different levels of abstraction. (*iv*) Formal software certification processes (e.g., DO-178B) usually also cover source code level, so certification support has to work on that level. (*v*) Finally, we are interested in the combination of certification and program synthesis [19], using certification (in a roundabout way) to increase confidence in our synthesis system, which generates source code and not object code.

The main contributions of this paper are as follows. First, we develop a general notion of safety property: we distinguish *stateless* properties, where safe execution can be defined in terms of the original operational semantics (i.e., execution traces), and *stateful* properties, where for book-keeping purposes the operational semantics must be augmented with a separate safety semantics. Second, we develop a *semantic* definition of safety, which lets us reason about the soundness and completeness of our safety policies. Third, we give a generic method of extending Hoare rules to incorporate an arbitrary safety property. In particular, our framework can serve as the basis for the implementation of a generic VCG.

In Section 2, we develop the basic theory of stateless safety properties, and then extend this in Section 3 to some examples of stateful safety. In Section 4 we present a general account of safety. Finally, Sections 5 and 6 discuss related

---

[2] This is related to the use of certification to enforce syntactic restrictions and coding standards.

work and draw some conclusions. Throughout this paper we assume a working familiarity with Hoare-style program correctness proofs (see [11], for example).

2 Stateless Safety Properties

We introduce our framework using the deliberately simplistic language $\mathcal{L}_0$ of *while*-programs as shown in Figure 3; it uses the unspecified sets *Var* and *Const* of variables and literal constants.

$$
\begin{array}{ll}
\mathit{Cmd} ::= \texttt{skip} & \mathit{Expr} ::= \mathit{Const} \\
\quad | \ \mathit{Var}\ \texttt{:=}\ \mathit{Expr} & \quad | \ \mathit{Var} \\
\quad | \ \texttt{if}\ \mathit{Expr}\ \texttt{then}\ \mathit{Cmd} & \quad | \ \mathit{Expr}\ \texttt{*}\ \mathit{Expr} \\
\quad | \ \texttt{while}\ \mathit{Expr}\ \texttt{do}\ \mathit{Cmd} & \quad | \ \mathit{Expr}\ \texttt{/}\ \mathit{Expr} \\
\quad | \ \mathit{Cmd}\ \texttt{;}\ \mathit{Cmd} & \quad | \ \mathit{Expr}\ \texttt{+}\ \mathit{Expr} \\
& \quad | \ \mathit{Expr}\ \texttt{-}\ \mathit{Expr} \\
& \quad | \ \mathit{Expr}\ \texttt{=}\ \mathit{Expr}
\end{array}
$$

Fig. 3. Syntax of *while*-language $\mathcal{L}_0$

Our initial safety property is *operator safety*, i.e., expression operators such as division are only applied to arguments within their respective domains. For $\mathcal{L}_0$, this boils down to the question of whether divisors are non-zero. However, even for this simple case we cannot naively define the safety of commands in terms of the safety of their subexpressions. Consider, for example, the commands

```
if false then x:=x+1/0        while true do skip; x:=x+1/0
```

which contain unsafe subexpressions but which we would nevertheless want to regard as safe (w.r.t. operator safety) because the division-by-zero exception will never be raised. Consider also the sequence `x:=y; w:=1/x` where safety of the subexpressions is not sufficient either because this does not incorporate the information that the division `1/x` is performed when `x` is bound to the value of `y`. Hence, we need an analysis of safety which takes into account the (operational) semantics of the programs.

2.1 Formulation of Safety Properties

A *safety property* is an operational characterization of the fact that "a program does not go wrong." We formalize safety properties as *judgements* of the form $\eta \vDash c$ safe, i.e., the command $c \in \mathit{Cmd}$ is safe under the environment $\eta \in \mathit{Env}$. As usual, we use environments $\eta : \mathit{Var} \rightharpoonup \mathit{Val}_\bot$ to record value bindings for the variables. Note that we use the bottom element $\bot$ only as an operational concept to denote and propagate the result of an undefined computation, but not to denote (un-) safety. In particular, a command can still be safe under an environment which contains a binding $x \mapsto \bot$; for example, `y:=x+1` is obviously still safe w.r.t. operator safety (i.e., division-by-zero free) simply because it does not contain any occurrence of the division operator. Conversely, unsafety does not necessarily manifest itself in a binding $x \mapsto \bot$.

We can then define the judgement safe_{op} which formalizes operator safety for $\mathcal{L}_0$-expressions in the expected way, as shown in Figure 4. We use the notation $J e K_\eta$ to denote evaluation of an expression $e \in \mathit{Expr}$ in an environment η.

$$\eta \vDash c \; \mathsf{safe}_{op}$$
$$\eta \vDash x \; \mathsf{safe}_{op}$$
$$\eta \vDash e_1 \; op \; e_2 \; \mathsf{safe}_{op} \; \text{iff} \; \eta \vDash e_1 \; \mathsf{safe}_{op} \; \text{and} \; \eta \vDash e_2 \; \mathsf{safe}_{op} \; \text{and} \; op \in \{\texttt{*},\texttt{+},\texttt{-},\texttt{=}\}$$
$$\eta \vDash e_1 \; / \; e_2 \; \mathsf{safe}_{op} \; \text{iff} \; \eta \vDash e_1 \; \mathsf{safe}_{op} \; \text{and} \; \eta \vDash e_2 \; \mathsf{safe}_{op} \; \text{and} \; J e_2 K_\eta \neq 0$$

Fig. 4. Operator safety for $\mathcal{L}_0$-expressions

Extending operator safety to commands requires an operational semantics for the commands; here, we assume the standard single-step operational semantics $\langle c, \eta \rangle \Rightarrow \langle c', \eta' \rangle$ for *while*-programs.[3][4] However, there are two different approaches to an extension. The first approach factors safety into two different judgements, $\mathsf{safestate}_{op}$ and safe_{op} (cf. Figure 5), where $\eta \vDash c \; \mathsf{safestate}_{op}$ formalizes the intuition that the immediately next command is safe to execute (i.e., all of the expressions which it would evaluate immediately are safe) and the reduction relation restricts the application of $\mathsf{safestate}_{op}$ to reachable commands and environments only. Hence, we have $\eta \vDash \texttt{while true do skip; x:=1/0} \; \mathsf{safe}_{op}$, as expected. This approach essentially mirrors the definition of what is called the safety policy in the syntactic FPCC-approach of Hamid et al. [6].

$$\eta \vDash \texttt{skip} \; \mathsf{safestate}_{op}$$
$$\eta \vDash x \; \texttt{:=} \; e \; \mathsf{safestate}_{op} \quad \text{iff} \quad \eta \vDash e \; \mathsf{safe}_{op}$$
$$\eta \vDash \texttt{if} \; b \; \texttt{then} \; c \; \mathsf{safestate}_{op} \quad \text{iff} \quad \eta \vDash b \; \mathsf{safe}_{op}$$
$$\eta \vDash \texttt{while} \; b \; \texttt{do} \; c \; \mathsf{safestate}_{op} \quad \text{iff} \quad \eta \vDash b \; \mathsf{safe}_{op}$$
$$\eta \vDash c_1 ; c_2 \; \mathsf{safestate}_{op} \quad \text{iff} \quad \eta \vDash c_1 \; \mathsf{safestate}_{op}$$

$$\eta \vDash c \; \mathsf{safe}_{op} \; \text{iff} \; \forall \langle c, \eta \rangle \Rightarrow^* \langle c', \eta' \rangle \cdot \eta' \vDash c' \; \mathsf{safestate}_{op}$$

Fig. 5. Operator safety for $\mathcal{L}_0$-commands

The second approach directly integrates the formulation of the $\mathsf{safestate}_{op}$-judgement into the operational semantics and has thus more of an abstract interpretation flavor (cf. Figure 6).

---

[3] $\langle x := e, \eta \rangle \Rightarrow \langle \texttt{skip}, \eta \oplus \{x \mapsto J e K_\eta\} \rangle$,
$\langle \texttt{skip} \; ; \; c_2, \eta \rangle \Rightarrow \langle c_2, \eta \rangle$,
$\langle c_1 \; ; \; c_2, \eta \rangle \Rightarrow \langle c'_1 \; ; \; c_2, \eta' \rangle$ if $\langle c_1, \eta \rangle \Rightarrow \langle c'_1, \eta' \rangle$,
$\langle \texttt{if} \; b \; \texttt{then} \; c, \eta \rangle \Rightarrow \langle c, \eta \rangle$ if $J b K_\eta = \mathit{true}$,
$\langle \texttt{if} \; b \; \texttt{then} \; c, \eta \rangle \Rightarrow \langle \texttt{skip}, \eta \rangle$ if $J b K_\eta = \mathit{false}$,
$\langle \texttt{while} \; b \; \texttt{do} \; c, \eta \rangle \Rightarrow \langle \texttt{if} \; b \; \texttt{then} \; (c; \texttt{while} \; b \; \texttt{do} \; c), \eta \rangle$

[4] We also use $\langle c, \eta \rangle \Downarrow \eta'$ to denote the result of a terminating evaluation of c, i.e., $\langle c, \eta \rangle \Downarrow \eta'$ iff $\langle c, \eta \rangle \Rightarrow^* \langle \texttt{skip}, \eta' \rangle$.

$\eta \vDash \mathtt{skip}\ \widehat{\mathsf{safe}}_{op}$

$\eta \vDash x := e\ \widehat{\mathsf{safe}}_{op}$ iff $\eta \vDash e\ \mathsf{safe}_{op}$

$\eta \vDash \mathtt{if}\ b\ \mathtt{then}\ c\ \widehat{\mathsf{safe}}_{op}$ iff $\eta \vDash b\ \mathsf{safe}_{op}$ and $J b K_\eta = \mathit{true}$ implies
$\eta \vDash c\ \widehat{\mathsf{safe}}_{op}$

$\eta \vDash \mathtt{while}\ b\ \mathtt{do}\ c\ \widehat{\mathsf{safe}}_{op}$ iff $\eta \vDash b\ \mathsf{safe}_{op}$ and $J b K_\eta = \mathit{true}$ implies ($\eta \vDash c\ \widehat{\mathsf{safe}}_{op}$ and
$\langle c, \eta \rangle \Downarrow \eta'$ implies $\eta' \vDash \mathtt{while}\ b\ \mathtt{do}\ c\ \widehat{\mathsf{safe}}_{op}$)

$\eta \vDash c_1; c_2\ \widehat{\mathsf{safe}}_{op}$ iff $\eta \vDash c_1\ \widehat{\mathsf{safe}}_{op}$ and $\langle c_1, \eta \rangle \Downarrow \eta'$ implies $\eta' \vDash c_2\ \widehat{\mathsf{safe}}_{op}$.

Fig. 6. Operator safety for $\mathcal{L}_0$-commands (structural definition)

For this alternative definition $\widehat{\mathsf{safe}}_{op}$ we first show by straightforward induction over commands that safety is preserved by reduction; in analogy to subject reduction[5] we call this property *safety reduction*. Note that safety reduction holds trivially for safe_{op} as defined in Figure 5.

Lemma 1. *(Safety Reduction)* $\eta \vDash c\ \widehat{\mathsf{safe}}_{op}$ *and* $\langle c, \eta \rangle \Rightarrow \langle c', \eta' \rangle$ *implies* $\eta' \vDash c'\ \widehat{\mathsf{safe}}_{op}$.

We can then show that both definitions are in fact equivalent. This is quite useful because the operational definition ($\widehat{\mathsf{safe}}$) is what we intuitively want but most proofs use the inductive definition (safestate).

Lemma 2. *For all* η, c: $\eta \vDash c\ \widehat{\mathsf{safe}}_{op}$ *iff* $\eta \vDash c\ \mathsf{safe}_{op}$.

Proof: Use Lemma 1, and the fact that $\eta \vDash c\ \widehat{\mathsf{safe}}_{op}$ implies $\eta \vDash c\ \mathsf{safestate}_{op}$. ∎

Both Lemma 1 and Lemma 2 are independent of the particular safety judgement and hold as long as command safety is derived from expression safety in the way described in Figure 6.

In the following we discuss arbitrary safety properties, which can be *any* mathematical relation between environments and expressions. We reserve the use of *safety judgement* for the semantic clauses defining the property. For commands, we define a safety property to be any relation, $\_ \vDash \_\ \mathsf{safe} \subseteq \mathit{Env} \times \mathit{Cmd}$, which is defined from expression safety, according to Figure 6 (cf. Definition 5 for the stateful case).

2.2 Formulation of Safety Policies

A *safety policy* is a set of proof rules and auxiliary definitions which are designed to show that safe programs satisfy the safety property of interest. The intention is that a safety policy enforces a particular safety property (see Section 2.1). For

---
[5] A system is said to satisfy *subject reduction* [11] if types are preserved by term reduction, i.e., if $M : \tau$ and $M \Rightarrow M'$ implies $M' : \tau$.

$$(skip)\ \overline{Q\ \{\texttt{skip}\}\ Q}$$

$$(assign)\ \overline{Q[e/x] \wedge safe_{op}(e)\ \{x := e\}\ Q}$$

$$(if)\ \frac{P \Rightarrow safe_{op}(b)\quad b \wedge P\ \{c\}\ Q\quad \neg b \wedge P \Rightarrow Q}{P\ \{\texttt{if}\ b\ \texttt{then}\ c\}\ Q}$$

$$(while)\ \frac{P \Rightarrow safe_{op}(b)\quad b \wedge P\ \{c\}\ P}{P\ \{\texttt{while}\ b\ \texttt{do}\ c\}\ \neg b \wedge P}$$

$$(comp)\ \frac{P\ \{c_1\}\ R\quad R\ \{c_2\}\ Q}{P\ \{c_1\ ;\ c_2\}\ Q}$$

$$(cons)\ \frac{P \Rightarrow P'\quad P'\ \{c\}\ Q'\quad Q' \Rightarrow Q}{P\ \{c\}\ Q}$$

Fig. 7. Hoare rules for $\mathcal{L}_0$ operator safety

$$safe_{op}(e) = \begin{cases} true & \text{if } e \in Var \text{ or } e \in Const \\ safe_{op}(e_1) \wedge safe_{op}(e_2) & \text{if } e \equiv e_1\ op\ e_2,\ op \in \{\texttt{*},\texttt{+},\texttt{-},\texttt{=}\} \\ safe_{op}(e_1) \wedge safe_{op}(e_2) \wedge e_2 \neq 0 & \text{if } e \equiv e_1/e_2 \end{cases}$$

Fig. 8. Safety formula for $\mathcal{L}_0$ operator safety

source-level safety properties, the proof rules can be formalized concisely using the usual Hoare triples $P\ \{c\}\ Q$. We also use the notation $\vdash^{\mathsf{safe}} P\ \{c\}\ Q$ to denote derivability of Hoare triples, given a set of Hoare rules. Figure 7 shows the Hoare rules for operator safety. The rules are a slight modification of the standard ones; the $(assign)$ axiom requires safety of the right-hand side expression, and the (if) and $(while)$ rules require the additional hypothesis that the guard is safe under the precondition P. Figure 8 shows the definition of the auxiliary predicate $safe_{op}$ used in the rules; note that $safe_{op}$ is not a judgement but a function which maps expressions into formulae.

The standard Hoare rules are well-understood, unlike extensions to deal with safety. Our aim is to show how such extensions can be made automatically, while ensuring soundness and completeness. We first need to modify the standard interpretation of Hoare triples (i.e., $\eta \vDash P\ \{c\}\ Q$ iff $\eta \vDash P$ and $\langle c, \eta \rangle \Downarrow \eta'$ together imply $\eta' \vDash Q$) to take a safety judgement into account.

Definition 1. $\vDash^{\mathsf{safe}} P\ \{c\}\ Q$ *holds iff for all* $\eta \in Env$, *if* $\eta \vDash P$, *then* $\eta \vDash c$ safe, *and if* $\langle c, \eta \rangle \Downarrow \eta'$, *then* $\eta' \vDash Q$.

Note that the proof rules inherit an underlying logic from a system given separately; in particular, they do not say anything about the definedness of the formulae P and Q used in the Hoare triples (e.g., $\vDash^{\mathsf{safe}} true\ \{x := 0\}\ 1/x \neq 100$ holds). Hence, logical definedness is unconnected to the safety policy.

2.3 Soundness and Completeness of Safety Policies

The crucial task is now to show that the proof rules of the safety policy are sound and complete w.r.t. the safety property of interest. Since we have defined semantic safety of a command with respect to an environment we need to show a theorem of the form $\eta \vDash c$ safe *iff* $\vdash^{\mathsf{safe}} P \{c\}$ *true*, for some P such that $\eta \vDash P$. The role of the proof obligation P is to collect all the safety information for c in η.

For the *only if* direction of the proof (i.e., completeness), we need the notion of *expressivity* [11] which postulates the existence of formulae which characterise particular sets of environments. More precisely, we *assume* the existence of weakest preconditions *wpc* for all statements. Formally, a (first-order) language $\mathcal{L}$ is called *expressive* if, for all commands $c \in Cmd$ and postconditions Q, there exists a formula $wpc(c, Q)$ such that $\eta \vDash wpc(c, Q)$ iff $\langle c, \eta \rangle \Downarrow \eta'$ implies $\eta' \vDash Q$. This is a nontrivial assumption as there is no reason why an arbitrary semantic condition should be expressible by a (first-order) formula. However, the assumption is required for proof purposes only and in practice *wpc*s can often be computed automatically. As usual, while-loops pose the real problem, and here loop invariants have to be given explicitly.

Unfortunately, this standard definition of expressivity is not strong enough to show safety in all cases. Consider the example

```
i:=0;
while true do
    x:=1/(a-i); i:=i+1
```

which is safe in environments where a is negative but where the weakest precondition of the non-terminating loop is *true*, telling us nothing about its safety. Indeed, examples can be given which have *no* first-order wspc. We thus introduce the notion of *weakest safety precondition* (*wspc*) to characterize safe environments.

Definition 2. *(Expressivity for commands) A command $c \in Cmd$ is called expressible w.r.t. a safety judgement* safe *if, for all postconditions Q, there exists a formula $wspc(c, Q)$ such that*

$$\eta \vDash wspc(c, Q) \text{ iff } (\eta \vDash c \text{ safe } and \langle c, \eta \rangle \Downarrow \eta' \text{ implies } \eta' \vDash Q).$$

A language $\mathcal{L}$ is called expressive for commands w.r.t. a safety judgement safe *if all commands are expressible.*

Now a consequence of the definition of *wspc* is that all intermediate commands are safe, by safety reduction. However, since there is no useful notion of safe environment, it is not sufficient to simply consider the environments in which c reduces to a safe environment, or for which all intermediate environments are safe. We also need to extend expressivity to the expression level; here it assumes the existence of safety formulae, $safe(e)$, compatible with the safety judgement safe.

Definition 3. *(Expressivity for expressions)* An expression $e \in \mathit{Expr}$ is called expressible w.r.t. a safety judgement safe if there exists a formula $\mathit{safe}(e)$ such that $\eta \models e$ safe iff $\eta \models \mathit{safe}(e)$.

By abuse of notation we will also call a given safety predicate $\mathit{safe}(\_)$ expressive for a safety judgement safe if it satisfies the condition of Definition 3. It is then easy to show by straightforward induction over expressions that safe_{op} is expressive for safe_{op}.

Lemma 3. *For all $e \in \mathit{Expr}$, $\eta \models e$ safe_{op} iff $\eta \models \mathit{safe}_{op}(e)$.*

We can now characterize the weakest safety preconditions wspc (w.r.t. operator safety) for each command of $\mathcal{L}_0$. Lemma 4 thus gives a recursive (but due to the while-case unfortunately not well-founded) definition of wspc.

Lemma 4. *Assuming all formulae exist, the following equivalences are sound:*

1. $\mathit{wspc}(\mathsf{skip}, Q) \iff \mathit{wpc}(\mathsf{skip}, Q)$
2. $\mathit{wspc}(x := e, Q) \iff \mathit{safe}_{op}(e) \wedge \mathit{wpc}(x := e, Q)$
3. $\mathit{wspc}(\mathsf{if}\, b\, \mathsf{then}\, c, Q) \iff \mathit{safe}_{op}(b) \wedge (b \Rightarrow \mathit{wspc}(c, Q)) \wedge (\neg b \Rightarrow Q)$
4. $\mathit{wspc}(\mathsf{while}\, b\, \mathsf{do}\, c, Q) \iff \mathit{safe}_{op}(b) \wedge (b \Rightarrow \mathit{wspc}(c, \mathit{wspc}(\mathsf{while}\, b\, \mathsf{do}\, c, Q))) \wedge (\neg b \Rightarrow Q)$
5. $\mathit{wspc}(c_1; c_2, Q) \iff \mathit{wspc}(c_1, \mathit{wspc}(c_2, Q)))$

The preceding lemma does not give a constructive definition of wspc, because of the recursion in the while-case.

Lemma 5. *(wspc properties) For all formulas P and Q, and commands, c:*

1. $\models^{\mathsf{safe}} \mathit{wspc}(c, Q)\, \{c\}\, Q$.
2. $\models^{\mathsf{safe}} P\, \{c\}\, Q$ implies $P \Rightarrow \mathit{wspc}(c, Q)$.

Proof: 1. By definition of wspc. 2. The implication is clearly true in the model. Provability follows from completeness of the underlying logic. ∎

We can now extend the definition of safety formulae to commands via a reduction to wspc. We define $\mathit{safe}_{op}(c) = \mathit{wspc}(c, \mathit{true})$, which also yields $\models^{\mathsf{safe}} \mathit{safe}_{op}(c)\, \{c\}\, \mathit{true}$, for all $c \in \mathit{Cmd}$, as a special case of Lemma 5. Moreover, we clearly have $\eta \models c\, \mathsf{safe}_{op}$ iff $\eta \models \mathit{safe}_{op}(c)$, so can factor wspc into a functional component expressed in terms of the standard precondition wpc and a safety component $\mathit{safe}_{op}(c)$.

Proposition 1. $\mathit{wspc}(c, Q) \iff \mathit{wpc}(c, Q) \wedge \mathit{safe}_{op}(c)$.

Note that we choose not to define wspc this way i.e., by giving a direct definition of $\mathit{safe}_{op}(c)$. The reason is that checking safety requires a similar recursive descent over the structure of a command, similar to computing the wpc, so it is more natural to combine them into a single definition. Similarly, it is not possible to give a neat definition of wspc from wpc and safety of expressions, for the reasons given in Section 2.

Theorem 1. *Suppose c is expressible. Then,* $\models^{\text{safe}} P \{c\} Q$ *iff* $\vdash^{\text{safe}} P \{c\} Q$.

Proof: Soundness is by induction over the derivation. For completeness, the proof structure follows that of the standard (relative) completeness proof for Hoare logic, using expressivity to get, in our case, the weakest safety preconditions which are needed to make the proof go through. The most interesting cases are for conditionals and `while`-loops.
(if) Let R denote $wspc(\text{if } b \text{ then } c, Q)$. Then:

$$\cfrac{\cfrac{R \Rightarrow safe(b) \;(1) \quad \cfrac{\overline{b \wedge R \Rightarrow wspc(c,Q)} \;(2) \quad \overline{wspc(c,Q) \{c\} Q} \;(3)}{b \wedge R \{c\} Q} \quad \overline{\neg b \wedge R \Rightarrow Q} \;(4)}{R \{\text{if } b \text{ then } c\} Q} \quad \overline{P \Rightarrow R} \;(5)}{P \{\text{if } b \text{ then } c\} Q}$$

The first, second, and fourth hypotheses follow from Lemma 4, the third and fifth follow from Lemma 5 (parts 1 and 2, respectively).
(while) Suppose $\models^{\text{safe}} P \{\text{while } b \text{ do } c\} Q$. Let R denote $wspc(\text{while } b \text{ do } c, Q)$. Then:

$$\cfrac{\cfrac{R \Rightarrow safe_{op}(b) \;(1) \quad \cfrac{\overline{b \wedge R \Rightarrow wspc(c,R)} \;(2) \quad \overline{wspc(c,R) \{c\} R} \;(3)}{b \wedge R \{c\} R}}{R \{\text{while } b \text{ do } c\} \neg b \wedge R} \quad \overline{\neg b \wedge R \Rightarrow Q} \;(4) \quad \overline{P \Rightarrow R} \;(5)}{P \{\text{while } b \text{ do } c\} Q}$$

The first, second and fourth hypothesis follow from Lemma 4, the third follows from the inductive hypothesis on c and Lemma 5(1); and the fifth follows from Lemma 5(2). ∎

Theorem 2. *Assume expressivity. Then,* $\eta \models c \; \mathsf{safe}_{op}$ *iff* $\vdash^{\text{safe}} \phi \{c\} \text{true}$ *for some ϕ such that $\eta \models \phi$.*

Proof: We show the left-to-right implication. We know that $\models^{\text{safe}} safe_{op}(c) \{c\} \text{true}$ by Lemma 5. Hence, by Theorem 1, we have that $\vdash^{\text{safe}} safe_{op}(c) \{c\} \text{true}$, and since $\eta \models c \; \mathsf{safe}_{op}$ by assumption, expressivity gives us $\eta \models safe_{op}(c)$. ∎

At this point it might look like we have built a formidable machinery to prove some less than formidable properties. However, subtle variations of the Hoare rules are possible, and finding the "right" rules (much less proving that they are right) is difficult without a formal framework like the one we have developed here. Consider, for example, the following variant of the *if*-rule

$$(if') \; \frac{safe_{op}(b) \wedge b \wedge P \{c\} Q \quad safe_{op}(b) \wedge \neg b \wedge P \Rightarrow Q}{P \{\text{if } b \text{ then } c\} Q}$$

in which the safety formula is "inlined" into the two hypotheses and not separated into a third hypothesis (cf. Figure 7). However, this rule variant allows safety information to be used to determine the control flow, which makes it potentially unsound. It allows us to derive the triple

$$\text{true} \; \{\text{if } 1/x \neq 1 \text{ then if } x \neq 0 \text{ then } y := 3\} \; x = 1 \vee y = 3$$

which on the surface seems reasonable: either x is one and nothing can be concluded about y, or x is non-zero and y is assigned, or x is zero, the outer guard is undefined, and hence, the statement causes an exception and does not terminate properly. However, it is exactly this third alternative which causes the trouble: if division by zero does *not* cause an exception but returns a defined value (e.g., *NaN*, "not a number"), we can no longer conclude at the inner guard that the safety formula on the outer guard holds.

We note in passing that the rules in this paper are different from those in [19]. However, we believe that the rules shown here are easier to implement and apply in practice.

3 Stateful Safety Properties

For operator safety, the property itself was defined in terms of the original environments only. Most safety properties, however, are not that simple and require additional information: memory safety requires information about the size of arrays or the number of variable accesses, domain-specific policies such as frame safety require additional typing information which is not part of the operational semantics of the language, and so on. We now extend our framework to deal with such safety properties.

Our basic idea is to introduce a distinct auxiliary (or *shadow*) variable $\overline{x} \in \overline{Var}$ for each variable $x \in Var$, which records the necessary safety information associated with x. We also introduce shadow environments $\overline{\eta} : \overline{Var} \rightharpoonup \overline{Val}$, where the shadow domain $\overline{Val}$ depends on the safety property of interest, and extend the operational semantics to include the effects the different commands have on the values of the shadow variables. We then modify the Hoare rules to ensure that $\overline{x}$ actually "shadows" x, i.e., that the information recorded in $\overline{x}$ is always current.

We already adopted part of this methodology in [19]; one motivation for the present work is to formally justify it. The methodology itself is quite flexible and allows us to encode different safety properties, using different shadow domains. We illustrate our approach first for memory safety (more precisely, array bounds checks), and then show how two other, less typical safety policies can be encoded.

3.1 Memory Safety

For memory safety, we need to extend our language $\mathcal{L}_0$ by simple arrays; here, we restrict ourselves to one-dimensional arrays with a fixed lower bound of zero to simplify the presentation. Figure 9 shows the syntax of the extended language $\mathcal{L}_1$. As usual, we add array updates to the commands and array selects to the expressions. However, we also require explicit array declarations of the form `var x[n]`, which declares an n-element array x.[6]

For memory safety, the shadow environment needs to record the size of each array; we thus have $\overline{\eta} : \overline{Var} \rightharpoonup I\!N$. Eventually, the shadow variables get their

---

[6] For consistency, we also add scalar declarations `var x`.

$$
\begin{aligned}
Cmd &::= \ldots \\
&\mid \textit{Var}\,[\textit{Expr}] := \textit{Expr} \\
&\mid \textit{Decl} \\[4pt]
Decl &::= \textbf{var}\ \textit{Var} \\
&\mid \textbf{var}\ \textit{Var}\,[\textit{Const}]
\end{aligned}
\qquad
\begin{aligned}
\textit{Expr} &::= \ldots \\
&\mid \textit{Var}\,[\textit{Expr}]
\end{aligned}
$$

Fig. 9. Syntax of extended *while*-language $\mathcal{L}_1$

values from the declarations. This differs from the usual approach where the array bounds are represented by an extra function $high(x)$ on the logical level.

Since we now have two environments, we have to slightly extend some parts of our machinery. This includes interpretations, the operational semantics, and the safety judgements. For interpretations, the only difference is in the case of variables, which need to be taken from the correct environment:

$$
\begin{aligned}
\mathrm{J}x\mathrm{K}_{\eta,\overline{\eta}} &= \eta(x) \\
\mathrm{J}x_{\mathrm{hi}}\mathrm{K}_{\eta,\overline{\eta}} &= \overline{\eta}(x_{\mathrm{hi}})
\end{aligned}
$$

In the operational semantics, the only case interesting for memory safety is the array declaration; all other constructs leave the shadow environment unchanged.[7]

$$
\begin{aligned}
\langle \textbf{var}\ x, \eta, \overline{\eta}\rangle &\Rightarrow \langle \textbf{skip}, \eta, \overline{\eta}\rangle \\
\langle \textbf{var}\ x[n], \eta, \overline{\eta}\rangle &\Rightarrow \langle \textbf{skip}, \eta, \overline{\eta} \oplus \{x_{\mathrm{hi}} \mapsto \mathrm{J}n\mathrm{K}_{\eta,\overline{\eta}}\}\rangle \\
\langle x[e_1] := e_2, \eta, \overline{\eta}\rangle &\Rightarrow \langle \textbf{skip}, \eta \oplus \{x \mapsto (x \oplus \{\mathrm{J}e_1\mathrm{K}_{\eta,\overline{\eta}} \mapsto \mathrm{J}e_2\mathrm{K}_{\eta,\overline{\eta}}\})\}, \overline{\eta}\rangle \\
\langle c, \eta, \overline{\eta}\rangle &\Rightarrow \langle c', \eta', \overline{\eta}\rangle,\ \text{if}\ \langle c, \eta\rangle \Rightarrow \langle c', \eta'\rangle
\end{aligned}
$$

As in the stateless case, we can then define the safety judgement for memory safety. Figure 10 shows both judgements for expressions and commands.

Again following the schema developed for the stateless case, we then formulate the Hoare rules of the safety policy, as shown in Figure 11; we have omitted the rules (*skip*), (*comp*), and (*cons*) which remain unchanged. In the rules (*assign*), (*if*), and (*while*), the safety predicate is changed. The (*update*)-rule is an appropriately modified version of McCarthy's original rule.

The lemmas and theorems of the previous section hold in a suitably modified form. The main change is to modify the expansions of *wspc*. The key cases are

$$
\begin{aligned}
wspc(\textbf{var}\ x[n], Q) &\iff Q[0/x_{\mathrm{hi}}] \\
wspc(x[e_1] := e_2, Q) &\iff Q[update(x, e_1, e_2)/x] \land \mathit{safe}_{\mathrm{mem}}(x[e_1]) \land \mathit{safe}_{\mathrm{mem}}(e_2).
\end{aligned}
$$

---

[7] We also need to specify how array selection and updates are modeled; however, this is a consequence of extending the language and is independent of any certification issues. Here, we model arrays as maps from naturals to values; hence: $\mathrm{J}x[e]\mathrm{K}_{\eta,\overline{\eta}} = (\eta(x))(\mathrm{J}e\mathrm{K}_{\eta,\overline{\eta}})$

$\eta, \overline{\eta} \vDash c$ safe$_{mem}$
$\eta, \overline{\eta} \vDash x$ safe$_{mem}$
$\eta, \overline{\eta} \vDash x[e]$ safe$_{mem}$ iff $0 \leq \text{JeK}_{\eta,\overline{\eta}} < \overline{\eta}(x_{hi})$ and $\eta, \overline{\eta} \vDash e$ safe$_{mem}$
$\eta, \overline{\eta} \vDash e_1$ op e_2 safe$_{mem}$ iff $\eta, \overline{\eta} \vDash e_1$ safe$_{mem}$ and $\eta, \overline{\eta} \vDash e_2$ safe$_{mem}$

$\eta, \overline{\eta} \vDash$ var x safestate$_{mem}$
$\eta, \overline{\eta} \vDash$ var $x[n]$ safestate$_{mem}$
$\eta, \overline{\eta} \vDash$ skip safestate$_{mem}$
$\eta, \overline{\eta} \vDash e_1 := e_2$ safestate$_{mem}$ iff $\eta, \overline{\eta} \vDash e_1$ safe$_{mem}$ and $\eta, \overline{\eta} \vDash e_2$ safe$_{mem}$
$\eta, \overline{\eta} \vDash$ if b then c safestate$_{mem}$ iff $\eta, \overline{\eta} \vDash b$ safe$_{mem}$
$\eta, \overline{\eta} \vDash$ while b do c safestate$_{mem}$ iff $\eta, \overline{\eta} \vDash b$ safe$_{mem}$
$\eta, \overline{\eta} \vDash c_1; c_2$ safestate$_{mem}$ iff $\eta, \overline{\eta} \vDash c_1$ safestate$_{mem}$

$\eta, \overline{\eta} \vDash c$ safe$_{mem}$ iff $\forall \langle c, \eta, \overline{\eta} \rangle \Rightarrow^* \langle c', \eta', \overline{\eta}; \rangle \cdot \eta', \overline{\eta}; \vDash c'$ safestate$_{mem}$

Fig. 10. $\mathcal{L}_1$ memory safety

$(decl)$ $\dfrac{}{Q \{\texttt{var } x\} Q}$

$(adecl)$ $\dfrac{}{Q[n/x_{hi}] \{\texttt{var } x[n]\} Q}$

$(assign)$ $\dfrac{}{Q[e/x] \wedge \textit{safe}_{mem}(e) \{x := e\} Q}$

$(update)$ $\dfrac{}{Q[update(x, e_1, e_2)/x] \wedge \textit{safe}_{mem}(x[e_1]) \wedge \textit{safe}_{mem}(e_2) \{x[e_1] := e_2\} Q}$

(if) $\dfrac{P \Rightarrow \textit{safe}_{mem}(b) \quad b \wedge P \{c\} Q \quad \neg b \wedge P \Rightarrow Q}{P \{\texttt{if } b \texttt{ then } c\} Q}$

$(while)$ $\dfrac{P \Rightarrow \textit{safe}_{mem}(b) \quad b \wedge P \{c\} P}{P \{\texttt{while } b \texttt{ do } c\} \neg b \wedge P}$

Fig. 11. Hoare rules for $\mathcal{L}_1$ memory safety

3.2 Memory Write Limits

Next, we consider a safety policy which limits the number of times values can be written into each memory location. Obviously, this is undecidable in general, but with appropriate annotations (i.e., loop invariants) it can still be very helpful. Such a policy can then be used to ensure that the physical limitations of non-volatile memory, as for example used in spacecraft, are not exceeded. For example, locations in flash memory can only be written to a finite number of times before wearing out.

We formalize this using shadow variables x_{wl} which are initialized with zero when x is declared and incremented each time it is assigned to. As in the case of memory safety, the abstract environments map the variables to naturals, $\overline{\eta}$: $\overline{Var} \rightharpoonup I\!N$. However, unlike in the case of memory safety, we now need (i) shadow variables for scalars as well, and (ii) a separate shadow variable for each element of an array. While the first point is straightforward to deal with, the second seems at first more complicated. However, by introducing a complete shadow

$$safe_{mem}(e) = \begin{cases} true & \text{if } e \in \mathit{Var} \text{ or } e \in \mathit{Const} \\ safe_{mem}(e_1) \wedge 0 \leq e_1 < x_{hi} & \text{if } e \equiv x\texttt{[}e_1\texttt{]} \\ safe_{mem}(e_1) \wedge safe_{mem}(e_2) & \text{if } e \equiv e_1 \text{ mem } e_2,\ op \in \{*,/,+,-,=\} \end{cases}$$

Fig. 12. Safety formula for $\mathcal{L}_1$ memory safety

array, we get around all these problems. In the operational semantics we then see a nice symmetry between the operations on the original value environment and on the shadow environment:

$$\begin{aligned}
\langle \texttt{var } x, \eta, \overline{\eta}\rangle &\Rightarrow \langle \texttt{skip}, \eta, \overline{\eta} \oplus \{x_{wl} \mapsto 0\}\rangle \\
\langle \texttt{var } x\texttt{[}n\texttt{]}, \eta, \overline{\eta}\rangle &\Rightarrow \langle \texttt{skip}, \eta, \overline{\eta} \oplus \{x_{wl} \mapsto \lambda i \cdot 0\}\rangle \\
\langle x \texttt{ := } e, \eta, \overline{\eta}\rangle &\Rightarrow \langle \texttt{skip}, \eta \oplus \{x \mapsto \mathrm{J}e\mathrm{K}_\eta\}, \overline{\eta} \oplus \{x_{wl} \mapsto \overline{\eta}(x_{wl}) + 1\}\rangle \\
\langle x\texttt{[}e_1\texttt{] := } e_2, \eta, \overline{\eta}\rangle &\Rightarrow \langle \texttt{skip}, \\
&\qquad \eta \oplus \{x \mapsto (x \oplus \{\mathrm{J}e_1\mathrm{K}_{\eta,\overline{\eta}} \mapsto \mathrm{J}e_2\mathrm{K}_{\eta,\overline{\eta}}\})\}, \\
&\qquad \overline{\eta} \oplus \{x_{wl} \mapsto (x_{wl} \oplus \{\mathrm{J}e_1\mathrm{K}_{\eta,\overline{\eta}} \mapsto x_{wl}(\mathrm{J}e_1\mathrm{K}_{\eta,\overline{\eta}}) + 1\})\} \\
&\qquad \rangle \\
\langle c, \eta, \overline{\eta}\rangle &\Rightarrow \langle c', \eta', \overline{\eta}\rangle,\ \text{if } \langle c, \eta\rangle \Rightarrow \langle c', \eta'\rangle
\end{aligned}$$

The safety judgement safe_{wl} obviously only needs to look at assignments; it just checks that the assignment counts are still below a fixed upper limit $\textsc{Maxwr}$. Since safety reduction holds trivially, we formulate safe_{wl} directly and not via safestate.

$$\begin{aligned}
\eta, \overline{\eta} \vDash x \texttt{ := } e \text{ safe}_{wl} &\quad \text{iff}\quad \overline{\eta}(x_{wl}) < \textsc{Maxwr} \\
\eta, \overline{\eta} \vDash x\texttt{[}e_1\texttt{] := } e_2 \text{ safe}_{wl} &\quad \text{iff}\quad (\overline{\eta}(x_{wl}))(\mathrm{J}e_1\mathrm{K}_{\eta,\overline{\eta}}) < \textsc{Maxwr}
\end{aligned}$$

Finally, we formulate the Hoare rules (cf. Figure 13); again, the only interesting cases are declarations and assignments. We thus omit an explicit definition of the safety formula and inline it instead. Note that we extend the logic for arrays by the construct $init(x, n, k)$ which denotes the array x of size n where every element is set to k. For this, we need the axiom $i < n \Rightarrow (init(x, n, k))(i) = k$ in the domain theory of the underlying logic (not shown here).

$$(decl)\ \frac{}{Q[0/x_{wl}]\ \{\texttt{var } x\}\ Q}$$

$$(adecl)\ \frac{}{Q[init(x_{wl}, n, 0)/x_{wl}]\ \{\texttt{var } x\texttt{[}n\texttt{]}\}\ Q}$$

$$(assign)\ \frac{}{Q[e/x, (x_{wl} + 1)/x_{wl}] \wedge x_{wl} < \textsc{Maxwr}\ \{x \texttt{ := } e\}\ Q}$$

$$(update)\ \frac{}{Q\begin{bmatrix}update(x, e_1, e_2)/x, \\ update(x_{wl}, e_1, x_{wl}\texttt{[}e_1\texttt{]}+1)/x_{wl}\end{bmatrix} \wedge x_{wl}\texttt{[}e_1\texttt{]} < \textsc{Maxwr}\ \{x\texttt{[}e_1\texttt{] := } e_2\}\ Q}$$

Fig. 13. Hoare rules for $\mathcal{L}_1$ write limits

Again, we can show that the system is sound and complete with respect to the corresponding semantics. The proofs follow the outline in Section 2.

3.3 Memory Read Limits

The final safety policy we consider in this paper limits the number of times memory locations can be read. Intuitively, this is the dual of the write limit policy considered above; formally, however, it is quite different. The reason for the difference (and the source of additional complexity) is that the updates of the shadow environment are now much less localized: the evaluation of each expression can potentially change the shadow environment. This problem is not restricted to read limits but occurs whenever expression evaluation can have side effects, either in the original environment, or in the shadow environment. We thus extend the evaluation notation for expressions to take the environments into account, i.e., $\langle e, \eta, \overline{\eta} \rangle \Downarrow \langle v, \eta', \overline{\eta}' \rangle$.

To simplify our notation we define a shadow environment update function $upd : Env \times \overline{Env} \times Expr \to \overline{Env}$ which examines the expression and adds the correct number of occurrences to the shadow environment; the notation $y \in_n e$ denotes that there are n occurrences of the variable y in e:

$$upd(\eta, \overline{\eta}, e) = \overline{\eta} \oplus \{x_{\mathrm{rl}} \mapsto \overline{\eta}(x_{\mathrm{rl}}) + n \mid x \in_n e\}$$
$$\oplus \{x_{\mathrm{rl}} \mapsto x_{\mathrm{rl}} \oplus \{\mathrm{Je'K}_{\eta,\overline{\eta}} \mapsto x_{\mathrm{rl}}(\mathrm{Je'K}_{\eta,\overline{\eta}}) + n\} \mid x\texttt{[}e'\texttt{]} \in_n e\}$$

We can then formulate the operational semantics concisely; the omitted cases follow easily.

$$\begin{aligned}
\langle \texttt{var } x, \eta, \overline{\eta} \rangle &\Rightarrow \langle \texttt{skip}, \eta, \overline{\eta} \oplus \{x_{\mathrm{rl}} \mapsto 0\} \rangle \\
\langle \texttt{var } x\texttt{[}n\texttt{]}, \eta, \overline{\eta} \rangle &\Rightarrow \langle \texttt{skip}, \eta, \overline{\eta} \oplus \{x_{\mathrm{rl}} \mapsto \lambda i \cdot 0\} \rangle \\
\langle x := e, \eta, \overline{\eta} \rangle &\Rightarrow \langle \texttt{skip}, \eta \oplus \{x \mapsto \mathrm{JeK}_{\eta,\overline{\eta}}\}, upd(\eta, \overline{\eta}, e) \rangle \\
\langle x\texttt{[}e_1\texttt{]} := e_2, \eta, \overline{\eta} \rangle &\Rightarrow \langle \texttt{skip}, \\
&\quad \eta \oplus \{x \mapsto (x \oplus \{\mathrm{Je_1K}_{\eta,\overline{\eta}} \mapsto \mathrm{Je_2K}_{\eta,\overline{\eta}}\})\}, \\
&\quad upd(\eta, upd(\eta, \overline{\eta}, e_1), e_2) \\
&\quad \rangle \\
\langle \texttt{if } b \texttt{ then } c, \eta, \overline{\eta} \rangle &\Rightarrow \langle c, \eta, upd(\eta, \overline{\eta}, b) \rangle \text{ if } \mathrm{JbK}_{\eta,\overline{\eta}} = \mathit{true} \\
\langle \texttt{if } b \texttt{ then } c, \eta, \overline{\eta} \rangle &\Rightarrow \langle \texttt{skip}, \eta, upd(\eta, \overline{\eta}, b) \rangle \text{ if } \mathrm{JbK}_{\eta,\overline{\eta}} = \mathit{false}
\end{aligned}$$

In effect, we can give the semantics in terms of the basic underlying semantics and the update function on the shadow environments: if $\langle c, \eta \rangle \Rightarrow \langle c', \eta' \rangle$, then $\langle c, \eta, \overline{\eta} \rangle \Rightarrow \langle c', \eta', upd(\eta, \overline{\eta}', e_1, \ldots, e_n) \rangle$ for immediate subexpressions $e_1, \ldots, e_n$ of c (extending upd to lists of expressions in the obvious way). We can also apply the same idea to the Hoare rules. Instead of an update function which is applied to the shadow environment we need an update substitution $\mathsf{Sub}(e)$ which is applied to the precondition; it is defined in the same way as the update function:

$$\mathsf{Sub}(e) = [x_{\mathrm{rl}} + n/x_{\mathrm{rl}} \mid x \in_n e] \cup [update(x_{\mathrm{rl}}, e', x_{\mathrm{rl}}\texttt{[}e'\texttt{]} + n)/x_{\mathrm{rl}} \mid x\texttt{[}e'\texttt{]} \in_n e]$$

We then define the safety formula $\mathit{safe}_{\mathrm{rl}}(e)$ in the same way: it checks that the occurrences in e do not exceed the limit MAXRL:

$$\mathit{safe}_{\mathrm{rl}}(e) = \bigwedge_{x \in_n e} x_{\mathrm{rl}} + n \leq \text{MAXRL} \ \land \bigwedge_{x\texttt{[}e'\texttt{]} \in e} (\mathit{fold}_{x\texttt{[}e'\texttt{]} \in_n e}(upd(n), x_{\mathrm{rl}}))\texttt{[}e'\texttt{]} \leq \text{MAXRL}$$

where the folded update of x_{r1} by all *literal* occurrences $x[e']$ in e is defined using:

$$upd(n)(x[e'], x_{r1}) = update(x_{r1}, e', x_{r1}[e'] + n).$$

The safety judgements are similar to those for write limits. The only change is that since expression evaluation can affect the shadow environment, we need to add the the safety condition outside the substitution. With this, we have all the pieces in place to formulate the Hoare rules. We only give a single rule for the `if`-statement; the other rules follow the same schema.

$$(if) \; \frac{b \wedge P \; \{c\} \; Q \quad \neg b \wedge P \Rightarrow Q}{\mathsf{Sub}^b(P) \wedge \mathit{safe}_{r1}(b) \; \{\texttt{if} \; b \; \texttt{then} \; c\} \; Q}$$

4 Automatic Derivation of Safety Policies

We now generalize the idea from Section 3.3 and derive a general way of formulating safety extensions to an operational semantics and Hoare logic, respectively, such that the results of the previous sections are preserved. The main idea is to develop a notion of *compositional* safety property, which then allows us to augment the Hoare rules in a similarly compositional manner.

We have seen that abstract environments describe how programs compute the abstract properties we are interested in for a given safety property. In order to reason about such properties in a safety policy, we need a notion of expressivity to relate environments to the logic.

Definition 4. *We say that a command $c \in \mathit{Cmd}$ is operationally expressive, if whenever $\langle c, \eta, \bar{\eta} \rangle \Rightarrow \langle c', \eta', \bar{\eta}' \rangle$, then for all $x \in (\eta' \cup \bar{\eta}')$, there exists an expression e, such that $\mathrm{J} e \mathrm{K}_{\eta, \bar{\eta}} = \mathrm{J} x \mathrm{K}_{\eta', \bar{\eta}'}$.* ■

This formalizes the idea that whatever change a command makes to the environments can be expressed in terms of substitutions. Clearly, the expression can only contain variables from the original environments.

We use the notation $\mathsf{Sub}_\theta^{e_1,\ldots,e_n}(P)$ to denote the substitution, applied to P, which expresses the change in environments effected by command type θ with immediate subexpressions $e_1, \ldots, e_n$. We are implicitly assuming particularly simple changes to the environment which can always be expressed this way, but this accounts for all our examples. For example, $\mathsf{Sub}_{\texttt{assign}}^{x,e}(P)$ is simply $P[e/x]$ for the assignment $x := e$.

In general, each command has its own notion of safety. However, we want to exclude pathological examples of safety properties, so we consider, now, what sort of properties are acceptable. For atomic commands, we allow an arbitrary condition on the environments and the component expressions. For example, the safety of the assignment $x := e$ can be any condition on x and e. We can express this as a predicate $P \subseteq \mathit{Env} \times \overline{\mathit{Env}} \times \mathit{Expr} \times \mathit{Expr}$. For compound commands, the key idea is that the basic data of a safety property consists of arbitrary predicates, Cond, on the immediately accessible subexpressions for each command. We will write $\eta, \bar{\eta} \models \textsf{Cond}(e_1, \ldots, e_n)$ to mean $\langle \eta, \bar{\eta}, e_1, \ldots, e_n \rangle \in$ Cond.

Definition 5. *A safety property on commands is* compositional, *if there exist predicates* $\textsf{Cond}_\theta$, *with the following properties:*

- $\eta, \bar{\eta} \models \textsf{var } x$ safe *iff* $\eta, \bar{\eta} \models \textsf{Cond}_\texttt{decl}(x)$
- $\eta, \bar{\eta} \models \textsf{var } x[n]$ safe *iff* $\eta, \bar{\eta} \models \textsf{Cond}_\texttt{adecl}(x, n)$
- $\eta, \bar{\eta} \models x := e$ safe *iff* $\eta, \bar{\eta} \models \textsf{Cond}_\texttt{assign}(x, e)$
- $\eta, \bar{\eta} \models x[e_1] := e_2$ safe *iff* $\eta, \bar{\eta} \models \textsf{Cond}_\texttt{update}(x, e_1, e_2)$
- $\eta, \bar{\eta} \models \textsf{skip}$ safe
- $\eta, \bar{\eta} \models \textsf{if } b \textsf{ then } c$ safe *iff* $\textsf{Cond}_\texttt{if}(b)$ *and* $\langle b, \eta, \bar{\eta} \rangle \Downarrow \langle true, \eta', \bar{\eta}' \rangle$ *implies* $\langle \eta', \bar{\eta}' \rangle \models c$ safe
- $\eta, \bar{\eta} \models \textsf{while } b \textsf{ do } c$ safe *iff* $\eta, \bar{\eta} \models \textsf{Cond}_\texttt{while}(b)$ *and* $\langle b, \eta, \bar{\eta} \rangle \Downarrow \langle true, \eta', \bar{\eta}' \rangle$ *implies* $(\langle \eta', \bar{\eta}' \rangle \models c$ safe *and* $\langle c, \eta', \bar{\eta}' \rangle \Downarrow \langle \eta'', \bar{\eta}'' \rangle$ *implies* $\langle \eta'', \bar{\eta}'' \rangle \models \textsf{while } b \textsf{ do } c$ safe).

For sequential composition, the safety of $c_1; c_2$ is defined as before. Although this looks fairly similar to Figure 6 it generalizes it by allowing arbitrary conditions on the expressions. Stateless safety follows as the special case where $\eta, \bar{\eta} \models \textsf{Cond}_\theta(e_1, \ldots, e_n)$ iff $\eta, \bar{\eta} \models e_i$ safe, for each i.

This notion of compositionality maintains the correspondence between **safe** and **safestate**, while allowing that safety of a command is arbitrarily expressed in terms of the safety of its subcommands. Now it should come as no surprise that we require the condition predicates to be expressible.

Definition 6. *We say that the n-ary predicate, P, is* expressible *when there exists formulas ϕ such that*

$$\langle e_1, \ldots, e_n \rangle \in P \text{ iff } \eta, \bar{\eta} \models \phi(e_1, \ldots, e_n).$$

Finally, we are in a position to state a general completeness theorem, which generalizes the theory of stateless safety developed in Section 2. We omit the details of the proof here and just state the theorem; the proof structure is the same as for the stateless case, making use of expressivity where appropriate.

Theorem 3. *Given (i) a set, $\overline{Val}$ (the shadow domain), (ii) an operational semantics, $\langle c, \eta, \bar{\eta} \rangle \Rightarrow \langle c, \eta', \bar{\eta}' \rangle$, and (iii) a compositional safety property, such that expressivity (operational, predicate, commands and expressions) holds, the* *following system is sound and complete with respect to the safety property:*

$$(decl) \quad \frac{}{\mathsf{Sub}^x_{\mathtt{decl}}(Q) \land \mathsf{Cond}_{\mathtt{decl}}(x) \ \{\mathtt{var}\ x\}\ Q}$$

$$(adecl) \quad \frac{}{\mathsf{Sub}^{x,n}_{\mathtt{adecl}}(Q) \land \mathsf{Cond}_{\mathtt{decl}}(x,n) \ \{\mathtt{var}\ x\mathtt{[}n\mathtt{]}\}\ Q}$$

$$(assign) \quad \frac{}{\mathsf{Sub}^{x,e}_{\mathtt{assign}}(Q) \land \mathsf{Cond}_{\mathtt{assign}}(x,e) \ \{x\ \mathtt{:=}\ e\}\ Q}$$

$$(update) \quad \frac{}{\mathsf{Sub}^{x,e_1,e_2}_{\mathtt{update}}(Q) \land \mathsf{Cond}_{\mathtt{update}}(x,e_1,e_2) \ \{x\mathtt{[}e_1\mathtt{]}\ \mathtt{:=}\ e_2\}\ Q}$$

$$(if) \quad \frac{b \land P\ \{c\}\ Q \quad \neg b \land P \Rightarrow Q}{\mathsf{Sub}^b_{\mathtt{if}}(P) \land \mathsf{Cond}_{\mathtt{if}}(b) \ \{\mathtt{if}\ b\ \mathtt{then}\ c\}\ Q}$$

$$(while) \quad \frac{b \land P\ \{c\}\ P}{\mathsf{Sub}^b_{\mathtt{while}}(P) \land \mathsf{Cond}_{\mathtt{while}}(b) \ \{\mathtt{while}\ b\ \mathtt{do}\ c\}\ Q}$$

(with the rules (skip) and (cons) as before). ∎

5 Related Work

A number of different techniques have been applied to program certification. The following list is certainly not exhaustive; we focus on static techniques and leave out dynamic techniques like runtime monitoring [5].

Certification tools based on static analysis are already commercially available, e.g., PolySpace [14], which uses abstract interpretation and constraint solving techniques to identify possible runtime errors. However, such tools usually have fixed built-in notions of safety and suffer from a high number of false positives.

Other approaches use expressive type systems to enforce safety policies. Rittri [16] and Kennedy [7] have extended type inference techniques to ensure the consistent use of physical dimensions in functional programs. However, both approaches exploit certain algebraic properties of dimensions and it is unclear how general they are. Xi and Pfenning [20] have used dependent types to show array bounds safety, again for functional programs. Using similar ideas, Walker [18] has developed a type system to express and enforce a number of security policies. Shankar et al. [17] have used type qualifiers [3] to detect vulnerabilities due to C's format strings. Their tainted and untainted qualifiers take the same role as the values in our shadow domains. In general, type-based approaches tend to scale better, although it is unclear when a specific expressive type inference algorithm becomes intractable in practice. Unlike the shadow variables, however, inferred types are static, i.e., the abstract value associated with a program cannot change during execution. Moreover, structured collections like arrays are usually modeled using a single type to keep inference tractable; this makes the analysis necessarily less precise. Experiments are thus required to compare the effects and trade-offs of the different approaches in practice.

Traditionally, program verification concentrates on showing full functional equivalence between specifications and programs. This is true especially for integrated development/proof environments as for example the KIV system [15]. However, Hoare-style verification has also been used in property-oriented certification as we investigate it here. Extended static checking (ESC) [8, 4] can be thought of as an "inference-based debugger": it uses Hoare rules, supported by program annotations, to detect a variety of potential errors, including division-by-zero and array-bounds violations. The more annotations the program contains, the more errors ESC can detect. Similarly, the SPARK Examiner [1] is a tool which uses Hoare rules to show exception freedom of Ada programs; this corresponds to a safety policy which combines more elaborate versions of operator safety (i.e., division-by-zero and overflow) and memory safety (i.e., array-bounds violations and overflow).[8] However, none of the systems deal with the question of correctness of their respective safety policies. Also, they typically only deal with one specific policy, whereas our framework is general.

6 Conclusions and Future Work

In this paper we have formalized a selection of safety properties using Hoare logic, and shown that they are sound and complete with respect to a semantic notion of safety. We have developed a generic method of doing this for arbitrary safety properties, thus showing how a safety policy can be automatically derived from a safety property and an operational semantics. The principal difficulty has been finding a general definition of safety property which enables this automatic derivation.

The rules we have presented show that safety rules can be quite complicated, even when dealing with a single policy at a time. The semantic framework developed in this paper serves as a structuring mechanism to deal with such complexity. The modularization of safety policies is a difficult problem but the present theory should serve as a starting point.

We are currently using this theory as the basis for the implementation of a VCG which is parametric with respect to a safety policy, and we are looking at a wide range of safety properties. Direct application of the theory should lead to a modular implementation.

The simple *while*-language studied here is sufficient for this because our aim is to certify synthesized code, and so we can control the language subset under consideration. Moreover, since we can generate loop invariants along with the synthesized code our safety logic need not be concerned with this.

On a theoretical side, we believe that the logical nature of Definition 5 points to some interesting connections to the theory of computation, and we are currently investigating this.

---

[8] Note that overflows can result from arithmetic operations as well as from inconsistent use of derived types (i.e., subtypes) and thus influence both operator safety and memory safety.

References

[1] P. Amey and R. Chapman. "Industrial Strength Exception Freedom". In: *2002 SIGAda Intl. Conf. on Ada*, pp. 1–9. ACM, 2002.
[2] A. Appel. "Foundational proof-carrying code". In: *LICS-16*, pp. 247–258. IEEE, 2001.
[3] J. S. Foster, M. Fähndrich, and A. Aiken. "A Theory of Type Qualifiers". In: *PLDI*, pp. 192–203. ACM, 1999.
[4] C. Flanagan, K. R. M. Leino, M. Lillibridge, G. Nelson, J. B. Saxe, and R. Stata. "Extended static checking for Java". In: *PLDI*, pp. 234–245. ACM, 2002.
[5] K. Havelund and G. Roşu. "Monitoring Java Programs with Java PathExplorer". In: *First Workshop on Runtime Verification, ENTCS* **55(2)**. Elsevier, 2001.
[6] N. A. Hamid, Z. Shao, V. Trifonov, S. Monnier, and Z. Ni. "A Syntactic Approach to Foundational Proof-Carrying Code". In: *LICS-17*, pp. 89–100. IEEE, 2002.
[7] A. Kennedy. *Programming Languages and Dimensions*. PhD thesis, University of Cambridge, April 1996.
[8] K. R. M. Leino and G. Nelson. "An extended static checker for Modula-3". In: *7th Intl. Conf. Compiler Construction, LNCS* **1383**, pp. 302–305. Springer, 1998.
[9] M. Lowry, T. Pressburger, and G. Rosu. "Certifying Domain-Specific Policies". In: *16th Intl. Conf. Automated Software Engineering*, pp. 118–125. IEEE, 2001.
[10] C. League, Z. Shao, and V. Trifonov. "Precision in Practice: A Type-Preserving Java Compiler". In: *12th Intl. Conf. Compiler Construction, LNCS* **2622**, pp. 106–120. Springer, April 2003.
[11] J. C. Mitchell. *Foundations for Programming Languages*. The MIT Press, 1996.
[12] G. C. Necula and P. Lee. "The Design and Implementation of a Certifying Compiler". In: *PLDI*, pp. 333–344. ACM, 1998.
[13] G. C. Necula and R. R. Schneck. "A Gradual Approach to a More Trustworthy, yet Scalable, Proof-Carrying Code". In: *CADE-18, LNCS* **2392**, pp. 47–62. Springer, 2002.
[14] PolySpace Technologies, 2002. http://www.polyspace.com.
[15] W. Reif. "The KIV Approach to Software Verification". In: *KORSO: Methods, Languages and Tools for the Construction of Correct Software, LNCS* **1009**, pp. 339–370. Springer, 1995.
[16] M. Rittri. "Dimension Inference Under Polymorphic Recursion". In: *7th Conf. Functional Prog. Languages Computer Architecture*, pp. 147–159. ACM, 1995.
[17] U. Shankar, K. Talwar, J. S. Foster, and D. Wagner. "Detecting Format String Vulnerabilities with Type Qualifiers". In: *10th Usenix Security Symposium*, 2001.
[18] D. Walker. "A Type System for Expressive Security Policies". In: *POPL-27*, pp. 254–267. ACM, 2000.
[19] M. Whalen, J. Schumann, and B. Fischer. "Synthesizing Certified Code". In: *FME, LNCS* **2391**, pp. 431–450. Springer, 2002.
[20] H. Xi and F. Pfenning. "Eliminating Array Bound Checking Through Dependent Types". In: *PLDI*, pp. 249–257. ACM, 1998.

A Topological Characterization of TCP/IP Security

Giovanni Vigna

Reliable Software Group
Department of Computer Science
University of California Santa Barbara
vigna@cs.ucsb.edu

Abstract. The TCP/IP protocol suite has been designed to provide a simple, open communication infrastructure in an academic, collaborative environment. Therefore, the TCP/IP protocols are not able to provide the authentication, integrity, and privacy mechanisms to protect communication in a hostile environment. To solve these security problems, a number of application-level protocols have been designed and implemented on top of TCP/IP. In addition, *ad hoc* techniques have been developed to protect networks from TCP/IP-based attacks. Nonetheless, a formal approach to TCP/IP security is still lacking. This work presents a formal model of TCP/IP networks and describes some well-known attacks using the model. The topological characterization of TCP/IP-based attacks enables better understanding of the vulnerabilities and supports the design of tougher detection, protection, and testing tools.

Keywords: Security, TCP/IP protocols, Network model, Topology.

1 Introduction

Security has become a major concern in the ever-growing Internet. Break-ins are becoming wide-spread and more sophisticated [6]. Some of these attacks either exploit or are based on some well-known flaws in the TCP/IP protocol suite [21, 4].

The TCP/IP protocol suite was designed more than twenty years ago [32] to provide a simple, efficient, open communication infrastructure in a collaborative and friendly environment. Little attention was paid to security issues, at that time. Therefore, the most used version of the TCP/IP protocol suite (namely, version 4) does not provide authentication, integrity, and privacy mechanisms to protect communication in a potentially hostile environment. To provide secure communication services, a number of secure higher-level protocols (e.g., Kerberos [17] and SSL [13]) have been designed and implemented on top of the TCP/IP stack. In order to protect TCP/IP networks from attacks based on those protocols *ad hoc* techniques (e.g., firewalls [8, 7]) have been developed. In addition, a secure version of the TCP/IP protocol suite (called version 6) has been designed. Nonetheless, the original (insecure) protocols are still widely used.

Even if in the last few years a more systematic approach to the problem has been followed, a formal approach to TCP/IP security is still lacking. This work presents a formal model of TCP/IP networks. The model is used to describe several well-known attacks that exploit vulnerabilities in the TCP/IP protocol suite. The analysis is carried out from a topological viewpoint aimed at identifying the prerequisites to mount a particular attack and the conditions that enable both detection and protection.

The examples included in the paper show that the model supports a precise description of the attacks and provides effective support to network security analysis. The network model described in this paper has been successfully used as the basis for intrusion detection sensor placement [30].

The rest of the paper is structured as follows. In Section 2 we shortly present the TCP/IP protocol suite. In Section 3 we present our model of TCP/IP networks. In Sections 4, 5, and 6 we describe some of the vulnerabilities of the TCP/IP protocol suite using the proposed model. In Section 7 we discuss how the outcomes of the previous sections can be used to protect TCP/IP networks. In Section 8 we draw some conclusions and outline future work.

2 The TCP/IP Protocol Suite

The Internet is a collection of computer networks, which share the same network protocol suite, namely TCP/IP. Networks participating in the Internet may adopt any protocol at the link layer (e.g., Ethernet, Token Ring, etc.), but they must adopt the TCP/IP protocol suite in the upper layers, i.e., the *Internet Protocol* (IP) at the network level, and the *Transmission Control Protocol* (TCP) or the *User Datagram Protocol* (UDP) at the transport level[1]. Since the TCP/IP protocol suite does not include any session and presentation layer protocols, application-level protocols (e.g., SSH or FTP) are based directly on TCP/UDP protocols.

2.1 Internet Protocol

The IP protocol [25] provides an unreliable, best-effort, connectionless packet delivery service. Each possible source or destination of a message in the network (i.e., each network interface) has a unique IP address, composed of 32 bits (e.g., 192.168.5.10). Hosts may have one or more network interfaces, and, therefore they may have more than one IP address.

An IP *datagram* is composed of a header and a payload. The header contains, among other fields, the source and destination IP addresses, the type of the payload and possible options. Every host in the Internet can communicate with every other host by sending an IP datagram containing the recipient IP address. The datagram is forwarded by a series of gateways until it reaches the intended destination.

---

[1] We adopt the ISO/OSI reference model [12].

The process of determining the path of a datagram in an internet is called *routing*. In the simplest case, both source and destination hosts reside in the same physical subnetwork, and, therefore, the datagram is delivered directly, encapsulating the IP datagram in a link-level message. However, if the source and destination hosts are in different subnetworks, the datagram must be delivered indirectly. In this case, the source host sends the datagram to a directly connected gateway. The gateway compares the destination IP address to its routing table and it decides if it can deliver the datagram directly or if it must send the datagram to another gateway. Routing tables entries are either static or defined dynamically by means of *routing protocols* (e.g., RIP [18], BGP [28]).

2.2 UDP

The User Datagram Protocol [24] relies on IP to provide an unreliable, best-effort, connectionless datagram delivery service. UDP datagrams are encapsulated in IP datagrams. A UDP datagram contains a source and destination port number and a payload. The port numbers are used to distinguish different datagram sources and destinations for a single IP address. UDP is used mostly for request/reply services (e.g., NFS [19]).

2.3 TCP

The Transmission Control Protocol [26] relies on IP to provide a reliable, best-effort, connection-oriented, full-duplex stream delivery service. The TCP protocol uses the port abstraction in order to distinguish among different virtual circuits between the same IP addresses. A virtual circuit is uniquely identified by the tuple *(source IP address, destination IP address, source TCP port, destination TCP port)*. TCP segments are encapsulated into IP datagrams. Each TCP segment has a header and a payload. The header contains the source and destination port numbers, which, together with the IP addresses of the enclosing IP datagram, identify the virtual circuit the segment belongs to. In addition, the TCP header contains a sequence number that identifies the position of the first byte of the payload with respect to the circuit's stream and an acknowledgment number that identifies the next byte that the segment source expects from the destination. Finally, the header contains a set of flags that are used during the setup and shutdown phase of the TCP virtual circuit.

The setup phase of a TCP virtual circuit is a three-way handshake between a client that performs an *active open* from port p_c and a server that performs a *passive open* at port p_s. The three-way handshake is performed according to the following steps:

1. the client sends a segment to the server with the SYN flag set and containing an initial sequence number s_c^0;
2. the server replies with a segment containing its initial sequence number s_s^0 and the acknowledgment of the client sequence number $a_s^0 = s_c^0 + 1$; the segment is marked with both the SYN and ACK flags;

3. the client sends a segment with the ACK flag set, containing the sequence number $s_c^1 = s_c^0 + 1$ and the acknowledgment number $a_c^1 = s_s^0 + 1$.

From this point on, the session is in an *established* state, and each of the communication partners can send a segment that will be acknowledged by the other. When one of the partners decides to stop transmitting data, it sends a segment marked with the FIN flag. The other partner acknowledges the message and eventually produces a similar segment, shutting down the connection. At any moment, both partners may send a segment marked with the RST flag to immediately shut down the connection.

2.4 Application Protocols

Application protocols can be implemented on top of either TCP or UDP, depending of the underlying requirements (e.g., reliability). For example, the Simple Mail Transfer Protocol (SMTP) [27] and the Hypertext Transfer Protocol (HTTP) [11] are both implemented on top of TCP, while the Domain Name System [20] is implemented on top UDP[2].

2.5 Security Issues

The TCP/IP protocol suite has been designed to deliver robust communication services in a cooperative, friendly network environment. As a consequence, the TCP/IP protocol suite is vulnerable to a number of attacks, such as spoofing, sniffing, and hijacking. In the following sections, we first introduce a model for networks and the TCP/IP protocol suite. Then, we use the model to describe some basic attacks against the TCP/IP protocol suite.

3 A Network Model

We model a *network* as a connected hypergraph [5] N on the set of *interfaces* $I = \{i_1, i_2, \ldots, i_n\}$. More precisely, a network is a family $N = \{E_1, E_2, \ldots, E_m\}$ where each E_i is a subset of I and it is called an *edge* of the hypergraph. The following statements hold:

$$E_i \neq \emptyset \qquad (i = 1, 2, \ldots, m), \tag{1}$$

$$\bigcup_{i=1}^{m} E_i = I.$$

We define a *route* between two interfaces i_j and i_k as a sequence of edges $r = \langle E_{r_1}, E_{r_2}, \ldots, E_{r_n} \rangle$ with $i_j \in E_{r_1}$, $i_k \in E_{r_n}$, and, $E_{r_l} \cap E_{r_{l+1}} \neq \emptyset$ for $l < n$. We call R the set of all routes.

---

[2] The DNS protocol can actually operate on top of both UDP and TCP.

We partition the set of edges N in two parts: the set *hosts* $H=\{H_1, H_2, \ldots, H_p\}$ and the set *links* $L = \{L_1, L_2, \ldots, L_q\}$. Hosts are edges (with at least one interface by (1)) which partition the set of interfaces, i.e.:

$$\bigcup_{i=1}^{p} H_i = I$$
$$H_i \cap H_j = \emptyset \qquad i, j \in \{1, 2, \ldots, p\} \text{ and } i \neq j. \tag{2}$$

Links are edges containing at least two interfaces. They also partition the set I:

$$\min_j |L_j| \geq 2$$
$$\bigcup_{i=1}^{q} L_i = I$$
$$L_i \cap L_j = \emptyset \qquad i, j \in \{1, 2, \ldots, q\} \text{ and } i \neq j. \tag{3}$$

From the previous formulas it follows that any route in the network alternates hosts and links[3].

We define a graphic representation for the entities of the model. Hosts are drawn as circles. Interfaces belonging to a host are drawn as dots inside the corresponding circle. Links are drawn as lines connecting interfaces belonging to the link. The network topology may also be described by using the *hosts matrix* HM and the *links matrix* LM. The hosts matrix has columns representing the network hosts $H_1, H_2, \ldots, H_p$ and rows representing the interfaces $i_1, i_2, \ldots, i_n$. Element e_k^j is 1 if $i_j \in H_k$ and 0 otherwise. The links matrix has columns representing the network links $L_1, L_2, \ldots, L_q$ and rows representing the interfaces $i_1, i_2, \ldots, i_n$. Element e_k^j is 1 if $i_j \in L_k$ and zero otherwise. The juxtaposition of HM and LM gives the incidence matrix IM of the network hypergraph.

Figure 1 shows a network with nine hosts, six links, and fifteen interfaces:

$$I = \{i_1, i_2, i_3, i_4, i_5, i_6, i_7, i_8, i_9, i_{10}, i_{11}, i_{12}, i_{13}, i_{14}, i_{15}\}$$
$$H = \{\{i_1\}, \{i_2, i_3, i_4, i_{15}\}, \{i_5\}, \{i_6, i_7\}, \{i_8\}, \{i_9\},$$
$$\{i_{10}, i_{11}\}, \{i_{12}\}, \{i_{13}, i_{14}\}\}$$
$$L = \{\{i_1, i_2\}, \{i_3, i_5\}, \{i_4, i_6\}, \{i_7, i_8, i_9, i_{10}\}, \{i_{11}, i_{12}, i_{13}\}, \{i_{14}, i_{15}\}\}$$
$$N = \{H_1, \ldots, H_9, L_1, \ldots, L_6\}.$$

The corresponding hosts and links matrices are shown in Figure 2.

A host H_i is *connected to* a link L_j iff $H_i \cap L_j \neq \emptyset$. A link L_j *connects* a set of hosts $C(L_j)$ with:

$$C(L_j) = \{H_i \in H \mid H_i \cap L_j \neq \emptyset\}.$$

---

[3] If not so, two hosts or two links may have a non-empty intersection, which is against (2) and (3), respectively.

A Topological Characterization of TCP/IP Security

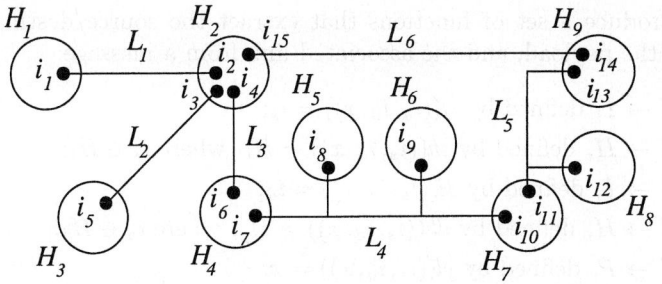

Fig. 1. A network hypergraph.

Two hosts H_i, H_j are said to be *connected by* a link L_k iff they both belong to the set of hosts the link connects, i.e., $H_i \in C(L_k) \wedge H_j \in C(L_k)$.

A *subnetwork* is a sub-hypergraph composed of a non-empty set of links $L_J = \{L_i \in L \mid i \in J \text{ and } J \subseteq \{1,2,\ldots,q\}\}$ together with the hosts they connect, i.e.:

$$N_J = L_J \cup \{H_i \in H \mid \exists j \in J \text{ such that } H_i \in C(L_j)\}.$$

A *message* $m \in M$ is a triple containing two interfaces i_s (the *source* interface) and i_d (the *destination* interface), and a payload $x \in X$ (for some set X, to be specified later) such that both interfaces belong to the same link, i.e.:

$$m = (i_s, i_d, x) \text{ such that } i_s \in L_i \text{ and } i_d \in L_i \text{ with } L_i \in L.$$

A message $m = (i_s, i_d, x)$ is said to be *between* hosts H_i (the *source* host) and H_j (the *destination* host), with $i_s \in H_i$ and $i_d \in H_j$, and it is said to *appear* on link L_i, if $i_s, i_d \in L_i$.

	H_1	H_2	H_3	H_4	H_5	H_6	H_7	H_8	H_9
i_1	1	0	0	0	0	0	0	0	0
i_2	0	1	0	0	0	0	0	0	0
i_3	0	1	0	0	0	0	0	0	0
i_4	0	1	0	0	0	0	0	0	0
i_5	0	0	1	0	0	0	0	0	0
i_6	0	0	0	1	0	0	0	0	0
i_7	0	0	0	1	0	0	0	0	0
i_8	0	0	0	0	1	0	0	0	0
i_9	0	0	0	0	0	1	0	0	0
i_{10}	0	0	0	0	0	0	1	0	0
i_{11}	0	0	0	0	0	0	1	0	0
i_{12}	0	0	0	0	0	0	0	1	0
i_{13}	0	0	0	0	0	0	0	0	1
i_{14}	0	0	0	0	0	0	0	0	1
i_{15}	0	1	0	0	0	0	0	0	0

	L_1	L_2	L_3	L_4	L_5	L_6
i_1	1	0	0	0	0	0
i_2	1	0	0	0	0	0
i_3	0	1	0	0	0	0
i_4	0	0	1	0	0	0
i_5	0	1	0	0	0	0
i_6	0	0	1	0	0	0
i_7	0	0	0	1	0	0
i_8	0	0	0	1	0	0
i_9	0	0	0	1	0	0
i_{10}	0	0	0	1	0	0
i_{11}	0	0	0	0	1	0
i_{12}	0	0	0	0	1	0
i_{13}	0	0	0	0	1	0
i_{14}	0	0	0	0	0	1
i_{15}	0	0	0	0	0	1

Fig. 2. Hosts and links matrices.

We introduce a set of functions that extract the source/destination interface/host, the payload, and the associated link from a message:

$si : M \to I$, defined by $si((i_s, i_d, x)) = i_s$;
$sh : M \to H$, defined by $sh((i_s, i_d, x)) = H_i$, where $i_s \in H_i$;
$di : M \to I$, defined by $di((i_s, i_d, x)) = i_d$;
$dh : M \to H$, defined by $dh((i_s, i_d, x)) = H_j$, where $i_d \in H_j$;
$pl : M \to P$, defined by $pl((i_s, i_d, x)) = x$;
$al : M \to L$, defined by $al((i_s, i_d, x)) = L_i$, where $i_s, i_d \in L_i$.

The use of hypergraphs to describe network topologies allows for intuitive modeling of networks based on shared bus technologies, e.g., Ethernet. In these technologies, hosts that are connected to a shared communication link may eavesdrop the messages exchanged using such link even if they are not directly involved in the communication.

Given a message m, we define the set of *listeners* of the message as the set of hosts connected to the link the message appears on, and owning neither of the interfaces used to send or receive the message:

$$ML(m) = \{H_i \in H \mid H_i \in C(al(m)) \land si(m), di(m) \notin H_i\}.$$

Current shared bus technologies provide mechanisms to prevent listeners to actively intercept traffic. For example, Ethernet switches propagate messages selectively to the intended destinations only. Unfortunately, the mechanisms implemented by these technologies can be easily bypassed (see for example [29]). Therefore, it is important to model shared bus technologies as hypergraphs to represent the fact that it is possible that, under certain conditions, a host not involved in the communication may access the messages. This is also true in the case of wireless networks, where the communication medium is physically shared.

Note that it is possible for a node to connect to a link and passively eavesdrop the traffic without ever participating in any message exchange. These nodes will never generate a message and may not even have an associated IP address. Therefore, such nodes are impossible to spot or detect reliably [22]. Nodes of this type are not taken into account in our model.

3.1 IP Networks

An IP network is a network with a injective function $addr : I \to A$ which is a mapping between IP addresses $A = \{a_1, a_2, \ldots, a_n\}$ and interfaces.

IP datagrams are exchanged between endpoints using a number of link-level messages. Therefore, we model an IP datagram $d \in D$, as a sequence of messages $\langle m_1, m_2, \ldots, m_n \rangle$ such that:

1. the payload x of each message m_i is a triple (a_s, a_d, x'), where $a_s \in A$ is the source address, $a_d \in A$ is the destination address and $x' \in X'$

(to be specified later) is the datagram payload. A datagram is said to be *between* hosts H_i (the source host) and H_j (the destination host), with $addr^{-1}(a_s) \in H_i$ and $addr^{-1}(a_d) \in H_j$. We introduce a set of functions to extract the source/destination addresses/hosts and the payload from a message m_i belonging to a datagram d:

$dsa : M \to A$, defined by $dsa((i_{s_i}, i_{d_i}, (a_s, a_d, x'))) = a_s$;
$dsh : M \to H$, defined by

$$dsh((i_{s_i}, i_{d_i}, (a_s, a_d, x'))) = H_i \in H, \text{ where } addr^{-1}(a_s) \in H_i;$$

$dda : M \to A$, defined by $dda((i_{s_i}, i_{d_i}, (a_s, a_d, x'))) = a_d$;
$ddh : M \to H$, defined by

$$ddh((i_{s_i}, i_{d_i}, (a_s, a_d, x'))) = H_j \in H, \text{ where } addr^{-1}(a_d) \in H_j;$$

$dpl : M \to P'$ defined by $dpl((i_{s_i}, i_{d_i}, (a_s, a_d, x'))) = x'$.

2. Given two consecutive messages m_j and m_{j+1} in a datagram d, the destination interface of m_j and the source interface of m_{j+1} belong to the same host H_f:

$$di(m_j) \in H_f \land si(m_{j+1}) \in H_f.$$

H_f is said to be a *forwarder* of d. We define the partial function *forw* that given two messages m_i and m_j returns the forwarder host if it exists, and otherwise returns $\bot$, which means "undefined":

$forw : M \times M \to H \cup \{\bot\}$, defined by

$$forw((i_{s_i}, i_{d_i}, x_i), (i_{s_j}, i_{d_j}, x_j)) = \begin{cases} H_f & \text{if } i_{d_i} \in H_f \land i_{s_j} \in H_f \\ \bot & \text{otherwise.} \end{cases}$$

In a datagram, the sequence of links and hosts generated analyzing the sequence of messages, must represent a route in the network. More precisely, the following sequence:

$$\langle L_{l_1} = al(m_1), H_{h_1} = forw(m_1, m_2), \ldots,$$
$$L_{l_i} = al(m_i), H_{h_i} = forw(m_i, m_{i+1}), L_{l_{i+1}} = al(m_{i+1}), \ldots,$$
$$L_{l_n} = al(m_n)\rangle \qquad (8)$$

is defined for each couple (m_i, m_{i+1}), has no repeated elements, and represents a route in the network, which is called the *datagram route*. We define a function *route* that given a datagram d returns its route:

$route : D \to E^+$, defined by

$$route(\langle m_1, m_2, \ldots, m_n \rangle) = \langle L_{l_1}, H_{h_1}, \ldots, H_{h_{n-1}}, L_{l_n} \rangle$$

as defined by (8).

A datagram $\langle m_1, m_2, \ldots, m_n \rangle$ is *well-formed* if the source interface of the first message and the destination interface of the last message are mapped respectively into the source and destination addresses contained in the message payload, i.e.:

$$addr(si(m_1)) = dsa(m_i) \text{ and } addr(di(m_n)) = dda(m_i).$$

For a given datagram d, we define the *listeners* of the datagram as the union of the listeners of every message of the datagram:

$$DL(\langle m_1, \ldots, m_n \rangle) = \bigcup_{j=1}^{n} ML(m_j).$$

In addition, we define the set of *forwarders* of a datagram d as the set of hosts that appear in the datagram route:

$$DF(d) = \{H_i \mid H_i \in route(d)\}.$$

We define a *session* s as a sequence of IP datagrams $\langle d_1, d_2, \ldots, d_n \rangle$ that represent a conversation between two IP addresses. Therefore, for each $d_i \in s$ with $i \neq n$, the following holds:

$$\forall m \in d_i, \forall m' \in d_{i+1} \; \{dsa(m), dda(m)\} = \{dsa(m'), dda(m')\}.$$

Note that datagrams belonging to the same session may follow different routes.

3.2 UDP Interactions

The UDP protocol provides an unreliable datagram delivery service over IP (see Section 2.2). A *UDP datagram* u is an IP datagram d whose (IP) payload x' is a tuple (p_s, p_d, x'') where $p_s, p_d \in \mathbb{N}$ represent the source and destination port respectively, and $x'' \in X''$ represents the (UDP) datagram payload.

There is no concept of a UDP session, but since a number of application protocols based on UDP (like DNS or NFS) follow a query/reply schema, we define a *UDP interaction* as an IP session composed of two UDP datagrams $\langle u^1, u^2 \rangle$, whose payloads are respectively: (p_s, p_d, x''^1) and (p_d, p_s, x''^2).

For example, a UDP interaction between the two endpoints specified by addresses/ports (a_i, p_i) and (a_j, p_j) is composed of two datagrams $d^1 = \langle m_1^1, m_2^1, \ldots, m_p^1 \rangle$ and $d^2 = \langle m_1^2, m_2^2, \ldots, m_q^2 \rangle$ such that:

$$pl(m_i^1) = (a_i, a_j, (p_i, p_j, x_i''^1)), \text{ and } pl(m_i^2) = (a_j, a_i, (p_j, p_i, x_j''^2)).$$

Note that UDP datagrams may be used outside UDP interactions, e.g., in multicast-based applications and SNMP traps. These datagrams can be easily modeled using the proposed formalism but are not described in details, for the sake of brevity.

3.3 TCP Sessions

The TCP protocol (see Section 2.3) provides a reliable stream delivery service, using the IP datagram delivery service. A *TCP segment* s is an IP datagram d whose payload x' is a tuple $(p_s, p_d, seq, ack, F, x'')$ where $p_s, p_d \in \mathbb{N}$ represent the source and destination ports, $seq, ack \in \mathbb{N}$ are the sequence and acknowledgment numbers, F is a subset of the set of *flags* $FLAGS = \{\mathsf{SYN}, \mathsf{ACK}, \mathsf{FIN}, \mathsf{RST}, \mathsf{PSH}, \mathsf{URG}\}$ representing the segment properties, and $x'' \in X''$ is the segment payload. The elements of X'' are unstructured sequences of bytes. Thus, the payload sets X and X' are defined by:

$$X = A \times A \times X'$$
$$X' = \mathbb{N} \times \mathbb{N} \times X'' \cup \mathbb{N} \times \mathbb{N} \times \mathbb{N} \times \mathbb{N} \times \wp(FLAGS) \times X''.$$

We define a *TCP session* between port p_c at address a_c of host H_c and port p_s at address a_s of host H_s as an IP session such that:

- the first three segments represent the connection setup handshake, which defines the initial sequence numbers:

$$s^1 = (a_c, a_s, (p_c, p_s, seq_c^1, 0, \{\mathsf{SYN}\}, x''_{empty}))$$
$$s^2 = (a_s, a_c, (p_s, p_c, seq_s^2, seq_c^1 + 1, \{\mathsf{SYN}, \mathsf{ACK}\}, x''_{empty}))$$
$$s^3 = (a_c, a_s, (p_c, p_s, seq_c^1 + 1, seq_s^2 + 1, \{\mathsf{ACK}\}, x''_{empty})),$$

where x''_{empty} represents a null payload;
- the subsequent segments are such that, having defined the function $size : P'' \to \mathbb{N}$ that given a TCP payload returns a natural number representing its size, we have:
  - given two consecutive segments:

$$s^i = (a_t, a_u, (p_t, p_u, seq_t^i, ack_t^i, flags_t^i, x''^i_t)), \text{ and}$$

$$s^{i+1} = (a_u, a_t, (p_u, p_t, seq_u^{i+1}, ack_u^{i+1}, flags_u^{i+1}, x''^{i+1}_u)),$$

the following holds:

$$seq_u^{i+1} \geq ack_t^i, \text{ and } ack_u^{i+1} \leq seq_t^i + size(x''^i_t).$$

In addition, if it is:

$$seq_u^{i+1} = ack_t^i, x''^{i+1}_t = x''_{empty}, ack_u^{i+1} = seq_t^i + size(x''^i_t), \text{ and}$$
$$\mathsf{ACK} \in flags_u^{i+1},$$

the session is in a "quiet" state, i.e., all the data exchanged between the communication partners have been acknowledged;

- given a segment:

$$s^i = (a_t, a_u, (p_t, p_u, seq^i_t, ack^i_t, flags^i_t, x''^i_t)),$$

the following segment of the session featuring the same source/destination addresses, i.e.:

$$s^{i+k} = (a_t, a_u, (p_t, p_u, seq^{i+k}_t, ack^{i+k}_t, flags^{i+k}_t, x''^{i+k}_t)),$$

must be such that:

$$seq^{i+k}_t = seq^i_t + size(x''^i_t), \text{ and } ack^{i+k}_t \geq ack^i_t;$$

- after a pair of consecutive segments:

$$s^f = (a_t, a_u, (p_t, p_u, seq^f_t, ack^f_t, \{\mathsf{FIN}\}, x''_{empty})), \text{ and}$$

$$s^{f+1} = (a_u, a_t, (p_u, p_t, ack^f_t, seq^f_t + 1, \{\mathsf{ACK}\}, x''_{empty})),$$

representing the shutdown of one direction of the connection, every following segment from a_t to a_u is just an acknowledgment of a previous segment from a_u to a_t and it has a null payload. This goes on until the active direction of the connection is shut down with a similar message exchange;
- after a segment with a RST flag, no other segment exists.

This is a simplified model of the TCP/IP protocol suite. We do not model fragmentation of IP datagrams, IP options, several TCP mechanisms like retransmission, windows, etc. We modeled just the features that are useful to describe the attacks that are the subjects of the next sections.

4 Sniffing

Sniffing is one of the most exploited techniques used in TCP/IP networks to obtain sensitive information about hosts and eventually breach their security.

Technically, sniffing consists in eavesdropping network traffic by using hosts connected to shared-bus networks or by placing sniffer programs on Internet gateways. In the first case, the attacker sets the network interface of its host in *promiscuous mode* reading all link-level messages that are transmitted on that link, regardless of their intended destination. In the second case, the attacker installs a program on the gateway so that every packet that the gateway forwards is logged to a file. In both cases, the sniffer program looks for IP datagrams containing sensitive information that are transmitted in unencrypted form and logs such information. A typical example is represented by Telnet connections. Sniffers wait for TCP packets directed to port 23 with the SYN bit set, which represent the request for the establishment of a new remote session. After the initial handshake and the presentation of the login banner, the connecting user must insert a user name and a password. Such information is transmitted in unencrypted form to the server host. The sniffer program extracts the characters inserted by the user from the segments transmitted from the client to the server host and logs the inserted user name and password. Eventually, the attacker is able to access the server host providing the stolen user name/password combination. In addition, the sniffer program is able to log the whole session, which could include sessions to other hosts and so on. In general, sniffing is used as a building block to mount more complex attacks.

In our model, given a datagram d between two hosts H_i and H_j, every host H_k which is a listener or a forwarder of d may mount a sniffing attack. Therefore, called $DS(d)$ the set of hosts that may sniff a datagram, we have:

$$DS(d) = DL(d) \cup DF(d).$$

Given a session $s = \langle d^1, d^2, \ldots, d^n \rangle$ the hosts that may access the whole information are:

$$SS(s) = \bigcap_{j=1}^{n} DS(d^j)$$

For example, in Figure 1, given the datagram

$$d = \langle (i_7, i_{10}, (a_7, a_{13}, p')), (i_{11}, i_{13}, (a_7, a_{13}, p')) \rangle$$

that represents a datagram from host H_4 to host H_9 along route $\langle L_4, H_7, L_5 \rangle$, it is: $SS(d) = \{H_5, H_6, H_7, H_8\}$.

5 Spoofing

When a host tries to impersonate another host in a communication, we are in presence of *spoofing* [9]. The impersonated host may have a privileged access to the attacked host or may be regarded as a source of sensitive information. For example, the *rsh* and *rlogin* protocols allow sessions to be established between hosts without the need to provide a password if the connecting host is *trusted*. This means that the name (or address) of the host is used as the only means of authentication. This is equivalent to induce the identity of the sender of a letter from the return address printed on the envelope rather then from the signature of the message.

5.1 Spoofing IP

At the IP level, a host H_i may impersonate another host[4] H_j toward a third host H_k by producing a *spoofed datagram* d. Such datagram contains, as its source address, the address associated to one of the interfaces of H_j even if the

---
[4] Actually spoofing is about impersonating *addresses* rather than *hosts*, but we will extend the expression in order to match the common use of the term.

first message of the datagram is generated from one of the interfaces of H_i, i.e., $d = \langle m_1, m_2, \ldots, m_n \rangle$ is spoofed if:

$$\forall m_i \in d, \; dsa(m_i) = a_s \text{ where } addr^{-1}(a_s) \in H_j, \text{ and } si(m_1) = i_s \in H_i \neq H_j$$

H_k receives just message m_n and considers the enclosed IP datagram as sent by H_j.

5.2 Spoofing UDP

The UDP protocol just adds the port concept to IP datagrams, and therefore spoofing single UDP datagrams is exactly as spoofing IP datagrams. But, since UDP is often used in request/reply protocols, it is useful to analyze how spoofing can be used to mount an attack in those cases. An host H_i may spoof a host H_j toward a third host H_k in a UDP interaction $\langle u^1, u^2 \rangle$ by creating a bogus request or a bogus reply. The latter case, also called *session hijacking*, will be described in Section 6.

In the former case, host H_i sends a spoofed UDP datagram u^1 in an attempt to access resources on the attacked host H_k available to the impersonated host H_j. If the spoofing host is not interested in the reply payload, it may perform plain IP spoofing. Differently, if the reply contains information that is the aim of the spoofing attack, the spoofing host must be a sniffer of the reply datagram, i.e., $H_i \in DS(u^2)$. In addition, if the attacker wants to avoid the reply packet to reach the spoofed host (e.g., to avoid detection), it must be a forwarder of the *hypothetical* reply datagram. Thus, considering the hypothetical reply datagram $u_h^2 = \langle m_1, \ldots, m_n \rangle$ between H_k and H_j it must be $H_i \in DF(u_h^2)$. The actual datagram will be: $u^2 = \langle m_1, \ldots, m_j \rangle$ with $j < n$ and such that $di(m_j) \in H_i$, i.e., the datagram is intercepted by H_i and it is not forwarded to H_j. In actual TCP/IP networks, attacks to routing mechanisms could be used in order to create this condition. Alternatively, the attacking host must make sure that the impersonated host is unable to process the reply datagram by waiting for the host being down or malfunctioning or by flooding the host with so much traffic that the datagram is dropped.

A protocol that is vulnerable to this attack is the NFS protocol [19]. NFS servers accept requests to access the exported file systems only from a restricted set of addresses. An attacker may use spoofing in order to impersonate an authorized address and therefore gain access to the exported file systems. In this case, if the attacker aims at obtaining some file contents, then it must be a sniffer of the reply. If the attack is aimed at executing some command (e.g., *delete* a file), and the attacker is not interested in the command results, then plain spoofing can be performed.

5.3 Spoofing TCP

A host H_i may try to impersonate another host H_j toward a third host H_k not just at the datagram level but for a whole TCP session. This attack has been discussed in [4, 21].

In order to successfully impersonate host H_j, H_i must be able to:

1. avoid that any segment sent by H_k during the session reaches the spoofed host H_j;
2. determine the first sequence number produced by the attacked host H_k.

The first problem arises because if replies to spoofed segments are delivered to H_j, H_j will induce that some error occurred and generate a reset segment directed to H_k, resulting in connection shutdown. This implies that H_i must be an "intended" forwarder of every segment of the session, i.e., given the set of hypothetical segments $\{s_h^1, \ldots, s_h^n\}$ from H_k to H_j, we have:

$$H_i \in \bigcap_{j=1}^{n} DF(s_h^j). \tag{12}$$

This means that all the segments, under normal circumstances, would follow a route that includes the attacking host. Alternatively, host H_i must make host H_j unable to process the reply segments. As said before, in an actual TCP/IP network there are a number of ways to achieve this effect.

The second condition is posed by the three-way handshake used to establish a TCP connection. The spoofing attack starts with host H_i sending a first spoofed segment requesting a connection to H_k and pretending to come from H_j:

$$s^1 = (a_j, a_k, (p_j, p_k, seq_j^1, 0, \{\mathsf{SYN}\}, x''_{empty})),$$

where $addr^{-1}(a_j) \in H_j$. Host H_k, at this point, sends a reply segment:

$$s_2 = (a_k, a_j, (p_k, p_j, seq_k^2, seq_j^1 + 1, \{\mathsf{SYN}, \mathsf{ACK}\}, x''_{empty})).$$

Thus, host H_i must send the segment:

$$s_3 = (a_j, a_k, (p_j, p_k, seq_j^1 + 1, seq_k^2 + 1, \{\mathsf{ACK}\}, x''_{empty}))$$

in order to complete the handshake. Therefore, H_i must know seq_k^2. This implies that H_i must be a sniffer of the second datagram, i.e., $H_i \in DS(s^2)$, or that it is able to "guess" the right sequence number. This ability can be achieved analyzing how H_k chooses its sequence numbers when setting up a TCP session, and predicting the value that will be used for the spoofed session. The TCP specification suggests that the number used to generate initial sequence numbers should be increased 250,000 times per second. Some implementations have chosen slower rates. For examples, as described in [21], 4.2 BSD Unix software increases the number used for new connections by 128 each second and by 64 after each new connection setup. Even if modern implementations use faster rates, the attack remains feasible as stated in [4]. A famous break-in [1] was based on this technique.

Once the handshake has been successfully carried out:

1. if the attacker is an "intended" forwarder of every segment between the attacked and the spoofed host, (see (12)) the session may continue seamlessly;

2. if the attacker is a listener of every reply segment between H_k and H_j, i.e., called RS the set of all replies from H_k and H_j, if:

$$H_i \in DL(s^i) \text{ for each } s^i \in RS$$

the session may continue provided that H_j is not able to process H_k's replies;
3. if the attacker cannot access H_k's replies (i.e., it is mounting a "guessing" attack) then, after the initial handshake, the session proceeds as follows:
   - segments from H_i to H_k:

$$s^{ik} = \langle m_1^{ik}, m_2^{ik}, \ldots, m_p^{ik} \rangle \text{ with}$$
$$pl(m^{ik}) = (a_j, a_k, (p_j, p_k, seq_j^{ik}, seq_k^2 + 1, flags_j^{ik}, x_j'''^{ik}))$$

   follow route r_{ik} from $si(m_1^{ik}) \in H_i$ to $di(m_p^{ik}) \in H_k$. Note that the acknowledgment number does not change since H_i does not know the amount of data that have been produced by H_k;
   - segments from H_k to H_j:

$$s^{kj} = \langle m_1^{kj}, m_2^{kj}, \ldots, m_q^{kj} \rangle \text{ with}$$
$$pl(m^{kj}) = (a_k, a_j, (p_k, p_j, seq_k^{kj}, ack_k^{kj}, flags_k^{kj}, x_k'''^{kj}))$$

   follow route r_{kj} from $si(m_1^{kj}) \in H_k$ to $di(m_q^{kj}) \in H_j$.
This communication is just one-way for the attacker, but, in most cases this is enough to breach the security of the attacked host.

6 Hijacking

While in spoofing attacks a malevolent host tries to pose as a different (trusted) host for a whole session, in the *hijacking* attack the host tries to interfere with an ongoing session in order to impersonate one partner of the communication with the other and/or vice versa.

6.1 Hijacking UDP Interactions

In a UDP hijacking attack a host H_i replies to a legitimate query from H_j to H_k, providing false information pretending to come from the host H_k.
There are two possibilities:

1. if the attacking host is a forwarder of the hypothetical request u_h^1 from H_j to H_k, then it may seamlessly impersonate H_k, by blocking the request and producing the bogus reply. Thus, if $H_i \in DF(u_h^1)$ the session would be as follows:

$$u^1 = \langle m_1^1, \ldots, m_p^1 \rangle \text{ with } pl(m_i^1) = (a_j, a_k, (p_j, p_k, x_j''^1)) \text{ and}$$
$$a_j = addr(si(m_1^1)), di(m_p^1) \in H_i;$$
$$u^2 = \langle m_1^2, \ldots, m_q^2 \rangle \text{ with } pl(m_i^2) = (a_k, a_j, (p_k, p_j, x_k''^2)) \text{ and}$$
$$si(m_1^2) \in H_i, a_j = addr(di(m_q^2));$$

2. if H_i is just a listener of the request u^1 from H_j to H_k (which is the same of u_h^1 above), then its bogus reply u_s^2 must reach the attacked host H_j before the legitimate reply u^2 from H_k. Unfortunately, in actual TCP/IP networks there are many denial-of-service attacks (e.g., flooding) that are able to slow down or completely block a host. Therefore, the problem is easily solved. In summary, if $H_i \in DL(u^1)$ the UDP interaction will be:

$$u^1 = \langle m_1^1, \ldots, m_p^1 \rangle \text{ with } pl(m_i^1) = (a_j, a_k, (p_j, p_k, x_j''^1)) \text{ and}$$
$$a_j = addr(si(m_1^1)), \ a_k = addr(di(m_p^1));$$
$$u_s^2 = \langle m_1^2, \ldots, m_q^2 \rangle \text{ with } pl(m_i^2) = (a_k, a_j, (p_k, p_j, x_k''^2)) \text{ and}$$
$$si(m_1^2) \in H_i, \ a_j = addr(di(m_q^2)).$$

An example of this attack applied to the Network Information System of Sun Microsystems is given in [14]. The NIS is used in a network of hosts in order to manage and distribute system maps, like host names and user passwords. In particular, when a user logs in a host providing a user name and password, the host's operating system queries the local NIS server in order to get the password file and authenticate the user. An attacker may race with the server and provide a modified password map in a spoofed UDP datagram allowing the user to be authenticated (possibly with extended privileges) with a password specified by the attacker. In another scenario, an attacker may impersonate a NFS server and provide modified version of files in order to breach security.

6.2 TCP Session Hijacking

In TCP session hijacking a host H_i tries to interfere with an *existing* TCP session between two hosts H_j and H_k. We can, at least, distinguish between two cases: *data injection* and *take over*.

Injection In the data injection attack, host H_i sends a single bogus TCP segment to one of the partners of the session (e.g., H_j) claiming to come from the other partner (i.e., H_k). The segment payload contains a higher-level protocol command that breaches H_k security. The command is interpreted as it was issued by H_j.

Let us suppose that the last two segments exchanged between H_k and H_j have been:

$$s^t = (a_j, a_k, (p_j, p_k, seq_j^t, ack_j^t, flags_j^t, x_j'''^t)),$$
$$s^{t+1} = (a_k, a_j, (p_k, p_j, ack_j^t, seq_j^t + size(x_j'''^t), \{ACK\}, x_{empty}''));$$

this means that the session is in a "quiet" state and the next segment between H_j and H_k should have the sequence number $seq_j^t + size(x_j''')$. Therefore, the attacker H_i produces the following segment:

$$s^{t+2} = (a_j, a_k, (p_j, p_k, seq_j^{t+2}, ack_j^{t+2}, flags_j^{t+2}, x_j'''^{t+2})),$$

where: $seq_j^{t+2} = seq_j^t + size(x_j'''^t)$, $ack_j^{t+2} = ack_j^t$, and $x_j'''^{t+2}$ represents some kind of action aimed at breaking into H_k. At this point, H_k replies with an acknowledgment segment:

$$s^{t+3} = (a_k, a_j, (p_k, p_j, ack_j^{t+2}, seq_j^{t+2} + size(x_j'''^{t+2}), \{\mathsf{ACK}\}, x''_{empty})).$$

If this segment reaches H_j, H_j will produce an acknowledgment message stating that the received segment has a wrong acknowledgment number. The message contains the sequence number H_j believes to be correct, namely, seq_j^{t+2}:

$$s^{t+4} = (a_j, a_k, (p_j, p_k, seq_j^{t+2}, ack_j^{t+2}, \{\mathsf{ACK}\}, x''_{empty})).$$

In turn, H_k sends another acknowledgment message containing the acknowledgment number that it considers correct:

$$s^{t+5} = (a_k, a_j, (p_k, p_j, ack_j^{t+2}, seq_j^{t+2} + size(x_j'''^{t+2}), \{\mathsf{ACK}\}, x''_{empty})).$$

This message exchange, called *acknowledgment storm*, goes on until a time out expires[5]. Nonetheless, any other attempt to exchange data between H_i and H_j on that session will fail and produce an acknowledgment storm.

In order to mount this attack, H_i must be a sniffer of the at least one of the first two segment in order to determine the correct sequence and acknowledgment numbers to be put in the bogus segment[6]. Therefore it must be: $H_i \in DS(s^t) \cup DS(s^{t+1})$.

Take Over In a *take over* attack a host H_i gains complete control over an existing session between two hosts H_j and H_k. In this attack, extensively described in [16], the attacker creates a *desynchronized* state in the TCP session. In a synchronized TCP session, when all data have been acknowledged, the client (say, H_j) sequence number is equal to the server (say, H_k) acknowledgment number and vice versa. In a stable desynchronized session the sequence and acknowledgment numbers of the involved parties do not correspond and therefore any data sent by one partner is refused by the other[7]. If the attacker knows the sequence numbers that the parties expect from each other it may filter all traffic by producing the right segments.

---

[5] Following the actual TCP specification, the process should go on indefinitely, but since acknowledgment messages with empty payloads are not retransmitted in case of errors, the storm stops when the traffic that has been produced leads to dropping some of the packets.

[6] From a theoretical point of view, this attack could be composed with the one described by Morris in [21] in order to be able to mount an attack from a host that it is not a listener of traffic between the attacked hosts. However, it would be rather difficult to guess the correct sequence number in an established session over which random traffic may occur.

[7] Actually the sequence number must be out of a *window* of acceptable values [26], but we will assume that the session is sufficiently desynchronized.

In [16], two ways to create a desynchronized state are described. In the first case, the attacker resets the current session between H_j and H_k and immediately opens a new connection with H_k. In this scenario, the three-way TCP setup handshake (see Section 2.3) and subsequent data exchange have determined the current sequence numbers seq_j and seq_k. Then, the attacker H_i sends a reset segment to H_k, immediately followed by a new connection request. Both segments appear to come from H_j:

$$s^t = (a_j, a_k, (p_j, p_k, seq_j, seq_k, \{\mathsf{RST}\}, x''_{empty}));$$
$$s^{t+1} = (a_j, a_k, (p_j, p_k, seq_j^{t+1}, 0, \{\mathsf{SYN}\}, x''_{empty}));$$

H_k then replies to s^{t+1} with an acknowledgment/synchronization segment (second step of the setup):

$$s^{t+2} = (a_k, a_j, (p_k, p_j, seq_k^{t+2}, seq_j^{t+1} + 1, \{\mathsf{SYN}, \mathsf{ACK}\}, x''_{empty})).$$

The attacker replies to this segment with the last step of the setup:

$$s^{t+3} = (a_j, a_k, (p_j, p_k, seq_j^{t+1} + 1, seq_k^{t+2} + 1, \{\mathsf{ACK}\}, x''_{empty})).$$

If segment s^{t+2} reaches H_j, it will start an acknowledgment storm between H_j and H_k:

$$s^{t+4} = (a_j, a_k, (p_j, p_k, seq_j, seq_k, \{\mathsf{ACK}\}, x''_{empty}));$$
$$s^{t+5} = (a_k, a_j, (p_k, p_j, seq_k^{t+2} + 1, seq_j^{t+1} + 1, \{\mathsf{ACK}\}, x''_{empty}));$$
$$\vdots$$

At this point the session is desynchronized. The attacker knows all the "right" sequence and acknowledgment numbers, and, therefore, he/she may filter/change all traffic. In fact, when H_j sends a segment:

$$s^l = (a_j, a_k, (p_j, p_k, seq_j, seq_k, flags_j^l, x'''_j)),$$

the segment is refused by H_k and generates an acknowledgment storm. But the attacker sends a modified version of s^l:

$$s^{l+1} = (a_j, a_k, (p_j, p_k, seq_j^{t+1} + 1, seq_k^{t+2} + 1, \{\mathsf{ACK}\}, x'''_j)),$$

which H_k happily accepts because it contains the right acknowledgment and sequence numbers. The acknowledgment of the segment is processed accordingly. Note that the users at the endpoints of the virtual circuit do not perceive any abnormal behavior. However, the attacker has complete control over the connection and can modify or insert data in the stream.

The second way to create a desynchronized connection consists in sending to the communication partners some data that increase the sequence numbers associated to the virtual circuit. Thus, once H_j and H_k have setup a session and exchanged some data so that their sequence numbers are seq_j and seq_k respectively, the attacker H_i sends to H_k:

$$s^t = (a_j, a_k, (p_j, p_k, seq_j, seq_k, flags_j^t, x_j'''^t)).$$

H_k will send an acknowledgment segment:

$$s^{t+1} = (a_k, a_j, (p_k, p_j, seq_k, seq_j + size(x_j'''^t), flags_k^{t+1}, x_k'''^{t+1})),$$

and start an acknowledgment storm. In the meantime, H_i sends some data to H_j pretending to come from H_k:

$$s^{t+2} = (a_k, a_j, (p_k, p_j, seq_k, seq_j, flags_k^{t+2}, x_k'''^{t+2})).$$

H_j will acknowledge the segment and start another storm. At this point, the session is desynchronized and the attacker may filter or inject any traffic. In order to make this attack less detectable, the data used to desynchronize the session, namely, $x_j'''^t$ and $x_k'''^{t+2}$, should have no effect on the upper-layer protocol (e.g., some kind of no-operation command).

In order to accomplish take over with both desynchronization methods, the attacker must be a sniffer of all the segments of the session between H_j and H_k, i.e., called *ES* the set of such segments, we must have: $H_i \in DS(s^i)$ for each $s^i \in ES$.

7 Using The Model

The proposed network model can be used to support network security analysis in a number of different ways.

- *Better understanding of the vulnerabilities*: modeling attacks it is possible to define formally the prerequisites to mount each type of attack and the messages produced during the attack.
- *Support for detection of attacks*: given a particular vulnerability, it is possible to devise which are the conditions sufficient to detect particular attack scenarios, and which are the patterns to be looked for.
- *Support for protection from attacks*: given a particular vulnerability it is possible to find which are the configurations that provide protection from attacks of the given type and if such configurations exist.
- *Support for testing and certification of networks*: given a particular network topology, the model can be used in order to automatically produce testing procedures that verify the existing protections. In addition, the model can be used by solution vendors to validate and certify security protections.

7.1 Detection

Defining exactly which messages are produced during attacks and where they appear provides hints for network intrusion detection systems [10, 2, 3]. The model allows the security designer to determine which are the message patterns that are to be looked for in order to flag out occurring intrusion attempts and where, in the network topology, probes have to be placed in order to detect the largest range of attacks. The model proposed here has been extensively used in designing and developing the STAT system [30, 31]. In the following, we describe how the model can be used to determine the conditions that are necessary to detect the attacks described before.

Spoofing As stated in Section 5.1, usually the receiver of a spoofed IP datagram is not able to detect the attack. In general, IP spoofing is detectable only in particular topologies. More precisely, given a single message belonging to a spoofed IP datagram, the corresponding datagram may be considered spoofed if, in the network obtained removing the message source interface from the corresponding link, there is no path between the interface corresponding to the datagram source address and the message source interface. Thus, given a network $N = (H_1, \ldots, H_p, L_1, \ldots, L_q)$ and a message $m_i \in d$, d can be considered spoofed if in:

$$N' = N - \{al(m_i)\} \cup \{al(m_i) - \{si(m_i)\}\}$$

there is no path between $addr^{-1}(dsa(m_i))$ and $si(m_i)$.

For example, consider Figure 3. Host H_1 tries to impersonate host H_3 toward host H_7 with the spoofed datagram $d = \langle m_1, m_2, m_3 \rangle$. Host H_4, that sees message m_2, is able to detect the occurring spoofing attack since in network N' there is no path between $i_3 = addr^{-1}(dsa(m_2))$ and $i_4 = si(m_2)$. On the contrary, host H_5 is not able to detect spoofing since it accesses only message m_3 and in network N'' there is a path between i_3 and i_7.

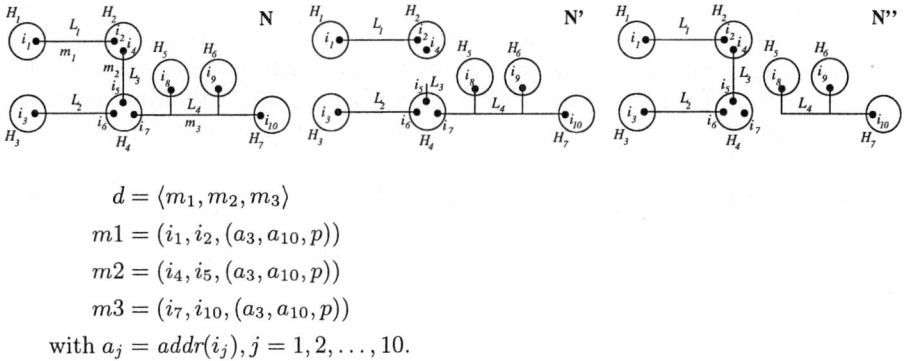

$$d = \langle m_1, m_2, m_3 \rangle$$
$$m1 = (i_1, i_2, (a_3, a_{10}, p))$$
$$m2 = (i_4, i_5, (a_3, a_{10}, p))$$
$$m3 = (i_7, i_{10}, (a_3, a_{10}, p))$$
with $a_j = addr(i_j), j = 1, 2, \ldots, 10$.

Fig. 3. IP spoofing example.

We define a *reachability* function *reach* that, given a network $N=\{E_1, \ldots, E_m\}$ and an interface $i_j \in E_l$ for some l, returns the set of interfaces that are reachable from i_j:

$reach : I \times \wp(\wp(I)) \to \wp(I)$, defined by
$$reach(i_j, \{E_1, E_2, \ldots, E_m\}) = \{i_k \mid \exists r = \langle E_{r_1}, E_{r_2}, \ldots, E_{r_n}\rangle \in R$$
such that $i_j \in E_{r_1} \wedge i_k \in E_{r_n}\}$

Given a host H_i, we can build its *spoofing detection matrix* $SDM(H_i)$ that has rows labeled with the links the host is connected to and columns labeled with all network addresses. The matrix contains, for each row, a 1 for every address whose spoofing the host can detect from messages appearing on that link and a 0 otherwise. Each row is built in the following way: given the associated link L_k, for each interface $i_j \in L_k \wedge i_j \notin H_i$ consider the network N_{jk} obtained removing i_j from L_k and associate a 0 to the columns corresponding to the elements of $Im_{addr_{|I_{jk}}}$ where $I_{jk} = reach(i_j, N_{jk})$.

For example, let us consider the network N in Figure 3. $SDM(H_4)$ is:

```
      a1 a2 a3 a4 a5 a6 a7 a8 a9 a10
L2    1  1  0  1  1  1  1  1  1  1
L3    0  0  1  0  1  1  1  1  1  1
L4    1  1  1  1  1  1  1  1  1
```

From the matrix above we can induce that host H_4 can detect every attempt coming from link L_4 to spoof any address.

A UDP or TCP spoofing attack may also be detected by means of *orphan datagrams*. Such datagrams appear when a host H_i is impersonating a host H_j toward a third host H_k (actually H_i is using its interface i_i to impersonate one of the addresses of H_j, say a_j, when communicating with one of the addresses of H_k, say a_k) and it is not able to block the reply traffic from H_k to H_j. Thus, there will be particular links or hosts on the network on which the interaction/session datagrams from H_k will appear and the ones from H_j will not[8]. More precisely, given the set R_{kj} of all routes from $i_k = addr^{-1}(a_k)$ to $i_j = addr^{-1}(a_j)$:

$$R_{kj} = \{\langle E_1, \ldots, E_n \rangle \in R \mid i_k \in E_1 \wedge i_j \in E_n\}, \tag{14}$$

we extract the subset E_{kj} of edges that are common to all routes:

$$E_{kj} = \bigcap_{r \in R_{kj}} r, \tag{15}$$

---

[8] Actually, in case of UDP spoofing, since there is no way to determine the membership of a single datagram to an interaction. The datagram must contain some kind of protocol-specific information that identifies the datagram as a reply in an interaction. For example, examining UDP datagrams of an NFS operation we can distinguish between request and reply messages.

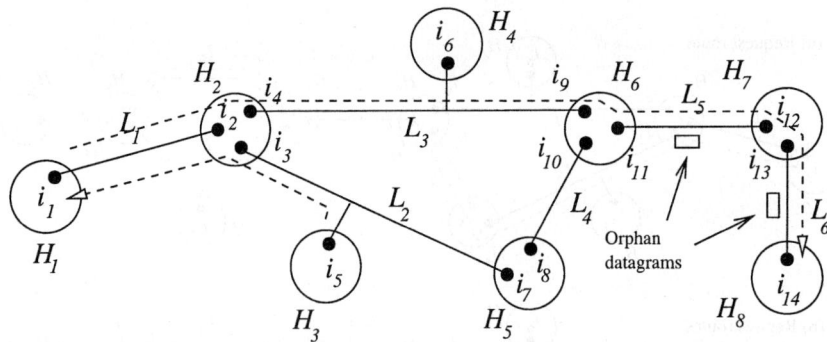

Fig. 4. Orphan datagrams.

and, given the set C_{ik} of all edges that appear at least in one route from i_i to i_k:

$$C_{ik} = \bigcup_{r \in R_{ik}} r, \text{where } R_{ik} \text{ is defined by (14)},$$

we obtain the set of edges O_{ijk}:

$$O_{ijk} = E_{kj} - C_{ik}.$$

Orphan datagrams can be detected by hosts that are in O_{ijk} or that are connected to a link in O_{ijk}:

$$H^o_{ijk} = \{H_o \in H \mid H_o \in O_{ijk} \vee \exists L_o \in O_{ijk} \text{ such that } H_o \in C(L_o)\}.$$

For example, let us consider Figure 4. Host H_3 is impersonating host H_8 toward host H_1. Spoofed traffic from H_3 to H_1 follows route $\langle L_2, H_2, L_1 \rangle$ while traffic from H_1 to H_8 follows route $\langle L_1, H_2, L_3, H_6, L_5, H_7, L_6 \rangle$. Orphan datagrams can be detected from hosts that belong to route $\langle L_5, H_7, L_6 \rangle$ or that are connected to links appearing in the route. Even if host H_4 is able to see replies from H_1 to H_8, it is not able to distinguish between orphan datagrams and replies to legitimate traffic that has followed a different route (e.g., $\langle L_6, H_7, L_5, H_6, L_4, H_5, L_2, H_2, L_1 \rangle$). Different, H_7 is able to identify datagrams as orphans since it can be sure that no traffic from H_8 to H_1 was generated before the orphan datagrams.

Hijacking In the case of UDP hijacking we have the dual situation with respect to spoofing: instead of "orphan" datagrams we have "twin" datagrams. These datagrams are the false reply (say, produced by the attacker H_i from its interface i_i) followed by the legitimate response (say, produced by the server H_k from the address a_k) that follow a request (say, produced by the attacked host H_j from its address a_j). Given the set E_{ij} of all edges that appear in all routes from i_i

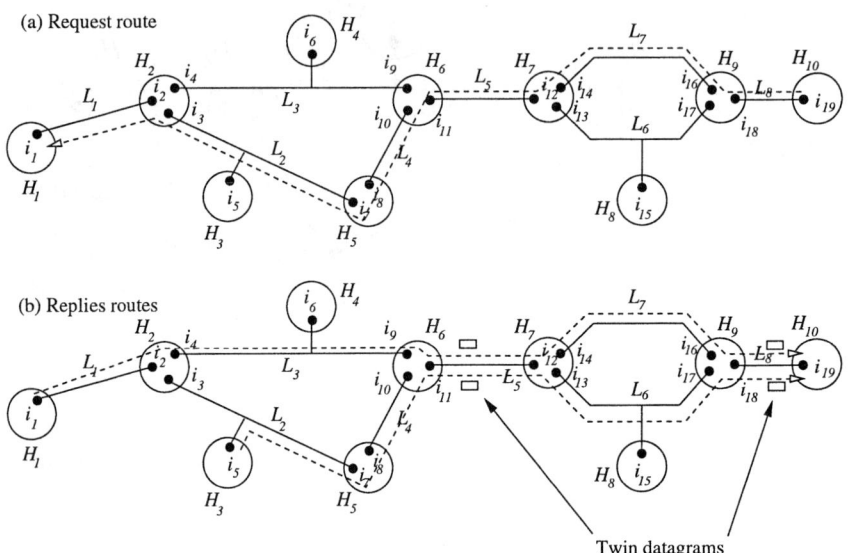

Fig. 5. Twin datagrams.

to $i_j = addr^{-1}(a_j)$ (defined by (15)) and the set E_{kj} of all edges routes from $i_k = addr^{-1}(a_k)$ to i_j, we consider the set: $T_{ijk} = E_{ij} \cap E_{kj}$.

Twin datagrams can be detected by hosts in T_{ijk} or connected to links in T_{ijk}, i.e.,:

$$H_{ijk}^t = \{H_t \in H \mid H_t \in T_{ijk} \vee \exists L_t \in T_{ijk} \text{ such that } H_t \in C(L_t)\}.$$

For example, suppose host H_{10} is requesting some kind of service to host H_1 (see Figure 5 (a)). Host H_3 hijacks the UDP interaction and produces a forged reply directed to H_{10} and pretending to come from H_1. In addition, H_1 sends the legitimate reply to H_{10}. As can be seen in Figure 5 (b), twin datagrams appear on links L_5 and L_8 and will be forwarded by hosts H_6, H_7, and H_9. Host H_8 does not see the twin datagrams since it is not connected to a link that is a forced passage from both H_1 and H_3 to H_{10}. In principle, if both twin datagrams would have followed the route than includes L_6, H_8 could have detected the hijacking.

Detecting TCP session hijacking attacks is easy because such attacks produce the *acknowledgment storms* that are easily detectable by every hosts that is a listener or forwarder of all the traffic occurring between the attacked hosts H_j and H_k. Therefore, assuming that the hijacked session is occurring between addresses $a_j = addr(i_j)$ of H_j and $a_k = addr(i_k)$ of H_k, the set of hosts that can detect the acknowledgment storm is:

$$J_{jk} = \{H_l \in H \mid H_l \in E_{jk} \vee \exists C_l \in E_{jk} \text{ such that } H_l \in C(L_l)\},$$

where E_{jk} is defined by (15).

7.2 Protection

The proposed formal model, defining the prerequisites to mount attacks and the conditions to be verified in order to be able to detect attacks, provides support to the design of security protections.

Sniffing The only effective means to protect from sniffing is the encryption of traffic. Such protection must be implemented at the application level (e.g., [33]), since the TCP/IP protocol suite does not provide any mechanisms to protect the transmitted data.

Nonetheless, the model may provide useful information. When sending a datagram to H_k, H_j (actually its network software) may use the network topology description in order to compute all possible routes to destination and the corresponding possible sniffers, following the procedures described in Section 3. Then, H_j may decide to choose a specific route (e.g., by using source routing) adopting some heuristics or quality-of-service parameter. For example, H_j may define a *listener vector* $SV(H_j)$ that for each host $H_i \neq H_j$ associates a value representing a certain level of trust. Then, when comparing the possible routes H_j may choose to maximize the average trust of the path or not to send the packet if hosts with a too low level of trust are listeners of the packet. The choice could also be supported by a security model of the transmitted data.

Spoofing The model can be used as a basis to build effective protections from spoofing attacks. For example, given a particular protocol (e.g., NFS) one can build the corresponding *trust vector* TM for a given host. The vector identifies the set of addresses that the host considers *trusted*, i.e., the set of addresses from which requests are accepted without further authentication. The trust vector can be used in conjunction with the SDM matrix of each host in order to determine which hosts can successfully build a spoofing attack for that particular protocol without being detected. For example, let us suppose that host H_7 in Figure 3 is an NFS server exporting its file systems to H_5, H_6 and H_1 (actually, to the addresses associated to their interfaces, namely $a_8 = addr(i_8)$, $a_9 = addr(i_9)$, and $a_1 = addr(i_1)$). Thus H_7's trust vector for the NFS protocol is:

$a_1\ a_2\ a_3\ i_4\ i_5\ i_6\ i_7\ i_8\ i_9\ i_{10}$
$1\ \ 0\ \ 0\ \ 0\ \ 0\ \ 0\ \ 0\ \ 1\ \ 1\ \ 0$

Given this scenario, we can analyze the spoofing detection matrix of all the hosts involved and find which is the most suitable host to detect spoofing attacks. In our case, host H_4 is able to detect every possible attempt to spoof addresses a_8 and a_9, but it is not able to detect the attempts to spoof address a_1 appearing on link L_3. Thus, in order to cover all possible attacks, we have to use both hosts H_2 and H_4 in order to protect the server.

Hijacking As in the case of sniffing, protection from hijacking attacks must be implemented at the application level. If the traffic is encrypted, the attacker can filter every byte exchanged between the partners of the communication but it is not able to insert meaningful commands aimed at breaking the security of the endpoints of the connection. Nonetheless, an attacker may use injection in order to realize a "denial of service" attack, preventing any information exchange.

7.3 Testing and Validation

Most testing of network security tools [23, 15] use *ad hoc* techniques that are based neither on a formal model nor on information as network topology and trust.

The proposed model can be used as a basis for the automatic generation of test cases for network security software (e.g., firewalls). Given a particular network topology and the types of protection implemented, the model can be used in order to determine a set of test attacks and from where such attacks must be carried out. In addition, the model can be used by solution vendors in order to certify the offered protections. The main problem for network security applications is that their certification is often done once for all and is not performed in the context of the particular network to protect. The model can support a sound, formal certification that is related to the particular topology of the protected network. This way, solution vendors could show that given the particular topology and a set of attacks described on the model, the network is immune to such attacks.

8 Conclusions and Future Work

Security is a growing concern. The Internet, the world-wide TCP/IP network, is becoming an important part of everyday life, and people rely on services offered by the TCP/IP protocol suite in order to carry out personal communication and commercial transactions. Despite its critical infrastructure role, the TCP/IP suite is insecure. There are many *ad hoc* techniques used to protect TCP/IP networks from known attacks, but still there is no underlying formal framework.

We have presented a formal model of networks and of TCP/IP networks in particular. We have used the model to describe some well-known vulnerabilities of the TCP/IP protocol suite, namely *sniffing*, *spoofing*, and *hijacking*. Then, we have shown how the model of the network and of the attacks can be used as a basis to perform network security analysis. In particular we showed how the topology constraints derived from the modeling of the attacks can be used to determine the placement of intrusion detection system and to identify flawed configurations.

Future work will be aimed to model more attack techniques, in particular those exploiting the vulnerability of routing protocols, where the topological characterization of the network is an integral part of the attack analysis. We are also working on extending the model in order to be able to describe some state associated to hosts (e.g., routing tables) and to take into account the dynamic aspects of networks (e.g., dynamically assigned addresses). We also plan to use the model as a basis to build toolsets for topology-aware testing of firewall systems.

Acknowledgments

Many thanks to Prof. Richard Kemmerer and Prof. Sebastiano Vigna for their comments on early versions of this paper.

This research was supported by the Army Research Office, under agreement DAAD19-01-1-0484. The U.S. Government is authorized to reproduce and distribute reprints for Governmental purposes notwithstanding any copyright annotation thereon.

The views and conclusions contained herein are those of the author and should not be interpreted as necessarily representing the official policies or endorsements, either expressed or implied, of the Army Research Office, or the U.S. Government.

References

1. T. Shimomura amd J. Markoff. *Takedown.* Hyperion, 1996.
2. S. Axelsson. Intrusion Detection Systems: A Taxomomy and Survey. Technical Report 99-15, Dept. of Computer Engineering, Chalmers University of Technology, Sweden, March 2000.
3. R. Bace and P. Mell. Special Publication on Intrusion Detection Systems. Technical Report SP 800-31, National Institue of Standards and Technology, November 2001.
4. S. Bellovin. Security Problems in the TCP/IP Protocol Suite. *Computer Communications Review,* 19(2), 1990.
5. C. Berge. *Hypergraphs.* North-Holland, 1989.
6. CERT. Cert advisories. http://www.cert.org, 2003.
7. B. Chapman and E. Zwicky. *Building Internet Firewalls.* O'Reilly & Associates, 1995.
8. W. Cheswick and S. Bellovin. *Firewalls and Internet Security: Repelling the Wily Hacker.* Addison-Wesley, 1994.
9. Computer Emergency Response Team. IP Spoofing Attacks and Hijacked Terminal Connections. CA-95:01, January 1995.
10. H. Debar, M. Dacier, and A. Wespi. Towards a taxonomy of intrusion-detection systems. *Computer Networks,* 31(8):805–822, 1999.
11. R. Fielding et al. Hypertext Transfer Protocol – HTTP/1.1. RFC 2616, June 1999.
12. International Organization for Standardization. Information Processing Systems - Open Systems Interconnection. International Standard, 1986.
13. A Freier, P. Karlton, and P. Kocher. The ssl protocol version 3.0. Internet draft `draft-freier-ssl-version3-02.txt`, November 1996.
14. D.K. Hess, D.R. Safford, and U.W. Pooch. A Unix Network Protocol Security Study: Network Information Service. Technical report, Texas A&M University, November 1992.
15. ISS. Realsecure 6.5. http://www.iss.net/, February 2002.
16. L. Joncheray. A Simple Active Attack Against TCP. Technical report, Merit Network Inc., April 1995.

17. J. Kohl and C. Neuman. The Kerberos Authentication Service (V5). RFC 1510, September 1993.
18. G. Malkin. Rip version 2. IETF RFC 2453, Nov 1998.
19. Sun Microsystems. NFS: Network File System Protocol Specification. RFC 1094, 1989.
20. P. Mockapetris. Domain Name System. RFC 1034, November 1987.
21. R.T. Morris. A Weakness in the 4.2BSD UNIX TCP/IP Software. Technical report, AT&T Bell Laboratories, February 1985.
22. Mudge. Antisniff 1.1. http://www.L0pht.com/antisniff/, May 2000.
23. Nessus homepage. http://www.nessus.org/, 2003.
24. J. Postel. User Datagram Protocol. RFC 768, August 1980.
25. J. Postel. Internet Protocol. RFC 792, 1981.
26. J. Postel. Transmission Control Protocol. RFC 793, September 1981.
27. J. Postel. Simple Mail Transfer Protocol. RFC 821, 1982.
28. Y. Rekhter and T. Li. A border gateway protocol 4 (bgp-4). IETF RFC 1654, Mar 1995.
29. D. Song. Dsniff version 2.3. http://naughty.monkey.org/ dugsong/dsniff/, Feb 2003.
30. G. Vigna and R.A. Kemmerer. NetSTAT: A Network-based Intrusion Detection System. *Journal of Computer Security*, 7(1):37–71, 1999.
31. G. Vigna, R.A. Kemmerer, and P. Blix. Designing a Web of Highly-Configurable Intrusion Detection Sensors. In W. Lee, L. Mè, and A. Wespi, editors, *Proceedings of the 4th International Symposiun on Recent Advances in Intrusion Detection (RAID 2001)*, volume 2212 of *LNCS*, pages 69–84, Davis, CA, October 2001. Springer-Verlag.
32. R. Zakon. Hobbes' internet timeline. http://www.zakon.org/robert/internet/timeline/, February 2003. Version 6.0.
33. Philip Zimmerman. *PGP User's Guide*, March 1993.

Author Index

Abrial, Jean-Raymond 51
Aguirre, Nazareno M. 678
Aldini, Alessandro 658
Armando, Alessandro 875
Atiya, Diyaa-Addein 617

Banach, Richard 814
Baum, Gabriel A. 678
Beek, Maurice H. ter 381
Bernardo, Marco 658
Bert, Didier 94
Boulmé, Sylvain 94
Bouquet, Fabrice 778
Boyer, Marc 264
Bozzano, Marco 208
Browne, James C. 582
Burdy, Lilian 422
Butler, Michael 855

Cavalcanti, Ana 301
Cavallo, Antonella 208
Chalin, Patrice 440
Charpentier, Michel 401
Chechik, Marsha 503
Chin, Wei-Ngan 282, 321
Cifaldi, Massimo 208
Compagna, Luca 875
Compare, Daniele 114

Denney, Ewen 894
Dong, Jin Song 321, 796
Duran, Adolfo 301

Eker, Steven 359

Fenkam, Pascal 636
Fidge, Colin J. 187
Fischer, Bernd 894
Frias, Marcelo F. 678
Futatsugi, Kokichi 7

Gall, Harald 636
Ganty, Pierre 875
Glesner, Sabine 758
Goldsmith, Michael 600
Gurfinkel, Arie 503

Hayes, Ian J. 154
Heimdahl, Mats P.E. 75
Henderson, Neil 244
Holzmann, Gerard J. 40

Inverardi, Paola 114

Jackson, Michael A. 154
Jazayeri, Mehdi 636
Jones, Cliff B. 154

King, Steve 617
Kishida, Kouichi 1, 7
Kleijn, Jetty 381
Kouchnarenko, Olga 341
Kuhn, Thomas A. 698
Kurshan, Robert P. 582

Laleau, Régine 834
Lanet, Jean-Louis 422
Lanoix, Arnaud 341
Lawford, Mark 133
Legeard, Bruno 778
Lettrari, Marc 462
Leuschel, Michael 855
Lincoln, Patrick 359
López Pombo, Carlos G. 678

Maibaum, Tom 678
Mammar, Amel 834
Marinescu, Maria-Cristina V. 482
Meseguer, José 359
Miller, Steven P. 75
Moffat, Nick 600
Morzenti, Angelo 542
Musset, Julien 562

Oheimb, David von 698

Pelliccione, Patrizio 114
Pietro, Pierluigi San 542
Poppleton, Michael 814
Potet, Marie-Laure 94
Pradella, Matteo 542

Qin, Shengchao 282, 321

Author Index

Randell, Brian 18
Requet, Antoine 94, 422
Rinard, Martin C. 482
Roscoe, Bill 600
Roşu, Grigore 359
Rusinowitch, Michaël 562
Rusu, Vlad 223

Sampaio, Augusto 301
Sawada, Toshimi 7
Schäfer, Andreas 522
Schellhorn, Gerhard 739
Sebastiani, Alessandra 114
Sighireanu, Mihaela 264
Spoletini, Paola 542
Stidolph, Donna C. 170
Sun, Jing 796

Teng, Jei-Wen 719

Thums, Andreas 739
Tribble, Alan C. 75
Tsay, Yih-Kuen 719

Valacca, Laura 208
Vigna, Giovanni 914
Villafiorita, Adolfo 208
Voisin, Laurent 94

Wang, Hai 796
Wassyng, Alan 133
Whitehead, James 170
Whitworth, Tim 600
Woodcock, Jim C.P. 617

Xie, Fei 582

Zakiuddin, Irfan 600

Lecture Notes in Computer Science

For information about Vols. 1–2704
please contact your bookseller or Springer-Verlag

Vol. 2705: S. Renals, G. Grefenstette (Eds.), Text- and Speech-Triggered Information Access. Proceedings, 2000. VII, 197 pages. 2003. (Subseries LNAI).

Vol. 2706: R. Nieuwenhuis (Ed.), Rewriting Techniques and Applications. Proceedings, 2003. XI, 515 pages. 2003.

Vol. 2707: K. Jeffay, I. Stoica, K. Wehrle (Eds.), Quality of Service – IWQoS 2003. Proceedings, 2003. XI, 517 pages. 2003.

Vol. 2708: R. Reed, J. Reed (Eds.), SDL 2003: System Design. Proceedings, 2003. XI, 405 pages. 2003.

Vol. 2709: T. Windeatt, F. Roli (Eds.), Multiple Classifier Systems. Proceedings, 2003. X, 406 pages. 2003.

Vol. 2710: Z. Ésik, Z, Fülöp (Eds.), Developments in Language Theory. Proceedings, 2003. XI, 437 pages. 2003.

Vol. 2711: T.D. Nielsen, N.L. Zhang (Eds.), Symbolic and Quantitative Approaches to Reasoning with Uncertainty. Proceedings, 2003. XII, 608 pages. 2003. (Subseries LNAI).

Vol. 2712: A. James, B. Lings, M. Younas (Eds.), New Horizons in Information Management. Proceedings, 2003. XII, 281 pages. 2003.

Vol. 2713: C.-W. Chung, C.-K. Kim, W. Kim, T.-W. Ling, K.-H. Song (Eds.), Web and Communication Technologies and Internet-Related Social Issues – HSI 2003. Proceedings, 2003. XXII, 773 pages. 2003.

Vol. 2714: O. Kaynak, E. Alpaydin, E. Oja, L. Xu (Eds.), Artificial Neural Networks and Neural Information Processing – ICANN/ICONIP 2003. Proceedings, 2003. XXII, 1188 pages. 2003.

Vol. 2715: T. Bilgiç, B. De Baets, O. Kaynak (Eds.), Fuzzy Sets and Systems – IFSA 2003. Proceedings, 2003. XV, 735 pages. 2003. (Subseries LNAI).

Vol. 2716: M.J. Voss (Ed.), OpenMP Shared Memory Parallel Programming. Proceedings, 2003. VIII, 271 pages. 2003.

Vol. 2718: P. W. H. Chung, C. Hinde, M. Ali (Eds.), Developments in Applied Artificial Intelligence. Proceedings, 2003. XIV, 817 pages. 2003. (Subseries LNAI).

Vol. 2719: J.C.M. Baeten, J.K. Lenstra, J. Parrow, G.J. Woeginger (Eds.), Automata, Languages and Programming. Proceedings, 2003. XVIII, 1199 pages. 2003.

Vol. 2720: M. Marques Freire, P. Lorenz, M.M.-O. Lee (Eds.), High-Speed Networks and Multimedia Communications. Proceedings, 2003. XIII, 582 pages. 2003.

Vol. 2721: N.J. Mamede, J. Baptista, I. Trancoso, M. das Graças Volpe Nunes (Eds.), Computational Processing of the Portuguese Language. Proceedings, 2003. XIV, 268 pages. 2003. (Subseries LNAI).

Vol. 2722: J.M. Cueva Lovelle, B.M. González Rodríguez, L. Joyanes Aguilar, J.E. Labra Gayo, M. del Puerto Paule Ruiz (Eds.), Web Engineering. Proceedings, 2003. XIX, 554 pages. 2003.

Vol. 2723: E. Cantú-Paz, J.A. Foster, K. Deb, L.D. Davis, R. Roy, U.-M. O'Reilly, H.-G. Beyer, R. Standish, G. Kendall, S. Wilson, M. Harman, J. Wegener, D. Dasgupta, M.A. Potter, A.C. Schultz, K.A. Dowsland, N. Jonoska, J. Miller (Eds.), Genetic and Evolutionary Computation – GECCO 2003. Proceedings, Part I. 2003. XLVII, 1252 pages. 2003.

Vol. 2724: E. Cantú-Paz, J.A. Foster, K. Deb, L.D. Davis, R. Roy, U.-M. O'Reilly, H.-G. Beyer, R. Standish, G. Kendall, S. Wilson, M. Harman, J. Wegener, D. Dasgupta, M.A. Potter, A.C. Schultz, K.A. Dowsland, N. Jonoska, J. Miller (Eds.), Genetic and Evolutionary Computation – GECCO 2003. Proceedings, Part II. 2003. XLVII, 1274 pages. 2003.

Vol. 2725: W.A. Hunt, Jr., F. Somenzi (Eds.), Computer Aided Verification. Proceedings, 2003. XII, 462 pages. 2003.

Vol. 2726: E. Hancock, M. Vento (Eds.), Graph Based Representations in Pattern Recognition. Proceedings, 2003. VIII, 271 pages. 2003.

Vol. 2727: R. Safavi-Naini, J. Seberry (Eds.), Information Security and Privacy. Proceedings, 2003. XII, 534 pages. 2003.

Vol. 2728: E.M. Bakker, T.S. Huang, M.S. Lew, N. Sebe, X.S. Zhou (Eds.), Image and Video Retrieval. Proceedings, 2003. XIII, 512 pages. 2003.

Vol. 2729: D. Boneh (Ed.), Advances in Cryptology – CRYPTO 2003. Proceedings, 2003. XII, 631 pages. 2003.

Vol. 2730: F. Bai, B. Wegner (Eds.), Electronic Information and Communication in Mathematics. Proceedings, 2002. X, 189 pages. 2003.

Vol. 2731: C.S. Calude, M.J. Dinneen, V. Vajnovszki (Eds.), Discrete Mathematics and Theoretical Computer Science. Proceedings, 2003. VIII, 301 pages. 2003.

Vol. 2732: C. Taylor, J.A. Noble (Eds.), Information Processing in Medical Imaging. Proceedings, 2003. XVI, 698 pages. 2003.

Vol. 2733: A. Butz, A. Krüger, P. Olivier (Eds.), Smart Graphics. Proceedings, 2003. XI, 261 pages. 2003.

Vol. 2734: P. Perner, A. Rosenfeld (Eds.), Machine Learning and Data Mining in Pattern Recognition. Proceedings, 2003. XII, 440 pages. 2003. (Subseries LNAI).

Vol. 2735: F. Kaashoek, I. Stoica (Eds.), Peer-to-Peer Systems II. Proceedings, 2003. XI, 316 pages. 2003.

Vol. 2736: V. Mařík, W. Retschitzegger, O.Štěpánková (Eds.), Database and Expert Systems Applications. Proceedings, 2003. XX, 945 pages. 2003.

Vol. 2737: Y. Kambayashi, M. Mohania, W. Wöß (Eds.), Data Warehousing and Knowledge Discovery. Proceedings, 2003. XIV, 432 pages. 2003.

Vol. 2738: K. Bauknecht, A M. Tjoa, G. Quirchmayr (Eds.), E-Commerce and Web Technologies. Proceedings, 2003. XII, 452 pages. 2003.

Vol. 2739: R. Traunmüller (Ed.), Electronic Government. Proceedings, 2003. XVIII, 511 pages. 2003.

Vol. 2740: E. Burke, P. De Causmaecker (Eds.), Practice and Theory of Automated Timetabling IV. Proceedings, 2002. XII, 361 pages. 2003.

Vol. 2741: F. Baader (Ed.), Automated Deduction – CADE-19. Proceedings, 2003. XII, 503 pages. 2003. (Subseries LNAI).

Vol. 2742: R. N. Wright (Ed.), Financial Cryptography. Proceedings, 2003. VIII, 321 pages. 2003.

Vol. 2743: L. Cardelli (Ed.), ECOOP 2003 – Object-Oriented Programming. Proceedings, 2003. X, 501 pages. 2003.

Vol. 2744: V. Mařík, D. McFarlane, P. Valckenaers (Eds.), Holonic and Multi-Agent Systems for Manufacturing. Proceedings, 2003. XI, 322 pages. 2003. (Subseries LNAI).

Vol. 2745: M. Guo, L.T. Yang (Eds.), Parallel and Distributed Processing and Applications. Proceedings, 2003. XII, 450 pages. 2003.

Vol. 2746: A. de Moor, W. Lex, B. Ganter (Eds.), Conceptual Structures for Knowledge Creation and Communication. Proceedings, 2003. XI, 405 pages. 2003. (Subseries LNAI).

Vol. 2747: B. Rovan, P. Vojtáš (Eds.), Mathematical Foundations of Computer Science 2003. Proceedings, 2003. XIII, 692 pages. 2003.

Vol. 2748: F. Dehne, J.-R. Sack, M. Smid (Eds.), Algorithms and Data Structures. Proceedings, 2003. XII, 522 pages. 2003.

Vol. 2749: J. Bigun, T. Gustavsson (Eds.), Image Analysis. Proceedings, 2003. XXII, 1174 pages. 2003.

Vol. 2750: T. Hadzilacos, Y. Manolopoulos, J.F. Roddick, Y. Theodoridis (Eds.), Advances in Spatial and Temporal Databases. Proceedings, 2003. XIII, 525 pages. 2003.

Vol. 2751: A. Lingas, B.J. Nilsson (Eds.), Fundamentals of Computation Theory. Proceedings, 2003. XII, 433 pages. 2003.

Vol. 2752: G.A. Kaminka, P.U. Lima, R. Rojas (Eds.), RoboCup 2002: Robot Soccer World Cup VI. XVI, 498 pages. 2003. (Subseries LNAI).

Vol. 2753: F. Maurer, D. Wells (Eds.), Extreme Programming and Agile Methods – XP/Agile Universe 2003. Proceedings, 2003. XI, 215 pages. 2003.

Vol. 2754: M. Schumacher, Security Engineering with Patterns. XIV, 208 pages. 2003.

Vol. 2756: N. Petkov, M.A. Westenberg (Eds.), Computer Analysis of Images and Patterns. Proceedings, 2003. XVIII, 781 pages. 2003.

Vol. 2758: D. Basin, B. Wolff (Eds.), Theorem Proving in Higher Order Logics. Proceedings, 2003. X, 367 pages. 2003.

Vol. 2759: O.H. Ibarra, Z. Dang (Eds.), Implementation and Application of Automata. Proceedings, 2003. XI, 312 pages. 2003.

Vol. 2761: R. Amadio, D. Lugiez (Eds.), CONCUR 2003 - Concurrency Theory. Proceedings, 2003. XI, 524 pages. 2003.

Vol. 2762: G. Dong, C. Tang, W. Wang (Eds.), Advances in Web-Age Information Management. Proceedings, 2003. XIII, 512 pages. 2003.

Vol. 2763: V. Malyshkin (Ed.), Parallel Computing Technologies. Proceedings, 2003. XIII, 570 pages. 2003.

Vol. 2764: S. Arora, K. Jansen, J.D.P. Rolim, A. Sahai (Eds.), Approximation, Randomization, and Combinatorial Optimization. Proceedings, 2003. IX, 409 pages. 2003.

Vol. 2765: R. Conradi, A.I. Wang (Eds.), Empirical Methods and Studies in Software Engineering. VIII, 279 pages. 2003.

Vol. 2766: S. Behnke, Hierarchical Neural Networks for Image Interpretation. XII, 224 pages. 2003.

Vol. 2769: T. Koch, I. T. Sølvberg (Eds.), Research and Advanced Technology for Digital Libraries. Proceedings, 2003. XV, 536 pages. 2003.

Vol. 2776: V. Gorodetsky, L. Popyack, V. Skormin (Eds.), Computer Network Security. Proceedings, 2003. XIV, 470 pages. 2003.

Vol. 2777: B. Schölkopf, M.K. Warmuth (Eds.), Learning Theory and Kernel Machines. Proceedings, 2003. XIV, 746 pages. 2003. (Subseries LNAI).

Vol. 2779: C.D. Walter, Ç.K. Koç, C. Paar (Eds.), Cryptographic Hardware and Embedded Systems – CHES 2003. Proceedings, 2003. XIII, 441 pages. 2003.

Vol. 2782: M. Klusch, A. Omicini, S. Ossowski, H. Laamanen (Eds.), Cooperative Information Agents VII. Proceedings, 2003. XI, 345 pages. 2003. (Subseries LNAI).

Vol. 2783: W. Zhou, P. Nicholson, B. Corbitt, J. Fong (Eds.), Advances in Web-Based Learning – ICWL 2003. Proceedings, 2003. XV, 552 pages. 2003.

Vol. 2786: F. Oquendo (Ed.), Software Process Technology. Proceedings, 2003. X, 173 pages. 2003.

Vol. 2787: J. Timmis, P. Bentley, E. Hart (Eds.), Artificial Immune Systems. Proceedings, 2003. XI, 299 pages. 2003.

Vol. 2789: L. Böszörményi, P. Schojer (Eds.), Modular Programming Languages. Proceedings, 2003. XIII, 271 pages. 2003.

Vol. 2790: H. Kosch, L. Böszörményi, H. Hellwagner (Eds.), Euro-Par 2003 Parallel Processing. Proceedings, 2003. XXXV, 1320 pages. 2003.

Vol. 2794: P. Kemper, W. H. Sanders (Eds.), Computer Performance Evaluation. Proceedings, 2003. X, 309 pages. 2003.

Vol. 2795: L. Chittaro (Ed.), Human-Computer Interaction with Mobile Devices and Services. Proceedings, 2003. XV, 494 pages. 2003.

Vol. 2796: M. Cialdea Mayer, F. Pirri (Eds.), Automated Reasoning with Analytic Tableaux and Related Methods. Proceedings, 2003. X, 271 pages. 2003. (Subseries LNAI).

Vol. 2803: M. Baaz, J.A. Makowsky (Eds.), Computer Science Logic. Proceedings, 2003. XII, 589 pages. 2003.

Vol. 2805: K. Araki, S. Gnesi, D. Mandrioli (Eds.), FME 2003: Formal Methods. Proceedings, 2003. XVII, 942 pages. 2003.

Vol. 2810: M.R. Berthold, H.-J. Lenz, E. Bradley, R. Kruse, C. Borgelt (Eds.), Advances in Intelligent Data Analysis V. Proceedings, 2003. XV, 624 pages. 2003.

Vol. 2817: D. Konstantas, M. Leonard, Y. Pigneur, S. Patel (Eds.), Object-Oriented Information Systems. Proceedings, 2003. XII, 426 pages. 2003.